SRI CHAITANYA & HIS ASSOCIATES

Swami B. B. Tirtha

MANDALA
SAN RAFAEL | LOS ANGELES | LONDON

MANDALA
Mandala Publishing
P.O. Box 3088
San Rafael, CA 94912
www.MandalaEarth.com

Find us on Facebook: www.facebook.com/mandalaearth
Follow us on Twitter: @mandalaearth

Other books by Swami B. B. Tirtha

Sages, Saints & Kings of Ancient India
A Taste of Transcendence
Suddha Bhakti: The Path of Pure Devotion
Dasavatara: The Ten Manifestations of Godhead
Hari Katha and Vaishnava Aparadha
The Holy Life of Srila B. D. Madhava Gosvami Maharaja
Sri Arcana Paddhati: The Puja Book
Affectionately Yours
Sri Guru-Tattva
The Philosophy of Love

Published by Mandala Publishing.

Library of Congress Cataloging-in-Publication Data available.
ISBN: 978-1-64722-676-3

Readers interested in this subject matter should visit these websites:
www.bbtirtha.org, www.sreecgmath.org

Printed in India

All Glories to Śrī Śrī Guru and Gaurāṅga!

Dedication

This volume is dedicated to the divine lotus feet of my gurudeva, Oṁ Viṣṇupāda Śrī Śrīmad Bhakti Dayita Mādhava Gosvāmī Mahārāja, and also to the lotus feet of my śikśā-guru, Oṁ Viṣṇupāda Śrī Srimad Bhakti Pramode Purī Gosvāmī Mahārāja, who greatly inspired this publication in English for the benefit of the devotees all over the world.

CONTENTS

FOREWORD	*xvi*
INTRODUCTION	*xxiii*
Śrī Abhirāma Ṭhākura (Śrī Rāma Dāsa)	146
Śrīla A. C. Bhaktivedanta Swami Prabhupāda	505
Śrī Acyutānanda	129
Śrīmad Advaita Ācārya	29
Śrīla Baladeva Vidyābhūṣaṇa	373
Śrī Bhagavān Ācārya	238
Śrīla Bhakti Dayita Mādhava Gosvāmī Mahārāja	458
Śrīla Bhakti Pramode Purī Gosvāmī Mahārāja	498
Śrīla Bhakti Rakṣaka Śrīdhara Deva Gosvāmī Mahārāja	501

Śrīla Bhakti Siddhānta Sarasvatī Gosvāmī Ṭhākura Prabhupāda 418

Śrīla Saccidānanda Bhaktivinoda Ṭhākura 383

Śrī Bijlī Khān (The Pāṭhāna Vaiṣṇava) 171

Śrī Buddhimanta Khān 82

Śrī Candraśekhara Ācārya 87

Śrī Dāmodara Paṇḍita 173

Śrī Devānanda Paṇḍita 106

Śrīla Dhanañjaya Paṇḍita 159

Śrī Gadādhara Dasa 141

Śrīla Gadādhara Paṇḍita Gosvāmī 76

Śrī Gaṅgā Dāsa Paṇḍita 59

Śrī Gaṅgā Mātā Gosvāminī 366

Śrīla Gaura Kiśora Dāsa Bābājī 407

Śrī Gaurī Dāsa Paṇḍita 144

The Ghoṣa Brothers 109

Śrīla Gopāla Bhaṭṭa Gosvāmī 294

Śrīla Gopāla Guru Gosvāmī 339

Śrī Gopīnātha Paṭṭanāyaka 245

Śrīla Nāmācārya Haridāsa Ṭhākura 43

Śrī Īśāna Ṭhākura 114

Śrī Īśvara Purīpāda 16

Śrī Jagadānanda Paṇḍita 178

Śrīla Jagadīśa Paṇḍita 25

Śrī Jagannātha Miśra 20

Śrīla Jagannātha Dāsa Bābājī Mahārāja 374

Śrīmatī Jāhnavā Devī 334

Śrī Jayadeva Gosvāmī 1

Śrīla Jīva Gosvāmī 311

Śrīla Kāśīśvara Paṇḍita 236

Śrī Kālī Dāsa & Jhāru Ṭhākura 136

Śrī Kālīya Kṛṣṇa Dāsa (Kāla Kṛṣṇa Dāsa) 158

Śrī Kamalākara Pippalāi 155

Śrīla Kṛṣṇadāsa Kavirāja Gosvāmī 329

Kavi Karṇapūra (Śrī Purī Dāsa) 324

Kūrma Vipra 163

Śrī Locana Dāsa Ṭhākura 326

Śrīla Lokanātha Gosvāmī & Bhūgarbha Gosvāmī 252

Śrī Mādhavendra Purī 7

Śrīla Maheśa Paṇḍita 144

Śrī Mīnaketana Rāma Dāsa 161

Śrī Mukunda Datta Ṭhākura 232

Śrī Murārī Gupta 70

Śrī Nandana Ācārya 83

Śrīla Narahari Sarakāra Ṭhākura 118

Śrīla Narottama Dāsa Ṭhākura 348

Śrī Paramānanda Purī 214

Śrī Parameśvara Dāsa Ṭhākura (Parameśvarī Dāsa) 148

Śrīla Prabodhānanda Sarasvatī 315

Śrī Pradyumna Brahmacārī (Nṛsiṁhānanda) 139

Śrī Pradyumna Miśra 241

King Śrī Pratāparudra Deva 195

Śrī Puṇḍarīka Vidyānidhi 90

Śrī Puruṣottama Dāsa 154

Śrī Raṅga Purī 19

Śrī Rāghava Paṇḍita 132

Śrīla Raghunandana Ṭhākura 121

Śrīla Raghunātha Bhaṭṭa Gosvāmī 291

Śrīla Raghunātha Dāsa Gosvāmī 299

Śrī Raghupati Upādhyāya 167

Śrī Rāmacandra Kavirāja 357

Śrī Rāmacandra Purī 247

Śrī Rāmānanda Rāya 204

Śrīla Rasikānanda Deva Gosvāmī 363

Śrīla Rūpa Gosvāmī 258

Śrī Sadāśiva Paṇḍita	98
Śrīla Sanātana Gosvāmī	272
The Sanoḍiya Vipra	168
Śrī Sāraṅga Ṭhākura	157
Śikhi Māhiti	243
Śrī Śivānanda Sena	123
Śrīdhara Paṇḍita	99
Śrīnivāsa Ācārya	343
Śrīvāsa Paṇḍita	62
Śrī Subuddhi Rāya	256
Śrī Śuklāmbara Brahmacārī	96
Śrī Sundarānanda Ṭhākura	160
Śrī Svarūpa Dāmodara	218
Śrī Śyāmānanda Prabhu	359
Śrī Uddhāraṇa Datta Ṭhākura	150
Śrī Uddhava Dāsa	163

Śrīla Vaṁśī Dāsa Bābājī	414
Śrī Vaṁsīvadanānanda Ṭhākura	116
Śrī Vakreśvara Paṇḍita	104
Śrī Vṛndāvana Dāsa Ṭhākura	321
Śrī Vāsudeva Datta Ṭhākura	74
Vāsudeva Sārvabhauma Bhaṭṭācārya	187
Śrī Vāsudeva Vipra	165
Śrī Vīracandra Prabhu (Vīrabhadra)	337
Śrīla Viśvanātha Cakravartī Ṭhākura	369
Śrīmatī Viṣṇupriyā Devī	111
INDEX OF ASSOCIATES	508
ABOUT THE AUTHOR	513

FOREWORD

by

Śrīla Bhakti Pramode Purī Gosvāmī Mahārāja

Our Divine Master, Oṁ Viṣṇupāda 108 Śrī Śrīmad Bhakti Siddhānta Sarasvatī Gosvāmī Ṭhākura, who has now entered into the eternal pastimes of the Supreme Lord, founded the Sree Chaitanya Math in Mayapur in Nabadwip, whose branch Gaudiya Maths have now spread throughout the world. His dear associate and successor in the disciplic succession, Śrīmad Bhakti Dayita Mādhava Gosvāmī Mahārāja, an exemplary monk in the Tridaṇḍi order, founded the Sree Chaitanya Gaudiya Math, which also has branches throughout India. After he went to join the pastimes of the Lord, he left his dear disciple Śrīmad Bhakti Ballabh Tīrtha Mahārāja as the current President and Ācārya of Sree Chaitanya Gaudiya Math.

In this jewel-like volume, the venerable Tirtha Mahārāja recounts the nectarean activities of the associates of Lord Gaurāṅga and the *ācāryas* of the Gauḍīya Vaiṣṇava religion. Tīrtha Mahārāja has previously written commentaries on the life of the devotee Dhruva, a guide to the Vṛndāvana *parikramā*, a summary of the procedures involved in deity worship as well as a biography in two volumes of his spiritual master, Śrīmad Mādhava Gosvāmī Mahārāja. These have all been published in Bengali. He is also the editor of the Sree Chaitanya Gaudiya Math's monthly magazine, *Śrī Caitanya Vāṇī*, in which his biography of Mādhava Mahārāja as well as the biographies found in this volume first appeared in installments.

Tirtha Mahārāja has shown a force of intelligence beyond the capacities of an ordinary man, for at seventy years of age he not only edits a monthly magazine and writes books such as this one, but takes the responsibility for managing a large organization like the Chaitanya Gaudiya Math, through which he preaches the gospel of Śrī Caitanya Deva to devotees speaking a variety of languages throughout India, from the Himalayas to Cape Comorin. Even at his advanced age, it has been possible for him to find the energy and the enthusiasm to apply himself to tasks that tax his body, mind, speech and intelligence, and he achieves unimaginable results.

This is proof that the inexhaustible affectionate blessings of the Supreme Lord, the guru and the Vaiṣṇavas have poured down upon him and that unlimited divine powers have descended upon him through their transcendental mercy. We pray to the lotus feet of Śrī Guru, the Vaiṣṇavas, and the Supreme Lord that he will live many more years so that he may continue to serve Kṛṣṇa and his devotees in the same enthusiastic and unyielding manner. We also humbly submit our prayer to the *Śrīmad Bhāgavatam* and the devotee Bhāgavata that these sweet biographies of Mahāprabhu's associates will flood the ears and touch the hearts of the devotees like a nectar tonic, bringing them all unending joy.

Lord Gaurasundara Mahāprabhu is the most generous *avatāra* who descended to bestow upon the world the unique love of Vraja, a mood of devotion to Himself which had never before been given. The lives of the saintly are rich with the sweetness of loving service and are worth repeated study because they are most dear to Gaurasundara. Without such study, we will never be able to understand the nature of devotional service. By relishing the lives of the great devotees, we become attracted by their compassion and develop affection without artifice for their lotus feet. Since the Lord is so kind to His devotees, this is the road to becoming the object of His mercy.

Scripture has said that the Lord's mercy follows that of His devotees. Lord Kṛṣṇa Himself has said in *Śrīmad Bhāgavatam* that the worship of His devotee is dearer to Him than His own worship (*mad-bhakta-pūjābhyadhikā*). Vṛndāvana Dāsa paraphrases this statement in the *Caitanya Bhāgavata:* "The worship of My devotee is even greater than the worship of Me; this has been confirmed by the Lord in the Vedas and *Śrīmad Bhāgavatam.*"

No matter how great a show of commitment one makes to Kṛṣṇa's worship, Kṛṣṇa will never pay the slightest attention to it if one disregards the service of His devotees. Indeed, Kṛṣṇa will refuse such worship because of the performer's pride. In no way can one be engaged in the worship of the Lord without following in the footsteps of the devotees. Thus, the scriptures have ordained that one should begin one's *pūjā* with the worship of the guru, who is the best of the devotees and most dear to Kṛṣṇa.

Kṛṣṇa stated as much to His foremost devotee and associate Uddhava, when He said, "O Uddhava! Know that it is I who am the *ācārya*. Never show disrespect for the *ācārya* by thinking that he is an ordinary man, for all gods reside within him." The compassion of the Lord has become incarnate in the form of the guru. Worship of the Lord can have no meaning if one disregards the spiritual master.

Tīrtha Mahārāja has gathered a great deal of information about the lives of the devotees from numerous sources and has made this information more relishable by virtue of his own insight. It is my wish that these biographies of Mahāprabhu's devotees will be read on their appearance and disappearance days, for this will bring great joy to both those who hear and those who read them. It is for this reason that we pray for the wide distribution of this work. In this English translation, it will be possible for devotees around the world to enjoy.

In this volume, the author delights in the life stories of Jagannātha Miśra, Mādhavendra Purī, Īśvara Purī, Advaita Ācārya, Śrīvāsa Paṇḍita, Candraśekhara Ācārya, Puṇḍarīka Vidyānidhi, Gadādhara Paṇḍita, Vakreśvara Paṇḍita, Gadādhara Dāsa, Śivānanda Sena, Paramānanda Purī, Murārī Gupta, and many others. Every letter of these accounts is drenched with the nectar of devotion. We will never be able to enter the transcendental kingdom or to advance in devotional life unless we also experience this delight. We should repeatedly discuss the lives of the devotees, as they are saturated with loving service to the Lord – this will melt our stone-like hearts. It will awaken in us a genuine remorse for all the wasted activities in which we have engaged outside the life of devotion, thus readying our minds for the mercy of the pure devotee, which enables our receptivity to devotion.

The devotees of the Lord are oceans of mercy; they feel distressed at the pain of others; they are endowed with amazing powers of forgiveness; their hearts are entirely pure, free from enviousness, hate and jealousy. When they see the misery of persons like me, the lowest of souls, who, bound by illusion and forgetful of their eternal identities, have become uninterested in Kṛṣṇa, they pray to Kṛṣṇa's lotus feet for their salvation, shedding tears in intense feelings of compassion. After hearing this prayer, Kṛṣṇa turns His merciful glance towards us. Śrīla Bhaktivinoda Ṭhākura has written:

vaiṣṇavera āvedane kṛṣṇa dayāmaya
mo hena pāmara prati habena sadaya

"The merciful Kṛṣṇa, upon hearing the Vaiṣṇava's supplications, will become merciful to those, who like me, are most fallen."

The Lord, the ocean of compassion, cannot resist the heart-rending tears of those whose lives are totally dedicated to Him. The Lord quickly appears in the world when he hears the intense pleas of the surrendered devotee. All the living beings attain the great fortune of the Lord's mercy through the mercy of such devotees. Therefore, one should take shelter of a pure devotee before doing anything else.

śuddha-bhakata-caraṇa-reṇu bhajana-anukūla
bhakata-sevā parama-siddhi prema-latikāra mūla

"The dust of the pure devotee's lotus feet has the most positive effect on one's worship of the Lord. Service to the devotee is the greatest perfection; it is the root of the creeper of love for Kṛṣṇa."

At the beginning of his collection of devotional songs, *Śaraṇāgati*, Bhaktivinoda Ṭhākura wrote: "Lord Śrī Kṛṣṇa Caitanya, out of compassion for the people of this world, descended into this world along with His eternal associates and His abode. In order to give *prema* most rare, He taught the process of surrender that is the life of devotion."

In every age for all eternity, the Lord descends in each of the unlimited universes. This does not cause a disruption in the Lord's eternal pastimes. Thus, when the Supreme Lord, the *līlā-puruṣottama*, son of Nanda, the king of Vraja, appears in Nabadwip as Gaurāṅga, the son of Jagannātha Miśra, all of His associates from His Vraja *līlā* join Him as companions for these pastimes. Narottam Dāsa Ṭhākura sings: "He who is the son of the King of Vraja has become the son of Śacī; Balarāma has become Nitāi."

Kṛṣṇadāsa Kavirāja states as much in the *Caitanya Caritāmṛta*: "Kṛṣṇa appeared with all of Vraja at the end of the Dvāpara-yuga of the twenty-eighth four-*yuga* cycle in the seventh Manvantara, named Vaivasvata." (1.3.9-10)

Jīva Gosvāmī explains the *Bhāgavata* verses which begins *kṛṣṇa-varṇaṁ tviṣākṛṣṇaṁ* (11.5.32) and *āsan varṇās trayo hy asya* (10.8.13) in his *Krama-sandarbha* commentary: "Thus, the same Kṛṣṇa who descended at the end of the Dvāpara-yuga appears as Gaura in the age of Kali that immediately follows it. From this understanding, it is evident that Gaurāṅga is a special *avatāra* of Kṛṣṇa. This is the only way to avoid contradictions in *Śrīmad Bhāgavatam* verses which state that 'in the Kali Age Kṛṣṇa appears in a color other than black,' and that He appears in the four ages in four colors: red, black, white and gold."

The Supreme Personality of Godhead Kṛṣṇa displays activities that are characterized by magnanimity (*audārya*) predominated by the character of *mādhurya*, sweetness. The pastimes of the Lord in Nabadwip, however, though non-different from those of Vraja, are characterized by *mādhurya* predominated by His magnanimity. Just as all of Kṛṣṇa's qualities are manifest in His devotees, so too are Gaura's qualities in their entirety manifest in His devotees. Since Gaura is the most magnanimous and generous *avatāra*, these qualities are the primary characteristics of His divine pastimes and are therefore also present in all the participants in His *līlā*.

It is thus natural that constant rereading of the activities of the devotees who have dedicated themselves to Gaura's service will wash all of the dirt and sin from our hearts and we will become free from envy, hatred and jealousy. Then, in the same way, that it is said of Gaura that "He taught the world by following the practices and principles Himself" (*Caitanya Caritāmṛta* 1.3.20, 1.4.41), we will be able to enthusiastically preach the message of Lord Caitanya to every corner of the world.

Should this happen, by the mercy of the beneficent Lord a supreme peace will be established everywhere, the victory banner of the Holy Name will fly, the skies of the world will ring with the glorious sound of Kṛṣṇa's name being sung, and the sweetness of the Holy Name, which Lord Caitanya Himself called out, will flood the world with divine love. For, as Bhaktivinoda Ṭhākura exclaimed, "What power is contained in the name of Kṛṣṇa!"

Bhakti Vāridhi Parivrājaka Mahārāja, a monk who is particularly dear to me, took on himself the responsibility for printing the Bengali edition of this book. He worked with dedication both day and night to finish the job, and even if I could sing his glories with a hundred tongues, I would not feel satisfied. He not only produced this volume, but works tirelessly and with unflagging enthusiasm to put out all of the Math publications. His gurus have noticed this service and will pour unlimited affectionate blessings on him. We pray to the Lord's lotus feet with all our heart that his eager efforts to serve the Lord, the guru and all the Vaiṣṇavas constantly increase, and that he receives their unlimited blessings and enjoy good health and long life.

Śrīla Prabhupāda Bhakti Siddhānta Sarasvatī Gosvāmī Ṭhākura used to call the printing press the big drum, the *bṛhad-mṛdaṅga*, because through books and magazines filled with the authoritative message of pure devotion, the worldwide preaching mission can have a stable and far-reaching effect. Therefore, the beating of the "big drum" is a major element in serving Mahāprabhu in preaching His teachings. Mahāprabhu Himself said, "Wherever you go, give the fruits of love to whomever you see." (*Caitanya Caritāmṛta* 1.9.36). "Those who have taken a human birth in India (Bhārata-bhūmi) should perfect their own lives and then do good for others." (*Caitanya Caritāmṛta* 1.9.41) "Spread this command of Mine wherever you go: 'Chant Kṛṣṇa, worship Kṛṣṇa, study Kṛṣṇa's teachings.'" (*Caitanya Bhāgavat* 2.13.7-8) "Explain Kṛṣṇa consciousness to whomever you meet." (*Caitanya Caritāmṛta* 2.7.128) "My name shall be heard in all the towns and villages of the world." (*Caitanya Bhāgavata* 3.4.126). As we try to fulfill these commands of the Lord in a sustained and far-reaching way as possible, we will get the most help from the "big *mṛdaṅga*."

Therefore, in making the preaching of Caitanya Mahāprabhu's message through printing books a prominent part of the Math's service activities, Parivrājaka Mahārāja and Bhakti Ballabh Tīrtha Mahārāja are ensuring that they will receive the affection of their gurus and all pure devotees, not only those who have preceded them, but those who will follow.

In conclusion, we would like to sincerely thank as much as possible all those who have aided through their financial contributions or volunteer work to help bring this and other books and magazines of the Math to publication. We humbly pray to everyone who reads this work to kindly forgive any errors that may have been missed in proofreading.

Praying for the dust of the pure devotees' lotus feet, I am the servant of the servant of the Vaiṣṇavas,

Śrī Bhakti Pramode Purī

23 Bhādra 1399 (Bengali year)
9 September 1992

INTRODUCTION

by

Śrīla Bhakti Ballabh Tīrtha Gosvāmī

The contents of this book first appeared as a series of articles in Śrī Caitanya Vāṇī ("The Gospel of Lord Caitanya"), a monthly magazine exclusively devoted to spiritual subject matters. Those articles have here been brought together to form a single book, though they were originally published in Bengali in two separate volumes. I hope that this publication will facilitate the devotees' relishing of the activities of the Lord's associates.

Śrī Gaurāṅga Mahāprabhu is the Supreme Truth, and His associates are also transcendental, beyond matter. They are thus not accessible to the material senses, mind and intelligence. Since the transcendental is by nature self-manifest, one can only understand Śrī Gaurāṅga's associates glories through their causeless mercy. Just as the glories of the Lord are unlimited, so too are the glories of His devotees without end. Those who are not surrendered have no right of entry into these mysteries.

Amongst those who have abandoned themselves to the Lord, there are varying degrees of surrender that produce diverse abilities to perceive the glories of devotees. The *jīva* who is covered by an assortment of *anarthas* cannot approach an understanding of the glories of Viṣṇu and the Vaiṣṇavas. Even when such person tries to glorify them, the inevitable result is a discourtesy. Nevertheless, if one recognizes one's own unworthiness and humbly glorifies them with a prayerful attitude, the Vaiṣṇavas will forgive any flaws in one's expression.

The satisfied glance of the Vaiṣṇavas frees the *jīva* from his *anarthas* and brings him all auspiciousness. Even though the neophyte devotee is inadequate in so many ways and is thus unable to glorify Kṛṣṇa and His devotees in a satisfactory manner, if he does not do so his inadequacies will remain. The only hope for the fallen souls is that the Vaiṣṇavas are merciful and not find any fault with them. Those who engage honestly in service find that by the mercy of the Vaiṣṇavas, all obstacles are eliminated, and all desired goals attained.

The pure devotee is very rare in this world; it is only due to great fortune that one can meet and associate with such a devotee. In the *Caitanya Caritāmṛta* (1.1.20-1), it is said, "By meditating on the guru, the Vaiṣṇava and the Lord, all obstacles are destroyed, and all desires are fulfilled. All perfections come from the mercy of the Vaiṣṇavas. I have heard from my guru and from the saintly persons that the jīva who glorifies the qualities of the devotees is liberated."

Caitanya Mahāprabhu's direct associates the Six Gosvāmīs daily paid thousands of obeisances to the Vaiṣṇavas. Indeed, one should spend some time meditating on the Vaiṣṇavas every single day. An important element of devotional service is the regular observance of Vaiṣṇavas' appearance and disappearance days. On these occasions, one should remember them, pray to them for their mercy and glorify their qualities in *kīrtana*. We at the Chaitanya Gaudiya Math annually publish a Vaiṣṇava calendar in which all the different fasting days and feasts are indicated; all the known appearance and disappearance days have been noted therein. The purpose of this book is to assist the devotees who wish to remember the Vaiṣṇavas, to pray to them and especially to glorify them in *kīrtana*.

We should chant the glories of the merciful devotees of Śrī Caitanya because we wish to rid ourselves of all tendencies that lead away from devotional service and to develop attachment for Kṛṣṇa. Sometimes, however, we find that there is absolutely no change in our nature. We do not attain the desired result because we are not able to adequately glorify them due to our incapacities. Nevertheless, one cannot but give it the effort because the lotus feet of the Vaiṣṇavas are the only recourse for the fallen.

In researching the holy activities of Caitanya's associates, I became aware that many details of their lives are unavailable. Many of their appearance and disappearance *tithis* (lunar dates) and years are unknown, as are their places of birth, the names of their parents and their ancestors. This information could thus not be given in all cases. Some readers may find that the language used to describe the devotees' lives is not sufficiently poetic and thus not find the joy in reading these accounts as they had hoped.

The chief editor and president of *Caitanya Vāṇī* magazine, the most venerable Bhakti Pramode Purī Gosvāmī Mahārāja, has rained down countless blessings on me to encourage me to perform this service. He has made many personal contributions, and in some instances adding new information about certain of the associates' lives.

We thank everyone who contributed for the publication of this book. I pray that the blessings of the guru, the Vaiṣṇavas and the Supreme Lord fall upon them.

I pay thousands of prostrated obeisances to the lotus feet of my most worshipable Gurudeva, the purifier of the sinful, to the lotus feet of my *parama gurudeva,* Śrīla Prabhupāda Bhakti Siddhānta Sarasvatī Ṭhākura, to the feet of my *śikṣā-guru*, Śrīla Bhakti Pramode Purī Gosvāmī Mahārāja, and to all the other disciples of Śrīla Prabhupāda, who are all *śikṣā-gurus*, and I pray for their causeless mercy and their blessings.

Servant of the servant
of the Vaiṣṇavas,

Bhakti Ballabh Tīrtha

Śrīla Bhakti Ballabh Tīrtha Gosvāmī Mahārāja

Śrīla Bhakti Dayita Mādhava Gosvāmī Mahārāja

Śrīla Bhakti Siddhānta Sarasvatī Ṭhākura Prabhupāda

Śrī Jayadeva Gosvāmī

Śrīla Jayadeva Gosvāmī appeared in either the eleventh or twelfth century of the Śaka era. There is a difference of opinions about the place of his birth. The majority opinion holds that he hailed from the village of Kenduvilva, presently in the district of Birbhum. Others hold that he was born in Odisha or in South India.

Kenduvilva is situated about twenty miles south of Siuri on the banks of the Ajay River. In the *Gauḍīya Vaiṣṇava Abhidhāna,* it is stated that Jayadeva Gosvāmī found his Rādhā Mādhava deities in this river's waters. It is also stated there that he used to rest and worship at the temple of Śiva known as Lord Kuśeśvara, which is also on the banks of the Ajaya Riveer. His father was Bhojadeva, and his mother, Vāmā Devī.

JAYADEVA GOSVĀMĪ'S LIFE IN NABADWIP

Jayadeva Gosvāmī lived for a long time in Nabadwip during the reign of the King of Bengal, Lakṣmaṇa Sena, making his home not far from the King's palace. At that time, the King's chief scholar was Govardhana Ācārya. According to Ashutosh Deb's *Bengali Dictionary*, Jayadeva Gosvāmī was Lakṣmaṇa Sena's court poet.

Śrīla Bhaktivinoda Ṭhākura wrote in his *Nabadvīpa-dhāma-māhātmya* that Lakṣmaṇa Sena was delighted when he heard Jayadeva Gosvāmī's hymn to the ten *avatāras*, the *Daśāvatāra-stotra.* When Govardhana Ācārya notified the King that it was Jayadeva Gosvāmī who had composed the hymn, he became desirous to meet the poet. He went incognito to Jayadeva Gosvāmī's house, and when he saw him, he noticed that Jayadeva Gosvāmī possessed the characteristics of a great and powerful spiritual personality. Greatly impressed and attracted by Jayadeva Gosvāmī, the King revealed his identity to him and invited him to come and live in the royal palace. Jayadeva Gosvāmī was leading a much-renounced life and was therefore unwilling to live in the opulent environment of the palace. He told the King that he preferred to live in Jagannatha Puri.

Lakṣmaṇa Sena was disappointed by Jayadeva Gosvāmī's intentions. He quickly suggested that he take up residence in the village of Champāhati, saying that it was a place suitable for a person who wished to lead a meditative life. He also promised him that he would never come to disturb him again. When Jayadeva Gosvāmī agreed, Lakṣmaṇa Sena had a cottage built for him in the village which was formerly known as Champākhatta, named after the beautiful garden of *Champā* trees and the village market where its flowers were sold. It was in this village that Mahāprabhu's associate Dvija Vāṇīnātha received a vision of Him in the Satya Yuga, seeing Him in the form of a *brāhmaṇa* whose skin was the color of a *Champā* flower. Similarly, Jayadeva Gosvāmī had a vision here, first of Rādhā Mādhava, then of Their combined form as the golden *Champā*-colored Gaurāṅga Mahāprabhu.

After the Lord gave Jayadeva Gosvāmī this vision, He told him to go to Jagannatha Puri. Although Jayadeva Gosvāmī was sad to leave the future abode of his Lord, he obeyed the Lord's command and made his way to Puri, where it is said that he was the court poet of the King of Odisha. He spent the remainder of his life in the abode of Lord Jagannātha, where he wrote the transcendental poem based on the sentiments of love in separation known as *Gīta*

Govinda or *Aṣṭapadī*. Indeed, Mahāprabhu told Jayadeva Gosvāmī while giving him the vision in Nabadwip that after appearing there, He would take *sannyāsa* and go to Jagannatha Puri where He would relish the *Gīta Govinda*.

Further information about the life of Jayadeva Gosvāmī is found in the preface to the Kolkata Basumati Sahitya Mandir's edition of *Gīta Govinda:* "Sometime prior to the Muslim conquest of Delhi, King Māṇikya Candra ordered the writing of the book *Alaṁkāra-śekhara,* in which Jayadeva Gosvāmī is mentioned as the court poet of the King of Odisha. Śrīdhara Dāsa, the son of one of the chief courtiers of Lakṣmaṇa Sena, included many of Jayadeva Gosvāmī's verses in his anthology *Sad-ukti-karṇāmṛta*, citing a work named *Amiyābha-kāvya.* The colophon to one ancient manuscript of the *Gīta Govinda* states, 'Jayadeva Gosvāmī had a great reputation as a poet during the time of Lakṣmaṇa Sena.' "

JAYADEVA GOSVĀMĪ'S MARRIAGE TO PADMĀVATĪ

According to legend, Lord Jagannātha Himself ordered Jayadeva Gosvāmī to marry his wife, Padmāvatī. The story is told in the *Viśvakoṣa* as follows: There once was a *brāhmaṇa* who was without offspring despite having worshipped Lord Jagannātha for many years in the hope of having a son. Finally, he and his wife had a daughter and they named her Padmāvatī. When she came of marriageable age, the *brāhmaṇa* brought her to Lord Jagannātha to offer her to His lotus feet.[1] When He saw them, Lord Jagannātha Himself said to the *brāhmaṇa*, "I have a servant whose name is Jayadeva Gosvāmī. He has given up family life and has dedicated himself to chanting My names. Give your daughter to him in marriage."

The *brāhmaṇa* took his daughter to Jayadeva Gosvāmī and asked him to marry his daughter. However, since Jayadeva Gosvāmī had no desire to get married, he refused to agree to any arrangement. Then the *brāhmaṇa* told him that it was Lord Jagannātha Himself who had arranged this marriage, and without another word, he left, leaving his daughter behind. Jayadeva Gosvāmī found himself totally unprepared for this situation and told the girl, "Tell me where you want to go, and I will take you and leave you there. You cannot stay here."

Padmāvatī started to cry and said, "My father brought me here to marry you on Jagannātha Deva's order. You are my husband, my all in all. If you do not accept me, then I will fall down at your feet and die right here. You are my only hope, my lord."

The poet and scholar Jayadeva Gosvāmī could not abandon her after such a heartfelt plea. So he became a householder.

THE LORD HELPS JAYADEVA GOSVĀMĪ WRITE GĪTA GOVINDA

Jayadeva Gosvāmī took up the worship of a Nārāyaṇa deity and in the waves of love he felt for Him, began writing *Gīta Govinda,* with incomparable ambrosia. It is said that though Jayadeva Gosvāmī is responsible for all the moods and sentiments that appear in the *Gīta Govinda,* he had some reticence about writing that Kṛṣṇa fell down at Rādhārāṇī's feet to beg Her forgiveness when She was angry with Him for having deceived Her.

On that day, when he left the house to take his bath in the ocean, Lord Jagannātha Himself

1 Many people in Odisha still follow the custom of offering their daughters in marriage to Lord Jagannātha before they marry anyone else.

came inside, disguised as Jayadeva Gosvāmī, opened his manuscript and completed the verse he had started, *smara-garala-khaṇḍanaṁ mama śirasi maṇḍanaṁ*, with the words *dehi pada-pallavam udāraṁ*: "Make the noble blossom of Your foot an ornament on My head, as it dispels the poison of love in separation." (*Gīta Govinda* 10.8)

Padmāvatī was surprised to see her husband back so soon from his bath and asked, "What are you doing here? You just left a minute ago." The disguised Lord Jagannātha answered, "I thought of something I had forgotten while on my way. I was afraid I might forget, so I came back to write it down."

Not long after Lord Jagannātha had left, the real Jayadeva Gosvāmī returned. This time, Padmāvatī was really astonished to see him. She said, "You just left to go and take your bath. Just a few moments ago you were writing your manuscript, and then you left. How could you have finished and come back so quickly? I am beginning to wonder who that was and who you are."

Jayadeva Gosvāmī was clever enough to guess what had happened, and he went and

looked at his unfinished text and saw the words that the Lord Himself had written. The hair stood on end all over his body, and tears came pouring from his eyes. He called Padmāvatī and said to her, "You are so fortunate. Your life has been made worthy. You have had the good fortune to see the Lord Himself. I am so lowly that I did not have that opportunity!"

LORD JAGANNĀTHA'S LOVE FOR GĪTA GOVINDA

There is a legend told in Jagannatha Puri that there was a flower gardener's daughter who had learned *Gīta Govinda* and would sing it with great emotion. Lord Jagannātha was attracted by her singing and would go to listen to her, only returning to the temple after she had finished singing.

One day, when the King of Odisha came to see the deity, he saw that the Lord's body was covered in dust and his clothes were filled with thorns. He asked the *pūjārīs* the reason for the Lord's disheveled condition, but no one could explain how it had come about. The servants of the deity were afraid that they would be punished, but that night, Lord Jagannātha appeared to the King in a dream and explained that no one was to blame for His clothes being soiled that day. He had gone to listen to the gardener's daughter and had become covered with dust and thorns while hiding in the garden.

The King was struck with wonder by his dream and immediately sent for the gardener's daughter to be brought to the court in a palanquin. After making inquiries from her, he decided that she should sing for Jagannātha in the temple, rather than obliging the Lord to leave the temple and get all dirty. This was the beginning of the tradition of the temple engaging girls, named *deva-dāsīs,* to sing *Gīta Govinda* for Jagannātha's pleasure.

MAHĀPRABHU APPRECIATES GĪTA GOVINDA

In the last twelve years of His pastimes, Mahāprabhu was absorbed in Rādhā's mood and constantly relished this hidden spirit of love. During this time, He would savor the songs of the *Gīta Govinda.*

Day and night, the Lord would speak as though He were Rādhā meeting Uddhava. He would also relish the poems of Caṇḍī Dāsa, Jayadeva Gosvāmī and Vidyāpati. (*Caitanya Caritāmṛta* 1.13.41-2)

Mahāprabhu was never pleased to hear books or verses that contradicted *siddhānta,* nor did He like hearing *rasābhāsa,* an improper mixture of devotional sentiments. It was the practice of Svarūpa Dāmodara Gosvāmī to examine all works of literature to find out whether their conclusions were correct. Only then would he allow them to be heard by the Lord. Śrī Svarūpa Dāmodara used to make Mahāprabhu very happy by singing the songs of Vidyāpati, Caṇḍī Dāsa and *Gīta Govinda.* (*Caitanya Caritāmṛta* 2.10.113-5)

Svarūpa Dāmodara would sing songs that reflected the moods of the Lord whenever they arose, while Rāmānanda Rāya selected verses from Vidyāpati, Caṇḍī Dāsa and *Gīta Govinda* according to the Lord's mood. (*Caitanya Caritāmṛta* 2.17.5-6)

The Lord returned to external consciousness for a moment and told Svarūpa to sing some sweet songs. Svarūpa sang one of Vidyāpati's songs and then songs from the *Gīta Govinda*, which were greatly appreciated by the Lord. (*Caitanya Caritāmṛta* 3.17.62)

caṇḍīdāsa vidyāpati rāyera nāṭaka gīti
karṇāmṛta śrī gīta govinda
svarūpa rāmānanda sane mahāprabhu rātri-dine
gāya, śune parama ānanda

"Day and night, Mahāprabhu ecstatically relished the songs of Caṇḍī Dāsa, Vidyāpati and Rāmānanda Rāya's plays, as well as *Kṛṣṇa-karṇāmṛta* and *Gīta Govinda* in the company of Svarūpa and Rāmānanda." (*Caitanya Caritāmṛta* 2.2.77)

JAYADEVA GOSVĀMĪ AND THE ROBBERS

Many other amazing and miraculous events were scattered through Jayadeva Gosvāmī's life. He used to serve his deities, Rādhā-Mādhava, in a trance of divine love. It is said that just as the devotee dedicates himself to the Lord, the Lord also dedicates Himself to His devotee. One day, Jayadeva Gosvāmī was thatching his roof under the merciless midday sun. Lord Jagannātha saw His devotee's discomfort and decided to help him finish the work quickly by handing him the rope needed to bale the straw and removing the finished bundles and placing them on the roof. Jayadeva Gosvāmī thought that Padmāvatī was helping him in this way. But when he came down from the roof after finishing much earlier than expected, he saw no one there. He asked his wife, and she told him that she had been busy elsewhere at the time. He was curious about what had happened but struck with wonder when he went into the deity room and saw that Mādhava's hands were black from handling the straw. He was thus able to understand that Lord Mādhava Himself had come to help him thatch the roof. He fell down before his Lord and started to cry.

On another occasion, Jayadeva Gosvāmī wished to put on a festival for his deities, Rādhā-Mādhava, but he was short of money. He decided to travel in order to collect some funds. On his return journey, he was stopped by a band of thugs who not only stole his money but cut off his hands and feet and threw him down a well to die. Despite the pain, Jayadeva Gosvāmī shouted out the names of the Lord loudly.

After Jayadeva Gosvāmī had spent three days in this way, the King happened to pass that way on a hunting expedition and heard the sound of the Holy Names coming from the hole in the ground. The King approached the sound out of curiosity and was horrified to see Jayadeva Gosvāmī in such a serious condition. He had him pulled out of the well and brought back to his palace, where he had him treated. Under the care of the King and the Queen, Jayadeva Gosvāmī was gradually returned to health.

Both the King and Queen were charmed by Jayadeva Gosvāmī's sweet singing of the *Gīta Govinda* as well as by his saintly character. They immediately sent for Padmāvati and had her brought to their palace. The royal couple heard about Kṛṣṇa from Jayadeva Gosvāmī and took initiation from him and started to make their lives successful by service of the Lord and His devotees. One day, the robbers who had attacked Jayadeva Gosvāmī came to the King's palace as guests in the guise of devotees. Even though Jayadeva Gosvāmī recognised who they were, he gave them the appropriate honor due to their outward appearance and arranged for the King's hospitality to be extended to them. The robbers, however, did not understand Jayadeva Gosvāmī's forgiving and generous nature and, fearing capture and punishment, thought it best to leave without accepting the royal invitation. Jayadeva Gosvāmī understood their fear and asked the King to give them a large sum of money, and an escort and send them on their way.

After they had gone a certain distance, the robbers said to the soldiers accompanying them, "You need not go any farther. However, we would like to tell you a secret message to convey to the King. Prior to becoming Vaiṣṇavas, we were the servants of a certain king who for a very good reason ordered us to murder this priest, Jayadeva Gosvāmī. That is why we cut off his hands and feet and left him to die. The priest gave us a lot of money and asked us to leave quickly because he was afraid that this secret would come out."

Unable to tolerate the telling of such a great lie, the earth herself opened up and swallowed the entire gang of thieves. The Goddess of the earth was unable to support the weight of these sinful liars, and so she swallowed them up. As they blasphemed the great devotee of the Lord, they met their doom in the bowels of the earth. When Śukrācārya, the guru of the demons, told Bali Mahārāja not to give the three steps of land demanded by Vāmana Deva, Bali answered that he was the grandson of Prahlāda Mahārāja. How could he go back on his word like a miser once he had committed himself to giving in charity? He substantiated this by quoting the earth goddess;

na hy asatyāt paro'dharmati hovāca bhūr iyam
sarvaṁ soḍhum alaṁ manye ṛte'līk-aparaṁ naram

"There is no greater irreligiousness than untruth," says the earth goddess, "I can bear any burden other than that of a person who constantly lies." (*Śrīmad Bhāgavatam* 8.20.4)

The servants of the King who had accompanied these robbers were amazed to see them punished for their offense to Jayadeva Gosvāmī right before their very eyes. They came back to the King's palace and told him everything they had witnessed. The King inquired from Jayadeva Gosvāmī about the robbers, and he told the entire story. He said, "O King! A saintly man does not seek revenge from those who have done evil toward him. He attempts to satisfy them with polite behavior. Even so, the Lord's flawless dispensation will make them suffer the consequences of their own sinfulness, as He did in this case."

PADMĀVATĪ IS TESTED

Jayadeva Gosvāmī's wife became a close friend of the Queen. In those days, the practice of sati, where the wife would enter the funeral pyre along with her husband, was an accepted custom. After her brother's death, the Queen was mortified that her sister-in-law would have to die on the funeral pyre with him. Padmāvatī said to the Queen, "A faithful wife's life airs leave her body the very moment her husband dies."

When the Queen heard this, she decided to test Padmāvatī herself. One day she announced to Padmāvatī that her husband Jayadeva Gosvāmī had suddenly died. As soon as this news entered her ears, Padmāvatī gave up her life. This shocked the Queen, and she began to cry out of a sense of guilt for having caused it. The King went to Jayadeva Gosvāmī and begged him to return the life to her. The great devotee Jayadeva Gosvāmī whispered the name of Kṛṣṇa into his wife's ear, and she opened her eyes as though she had just awakened. Upon seeing this manifestation of both Jayadeva Gosvāmī and Padmāvatī's glories, the King and Queen along with their courtiers and servants paid their obeisances at their feet.

JAYADEVA GOSVĀMĪ GOES TO VRINDAVAN

After this, Jayadeva Gosvāmī wished to see Vrindavan. He took leave of the King and Queen and then, taking his deities, Rādhā-Mādhava with him, set off on the long journey. Once in Vrindavan, he began to serve his deities in a spot near Keśī Ghāṭa. When the residents of the Dhāma heard Jayadeva Gosvāmī sing the *Gīta Govinda* in his sweet voice, they were entranced. One merchant built a large temple for the deities on that site.

It is said that Jayadeva Gosvāmī returned to his birthplace in Kenduvilva after living in Vrindavan for many years. He spent the rest of his life there, performing his *bhajana*. He would make the long walk to the Ganges every day to take his bath there. One day, for some reason or other, he was unable to make it. Gaṅgā Devī was so kind to him that she came personally to the village of Kenduvilva so that he could bathe in her holy waters. It is said that he left the body in Kenduvilva, and every year on the first day of the month of Māgha a large festival is held there in his memory.

There is a difference of opinions about where Jayadeva Gosvāmī left this body. Though some say he returned to Kenduvilva, others claim it was Puri, and still others say that he went to Vrindavan. Śrīla Bhaktisiddhānta Sarasvatī Gosvāmī Ṭhākura has stated his opinion that Jayadeva Gosvāmī left this world from Jagannatha Puri. Though some people say that Jayadeva Gosvāmī returned to Kenduvilva to spend his last days, there is no indication anywhere that he brought his Rādhā-Mādhava deities with him. In fact, these deities were taken by the King of Jaipur to a place named Ghati sometime after Jayadeva Gosvāmī's passing away, and they are still being served in the Jaipur area. Jayadeva Gosvāmī's disappearance day is on the sixth day of the waning moon of the month of *Pauṣa*.

Śrī Mādhavendra Purī

Mahāprabhu's seniors, including His parents and gurus, are all his servants and eternal associates, and they take their birth prior to His appearance in order to serve Him in their own way.

Whenever Kṛṣṇa descends to the earth, He first sends down His elders. These include His father, mother, guru and all the other persons He considers to be the objects of His respect. He arranges that these persons should take birth before He does. Mādhavendra Purī, Īśvara Purī, Śacī, Jagannātha Miśra and Advaita Ācārya are amongst those who appeared in this way. (*Caitanya Caritāmṛta* 1.3.92-4)

Later in the *Caitanya Caritāmṛta* (1.13.52-55), the same thing is described in the following way:

"Whenever the son of the king of Vraja decides to appear on earth in order to fulfill a particular desire, then He first sends down His seniors. I will briefly name some of them ,as it is not possible to mention everyone: Śacī Devī, Jagannātha Miśra, Mādhava Purī, Keśava Bhāratī, Īśvara Purī, Advaita Ācārya, Śrīvāsa Paṇḍita, Ācāryaratna, Puṇḍarīka Vidyānidhi, and Haridāsa Ṭhākura."

THE DISCIPLIC SUCCESSION

Śrīla Mādhavendra Purī appeared in the fourteenth century. He was a guru of the Brahma or Madhva *sampradāya*, one of the four (Brahmā, Śrī, Rudra and Sanaka) Vaiṣṇava lineages that purify the world in the Age of Kālī. The Madhva lineage has been described in books like *Gaura-gaṇoddeśa-dīpikā*, *Prameya-ratnāvalī* and the writings of Gopāla Guru Gosvāmī. The mention of this lineage is also to be found in the *Bhakti-ratnākara* (5.2149-2162). The following is taken from the *Gaura-gaṇoddeśa-dīpikā*:

paravyomeśvarasyāsīc chiṣyo brahmā jagat-patiḥ
tasya śiṣyo nārado'bhūt vyāsas tasyāpa śiṣyatām
śuko vyāsasya śiṣyatvaṁ prāpto jñānāvabodhanāt
vyāsāl labdha-kṛṣṇa-dīkṣo madhvācāryo mahāyaśaḥ
tasya śiṣyo'bhavat padmanābhācāryo mahāśayaḥ
tasya śiṣyo naraharis tacchiṣyo mādhava-dvijaḥ
akṣobhyas tasya śiṣyo'bhūt tac-chiṣyo jayatīrthakaḥ
tasya śiṣyo jñāna-sindhus tasya śiṣyo mahānidhiḥ
vidyānidhis tasya śiṣyo rājendras tasya sevakaḥ
jayadharmā munis tasya śiṣyo yad-gaṇa-madhyataḥ
śrīmad-viṣṇu-purī yas tu bhaktiratnāvalī-kṛtiḥ
jayadharmasya śiṣyo'bhūd brahmaṇyaḥ puruṣottamaḥ
vyāsatīrthas tasya śiṣyo yaś cakre viṣṇusaṁhitām
śrīmān lakṣmīpatis tasya śiṣyo bhaktirasāśrayaḥ
tasya śiṣyo mādhavendro yad-dharmo'yaṁ pravartitaḥ
tasya śiṣyo 'bhavat śrīmān īśvarākhya-purī-yatiḥ
kalayāmāsa śṛṅgāraṁ yaḥ śṛṅgāra-phalātmakaḥ
advaitaḥ kalayāmāsa dāsya-sākhye phale ubhe
īśvarākhya-purīṁ gaura urarīkṛtya gaurave
jagad āplāvayāmāsa prākṛtāprākṛtātmakam

"Brahmā, the master of this universe, was the disciple of the Lord of the spiritual world. His disciple was Nārada, and Vyāsa became the disciple of Nārada. Śuka became the disciple of Vyāsa through the endowment of spiritual knowledge. Madhvācārya took initiation in the Kṛṣṇa *mantra* from Vyāsa. His disciple was Padmanābhācārya, whose disciple was Narahari, who was followed by Mādhava Dvijaḥ. Akṣhobhya was his disciple; then Jayatīrtha, Jñānasindhuḥ, Mahānidhi, Vidyānidhiḥ and Rājendra followed. Jayadharmā Muni was one of Rājendra's many disciples, and Viṣṇu Purī, the author of *Bhakti-ratnāvalī*, and Puruṣottama, the lover of *brāhmaṇa* culture became his disciples. Vyāsa Tīrtha, the author of *Viṣṇu-saṁhitā*, was the disciple of Puruṣottama. Lakṣmīpati Tīrtha, a reservoir of devotion, was the disciple of Vyāsa Tīrtha. Mādhavendra Purī was the disciple of Lakṣmīpati, and it is by him that this religion was founded. His disciple the *sannyāsī* Īśvara Purī took up the mood of conjugal devotion, while Advaita Ācārya [also the disciple of Mādhavendra Purī] took up the moods of servitude and friendship. Gaura accepted Īśvara Purī as His guru, and then flooded the material and spiritual worlds [with love]."

Thus, Mādhavendra Purī was the disciple of Lakṣmīpati Tīrtha. Mādhavendra Purī's disciples included Īśvara Purī, Advaita Ācārya, Paramānanda Purī (a *brāhmaṇa* from the Tirhut area), Brahmānanda Purī, Śrī Raṅga Purī, Puṇḍarīka Vidyānidhi, Raghupati Upādhyāya and others. Nityānanda Prabhu is said by some to be Mādhavendra Purī's disciple, others say that Lakṣmīpati was his guru, while in the *Prema-vilāsa* it is said that he was Īśvara Purī's disciple.

Bhaktivinoda Ṭhākura writes: "Mādhavendra Purī was a well-known *sannyāsī* of the Madhva-*sampradāya*. His grand-disciple is Śrī Caitanya Mahāprabhu. Prior to Mādhavendra Purī's appearance, there was no evidence of *prema bhakti* in the Madhva line. In his verse, *ayi dīna-dayārdra-nātha* (*Caitanya Caritāmṛta* 2.4.197), the seed of the religious doctrines of Caitanya Mahāprabhu can be found."

To this, Bhakti Siddhānta Sarasvatī Gosvāmī Prabhupāda adds, "Mādhavendra Purī was the first shoot of the desire tree of divine love which came out of the Madhva lineage. Prior to his appearance, there was no sign of the conjugal mood of devotion in the Madhva line."

MĀDHAVENDRA AND NITYĀNANDA PRABHU

Nityānanda Prabhu met Mādhavendra Purī while wandering through the pilgrimage sites in western India. As soon as they saw each other, they were overcome with the symptoms of ecstatic love. This event is described in the ninth chapter of the *Ādi-khaṇḍa:*

"As Nityānanda Prabhu was wandering (through southern India) in this way, he suddenly encountered Mādhavendra Purī. Mādhavendra Purī was the embodiment of love, as were all his associates. He consumed nothing other than Kṛṣṇa *rasa*, and Kṛṣṇa dwelt in his body. How can I sufficiently glorify him whose disciple was Advaita Ācārya?
When Nityānanda Prabhu saw Mādhavendra Purī, he fainted and became motionless with love. As soon as Mādhava Purī saw Nityānanda Prabhu, he too completely forgot himself and lost consciousness. No wonder Gaurāṅga repeatedly said that Mādhavendra Purī was the harbinger of the ecstatic mood of devotion.

"Nityānanda Prabhu said, 'I have visited many holy sites, but today I have been fulfilled by the sight of Mādhavendra Purī. I have finally achieved the true reward of visiting the holy places. I have never seen the symptoms of such divine love anywhere else. Mādhavendra loses consciousness simply upon seeing a cloud in the sky.'

"Mādhavendra Purī embraced Nityānanda Prabhu and wet him with his tears. He began to describe Nityānanda Prabhu's glories and became completely absorbed in this description. He took Nityānanda Prabhu to his chest, his throat so choked with tears that he could not speak. He felt such deep affection for Nityānanda Prabhu that he would not let him go. He finally spoke, saying, 'I know that Lord Kṛṣṇa is merciful to me, for He has given me a companion like Nityānanda Prabhu. Anyone who feels even the slightest enmity for Nityānanda Prabhu can never be dear to Kṛṣṇa, no matter how much of a devotee he appears to be.' " (*Caitanya Bhāgavata* 1.9.154-169)

The *Bhakti-ratnākara* also describes the glories of Mādhavendra Purī and states that Nityānanda Prabhu treated him as a guru:

"Mādhavendra Purī is the embodiment of ecstatic loving devotion; simply by remembering his name, all perfections are achieved. Īśvara Purī, Raṅga Purī and so many of his other disciples were intoxicated with the loving devotion in the way he was. Mādhavendra Purī had many disciples throughout Bengal and Odisha, all of whom were devotees and fixed in *prema bhakti.*" (*Bhakti-ratnākara* 5.2272-4)

"A few days later, in a holy place on the west coast of India, Nityānanda Prabhu met Mādhavendra Purī. Who can describe the manifestations of love that arose upon their meeting? Only those who were there can know. Mādhavendra Purī treated Nityānanda Prabhu as a friend, an equal, but Nitāi treated him like a superior. Mādhavendra Purī said, 'I know that Kṛṣṇa has been merciful toward me, for he has given me a companion like Nityānanda Prabhu.' On the other hand, Nityānanda Prabhu never treated him as anything but a guru." (*Bhakti-ratnākara* 5.2330-2334)

GIRIDHĀRĪ GOPĀLA

After taking *sannyāsa* in Katwa, Mahāprabhu went to Shantipur and spent some time at Advaita Ācārya's house. Then he proceeded from there to Śrī Puruṣottama (Puri), following the path through Chatrabhoga along the banks of the Ganges. He traveled through Āṭisāra, Pāṇihāṭī, and Varāhanagara until finally He arrived at the border of the kingdom of Utkala (Odisha), at the place called Vṛddha Mantreśvara. Nityānanda Prabhu, Mukunda Datta, Jagadānanda Paṇḍita and Dāmodara Paṇḍita were His companions on this journey. They came to the town of Remuna in the district of Baleshwar, where they visited the deity Kṣīracorā Gopīnātha. Afterward, Mahāprabhu recounted to His companions the story of Mādhavendra Purī as He had heard it from His guru, Īśvara Purī, at the same time telling how Kṣīrcorā Gopīnātha had earned His name:

One day Mādhavendra Purī was circumambulating Govardhan in a state of total intoxication and absorption in love for Kṛṣṇa. When he arrived at Govinda Kuṇḍa, he took his bath and sat down beneath a nearby tree to perform his evening *sandhyā* meditation and rituals. While he was so doing, a young cowherd boy carrying a pot of milk approached him and said with a smile, "What have you been thinking? Why don't you ask for something to eat? I have brought you some milk. Drink it."

When Mādhavendra Purī saw the beautiful lad, he was so amazed that he completely forgot his hunger and thirst. Instead, he asked him, "Who are you? Where do you live? How did you know that I had not eaten?" The cowherd boy answered, "I am a cowherd and I live in this village. In our village, no one ever goes hungry. Some people beg for food, but if someone doesn't ask, then I bring him something to eat. The womenfolk came here to fetch water and saw that you had not eaten. They sent me here with this milk for you. But it is nearly milking time and I will have to leave. I'll come back later to fetch the pot."

Mādhavendra Purī was astonished to see the boy walk away and disappear. He drank the milk and then washed the pot and put it aside, waiting for the cowherd boy to return. He sat under the tree chanting the Holy Names until the end of the night, when he started to doze. While asleep, he had a dream in which the cowherd boy came to him and led him by the hand to a wooded bower. The boy said, "I live here in this bower, but I am very uncomfortable due to the summer heat, the rains and the winter cold. Go and tell the village folk to help you uncover Me, and take Me to the top of the hill and build a shelter for Me. Then bathe me with cool, clear water. I have been waiting for you for a long time, wondering when you would come to serve me. I was waiting for your loving service so that I could show Myself and thereby save the entire universe."

"My name is Gopāla, the lifter of Govardhan. Kṛṣṇa's great grandson, Aniruddha's son Vajra, established My service so many years ago, but the *pūjārī* in charge of My service hid me here when he fled out of fear of the Muslims. Since then I have been here. It is good that you have finally come here. Now please dig Me up."

When Mādhavendra Purī awoke, he began to cry from his intense feelings of love, thinking, "Alas! Kṛṣṇa Himself came to me in the form of a cowherd boy, and I was unable to recognize him!" However, after a few moments he brought himself under control in order to carry out Gopāla's orders. He took his morning bath and then gathered the village folk together and said, "Gopāla, the lifter of Govardhan, is the deity of this village, but He is buried in this bower. Go and bring axes and shovels; we have to dig Him up and release Him."

The village people enthusiastically started to clear the bower and soon discovered a large deity who was covered in earth and weeds. The strongest of the local people lifted the deity up and carried Him to the top of the hill, where they placed Him on a large rock throne. In order to carry out the grand *abhiṣeka* ceremony, the local *brāhmaṇas* had water from Govinda Kuṇḍa filtered and carried to the site in a hundred new jugs. When word got out of the discovery of the deity and it was announced that His *pūjā* and *abhiṣeka* would soon be held, a joyful noise arose in all directions, musicians played on their instruments and the people danced and sang. The mountain was covered with all kinds of offerings, including ghee, milk, yogurt and *sandeśa*, all gifts from the local people.

Mādhavendra Purī himself performed the *abhiṣeka* bathing ceremony. First of all, he cleaned the accumulated dirt from the body of the deity according to the regulations. [The scriptures say that barley and wheat flour, a powder made from *symplocos racemosa*, as well as the powder of pistachio nuts, saffron and pulses, are to be used to clean the deity's body. A brush made from long *uṣīra* grasses and the hair of a cow's tail can also be used.] Afterwards, Gopāla's body was made shiny with oil, and then He was bathed again, first in *pañca-gavya* (milk, yogurt, clarified butter, cow's urine and dung) and then in *pañcāmṛta* (milk, yogurt, clarified butter, honey and sugar). This procedure is described in the *Hari-bhakti-vilāsa*'s sixth chapter, where it is said,

tataḥ śaṅkhabhūtenaiva
kṣīreṇa snapayet kramāt
dadhnā ghṛtena madhunā
khaṇḍena ca pṛthak pṛthak

"First bathe the deity with milk poured from a conch shell, then with yogurt, clarified butter, honey and finally sugar, each one separately." (*Hari-bhakti-vilāsa* 6.30)

After this, Gopāla was bathed with a hundred jugs of water. This was the great bathing ceremony – the *mahā-snāna* – in which ghee and water are used in equal parts, and a total of a hundred seers [approximately a litre] of water are needed. After bathing the deity in this way and then oiling Him once again, Mādhavendra Purī bathed Him in water scented with sandalwood and perfumes poured from a conch. The *Hari-bhakti-vilāsa* prescribes 100 palas[2] of water for the bath, another 25 of oil for the body, and then 2,000 palas for the *mahā-snāna*.

After the *mahā-snāna*, or great bath, was completed, the entire body of the deity was dried with a cloth, and He was dressed in a clean cloth and decorated with sandalwood, Tulasī and flower garlands. Just as Kṛṣṇa instructed the cowherds at the end of the Dvāpara yuga to worship Govardhan with a mountain of foodstuffs, so in the Kālī Yuga, Mādhavendra Purī ordered a mountain of food to be prepared for Giridhārī Gopāla. Ten *brāhmaṇas* were engaged in preparing the rice, another five in cooking vegetable preparations, another five or six *brāhmaṇas* prepared various types of bread, which was all brought together in one place to be heaped up in the shape of a mountain. A pile of rice was surrounded by many clay pots filled with soups, cooked vegetable preparations, milk, yogurt, whey, *śikhariṇī* (a drink made of yogurt, milk, sugar, camphor and pepper), rice pudding, butter, cream, etc. When the mountain of food was ready, Mādhavendra Purī made the offering along with many jugs filled with water. Gopāla, who had not eaten for such a long time, hungrily ate everything He was offered. Even so, by His merciful touch all the pots were again filled. Only Mādhavendra Purī saw how the Lord did this.

Afterwards, Mādhavendra Purī offered the deity a mouthwash and then betel leaf. Then he performed the *ārati* ceremony, after which he brought a new bed for Gopāla to rest upon. When Gopāla was finally taking rest, Mādhavendra Purī fed the *prasāda* of the *anna-kūta* festival, first to all the *brāhmaṇas* and then to all the men, women and children, of the village.

Word spread to all the villages of the area that Gopāla had made His appearance, and people from each village took turns having their own feast on different days in His honor. "The people of Vraja are naturally affectionate

2 A pala is a smaller measure of weight, about equal to 1.5 oz. or 45 grams. 25 palas of oil or ghee is thus about a liter, 2000 palas of water about 80 liters.

toward Kṛṣṇa. And Kṛṣṇa, too, is affectionate to them." (*Caitanya Caritāmṛta* 2.4.95)

In time, the rich *kṣatrīyas* had a temple built for Gopāla and gave Him ten thousand cows. Mādhavendra Purī remained there for two years in Gopāla's service, until one day he again had a dream in which Gopāla told him that He still suffered from the heat and that it was only by smearing Malayaja[3] sandalwood that He would be freed of the problem. Mādhavendra Purī was overjoyed to receive the Lord's direct order and after engaging a qualified person to serve Him, started off on a journey to the east to find Malayaja sandalwood.

Malaya refers to the Malabar Coast in Kerala at the very south of India, in what is known as the Western Ghats. This area is also known as Nilgiri or Malaya Parvata. Sandalwood is so closely associated with this area that the word *malayaja* ("born of Malaya") is a synonym for the perfumed wood.

THE STORY OF KṢĪRACORĀ GOPĪNĀTHA

While on his way to the South, Mādhavendra Purī stopped at Advaita Ācārya's house in Shantipur and initiated him. From there he went on until he arrived at Remuna. Seeing the beautiful deity of Gopīnātha in Remuna, Mādhavendra Purī was overwhelmed with love, and started singing His names and danced for some time in ecstasy. Being extremely satisfied with the exquisite offerings to Gopīnātha, he asked one of Gopīnātha's *brāhmaṇa* servants what foods were offered to the deity. The *brāhmaṇa* answered: "In the evening we give Gopīnātha twelve bowls of *amṛta-keli*, a thickened milk preparation that is like the nectar of the gods. This *kṣīra* is famous everywhere as Gopīnātha's *kṣīra*, and no offering anywhere in the world is its equal." (*Caitanya Caritāmṛta* 2.4.119)

As the *brāhmaṇa* spoke, other servants of Gopīnātha started to make the *amṛta-keli* offering to the deity. Mādhavendra Purī thought that if he could just get a taste of this preparation unsolicited, he would be able to one day make it himself and offer this *kṣīra* to his own Gopāla. However, this very thought of eating the *kṣīra* shamed him. After watching the *ārati* ceremony, Mādhavendra Purī went outside and sat in the empty marketplace, chanting the Holy Names. Mādhavendra Purī followed *ayācaka-vṛtti*, which means that he would never ask for food from anyone and only accepting the food that was spontaneously offered him. He was able to do this because he never felt hunger or thirst, as he was constantly engaged in drinking the nectar of *prema*, and that kept him satisfied.

In the meantime, the *pūjārī* had finished his duties and was taking rest when he had a vision of the deity in a dream. The deity told him,, "Get up! Open the door. I have put a bowl of *kṣīra* aside for the *sannyāsī*. It is hidden

3 Malayaja – Sandalwood from the Malaya mountains, the part of the Western Ghats lying south of Mysore and east of Travancore, the region of Malabar.

behind the pleats of My dhoti. You did not see Me hide the bowl there because of My *māyā*. The *sannyāsī*, whose name is Mādhava Purī, is sitting in the marketplace. Quickly take this *kṣīra* to him." (*Caitanya Caritāmṛta* 2.4.127-129)

The *pūjārī* was startled by the dream and immediately got up. He bathed, opened the door to the altar and found a bowl of the *kṣīra* behind the deity's cloth, just as he had been told. He took the bowl and went to find Mādhavendra Purī. He wandered through the market, shouting, "I have *kṣīra* here for Mādhava Purī. Gopīnātha has stolen it for you. Take it and eat it with joy, for there is no person as fortunate as you in the three worlds." (*Caitanya Caritāmṛta* 2.4.133)

When Mādhavendra Purī heard the *pūjārī* shouting in this way, he approached him and identified himself. The *pūjārī* gave him the *kṣīra* and then fell at his feet. He recounted the whole story to Mādhavendra Purī, sending him into paroxysms of divine love for Lord Kṛṣṇa. He respectfully ate the *prasāda* and then, after washing the clay bowl, broke it into many small pieces and wrapped them up in his outer garment. Each day thereafter, he would eat a piece of the clay bowl and once again feel the same ecstatic love. Knowing that word of this miracle would spread by morning, Mādhavendra Purī became fearful of the celebrity that would inevitably befall him and the crowd of people that would then surround him. So, he paid his obeisance to Gopinātha from that very place and left for Purī before dawn.

When Mādhavendra Purī arrived in Jagannātha Purī, he visited Lord Jagannātha and became ecstatic with love at seeing Him. News of the miracle at Remuna had reached Purī even before he had, and countless people came to see him and pay him their respects. "The nature of fame in this world is well known: even if one does not seek it, it comes anyway as a result of one's destiny. Though Mādhavendra Purī was afraid of being distracted by celebrity and ran away from it, when one has love for God, then celebrity comes flowing to him without being sought." (*Caitanya Caritāmṛta* 2.4.146)

Even though Mādhavendra Purī wanted to flee from there because people were honoring him as a great devotee, he was unable to do so because he was committed to finding the sandalwood he had promised to bring Gopāla. He went to the servants and directors of the Lord Jagannātha temple and explained his mission. Those who had contacts with the king interceded and collected both sandalwood and camphor on Mādhavendra Purī's behalf. They then arranged for another *brāhmaṇa* and a servant to travel with him and to help him carry the load. The king also gave him an official exemption paper to help him avoid customs duties.

On his return route, Mādhavendra Purī stopped in Remuna again. Once again, he danced and sang *kīrtana* before Gopīnātha in a state of loving absorption and accepted the *kṣīra prasāda* from the *pūjārī*. That night he slept in the temple. Once again, he had a vision of Gopāla, who spoke to him as follows: "Listen, Mādhava. I have already received all the sandalwood and camphor. Now grind it into a paste and smear it on Gopīnātha's body. Gopīnātha and I are one and the same person; if you give Him the sandalwood, I will feel the cooling effect. Don't hesitate; don't doubt this message at all. Just believe Me and give Gopīnātha the sandalwood on My order." (*Caitanya Caritāmṛta* 2.4.158-161)

After having this dream, Mādhavendra Purī summoned the servants of Gopīnātha to let them know what Gopāla had told him. The *pūjārīs* were very happy to hear that Gopīnātha would be getting sandalwood paste, as it was the middle of summer. Mādhavendra Purī had his two companions, as well as two other persons from the temple, daily grind the sandalwood into a paste. He stayed in Remuna until it had been used up in Gopīnātha's service. At the end of the summer season, with the coming of the rains, Mādhavendra Purī returned to Purī, where he observed *Cāturmāsya* and demonstrated the exemplary character of his love for Kṛṣṇa.

Gopāla gave Mādhavendra Purī the order to bring sandalwood paste to show the world the depth of his love. It was a great effort for Mādhavendra Purī to bring the sandalwood as far as Remuna, but he experienced it as a joy, not a difficulty. Gopāla gave Mādhavendra Purī this commission in order to test him; but when he passed the test, He was merciful to His devotee. (*Caitanya Caritāmṛta* 2.4.187-189)

THE SANOḌIYA BRĀHMAṆA

Śrī Mādhavendra Purī mercifully bestowed love for Kṛṣṇa on a Sanoḍiya *brāhmaṇa*[4] in Mathura. He accepted food from this *brāhmaṇa*, knowing him to be a Vaiṣṇava. By this, he showed how the *daiva-varṇāśrama* system is meant to operate.

Later on, when Mahāprabhu was traveling in northern India, He went to take food at this Sanoḍiya *brāhmaṇa*'s house between His visits to Kashi and Prayag because he knew that Mādhavendra Purī had been merciful to him. He even showed him the respect that was dueto a senior person, saying, "You are my guru, and I am practically your disciple. It is not fitting for a guru to pay obeisance to a disciple." (*Caitanya Caritāmṛta* 2.17.170)

This was the example that Mahāprabhu exhibited.

ŚRĪ MĀDHAVENDRA PURĪ AND ŚRĪ ĪŚVARA PURĪ

There is another important incident from Mādhavendra Purī's immaculate life left to be told. Rāmacandra Purī and Īśvara Purī were two of Mādhavendra Purī's initiated disciples. However, Rāmacandra Purī was unable to receive his spiritual master's mercy because he showed him disrespect, whereas Īśvara Purī was blessed through his single-minded devotion to him and was thus able to attain the highest level of pure love for Kṛṣṇa. Rāmacandra Purī was unable to understand the sweetness and supremacy of his Gurudeva's feelings of separation and had the audacity to give him advice based on knowledge of Brahman. Mādhavendra Purī became so angry that he shunned him completely. Even though he was such a great loving devotee, Mādhavendra Purī became angry with his own disciple when he became offensive, chastised him severely, using harsh words. When Rāmacandra Purī told him to remember that he was a spiritual being, Mādhavendra Purī became extremely angry and said: "Get away from me, you most sinful rascal! I am dying from the distress of not having received Kṛṣṇa's mercy, of not having attained Mathura, and you come to add to my

4 According to Śrīla Bhaktivinoda Ṭhākura, members of the business community (*vaiśyas*) in the west of India are divided into several castes: Agarwals, Kanwars, and Sanwars. Of these, the Agarwals are considered to be very pure, while the two other groups, who are gold and jewelry merchants, are considered fallen as a result of their own actions. Those *brāhmaṇas* who perform the ritual activities for the Kanwars and Sanwars are known as Sanoḍiya *brāhmaṇas*. Because of their association with these lower castes, they are also considered to be fallen as a caste and *sannyāsīs* refuse to accept food in their homes.

misery! Go wherever you like, but don't show your face to me again! If I see you while I am dying, I will take a lower birth. I am dying from the distress of not having attained Kṛṣṇa, and this lowly fool is teaching me about Brahman."

As a result, Mādhavendra Purī withdrew his blessings from his disciple, who then started to develop *vāsanā* (referring to "the desire for dry knowledge that leads to the tendency to criticize the devotees"). He became a dry philosopher without any interest in Kṛṣṇa. Not only that, but he became critical of everyone, devoting himself to faultfinding. (*Caitanya Caritāmṛta* 3.8.20-25)

Śrīla Prabhupāda Bhakti Siddhānta Sarasvatī Ṭhākura comments on this incident in his *Anubhāṣya*, "Even though Rāmacandra Purī saw his own guru suffering of separation from Kṛṣṇa, he was incapable of recognizing the transcendental nature of his transport of emotions. He judged his guru to be an ordinary man and took his mood to be material, the result of some material insufficiency. As a result, he tried to explain to him the value of experiencing the oneness of Brahmaṇ. Mādhavendra Purī reacted unfavorably to his disciple's stupidity and disregard for his teachings and thus stopped wishing for his well-being. He abandoned him and drove him away."

On the other hand, Īśvara Purī not only adhered to his guru's teaching but served him physically and thus received his mercy. He served the lotus feet of his spiritual master, even to the point of personally cleaning his urine and excrement, as well as helping him to perform *śravaṇa* of Kṛṣṇa's name and pastimes. In this way, he satisfied him completely.

He continuously repeated the name of Kṛṣṇa and recounted Kṛṣṇa's pastimes to him. Mādhavendra Purī was so pleased with Īśvara Purī that he embraced him and blessed him, saying, "May you have the wealth of love for Kṛṣṇa!"

From that time onward, Īśvara Purī became an ocean of love for Kṛṣṇa, while Rāmacandra Purī became a mine of insults. These two personalities thus bear witness to the results of pleasing or displeasing a great soul. Mādhavendra Purī taught this truth through them.

He was the spiritual master of the whole world, and he gave the gift of love of God. He left this world while repeating this verse (from *Padyāvalī*):

ayi dīnadayārdra nātha he
mathurānātha kadāvalokyase
hṛdayaṁ tvad-aloka-kātaraṁ
dayita bhrāmyati kiṁ karomy aham

"O Lord, whose heart softens at seeing the condition of the unfortunate! O Lord of Mathurā, when will I see you? My heart is filled with pain from not seeing you, my love, and I am confused. What can I do?" (*Caitanya Caritāmṛta* 3.8.26-32)

When Mahāprabhu recited this verse, He became so intoxicated with love that Nityānanda Prabhu had to hold Him to calm Him down.

Prabhupāda Bhakti Siddhānta Sarasvatī writes, "The feeling of separation from Kṛṣṇa, or transcendental *vipralambha,* is the only practice by which the spirit soul can achieve perfection. Material feelings of separation give rise to a despondency which reveals the attachment that one has for matter, whereas the despondency that results from the feelings of separation for Kṛṣṇa is the best proof of one's desire to bring pleasure to His senses. The desire to bring pleasure to Kṛṣṇa's senses shown by Mādhavendra Purī, the great soul who is the root of this movement, is the ideal example to follow for anyone who wishes to serve the Lord. It is especially worth remarking that Mahāprabhu and His closest followers later adopted this example and made it their standard."

Mādhavendra Purī's disappearance day is the Śukla Dvādaśī of the month of Phālguna.

Śrī Īśvara Purīpāda

Īśvara Purī was born in the town of Kumar Hatta on the full-moon day of the month of Jyaiṣṭha to a family of *brāhmaṇas* hailing from Rāḍha. Kumar Hatta is in the 24 Paragaṇās district about two miles west of the Hāliśahara train station. Some local people indicate his appearance place to be near the Kālī temple in Mukhopādhāyay Para of Kumar Hatta. Śrīvāsa Paṇḍita and his brothers moved here after Mahāprabhu took *sannyāsa* because they were unable to tolerate all the painful reminders of Him in Nabadwip. The temple ,not far from Caitanya Ḍobā, is indicated to be their residence.

Īśvara Purī's birthplace is popularly known by the name "Caitanya Ḍobā." The word *ḍobā* means "a pool of water." When Caitanya Mahāprabhu passed through Kumar Hatta on His way to Purī, He showed respect for His spiritual master by picking up some earth from the place of his birth, wrapping it in His cloth and taking it with Him. Thousands of pilgrims have since followed His example, thus forming a pit that has since filled with water.

THE MERCY OF THE SPIRITUAL MASTER

Īśvara Purī is a *sannyāsa* name. His name prior to taking *sannyāsa* is unknown. His father's name was Śyāmasundara Ācārya. Īśvara Purī took initiation from Mādhavendra Purī, the embodiment of nectarine devotional love. Mādhavendra Purī was pleased with Īśvara Purī's guileless, sincere and loving service and thus showered him with blessings so that he too became immersed in the ocean of love for Kṛṣṇa. If a disciple can satisfy his spiritual master, then he will be fortunate and attain all auspiciousness and the fulfillment of all his desires. On the other hand, if the guru is unhappy with his disciple, then he will only know inauspiciousness. These teachings have been highlighted in the exemplary life of Mādhavendra Purī.

Rāmacandra Purī was another of Mādhavendra Purī's initiated disciples, but because of his arrogance, he was bereft of his guru's grace. Kṛṣṇadāsa Kavirāja has described the incident with great beauty in the *Caitanya Caritāmṛta* (3.8.16-30) as follows:

Previously, when Mādhavendra Purī was showing pastimes of sickness, Rāmacandra Purī came to see him. Mādhavendra Purī was singing the names of the Lord and crying out, "I have not attained Mathura!" Rāmacandra then began to instruct him without compunction even though he was a disciple. He said, "Remember that you are completely full of the bliss of Brahman. Why are you crying like this despite being knowledgeable of your own Brahman nature?"

When Mādhavendra Purī heard this, he became angry and began to rebuke Rāmacandra, saying, "Get away, get away, you most sinful rascal! I am dying from the distress of not having received Kṛṣṇa's mercy, of not having attained Mathura, and you come to add to my misery! Go wherever you like, but don't show your face to me again! If I see you while I am dying, I will take a lower birth. I am dying from the distress of not having attained

Kṛṣṇa and this lowly fool is teaching me about Brahman."

As a result, Mādhavendra Purī withdrew his blessings from his disciple, who thenceforth started to develop material desires. He became a dry philosopher without any interest in Kṛṣṇa. Not only that, but he became critical of everyone and devoted himself to faultfinding.

Īśvara Purī, on the other hand, served his guru, even personally cleaning his urine and faeces. He continuously repeated the name of Kṛṣṇa and recounted Kṛṣṇa's pastimes. Mādhavendra Purī was so pleased with Īśvara Purī that he embraced and blessed him, saying, "May you have the treasure of love for Kṛṣṇa!"

From that time onward, Īśvara Purī became an ocean of love for Kṛṣṇa, while Rāmacandra Purī became a mine of insults. These two personalities thus bear witness to the results of pleasing or displeasing a great soul. Mādhavendra Purī taught this truth through them.

In this connection, Śrīla Bhakti Siddhānta Sarasvatī Gosvāmī Prabhupāda has written in his *Anubhāṣya*, "Even though Rāmacandra Purī saw his own guru suffering of separation from Kṛṣṇa, he was incapable of recognizing the transcendental nature of this transport of emotions. He judged his guru to be an ordinary man and took his mood to be mundane, the result of some material insufficiency. As a result, he tried to explain to him the value of experiencing the oneness of Brahman. Mādhavendra Purī reacted to his disciple's stupidity and disregard for his instructions and thus stopped wishing for his welfare. He abandoned him and drove him away."

MAHĀPRABHU TAKES INITIATION FROM ĪŚVARA PURĪ

Mahāprabhu is the Supreme Personality of Godhead and has no need of any teacher. Even so, He wishes to teach that it is absolutely necessary to take shelter of a bona fide spiritual master. For this reason, He played the role of a disciple, taking initiation from Īśvara Purī when He met him at Gaya. This in itself shows beyond a doubt Īśvara Purī's greatness and importance.

"Then the Lord went to Gaya, where He met Īśvara Purī. After taking initiation from him, He started to display the signs of love of God, and when He returned to His homeland, He began to engage in the pastimes of divine love." (*Caitanya Caritāmṛta* 1.17.8-9)

When they met, Mahāprabhu and Īśvara Purī were overcome by the ecstasy of love and drenched each other in the tears of *prema* that fell from their eyes. The Lord said, "My pilgrimage to Gaya is successful, for today I have seen your lotus feet. When one makes the *piṇḍa* (offering to the ancestors at a holy place), then that ancestor is delivered. But simply by one's seeing you, ten million ancestors are delivered from all forms of bondage in a single moment. Therefore, no holy place is your equal, and you are the primary source of auspiciousness for even the holy places. Please lift Me up from the ocean of material suffering; I offer this body up to your service. The only gift I ask for

is that you give Me the nectar of Kṛṣṇa's lotus feet to drink." (*Caitanya Bhāgavata* 1.17.49-55)

Mahāprabhu was acting the role of an ordinary mortal, a pilgrim who had come to Gaya to offer the *śrāddha* oblations for His deceased father. On the day that He had performed these rituals, He returned to His room and began to cook. When Īśvara Purī came and placed his holy feet in Mahāprabhu's room, Mahāprabhu personally served him the rice and vegetables that He Himself had cooked with great satisfaction. In so doing, Mahāprabhu demonstrated most perfectly how to serve the guru.

ĪŚVARA PURĪ IN NABADWIP

Īśvara Purī had met Mahāprabhu in Nabadwip even prior to giving him the ten-syllable *mantra* in Gaya. He had also met with Advaita Ācārya, who had similarly played the role of Mādhavendra Purī's disciple. Vṛndāvana Dāsa Ṭhākura has described this meeting in the *Caitanya Bhāgavata.*

Once Īśvara Purī passed through Nabadwip when Nimāi was still engaged in His pastimes as a student. He stayed there for a few months in the house of Gopīnātha Ācārya as his guest. One day he saw Nimāi and was most impressed and attracted by His bodily beauty. Nimāi invited Īśvara Purī to His house to eat and had His Mother Śacī cook and serve him Kṛṣṇa *prasāda.* Then He and Īśvara Purī began talking about Kṛṣṇa.

Īśvara Purī also met Gadādhara Paṇḍita and was pleased when he saw the depth of his renunciation and pure love for Kṛṣṇa. He started to affectionately give him lessons from *Śrī-Kṛṣṇa-līlāmṛta,* a book of his own composition. Nimāi would also come daily to visit Īśvara Purī while he was teaching Gadādhara and offer him His obeisance. One day, Īśvara Purīpāda asked Nimāi to correct any mistakes that were in his book. Nimāi answered:

"Anyone who finds any fault with a devotee's description of Kṛṣṇa is a sinner. If a devotee writes a poem, no matter how poorly he does it, it will certainly contain his love for Kṛṣṇa. A fool says *viṣṇāya* while a scholar knows the correct form is *viṣṇave,* but Kṛṣṇa accepts the sentiment in either case. If anyone sees a fault in this, the fault is his, for Kṛṣṇa is pleased with anything the pure devotee says. You too describe the Lord with words of love, so what arrogant person would dare criticize anything that you have written?" (*Caitanya Bhāgavata* 1.11.105-110)

The same incident is described in the *Bhakti-ratnākara* (12.2205-7) in the following way:

"Look here; this is the house of Gopīnātha Ācārya, where Viśvambhara would visit from time to time. Īśvara Purī stayed here for a while and composed his book *Śri-Kṛṣṇa-līlāmṛta.* He had great affection for Gadādhara Paṇḍita, and when he saw the symptoms of love for Kṛṣṇa in him, he taught him that book."

"When Nityānanda Prabhu was traveling in the west of India, he incidentally met Mādhavendra Purī. When the two met, they fainted. Nityānanda Prabhu was overcome by love and started to describe Mādhavendra Purī's glories, and Mādhavendra Purī himself embraced Nityānanda Prabhu and wet him with his tears. Īśvara Purīpāda understood that Nityānanda Prabhu was extremely dear to his spiritual master and so, like his guru's other disciples, held him in great affection and felt a deep love for him."

"All glories to Mādhava Purī, the ocean of love for Kṛṣṇa! He was the first shoot of the desire tree of devotion. That first shoot was nourished and grew in the form of Īśvara Purī, and from him the thick trunk of Caitanya *līlā* took shape. (*Caitanya Caritāmṛta* 1.9.10-11)

Before he left this world, Īśvara Purī sent two of his disciples, Kāśīśvara and Govinda, to serve Mahāprabhu. Even though they were His godbrothers, Mahāprabhu still obeyed the order of His spiritual master and accepted them as His servants.

Śrī Raṅga Purī

"Mahāprabhu met Śrī Raṅga Purī and put an end to the sufferings of Rāma Dāsa." (*Caitanya Caritāmṛta* 2.1.113)

During His travels through South India, Mahāprabhu came to the town Pandarpur on the banks of the Bhima River. Pandarpur is in the Sholapur district of Maharashtra about 38 miles west of Sholapur and is the home of the four-armed deity of Nārāyaṇa, Vitṭhala, or Viṭhavā deva. Pandarpur is also well known as the home of the famous Vaiṣṇava saint Tūkārāma, who lived there in the fifteenth century of the Śaka era. (*Anubhāṣya* 2.9.282)

While in Pandarpur, Mahāprabhu was invited by a *brāhmaṇa* to his home, where He was lavishly fed. While there, He heard that Mādhavendra Purī's disciple Śrī Raṅga Purī was staying nearby in another *brāhmaṇa's* house. Mahāprabhu immediately went there to meet him. He prostrated Himself before his guru's godbrother and was immediately inspired by a mood of ecstatic love. Śrī Raṅga Purī was also impressed by the sight of Mahāprabhu's ecstatic symptoms and guessed that the Lord must have some relation to the spirit of devotion promulgated by his own spiritual master, without which such symptoms would be impossible. He lifted the Lord up and embraced Him, and the two of them began to cry in devotional ecstasy.

Kṛṣṇadāsa Kavirāja's account of this meeting is given as follows:

"From there Śrī Caitanya Mahāprabhu went to Pandarpur, where He joyfully saw the deity of Vitṭhala Ṭhākura. A local *brāhmaṇa* was delighted when he saw the Lord chanting and dancing in ecstatic love and invited Him to his home for lunch. The *brāhmaṇa* offered Mahāprabhu food with great respect and love. After the Lord finished His lunch, He heard the auspicious news that Śrī Raṅga Purī, one of Śrī Mādhavendra Purī's disciples, was currently residing at the home of another *brāhmaṇa*. The Lord immediately went to that *brāhmaṇa's* home and, upon entering, saw Śrī Raṅga Purī. He was overwhelmed with ecstatic love and prostrated Himself in obeisance. All the symptoms of ecstatic transformation were visible in His body – tears, jubilation, trembling and perspiration." (*Caitanya Caritāmṛta* 2.9.282-7)

Upon learning that Mahāprabhu was Īśvara Purīpāda's disciple, Śrī Raṅga Purī was filled with great affection for him. Just by touching each other, they were both flooded with ecstatic feelings. They passed seven days together in discussions of Kṛṣṇa consciousness. Śrī Raṅga Purī was overjoyed to hear that the Lord's birthplace was in Nabadwip. He told the Lord that he had previously been to Nabadwip with his spiritual master and that they had eaten at Jagannātha Miśra's house. He recalled that Jagannātha Miśra's wife, Śacī had fed them a delicious banana flower curry. The Mother of the Universe, Śacīdevī, had served the *sannyāsīs* as though they were her own sons. Śrī Raṅga Purī continued to tell Mahāprabhu that Śacī Devī and Jagannātha Miśra had a worthy son who had taken *sannyāsa*, taking on the name Śaṅkarāraṇya, but who had left the body in Pandarpur.

Upon hearing all this, Mahāprabhu was overcome with feelings of separation, and He told Śrī Raṅga Purī that Śaṅkarāraṇya was His very own elder brother and that Jagannātha Miśra and Śacī Devī were His father and mother. Mahāprabhu and Śrī Raṅga Purī discussed their favorite topics (*iṣṭagoṣṭhī)* for several days. Śrī Raṅga Purī went on to Dwarka after that.

"Mādhavendra Purī is an abode of divine loving sentiments. Simply by remembering his name one achieves all perfection. All of his disciples, such as Īśvara Purī and Śrī Raṅga Purī, were similarly intoxicated with moods of sacred rapture." (*Bhakti-ratnākara* 5.2272-3)

Some people say that Śrī Raṅga Purī later came to Jagannatha Puri to join the Lord and spend the remainder of his life in His association.

Śrī Jagannātha Miśra

Jagannāth Miśra was born in the village of South Dhaka in Sylhet. His grandfather, Madhu Miśra, had four sons: Upendra, Raṅgada, Kīrtida and Kīrtivāsa. His father and mother, Upendra Miśra and Kalāvātī, had seven sons: Kaṁsāri, Paramānanda, Padmanābha, Sarveśvara, Jagannātha Miśra, Janārdana and Trailokyanātha. (*Prema-vilāsa*, 24)

purā yaśodā-vrajarāja-nandau
vṛndāvane prema-rasākarau yau
śacī-jagannāth-purandarābhidhau
babhūvatus tau na ca saṁśayo'tra
amū āviśatām eva devāvaditi-kaśyapau
śrī-kauśalyā-daśarathau tathā śrī-pṛṣṇi-tatpatī
(*Gaura-gaṇoddeśa-dīpikā* 37-8)

According to the *Gaura-gaṇoddeśa-dīpikā*, Upendra Miśra was formerly Kṛṣṇa's grandfather, the cowherd Parjanya. Jagannātha Miśra was Nanda Mahārāja in Kṛṣṇa's Vraja pastimes, and he was Kāśyapa, Daśaratha, Sutapā and Vasudeva in the other *avatāras* of the Lord.

"The King of Vraja has become Caitanya's father, Jagannātha Miśra; the Queen of Vraja is His mother, Śacī. The son of Nanda is Caitanya Gosāi, and His brother, Baladeva, is Nityānanda Prabhu." (*Caitanya Caritāmṛta* 1.17.294-295)

Caitanya Caritāmṛta also states that Jagannātha Miśra, an ocean of virtues, was also known by his title Purandara, which is an epithet of Indra. His devoted wife Śacīdevī's father was Nīlāmbara Cakravartī. (*Caitanya Caritāmṛta* 1.13.59-60)

THE APPEARANCE OF MAHĀPRABHU

At first, eight baby girls were born to Jagannātha Miśra and Śacīdevī, but each of them died at birth. Jagannātha Miśra then performed a special ceremony to have a son, and not long afterwards a boy, Viśvarūpa, appeared. Viśvarūpa is a manifestation of Baladeva and belongs to the same ontological category, named Saṅkarṣaṇa, in the spiritual world. Viśvarūpa took *sannyāsa* at the age of twelve, adopting the name Śaṅkarāraṇya. He left this world in the year 1510 in Pandarpur, in the Solapur district of Maharashtra.

Jagannātha Miśra and Śacīdevi are eternally liberated companions of Kṛṣṇa; thus, it is clear that their heart and body are made of pure goodness, or *śuddha-sattva*. Another name for pure goodness is *vasudeva*. Kṛṣṇa is named Vāsudeva because He takes pleasure in the spiritual nature and makes His appearance through pure goodness, or *vasudeva*.

At sundown on the full-moon day of the month of Phālguna in 1486, at the auspicious moment of a lunar eclipse, amidst the joyful sounds that filled the sky the cries of "Hari!" and "Kṛṣṇa!" made by the town people, the *ulu-dhvanī* of the womenfolk and the divine

instruments of the gods in heaven – Gaurāṅga Mahāprabhu accepted Jagannātha Miśra and Śacīdevī as His father and mother and appeared in the holy *dhāma* of Śrī Mayapur.

It is said that witches, evil female spirits and other powerful demonic spectres cannot go near a neem tree. Out of their feelings of maternal love, Śacī and the other women named the Lord Nimāi in order that He be protected from any inauspiciousness. Later, when Nimāi took the renounced order of life, he was given the name Śrī Kṛṣṇa Caitanya. Some of the other names by which He is known are Viśvambhara, Nabadwip Candra, Gaura Hari, and Gaurāṅga.

When Śacī and Jagannātha Miśra saw their child's face, they forgot themselves in their excitement. Nīlāmbara Cakravartī was a great astrologer, and when he examined the constellations at the baby's birth, he announced that He would be a king among kings, that He would possess all divine virtues, indeed that He is Nārāyaṇa Himself. Jagannātha Miśra and his entire household were immersed in the ocean of ecstasy upon hearing these predictions.

This ocean only increased in fullness as the baby Nimāi began to display His childhood pastimes. Whenever Nimāi cried, the adults would sing the Holy Names in order to pacify Him. When He was only four months old, He started throwing various household articles about, but as soon as He caught sight of His Mother He would lie down and start to cry. Mother Śacī would sing the Holy Names to stop Him from crying, and only when He had stopped would she notice the mess the baby had made of the room. Because He was so young, she never suspected him of creating the disorder; rather, she thought that it must have been some evil spirit whose efforts to harm the baby had failed due to the protective incantations she was always making over Him.

When the time came for Nimāi's name-giving ceremony, Nīlāmbara Cakravartī and other learned men in the community called Him Viśvambhara, which is thus His principal name, while the women gave Him the name Nimāi. This latter name was given because neem leaves have a bitter taste and are said to keep death away, and they wished to bless Nimāi with a long life. The name-giving ceremony is also the occasion when a child's tastes and tendencies are tested. Jagannātha placed rice, puffed rice, gold, silver and a manuscript of the *Śrīmad Bhāgavatam* before the child, who ignored everything to reach out for the holy scripture. All were delighted by Nimāi's choice. The learned scholars began to say, "Viśvambhara will become a great Vaiṣṇava in the future, and by His ascendancy in Viṣṇu *bhakti,* He will attain exceptional scholarship in all the scriptures." The womenfolk began to say, "Nimāi will be a great scholar." In fact, Nimāi wished to show, even at this young age, that *Śrīmad Bhāgavatam* is the supreme authority in spiritual matters. This is the teaching hidden within this pastime.

NIMĀI'S CHILDHOOD

As Nimāi grew, He began to crawl, giving pleasure to His mother and father and all their neighbors. One day, the child saw Lord Śeṣa in the form of a cobra in the garden. He played with him for a while in the mood of Gaura Nārāyaṇa, and then like Śeṣaśāyī curled up on the coiled snake and fell asleep. When Jagannātha Miśra came upon this scene, he feared the worst for the child and started to shout and cry, frightening the serpent, which then slithered away. Nevertheless, Śacī and Jagannātha Miśra had seen the wondrous form that the child had displayed and became convinced that He was a divine personality.

The neighborhood women found that whenever they loudly chanted the names of the Lord, Nimāi would stop crying and start dancing in ecstasy, even rolling about in the dust. So every morning they would surround Him and sing the Holy Names. Whether they knew Him or not, people would be attracted by His beautiful appearance and would affectionately give Him *sandeśa* sweets or bananas. Nimāi would take all these sweets and fruits and give them as *prasāda* to the women who sang for Him.

When Nimāi was able to walk, He would go into the neighbors' houses and take milk and rice, and if He found nothing to eat, He would break various household items. This naughty behavior is a source of delight for His devotees. On one occasion, as Nimāi was playing in front of Jagannātha Miśra's house, two thieves saw that He was wearing valuable ornaments and became greedy. They charmed the child by offering Him a ride on their shoulders and then started to carry Him away. However, they were bewildered by Viṣṇu's illusory power and shortly they found themselves back in front of Nimāi's own home. Frightened by this unexpected turn of events, the two scoundrels ran away. Meanwhile, Jagannātha Miśra had been searching anxiously for Nimāi. When he saw that his child had returned, he held Him tightly to his heart and felt as though his life had also been returned to him.

One day, Jagannātha Miśra asked Nimāi to bring him a book from inside the house. When Nimāi ran to fetch it, Śacī and Jagannātha Miśra were surprised to hear the wondrous jingling of ankle bells. After Nimāi had given His father the book and gone off to play, they were amazed to see that His footprints held the auspicious signs of the flag, the lightning bolt, the elephant rod and banner. Under the influence of their parental love, Jagannātha

Miśra and Śacī were not able to accept that these were Nimāi's own footprints, but took them rather be the traces of Dāmodara, their household Śālagrāma-śilā deity, and so they did a special ceremony for the deity, bathing Him, performing the *pūjā* and offering food.

BABY NIMĀI STEALS GOPĀLA'S OFFERINGS

On another day, a *brāhmaṇa* pilgrim passed through Nabadwip with Bāla Gopāla, his deity of the baby Kṛṣṇa. Jagannātha Miśra offered the *brāhmaṇa* a place to perform his *pūjā* as well as food to cook for an offering. When the pilgrim had finished cooking, he sat down to offer the *bhoga* to his deity. But as soon as he started meditation on his *mantra*, Nimāi came and began eating the offering. The *brāhmaṇa* saw this and started to shout in distress. Jagannātha Miśra was extremely disturbed by the incident, and the *brāhmaṇa* had to intercede to stop him from giving the child a spanking.

Although the *brāhmaṇa* did not want to cook again, Jagannātha Miśra begged him to do so. Before he recommenced preparing the offering, Jagannātha Miśra took Nimāi to a neighbor's house so that He would not do any more mischief. Once again, when the *brāhmaṇa* sat down to meditate on his Bāla Gopāla *mantra* to make his offering, Gaura Gopāla appeared out of nowhere and started to enjoy the foodstuffs. The *brāhmaṇa* again began to shout in frustration, "Everything's ruined. Everything's ruined!" For a second time, Jagannātha Miśra was devastated and once again was about to punish the child, only to be stopped by his guest. The *brāhmaṇa* said, "He's only a child and doesn't understand anything. It's not His fault. It seems that it is not my destiny to eat today."

This time, Nimāi's older brother, Viśvarūpa, begged the *brāhmaṇa* to try a third time, and so finally, on his insistence, he began to cook again. This time it was quite late at night and Nimāi was fast asleep in His room, so no one suspected any trouble. Even so, the *brāhmaṇa* waited until the entire household had gone to bed before making his offering; but once again, contrary to all expectation, Gaura Gopāla came to accept the offering. This time, however, He gave the *brāhmaṇa* a vision of an extraordinary eight-armed form. In four of these hands, He held the conch, discus, mace and lotus flower of Nārāyaṇa; but in the palm of another hand, He held a lump of butter from which He was taking morsels with another hand. The last two hands were engaged in playing the flute. When the pilgrim *brāhmaṇa* saw this wonderful vision, he fainted away completely.

When he came to consciousness, Nimāi told him not to reveal this pastime to anyone. He told him, "You have been My servant for many, many births. This very same pastime also took place at Nanda's house in Gokula."

Every day after finishing his daily activities, he would return to Nimāi's house to behold his worshipable Lord.

NIMĀI'S EDUCATION

Nimāi underwent the three rituals (*saṁskāras*) in which a child's ears are pierced, his hair is shorn and his education is begun. It took Nimāi only three days to learn the entire alphabet, and He started to read and write all of Kṛṣṇa's names.

Little Gaura Gopāla would often ask His parents to bring Him birds, even the stars or the moon, and would cry if they could not do so. When they chanted the Holy Names, He would stop crying; otherwise, there was no way to quiet Him. One day, however, though they repeatedly sang the names of Hari, the child's tears did not stop flowing. When pressed to tell them why He was crying so insistently, Nimāi said that though it was *Ekādaśī*, He wanted to eat the offerings that the *brāhmaṇas* Jagadīśa and Hiraṇya had made to their Viṣṇu deity. Jagannātha Miśra was astonished to hear this unusual request but went to the house of his two friends. He told them the whole story, and they were delighted to give him the offering. When Jagannātha Miśra brought the offering home and gave it to Nimāi, He finally stopped crying.

Nimāi continued His naughty behavior, and the gents in the community reported it to His father, while the girls and women would complain to Śacī. Though His father would be angry and want to punish his child, he would be quite astonished to see Him completely calm and free from any guilty demeanor. Both parents wondered, "Who is this child? Has Nandanandana Kṛṣṇa secretly appeared here as our son?"

Viśvambhara's older brother, Viśvarūpa, had been indifferent to material life since his childhood. After studying at Advaita Ācārya's school (*tol*), he came to understand that the ultimate conclusion of the scriptures was devotion to Kṛṣṇa. When he was twelve years old, his parents started making arrangements for his marriage, so he left home and was initiated as a *sannyāsī*, taking the name Śaṅkarāraṇya. This event traumatized Śacī and Jagannātha Miśra, who were greatly pained by their separation from their oldest son. As a result, Jagannātha Miśra was afraid that Nimāi too would become indifferent to family life through studying the scriptures, so he stopped His education. Better that He should remain a fool at home than become a scholar only to abandon His family!

This decision did not please Nimāi, and He started to misbehave again. One day, He went and sat down in the rubbish heap where used and contaminated pottery was thrown. When Śacī saw this, she became angry and told Him several times to leave that filthy area. Nimāi answered her in the spirit of the divine master Dattātreya; "How can a fool tell the difference between what is pure and what is not? How can the pots that have been used to cook for Viṣṇu possibly be contaminated? What is more, how can any place be impure if I am there? Ideas of purity and impurity from the *karma-kāṇḍa* that lack devotion to the Lord is just the imagination of materialistic people."

Seeing that the boy would in no way heed her order to leave the unclean spot, Śacī finally dragged Him away and made Him bathe and then took a bath herself. After this, she and other members of the community approached Jagannātha Miśra and entreated him to allow Nimāi to resume His studies. Thus Jagannātha Miśra was forced to relent.

Sometime after this, Nimāi's sacred thread ceremony was held. After the fire sacrifice, Nimāi went out to beg alms, just as Lord Vāmana did earlier. Jagannātha Miśra then entrusted Him to Gaṅgā Dāsa Paṇḍita, who is none other than the same Sāndīpani Muni who gave Kṛṣṇa His education. Gaṅgā Dāsa Paṇḍita was overjoyed to accept the handsome and virtuous child as his student. Nimāi would ask him and his fellow students trick questions based on logic, and the ensuing arguments would be a source of amazement to everyone.

Jagannātha Miśra was pleased to see his son take up a disciplined life in which He would bathe daily in the Ganges, perform *pūjā* to Viṣṇu strictly according to the regulations, and offer water to the sacred Tulasī plant before finally taking *prasāda*. Nimāi would then go to a place where He could be undisturbed and study. Jagannātha Miśra prayed to Kṛṣṇa for Nimāi's continued welfare, but at the same time was always afraid that He would come to understand the emptiness of the cycle of *saṁsāra* and eventually leave home. One day, Jagannātha Miśra had a dream in which he saw Mahāprabhu's beautiful form as a *sannyāsī*, performing *saṅkīrtana*, dancing, singing, laughing and crying, while surrounded by His devotees. After this, he began to think it inevitable that Nimāi would one day leave home. Śacīdevī tried to convince Jagannātha Miśra that because Nimāi had become so attached to His studies, He would never leave, but she failed. As it happened, Nimāi's father left this world before He became a *sannyāsī*. On the disappearance of His father, Gaurasundara lamented just as Rāmacandra did upon hearing of the disappearance of King Daśaratha (due to separation from a devotee), but still showed great strength of character to console His heartbroken mother.

Śrīla Jagadīśa Paṇḍita

apare yajña-patnau śrī-jagadīśa-hiraṇyakau
ekādaśyāṁ yayor annaṁ
prārthayitvā'ghasat prabhuḥ

"The wives of the sacrificing *brāhmaṇas* in Vraja took birth as Jagadīśa and Hiraṇya. The Lord (Mahāprabhu) asked for and ate their *prasāda* on the Ekādaśī day." (*Gaura-gaṇoddeśa-dīpikā* 192)

āsīd vraje chandrahāso nartako rasa-kovidaḥ
so'yaṁ nṛtya-vinodī śrī-jagadīśākhyaḥ paṇḍitaḥ

"In Vraja, there was a dancer named Candrahāsa who was very expert in the tasting of *rasa*. In Caitanya *līlā*, he became Jagadīśa Paṇḍita who also took great pleasure in dancing for the Lord." (*Gaura-gaṇoddeśa-dīpikā* 143)

Jagadīśa Paṇḍita is considered to be simultaneously both Nityānanda-*śākhā* and Caitanya-*śākhā*, a branch of both Caitanya as well as Nityānanda Prabhu in the desire tree of devotion. He was born in the town of Guwahati (Pragjyotishpur) in East India. His father's name was Kamalākṣa Bhaṭṭa. Both of his parents were devotees of Viṣṇu. When they left the world, he came with his wife, Duḥkhinī, and his brother Hiraṇya to Mayapur, on the shores of the Gaṅgā, where they built a home near that of Jagannātha Miśra. Jagadīśa Paṇḍita was a very close friend of Jagannātha Miśra.

Jagadīśa and his wife, Duḥkhinī, had the same kind of parental affection for the little Nimāi as Jagannātha Miśra and Śacī Devī themselves. Duḥkhinī was like a mother to Him and even sometimes acted as His wet-nurse. Nimāi, the son of Śacī, is none other

than the son of Yaśodā, the Supreme Lord Kṛṣṇa. It is not possible for anyone but an eternal associate of the Lord to have the good fortune to treat Him like a son in this way.

NIMĀI BEGS FOR JAGADĪŚA'S OFFERING

Mahāprabhu showed through His pastimes just how dear He considered Jagadīśa Paṇḍita to be. Śrīmān Mahāprabhu is the father of *saṅkīrtana*, and even as a child He tricked everyone into chanting the Holy Names. Śacī and all the other neighbors would clap their hands and sing the names of the Lord in order to make Him stop crying. On Ekādaśī day, however, Nimāi kept on crying despite Śacī Mātā and Jagannātha Miśra's chanting the Names in the usual way. Confused and anxious, His parents finally asked Him out of desperation, "What do You want, child? What must we give You to make You stop crying?"

Nimāi answered, "They have made a rice offering to Lord Viṣṇu at Jagadīśa Paṇḍita's house. I want to eat some of that *prasāda*. Give Me some of that *prasāda*, and I will stop crying."

Jagannātha Miśra was amazed to hear Nimāi say such things. How could He know that Jagadīśa Paṇḍita was making a rice offering on Ekādaśī? Jagannātha Miśra immediately went to his neighbor's house and was surprised to see that a large offering of rice and other dishes had indeed been made to their Viṣṇu deity. Jagannātha Miśra told Jagadīśa Paṇḍita of Nimāi's request, adding that he was worried that it would not be correct for Him to eat rice on Ekādaśī day. But Gaurāṅga's eternal associate Jagadīśa Paṇḍita knew that this was little Gopāla in the form of Nimāi who was hungry. Without any hesitation, he gave the entire offering to Jagannātha Miśra. As soon as Nimāi received the plate, He immediately stopped crying and joyfully started to eat.

"The merciful Lord gave Jagadīśa Paṇḍit and Hiraṇya Paṇḍita His grace when He was a little boy. He ate the offerings to Viṣṇu at their house on the Ekādaśī day." (*Caitanya Caritāmṛta* 1.10.70-71)

"Jagadīśa Paṇḍita purifies the entire universe because the nectar of love for Kṛṣṇa pours from him like torrents of rain." (*Caitanya Caritāmṛta* 1.11.30)

The above-mentioned pastime is described in the *Caitanya Bhāgavata*, *Ādi-khaṇḍa*, chapter 4.

The Lord grabs the things of the devotee even if he doesn't offer them, but He shows no interest whatsoever in the gifts of the nondevotee.

Just as Mahāprabhu was conquered by the devotion of Jagadīśa Paṇḍita, so too was His dearest companion Nityānanda *Prabhu* who considered him to be one of His own intimate associates. Nityānanda Prabhu was Jagadīśa Paṇḍitas' life and soul. Jagadīśa Paṇḍita was present in Panihati for the Ciḍa-dadhi Mahotsava (the great-chipped rice and yogurt festival).

JAGADĪŚA AND LORD JAGANNĀTHA

Before taking *sannyāsa*, Mahāprabhu ordered Jagadīśa Paṇḍita to go to Nilachal to preach Kṛṣṇa *bhakti* and the religious practice of the age, *harināma-saṅkīrtana*. The son of Nanda, Śrī Kṛṣṇa, and the son of Jagannātha Miśra, Śrī Gaurasundara, are the same supreme divinity as Lord Jagannātha. When Jagadīśa Paṇḍita arrived in Puri, he went for Lord Jagannātha's *darśana* and melted with love when he saw Him. On his way back to Bengal, however, he felt extreme separation from Lord Jagannātha. Thousands and thousands of people go on pilgrimage to Puri every single day. All of them take *darśana* of Lord Jagannātha, but how many of them are overcome by feelings of separation when returning home? Perhaps once in a while, some fortunate individual is able to feel such emotions. If one truly feels such pangs of separation, then this is a sign of Lord Jagannātha's mercy; if not, then one has not truly received the grace of the Lord.

Lord Jagannātha saw Jagadīśa Paṇḍita crying and so mercifully appeared to him in a dream and told him to serve His vigraha. Simultaneously, He appeared to the King of Odisha and ordered him that at the time of the *nava-kalevara,* when the wooden deity of Lord Jagannātha is renewed, the outgoing form should be given to Jagadīśa Paṇḍita. As a result of this dream, the King felt greatly honored to meet Jagadīśa Paṇḍita and gave him Lord Jagannātha's outgoing form, which is known as the *samādhi-stha-vigraha.*

Jagadīśa Paṇḍita prayed to Lord Jagannātha, asking Him just how he could possibly carry the heavy figure of the deity all the way back to Bengal. Lord Jagannātha answered him that for his sake He would become as light as a cork. Then Jagadīśa was to cover Him with a new cloth and then carry Him suspended at the end of a staff. Lord Jagannātha farther told him that he would have to make permanent arrangements to stay wherever He was set down on the ground. Jagadīśa Paṇḍita Prabhu took the aid of two *brāhmaṇas* to carry Lord Jagannātha as far as the village of Jashora, on the banks of the Ganges, near the town of Chakdah. Jagadīśa Paṇḍita left Lord Jagannātha with one of the *brāhmaṇas* and went to take his bath in the Ganges and to perform oblations of Gaṅgā water. While he was gone, the *brāhmaṇa* found that Lord Jagannātha was suddenly becoming very heavy and that he was no longer able to hold Him up. When Jagadīśa Paṇḍita came back from his bath, he saw Lord Jagannātha sitting on the ground and realized that the Lord wanted to stay in that very spot.

Chakdah is a historical site and an ancient holy place. During the Purāṇic age, it was known as Rathavarma. Śrī Kṛṣṇa's son Pradyumna killed the demon Śambarā there at the end of the Dvāparā age and since then it was known as Pradyumna-nagar. Later when Bhagiratha was bringing down the Gaṅga in order to save the Sagara dynasty, the wheel of his chariot got stuck here. Thus the town has come to be known as Chakradah, which in time has been changed into Chakdah. When the local people heard that the Lord Jagannātha deity from Puri had come to stay in Jashora, they flocked there in thousands to seek His *darśana.* This is how Jagadīśa Paṇḍita decided to remain in Jashora rather than return to his home in Mayapur.

Being attracted by the parental devotion of Jagadīśa Paṇḍita and his wife, Nityānanda Prabhu and Caitanya Mahāprabhu visited the Lord Jagannātha temple in Jashora on two different occasions. The two Prabhus held *saṅkīrtana* and a feast both times. As the Lord was about to leave Jashora to go to Puri, Duḥkhinī began to cry from the imminent separation so intensely that the Lord agreed to remain behind in the form of the Śrī Gaura-Gopāla deity. In the course of the couple's householder life, they had a son named Rāmabhadra.

THE JASHORA TEMPLE AFTER JAGADĪŚA PAṆḌITA

At first, the Jagannātha deity was kept under a *baṭa* tree near the Ganges, and later the King of Krishnanagar, Krishna Chandra, had a temple built there for Him. When the temple became old and dilapidated, Umeśa Candra Majumdar's wife, Mokṣadā Devī, arranged for repairs to be made. The temple building has no spire but has been constructed in the manner of an ordinary house. Along with Lord Jagannātha, it houses Śrī Śrī Rādhā Vallabha and Gaura-Gopāla deities. The staff that Jagadīśa Paṇḍita used to carry the deity from Purī continues to be kept there. For the service of the Lord Jagannātha deity, devotees donated a large amount of land, but over the course of time, Jagadīśa Paṇḍita's descendants sold it off in order to keep the service of the deity alive. No Rathayātrā festival is held here, though His Snāna-yātrā is celebrated with great pomp. On that occasion, the deity is carried from the temple to an altar built in a large field not far from the temple for the purpose of the bathing ritual. A *melā,* or fair, is also held in the field, attracting countless people. This Jashora Lord Jagannātha Snāna-yātrā fair is still very well known. There is also a 500-year-old dais (wooden platform) for Dolayātrā at the site that is used to swing Rādhā Vallabha on Phālgunī Pūrṇimā.

Siddha Bhagavāna Dāsa Bābājī of Kalna stayed in Jashora for some time to do his *bhajana.* There is an annual festival celebrating Jagadīśa Paṇḍita's disappearance day on the third day of the waxing moon *(śukla tṛtīyā)* in the month of *Pauṣa* (December-January). His appearance day is the twelfth day of the waxing moon *(śukla dvādaśī)* in the same month.

Jagadīśa Paṇḍita's temple is currently under the management of the Sri Chaitanya Gaudiya Math. How this came to pass was described in *Caitanya Vāṇī* magazine (2.9) in the following way:

"The Supreme Lord is most affectionate to His devotees and is conquered by their love. How many different stratagems He engages in just to accept the service of His devotee! Though served in Goloka by hundreds of thousands of goddesses of fortune, Govinda still seems not to have enough people to serve Him. It is as though He feels the service is not being conducted as it should. How many tricks He plays in order to engage the devotee He wants in His service!

"Just look at the ploy that Govardhan-dhārī Gopāla used to engage Mādhavendra Puri. Lord's previous *pūjārī* had hidden Him in the jungle on top of Govardhan out of his fear of Muslim marauders. Gopāla waited there patiently until Purīpāda happened by. He said to him, 'I have been waiting impatiently for you for many days, just wondering when Mādhavendra Purī will come to render Me service?' The Lord is playing His cosmic game, and these are all different aspects of His pastimes.

So now, the very same Lord Jagannātha and Gaura Gopāla deities who were worshipped by Nityānanda Prabhu's dear associate Jagadīśa Paṇḍita have similarly displayed the wonderful pastime of voluntarily offering Themselves to the great devotee Tridaṇḍi Swāmī Śrīmad Bhakti Dayita Mādhava Mahārāja in order to accept his service."

Due to increasing monetary difficulties, three of Jagadīśa Paṇḍita's descendants, Viśvanātha Gosvāmī, Sambhunātha Mukhopādhyaya, and Mṛtyunjaya Mukhopādhaya, had come to realize that they were no longer able to maintain the day-to-day service or undertake the annual festivals of their ancestral deities. The condition of the temple buildings had also deteriorated, and they were unable to make the necessary repairs. As a result, they decided to take the counsel of Śrī Pañcu Ṭhākura of Jashora and Santoṣa Kumāra Mallika of Ranaghat, and eventually surrender the temple, without conditions, to our most revered spiritual master, the founder-*ācārya* of Śrī Chaitanya Gaudiya Math, Oṁ 108 Śrī Śrīmad Bhakti Dayita Mādhava Gosvāmī Mahārāja. Guru Mahārāja immediately spent a large sum of money on making the needed repairs and improvements to the temple, adding electric lighting and a new hostel building.

In the first year after taking over Lord Jagannātha's service, Guru Mahārāja came to the annual festival and personally sat several thousand men and women in the neighboring field and fed them with *mahā-prasāda*. Whoever witnessed that event still feels horripilation when they remember the ecstasy that flooded over Jashora on that day.

Śrīmad Advaita Ācārya

vraje āveśa-rūpatvād vyūho yo'pi sadāśivaḥ
sa evādvaita-gosvāmī caitanyābhinna-vigrahaḥ
yaś ca gopāla-dehaḥ san vraje kṛṣṇasya sannidhau
nanarta śrī-śivā-tantre bhairavasya vaco yathā
ekadā kārttike māsi dīpa-yātrā-mahotsave
sa-rāmaḥ saha-gopālaḥ kṛṣṇo nṛtyati yatnavān
nirīkṣya mad-gurur devo gopa-bhāvābhilāṣavān
priyeṇa nartitum ārabdhaś cakra-bhramaṇa-līlayā
śrī-kṛṣṇasya prasādena dvi-vidho'bhūtat sadāśivaḥ
ekas tatra śivaḥ sākṣād anyo gopāla-vigrahaḥ

"Sadāśiva, formerly an *āveśa* incarnation of the Supreme Lord in Vraja, is known as Advaita Ācārya in Lord Caitanya's pastimes. He is nondifferent from Lord Caitanya Himself. In Vraja, Sadāśiva took the form of a cowherd boy and danced alongside Kṛṣṇa. This is stated by Bhairava in the *Śivātantra*: 'Once, during the Diwali festival in the month of Kārtika, my guru Śaṅkaradeva saw Kṛṣṇa dancing with Balarāma and the cowherd boys. He became desirous of becoming a cowherd boy himself, and he began to dance, spinning like a whirling wheel for Kṛṣṇa's pleasure.' Thus, by Kṛṣṇa's mercy, Sadāśiva plays two different roles in Vraja, in one he is Śiva himself, in the other, he is a cowherd boy." (*Gaura-gaṇoddeśa-dīpikā* 76-80)

ADVAITA-TATTVA

In *Caitanya Caritāmṛta*, Kṛṣṇadāsa Kavirāja Gosvāmī quotes the following evidence from the diary of Svarūpa Dāmodara to describe the ontological principle of Advaita Ācārya:

mahā-viṣṇur jagat-kartā māyayā yaḥ sṛjaty adaḥ
tasyāvatāra evāyam advaitācārya īśvaraḥ
advaitaṁ hariṇādvaitād ācāryaṁ bhakti-śaṁsanāt
bhaktāvatāram īśaṁ tam advaitācāryam āśraye

"Mahā-Viṣṇu is the master of the universe, which He creates through His power of *māyā*. Lord Advaita Ācārya is the *avatāra* of this form of the Supreme Lord. He is known as Advaita because He is none other than Hari, and as Ācārya because He is the preceptor of devotion. I take shelter of the Supreme Lord Advaita Ācārya, who is the *avatāra* of a devotee." (*Caitanya Caritāmṛta* 1.1.12-13)

Śrīla Bhaktivinoda Ṭhākura has written, "*māyā* has two functions, and Mahā-Viṣṇu appears in two ways according to those functions. When He is within the material world as creator, He is the universe's effective cause (*nimitta-kāraṇa*) in His form as Viṣṇu.

In the unmanifest material energy (*pradhāna*), appearing in the form of Rudra, He has a second identity as Advaita."

Bhakti Siddhānta Sarasvatī Gosvāmī Ṭhākura has also written about Advaita Ācārya in his *Anubhāṣya* to *Caitanya Caritāmṛta* 1.6.12: "Lord Advaita Ācārya is Mahā-Viṣṇu. He is the supreme preceptor. Viṣṇu's activities are auspicious because of His existence as the owner or master of the universe. He is the root source of all auspiciousness. Those who are entangled in the material hankerings, which are like garbage, cannot understand this greatest auspiciousness, which is pure, eternal, complete and fully liberated. Thus they remain deprived of their true spiritual activity, devotion to Kṛṣṇa."

Advaita Ācārya was also known as Kamalākṣa:

"Advaita embodies universal welfare. He is the abode of all auspicious qualities. His activities are the eternal source of the world's well-being, and so is His name." (*Caitanya Caritāmṛta* 1.6.12)

"Advaita, the abode of virtue, is a portion (*aṁśa*) of Mahā-Vishṇu. Because He is not different from Viṣṇu, Advaita is His most perfect name." (*Caitanya Caritāmṛta* 1.6.26)

"He is the noblest personality in the universe, the spiritual master of the Vaiṣṇavas; by a combination of these two names, His name is Advaita Ācārya. Since He is a limb or part of the lotus-eyed Supreme Lord, He also has the name Kamalākṣa." (*Caitanya Caritāmṛta* 1.6.30-31)

Śrīla Vṛndāvana Dāsa Ṭhākura has also described Advaita Ācārya as both the foremost of the Vaiṣṇavas and as Śiva:

"Residing in Nabadwip is the foremost and the most fortunate of all the Vaiṣṇavas, Śrī Advaita Ācārya. He heads all spiritual masters in knowledge, devotion and renunciation. He especially teaches devotion to Kṛṣṇa in the same way that Lord Śaṅkara did." (*Caitanya Bhāgavata* 1.2.78-9)

ADVAITA ĀCĀRYA'S APPEARANCE

Advaita Ācārya appeared in the village of Navagrama near the city of Sylhet as the son of the Vārendra *brāhmaṇa* Kuvera Paṇḍita and his wife, Nābhā Devī, on the seventh day of the waxing moon in the month of Māgh. Kuvera Paṇḍita is identified in the *Gaura-gaṇoddeśa-dīpikā* (v. 91) with the god Kuvera, Mahādeva's friend and the leader of the Guhyakas.

"Kuvera Paṇḍita, a devotee of Nṛsiṁha, resided in the village of Navagrama near Sylhet in Bangladesh. He was a greatly fortunate follower of the path of devotion; he knew nothing other than the lotus feet of Kṛṣṇa. His devoted and faithful wife was named Nābhā Devī. She is worshipable for the whole world for she is the mother of Advaita Prabhu." (*Bhakti-ratnākara* 5.2041-3)

"On the seventh day of the waxing moon in the month of Māgha, the great ocean of joy overflowed. In that auspicious moment, the moon of Advaita descended in the blessed womb of Nābhā Devī. In his ecstasy, Kuvera Paṇḍita made gifts to the *brāhmaṇas* and the poor. He tiptoed to the room where the child was delivered, and his heart was filled with gladness upon seeing his son's face. All the villagers came running to his house and said to each other, 'What pious works did this brāhmaṇa do that in his old age he has been blessed with such a jewel of a son?' The gods rained down flowers without being seen. There is nothing with which this scene can compare. Ghanaśyāma sings of this great auspicious occasion when a joyous uproar rang around the earth." (*Bhakti-ratnākara* 12.1759-62)

In the *Gauḍīya Vaiṣṇava Abhidhāna*, Advaita's birthplace is given as Laura near Sylhet. It is also said there that Advaita Prabhu left Laura to reside in Navahat and then from there moved to Shantipur. He also had a home in Nabadwip. His full name was Śrī Kamalākṣa or Kamala Kānta Vedapañcānana. He appeared in 1434 A.D., and he disappeared in the year 1559, at the age of 125 years. In the *Advaita-vilāsa* it is written, 'The Lord remained on this earth for a century and a quarter, performing unlimited pastimes.' "

Jāhanavā Mātā's *dīkṣā* disciple Nityānanda Dāsa gives a third opinion in his *Prema-vilāsa* that Advaita Ācārya was born in Shantipura. He writes that He studied the Veda and other scriptures with the scholar Śāntācārya, who lived in the Phullabati section of Shantipur and earned the title *ācārya*.

Advaita Ācārya's holy life has been described in several Bengali books, including *Advaita-maṅgala*, *Advaita-vilāsa* and *Sītācaritra*. The great scholar Sārvabhauma Bhattācārya also wrote several Sanskrit poems glorifying Advaita – *Advaita-dvādaśa-nāma-stotra*, *Advaitāṣṭakama* and *Advaitāṣṭottara-śata-nāma-stotra*.

ADVAITA ĀCĀRYA INITIATED

When Kuvera Paṇḍita and Nābhā Devī disappeared, Advaita Ācārya went to Gayā on the pretext of performing the appropriate rituals of mourning, and thence continued on a pilgrimage of all of India's holy places. When He came to Vrindavan, He became absorbed in the worship of Kṛṣṇa, but through His meditation, He was able to understand that Kṛṣṇa was about to appear in Nabadwip. While on this pilgrimage, He stopped in Mithila where, He met the poet Vidyāpati. This encounter is beautifully described in *Advaita-vilāsa*. Advaita Prabhu finally returned from Vrindavan to Shantipur after spending several days in Nabadwip. The people of Shantipur had been suffering from His separation for a long time and were very happy to see Him back.

Lord Viṣṇu is always accompanied by three energies, or *śaktis* – Śrī, Bhū and Nīla (Līlā). Advaita Ācārya's own divine persona would not be fully manifest without all these three energies of His identity. Therefore, Advaita Ācārya accepted two wives; one was named Śrīdevī, the other Sītādevī. Both appeared as daughters of the great *brāhmaṇa* devotee Śrī Nṛsiṁha Bhāduṛī. In the *Gaura-gaṇoddeśa-dīpikā*, it is written that the divine Yogamāyā took the form of Advaita Prabhu's wife Sītā and that Śrī is her *prakāśa* expansion.

Advaita Ācārya had two residences, one in Shantipur, the other not far from Śrīvāsa's home in Nabadwip-Mayapur. His heart was greatly pained at seeing that the people of the world were devoid of any devotion to Viṣṇu and as a consequence greatly suffering the torments of material life. Overwhelmed with compassion, He began to teach the *Bhāgavad-gītā* and *Śrīmad Bhāgavatam*, explaining that the purport of the scriptures was to engage in devotional service to Kṛṣṇa.

At about the same time, Mādhavendra Purī had a dream in which Govardhan Dhārī Gopāla commanded him to find sandalwood paste for the deity service. Mādhavendra Purī then started out for Puri, taking the road through western Bengal. While there, he stopped at Advaita Ācārya's house in Shantipur. Advaita Prabhu became convinced that Mādhavendra Purī was His guru when he saw his devotional ecstasies. Even though He Himself is an expansion of the Supreme Lord, He underwent the ritual of initiation in order to demonstrate to the conditioned souls the necessity of accepting a spiritual master.

"Mādhavendra Purī arrived at Advaita Ācārya's house. When Advaita Ācārya saw Purīpāda's *prema*, He felt a deep inner joy. He begged to be initiated by him, after which Mādhavendra Purī left to continue his voyage to the south." (*Caitanya Caritāmṛta* 2.4.110-1)

It is said that Mahāprabhu is the main trunk of the wish-fulfilling tree of devotion, as well as the gardener who enjoys and distributes the tree's fruits. Though the tree was planted in Nabadwip, it grew in *Puruṣottama dhāma* (Puri) and Vrindavan, expanding into an entire orchard producing many, many fruits of love. Mādhavendra Purī is said to be the first seedling, which eventually grew into this tree. Īśvara Purī was the sprouted form of this seedling. Mahāprabhu, though Himself the gardener, also became the tree's main trunk through His inconceivable energies. Advaita Prabhu and Nityānanda Prabhu were the two secondary trunks into which the main trunk divided. (*Caitanya Caritāmṛta* 1.9.21)

THE CAUSE OF THE LORD'S DESCENT

Śrī Kṛṣṇa Caitanya Mahāprabhu is the main body of the devotional movement, and Advaita Ācārya and Nityānanda Prabhu are His principal limbs, whereas Śrīvāsa and other devotees are His secondary limbs. All of them advented in order to preach devotion to Hari. All those who were senior to Gaurāṅga appeared on this earth prior to Him. Advaita Prabhu appeared along with the other elder members of Caitanya's retinue, and when He did so, He observed that the sinfulness of the Age of Kālī had reached a disturbing extreme and that the world was entirely devoid of devotion to Lord Kṛṣṇa. He thought that a partial *avatāra* of the Lord would not be sufficient to completely remedy the situation.

He thought, "The world will only benefit if the Supreme Personality of Godhead Himself descends to the earth." So He began to worship Kṛṣṇa's lotus feet with Ganges water and Tulasī leaves, shouting and pleading to the Lord to descend. With roars of love (*prema-huṅkāra*)

Advaita Ācārya showed His desire for the Lord of Goloka to descend to the earth.

He constantly offered water from the Ganges and Tulasī *mañjarīs* while meditating on Kṛṣṇa's lotus feet, at the same time calling to Kṛṣṇa with loud roars. This is the way that He brought about Kṛṣṇa's descent. This plea by Advaita Ācārya is the chief reason for Kṛṣṇa Caitanya to descend on earth. The Lord, the protector of religion, descends at the wish of His devotee. (*Caitanya Caritāmṛta* 1.3.107-9)

"Advaita Ācārya lived in Shantipur. His body is the reservoir of devotional nectar and is not different from that of Caitanya Mahāprabhu. He whose spotless fame has filled the world brought Śrī Kṛṣṇa Caitanya down to this earth. My Advaita Prabhu is not different from Gaurāṅga, and His wife Sītā is the mother of the universe. First He brought Gaurāṅga into this world with His roars, and then He glorified Him everywhere." (*Bhakti-ratnākara* 12.3753-6)

"All glories to Advaita Ācārya, the most merciful, whose roars brought about Gaurāṅga's *avatāra*. Whoever takes shelter of His lotus feet will obtain the great wealth of love for Gaura." (*Bhakti-ratnākara* 12.3761, 3764)

"He constantly served Kṛṣṇa with great enthusiasm, offering Ganges water and Tulasī *mañjarīs*. Absorbed in thoughts of Kṛṣṇa, He worshipped Him by roaring His name, the sound of which filled the entire universe, reaching up to Vaikuṇṭha. Lord Kṛṣṇa heard the sound of these roars of love and appeared Himself, for He is controlled by His devotee." (*Caitanya Bhāgavata* 1.2.81-3)

Nityānanda Prabhu, the nondifferent manifestation of Lord Balarāma, also descended prior to Mahāprabhu's appearance, on the thirteenth day of the waxing moon in the month of Māgha, into the family of Haṛāi Paṇḍita and Padmāvatī in the village of Ekachakra in Rarha, bestowing upon them the opportunity to serve Him in the *vātsalya-rasa*. Meanwhile, eight daughters were born to Jagannātha Miśra and Śacī Devī, all of whom died before their son Viśvarūpa, Nityānanda Prabhu's other self, appeared. Subsequently, on the full-moon evening of the month of Phālguna, the source of all avatars and the father of the *saṅkīrtana* movement, Gauracandra, made His appearance amidst Kṛṣṇa *saṅkīrtana* that people in Nabadwip were performing on the pretext of a lunar eclipse. After the appearance of Śrī Caitanya, Sītā Devī took Advaita Ācārya's permission to come with gifts to Nabadwip from Shantipur to see the most wonderful child. When she saw Him, she blessed Him by placing paddy and *dūrvā* grass on His head.

"After taking permission from her husband Advaita Ācārya, Sītā Ṭhākurāṇī, the most respectable and noble lady, went to Nabadwip bearing gifts to see the crown jewel of infants." (*Caitanya Caritāmṛta* 1.13.112)

Advaita Ācārya established a *tol* (school) for teaching Sanskrit in Nabadwip-Mayapur and started to engage in a deep study of the scriptures. Every day, after bathing in the Ganges, Mahāprabhu's older brother, Viśvarūpa used to go to Advaita Ācārya's house to listen to Him lecture. When Advaita Ācārya Prabhu was engaged in performing His *pūjā*, Viśvarūpa, would explain to everyone present there that devotion to Kṛṣṇa is the ultimate purport of all the scriptures. When Advaita Ācārya heard him speaking in this way, He got up from worshipping His deity and embraced him. Śacī regularly sent young Nimāi at noon with something for Viśvarūpa's lunch. When Advaita Prabhu saw Nimāi's beautiful face, He became enchanted but was unable to recognize

Him as His worshipable Lord, the Supreme Truth.

In the meantime, Viśvarūpa had secretly decided that he would renounce family life in the knowledge that the material world is temporary and that a human being's only real duty is to worship the Lord. When he saw that his parents were starting to make wedding plans for him, he quickly left home and took *sannyāsa*, after which he was known by the name Śaṅkarāraṇya. Śacī, Jagannātha Miśra and other devotees all lamented his loss. Advaita Prabhu too was pained by Viśvarūpa's departure but pacified everyone by saying that Kṛṣṇa Himself would appear soon to eradicate everyone's distress.

After Viśvarūpa left home, Śacī and Jagannātha Miśra feared that Nimāi would follow his example, and so they put a stop to His education. Later, however, when they heard Nimāi speaking sweetly in the mood of Dattātreya, they decided it would be better to send Him back to school. Jagannātha Miśra left this world not long after Nimāi was given the sacred thread and had become fully absorbed in His studies.

While Mahāprabhu was still fully devoted to His pastimes as a scholar, His mother arranged His marriage to Lakṣmīpriyā, the daughter of Ballabha.

In those days, Advaita Ācārya was holding *Bhāgavata* lectures and *kīrtana* at His house in Nabadwip. All the devotees including, Advaita Ācārya, were very enthused about the singer Mukunda Datta's fine voice. On one occasion Īśvara Purī came to Advaita Ācārya's house while visiting Nabadwip. From his vigorous appearance, Advaita Ācārya was able to recognize that he was a Vaiṣṇava *sannyāsī*. Later, Gaurāṅga also met Īśvara Purī there.

"At that time, Īśvara Purī arrived in Nabadwip incognito. Īśvara Purī was single-minded in his constant preoccupation with relishing Kṛṣṇa devotion; he was dear to Kṛṣṇa and compassionate. No one was able to recognize him because he was not dressed like a devotee until he arrived by chance one day at Advaita Ācārya's house." (*Caitanya Bhāgavata* 1.11.70-72)

ADVAITA TESTS MAHĀPRABHU

Advaita Ācārya, Śrīvāsa Paṇḍita and the other devotees were overjoyed to see the mood of extreme eagerness coming out of separation from Śrī Kṛṣṇa and the transcendental ecstatic feelings in Gaurāṅga Mahāprabhu after His return from Gaya. In due course, Nityānanda Prabhu arrived in Nabadwip after having toured the sacred pilgrimage sites, and there He met Nimāi. One day at Śrīvāsa's house, Mahāprabhu indicated that He wanted to perform the Vyāsa Pūjā to Nityānanda Prabhu. On the eve of this *pūjā*, Mahāprabhu showed everyone that Nityānanda Prabhu was Baladeva and then, repeating the words "*Nāṛā, Nāṛā,*" revealed that Advaita Prabhu had caused Him to descend to the earth by calling Him.

"It is due to Advaita Ācārya that I have descended, for Nāṛā's roars rang in My ears. I was lying in the Milk Ocean, but Nāṛā's roar woke Me up and brought Me down here." (*Caitanya Bhāgavata* 2.9.297-8)

After the Vyāsa Pūjā had come to an end, Mahāprabhu took on the mood of the Supreme Lord and sent Rāmāi Paṇḍita, Śrīvāsa Paṇḍita's brother, to fetch Advaita Prabhu from His house in Shantipur. He told him of the Lord's divine manifestation: "Advaita Prabhu has brought Hari, the Lord of Goloka, to this earth by His cries and by worshipping Him with Ganges water and Tulasī. Nityānanda Prabhu has also made His auspicious arrival in Nabadwip. So Advaita Ācārya and his wife should immediately come to Śrīvāsa Aṅgana, bringing all the paraphernalia for worship." Rāmāi Paṇḍita promptly carried out Mahāprabhu's order and took His message to Advaita Prabhu.

As soon as Advaita heard that Mahāprabhu had publicly revealed His divinity, He and Sītā Devī immediately set off, bringing their son Acyutānanda and some other associates. But rather than going directly to Śrīvāsa's house, Advaita decided to test Mahāprabhu by hiding in Nandana Ācārya's house. He told Rāmāi Paṇḍita not to tell Mahāprabhu, but the Lord, who knows the heart of all, was able to see through Advaita Ācārya's plan. As Mahāprabhu sat on the altar and revealed to everyone His divine identity, Nityānanda Prabhu held the royal parasol while Gadādhara Paṇḍita and the other devotees engaged in a variety of services. This time, when Mahāprabhu sent Rāmāi to Nandana Ācārya's house to fetch Advaita Ācārya, Advaita Ācārya realized that Mahāprabhu was omniscient and hesitated no longer.

Advaita Ācārya joyfully prostrated Himself before the Lord, stunned by the sight of the Lord's divine power. He washed the Lord's lotus feet and then worshipped Him with the five ingredients (*pañcopacāra*), using the following *mantra* to do so:

namo brahmaṇyadevāya go-brāhmaṇa-hitāya ca
jagad-dhitāya kṛṣṇāya govindāya namo namaḥ

"I offer my respectful obeisances unto Lord Kṛṣṇa, who is the worshipable Deity for all *brāhmaṇas*, the well-wisher of the cows and the *brāhmaṇas*, and the benefactor of the whole world. I offer my repeated obeisances to the Personality of Godhead, known as Kṛṣṇa and Govinda."

Mahāprabhu then commanded Advaita Prabhu to dance. Advaita Ācārya started to dance madly, until he was completely intoxicated in a way that astonished all the devotees.

Kṛṣṇadāsa Kavirāja has written: "There is one Mahāprabhu or Supreme Lord, and two other Prabhus, or masters. The two other Prabhus serve the lotus feet of Mahāprabhu. These three personalities belong to the category of the all-worshipable; the fourth category is the devotee, who is the worshipper. Śrīvāsa and the millions of other devotees belong to the category of the pure devotees. Gadādhara Paṇḍita and others are considered to be *avatāras* of the Lord's energies, or *śaktis*. They are counted as His most intimate devotees." (*Caitanya Caritāmṛta* 1.7.94-7)

Pañca Tattva, the five–fold aspect of divinity, includes Gaurāṅga Mahāprabhu, who accepted the form of a devotee; Nityānanda Prabhu, who is the manifestation of a devotee; and Advaita Ācārya, the Lord's *avatāra* as a devotee. These three are considered to be *prabhu-tattva*, or *Viṣṇu-tattva*, the ontological category of Godhead. Advaita Ācārya is an *avatāra* of Mahā Viṣṇu, so belongs to the category of *Viṣṇu-tattva*, but because He took on the mood of a devotee, He is called

bhaktāvatāra, "the Lord's *avatāra* of a devotee." Because Gaurāṅga Mahāprabhu, Nityānanda Prabhu and Advaita Ācārya all belong to the category of Viṣṇu-tattva, Tulasī leaves are offered to Their feet. Without Advaita Ācārya's mercy, one can never attain the service of Caitanya and Nityānanda Prabhus.

dayā koro sītāpati advaita gosāi
tava kṛpābale pāi caitanya-nitāi

"Be merciful, Advaita Prabhu, husband of Sītā! On the strength of Your mercy, I will attain Caitanya and Nitāi." (Narottama Dāsa Ṭhākura)

Advaita Ācārya's glories and His activities have been extensively described in Kṛṣṇadāsa Kavirāja Gosvāmī's *Caitanya Caritāmṛta*, Vṛndāvana Dāsa Ṭhākura's *Caitanya Bhāgavata*, Narahari Cakravartī's *Bhakti-ratnākara, and in Advaita Vilāsa* and other works. Those who wish to have a deeper knowledge of His life should consult these books. We can only give an abbreviated biography in this book, and such an extensive account cannot be given here. We have only set out to remember the main pastimes of Śrī Advaita.

ADVAITA AND HARIDĀSA ṬHĀKURA

By his deeds, Advaita Prabhu revealed that a Vaiṣṇava is worthy of praise and worship regardless of his family background. Nāmācārya Haridāsa Ṭhākura was born in a Muslim family in Buṛhan village in the district of Jessore. Later he came to live in the village of Phuliya and was staying in a grotto engaged in solitary devotional practices, but would sometimes come to associate with Advaita Prabhu in nearby Shantipur. This was after he had spent time preaching the glories of the Holy Names at the Chandpur house of Raghunātha Dāsa Gosvāmī's father and uncle, Govardhana and Hiraṇya Majumadāra. Advaita used to invite Haridāsa Ṭhākura to come to his house in Shantipur to take *prasāda*. This made Haridāsa Ṭhākura feel somewhat uneasy. However, Advaita Prabhu, the world teacher, claimed that his behavior conformed with all the scriptures, for to feed a great devotee like Haridāsa Ṭhākura is equal to feeding millions of *brāhmaṇas*. In order to demonstrate this, he honored Haridāsa Ṭhākura by giving him the plate offered in the *śrāddha* ceremony. On the annual date set aside for offering oblations to the forefathers, householder Vaiṣṇavas offer all kinds of foodstuffs to the Lord. They then invite *brāhmaṇas* and Vaiṣṇavas to honor *prasāda*. The *mahā-prasāda* is given to the guest of honor, and Advaita Prabhu chose Haridāsa Ṭhākura for this special treatment, considering him to be a transcendental *brāhmaṇa* guru.

"Advaita said to Haridāsa Ṭhākura, 'Please don't be afraid. I shall only do what is accepted in scripture. If you accept this *prasāda* it is as though I had fed ten million *brāhmaṇas*.' After saying these words, he gave him the *śrāddha* plate to eat." (*Caitanya Caritāmṛta* 3.3.219-20)

"One of the branches of the Caitanya tree is Haridāsa Ṭhākura, whose activities are amazing. He would unfailingly chant 300,000 names of the Lord every day. I only give an indication here of his unlimited virtues; Advaita Ācārya honored him by giving him the *śrāddha* plate." (*Caitanya Caritāmṛta* 1.10.43-4)

THE SONS OF ADVAITA

Although six sons were born to Advaita Ācārya, the *avatāra* of Mahā-Viṣṇu, He indicated that some of them had understood the essence of spiritual life and some had not. Those who simply claimed to be his followers but showed no affection for Gaurāṅga were the latter; those who were attached to Mahāprabhu in ever-increasing affection were the former. These included Acyutānanda, Śrī Kṛṣṇa Miśra and Gopāla Miśra, while Balarām, Svarūpa and Jagadīśa belonged to the category of those who did not give recognition to Śrī Caitanya. Acyutānanda was the oldest brother, and Śrī Kṛṣṇa Miśra and Gopāla Miśra followed his lead. Caitanya Caritāmṛta (1.12.12) compares the two groups to wheat and chaff.

Śrīla Bhakti Siddhānta Sarasvatī Ṭhākura also writes in his *Gauḍīya-bhāṣya* to the *Caitanya Bhāgavata* (2.10.162), "If someone takes Advaita Ācārya to be the best of all the Vaiṣṇavas, then he can be called a Vaiṣṇava. On the other hand, if someone considers Him to be the object of all religious life, the *viṣaya* Kṛṣṇa, and Śrī Kṛṣṇa Caitanya Mahāprabhu to be His devotee, or *āśraya*, then he will never be able to attain Kṛṣṇa's lotus feet."

THE LORD PUNISHES ADVAITA ĀCĀRYA

It is also said that Mahāprabhu taught Advaita Ācārya the real meaning of the *Bhagavad-gītā*.

"Viśvambhara explained the true understanding of the *Gita* to Advaita Ācārya, withdrawing the gates that conceal the nature of *bhakti*." (*Caitanya Bhāgavata* 2.10.166)

Another wonderful pastime was prepared by Advaita Ācārya in order to show the fallen *jīvas* how auspicious it is to receive punishment from the Lord, the guru or a Vaiṣṇava. How fortunate is a devotee who is chastised by his guru! This is described in the seventeenth chapter of the *Caitanya Caritāmṛta*, *Ādi-līlā*, where Śrīla Bhaktivinoda Ṭhākura has made the following comments in his *Amṛta-pravāha-bhāṣya*: "Advaita Ācārya is the godbrother of Mahāprabhu's guru, Īśvara Purī. For this reason, Mahāprabhu treated Advaita Ācārya as his elder and spiritual master, even though Advaita Ācārya considered Himself to be Mahāprabhu's servant. Advaita Ācārya was pained to see Mahāprabhu treat Him with such respect and so, in order to seek out the merciful punishment of the Lord, returned to Shantipur and began to explain the path of knowledge to a few unfortunate individuals. When the Lord caught wind of this, He became extremely angry and went to Shantipur to give Him a good thrashing. When He was chastised in this way, Advaita Ācārya danced in joy, saying, "Just see, My desires have been fulfilled today! Mahāprabhu was previously miserly with Me, treating Me as His respectful elder. Now He has acted toward me as though I were His servant or disciple, by trying to save Me from the heresy of *māyāvāda*." When the Lord understood that this had all been a ruse on Advaita Ācārya's part, He was embarrassed but pleased with Him.

"The Lord treated Advaita with the respect deserved by a guru. This caused the Ācārya great distress, so He adopted a ruse of teaching the path of knowledge. Mahāprabhu became angry and scorned Advaita Ācārya, causing Him great bliss. When He saw His satisfaction with the turn of events, the Lord became ashamed and was merciful to Him." (*Caitanya Caritāmṛta* 1.17.66-8)

"Previously Mahāprabhu would honor Me. This made Me unhappy, so I thought that if I start giving lectures on the *Yoga-vaśiṣṭha*, explaining *mukti* as the supreme goal of life, the Lord would become angry and insult Me." (*Caitanya Caritāmṛta* 1.12.39-40)

ŚACĪ DEVĪ AND ADVAITA ĀCĀRYA

Mahāprabhu could not forgive even His mother when she looked askance at Advaita Ācārya, who is compassionate for the plight of the conditioned souls. On one occasion, through chastising her, He warned all devotees of the danger of offenses to the Vaiṣṇavas. If Śacī Devī, who is the essence of motherly affection, the *avatāra* of Yaśodā Devī, cannot be forgiven an offense to the Vaiṣṇava, then what chance do others have? By the same pastime, Caitanya Mahāprabhu also showed that in order to become free of Vaiṣṇava *aparādha*, one should beg for forgiveness from the Vaiṣṇava one has offended.

When Viśvarūpa came to the conclusion, after studying with Advaita Prabhu, that the world is a temporary place and that the only real duty of humankind is to worship the Supreme Lord, he left home and took *sannyāsa*. Śacī Mātā, though troubled by his departure, was wary of insulting Advaita Ācārya for the role he had played in it, knowing Him to be a Vaiṣṇava, and took solace in Nimāi's presence at home. But when she saw that Nimāi too was constantly going to associate with Advaita Ācārya, leaving his wife, Lakṣmīpriya, alone at home, she began to think that Advaita's name was really unsuitable, that rather than unifying people as it would indicate, He split them apart. *Dvaita* would thus be a more appropriate name, she thought. "This old *gosāi* goes by the name Advaita, but He should be called Dvaita. One son of mine, as beautiful as the moon, has left home because of Him, and He hasn't let me keep the other one settled. No one has mercy on me; I am now alone in this world. He may be one (*advaita*) with the world, but I see Him as *māyā* (*dvaita*)." (*Caitanya Bhāgavata* 2.22.114-6)

Because of her affection for her son, Śacī Mātā mentally criticized Advaita Ācārya in this way, and no one knew except for her son, Gaura Hari, who is the indweller of all beings. On the day of the *mahā-prakāśa* in the house of Śrīvāsa Paṇḍita, when Mahāprabhu was fulfilling the desires of every one of His devotees by allowing them to see His divine form for twenty-one hours, Śrīvāsa Paṇḍita asked Him whether Śacī Devī could also be blessed with this divine vision. Mahāprabhu answered, "My mother has committed an offense against Advaita Prabhu, so I will not show her this form."

When the devotees told Śacī what her son had said, she immediately went to Advaita Ācārya and begged Him for forgiveness. After Advaita Ācārya had heard Śacī Mātā's confession, He began to glorify her as the one who had carried the Supreme Lord of all creation in her womb. He continued to do so until He became unconscious from the overwhelming love that He felt. Only when He fell unconscious could Śacī Devī finally take the dust of His lotus feet and thus be free from her offense. Mahāprabhu was satisfied with His mother and showed her His glorious, divine form. Another important lesson we can draw from this story is that Vaiṣṇavas are never proud. Even though she had given birth to Lord Gaurahari, Śacī Devī felt no pride in her exalted status. As soon as she became aware of having committed an offense, she went to Advaita Ācārya without any hesitation and prayed to be pardoned.

THE LORD COMES TO SHANTIPUR

Advaita Ācārya was Mahāprabhu's associate in *saṅkīrtana*, both in Śrīvāsa's house and in the streets of Nabadwip, and along the shores of the Ganges.

"Everyone joyfully sang in unison, 'Kṛṣṇa, Rāma, Mukunda, Murārī, Vanamālī!' Holding on to Nityānanda Prabhu and Gadādhara Paṇḍita, Advaita Ācārya ran in every direction like a lion." (*Caitanya Bhāgavata* 2.23.29-30)

"The Lord danced along the banks of the Bhāgīrathī while around Him all the people sang the names of Hari. Advaita Ācārya preceded Him, dancing ecstatically with a small group of devotees. " (*Caitanya Bhāgavata* 2.23.202-3)

After Mahāprabhu had taken *sannyāsa* from Keśava Bhāratī in Katwa, He became overwhelmed with love for Śrī Kṛṣṇa and started to run toward Vrindavan. With the help of some cowherd boys, Nityānanda Prabhu tricked Him into coming to the banks of the Ganges. Nityānanda Prabhu wanted to show the wonderful *sannyāsa* form of Mahāprabhu to the people of Nabadwip and brought Him to Shantipur. When Mahāprabhu saw the Ganges, He thought that the river was the Yamuna and became overwhelmed with ecstasy. Meanwhile, Advaita Ācārya heard that Nityānanda Prabhu had brought Mahāprabhu there and came by boat across the river with new clothes for Him. Mahāprabhu was astonished to see Advaita Ācārya, wondering how He could have known that He was in Vrindavan. Advaita Ācārya answered by saying that Vrindavan was wherever Mahāprabhu went and that the northen flow of the Ganges was the Yamuna. When He heard these words, Mahāprabhu realized that He had been tricked into coming to the northen bank of the Ganges across from the town of Shantipur. Advaita Ācārya had Mahāprabhu take a bath and dressed Him in the new cloth and then took Him to His house where the Lord stayed for several days.

When Śacī Devī and the people of Nabadwip heard that Gaurahari was at Advaita Prabhu's house, they all came there to visit Him. Seeing Him in His dress as a *sannyāsī*, they felt joy mixed with separation. Sītā Ṭhākurāṇī prepared an immense meal and served it on whole leaves from seed-banana trees for Mahāprabhu and Nityānanda Prabhu. At that time there were many joking exchanges between Advaita Prabhu and Nityānanda Prabhu. This has been extensively described in the *Caitanya Caritāmṛta*'s *Madhya-līlā*, chapter 3. Mahāprabhu afterwards also ate foodstuffs prepared by His mother, Śacīdevī in order to ease the suffering He had caused her by His departure. The reunion of devotees turned into a great festival, and Advaita Ācārya's house in the town of Shantipur was transformed into Vaikuṇṭha.

"Everyone was dancing and singing the names of Hari. Advaita Ācārya's house became Vaikuṇṭha Purī." (*Caitanya Caritāmṛta* 2.3.156)

ADVAITA GOES TO PURI ON THE ANNUAL PILGRIMAGE

After Mahāprabhu said His goodbyes to the devotees, He set off to Puri or Nilachal to live there at the behest of His mother. Advaita Ācārya and the residents of Nabadwip were once again hurled into the ocean of separation from their lord. These events took place in the year 1510. It was probably three more years before the devotees went to Puri during the *Cāturmāsya* period to visit Him there at the time of the Rathayātrā.

The first year Advaita Ācārya and the other devotees went to Nilachal to see Mahāprabhu, they witnessed the Rathayātrā and then stayed for four months, passing the time in *kīrtana* and dancing in great joy. When the time came for them to depart, the Lord told everyone to return every year to see the Rathayātrā festival. And so the yearly trips to Puri to see the Lord became a tradition. (*Caitanya Caritāmṛta* 2.1.46-49)

Of the last twenty years of Mahāprabhu's pastimes, six were spent in traveling to and from Puri, while He spent the eighteen in Puri without ever leaving. During the six years that He spent traveling, the Bengali devotees would visit Puri after they found out that He was present in Puri. During the eighteen years of Mahāprabhu's permanent stay in Puri, the annual trips became an annual event.

"After Mahāprabhu arrived in Puri from Vrindavan, He never again left in the eighteen remaining years of His pastimes. The devotees came from Bengal every year, meeting with the Lord and staying for the four months of the rainy season." (*Caitanya Caritāmṛta* 2.1.249-50)

"All of Mahāprabhu's associates, Advaita Ācārya, Nityānanda Prabhu, Mukunda, Śrīvāsa, Vidyānidhi, Vāsudeva and Murāri, went every year to meet with the Lord, staying in Puri for four months. The Lord enjoyed a multitude of pastimes with these devotees during this time." (*Caitanya Caritāmṛta* 2.1.255-6)

"The time for Rathayātrā came again, and the devotees started off on the annual pilgrimage to Nilachal. They were following the Lord's order to come every year to see the Rathayātrā festival. With Advaita Ācārya at their head, all the devotees set off toward Nilachal." (*Caitanya Caritāmṛta* 3.8.4-6)

Advaita Ācārya would go every year to Puri and stay for the full four months, participating with Mahāprabhu in pastimes such as the cleaning of the Guṇḍicā temple, the water sports in Narendra Sarovara, and Lord Jagannātha's Rathayātrā. The best of Advaita's three orthodox sons, Acyutānanda, who was totally devoted to Gaurāṅga, was also present there, as is attested by the mentioning of him as the leader of the sixth *kīrtana* group at the Rathayātrā, which was from Shantipur. Advaita himself was the principal dancer in the first *kīrtana* group, led by Svarūpa Dāmodara Prabhu.

In the third year of this tradition, the wives of the Bengal devotees accompanied them, bringing various gifts for Mahāprabhu's service.

"In the third year, all the devotees from Bengal decided to go to Nilachal. They went in a group to Advaita Ācārya's house, and He happily agreed to go with them to see the Lord. That year, all the wives of these saints went also, the mother of Acyuta accompanying Advaita Ācārya." (*Caitanya Caritāmṛta* 2.16.12-13, 21)

"Advaita went first to Śacī Mātā's house to take leave. Then He departed with the assembly of devotees. They brought with them all the edibles they knew formerly brought pleasure to the Lord. They performed *saṅkīrtana* the entire length of the route, purifying everything and everyone on their path. All the people of the three worlds were sanctified by the devotees' joyful calls of 'Hari! Hari!' In a mood of ecstasy, they were all going to see Caitanya Mahāprabhu, accompanied by their sons and their wives, their male and female servants." (*Caitanya Bhāgavata* 3.8.39-43)

Kṛṣṇadāsa Kavirāja Gosvāmī has written about a wonderful pastime with Advaita Ācārya's son Gopāla Miśra in the twelfth chapter of *Caitanya Caritāmṛta*'s *Ādi-līlā*. During the cleaning of the Guṇḍicā temple, both Advaita Ācārya and Mahāprabhu were satisfied to see Gopāla's deep absorption in dancing and singing before Them. When Gopāla Miśra suddenly fell unconscious, Advaita Ācārya became very anxious and took his inert body in His lap, chanting the Nṛsiṁha *mantra*. Despite the various *mantras* that Advaita Ācārya uttered, Gopāla did not return to consciousness. All the devotees began to cry for him, but Mahāprabhu, who takes away the distress of His devotees, touched Gopāla over the heart and said, "Get up, Gopāla, and chant Hari Hari!" Gopāla immediately awoke and stood up. The devotees shouted the names of the Lord in relief and joy.

KAMALĀ KĀNTA VIŚVĀSA

Advaita Ācārya had a disciple named Kamalā Kānta Viśvāsa, who wrote to King Pratāparudra explaining that Advaita Ācārya was the Supreme Lord but that He was in debt and needed money. He asked Pratāparudra to give Advaita Ācārya the amount needed to pay his creditors. When Mahāprabhu heard about this, He punished Kamalā Kānta by refusing him access to the Gambhīrā. Kamalā Kānta was disturbed by this punishment, but Advaita Ācārya explained to him that to be punished by Mahāprabhu was a cause for rejoicing and that he was most fortunate.

Bhaktivinoda Ṭhākura has made the following comment on this story, which is found in the twelfth chapter of the *Ādi-līlā*: "Kamalā Kānta first proved that Advaita Ācārya was the Supreme Lord, but then begged for money from the King on Advaita Ācārya's behalf. This action was very displeasing to Mahāprabhu. Even though Advaita Ācārya is God Himself, He is in this world playing the part of a man in order to teach. For an *ācārya* to beg from a king in order to free himself from a debt is considered to be a shameless behavior. One should entirely abandon the desire for material gain, and if the desire for material well-being is taken to the point of begging from a foreign king in order to become free of a debt, then one's spiritual life will certainly go to ruin. kings are by nature materialistic. If one eats the food of a materialistic person, his mind becomes polluted. With the polluted mind one can no longer remember Kṛṣṇa, and his life is wasted.

"Such begging from materialistic men is therefore prohibited for everyone, but it is especially so for those who are in the position of *ācārya*. It is the *ācārya*'s duty to instruct people in the Holy Names, but he should not take money in return for such instruction. If he does so, he becomes an offender to the Holy Name rather than an initiator in the Name. If an instructor of the Holy Names becomes a money collector, then it is a matter of shame, and his religious reputation will be ruined."

MAHĀPRABHU GLORIFIES ADVAITA PRABHU

In the third year, when the Bengal devotees came with their wives and gifts of various food preparations dear to the Lord, He mercifully ate all these offerings out of His affection for them. One day, Mahāprabhu was invited to eat at Advaita Ācārya's residence. This time, Advaita Ācārya himself did the cooking, and his wife assisted Him by cutting the vegetables and gathering the ingredients. It was Advaita Ācārya's secret wish to be able to feed Mahāprabhu alone. It so happened that on that day the weather turned bad and due to a storm, all the *sannyāsīs* who normally came with Mahāprabhu on such occasions were unable to accompany Him. Mahāprabhu thus arrived by Himself, to Advaita Ācārya's great satisfaction, for He was thus able to serve Him the meal in complete privacy. He praised the god Indra as a servant of Kṛṣṇa for he fulfilled Ācārya's wishes. Mahāprabhu was aware of Advaita Ācārya's mood and praised Him by saying, "Kṛṣṇa Himself fulfills Your desires, and so what is unusual about Indra carrying out Your orders?" (*Caitanya Bhāgavata* 3.9.60-72)

On another occasion, Mahāprabhu glorified Advaita Ācārya and described the underlying truth of His nature in the following way:

"Advaita Ācārya is God Himself. As a result of His association, I have become purified. Because there is no one equal to Him in devotion to Kṛṣṇa, nor in knowledge of the scriptures, He is called Advaita Ācārya. By His mercy, even the immoral and evil persons (*mlecchās*) become devotees of Kṛṣṇa. Who can describe the extent of His powers or devotion?" (*Caitanya Caritāmṛta* 3.7.17-9)

Mahāprabhu had Rūpa and Sanātana Gosvāmīs meet with Śrī Advaita and Nityānanda Prabhus in Puri and asked Them to bless the brothers. Raghunātha Dāsa Gosvāmī received Mahāprabhu's leftovers by the grace of Advaita Prabhu. He was the object of Advaita Ācārya's affection because his father, Govardhana Majumadāra, had served Him honestly.

"His father always rendered service to Advaita Ācārya; therefore the *ācārya* was pleased with him. By the grace of the *ācārya*, Raghunātha obtained the Lord's leftover plate and was able to have *darśana* of the Lord for five or six days." (*Caitanya Caritāmṛta* 2.16.225-6)

The words that Mahāprabhu spoke to Advaita Ācārya when He was about to leave Puri show just how much affection He had for Him:

"Ācārya Gosāi came here to show Me His mercy. I am bound in debt to His love, and there is no way that I can repay Him. He left His wife, children and home for My sake, traveling a long and difficult way to come here. I am living here in Nilachal without moving. I make no effort on your behalf. I am a monk and I have no wealth–what could I give all of you to make good on My debt? My only possession is My body, which I give you. I will sell it to whomever you wish." (*Caitanya Caritāmṛta* 3.12.70-74)

ADVAITA'S RIDDLE

When Advaita Ācārya returned to Nabadwip from Puri, he met Jagadānanda Paṇḍita, who had been sent there earlier by Mahāprabhu. Advaita Ācārya was very happy to have his association. When Jagadānanda Paṇḍita finally asked permission of Advaita Prabhu to return to Nilachal, Advaita Ācārya gave him a message in the form of a riddle to take back to Mahāprabhu. The riddle was comprehensible to no one but Mahāprabhu Himself. The message read as follows:

"Convey My obeisance hundreds and thousands of times unto Śrī Caitanya Mahāprabhu and then offer this petition at His feet. Please inform Mahāprabhu, who is acting like a madman, that everyone here has become mad like Him. Inform Him also that in the marketplace rice is no longer in demand. Further, tell Him that those now mad in ecstatic love are no longer interested in the material world. Also, tell Śrī Caitanya Mahāprabhu that one who has also become a madman in ecstatic love [Advaita Prabhu] has spoken these words." (*Caitanya Caritāmṛta* 3.19.19-21)

Bhaktivinoda Ṭhākura explains this riddle in this way: "Tell Mahāprabhu that everyone has become intoxicated with love for Kṛṣṇa and so in the marketplace of love, no one is buying the rice of Kṛṣṇa *prema* any longer. Tell Mahāprabhu that the crazies (*āul*) are so intoxicated with love that they are no longer doing their material duties. Tell Mahāprabhu that Advaita said this in a state of complete intoxication with *prema*. In short, the message was that the purpose for which Advaita Ācārya had called Mahāprabhu to earth had been achieved. Now the Lord may do as He wishes."

Advaita Ācārya, the *avatar* of Mahā-Viṣṇu, appeared in this world on the seventh day of the waxing moon in the month of Māgha. This *tithi* is also known as *Advaita-saptamī*.

Śrīla Nāmācārya Haridāsa Ṭhākura

ṛcīkasya muneḥ putro nāmnā brahmā mahātapāḥ
prahlādena samaṁ jāto haridāsākhyako'pi san
murāri-gupta-caraṇaiś caitanya-caritāmṛte
ukto muni-sutaḥ prātastulasi-patram āharan
adhautam abhiśaptas taṁ pitrā yavanatāṁ gataḥ
sa eva haridāsaḥ san jātaḥ parama-bhaktimān

"Haridāsa Ṭhākura is a combined *avatāra* of Ricīka Muni's son Brahmā Mahātapā and Prahlāda. The respected Murāri Gupta has written in his *Caitanya Carita Mahākāvya* that this *muni's* son picked a Tulasī leaf and offered it to Kṛṣṇa without having washed it first. His father then cursed him to become a *mlecchā* in his next life. He was thus born as Haridāsa, a great devotee." (*Gaura-gaṇoddeśa-dīpikā* 93-95)

HARIDĀSA ṬHĀKURA'S BIRTH AS A MUSLIM

In his book *Navadvīpa-dhāma-māhātmya*, Śrīla Bhaktivinoda Ṭhākura has written the following account of how Brahmā became Haridāsa Ṭhākura: Once, in the Dvāpara Yuga, when Nandanandana Śrī Kṛṣṇa was herding the cows through Vraja dhāma in the company of His cowherd boyfriends, Brahmā desired to see the actual identity of Śrī Kṛṣṇa and decided to test Him. He stole Kṛṣṇa's calves as well as His friends and hid them for a year in the caves of Sumeru Mountain. But when Brahmā returned to Vraja a year later, he was astonished to see that Kṛṣṇa was still there with both His friends and His calves. Realizing his foolishness, Brahmā regretted by falling down at Kṛṣṇa's feet and begged for forgiveness; Kṛṣṇa responded by mercifully revealing His divine opulence.

He who appears in the Dvāpara-yuga as Nandanandana Śrī Kṛṣṇa descends again in the Kālī Yuga as the most munificent form Gaurāṅga, taking on the mood and bodily luster of Rādhārāṇī. Brahmā was afraid that he might commit the same offense during the Gaura incarnation, so he went to Antardwip, the central island of Nabadwip, and began to meditate. The Lord was able to understand his mind and so came to him in the form of Gaurāṅga and said, "During My *avatāra* as Gaura, you will be born in a family of *mlecchās* and will preach the glories of the Holy Name and bring auspiciousness to all the living beings." From this above description, it is understood that Haridāsa Ṭhākura was an *avatāra* of the creator Lord Brahmā. It is said that in order to avoid committing offense by coming under the influence of false ego in Gaurāṅga pastimes, he prayed to Kṛṣṇa to take birth in a lowly family. This description is also seen in *Advaita-vilāsa*.

A Vaiṣṇava may appear in any family in any class of society. Mahāprabhu wished to show that even though he may be born in a lowly family, a Vaiṣṇava is the best among others. In order to do so, He had His associates appear in a variety of castes. Śrī Vṛndāvana Dāsa Ṭhākura has written the following in *Caitanya Bhāgavata*:

"Haridāsa Ṭhākura was born in a low-caste family on the Lord's order in order to show that caste and class have no importance at all. All the scriptures say that a devotee of Viṣṇu, though born in a lowly family, is still worshipable by all. What will one's pedigree do for one who is born in a high caste but does not worship Kṛṣṇa? He will go to hell in spite of his noble birth. Haridāsa took a low birth just to bear witness to these scriptural statements. He is comparable to Prahlāda, who was born in a family of demons, or Hanumān, who was born a monkey. They only superficially belong to low classes." (*Caitanya Bhāgavata* 1.16.237-240)

Nāmācārya Haridāsa Ṭhākura appeared in Burhan village. Burhan is currently an administrative region having sixty-five blocks (groups of villages) in the Satkhira subdivision of Khulna in Bangladesh. It is not clear exactly where Burhan village itself lies. Some people hold that it is in West Bengal in the district known as 24 Paraganas, while others say that it is in the Jessore district in Bangladesh. Benapole, where many of Haridāsa Ṭhākura's pastimes took place, is the first railway station after Bongaon on the line to Khulna on the Bangladesh side of the border. It is thus likely that Burhan is also on the Bangladesh side of the border.

According to some sources, Haridāsa Ṭhākura was born in a *brāhmaṇa* family. His father's name was Sumati, and his mother's was Gaurī. His parents died when he was young, so he went to live in the house of a Muslim named Khan in the village of Halimpur, about five miles from his birthplace, on the other bank of the Salai River. According to the *Advaita-vilāsa*, however, Haridāsa Ṭhākura was born in 1372 of the Śāka era (1451 A.D.) in the month of Agrahāyaṇa, and his father's name was Khānaulla Kājī. However, Haridāsa Ṭhākura became an orphan at a young age according to this version as well.

HARIDĀSA ṬHĀKURA'S PARTICIPATION IN THE SAṄKĪRTAN MOVEMENT

It was Mahāprabhu's wish that Haridāsa Ṭhākura should appear long before He did. According to *Advaita-vilāsa*, Haridāsa was thirty-five years older than Mahāprabhu, who was born in 1407 Śaka. Nityānanda Prabhu was twelve years older than Mahāprabhu, so Haridāsa Ṭhākura was also twenty-three years older than He. Haridāsa Ṭhākura first entered into Mahāprabhu's association when the Lord returned to Nabadwip after being initiated by Śrī Iśvara Puri in Gaya and had begun preaching the *saṅkīrtana* movement. Mahāprabhu began His *saṅkīrtana* pastimes in Nabadwip in His adolescence. From this, we can reckon that Haridāsa Ṭhākura was about fifty years old when he first met the Lord. Even before meeting the Lord, however, Haridāsa Ṭhākura had already started to reveal the glories of the Holy Names in many wondrous ways. He is one of the Lord's most important associates in his role as the initiator of the *yuga dharma*, which is *harināma saṅkīrtana*. Śrī Vṛndāvana Dāsa Ṭhākura has described Haridāsa Ṭhākura's spotless and glorious pastimes extensively in his *Caitanya Bhāgavata*. Śrī Kṛṣṇadāsa Kavirāja Gosvāmī has supplemented this with some extra information about his life and character.

"Haridāsa Ṭhākura was an extraordinary personality and a major branch of the desire tree of devotion. He would unfailingly chant 300,000 names of the Lord each day. His virtues are unlimited, and I can only give a brief summary here. Advaita Ācārya gave him the place of honor at his father's *śrāddha* ceremony. Haridāsa Ṭhākura possessed the same qualities as Prahlāda, being undisturbed even when being beaten by the Muslims. When he entered the Lord's eternal pastimes, Mahāprabhu danced ecstatically with Haridāsa Ṭhākura's body in His arms. Vṛndāvana Dāsa Ṭhākura has described his pastimes extensively. I will simply take up what he has left unsaid." (*Caitanya Caritāmṛta* 1.10.43-47)

It is not known exactly when Haridāsa Ṭhākura performed the various *līlā's* which have been described; nevertheless, we will try to follow a chronological order as far as possible. In the *Ādi-khaṇḍa* of the *Caitanya Bhāgavata*, Vṛndāvana Dāsa Ṭhākura writes about Mahāprabhu's life from His birth until the return from Gaya. Some of Haridāsa's pastimes before meeting Mahāprabhu are described there. The *Madhya-khaṇḍa* describes the period after He came back from Gaya, His ecstatic transformations in separation from Kṛṣṇa, His Kṛṣṇa conscious instructions to His students, His beginning the *saṅkīrtana* movement with His students, His *kīrtana* pastimes in the houses of Candraśekhara Ācārya and Śrīvāsa Paṇḍita, and other activities up until He took *sannyāsa*.

Haridāsa Ṭhākura is an eternal associate of the Lord, and he appeared in a Muslim household in order to serve Him. From a very early age, he showed a proclivity for the chanting of the Holy Names. His life gives a brilliant example of how a devotee who chants constantly without ulterior motivation and without offenses cannot be swayed from his goal of attaining pure devotional service by any kind of worldly temptation, not even if Māyā Devī herself comes to lure him. We summarize what Kṛṣṇadāsa Kavirāja Gosvāmī has written in the third chapter of the *Antya-līlā* of *Caitanya Caritāmṛta*, where he mentions the glories of Haridāsa Ṭhākura sung by Mahāprabhu Himself to His associates.

TEMPTATION BY THE PROSTITUTE LAKṢAHĪRĀ

After Haridāsa Ṭhākura had left his home in Burhan, he came to the Benapole jungle, which after the pastime about to be described was given the name "the prostitute Hīrā's jungle." Haridāsa would have been in his early youth at this time, and these events took place before Mahāprabhu had appeared. He took up residence in a cottage in a secluded part of the jungle, worshipping Tulasī Devī and daily chanting 300,000 Holy Names. He would beg for food at a *brāhmaṇa's* house. All the people of the surrounding country observed Haridāsa Ṭhākura's spotless character and staunch devotion to the Holy Name and gave him their respect.

At that time, an atheistic Vaiṣṇava hater named Rāmacandra Khān was the area's principal landowner. He became jealous of Haridāsa Ṭhākura's increasing reputation and decided to ruin it by showing a flaw in his character. To this end, he devised numerous tactics, none of which were successful. Finally, he called some prostitutes together and asked them to seduce Haridāsa Ṭhākura. One of these prostitutes, a very beautiful young girl named Lakṣahīrā, claimed to be able to accomplish the task within three days. Hence, Rāmacandra engaged her in this mission.

Rāmacandra Khān proposed sending an armed guard with Lakṣahīrā to arrest Haridāsa Ṭhākura as soon as he was seen uniting with her, but she refused, saying that it would be better to wait until she was sure that Haridāsa Ṭhākura was ready to succumb. That night, she dressed and decorated herself in a most attractive manner and went to Haridāsa Ṭhākura's hut. The first thing she did was to pay obeisances to the Tulasī, showing that she was still influenced by her pious Hindu upbringing.

She then went and stood beside Haridāsa Ṭhākura. She began to use all the wiles at her command, flirting with him by saying, "You are a very handsome man, Ṭhākura, in the full bloom of youth. What woman would be able to resist you? I have come here because I am filled with desire for you. If I don't obtain you, I will kill myself."

In answer to this, Haridāsa Ṭhākura said, "I have just begun chanting my regular number of Holy Names. As soon as I am finished, I will do whatever you wish. In the mean time, please sit down and wait and listen to the chanting of the Holy Name." He kept chanting until morning, when the prostitute finally became impatient and left. She returned to Rāmacandra Khān and reported what had happened.

That night she returned to Haridāsa Ṭhākura's hut, and he expressed his regret at having been unable to fulfill her desires due to his inability to complete his quota of Holy Names. Once again, however, he assured her that as soon as he was finished, he would do as she wished. Lakṣahīrā paid her obeisances to Tulasī Devī as she had the previous evening and sat down. Once again she spent the night waiting for Haridāsa Ṭhākura to finish his chanting. In spite of her wily tricks to make Haridāsa Ṭhākura impatient, he continued to chant the Holy Name unperturbed. When morning came, she again grew restless. Haridāsa Ṭhākura said to her, "I have taken a vow that I will chant 10 million Holy Names before the end of the month. I have almost completed this number. As a matter of fact, I should finish it this very night. Don't worry; as soon as I have fulfilled my obligation, I will be able to fulfill your desire."

On the third night, Lakṣahīrā returned, again paying obeisances to the Tulasī and sitting down beside Haridāsa Ṭhākura to listen to him chant. As she continued to listen to him repeat the Holy Names, the contaminations in her mind began to melt away and she began to regret her mission. She finally fell down at his feet and begged forgiveness of him. She told him all about Rāmacandra Khān's evil intentions, but Haridāsa Ṭhākura answered her, "I know all about them. I would have left here on the very first day you came, but I wanted to bestow mercy to you, so I stayed for three days."

Lakṣahīrā then asked him to instruct her so that she might be saved. He told her that whatever money she had earned by sinful means should be given in charity to the *brāhmaṇas*, and then she should come and take up residence in his hut, where she should worship Tulasī Devī and chant the Holy Names constantly.

Lakṣahīrā did exactly as her guru instructed her, giving all her riches to the *brāhmaṇas* and shaving her head before returning to the hut dressed in a single piece of cloth. She then started to chant 300,000 names every day. By virtue of her service to Tulasī and her

chanting of the Holy Name, she became much renounced. All her senses were conquered, and she attained pure love for Kṛṣṇa. Through Haridāsa Ṭhākura's mercy, the prostitute had become a great Vaiṣṇavī.

"The prostitute became a celebrated devotee and very advanced in spiritual life. Many stalwart Vaiṣṇavas would come to see her." (*Caitanya Caritāmṛta* 3.3.141)

Śrīla Bhakti Siddhānta Sarasvatī Gosvāmī Ṭhākura has commented on Haridāsa Ṭhākura's instructions to Lakṣahīrā in the following way: "Even though the guru has a legitimate claim on all of his disciple's worldly possessions, a Vaiṣṇava guru does not ask for them for his own use. Those who take *dakṣiṇā*, or alms, are opening the door to the house of Yamarāja. A Vaiṣṇava guru is not bound for the house of Yama, but is a traveler on a higher road. For this reason, there is an arrangement for giving donations to *brāhmaṇas* on the *karma-mārga*. By not accepting his disciple's possessions, which are after all intended for sense gratification, the Vaiṣṇava guru remains independent of his disciple and does not compromise his integrity. He renounces them because he knows that they will awaken in him a lack of interes in the service of the Lord. Haridāsa Ṭhākura's teaching here is that the duty of a bona fide guru is to rid his disciple of his mundane pride and not himself accept the material possessions his disciple has renounced." (*Anubhāṣya* to *Caitanya Caritāmṛta* 3.3.139)

THE FATE OF RĀMACANDRA KHĀN

A Vaiṣṇava does not take offense from anyone, for he does not even consider himself to be a Vaiṣṇava. He accepts that all the suffering he undergoes is a result of his own sinful past and thus does not blame anyone else. Nevertheless, he is so dear to Kṛṣṇa that the Lord never tolerates offenses to his feet. The Lord never forgives offenses at the feet of a devotee who is free from defects and constantly engaged in acts that benefit all living beings. As a result, there is no other source of self-destruction and misfortune more powerful than offense to a Vaiṣṇava. The results of such offenses may come immediately, or they may be delayed, but they are inevitable.

In the case of Rāmacandra Khān, the seeds he had sown in committing offenses to Haridāsa Ṭhākura grew into a great tree that bore fruit one day when Nityānanda Prabhu along with His associates came to his house during a preaching tour in the area. As the indwelling soul of all beings, Nityānanda Prabhu was perfectly aware of Rāmacandra Khān's record and had, in fact, come to his house because he was angry and intended to punish him. Though Nityānanda Prabhu is known to be the most compassionate, merciful to even the lowliest people, saving sinners like Jagāi and Mādhāi and giving them love of God, He too becomes angry with one who offends a Vaiṣṇava.

As a result of his offenses to Haridāsa Ṭhākura, Rāmacandra Khān had become a complete demon. He could not give Nityānanda Prabhu and His companions the respect due to such exalted guests but arranged quarters for them in a cowshed. Nityānanda Prabhu became even more displeased with Rāmacandra Khān as a result of this insult and immediately left the place. He said, "This place is not fit for us, but for cow-slaughtering meat-eaters." Not long thereafter, the Muslim revenue officer came with his soldiers to collect overdue taxes. He and his men stayed in the Dūrga Maṇḍapa at Rāmacandra Khān's house and killed a cow there. They arrested him and his family and looted the house and village, destroying his caste, his wealth and his family in one fell swoop.

"Any town or country in which a great soul is insulted, even if by only one of its inhabitants, is destroyed on account of that offense." (*Caitanya Caritāmṛta* 3.3.163)

HARIDĀSA ṬHĀKURA IS IMPRISONED AND TORTURED

From Śrīla Vṛndāvana Dāsa Ṭhākura's *Caitanya Bhāgavata* it is known that before meeting Advaita Prabhu in Shantipur, Haridāsa Ṭhākura lived in Phuliya. Phuliya is on the Eastern Railway line in Nadia district between Ranaghat and Shantipur, about five miles north of Ranaghat. When the *brāhmaṇas* of the village saw his dedication to the chanting of the Holy Names as well as his ecstatic symptoms of love, they respected him as a Vaiṣṇava of the highest order.

The local magistrate (Kājī), however, knowing that Haridāsa Ṭhākura had been born in a Muslim household and now was showing such a taste for chanting the Holy Names of Kṛṣṇa, began to fear that he might convert others to Vaiṣṇavism. He took his complaint to the governor (Nawab), suggesting that Haridāsa Ṭhākura be punished as soon as possible. The governor ordered his officers to place Haridāsa Ṭhākura under arrest. The other prisoners already knew Haridāsa Ṭhākura's glories and thought that the sight and blessings of such a great spiritual personality would surely bring them merit to insure their early release from jail. But Haridāsa Ṭhākura told them that they were better off in jail and he blessed them that they stay there. The prisoners were naturally unhappy to hear such a "benediction," but then Haridāsa Ṭhākura explained it to them:

"I don't mean to say that you should remain prisoners, but that you forget sense gratification and chant the names of Hari. This was the meaning of my blessing; please don't be troubled for a moment on that account." (*Caitanya Bhāgavata* 1.16.63-64)

In other words, while in jail, the prisoners could forget the entanglements of material life and simply concentrate on chanting the Holy Name.

One day, the Nawab asked Haridāsa why he had abandoned the pure religion of Islam to embrace Hinduism. Haridāsa Ṭhākura answered, "God is one. He is in the same for everyone; He is the nondual Absolute Truth. In the different faiths, it is simply the name that differs, but on the absolute plane, there is no distinction. The same God sits in the heart of every single living being and engages everyone in His service in different ways. We all worship in the way we are made to worship by Him. Some Hindu *brāhmaṇas* convert to Islam. In the same way, though I was born in a Muslim family, the Lord has engaged me in chanting the Holy Names of Kṛṣṇa. The living being has no independence in such matters. If this is a fault, then please punish me."

The Nawab rebuked Haridāsa, saying, "Chant the names of God as they are found in your own religion and stop practicing that of other people. If you don't, you will have to face a very severe punishment." Haridāsa Ṭhākura answered with conviction:

khaṇḍa khaṇḍa haṣ deha jāy jadi prāṇa
tabu āmi vadane nā chāṛi hari-nāma

"You may cut my body to pieces, and the life may leave it. But I will never abandon the Holy Name, which my tongue will ever continue to chant." (*Caitanya Bhāgavata* 16.91)

This statement demonstrated Haridāsa Ṭhākura's unswerving determination in his worship of the Name. The ordinary living entity is bound up in *māyā* and so considers the well-being of the body and mind to be more important than worshipping the Lord. Those who are transcendentalists recognize that the body and its interests are fleeting, and so they put them aside and concentrate on their real self-interest, that of the soul, and worship the Lord.

When the Nawab saw that Haridāsa Ṭhākura's determination to continue chanting the names of Kṛṣṇa was unbreakable, he asked the Kājī what should be done. The Kājī answered, "He should be given such a severe punishment that other Muslims will be afraid to convert. He should be flogged publicly in twenty-two marketplaces until he is dead. If he is still alive after that, we will know that he is a genuine saint!"

The Nawab gave the order, and several infantrymen took Haridāsa Ṭhākura from one marketplace to another, giving him a cruel flogging with a cane in each one. Even so, he did not die. Just like Prahlāda, Kṛṣṇa's mercy protected him and kept him conscious only of the joys of the Holy Name, and so he did not feel the slightest pain. The pious people of the area who witnessed the merciless beating of Haridāsa Ṭhākura were greatly distressed, but he himself prayed to the Lord for the well-being of his torturers despite being ruthlessly flogged by them.

"Be merciful to all these poor souls, O Lord! Though they treat me like an enemy, do not consider this to be an offense." (*Caitanya Bhāgavata* 16.110)

Normally, the type of beating that was being given to Haridāsa Ṭhākura would have killed an ordinary man after only two or three marketplaces. When his torturers saw that he was still alive after twenty-two, they began to worry. The Kājī would not believe that they had really flogged him if Haridāsa Ṭhākura remained alive, and would order them to be killed in punishment for their failure. When Haridāsa Ṭhākura saw that they were inconvenienced by his remaining alive, he went into a deep trance of meditation on Kṛṣṇa, appearing to everyone as though dead.

The infantrymen took the body to the Nawab, who ordered it to be buried. But the Kājī objected, saying that because Haridāsa Ṭhākura had engaged in such reprehensible activities, he should not be given a Muslim burial but thrown into the water. So, on the Kājī's order, the soldiers flung Haridāsa Ṭhākura's body into the Ganges. To everyone's surprise, Haridāsa Ṭhākura floated to the other shore, where he climbed onto dry land and started walking in the direction of Phuliya, chanting the Holy Names in a loud voice. Both the Nawab and the Kājī realized that he was a real saint, or *pīr*, and they fell to the ground in obeisances and begged him for forgiveness. By Haridāsa Ṭhākura's grace, they were freed of their wicked misdeeds. The Nawab gave Haridāsa Ṭhākura official permission to go wherever he pleased and to chant the Holy Names.[5]

5 In *Śrī Caitanya Bhāgavata*'s tenth chapter of the *Madhya-khaṇḍa*, Vṛndāvana Dāsa Ṭhākura

The *brāhmaṇas* of Phuliya were overjoyed to see Haridāsa Ṭhākura again. They had been paralyzed by the news that he was being flogged in all the district marketplaces. Haridāsa Ṭhākura comforted them by saying that he had to submit to these events for the offense of hearing the blasphemy of Vaiṣṇavas. Indeed, the punishment that he had received could be considered minimal.

HARIDĀSA ṬHĀKURA MEETS ADVAITA ĀCĀRYA

Later, Haridāsa met Advaita Ācārya[6]. In recognition of his exalted status, Advaita Prabhu gave Haridāsa Ṭhākura the *śrāddha* plate that was normally given only to *brāhmaṇas*. When Haridāsa Ṭhākura objected to the honor, Advaita Ācārya said, "Feeding you is the equivalent of giving thousands of *brāhmaṇas* food to eat." Hence forward, Haridāsa Ṭhākura daily took his midday meal at Advaita Ācārya's house at his invitation. From Kṛṣṇadāsa Kavirāja Gosvāmī's account, it is apparent that these events took place before Mahāprabhu's appearance. The primary reason for Mahāprabhu's *avatāra* was the devotion and the heartfelt prayers of both Advaita Ācārya and Haridāsa Ṭhākura.

"Advaita Ācārya began to wonder how the world could be saved. How could this world ever achieve liberation without devotion for the Supreme Lord? Determined to make Kṛṣṇa descend, He worshipped Kṛṣṇa with Ganges water and Tulasī leaves. Meanwhile, Haridāsa Ṭhākura was in his grotto chanting the Holy Names and praying for Kṛṣṇa to appear. Caitanya Mahāprabhu's appearance, by which He saved the world through preaching the chanting of the Holy Names and love of Kṛṣṇa, was the result of both these persons' devotion." (*Caitanya Caritāmṛta* 3.3.221-4)

MĀYĀ DEVĪ TRIES TO TEMPT HARIDĀSA ṬHĀKURA

While Haridāsa Ṭhākura was sitting in solitude in his grotto on the banks of the Ganges in Shantipur and chanting the Holy Names with exclusive devotion, Māyā Devī, the presiding deity of the material manifestation, the Lord's illusory potency, came herself to test him. She took on the form of a beautiful woman and called out to him in a sweet voice that would have shaken the resolve of even great sages, imploring him to embrace her. Once again, Haridāsa Ṭhākura told her that he would complete his vow of chanting a fixed number of *harināma*, and only then would he satisfy her desires. Although she came three nights in a row, Māyā Devī was astonished to see that there was not the slightest wavering in Haridāsa Ṭhākura's resolve to chant the Holy Name. She admitted defeat and prayed to him for his mercy.

---

writes that while Haridāsa Ṭhākura was being cruelly beaten, Mahāprabhu descended with His discus, intending to destroy the demons, but was unable to do so on account of Haridāsa Ṭhākura's prayers. So He shielded Haridāsa Ṭhākura's body with His own. As a result, the marks of the cane were seen on His own back. The main reason for the Lord's appearance is His devotee. When such an outrage was being perpetrated on His devotee, He immediately appeared to protect him.

When Haridāsa Ṭhākura heard the Lord recount this story, he immediately fainted. The Lord then showed him His divine form. The Lord glorified Haridāsa Ṭhākura: "Anyone who even sees Haridāsa Ṭhākura becomes free from all bondage. Even great demigods like Brahmā and Śiva desire Haridāsa Ṭhākura's company. Even the Ganges desires his touch."

6 Advaita was born in 1434, 52 years before the appearance of Caitanya Mahāprabhu, so he was 17 years older than Haridāsa Ṭhākura.

"Previously I received the name of Lord Rāma from Lord Śiva, but I had the desire to hear the name of Lord Kṛṣṇa from you. Lord Rāma's name awards liberation, whereas Kṛṣṇa's name simultaneously awards *prema* also. Please bless me by initiating me in Kṛṣṇa's name, so that I may float in the flood of love for Him." (*Caitanya Caritāmṛta* 3.3.254-6)

Haridāsa Ṭhākura gave her initiation in the *mahā-mantra,* and thus Māyā Devī left, feeling that she had been fulfilled.

A devotee who one-pointedly chants the Holy Name without artifice cannot be swayed from the path of pure devotion, not even by the personification of *māyā* herself. Once again, Haridāsa Ṭhākura is an outstanding example. There was no object of enjoyment in this entire world that could tempt him. If one sees someone who is apparently taking shelter of the Holy Name, but at the same time succumbs to the temptations of women, wealth and prestige, it can be understood that he is not truly surrendered to the Holy Name. *Phalenā phalakāraṇam anumīyate:* one can figure out the cause by examining the results. Although one sees the Holy Names being chanted in many places, we do not often see the desired results. The reason is that those who are chanting are not doing it in a fashion that is sincere, single-minded and offenseless.

HARIDĀSA, THE SNAKE AND THE SNAKE-CHARMER

In the grotto in Phuliya on the banks of the Gaṅgā where Haridāsa performed his *bhajana* lived a poisonous snake. Those who came to visit Haridāsa Ṭhākura's residence were placed in some discomfort because of the poisonous fumes emanating from this beast. Some local doctors, who were particularly expert in dealing with snakebite, warned Haridāsa Ṭhākura of the danger and advised him to leave his place of worship. At the consistent pleadings of all the people, Haridāsa Ṭhākura finally agreed to move. However, just before sunset, the great serpent left the grotto of its own accord.

Another lesson that can be taken from Haridāsa Ṭhākura's holy life is that making a public display of love of Kṛṣṇa in order to gain public prestige is very detrimental to one's devotional life. One day, a snake charmer from Phuliya village went to a rich man's house to sing Kṛṣṇa's pastime of taming the serpent Kāliya. Haridāsa Ṭhākura was present, and when he heard the *līlās* of Kṛṣṇa he became so affected by love that he fainted in the assembly and the various manifestations of ecstatic love became visible on his body. All the people present took the dust of Haridāsa Ṭhākura's feet and smeared it on their bodies.

A certain *brāhmaṇa* who was present there saw the respect that the people were showing to Haridāsa Ṭhākura and became jealous. The shameless fellow had such a strong desire for prestige that when the snake charmer continued his song, he too fell to the ground and started to make a show of all kinds of false ecstasies. The snake charmer could recognize the faker for what he was and started to hit him with a cane. The *brāhmaṇa* began to scream and plead and then ran away. The snake charmer explained to everyone present the spontaneity of Haridāsa Ṭhākura's love and the falseness of the *brāhmaṇa*'s pretence. This particular pastime shows that even a humble snake charmer can have enough common sense to distinguish between real and faked ecstatic symptoms.

THE LOUD CHANTING OF THE HOLY NAMES

Haridāsa Ṭhākura constantly chanted the Holy Name and called to the Lord in a loud voice. At that time, not many people were able to understand the value of this practice. Prior to Gaurāṅgasundara's appearance, most people were simply interested in sense gratification and were inimical to devotion for Kṛṣṇa and the chanting of His Holy Names. Advaita Ācārya and Haridāsa Ṭhākura were saddened by this terrible situation. When the nondevotees heard them chanting loudly, they would say, "The Lord sleeps during the four months of the rainy season. If you call Him out loud in this way, you will wake Him up, and that will be a grave offense. There will be famine in the country if you keep on with it. Some *brāhmaṇas* have taken up this chanting business as a way of worshipping their own bellies, no doubt." They would criticize Haridāsa Ṭhākura and Advaita Ācārya by joking in this way. Even though such statements pained Haridāsa Ṭhākura, he never stopped chanting the Lord's Names in a loud voice.

One day, a rascal *brāhmaṇa* from a village named Harinadi in the Jessore district started a debate with Haridāsa Ṭhākura on this subject. He argued that the names of the Lord should be meditated upon and that there was no reason to chant them aloud. He wanted to know in which scripture it was stated that one should chant aloud. In answer to these questions, Haridāsa Ṭhākura gave a detailed account of the glories of the Holy Name. He said that loud chanting of the Holy Names was a hundred times more powerful than *japa*. Through the loud chanting of the Names, even the birds, animals and other creatures are also saved.

"Animals, birds, insects and other creatures cannot utter the Holy Name, but if they just hear the Holy Name, they can all cross over the ocean of nescience. If you chant the Holy Names silently, then you yourself will be saved, but if you chant aloud, then you will benefit others. Therefore, all the scriptures state that by the loud chanting of the Name, a hundred times greater result can be obtained." (*Caitanya Bhāgavata* 1.16.280-2)

japato harināmāni
sthāne śata-guṇādhikaḥ
ātmānaṁ ca punāty uccair
japan śrotṛn punāti ca

" 'Someone who chants the Holy Names aloud is a hundred times better than one who performs *japa* because the one who chants *japa* silently simply benefits himself, while the person who chants aloud not only does good for himself, but for all those who hear him as well.' (*Nāradīya Purāṇa*)"

Who is better, the person who earns money and spends it all on himself, or the one who uses his money to support a thousand others? Through silent *japa*, one takes care of his own spiritual needs, whereas all living beings are benefited through loud *saṅkīrtana*. This is why it is considered to be superior.

Even though he heard Haridāsa quote scripture in support of his idea, the *brāhmaṇa* from Harinadi village was unconvinced. Indeed, he became angry and began to verbally abuse Haridāsa Ṭhākura by bringing up his low birth. He said, "If everything that you say about the Holy Name is not found in scripture, then I will publicly cut off your nose and ear as a punishment." As a result of this offensive behavior, the *brāhmaṇa* contracted smallpox not long afterward, and his own nose and ear fell off.

THE OFFENSES OF GOPĀLA CAKRAVARTĪ

Once Haridāsa Ṭhākura came to Hoogly and stayed in the village of Chandpur, near Saptagram-Triveni, at the house of Hiraṇya and Govardhana Majumadāra's family priest,

Balarāma Ācārya. He was given a straw hut to live in, and there he chanted the Holy Names all day long, taking food at Balarāma Ācārya's house. Goverdhana Majumdāra's son Raghunātha Dāsa Gosvāmī was a young boy at the time and would often visit Haridāsa Ṭhākura, whose merciful glance made it possible for him to eventually come into Mahāprabhu's direct company.

Hiraṇya and Govardhana Majumadāra would regularly arrange for discussions of the *Bhāgavata* and other scriptures at their house. One day Balarāma Ācārya brought Haridāsa Ṭhākura to this assembly. When Raghunātha's father and uncle heard about Haridāsa Ṭhākura's various qualities and that he chanted 300,000 names every day, they were very impressed.

While discussing the scriptures at the meeting, the scholars present brought up the subject of the glories of the Holy Names. One Paṇḍita said that the Holy Name destroys sins; another claimed it bestows liberation. Haridāsa Ṭhākura said that the primary fruit of chanting the Holy Name is love for the lotus feet of Śrī Kṛṣṇa, and the destruction of accumulated sinful *karmas* and liberation from the material condition are only its secondary effects. He gave the following example: with dawn's first light, the darkness is dissipated and with it the fear of thieves, ghosts and demons. With the full rising of the sun, one can set about doing one's religious activities and regulative duties. Similarly, even before one has experienced the full manifestation of the Holy Name, one's sins are destroyed and one becomes liberated. With its full manifestation, one attains Kṛṣṇa *prema*. The glimpse of the Holy Name (*nāmābhāsa*) brings liberation, but the devotee considers liberation such an inconsequential benefit that he does not accept it even if the Lord wants to give it to him.

One of the people who heard Haridāsa Ṭhākura speak was a *brāhmaṇa* named Gopāla Cakravartī, a handsome and learned young scholar who worked as a tax collector in Bengal. When he heard that simply the glimpse of the Holy Name could bring liberation, he got angry and said, "Fellow scholars! These are the statements of a sentimentalist. After millions of births of cultivating knowledge one still may not attain liberation. Yet this fellow says that just a glimpse of the Holy Name will bring that result!"

Haridāsa Ṭhākura answered, "The pleasure of liberation is insignificant when compared to the ecstasy of devotion. Just a glimpse of devotion or a glimpse of the Holy Name will easily produce liberation."

The *brāhmaṇa* became even angrier and said, "Haridāsa Ṭhākura must swear that he will cut off his nose if one is not liberated by *nāmābhāsa*."

Haridāsa Ṭhākura had no trouble agreeing to this, but the rest of the people in the assembly were shocked by Gopāla's breach of the proper etiquette toward a great spiritual personality. Hiraṇya and Govardhana Majumadāra rebuked him. Balarāma Ācārya also chastised him, saying, "You are a foolish logician. What do you know about devotion? You have insulted Haridāsa Ṭhākura. You will be ruined on account of it. You shall remain deprived of auspiciousness." All the other members of the assembly fell at Haridāsa Ṭhākura's feet and asked for forgiveness for Gopāla's behavior, but he only said, "Neither he nor you are at fault. The *brāhmaṇa* is ignorant and addicted to arguing. One cannot understand the glories of the Holy Name through logic. May the Lord bless you all. Don't worry about me." The Majumdar brothers ostracized Gopāla Cakravartī, banning him from their home.

Though Haridāsa Ṭhākura took no offense at Gopāla Cakravartī's words, and even forgave him, Kṛṣṇa does not take the blasphemy of a devotee lightly, and so He punished the *brāhmaṇa*. Three days later he contracted leprosy, and his very prominent nose decayed and melted off. Everyone was terrified by the *brāhmaṇa*'s misfortune and glorified Haridāsa Ṭhākura's spiritual power, but it was a source of distress to Haridāsa himself.

HARIDĀSA COMES TO NABADWIP

After this, Haridāsa Ṭhākura went to live in Nabadwip out of a desire to be with pure devotees like Advaita Ācārya. He was thus present there when Mahāprabhu began the *saṅkīrtana* movement. Haridāsa's participation in these pastimes is described in the *Madhya-khānda* of *Śrī Caitanya Bhāgavata* where it is said that he was a participant in the *saṅkīrtana* festivities in the houses of Candraśekhara Ācārya and Śrīvāsa Paṇḍita.

"When the Vaiṣṇavas heard that the Lord had begun His *saṅkīrtana* pastimes, they all were overjoyed. Every night He would hold *kīrtana* in the house of Śrīvāsa Paṇḍita, or sometimes at the house of Candraśekhara Ācārya. Nityānanda Prabhu, Gadādhara Paṇḍita, Advaita Ācārya, Śrīvāsa Paṇḍita, Vidyānidhi, Murārī Gupta, Hiraṇya and Haridāsa Ṭhākura were all there." (*Caitanya Bhāgavata* 2.8.110-112)

Haridāsa Ṭhākura and Nityānanda Prabhu were the first preachers of the Holy Name. Mahāprabhu ordered Haridāsa Ṭhākura and Nityānanda Prabhu to go from door to door to beg people to chant the names of Kṛṣṇa, to worship Him and to learn about Him.

One day, the Lord suddenly had an idea, and He called Nityānanda Prabhu and Haridāsa Ṭhākura to tell them: "Listen, listen, Nityānanda Prabhu. Listen, Haridāsa. I wish you to go and tell everyone about My order. Knock on every door and beg people to chant the names of Kṛṣṇa, worship Kṛṣṇa and learn about Kṛṣṇa. Speak of nothing but this and inspire others to do the same. At the end of the day, come here and tell me the results of your preaching. If people do not comply with you, implore them in this way – tell them I will come and destroy them with My *chakra* in My hand." (*Caitanya Bhāgavata* 2.13.7-11)

Nityānanda Prabhu and Haridāsa Ṭhākura followed the Lord's order and began preaching throughout Nabadwip town. One day they went up to two dreadful drunken bandits named Jagāi and Mādhāi. Seeing their fallen condition, Nityānanda Prabhu was particularly merciful toward them, but Jagāi and Mādhāi were so inebriated that they simply became angry when they heard his appeal, and turned on him and Haridāsa Ṭhākura, intending to give them a beating. They both started to run away, but Haridāsa Ṭhākura, being already quite advanced in age, was unable to keep up with Nityānanda Prabhu. Nevertheless, he somehow managed to escape with his life.

That evening, Haridāsa Ṭhākura told Advaita Ācārya about the day's events, saying that he would not go out preaching with Nityānanda Prabhu anymore since His behavior was unpredictable. The all-powerful Lord Nityānanda Prabhu's running away is certainly a mysterious pastime, but it is to be remembered that He later went out on His own and managed to deliver the two bandits, Jagāi and Mādhāi.

Haridāsa Ṭhākura also engaged in water sports with Mahāprabhu in Nabadwip. One day, overcome by a mood of love, the Lord jumped in the Ganges; then Haridāsa Ṭhākura and Nityānanda Prabhu lifted Him from the water. They then arranged to hide Mahāprabhu in the house of Nandan Ācārya because of His wish for seclusion. When Advaita Ācārya and the other devotees felt the distress of separation from the Lord, Haridāsa Ṭhākura went and brought Śrīvāsa Paṇḍita to Nandana Ācārya's house, bringing about the reunion of the devotees and the Lord.

When Mahāprabhu put on a play about Kṛṣṇa's Vrindavan pastimes in the house of Candraśekhara Ācārya, Haridāsa Ṭhākura played the part of a watchman. He came onto the scene, dressed as a guard, carrying a stick in his hand. The other actors in the play were Mahāprabhu as Ādyāśakti, Nityānanda Prabhu as an old cowherd woman, Advaita Ācārya as the clown, Gadādhara Paṇḍita as a cowherd girl, and Śrīvāsa Paṇḍita as Nārada Muṇi. Haridāsa Ṭhākura's duty in the play was to awake everyone for the service of Śrī Kṛṣṇa. He cried out, "Wake up! Wake up! Wake up!" And Śrīvāsa Paṇḍita would dance dressed as Nārada Muṇi. (*Caitanya Bhāgavata* 2.18.100)

When the Lord took His *saṅkīrtana* party along the banks of the Bhagīrathī, Haridāsa Ṭhākura joined Him.

"Then Haridāsa Ṭhākura, the ocean of Kṛṣṇa *rasa* danced beautifully on Mahāprabhu's order." (*Caitanya Bhāgavata* 2.23.204)

The night before Mahāprabhu left to take *sannyāsa*, Haridāsa Ṭhākura was staying at His home. He and all the other devotees were devastated by the Lord's intention to take the renounced order. Not long after the Lord went to Puri. Haridāsa Ṭhākura followed Him in order to participate in the Rathayātrā festival.

HARIDĀSA ṬHĀKURA IN PURI

While at Puri, after the Snāna-yātrā, when Lord Jagannātha was absent from the temple (*anavasara-kāla*) Mahāprabhu felt separation so intensely that He went to stay in Alalanatha. However, when Mahāprabhu heard that more than two hundred devotees from Bengal had arrived, He returned to Puri, where He met them at Kāśī Miśra's house. At first, He did not see Haridāsa Ṭhākura, and so He inquired after him. In fact, Haridāsa Ṭhākura was standing in the roadway, paying his obeisances from there. The devotees went to Haridāsa Ṭhākura and told him that Mahāprabhu wanted to see him, but Haridāsa Ṭhākura answered:

"I am a low-born person with no good qualities. I have no right to go near the temple. If I can find a solitary place to stay in some garden somewhere, then I will pass my time there alone. That way there is no danger that the servants of Lord Jagannātha will accidentally touch me. This is my wish." (*Caitanya Caritāmṛta* 2.11.165-7)

The devotees came back to Mahāprabhu to report what Haridāsa Ṭhākura had said, and his wish pleased Him. He asked Kāśī Miśra to arrange for a solitary cottage for Haridāsa Ṭhākura in a garden not far from His own place of worship. Kāśī Miśra was happy to have the chance to serve the Lord by making these arrangements according to His order.

Later the Lord went to see Haridāsa Ṭhākura, who immediately fell to the ground in respectful obeisances. The Lord lifted him from the ground and embraced him, but Haridāsa Ṭhākura said, "I am an untouchable. You should not touch me." The Lord answered:

"I touch you for My own purification, for you have reached a level of holiness that I haven't. At every moment you are engaged in every pious activity; you are constantly bathing in the water of every holy place; you are constantly engaged in all the sacrifices, penances and charity. You are constantly studying the Vedic scriptures. You are thus holier than any *brāhmaṇa* or *sannyāsī*."

After saying this, the Lord took him to the flower garden and gave him the solitary room there as a place to stay. "Stay here and chant the Holy Names. I will come every day to visit you. You can see the discus (*cakra*) on the pinnacle of the temple tower from here. Pay your obeisances when you see it. I will arrange for Lord Jagannātha's *prasāda* to be brought to you here every day." (*Caitanya Caritāmṛta* 2.11.189-95)

This flower garden is now known as Siddha Bakul. Previously it was named Mudra Math. There is a legend connected with the Siddha Bakul tree. Lord Jagannātha's *pūjārīs* have a tradition of giving some fortunate person the twig used to clean Lord Jagannātha's teeth as *prasāda*. One day they gave Mahāprabhu a twig that had so been used. The Lord planted this twig in the ground at Haridāsa Ṭhākura's place of *bhajana*. This twig eventually grew into a large tree. It is said that the Lord planted the twig on the first day of the month of Caitra, also known as *Mahā-Viṣnu Saṅkrānti*, i.e., the day when the sun enters into the sign of Aries. For this reason, a festival named the Danta-kāṣṭha-ropaṇa Mahotsava is held every year on that day to celebrate the occasion.

Though Haridāsa Ṭhākura was not officially banned from going into the Lord Jagannātha temple or the house of Kāśī Miśra (where Mahāprabhu was staying), he never went there out of humility at his lowly birth. Like Haridāsa Ṭhākura, Rūpa Gosvāmī and Sanātana Gosvāmī never entered the Lord Jagannātha temple. Even though they were born in a very high-caste *brāhmaṇa* family, Rūpa Gosvāmī and Sanātana Gosvāmī considered themselves to be no better than *mlecchās* because of their long association with the Muslim court. When in Puri, they would stay with Haridāsa Ṭhākura. Mahāprabhu Himself would go to see them every day.

"Haridāsa Ṭhākura, Rūpa Gosvāmī and Sanātana Gosvāmī never entered the Lord Jagannātha temple, but when Mahāprabhu went to see the Upala-bhoga in the morning, He would regularly go to Haridāsa Ṭhākura's cottage, where they were staying. It was the Lord's regular practice to visit Rūpa Gosvāmī and Sanātana Gosvāmī whenever they were staying in Puri." (*Caitanya Caritāmṛta* 2.1.63-65)

Śrīla Haridāsa Ṭhākura participated in the *kīrtana* during the Rathayātrā festival as the main dancer in one of the seven *kīrtana sampradāyas*. He was in the third group, whose lead singer was Mukunda Datta.

HARIDĀSA ṬHĀKURA'S TEACHINGS ON THE HOLY NAME

Mahāprabhu taught the glories of the Holy Name through Haridāsa Ṭhākura. One day, the Lord was feeling particularly unhappy about the lot of the conditioned souls. He came to Siddha Bakul and said to the Ṭhākura: "Haridāsa, in the Age of Kālī, the non-Hindus kill the cow and are inimical to the *brāhmaṇas*. How will these Muslims ever be saved?" Haridāsa Ṭhākura answered, "Don't be distressed at seeing the pitiable condition of the Muslims. They will be liberated by the *nāmābhāsa*, the shadow of the Holy Name, whenever they say *hārām*[7]. In the *Nṛsiṁha-purāṇa* it is said,

daṁṣṭri-daṁṣṭrāhato mleccho
hārāmeti punaḥ punaḥ

7 The Arabic word *harām* (*hārām* in Bengal) means anything which is impure according to Islamic religion. For Bengali Muslims, it particularly refers to the pig or boar which is an untouchable animal in Islam.

uktvāpi muktim āpnoti kiṁ
punaḥ śraddhayā gṛṇan

"When wounded by the tusks of a boar, the Muslim cries out 'Hārāma, Hārāma!' again and again. If he attains liberation by so doing, then just think what will be the result if one chants the name of Rāma with faith." (*Caitanya Caritāmṛta* 3.3.56)

Bhaktivinoda Ṭhākura says that if any Muslim dies while saying this word, he is immediately liberated. This is *nāmābhāsa* or *nāma-saṅkeṭa* because the speaker makes the correct sound even though he does not intend calling for Lord Rama. When the Holy Name is such a powerful sound, it is impossible to say just what fruits await the sincere and faithful chanter. The example is given of Ajāmila, who called the name of his son Nārāyaṇa as he was dying but attained liberation through this *nāmābhāsa*.

When He heard Haridāsa Ṭhākura's explanation, Mahāprabhu was very pleased, but again He asked him, "But how will the dumb animals and the trees and the plants be delivered?" Haridāsa Ṭhākura answered:

"You Yourself have instituted the loud chanting of the Holy Names, which both the moving and nonmoving creatures can hear. The mobile creatures are freed from their bondage to repeated birth and death by hearing the Holy Name. As for the immobile, they perform *kīrtana* themselves by echoing the sounds. By your indescribable mercy, the entire universe is engaged in *kīrtana*, and the mobile and immobile beings dance when they hear it. You preached the loud chanting of the Holy Names, by which the repeated births and deaths of all living beings come to an end." (*Caitanya Caritāmṛta* 3.3.68-71, 75)

THE DISAPPEARANCE OF HARIDĀSA ṬHĀKURA

Rūpa Gosvāmī and Sanātana Gosvāmī first met Nityānanda Prabhu and Haridāsa Ṭhākura when they accompanied Mahāprabhu to Ramakeli *grama* in the Maldaha district. They thus knew each other's virtues quite well. One day in Puri, Haridāsa Ṭhākura recited the glories of Sanātana Gosvāmī. Sanātana Gosvāmī, in turn, praised him as follows:

"Who is equal to you? You are the most fortunate member of Mahāprabhu's entourage. The purpose of the Lord's descent is the preaching of the Holy Name, but He accomplishes His personal mission through you. Every single day you chant 300,000 Holy Names, and you glorify the Holy Name to everyone you meet. Some people act properly but do not deliver the message of Kṛṣṇa *bhakti*, while others preach but do not meet the behavioral standards. You demonstrate ideal behavior as well as preach the chanting of the Holy Names. You are the most advanced in the world and the spiritual master of everyone in the universe." (*Caitanya Caritāmṛta* 3.4.99-103)

In the eleventh chapter of the *Caitanya Caritāmṛta*'s *Antya-līlā*, Kṛṣṇadāsa Kavirāja Gosvāmī describes Haridāsa Ṭhākura's disappearance in a most captivating way. The account should be read in its entirety to commemorate that day. A brief summary is given here:

namāmi hari dāsaṁ taṁ caitanyaṁ
taṁ ca tat-prabhum
saṁsthitām api yan-mūrtiṁ
svāṅke kṛtvā nanarta yaḥ

"I offer my obeisances to Haridāsa Ṭhākura as well as to his worshipable Lord, Caitanya

Mahāprabhu, who placed his body on His lap and danced." (*Caitanya Caritāmṛta* 3.11.1)

As Haridāsa Ṭhākura grew old, it became more and more difficult for him to maintain his vow of chanting 300,000 Names every day. Thus, he had no appetite when Govinda came with Lord Jagannātha's *prasāda* and would eat only a single grain of rice just to avoid disrespecting the holy food. Out of His affection for Haridāsa Ṭhākura, Mahāprabhu told him that he was a perfected being and that there was no need for him to show such attachment for devotional service in practice; he could thus reduce the number of Holy Names that he chanted every day.

Haridāsa Ṭhākura knew that Mahāprabhu would soon be ending His pastimes in this world, and he wished to leave before Him. The affectionate Lord granted Haridāsa Ṭhākura his wish, even though He felt desolate at the prospect of losing his company.

Haridāsa Ṭhākura sat in front of Mahāprabhu and gazed at His lotus face. As the tears flowed from his eyes, he took the Lord's lotus feet on his chest and, with the names "Kṛṣṇa Caitanya" on his lips, voluntarily left his body like Bhīṣma.

All around them, the devotees were being swept away by a *kīrtana* that grew louder and louder. The Lord spontaneously lifted Haridāsa Ṭhākura's body and started to dance around the courtyard, holding him to His chest. To the accompaniment of the loud singing of the Holy Names, He and the devotees took Haridāsa Ṭhākura's body to the beach. There they bathed the body in the sea and then dug a hole in the sand, where they placed it. Mahāprabhu was the first to offer sand into the *samādhi*. This was the *samādhi* ritual of Haridāsa Ṭhākura, and the seashore has become a great place of pilgrimage.

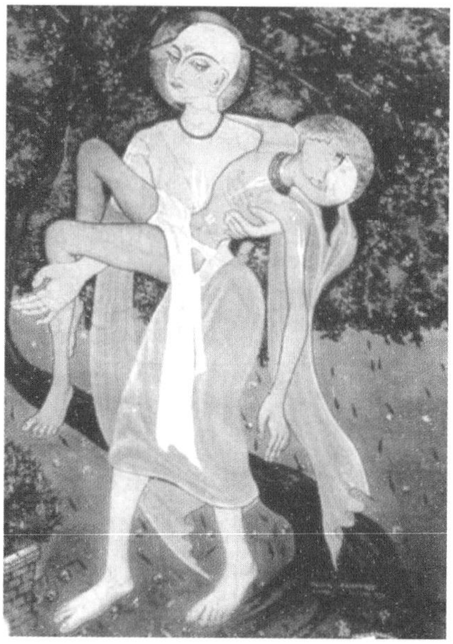

Mahāprabhu circumambulated the burial place and then went personally to the Jagannātha temple to beg for *prasāda* for a feast in honor of Haridāsa Ṭhākura. Svarūpa Dāmodara Gosvāmī would not let Mahāprabhu carry the *prasāda*, but took personal responsibility for organizing the festival. At the feast, all the devotees were given enough food to eat to their fill. In a mood of absorption in divine love, Mahāprabhu said to them:

"All those who witnessed Haridāsa Ṭhākura's disappearance festival, who participated in it by dancing or singing the Holy Names, who offered sand on his *samādhi* or took *mahā prasāda* on this occasion, will quickly attain Kṛṣṇa. This is the fruit of seeing a great personality like Haridāsa Ṭhākura. The Supreme Lord is so merciful that He gave Me Haridāsa's association, and now the independent Lord has again wished to deprive Me of that association. When Haridāsa decided that he wanted to leave, there was nothing I could do to keep him back. He left his body at the very moment that he desired to do so, just as we have heard that Bhīṣma did. Haridāsa was the exemplar of humanity in this world, and now that he is gone, the world has lost a jewel. All glories to Haridāsa Ṭhākura! Sing the Lord's names!" Having finished His eulogy, the Lord began to dance once again. (*Caitanya Caritāmṛta* 3.11.91-98)

Haridāsa Ṭhākura's *tirodhāna-līlā* (disappearance pastime) took place on the fourteenth day of the waxing moon in the month of Bhādra.

Gaṅgā Dāsa Paṇḍita

purāsīd raghunāthasya yo vaśiṣṭha-munir guruḥ
sa prakāśa-viśeṣeṇa gaṅgādāsa-sudarśanau

"Lord Rāmacandra's guru, Vaśiṣṭha Muni, appeared in two expansions in Gaura *līlā* as Gaṅgā Dāsa Paṇḍita and Sudarśana." (*Gaura-gaṇoddeśa-dīpikā* 53)

ācāryaḥ śrī-jagannātho gaṅgādāsaḥ prabhu-priyaḥ
āsīn nidhuvane prāg yo durvāsā gopikā-priyaḥ

"Jagannātha Ācārya and Gaṅgā Dāsa Paṇḍita, the dear associates of the Lord, were previously Durvāśa, who was so dear to the *gopīs* in Nidhuvan." (*Gaura-gaṇoddeśa-dīpikā* 111)

"Gaṅgā Dāsa Paṇḍita was very dear to Lord Caitanya Mahāprabhu. Anyone who remembers him will be freed from all material bondage." (*Caitanya Caritāmṛta* 1.10.29)

In his *Caitanya Bhāgavata,* Vṛndāvana Dāsa Ṭhākura identifies Gaṅgā Dāsa Paṇḍita with Kṛṣṇa's guru, Sāndīpani Muni:

"There was a wonderful professor in Nabadwip named Gaṅgā Dāsa Paṇḍita, who resembled Kṛṣṇa's guru, Sāndīpani Muni." (*Caitanya Bhāgavata,* 1.8.26)

The author of the *Gauḍīya Vaiṣṇava Abhidhāna* suggests that Lord Rāmacandra's guru Vaśiṣṭha Muni entered into Sāndīpani Muni during Kṛṣṇa *līlā*. Thus, he reconciled the apparently conflicting statements of *Gaura-gaṇoddeśa-dīpikā* and *Caitanya Bhāgavata.* In verse 52 of *Gaura-gaṇoddeśa-dīpikā*, however, Kavi Karṇapūra identifies Sāndīpani Muni with Keśava Bhāratī.

Advaita Ācārya, the *avatāra* of Mahā-Viṣṇu, prayed and called to Kṛṣṇa to descend to this earth out of a desire to see the salvation of all creatures in this world. Indeed, it was through the heartfelt cries of Advaita Ācārya that Caitanya Mahāprabhu felt obliged to descend. It was the Lord's desire that all His eternally perfected associates from His previous *avatāras* who played the role of His seniors descend prior to His own appearance. Gaṅgā Dāsa Paṇḍita was one of these elders (*guruvarga*) who preceded the Lord.

"Nityānanda Prabhu appeared in Rāḍhadeśa while Gaṅgā Dāsa Paṇḍita, Murāri Gupta and Mukunda also appeared elsewhere." (*Caitanya Caritāmṛta* 1.13.61)

"Many other associates of the Lord remained hidden in Nabadwip, taking birth there prior to Him on His order. They included Candraśekhara, Jagadīśa, Gopīnātha, Śrīmān, Murāri, Śrī Garuḍa and Gaṅgā Dāsa." (*Caitanya Bhāgavata* 1.2.98-9)

NIMĀI'S STUDENT LIFE

Jagannātha Miśra took little Nimāi to Gaṅgā Dāsa Paṇḍita when the child expressed his desire to study with him. Gaṅgā Dāsa Paṇḍita lived in the neighborhood known as Gaṇgānagar. It is said that when Bhagīratha brought down the Ganges, the goddess waited on this spot for the arrival of Gaurāṅga Mahāprabhu and hence the name. During the *parikramā* of Nabadwip *dhāma*, the devotees sit down at a spot near the Yogapīṭha temple to hear the glories of Ganganagar, even though it is in fact situated in Simantadwip.

In his commentary to *Caitanya Bhāgavata* (1.8.25), Śrīla Bhakti Siddhānta Sarasvatī Gosvāmī Ṭhākura writes: "Śrī Gaura-Nārāyaṇa is the Lord of Vaikuṇṭha, the Supreme Personality of Godhead. He is therefore the only reservoir of all scriptural knowledge, opulence and wisdom. Even so, during His earthly pastimes He desired to learn grammar and other arts and sciences just as Kṛṣṇa did when He studied with Sāndīpani Muni. He did this to show that those who make a living as teachers should have genuine learning and not make a pretense of possessing knowledge."

When Jagannātha Miśra brought Nimāi to Gaṅgā Dāsa Paṇḍita, the scholar was overjoyed to accept Him as his student. He began to teach Him with as much care as if He were his own son. He was astounded by Nimāi's powerful memory and intelligence. Though he had taught thousands of students, he had never had a pupil of such caliber. A student of quality brings glory to his teacher. Gaṅgā Dāsa Paṇḍita considered Nimāi to be the best among his students.

Nimāi would ask tricky questions to His fellow students Murāri Gupta, Kṛṣṇānanda, Kamalā Kānta and others. He was able to explain a *sūtra* in one way, then refute it Himself and then again reestablish the previous, explanation in a completely different way, baffling His classmates while impressing them with His scholarship. Thus, the Lord's education pastimes took place in the home of Gaṅgā Dāsa Paṇḍita.

"This is the house of Gaṅgā Dāsa Paṇḍita, where the son of Śacī studied grammar. He took delight in study daily, even making His own explanatory comments on the *sūtras*. In great jubilation, He would ask tricky questions to Murāri Gupta, Kṛṣṇānanda, and Kamalā Kānta. Gaurasundara thus immersed Himself completely in the joys of learning – such pastimes are beyond the understanding of the great demigods, headed by Brahmā." (*Bhakti-ratnākara* 12.2185-8)

"The Lord studied grammar from Gaṅgā Dāsa Paṇḍita. He would only have to hear a lesson once in order to learn both the *sūtra* and its explanation." (*Caitanya Caritāmṛta* 1.15.5)

MAHĀPRABHU AFTER HIS RETURN FROM GAYA

After Mahāprabhu's return from Gaya, Śrīvāsa Paṇḍita, Śrīmān Paṇḍita, Gadādhara Paṇḍita, Sadāśiva, Śuklāmbara Brahmacārī, and other devotees were amazed to see the transcendental symptoms out of the feelings of separation from Kṛṣṇa in Him. They also felt great joy to see how He had abandoned His attachment to studies to turn to Kṛṣṇa *bhakti*.

On His return, Mahāprabhu continued to set the proper example of how to serve one's teacher, going to Gaṅgā Dāsa Paṇḍita's house and paying obeisances to his feet. Gaṅgā Dāsa Paṇḍita also displayed the suitable behavior of a guru toward his dear disciple by embracing Him with respect and affection. If one's education does not lead to devotion to Kṛṣṇa, then his human birth becomes meaningless. Through devotion to Kṛṣṇa, one's ancestors are delivered. Gaṅgā Dāsa Paṇḍita was also happy to see Nimāi's transformation, and ordered Him to continue teaching.

Nimāi's guru said, "Your life is blessed, my child. Your mother and father's forefathers have all been delivered. Your students do not want to study under any teacher other than You, even if Brahmā himself orders them to do so. You have come now, and everyone has seen You, so go home for today. Come back tomorrow, however, and continue teaching." (*Caitanya Bhāgavata* 2.1.122-4)

"I pay obeisances to Gaṅgā Dāsa Paṇḍita's feet, for he has the Lord of the Vedas and the husband of the goddess of learning as his disciple. What goals are left for Gaṅgā Dāsa Paṇḍita to achieve, for his disciple is worshipable to the fourteen worlds?" (*Caitanya Bhāgavata* 2.1.283-4)

GAṆGĀ DĀSA AT ŚRĪVĀSA AṆGANA

Nityānanda Prabhu, the savior of the most fallen, also visited Gaṅgā Dāsa Paṇḍita one day after having been worshipped in Śrīvāsa Paṇḍita's house. At the time He was wandering through Nabadwip in the mood of a child, playing with the boys of the town.

On the day that Mahāprabhu sat on Viṣṇu's throne in the house of Śrīvāsa Paṇḍita, displaying His effulgent form for twenty-one hours in the *Mahā-prakāśa,* He called all His devotees one by one to give them His blessings. On this occasion He called Gaṅgā Dāsa Paṇḍita as well, reminding him of the following event from the past.

One day, Gaṅgā Dāsa Paṇḍita had left his home with his wife and children due to fear of the Muslim rulers. He was standing by the banks of the Ganges with his family, waiting for a ferry to come to take them across the river, but none came. This was causing him no small amount of anxiety, but even after they had waited almost the whole night, no ferry docked at the quay. He began to cry in the fear that the Muslims would touch his family members and contaminate them. He thought that he would drown himself in the Ganges and give up his body.

At that very moment, Mahāprabhu Himself took the form of a ferryman and arrived at the riverbank. Gaṅgā Dāsa Paṇḍita was so glad to see Him that he said:

"O brother! Please save me this time. My caste, my life, my wealth and my body are all dependent on You. Help me by taking my family and me across the river. I will give You a silver coin and a pair of new garments." (*Caitanya Bhāgavata* 2.9.116)

The Lord then took them on board and across the river, after which He returned to His abode in Vaikuṇṭha. When Gaṅgā Dāsa Paṇḍita heard the Lord recount this event, he fainted in ecstasy.

GAṆGĀ DĀSA PAṆḌITA IN PURI

After the Lord took *sannyāsa* at Katwa, Nityānanda Prabhu tricked Him into going to Advaita Ācārya's house in Shantipur. Gaṅgā Dāsa Paṇḍita came to see Him along with the rest of the Nabadwip devotees. He was also one of the first Bengali devotees to go to Puri to see the Lord there. The first time that the devotees went to Puri, the Lord was in Alalanath due to His feelings of separation from Lord Jagannātha, who cannot be seen for a period following the Snāna-yātrā. On hearing that the Bengali devotees had come, the Lord immediately returned to Puri to meet them. Sārvabhauma Bhaṭṭācārya pointed out these devotees to King Pratāparudra, naming them one by one, including Gaṅgā Dāsa Paṇḍita. (*Caitanya Caritāmṛta* 2.11.85)

"The Lord met Gaṅgā Dāsa Paṇḍita and several other devotees on that occasion. He praised each one of them and repeatedly embraced them in honor." (*Caitanya Caritāmṛta* 2.11.159-60)

Gaṅgā Dāsa Paṇḍita also participated in the *kīrtana* before the Lord Jagannātha cart as a member of the chorus in the second *kīrtana* group, which had Śrīvāsa Paṇḍita as the lead singer and Nityānanda Prabhu as the chief dancer. Haridāsa Ṭhākura, Śrīmān Paṇḍita, Śubhānanda, Śrīrāma Paṇḍita were some of the others in the same group. (*Caitanya Caritāmṛta* 2.13.38-9)

Śrīvāsa Paṇḍita

śrīvāsa-paṇḍito dhīmān yaḥ purā nārado muniḥ
parvatākhyo muni-varo ya āsīn nārada-priyaḥ
śri-rāma-paṇḍitaḥ śrīmān tat-kaniṣṭha-sahodaraḥ
nāmnāmbikā vraje dhātrī stanya-dātrī sthitā purā
saiveyaṁ mālinī nāmnī śrīvāsa-gṛhiṇī matā

"Nārada Muni in Kṛṣṇa's *līlā* has become Śrīvāsa Paṇḍita in Gaura *līlā*. Nārada Muni's friend Parvata Muni appeared as Śrīvāsa Paṇḍita's younger brother Śrī Rāma Paṇḍita. Śrīvāsa Paṇḍita's wife, Mālinī Devī, is Ambikā, Kṛṣṇa's wet nurse in Vraja." (*Gaura-gaṇoddeśa-dīpikā* 90)

THE PAÑCA TATTVA

pañca-tattvātmakaṁ kṛṣṇaṁ
bhaktarūpa-svarūpakam
bhaktāvatāraṁ bhaktākhyaṁ
namāmi bhakta-śaktikam

"I pay obeisances to the Supreme Lord Śrī Kṛṣṇa, who has appeared in five aspects: as a devotee, as the expansion of a devotee, as the *avatāra* of a devotee, as a pure devotee and as the devotional energy." (*Caitanya Caritāmṛta* 1.1.14)

The supremely potent is revealed in five different manifestations according to His desire to experience five different pastimes. Ontologically there is no difference between them: they are one truth expressed according to five dispositions. Thus, Śrī Gaurāṅga, Śrī Nityānanda Prabhu, Śrī Advaita Ācārya, Śrī Gadādhara Paṇḍita and Śrīvāsa Paṇḍita and the other devotees are ontologically nondifferent from one another. Nevertheless, that one truth is manifest as a devotee (*bhakta-rūpa*), the expansion of a devotee (*bhakta-svarūpa*), the *avatāra* of a devotee (*bhaktāvatāra*), the energy of a devotee (*bhakta-śakti*) and the pure devotee (*bhaktākhya*), according to the desire to relish different tastes of divine relationship.

Of these five truths, the Supreme Lord Himself, the son of Nanda, takes on the devotional mood to become *bhakta-rūpa*. His full expansion (*svayaṁ prakāśa*), Balarāma, takes on the devotional mood and appears as the *bhakta-svarūpa*, Nityānanda Prabhu. Mahā-Viṣṇu takes on the devotional mood and appears as the *bhaktāvatāra*, Advaita Ācārya. These three are Viṣṇu-tattva. The devotional energy (*bhakta-śakti*) and the pure devotee (*śuddha-bhakta*) are classified as energies of Viṣṇu-tattva, which are considered nondifferent because of their dependent relationship.

The principal devotional energies are Gadādhara Paṇḍita, Svarūpa Dāmodara Gosvamī, and Rāmānanda Rāya. The pure devotees include Śrīvāsa Paṇḍita and others who are in the moods of friendship or servitude. Śrīvāsa Paṇḍita is thus a member of the Pañca Tattva.

ŚRĪVĀSA PAṆḌITA'S ORIGINS

Śrīvāsa Paṇḍita hailed from Sylhet. He later came to live in Nabadwip, where he became instrumental in enhancing the Gaurāṅga *līlā*. From the *Caitanya Bhāgavata* and *Caitanya Caritāmṛta*, we learn that Śrīvāsa and his three brothers, Śrīrāma Paṇḍita, Śrīpati Paṇḍita and Śrīkānta (or Śrīnidhi Paṇḍita) were, all participants in Mahāprabhu's *līlā*.

Gauḍīya Vaiṣṇava Abhidhāna cites *Prema-vilāsa* as saying that Śrīvāsa Paṇḍita's father was a Vedic *brāhmaṇa* of the name Śrī Jaladhara Paṇḍita. Śrīvāsa Paṇḍita was the second of five sons. The eldest son, named Śrī Nalina Paṇḍita, had a daughter named Nārāyaṇī Devī, mother of the author of the *Caitanya Bhāgavata*, Vṛndāvana Dāsa. Nārāyaṇī Devī's husband, Vaikuṇṭha Dāsa Vipra, died while she was pregnant with Vṛndāvana Dāsa, so she left her husband's house in Kumarahatta (Halisahar) and came to live with Śrīvāsa Paṇḍita in Nabadwip.

ŚRĪVĀSA PAṆḌITA AND NIMĀI PAṆḌITA

During his student life, Nimāi would engage Gadādhara, Mukunda and other devotees in debate, first defeating all their arguments and then showing how they could have been defended. The devotees were astonished at His prowess but thought that His learning would bear fruit only if He became a devotee of Kṛṣṇa. Nimāi would pay obeisances to devotees such as Śrīvāsa Paṇḍita whenever He saw them, and they, in turn, would bless Him, saying, "May You have devotion to Kṛṣṇa."

One day Śrīvāsa Paṇḍita was out walking when he encountered Nimāi on the street. He said, "People study in order to become devotees of Kṛṣṇa. What is the use of all their studies if they don't become devotees? Don't waste Your time. Start worshipping Kṛṣṇa as soon as possible."

Mahāprabhu felt great joy upon hearing such words from the mouth of His own devotee and answered, "You are a devotee. By your mercy, I will surely have devotion for Kṛṣṇa someday." Even though they could not help but be attracted to Nimāi, the devotees were unable to recognize Him as their own worshipable Lord due to the influence of His Yogamāyā *līlā-śakti*. This is a most astonishing and attractive pastime.

NIMĀI BECOMES A DEVOTEE

When Mahāprabhu returned from Gaya, He began to display all the symptoms of one who is intoxicated with love of God. Śacī Mātā became terrified, thinking that her son had gone mad. When Śrīvāsa Paṇḍita came to see Mahāprabhu, He said, "Everyone thinks that I have gone crazy. What do you think has happened to Me?" Śrīvāsa Paṇḍita laughed and answered:

"Your madness is good madness. I want the same for myself. I see the signs of ecstatic love for Kṛṣṇa in Your body. Lord Kṛṣṇa is very merciful to You."

A relieved Mahāprabhu embraced Śrīvāsa Paṇḍita and said, "If you too had said that I was going mad, I would have drowned Myself in the Ganges." (*Caitanya Bhāgavata* 2.2.113-7)

When Mahāprabhu instituted the loud chanting of the Holy Names in His own house and in that of Śrīvāsa Paṇḍita, all the atheistic neighbors began to complain that they were losing sleep because of the noise. They looked for ways to counter the movement and even started false rumors that the King would come soon to punish the devotees. The naive Śrīvāsa Paṇḍita believed these stories and was filled with anxiety. He began to worship Nṛsiṁhadeva for protection.

Understanding that Śrīvāsa Paṇḍita was afraid, the Lord, who takes away the distress of His devotees, went to his house. He kicked open the door and said, "Who are you worshipping? Who are you meditating on? Behold! He whom you are worshipping is standing before you! I will save the righteous and destroy the wicked. You should worry no longer!" So saying, He sat down in the heroic posture (*vīrāsana*) and revealed the divine form of Lord Nṛsiṁha, holding the conch, discus, club and lotus.

When Śrīvāsa Paṇḍita saw this extraordinary manifestation of the Lord, he was overcome with feelings of love and began to recite hymns of praise. Mahāprabhu was pleased with Śrīvāsa Paṇḍita's recital and told him to call his wife and family members to see His divine form. He gave His *prasāda* to Nārāyaṇī Devī and showed His mercy to her by making her utter the Holy Name. Just as the devotee is dear to the Lord, the Lord is also dear to His devotee.

NITYĀNANDA PRABHU'S VYĀSA PŪJĀ

When Nityānanda Prabhu came to Nabadwip, Mahāprabhu knew that He was staying at Nandana Ācārya's house, and so He went there in the company of the devotees. There They met for the first time. In order to reveal Nityānanda Prabhu's glories to His associates, He had Śrīvāsa Paṇḍita recite a verse from *Śrīmad Bhāgavatam*:

barhāpīḍaṁ naṭavaravapuḥ
karṇayoḥ karṇikāraṁ
vibhradvāsaḥ kanaka-kapiśaṁ
vaijayantīṁ ca mālām
randhrān veṇor adhara-sudhayā
pūrayan gopa-vṛndair
vṛndāraṇyaṁ svapada-ramaṇaṁ
prāviśad gīta-kīrtiḥ

"Kṛṣṇa was dressed as a dancing performer, ornamented with a peacock feather on His topknot, *karṇikāra* flowers on His ears, wearing a yellow garment as brilliant as gold, and a Vaijayantī garland around His neck. He entered the forest of Vrindavan, the pleasure garden of His auspiciously marked feet, while filling the holes of His flute with the nectar of His lips. The cowherd boys began to sing His glories." (*Śrīmad Bhāgavatam* 10.21.5)

As soon as Nityānanda Prabhu heard the verse, He fainted, and the eight ecstatic symptoms appeared on His body. Viśvambhara clasped Nityānanda Prabhu to His bosom. A few days later, Mahāprabhu indicated that He wished Nityānanda Prabhu to perform the Vyāsa Pūjā ceremony, so preparations were made for this ritual to be held at Śrīvāsa Paṇḍita's house. On the eve of the ceremony, when the *adhivāsa kīrtana* was being sung, Mahāprabhu Himself was possessed by the spirit of Baladeva, thus revealing Nityānanda Prabhu's identity with Balarāma. Then He called out Advaita Ācārya's name "*Nāṛā, Nāṛā!*" ("one who makes something move"), revealing how Advaita Ācārya had made Him descend by His prayers.

On the following day, Śrīvāsa Paṇḍita, took the role of the ceremony's *ācārya*. After completing the *pūjā*, he placed a flower garland in Nityānanda Prabhu's hand and told him to offer it to Vyāsadeva while chanting the appropriate *mantras*. Nityānanda Prabhu, however, put the garland around Mahāprabhu's neck.

Mahāprabhu immediately gave Nityānanda Prabhu a vision of a six-armed form.

At the end of the Vyāsa Pūjā, Mahāprabhu ordered the devotees to sing the Holy Names. Later He asked Śrīvāsa Paṇḍita for the *prasāda* of Vyāsadeva, which He personally distributed to all the devotees, as well as to Śrīvāsa Paṇḍita's servants. Everyone ate the offerings with great pleasure.

When Mahāprabhu saw Śrīvāsa Paṇḍita's devotion to Nityānanda Prabhu, He blessed him, saying that there would never be any poverty in his house and that even the dogs and cats in his house will have steady devotion to the Lord.

KĪRTANA AT ŚRĪVĀSA AṄGANA

When Mahāprabhu desired to begin His *saṅkīrtana* pastimes, He held them in the house of Śrīvāsa Paṇḍita with only His intimate associates present. When the *kīrtana* began on an Ekādaśī, Mahāprabhu revealed many transformations of ecstatic love as soon as the chanting began.

śrī hari vāsare hari-kīrtana vidhāna
nṛtya ārambhilā prabhu jagatera prāṇa
puṇyavanta śrivāsāṅgane śubhārambha
uṭhila kīrtana-dhvani "gopāla! govinda!"

"The scriptural injunction is that one should engage in *hari-kīrtana* on Ekādaśī, also known as Hari-vāsara. That evening, Mahāprabhu, the life of the world, began to dance. This auspicious beginning of the *saṅkīrtana* movement took place in the pious Śrīvāsa Paṇḍita's courtyard, where the sound of Kṛṣṇa's names Gopāla and Govinda rose to the sky." (*Caitanya Bhāgavata* 2.8.138)

Mahāprabhu ordered that the doors should remain closed, and the wicked and hard-hearted persons who were refused entry began to criticize Mahāprabhu and His devotees. Mahāprabhu's followers ignored their insults and continued to ecstatically sing the Holy Names. Just as the long night of the *rāsa-līlā* seemed to the *gopīs* to last only a few moments, the nights of *kīrtana* at Śrīvāsa Paṇḍita's house seemed brief to Mahāprabhu and His followers.

At the end of one such night, Mahāprabhu placed all the Śālagrāma-śilās on His lap and sat down on the altar, where He revealed His divine nature in a wonderful form and accepted all the food offerings given to Him by His devotees.

On another occasion, Mahāprabhu exhibited *Mahā-prakāśa-līlā*, "the pastime of the great epiphany," at Śrīvāsa Aṅgana. This is recounted in chapter nine of *Caitanya Bhāgavata*'s *Madhya-khaṇḍa*. On that occasion, He withdrew His devotional mood, stopped all His divine trances and openly revealed His divinity, sitting on Viṣṇu's throne for twenty-one hours. At His signal, the devotees performed the *abhiṣeka* ceremony reserved for the king of kings according to the scriptural regulations. The devotees made their offerings of flowers and gifts and Mahāprabhu stretched out His feet and, accepted them without artifice. He then gave all present a blessing, fulfilling their personal desires. In the course of this twenty-one-hour *Mahā-prakāśa-līlā*,

Mahāprabhu appeared in the forms of all the previous *avātaras*.

One evening, Śrīvāsa's mother-in-law hid in a corner of the courtyard from where she hoped to be able to see the Lord's *saṅkīrtana* pastimes. Being the indweller of all beings, the Lord was aware of her presence and kept repeating to His companions that on that day He felt no joy in the singing of the Holy Name. This was very disquieting to the devotees, who, suspecting that some outsider might be hiding there, started to search through the house. When Śrīvāsa Paṇḍita found his mother-in-law, he was mortified and, taking her by the hair, led her out of the courtyard. Only those who have received the mercy of Śrī Caitanya Mahāprabhu have the right to witness His pastimes.

On another occasion, a certain *brahmacārī* who subsisted on milk alone asked Śrīvāsa Paṇḍita for permission to see Mahāprabhu's *kīrtana*. Śrīvāsa Paṇḍita knew that he was *sāttvika* in his habits, and so he invited him in. Śrīvāsa Paṇḍita had the *brahmacārī* hide inside the house, but Mahāprabhu, the indweller of all beings, was well aware of what was taking place. He said, "I don't know what is wrong with the *kīrtana* today; I am feeling no pleasure in it. I think that there must be an outsider here somewhere." Śrīvāsa Paṇḍita became afraid and said, "A *brahmacārī* who takes only milk asked if he could watch You dance. He was so eager, and I knew him to be austere, so I let him in." Mahāprabhu became angry and answered, "One cannot attain devotion to Kṛṣṇa without surrendering to Him, and certainly not by drinking a milk diet and engaging in other superficial austerities. Make him leave." The *brāhmaṇa* fearfully left the house, but still asked if he could have a partial look at the Lord. The most merciful Lord called him to His side and placed His lotus feet on his head, telling him not to make a show of his austere practices out of pride.

When Mahāprabhu put on a play about His Vrindavan pastimes at Candraśekar's house in Mayapur, Śrīvāsa Paṇḍita played the part of Nārada Muni. Advaita Ācārya took on the role of the clown, or *vidūṣaka*, and Haridāsa Ṭhākura played the police officer. Mahāprabhu Himself first played Rukmiṇī and then the *Ādyā-śakti*, while Nityānanda Prabhu played the part of an old woman. The Lord again sat on the altar in the mood of the goddess of fortune, Lakṣmī Devī. As the mother of the universe and in a spirit of affection for His devotees, He fed them breast milk.

OFFENSES TO ŚRĪVĀSA

Mahāprabhu's *kīrtanas* went on at Śrīvāsa Paṇḍita's house with the doors locked every night for a full year. During this time, many nondevotee *brāhmaṇas* tried to make fun of Mahāprabhu and His associates. Several of these nondevotees became envious because they were unable to see what was going on and insulted the devotees. One of them was a Bhaṭṭācārya *brāhmaṇa* named Gopāla Cāpāla, who decided to destroy Śrīvāsa Paṇḍita's reputation by placing a plate of offerings intended for Kālī on his doorstep. These included liquor and meat, red hibiscus (*jabā phūl*) flowers, and red sandalwood. In the morning, when Śrīvāsa Paṇḍita opened the door, he saw these items and started to laugh. He loudly proclaimed, "Look everyone! I am a *śākta*. I have been worshipping the Goddess all night long." His better-behaved neighbors were pained to see what had taken place, and they removed the offending items and purified the doorstep with cow dung.

As a result of this offense to Śrīvāsa Paṇḍita, Gopāla Cāpāla was afflicted with leprosy. One day, when Mahāprabhu came to the banks of the Ganges to bathe, Gopāla Cāpāla approached Him and prayed to be freed from his disease. Mahāprabhu angrily answered him:

"O sinner! Envious of the devotees! I will not save you. I will have you eaten by worms like this for a million births. You made it seem as though Śrīvāsa Paṇḍita had worshipped Kālī, so you will dwell for a million lifetimes in the hell known as Raurava." (*Caitanya Caritāmṛta* 1.17.51-2)

When Mahāprabhu had taken *sannyāsa*, He came once to Kuliya, the site where offenses are forgiven. Kuliya is the present-day town of Nabadwip, also known as Koladwip. This time, when Gopāla Cāpāla begged Him again to be forgiven, Mahāprabhu was compassionate and told him to ask forgiveness of Śrīvāsa Paṇḍita. One must ask forgiveness of the very devotee one has offended if one wishes to be freed from offense. When Śrīvāsa forgave Gopāla Cāpāla, he was liberated from the effects of his offense.

The unfortunate Devānanda Paṇḍita, though a great lecturer in the *Śrīmad Bhāgavatam*, was devoid of devotion. One day, Śrīvāsa Paṇḍita went to listen to him lecture and, being a great devotee, was deeply affected by the *Bhāgavata's* verses, and tears started to flow from his eyes in midst of the assembly. Devānanda Paṇḍita's students, who were all *pāṣaṇḍīs*, forcibly dragged Śrīvāsa Paṇḍita outside for disturbing the audience. Even though he saw his students acting in this way, Devānanda Paṇḍita did nothing to stop them. Thus, he too became an offender to a Vaiṣṇava. Mahāprabhu later roundly rebuked Devānanda Paṇḍita for his inaction on this occasion. Later on, Devānanda Paṇḍita had the good fortune to come into the association of Vakreśvara Paṇḍita, who taught him Caitanya Mahāprabhu's true identity. He thus became sorry for the offense he had committed and received Mahāprabhu's mercy. According to *Gaura-gaṇoddeśa-dīpikā*, Devānanda is Nanda Mahārāja's court *paṇḍita* Bhāguri Muni in Vraja līlā.

THE KĀJĪ TRIES TO BREAK UP THE KĪRTANA

In the mood of *amānī mānada* – one who does not ask for any respect for himself but always respect others – Mahāprabhu would embrace everyone and with a great urge beg them to chant the names of the Lord. These followers would then engage in the loud chanting of the Holy Names in the accompaniment of *mṛdaṅga* and conch shells. Materialistic persons considered them to be nothing other than musicians and dancers who were worshipping Mahāmāyā in the wrong way and would insult them with various blasphemous statements. One day the local magistrate, or Kājī, known as Sirājauddīna Cāṇḍa Kājī, was walking by and saw the scene. Hearing the loud noise of the *kīrtana*, he became irritated and angry. He went to Śrīvāsa Paṇḍita's house and broke the *mṛdaṅga* and had some of the devotees beaten as a warning. He said, "If anyone does this *saṅkīrtana* again, he will be punished even more severely." This brought great satisfaction to all the nondevotees of the town, and they joyfully continued to mock the devotees.

When Mahāprabhu received word of the incident, He became very angry. He ordered the devotees to take torches and musical instruments and to join Him fearlessly for *saṅkīrtana*. He divided the devotees into several groups and then led the procession along the banks of the Ganges, Himself dancing at its lead. Thousands of men, women and children put aside their housework to join Him and follow the *saṅkīrtana* procession. When the miscreants heard the sound of the *kīrtana*, their hearts began to tremble. Meanwhile, when Cāṇḍa Kājī heard that thousands of

Hindus were approaching his house, he ran inside to hide, trembling with fear.

Upon His arrival, Mahāprabhu asked some respectable persons from the neighborhood to kindly inform the Kājī that He was there and that He meant him no harm. When the Kājī heard the polite way in which Mahāprabhu had addressed him, he was attracted and came outside. He addressed Mahāprabhu as "nephew," since by village relationship he was Nīlāmbara Cakravartī's brother. After a few moments of cordial conversation, the Kājī recounted the following story: "The night after I broke the mṛdaṅga, I had a dream in which I saw a most frightening figure, half-man, half-lion. He came and sat on my chest and threatened to rend it asunder in the way that I had broken the drum. When he saw how afraid I was, He calmed me down and told me that He would forgive me if I promised never to interfere with *kīrtana* again."

Cāṇḍa Kājī then showed the scratch marks that had been imprinted on his chest by Nṛsiṁhadeva's claws. He then promised that neither he nor anyone from his family would ever stop *saṅkīrtana* again. He also became Mahāprabhu's devotee. The tomb of Cāṇḍa Kājī is in Brahmana Pushkarini, the present-day Baman Pukur, by which stands a very old Goloka Cāṇpā tree. Both Hindus and Muslims offer their respects to the tomb of the Cāṇḍa Kājī.

MORE KĪRTANA PASTIMES AT ŚRĪVĀSA AṄGANA

After a night of *kīrtana* at Śrīvāsa Paṇḍita's house, when Mahāprabhu returned to external awareness He would go with all the devotees to bathe in the Ganges. Sometimes the devotees would ceremonially bathe the Lord at Śrīvāsa Aṅgana. One of Śrīvāsa Paṇḍita's servant girls, named Dukhī, would watch Mahāprabhu's ecstatic dancing with tears in her eyes. She also performed the service of filling jugs of water from the Ganges for Mahāprabhu's morning bath. Mahāprabhu observed her devotion and was pleased; He changed her name from Dukhī (unhappy) to Sukhī (happy).

One day, Śrīvāsa Paṇḍita's only son died as *kīrtana* was being performed in his house. Śrīvāsa Paṇḍita was afraid that the sounds of mourning from the women's quarters would disturb Mahāprabhu while He was engaged in singing the Holy Names. So he swiftly went inside the house and tried to quiet the women by explaining spiritual truths to them. When they still didn't stop their loud lamentations, Śrīvāsa Paṇḍita threatened to throw himself into the river and drown if they did not stop making noise. This had the desired result.

Mahāprabhu performed *kīrtana* until late night and later said, "Something doesn't seem right. Has some tragedy taken place in the Paṇḍita's house?" Śrīvāsa Paṇḍita answered, "How can anything be wrong when I have Your smiling face in my home?"

However, some of the other devotees said, "Prabhu, Śrīvāsa Paṇḍit's only son died in the evening about an hour after sunset."

Mahāprabhu asked, "Why did no one say anything before now?"

The devotees answered, "Lord, Śrīvāsa Paṇḍita told us not to because he was afraid that it would interfere with Your pleasure in *kīrtana*."

Mahāprabhu said, "How could I ever abandon devotees who love Me to this extent!" and started to shed tears.

After this, Mahāprabhu went inside and sat beside the child's dead body and brought him back to consciousness. He asked, "Child! Why do you want to leave the house of such a devotee as Śrīvāsa?"

The dead child answered, "The few days that I was to spend in Śrīvāsa Paṇḍita's house are over; now I am following Your wish in going elsewhere. I am a living being without independence; I cannot go against Your wishes. Please be merciful to me that I never forget Your lotus feet, wherever I go."

When Śrīvāsa Paṇḍita's family members heard the child speak such wisdom, they immediately forgot their distress and stopped mourning. Mahāprabhu said to Śrīvāsa Paṇḍita, "From this day on, Nityānanda Prabhu and I will be your sons. We will never leave you."

ŚRĪVĀSA PAṆḌITA'S VISITS TO PURI

After Mahāprabhu had taken *sannyāsa* and was living in Puri, Śrīvāsa Paṇḍita would come with the other devotees each year to stay with Him for the four months of the rainy season.

"Advaita, Nityānanda Prabhu, Mukunda Datta, Śrīvāsa Paṇḍita, Vidyānidhi, Vāsudeva Datta, Murāri Gupta and all of Mahāprabhu's other devoted servants met with Him in Puri every year and stayed four months. Mahāprabhu engaged in various pastimes in their company." (*Caitanya Caritāmṛta* 2.9.255-6)

Śrīvāsa Paṇḍita was a participant with Mahāprabhu in His pastimes of cleaning the Guṇḍicā temple and Rathayātrā. He was the principal singer in the second *kīrtana* group, or *sampradāya*, whose chief dancer was Nityānanda Prabhu Himself. Śrī Svarūpa Dāmodara was the lead singer and Advaita Ācārya the dancer in the first *kīrtana* group; in the third, Mukunda Datta was the principal singer, while Haridāsa Ṭhākura danced. Govinda Ghoṣa the lead singer in the fourth, with Vakreśvara Paṇḍita dancing. The fifth *sampradāya* came from the village of Kulina, and Rāmānanda Rāya and Satyarāja were its principal dancers. The sixth group, in which Acyutānanda danced, was from Shantipur. The seventh group was composed of the residents of Srikhanda, of whom Narahari and Raghunandana took the lead roles.

When Mahāprabhu wished to dance, all the seven groups came together. On one such occasion, King Pratāparudra was watching Mahāprabhu's energetic dancing while leaning on his servant Harichandana's shoulder. In the meantime, Śrīvāsa Paṇḍita came and stood in front of Harichandana to watch Mahāprabhu dance. The King's servant kept pushing the deeply absorbed Śrīvāsa Paṇḍita, telling him to move so that the King could see. Śrīvāsa Paṇḍita became irritated at the repeated disturbance and finally turned around and slapped Harichandana. Harichandana became angry and was about to hit him back when the King stopped him, telling him how fortunate he was to have been touched by the hand of a devotee such as Śrīvāsa Paṇḍita.

One day, Śrīvāsa Paṇḍita and the other devotees, led by Advaita Prabhu were joyfully glorifying Mahāprabhu's name, form, qualities and activities in Puri. Mahāprabhu became angry and left the scene, but later accepted defeat and acquiesced to their desire to glorify Him.

ŚRĪVĀSA PAṆḌITA MOVES TO KUMARAHATTA

After Mahāprabhu took *sannyāsa* in Katwa, Śrīvāsa Paṇḍita found it impossible to remain in Nabadwip, where everything was full of painful reminders of the Lord. He and his brothers moved to Kumarahatta (Halisahar), the birthplace of Īśvara Puri. Even so, Śrīvāsa Paṇḍita and his brothers made annual trips from Kumarahatta to Nilachal to see Mahāprabhu and to Mayapur to visit Śacī Mātā.

On one occasion Mahāprabhu came to His guru's birthplace and showed His respects by taking some dust and wrapping it in His cloth. After that, pilgrims went to that place and took the dust from there with great veneration. Consequently, a pool (*doba*) was created which is famous as Chaitanya Doba.

Śrīvāsa Paṇḍita's house is very close to Chaitanya Doba. Mahāprabhu visited the house of Śrīvāsa Paṇḍita along with His associates on that occasion. All the members of the household joyfully received Him and His companions and became absorbed in their service. Mahāprabhu noticed this and said to Śrīvāsa Paṇḍita, "You are a householder with a large family. You have to earn money in order to maintain your family; otherwise, how will you be able to do so?" Śrīvāsa Paṇḍita first replied that he had no wish to make money and then clapped his hands three times. Mahāprabhu asked him what he meant by clapping his hands, and Śrīvāsa Paṇḍita answered, "I will fast one, two, three days. Then if I still get nothing to eat, I will tie a jug to my neck and jump in the Ganges." Mahāprabhu responded to Śrīvāsa Paṇḍita's statement by giving a roar and repeated the blessing He had given before in Nabadwip: "Even if the goddess of fortune has to go begging, you will never have any poverty in your home. Lord Kṛṣṇa Himself provides everything that His exclusive devotees need."

Śrīvāsa Paṇḍita's appearance day is the eighth day of the waning moon *(Kṛṣṇa Aṣṭamī)* in the month of Caitra, and his disappearance day is celebrated on the tenth day of the waning moon *(Kṛṣṇa Daśamī)* in Āṣāḍha.

Śrī Murāri Gupta

murāri-gupto hanumān
aṅgadaḥ śrī-purandaraḥ
yaḥ śrī-sugrīva-nāmāsīd
govindānanda eva saḥ

"Murāri Gupta is Hanumān in Rāmacandra's līlā; Purāndara is Aṅgada, and Govindānanda is Sugrīva." (*Gaura-gaṇoddeśa-dīpikā* 91)

"The word *gupta* means 'hidden,' so the name Murāri Gupta indicates that Murāri (Śrī Caitanya Deva) had secretly taken up permanent residence in his heart." (*Caitanya Bhāgavata* 2.10.31)

Murāri Gupta took birth in a family of Ayurvedic physicians in the district of Sylhet.

"Murāri Gupta is a physician for the disease of material life. He was amongst the many associates of Mahāprabhu who appeared in Sylhet." (*Caitanya Bhāgavata* 1.2.35)

"Murāri would cure anyone who came to him, whether their disease was of the body or the soul." (*Caitanya Caritāmṛta* 1.10.51)

The names of Murāri's parents are unknown. He was somewhat older than Mahāprabhu. *Caitanya Bhāgavata* includes his name in the list of associates who appeared prior to Mahāprabhu.

"There were many devotees hidden in Nabadwip who had previously taken birth at the Lord's command. They included Śrī Candraśekhara, Jagadīśa, Gopīnātha, Śrīmān, Murāri, Śrī Garuḍa and Gaṅgā Dāsa." (*Caitanya Bhāgavata* 1.2.98-99)

When Murāri's family moved from Sylhet to Nabadwip, they lived in the neighborhood of Mahāprabhu, so Murāri was Nimāi's companion in many of His childhood pastimes. It is also written in the *Caitanya Caritāmṛta* that Murāri witnessed Mahāprabhu's childhood pastimes. He authored the scripture *Śrī Caitanya Carita*.

MURĀRI'S STUDENT LIFE IN NABADWIP

Murāri Gupta was also a student at Gaṅgā Dāsa Paṇḍita's *ṭola* (school) along with Nimāi. When the Lord was engaged in His pastimes of learning and study, He would often debate and joke with Murāri. Mahāprabhu would be pleased with Murāri's interpretations. Murāri Gupta was also amazed at Mahāprabhu's wonderful intelligence and learning. He also observed that just the touch of Nimāi's hand would immerse him in ecstasy. All these things convinced him early on that Nimāi was no ordinary human being.

"Murāri Gupta became a good scholar by the Lord's mercy. One day, Nimāi was pleased with the explanations of Murāri Gupta to a certain problem. He touched Murāri with His lotus hand, filling His companion's entire body with ecstasy. Murāri Gupta thought privately that this person could in no way be an ordinary human being. Can an ordinary human attain such scholarship so quickly and his mere touch bring such ecstatic pleasure?" (*Caitanya Bhāgavata* 1.10.30-33)

The Vaiṣṇava's ornament is humility. Mahāprabhu's heart would melt when He saw this quality in Murāri Gupta.

"Murāri Gupta, the twenty-first branch of the Caitanya tree, was a storehouse of love. The Lord's heart would melt when He saw Murāri's meekness and humility." (*Caitanya Caritāmṛta* 1.10.49)

MAHĀPRABHU'S SPECIAL MERCY TO MURĀRI

When Mahāprabhu returned from Gaya, He saw Murāri at the house of Śuklāmbara Brahmacārī. Murāri had heard of Mahāprabhu's ecstatic feelings from Śrīmān Paṇḍita. Mahāprabhu was pleased with Murāri and one day gave him a vision of His form as the Varāha avātara; the Lord lifted Murāri's water jug on His nose as He gave a loud roar. Murāri considered his life to have been fulfilled by this vision, and he sang a hymn in glorification of the Lord. This event has been beautifully described by Vṛndāvana Dāsa Ṭhākura in the *Caitanya Bhāgavata, Madhya-khaṇḍa*, chapter 3.

"The Lord took on the mood of Varaha in the house of Murāri. The Lord climbed on his shoulders and danced in the courtyard." (*Caitanya Caritāmṛta* 1.17.19)

Murāri Gupta was a worshipper of Lord Rāmacandra, and Mahāprabhu's affection for him resembled that of Lord Rāma for His servant Hanumān.

"Lord Gaurahari felt great love for Murāri Gupta. It was just like Lord Rāmacandra's love for Hanumān." (*Caitanya Bhāgavata* 2.3.19)

During the twenty–one-hour great epiphany (*Mahā-prakāśa*) at Śrīvāsa Aṅgana, the Lord gave Murāri a vision of Himself as Lord Rama. When he saw his worshipable deity before him, Murāri fainted away. He then glorified the Lord in a way that so much pleased

Him that He gave Murāri the benediction to have all his desires fulfilled.

"Mahāprabhu ordered Murāri: 'Behold My form!' Lo! Murāri saw the form of Raghunātha directly before him. He saw the Lord of the universe with the swarthy color of *durba* grass, sitting in the *vīrāsana*, the posture of a great bowman. He saw Sītā and Lakṣmaṇa standing on both sides of Him, and His army of monkeys surrounding Him singing hymns of praise. It seemed to Murāri that he was himself one of the monkeys, and as soon as he saw this, he fainted. The best of the physicians, Murāri, lay unconscious on the ground, completely under Mahāprabhu's spell." (*Caitanya Bhāgavata* 2.10.7-11)

"On one occasion, when Mahāprabhu heard Murāri Gupta recite the glories of Rāmacandra, He wrote Rāma Dāsa, 'servant of Lord Rāma' ", on his forehead." (*Caitanya Caritāmṛta* 1.17.69)

On another occasion, Mahāprabhu displayed a four-armed Nārāyaṇa form in the house of Śrīvāsa Paṇḍita and began calling the name of Garuḍa. Murāri Gupta heard the call, and, giving a loud roar, took the form of the king of birds. Mahāprabhu then climbed on his shoulders. This *līlā* is described both in the twentieth chapter of the *Madhya-khaṇḍa* of *Caitanya Bhāgavata* and in the twelfth wave of *Bhakti-ratnākara.*

MURĀRI AND NITYĀNANDA PRABHU

Mahāprabhu taught the spiritual truths about Himself, Nityānanda Prabhu and matters of etiquette through Murāri. One day, Murāri Gupta came to Śrīvāsa Paṇḍita's house. Upon arriving, he first paid obeisances to Mahāprabhu and then to Nityānanda Prabhu, but Mahāprabhu told him that he had not followed the proper procedure. Murāri could not understand what He meant. That night when he returned home, he had a dream in which he saw Nityānanda Prabhu as Balarāma and Mahāprabhu as Kṛṣṇa with a peacock feather. Murāri then understood what Mahāprabhu had been telling him. The next day he paid obeisances first to Nityānanda Prabhu and afterwards to Mahāprabhu.

Śrīla Bhakti Siddhānta Sarasvatī Gosvāmī Ṭhākura writes in his *Gauḍīya-bhāṣya,* "Śrī Murāri was a worshipper of Balarāma. Therefore to worship the Supreme Lord without first worshipping the guru and *jagad-guru* is an error of protocol."

"The lotus-eyed Mahāprabhu was sitting down with the smiling Nityānanda Prabhu at His right-hand side. Murāri paid obeisances first to Nityānanda Prabhu and then to the feet of Viśvambhara." (*Caitanya Bhāgavata* 2.20.22-3)

THE LORD GIVES MURĀRI HIS BETEL LEAF

Mahāprabhu had great affection for Murāri Gupta and so would give him His own *pan* (betel leaf), which Murāri would eat with relish. When Mahāprabhu told Murāri to wash his hands, Murāri would simply wipe his hands on his head. It was at this time that Mahāprabhu suddenly began to criticize the false views of the *smārta brāhmaṇas* and Prakāśānanda's *māyāvāda* philosophy.

"The Lord said, 'O foolish one, you have lost your caste status. My remnants are all over your body.' As He spoke, the Lord went into a trance in which He took on His identity as the Supreme Person. He ground His teeth and started to say something special. 'There is a *sannyāsī* named Prakāśānanda in Kashi who is cutting Me into little bits. He teaches the Vedānta but does not accept My form. I have caused him to become leprous, but still, he does not understand. The fool does not realize that the unlimited universes are contained within My body. What arrogance that he should deny it! I tell you the truth, Murāri, for you are My servant: anyone who does not accept My form is bound for ruin." (*Caitanya Bhāgavata* 2.20.31-36)

MURĀRI CURES THE LORD'S INDIGESTION

"The Lord is very happy to accept a devotee's offering, no matter how it is made. One day Murāri returned home and told his wife that he wished to eat. His devoted wife carefully prepared rice with ghee and gave them to her husband. But Murāri, absorbed in contemplation on Kṛṣṇa, took handful after handful of the food and put it on the ground, offering it to the Lord in this way. The amazing thing is that even though Mahāprabhu was not physically present there at that time, He accepted the offering. The next day He came to Murāri's house at the dawn and said to him, 'I have come to you for medicine. Yesterday you kept insisting that I eat. You made me eat so much that now I have indigestion. You must give Me some water; that will be the remedy for My stomach problem.' Mahāprabhu took water from a jug in Murāri's house, drinking down its entire contents. Seeing this, Murāri fainted, and all the devotees began to cry in deep love." (*Caitanya Bhāgavata* 2.20.69-71)

MURĀRI'S FEAR OF THE LORD'S DEPARTURE

Murāri Gupta analyzed the many *avatāras* of the Lord and came to the conclusion that these *avatāras* manifest pastimes and at one point conceal them. Lord Rāmacandra destroyed Rāvaṇa to save Sītā, but then He abandoned her. Kṛṣṇa arranged for the destruction of the Yadus. Thus, Mahāprabhu too would inevitably be disappearing at a certain moment, so it would be better for him to depart before that day arrived, for it would be far too painful for him to witness such an event. For this reason, Murāri purchased a sharp chopper and kept it hidden in his home. The Lord knew of his intention and immediately came to his house and asked Murāri to hand over the chopper. Both the above-mentioned pastimes are described in the *Bhakti-ratnākara's* twelfth wave.

Murāri Gupta would also go on the annual pilgrimage with other devotees to see Mahāprabhu in Puri. Accompanied by his wife, he would offer Mahāprabhu many preparations they had prepared themselves. Murāri would participate in the Rathayātrā festival as a member of the third *saṅkīrtana* group, in which Mukunda Datta was the lead singer and Haridāsa Ṭhākura danced.

MURĀRI'S EXCLUSIVE DEVOTION TO RĀMA

Mahāprabhu taught the principle of devotion to one's worshipable deity through Murāri Gupta. One cannot advance in devotional service without a particular devotion to a worshipable deity, or *iṣṭa-devatā*. Murāri is an *avatāra* of Hanumān, and he saw Caitanya Mahāprabhu as Rāmacandra. On one occasion, Mahāprabhu desired to test his loyalty to his worshipable deity, Lord Rāma, by telling him to worship Kṛṣṇa instead. He explained to Murāri that Kṛṣṇa is the Supreme Personality of Godhead, the fountainhead of all the other *avatāras*. Because Vrajendranandana Śrī Kṛṣṇa is the ocean of all the devotional mellows, the joy to be had in worshipping Him cannot be had in the service of any other form of the Lord. Murāri promised Mahāprabhu that he would do as He advised and worship Kṛṣṇa, but when he returned to his home, he could not give up the lotus feet of Rāmacandra. Just the thought of it made him upset, and he stayed awake the entire night. In the morning, he went to Mahāprabhu and fell at His feet with tears in his eyes and made the following humble submission:

"I have sold my head to Rāmacandra. I cannot remove it from His feet, for as soon as I try, it causes me great pain. I cannot give up the lotus feet of Raghunātha, even though this means disobeying You. What can I do? O merciful one, please allow me to give up my life here before You rather than suffer this fate." (*Caitanya Caritāmṛta* 2.15.149-151)

Hanumān is famous for a verse, in which he shows his single-minded devotion for Rāma.

śrī-nāthe jānakī-nāthe
cābhede paramātmani
tathāpi mama sarvasvaḥ
rāmaḥ kamala-locanaḥ

"Both Nārāyaṇa, the husband of Lakṣmī, and Rāmacandra, the husband of Sītā, are equally the Supreme Personality of Godhead. Even so, the lotus-eyed Rāma alone is everything to me."

Mahāprabhu was greatly satisfied to hear this exclusive devotional attitude to the worshipable deity. He said, "You are Hanumān himself, the eternal servant of Rāmacandra. Indeed, why should you give up worshipping His feet?"

Śrī Jīva Gosvāmī's father, Anupama, was similarly devoted to Rāma. Mahāprabhu compared him to Murāri. "Previously, I tested Murāri Gupta and found him to be devoted to Rāma in the same way. That devotee who does not abandon his worshipable deity's lotus feet is truly glorious. Glorious too is that Lord who does not abandon His devotee." (*Caitanya Caritāmṛta* 3.4.45-46)

Murāri Gupta disappeared on the same full-moon day as the autumn *rāsa-līlā* festival, *Śarat Pūrṇimā*.

Śrī Vāsudeva Datta Ṭhākura

vraje sthitau gāyakau yau
madhukaṇṭhamadhuvratau
mukundavāsudevau tau
dattau gaurāṅgagāyakau

"In Vraja there were two singers named Madhukaṇṭha and Madhuvrata. They appeared as singers in Caitanya *līlā* as Mukunda and Vāsudeva Datta." (*Gaura-gaṇoddeśa-dīpikā* 140)

VĀSUDEVA'S FAMILY BACKGROUND

Śrī Vāsudeva Datta was born in the Chittagong district of modern Bangladesh, in the village of Chanhara, which is under the jurisdiction of the police station named Patiya. This village is situated ten *kosas*, or about twenty miles, from the village of Mekhala, where Puṇḍarīka Vidyānidhi made his home. Mahāprabhu's associate Mukunda Datta was Vāsudeva Datta's younger brother.

In the book *Prema-vilāsa*, it is said that Vāsudeva was the older of the two and that they were born in an Ambaṣṭha family:

"In the district of Chittagong, there is a village named Chakrashala, where lives a respectable family of *Ambaṣṭha* physicians named Datta. Two great devotees named Mukunda Datta and Vāsudeva Datta were born into this family. Both Vāsudeva, the elder and Mukunda, the younger, came to Nabadwip to live."

VĀSUDEVA THE KĪRTANĪYĀ

Vāsudeva Datta Ṭhākura had a beautiful voice and was also well versed in the *Saṅgīta-śāstra*. He was one of the chief associates of Mahāprabhu, participating in *saṅkīrtana* in the home of Śrīvāsa Paṇḍita and the streets of Nabadwip. Mahāprabhu enjoyed his association because of his Vaiṣṇava qualities.

"Vāsudeva Datta is a respected servant of the Lord. A thousand tongues are insufficient to sing his glories." (*Caitanya Caritāmṛta* 1.10.41)

Mahāprabhu said, "Even though Mukunda has been My companion since childhood, I get even more pleasure when I see you." (*Caitanya Caritāmṛta* 2.11.138)

Vāsudeva had a particularly close friendship with Śrīvāsa Paṇḍit and Śivānanda Sena. He lived near Kumarahatta and Kanchra Para, which were the homes of these two great associates of the Lord. Vāsudeva was very generous by nature. Never thinking of himself, he spent his money liberally for others. Mahāprabhu saw this and asked Śivānanda Sena to become his *sarakhela (secretary)* and supervise his affairs.

VĀSUDEVA'S COMPASSION

Vāsudeva was so distressed by the suffering of the living beings that he was ready to accept their sins and suffer in hell, and he prayed to Mahāprabhu for such a boon:

"My Lord! You have appeared in this world to save it, so please accept my prayer. You are omnipotent and all-merciful, so if You agree to fulfill my request, it can be easily done. When I see the suffering of the world, my heart is torn apart. So I ask You, Lord, give their sins to me. I will take their sins and suffer in hell on their behalf, but please deliver them from their material disease." (*Caitanya Caritāmṛta* 2.15.160-163)

"He wished to take the sins of every single living being and suffer in hell in their place so that they could be liberated." (*Caitanya Caritāmṛta* 1.10.42)

When Mahāprabhu heard this heartfelt plea on behalf of the living beings of the world, He said to Vāsudeva:

"If you desire the deliverance of all living entities within the universe, then all of them can be delivered even without your undergoing the tribulations of sinful activity. Kṛṣṇa is not incapable, for He has all potencies. Why would He induce you to suffer the sinful reactions of other living entities? Whosever welfare you desire immediately becomes a Vaiṣṇava, and Kṛṣṇa delivers all Vaiṣṇavas from the reactions of their past sinful activities." (*Caitanya Caritāmṛta* 2.15.167-169)

Śrīla Bhakti Siddhānta Sarasvatī Gosvāmī Ṭhākura writes in his *Anubhāṣya* to this verse of the *Caitanya Caritāmṛta*: "In the Western world, Christians believe that only their guru, Jesus Christ, appeared in this world out of a desire to suffer on behalf of the people of the world by accepting their sins. But here we see that amongst Mahāprabhu's associates, Vāsudeva Datta Ṭhākura showed great compassion like Haridāsa Ṭhākura or even more, as he was willing to suffer in the place of all creatures in the universe. By so doing, he taught the world the unlimited nature of the Vaiṣṇava's selfless love."

Raghunātha Dāsa Gosvāmī's *dīkṣā* guru, Yadunandana Ācārya, was blessed by Vāsudeva Datta. The author of *Caitanya Bhāgavata*, Vṛndāvana Dāsa Ṭhākura, was born in Mamgachi in Modadrumadwip, one mile from the Purbasthali station on the Howrah-Katwa line of the Eastern Railway. Vāsudeva Datta consecrated the worship of the Madana Gopāla deity that is still being worshipped at that place.

We can see just how dear Vāsudeva Datta was to Mahāprabhu by the Lord's statements made when He was visiting Śrīvāsa Paṇḍita's house in Kumarahatta:

"Gauracandra repeated again and again, 'This body of Mine belongs to Vāsudeva. If he wants to sell Me, I allow Myself to be sold; I will not do otherwise. I announce this truth to all of you. If someone has even come into the briefest contact with Vāsudeva Datta, he will be protected by Kṛṣṇa. Listen all you Vaiṣṇavas! I tell you the truth: My body belongs to Vāsudeva alone.' " (*Caitanya Bhāgavata* 3.5.27-30)

Śrīla Gadādhara Paṇḍita Gosvāmī

śrī-rādhā-prema-rūpā yā purā vṛndāvandeśvarī
sā śrī-gadādharo gaura-vallabhaḥ paṇḍitākhyakaḥ
nirṇītaḥ śrī-svarūpair yo vraja-lakṣmītayā yathā
purā vṛndāvane lakṣmīḥ śyāmasundara-vallabhā
sādya gaura-prema-lakṣmīḥ śrī-
gadādhara-paṇḍitaḥ
rādhām anugatā yat tal lalitāpy anurādhikā
ataḥ prāviśad eṣā taṁ gaura-candrodaye yathā

"The *avatāra* of love who was previously the Queen of Vrindavan, Rādhā, is now the beloved of Gaura named Śrī Gadādhara Paṇḍita. Svarūpa Dāmodara Gosvāmī himself indicated that Gadādhara was Vraja's goddess of fortune, the Lakṣmī who was previously the beloved of Syāmasundara in Vrindavan. She has today become the goddess of fortune and love for Gaura and is known as Śrī Gadādhara Paṇḍita. Lalitā, who is also known as Anurādhā, is Rādhā's closest friend and confidante. She has also entered into Gadādhara, as was shown in the play *Caitanya-candrodaya*." (*Gaura-gaṇoddeśa-dīpikā* 147-150)

GADĀDHARA-TATTVA

gadādhara paṇḍitādi prabhura nija-śakti
tān sabāra caraṇe mora sahasra praṇati

"Gadādhara Paṇḍita and others are the Lord's own energies. I pay thousands of obeisances to their feet." (*Caitanya Caritāmṛta* 1.1.41)

"Caitanya Mahāprabhu appears in six features, namely as the two types of guru, the devotees of the lord, the Lord himself, His *avatāra*, His expansion and His energy.

According to the principle of simultaneous oneness and difference, they are all identified with Caitanya Mahāprabhu Himself." (*Anubhāṣya* to *Caitanya Caritāmṛta* 1.1.37-45)

She who was Rādhā in Kṛṣṇa's pastimes became Śrī Gadādhara Paṇḍita Gosvāmī in Gaura *līlā*. When Gaura manifests His identity with Nārāyaṇa, His *śaktis* are His wives Lakṣmīpriya and Viṣṇupriya. When identifying with Kṛṣṇa, His *śakti* is Śrī Gadādhara Paṇḍita Gosvāmī.

pañca-tattvātmakaṁ kṛṣṇaṁ
bhakta-rūpa-svarūpakam
bhaktāvatāraṁ bhaktākhyaṁ
namāmi bhakta-śaktikam

"I offer my obeisances to Kṛṣṇa who appears in five features, as a devotee, as the expansion of a devotee, as an *avatāra* of a devotee, as the pure devotee and as the devotional energy."

These five features all appeared with Caitanya Mahāprabhu in His *avatāra*, and in their association He joyfully performed the congregational chanting of the Holy Names. Though He appears in these five forms, there is in fact no difference between them. The distinctions arise due to His desire to relish different devotional flavors.

Śrī Gaurāṅga, Nityānanda Prabhu, Advaita Ācārya, Gadādhara Paṇḍita and Śrīvāsa Paṇḍita, etc., make up the Pañca Tattva, and there is spiritually no difference between them. The Supreme Truth has unlimited pastimes in order to relish the different tastes of transcendental relationship, and thus He separates into these five forms as the form of devotee, the devotional manifestation, the devotional *avatāra*, the devotional energy and the pure devotee.

jaya jaya nityānanda-gadādharera jīvana
jaya jaya advaitādi bhaktera śaraṇa

"All glories, all glories, to the life of Nityānanda Prabhu and Gadādhara!

"All glories, all glories, to the shelter of all the devotees, headed by Advaita!"

Śrīla Bhakti Siddhānta Sarasvatī Gosvāmī Ṭhākura comments on words "the life of Gadādhara" as follows: "Śrīla Gadādhara Paṇḍita Gosvāmī is chief amongst the most intimate devotees of Śrī Caitanya. He is the fountainhead of the entire *śakti-tattva* and is thus present equally in Mahāprabhu's *līlās* in Nabadwip and in Nilachal. His childhood home was in Nabadwip; later he took *kṣetra sannyāsa* in Jagannatha Puri and lived in a garden, or *toṭā*, by the seashore. Pure devotees who wish to enter into the *madhura-rasa* of Śrī Rādhā-Govinda take shelter of Gadādhara Paṇḍita and only then they will come to be known as Gaurāṅga Mahāprabhu's intimate devotees. Those devotees who are not so inclined to the *madhura-rasa* take shelter of Nityānanda Prabhu and engage in pure devotional service. Some of Mahāprabhu's devotees, such as Narahari, were followers of Śrī Gadādhara Paṇḍita Gosvāmī. They took refuge in him because they knew him to be Mahāprabhu's dearest associate. Some devotees, therefore, call Caitanya 'the life of Nityānanda Prabhu' while others called Him the life of Gadādhara."

GADĀDHARA PAṆḌITA'S EARLY LIFE

Gadādhara Paṇḍita appeared in the village of Beleti Grama in the Chittagong district of modern Bangladesh in 1408 of the Śaka era (1487 A.D.) on the dark-moon day of the month of Vaiśākha. His father was Mādhava Miśra, a Vārendra *brāhmaṇa* in the Kāśyāpa *gotra*, and his mother was Ratnavatī Devī. He also had a younger brother named Vāṇīnātha. The family lived in Beleti Gram until Gadādhara was twelve and then moved to Nabadwip.

Gadādhara Paṇḍita was a *brahmacārī* for his entire life. Indeed, his indifference to the pleasures of the world was such that Īśvara Purīpāda was very impressed when he visited Nabadwip. Īśvara Purī gave Gadhādara Paṇḍita instruction in a book he had himself written, *Kṛṣṇa-līlāmṛta.*

While Mahāprabhu was delighting in His pastimes as a student, there was no scholar in the town of Nabadwip who was unafraid of entering into debate with Him. Mahāprabhu would defeat one's position and then show how the same position could be defended. Mukunda Datta, Śrīvāsa Paṇḍita and others who knew the joys of the devotional sentiment were afraid of getting involved in such useless debates with Nimāi Paṇḍita, and so they would avoid Him. One day, Nimāi Paṇḍita saw Gadādhara Paṇḍita and asked him to give the definition of liberation. Gadādhara Paṇḍita answered according to the *Nyāya* school that liberation consisted in the final eradication of all miseries (*ātyantika duḥkha-nivṛtti*). Nimāi Paṇḍita then proceeded to show how this definition was inadequate. The other devotees who were listening to Him speak thought how wonderful it would be if such a brilliant scholar would only become a devote.

When Mahāprabhu returned from Gaya, He began to reveal the transformations of divine love that amazed the devotees. Śrīmān Paṇḍita was the first to see Mahāprabhu's ecstatic symptoms, and he reported what he had seen to all the other devotees, who were overjoyed at the news. When Mahāprabhu decided to reveal His true identity to the devotees, He told them to come to the house of Śuklāmbara Brahmacārī. Gadādhara Paṇḍita was amongst those who went there, but remained discreet about his presence. When he saw Mahāprabhu become intoxicated with the power of the Holy Names, Gadādhara Paṇḍita fainted. Mahāprabhu then said to him:

"Gadādhara! You have such good fortune. From your early childhood, your mind has been fixed on Kṛṣṇa's lotus feet. Meanwhile, I have been wasting My life in useless activities. Despite obtaining the great treasure of a human birth, by My misfortune I was able to make no use of it." (*Caitanya Bhāgavata* 2.1.98-99)

Subsequently, Gadādhara Paṇḍita would calm Mahāprabhu whenever He was overly affected by His ecstasies. One day, Gadādhara Paṇḍita said to Mahāprabhu, "Your Lord Kṛṣṇa is hidden in Your heart." As soon as He heard this, Mahāprabhu began to claw at His chest, but Gadādhara Paṇḍita stopped Him from doing so. When Śacī saw how clever Gadādhara Paṇḍita was in handling her son, she asked him to always stay near Nimāi to protect Him. (*Caitanya Bhāgavata* 2.2.198-210)

GADĀDHARA PAṆḌITA TAKES INITIATION FROM PUṆḌARĪKA

Once, Mahāprabhu suddenly started calling out the name of His dear associate Puṇḍarīka Vidyānidhi, saying, "Puṇḍarīka, My father!" and crying. None of the devotees who were present knew Puṇḍarīka Vidyānidhi, who was formerly Rādhārāṇī's father, Vṛṣabhānu, and were thus unable to understand what the Lord meant. When they asked Him, He glorified Puṇḍarīka Vidyānidhi and told them that he would shortly be coming to Nabadwip-Mayapur. However, when Puṇḍarīka Vidyānidhi arrived in Nabadwip, no one recognized him because he disguised himself as a great sense enjoyer in order to mask his profound devotional feeling.

Mukunda Datta and Vāsudeva Datta were former residents of Chittagong and knew Puṇḍarīka Vidyānidhi very well. One day, Mukunda Datta told Śrī Gadādhara Paṇḍita Gosvāmī that he wanted to introduce him to a very advanced Vaiṣṇava and took him to Puṇḍarīka Vidyānidhi's house. Mukunda introduced the two of them, and Vidyānidhi happily engaged Gadādhara Paṇḍita in conversation. Gadādhara Paṇḍita, however, who had been indifferent to sensual pleasures since he was very young, could not help doubting Puṇḍarīka Vidyānidhi when he saw the expensive furnishings by which he was surrounded, from the fine silk sheets as white as milk foamto the perfumes in the air to the *pan* (betel) he was chewing. Mukunda saw the doubt written on Gadādhara Paṇḍita's face and decided to reveal Puṇḍarīka Vidyānidhi's true devotional nature to him. He recited the following two verses in glorification of Kṛṣṇa from *Śrīmad Bhāgavatam*:

aho bakīyaṁ stana-kāla-kūṭaṁ
jighāṁsayāpāyayad apy asādhvī
lebhe gatiṁ dhātry-ucitāṁ tato'nyaṁ
kaṁ vā dayāluṁ śaraṇaṁ vrajema

"How truly amazing! The sister of Bakāsura, the evil Putanā, was sent on a mission to kill Kṛṣṇa. Despite her evil intentions, He drank the *kālakūṭa* poison that was mixed with her breast milk and awarded her the position of a wet nurse [as Ambikā and Kilimbā in Goloka]. Is there anyone else I can take shelter of who is more merciful than this Kṛṣṇa?" (*Śrīmad Bhāgavatam* 3.2.23)

pūtanā loka-bāla-ghnī
rākṣasī rudhirāśanā
jighāṁsayāpi haraye
stanaṁ dattvāpa sad-gatim

"Putanā was always hankering for the blood of human children, and with that desire, she came to kill Kṛṣṇa; but because she offered her breast to the Lord, she attained the greatest achievement." (*Śrīmad Bhāgavatam* 10.6.35)

The instant that Puṇḍarīka Vidyānidhi heard these verses, he began to cry, "*Ha* Kṛṣṇa!" and fell to the ground in a faint. Extraordinary ecstatic symptoms began to show on his body. Śrī Gadādhara Paṇḍita Gosvāmī was amazed to see this reaction and began to regret the offensive thoughts he had been having just moments before. Later, Mahāprabhu advised Gadādhara Paṇḍita that the best way to become free of this offense was to ask Puṇḍarīka Vidyānidhi for initiation. So this is how Gadādhara Paṇḍita became his disciple.

THE LORD'S CONSTANT COMPANION

Śrī Gadādhara Paṇḍita Gosvāmī was Mahāprabhu's constant companion. He participated in Mahāprabhu's water sports after the conversion of Jagāi and Mādhāi; he acted in the play about Kṛṣṇa *līlā* in Candraśekhara's house; he observed the great epiphany (*mahā-*

prakāśa) in Śrīvāsa Aṅgana; he was there when the Kājī was converted and when Mahāprabhu took *sannyāsa*; he accompanied Mahāprabhu to Puri where he joined Him in cleaning the Guṇḍicā temple and then bathing in Narendra Sarovara; and in so many other pastimes.

At Candraśekara Ācārya's house, in the first act of the play about Kṛṣṇa's pastimes in Vrindavan that Mahāprabhu staged, Haridāsa Ṭhākura played the part of the village constable, Śrīvāsa Paṇḍita played Nārada Muni, and Mahāprabhu played Rukmiṇī. In the second act, Gadādhara Paṇḍita also dressed as a woman, at which time Mahāprabhu said, "Gadādhara is a part of my Vaikuṇṭha family." Afterward, Mahāprabhu dressed as the primal energy and gave joy to everyone in the form of the mother of the universe; the devotees too glorified Him with hymns addressed to the Divine Mother.

GADĀDHARA PAṆḌITA'S KṢETRA SANNYĀSA

Śrī Gadādhara Paṇḍita Gosvāmī went to live in Puri as a *kṣetra-sannyāsī*. Mahāprabhu gave him the service of the Toṭā Gopīnātha deity and told him to live in the Yameśvara Toṭā, or garden adjoining the Yameśvara Śiva temple. On one occasion, when Gadādhara Paṇḍit heard that Nityānanda Prabhu had come to Puri, he invited Him to come and take Toṭā Gopīnātha's *prasāda*. Nityānanda Prabhu accepted his invitation and brought some fine rice from Bengal as an offering for Gopīnātha. Gadādhara Paṇḍita cooked the rice along with leaves and vegetables from the Yameśvara garden. When he was offering the foodstuffs to the deity, Mahāprabhu also appeared there, giving him great pleasure. The three of them joyfully took *prasāda* together. (*Caitanya Bhāgavata, Antya* 10)

When Mahāprabhu wanted to go to Vrindavan, Rāmānanda Rāya and Sārvabhauma Bhaṭṭācārya used all the means at their disposal to make Him stay in Puri. On the third *Cāturmāṣya* after His departure from Nabadwip, all the Bengali devotees came to Puri with their wives to see Him. After the Guṇḍicā temple cleansing and the Rathayātrā, the devotees returned home. As they were leaving, the devotees from Kulina village asked Mahāprabhu to describe the characteristics of a devotee. Mahāprabhu then described the differences between a Vaiṣṇava, a more advanced Vaiṣṇava and the most advanced Vaiṣṇava. (*Caitanya Caritāmṛta* 2.16.69-75)

When Mahāprabhu showed even more determination to go to Vrindavan, the devotees finally gave Him permission to leave after Vijaya-daśamī. King Pratāparudra gave a great deal of official help to smooth His journey. When Mahāprabhu crossed the Chitrotpala River to leave Puri, Rāya Rāmānanda, Maṅgalarāja, and Haricandana continued on in His company. Because of his *kṣetra-sannyāsa*, Śrī Gadādhara Paṇḍita Gosvāmī was not permitted to go any farther. He was unable to tolerate the idea of separation from the Lord, however, and wanted to continue on with Him. Mahāprabhu had to remind him of his vow to remain in Jagannatha Puri and forbade him to go onward to Vraja. Gadādhara Paṇḍita retorted, "To hell with my vows to remain in Puri. As far as I am concerned, Jagannatha Puri is wherever You are." Mahāprabhu insisted and told Gadādhara Paṇḍita not to abandon his service to Gopīnātha. Gadādhara Paṇḍita stubbornly argued, "Just seeing Your lotus feet is worth a million times more than any service to Gopīnātha."

When Mahāprabhu said, "If you abandon your duties to Gopīnātha, then it will be considered My fault." Gadādhara said, "No, I will take all the responsibility for any offense for abandoning the service to Gopīnātha and for breaking the vow of *kṣetra-sannyāsa*. I will be going alone without disturbing You. I am going to Bengal to see Śacī Mātā." Other than Mahāprabhu's intimate associates, no one will be able to understand the extent of Gadādhara Prabhu's devotion to Gaurāṅga. Love on the path of spontaneous devotion is not easy to comprehend. Gadādhara Paṇḍita was ready to abandon his vows, his service, everything for the sake of Mahāprabhu.

When Mahāprabhu's party arrived at Cuttack, a hundred kilometers north of Puri, Mahāprabhu called Gadādhara Paṇḍita and said, "You have realized your objective to break your vows and leave your service. If you come with Me, that will make you happy. But do you want your own happiness or Mine? It will make Me unhappy if your vows to remain in Puri and to serve Gopīnātha are broken. If you want My happiness, return to Puri. That is all I have to say."

When he heard Mahāprabhu's words, Gadādhara Paṇḍita fell to the ground and fainted. By the order of Mahāprabhu Sārvabhauma Bhaṭṭācārya comforted Gadādhara Paṇḍita and accompanied him back to Puri.

GADĀI-GĀURĀṄGA

Due to her submissiveness and simplicity, Kṛṣṇa's wife Rukmiṇī was not always able to understand His joking words and would become frightened. Like her, Gadādhara Paṇḍita was also unable to always understand Mahāprabhu's witticisms or His feigned indifference, all of which would cause him anxiety. Śrī Gadādhara Paṇḍita Gosvāmī was by nature simple and pleasant. On one occasion, when Vallabha Bhaṭṭa came to see Mahāprabhu, He saw that Vallabha Bhaṭṭa was proud of his scholarship and ridiculed him. Mahāprabhu pointed out flaws in his philosophical understanding and ignored him.

Vallabha Bhaṭṭa responded to Mahāprabhu's indifference by starting to visit Gadādhara Paṇḍita and making a show of attachment to him. Mahāprabhu did not particularly like Gadādhara Paṇḍita's relation with Vallabha Bhaṭṭa and began to demonstrate a certain coolness toward him also. This behavior made Gadādhara Paṇḍita fear that Mahāprabhu would ostracize him, and so he came and fell at Lord's feet and started to cry. Mahāprabhu laughed and embraced Gadādhara Paṇḍita. He said,

"I wanted to tease you, but you were not flustered. You said nothing in anger but patiently bore everything. Your mind was not agitated by My tricks. By remaining fixed in your simple nature, you have purchased Me." No one can fully describe the nature of Gadādhara Paṇḍita's ecstatic love. Mahāprabhu has thus been given the name *Gadādhara-prāṇanātha*, "Gadādhara's life and soul." No one can describe the Lord's mercy toward Gadādhara Paṇḍita; thus people sing Their names together: Gadāi-Gaurāṅga."
(*Caitanya Caritāmṛta* 3.7.157-160)

Śrī Gadādhara Paṇḍita Gosvāmī remained on this earth only eleven months after Mahāprabhu's disappearance. In *Bhakti-ratnākara*, Narahari Cakravartī has described the terrible suffering of Gadādhara Paṇḍita in Mahāprabhu's separation. He remained alive only in order to be able to see Śrīnivāsa Ācārya.

"As he repeated the name of Gaurasundara with his eyes closed, his sighs were as hot as flames. No one but the Lord can know how Gadādhara Paṇḍita suffered in His absence. His motionless body remained alive only so that he could bestow his mercy on Śrīnivāsa Ācārya." (*Bhakti-ratnākara* 3.142-4)

Śrī Gadādhara Paṇḍita Gosvāmī disappeared at Puri on the dark-moon day of Jyaiṣṭha in 1456 of the Śaka era (1535 A.D.).

Śrī Buddhimanta Khān

"Buddhimanta Khān was very dear to Lord Caitanya Mahāprabhu. He was one of the Lord's greatest servants, and he obeyed Him from the time of his birth." (*Caitanya Caritāmṛta* 1.10.74)

BUDDHIMANTA'S PREVIOUS LIFE

Buddhimanta Khān is considered to be one of Caitanya's branches. In his *Navadvīpa-dhāma-māhātmya*, Śrīla Bhaktivinoda Ṭhākura has written the following in connection with the village of Suvarna Vihara in Godrumdwip: "In the Satya Yuga, a pious king named Suvarṇa Sena lived in this village of Suvarna Vihara. Through the blessings of Nārada Muni, this king obtained love for Rādhā and Kṛṣṇa as well as for Their combined manifestation, Śrī Gaurāṅga Mahāprabhu. One night, Suvarṇa Sena saw Gaura and Gadādhara with all their associates in a dream. When he awoke, the King cried out in distress from the loss of the vision. Suddenly, he heard a voice from the sky which told him that when Mahāprabhu would appear again in the Age of Kālī, then the King would also take birth as Buddhimanta Khān in order to expand the Lord's pastimes."

BUDDHIMANTA'S CHARITABLE WORKS

Buddhimanta lived in Nabadwip. He and Mukunda Sañjaya were amongst the richest people in the town. They performed charitable works such as providing medicines and treatment for the poor who fell ill. Once, when Mahāprabhu was still exhibiting the pastimes of a householder, He was undergoing ecstatic transformations of love for Kṛṣṇa. His relatives and friends thought that He had been afflicted by some kind of mental disorder and called Buddhimanta Khān to see to His treatment.

Buddhimanta paid for all the costs of Mahāprabhu's wedding when He married for the second time, to Viśṇupriyā, the daughter of a local zamindar's priest, Sanātana Miśra. Buddhimanta also participated in all of Mahāprabhu's Nabadwip pastimes – in the *kīrtanas* at Śrīvāsa Aṅgana, at Candraśekhara's house and on the streets of Nabadwip, and in the water sports in the Ganges along with His associates after the deliverance of Jagāi and Mādhāi.

BUDDHIMANTA AT CANDRAŚEKHARA'S HOUSE

One day Mahāprabhu revealed His desire to put on a play about Vraja *līlā* and dance in the mood of Mahālakṣmī. He told Buddhimanta Khān that He wanted him to take responsibility for the costumes and decorations. Buddhimanta himself dressed Mahāprabhu.

"Mahāprabhu said, 'Buddhimanta Khān! Go quickly and arrange for costumes for today I shall dance.' Upon receipt of the order, Sadāśiva and Buddhimanta Khān immediately returned home, feeling unlimited joy. The devotees quickly put up an awning of bamboo and cloth and there started dressing the actors for the play. Buddhimanta brought the costumes and presented them to the Lord." (*Caitanya Bhāgavata* 2.18.13-16)

"Look here. This is the house of Candraśekhara Ācārya. The Lord came here with His dearest associates. Sadāśiva and Buddhimanta Khān took charge of the costumes and dressing the actors." (*Bhakti-ratnākara* 12.2902-3)

After Mahāprabhu took *sannyāsa* in Katwa, He went to Shantipur, where He met with all the Nabadwip devotees, including Buddhimanta Khān. Buddhimanta also accompanied the Bengali devotees to Puri to see the Lord. The Lord also lovingly accepted his and the Bengali devotees' gifts of foodstuffs, which they brought to Puri for Him.

"Buddhimanta Khān, whose only interest from his very birth had been to serve the Lord's order, also went [on the pilgrimage to Puri]." (*Caitanya Bhāgavata* 3.8.30)

Śrī Nandana Ācārya

According to both scriptures, the *Caitanya Bhāgavata* and the *Caitanya Caritāmṛta*, Nandana Ācārya's father was named Caturbhuja Paṇḍita and he had two brothers, Viṣṇu Dāsa and Gaṅgā Dāsa.

"Lord Nityānanda performed pastimes in the house of Caturbhuja Paṇḍita's son Gaṅgā Dāsa." (*Caitanya Bhāgavata* 3.5.74)

"Lord Nityānanda stayed in the house of the three brothers Viṣṇu Dāsa, Nandan and Gaṅgā Dāsa." (*Caitanya Caritāmṛta* 1.11.43)

They were a family of Bhattācārya *brāhmaṇas* residing in Nabadwip. Both Viṣṇu Dāsa and Gaṅgā Dāsa stayed in Nilachal with Mahāprabhu for a while. Mahāprabhu, Nityānanda Prabhu and Advaita Ācārya all hid in Nandana Ācārya's house at one time or another as a part of Their pastimes. Nityānanda Prabhu stayed at his house while at Nabadwip.

"Nandana Ācārya is a branch of the Caitanya tree that is celebrated throughout the world because the two Prabhus hid in his house." (*Caitanya Caritāmṛta* 1.10.39)

In the *Gauḍīya Vaiṣṇava Abhidhāna,* a different family tree is given for Nandana Ācārya. The author of that dictionary writes: "Nandana Ācārya came from a family of astrologer *brāhmaṇas*. His father's name was Lakṣmī Nārāyaṇa. Lakṣmī Nārāyaṇa had two sons: Nandana Ācārya and Bhagavān Adhikārī Sārvabhauma. Lakṣmī Nārāyaṇa had a reputation as a seer and astrologer. He was present when Mahāprabhu was born. Nandana Ācārya is included as a branch of the Caitanya tree. He was lame. When Mahāprabhu returned from South India, all the devotees were overjoyed to see Him. Even though Nandana Ācārya was lame, he went ahead of everyone else to perform *pūjā* to the Lord.

"Śrī Nandana Ācārya came from a family of Śākadvīpī *brāhmaṇas* descended from Śanti Muni, the son of Parāśara. He belonged to the Bharata branch of the Vatsya *gotra* from Rarha. He lived for some time in Bahirkhanda village near Tarakeswar in present-day Birbhum before moving to Nabadwip, where he made his home in Srihatta or Dakshin Para."

It is also written in the *Gauḍīya Vaiṣṇava Abhidhāna*: "The Nandana mentioned in the *Caitanya Caritāmṛta* as the brother of Gaṅgā Dāsa and Viṣṇu Dāsa is a different person. He is counted as a branch of Nityānanda Prabhu. He is a writer of poetry and songs, but little else is known about him. He is not Nandana Ācārya."

NITYĀNANDA PRABHU IN THE HOUSE OF NANDANA ĀCĀRYA

When Śrīmān Nityānanda Prabhu was in a mood of separation, he wandered all over India looking for Kṛṣṇa until finally he came to Vrindavan. There He heard that Kṛṣṇa had already appeared in Nabadwip-Mayapur: the son of Nanda, Śrī Kṛṣṇa, had appeared as Gaurahari, the son of Śacī. Nityānanda Prabhu, who is none other than Balarāma Himself, quickly came to Nabadwip and started to live incognito in the house of Nandana Ācārya. Nandana Ācārya felt that his life had been fulfilled. Mahāprabhu knew of Nityānanda Prabhu's coming through a dream. He told the other devotees that Nityānanda Prabhu had arrived in town and sent Śrīvāsa Paṇḍita and Haridāsa Ṭhākura out to look for Him. These two searched through the entire town but could not find Him anywhere. When Mahāprabhu heard from Śrīvāsa Paṇḍita and Haridāsa Ṭhākura that Nityānanda Prabhu was not in Nabadwip, He slightly smiled in His omniscience and took the devotees with Him to Nandana Ācārya's house.

The devotees were astonished to behold a personality as effulgent as a million suns. In order to reveal Nityānanda Prabhu's true identity to all His devotees, Mahāprabhu signaled Śrīvāsa Paṇḍita to sing a verse from *Śrīmad Bhāgavatam* (10.21.5):

barhāpīḍaṁ naṭa-vara-vapuḥ
karṇayoḥ karṇikāraṁ
vibhrad-vāsaḥ kanaka-kapiśaṁ
vaijayantīṁ ca mālām
randhrān veṇor adhara-sudhayā
pūrayan gopa-vṛndai-
vṛnāraṇyaṁ sva-pada-ramaṇaṁ
prāviśad gīta-kīrtiḥ

"Kṛṣṇa, whose glories are sung by the cowherd boys, dressed as a dancing performer, a peacock feather decorating His topknot, *karṇikāra* flowers behind His ears, wearing a yellow garment as brilliant as gold and a *vaijayantī* garland around His neck. In this costume, He entered the forest of Vrindavan, the pleasure garden of His auspiciously marked feet, while filling the holes of His flute with the nectar of His lips."

As soon as He heard this verse, Nityānanda Prabhu uttered the words "*Ha Kṛṣṇa!*" and fainted, the eight ecstatic symptoms manifesting in His body. Mahāprabhu was eager to be reunited with His brother, and thus, after He revealed the identity of Nityānanda Prabhu to the assembled devotees, He clutched Nitāi to His bosom.

"Śrī Nandana Ācārya was fortunate, indeed. Just look, Śrīnivāsa; this is his home. The Lord came to this house with all the devotees and found Nityānanda Prabhu sitting here in meditation. The devotees stood here gazing upon His incomparable beauty." (*Bhakti-ratnākara* 12.2422-4)

ADVAITA ĀCĀRYA HIDES IN ŚRĪ NANDANA ĀCĀRYA'S HOUSE

When the Vyāsa Pūjā at Śrīvāsa Aṅgana had been completed, Mahāprabhu, Nityānanda

Prabhu and Their other associates became fully absorbed in the ecstasies of *saṅkīrtana*. One day, Mahāprabhu, in His identity as the Supreme Person, ordered Rāmāi Paṇḍita to go to Advaita Ācārya's house and tell Him that He had manifested His presence. He also said to Ramai, "Śrī Advaita Ācārya called to the Lord of Goloka in order to bring Him down to this earth, while performing *pūjā* with Ganges water and Tulasi leaves. This Lord has now appeared in Navadvīpa along with Nityānanda Prabhu. Therefore, Advaita Ācārya should immediately come to Śrīvāsa Aṅgana with his wife and all the paraphernalia needed to worship Him."

Rāmāi acted according to Mahāprabhu's instruction and went to Advaita Ācārya's house. Advaita Ācārya, through His omniscience, understood the purpose of his arrival. Nevertheless, He inquired the matter from Rāmāi. When Advaita Ācārya heard from him that Mahāprabhu had manifested in Nabadwip, He and His wife, Sītādevī, His son Acyutānanda, and a number of His other followers all shed tears of joy. Advaita Ācārya did as He had been instructed, gathering up the paraphernalia for worship and traveling to Nabadwip with His entourage. Even so, He wished to test Mahāprabhu first, and so He stopped at Nandana Ācārya's house and waited there. He sent Rāmāi ahead but told him to keep his presence at Nandana's house secret and to tell Mahāprabhu instead that he had refused to come.

As the Supersoul, Viśvambhara Mahāprabhu could understand exactly what Advaita Ācārya was trying to do. He revealed a majestic divine form on the altar of Śrīvāsa Paṇḍita's house. He indicated to Nityānanda Prabhu to hold the parasol over His head and to the other devotees to engage in various services. Mahāprabhu then announced to all the devotees, "Advaita Ācārya has decided to test Me. He is hiding at Nandana Ācārya's house with all the paraphernalia for My *pūjā*." He again sent Rāmāi to tell Him that He was aware of his plan and to tell him to quickly come. When Advaita Ācārya got the direct order from Mahāprabhu a second time, He joyfully went to Śrīvāsa Paṇḍita's house. As soon as He saw the Lord, he fell to the ground at some distance to pay obeisance to His lotus feet and began to recite hymns of glorification. Seeing the Lord's opulent form, Advaita Ācārya became motionless and then began to praise the unequalled mercy of the Lord. Advaita Ācārya then washed the Lord's lotus feet and then worshipped Him with the five ingredients (*pañcapocāra*), using the following *mantra* to do so:

namo brahmaṇya-devāya go-brāhmaṇa-hitāya ca
jagad-dhitāya kṛṣṇāya govindāya namo namaḥ

"I pay my obeisances to Kṛṣṇa Govinda, the Lord of the brahminical society, to Him who is the source of the cows' and the *brāhmaṇas*' welfare, and who is the source of the welfare of the entire universe."

Mahāprabhu then commanded Advaita Prabhu to get up and dance. Advaita Ācārya started to dance madly until He became completely intoxicated, immersing all the watching devotees in a flood of ecstasy.

MAHĀPRABHU HIDING IN THE HOUSE OF NANDANA ĀCĀRYA

The local atheists started to plot against Mahāprabhu after having been beaten in debates by His talent and learning. They fabricated complaints and went to the local administrator. That day, when He returned home, Mahāprabhu started *saṅkīrtana* in order to put an end to the atheists' blasphemous ways.

However, on that day, Mahāprabhu noticed that He was not feeling the usual ecstasy in the divine names and expressed His distress. Advaita Ācārya gave the following reasons for His lack of ecstasy on that day: "You have made Nityānanda Prabhu the keeper of the storehouse of love. You have deprived Śrīvāsa and Me of this love. On the other hand, You have given it to everyone else, even to those in the lower castes. So, I have dried up the ocean of Your *prema*. That is why You are not feeling anything today."

When Mahāprabhu heard this, He decided that He could not bear to live another minute in a useless body devoid of *prema*, and so He went and jumped into the Ganges, intending to drown Himself. Nityānanda Prabhu and Haridāsa Ṭhākura immediately jumped in after Him and pulled Him out. Mahāprabhu then revealed to these two His intention to go and stay for a while at Nandana Ācārya's house, out of sight of the other devotees. Nityānanda Prabhu and Haridāsa Ṭhākura were thus the only ones to know that He was staying there.

The other devotees found no sign of Mahāprabhu anywhere and began to cry in intense separation from Him. Advaita Prabhu even undertook a fast. Meanwhile, Mahāprabhu sat down on the deity's throne in the house of Nandana Ācārya and engaged him in various kinds of service. Mahāprabhu also instructed him not to tell anyone that He was at his place, but Nandana answered, "You are the wealth of the devotees' hearts. The devotees are the ones who reveal You to the world. How will You ever manage to remain hidden from them?"

Indeed, the Lord was aware that the devotees were unable to tolerate the pain of His absence, and so He asked Nandana Ācārya to bring Śrīvāsa Paṇḍita there. Śrīvāsa Paṇḍita described how upset Advaita Prabhu was and that He was fasting. Mahāprabhu immediately accompanied Śrīvāsa Paṇḍita to Advaita Ācārya's residence, and when He saw Him lying faint and weak on the floor, He felt Himself to be a great offender. Advaita Ācārya rose up from His transcendental unconscious state and prayed to the Lord again and again to be forgiven for His rash statements and begged a place at the Lord's lotus feet so that He could serve Him birth after birth.

NANDANA ĀCĀRYA'S PARTICIPATION IN OTHER LĪLĀS

After taking *sannyāsa* in Katwa, Mahāprabhu was brought to the house of Advaita Ācārya in Shantipur by Nityānanda Prabhu's trickery. Śacī Mātā and other residents of Nabadvīpa came to see Him there; Nandana Ācārya was amongst them. The year that Rāghava Paṇḍita first brought his famous bags of food (*rāghavera jhāli*) to Mahāprabhu in Puri, Nandana Ācārya and many other Bengal devotees also gave the Lord some food preparations that pleased Him greatly. Nandana Ācārya was also among those devotees whose invitations to lunch were accepted by the Lord at Puri. His name was also mentioned by Sārvabhauma Bhaṭṭācārya when he described the Lord's devotees to King Pratāparudra; "Here is Rāghava Paṇḍita, here is

Nandana Ācārya, there is Śrīmān Paṇḍita, and here are Śrīkānta and Nārāyaṇa." (*Caitanya Caritāmṛta* 2.11.89).

Nandana Ācārya was also amongst the participants in the nightly *kīrtana* at Śrīvāsa Aṅgana, at Śrīdhara Aṅgana and in the procession to the Kājī's house. In Puri, he participated in the cleaning of the Guṇḍicā temple and the Nṛsiṁha temple and the Lord's bathing pastimes in Indradyumna Sarovara. He also took part in the feast in the Āi Toṭā gardens and, of course, the Rathayātrā festival.

Śrīla Bhakti Sāraṅga Gosvāmī Mahārāja, the founder of the Sri Gaudiya Sangha and who has now entered the eternal pastimes of the Lord, constructed a temple at the site of Nandana Ācārya's house in Ishodyan, Mayapur. The temple houses deities of Śrī Caitanya Mahāprabhu and Nityānanda Prabhu.

The date and places of Nandana Ācārya's appearance and disappearance are unknown.

Candraśekhara Ācārya

candraśekhara ācāryaś
candro jñeyo vicakṣaṇaiḥ
śrīmān uddhavadāso'pi
candrāveśāvatārakaḥ

"The wise know Candraśekhara Ācārya and Uddhava Dāsa to be the partial manifestations of the moon god." (*Gaura-gaṇoddeśa-dīpikā* 112)

"One of the great branches of the Caitanya tree is called Ācāryaratna, also known as Candraśekhara; his associates are its sub-branches. Mahāprabhu danced in his house in the mood of the goddess of fortune." (*Caitanya Caritāmṛta* 1.10.12-13)

Śrīla Bhakti Siddhānta Sarasvatī Gosvāmī Ṭhākura writes: "Candraśekhara was one of the nine treasures or the god Candra. His home is known as Vraja-pattana [or the place where Mahāprabhu enjoyed His pastimes of putting on a play about Vrindavan]."

Śrīla Bhaktivinoda Ṭhākura writes in his *Amṛta-pravāha-bhāṣya* that according to some sources, Ācāryaratna was the husband of the sister of Caitanya Mahāprabhu's mother. The *Gauḍīya Vaiṣṇava Abhidhāna* explains that he married Śacī Devī's sister Sarvajayā Devī.

In the book called *Śākhā-nirṇayāmṛta* by Śrīla Gadādhara Paṇḍita Gosvāmī's disciple Yadunātha Dāsa, Candraśekhara Ācārya's identity is revealed in the following way:

paurṇamāsī-pṛthu-prema-
pātraṁ śrī-candraśekharam
apāra-karuṇā-pūra-
paurṇamāsīti saṁjñakam

"Candraśekhara was the recipient of Paurṇamasī Devī's deepest love. He is known as the full-moon of unlimited compassion."

Candraśekhara Ācārya was born in the modern Sylhet (Srihatta).

"Śrīvāsa Paṇḍita, Śrī Rāma Paṇḍita and Candraśekhara Deva are worshipable throughout the three worlds; they, as well as Murāri Gupta, the physician who cures one of the disease of worldliness, all appeared in Sylhet." (*Caitanya Bhāgavata* 1.2.34-5)

All of Mahāprabhu's elders appear on this earth prior to His birth.

"There were many devotees hidden in Nabadwip who had previously taken birth at the Lord's command. They included Candraśekhara, Jagadīśa, Gopīnātha, Śrīmān, Murāri, Śrī Garuḍa, and Gaṅgā Dāsa." (*Caitanya Bhāgavata* 1.2.98-9)

Śrī Candraśekhara lived in the neighborhood of Śrī Jagannātha Miśra in

Mayapura. The Caitanya Maṭha established by Śrīla Bhakti Siddhānta Sarasvatī Gosvāmī Ṭhākura now stands on this site. After Mahāprabhu's appearance, Candraśekhara Ācārya and his wife would visit the Miśra's household regularly to see Him and also looked after Him. When Jagannātha Miśra departed from this world, Candraśekhara Ācārya took complete responsibility for Śacī Devī's household affairs.

PASTIMES IN CANDRAŚEKHARA'S HOUSE

After Mahāprabhu's return from Gaya, when He commenced His *saṅkīrtana* movement in the company of His devotees, He would sometimes hold His nightly *kīrtanas* in the house of Candraśekhara, just as He would in the house of Śrīvāsa Paṇḍita.

"All the Vaiṣṇavas felt great enthusiasm when they heard that Mahāprabhu had begun His *saṅkīrtana* movement. Every night, these *kīrtanas* took place in the house of Śrīvāsa Paṇḍita, and on certain occasions, in the house of Candraśekhara Ācārya." (*Caitanya Bhāgavata* 2.8.110-1)

Jagāi and Mādhāi were two brothers who, though born in a high-caste *brāhmaṇa* family, had nevertheless adopted robbery as their livelihood. By Mahāprabhu's causeless mercy, all of their sins were cleansed and they were given the opportunity to engage in *saṅkīrtana* with the rest of His devotees. Candraśekhara Ācārya was amongst the associates of the Lord who witnessed these wonderful events. "Vakreśvara Paṇḍita and Candraśekhara Ācārya both know all the glories of Caitanya Mahāprabhu." (*Caitanya Bhāgavata* 2.13.240)

Mahāprabhu put on a play about Vraja *līlā* in the house of Candraśekhara Ācārya. This *līlā* has been described in great detail by Vṛndāvana Dāsa Ṭhākura in his *Caitanya Bhāgavata*, in the eighteenth chapter of the *Madhya-khaṇḍa*. Kṛṣṇadāsa Kavirāja Gosvāmī has briefly mentioned the event in his *Caitanya Caritāmṛta*:

"Then Mahāprabhu performed Kṛṣṇa *līlā* in the house of Candraśekhara Ācārya. He Himself took on the role of Rukmiṇī. He sometimes became Durgā, Lakṣmī or the Divine Energy. Then He sat down on the deity throne and distributed love of God to all the assembled devotees." (*Caitanya Caritāmṛta* 1.17.241-2)

"Then Śacī's son, completely absorbed in the *kīrtana* of the Lord's names, called out to Sadāśiva and Buddhimanta Khān. 'Today I will go to Candraśekhara's house, where I will dance in the dress of Lakṣmī. Arrange for conch bracelets, saris, bodices, golden ornaments and other paraphernalia that will be suitable for our costumes.' Having so ordered him, Mahāprabhu and His companions went down the path which led to Candraśekhara's house." (*Bhakti-ratnākara* 12.1949-52)

Here is a brief summary of the story as found in the *Caitanya Bhāgavata*: One day Mahāprabhu revealed His desire to put on a play with His devotees about His pastimes in Vrindavan. He told Sadāśiva and Buddhimanta Khān who would play which role and what they should wear.

According to His instruction, Buddhimanta then arranged for appropriate dress and makeup for those who would be in the play, pleasing Mahāprabhu immeasurably. Mahāprabhu announced that He would dance in the role of Lakṣmī, but that only those whose senses were controlled would be able to sit in the audience. Advaita Ācārya, Śrīvāsa Paṇḍita and others sadly said that since they had no control over their senses they would be ineligible to watch. Mahāprabhu laughed slightly at hearing this and said that everyone would become a great yogi and would not be bewildered by His performance.

Śacī Mātā and Viṣṇupriyā Devī also came to see Mahāprabhu dance as Lakṣmī, and so did all the other devotees with their families. Advaita Ācārya took the role of the *vidūṣaka*, or clown, while Haridāsa Ṭhākura played the role of the town constable and Śrīvāsa Paṇḍita dressed up as Nārada Muni. The performance began when Mukunda sang Kṛṣṇa *kīrtana*. Haridāsa Ṭhākura came dancing in, twirling his baton, and he told everyone to watch the play and the Lord's dancing attentively.

Śrīvāsa Paṇḍita in the role of Nārada Muni said, "I have been wandering through the universes hoping to get a glimpse of Kṛṣṇa. I went to Vaikuṇṭha, but found the door closed and the house empty. Then I heard that Kṛṣṇa had come to Nadia and had dressed up as Lakṣmī." When Śacī saw Śrīvāsa in his identity as Nārada, she fainted in her amazement, but the other women brought her back to consciousness by chanting the name of Kṛṣṇa.

In the next act, Mahāprabhu came out dressed as Rukmiṇī. Totally absorbed in the mood of Rukmiṇī, He recited from *Bhāgavatam* the letter she wrote to Kṛṣṇa, and as He did so, He cried and wrote on the ground with His toes. When the Vaiṣṇavas saw this scene, they were overwhelmed by the ecstasy of divine love.

Later on in the evening, Śrīla Gadādhara Paṇḍita Gosvāmī came onto the stage dressed as a *gopī* and began to dance like a woman in love. Mahāprabhu and Nityānanda Prabhu then entered the stage area, Mahāprabhu in the dress of the *ādyā śakti* and Nityānanda Prabhu as an old woman, Rādhā's maternal grandmother. As the members of the audience looked at Mahāprabhu, each beheld Him according to his or her own mood: some as Kamalā, some as Lakṣmī, others as Sītā and yet others as Mahāmāyā. Even those who had known Nimāi since His birth, including Śacī, were unable to recognize Him. In the guise of playing the roles of all the different goddesses, Mahāprabhu revealed His divine energies and taught the proper respect due to each one of them. While the Lord was thus dancing as the *ādyā śakti*, Nityānanda Prabhu fainted, and all the other devotees began to cry loudly.

Then the Lord revealed another amazing pastime: He took on the mood of Mahālakṣmī, sat down on the deity throne and placed the Gopīnātha deity on His lap. When the devotees saw this they began to sing hymns of praise to Mahālakṣmī. As this was going on, day suddenly broke and the devotees were saddened to know that the wonderful night had come to an end. When the Lord saw their sadness, He took the form of the mother of the universe and one by one, took all the devotees on His lap and fed them with His breast milk. The devotees' sadness disappeared in a moment.

By the Lord's inconceivable potencies, there remained a divine light in Candraśekhara's house for seven days and nights afterward. It was so bright that people were not able to open their eyes to look at it. When people asked what this light was, the Vaiṣṇavas would only smile in response.

PARTICIPATION IN OTHER PASTIMES

Candraśekhara Ācārya was also present in the *saṅkīrtana* procession Mahāprabhu led through Nabadwip to Cāṇḍa Kājī's house to deliver him. He was also present when Mahāprabhu took *sannyāsa* in Katwa, and he performed all the rituals on His behest at that time.

"So saying, Keśava Bhāratī went to Katwa. Mahāprabhu followed later to take *sannyāsa*. Nityānanda Prabhu, Mukunda Datta and Candraśekhara Ācārya accompanied Him and performed all the rituals." (*Caitanya Caritāmṛta* 1.17.272-3)

Afterwards, Mahāprabhu became frantic to see Vrindavan and set off in that direction. However, Nityānanda Prabhu tricked Him into going to the bank of the Ganges opposite Shantipur. Candraśekhara Ācārya gave the message of Mahāprabhu's *sannyāsa* for the people of Nabadwip and Shantipur.

"The children showed Mahāprabhu the way to the Ganges, and He set off in that direction, completely absorbed in the consciousness of Kṛṣṇa. Nityānanda Prabhu said to Candraśekhara, 'Go immediately to Advaita Ācārya and tell Him that I am coming there with the Lord. Tell Him to wait for us with a boat at the bank. Then go to Nabadwip and fetch Śacī Mātā and the devotees.' (*Caitanya Caritāmṛta* 2.3.19-22)

Candraśekhara Ācārya did as he was commanded and brought Śacī Mātā to Advaita Ācārya's house in a palanquin. The Nabadwip devotees also accompanied them.

"In the morning, Ācāryaratna put Śacī in a palanquin and set off to Shantipur in the company of the other devotees." (*Caitanya Caritāmṛta* 2.3.137)

Later, when Mahāprabhu came back from South India to Puri, He sent Kāla Kṛṣṇadāsa (whom He had rescued from the *bhaṭṭahāri* women) with Nityānanda Prabhu and some other devotees to inform the Bengali Vaiṣṇavas of His return. Kāla Kṛṣṇadāsa met with Candraśekhara on that occasion. Candraśekhara also regularly accompanied the other devotees to Puri to spend *Cāturmāsya* with Mahāprabhu. He participated with Him in all the pastimes there, such as cleaning the Guṇḍicā temple and playing water sports in Narendra Sarovara.

Śrī Puṇḍarīka Vidyānidhi

vṛṣabhānutayā khyātaḥ purā yo vraja-maṇḍale
adhunā puṇḍarīkākṣo vidyānidhi-mahāśayaḥ
svakīya-bhāvam āsvādya rādhā-viraha-kātaraḥ
caitanyaḥ puṇḍarīkākṣam aye tātāvadat svayam
prema-nidhitayā khyātiṁ gauro
yasmai dadau sukhī
mādhavendrasya śiṣyatvāt gauravaṁ ca sadākarot
tat-prakāśa-viśeṣo'pi miśraḥ śrī-mādhavo mataḥ
ratnāvatī tu tat-patnī kīrtidā kīrtitā budhaiḥ

"He who was previously known in Vraja as Vṛṣabhānu is known here as Śrī Puṇḍarīkākṣa Vidyānidhi. When Mahāprabhu was afflicted by the feelings of Śrīmatī Rādhā's intense love in separation from Śrī Kṛṣṇa, He would call him 'Father!' Gauracandra was very pleased with Puṇḍarīka Vidyānidhi and entitled him Premanidhi, or "the treasure house of love." Mahāprabhu always treated him with respect because he was the disciple of Mādhavendra Purī. Mādhava Miśra is said to be his expansion. Vidyānidhi's wife, Ratnāvatī, was Kīrtidā in Vraja." (*Gaura-gaṇoddeśa-dīpikā* 54)

Puṇḍarīka Vidyānidhi's father was named Bāṇeśvara[8] and his mother, Gaṅgā Devī. He was born on *Vasanta-pañcamī*, the fifth day of the waxing moon in the month of Māgha, in Chakrashala in Chittagong. His home, or Sripat, used to stand in the village of

8 According to some others Śuklāmbara Brahmacārī was the father of Puṇḍarīka Vidyānidhi. Śrī Bāṇeśvara was the descendent in the family lineage of Śivarāma Gaṅgopādhyāya.

Mekhala, two miles east of the Hata Hajari police station, about twelve miles north of the city of Chittagong. Vidyānidhi's father was a Vārendra *brāhmaṇa* who hailed from the town of Baghiya in the district of Dhaka. Puṇḍarīka Vidyānidhi himself was a wealthy landowner in Chakrashala.

"He is an extremely rich zamindar from Chakrashala but is very pure in his action. He is a Vārendra *brāhmaṇa*, whose lineage is extremely respectable. His name is Śrī Puṇḍarīka Vidyānidhi. Sometimes he stays in Chittagong, and sometimes in Nabadwip. He is a disciple of Mādhavendra Purī." (*Prema-vilāsa*, 22)

THE LORD GLORIFIES PUṆḌARĪKA

Śrī Puṇḍarīka Vidyānidhi came to Nabadwip because he wished to live by the banks of the Ganges. Mahāprabhu, the indweller of all beings, knew prior to his coming that he had such a desire, and one day in the assembly of devotees started calling out, "Puṇḍarīka, My friend, My father!" and crying.

When His associates asked Him why He was crying in this way, the Lord described Puṇḍarīka Vidyānidhi to them in the following way: "His character is quite extraordinary. Just by hearing his name, the whole world is purified, but he dresses and looks just like a materialistic person in the midst of the accouterments of the life of pleasure. No one is able to recognize him as a Vaiṣṇava, yet he remains constantly merged in the deep ocean of devotion for Kṛṣṇa. He never bathes in the Ganges because he is afraid to touch the holy waters with his feet, which would show disrespect. He only goes to take *darśana* of the Ganges at night and from a distance. He cannot bear to see people engaged in offensive behavior to the Ganges by gargling, cleaning their teeth, washing their hair in her waters, so he never goes there during the daytime. He never engages in worship of the deity without having taken a drink of Ganges water. He has homes in both Chittagong and Nabadwip and will soon be arriving here. Because of his apparently materialistic behavior, you will not be able to recognize him, but I feel unwell because I am not able to see him."

"The Supreme Lord appeared in Nabadwip. He heaved long sighs because He was unable see Puṇḍarīka Vidyānidhi. One day, after dancing, Lord Gaurāṅga sat down calling out loudly, 'Puṇḍarīka, My father! Puṇḍarīka, My friend, My father! When will I see you?' and wept." (*Caitanya Bhāgavata* 2.7.11-3)

It is supposed that Puṇḍarīka Vidyānidhi took initiation from Mādhavendra Purīpāda at the same time that Advaita Ācārya did. Mahāprabhu always showed him the respect that was due the godbrother of His own guru. In the *Caitanya Caritāmṛta*, Kṛṣṇadāsa Kavirāja Gosvāmī writes:

"I know Śrī Puṇḍarīka Vidyānidhi to be a major branch of the Caitanya tree, for the Lord Himself cried while spontaneously calling out his name." (*Caitanya Caritāmṛta* 1.10.14)

GADĀDHARA BECOMES PUṆḌARĪKA'S DISCIPLE

Śrīla Gadādhara Paṇḍita Gosvāmī, Mukunda Datta and Vāsudeva Datta were also originally from Chittagong, and so they were acquainted with Puṇḍarīka Vidyānidhi. Indeed, Gadādhara Paṇḍita's father, Mādhava Miśra, was his good friend. Mukunda Datta knew his transcendental personality and that he was a Vaiṣṇava, but Gadādhara did not, even though he was from the same town. This was, of course, a pretense for the sake of the *līlā*.

When Puṇḍarīka Vidyānidhi was living in Nabadwip, Mukunda Datta told Gadādhara Paṇḍita one day that he wanted to introduce him to a great Vaiṣṇava. Śrīla Gadādhara Paṇḍita Gosvāmī was a *brahmacārī* from childhood and extremely detached from the senses and ascetic in his lifestyle. When he saw Puṇḍarīka Vidyānidhi sitting on comfortable cushions covered in sheets as white as the foam of milk, wearing very expensive clothes and perfumes, smoking from a hookah, and generally surrounded by all the trappings of a sensual lifestyle, he was unable to recognize him as a Vaiṣṇava. Indeed, he felt let down.

Mukunda Datta could see from Gadādhara Paṇḍita's face what was going through his head, and in order to bring out Puṇḍarīka Vidyānidhi's inner mood, recited two verses from *Śrīmad Bhāgavatam* that ignited flames of love for Kṛṣṇa.

aho bakīyaṁ stana-kāla-kūṭaṁ
jighāṁsayāpāyayad apy asādhvī
lebhe gatiṁ dhātry-ucitaṁ tato'nyaṁ
kaṁ vā dayāluṁ śaraṇaṁ vrajema

"How truly amazing! The sister of Bakāsura, the evil Putanā, was sent on a mission to kill Kṛṣṇa. He drank the *kālakūṭa* poison mixed with her breast milk, and despite her evil intentions, awarded her the position of a wet nurse [as Ambikā and Kilimbā in Goloka]. Is there anyone else I can take shelter of who is more merciful than Him?" (*Śrīmad Bhāgavatam* 3.2.23)

pūtanā lokabālaghnī rākṣasī rudhirāśanā
jighāṁsayāpi haraye stanaṁ dattvāpa sad-gatim

"That she-demon Putanā was a blood-drinking killer of infants. Even though she wanted to kill Kṛṣṇa, she attained the auspicious goal of a nurse in Goloka because she had given Him her breast to drink." (*Śrīmad Bhāgavatam* 10.6.35)

As soon as he heard these two verses in glorification of Kṛṣṇa's mercy, Śrī Puṇḍarīka Vidyānidhi cried out "*Ha* Kṛṣṇa!" and fell to the floor in a swoon. He began to roll on the floor in ecstasy, knocking over the hookah and tearing his clothes.

When he saw these transcendental symptoms of love on Puṇḍarīka Vidyānidhi's body, Gadādhara Paṇḍita realized that he had committed an offense, which he began to regret. He decided that the only way to rid himself of this offense would be to take initiation from Puṇḍarīka, and he related this idea to Mukunda. Mukunda Datta then communicated his desire to Puṇḍarīka Vidyānidhi Prabhu, who happily set a date for the auspicious act. Mahāprabhu also gave His approval, and so Gadādhara Paṇḍita took *mantra* initiation from Puṇḍarīka Vidyānidhi.

In Kṛṣṇa *līlā*, Śrī Puṇḍarīka Vidyānidhi is King Vṛṣabhānu and, Śrīla Gadādhara Paṇḍita Gosvāmī is Rādhā. Because of Puṇḍarīka Vidyānidhi's identity as Vṛṣabhānu,

Mahāprabhu would call out to him as "Father!" when He was Himself in the mood of Śrīmatī Rādhārāṇī. The deep affection from their previous life's relation became apparent between Puṇḍarīka Vidyānidhi and Gadādhara Paṇḍita. No one can understand the pastimes of the Vaiṣṇavas without their mercy.

vaiṣṇava cinite nāre devera śakati
mui kon chāra śiśu alpamati

"Even the gods are unable to recognize a Vaiṣṇava, so how can a foolish, fallen child like myself do so?"

Even though Puṇḍarīka Vidyānidhi was a great Vaiṣṇava, he kept it a secret and went about just like a materialistic person. Śrīla Bhakti Siddhānta Sarasvatī Gosvāmī Ṭhākura warns in his *Gauḍīya-bhāṣya* to the *Caitanya Bhāgavata* that one cannot recognize. One cannot recognize a Vaiṣṇava through any superficial examination. "Kṛṣṇa *līlā* is not accessible to limited sensory understanding. Kṛṣṇa's servants occasionally go unrecognized by an external display of materialistic surroundings. In this way they deceive the conditioned souls. Ignorant critics take Kṛṣṇa's activities to be those of a material hero because of their materialistic vision, and thus they have no faith in Him. Others consider Kṛṣṇa to be an ordinary man who is born, undergoes transformation and dies; thus they have no idea of who He really is. Kṛṣṇa's devotees are also sometimes reluctant to reveal their real selves to the unworthy and thus make a pretense of being ordinary materialistic persons. Gaurāṅga Mahāprabhu is also sometimes called the *pracchanna-avātara*, or hidden *avatāra*. In the same spirit, Puṇḍarīka Vidyānidhi put on the show of being sensualist for those who were capable of being deceived by someone's external appearance."

Once Puṇḍarīka Vidyānidhi came to see Mahāprabhu when it was already quite late at night. As soon as he saw the Lord, he was so overcome by love that he could not even pay his obeisances. Mahāprabhu was similarly anxious to see His most dear devotee Puṇḍarīka Vidyānidhi, and He immediately took him to His chest and washed him with tears of love. When the other devotees heard Mahāprabhu cry and call Puṇḍarīka "father" and "treasure of love", they knew just how dear he was to Him. Puṇḍarīka Vidyānidhi was also known to Mahāprabhu's associates as Ācāryanidhi.

The Supreme Lord cried and called out "Puṇḍarīka! Father! Today I have seen My own father! Today I rose from My sleep at an auspicious moment, and I saw Premanidhi standing before Me." (*Caitanya Bhāgavata* 2.7.131, 143)

Śrī Puṇḍarīka Vidyānidhi participated in the nightly *saṅkīrtana* festival in Śrīvāsa Paṇḍita's house along with Mahāprabhu and His other associates. On Mahāprabhu's order, Nityānanda Prabhu and Haridāsa Ṭhākura went door to door to spread the chanting of the Holy Names and thus to liberate the conditioned souls, succeeding in converting Jagāi and Mādhāi. Later, when Jagāi and Mādhāi were sitting amongst the devotees before Mahāprabhu, they also displayed the ecstatic symptoms of *prema*. Śrī Puṇḍarīka Vidyānidhi was also present there, and he became completely submerged in loving ecstasy to see their great fortune. It is stated in the *Bhakti Ratnākara* that Mahāprabhu celebrated the appearance day of Rādhārāṇī at Śrī Puṇḍarīka Vidyānidhi's house. (*Bhakti Ratnākara* 12.3177)

PUṆḌARĪKA IN PURI

On Mahāprabhu's order, the devotees led by Advaita Ācārya went each year to see the

Rathayātrā. Puṇḍarīka Vidyānidhi was one of those principal associates of Mahāprabhu among the party of pilgrims that visited Puri *dhāma* annually.

"All of Mahāprabhu's servants, such as Advaita Ācārya, Nityānanda Prabhu, Mukunda, Śrīvāsa, Vidyānidhi, Vāsudeva and Murāri, came together each year to meet with Him, and they would stay four months. The Lord enjoyed many pastimes in their company." (*Caitanya Caritāmṛta* 2.1.255-6)

Śrī Puṇḍarīka Vidyānidhi was also present at Lord Jagannātha's Candana Yātrā festival when Mahāprabhu and all His devotees played in the water of Narendra Sarovara, also known as Chandana Pukura. Puṇḍarīka Paṇḍita and Svarūpa Dāmodara Gosvāmī were close friends, and they laughed and joyfully splashed water on each other as a part of these pastimes. (*Caitanya Bhāgavata* 3.8.124)

Puṇḍarīka Vidyānidhi also participated with Mahāprabhu and His associates in the cleaning of the Guṇḍicā temple, relishing *mahā-prasāda* with them afterwards.

GADĀDHARA WISHES TO RECEIVE THE MANTRA AGAIN

One day, Śrīla Gadādhara Paṇḍita Gosvāmī asked Mahāprabhu if he could hear his initiation *mantra* from Him. He said:

" 'Ever since I repeated my *iṣṭa-mantra* to someone, I have been unable to concentrate when I chant. Please repeat the *mantra* to me; then my mind will be calmed.'

"Mahāprabhu answered, "You already have a *guru*. Be careful, otherwise you will become an offender to him. Everything I have is yours, even My life, what to speak of the *mantra*. But as long as your guru is alive it is improper for Me to repeat it to you.' " (*Caitanya Bhāgavata* 3.10.23-6)

Gadādhara answered, saying, "He isn't here. Please do it in his place."

Mahāprabhu replied: "Destiny will bring your guru, Vidyānidhi ,to you." The omniscient Mahāprabhu continued, "Śrī Puṇḍarīka Vidyānidhi will be coming to Puri to see Me, and will be here in ten days." And that is what came to pass. Mahāprabhu became ecstatic, crying, "Father has come! Father has come!" Gadādhara went to Vidyānidhi upon his arrival.

"Gadādhara asked Premanidhi to again initiate him in the *iṣṭa-mantra,* which he lovingly did. How can I sufficiently glorify Śrī Puṇḍarīka Vidyānidhi, who has a loving disciple like Gadādhara Paṇḍita!" (*Caitanya Bhāgavata* 3.10.79-80)

Our most worshipable Śrīla Prabhupāda commented on the above verse (3.10.24) in the following way: "The *mantra* is *śabda brahma,* the divine sound that destroys the mental aptitude for sense gratification. If one instructs a faithless person in the divine sound, the instructor's mind becomes contaminated. If one's divine knowledge (*divya-jñāna*) is lost due to bad association, then one must seek the same again. Gadādhara Paṇḍita understood this, and so he asked Gaurasundara Mahāprabhu to reinitiate him. Mahāprabhu's instruction, however, was that he should go to his own guru to hear the *mantra* again."

The lesson to be learned here is this: Śrīla Gadādhara Paṇḍita Gosvāmī is Mahāprabhu's eternal associate; it is thus impossible that any contamination could have entered his mind. Through Gadādhara Paṇḍita, Mahāprabhu was instructing those who would be a guru that if one instructs an unqualified person in the *mantra*, it loses its potency and no longer brings the same joy to the heart of the practitioner. When this happens, it is necessary to go to the guru and hear the *mantra* from him again. It is against custom to hear the *mantra* again from someone who is not one's guru because one cannot change initiating spiritual masters in this way. Gadādhara Paṇḍita was only saying "I cannot concentrate like before" (*nā sphure bhālo mati*), i.e., "The ecstatic feelings no longer come when I chant," out of an exemplary humility designed to teach humanity how to act.

LORD JAGANNĀTHA SLAPS PUṆḌARĪKA

On the Oḍana Ṣaṣṭhī festival, Lord Jagannātha's servants dress Him in a cloth which still has starch in it.[9] Śrī Puṇḍarīka Vidyānidhi was a pure *sad-ācārī*, i.e., attached to the proper etiquette of Vaiṣṇavism. When he observed this custom, he did not feel happy about it and said to his friend Svarūpa Dāmodara Paṇḍita, "Why do they give this unwashed cloth to the Lord? The people of this country know the rules in the *smṛtis* and the *śrutis*, so why do they give this *māṛuwā* cloth to the Lord?"

Svarūpa Dāmodara Prabhu answered that the Supreme Lord is beyond the customary rules and regulations of the scriptures and that therefore there was no fault. Vidyānidhi did not find this conclusion satisfying, and he countered by saying, "That may be true for the Lord Himself. But His servants should follow the rules of the scripture. The *śrī-vigraha* of the Lord is beyond the material qualities, so you can say this of Him, but His servants are not of the same nature as He. So they have to judge whether or not it is proper to offer a particular object in the service."

Vidyānidhi is Mahāprabhu's dear associate and beyond any fault, but once again we see that the Lord teaches particular lessons through His devotees. Here He wished to show that we have no right to make judgments or to find fault with the behavior of Lord Jagannāth's devotees. That night Mahāprabhu entered in the dream of Puṇḍarīka Vidyānidhi as Lord Jagannātha. Vidyānidhi was frightened when he saw the anger of the Lord. He saw both Lord Jagannātha and Lord Balarāma slap him on each of his cheeks, and he started to cry out in distress, "Kṛṣṇa, save me! Kṛṣṇa, save me! Forgive me my offense!" Lord Jagannātha said:

"There is no end to your offensiveness. Just as there is no question of pure and impure in My case, the same holds true for My servants. You are staying here; you should know all this. If you thought that it was impure, then why did you stay at all? Go home and maintain your purity." (*Caitanya Bhāgavata* 3.10.131-3)

When Puṇḍarīka Vidyānidhi woke up in the morning, the devotees saw the marks of the Lords' slaps on his cheeks, which had swollen as a result, and they started to laugh. This pastime shows just how dear Śrī Puṇḍarīka Vidyānidhi was to Lord Jagannātha and to Mahāprabhu, for the Lord only comes to His dearest devotees to personally punish them in this way.

"That night Lord Jagannātha and Balarāma came to him and, laughing all the while, slapped him on the cheeks. Puṇḍarīka Vidyānidhi felt a secret joy at his swollen cheeks, as has been described by Vṛndāvana Dāsa in detail." (*Caitanya Caritāmṛta* 2.16.80-1)

9 According to Bhaktivinoda Ṭhākura, Oḍana Ṣaṣṭhī takes place at the beginning of winter. This is the first day that Lord Jagannātha is dressed in winter clothes. The winter cloth still has *māṛa* (weaver's starch) in it and has not been washed. Puṇḍarīka Vidyānidhi did not approve of this unwashed cloth being given to the deity and so felt a dislike for the people of Utkala as a result. He had to suffer the consequences.

Vṛndāvana Dāsa Ṭhākura concludes the *Caitanya Bhāgavata* with the following glorification of Śrī Puṇḍarīka Vidyānidhi:

"The Supreme Lord Gaurāṅga called out the name of this devotee, crying, 'Puṇḍarīka, My father.' Anyone who hears about his life and activities will undoubtedly attain Kṛṣṇa's lotus feet." (*Caitanya Bhāgavata* 3.10.183-4)

Śrī Śuklāmbara Brahmacārī

śuklāmbaro brahmacārī purāsīd yajñapatnikā
prārthayitvā yad-annaṁ śrī-
gaurāṅgo bhuktavān prabhuḥ
kecid āhur brahmacārī yājñika-brāhmaṇaḥ purā

"Śuklāmbara Brahmacārī was previously one of the wives of the sacrificial *brāhmaṇas* in Vraja. Mahāprabhu requested food from him and ate it. Some people say that he was one of the sacrificial *brāhmaṇas*." (*Gaura-gaṇoddeśa-dīpikā* 191)

ŚUKLĀMBARA BRAHMACĀRĪ, A POOR MENDICANT

Śuklāmbara Brahmacārī is counted among the branches of Caitanya Mahāprabhu. He was a resident of Nabadwip town, manifesting the pastimes of a poor *brāhmaṇa* who begged for a living. Nevertheless, he had an abiding affection for the Lord. Though to an ordinary conditioned soul he appeared to be a poverty-stricken mendicant, to transcendental eyes he was rich because of his love for Mahāprabhu.

prema-dhana vinā vyartha daridra jīvana
dāsa kari vetana more deha prema-dhana

"Without the wealth of love of God, my life is poverty-stricken and worthless. Employ me as Your servant, and pay me with the salary of ecstastic love of God." (*Caitanya Caritāmṛta* 3.20.37)

When Mahāprabhu returned from Gaya, He first met with the devotees in Śuklāmbara Brahmacārī's house.

"Śrīmān Paṇḍita then left along the banks of the Ganges to the house of Śuklāmbara Brahmacārī. Having heard the news, Gadādhara Paṇḍita quickly followed him there. He hid in Śuklāmbara's house, thinking that he would eavesdrop as to what Mahāprabhu would talk about Kṛṣṇa. All the loving devotees of the Lord, such as Sadāśiva, Murāri, Śrīmān and Śuklāmbara, had gathered there when Viśvambhara, the jewel of the *brāhmaṇas*, came and met them." (*Caitanya Bhāgavata* 2.1.78-82)

Śrīla Gadādhara Paṇḍita Gosvāmī, Sadāśiva, Murāri, Śrīvāsa Paṇḍita, Śrīmān Paṇḍita and others were amazed to witness the Lord's ecstatic transformations in Śuklāmbara's house.

THE LORD SNATCHES RICE FROM ŚUKLĀMBARA'S BEGGING BAG

"Śuklāmbara Brahmacārī was very fortunate, for the Lord snatched food from him and ate it Himself." (*Caitanya Caritāmṛta* 1.10.38)

Śuklāmbara Brahmacārī kept body and soul together by offering and eating the foodstuffs which he daily accumulated by begging. Since he was constantly absorbed in the joys of chanting the names and qualities of the Lord, he never suffered from his poverty. Ignorant people thought he was just an ordinary beggar. No one can recognize Mahāprabhu's servants unless they receive the Lord's mercy.

One day, Mahāprabhu was sitting alone in a devotional trance when Śuklāmbara Brahmacārī happened by, his begging bag flung over his shoulder. When he saw the Lord, he started to dance ecstatically. The Lord was pleased to see the depth of Śuklāmbara's feeling, and He began to glorify him. He then plucked a handful of the dry rice from his bag and began to chew it. Śuklāmbara Brahmacārī was troubled to see the Lord eating the uncleaned and broken fragments of low-quality rice and felt that he had committed an offense. The Lord calmed him and said that He always ate His devotee's food with great enthusiasm, but that He had no interest whatsoever in the finest foods of the nondevotee. The devotees were delighted to see the Lord's mercy on Śuklāmbara Brahmacārī, who was then given a blessing by the Lord.

"The Lord said, 'Listen, Śuklāmbara Brahmacārī. I reside permanently in your heart. Whenever you eat, I eat. When you go on your begging rounds, I accompany you. I have descended to distribute love of Godhead, and you are My affectionate servant, lifetime after lifetime. I hereby bestow upon you *prema bhakti*, which is My very soul.' When the devotees heard the Lord's blessing, they made a joyful noise, shouting 'Jaya, jaya!' " (*Caitanya Bhāgavata* 2.16.133-8)

Śrīla Bhakti Siddhānta Sarasvatī Gosvāmī Ṭhākura paraphrases Mahāprabhu's blessing in his *Gauḍīya-bhāṣya:* "You are My poor servant lifetime after lifetime. You have no desire to enter into family life to become an enjoyer. Rather, you remain a bachelor and beg from house to house, making an offering to Me of whatever you amass in this way. Your vow of celibacy is unbreakable. You are free of the mundane egoism that is prominent in householders and retired householders. You are thus factually fixed in the highest state of spiritual life, the highest stage of the renounced order. You are a de facto *sannyāsī*, a completely surrendered carrier of the triple staff, because you have successfully engaged every action of your body, mind and speech in My service. I pray constantly for your offerings, for you offer everything to Me and have no interest in enjoying anything. It is for this reason that I have forcefully taken everything away from you, making you poor." (*Caitanya Bhāgavata* 2. 16.122-3)

"The Lord was sitting here on this altar of Viṣṇu, absorbed in the sound of the Holy Name, when Śuklāmbara Brahmacārī passed by on his begging rounds. Mahāprabhu lovingly put His hand in Śuklāmbara's begging bag and took a handful of unwashed rice, calling him Sudāmā. With extreme humility, Śuklāmbara Brahmacārī danced charmingly in the *kīrtana* with the bag still on his shoulder. The Lord and His devotees felt the intensity of their bliss increase as they watched Śuklāmbara's ecstatic transformations. This is one of the pastimes of the Lord in the house of Śrīvāsa Paṇḍita, after which He went through the town back to His own house." (*Bhakti-ratnākara* 12.2754-8)

THE LORD EATS AT ŚUKLĀMBARA'S HOUSE

In the twenty-sixth chapter of the *Caitanya Bhāgavata*'s *Madhya-khaṇḍa*, it is also said that Mahāprabhu ate cooked food in the house of Śuklāmbara Brahmacārī, being attracted by his love. When the Lord announced to Śuklāmbara that He wished to eat at his house, the *brahmacārī* felt nervous because he was afraid that he was unable to provide suitable fare for the Lord with his begged rice. However, the Lord repeatedly told him that this was indeed His desire, and so Śuklāmbara went to the other devotees to ask their advice.

The devotees praised his fortune and suggested that he cook without touching the food.

After taking bath, Śuklāmbara lit the stove and put water to boil. Then, without touching the rice, he poured it into the water along with the core of the plantain tree (*thoṛ*), while remaining completely absorbed in chanting the Lord's names. At that moment, Lakṣmī Devī blessed the food cooked by the devotee by glancing at it. When Mahāprabhu came to Śuklāmbara's house with His associates, He offered the rice and vegetables to Lord Viṣṇu by His own hand. When it came time to eat it, He praised its wonderful taste. Once again the devotees cried at the sight of the Lord's merciful attitude to Śuklāmbara.

"When the devotees saw the wealth of blessings of the Lord to Śuklāmbara Brahmacārī, they all began to cry. The Lord continued to eat joyfully, greatly relishing its taste. May all the rich millionaire nondevotees observe the mercy received by the beggar Śuklāmbara. No one can attain the Lord's mercy through wealth, high birth or scholarship. The scriptures repeatedly tell us that the Lord is only attracted by the taste of devotion." (*Caitanya Bhāgavata* 2.26.28-31)

Śrīla Bhakti Siddhānta Sarasvatī Gosvāmī Ṭhākura comments on this in *Gauḍīya-bhāṣya*: "Viṣṇu is the lord of the sacrifice who only eats that which is offered in the sacrifice of Brahman. Śuklāmbara Brahmacārī gathered rice by begging from a variety of households. Householder *brāhmaṇas* thus normally consider them contaminated and refuse to accept it. However, Vaiṣṇavas hold that rice received from begging is superior to any other rice because it has been obtained by the mercy of the Lord. Though superficially this rice appears to be contaminated by the touch of nondevotees and offering it is thus a deviation from the usual rules and regulations, in Mahāprabhu's path the purity of a devotee's heart is the most important ingredient in *mahā-prasāda*. One should not think that a millionaire is the only person who can offer foods suitable for the Lord. Śuklāmbara was poverty-stricken, but the Lord was satisfied with the food that he had gathered through begging. Those who are sinful and without an aptitude of service cannot understand this at all."

"One day, the Lord asked Śuklāmbara to cook lunch for him and took this path to his house along with devotees. What can I say? The Lord ate Śuklāmbara's cooking, and a wonderful pastime took place there." (*Bhakti-ratnākara* 12.3467-8)

Śuklāmbara is also named in the *Caitanya Bhāgavata* as being amongst the Bengali devotees who went to Puri on the annual pilgrimage. "Śuklāmbara Brahmacārī, whose rice had been eaten by Lord Gaurasundara, joyfully went along." (*Caitanya Bhāgavata* 3.8.23)

Śrī Sadāśiva Paṇḍita

Sadāśiva Paṇḍita is considered a Caitanya branch of the tree of divine love. He was a resident of Nabadwip who participated in the beginnings of the *saṅkīrtana* movement. When Nityānanda Prabhu first arrived in Nabadwip, He stayed in his house.

"Sadāśiva Paṇḍita placed all his hopes at the Lord's feet. His house was Nityānanda Prabhu's first residence in Nabadwip." (*Caitanya Caritāmṛta* 1.10.34)

"Sadāśiva Paṇḍita, in whose home Nityānanda Prabhu had previously been domiciled, also went [with the party of devotees to Jagannatha Puri]." (*Caitanya Bhāgavata* 3.8.19)

In Vṛndāvana Dāsa Ṭhākura's *Caitanya Bhāgavata*, Sadāśiva Paṇḍita's name is included in the list of devotees who were present in the *kīrtana* in the house of Śrīvāsa Paṇḍita, along with Gopīnātha, Jagadīśa, Śrīmān, Śrīdhara, Vakreśvara, Śrīgarbha and Śuklāmbara. (*Caitanya Bhāgavata* 2.8.115)

He was also one of the Lord's companions when He engaged in water sports in the Ganges. He was also one of the first to witness the Lord's displays of ecstatic love after He returned from Gaya. Mahāprabhu also ordered Sadāśiva Paṇḍita and other devotees to assemble in the house of His dear associate Śuklāmbara Brahmacārī.

"[The Lord said,] 'You [Śrīmān Paṇḍita] and Sadāśiva Paṇḍita should also come tomorrow to Śuklāmbara's house.' " (*Caitanya Bhāgavata* 2.1.40)

"Sadāśiva, Murāri, Śrīmān, Śuklāmbara, and all the Lord's other devoted followers assembled there." (*Caitanya Bhāgavata* 2.1.81)

On the same occasion, the Lord revealed to the world how dear He considered Sadāśiva by unveiling His heart's sadness to him.

"I will reveal all my sadness to you [Śrīmān Paṇḍita], Sadāśiva and Murāri Gupta." (*Caitanya Bhāgavata* 2.1.70)

When Mahāprabhu decided to put on a performance of Vraja *līlā* in the house of Candraśekhara Ācārya, He gave the responsibility for costumes and makeup to Sadāśiva and Buddhimanta Khān. Sadāśiva was ecstatic to receive this order from the Lord.

"The Lord called Buddhimanta Khān and Sadāśiva and told them to go immediately to arrange for the actors' costumes." (*Caitanya Bhāgavata* 2.18.7)

"Overjoyed, Buddhimanta and Sadāśiva immediately went home to fulfill the duties given to them by the Lord." (*Caitanya Bhāgavata* 2.18.14)

"Here [at the house of Candraśekhara Ācārya], Buddhimanta Khān and Sadāśiva Paṇḍita made all kinds of costume arrangements to help Lord Gaurāṅga put on a performance as Lakṣmī so that the entire universe would become intoxicated by the singing of the Holy Names." (*Bhakti-ratnākara* 12.2903-4)

Śrīdhara Paṇḍita

One of the twelve Gopālas in Kṛṣṇa *līlā* is named Kusumāsava. He appeared in Gaura *līlā* as Śrīdhara Paṇḍita.

kholā-becatāyā khyātaḥ paṇḍitaḥ śrīdharo dvijaḥ
āsīd vraje hāsya-karo yo nāmnā kusumāsavaḥ

"The cowherd boy named Kusumāsava, who joked with Lord Kṛṣṇa and made Him laugh in Vrajabhūmi, appeared in Lord Gaurāṅga's pastimes as the learned *brāhmaṇa* named *kholā-becā* (bark seller) Śrīdhara." (*Gaura-gaṇoddeśa-dīpikā* 133)

Śrīdhara Paṇḍita was a resident of Nabadwip. Nabadwip is composed of nine islands, of which the central island is known as Antardwip. He used to live at the northern extremity of Mayapur and to the southeast of the Cāṇḍa Kājī's *samādhi*, in the place that now goes by the name of Śrīdhara Aṅgana. During his lifetime, it was a banana orchard, which nowadays is no longer the case, at least not to our mortal eyes. During these pastimes, Śrīdhara Paṇḍita played the role of a poor *brāhmaṇa* who made his living selling the produce of his banana garden. In order to keep the memory of Śrīdhara Paṇḍita alive, the founder of the world-wide Chaitanya Maths and Gaudiya Maths, Nitya-līlā-praviṣṭa Oṁ Viṣṇupāda Śrīla Bhakti Siddhānta Sarasvatī Gosvāmī Prabhupāda, discovered and revealed Śrīdhara Aṅgana. Deity worship was established there and it continued until after Śrīla Bhakti Siddhānta Sarasvatī Gosvāmī Ṭhākura's disappearance. Now, because of problems with local people, the beauty of this place is once again being covered over. Even so, during the Nabadwip *parikramā*, devotees still pay their obeisances to the memory of Śrīdhara Paṇḍita at that spot.

Śrīla Bhaktivinoda Ṭhākura says in his *Nabadvīpa-dhāma-māhātmya* that "Śrīdhara's house was on the other side of the weaver district. Mahāprabhu often stopped the *kīrtana* here so that the devotees could rest. Nityānanda Prabhu says the following to Jīva Gosvāmī:

" 'Out of His mercy, Mahāprabhu Gaurāṅga Hari would end the *kīrtana* here so that the devotees could rest. It is therefore known as *viśrāma-sthāna* or the Lord's place of rest. So let us also repose a while here at the house of Śrīdhara Paṇḍita.' " (*Nabadvīpa-dhāma-māhātmya*)

According to Śrīla Bhaktivinoda in the same book, there was previously a large pond near Śrīdhara's banana orchard, but this too is no longer visible.

ŚRĪDHARA'S POVERTY

Material wealth and prosperity are not the truest signs of the Lord's mercy on someone. Those who worship the gods and goddesses are generally seen to prosper materially, but one who is rich in the wealth of devotion to the Lord is the one who has truly benefited from His mercy. Mahāprabhu gave this teaching to the world through His associate Śrīdhara Paṇḍita: a devotee of Viṣṇu is free from attachments to material possessions and enjoyments.

One day, the Lord went to Śrīdhara's place and asked him why he was so poor. He was worshipping the husband of the goddess of fortune, Lakṣmī, and yet he never had enough money for food or clothing, and his house was dilapidated. On the other hand, those who worshipped Kālī always seemed to have an abundance of material wealth. Śrīdhara answered that a bird who made its nest in the trees and wandered from place to place to find food was passing the time of day in the same way as a king in his palace who enjoyed the best objects of gratification. There was no difference of degree or amount of pleasure experienced by the two. The Lord then said to Śrīdhara, "Externally, though you appear to be poor, you are actually the truly rich man. I will shortly reveal to the entire foolish world that devotees are qualified to possess the greatest wealth; indeed they are the owners of all things."

Generally, we call someone deprived of wealth and possessions "poor" or "unfortunate". One who has these things is called rich or fortunate. In reality, however, it is not so. People try to accumulate wealth in order to find happiness, not distress. But happiness is the real wealth, not the external possessions, through which they hope to find it. Śrī Kṛṣṇa is the personification of happiness. The real difference between wealth and poverty is that one who has love for Kṛṣṇa is rich; one who does not is poor. By way of example, during Kṛṣṇa's *līlā*, Vidura played the part of a poor man, but one who was rich in love for Kṛṣṇa. On the other hand, Duryodhana possessed unlimited riches but had no love for Kṛṣṇa, and thus was truly poor. The Supreme Lord used *kholā becā* Śrīdhara to show the world who was truly wealthy and fortunate. The Lord is conquered by loving devotion alone, and by nothing else.

bhaktyāham ekayā grāhyaḥ
śraddayātmā priyaḥ satām
bhaktiḥ punāti man-niṣṭhā
śvapākān api sambhavāt

"I, who as the supreme soul am the ultimate object of affection and love, can be attained only through exclusive devotion born of faith. Such devotion performed with single-minded attention purifies even a dog-eater and outcaste." (*Śrīmad Bhāgavatam* 11.14.21)

patraṁ puṣpaṁ phalaṁ toyaṁ yo
me bhaktyā prayacchati
tad ahaṁ bhakty-upahṛtam
aśnāmi prayatātmanaḥ

"I accept whatever anyone offers Me with devotion, whether it be a leaf, a flower, a fruit or water, because of his pure consciousness." (*Bhagavad-gītā* 6.26)

The Lord accepts and eats whatever is given to Him with devotion but does not accept things given to Him by a nondevotee. He would not accept the invitation to eat the finest, most expensive foods with Duryodhana in order to take a humble meal prepared for Him by Vidura and his wife.

THE LORD STEALS ŚRĪDHARA'S GOODS

The Lord will grab food from His devotee, but He will not even glance at anything offered by a nondevotee. The Supreme Lord Caitanya Mahāprabhu showed the charming pastime of hungrily taking Śrīdhara's foodstuffs without being invited to do so. While the Lord was still a student, Śrīdhara used to make his living by selling bananas, their flowers (*mocā*) and the core of the banana plant (*thoṛa*). He would spend half of whatever little money he made in this way on worshipping the Ganges, the other half on his own necessities. Like Yudhiṣṭhira, he was a great devotee of the truth and would always tell the real price of the items he sold. Everyone in Nabadwip knew this and so would not haggle with him. But Mahāprabhu would come to Śrīdhara and give him only half the amount he was asking for his bananas, banana flowers or *thoṛa* and then walk off with them. Every day, the two of them would pull back and forth on a bunch of bananas or something else, arguing for an hour or more over the price that was to be paid.

"Every day they would argue for an hour and a half; then finally Mahāprabhu would walk away with the goods, leaving only half the asked price. Śrīdhara would always tell the truth and give the real price of each item, but the Lord would still only give him half of the amount he asked for and then take it. Śrīdhara would jump up and grab the item, trying to take it back, even pushing and shoving the Lord." (*Caitanya Bhāgavata* 2.9.163-5)

Even though the Lord argued with Śrīdhara, He saw that Śrīdhara would not become angry and hence took his wares. From a superficial point of view, it appears that Mahāprabhu was mistreating Śrīdhara by stealing from him, but the fact of the matter is that Śrīdhara allowed Him to get away with it. Upon seeing the

Lord's beauty, he would become completely enchanted and immersed in an ocean of joy, so how could he get angry with Him? While arguing with him, Mahāprabhu would delight in calling him names and insulting him, and sometimes even hinted at His own divine identity:

"Every day you buy things to offer to the Gaṅgā. Why don't you just give something to Me without charging anything? Don't you know that I am the father of the Gaṅgā that you worship? I assure you that this is the absolute truth!" (*Caitanya Bhāgavata* 2.9.178-9)

They finally came to a settlement, and Śrīdhara agreed to daily give Mahāprabhu some bananas or other items from the banana tree for free. From then on, the Lord daily ate with great satisfaction from the little bowls made of banana bark given him by Śrīdhara.

"The Lord said, 'Very well. There is no reason for you to give Me anything else.'And from that day on, He ate with great contentment on banana leaves Śrīdhara had given Him. The Lord thus eats anything that the devotee offers Him, but He rejects even luxurious items given Him by a nondevotee." (*Caitanya Bhāgavata* 2.9.184-5)

ŚRĪDHARA BLESSED AT THE MAHĀ-PRAKĀŚA

On that eventful night, the Lord sat on the altar in Śrīvāsa's home and revealed His divine form to His devotees for twenty-one hours. After showing them all the different *avatāras* of Viṣṇu, one after the other, He ordered them to summon Śrīdhara also. Śrīdhara would regularly stay up the whole night chanting the Holy Names and calling out to the Lord. This was a source of happiness to the devotees, but the nondevotees would complain that he was keeping them awake with his noise and would regularly criticize and rebuke him. As the devotees were going to his house on the Lord's order, they could hear his loud chanting from a considerable distance.

When Śrīdhara arrived at Śrīvāsa Aṅgana, he beheld the Lord's glorious form and fell to the ground in a faint. He was brought back to consciousness by the Lord's voice and then, with the power that was given to him through the Lord's mercy, began to recite hymns of glorification. Satisfied with Śrīdhara's hymns of praise, Mahāprabhu offered him the eight mystic powers[10] as a benediction, but Śrīdhara refused, saying that he only wanted service to the Lord's lotus feet.

"Lord Viśvambhara repeatedly urged Śrīdhara to ask for a boon. Finally, Śrīdhara said, 'Lord, if You must give me something, then I ask for this: May that *brāhmaṇa* boy who used to pinch my banana leaves and bark be my Lord, lifetime after lifetime. May I ever serve the lotus feet of that *brāhmaṇa* boy who always used to argue with me.' " (*Caitanya Bhāgavata* 2.9.223-5)

Who can recognize all these servants of the Lord who want nothing of wealth, followers, or scholarship? Of what use are learning, wealth, beauty, fame or high birth? All of these things

---

10 The eight mystic powers, or *siddhis* are listed in the *Nārada-pañcarātra*: *aṇimā laghimā vyāptiḥ prākāmyā mahimā tathā / īśitvaṁ ca vaśītvaṁ ca tathā kāmāvasāyitā //* Three of these mystic powers are physical: becoming very small (*aṇimā*), light (*laghimā*) or large (*mahimā*); *vyāpti* means to possess the powers of the tutelary deities of the senses; *prākāmya* is the power to do anything within the scope of the material nature; *īśitva* is the perfection through which one can control the *māyā* energy; *vaśitā* is the perfection of detachment from sense enjoyment; *kāmāvasāyitā* is the power to be able to enjoy anything that one can imagine through his desires.

simply increase one's pride and are ultimately valueless. A millionaire may try for millions of years to achieve what Śrīdhara did while selling bananas and banana products, and still not be able to do so." (*Caitanya Bhāgavata* 2.9.233-5)

Śrīla Bhakti Siddhānta Sarasvatī Gosvāmī Ṭhākura comments on these verses as follows: "Through empirical knowledge or external analysis, no one can recognize the true character of a devotee. It should not be thought that the ability to collect great amounts of money is a function of devotion, nor that someone who is able to accumulate a great number of followers is a better Vaiṣṇava than someone who cannot. Furthermore, even if someone is a great religious scholar, this does not mean that he is a devotee of the Lord. A servant of Śrī Caitanya might have very little money, may show no signs of having a great number of followers, and have no talent for argument or debate. Ordinary people are unable to understand why he is indifferent to these externals. The answer is that these devotees consider service to Śrī Caitanya to be something more valuable than the accumulation of wealth, followers or learning. Thus, there is no possibility of the depth of their wisdom, their glories and their superiority being perceived by the general public."

"Who is capable of recognizing a devotee? He may possess all perfections, but we see only his poverty. The seller of banana products, Śrīdhara Paṇḍita, is a living example of this. He disregarded the eight mystic perfections in order to accept only devotion as a benediction. However much misery you see in a devotee's life, you should know that in fact, he is blissful in devotional service. Those who are absorbed in sense gratification and intoxicated by learning or wealth can never recognize a Vaiṣṇava." (*Caitanya Bhāgavata* 2.9.238-41)

MAHĀPRABHU DRINKS FROM ŚRĪDHARA'S WATERPOT

On the day Mahāprabhu delivered Cāṇḍa-Kājī and led His *saṅkīrtana* party through the conch shell merchant area and weaver districts to Śrīdhara Paṇḍita's house. There He took a drink of water from Śrīdhara's old, beaten iron water pot with great satisfaction. When Śrīdhara saw Mahāprabhu do this, he cried loudly and fell unconscious.

Mahāprabhu's action was meant to teach us that we can attain devotion by drinking a devotee's water. He wanted to show that the water from a devotee's water jug, even though it is old and rusty, is still like nectar to the Supreme Lord Himself. By way of contrast, He ignores the proud nondevotee's water, even if offered in a jewelled goblet.

"When the Lord saw Śrīdhara's tumbledown shack of a home from a distance, He laughed quietly from the inner joy He felt. He led the company of devotees along the path to Śrīdhara's hut, where He spotted an iron water pot full of holes. There was still a little water in it, and the Lord drank it thirstily. The Lord is *bhakta-vatsala*, ever affectionate toward His devotees, and this act overwhelmed Him with feelings of love. Tears poured from His eyes like the currents of the Ganges, and a wonderful *kīrtana* began in Śrīdhara's courtyard in which all the devotees, led by Nityānanda Prabhu and Advaita Prabhu were crying. Ah, my heart breaks when I think of the great joy they all experienced on that day here at Śrīdhara's house." (*Bhakti-ratnākara* 12.3136-41)

"The Lord drank water from Śrīdhara's iron water pot and then fulfilled the desires of every single devotee." (*Caitanya Caritāmṛta* 1.17.70)

On the very day before He took *sannyāsa*, Mahāprabhu happily accepted a gift of a gourd from Śrīdhara. Śacī Mātā cooked the gourd with milk, making one of the Lord's favorite preparations.

"The pious Śrīdhara came to see the Lord carrying a gourd (*lāu*). When Gaurasundara saw the gift, He laughed and asked, 'Where did you get it?' He knew that He would be leaving the next day and would not be able to eat it after He had gone. He did not want to see the gift go unused and so determined to have it prepared that very day." (*Caitanya Bhāgavata* 2.28.33-6)

After taking *sannyāsa*, Mahāprabhu wandered in the land of Rarha for three days in an intoxicated state of love for Kṛṣṇa until Nityānanda Prabhu tricked Him into coming to Shantipur, to Advaita Ācārya's house. When the Lord met Śacī Mātā and the other Nabadwip devotees, He also met with Śrīdhara. Śrīdhara came every year to Puri to meet with the Lord at the time of the Rathayātrā.

Śrī Vakreśvara Paṇḍita

vyūhas turyo'niruddho yaḥ sa vakreśvara-paṇḍitaḥ
kṛṣṇāveśaja-nṛtyena prabhoḥ sukham ajījanat
sahasra-gāyakān mahyaṁ dehi tvaṁ karuṇā-maya
iti caitanya-pāde sa uvāca madhuraṁ vacaḥ
sva-prakāśa-vibhedena śaśirekhā tam āviśat

"Vakreśvara Paṇḍita is the fourth member of the *catur-vyūha*, Aniruddha. He brought happiness to the Lord by dancing in the absorption of Kṛṣṇa. He would sweetly say to Mahāprabhu, 'O merciful Lord! Give me a thousand singers so that I can dance.' Rādhā's dear *sakhī* Śaśirekhā also entered into him." (*Gaura-gaṇoddeśa-dīpikā* 71)

Śrī Vakreśvara Paṇḍita appeared in Guptipara near Triveni on the fifth day of the waning moon in the month of Āṣāḍha.

Śrī Vakreśvara Paṇḍita revealed such great potency that he danced nonstop for three days. Kṛṣṇadāsa Kavirāja Gosvāmī wrote the following summary of Vakreśvara Paṇḍita:

"Vakreśvara Paṇḍita is the Lord's dear servant. He danced without rest for seventy-two hours. Mahāprabhu personally sang when Vakreśvara Paṇḍita danced, and thus Vakreśvara Paṇḍita fell down at the Lord's feet and said, 'O moon-faced Lord! Give me ten thousand Gāndharvas! It will make me happy if I can dance as they sing. The Lord answered, "I have only one wing like you. If I had another, I could fly in the sky!' " (*Caitanya Caritāmṛta* 1.10.17-20)

VAKREŚVARA AND DEVĀNANDA PAṆḌITA

Vakreśvara was also present in the *kīrtanas* at the houses of Śrīvāsa and Candraśekhara, where he would dance ecstatically. Vakreśvara Paṇḍita was so dear to Mahāprabhu that Devānanda Paṇḍita was freed of his offenses to Śrīvāsa Paṇḍita and received Mahāprabhu's mercy through serving him. In answer to a *brāhmaṇa*'s question, Mahāprabhu explained how to atone for offenses to the Vaiṣṇavas:

"Listen, *brāhmaṇa*. If you want to be cured after consuming poison, you must ingest ambrosia through the very same mouth that took the poison. That way, not only will the poison be digested, but your body will become immortal through ambrosia's divine power. Now let Me answer your question. Whatever blasphemies you have unknowingly made are exactly like the poison that you have eaten. Now you must use the same mouth to constantly glorify Kṛṣṇa's name and qualities, which are like ambrosia. You have used your tongue to insult the devotees; now use it to glorify them. Glorify the devotees in songs and poetry as the best of humanity. I will destroy all the poison of blasphemy through the ambrosia of the ecstasies of Kṛṣṇa's glories. Everyone has unknowingly committed offenses; this is the truth. If you should stop all kinds of offensive activity and simply engage in praising Kṛṣṇa and His devotees, then you will be free from all the sins you have committed, however numerous they may be. You will not be able to achieve the same results through millions of atonements." (*Caitanya Bhāgavata* 3.3.449-458)

Śrīla Bhakti Siddhānta Sarasvatī Gosvāmī Ṭhākura comments: "An offensive person will only attain the ultimate good by using the tongue with which he made his blasphemous comments to acknowledge his offense and then to glorify Kṛṣṇa's devotees. If you take poison it will disrupt the body's functioning, but you can remedy the situation by taking a medicine that destroys its effects. Similarly, the way to become free from the effects of offenses to Vaiṣṇava is to first of all stop the poisonous activity; then, rather than performing thousands of other ineffective atonement rituals, one should glorify the Vaiṣṇava.

"Through serving the devotee, Kuliya's Devānanda Paṇḍita became a believer in Mahāprabhu's lotus feet. This good fortune visited him when Vakreśvara came to stay in his house. Devānanda Paṇḍita was a follower of the *smārta* path but was nevertheless a great scholar and very renounced. He read no scripture other than the *Śrīmad Bhāgavatam*. He was devoted to the Supreme Lord and was free from the domination of his senses. Nevertheless, he was not a believer in Śrī Caitanya Mahāprabhu. By Vakreśvara's mercy, this foolish misunderstanding was dispelled, and he developed faith in the Lord." (*Gauḍīya-bhāṣya* to *Caitanya Bhāgavata* 3.3.453, 481)

"Vakreśvara Paṇḍita was very dear to Caitanya Mahāprabhu. His remembrance will purify the entire creation. He is the embodiment of Kṛṣṇa *prema*. He was always in ecstasy, and both gods and demons are enchanted by his dancing." (*Caitanya Bhāgavata* 3.3.469-70)

Mahāprabhu Himself described Vakreśvara Paṇḍita's glories to Devānanda Paṇḍita:

"The Lord said, 'You have served Vakreśvara and have thus come into My presence. Vakreśvara Paṇḍita is the Lord's complete energy, so whoever pays homage to him attains Kṛṣṇa. Kṛṣṇa has made His home in Vakreśvara's heart. Kṛṣṇa dances in order to make Vakreśvara dance. If any place becomes associated with Vakreśvara, it immediately becomes the equivalent of Vaikuṇṭha and equal to all the holy places.' " (*Caitanya Bhāgavata* 3.3.493-6)

After Mahāprabhu had absolved Devānanda Paṇḍita of his offenses, He affectionately gave him many instructions:

"Those vain egoists who are proud of their scholarship cannot understand the meaning of *Śrīmad Bhāgavatam*; that is the prerogative of the surrendered devotee, the *śaraṇāgata.* The only object of the scriptural *Bhāgavatam* is to elucidate pure devotion; so it is not different from the pure devotee. One who speaks from *Śrīmad Bhāgavatam* with this knowledge will attain the supreme auspiciousness.

"One who thinks, "I understand *Śrīmad Bhāgavatam*" does not really know *Śrīmad Bhāgavatam's* central meaning. On the other hand, an ignorant person who takes shelter of *Śrīmad Bhāgavatam* will directly perceive its meaning. Śrīmad Bhāgavatam is pure love and Lord Kṛṣṇa Himself. *Śrīmad Bhāgavatam* recounts Kṛṣṇa's most intimate activities. After recounting the Vedas and the *Purāṇas*, Vedavyāsa felt unsatisfied, but as soon as *Śrīmad Bhāgavatam* manifested on his tongue, his mind was immediately satisfied." (*Caitanya Bhāgavata* 3.3.514-8)

GOPĀLA GURU GOSVĀMĪ

When Vakreśvara came to live at Puri, he would accompany Mahāprabhu, Advaita Ācārya and other devotees to Toṭā Gopīnātha to hear Gadādhara Paṇḍita give discourses on *Śrīmad Bhāgavatam*. One should hear the book *Bhāgavatam* from the devotee *Bhagavatam*.

Gopāla Guru Gosvāmī, whose previous name was Makaradhvaja Paṇḍita, was Vakreśvara Paṇḍita's disciple. In his childhood, Gopāla Guru personally served Caitanya Mahāprabhu. It is said that he also displayed extraordinary powers. When Abhirāma Ṭhākura came to pay him obeisances, Mahāprabhu took Gopāla on His lap to protect him. Mahāprabhu gave Gopāla the name Guru because he instructed people to chant Kṛṣṇa's names in all circumstances, whether pure or impure.

Before leaving his body, Gopāla Guru turned over the service of his Rādhākānta deity to his disciple Dhyānacandra Gosvāmī. After his disappearance, when Gopāla Guru's body was taken to the Svarga-dvāra to be cremated, some representatives of the king came and closed the Rādhākānta Math. Dhyānacandra was so distressed that he began to cry aloud. Gopāla Guru arose from the funeral pyre, returned to Rādhākānta's temple and resolved the problem before going back to the crematorium. Even after that, however, Gopāla Guru appeared in Vrindavan, where devotees were amazed to witness him engaged in his devotions. A deity of Gopāla Guru is still worshipped at Rādhākānta Math. Many people in Odisha are initiated in Vakreśvara Paṇḍita's line and consider themselves to be Gauḍīya Vaiṣṇavas.

During Rathayātrā at Puri, Vakreśvara was the chief dancer in the fourth *kīrtana sampradāya,* whose lead singer was Govinda Ghoṣa. He is sometimes described as a branch of Caitanya, or alternatively as a branch of Gadādhara Paṇḍita.

Vakreśvara's disappearance day is the sixth day of the waxing moon *(śukla ṣaṣṭhī)* in the month of Āṣāḍha.

Śrī Devānanda Paṇḍita

purāṇānām artha-vettā śrī devānanda-paṇḍitaḥ
purāsīn nanda-pariṣat-paṇḍito bhāgurir muniḥ

"The scholar Devānanda Paṇḍita knew the meaning of all the *Purāṇas*. Previously, he was Bhāguri Muni, the scholar in

Nanda Mahāraja's court." (*Gaura-gaṇoddeśa-dīpikā* 106)

"Sārvabhauma Bhaṭṭācārya's father was named Maheśvara Viśārada. Mahāprabhu visited his house, which was situated on an embankment. Devānanda Paṇḍita, a peaceful *brāhmaṇa* who desired liberation, made his home nearby." (*Caitanya Bhāgavata* 2.21.6-7)

"The Lord delivered Devānanda Paṇḍita in the town of Kuliya." (*Caitanya Caritāmṛta* 2.1.153)

According to Bhakti Siddhānta Sarasvatī Prabhupāda, Kuliya was a suburb of Nabadwip, situated on the west bank of the Ganges. In that time, the central part of the town of Nabadwip, also known as Mayapur, was situated on the eastern bank of the river. The modern city of Nabadwip stands on the site of the former Kuliya, which is known as the place where offenses are forgiven (*aparādha-bhañjanera pāṭa*). Proof of this is found in the old names of many neighborhoods, such as Koler Ganj, Koler Daha and Gadkhali Kol. (*Gauḍīya-bhāṣya* to *Caitanya Bhāgavata* 2.9.98)

Each of the nine islands of Nabadwip *dhāma* represents one of the nine types of devotional service. Koladwip is the island of service to the Lord's lotus feet (*pādasevana*). The word *kola* has been distorted in the popular speech as *kuliya*. The word *kol* also means a boar (*varāha*). The Lord revealed His Varāha form to Vāsudeva *vipra* in Satya Yuga.

"Just look – this is Viśārada's embankment. Here the Lord met Devānanda Paṇḍita. He chastised him for the offense he had committed to Śrīvāsa Paṇḍita, which caused him to repent." (*Bhakti-ratnākara* 12.2976-7)

From the above evidence from *Caitanya Bhāgavata*, *Caitanya Caritāmṛta* and *Bhakti-ratnākara*, it is clear that Devānanda Paṇḍita's house was somewhere near to the house of Sārvabhauma Bhaṭṭācārya's father, Maheśvara Viśārada. It is thus clearly indicated that his school (*ṭol*) was situated somewhere in Kuliya village.

DEVĀNANDA'S OFFENSE

Devānanda Paṇḍita was a scholar and an ascetic who had been indifferent to the world from an early age. Although he had won a reputation for his erudition, he nevertheless had no feeling of devotion to Kṛṣṇa and so failed to understand that *bhakti* is the ultimate purport of the *Śrīmad Bhāgavatam*. Being a *mumukṣu*, or one who seeks impersonal liberation, *mokṣa*, Devānanda Paṇḍita praised dry austerities and renunciation and did not speak devotional purports to *Śrīmad Bhāgavatam*.

One day, Śrīvāsa Paṇḍita came to hear a *Bhāgavatam* recital at Devānanda Paṇḍita's house. As he listened to the text of *Śrīmad Bhāgavatam*, Śrīvāsa Paṇḍita became absorbed in a mood of loving devotion and started to cry. Devānanda Paṇḍita's faithless disciples threw him out of the assembly for causing a disturbance. Since Devānanda Paṇḍita did not object to the action of his students, he was responsible for their offense to a devotee. For this reason, Mahāprabhu was thus angry with him.

"The Lord said: 'Whoever recites *Śrīmad Bhāgavatam* without glorifying devotional service is an ignorant fool who knows nothing. This rascal recites *Śrīmad Bhāgavatam* and never mentions *bhakti*. I will go and tear up his manuscript; just watch Me.' " (*Caitanya Bhāgavata* 2.21.20-21)

Śrīla Bhakti Siddhānta Sarasvatī Gosvāmī Ṭhākura comments on this verse as follows: "When those bereft of devotion forget their actual identity, they become completely indifferent to the service of the Lord. When they identify this indifference as the ultimate goal of life, they become a source of great displeasure to the Lord, even though He is by nature supremely merciful. Here Lord Gaurasundara shows His dissatisfaction and informs us that this attitude of the nondevotee is not only unnecessary but reprehensible. He also indicates that both the acts of enjoying and renouncing the fruits of material actions are improper. The devotees find great satisfaction in seeing the Lord become angry in this way."

DEVĀNANDA GAINS FAITH IN THE LORD

Sometime after Devānanda Paṇḍita committed this offense to Śrīvāsa Paṇḍita, Mahāprabhu passed near his house and saw that he was engaged in giving a discourse on *Śrīmad Bhāgavatam.* He became angry and rebuked him severely for his lack of faith in the Vaiṣṇavas. Just as blasphemy of the devotees makes one deprived of the Lord's mercy and destined for downfall, glorifying them and engaging in their service is the best way to find the mercy of the Lord and become freed from all sinful and offensive activity.

"Listen, *brāhmaṇa.* If you want to be cured after consuming poison, you must ingest ambrosia through the very same mouth that took the poison. In this way, not only will the poison be digested, but your body will become immortal through the ambrosia's divine power." (*Caitanya Bhāgavata* 3.3.449-50)

Through great good fortune, Mahāprabhu's dear associate Vakreśvara Paṇḍita came to stay at Devānanda Paṇḍita's house. Because Devānanda took excellent care of Vakreśvara Paṇḍita, Mahāprabhu softened towards him. Previously, Devānanda Paṇḍita had been completely lacking faith in the Lord, but when he heard of Mahāprabhu's glories from Vakreśvara Paṇḍita, his attitude changed. Through the association of the Lord's devotee, he began to develop a taste for pure devotional service.

Śrīla Bhakti Siddhānta Sarasvatī Gosvāmī Ṭhākura writes in this regard: "For Devānanda Paṇḍita of Kuliya, the fruit of service to the Vaiṣṇava was faith in Mahāprabhu's lotus feet. Vakreśvara Paṇḍita's visit to his house was the source of this auspiciousness. Although Devānanda Paṇḍita was a *smārta,* he was a great scholar and self-controlled. He studied nothing but the *Śrīmad Bhāgavatam.* He believed in God and had control of his senses. All he lacked was faith in Mahāprabhu. By the grace of Vakreśvara Paṇḍita, this faulty intelligence was wiped away and he became a believer in Lord Gaurasundara."

"Devānanda was a scholar of *Śrīmad Bhāgavatam,* but it was through Vakreśvara's mercy that he was able to understand its meaning from Mahāprabhu." (*Caitanya Caritāmṛta* 1.10.77)

Mahāprabhu told Devānanda to explain *Śrīmad Bhāgavatam* in terms of devotional service. It was Devānanda Paṇḍita's great fortune that he was able to receive the mercy of the Lord in the form of a chastisement.

"Devānanda Paṇḍita was a great pious soul, for Mahāprabhu verbally punished him. The chastisement of Caitanya Mahāprabhu is the greatest pious act. Even if one should die as a result of the Lord's punishment, he still goes to Vaikuṇṭha." (*Caitanya Bhāgavata* 2.21.77-8)

Devānanda Paṇḍita received this mercy due to living in Kuliya, or Koladwip, the place where offenses are forgiven. Gopāla Cāpāla was also forgiven his offenses in Kuliya.

Devānanda Paṇḍita's disappearance day is celebrated on the *kṛṣṇa ekādaśī* of the month of Pauṣa.

The Ghoṣa Brothers

kalāvatī rasollāsā guṇatuṅgā vraje sthitāḥ
śrī-viśākhā-kṛtaṁ gītaṁ gāyanti smādya tā matāḥ
govinda-mādhavānanda-vāsudevā yathā-kramam

"Govinda, Mādhavānanda and Vāsudeva were *gopīs* in Vraja, namely Kalāvatī, Rasollāsā and Guṇatuṅgā, who used to sing the songs composed by Viśākhā." (*Gaura-gaṇoddeśa-dīpikā* 188)

These three Ghoṣa brothers were born in an upper-class *kāyastha* family from northern Rarha. They hailed from Agradwip. All three were singers famed for the sweetness of their voices.

"The meritorious Mādhava Ghoṣa devoted himself to *kīrtana*. There was no singer on earth who was his equal. It was said of him that he was a singer from Vrindavan. He was most dear to Nityānanda Prabhu. The three brothers Govinda, Mādhava and Vāsudeva sang while Lord Nityānanda Prabhu danced." (*Caitanya Bhāgavata* 3.5.257-9)

"Caitanya Mahāprabhu and Nityānanda Prabhu danced to the *kīrtana* of the three brothers Govinda, Mādhava and Vāsudeva." (*Caitanya Caritāmṛta* 1.15.115)

"When Nityānanda Prabhu returned from Puri to preach in Bengal, he was accompanied by Vāsudeva and Mādhava Ghoṣa, while Govinda remained with Mahāprabhu and thus felt great satisfaction." (*Caitanya Caritāmṛta* 1.10.118)

GOVINDA GHOṢA

Govinda is counted amongst Caitanya Mahāprabhu personal branches. Eventually, he made his home in Agradwip, Vāsudeva in Tamluk, and Mādhava Ghoṣa in Dain Hat.[11] Govinda Ghoṣa Ṭhākura's house is not far from Agradwip in Kashipur Vishnutala. Some are of the opinion that Vishnutala was his birthplace. Govinda Ghoṣa participated in Mahāprabhu's *līlās* in Śrīvāsa Aṅgana, in the *nagara-saṅkīrtana* to the Kājī's house, and in the house of Rāghava Paṇḍita. During the Rathayātrā festival, he was the lead singer in the fourth *kīrtana* group, accompanied by his two brothers, by Chota Haridāsa, Viṣṇu Dāsa and Rāghava Paṇḍita. Vakreśvara Paṇḍita joined this group as the principal dancer.

On Mahāprabhu's direction, Govinda revealed the Gopīnātha deity from a black stone in Agradwip. Mahāprabhu also instructed him to get married. There is a legend that Govinda Ghoṣa's wife and son both died untimely. As he grew older, Govinda

11 Agradwip and Dain Hat are villages lying between Nabadwip and Katwa, while Tamluk is in Mednipur.

began to wonder who would perform his last rites (as it is considered important to have a son who can do the *śrāddha* ceremony on one's behalf). Govinda had a dream in which Gopīnātha appeared to him and said, "Don't worry about this. I will perform the *śrāddha* ceremony for you Myself."

When Govinda Ghoṣa left this world, Gopīnātha was true to His word and offered his *piṇḍa*. Gopīnātha continues to perform this ceremony every year on the anniversary of Govinda Ghoṣa's departure from the world. This takes place on the waning moon (*kṛṣṇa dvādaśī*) of the month of Caitra. Vāsudeva Ghoṣa's disappearance day is on the second day of the waxing moon *(śukla dvitīyā)* in the month of Kārtika.

Two songs written by Govinda Ghoṣa

prāṇera mukunda he!
ki āji śunilu ācambita?
kahite parāṇa jāya mukhe nāhi bāhirāya
śrī gaurāṅga chāṛibe nabadvipa

ihāto nā jāni morā sakāle milinuṅ gorā
avanata māthe āche basi
nijhare nayana jhare buka bahi dhārā paṛe
malina haiyāche mukha śaśi

dekhite takhāna prāṇa sadā kare āna cāna
sudhāite nāhi avasara
kṣaṇeke sambita haila tabe mui nivedila
śuniyā dilena e uttara

āmi ta vivaśa haiyā tāre kichu nā kahiyā
dhāiyā āiluṅ tuwā pāśa
ei ta kahiluṅ āmi je karite pāra tumi
mora nāhi jivanera āśa

śuniyā mukunda kānde hiyā thira nāhi bāndhe
gadādharera vadana heriyā
e govinda ghoṣa kaya ihā jena nāhi haya
tabe mui jāinu mariyā

[Gadādhara says,] "O Mukunda! My life! Did I really hear what I think I heard today? If I say it I will die. The words do not want to come out of my mouth. Gaurāṅga is really going to leave Nabadwip.

"I had no idea, but when I saw Gaura this morning, He was sitting with His head bowed in thought. Streams of tears flowed from His eyes and washed over His chest; His moon-like face had lost its luster.

"When I saw Him like that, my own heart fluttered and I could not ask Him anything. For a moment I regained consciousness and humbly asked Him the question, and that is what He told me.

"I was so disturbed that I ran here to you right away without saying anything farther to Him. I have told you this, and now do what you can. I don't think that I have any hope of continuing to live."

When he heard this news, Mukunda started to cry. He could no longer keep his composure when he looked at Gadādhara. Govinda Ghoṣa says, "Let it not be, for if He leaves, I will die."

hede re nadīyā vāsī kāra mukha cāo
bāhu pasāriyā gorācāṅde phirāo
to sabāre ke āra karibe nija kore
ke jāciyā dibe prema dekhiyā kātare
ki śela hiyāya hāya ki śela hiyāya
parāṇa putalī nabadvipa chāṛi jāya
āra nā jāiba morā gaurāṅgera pāśa
āra nā kariba morā kīrtana vilāsa
kāṅdaye bhakata-gaṇa buka vidāriyā
pāṣāṇa govinda ghoṣa nā jāya miliyā

O people of Nabadwip, who are you staring at? Spread your arms to stop Gauracandra; make Him come back! Who is there now who will clasp you to His chest? Who will come and beg you to take love of Kṛṣṇa? I have been stabbed in the heart! I have been stabbed in the heart! The beloved of my life has abandoned Nabadwip and gone. No longer will we be able to go and sit with Gaurāṅga; no longer will we be able to enjoy *kīrtana* the way we did. All the devotees are crying; their hearts are bursting and, like a stone, Govinda Ghoṣa does not go to join them.

Śrīmatī Viṣṇupriyā Devī

śrī-sanātana-miśro'yaṁ purā satrājito nṛpaḥ
viṣṇupriyā jagan-mātā yat-kanyā bhū-svarūpiṇī

"King Satrājit in Kṛṣṇa *līlā* became Sanātana Miśra in Caitanya *līlā*. The mother of the universe, the *avatāra* of the Lord's *bhū-śakti*, is his daughter Viṣṇupriyā." (*Gaura-gaṇoddeśa-dīpikā* 47)

Kṛṣṇa married Satyabhāmā, the daughter of King Satrājit and a Yadu princess. In Gaura *līlā*, this same Satrājit became Sanātana Miśra, and she became Viṣṇupriyā Devī. All manifestations of Viṣṇu-tattva have three energies, known as Śrī, Bhū and Nīlā (or Līlā). Lakṣmīpriyā Devī is the *śrī-śakti* of Mahāprabhu in His majestic Gaura-Nārāyaṇa attitude; Viṣṇupriyā is His *bhū-śakti* or *bhakti-śakti* and Nabadwip Dhāma is His *līlā-śakti*. Śrīla Gadādhara Paṇḍita Gosvāmī is the *śakti* of Gaura-Kṛṣṇa, or Mahāprabhu in the mood of Kṛṣṇa.

Knowledge is of two kinds, *aparā vidyā*, or material knowledge, and *parā vidyā*, or transcendental knowledge. Viṣṇupriyā Devī is the personification of transcendental knowledge. Devotees worship her on her appearance day on the *śukla pañcamī* of the month of Māgha. On the same day, materialistic persons seeking the perfection of worldly knowledge worship the goddess of learning, Sarasvatī.

Viṣṇupriyā Devī's grandfather was Durgā Dāsa Miśra. Some people believe that Durgā Dāsa was Viṣṇupriyā Devī's father. In the *Prema-vilāsa*, the family of Durgā Dāsa Miśra's descendants through Yādavācārya is known as Viṣṇupriyā's *parivāra*.

MAHĀPRABHU'S MARRIAGE TO VIṢṆUPRIYĀ DEVĪ

Vṛndāvana Dāsa Ṭhākura describes the birth of Gaura-Nārāyaṇa's *śakti*, Viṣṇupriyā Devī, in his *Caitanya Bhāgavata*. Kṛṣṇadāsa Kavirāja Gosvāmī has also mentioned the event in his *Caitanya Caritāmṛta*.

In the *Ādi-khaṇḍa*, the disappearance of Mahāprabhu's first wife, Lakṣmīpriyā Devī, is described, and then his second marriage, to Viṣṇupriyā Devī, the daughter of the court Paṇḍita. (*Caitanya Bhāgavata* 1.1.110)

"Then the Lord was married to Viṣṇupriyā Ṭhākurāṇī, after which He defeated the Digvijayī Paṇḍita." (*Caitanya Caritāmṛta* 1.16.25)

For the materialistic person, the marriage of a man and woman is the source of bondage. When the Lord marries in imitation of ordinary mortals, it becomes something quite different: it is a transcendental affair. By chanting and hearing about the union of the Supreme Lord with His divine energy, one is liberated from the material world.

"Whoever hears about the holy pastime of the Lord's marriage will be liberated from his bondage to this world. Lakṣmī sat beside the Lord, and the house of Śacī was filled with light." (*Caitanya Bhāgavata* 1.10.110-1)

"All who saw the Lord's marriage on that day were freed from their sins and attained Vaikuṇṭha *dhāma*. This is why the Lord is known as merciful (*dayāmaya*) and the master of the fallen (*dīna-nātha*)." (*Caitanya Bhāgavata* 1.15.216-7)

Mahāprabhu's first wife, Lakṣmīpriyā, left the world early. In order to support her and his mother, Mahāprabhu made a trip to eastern Bengal to teach some students. However, He was away longer than planned, and Lakṣmīpriyā Devī found it impossible to tolerate His absence. So, meditating on His lotus feet, she departed from this world. When Mahāprabhu finally arrived back in Nabadwip, He found His mother grieving for her daughter-in-law and consoled her.

Though Mahāprabhu consoled her, soon afterwards Śacī Mātā started looking for another wife for her son. For that purpose, she consulted Kāśīnātha Paṇḍita, a well-known matchmaker described in *Gaura-gaṇoddeśa dīpikā* (50) as having been Kulakaḥ in Kṛṣṇa *līlā*. Kulakaḥ was the *brāhmaṇa* who was sent by Satrājit to arrange the marriage between his daughter Satyabhāmā and Kṛṣṇa. Kāśīnātha went to court *paṇḍita* Sanātana Miśra to arrange for a marriage between Mahāprabhu and his daughter, the devotionally minded Viṣṇupriyā. Kāśīnātha persuaded Sanātana Miśra with the following words:

"Give your daughter to Viśvambhara Paṇḍita. In every way they are a perfect match. She alone is suitable of such a divine husband, while He deserves just such a pious and chaste wife. Viṣṇupriyā and Nimāi Paṇḍita are right for each other, just as Rukmiṇī and Kṛṣṇa were." (*Caitanya Bhāgavata* 1.15.57-59)

From her early childhood, Viṣṇupriyā Devī had been deeply devoted to her parents and to Viṣṇu. She would take bath in the Ganges three times daily. Śacī Mātā would see her there and bless her when she saw her pay obesciences. Śacī thus already knew Viṣṇupriyā's good qualities and happily agreed to accept her as a wife for her son.

Buddhimanta Khān was a rich and wise friend of Nimāi's family who volunteered to bear the entire expense of His marriage. Once it had been decided that Viṣṇupriyā and Viśvambhara would be married, an auspicious day and moment were fixed for the ceremony. With great pomp, the *adhivāsa* rituals were carried out on the eve of the marriage. The Lord arrived at Sanātana Miśra's house in a palanquin at dusk, and Gaura and Viṣṇupriyā's wedding ceremony was performed according to both scriptural and popular traditions.

On the following day in the forenoon, Viṣṇupriyā joined the Lord on the palanquin and arrived with Him to His house. Those who hear the eternal pastime of the wedding of Lakṣmī and Nārāyaṇa lose their desire for a material relationship of enjoyer and enjoyed, for one comes to understand that Nārāyaṇa alone is the supreme enjoyer of the entire universe. For his service, Buddhimanta Khān received Mahāprabhu's embrace and mercy.

Vṛndāvana Dāsa Ṭhākura describes how the pious women who saw the newlyweds compared them to various divine couples: "Some said, 'They remind me of Gaurī and Śiva.' Others said, 'It seems that they are Lakṣmī and

Nārāyaṇa.' Yet others said, 'No, they rather resemble Rati and Kāmadeva.'Some compared them to Indra and Śacī, and others to Rāma and Sītā." (*Caitanya Bhāgavata* 1.15.205-8)

VIṢṆUPRIYĀ DEVĪ AFTER NIMĀI'S SANNYĀSA

Mahāprabhu took *sannyāsa* from Keśava Bhāratī in Katwa when He was only twenty-four years old. In the *Caitanya Maṅgala* Locana Dāsa Ṭhākura has described Viṣṇupriyā Devī's terrible feelings of separation in the days that followed His departure:

"The earth split from the sound of Viṣṇupriyā's crying. The birds and beasts, even the trees and stones shed tears when they heard it. Falling to the ground she would lament, crying out, 'Why does my sinful life not end?'In separation, her breath was like fire, drying her lips and her body trembled constantly." (Caitanya *Maṅgala* 2.14.15-6)

The *Advaita-prakāśa* also describes how Viṣṇupriyā Devī lived her life in terrible separation from the Lord after His departure. Every morning, she would go for her bath in the Ganges with mother Śacī, after which she spent the entire day inside the house, never allowing the moon or the sun to see her. Not even the devotees were allowed to see anything more than her feet, nor hear her voice. Constantly shedding tears and eating only Mother Śacī's remnants, she became pale and thin. She took intense delight in the Holy Name, chanting all day long in solitude before a deity of Gaurāṅga and serving it and surrendering herself to His lotus feet. In this way, she demonstrated the ideal character of a devoted wife as well as the forbearance spoken of by the Lord in His verse *tṛṇād api sunīcena taror iva sahiṣṇunā*.

Śrīnivāsa Ācārya received Viṣṇupriyā Devī's blessing. He personally witnessed her devotion to Mahāprabhu in separation. Narahari Cakravartī has described this in his *Bhakti-ratnākara*:

"Every day Śrīnivāsa would come to see her. He observed her daily activities, which are beyond description. She had renounced sleep, and if ever she slept, she would do so on the bare ground. Her bodily luster, which had formerly glowed more brilliantly than gold, had become dull, and she was as thin as the waning moon on its fourteenth day. She set aside grains of rice to count the Holy Names she chanted, and would cook only this rice and offer it to her Lord. Of this amount, she would only eat a small portion. No one understood how she managed to stay alive." (*Bhakti-ratnākara* 4.47-51)

Jāhnavā Devī's disciple Nityānanda Dāsa has also described the standard Viṣṇupriyā Devī set for *bhajana* in his *Prema-vilāsa*.

"Listen, brothers, to the way in which Iśvarī Viṣṇupriyā would take the names of the Lord. By listening to this, you will get a feeling for the *līlā*. Every day she would place one clay pot on either side of her, one filled with uncooked rice, the other empty. Each time she completed one *mantra* of sixteen names and thirty-two syllables, she would joyfully place a grain of rice into the empty container. She would chant in this way until noon, and then would take whatever rice had accumulated and cook it. This is the only food that she prepared, drenching it with her tears before she offered it to the Lord."

It is not possible to estimate how many names Mahāprabhu Himself chanted, for He chanted all day and night. Similarly, His beloved wife Viṣṇupriyā chanted incessantly through the day and the night. Such dedication to the Holy Name was not impossible for her, for the Lord had planted the seed of His power in her.

It is said that Viṣṇupriyā Devī was the first to establish the worship of a *mūrti* of Gaurāṅga. This has been stated in Murāri Gupta's dairy, *kaṛacā:*

prakāśa-rūpeṇa nija-priyāyāḥ
samīpam āsādya nijāṁ hi mūrtim
vidhāya tasyāṁ sthita eṣaḥ kṛṣṇaḥ
sā lakṣmī-rūpā ca niṣevate prabhum

"Kṛṣṇa came to His beloved wife in this expansion form to remain by her side as the Mahāprabhu deity. Thus she, the *avatāra* of the goddess of fortune, was able to serve Him constantly."

The devotees of Mahāprabhu sometimes said that just as Rāmacandra, who had taken

the vow of monogamy, performed a sacrifice by seating Sītā Devī's deity made out of gold next to Him during her exile in the forest rather than marry a second time, so Viṣṇupriyā repaid her debt to her Lord in the pastimes of Gaura-Nārāyaṇa by serving the deity of Mahāprabhu. This deity is still present and worshipped in Nabadwip.

Śrī Vaṁśīvadana Ṭhākura and Śrī Iśāna Ṭhākura were blessed by the service of caring for Śrīmati Viṣṇupriyā Devī and Śrīmati Śacī Devī after Mahāprabhu took *sannyāsa*.

Śrī Iśāna Ṭhākura

"Iśāna Ṭhākura is counted as one of Caitanya Mahāprabhu's branches: Śrīnātha Miśra, Śubhānanda, Śrī Rāma, Iśāna, Śrīnidhi, Śrī Gopīkānta, and Bhagavān Miśra [were branches of Caitanya's tree]." (*Caitanya Caritāmṛta* 1.10.110)

Iśāna Ṭhākura[12] was Jagannātha Miśra's household servant. Only an eternal associate of the Supreme Lord could have the good fortune to render Him personal service in His own home. The Lord accepts the service of His own confidential associates. When Mahāprabhu was born, Iśāna had the chance to take the Lord on his lap and hold Him affectionately. He tolerated all of little Nimāi's childhood pranks and answered His every whim. Nimāi

12 Other than this Iśāna, there were several other associates of the Lord who had the same name. (1) Sanātana Gosvāmī's servant was named Iśāna. (2) There was a devotee in Vrindavan of that name. He was a member of the party of devotees who accompanied Rūpa Gosvāmī to the house of Viṭṭhaleśara to have *darśana* of Govardhanadhārī Gopāla. He also is said to have blessed Śrīnivāsa Ācārya, Narottam Dāsa Ṭhākura and Śyāmānanda *Prabhu* when they started their voyage to Bengal with the Gosvāmīs' books. (3) In the *Gauḍīya Vaiṣṇava Abhidhāna*, there is mention of a certain Iśāna Ācārya who is identified as Vraja's Yauna Mañjarī. (4) The author of the *Advaita-Prakāśa* was named Iśāna Nāgara.

was unable to go without Iśāna for even a moment.

"How can I understand the activities of Iśāna Ṭhākura, whom Nimāi used to lovingly call 'Father?' The son of Śacī, Nimāi Cāṇḍa, was his very life, and Nimāi would not go anywhere without him. In His childhood, Nimāi was very naughty and would make all kinds of capricious demands that Iśāna would do his best to fulfill." (*Bhakti-ratnākara* 12.95-7)

"Iśāna Ṭhākura also had the chance to serve Nityānanda Prabhu, Śrī Caitanya Mahāprabhu's other self. The Lord would plead with His mother to be able to invite Nitāi, and upon her consent would go Himself to invite Him. Before the two sat down to eat in Śacī's house, Iśāna Ṭhākura would bring water to wash Their feet." (*Caitanya Bhāgavata* 2.8.59)

As one of the Lord's eternal associates, Iśāna Ṭhākura was fully aware of devotional truths. He knew that the worship of the devotee is more important than even the worship of the Lord Himself. Thus he performed all kinds of service in the house of Śacī Devī, who is none other than Yaśodā Devī, and was blessed by her affection. The Lord also blesses one through His devotee's merciful attitude. The Lord's mercy follows upon the mercy of the devotee.

Iśāna Ṭhākura's glories are described in the work known as the *Vaiṣṇava-vandanā*:

vandiba īśāna-dāsa kara-joṛa kari
śacī-ṭhākurāṇī yāre sneha kaila vaṛi

"I pay obeisances to Iśāna Dāsa with folded hands, for Śacī Ṭhākurāṇī was very affectionate towards him." (*Bhakti-ratnākara* 12.94)

"The *brāhmaṇa* said, 'I am just returning after visiting Iśāna. What can I say, no one really understands his great qualifications. He has the reputation of knowing all the truths about the Lord, and he served Śacī Devī by doing whatever she needed. Because he rendered such constant service to the Lord's mother, Iśāna is uniquely fortunate in the fourteen worlds. Even though I saw with my own eyes the affection she had for him, I am unable to find words to describe it.' " (*Bhakti-ratnākara* 12.90-3)

"Iśāna, who was most fortunate in the fourteen worlds, served the Lord's mother constantly." (*Caitanya Bhāgavata* 2.8.74)

When Mahāprabhu took *sannyāsa* and left for Puri, Iśāna was left with the responsibility of taking care of His mother, Śacī, and his wife Viṣṇupriyā Devī, and supervising their household. In his commentary to the *Caitanya Bhāgavata* (2.8.73), where it is said that Iśāna Ṭhākura did all the cleaning of the house and later took the remnant *prasāda*, Śrīla Bhakti Siddhānta Sarasvatī Gosvāmī Ṭhākura writes: "Iśāna was the servant in Mahāprabhu's house. He gathered up the rice that had been thrown all over [by Nityānanda Prabhu] and made the house proper. There was no limit to Iśāna's good fortune. He rendered service to the Lord's mother throughout his entire life. Even after the Lord took *sannyāsa*, he was engaged in the service of the Lord's mother and wife, showing the extent of the blessings he had received. He is therefore described as 'most blessed' or 'the most fortunate among the blessed.'"

Iśāna Ṭhākura lived a very long life. He was still living even after the disappearance of Viṣṇupriyā Devī and all the other devotees of Mahāprabhu in Nabadwip. Thus when Śrīnivāsa Ācārya, Narottama Ṭhākura and Rāmacandra Kavirāja came to Nabadwip on pilgrimage, only Iśāna was able to show them where all the places of the Lord's pastimes were. In the *Bhakti-ratnākara*, it is said that when Iśāna showed these devotees the holy places, they were already old and in a state of disrepair. This gives some idea of how old he must have been.

Nearly everyone has disappeared from Nabadwip. No one but the Lord's servant Iśāna lived. (*Bhakti-ratnākara* 11.721)

"Śrīnivās Ācārya, Narottama Ṭhākura and Rāmacandra Kavirāja received Iśāna Ṭhākura's blessings in Nabadwip *dhāma* and were embraced by him before leaving to visit Srikhanda, where they met with Raghunandana Ṭhākura. When they arrived there, they received the news that Iśāna had left the world."

"I heard from some people while on my way here that Iśāna has disappeared." (*Bhakti-ratnākara* 13.21)

After Mahāprabhu and Śacī Mātā had disappeared, Vaṁśīvadanānanda Ṭhākura served Viṣṇupriyā Devī and Iśāna Ṭhākura.

Śrī Vaṁśīvadanānanda Ṭhākura

vaṁśī kṛṣṇa-priyā yāsīt sā vaṁśī-dāsa-ṭhakuraḥ

"Vaṁśīvadanānanda Ṭhākura was Kṛṣṇa's dear flute in Vraja." (*Gaura-gaṇoddeśa-dīpikā* 179)

The *gopīs* praised the good fortune of Kṛṣṇa's flute, for He was able to constantly drink the nectar of Kṛṣṇa's lips. Everything in Vraja is spiritual, i.e., conscious, and so the flute could take human form as Śrī Vaṁśīvadanānanda Ṭhākura. His life story has been recounted by his great-grandson Śrī Ballabha Dāsa in the book *Vaṁśī-vilāsa*. Other books which contain details of his life are *Śrīpāṭa-paryaṭana* and *Bhakti-ratnākara*, and the *Gauḍīya Vaiṣṇava Abhidhāna* also gives a brief biography.

Vaṁśīvadanānanda Ṭhākura was known by five names in Gauḍīya Vaiṣṇava society: Vaṁśīvadana, Vaṁśī Dāsa, Vaṁśī, Vadana, and Vadanānanda. He was a well-known writer of devotional songs. His appearance took place on the day of the spring full-moon (in the month of Caitra) in either 1416 (according to *Vaṁśī-śikṣā*) or 1427 of the Śaka era (1495 or 1506 A.D.).

VAṀŚĪVADANĀNANDA'S HOME IN NABADWIP

In the *Śrīpāṭa-paryaṭana*, the following information is given:

The two villages known as Kuliya and Paharpur were side by side. Vaṁśīvadana, Kavidatta and Sāraṅga Ṭhākura lived there. As the town grew, it was known as Kuliya Paharpur.

Vaṁśīvadanānanda Ṭhākura's home was in Koladwip, i.e., the present-day town of Nabadwip, formerly known as Kuliya Paharpur. Chakaṛi Caṭṭopādhyāya[13] was Vaṁśīvadana's father. His mother's name was Candrakalā Devī.

It is said that both Mahāprabhu and Advaita Ācārya were present when Vaṁśīvadanānanda

13 Kuliya had four neighborhoods, known as Teghari, Bechiara, Bedara Para and Chine Danga. Śrīkara Caṭṭopādhyāya came from Bilwagram to live in Bechiara. Amongst the descendants of Śrīkara Caṭṭopādhyāya was Yudhiṣṭhira Caṭṭopādhyāya ,who had three sons: Mādhava Dāsa (nicknamed Chakaṛi), Hari Dāsa (Tinakaṛi) and Kṛṣna Sampatti (Dukaṛi) Caṭṭopādhyāya.

Mahāprabhu stayed at Chakaṛi Caṭṭopādhyāya's house for seven days. During this time, He gave His blessings to all the residents of Nabadwip and instructions to Devānanda Paṇḍita. This information comes from Kavi Karṇapūra's *Caitanya-candrodaya Nāṭaka*.

was born. After Mahāprabhu took *sannyāsa*, Vaṁśīvadanānanda was engaged as Śacī Mātā and Viṣṇupriyā's servant and protector. On one occasion, Vaṁśī embraced Śrīnivāsa Ācārya emotionally and then went to Viṣṇupriyā and Śacī Mātā. This is described in the *Bhakti-ratnākara*:

"Though he had not been introduced, Vaṁśīvadanānanda guessed that this must be Śrīnivāsa. He approached him and asked him who he was. Śrīnivāsa told him everything about himself. Vaṁśīvadanānanda embraced him and washed his body with his tears. Śrīnivāsa wanted to fall to the ground and pay obeisances to Vaṁśī Ṭhākura, but Vaṁśī would not free him from his embrace. He then went and told Viṣṇupriyā and Śacī Māta that Śrīnivāsa had come." (*Bhakti-ratnākara* 4.20-4)

Vaṁśīvadanānanda Ṭhākura lived as a householder. He had two sons, Caitanya Dāsa and Nityānanda Dāsa. His deity's name was Prāṇavallabha. Later, at Viṣṇupriyā Devī's request, he established the worship of the Mahāprabhu deity. He also worshipped his forefathers' Gopīnātha deity. He spent the last part of life in his ancestral village of Bilwa Gram. The Bhaṭṭācāryas of that village are said to be his descendants.

RĀMĀI ṬHĀKURA

Vaṁśīvadanānanda Ṭhākura's grandson, the son of Caitanya Dāsa, was named Śrī Rāmacandra or Rāmāi Ṭhākura. He found Rāma and Kṛṣṇa deities at Praskandan Tirtha[14] in Vrindavan and then brought them to Baghna Para in the Burdwan district. They are known as Śrī-Rāma-Kānāi.

Vaṁśīvadanānanda Ṭhākura's family received the mercy of Jāhnavā Ṭhākurāṇī. The following comment is found in the *Gaudiya* magazine (22.30-7): "Jāhnavā Mātā, the potency of Śrīmān Nityānanda Prabhu, asked for Rāmacandra to be given to her. She gave him initiation and then took him to Khardah, where she taught him Vaiṣṇava philosophy."

A SONG BY VAṀŚĪVADANĀNANDA

The following is a song written by Vaṁśīvadanānanda Ṭhākura:

āra nā heriba prasara kapāle alakā tilaka kāca
āra nā heriba sonāra kamala
nayana khañjana nāca
āra nā nācibe śrīvāsa mandire
bhakata cātaka laiyā
āra nā nācibe āpanāra ghare āmarā dekhiba cāiyā
āra ki du' bhāi nimāi nitāi nācibe ek ṭhāñi
nimāi kariyā phukari sadāi nimāi kothāo nāi
nidaya keśava bhāratī āsiyā māthāya paṛila bāja
gaurāṅga sundara nā dekhi
kemane rahiba nadīyā māja
kebā hena jana ānibe ekhāna
āmāra gaurāṅga rāya
śāśuṛī vadhūra rodana śuniyā vaṁśī gaṛāgaṛi jāya

"No more will I see His broad forehead, decorated with *tilaka* and sandalwood dots; no more will I see His eyes dance like hummingbirds in the golden lotus of His face. No longer will He dance in Śrīvāsa's house with His *cātaka*-like devotees; no more will He dance in His own home while looking upon me. Will

14 Praskandana Tirtha is the Yamuna ghat which is not far from Dwadashaditya Ṭila. It is said that when Kṛṣṇa fought with Kālīya in the middle of the Yamuna, He became cold in the water. When He came out, all the twelve Ādityas appeared simultaneously and warmed Him up. Kṛṣṇa became so hot that He started to sweat. His sweat flowed down and merged with the water of the Yamuna. The place where this happened is known as Praskandana Tirtha.]

Nimāi and Nitāi, those two divine brothers ever dance together again? I constantly call out Nimāi's name, but Nimāi is nowhere to be seen. The heartless Keśava Bhāratī came and threw a thunderbolt on all of our heads. How can we now stay in Nabadwip, now that we cannot see Gaurāṅga here? Who here can now bring my Gaurāṅga back? When Vaṁśī hears the Lord's young wife and her mother-in-law crying, he rolls on the ground in pain."

Śrīla Narahari Sarakāra Ṭhākura

purā madhumatī prāṇa-sakhī vṛndāvane sthitā
adhunā narahary-ākhyaḥ
sarakāraḥ prabhoḥ priyaḥ

"Narahari Sarakāra, the Lord's dear associate, was previously Rādhā's intimate girlfriend named Madhumatī. (*Gaura-gaṇoddeśa-dīpikā* 117)

Śrīla Narahari Sarakāra Ṭhākura is counted as one of Caitanya's branches on the desire tree of pure devotional service. By Mahāprabhu's desire, he took birth in a physician (*vaidya*) family, blessing his family when he did so. He was foremost among the Lord's associates of the village of Srikhanda. Narahari's home is about one mile from the Srikhanda railway station near Katwa in the Burdwan district. Some of the other prominent residents of Srikhanda who were devotees of Lord Caitanya were Śrī Mukunda, Śrī Raghunandana, Śrī Cirañjīva, Śrī Sulocana, Śrī Dāmodara Kavirāja, Śrī Rāmacandra Kavirāja, Śrī Govinda Kavirāja, Śrī Balarāma Dāsa, Śrī Ratikānta, Śrī Rāmagopāla Dāsa, Śrī Pītāmvara Dāsa, Śrī Śacīnandana and Śrī Jagadānanda. Kṛṣṇadāsa Kavirāja Gosvāmī mentions many of these names as Caitanya's branches that generously distributed the fruits of love of God. (*Caitanya Caritāmṛta* 1.10.78-9)

The scholar Bharat Mallik has written the following Sanskrit verses about Narahari's appearance in a *vaidya* family in his book *Candra-prabhā:*

śrīkhaṇḍa-nāma-nagarī rāḍhe baṅgeṣu viśrutā
sarveṣām eva vaidyānām āśrayo yatra vidyate
yatra goṣṭhī-bhūtā vaidyā yaḥ
khaṇḍo'bhūd bhiṣak-priyaḥ
viśeṣataḥ kulīnānāṁ sarveṣām eva vāsa-bhūḥ

"In Bengal, in the area known as Rarha (Burdwan, Birbhum), there is a famous town known as Srikhanda that gave shelter to all the physician clans. Since *vaidyas* gathered there, it became a favored residence for them, especially those who were of the noblest birth."

In the *Gauḍīya Vaiṣṇava Abhidhāna,* it is stated that Narahari Sarakāra Ṭhākura appeared in either the Śaka year 1401 or 1402 (1480-81 A.D.). His father's name was Śrī-Nārāyaṇa Dāsa, his mother's Śrī Goyī. Goyī was the daughter of Murāri Sena. Nārāyaṇa Dāsa had three sons, Mukunda, Mādhava and Narahari. Raghunandana Ṭhākura, whose *darśana* would drive away all the material afflictions, was Mukunda's son. (*Bhakti-ratnākara* 11.730-1)

The author of *Caitanya Maṅgala,* Locana Dāsa, who came from a remote village near Jhamaṭpur, was Narahari's disciple. For this reason, Locana Dāsa writes that Śrī Gadādhara Dāsa and Narahari Sarakāra Ṭhākura were Mahāprabhu's dearest associates. On the other hand, in *Caitanya Bhāgavata,* Vṛndāvana Dāsa Ṭhākura has not spoken at any length about the devotees of Srikhanda.

Śrīla Locana Dāsa Ṭhākura has written the following about his guru in *Caitanya-maṅgala:*

"Narahari Dāsa Ṭhākura is my worshipable master. He descended from an esteemed line of physicians; his body was permeated by love for Kṛṣṇa, and he taught his disciples nothing other than Kṛṣṇa *prema*. He was previously known as Madhumatī, one of Rādhā's dearest *sakhīs* in Vrindavan, a storehouse of sweetness. Now in the age of Kali, along with Gaurāṅga, he has become the keeper of the storehouse of love for Rādha and Kṛṣṇa."

After the death of his father, Nārāyaṇa Dāsa, Narahari's older brother Mukunda arranged for him to study in Nabadwip. It is said that, in fact, Mukunda also worked as a physician to the Badshah in order to meet his family expenses. Narahari quickly became very learned as well as a connoisseur of the flavors of devotional sentiment. Even before becoming Mahāprabhu's associate, he composed songs glorifying Rādhā and Govinda's pastimes. When Śrīla Gadādhara Paṇḍita Gosvāmī was constantly by the Lord's side, engaged in His service, Narahari had the good fortune to enter into his association. Narahari Sarakāra Ṭhākura's personal service was to fan the Lord with the yak-tail whisk. Śrīla Bhaktivinoda Ṭhākura, Mahāprabhu's personal associate, confirmed this in his *Gaura-ārati*:

narahari ādi kari cāmara ḍhulāy
sañjaya, mukunda, vāsu ghoṣa ādi gāy

"Narahari and the other residents of Srikhanda fanned with the *cāmara*, while Sañjaya, Mukunda and Vāsu Ghoṣa sang."

Narahari wrote several books, including *Bhakti-candrikā-paṭala*, *Śrī-Kṛṣṇa bhajanāmṛta*, *Śrī-caitanya-sahasranāma*, *Śrī-Śacīnandanāṣṭaka*, *Śrī-Rādhāṣṭaka*, etc. All of these are well known and thought of highly by the devotees.

The following story is told about Narahari: Once when Mahāprabhu and Nityānanda Prabhu came to his house in Srikhanda, they suddenly expressed a desire for honey. Narahari demonstrated his miraculous powers by transforming the water in a pond near his house into honey. Ever since he quenched the Lord's desire for honey with water from this pond, it has been known as Madhu-puṣkariṇī. The Lord gave Narahari the order in a dream to install three deities of Himself, which are currently worshipped in Srikhanda, Katwa and Ganganagar.

Narahari Sarakāra Ṭhākura also participated in the Lord's activities in Puri. He and the other residents of Srikhanda were amongst those who went every year with Śivānanda Sena (*Caitanya Caritāmṛta* 2.1.132). When Mahāprabhu returned to Puri after His pilgrimage to South India, where He had saved so many people by giving them love for Kṛṣṇa, Nityānanda Prabhu sent Kāla Kṛṣṇadāsa back to Bengal to tell everyone that Mahāprabhu was back. The Bengali devotees immediately made arrangements to go to Jagannatha Puri to see the Lord. The residents of Srikhanda (the Khaṇḍa-vāsīs) were counted amongst them.

"Mukunda, Narahari and Raghunandana from Srikhanda arrived at Advaita Ācārya's house to go to Nilachal." (*Caitanya Caritāmṛta* 2.10.90)

After the Snāna Yātrā, Lord Jagannātha would not be available for *darśana*. Out of separation from the Lord, Mahāprabhu would go to Alalanatha and returned to Puri when He heard that the devotees from Bengal were arriving there. When Sārvabhauma Bhaṭṭācārya asked Gopīnātha Ācārya to identify the Lord's devotees, he mentioned the names of Narahari, Mukunda Dāsa, Raghunandana, Cirañjīva, Sulocana and other Khaṇḍa-vāsīs as most dear to Caitanya Mahāprabhu. (*Caitanya Caritāmṛta* 2.11.92-3)

During the Rathayātrā festival, the Lord formed seven *kīrtana* groups with the devotees from Bengal. One of these was composed uniquely of the devotees from Srikhanda. Kṛṣṇadāsa Kavirāja Gosvāmī writes that Narahari Sarakāra Ṭhākura and Raghunandana were the dancers for this group. (*Caitanya Caritāmṛta* 2.13.46)

When the Lord gave Mukunda, Raghunandana and Narahari directions for service, He told Narahari to remain in the association of devotees. (*Caitanya Caritāmṛta* 2.15.132)

Many people confuse Narahari Sarkar Ṭhākura with the author of *Bhakti-ratnākara*, Narahari Cakravartī. The latter, who is also known as Ghanaśyāma Dāsa, was born in the district of Murshidabad. His father's name was Jagannātha Cakravartī and was a disciple of Viśvanātha Cakravartī. On Govindajī's order, he was engaged as the cook for the Govinda temple and was known as the "cooking *pūjārī*" (*rasuiyā pūjārī*) in Vraja.

IF GAURA CAME BACK TO NADIA TOWN

The following is one of the many delectable songs composed by Narahari Sarakāra Ṭhākura:

āola gaura punahi nadīyā pura
hoyata manahi ullāsa
aiche ānanda kanda kiye heraba
karabahi kīrtana vilāsa

hari hari,
kaba hāma heraba so mukha-cāṅda
viraha payodhi kabahu dina pāṅ raba
ṭuṭaba hṛdayaka bāṅdha

kundana kanaka pāṅti keba heraba
yajña ki sutra virāja
bāhu-jugala tuli hari hari bolaba
naṭana bhakata-gaṇa mājha

eta kahi nayana mudi bahu saba jana
gaura prema bhela bhora
narahari dāsa āśa kaba pūraba
heraba gaura-kiśora

"If Gaura came back to Nadia town, my mind would be filled with joy. Then I would see Him, the source of all joy, performing His *kīrtana* pastimes.

"Hari Hari! When will I again gaze upon that moon-like face? When will that day come when the dam holding the ocean of separation in my heart breaks?

"When will I see the golden form of the Lord, wrapped in His *yajña-sūtra*? Lifting my arms in the air, I will shout 'Hari! Hari!' and dance in the midst of the devotees.

"Saying such things, many of Gaura's devotees close their eyes and merge into love for Him. When will Narahari's desires be fulfilled? When will he gaze again upon the form of the young Gaura?"

Narahari disappeared in around 1540 A.D. in the month of Agrahāyaṇa on the kṛṣṇa *ekādaśī* day. Śrīnivāsa Ācārya officiated at his funeral ceremony. Nityānanda Prabhu's son Vīrabhadra Gosvāmī and many other important Vaiṣṇavas were in Srikhanda to celebrate Narahari's disappearance feast, which is described in *Bhakti-ratnākara*:

"Some people said, 'Brothers! Do not leave right away. An ocean of *prema* will flood over in Srikhanda in a few days. On the eleventh day of the waning moon of Agrahāyaṇa, when Narahari Ṭhākura disappeared, a great festival will be held here. See this festival that is going to start in the next three or four days to the full satisfaction of your eyes.' " (*Bhakti-ratnākara* 9.512-4)

Śrīla Raghunandana Ṭhākura

vyūhas tṛtīyaḥ pradyumnaḥ priya-narma-sakho'bhavat
cakre līlā-sahāyaṁ yo rādhā-mādhavayor vraje
śrī-caitanyādvaita-tanuḥ sa eva raghunandanaḥ

"The third member of the *catur-vyūha*, Pradyumna, took part in Rādhā Mādhava's *līlā* in Vraja as Kṛṣṇa's intimate friend, or *priya-narma-sakhā*. He has now appeared as Raghunandana, whose body is not different from that of Śrī Caitanya." (*Gaura-gaṇoddeśa-dīpikā* 70)

RAGHUNANDANA'S FATHER, MUKUNDA DĀSA

Raghunandana was born into a family of physicians[15] in the Śaka year 1432 (1511 A.D.). His father's name was Mukunda Dāsa; his mother's name is unknown. Mukunda Dāsa was Narahari Sarakāra Ṭhākura's older brother. In the fifteenth chapter of the *Madhya-līlā* of *Caitanya Caritāmṛta*, it is clearly said that Mukunda Dāsa was a physician to the king.

"Externally, he appears to be engaged in government service as a physician to the king. But in his inner life, he is filled with divine love. Who can know the extent of his love?" (*Caitanya Caritāmṛta* 2.15.120)

Once when Mukunda Dāsa was engaged in treating the king, he saw a peacock feather and fainted. This incident is also described in the *Caitanya Caritāmṛta* (2.15.121). On the Burdwan-Katwa rail line, Sripat Srikhanda station comes first, and then the Srikhanda. Mukunda Dāsa's home is about one mile from the Srikhanda station. Raghunandana Ṭhākura took birth on the Vasanta Pañcamī day. His uncle Narahari took a great deal of interest in raising Raghunandana, for whom he had much affection.

Caitanya Mahāprabhu indicated that one's seniority depends on the depth of devotion, by telling Mukunda Dāsa's son to be really his father.

The three most important devotees from Srikhanda were Mukunda Dāsa, Raghunandana and Narahari. Mahāprabhu asked Mukunda Dāsa, "Are you Raghunandana's father and he your son? Or is he your father and you his son? Tell me so that I can put my doubts to rest." Mukunda answered, "Raghunandana is my father and I am his son, rest assured. Whatever devotion we have comes from him; therefore I see him as my father." When he heard Mukunda Dāsa's answer, Mahāprabhu was thrilled and said, "He from whom we imbibe devotion should always be considered our senior." (*Caitanya Caritāmṛta* 2.15.112-117)

RAGHUNANDANA AND THE GOPĪNĀTHA DEITY

"Mahāprabhu gave Raghunandana the service of deity worship. He constantly engaged in the service of Śrī Kṛṣṇa. He had no other intentions." (*Caitanya Caritāmṛta* 2.15.131)

From his early childhood, Raghunandana Ṭhākura would feed the family's Gopīnātha deity *lāḍḍus*. Uddhava Dāsa has written a song in which this *līlā* is described:

Mukunda Dāsa lived in the village of Srikhanda with his household deity Gopīnātha. One day he had to go somewhere for work, and he called Raghunandana to do the service.

He said, "In this house we worship Kṛṣṇa, so I want you to be sure to give Him something

15 See chapter on Narahari Sarakāra Ṭhākura.

to eat." And then he left. Raghunandana did as his father had ordered and made the offering to the deity.

Raghunandana was just a child, and in his simplicity he said to Gopīnātha, "Eat! Eat!" Kṛṣṇa is controlled by love, and so He did as the child told Him and ate everything on the plate without leaving a grain of rice.

When Mukunda Dāsa returned, he asked the boy to bring him the *prasāda* from the offering he had made. The child answered, "Father, He ate everything and left no remnants."

Mukunda was so astonished at his child's wondrous words that he asked him to make another offering. This time after he left the house, he returned and hid to watch what his son did.

Raghunandan joyfully placed a *lāḍḍu* in Kṛṣṇa's hand and said in a commanding voice, "Eat! Eat!" When Kṛṣṇa had eaten half of the *lāḍḍu*, Mukunda Dāsa came in the doorway. Mukunda saw that Kṛṣṇa did not take another bite and that the half-eaten *lāḍḍu* remained in His hand. This caused him to be filled with love. He embraced his child and as tears of joy rained from his eyes, spoke to him in a broken voice.

To this day, fortunate people come to Srikhanda to see the half-eaten *lāḍḍu* in Gopīnātha's hand. Raghunandana is not different from Cupid himself, says Uddhava Dāsa with great feeling.

[All the *mahantas*] felt fascinated to see the Gopīnātha deity whom Raghunandana had fed *lāḍḍus*. (*Bhakti-ratnākara* 9.525)

OTHER MIRACULOUS EVENTS

Narahari Sarakāra Ṭhākura gave honey to Nityānanda Prabhu and Mahāprabhu from a pond right next to his home. This pond became known as Madhu Puṣkariṇī. The legend is told that a *kadamba* tree which grew right next to this pond always had two flowers blooming regardless of the season by Raghunandana's miraculous powers.

According to the *Gauḍīya Vaiṣṇava Abhidhāna*, another miraculous event took place in Raghunandana's life: One day, Abhirāma Ṭhākura came to Srikhanda and paid his obeisances to Raghunandana. Then he embraced him and melted with feelings of *prema*. Raghunandana started to dance and sing *kīrtana*, and while doing so, one of his ankle bells slipped from his foot and went flying off, landing four miles away in Akai Hat near his disciple Kṛṣṇadāsa's house. Later, in order to commemorate the event, a tank was excavated in that village and given the name Nūpura Kuṇḍa.

Mahāprabhu, the father of *saṅkīrtana*, gave His adopted son Raghunandana Ṭhākura the authority to offer the garland on the day before the *saṅkīrtana yajna* (the *adhivāsa*) and to make the final offering at the yajna's end.

Raghunandana Ṭhākura accompanied the Bengali devotees to Puri every year during the *cāturmāsya.* He would dance with his uncle Narahari at the Rathayātrā festival in the group formed by the residents of Srikhanda.

He participated in the Kheturi festival organized by Narottama Dāsa Ṭhākura, at Gadādhara Dāsa's festival in Katwa and at the commemorative festival for Narahari Sarakāra Ṭhākura in Srikhanda.

"Some people said, 'Anyone who is dear to Raghunandana will win Mahāprabhu's mercy for life after life.' Others said, 'Raghunandana is so merciful that he gives life to the humblest and fallen.' Some said, 'What humility! There is no one who is his equal.' And others, 'He is as beautiful as Cupid himself!' " (*Bhakti-ratnākara* 9.660)

Śrīla Raghunandana Ṭhākura had great affection for Śrīnivāsa Ācārya. Prior to his disappearance he consoled Śrīnivāsa Ācārya that despite the difficult times, he would be able to spread Vaiṣṇavism in the future:

"A difficult time is coming in which people will succumb to various doubts. Narahari Prabhu wrote in his *Śrī-Kṛṣṇa-bhajanāmṛta*:

kṛṣṇa-caitanya-candreṇa nityānandena saṁhṛte
avatāre kalāv asmin vaiṣṇavāḥ sarva eva hi
bhaviṣyanti sadodvignāḥ kāle kāle dine dine
prāyaḥ sandigdha-hṛdayā uttametara-
madhyamāḥ (verses 3-4)

" 'Once our Lord Kṛṣṇa Caitanya and His companion Nityānanda Prabhu have completed their pastimes in the material world, the Vaiṣṇavas in this Age of Kālī will become more anxious with every passing day. Whether very advanced, somewhat advanced or neophyte, their hearts will nearly always be filled with doubt.'

"But don't let this worry you. Lord Gaurāṅga will accomplish many great works through you. I bless you that you remain long on this earth and that you and your followers protect our Lord's religion. Those who are opposed to devotion to Kṛṣṇa will become devotees by your influence, and they will take shelter of you." (*Bhakti-ratnākara* 13.174-9)

Raghunandana Ṭhākura bequeathed the service of his Gaura-Gopāla deity to his son Kānāi Ṭhākura and then left this world on the fourth day of the waxing moon (*śukla caturthī)* in the month of Śrāvaṇa. Kānāi Ṭhākura gave a feast as a part of his father's last rites:

"Raghunandana slowly became hidden to mortal eyes while repeating the names of Śrī Kṛṣṇa Caitanya again and again. How glorious is that day of Śrāvaṇa *śukla caturthī*! Will anyone not sing the glories of Raghunandana Ṭhākura?" (*Bhakti-ratnākara* 13.183-4)

Śrī Śivānanda Sena

purā vṛndāvane vīrā dūtī sarvāś ca gopikāḥ
nināya kṛṣṇa-nikaṭaṁ sedānīṁ janako mama

"The go-between Vīrā, who previously brought all the *gopīs* to Kṛṣṇa, has now become my father." (*Gaura-gaṇoddeśa-dīpikā* 176)

ŚIVĀNANDA'S HOME AND FAMILY

Śivānanda Sena's son Paramānanda Sena, also known as Kavi Karṇapūra, wrote the above verse in his *Gaura-gaṇoddeśa-dīpikā.* Just as Vīrā Dūtī acted to enrich the pastimes of Kṛṣṇa and the *gopīs*, Śivānanda Sena appeared to enrich Gaura Hari's *līlā*. A Vaiṣṇava may take birth in any family. Śivānanda Sena manifested his *līlā* of being born in the *vaidya*, or physician, caste to increase its glory. The names of his parents are not known, nor that of his wife. He had three sons: Śrī Caitanya

Dāsa, Śrī Rāma Dāsa and Śrī Paramānanda (Kavi Karṇapūra).

Śivānanda Sena made his home in the present-day city of Halisahar, in Kumarahatta near Kanchra Para. This is the same town where Īśvara Purī, Mahāprabhu's guru, was born. Mahāprabhu took some earth from Īśvara Purī's birthplace. Ever since, devotees have been taking earth from that spot, leaving a hole in the ground big enough to form a pool that has taken the name Śrī Caitanya Ḍobā.

After Mahāprabhu took *sannyāsa*, Śrīvāsa Paṇḍita and his family found it impossible to remain in Nabadwip and so moved to Kumarahatta. Other notable residents of the town were Vāsudeva Datta Ṭhākura, Śrī Khañja Bhagavān Ācāya and others. According to *Caitanya Bhāgavata*, Śivānanda Sena was present when Mahāprabhu came to visit Śrīvāsa Paṇḍita's house in Kumarahatta:

"Vāsudeva Datta came immediately, as did Śivānanda Sena and his family members." (*Caitanya Bhāgavata* 3.5.18)

ŚIVĀNANDA'S SERVICE

Śivānanda was best known for managing the yearly trips to Puri when the Bengali devotees went on a pilgrimage to see Mahāprabhu. He would take responsibility for the route they took, the costs of both coming and going, their lodgings, etc.

"On the Lord's order, every single year all the devotees came to see the Rathayātrā. Amongst them were Kṛṣṇa's own singer Mukunda Datta, and, Śivānanda Sena and others, who were accompanied by their family members." (*Caitanya Bhāgavata* 3.8.5, 15)

"Śivānanda Sena took care of paying the customs duties and ferry fees for the group. He took personal care of everyone in the pilgrimage. He saw to all the devotees' necessities, especially making lodging arrangements. He knew the roads through Odisha and would show the way." (*Caitanya Caritāmṛta* 2.16.19-20)

In the third year, when Mahāprabhu's associates took their wives with them, Śivānanda Sena also took his wife and son, Śrī Caitanya Dāsa. *Caitanya Caritāmṛta's* description of that trip is as follows:

"Mālinī accompanied Śrīvāsa Paṇḍita, Śivānanda Sena's wife traveled with him. Śivānanda's little boy named Caitanya Dāsa also jubilantly came along with them to see the Lord. Śivānanda Sena dealt with customs officials and made eating and lodging arrangements, ecstatically going on the road to see Mahāprabhu." (*Caitanya Caritāmṛta* 2.16.22-3, 26-7)

One of Mahāprabhu's dear devotees was Vāsudeva Datta from Chittagong. He was very generous and somewhat prodigal in his spending. Mahāprabhu told Śivānanda Sena to take charge of his affairs to help him cut back on his expenses, giving practical instructions on the necessity of saving money to run a household.

"He respectfully said to Śivānanda Sena, 'Please take Vāsudeva Datta to hand. He is too generous. He spends whatever he earns the very day he earns it. He is a householder, he has to save some money; if he doesn't, he will not be able to maintain his wife and family. I want you to supervise his income and expenditures. Be his manager and make proper adjustments.' " (*Caitanya Caritāmṛta* 2.15.93-6)

ŚIVĀNANDA SENA AND THE DOG

Kṛṣṇadāsa Kavirāja Gosvāmī has recounted an anecdote in the *Caitanya Caritāmṛta* about the amazing relationship between Śivānanda Sena and a dog.

One year, as the pilgrimage party made their way to Puri, a stray dog began to tag along behind them. When they had to cross a certain river, the ferryman refused to allow the dog to get on board. Śivānanda Sena paid the ferryman ten *paṇas* of cowry shells to get it across. One day, his servant forgot to feed the dog its rice and it disappeared. Śivānanda was so upset that he did not eat his meal that evening.

As they approached Puri, the devotees became increasingly anxious to see Mahāprabhu, and on their arrival, they went straight to His residence even before going to the temple to see Lord Jagannātha. They then went to take their meal with Mahāprabhu, who at the end of the meal sent them all to their lodgings to rest.

The next day, when the devotees came to see Mahāprabhu, they were astonished to see the dog there. Mahāprabhu was laughing and feeding it coconut *prasāda* and saying, "Chant Kṛṣṇa *harināma*!" The dog was clearly chanting out the divine names and eating the *prasāda* given him by the Lord. Everyone was completely amazed to see this extraordinary event. Śivānanda Sena prostrated himself on the ground in obeisances to the dog and begged him for forgiveness. The next day, the dog had disappeared once more and was never seen again. By Mahāprabhu's mercy, the dog had taken a spiritual body and gone to Vaikuṇṭha.

"These are the transcendental pastimes of Lord Śacīnandana: He made a dog say the names of Kṛṣṇa and then sent it to the spiritual world." (*Caitanya Caritāmṛta* 3.1.33)

ŚIVĀNANDA SENA AND NAKULA BRAHMACĀRĪ

During the period of Muslim rule, the county courthouse in the town of Ambika was in the neighborhood named Kalna in the district of Burdwan. This was known then as Ambua Muluk, today as Pyari Ganj. A great Vaiṣṇava named Nakula Brahmacārī lived there. Mahāprabhu entered into Nakula's heart out of His desire to deliver the people of Bengal. The *brahmacārī* began to behave just like someone possessed by celestial influences and would dance, sing and shout in a deep mood of divine love. Both his inner mood and his physical appearance took on Mahāprabhu's qualities.

When people heard about the miraculous occurrences surrounding Nakula Brahmacārī, they gathered to see him. In his presence everyone would be influenced by his absorption in Mahāprabhu's mood; they would sing Kṛṣṇa's names and begin to experience the taste of Kṛṣṇa *prema*.

When he heard about all this, Śivānanda Sena could not at first believe that it was true, and he decided to test Nakula Brahmacārī to eradicate his doubts. He came to Ambika but kept himself at some distance from the *brahmacārī*. His idea was that if Nakula were truly possessed by Mahāprabhu, he would call out to him and tell him what his own secret *mantra* was. In spite of the fact that Śivānanda was invisible in the great crowd of countless devotees, Nakula called out his name and sent people to look for him. When he heard his name being called, Śivānanda came forth and paid his obeisance to Nakula. The *brahmacārī* said:

"You doubted me; so listen carefully and I will put an end to your doubts. Your worshippable *mantra* is the four-syllable Gaura-Gopāla *mantra*. Give up the uncertainty you held in your heart." (*Caitanya Caritāmṛta* 3.2.30-1)

When he heard this, Śivānanda became convinced that Nakula Brahmacārī was indeed filled with the presence of Mahāprabhu. He paid his prostrated obeisances to him and acknowledged his faith in and devotion to him. This is just one example of Mahāprabhu's inconceivable potencies.

ŚIVĀNANDA SENA AND NṚSIṀHĀNANDA BRAHMACĀRĪ

Śivānanda Sena had a nephew, Śrīkānta Sena, who was so eager to see the Lord that one year he went to Puri alone. Mahāprabhu treated him warmly and kept him for two months before instructing him to return to Bengal. He told him to convey the message to the Bengali devotees that there was no need for them to come to Puri that year, for He Himself would be visiting Bengal in the month of Pauṣa. He would then meet with them all and eat at Jagadānanda Paṇḍita's house. When Śrīkānta returned with the news, everyone was jubilant in expectation of the Lord's visit. But when the time of Mahāprabhu's expected arrival came, Śivānanda, Jagadānanda Paṇḍita and the others who had been waiting anxiously for Him were distressed to see that He did not come.

At that time, Pradyumna Brahmacārī (who had been given the name Nṛsiṁhānanda by Mahāprabhu) happened by and asked them why everyone was so unhappy. When he heard about their disappointment over Mahāprabhu's not arriving, he assured them that he would bring Mahāprabhu there within three days. Everyone knew of Pradyumna's spiritual powers, and so they believed that he could do it.

Pradyumna sat down in meditation. After two days, he said, "Mahāprabhu has arrived in Panihati. By midday tomorrow he will be at Śivānanda's house." Without showing the slightest doubt, he ordered Śivānanda Sena to start making preparations for a feast in honor of Mahāprabhu's arrival. Pradyumna personally started cooking early in the morning and made a large variety of preparations, which he distributed onto three plates to make offerings to Lord Jagannātha, Nṛsiṁhadeva and to Mahāprabhu. As soon as he sat down in meditation for the offerings, Mahāprabhu personally appeared and ate all three offerings, without leaving any remnants.

Pradyumna was overjoyed to see the Lord accept his offerings. Nevertheless, though he well knew that on a higher level there is no distinction between Mahāprabhu, Nṛsiṁhadeva and Lord Jagannātha, in order to demonstrate the principle of devotion to one's personal worshipable deity, he said, "Nṛsiṁhadeva has not eaten anything today." Śivānanda asked why this was so, and Pradyumna Brahmacārī answered:

"Mahāprabhu ate the offerings intended for all three deities. Therefore Nṛsiṁhadeva and Lord Jagannātha have gone hungry." (*Caitanya Caritāmṛta* 3.2.71)

When he heard this, Śivānanda felt a twinge of doubt. Nevertheless, he furnished Pradyumna with more raw foodstuffs so that he could prepare another offering for Nṛsiṁhadeva. The next year, when Śivānanda came to Nilachal, Mahāprabhu one day started to glorify Nṛsiṁhānanda's virtues to all the devotees.

"Last year in the month of Pauṣa, he gave Me such a nice meal. I have never tasted such delicious rice and vegetables!" (*Caitanya Caritāmṛta* 3.2.77)

All the devotees were struck with wonder at hearing this, and Śivānanda himself became confident that the incident was true. This is another example of Mahāprabhu's mercy to Śivānanda.

NITYĀNANDA PRABHU PUNISHES ŚIVĀNANDA

Śivānanda Sena also received much mercy from Nityānanda Prabhu. One day Nityānanda Prabhu kicked Śivānanda, who thus received the touch of his lotus feet, a rare attainment for even Brahmā and the demigods. Srila Kṛṣṇadāsa Kavirāja Gosvāmī has described this incident in the twelfth chapter of the *Caitanya Caritāmṛta*'s *Antya-līlā*.

After the disappearance of Haridāsa Ṭhākura, Mahāprabhu's ecstatic transformations increased day by day. That year, the devotees gathered in Nabadwip as usual in preparation for the journey to Puri. Nityānanda Prabhu also joined the party, even though Mahāprabhu had expressly forbidden him to come to Puri. Śivānanda Sena was in charge of the party and would take care of the customs agents and toll collectors along the way. On this occasion, he was accompanied by his wife and three sons.

Normally, Śivānanda would cross a given toll gate last, after first ensuring that all members of the party had gone through. On one occasion, the procedure took longer than usual, and since Śivānanda had not arranged for lodgings for the company in the nearby village, the devotees were obliged to loiter about under a tree. While waiting for Śivānanda to come through the toll gate, Nityānanda Prabhu appeared to take on the mood of a cowherd boy from Vraja overcome by hunger. He made a pretence of being angry at Śivānanda, complaining, "Śiva has still not come and arranged for a place for us to stay, and I am dying of hunger. I curse his three sons to die."

On hearing Nityānanda Prabhu make such a curse, Śivānanda's wife started to cry. When Śivānanda finally returned he went to see Nityānanda Prabhu, who kicked him in the head as he paid his obeisances. Śivānanda was overjoyed to receive the merciful touch of the Lord's foot and immediately went to arrange quarters for the night in the house of a milkman. When Śivānanda had brought Nityānanda Prabhu to his lodgings, he glorified Him and prayed to receive the touch of His feet again and again. He said:

"Today You have accepted me as Your servant, for You have punished me as You would Your own servant. You are so compassionate that even Your punishments are a sign of Your causeless mercy. Who in the three worlds can understand Your personality? The dust of Your feet is unattainable by even Brahmā, yet it has fallen on my wretched body. My life, my family and my service have all become perfected today. Today I have attained devotion to Kṛṣṇa, as well as all the other goals of human life." (*Caitanya Caritāmṛta* 3.12.27-30)

Nityānanda Prabhu was so pleased by Śivānanda's prayers that He embraced him. However, Śrīkānta, Śivānanda's nephew, had been upset by Nityānanda Prabhu's behavior. He thought, "Śivānanda is Mahāprabhu's dear associate and respected by all the devotees, and yet Nityānanda Prabhu has kicked him in the head." He left the party and went ahead to Puri on his own. Upon his arrival, he went to Mahāprabhu and paid his prostrated obeisances. Mahāprabhu's servant Govinda told Śrīkānta to take off his upper garments when paying obeisances. However, knowing his thoughts, Mahāprabhu said to His associates:

"Śrīkānta has come on his own because of some great mental distress. Don't tell him what to do, but allow him to do as he pleases." (*Caitanya Caritāmṛta* 3.12.38)

From these words, Śrīkānta could understand that Mahāprabhu is all-knowing and so said nothing about the incident to anyone. The Lord is so affectionate to His devotees that even their friends and relations are also dear to Him.

ahaṁ bhakta parādhīno
hy asvatantra iva dvija
sādhubhir grasta-hṛdayo bhaktair
bhakta-jana-priyaḥ

"O *brāhmaṇa*, I am under the control of My devotees, as though I were completely lacking any independence. The saintly devotees have taken possession of My heart, for I am dear to them and they to Me." (*Śrīmad Bhāgavatam* 9.4.63)

MAHĀPRABHU'S MERCY TO ŚIVĀNANDA'S FAMILY

Due to their relation to Śivānanda, his wife and three sons also received the Lord's unlimited mercy. He had named his youngest son Paramānanda Dāsa in accordance with Mahāprabhu's instruction. Mahāprabhu would jokingly call the child "Puri Dāsa." When Śivānanda presented the baby to Him, the Lord affectionately allowed him to suck on His toe.

"Who can find the limits of the ocean of Śivānanda's good fortune? The Lord accepted his entire family as His own. The Lord sat down and ate with all the devotees. As He washed His mouth and hands after the meal, He instructed Govinda to give Śivānanda Sen, his wife and children His remnants every day for as long as they stayed in Puri." (*Caitanya Caritāmṛta* 3.12.51-3)

Mahāprabhu's unlimited mercy on Śivānanda's youngest son, Purī Dāsa, is described in the sixteenth chapter of the *Caitanya Caritāmṛta, Antya-līlā*. One year, when Śivānanda and his wife were in Puri for the Rathayātrā, Mahāprabhu said to the little boy, "Say Kṛṣṇa, say Kṛṣṇa!" Though the Lord repeatedly asked him to chant, the boy did not do so. His embarrassed father also tried to get him to chant, but Purī Dāsa was steadfast in not uttering the Holy Name. Mahāprabhu said, "I have induced everyone in the universe, even including the nonmoving creatures, to chant the names of Kṛṣṇa, but was unable to make this little child do so. Whatever is the reason for this?"

Svarūpa Dāmodara ascertained: "You have instructed him in the *mantra* consisting of Kṛṣṇa's name. Now that he has received the *mantra*, he will not reveal it publicly but only chants it mentally. That is my guess."

In his *Anubhāṣya*, Śrīla Bhakti Siddhānta Sarasvatī Gosvāmī Ṭhākura has written: "The *mantra* which one has received from his guru is not to be revealed to anyone else; otherwise it will lose the potency. We have seen this previously from the story about Gadādhara Paṇḍita."

Another day, Mahāprabhu asked Purī Dāsa to recite a verse. Purī Dāsa broke his silence and recited a verse of his own composition that astonished all those who heard it. He was only a seven-year-old boy with a little or no learning. Even Brahmā and the gods cannot understand the glories of Mahāprabhu's mercy. Purī Dāsa (Kavi Karṇapūra's) verse:

śravasoḥ kuvalayam akṣṇor añjanam
uraso mahendra-maṇi-dāma
vṛndāvana-ramaṇīnāṁ maṇḍanam
akhilaṁ harir jayati

"All glories to Hari, the ornament of all the lovely ladies of Vrindavan – a blue lotus for their ears, black collyrium for their eyes, and a necklace of blue sapphires to decorate their breasts." (*Caitanya Caritāmṛta* 3.16.74)

ŚIVĀNANDA AND RAGHUNĀTHA DĀSA GOSVĀMĪ

When Raghunātha Dāsa Gosvāmī left home, using an errand for guru Yadunandana Ācārya as a pretext, his father, Govardhana Majumadāra, sent ten men to Śivānanda, who was already on his way to Puri, asking him to send Raghunātha Dāsa back. They did not find Raghunātha Dāsa with Śivānanda, however, and returned empty-handed. At the end of the rainy season, when Śivānanda and the other devotees returned from Puri, Govardhana Majumadāra heard from some of them that Raghunātha Dāsa was engaged in strict austere practices and begging near the Siṁha Dvāra of the Lord Jagannātha temple. Raghunātha's parents were greatly distressed by this news, and the next year, Govardhana Majumadāra entrusted four hundred coins, two servants and a *brāhmaṇa* cook to Śivānanda for his son. Raghunātha refused to accept this money for himself, however. Śivānanda Sena's son Kavi Karṇapūra has glorified Raghunātha Dāsa extensively in his play *Caitanya candrodaya.*

The dates of Śivānanda Sena's appearance and disappearance are not known. The Gaura Gopāla deity he installed is still being worshipped in the Kṛṣṇa Rāya temple in Kanchra Para.

Śrī Acyutānanda

yogamāyā bhagavatī gṛhiṇī tasya (advaitasya) sāmpratam
sītārūpeṇāvatīrṇā śrī-nāmnā tat-prakāśataḥ
tasya putro'cyutānandaḥ kṛṣṇa-caitanya-vallabhaḥ
śrīmat-paṇḍita-gosvāmi-śiṣyaḥ priya iti śrutaṁ
yaḥ kārttikeyaḥ prāg āsīd iti jalpanti kecana
kecid āhū rasavido 'cyutā-nāmnī tu gopikā
ubhayantu samīcīnaṁ dvayor ekatra saṅgatāt
kārttikeyaḥ kṛṣṇa-miśras tat-sāmyād iti kecana

"The goddess Yogamāyā appeared as Advaita Ācārya's wife, Sītā, whose expansion was Śrī. Advaita Ācārya's son Acyutānanda was very dear to Śrī Kṛṣṇa Caitanya. He became a dear disciple of Śrīla Gadādhara Paṇḍita Gosvāmī. Those who are knowledgeable about sacred rapture say that Kārttikeya and the *gopī* named Acyutā are both joined in him. Some people hold that his brother Kṛṣṇa Miśra was also Kārttikeya." (*Gaura-gaṇoddeśa-dīpikā*, 86-8)

Acyutānanda was born as the son of Advaita Ācārya and Sītādevi in the town of Shantipur in the year 1428 Śaka (1507 A.D.). He was Advaita Ācārya's oldest son and is counted as a Caitanya branch of the tree of devotion.

śrī-caitanyāmarataror
dvitīya-skandha-rūpiṇaḥ
śrīmad-advaita-chandrasya
śākhā-rūpān gaṇān numaḥ

"I offer my obeisances to all the branches of Śrī Advaita Candra, who is the second trunk of the eternal Caitanya tree." (*Caitanya Caritāmṛta* 1.12.3)

"Acyutānanda was one of Advaita Prabhu's major branches; from his very birth, he served Caitanya's lotus feet." (*Caitanya Caritāmṛta* 1.12.13)

ADVAITA'S SIX SONS

Advaita Ācārya had six sons, of whom three, Acyutānanda, Kṛṣṇa Miśra and Gopāla Dāsa, are considered to have understood the essence of spiritual life, while the other three, Balarāma, Svarūpa and Jagadīśa, did not. The book *Advaita-carita* describes this as follows:

acyutaḥ kṛṣṇa-miśraś ca
gopāla-dāsa eva ca
ratna-trayam idaṁ proktaṁ
sītā-garbhādi-sambhavam
ācārya-tanayeṣvete
trayo gaura-gaṇāḥ smṛtāḥ
caturtha balarāmaś ca
svarūpaḥ pañcamaḥ smṛtaḥ
ṣaṣṭhas tu jagadīśākhya
ācārya-tanaya hi ṣaṭ

"The three sons Acyuta, Kṛṣṇa Miśra and Gopāla Dāsa were born in the womb of Sītādevi and are called the three jewels. Amongst Advaita Ācārya's sons, these three were members of Gaura's inner circle. His fourth son was Balarāma, his fifth son Svarūpa, and the sixth Jagadīśa.

"Śrīla Bhaktivinoda Ṭhākura paraphrases Kṛṣṇadāsa Kavirāja's explanation of this problem in his *Amṛta-pravāha-bhāṣya*: "In the beginning, all of Advaita Prabhu's followers shared a common understanding, but in the course of time some unfortunately adopted differing doctrines. Those who followed the opinions of Advaita Ācārya Himself are considered to be pure Vaiṣṇavas, but those who under some fateful influence rejected his teachings and invented a new doctrine are considered unworthy. We have no need of knowing the names of the unworthy sons of Advaita Prabhu but have listed them together in order to be able to distinguish them. Just as the useful rice grain is separated from the chaff by winnowing, so have the noble sons of Advaita been separated from the unworthy."

"The doctrines of Advaita Ācārya are the essential teachings of spiritual life; those who ignored His orders became useless." (*Caitanya Caritāmṛta* 1.12.10)

"All those who took Acyutānanda's opinion belong to the group of Advaita Ācārya's associates. They are great devotees who received His mercy and easily attained the lotus feet of Caitanya Mahāprabhu." (*Caitanya Caritāmṛta* 1.12.73-4)

MAHĀPRABHU'S MERCY ON THE CHILD ACYUTĀNANDA

When Mahāprabhu came to Advaita Ācārya's house in Shantipur after taking *sannyāsa* in Katwa, Acyutānanda was around three or five years old at that time.

"Advaita's effulgent son Acyutānanda, was a small boy, still young enough to go about without any clothes. He glowed with good fortune. He was omniscient, greatly fortunate and had inconceivable power; he was Advaita's worthy heir. His entire body was covered with dust, but on hearing that the Lord had arrived, he came to see Him with a smile on his face. He fell at the Lord's feet, and the Lord picked up the dust-covered child and held him on His lap." (*Caitanya Bhāgavata* 3.1.213-6)

While holding him, Mahāprabhu said to Acyutānanda, "Since Advaita is My father, you are My brother." When he heard this, Acyutā responded by displaying a profound understanding of Mahāprabhu's spiritual identity. He said, "You are the friend of every single living being, and the scripture says that You are the father of all creation." The devotees were astonished when they heard Acyutā show this understanding of the Lord's identity.

THE WISDOM OF ACYUTĀNANDA AT FIVE

In the fourth chapter of the *Antya-khaṇḍa* of *Caitanya Bhāgavata*, Vṛndāvana Dāsa Ṭhākura writes about Acyutānanda's single-minded devotion to Caitanya Mahāprabhu in the following way: One day, a *sannyāsī* came to visit Advaita Prabhu's house and asked him what the relationship between Caitanya Mahāprabhu and Keśava Bhāratī was. Advaita Ācārya answered in a conventional way that Keśava Bhāratī was the Lord's guru. The five-year-old child interjected angrily, "The Lord is the spiritual master of all the gurus of the world; He is the Supreme Lord Himself. How could anyone be His guru?" When Advaita Ācārya heard this wisdom from the mouth of His child, He said, "This boy is My father and I am his son!" And He asked His son forgiveness for His offense – causing the lad to hang his head in embarrassment. Kṛṣṇadāsa Kavirāja Gosvāmī has also summarized this story beautifully:

"When Acyutānanda heard from his father that Keśava Bhāratī was Lord Caitanya Mahāprabhu's spiritual master, he was very unhappy. He told his father, 'Your teaching about the supreme spiritual master, Caitanya Mahāprabhu, will wreak havoc in the country. Lord Caitanya Mahāprabhu is the teacher of the fourteen worlds, but You say that someone else is His spiritual master. This is not supported by any revealed scripture.' Advaita Ācārya felt great satisfaction to hear His five-year-old son Acyutānanda display such an understanding of doctrine." (*Caitanya Caritāmṛta* 1.12.14-7)

Mahāprabhu appeared at Advaita Ācārya's house just when the entire household and other devotees were becoming aware of Acyutānanda's spiritual intelligence and gave him His blessings.

Acyutānanda had seen Mahāprabhu's glories at His great epiphany (*mahā-prakāśa*), for when the Lord had summoned Advaita Ācārya through Śrīrāma Paṇḍita, Acyutānanda had accompanied Him to Nabadwip.

Acyutānanda also witnessed the Lord's punishment of his father for teaching impersonalism. Śrīla Bhakti Siddhānta Sarasvatī Gosvāmī Ṭhākura writes the following in his *Anubhāṣya*: "Śrī Acyutā was the Lord's devotee from childhood. There is no information on whether Acyutānanda ever married, but he is described as the foremost of Advaita Ācārya's disciples. On the other hand, in Yadunandana Dāsa's book describing the disciples of Gadādhara Paṇḍita Gosvāmī, *Śākhānirṇayāmṛta*, it is said that Acyutānanda was a disciple and branch of Gadādhara Paṇḍita. The passage there is as follows:

mahārasāmṛtānandam
acyutānanda-nāmakam
gadādharaṁ-priyatamaṁ
śrīmad-advaita-nandanam

"[I offer obeisances to] Advaita Ācārya's son named Acyutānanda, who takes great joy in the ocean of nectarean sacred rapture. He is Gadādhara's dearest disciple."

ACYUTĀNANDA IN PURI

Near the end of Mahāprabhu's life, Gadādhara Paṇḍita remained permanently in Jagannatha Puri. Acyutānanda and Advaita Ācārya's other worthy sons also came to stay in Puri to be near Him.

"Acyutānanda, the son of Advaita Ācārya, lived in Jagannatha Puri, taking shelter of Lord

Caitanya Mahāprabhu." (*Caitanya Caritāmṛta* 1.10.150)

Acyutānanda came to Puri every year to celebrate the Rathayātrā festival, during which he danced in the sixth *kīrtana* group which came from Shantipur,(*Caitanya Caritāmṛta* 2.13.45). He also participated as a dancer in the *beṛā-saṅkīrtana*, when Mahāprabhu danced in front of Lord Jagannātha.

"The *kīrtana* around the temple started, and the seven groups began to sing. In each of the seven groups, one devotee was the designated dancer: Advaita Ācārya, Nityānanda Prabhu, Vakreśvara, Acyutānanda, Śrīvāsa Paṇḍita, Satyarāja Khān, and Narahari Dāsa. The Lord wandered from group to group, but all the devotees thought that He was with them alone." (*Caitanya Caritāmṛta* 3.10.58-61)

Acyutānanda also participated in the cleaning of the Guṇḍicā temple. When Lord Jagannātha was in the Guṇḍicā temple, Mahāprabhu would go there with the devotees to see Him after His morning bath. They would go three times a day and perform *saṅkīrtana* in the Guṇḍicā temple courtyard. At the Lord's behest, either Advaita Ācārya, Nityānanda Prabhu, Vakreśvara Paṇḍita, Acyutānanda, Haridāsa Ṭhākura or other devotees would dance.

"After bathing in the morning, the Lord would go to see Lord Jagannātha, taking the devotees and dancing in *saṅkīrtana*. He would sometimes make Advaita Ācārya dance, sometimes Nityānanda Prabhu, sometimes Haridāsa, sometimes Acyutānanda, sometimes Vakreśvara and sometimes other devotees. The Lord performed *saṅkīrtana* three times a day in the courtyard of the Guṇḍicā temple." (*Caitanya Caritāmṛta* 2.14.70-2)

According to Narahari Cakravartī's *Narottama-vilāsa*, Acyutānanda remained in Puri until Mahāprabhu's disappearance, after which he spent the rest of his life living at the family home in Shantipur. He also participated in the Khetari festival.

Śrī Rāghava Paṇḍita

dhaniṣṭhā bhakṣya-sāmagrīṁ
kṛṣṇāyādād vraje'mitām
saiva sāmpratam gaurāṅga-
priyo rāghava-paṇḍitaḥ
guṇamālā vraje yāsīd
damayantī tu tat-svasā

"The *gopī* Dhaniṣṭhā, who brought unlimited amounts of food to Kṛṣṇa in Vraja, has now become Gaurāṅga's dear servant Rāghava Paṇḍita. His sister Damayantī was Guṇamālā in Kṛṣṇa *līlā*." (*Gaura-gaṇoddeśa-dīpikā* 166-7)

In Kṛṣṇa *līlā*, Dhaniṣṭhā Devī would take Kṛṣṇa's *prasāda* to Rādhārāṇī on Yaśodā Mātā's order. Rādhārāṇī would then lovingly eat the *prasāda*. Bhaktivinoda describes this in his *bhoga ārati*:

yaśomati ājñā peye dhaniṣṭhā ānīta
śrī-kṛṣṇa-prasād rādhā bhuñje haye prīta

Mahāprabhu, who was none other than Nanda-nandana Kṛṣṇa, similarly accepted the food offerings made by Dhaniṣṭhā's *avatāra*, Rāghava Paṇḍita, being absorbed in the mood of Rādhārāṇī.

MAHĀPRABHU RESIDES PERMANENTLY IN RĀGHAVA'S HOUSE

Rāghava Paṇḍita's home was in the town of Panihati. Panihati is on the bank of the

Ganges, one mile east of the Sodpur station, which is on the Eastern Railway line north of Sealdah. Kṛṣṇadāsa Kavirāja Gosvāmī has written that Mahāprabhu was a permanent resident in the house of Rāghava Paṇḍita.

The Lord's manifestations took place in the home of Śacī, during Nityānanda Prabhu's dancing, in Śrīvāsa' *kīrtana*, and in the house of Rāghava Paṇḍita always. It is the Lord's nature to be attracted by His devotee's love. (*Caitanya Caritāmṛta* 3.2.34-5)

Vṛndāvana Dāsa Ṭhākura's biography of the Lord indicates clearly how dear Rāghava Paṇḍita was to Mahāprabhu. When Rāghava saw the Lord of his life coming from Śrīvāsa' house in Kumarahatta toward his own home he fell down at His feet, overcome by love.

When the Lord of Vaikuṇṭha saw Rāghava Paṇḍita's devotion, He blessed him with a look of favor. The Lord said, "I have come to Rāghava's house and forgotten all distress simply by seeing him. I feel the same pleasure coming here as I do by taking a refreshing bath in the Ganges." (*Caitanya Bhāgavata* 3.5.81-3)

The Lord often told Rāghava Paṇḍita to cook for Him because He enjoyed accepting his preparations, imbued as they were with deep devotion. Rāghava Paṇḍita cooked several items and fed the Lord with great enthusiasm. Balarāma's other form, Nityānanda Prabhu, would also come to eat at Rāghava Paṇḍita's house with his companions and all would praise his cooking. Mahāprabhu especially enjoyed his *śāka* (spinach).

While the Lord was there, Gadādhara Dāsa, Purundara Paṇḍita, Paramesvarī Dāsa, Raghunātha Vaidya and other great Vaiṣṇavas came to Rāghava Paṇḍita's house in Panihati in accordance with His desire. The Lord took Rāghava Paṇḍita aside in order to explain to him His oneness with Nityānanda Prabhu. Mahāprabhu once told Makaradhvaja Kara that service to Rāghava Paṇḍita was the same as service to Himself.

RĀGHAVERA JHĀLI

Rāghavera jhāli, or "Rāghava's bags," were filled with various preparations for the entire year that his sister Damayantī made for Mahāprabhu. They have been mentioned in Abhirāma Dāsa Ṭhākura's *Pāṭa-paryaṭana* and in the *Caitanya Caritāmṛta*.

"Rāghava and Damayantī lived in Panihati. They were famous for the bags of food known as *Rāghavera jhāli*." (*Pāṭa-paryaṭana*)

"Rāghava Paṇḍita, Mahāprabhu's primary follower, is the Lord's seventh branch. An important sub-branch, Makaradhvaja Kara, proceeded from him. His sister Damayantī was the Lord's dear servant. Throughout the year she gathered various ingredients for the Lord's bhoga. Rāghava filled bags with the foods Damayantī prepared and secretly carried them to Puri for the Lord. The Lord then ate these gifts of food for an entire year. Those bags are still celebrated as *Rāghavera jhāli*."(*Caitanya Caritāmṛta* 1.10.24-27)

"The generous Rāghava Paṇḍita, in whose house Mahāprabhu secretly stayed, also went with them." (*Caitanya Bhāgavata* 3.8.32)

Kṛṣṇadāsa Kavirāja Gosvāmī writes a complete description of these bags in his *Caitanya Caritāmṛta* (*Antya-līla*, Chapter 10). Kṛṣṇa's devotees in Vraja have no sense of awe and reverence in their transcendental pure love to the Lord. Damayantī would prepare *śuktā* for the Lord because she worried that He might have problems with His digestion. Mahāprabhu was overjoyed to receive these preparations because they were offered with such natural affection.

"Rāghava Paṇḍita came with bags full of condiments prepared very nicely by his sister, Damayantī. Damayantī made a variety of unparalleled culinary concoctions suitable for the Lord. The Lord would then enjoy them for the entire year that followed. Since Caitanya Mahāprabhu is the Supreme Lord, He takes the spirit in which things are done, accepting the love in which a gift is given. He therefore derived great pleasure even from the dried bitter leaves of *śuktā* and from *kāśandi* (mustard sauce). Because of her natural love for Mahāprabhu, Damayantī considered Him to be an ordinary human being and therefore worried that He might become sick from overeating and get dysentery. She prepared *śuktā* for Him, since it diminishes the mucus that accumulates in the digestive system and causes dysentery. Damayantī's affectionate attitude brought great pleasure to the Lord." (*Caitanya Caritāmṛta* 3.10.13,14,18-20)

"Makaradhvaja Kara, a *kāyastha* who also lived in Panihati, was Rāghava Paṇḍita's initiated disciple. It was he who annually carried to Puri the bags of food that his spiritual master prepared for the Lord. He was named the *munsib*, or superintendent, of these bags." (*Caitanya Caritāmṛta* 3.10.40).

RĀGHAVA PAṆḌITA'S STRICT CLEANLINESS

To His entourage in Puri, Mahāprabhu joyfully praised the extent of Rāghava Paṇḍita's devotion, especially talking about his coconut offerings. Though Rāghava Paṇḍita owned an orchard with hundreds of coconut trees, he would have more expensive coconuts brought from afar in order to offer its water and pulp to the Lord. Mahāprabhu happily accepted them.

Rāghava Paṇḍita never offered anything to the Lord that was not pure and not of the highest quality. Paying high prices for the best possible produce, he had mangoes, jackfruit, bananas and other fruit brought from distant villages to be offered to Mahāprabhu. One day a servant touched the coconut offering after his hand had brushed against the doorframe. Rāghava worried that dust from people's feet had contaminated the foodstuffs. Thus, he rejected them as unsuitable for the offering and threw them away.

Should anyone criticize Rāghava Paṇḍita for throwing fruit away, Śrīla Bhakti Siddhānta Sarasvatī Gosvāmī Ṭhākura has warned, "Rāghava Paṇḍita was an eternally perfected servant of Kṛṣṇa and not some person with an obsessive-compulsive neurosis about cleanliness. Nor was he a low-level devotee who artificially projected transcendental qualities on matter. He served the object of his worship without the slightest hint of any materialistic attitude, completely absorbed in a transcendental mood of service." (*Anubhāṣya*, *Caitanya Caritāmṛta* 2.14.83)

NITYĀNANDA VISITS PANIHATI

Following the order of Mahāprabhu, Nityānanda Prabhu along with his associates left Puri to preach pure devotion in Bengal. While wandering through the Ganges valley, Nitāi was attracted by Rāghava Paṇḍita's pure devotional attitude and came to his house in Panihati. Along with Him came the three Ghoṣa brothers, Govinda, Mādhava and Vāsudeva, who were known for their abilities as *kīrtanīyas*. When they started singing, Nityānanda Prabhu fell into a trance-like state and started to dance. When He had finished dancing, He sat on the deities' altar; Nityānanda Prabhu's entourage and Rāghava Paṇḍita performed an elaborate *abhiṣeka* ceremony to honor Him. After the bathing ceremony, they dressed and garlanded Him, whereupon Nityānanda Prabhu sat down again on the deities' throne while Rāghava Paṇḍita held the parasol.

At this moment, a miraculous event occurred. Nityānanda Prabhu, still in a trance-like state, ordered Rāghava Paṇḍita to quickly bring him a garland of *kadamba* flowers. Rāghava answered that *kadamba* trees were not yet in flower. Nityānanda Prabhu told him to look around the grounds of his house and he would find the flowers. As Rāghava searched, he was amazed to find *kadamba* flowers blossoming on a lime tree. He quickly picked the flowers and made a garland, which he placed around Nityānanda Prabhu's neck.

A few moments later, the house was filled with the fragrance of *damanaka* flowers. Nityānanda Prabhu said that Mahāprabhu Himself had come from Puri wearing a *damanaka* garland to hear the *kīrtana*. Śrī Narahari Cakravartī Ṭhākura mentions this dance and *kīrtana* in his *Bhakti-ratnākara*:

"First Nityānanda Prabhu came to Panihati with His associates. Rāghava Paṇḍita, Makaradhvaja Kara and the other devotees of the village were overjoyed to see them. Who can describe the wonderful dancing and *kīrtana* that took place in Rāghava Paṇḍita's house?" (*Bhakti-ratnākara* 12.3645-7)

Nityānanda Prabhu came to Panihati along with Rāma Dāsa and Gadādhara Dāsa, where He first visited Rāghava Paṇḍita's house. The *kīrtana* that they began there filled the entire universe with transcendental joy. Panihati is the birthplace of the great devotee Rāghava Paṇḍita. There is no limit to the glories of a great devotee's birthplace." (*Bhakti-ratnākara* 8.156-8)

CIḌĀ-DADHI MAHOTSAVA

While Nityānanda Prabhu was there in Panihati, He ordered Raghunātha Dāsa Gosvāmī to put on a feast of chipped rice and yogurt for His entourage. Rāghava Paṇḍita also participated by contributing various foods that had not been contaminated by the touch of cooked rice. He thus witnesed, in a mood of great amazement, Nityānanda Prabhu's *līlā* of picnicking by the riverbank. After resting in the afternoon by the Ganges, Nityānanda Prabhu went and spent the evening at Rāghava Paṇḍita's house in *kīrtana* and dance. Mahāprabhu Himself manifested there, being attracted by Nityānanda Prabhu's dancing. In order to reveal the extent of Rāghava Paṇḍita's good fortune, Mahāprabhu and Nityānanda Prabhu sat down together and with great satisfaction accepted his offerings of fine rice and various vegetable preparations, as well as cakes and sweet rice, all of which were like the nectar of the gods. Overcome with affection for Raghunātha Dāsa, Rāghava Paṇḍita gave him Mahāprabhu's remnants.

On occasion, Rāghava Paṇḍita visited Puri, where he participated with Mahāprabhu in the cleaning of the Guṇḍicā temple, the Rathayātrā festival, water sports in the Indradyumna Sarovara, and many others. Among the seven groups that performed *kīrtana* in front of Jagannātha's cart, Rāghava Paṇḍita sang in the chorus with the first group of singers, who were led by Svarūpa Dāmodara and in which Advaita Ācārya was the principal dancer.

Śrīla Bhakti Siddhānta Sarasvatī Gosvāmī Ṭhākura has written a few words about Rāghava Paṇḍita's *samādhi*: "A high platform was built over Rāghava Paṇḍita's *samādhi* and it is now overgrown with vines. To the north of the *samādhi* is a broken-down building in which his Madana Mohana deities are present, but much neglected. The service is managed by the principal landlord of Panihati, named Śivacandra Rāya Caudhurī." (*Anubhāṣya, Caitanya Caritāmṛta* 1.10.24). Śrīla Prabhupāda wrote these lines in 1932. Sixty years later, it appears that the situation has changed. A new temple and residential building have now been constructed on the site of Rāghava Paṇḍita's home.

Śrī Kālī Dāsa & Jhāru Ṭhākura

pulinda-tanayā mallī kālidāso'dhunābhavat

"Kālī Dāsa was previously the tribal girl named Mallī in Vraja." (*Gaura-gaṇoddeśa-dīpikā* 190)

Mahāprabhu's devotee Kālī Dāsa appeared in a *kāyastha* family. His home was in the village of Bheda, or Bhaduwa. This village is about three miles south of Raghunātha Dāsa Gosvāmī's birthplace in Saptagram Krishnapur (in the Hoogly district) and one mile west of the present-day Bandel Junction train station. Jharu Ṭhākura, who appeared in a sweeper caste (*bhuṅi-mālī*), lived in the same village. These places are served by the Devanandapura post office. Kālī Dāsa's deities used to be worshipped in Sankhanagar village, but they have since been moved to Triveni. Jhāru Ṭhākura's deity was named Madana Gopāla and is still being worshipped in Bhaduwa.

Kṛṣṇadāsa Kavirāja Gosvāmī has glorified these two devotees in his *Caitanya Caritāmṛta*, in the sixteenth chapter of the *Antya-līlā*. There we learn that Kālī Dāsa was related to Raghunātha Dāsa Gosvāmī as a distant uncle.

"He was related to Raghunātha Dāsa as an uncle, and he made a vow of eating the remnants of the Vaiṣṇavas throughout his life." (*Caitanya Caritāmṛta* 3.16.8)

KĀLĪ DĀSA' DEVOTION TO THE REMNANTS OF THE DEVOTEES

Kālī Dāsa was a great devotee who constantly chanted the Holy Names of Kṛṣṇa. He used the words "Hare Kṛṣṇa" throughout all his activities. His devotion to eating the remnants of the Vaiṣṇavas resulted in his receiving extraordinary blessings from Śrī Caitanya Mahāprabhu. The Lord gives so much mercy to anyone who has faith in the Vaiṣṇavas and eats their remnants that He has nothing left to give.

"Therefore, set aside your shame and disgust and eat the Vaiṣṇavas' remnants, for by so doing you will be able to fulfill all your desires. The remnants of Kṛṣṇa's food are called *mahā-prasāda*, but the remnants of the devotee are given the name *mahā-mahā-prasāda*. The dust of a devotee's feet, the water that has washed his feet, and the remnants of his food are three very powerful aids to spiritual practice. All revealed scriptures loudly declare again and again that one can attain the supreme goal of ecstatic love for Kṛṣṇa through the grace of these three substances. So, my dear devotees, please listen to me, for I insist on this point: keep faith in these three substances and render service to them with complete faith. Through these three substances, you will taste the joy of sacred love which is found in the Holy Name of Kṛṣṇa and you will win Kṛṣṇa's pleasure. This has been proved by the experience of Kālī Dāsa. (*Caitanya Caritāmṛta* 3.16.58-63)

While living in Bengal, Kālī Dāsa ate the remnants of all devotees, without taking their caste status into consideration. He would go to their houses with gifts of the finest foodstuffs. After they had finished eating, he would ask for their remnants. If any of them were unwilling to give him their remnants, he would take them without their knowledge. He would hide and wait for them to throw away the leaf-plates on which they had eaten and lick them clean.

KĀLĪ DĀSA VISITS JHĀRU ṬHĀKURA

All Vaiṣṇavas are worshipable, regardless of the caste in which they have been born. A Vaiṣṇava is beyond the material qualities and thus is not to be identified with his nationality or caste. Anyone who makes a judgment of a devotee on the basis of caste is said to have a hellish mentality. Though Jhāru Ṭhākura was born into the Bhuṅi-mālī caste, he was a great devotee.

One day, Kālī Dāsa went to Jhāru Ṭhākura's house and paid him and his wife obeisances. He then made them a gift of ripe, sweet mangoes. Jhāru Ṭhākura recognized Kālī Dāsa to be a guest of the highest order. He showed him the appropriate respect and said, "Dear sir, I am of a low caste. Please let me know how I can serve you. Just say the word and I will arrange for food to be cooked for you in a *brāhmaṇa*'s house. If you take *prasāda* there, I will consider myself most fortunate."

Kālī Dāsa recognized Jhāru Ṭhākura's humility as being appropriate to a Vaiṣṇava and said, "I am extremely fallen. It is only as a result of great good fortune that I have been able to meet you today. If you would only be so kind, please place the dust of your feet on my head."

Jhāru Ṭhākura was embarrassed and felt uneasy. Kālī Dāsa recited a few verses that glorify the devotees of the Lord:

na me 'bhaktaś caturvedī
madbhaktaḥ śvapacaḥ priyaḥ
tasmai deyaṁ tato grāhyaṁ
sa ca pūjyo yathā hy aham

"A scholar learned in the four Vedas is not dear to Me if he is not My devotee, whereas someone born as a dog-eater who is devoted to Me is very dear to Me. All respect should be given to such a person, and one should accept his gifts, for such a devotee is as worshipable as I am." (*Hari-bhakti-vilāsa* 10.29, *Caitanya Caritāmṛta* 3.16.25)

viprād dvi-ṣaḍ-guṇa-yutād aravindanābha
pādāravinda-vimukhāt śvapacaṁ variṣṭham
manye tad-arpita-mano-vacanehitārtha
prāṇaṁ punāti sa kulaṁ na tu bhūrimānaḥ

A person born in a *brāhmaṇa* family and possessing all twelve brahminical qualities, but averse to the lotus-naveled Lord Kṛṣṇa's lotus feet, is inferior to a dog-eater who has dedicated his mind, words, activities, wealth and life to the service of the Lord. Such a person purifies not only his own being but that of his entire family, whereas one who is proud of his qualifications cannot purify anything." (*Śrīmad Bhāgavatam* 7.9.10, *Caitanya Caritāmṛta* 3.16.26)

aho bata śvapaco'to garīyān

yaj-jihvāgre vartate nāma tubhyam
tepus tapas te juhuvuḥ sasnur āryā
brahmānūcur nāma gṛṇanti ye te

"How wonderful it is! Even a dog-eater who always keeps Your Holy Name on his tongue is greater than a *brāhmaṇa*! Despite his low caste, anyone who chants Your names is understood to have performed all kinds of austerities and the great Vedic sacrifices, to have studied all the Vedas, and to have bathed in all the holy places of pilgrimage. Such people belong to the truly noble class of man." (*Śrīmad Bhāgavatam* 3.33.7, *Caitanya Caritāmṛta* 3.16.27).

Though Jhāru Ṭhākura accepted the truth of these scriptural statements, he humbly stated that they were not applicable to him. Kālī Dāsa respectfully paid his obeisances and withdrew, and Jhāru Ṭhākura politely followed him a short distance before returning to his home. Kālī Dāsa took this opportunity to take the dust from the Jhāru Ṭhākura's footprints and smeared it over his entire body. Desiring to take the Ṭhākura's remnants, he then hid not far from his house.

When Jhāru Ṭhākura entered his house, he placed the mangoes in a banana-bark bowl and mentally offered them to Kṛṣṇa. His wife then took the mango *prasāda* from the bowl and gave it to her husband. Jhāru Ṭhākura ate the mangoes, and after sucking the seeds, placed them back in the bowl. She, being a chaste and devoted wife, took his remnants and then took the mango seeds and skins and threw the bowl into the refuse pit. When she had gone, Kālī Dāsa came and sucked on the seeds and even licked the outside of the skins. As he tasted the remnants of the Vaiṣṇavas, Kālī Dāsa was overwhelmed with ecstatic symptoms.

This, then, was Kālī Dāsa's procedure as he paid obeisances to all the Vaiṣṇavas in Bengal and ate their food remnants.

KĀLĪ DĀSA RECEIVES MAHĀPRABHU'S MERCY IN PURI

Every year, the Bengali devotees went to Puri to visit Mahāprabhu. Kālī Dāsa went in the second year of this institution. As the Supersoul, the Lord knew of Kālī Dāsa's dedication to the devotees' remnants, and so He bestowed profuse blessings upon him. When Mahāprabhu went on His daily visit to the Lord Jagannātha temple, He would be accompanied by Govinda, who carried his *kamaṇḍalu* (water pot). Mahāprabhu would wash His feet before entering the temple, and the water would run off into a pool situated at the bottom of the twenty-two steps at the northern entrance at the Siṁha Dvāra. Mahāprabhu gave Govinda the strict order to not allow anyone to touch the water that had washed His feet. Everyone knew this, so no one dared to make the attempt. Only a few intimate devotees found ways to get some of this holy liquid.

One day, as Mahāprabhu was washing His feet as usual, Kālī Dāsa came there and stretched out his hand to take some of the water. He drank not once, not twice, but three times as Mahāprabhu looked on. The Lord only stopped him when he cupped his hands for the fourth time.

"The all-knowing Supreme Lord, Caitanya Mahāprabhu, knew of the faith that Kālī Dāsa had in the Vaiṣṇavas. Happy with him for this great virtue, He allowed him to win a blessing unavailable to anyone else." (*Caitanya Caritāmṛta* 3.16.48-9)

After visiting Lord Jagannātha, Mahāprabhu returned to Kāśī Miśra's house to take His midday meal, Kālī Dāsa sat outside the door, hoping to receive some of the Lord's remnants. The Lord knew of his desire, and after He had finished eating, He signaled Govinda to bring him His remnants.

"This is the wonderful result of eating Vaiṣṇavas' remnants: through so doing, Kālī Dāsa attained Caitanya Mahāprabhu's supreme mercy. Therefore, set aside your shame and disgust and eat the Vaiṣṇavas' remnants, for by so doing you will be able to fulfill all your desires." (*Caitanya Caritāmṛta* 3.16.57-8)

Śrī Pradyumna Brahmacārī (Śrī Nṛsiṁhānanda)

āveśaś ca tathā jñeyo miśre pradyumna-sañjñake

"The Lord's *āveśa* manifestation took place in Pradyumna Miśra." (*Gaura-gaṇoddeśa-dīpikā* 74)

Śrīla Bhakti Siddhānta Sarasvatī Gosvāmī Ṭhākura has quoted the above verse in connection with Pradyumna Brahmacārī and not for the Odishan Pradyumna Miśra (who will be described later in this book). The *Gauḍīya Vaiṣṇava Abhidhāna* has also taken the same position, stating that Pradyumna Brahmacārī was an *āveśa* of Gaurāṅga.

THE LORD'S ĀVIRBHĀVA

"The Lord delivered the fallen souls in some places by meeting them directly, and in other places by empowering a pure devotee. In still other places, He personally appeared, which was the case with Nṛsiṁhānanda Brahmacārī. It is the Supreme Lord's nature to declare, 'I shall deliver the people of the world.' " (*Caitanya Caritāmṛta* 3.2.4, 6)

THE NAME NṚSIṀHĀNANDA

Mahāprabhu gave Pradyumna Brahmacārī the epithet Nṛsiṁhānanda because of his absorption in the service of Nṛsiṁha. He is considered to be one of Caitanya's own branches. (*Caitanya Caritāmṛta* 1.10.35, 3.2.53)

"Pradyumna Brahmacārī considered himself to be the servant of Nṛsiṁha, for Nṛsiṁhadeva manifested Himself in his body. He remained by Mahāprabhu's side in the consciousness that Nṛsiṁha Himself had appeared in the form of a *sannyāsī*." (*Caitanya Bhāgavata* 3.3.286-7)

Vṛndāvana Dāsa Ṭhākura writes in the *Caitanya Bhāgavata* that Pradyumna Brahmacārī conversed directly with Nṛsiṁhadeva. This is mentioned particularly when Pradyumna Brahmacārī joined the company of devotees on the annual pilgrimage to Jagannatha Puri.

"Pradyumna Brahmacārī, who talked directly to Lord Nṛsiṁha, walked along as a part of the company of devotees." (*Caitanya Bhāgavata* 3.8.92)

All those people who think that the body of the Lord is a product of the material nature are atheists who have been bewildered by the Lord's illusory energy. They think that these accounts are tall stories they can criticize out of their false sense of being learned. Anyone who lacks faith in the Supreme Lord is an unfortunate beggar who remains deprived of the actual welfare, and who gains nothing but the birth and death that is the lot of the conditioned soul.

THE POWER OF PRADYUMNA'S MEDITATION

When Mahāprabhu took *sannyāsa* in Katwa, he made off for Vrindavan, but Nityānanda Prabhu tricked him into coming back to Shantipur on the banks of the Ganges.

Afterwards, the Lord continued to Puri in the company of Nityānanda Prabhu, Jagadānanda Paṇḍita, Mukunda Datta and Dāmodara Paṇḍita. Shortly thereafter, He left Puri on a pilgrimage through southern India. On His return from South India, He planned a trip to Vrindavan that would take Him on the route along the Ganges through Bengal. On this trip, He stopped at the house of Sārvabhauma Bhaṭṭācārya's brother, Vidyā Vācaspati, in Vidyanagar, delivered Devānanda Paṇḍita and Gopāla Capala from their offenses in Kuliya village, and then met Rūpa Gosvāmī and Sanātana Gosvāmīs in the village of Ramakeli.

As Mahāprabhu made this trip, Pradyumna Brahmacārī, in his meditation, visualized himself placing jewelled bricks on the road the Lord was following to make His journey more agreeable. When the Lord reached Kanair Natshala, about 202 miles from Kolkata in the Santal Paragana in the Dumka district of Bihar state, five miles from the town of Rajmahal, Pradyumna could not prepare the road farther as his meditation suddenly broke. He was immediately able to understand that the Lord would only go as far as Kanair Natshala on this occasion and no farther.

It is said that mental service like that performed by Nṛsiṁha Brahmacārī in his meditation is superior to service performed with actual ingredients. There is evidence of this in *Purāṇas*, where the example of a poor *brāhmaṇa* from Pratishthanpur who attained the association of Nārāyaṇa in Vaikuṇṭha as a result of mental service, or *mānasī sevā*, is mentioned.

PRADYUMNA BRINGS THE LORD TO KUMARAHATTA

On one occasion, Mahāprabhu was attracted by Nṛsiṁhānanda's love to come to Kumarahatta and to appear in the house of Śivānanda Sena. This story has been told beautifully by Kṛṣṇadāsa Kavirāja Gosvāmī in the second chapter of the *Antya-līlā* of his *Caitanya Caritāmṛta*.

One year, as Śivānanda Sena's nephew Śrīkānta Sena left Puri, Mahāprabhu told him to convey the message to the Bengali devotees that there was no need for them to come to Puri that year, for He Himself would be visiting Bengal in the month of Pauṣa (December-January). When Śrīkānta came with this news, all the devotees were jubilant in expectation of the Lord's visit. But when the month of Pauṣa had almost come to an end and there was no sign of Mahāprabhu, Śivānanda Sena, Jagadānanda Paṇḍita and the others who had been waiting anxiously were disheartened by not seeing Him.

At that time, Nṛsiṁhānanda happened by and asked everyone the reason for their unhappiness. When he heard that they were disappointed that the Lord had not come, he assured them that he would make Mahāprabhu appear there on the third day. Since Śivānanda and Jagadānanda Paṇḍita knew Nṛsiṁhānanda's spiritual powers, they believed him.

Nṛsiṁhānanda sat down and stayed absorbed in meditation for two days, after which he told Śivānanda that Mahāprabhu had arrived in Panihati and that by noon of the next day He would be in Śivānanda's house. He ordered Śivānanda Sena to supply him with the ingredients for a feast in honor of the Lord. He personally started cooking early in the morning and made a large variety of preparations that he distributed onto three plates to make offerings to Lord Jagannātha, Nṛsiṁhadeva and Mahāprabhu. As soon as he sat down in meditation for the offerings,

Mahāprabhu personally appeared and ate all three plates, leaving no remnants.

Although Nṛsiṁhānanda was overjoyed to see the Lord accept his offerings, he made a pretence of disappointment. He said that since Mahāprabhu and Lord Jagannātha are ontologically nondifferent, there was no fault in His eating the plate set out for Lord Jagannātha. But why had He taken the offering intended for Nṛsiṁha? "Nṛsiṁhadeva has fasted today," He said. Indeed, the Lord performed this pastime in order to show that He is not different from Lord Jagannātha or Nṛsiṁhadeva.

After eating, Mahāprabhu left for Panihati. Nṛsiṁhānanda cried out in distress, causing Śivānanda to inquire the cause of his troubles. Nṛsiṁhānanda answered that the Lord had alone eaten all three plates, leaving Lord Jagannātha and Nṛsiṁhadeva to fast. Śivānanda Sena had some doubts, but on his request provided him with foodstuffs to prepare another offering. The *brahmacārī* cooked once again and made an offering to Nṛsiṁhadeva.

The next year, when Śivānanda Sena went with the Bengali devotees to Puri, everyone was duly astonished to hear the Lord Himself volunteer the information that He had been to Śivānanda's house in the month of Pauṣa and had eaten the delicious offerings made by Nṛsiṁhānanda.

"One day, the Lord was engaged in conversation in the presence of all the devotees and suddenly began to praise Nṛsiṁhānanda's qualities. He said, 'Last year in the month of Pauṣa, Nṛsiṁhānanda gave Me delicious sweetmeats and vegetables such as I had never eaten.' Hearing this, all the devotees were struck with wonder, and Śivānanda was finally convinced that the incident was true." (*Caitanya Caritāmṛta* 3.2.76-78)

Śrī Gadādhara Dāsa

rādhā-vibhūti-rūpā yā chandrakāntiḥ purā sthitā
sādya gaurāṅga-nikaṭe dāsa-vaṁśyo gadādharaḥ
pūrṇānandā vraje yāsīd baladeva-priyāgraṇīḥ
sāpi kārya-vaśād eva prāviśat taṁ gadādharaṁ

"She who during Kṛṣṇa's *avatāra* was Candrakānti, the manifestation of Rādhārāṇī's ornaments, has become Gadādhara Dāsa by Gaurāṅga's side. Balarāma's beloved Pūrṇānandā has also entered into him for some special purpose." (*Gaura-gaṇoddeśa-dīpikā* 154-155)

Śrīla Bhakti Siddhānta Sarasvatī Gosvāmī Prabhupāda has commented on Gadādhara Dāsa's identity in Kṛṣṇa *līlā*: "He is Śrīmatī Rādhārāṇī's effulgence. Just as Śrīla Gadādhara Paṇḍita Gosvāmī is Śrīmatī Rādhārāṇī Herself, so Gadādhara Dāsa is an *avatāra* of Her bodily luster. In the Lord's *avatāra* as Kṛṣṇa with the emotions and bodily luster of Śrīmatī Rādhārāṇī, he is that bodily luster. In the *Gaura-gaṇoddeśa-dīpikā*, he is said to be the manifestation of Rādhā's opulence. He is counted amongst the followers of both Gaura and Nityānanda Prabhu. The followers of Gaura relish the mood of conjugal love while the followers of Nityānanda Prabhu are in the mood of pure devotional service in friendship. Although Gadādhara Dāsa was an associate of Nityānanda Prabhu, he was not in the mood of friendship as a cowherd boy but is in the conjugal mood. He established the temple of Gaurāṅga in Katwa." (*Anubhāṣya* to *Caitanya Caritāmṛta* 1.10.53)

Gadādhara Dāsa's home was in Eriyadaha, a village situated eight miles north of Kolkata on the banks of the Bhagirathi River. After Mahāprabhu's disappearance, he moved from Nabadwip to Katwa, and then later to Eriyadaha. In the *Gauḍīya Vaiṣṇava Abhidhāna*, it is said that Gadādhara Dāsa supervised Śacī Mātā and Viṣṇupriyā Devī's affairs. When they disappeared, he moved to Katwa, where he established the worship of the Gaurāṅga deity. The temple is currently known in Katwa as Mahaprabhu Bari.

Gadādhara Dāsa met with Mahāprabhu when the Lord was making His initial attempt to travel to Vrindavan by taking the route through Bengal, first stopping in Shantipur, then Kumarahatta and then Rāghava Paṇḍita's house in Panihati. Mahāprabhu affectionately placed His lotus feet on Gadādhara Dāsa's head:

"When Gadādhara Dāsa heard that Mahāprabhu had arrived at Rāghava Paṇḍita's house, he ran to see Him. Gadādhara Dāsa is extremely dear to Mahāprabhu; his body is charged with the joy of devotion. When the Lord saw the pious Gadādhara, He lifted His feet and placed them on his head." (*Caitanya Bhāgavata* 3.5.92-4)

When Mahāprabhu sent Nityānanda Prabhu from Puri to Bengal to distribute divine love, Gadādhara Dāsa, Rāma Dāsa, Kṛṣṇadāsa Paṇḍita, Parameśvarī Dāsa, Purandara Paṇḍita, Raghunātha Vaidya and others accompanied Him. On the road from Nilachal, Nityānanda Prabhu and His associates made various extraordinary displays of divine love. Gadādhara Dāsa, the eternal resident of Vraja, took on the transcendental mood of Śrīmatī Rādhārāṇī, and in the ecstasy of a cowherd girl began to laugh and shout, "Yogurt for sale! Yogurt for sale! Does anyone want to buy some yogurt?" In the mood of a cowherd boy, Abhirāma Dāsa Ṭhākura stood for nine hours in the threefold bending form. Kṛṣṇadāsa and Parameśvarī Dāsa also took the mood of cowherd boys, shouting "*Hoi! Hoi!*" as though they were herding the cattle. Purandara Paṇḍita climbed up a tree and shouted, "I am Aṅgada!" and then jumped down to the ground.

"The mood of Rādhikā descended on Gadādhara Dāsa. He began to call, 'Who will buy yogurt?' and burst out laughing. Kṛṣṇadāsa and Parameśvarī Dāsa both shouted '*Hoi! Hoi!*' in the spirit of the cowherd boys." (*Caitanya Bhāgavata* 3.5.238, 240)

When Nityānanda Prabhu arrived in Bengal, He visited villages on both banks of the Ganges. Gadādhara Dāsa was experiencing *gopī-bhāva* and took a jug full of Ganges water and called out to everyone, "Milk! Who wants to buy milk?" When Nityānanda Prabhu saw Gadādhara Dāsa's *bhāva*, He took the Gopāla deity from his house and danced, holding the deity to His chest.

"In the mood of a *gopī*, Gadādhara Dāsa had no consciousness of external reality. He constantly referred to himself as a *gopī*." (*Caitanya Bhāgavata* 3.5.381)

Śrīla Bhakti Siddhānta Sarasvatī Gosvāmī Ṭhākura writes in his commentary to this verse that though Gadādhara Dāsa considered himself to be a *gopī*, he did not dress like a woman. His mood was expressed internally, and he did not make any artificial, external display.

One day, Nityānanda Prabhu was in the audience at a performance of Kṛṣṇa's *dāna-khaṇḍa-līlā* by Mādhavānanda Ghoṣa at the house of Gadādhara Dāsa, and He went into a deep trance. For this reason, Gadādhara's house is also known as the place of the *dāna-līlā*. The *dāna-līlā* is described elaborately in Rūpa Gosvāmī's *Dāna-keli-kaumudī*.

In Gadādhara Dāsa's village of Eriyadaha, there was a very powerful Kājī antagonistic to religion who hated the very sound of the congregational chanting of Kṛṣṇa's names. One day, Gadādhara Dāsa was in an ecstatic mood and walked right into the house of this Kājī, singing the Holy Names at the top of his voice. The Kājī was sitting there in the company of his inner circle. Gadādhara Dāsa ordered him to chant the Holy Names. The Kājī became very angry at the affront, but when he saw that Gadādhara Dāsa was in a trance-like state, he calmed down and asked him why he had come. Gadādhara Dāsa answered, "Caitanya Mahāprabhu and Nityānanda Prabhu have descended to this earth to make everyone chant the Holy Names. Only you have not yet done so, so I have come here to make you chant the name of Kṛṣṇa. If you chant the Holy Names, all your sins will be eradicated."

Although the Kājī was by nature cruel, he laughed and said, "All right, I will chant Kṛṣṇa's name tomorrow. Now go home." Gadādhara Dāsa danced jubilantly and said, "Why tomorrow? You have just uttered the name of Kṛṣṇa now! Now that you have taken the name of Hari, you will never again know any inauspiciousness!" (*Caitanya Bhāgavata* 3.5.409-10)

Gadādhara Dāsa thus converted the irascible Kājī through his divine power. This impossible task became possible because his body had become possessed by Kṛṣṇa.

"This is the glory of Gadādhara Dāsa, who has been counted as one of Caitanya Mahāprabhu's intimate associates. Just seeing him, who is constantly in a ecstatic devotional mood, erases all of one's sinful reactions." (*Caitanya Bhāgavata* 3.5.413, 727)

Kṛṣṇadāsa Kavirāja Gosvāmī has also written the following about Gadādhara Dāsa in the *Caitanya Caritāmṛta*:

"Śrī Rāma Dāsa and Śrī Gadādhara Dāsa were both devotees of Śrī Caitanya Mahāprabhu and stayed with Him. When the Lord ordered Nityānanda Prabhu to return to Bengal, he told both of them to accompany Him. Gadādhara Dāsa was always in an ecstatic state in the devotional mood of a *gopī*. Nityānanda Prabhu put on the *dāna-līlā* performance in his house." (*Caitanya Caritāmṛta* 1.11.13, 14, 17)

Gadādhara Dāsa was also present when Raghunātha Dāsa Gosvāmī put on the yogurt and chipped-rice festival in Panihati on Nityānanda Prabhu's order. Yadunandana Dāsa was Gadādhara Dāsa's disciple. This is stated in the *Bhakti-ratnākara*:

"Yadunandana Cakravartī was a very learned scholar whose guru and worshipable lord was Gadādhara Dāsa." (*Bhakti-ratnākara* 9.352)

Gadādhara Dāsa's disappearance day is on the eighth day of the waning moon (*kṛṣṇa aṣṭamī*) of the month of Kārtika. Śrīnivāsa Ācārya put on a huge festival on the occasion of Gadādhara Dāsa's disappearance day, in which many exalted Vaiṣṇavas participated. Like the one at Khetari, this festival was greatly renowned throughout the Vaiṣṇava community.

"What can I say about Kārtika *kṛṣṇa aṣṭamī*? My *prabhu* disappeared here on that day." (*Bhakti-ratnākara* 9.362)

Gadādhara Dāsa's *samādhi* tomb is situated on the grounds of the Mahāprabhu Bari temple in Katwa close to Keśava Bhāratī's *samādhi* tomb.

Śrīla Maheśa Paṇḍita

maheśa-paṇḍitaḥ śrīman-mahābāhur vraje sakhā

"In Vraja, Maheśa Paṇḍita is Kṛṣṇa's cowherd friend Mahābāhu." (*Gaura-gaṇoddeśa-dīpikā* 129)

Maheśa Paṇḍita is Mahābāhu Sakhā, one of the *dvādaśa-gopāla*, or twelve cowherd boys. His home (Sripat) was first situated in Masipur across the river from Jirat on the eastern bank of the Ganges. When Masipur fell into the river, the Sripat was moved to Beledanga near Sukhasagar. Here too, when the Sripat fell into the river it was moved, this time to its present location in Palpara. This last move took place in the Bengali year 1334, or 1927 A.D. Palpara is situated within the Pachanagar administrative block. Śrīla Bhakti Siddhānta Sarasvatī Gosvāmī Ṭhākura mentions in his commentary to *Caitanya Caritāmṛta* 1.11.32 that this final resting place for Maheśa Paṇḍita's Sripat is in Kathal Puli near Chakdah.

Maheśa Paṇḍita is considered to be a branch of both Nityānanda Prabhu and Caitanya Mahāprabhu. Some people say that he was the youngest brother of Jagadīśa Paṇḍita, whose Sripat is in Jashra. According to this opinion, there were three brothers in the family, Jagadīśa, Hiraṇya and Maheśa.

Maheśa Paṇḍita's Sripat is a small construction in the style of an ordinary residential building. It houses Gaura-Nityānanda Prabhu deities, as well as Śrī Gopīnātha, Madana Mohana, Rādhā Govinda and a *śālagrāma-śilā*. In front of the temple building is a memorial to Maheśa Paṇḍita, his *puṣpa-samādhi*.

Śrī Maheśa Paṇḍita participated in the Ciḍā-dadhi Mahotsava (the festival of chipped rice and yogurt) in Panihati, after which he followed Nityānanda Prabhu to Saptagram. He was present in Khardaha when Narottama Dāsa Ṭhākura came there to pay a visit. With great affection, Maheśa Paṇḍita bade farewell to Narottama Ṭhākura and became sad in his separation (*Bhakti-ratnākara* 8.220). Maheśa Paṇḍita, an associate of Nityānanda Prabhu, resembled Him in being extremely magnanimous and devoted to the salvation of all the fallen living beings. In his ecstasies of devotional love, he would dance madly.

"Maheśa Paṇḍita was a magnanimous cowherd boy of Vraja. In his love for Kṛṣṇa, he would dance to the sound of kettledrums like a madman." (*Caitanya Caritāmṛta* 1.11.32)

His name is also mentioned in *Caitanya Bhāgavata*; Vṛndāvana Dāsa Ṭhākura calls him a great soul, *parama-mahanta*. (*Caitanya Bhāgavata* 3.6).

His disappearance day is celebrated on the thirteenth day of the dark moon (*kṛṣṇa trayodaśi*) in the month of Pauṣa.

Śrī Gaurī Dāsa Paṇḍita

subalo yaḥ priya-śreṣṭhaḥ sa gaurīdāsa-paṇḍitaḥ

"In Vraja, Gaurī Dāsa Paṇḍita is Subala, one of the twelve *gopālas*. He is one of Nityānanda Prabhu's dearest associates." (*Gaura-gaṇoddeśa-dīpikā* 128)

"Gaurī Dāsa Paṇḍita was most fortunate. His body, mind and soul were all devoted to Nityānanda Prabhu." (*Caitanya Bhāgavata* 3.5.730)

GAURĪ DĀSA'S TEMPLE IN AMBIKA

Gaurī Dāsa's first residence was in the village known as Shaligram, not far from Muragacha. Later he moved to Ambika Kalna in the Burdwan district for longtime residence. There his Sripat is extremely well known. His father's name was Kaṁsāri Miśra. Kaṁsāri Miśra belonged to the Vātsa *gotra*, and their family name was Gośāla. Gaurī Dāsa was the fourth of six sons. His three older brothers were named Dāmodara, Jagannātha and Sūrya Dāsa. Sūrya Dāsa, whose title was Sarakhela, gave his two daughters, Vasudhā and Jāhnavā, in marriage to Nityānanda Prabhu. Gaurī Dāsa Paṇḍita's younger brothers were named Kṛṣṇadāsa Sarakhela and Nṛsiṁha Caitanya.

"Paṇḍita Sūrya Dāsa Sarakhela was a very magnanimous person. His younger brother was named Gaurī Dāsa. Gaurī Dāsa Paṇḍita took permission from his older brother before moving from Shaligram to Ambika. (*Bhakti-ratnākara* 7.330-1)

Gaurī Dāsa and his disciple Hṛdaya Caitanya left only a line of initiated disciples and not one of family descendant. According to the *Gauḍīya Vaiṣṇava Abhidhāna*, Gaurī Dāsa Paṇḍita and his wife, Bimalā Devī, had two sons, Balarāma and Raghunātha. Śrīla Bhakti Siddhānta Sarasvatī Gosvāmī Ṭhākura, however, did not accept this family connection due to the lack of authenticity. He has written as follows in his *Anubhāṣya:* "Gaurī Dāsa Paṇḍita's disciple was named Hṛdaya Caitanya Dāsa. His disciple was the son of Annapūrṇā Devī, Gopīramaṇa. It is the family descendants of this Gopīramaṇa who are the current owners of the Ambika Sripat." (*Anubhāṣya* to *Caitanya Caritāmṛta* 1.11.26)

The current temple at Ambika houses deities of Gaurī Dāsa, Rādhā-Kṛṣṇa, Gaura-Nityānanda, Jagannātha, Balarāma, and Sītā-Rāma. As one enters the temple grounds, there is a large tamarind tree. It is said that Mahāprabhu and Gaurī Dāsa met under this very tree. Other valuable items held in the temple are a paddle said to be used by Mahāprabhu Himself and a *Bhagavad-Gītā* said to have been hand-copied by the Lord.

Gauracandra, the Lord of lords, resides in the temple of Gaurī Dāsa in Ambika. Towards the north of Ambika is a place called Kalna; together they have become Ambika Kalna.

"One day Gaurāṅga crossed the Ganges from Shantipur to visit Ambika. He told Gaurī Dāsa Paṇḍita, 'I was in Shantipur, and from there I went to Harinadi village and took a boat to come here. I have brought one of the paddles with me – here, take it. Use it to take the fallen living beings across the river of material 'suffering.' So saying, the Lord embraced him." (*Bhakti-ratnākara* 7.333-6)

"Fortunate souls can still see the *Gita* that the Lord gave to Gaurī Dāsa, as well as the paddle, when they visit the deities in Ambika." (*Bhakti-ratnākara* 7.341)

Nityānanda Prabhu made no distinctions between those who were qualified or unqualified but simply gave Kṛṣṇa *prema* to everyone as though intoxicated. His intimate associate Gaurī Dāsa Paṇḍita similarly displayed a great power in preaching.

"Gaurī Dāsa possessed the highest order of loving devotion. He had a great ability to deliver and receive Kṛṣṇa *prema*. He surrendered everything he had, including his own clan, to

Nityānanda Prabhu and made Mahāprabhu and Nityānanda Prabhu the masters of his life and soul." (*Caitanya Caritāmṛta* 1.11.26-7)

Sūrya Dāsa Sarakhela's house and temple are also in Ambika, a little to the west of Gaurī Dāsa Paṇḍita's Sripat. Bhagavāna Dāsa Bābājī's *āśrama* is also a little farther west of there.

MAHĀPRABHU VISITS KALNA

A wonderful story is told about Gaurī Dāsa Paṇḍita in Ambika Kalna. It is said that on the day that Mahāprabhu paddled across the Ganges to come to visit Gaurī Dāsa, He sat under the tamarind tree in the courtyard. Gaurī Dāsa asked for Mahāprabhu to stay permanently with him in Ambika. In order to fulfill His devotee's desire, Mahāprabhu manifested His and Nityānanda Prabhu's deities from a nearby neem tree. It is also said that Nityānanda Prabhu was physically present when the deities were being carved.

When Mahāprabhu and Nityānanda Prabhu were about to leave, Gaurī Dāsa in deep mental anguish held Them back. Mahāprabhu calmed him by saying, "Nityānanda Prabhu and I are present here in person as well as in these deity forms. You can either tell the deities to go, or We can leave. You choose." Gaurī Dāsa chose the Gaura-Nitāi in person to stay and said that the deities could leave. So the deities walked away, and Gaura-Nitāi entered the temple room.

nāma vigraha svarūpa, tina eka-rūpa
tine bheda nāhi tina cidānanda-rūpa

"These three – the name, the deity form and the original form of the Lord – are all one. No distinction should be made between Them, for all three are of transcendental, spiritual nature." (*Caitanya Caritāmṛta* 2.17.131)

Subsequently, conquered by Gaurī Dāsa's love for Them, the deities would physically eat everything that he offered to Them.

Gaurī Dāsa Paṇḍita Gosvāmī disappeared in the month of Śrāvaṇa on the *śukla dvādaśī*, the twelfth day of the waxing moon. His *samādhi* is in Vrindavan.

"When Jāhnavā Devī saw Gaurī Dāsa Paṇḍita's *samādhi*, torrents of tears fell from her eyes, and she could do nothing to stop them." (*Bhakti-ratnākara* 11.259)

Śrī Abhirāma Ṭhākura (Śrī Rāma Dāsa)

Śrī Nityānanda Prabhu was Abhirāma Thakur's life and soul. He was Śrīdama, one among the twelve cowherd boys in Vraja.

purā śrīdāma-nāmāsīd abhirāmo'dhunā mahān
dvātriṁśatā janair eva vāhyaṁ kāṣṭham uvāha saḥ

"He who was previously known as Śrīdāma is today Abhirāma Ṭhākura. He picked up a piece of wood that took thirty-two men to lift." (*Gaura-gaṇoddeśa-dīpikā* 126)

Abhirāma Ṭhākura lived with his wife, Mālinī Devī, in the village of Khanakul Krishnanagar in the Hooghly district. Khana refers to the Dwarakeshwar River, *Kūla* means banks; thus, the village of Krishnanagar on the banks of the Dwarakeshwar River is also known as Khanakul Krishnanagar. At the doors of his temple stands a large *bakula* tree, and the place is popularly called Siddha-bakula Kuñja. This is the place where Abhirāma Ṭhākura first sat down when he arrived in the village. The Gopīnātha deity was found when digging for a pond first began. This pond goes by the name of Śrī Abhirāma Kuṇḍa. The temple also houses the deities of Vrajavallabha, Gopāla and a *śālagrāma-śilā*.

Śrī Abhirāma Ṭhākura was a very vigorous and powerful *ācārya*. He engaged in preaching on the orders of Lord Nityānanda Prabhu and saved many atheists and people opposed to the Vaiṣṇava religion.

"Abhirāma Gosvāmī possessed tremendous spiritual power. The atheists trembled whenever they saw him. He was intoxicated as though he had been possessed by Nityānanda Prabhu, and his enchanting mercies are famed throughout the world." (*Bhakti-ratnākara* 4.103-4)

"Abhirāma Dāsa was fully absorbed in the mood of friendship. He lifted a stick that contained sixteen knots and prepared a flute out of it." (*Caitanya Caritāmṛta* 1.10.116)

This *Caitanya Caritāmṛta* verse is making reference to the same piece of wood that according to the *Gaura-gaṇoddeśa-dīpikā* would have taken hundreds of people to pick it up. After Abhirāma Dāsa lifted it, he held it like a flute.

"He held in his hands a piece of wood that a hundred men could not move, in the way one holds a flute." (*Bhakti-ratnākara* 4.123)

The devotees were greatly astonished when they saw him perform such superhuman feats. According to one legend, whenever Abhirāma Ṭhākura paid his obeisances to a stone or statue, if it was not a Viṣṇu-śīlā or a consecrated deity, it would crack or be reduced to powder. Nondevotees were also unable to tolerate his *praṇāmas*. Nityānanda Prabhu's son Vīracandra Gosvāmī and Gaṅgāmātā Gosvāminī survived his obeisances, which confirmed their divinity. These things are written in *aṣṭakas* (eight-verse Sanskrit hymns) composed by Abhirāma Ṭhākura in their name.

Śrīla Abhirāma Ṭhākura possessed an amazing whip which he named Jaya-maṅgala. Anyone touched by this whip would immediately experience the transcendental ecstasies of *prema*. One day Śrīnivāsa Ācārya visited Abhirāma Ṭhākura, who touched the whip to the body of Śrīnivāsa Ācārya. Abhirāma's wife, Mālinī, stopped her husband from doing so again, saying that Śrīnivāsa was just a young lad who wouldn't be able to tolerate the effects of divine love. Nevertheless, Śrīnivāsa Ācārya was very dear to Abhirāma and received many blessings from him. Though not his initiated disciple, he was like a disciple to him. The Jaya-maṅgala whip is still held in a chest in Krishnanagar temple.

In the *Bhakti-ratnākara*, the following statement is also made:

"O Śrīnivāsa! How much more can I say? Abhirāma descended into this world in order to deliver it. Appearing in a *brāhmaṇa* family, he became a scholar in all the scriptures and an unequalled musician, not only in song and playing musical instruments, but in dance also. He married at Nityānanda Prabhu Balarāma's request. His wife, Mālinī, is also indescribably powerful." (*Bhakti-ratnākara* 4.105-8)

Many people say that the Bali Math in Puri was established by Abhirāma Ṭhākura. An annual festival is held in Khanakula Krishnanagar on his disappearance day, i.e., the Caitra *kṛṣṇa saptamī.*

Our *parama-guru*, Jagad-guru Śrīla Bhakti Siddhānta Sarasvatī Gosvāmī Prabhupāda, visited this site along with his associates when traveling on the *parikramā* of Śrī Gaura Maṇḍala. At that time, the devotees in charge of the temple greeted him with great hospitality and honored him and his followers with special treatment.

Śrī Parameśvara Dāsa Ṭhākura (Śrī Parameśvarī Dāsa)

nāmnārjunaḥ sakhā prāg yoḥ dāsaḥ parameśvaraḥ

"Parameśvara Dāsa Ṭhākura was previously Arjuna, one of Kṛṣṇa's twelve cowherd boyfriends." (*Gaura-gaṇoddeśa-dīpikā* 132)

Śrīla Parameśvarī Ṭhākura appeared in a Vaidya family. He made his home in Antpur, a village which was previously known as Bishkhali. His Sripat is close to the Antpur station on the Champādanga branch of the Howrah-Amta rail line and near the old Rādhā Govinda temple established by Kṛṣṇarāma Mitra, the late diwan (chief minister) of Burdwan's king, Tej Bahadur.

After the Lord took *sannyāsa* in Katwa, He headed for Vrindavan in a state of divine intoxication before being diverted to Advaita Ācārya's house in Shantipur by Nityānanda Prabhu. Śacī Mātā and the other devotees from Nabadwip all came to see the Lord there. At His mother's request, Mahāprabhu agreed to stay in Puri and took the path through Chatrabhoga to Nilachal in the company of Nityānanda Prabhu, Mukunda, Jagadānanda Paṇḍita and Dāmodara Paṇḍita.

The first time that the Lord wished to go to Vrindavan from Nilachal, He came through Bengal. Though He was eventually unsuccessful, He passed through Panihati, Kumarahatta, Kuliya, Ramakeli, Kanair Natshala, Shantipur before returning to Puri. When Nṛsiṁhānanda Brahmacārī heard that Mahāprabhu was going to Vrindavan, he meditated on the Lord's route, imagining a road of jewels as far as Kanair Natshala, when he realized that this was as far as the Lord would go and that He would not make it to Vrindavan this time. Thousands of people were accompanying the Lord at this time. When He arrived at Kanair Natshala, He remembered Sanātana Gosvāmī's advice:

"To go on pilgrimage with such a large company of devotees is not recommended." (*Caitanya Caritāmṛta* 2.1.224)

On His way back to Nilachal, Mahāprabhu stopped at Advaita's house in Shantipur. This time He was accompanied by Balabhadra Bhattācārya and Dāmodara Paṇḍita. When the Lord returned from Gaya, He also went as far as Kanair Natshala, where He had a vision of Muralīdhara Śrī Kṛṣṇa, who embraced Him before He disappeared. (*Caitanya Bhāgavata* 2.2.179-85) Once He returned to Nilachal, Mahāprabhu told Nityānanda Prabhu to go with Nityānanda' own associates to Bengal to deliver the lowborn, foolish and fallen people. Amongst His associates at that time were Śrī Rāma Dāsa, Gadādhara Dāsa, Raghunātha Vaidya, Kṛṣṇadāsa Paṇḍita, Parameśvarī Dāsa and Purandara Paṇḍita. While traveling with Nityānanda Prabhu, these devotees displayed various ecstatic moods. These are described in the *Caitanya Bhāgavata*:

"Kṛṣṇadāsa Paṇḍita, Parameśvarī Dāsa and Purandara Paṇḍita were all enthusiastic to join Nityānanda Prabhu. So all of His personal associates accompanied Him on this journey back to Bengal. Before starting off, Nityānanda Prabhu first empowered them by saturating them with Kṛṣṇa *prema*. They all completely forgot their external identities. There was no end to the varicty of ecstatic moods that manifested in each one of their bodies."(*Caitanya Bhāgavata* 3.5.232-5)

"Parameśvarī Dāsa and Kṛṣṇadāsa both shouted "*Hoi! Hoi!*" in the spirit of cowherd boys." (*Caitanya Bhāgavata* 3.5.240)

Parameśvarī Dāsa was one of the most important of Nityānanda Prabhu's companions; he appeared specifically to enrich His pastimes. Nityānanda Prabhu considered him to be His very own life. This too is stated in the *Caitanya Bhāgavata*:

"Parameśvarī Dāsa is Nityānanda Prabhu's life. Nityānanda Prabhu used his body as an extension of His own." (*Caitanya Bhāgavata* 3.5.732)

It is also stated in the *Caitanya Bhāgavata* that Mahāprabhu manifested Himself in the Gaurāṅga deity Parameśvarī Dāsa worshipped in Antpur.

"Purandara Paṇḍita and Parameśvarī Dāsa both saw the manifestation of Gauracandra in the deity. As soon as they saw Him, they ran towards Him and fell down, crying in the ecstasy of love." (*Caitanya Bhāgavata* 5.95-6)

It is said in the *Bhakti-ratnākara* that Parameśvarī Dāsa was in the entourage of Nityānanda Prabhu's *śakti*, Jāhnavā Mātā, when she went to the Khetari festival.

"Jāhnavā Iśvarī happily walked in the company of Gaurāṅga, Nakaṛi Kṛṣṇadāsa, Dāmodara, Parameśvarī, the learned Balarāma, Mukunda, Vṛndāvana Dāsa, etc." (*Bhakti-ratnākara* 10.376-7)

Śrī Parameśvarī Dāsa Ṭhākura also accompanied Jāhnavā Mātā on her trip to Vraja *dhāma* and by her mercy, witnessed the meeting of Śrīmatī Rādhikā with Gopīnātha and was flooded in ecstasy. In *Bhakti-ratnākara* (10.245-6) it is stated that on Jāhnavā's order, he established the worship of Rādhā-Gopīnātha deities in Antpur.

Once back from Vraja, Parameśvarī Dāsa stayed for some time in Khardah and Garalagacha village in Puri district. When Narottama Dāsa came to Khardah, Parameśvarī Dāsa gave him directions to Puri.

In *Caitanya Caritāmṛta*, it is written that just by remembering Parameśvarī Dāsa one can attain love for Kṛṣṇa.

"Parameśvarī Dāsa took exclusive shelter of Nityānanda Prabhu. Whoever remembers him attains devotion to Kṛṣṇa." (*Caitanya Caritāmṛta* 1.11.29)

Śrī Parameśvarī Dāsa had miraculous powers. On one occasion, he was dancing in ecstasy during *harināma-saṅkīrtana* at the house of Kamalākara Pippalāi in the town of Aknamahesh, which is situated near Serampore. Hearing the sounds of the *kīrtana* and seeing the ecstatic dancing caused some of the local atheists to become very envious. They decided to pollute the *kīrtana* area and teach the devotees a lesson, so they threw a dead jackal in the midst of the *kīrtana* group. But Parameśvarī did not stop *saṅkīrtana* for a moment. By the power of his *kīrtana*, the jackal came back to life and participated in the *kīrtana*. The other devotees were astonished by this display of power and were overcome by transcendental joy. This has been mentioned in the *Vaiṣṇava-vandanā*:

"I very attentively worship Parameśvarī Dāsa, who made a jackal come back to life during *saṅkīrtana*."

In front of the temple in Antpur there are two huge *bakula* trees and a *kadamba* tree. Between them is the *samādhi* of Parameśvarī Dāsa, over which is a Tulasī altar. It is said that *bakula* trees grew from the branches of the two trees that grew there during the time of Parameśvarī Ṭhākura. Every year, the *kadamba* tree produces a flower that is used for the worship of the deities. Parameśvarī Ṭhākura's *tirobhāva* (disappearance) festival is held every year on the *vaiśākhī pūrṇimā*.

Śrī Uddhāraṇa Datta Ṭhākura

"Uddhāraṇa Datta was the best of the *bhāgavatas* He served Nityānanda Prabhu's lotus feet in every way possible." (*Caitanya Caritāmṛta* 1.11.41)

Whenever the Supreme Lord Nanda-nandana Śrī Kṛṣṇa adopts the devotional mood and bodily luster of Śrīmatī Rādhārāṇī in order to become Śrī Kṛṣṇa Caitanya in the house of Śrī Jagannātha Miśra in Śrīdhāma Mayapur, He is always accompanied by His eternal associates, who join Him to enrich His pastimes. Thus, Kṛṣṇa's primary expansion, or *prakāśa*, Baladeva, accepts the attitude of a devotee as Śrī Nityānanda Prabhu, appearing in Ekachakra village in order to embellish Mahāprabhu's *līlā*. He too has His entourage of personal confidantes who descend to this earth to assist Him in playing His role. Nityānanda Prabhu is Baladeva *tattva*: He is none other than Lord Śeṣa, the source of the three *puruṣāvatāras*, Mahā Saṅkarṣaṇa's causal form, or *mūla* Saṅkarṣaṇa. His chief companions are known as the *dvādaśa-gopālas*, or twelve cowherds. Thus it is stated in the *Gaura-gaṇoddeśa-dīpikā* (129):

subāhur yo vraje gopo datta uddhāraṇākhyakaḥ

"The cowherd named Subāhu became Uddhāraṇa Datta."

Uddhāraṇa Datta Ṭhākura is thus one of the twelve *gopālas*. In order to assist Nityānanda Prabhu's pastimes, he appeared in the town of Saptagram in the year 1481 A.D. Saptagram is in the Hooghly district, near the Trishbigha railway station. His parents were named Śrīkara and Bhadrāvatī, and they belonged to the gold-merchant class. Any caste in which a Vaiṣṇava appears is holy. The earth itself is blessed by the appearance of a Vaiṣṇava, and his or her mother has achieved the perfection of motherhood. Vṛndāvana Dāsa has written:

"Nityānanda Prabhu remained a few days in Khardah and then went on to Saptagram with his troupe of associates. The Lord stayed at the home of the fortunate Uddhāraṇa

Datta on the banks of the Triveni. Completely surrendered to the feet of Nityānanda Prabhu, Uddhāraṇa Datta worshipped Him without any false pretence. The entire caste of gold merchants was purified by the presence of Uddhāraṇa Datta in its midst; of this, there can be no doubt." (*Caitanya Bhāgavata* 3.5.443, 449-50, 453)

jāti-kula saba nirarthaka jānāite
janmāilena haridāse mleccha-kulete

"In order to show that one's caste and family background are completely irrelevant, Haridāsa Ṭhākura took birth in an outcaste family."

Śrī Kṛṣṇa Caitanya and Nityānanda Prabhu wanted to teach that a great devotee may appear in any family in any caste, and so They had some of Their devotees take birth in such households.

"One who takes birth in a low-class family is not disqualified from performing devotional service, nor is one who born in a pure, high-class brahminical family automatically qualified for such service. Whoever engages in the worship of the Lord is a great person; one who does not worship is rejected." (*Caitanya Caritāmṛta* 3.4.66-7)

arcye viṣṇau śīladhīr guruṣu nara-
matir vaiṣṇave jāti buddhi
viṣṇor vā vaiṣṇavānāṁ kalimala-
mathane padatīrthe 'mbubuddhiḥ
śrī viṣṇor nāmni mantre sakala-
kaluṣa he śabda-sāmānya-buddhir
viṣṇau sarveśvareśe tad-itara-
samadhīr yasya vā nārakī saḥ

"Anyone who considers the deity to be nothing but stone, the guru to be an ordinary human being, or the Vaiṣṇava to be a member of a particular caste or race, who takes the holy water which has washed Viṣṇu or the Vaiṣṇava's feet and can destroy all the sins of the Age of Kālī to be ordinary water, who thinks that the name or *mantra* of Viṣṇu, which destroys all evils, is the same as any other sound, or who takes Viṣṇu to be equal to anything other than Him is a resident of hell." (*Padma purāṇa*)

Anyone who sees a Vaiṣṇava in terms of his material birth is destined for a hellish existence. Subāhu took birth in a family of gold merchants, but this does not mean that he was a gold merchant – hc was an eternal associate of the Lord, beyond the material qualities. One cannot understand the underlying nature or ontological aspect of the Lord and His devotees by using the gross or subtle material senses; one can only get a superficial understanding of their morphological or external aspect. The true nature of the devotee and the Supreme Lord is revealed to the surrendered heart. If Uddhāraṇa Datta Ṭhākura is merciful, one can understand his transcendental nature and his divine glories.

Amongst *devatās*, Viṣṇu is supreme. Only by uttering the name of Viṣṇu can all of one's sins be burned up, all inauspiciousness in one's destiny destroyed and auspiciousness gained. A single utterance of the name of Rāma equals a thousand repetitions of the name of Viṣṇu.

rāma rāmeti rāmeti rame rāme manorame
sahasra-nāmabhis tulyaṁ rāmanāma varānane

"Oh sweet-faced Durgā, I take great pleasure in chanting the names of Rāma, Rāma, Rāma. A single utterance of the name of Rāma is equivalent to a recital of the thousand names of Viṣṇu." (*Padma purāṇa, Uttara-khaṇḍa,* 72.335; *Caitanya Caritāmṛta* 2.9.32)

sahasra-nāmnāṁ puṇyānāṁ
trirāvṛttyā tu yat phalam
ekāvṛttyā tu kṛṣṇasya
nāmaikaṁ tat prayacchati

"The fruits of three recitations of the thousand names of Lord Viṣṇu are attained by a single utterance of the name of Kṛṣṇa." (*Brahmaṇḍa Purāṇa, Laghu-bhāgavatāmṛta* 1.631, *Caitanya Caritāmṛta* 2.9.33)

Even though the name of Kṛṣṇa and the Kṛṣṇa *mantra* are supremely powerful, offenses are taken into consideration in the chanting of Kṛṣṇa's name. Even the glow of the Holy Name (*nāmābhāsa*) can destroy all sins and give one liberation. Nevertheless, if one commits offenses, the benefits of *nāmābhāsa* are lost. Lord Kṛṣṇa withholds His mercy from the offensive person. The difference between a sin (*pāpa*) and an offense (*aparādha*) is the following: an improper act committed toward a conditioned embodied being is a sin, whereas a similar improper act committed toward Viṣṇu or the Vaiṣṇava is an offense. An offense has graver consequences than a sin. Ajāmila was a great sinner, but because he had committed no offenses, he was delivered by the power of *nāmābhāsa*. Lord Śrī Caitanya Mahāprabhu and Nityānanda Prabhu delivered everyone, both sinners and offenders.

"There are offenses to be considered while chanting Kṛṣṇa's name. Therefore simply by chanting His name, the offender does not become ecstatic. But these considerations do not exist where Lord Caitanya and Nityānanda Prabhu are concerned. So as soon as one chants the name, he feels the ecstasy of love for God." (*Caitanya Caritāmṛta* 1.8.24, 31)

Kṛṣṇadāsa Kavirāja Gosvāmī has glorified Nityānanda Prabhu's quality of being merciful to the most fallen in the following words:

"Nityānanda Prabhu is the *avatāra* of mercy; He is so intoxicated by ecstatic love that He does not discriminate between the good and the bad. He delivers anyone who falls down before Him. Therefore He has delivered such a sinful and fallen person as me." (*Caitanya Caritāmṛta* 1.5.208-9)

Śrīla Vṛndāvana Dāsa Ṭhākura has particularly given extensive glorifications of Nityānanda Prabhu. The sinful and offensive living beings of this world have no alternative but the mercy of Nityānanda Prabhu if they want to be delivered. Even though Nityānanda Prabhu is *bhagavat-tattva*, He behaves as a devotee. All of His associates are expansions of His mercy. Nityānanda Prabhu is said to be the deliverer of the most fallen; His companions seek out even more fallen souls to deliver. In fact, Nityānanda Prabhu distributes His mercy to the conditioned souls through his devotees.

As one of Nityānanda Prabhu's closest confidantes, Uddhāraṇa Datta Ṭhākura is called *parama-parama-patita-pāvana*, "the deliverer of the most fallen amongst the most fallen." Thus any *jīva* who takes shelter of Uddhāraṇa Datta Ṭhākura is quickly delivered from his material entanglements and attains the service of Nityānanda Prabhu and Gaurāṅga Prabhu's lotus feet. Therefore Kṛṣṇadāsa Kavirāja Gosvāmī describes him as the best of the *mahā-bhāgavatas*, and Vṛndāvana Dāsa Ṭhākura writes in the *Caitanya Bhāgavata*:

"Uddhāraṇa Datta is a great and magnanimous Vaiṣṇava who has a title to the service of Nityānanda Prabhu."

From a superficial point of view, Uddhāraṇa Datta worked as the manager of a big zamindar (Nairaja) of Naihati. The relics of this wealthy family are still visible not far from the Dain Hat station. The village where Uddhāraṇa Datta Ṭhākura lived while acting as the manager of the estate was named Uddharanapura.

Though he possessed a vast fortune, Uddhāraṇa Datta renounced all sense gratifications, dedicating all of his sense activities to the service of Nityānanda Prabhu. Being controlled by the love of His devotee,

Nityānanda Prabhu enjoyed the foodstuffs that Uddhāraṇa had cooked.

bhaktera dravya prabhu kāri kāri khāya
abhaktera dravya-pāne ulati na cāya

"The Lord will grab food from His devotee, but He will not even glance at anything offered by a nondevotee."

At Uddhāraṇa Datta's Sripat in Saptagram, which stands on the banks of the Sarasvatī River, one can still see the six-armed form of Mahāprabhu that he personally worshipped. On the right side of Śrī Caitanya Mahāprabhu is a deity of Śrī Nityānanda Prabhu, and on the left side is the deity of Śrī Gadādhara Paṇḍita. On another altar are the deities of Rādhā Govinda and a *śālagrāma-śilā*, and below the throne is a picture of Śrī Uddhāraṇa Datta Ṭhākura. After Uddhāraṇa Datta disappeared, Jāhnavā Devī made an auspicious visit to his home.

Śrīla Kṛṣṇadāsa Kavirāja Gosvāmī writes in the *Caitanya Caritāmṛta* that his brother did not have as much faith in Nityānanda Prabhu as he had in Caitanya Mahāprabhu. This was the cause of an argument between his brother and Nityānanda Prabhu's follower Mīnaketana Rāma Dāsa. Śrīla Kavirāja Gosvāmī took Rāma Dāsa's side in this argument and rebuked his brother. Nityānanda Prabhu was pleased with Śrīla Kavirāja Gosvāmī just because he supported His devotee. Nityānanda Prabhu gave him a vision of Himself, the right to live in Vrindavan and service to the lotus feet of Rādhā and Kṛṣṇa. The conclusion is that if we worship Uddhāraṇa Datta Ṭhākura, serving him and trying to please him, we will quickly be able to get the mercy of Lord Nityānanda Prabhu, through which we will become eligible to attain love for Kṛṣṇa and thus perfect our lives. In order to attract people allow them to benefit from Uddhāraṇa Datta's Sripat, it is necessary to make repairs to the buildings on the site. Through this, people will become aware of his glories and will seek his mercy and become blessed. If one makes an effort to serve, the object of worship will give the commensurate power to serve.

In front of the Saptagram temple, a large hall has been constructed, in front of which is a shady and cool terrace covered by a *madhavi* creeper.

Śrīnivāsa Datta Ṭhākura was Uddhāraṇa Datta's son. Their descendants have spread into many branches and today live in Kolkata, Hooghly and many other places. Those who have taken birth in this family are doubtlessly very fortunate individuals. We pray that they abandon the superficial illusory family connection and establish their transcendental relation with him and take care of developing the birthsite of Śrī Uddhāraṇa Datta Ṭhākura.

Uddhāraṇa Datta Ṭhākura left this world in the Śaka year 1463 (1551 A.D.), on the *kṛṣṇa trayodaśī* of the month of Pauṣa.

Śrī Puruṣottama Dāsa

sadāśivasuto nāmnā nāgaraḥ puruṣottamaḥ
vaidya-vaṁśodbhavo nāmnā dāma yo vallavo vraje

"Nāgara Puruṣottama was previously the cowherd named Dāma in Vraja. He is now born in a *vaidya* family as the son of Sadāśiva." (*Gaura-gaṇoddeśa-dīpikā* 131)

Dāma was one of the twelve gopālas and a companion of Kṛṣṇa in His childhood pastimes in Vraja. In the eleventh chapter of the *Ādi-līlā* of *Caitanya Caritāmṛta*, Kṛṣṇadāsa Kavirāja Gosvāmī has listed Puruṣottama Dāsa amongst the foremost devotees of Lord Nityānanda Prabhu.

"Sadāśiva Kavirāja was a great personality. Puruṣottama Dāsa was his son. From birth, Puruṣottama Dāsa was absorbed in the service of the lotus feet of Lord Nityānanda Prabhu, and he always engaged in childlike play with Lord Kṛṣṇa. His son was named Śrī Kānu Ṭhākura, a very respectable gentleman. His body was saturated with the nectar of love for Lord Kṛṣṇa." (*Caitanya Caritāmṛta* 1.11.38-40)

Vṛndāvana Dāsa Ṭhākura has also named Puruṣottama Dāsa as one of Nityānanda Prabhu's chief associates.

"Sadāśiva Kavirāja was very fortunate to have a son like Puruṣottama Dāsa. Puruṣottama Dāsa had no external consciousness of his body, for Nityānanda Prabhu dwelled in his heart." (*Caitanya Bhāgavata* 3.5.741-2)

For four generations, the family of Puruṣottama Ṭhākura consisted of eternally perfect direct associates of Mahāprabhu: Kaṁsāri Sen, Sadāśiva Kavirāja, Puruṣottama Ṭhākura and Kānu Ṭhākura. Such a thing is quite uncommon. The *Gaura-gaṇoddeśa-dīpikā* (156) identifies Kaṁsāri Sena as Ratnāvalī and Sadāśiva Kavirāja as Candrāvalī.

Puruṣottama Ṭhākura's wife was named Jāhnavā Devī. She died while her son, Kānu Ṭhākura, was just a young child. Nityānanda Prabhu named the boy Śiśu Kṛṣṇadāsa. It is said that Nityānanda Prabhu's wife Jāhnavā Devī adopted Kānu and took him with her to Vrindavan. Some say that he was also one of the twelve gopālas. Once while in Vrindavan, when, Kānu Ṭhākura was dancing in *kīrtana* his ankle bell flew off. He vowed that he would make his residence wherever the ankle bell was recovered. The ankle bell was found in the town of Bodhakhānā in the Jessore district, and so he established his Sripat there. Madhavācārya (Mādhava Caṭṭopadhyāya) of Jirat was Puruṣottama Ṭhākura's disciple.

Śrīla Bhakti Siddhānta Sarasvatī Gosvāmī Ṭhākura has the following to say about Puruṣottama Ṭhākura's Sripat: "Puruṣottama Dāsa Ṭhākura lived at Sukhasagar, midway between Chakdah and Simurali of the Nadia district. The deities he served were formerly in Beledanga village, but when the temple fell into the river, the deities were taken to Sukhasagara. That temple was also swallowed by the Ganges, and so the deities were brought with Jāhnavā Mātā's deity to Sahebdanga Berigram. Since that place was also destroyed, all the deities were again moved about three or four miles to the village named Chanduregram, on the banks of the Ganges about one mile up from Palpara." (*Anubhāṣya* 1.11.39)

Devakīnandana Dāsa, the author of the *Vaiṣṇava-vandanā*, was Puruṣottama Ṭhākura's disciple. There he writes:

"I worship Sadāśiva Kavirāja with great attentiveness. He was constantly intoxicated with love and had no external consciousness. I worship my worshipable lord, Puruṣottama Ṭhākura. Who can list his incomparable qualities? He was merciful to those who were devoid of virtue, displaying the natural power of his compassion. When only seven years old, he was so intoxicated with love for Kṛṣṇa that he danced in a way that enchanted the entire world."

The following supplementary information is given in the *Gauḍīya Vaiṣṇava Abhidhāna*:

"Some people say that Puruṣottama's surname was Nāgara. While others say that the name Nāgara comes from the name of the area where he lived. Since fourteen villages – Beledanga, Berigram, Sukhasagar, Chandure, Manasapota Palpara etc. – are under one administrative unit of Pancanagara, this area is sometimes called Nagaradesh. Puruṣottama ate snake poison when in a trance state without experiencing any ill effects. This was a source of great astonishment to all those who witnessed it. Many of Nityānanda Prabhu's associates often displayed such miraculous powers."

Śrī Kamalākara Pippalāi

kamalākaraḥ pippalāi-nāmnāsīd you mahābalaḥ

"Nityānanda Prabhu's associate Kamalākara Pippalāi was one of the twelve *gopālas*. He formerly known as Mahābala." (*Gaura-gaṇoddeśa-dīpikā* 128)

"Kamalākara Pippalāi's behavior and his love of God were uncommon.Thus his fame spread around the world." (*Caitanya Caritāmṛta* 1.11.24)

"The cowherd boy who was known as Mahābala in Vrindavan is now known as Kamalākara Pippalāi. Day and night he sang the glories of Rādhā and Kṛṣṇa and is counted as one of Nityānanda Prabhu's branches. He lived in Mahesh on the west bank of the Ganges, where he served a deity of Lord Jagannātha." (*Vaiṣṇavācāra-darpaṇa*)

In the *Gauḍīya Vaiṣṇava Abhidhāna*, Kamalākara Pippalāi's birth year is given as 1492 A.D. According to *Sripat-paryatana*, he was born in Akna Mahesh and lived in Jageshwar, but according to other sources he was born in the village known as Khalijhuli in the Sundarban area. His father was a rich landlord who belonged to a *brāhmaṇa* family of the Rarha branch. He had a younger brother named Śrīnidhipati Pippalāi.

Though born in Khalijhuli, Kamalākara moved to the village of Mahesh, which is about two and a half miles from the Serampore railway station in Hooghly. The famous Jagannātha deity in Mahesh was consecrated by him. Prior to Kamalākara's arrival, the area around Mahesh was nothing but jungle, but later it turned into a beautiful village whose fame spread everywhere.

Śrīla Bhakti Siddhānta Sarasvatī Gosvāmī Ṭhākura has told two stories about Kamalākara Pippalāi in his *Anubhāṣya* to the *Caitanya Caritāmṛta*:

(1) When Kamalākara Pippalāi left home, his younger brother, Śrīnidhipati Pippalāi, searched for him and in due course of time found him in the village of Mahesh. When his brother refused to return despite his remonstrance, Śrīnidhipati Pippalāi came to live in Mahesh with all his family members. His descendants still reside in the Mahesh area, numbering some twenty households.

(2) There was once a highly detached Vaiṣṇava named Dhruvānanda who went on a pilgrimage to Puri. It was his strong desire to offer Lord Jagannātha food that he had cooked with his own hands. Lord Jagannātha appeared to him in a dream one night and ordered him

to go to Mahesh on the bank of Ganges, install His deity there and make an offering to him. When Dhruvānanda came to Mahesh, he saw Lord Jagannātha, Balarāma and Śubhadrā floating in the river. He picked them out of the water and had a small hut built where he could shelter and worship Them. As he was worried about a suitable person to take care of the deities after him, Lord Jagannātha once again appeared to him in a dream and said, "My devotee, a great Vaiṣṇava named Kamalākara Pippalāi lives in the village of Khalijuli in the Sundarban. I have ordered him in a dream to come here and take over My service. When he comes, you should turn the responsibility for caring for Me over to him."

The next morning, Kamalākara Pippalāi, who had indeed had such a dream, arrived there, and Dhruvānanda immediately gave him charge of the worship of Jagannātha, Baladeva and Śubhadrā. Having been empowered in this way to serve the Lord, Kamalākara Pippalāi took the title Adhikārī, and this title has been used as the family name ever since. The Pippalāi name belongs to one of the fifty-five branches of the Rarha *brāhmaṇas*.

A devotee is always anxious to serve the Lord, so the Lord gives him directions for service. He never does this for a nondevotee. Kamalākara was gratified to have received Lord Jagannātha's order and immediately abandoned his home and family to go to Mahesh. The conditioned souls are normally so attached to the pleasures of their gross and subtle senses that the mere mention of service to Kṛṣṇa and the Vaiṣṇavas fills their hearts with fear. They consider it to be a burden and look for any excuse to avoid such service. Because it does not contribute to the gratification of the senses, they do not consider service to Viṣṇu and the Vaiṣṇavas to be a wealth or a source of profit in the way that a Vaiṣṇava does. In the eyes of the world, a Vaiṣṇava may be playing the role of a family man, but he is not of the same order as a worldly householder. Sometimes by the Lord's wish, a devotee may enter family life, but his mind is constantly absorbed in feelings of separation from the Lord. Thus, as soon as he receives direction from the Lord, he enthusiastically abandons his material connections and becomes fully engaged in the Lord's service. This renunciation of family life is not painful as it is for one on the *jñāna-yoga* path but is natural and spontaneous.

The *Vijaya-khaṇḍa* says that Nityānanda Prabhu gave Panihati over to Kamalākara.

Śrīla Bhakti Siddhānta Sarasvatī Gosvāmī Ṭhākura has noted a few of the generations that descended from Kamalākara. He had a son named Caturbhuja, who in turn had two sons, Nārāyaṇa and Jagannātha. Nārāyaṇa's son was named Jagadānanda, whose son was Rājīvalocana. During Kamalākara's lifetime, service to the Lord Jagannātha deity was at first hampered by a shortage of finances. Later when the glories of Lord Jagannātha of Mahesh were spread, the Nawab of Dhaka, Wali Shah Suja, donated 1185 *bighas* of land in the Bengali year 1060 (1653 A.D.). This land is found in the area of Jagannathpur, about 1.5

krośas west of Mahesh. The village was named Jagannathpur after the deity.

The *Gauḍīya Vaiṣṇava Abhidhāna* cites the following verses from *Nityānanda Prabhu-vaṁśa-vistāra*:

"A pure-hearted *brāhmaṇa* who regularly worshipped Viṣṇu and the Vaiṣṇavas lived in the town of Mahesh. He was Pippalāi's son-in-law named Sudhāmaya. His wife was Vidyunmālā."

Thus, Vidyunmālā, Kamalākara Pippalāi's daughter, married Sudhāmaya Cattopādhyāya. They had a daughter named Nārāyaṇī Devī. Vīrabhadra Prabhu later married this Nārāyaṇī Devi. The descendants of the Pippalāi family in Mahesh say that this girl's name was Rādhārāṇī. On the other hand, Śrīla Bhakti Siddhānta Sarasvatī Gosvāmī Ṭhākura has said that Vīrabhadra Prabhu married Śrīmatī, who was the daughter of Yadunātha Ācārya and Vidyunmālā of Jhamatpur village in the Hoogly district, as well as their adopted daughter, Nārāyaṇī.

The *Vaiṣṇavācāra-darpaṇa*, however, gives contradictory information. It says Vidyunmālā married a highly qualified *brāhmaṇa* named Yadunandana, "who thus had as his father-in-law a great devotee of Lord Jagannātha, who knew nothing but the desire to serve Lord Jagannātha."

Kamalākara Pippalāi was present in Panihati at the *Daṇḍa-mahotsava* of Raghunātha Dāsa in 1517 A.D. He also came to the renowned festival at Kheturī and the festival offered by Gadādhara Dāsa at Katwa. When Jāhnavā Devī came along with her associates from Khardah to attend the Kheturī festival, Kamalākara Pippalāi was also present. His name is mentioned in this connection in *Bhakti-ratnākara* (10.375).

According to the *Vaiṣṇavācāra-darpaṇa*, Kamalākara left for Vrindavan after giving his daughter away in marriage and lived there until the completion of his pastimes. According to his descendants in Mahesh, Kamalākara Pippalāi made his disappearance at the age of seventy-one on Caitra *śukla-trayodaśī* of the year 1563 A.D.

Śrī Sāraṅga Ṭhākura

Kavi Karṇapura, the youngest son of Śrī Śivānanda Sena, writes in his *Gaura-gaṇoddeśa-dīpikā* 172:

vraje nāndīmukhī yāsīt sādya sāraṅga-ṭhākura
prahlādo manyate kaiścin matpitrā sa na manyate

"Vraja's Nāndīmukhī became Sāraṅga Ṭhākura in Gaura *līlā*. Some people say that he is Prahlāda, but that is not the opinion held by my father."

Śrī Sāraṅga Ṭhākura is mentioned in the listing of branches of the Caitanya trunk of the tree of devotional service along with Rāma Dāsa, Kavidatta, Gopāla Dāsa and Bhāgavata Ācārya (*Caitanya Caritāmṛta* 1.10.113). He is also known as Śārṇga Ṭhākura, Śārṅgadhara and Śārṅgapāṇi. He used to live in Modadrumdwip, which is the island in Nabadwip that represents, of the nine types of devotional service, the service attitude. The name of the town is Mamgachi. He would sit in a secluded place by the banks of the Ganges to perform intense *bhajana*. Through these practices, he obtained many miraculous powers.

At first, Sāraṅga Ṭhākura did not want to make any disciples for fear of disturbances to his *bhajana*, but Mahāprabhu repeatedly encouraged him to do so. The following account is given in the *Gauḍīya Vaiṣṇava Abhidhāna:*

"When the Lord was returning after criticizing Devānanda Paṇḍita for having offended Śrīvāsa Paṇḍita, Sāraṅga Ṭhākura met Him on the streets of Nabadwip. Mahāprabhu ordered him to give up his determination to never take disciples."

Śrīla Bhakti Siddhānta Sarasvatī Gosvāmī Prabhupāda writes in his *Anubhāṣya* in *Caitanya Charitamṛta*: "Having been ordered by Mahāprabhu to take disciples, Sāraṅga Ṭhākura decided that he would make a disciple of the first person that he met the following morning. As fate would have it, the next morning a dead body washed up against him while he was taking bath in the Ganges. He revived the corpse and made him his disciple. This disciple was known as Ṭhākura Murāri, or sometimes as Sāraṅga Murāri."

In the *Gauḍīya Vaiṣṇava Abhidhāna,* it is farther said that Murāri was a boy who had been killed by a snake bite and his parents had set his uncremated body afloat on a raft in the Ganges, as was the custom in that time. Sāraṅga Ṭhākura revived him by giving initiation to him. Thus, his name became Sāraṅga Murāri. He became an empowered preacher of Mahāprabhu's *dharma* by guru's grace. Descendents of Sāraṅga Murāri's disciples still live in a village named Shav.

Sāraṅga Ṭhākura's deities were served in the town of Mamgachi. The original temple was built in front of a *bakula* tree. The deities of Rādhā Gopīnātha worshipped by him can be seen in this temple, as can the deity of Mahāprabhu's associate Vāsudeva Datta Ṭhākura, Śrī Madana Gopāla. The devotees who do *parikramā* of Nabadwip Dhāma visit this temple for *darśana*. Śrīla Bhakti Siddhānta Sarasvatī Gosvāmī Ṭhākura established a temple not far from the above-mentioned home of Sāraṅga Murāri at the birthplace of Vṛndāvana Dāsa Ṭhākura.

Sāraṅga Ṭhākura disappeared on the thirteenth day of the waning moon (*kṛṣṇa trayodaśī*) in the month of Agrahāyaṇa. An alternative opinion is that he disappeared on the Āṣāḍha *kṛṣṇa caturdaśī.*

Śrī Kāliyā Kṛṣṇa Dāsa (Kāla Kṛṣṇa Dāsa)

kālaḥ śrī-kṛṣṇadāsaḥ sa yo lavaṅgaḥ sakhā vraje

"In Vraja, Kāla Kṛṣṇadāsa was Kṛṣṇa's cowherd friend named Lavaṅga." (*Gaura-gaṇoddeśa-dīpikā* 132)

"Kāliyā Kṛṣṇadāsa was known throughout the three worlds. One can attain Gauracandra through remembrance of him." (*Caitanya Bhāgavata* 3.5.740)

The Sripat of Kāliyā Kṛṣṇadāsa is in the town of Akai Hat, within the jurisdiction of Katwa just off the road that leads to Nabadwip. It is about two miles south of the Katwa train station and one mile north of Dain Hat station.

Near the Sripat is a pond called Nupural Kuṇḍa. It is said that the ankle bell of Raghunandana Ṭhākura, the son of Khandavasi Mukunda, fell here. Others say that it was Nityānanda Prabhu's ankle bell. Even today one can get to see the Sripat's homestead, including bricks and the bank of the pond.

In his *Anubhāṣya* commentary to the *Caitanya Caritāmṛta*, Śrīla Bhakti Siddhānta Sarasvatī Gosvāmī Ṭhākura has written: "In the opinion of the Gosvāmīs of the Sonatala village on the north bank of the Icchamati River about three miles west of Bera Bandar in the Pabna district, Kāla Kṛṣṇadāsa was a *brāhmaṇa* of the Vārendra group, of the Bharadwaj Gotra in the village Bhadara. Kāla Kṛṣṇadāsa went to Pabna from Akai Hat to preach the chanting of the Holy Names. There are still the ruins of the buildings where he built his *āśrama*. Later, members of his family came to live there. Since there were no other *brāhmaṇas* of the Vārendra group in Akai Hat, he came there to marry. Afterwards, he returned to Akai Hat and also went to Vrindavan."

He had two sons, named Śrī Mohana Dāsa and Śrī Gaurāṅga Dāsa, or Vṛndāvana Dāsa. Their descendants still live in the Sonatala village. There they celebrate Kāla Kṛṣṇadāsa's disappearance day on the twelfth day of the waning moon in the month of Agrahāyaṇa. The deity which he worshipped was named Kāla Cāṇḍa.

"Kāla Kṛṣṇadāsa took birth in Rarhadesh. He was a great servant of Lord Nityānanda and was the best of the Vaiṣṇavas. He knew nothing other than Nityānanda Prabhu's lotus feet." (*Caitanya Caritāmṛta* 1.11.36-7)

When Jāhnavā Devī came to Katwa, Kāla Kṛṣṇadāsa was in her entourage.

"They all arrived in Kaṇṭaka Nagara (Katwa) in the company of many devotees, including Kāla Kṛṣṇadāsa from Akai Hat." (*Bhakti-ratnākara* 10.409)

"The Kāla Kṛṣṇadāsa who accompanied Śrī Caitanya Mahāprabhu to Southern India was not the same personality. (*Caitanya Caritāmṛta, Anubhāṣya,* 2.7.39)

Śrīla Dhanañjaya Paṇḍita

vasudāmā sakhā yaś ca paṇḍitaḥ śrī-dhanañjayaḥ

"The cowherd Vasudāmā became Dhanañjaya Paṇḍita in Gaura *līlā*." (*Gaura-gaṇoddeśa-dīpikā* 127)

Dhanañjaya Paṇḍita, the dear associate of Lord Nityānanda, was previously Vasudāma, one among the twelve bosom friends of Lord Baladeva.

"Dhanañjaya Paṇḍita was Nityānanda Prabhu's dear servant; he was very renounced and full of love for Kṛṣṇa." (*Caitanya Caritāmṛta* 1.11.31)

Opinions vary about Dhanañjaya Paṇḍita's birthplace and his parentage. In the *Gauḍīya Vaiṣṇava Abhidhāna*, it is said that he was born in the village of Jhargram in the Chittagong district on the fifth day of the waxing moon in the month of Caitra, 1484 A.D. His father's name was Śrīpati Bandopādhyāya; his mother's was Kālindī Devī. His wife was Haripriyā.

In the book *Gaurāṅga-mādhurī*, another version is given: He was born in the village of Siyan Muluk, near Bolpur in the Birbhum district. His father's name was Ādideva Vācaspati, and his mother's mane was, Dayāmayī Devī. Śrīla Bhakti Siddhānta Sarasvatī Gosvāmī Ṭhākura subscribes to the former view in his *Anubhāṣya*.

Dhanañjaya Paṇḍita's primary home was in the village of Shital Gram, which is served by the Kaichar post office in the precinct of Mangalkot in the Burdwan district. Shital Gram is about one mile northeast of the Kaichar railway station, which is nine miles from the Katwa railway station. He is also said to have had homes in the Sanchra Panchra and Jalandi villages. The first of these villages lies two miles south of Satdeula Tejapur, which is four miles from the Memari train station. Jalandi is about ten miles east of the city of Burdwan and is served by the Lokanagara post office. Also found in this village is the home of Sañjaya Paṇḍita, who is said by some to have been Dhanañjaya's brother and by others his disciple. Dhanañjaya had no offspring. Those who supervise the Shital Gram temple are descendants of his disciples.

Both the *Gauḍīya Vaiṣṇava Abhidhāna* and *Gaurāṅga-mādhurī* agree that Dhanañjaya Paṇḍita was married and that his wife's name was Haripriyā. It is also mentioned that he would prostrate himself in obeisances before Tulasī Devī three times a day. He was married when very young, but this did not stop him from leaving on a pilgrimage shortly after his wedding. His wealthy father gave him money for traveling expenses, but Dhanañjaya gave it all to Mahāprabhu and carried only a begging bowl. This particular action has been recalled by the author of the *Vaiṣṇava-vandanā*:

vilāsī vairāgī vandoṅ paṇḍita dhanañjaya
sarvasva prabhure diyā bhāṇḍa hāte laya

Dhanañjaya's main home or Sripat was in Shital Gram. The deities of Gopīnātha, Nitāi-Gaurāṅga and Dāmodara worshipped by him are still being served there. These deities are brought into a field not far from the temple where the disappearance-day festival is held annually in the middle of Māgha.

Dhanañjaya Paṇḍita participated for a few days with Mahāprabhu in His *saṅkīrtana* pastimes in Nabadwip. From there he returned to Shital Gram, whence he went on a pilgrimage to Vrindavan. Before traveling to Vrindavan, he stayed for a few days in Sanchra Panchra, leaving a disciple who was traveling with him in charge of the deity service. At present, there is no farther sign of this temple in Sanchra Panchra.

Nityānanda Prabhu delivered the most fallen and crushed the atheistic. These powers were manifest in his dear devotee Dhanañjaya. Dhanañjaya Paṇḍita converted many robbers and atheists in the Shital Gram area.

"Dhanañjaya Paṇḍita was an extraordinarily great Vaiṣṇava. Nityānanda Prabhu took up permanent residence in his heart." (*Caitanya Bhāgavata* 3.5.773)

As one enters the Shital Gram temple, a small Tulasī altar stands on the left. This is the site of Dhanañjaya Paṇḍita's *samādhi*.

His disappearance day is the *kṛṣṇa-aṣṭamī* of Kārtika month.

Sundarānanda Ṭhākura

purā sudāma-nāmāsīd adya sundara-ṭhakuraḥ

"Sundarānanda Ṭhākura was previously one of the twelve *gopālas* known as Sudāma." (*Gaura-gaṇoddeśa-dīpikā* 127)

"Sundarānanda, a true servant, is counted amongst the branches of Nityānanda Prabhu. Nityānanda Prabhu joked with him in the Vrindavan mood." (*Caitanya Caritāmṛta* 1.11.23)

"Sundarānanda is an ocean of sacred rapture. He is chief amongst the associates of

Nityānanda Prabhu." (*Caitanya Bhāgavata* 3.5.728)

His home was in the village of Maheshpur in the Jessore district. Maheshpur stands on the Betravati River, fourteen miles east of the Mazdia railway station. Only his place of birth remains there at present.

His deities were named Śrī Rādhā-Vallabha and Śrī Rādhā-Ramaṇa. Their priests later moved these deities to Sayyidabad, and later a wooden deity was installed in Maheshpur.

Sundarānanda never married and thus has no descendants. Descendants of his disciples continue to maintain the site in Maheshpur. Some of his relatives live in Mangaldihi in the Birbhum district.

Sundarānanda possessed great mystic powers. He made *kadamba* flowers bloom on a lime tree, He later used the flower in the service of Rādhā-Ramaṇa, as is stated in the *Vaiṣṇava-vandanā:*

sundarānanda ṭhākura vandibo bara āśe
phutālo kadamba-phula jabīrera gāche

"In great hope, I worship Sundarānanda Ṭhākura who made a *kadamba* flower bloom on a lime tree."

On another occasion, he dove into a river and pulled a crocodile out. He resembled Nityānanda Prabhu as being a savior of the most fallen.

His disappearance took place on the full-moon day of Kārtika month.

Śrī Mīnaketana Rāma Dāsa

amuṁ prāviśatāṁ kāryāt sahajau niśaṭholmukau
mīnaketana-rāmādir vyūhaḥ saṅkarṣaṇo'paraḥ

"The two brothers Niśaṭha and Ulmuka entered into the expansions of Nityānanda Prabhu as Mīnaketana and Rāma." (*Gaura-gaṇoddeśa-dīpikā* 68)

RĀMA DĀSA, A DEVOTEE OF NITYĀNANDA

Though the *Gaura-gaṇoddeśa-dīpikā* here indicates that Mīnaketana and Rāma Dāsa are two different people, it is clear from the *Caitanya Caritāmṛta* and the *Bhakti-ratnākara* that Mīnaketana Rāma Dāsa is one single individual. Perhaps both Niśaṭha and Ulmuka, participants in Baladeva *līlā*, entered into the body of Mīnaketana Rāma Dāsa during Gaura *līlā*.

Nothing is known about the details of Mīnaketana Rāma Dāsa's birthplace or his parents. From the account of Kṛṣṇadāsa Kavirāja Gosvāmī, it would appear that his residence was somewhere in the vicinity of Kavirāja Gosvāmī's home in Jhamatpur.

He was one of the associates of Nityānanda Prabhu who went to Khetari with Jāhnavā Devī. Narahari Cakravartī writes that the three worlds are purified by the sight of Vaiṣṇavas like Mīnaketana Rāma Dāsa:

"All the great devotees gathered to go to Khetari. Seeing them, the entire universe is sanctified. Mīnaketana Rāma Dāsa, Abhirāma Ṭhākura, Murāri Caitanya, Jñāna Dāsa, Mahīdhara, Śaṅkara, Kamālākara Pippalāi, Nṛsiṁha Caitanya, Jīva and Kānāi Paṇḍita." (*Bhakti-ratnākara* 10.372, 374-5)

Kṛṣṇadāsa Kavirāja Gosvāmī recounts some details about Mīnaketana Rāma Dāsa in his *Caitanya Caritāmṛta* in the course of glorifying Nityānanda Prabhu. Just as Nityānanda Prabhu was an *avadhūta*, his follower Mīnaketana also behaved in the manner of an *avadhūta*. Śrīla Bhakti Siddhānta Sarasvatī Gosvāmī Ṭhākura discusses the word in his commentary: "The word *avadhūta* is defined by Śrīdhara Svāmī in his commentary to *Bhāgavatam* 3.1.19 by the words *asaṁskṛta-deha*, or "one who does not take care of his body." Nityānanda Prabhu is an *avadhūta*, and his disciple is also an eternally perfect, *mahā-bhāgavata paramahaṁsa* like him – beyond the *varṇāśrama* system. As a result, none of the characteristics of any of the castes or states of life were manifest in his body. He was completely absorbed in the mood of Vraja and had no consideration whatsoever for the duties of the body." (*Anubhāṣya*, 1.5.161).

RĀMA DĀSA AT JHAMATPUR

On one occasion, Mīnaketana Rāma Dāsa was invited to attend an all-night *kīrtana* at Kṛṣṇadāsa Kavirāja's home in Jhamatpur. The other guests were impressed by his appearance and his display of transcendental emotions and came to pay their obeisances to his feet. In his ecstatic mood, he would sometimes hit the person prostrated before him with his flute, sometimes slap him. Occasionally, he would even climb onto some other devotees' shoulders. Tears poured from his eyes like the uninterrupted flow of a river. Seeing this, other devotees also felt their eyes fill with tears. All the eight amazing manifestations of ecstatic love appeared in his body. When he shouted the name of Nityānanda Prabhu in this state, all the devotees felt their hearts become full with divine ecstasy.

Guṇārṇava Miśra was engaged as a *pūjārī* in Kavirāja Gosvāmī's house. This *brāhmaṇa* was a *kaniṣtha adhikārī* and had faith in the deity but did not have much enthusiasm to pay him proper respect. Mīnaketana Rāma Dāsa was able to understand that this Guṇārṇava Miśra had no faith in Nityānanda Prabhu and that for this reason he was deliberately ignoring him because he was Nityānanda Prabhu's disciple. In order to teach the world, Rāma Dāsa said,

"Just look! A second Romaharṣaṇa Sūta who did not come forward to show respect when he saw Balarāma!" (*Caitanya Caritāmṛta* 1.5.170)

Romaharṣaṇa Sūta was seated on the *vyāsāsana* and engaged in reciting the *Bhāgavata* at the request of the assembled sages in Naimiṣaraṇya when Lord Baladeva Himself appeared there. All the other sages stood up to show Lord Balarāma the appropriate respect, with the exception of Romaharṣaṇa. For this, he was punished. Someone who is proud has no authority to speak on the *Bhāgavata*, nor, for that matter, is he authorized to worship the deity. The Bhāgavata is identical to Kṛṣṇa himself. However, in this case, the *pūjārī* Guṇārṇava Miśra did not object to Rāma Dāsa's chastisement, and he performed all the services that he was supposed to do.

At the end of the *kīrtana* festival, after the *pūjārī* left, however, Mīnaketana Rāma Dāsa got into an argument with Kṛṣṇadāsa Kavirāja's brother. Kavirāja Gosvāmī's brother had strong faith in Caitanya Mahāprabhu, but lacked such faith in Nityānanda Prabhu. When Rāma Dāsa discovered this, he broke his flute in anger and left the place. The result of this curse was that Kavirāja Gosvāmī's brother was doomed to destruction. Kavirāja Gosvāmī's himself rebuked his brother, an act which pleased Lord Nityānanda Prabhu, who came to him in a dream and told him to go to live in Vrindavan.

The above account reveals how dear Mīnaketana Rāma Dāsa was to Nityānanda Prabhu. Nityānanda Prabhu's followers are like Him: they are deliverers of the most fallen and capable of fulfilling all desires.

Śrī Uddhava Dāsa

śrīmān uddhava-dāso'pi candrāveśāvatārakaḥ

"Uddhava Dāsa is an *āveśa* avatāra of the moon god." (*Gaura-gaṇoddeśa-dīpikā* 192)

In the *Caitanya Caritāmṛta* (1.12.83), it is said that Uddhava Dāsa is a branch of Gadādhara Paṇḍita Gosvāmī. As such, he is mentioned by Yadunātha Dāsa, a disciple of Gadādhara Paṇḍita Gosvāmī, in the *Śākhā-nirṇayāmṛta* (35):

ati-dīna-jane pūrṇa
prema-vitta-pradāyakam
śrīmad-uddhava-dāsākhyaṁ
vande 'haṁ guṇa-śālinam

"I venerate the highly virtuous Uddhava Dāsa, who gave the wealth of love to those who were most fallen."

When Rūpa Gosvāmī was old and living in Vrindavan, he was desperate to see Mādhavendra Purī's Gopāla deity, but unable to go to Govardhan because of his advanced years. At this time, Gopāla came to stay in Mathura at the house of Viṭṭhalnātha, the youngest son of Vallabhācārya, ostensibly out of fear of possible attacks by the Muslim iconoclasts. Rūpa Gosvāmī thus had the opportunity to take His darśana. Uddhava Dāsa was amongst the devotees who stayed with Rūpa Gosvāmī at Viṭṭhalnātha's house for an entire month on this occasion." (*Caitanya Caritāmṛta* 2.18.51, *Bhakti-ratnākara* 5.1333)

Uddhava Dāsa lived in Vrindavan. When Śrīnivāsa Ācārya and Rāghava Gosvāmī were touring Vraja *dhāma*, they came to his cottage. He greeted them with enthusiastic hospitality. Uddhava Dāsa was amongst the devotees who bade farewell to Śrīnivāsa Ācārya, Narottama Dāsa Ṭhākura and Śyāmānanda Prabhu as they set off to Bengal with the books which had been given to them by Jīva Gosvāmī. (*Bhakti-ratnākara* 6.514)

According to the *Gauḍīya Vaiṣṇava Abhidhāna*, there are two more devotees named Uddhava Dāsa. One was a follower of Sanātana Gosvāmī who performed *bhajana* in Nandagaon on the banks of Pavana Sarovara; another was an initiated disciple of Rādhā Mohana Ṭhākura who was a famous poet. He lived in the Murshidabad district in the village of Teyagram. His real name was Kṛṣṇa Kānta Majumdāra.

Kūrma Vipra

When Mahāprabhu decided to deliver the people of the south, He left Puri on the pretext of going on pilgrimage in the month of Vaiśākha. At Nityānanda Prabhu's request, He accepted the *brāhmaṇa* Kṛṣṇadāsa as a servant. Distributing *prema* to all as He passed, He arrived in the place known as Kurmasthan (or Kurma Kshetra) where he bestowed his blessings on the Vedic *brāhmaṇa* also named Kūrma.

Kṛṣṇadāsa Kavirāja Gosvāmī has not given anything more than this *brāhmaṇa*'s name in his account of this event in his *Caitanya Caritāmṛta*. Though many devotees descended to this world to participate in the Lord's pastimes, the worldly identity of many of them, unfortunately, remains unknown. There is not much possibility that historians will ever be able to unearth any more information about any of the devotees who are by nature transcendental. Detailed knowledge of the Lord's associates' worldly identities is far less important, however, than the lessons which we are taught through their saintly lives.

Mahāprabhu was subjugated by the intense devotion of Kūrma Vipra to accept his service. He was fortunate enough to be able to take the Lord to his house, where he washed His feet and gave the holy water to all his family members to drink. He gave the Lord food to eat and took His remnants.

"In that village, there was a Vedic *brāhmaṇa* named Kūrma. He respectfully invited Lord Caitanya Mahāprabhu to his home. He washed the Lord's lotus feet and drank the water with his family members. With great affection and respect, he gave Mahāprabhu all kinds of food to eat. After that, all the members of the family shared His remnants." (*Caitanya Caritāmṛta* 2.7.121-3)

The *brāhmaṇa* glorified Mahāprabhu, pleasing Him, but as the Lord left he was unable to bear the thought of being separated from Him. He asked the Lord for permission to accompany Him, but the Lord denied it, telling him to stay at home and chant the names of Kṛṣṇa and then to take the role of an *ācārya* and preach the Holy Names to others.

[The Lord said,] "Never make this suggestion again. You should rather remain at home and constantly chant the holy name of Kṛṣṇa. Instruct whomever you see to follow the orders of Kṛṣṇa. Become a spiritual master on my order and deliver everyone in this land. Do this and you will never be entangled in the waves of materialistic life. Indeed, you will have My company again, here in this very place." (*Caitanya Caritāmṛta* 2.7.127-9)

Śrīla Bhakti Siddhānta Sarasvatī Gosvāmī Ṭhākura has elaborated on this instruction to Kūrma Vipra in his *Anubhāṣya* as follows: "For those who are determined to abandon everything to take shelter of the Supreme Lord Śrī Caitanya Mahāprabhu and serve Him exclusively, the Lord here gives the instruction to remain in the home, that is, to give up the pride of being a heroic performer of *bhajana* and to adopt a regular practice of chanting the Holy Name of Kṛṣṇa in the home and, with the humility that is characterized by remaining in the householder life, instruct others in chanting the Holy Names. If one chants the Holy Name with humility and takes up the duties of a spiritual master to propagate its glories, he will never become entangled in the 'waves of materialistic life' in the form of the desire for self-aggrandizement.

Many foolish people think that it is an impediment to spiritual practice to teach through writing books as Rūpa Gosvāmī, Sanātana Gosvāmī, Jīva Gosvāmī or Raghunātha Dāsa Gosvāmī have done, or that to accept large numbers of disciples like Madhvācārya, Rāmānujācārya or Narottama Dāsa Ṭhākura. Indeed, these less-intelligent persons even claim that such activities are material entanglements. By adhering to these erroneous ideas, they become offenders to such genuine unalloyed devotees. Such devotees understand Lord Gaurāṅga's teachings very well and give up their false pride and the show of humility and do not demonstrate inimical attitude towards those who are devoid of devotion to the Lord. They thus follow the order of Mahāprabhu for their own advancement in *bhajana*."

FRIENDSHIP WITH VĀSUDEVA VIPRA

While in Kurmasthan, Mahāprabhu was also attracted by the heartfelt devotion of the leper Vāsudeva Vipra. He delivered him and embraced him, transforming him into a handsome man. Vāsudeva said:

"Listen, O merciful one! The qualities You possess could not possibly manifest in an ordinary living being. The lowest of the low run away at the sight and smell of my body, yet You touched and embraced me! You are the supremely independent Lord. But I was well off in my humble state. By transforming me, You have put me at risk of becoming proud." (*Caitanya Caritāmṛta* 2.7.144-6)

The pleased Lord then gave him assurances that even though his body had been made handsome, he would not become entangled in the egoism that physical beauty usual brings. He also told him to help others by teaching them to chant the Holy Names of Kṛṣṇa.

The mercy of the Lord and His devotees upon seeing the distress of the conditioned souls is demonstrated by these words of the Lord and the above quotation from the writings of Śrīla Bhakti Siddhānta Sarasvatī Gosvāmī Ṭhākura. As Mahāprabhu left the pilgrimage town of Kurma Kshetra, Kūrma Vipra and Vāsudeva embraced each other and sang His glories, while absorbed in transcendental divine love.

Through this pastime, the Lord instructs everyone that He cannot be won over by any material qualities and that only exclusive devotion can please Him. He does not consider the external appearance of a one-pointed devotee.

Śrī Vāsudeva Vipra

"Then Mahāprabhu set off for South India. In Kurma Kshetra, he liberated Vāsudeva Vipra." (*Caitanya Caritāmṛta* 2.1.103)

Śrīla Bhakti Siddhānta Sarasvatī Gosvāmī Prabhupāda has written the following comments on Kurma Kshetra, or Kurmasthan. "On the BNR railroad line, there is a station named Chikakol Road in the district of Ganjam. Eight miles east of this station is a place known as Kurmachalam (Kūrma's mountain) or Sri Kurmam. This place, where Śrī Kūrmadeva is worshipped, is the most popular pilgrimage site for those who speak the Telugu language. When Rāmānuja was flung there by Lord Jagannātha in the eleventh century of the Śaka era, he thought that the Kūrma deity was a Śiva-liṅga and so started a fast. Later, when he learned that the deity was in fact of Viṣṇu, he arranged the worship."

Ganjam is a district of Odisha. Today, the Chikakol Road station is found in the state of Andhra Pradesh and has been renamed Sri Kakulam Road. The BNR railway line is now India's South Eastern Railway.

THE LORD'S MERCY TO VĀSUDEVA

Vāsudeva Vipra was a great devotee of Mahāprabhu in South India. It is very difficult to recognize a devotee. When a devotee is very poor and materially undistinguished, it is very hard for an ordinary mundane person to recognize him. Mahāprabhu revealed Vāsudeva Vipra's glories to the world. While wandering through South India, Mahāprabhu blessed a *brāhmaṇa* named Kūrma. Vāsudeva Vipra was a leper who upon learning that Mahāprabhu was at Kūrma's house, went there in the hope of getting a glance of Him. He learned from Kūrma, however, that the Lord had already departed. Vāsudeva was so disappointed at this news that he he fainted and fell on the ground.

The all-knowing and most merciful Lord is so affectionate to His devotees that even though He had already walked a good distance from there, He returned to grant His *darśana* to Vāsudeva and embraced him. Mahāprabhu's touch immediately cured him of his leprosy and turned him into a healthy and handsome young man. The Lord is everywhere. If one is eager to attain Him, one can attain Him. The Lord can only be won over by devotion. He takes no notice of any mundane qualification or virtue. He took no notice of Vāsudeva's advanced case of leprosy but embraced him out of His affection for him as a devotee.

"Vāsudeva was an incredible individual. The open sores of his body were home to maggots, which fed off the puss and blood that oozed from them. If one of them should fall from the wound, Vāsudeva would pick it up off the ground and put it back." (*Caitanya Caritāmṛta* 2.7.136-7)

When Vāsudeva Vipra saw the limitless mercy of the Supreme Lord, he responded in his amazement with a verse spoken by Sudāmā Vipra from *Śrīmad Bhāgavatam*:

kvāhaṁ daridraḥ pāpīyān
kva kṛṣṇaḥ śrī-niketanaḥ
brahma-bandhur iti smāhaṁ
bāhubhyāṁ parirambhitaḥ

"I am sinful, poor and the lowest of *brāhmaṇas*, whereas Śrī Kṛṣṇa is an abode of the goddess of fortune. Though I am an unqualified *brāhmaṇa*, He has embraced me in His arms. This is truly astonishing." (*Śrīmad Bhāgavatam* 10.89.16)

Such mercy could never be found in an ordinary human being. Ordinary people would stay far away from Vāsudeva, being disgusted by the foul odor of his disease, but Mahāprabhu, the independent Lord, not only touched him but embraced him.

A VAIṢṆAVA'S BODY IS NEVER MATERIAL

It should be remembered that a Vaiṣṇava's body is never material. It is transcendental and completely pure. Mahāprabhu's unparalleled affection for His devotees was displayed through the following conversation with Haridāsa Ṭhākura, which has been described in the *Caitanya Caritāmṛta* as follows:

Haridāsa said, "You are the merciful Supreme Lord; no one can understand the depths of Your heart. Vāsudeva had such terrible leprosy that his gaping wounds were full of maggots, yet you are so merciful that You embraced him in spite of it. Your embrace turned him into a young man as beautiful as Cupid. No one can understand the waves of Your mercy."

The Lord answered, "A devotee's body is never material. The devotee's transcendental body is made of divine and ecstatic spiritual substance." (*Caitanya Caritāmṛta* 3.4.188-191)

A person who is averse to Śrī Kṛṣṇa sees a Vaiṣṇava's body only externally and thus is deprived of the vision of his spiritual form.

THE LORD'S INSTRUCTION
TO VĀSUDEVA

When Vāsudeva became a beautiful young man by the Lord's miraculous touch, he became afraid that he would become vain and that would be his downfall. Those who are proud and vain are deprived of the Lord's mercy and are not even qualified to chant the names of the Lord.

Mahāprabhu considered Vāsudeva Vipra to be most qualified and instructed him to act as an *ācārya* :

[The Lord said,] "You will never become vain if you constantly chant Kṛṣṇa's name. Deliver the fallen souls by instructing them about Kṛṣṇa, and Kṛṣṇa will very quickly accept you." (*Caitanya Caritāmṛta* 2.7.147-8)

Śrī Raghupati Upādhyāya

Śrī Raghupati Upādhyāya was a *brāhmaṇa* who originated from the region of Mithila. He was born in Tirhut, in the Sitamari subdivision of the Dvarbhanga district in Bihar state. Tirhut, or Tiruhita, was also the name for a kingdom which included the four modern districts of Dvarbhanga, Saran, Muzaffarpur and Champaran in northwestern Bihar. Paramānanda Purī also came from Tirhut.

When Mahāprabhu heard Raghupati Upādhyāya's verses that are fully enriched with devotional mellows, He became overwhelmed with feelings of ecstatic love. Śrīla Rūpa Gosvāmī later included several of these verses in his *Padyāvalī*. Kṛṣṇadāsa Kavirāja Gosvāmī has recounted the meeting of Raghupati with the Lord in his *Caitanya Caritāmṛta*, *Madhya-līlā*, Chapter 19. This meeting took place when Mahāprabhu was staying in the house of Vallabhācārya in Prayag. [See the Chapter on Rūpa Gosvāmī.]

"At that time Raghupati Upādhyāya arrived there. He was from the Tiruhit district, a learned scholar, a Vaiṣṇava and a gentleman. He offered his respects to Śrī Caitanya Mahāprabhu, and the Lord blessed him, saying, 'May you always remember Kṛṣṇa.' " (*Caitanya Caritāmṛta* 2.19.92-3)

When Mahāprabhu asked Raghupati to speak to Him about Kṛṣṇa, Raghupati recited a verse of his own composition:

śrutim apare smṛtim itare
bhāratam anye bhajantu bhava-bhītāḥ
aham iha nandaṁ vande
yasyālinde paraṁ brahma

"Let those afraid of material existence worship the Vedas and *Upaniṣadas*, the *smṛtis* and *purāṇas*, or the *Mahābhārata*, as they wish. I, on the other hand, shall simply worship Mahārāja Nanda, in whose courtyard plays the Supreme Divinity Kṛṣṇa." (*Padyāvalī*, 126)

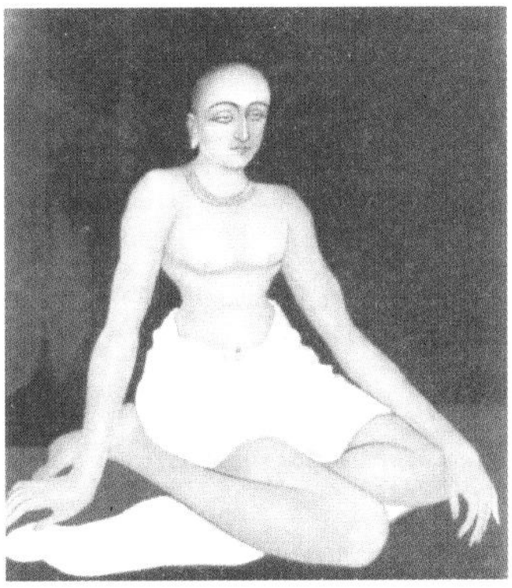

Mahāprabhu was ecstatic upon hearing this beautiful verse and asked to hear more. Raghupati acquiesced by reciting another verse he had written:

kaṁ prati kathayitum īśe
samprati ko vā pratītim āyātu
gopatitanayākuñje
gopavadhūṭīviṭaṁ brahma

"Who will believe me when I say that the Supreme Truth Kṛṣṇa is lusting after the young cowherd girls in the bushes by the banks of the River Yamuna?" (*Padyāvalī*, 98)

As the Lord heard more and more of Raghupati's compositions, which stimulate the remembrance of Kṛṣṇa's pastimes, He went deeper and deeper into a trance of *prema*, demonstrating powerful ecstatic symptoms which made a great impression on Raghupati Upādhyāya, leading him to believe that Mahāprabhu is Kṛṣṇa Himself.

When Mahāprabhu asked Raghupati which of Kṛṣṇa's many forms is the best, he replied, "The Lord's blackish form is supreme." Mahāprabhu then asked, "Which abode of the Lord is the best?" Raghupati answered, "Mathura is the best city." In response to Mahāprabhu's question about Kṛṣṇa's best age, he answered that it is His adolescence. And then to the question about the best amongst the *rasas*, Raghupati stated that the primary *rasa*, or the conjugal love, is supreme. The complete verse is found in the *Padyāvalī* (82):

śyāmam eva paraṁ rūpaṁ
purī madhupurī varā
vayaḥ kaiśorakaṁ dhyeyam
ādya eva paro rasaḥ

Mahāprabhu embraced Raghupati in His ecstasy, and then Raghupati began to dance. Vallabha Bhaṭṭa and all the members of his household were astounded by Raghupati Upādhyāya's great fortune.

The Sanoḍiya Vipra

Kṛṣṇadāsa Kavirāja Gosvāmī tells about Mahāprabhu's meetings with the Sanoḍiya *brāhmaṇa* in the seventeenth and eighteenth chapters of *Caitanya Caritāmṛta's Madhya-līlā*. Nothing is known about this *brāhmaṇa*'s family background – even his name is unknown. What we are concerned with here is the teachings which are to be found through his example.

MAHĀPRABHU MEETS THE SANOḌIYA BRĀHMAṆA

When Mahāprabhu arrived in Mathura after passing through Kashi and Prayag, He first came to the Vishram Ghat in Mathura, where He bathed. Then He visited Kṛṣṇa's birthplace and the deity of Ādi Keśava, dancing before Him in ecstatic love. Other visitors to the temple were amazed and charmed by the Lord's ecstatic dancing. At the same time, a certain *brāhmaṇa* fell at the Lord's feet then started to dance with Him, joining the Lord in His trance of divine love. They embraced each other and then raised their arms and while singing the Holy Names of Hari and Kṛṣṇa. A great tumult arose within the Ādi Keśava temple when everyone present joined the loud chanting of *kīrtana*. When the *kīrtana* finished, Mahāprabhu took the *brāhmaṇa* aside and asked him:

"You are a sincere and respectable elderly *brāhmaṇa*. Tell me where you got this wealth of love for Kṛṣṇa." (*Caitanya Caritāmṛta* 2.17.155)

In reply, the *brāhmaṇa* said, "While on his tour, Mādhavendra Purīpāda came to Mathura. He blessed me by setting foot in my humble abode. He initiated me by giving me the *mantra* and farther blessed me by accepting food which I had cooked. He uncovered the Gopāla deity which is still being worshipped to this day in Govardhan."

As soon as He learned of the elderly *brāhmaṇa*'s relationship to Mādhavendra Purī, the Lord fell at his feet. The *brāhmaṇa* became afraid at this action of the Lord and himself touched the Lord's feet. To teach that the spiritual master's godbrothers are worshipable by the disciple, the Lord said, "You are my guru, and I am practically your disciple. It is not fitting for a guru to pay obeisances to a disciple." (*Caitanya Caritāmṛta* 2.17.170)

The *brāhmaṇa* was astonished by the Lord's humility and said, "You are a *sannyāsī*; it is not proper for a *sannyāsī* to pay obeisances to a fallen person like myself." But the *brāhmaṇa* had also determined from the Lord's ecstatic symptoms that He too had some relationship to Mādhavendra Purī. He asked the Lord's traveling companion, Balabhadra Bhattācārya, the name of the Lord's guru. Upon learning that his guess had been correct, he was overjoyed.

The *brāhmaṇa* then invited the Lord to his house and the Lord accepted. Thus the *brāhmaṇa* got the opportunity to personally render Him various kinds of service.

THE LORD ACCEPTS THE BRAHMIN'S INVITATION

When it was time, the *brāhmaṇa* asked Balabhadra Bhattācārya to cook the Lord's lunch, but Mahāprabhu intervened. He said, "Puri Gosai ate your cooking, so you should cook for Me too. This is what I have learned from his example."

The Lord's host belonged to the Sanoḍiya community of *brāhmaṇas*. According to Śrīla Bhaktivinoda Ṭhākura, members of the business community (*vaiśyas*) in the north of India are divided into several castes: Agrawalas, Kalwars, Sanwars, etc. Of these, the Agrawalas are considered to be very pure, while the two other groups are considered fallen as a result of their own *karma*. Those *brāhmaṇas* who perform the ritual activities for the gold and jewellery merchants (Sanwars) are known as Sanoḍiya *brāhmaṇas*. Normally, because of these low-caste associations, they are considered to be fallen as a caste. *Sannyāsīs* thus refuse to accept food in their homes.

Śrīla Bhakti Siddhānta Sarasvatī Gosvāmī Ṭhākura adds to this the following analysis based on pure devotion. "The Sanoḍiya *brāhmaṇa* was a pure devotee, and although even drinking water from his hand was prohibited due to his caste status, he nevertheless was fixed in the *daiva-varṇāśrama* system and the Absolute Truth, both of which favor pure devotion. Those who judged devotees in terms of their mundane caste status (the *adaiva-varṇāśrama*) or who cast aspersions on *mahā-prasāda* were unhesitatingly identified as wicked fools by the Lord."

Though *sannyāsīs* generally do not accept food from members of the Sanoḍiya caste, Mādhavendra Purī did not hesitate to do so. Judging this *brāhmaṇa* to have the qualities of a Vaiṣṇava, Purīpāda gave him initiation and then ate in his house. In spite of that, the Sanoḍiya *brāhmaṇa* himself was simply taking consideration of the Lord's reputation, which would be subject to criticism if He ignored caste rules prevalent at that time. The Lord explained that since there may be some difference of opinion between the various scriptures and the seers, the best course of action was to follow the example set by those saintly persons who establish the principles of religion. Finally, the *brāhmaṇa* could understand the desire of the Lord, and he personally cooked for Him.

SAVING THE LORD'S COMPANIONS FROM DANGER

As the Lord traveled from Puri to Mathura, His absorption in ecstatic love increased a hundred fold over that which He experienced in Puri. Upon arriving in Mathura, it increased a thousand-fold, and when He went through the twelve forests of Vraja, it increased a hundred-thousand fold. Before He left Nilachal, Rāmānanda Rāya and Svarūpa Dāmodara Gosvāmī had arranged for two people to accompany Him, Balabhadra Bhattācārya and another *brāhmaṇa* servant.

While He was wandering through the twelve forests, a Rājaputa, Kṛṣṇadāsa, was attracted by the Lord and joined Him and His companions. When the Lord came to Akrura Ghat, He jumped into the Yamuna in a transport of ecstasy and remained submerged for a long period of time. Kṛṣṇadāsa became afraid that the Lord had drowned and started to cry out for help. Balabhadra Bhattācārya heard his shouts and immediately went into the water to pull the Lord out.

Balabhadra was anxious about the Lord's distraction from the normal state due to His absorption in divine ecstasy, and so he discussed with Mādhavendra Purī's disciple the Sanoḍiya *brāhmaṇa* about what could be done to protect Him. After some discussion, they decided that it was not wise to allow the Lord to stay any longer in Vraja-mandala. Rather, by telling Him of the full-moon bath at the end of the month of Māgha, known also as Makara-saṅkrānti, they should incite Him to go to Soro Kshetra on the banks of the Ganges, whence they could go on to Prayag. Since the Sanoḍiya *brāhmaṇa* was the worshipable godbrother of His guru, the Lord was not able to refuse him when he made the suggestion to leave Vraja.

Though the Lord's body left the boundaries of Vrindavan, His consciousness remained fixed in love for Kṛṣṇa, and His ecstatic trance remained unbroken. As He became tired from walking, the Lord sat down underneath a tree. Nearby, a herd of cows was grazing, which reminded Him of Kṛṣṇa's Vraja *līlā*. All of a sudden, a cowherd began to play his flute, causing Mahāprabhu to faint in an ecstasy of love. The Lord fell to the ground, His breathing stopped and foam accumulated around His mouth. At this very moment, the Muslim soldier Bijlī Khān was passing by with a troop of ten cavalrymen. On seeing the Lord's condition, Bijlī Khān immediately became suspicious that foul play was afoot. He thought that the four men accompanying the Lord had poisoned Him with *dhuturā* in order to steal gold He had in His possession.

The Pāṭhāna immediately made prisoners of the Lord's four companions with the intention of killing them. The two Bengali *brāhmaṇas* began to tremble in fear; the two others, however, were fearless and able to think on their feet. The Sanoḍiya *brāhmaṇa* tried to explain to the Pāṭhana by saying: "This *sannyāsī* is my guru, and He happens to have an illness which makes Him faint from time to time. Go ahead and tie us up and wait for a few minutes. My guru will soon regain consciousness, and you will be able to understand the truth. I know hundreds of people in the Emperor's court."

Bijlī Khān listened to the Sanoḍiya *brāhmaṇa* speak fearlessly and began to doubt his understanding of the situation. He replied, "I can recognize from your speech that you are from Mathura, but these two people are foreigners. They are also trembling, so they must be guilty of something."

The Rājaputa Kṛṣṇadāsa sensed that the situation was becoming more dangerous and said brazenly, trying to frighten the Pāṭhāna, "I live in the neighboring village. I have two hundred soldiers with a hundred cannons. I only have to shout and they will come here and take your horses and equipment. I think that you must be the real highwaymen and not these two Bengalis."

The Muslim cavalrymen were cast into fear by the Rājaputa's fearless words. Meanwhile, the Lord came back to consciousness and in a transport of ecstasy, loudly cried out the names "Hari! Hari!" and began to dance. The Pāṭhāna soldiers were overcome by fear when they heard the Lord bellow and saw His ecstatic dancing. They immediately liberated their four prisoners so that the Lord did not see His devotees tied up. The Muslims were attracted by the Lord's physical beauty and spiritual mood and submitted their doubts in front of him.

The Lord answered, "I have no wealth. These four men are My companions. I sometimes suffer from epilepsy and fall unconscious as a result. These four companions mercifully stay with Me when this happens to protect Me and take care of Me."

ONWARD TO PRAYAG

Upon His arrival at Soro Kshetra, Mahāprabhu took His bath in the Ganges and then desired to set off for Prayag along the banks of the holy river. He turned to the Sanoḍiya *brāhmaṇa* and the Rājaput Kṛṣṇadāsa. "You have taken such trouble to come all this way from Mathura just to show us the way. I do not wish you to trouble yourselves any farther. Please go back now."

They answered, "We don't know when we will have the good fortune of Your company again. There is a great likelihood of danger on the highways of this country, which is dominated by unscrupulous persons. Balabhadra Bhattācārya does not know the local language. We think that these are good reasons for us to accompany You as far as Prayag."

The Lord approved their desire by His mild laugh.

Śrī Bijlī Khān (The Pāṭhāna Vaiṣṇava)

Śrī Bijlī Khān was a Pāṭhāna Muslim. Even so, after receiving Mahāprabhu's mercy, he became well known as a Vaiṣṇava. He was a contemporary of Mahāprabhu. His father was a rich man. Kṛṣṇadāsa Kavirāja Gosvāmī has described how he met the Lord and received His mercy in the eighteenth chapter of *Caitanya Caritāmṛta's Madhya-līlā.*

MAHĀPRABHU LEAVES VRAJA

That year, Mahāprabhu took the deserted Jharikhand route to Vrindavan after the Rathayātrā festival. Rāmānanda Rāya and Svarūpa Dāmodara Gosvāmī arranged for two people to accompany Him, Balabhadra Bhattācārya and another *brāhmaṇa* servant. As He traveled, His absorption in ecstatic love increased a hundred-fold over that which He experienced in Puri. Upon arriving in Mathura, it increased a thousand-fold, and when He went through the twelve forests of Vraja, it increased a hundred-thousand fold.

As He was wandering through the twelve forests, the Lord came to the place known as Akrura Ghat on the Yamuna. The Lord jumped into the water and remained immersed for a long time. Kṛṣṇadāsa, a Rājaputa who had been attracted by the Lord after seeing Him in Vrindavan and was accompanying Him, became afraid that the Lord had drowned and started to cry out for help. Balabhadra Bhattācārya heard his shouts and quickly dove into the water to pull Him out.

Balabhadra was anxious about the Lord's great distraction due to His divine ecstasies, and so he discussed with Mādhavendra Purī's disciple the Sanoḍiya *brāhmaṇa* about what could be done to protect Him. After some discussion, they decided that the best thing to do was to propose to Mahāprabhu that He go to Soro Kshetra on the banks of the Ganges for the full-moon bath at the end of the month of Māgha, known also as Makara-saṇkrānti. From there, they could take Him on to Prayag. The Rājaputa Kṛṣṇadāsa and the Mathura *brāhmaṇa* were well acquainted with the route along the Ganges, and so they remained with the Lord and the two *brāhmaṇas* as guides.

As they tired from walking, the Lord sat down underneath a tree. Nearby, a herd of cows was grazing, which reminded the Lord of Kṛṣṇa's Vraja *līlā*. Suddenly, the cowherd began to play his flute, causing Mahāprabhu to faint in ecstasy. He fell to the ground, His breathing stopped and foam accumulated around His mouth.

BIJLĪ KHĀN TIES UP THE LORD'S COMPANIONS

At this very moment, the Muslim soldier Bijlī Khān was passing by with a troop of ten cavalrymen. His immediate suspicion on seeing the Lord's condition was that the four men accompanying Him (Kṛṣṇadāsa Rājaputa, the Sanoḍiya *brāhmaṇa* who was a disciple of Śrī Mādhavendra Purī, Balabhadra Bhattācārya and a *brāhmaṇa*) had poisoned Him with *dhuturā* in order to steal His money.

The Pāṭhāna immediately bound the Lord's four companions, causing the two Bengali *brāhmaṇas* to tremble in fear. The two others, however, were fearless and quickly thought of a way out of the situation. The Sanoḍiya *brāhmaṇa* explained to the Pāṭhāna as follows: "I am a *brāhmaṇa* from Mathura and I know hundreds of people in the Emperor's court. This *sannyāsī* is my guru, and He happens to be ill, which makes Him faint from time to time. Tie us up and wait for a few minutes. He will regain consciousness and you will know the truth for yourself."

The Pāṭhāna listened and said, "I can understand what you two are saying. You are from Mathura, but these two Bengalis are trembling with guilt. They must have done something wrong."

The Rājaputa Kṛṣṇadāsa was acutely aware of the danger of the situation and said, "I live in the neighboring village. I have two hundred soldiers with a hundred cannons at my command. I only have to shout and they will come here and take your horses and equipment. I think that you must be robbers, not these two Bengalis. You are only interested in robbing pilgrims like us."

The Muslim cavalrymen were cast into doubt and fear by these fearless words. Meanwhile, the Lord came back to consciousness and in a transport of ecstasy, shouted out the names "Hari! Hari!" and began to dance. The Pāṭhāna soldiers were overcome by fear when they heard the Lord roar and saw His ecstatic dancing. They immediately liberated their four prisoners, and the Lord never saw His devotees tied up. Balabhadra Bhaṭṭācārya consoled the Lord and made Him sit, and the Lord came back to external awareness upon seeing the Muslims in front of Him. They were attracted by the Lord's physical beauty and by His spiritual mood, and they asked Him the question that had been troubling them.

The Lord answered, "I am a *sannyāsī* and I have no wealth. These four men are my companions. I sometimes suffer from epilepsy and fall unconscious as a result. These four companions mercifully stay with Me when this happens to protect Me and take care of Me."

THE LORD DISCUSSES RELIGION WITH A SUFI

In the group of cavalrymen, one Muslim dressed all in black introduced himself as a saintly person. He was pleased by the Lord's appearance and wished to discuss scriptures with Him. He established that the Supreme Truth was impersonal on the basis of the Islamic scriptures. The Lord, however, demonstrated the invalidity of the Sufi's arguments by giving evidence from the Koran, establishing the personal nature of the Supreme Truth and the Supreme Lord's transcendental qualities. Then the Lord went on to refute the philosophies of *karma*, *jñāna* and *yoga* and established pure love of God as the supreme goal of life.

All the Pāṭhānas were enchanted by the Lord's physical appearance and were even more attracted when they heard Him speak on the goal of spiritual life. The Sufi Pāṭhāna began spontaneously to chant the names of Kṛṣṇa. When Mahāprabhu heard the saintly Muslim chant the Lord's names, He was pleased and said that all the sins that he had accumulated over millions of births had been destroyed and that he had been purified. The Lord told them all to chant, which they did. He initiated the Sufi Pāṭhāna in the Holy Name and gave him the name Rāma Dāsa. When the prince Bijlī Khān saw the good fortune of his own servant, he fell down at the Lord's feet and repeated the name "Kṛṣṇa, Kṛṣṇa." The Lord also blessed him.

"After bestowing His mercy upon them in this way, Mahāprabhu continued on His way. All the Muslim soldiers then became mendicants and were celebrated as the 'Pāṭhāna Vaiṣṇavas.' They toured all over the country, glorifying Mahāprabhu's activities. Bijlī Khān became a greatly advanced devotee, and his fame was sung at every holy place of pilgrimage." (*Caitanya Caritāmṛta* 2.18.210-2)

Śrī Dāmodara Paṇḍita

śaivya yāsīd vraje caṇḍī sa dāmodara-paṇḍitaḥ
kutaścit kāryato devī prāviśat taṁ sarasvatī

"The hot-tempered *gopī* named Śaibyā became Dāmodara Paṇḍita in Gaura *līlā*; the goddess Sarasvatī also entered into him for some special purpose." (*Gaura-gaṇoddeśa-dīpikā* 159)

Dāmodara Paṇḍita is considered to be one of Caitanya Mahāprabhu's branches.

"Dāmodara Paṇḍita, one of the branches of the Caitanya tree, was so elevated in love of Lord Caitanya that he once unhesitatingly chastised the Lord with strong words. The Lord, being very much satisfied by this chastisement, sent Dāmodara Paṇḍita to Nabadwip." (*Caitanya Caritāmṛta* 1.10.31-2)

DĀMODARA PAṆḌITA ACCOMPANIES THE LORD TO PURI

After the Lord took *sannyāsa* in Katwa, Nityānanda Prabhu tricked Him into coming to Advaita Prabhu's house in Shantipur. Many people came from Nabadwip to see Him there, one of whom was Dāmodara Paṇḍita. Mahāprabhu stayed ten days in Shantipur, after which He was asked by His mother to make His home in Puri. Dāmodara Paṇḍita was one of the devotees who accompanied the Lord on His trip to Jagannatha Puri. The others were Nityānanda Prabhu, Mukunda Datta and Jagadānanda Paṇḍita.

When Mahāprabhu arrived in Puri, He immediately went to the Jagannātha temple, where He fainted in ecstasy upon seeing Lord Jagannātha. Vāsudeva Sārvabhauma then took Him to his own house to take care of Him.

At that time, Sārvabhauma was convinced of the Māyāvāda philosophy, but by Caitanya Mahāprabhu's mercy, he gave up his predilection for this doctrine and took up the path of devotion. He then wrote two verses (*vairāgya-vidyā-nija-bhakti-yoga...*, *kālān naṣṭaṁ bhakti-yogaṁ nijaṁ yaḥ...*) glorifying Mahāprabhu on a palm leaf and gave it to Jagadānanda Paṇḍita and Dāmodara Paṇḍita to show to the Lord. Mukunda Datta copied the two verses down on the wall in front of the Lord's residence before Jagadānanda Paṇḍita carried it in to show Him. As soon as Mahāprabhu saw the verses, He tore up the palm leaf, but because Mukunda had preserved the verses,[16] the devotees were able to memorize them.

Mahāprabhu took *sannyāsa* during the fortnight of the waxing moon of Māgha. He arrived in Puri in the month of Phālguna and delivered Sārvabhauma Bhaṭṭācārya in the following month of Caitra. He decided to depart alone on His pilgrimage to southern India in the month of Vaiśākha. Nityānanda Prabhu and the other devotees suffered greatly in anticipation of His separation. Nityānanda Prabhu wanted to accompany the Lord, who then apparently criticized them, while in fact praising them. Of Dāmodara Paṇḍita He said:

"Even though I am a *sannyāsī* and Dāmodara Paṇḍita just a *brahmacārī*, he is always telling Me what to do, holding the rod of chastisement over Me. He does not like Me to act independently, and so I do not know how to behave in front of him. By Kṛṣṇa's mercy, he does not care for public opinion, whereas I cannot be indifferent to what people think." (*Caitanya Caritāmṛta* 2.7.25-7)

When Mahāprabhu returned from South India, getting as far as Alalanatha, He sent His servant companion Kṛṣṇadāsa to inform Nityānanda Prabhu and the other devotees that He had arrived. Dāmodara Paṇḍita joined Jagadānanda Paṇḍita, Nityānanda Prabhu and Mukunda and joyfully rushed onto the main road where they met Him.

"As soon as He heard that the Lord had arrived, Nityānanda Prabhu got up and started off to meet Him, as nothing could hold back His love. Jagadānanda Paṇḍita, Dāmodara Paṇḍita and Mukunda all danced down the

16 The verses are as found in the chapters on Jagadānanda Paṇḍita and Sārvabhauma Bhaṭṭācārya.

road, bursting with joy." (*Caitanya Caritāmṛta* 2.9.339-40)

After Mahāprabhu returned to Puri, He told Sārvabhauma Bhaṭṭācārya about the behavior of Kāla Kṛṣṇadāsa. While in the south, Kāla Kṛṣṇadāsa had left the company of Mahāprabhu, being allured by a group of bhaṭṭathāri women. Mahāprabhu somehow managed to free him from their clutches and brought him back to Puri. He then told him that he was free to go wherever he liked as he was no longer welcome to stay in His company. Kāla Kṛṣṇadāsa started to cry at this rejection, and out of sympathy for him, Nityānanda Prabhu, Dāmodara Paṇḍita, Jagadānanda Paṇḍita and Mukunda discussed what to do with him. Finally, they recommended to the Lord that he be sent to Nabadwip with news of the Lord's return from His pilgrimage. The Lord approved the proposal, and Kāla Kṛṣṇadāsa set off, delighting everyone in Bengal with the good news. Later, when Dāmodara Paṇḍita went back to Bengal himself, he met Kāla Kṛṣṇadāsa.

DĀMODARA PAṆḌITA'S BROTHER ŚAṄKARA PAṆḌITA

Mahāprabhu had a mixture of respect and affection for Dāmodara Paṇḍita. Towards Dāmodara's younger brother Śaṅkara Paṇḍita, however, He had pure affection unseparated by any distance. However, for his own good, He put Śaṅkara Paṇḍita in the care of his older brother because he knew that Dāmodara Paṇḍita would keep him under strict discipline.

"Seeing Śaṅkara, the Lord turned to Dāmodara Paṇḍita and said, 'My love for you is mixed with reverence, whereas I love Śaṅkara with all My heart. For this reason, I am putting him under your care.' " (*Caitanya Caritāmṛta* 2.11.146-7)

During Mahāprabhu's later pastimes, Śaṅkara Paṇḍita stayed in His direct association, sleeping in the same room. The Lord would even sleep sometimes with His feet resting on Śaṅkara Paṇḍita's body.

DĀMODARA PAṆḌITA'S TENDENCY TO CRITICIZE THE LORD'S BEHAVIOR

One day, the Lord Himself began serving *prasāda* to His devotees. Since He was engaged in serving, He was not eating. The other devotees raised their hands and sat silently, refusing to eat until the Lord did so. Finally, Svarūpa Dāmodara asked the Lord to sit down with Nityānanda Prabhu and to take *prasāda*. Svarūpa Dāmodara, Jagadānanda Paṇḍita, Dāmodara Paṇḍita and others then served.

When the Lord returned from the south, Mahārāja Pratāparudra became extremely desperate for a meeting with Him, in the absence of which he was ready to give up his kingdom and become a beggar. The Lord's devotees were all impressed by the King's show of devotion. Sārvabhauma Bhaṭṭācārya suggested to Nityānanda Prabhu and others that instead of directly asking the Lord to meet with the King, they should simply praise his faith and devotion. Following this policy, Nityānanda Prabhu told the Lord of the King's profound devotion and his intention to become a beggar if he could not have a personal audience with Him. Mahāprabhu was somewhat mollified upon hearing this but nevertheless maintained a hardline attitude. He also named Dāmodara Paṇḍita as one of the reasons for such strict behavior:

"It is your wish to take Me to Cuttack to meet with the King. Not only will my spiritual practice be affected by such an action, but people will criticize Me. Let alone what others say, Dāmodara will chastise Me. I will not go to meet the King on your order alone. I will only go if Dāmodara tells Me to." (*Caitanya Caritāmṛta* 2.12.23-5)

Śrīla Bhaktivinoda Ṭhākura comments on these verses in the following way: "Mahāprabhu said, 'I will not grant an audience to the King on your order alone. Only if Dāmodara commands Me shall I consider it.' These words had a particular significance: though the Lord appreciated Dāmodara's devotion, his criticisms of the Lord's behavior were often unnecessary. The Lord was thus hinting that Dāmodara should stop this tendency of unnecessary criticism." (*Amṛta-pravāha-bhāṣya*, 2.12.25)

When Dāmodara Paṇḍita heard the Lord's words, he muttered in response, "Mahāprabhu is the supremely independent Lord. He knows what should or should not be done. No insignificant *jīva* can dictate to Him what to do. The Lord is subject to devotion, and the King is devoted to Him, so He will surely meet with him someday. He may be supremely independent, but He is controlled by His devotee's love."

OTHER PASTIMES IN PURI

Dāmodara Paṇḍita was also the Lord's companion during the Rathayātrā festival. He was one of the five chorus singers in the first of the seven *kīrtana* groups, where Svarūpa Dāmodara was the lead singer. Advaita Ācārya danced in the same group.

When Mahāprabhu set off for Vrindavan through Bengal with many of His associates, Dāmodara Paṇḍita also joined Him. On this occasion, the Lord did not make it all the way to Vraja, as He changed His mind on Sanātana Gosvāmī's advice.

The following year, Mahāprabhu traveled through northern India, going as far as Vrindavan. He then returned to Puri with Balabhadra Bhaṭṭācārya on the path through Jharikhand. When they received the news of the Lord's arrival at Atharo Nala, all the Lord's devotees were extremely joyed and rushed to Narendra Sarovara to welcome Him back. Mahāprabhu paid obeisances to all those who were His elders. At that time, Dāmodara Paṇḍita received His embrace.

MAHĀPRABHU AND THE WIDOW'S SON

A certain beautiful Odishan *brāhmaṇa* widow was living in Puri while Mahāprabhu was there. She had a handsome young son who would come to visit the Lord daily. He would pay his obeisances to the Lord and then engage Him in a lengthy, affectionate conversation. The boy had also become very dear to the Lord, and he was not able to go through a day without seeing Him. The Lord also treated the boy with great warmth. Dāmodara Paṇḍita, however, could not tolerate seeing the affectionate relationship between the Lord and this boy. Though he repeatedly forbade him, the boy continued to come to see the Lord. A child will naturally go where he receives affection, and the Lord was indeed very affectionate to him.

One day, Dāmodara Paṇḍita finally exploded and said sarcastically to the Lord,

"Everyone says You are very learned because of the instructions You so generously give to others. I shall see what kind of master You really are. Now people will glorify You for being a great master, and You will truly be famous as a master throughout Puri." (*Caitanya Caritāmṛta* 3.3.11-12)

The Lord did not understand at first what Dāmodara Paṇḍita was getting at and made him explain himself. The Paṇḍita made himself more explicit: "Lord, You do as You like. No one has the authority to dictate to You. Even so, this is a world full of gossips whose speech no one can stifle. You are learned, so why don't You see the implications of Your acts? Why do You behave so affectionately towards a widow's child? She may be an austere and chaste *brāhmaṇa* woman, but she has the fault of being young and beautiful. You too are a young and handsome man. Such a close relationship with her son gives the world occasion to whisper. Do you think that this is intelligent behavior?"

With that, Dāmodara Paṇḍita fell silent. Mahāprabhu was satisfied with his sentiments and said:

"This is what I call a wave of pure love! No one of My associates is as uninhibited as Dāmodara." (*Caitanya Caritāmṛta* 3.3.19)

MAHĀPRABHU SENDS DĀMODARA PAṆḌITA TO NADIA

One day Mahāprabhu called Dāmodara Paṇḍita and asked him to go to Śacī Mātā in Nabadwip and help supervise her material affairs.

"No one is more suited than you to act in her protection, for you have put even Me on My guard. Amongst My associates, no one is as impartial as you. Religious principles can only be defended by someone who is free from bias or prejudice." (*Caitanya Caritāmṛta* 3.3.22-3)

After telling Dāmodara Paṇḍita to go to Nabadwip, He then consoled him by telling him to return to Puri from time to time. He also told him to pay repeated obeisances to His mother and gave him a confidential message to deliver to her:

"I come to her home repeatedly to eat all the sweetmeats and vegetables she offers. She experiences my coming and eating of the offerings to be real, but because of external separation, she thinks that it is nothing but a dream. During the last Māgha Saṅkrānti festival, she offered the food to the Lord, and while, in meditation, I ate everything in the condition of external separation, she again became bewildered, thinking that she had not offered any food to the Lord. So she cleansed the altar and made the offering once again. This is how I come again and again to eat everything she offers Me. I am attracted by her pure love and thus stay near her always."

Mahāprabhu then gave some Jagannātha *prasāda* to Dāmodara Paṇḍita and told him to give it to Śacī Mātā and the other Nabadwip devotees. Dāmodara set off and carried out the Lord's instructions to the letter. With the Paṇḍita there in Nabadwip, the devotees became very careful about their behavior. No one dared to act in an independent manner. If any one of Mahāprabhu's followers made even the slightest transgression in etiquette, Dāmodara Paṇḍita would establish the standards of behavior by verbally punishing the offender.

"The ignorance of atheism will flee from anyone who hears this history of Dāmodara Paṇḍita's chastisement of the Lord which has just been described." (*Caitanya Caritāmṛta* 3.3.46)

Dāmodara Paṇḍita is thus one of the great devotees through whose preaching the glories of the Holy Name have spread throughout the universe. Mahāprabhu glorified these great souls when He said:

"I have come to possess devotion to Kṛṣṇa through the grace of all these great devotees who have preached love for the Holy Name throughout the world." (*Caitanya Caritāmṛta* 3.7.50)

In the *Bhakti-ratnākara*, Narahari Cakravartī says that Narottama Dāsa Ṭhākura met Dāmodara Paṇḍita in Srīdhāma Mayapur. Narottama Ṭhākura paid his obeisances to his feet in excitement at meeting a direct associate of the Lord. (*Bhakti-ratnākara* 8.93)

Śrī Jagadānanda Paṇḍita

kenāvāntara-bhedena bhedaṁ kurvanti sātvatāḥ
satyabhāmā-prakāśo 'pi jagadānanda-paṇḍitaḥ

"Satyabhāmā in Kṛṣṇa-*līlā* has become Jagadānanda Paṇḍita in Gaura *līlā*." (*Gaura-gaṇoddeśa-dīpikā* 51)

"Jagadānanda Paṇḍita is the very life of the Lord. He is known everywhere as being a manifestation of Satyabhāmā." (*Caitanya Caritāmṛta* 1.10.21)

"All glories to Gaurāṅga, the life of Jagadānanda and Śrī Garbha!

"All glories to the wealth of Puṇḍarīka Vidyānidhi!" (*Caitanya Bhāgavata 2.7.3)*

The parentage, date and place of birth of Jagadānanda Paṇḍita are unknown. Devotees who are seeking devotion as the goal of their lives do not consider detailed information about material identity to be essential. From *Caitanya Bhāgavata* we learn that Jagadānanda Paṇḍita was present at Śrīvāsa Aṅgana and at Candraśekhara's house after Mahāprabhu returned from Gaya and participated in the *saṅkīrtana* movement.

"All the Vaiṣṇavas felt great enthusiasm when they heard that Mahāprabhu had begun His *saṅkīrtana* movement. Every night, these *kīrtanas* took place in the house of Śrīvāsa Paṇḍita, and on certain occasions, in the house of Candraśekhara Ācārya. Nityānanda Prabhu, Gadādhara, Advaita, Śrīvāsa, Vidyānidhi, Murāri, Hiraṇya Haridāsa, Gaṅgā Dāsa, Vanamālī, Vijaya Nandana, Jagadānanda, Buddhimanta Khān, Nārāyaṇa – these were some of the personalities who accompanied the Lord as He danced. Other than such intimate associates, no one was allowed entrance into the *saṅkīrtana*." (*Caitanya Bhāgavata* 2.8.110-113, 117)

Thus from Vṛndāvana Dāsa's account we know that Jagadānanda Paṇḍita is an eternal associate of the Lord and participated with Him in His Nabadwip *saṅkīrtana* pastimes. From this we can surmise that he was born somewhere in Bengal.

JAGADĀNANDA PAṆḌITA ACCOMPANIES THE LORD TO PURI

According to the *Caitanya Bhāgavata*, Jagadānanda Paṇḍita was in the group of devotees who accompanied Mahāprabhu from Shantipur to Puri after He took *sannyāsa*, the others being Nityānanda Prabhu, Gadādhara Paṇḍita, Mukunda Datta, Govinda and Brahmānanda. The *Caitanya Caritāmṛta* version has described the Lord as being accompanied by Nityānanda Prabhu, Jagadānanda, Dāmodara and Mukunda.

On their way to Puri, as they traveled through Atisara, Chatrabhog, northern Odisha, Suvarnarekha, Jaleshwar, Remuna, Jajpur, Vaitarani, Cuttack, Sakshi Gopal, Bhubaneshwar, Kamalpur and Atharo Nala, Mahāprabhu gave His companions many lessons in being impartial and desireless, depending absolutely on the Lord and other such matters. In one place named Ganga Ghata, just across the frontier into Odisha, Mahāprabhu Himself told His companions to wait in a temple while

He went to the village to beg. He came back with rice and vegetables in His cloth and gave them to Jagadānanda Paṇḍita to cook. When he had finished preparing the meal, Mahāprabhu and His other companions ate his cooking with great relish.

According to the *Caitanya Bhāgavata*, Jagadānanda Paṇḍita carried Mahāprabhu's *daṇḍa* (staff) as they walked. One day, Jagadānanda Paṇḍita gave the *daṇḍa* to Nityānanda Prabhu to hold as he went to collect foodstuffs. Nityānanda Prabhu is nondifferent from Balarāma, and He took this opportunity to break Mahāprabhu's staff into three pieces, so teaching His followers to take the *tridaṇḍa* – a staff of three branches signifying the acceptance of Vaiṣṇava *tridaṇḍi sannyāsa* – and threw it in Bhargi River. Jagadānanda Paṇḍita took the broken staff to Mahāprabhu, who was extremely unhappy to have lost His one and only possession. Mahāprabhu told His companions that He wished to travel alone, giving them the choice of whether they would walk in front or after Him. The devotees answered that they would follow Him, not go in front.

"Leaving Nityānanda Prabhu in one place, Jagadānanda Paṇḍita went to look for food. Jagadānanda Paṇḍita carried the Lord's *daṇḍa*, and he left it with Nityānanda Prabhu when he went. He said, 'Take care of the Lord's *daṇḍa*. I will be right back after begging foodstuffs.' " (*Caitanya Bhāgavata* 3.2.202-4)

While walking in front of the other devotees, when He arrived at Atharo Nala Mahāprabhu saw a vision of Kṛṣṇa playing His flute on the pinnacle of the Jagannatha Puri temple. He ran toward the temple and entered to behold the form of Jagannātha, whereupon He fell unconscious. Sārvabhauma Bhaṭṭācārya noticed Him and took Him to his own house, where he saw to His care. Nityānanda Prabhu, Jagadānanda, Mukunda and Dāmodara arrived at the Jagannātha temple not long afterwards. There they heard that the Lord was at Sārvabhauma Paṇḍita's residence and immediately went there. This was Jagadānanda Paṇḍita's first meeting with Sārvabhauma Bhaṭṭācārya.

A PERMANENT ASSOCIATE OF THE LORD AT PURI

The first time that Mahāprabhu wished to go to Vrindavan, He came to Gauḍa-maṇḍala from Puri. He stayed in Vidyanagar for five days; from there He went on to Kuliya, and then through the Maldah district to the village of Ramakeli, where He met with Rūpa Gosvāmī and Sanātana Gosvāmī. Jagadānanda Paṇḍita was amongst the associates of Mahāprabhu present on that occasion along with Nityānanda Prabhu, Haridāsa, Śrīvāsa, Gadādhara, Mukunda, Murāri and Vakreśvara. (*Caitanya Caritāmṛta* 2.1.219)

Jagadānanda Paṇḍita was a permanent associate of the Lord at Puri:

"Gadādhara Paṇḍita, Vakreśvara Paṇḍita, Dāmodara Paṇḍita, Śaṅkara Paṇḍita, Haridāsa, Jagadānanda Paṇḍita, Bhavānanda, Govinda, Kāśīśvara, Paramānanda Purī and Svarūpa Dāmodara all came and made their residence in Puri. They, along with Rāmānanda Rāya and other long-time residents of Sri Kshetra, were Mahāprabhu's permanent companions." (*Caitanya Caritāmṛta* 2.1.252-4)

Jagadānanda Paṇḍita's mood was primarily that of *madhura rasa*, which was very pleasing to Mahāprabhu and won His heart. In the *Caitanya Caritāmṛta* this is described as follows:

"Paramānanda Purī had parental affection for Mahāprabhu, Rāmānanda Rāya experienced love for Him in pure friendship, and Govinda Dāsa's love for Him was as a servant. Gadādhara, Jagadānanda and Svarūpa Dāmodara worshipped in the ecstasy of the chief *rasa*. Mahāprabhu heart was won by these four different loving attitudes." (*Caitanya Caritāmṛta* 2.2.78)

By Mahāprabhu's mercy, Sārvabhauma Bhaṭṭācārya gave up his predilection for the impersonal philosophy of Māyāvāda and took up the path of devotion. He then had a vision of Mahāprabhu in a six-armed form. Later he composed a Sanskrit hymn to the Lord in a hundred verses. He wrote the first two verses glorifying Mahāprabhu on a palm leaf and gave it to Jagadānanda Paṇḍita to show the Lord. Mukunda Datta was there when Jagadānanda Paṇḍita came from Sārvabhauma's house, carrying Jagannātha *prasāda* and the palm leaf. He took the precaution of copying the two verses down on the wall in front of the Lord's residence before Jagadānanda Paṇḍita carried it in to show Him. As soon as Mahāprabhu saw the verses, which glorified Him as an *avatāra* of the Supreme Lord, He tore up the palm leaf. Fortunately, as a result of Mukunda's foresight, the devotees were able to relish the joy of reading the verses. They are as follows:

vairāgya-vidyā-nija-bhakti-yoga-
śikṣārtham ekaḥ puruṣaḥ purāṇaḥ
śrī-kṛṣṇa-caitanya-śarīra-dhārī
kṛpāmbudhir yas tam ahaṁ prapadye

kālān naṣṭaṁ bhakti-yogaṁ nijaṁ yaḥ
prāduṣkartuṁ kṛṣṇa-caitanya-nāmā
āvirbhūtas tasya padāravinde
gāḍhaṁ gāḍhaṁ līyatāṁ citta-bhṛṅgaḥ

"Let me take shelter of the Supreme Personality of Godhead, the ocean of transcendental mercy, Śrī Kṛṣṇa, who has descended in the form of Lord Caitanya Mahāprabhu to teach us detachment, real knowledge and His own devotional service.

"The Supreme Personality of Godhead, who has taken the name of Śrī Kṛṣṇa Caitanya, has appeared to reinstate the devotional service to Himself which had almost been lost due to the influence of time. I pray that the honeybee of my mind will drink deeply of the honey of His lotus feet." (*Caitanya Caritāmṛta* 2.6.254-5; *Caitanya-candrodaya-nāṭaka* 6.74)

Mahāprabhu took *sannyāsa* during the fortnight of the waxing moon of the month of Māgha (January-February). He arrived in Nilachal in the month of Phālguna (February-March). In the month of Caitra (March-April), He converted Sārvabhauma Bhaṭṭācārya to Vaiṣṇavism. In the month of Vaiśākha (April-May), He left for his pilgrimage to the south of India. When Mahāprabhu said that He wanted to go on this pilgrimage alone, Nityānanda Prabhu tried to convince Him that He should take a companion and suggested that He would accompany Him. At this time, Mahāprabhu showed His great affection for His companions (Nityānanda Prabhu, Dāmodara Paṇḍita,

Jagadānanda Paṇḍita) by remonstrating with them and refusing their company. For Jagadānanda Paṇḍita, He said:

"Jagadānanda wants Me to enjoy sense gratification. I try to do whatever he tells Me because I am afraid of him. Whenever I act contrary to his wishes, he gets angry and stops talking to me for three days at a time." (*Caitanya Caritāmṛta* 2.7.21-22)

While Mahāprabhu was traveling in the south, the devotees waited for Him, feeling great distress on account of His absence. The deeper one's love, the more one feels the pain of separation. The sign of real love is the intensity of the joy one feels at being united after separation. After traveling for several months, the Lord arrived in Alalanatha, near Puri, and sent His servant Kāla Kṛṣṇadāsa to tell Nityānanda Prabhu and the other devotees that He had returned. The enthusiasm that they all felt for seeing Him again knew no bounds, and they all rushed to Alalanatha. Kṛṣṇadāsa Kavirāja Gosvāmī describes their reaction to the news of His arrival in his *Caitanya Caritāmṛta* as follows:

"As soon as Nityānanda Prabhu heard of Mahāprabhu's arrival, He immediately set off to see Him. Indeed, His love for the Lord made Him very impatient. Jagadānanda, Dāmodara Paṇḍita and Mukunda danced as they went to greet the Lord, their bodies unable to hold back their ecstasy." (*Caitanya Caritāmṛta* 2.9.339-40)

Nityānanda Prabhu, Jagadānanda Paṇḍita and the others advised Mahāprabhu to send Kāla Kṛṣṇadāsa to Bengal to tell Mother Śacī that He had returned from the pilgrimage to South India. Mahāprabhu approved of the idea. While in Puri, Jagadānanda Paṇḍita gradually met with all of Mahāprabhu's devotees, including Svarūpa Dāmodara, Rāya Rāmānanda, and Haridāsa Ṭhākura. One of Jagadānanda Paṇḍita's most pleasurable services to the Lord and His devotees was to satisfy them with the foodstuffs that he had himself cooked.

The Bengal devotees came annually during the *Cāturmāsya* period to be with the Lord in Nilachal. They did this three years in a row before Mahāprabhu announced His determination to go to Vrindavan. On this occasion, Jagadānanda Paṇḍita was amongst His companions as He traveled through Odisha and Gaudadesh. They went to Panihati, Kumarahatta, Kuliya village, and Ramakeli, before finally turning back from the village of Kanair Natshala to return to Puri, abandoning the pilgrimage to Vrindavan because of the large crowd of devotees that had gathered around Him. The Lord vowed that the next time He would travel to Vrindavan alone. Indeed, the next time He went, He took the path through the Jharikhand jungles, accompanied only by a servant named Balabhadra Bhaṭṭācārya. When Mahāprabhu returned by the same path, He was once again reunited with His loving devotees, including Jagadānanda Paṇḍita, who had once again been suffering greatly in His absence. This reunion was so joyful that it is beyond description.

SANĀTANA GOSVĀMĪ COMES TO PURI

On one occasion, Sanātana Gosvāmī took the Jharikhand route to Nilachal from Vraja. On the way, he developed blistering sores all over his body due to drinking bad water and fasting. Sanātana Gosvāmī became extremely troubled by the disease because his physical impurity would make him an obstacle to the servants of Lord Jagannātha. In view of this potential offense, he decided that he would throw himself under the wheels of Lord Jagannātha's chariot during the Rathayātrā festival. Mahāprabhu, the indweller of all beings, knew that he had made this decision and said to him, "You cannot attain Kṛṣṇa through suicide. You can only attain Him through *bhajana*. You have no right to destroy the body which has been given to you so that you can render service."

Through these instructions, the Lord changed the mind of Sanātana Gosvāmī. The Lord does not concern Himself with the purity or impurity of a devotee's external body; He is attracted by the inner purity of one's desire for service. Therefore Mahāprabhu did not hesitate to embrace Sanātana Gosvāmī, again and again. When He did so, the pus leaking from Sanātana Gosvāmī's sores touched the Lord's body and embarrassed and shamed Sanātana Gosvāmī turned to Jagadānanda Paṇḍita for advice, and Jagadānanda Paṇḍita told him that he should leave for Vrindavan immediately after the Rathayātrā. Sanātana Gosvāmī thought that this was the best solution and went to Mahāprabhu to ask Him permission to depart. When Mahāprabhu heard this, He became angry and chastised Jagadānanda Paṇḍita, saying:

"Jagadānanda is just a newcomer, a boy. Yet he has become so proud that he thinks that he can give even you advice. You are his guru in every respect, both in material and spiritual terms. Yet he gives you counsel? Doesn't he know his own worth? You are My teacher; you are an authority to even Me. And yet, like an impudent child, he is giving instruction to one as qualified as you." (*Caitanya Caritāmṛta* 3.4.158-60)

The devotee and the Lord occasionally chastise their intimates. Only due to great good fortune does one gets chastised by the Lord and His devotees. Sanātana Gosvāmī reacted to Mahāprabhu's criticism of Jagadānanda Paṇḍita as a sign of his great fortune and his own misfortune. He said, "You accept Jagadānanda Paṇḍita into Your inner circle, while You treat me with veneration. It is as though you were giving him ambrosia to drink and me the bitter juice of neem and *niśindā* leaves." (*Caitanya Caritāmṛta* 3.4.163)

Even though Mahāprabhu had long been won over by Jagadānanda Paṇḍita's devotion to Him, through him He made a point of teaching all His followers Vaiṣṇava etiquette and the importance of offering the proper respect to senior Vaiṣṇavas such as Sanātana Gosvāmī. He said,

"Jagadānanda Paṇḍita is not dearer to Me than you are, but I cannot tolerate transgressions of etiquette." (*Caitanya Caritāmṛta* 3.4.166)

Later, when Mahāprabhu was telling Vallabha Bhaṭṭa about the greatness of devotees, He said that one could attain devotion to Kṛṣṇa through the association of preachers of the Holy Name like Jagadānanda Paṇḍita.

"Ācāryaratna, Ācāryanidhi, Gadādhara Paṇḍita, Jagadānanda, Dāmodara, Śaṅkara, Vakreśvara, Kāśīśvara, Mukunda, Vāsudeva, Murāri and so many other great devotees have appeared in Bengal. They have preached the glories of the Holy Name throughout the world. Whatever little devotion I have for Kṛṣṇa is through their association." (*Caitanya Caritāmṛta* 3.7.48-50)

Kṛṣṇadāsa Kavirāja Gosvāmī contrasts the sincere loving attitude of Jagadānanda Paṇḍita with the hypocrisy of Rāmacandra Purī in the beginning of the eight chapter of *Caitanya Caritāmṛta*'s *Antya-līlā*. Even though Rāmacandra Purī was officially a disciple of Mādhavendra Purī, he had no proclivity for service. Because of his lack of sincerity and hypocrisy, he was ultimately deprived of his guru's mercy. Jagadānanda Paṇḍita was also present at Haridāsa Ṭhākura's funeral celebration, serving *prasāda* to the chief associates of the Lord. By his behavior, he showed that giving *prasāda* to the devotees is an important element of devotional service.

JAGADĀNANDA PAṆḌITA AS SATYABHĀMĀ

Jagadānanda Paṇḍita is the *avatāra* of Satyabhāmā; thus because of his refractory nature, he would often quarrel with Mahāprabhu.

"Jagadānanda Paṇḍita had a deep and pure love for the Lord, like that of Satyabhāmā for Kṛṣṇa. He was moody, being possessed of the *vāma* nature. He would repeatedly provoke loving arguments with the Lord, and there always seemed to be some disagreement between them." (*Caitanya Caritāmṛta* 3.7.142-3)

During the *Cāturmasya* all the devotees would come to meet the Lord in Nilachal and would return home at the end of the four-month period. In the same year that Mahāprabhu told Nityānanda Prabhu not to come to Puri, He also sent Jagadānanda Paṇḍita to Nabadwip with a message for His mother. Jagadānanda Paṇḍita related all that Mahāprabhu had told him about the exact times when He personally visited Śacī Mātā's house and accepted her food offerings. When she heard this from Jagadānanda Paṇḍita, she understood that these secret visits had not been dreams or hallucinations, but in fact real. When the other devotees in Mahāprabhu's hometown met His intimate associate Jagadānanda Paṇḍita, they all were immersed in an ocean of happiness.

Jagadānanda Paṇḍita went to Śivānanda Sena's house, where he collected a fragrant sandalwood oil for rubbing on Mahāprabhu's head. He filled an earthen jug with the oil and brought it back to Puri, where he gave it to Govinda, the Lord's servant. Govinda told Mahāprabhu, "Jagadānanda Paṇḍita has brought aromatic sandalwood oil back from Gaudadesh with him. If you rub it on Your head, it will relieve the symptoms of disturbed bile and wind."

In order to set a proper example for all, Mahāprabhu answered, "*Sannyāsīs* are forbidden the use of body oils. It is even more reprehensible to use aromatic oils. Since Jagadānanda has gone to the trouble of bringing the oil all the way here, you can give it to the Lord Jagannātha temple. They can use the oil to light lamps for the Deity. That will make all his troubles worthwhile."

Govinda told Jagadānanda Paṇḍita of Mahāprabhu's decision. Jagadānanda Paṇḍita began to sulk and stopped talking. After ten days, Govinda told Mahāprabhu that Jagadānanda Paṇḍita still wished Him to use the oil. Mahāprabhu became angry and in order to teach the world, said:

"Why don't we hire a masseur to give Me massage? Are these the pleasures for which I have taken the renounced order? It will no doubt amuse you all to see My downfall. As I walk along the road, people will get a whiff of My perfumes and say, 'There goes a womanizing monk.'" (*Caitanya Caritāmṛta* 3.12.112-4)

Govinda was speechless at Mahāprabhu's tirade. When Jagadānanda Paṇḍita came to visit Mahāprabhu the next morning, the Lord said, "A *sannyāsī* should not use fragrant oils. The best thing to do is to offer it to Lord Jagannātha for His service." Jagadānanda Paṇḍita became angry and sulkily retorted, "Who told You I brought this oil all the way from Gaudadesh? It's a lie." With that, he threw down the earthen jug in the courtyard and broke it. Then he went to his own room, locked the door and lay down.

Mahāprabhu, conquered by Jagadānanda Paṇḍita's love, went to assuage his anger, knocking on his door and saying gently, "Jagadānanda! Open the door. I am going now to bathe and then to the temple for *darśana* of Lord Jagannātha. When I come back I will take whatever food you have prepared for Me. So start cooking."

Out of his love for the Lord, Jagadānanda Paṇḍita immediately got up, bathed and started preparing the Lord's lunch. After performing His noonday rituals, the Lord returned, let Jagadānanda Paṇḍita wash His feet and then sat down to eat. Jagadānanda Paṇḍita set a banana leaf before Him and then covered it with fine rice soaked in clarified butter, numerous vegetable preparations and then cakes and sweet rice. Mahāprabhu told Jagadānanda Paṇḍita to set another banana leaf and fill it with food as he had done so that he could eat beside Him. He lifted His hands in the air and refused to eat a bite until Jagadānanda Paṇḍit sat down and ate with Him. Finally, Jagadānanda Paṇḍita's pride melted, and he agreed to take the Lord's *prasāda* once He had finished. As He ate, Mahāprabhu repeatedly praised the food that Jagadānanda Paṇḍita had cooked in his loving anger.

"This is the kind of nectar that you offer to Kṛṣṇa. Who can estimate the extent of your good fortune?" (*Caitanya Caritāmṛta* 3.12.133)

Jagadānanda Paṇḍita kept serving more and more vegetables to the Lord, who out of fear refused nothing, eating everything that He was given. He was afraid that if He refused even a single preparation, Jagadānanda Paṇḍita would again start fasting, so on that day He ate ten times as much as He did normally. After the meal, Jagadānanda Paṇḍita gave Him some aromatic spices, sandalwood and a garland. Mahāprabhu then insisted that he sit down and take his meal in front of Him. Jagadānanda Paṇḍita pleaded with Mahāprabhu to go and rest, as he was well aware of the demands of etiquette. Rāmāi and Raghunātha Bhaṭṭa had also helped with the cooking, so he wanted them to eat also before sitting down himself, but he assured the Lord that he would. Mahāprabhu was still not convinced, and so he told Govinda to remain there and report to Him whether or not Jagadānanda Paṇḍita had eaten. But Jagadānanda Paṇḍita immediately told Govinda to go and massage the Lord's feet. After he had served Rāmāi, Nandāi, Govinda and Raghunātha Bhaṭṭa *prasādam*, Jagadānanda Paṇḍita himself took the remnants of Mahāprabhu's plate. When Mahāprabhu heard that Jagadānanda Paṇḍita had finally eaten, He was able to rest peacefully.

"Jagadānanda's love for the Lord was just like the descriptions of Satyabhāmā's love for Kṛṣṇa in the *Bhāgavata*. Who can describe the extent of Jagadānanda's good fortune? He himself is an example of his own good fortune. Anyone who hears about the loving exchanges (*prema-vivarta*) between Jagadānanda Paṇḍita and Śrī Caitanya Mahāprabhu will know the characteristics of *prema* and will attain the wealth of pure love." (*Caitanya Caritāmṛta* 3.12.152-4)

Śrīla Bhakti Siddhānta Sarasvatī Gosvāmī Ṭhākura writes that the words *prema-vivarta* in this verse can mean (1) the apparent anger in Jagadānanda Paṇḍita's great loving dealings with the Lord or (2) the book of that name which he authored.

THE LORD SLEEPS ON PLANTAIN BARK

Due to His intense feelings of separation from Kṛṣṇa, Mahāprabhu took up severe austerities and started to sleep on a bed of dried plantain bark, which caused pain by rubbing against His bones. The devotees were greatly distressed to see the Lord's suffering. Jagadānanda Paṇḍita decided to take steps to alleviate the Lord's pain by getting some cloth and dying it saffron, and then filling it with cotton from the silk-cotton tree. In this way, he made both a mattress and a pillow for the Lord's comfort. Jagadānanda Paṇḍita then asked Govinda to give the mattress and pillow to the Lord and asked Svarūpa Dāmodara to convince Him to use them. When it was time for the Lord to go to bed, He saw the cotton pillow and became angry. When He heard that Jagadānanda Paṇḍita had given it, however, He hesitated. He made a pretence of anger. "A mattress and pillow? Why don't you just go and get me a bed? A *sannyāsī* is supposed to sleep on the ground. Jagadānanda Paṇḍita wants Me to become a sense enjoyer. This is shameful."

Jagadānanda Paṇḍita was saddened when he heard from Svarūpa Dāmodara that Mahāprabhu had refused the bedding. However, Svarūpa Dāmodara cleverly made some bedding out of dried banana leaves which the Lord accepted. This satisfied all the devotees with the exception of Jagadānanda Paṇḍita.

Though he said nothing about it, Jagadānanda Paṇḍita was angry and asked Mahāprabhu for permission to go to Vrindavan. The Lord was able to understand the real reason for his dissatisfaction and said to him in a consoling voice, "You are angry and blame Me for it. And so you want to go to Mathura and become a beggar?" The petulant Jagadānanda Paṇḍita hid his true feelings and simply said, "I have wanted to go to Vrindavan for a long time. Previously You wouldn't give me permission, so I could not."

Mahāprabhu, out of His affection for Jagadānanda Paṇḍita, would not allow him to leave, even though he asked Him repeatedly. Finally, Jagadānanda Paṇḍita asked Svarūpa Dāmodara to intercede on his behalf and get the Lord's permission to go. Svarūpa Dāmodara went to Mahāprabhu and said, "Jagadānanda's desire to see Vrindavan is very strong. I think it would be a good idea if You sent him to Vrindavan just as You previously sent him to Nabadwip with a message for Śacī Mātā." Mahāprabhu finally allowed Himself to be persuaded and accorded permission to Jagadānanda Paṇḍita to go to Vraja. Out of His affection for him, however, He gave him elaborate instructions for his voyage. "The road up to Benares is free from any problems. After Benares, however, the road is full of robbers, so be careful. You should take some soldiers with you for protection. If the highwaymen see a single Bengali on the road, they will be sure to attack and loot him. When you get to Mathura, first go and see Sanātana. Offer your respects to the Chaube *brāhmaṇas* of Mathura, but don't associate with them. You will not be able to understand their behavior, so respect them at a distance. Perform *parikramā* of Vraja-mandal with Sanātana; do not leave his side for even a moment. Don't climb Govardhan to see Gopāla. Don't stay in Vraja for a long time. Hurry back." (*Caitanya Caritāmṛta* 3.13.39)

JAGADĀNANDA PAṆḌITA CHASTISES SANĀTANA

Jagadānanda Paṇḍita paid his obeisance to the Lord and left on foot for Benares where he met with Tapana Miśra and Candraśekhara. From there he went on to Mathura, where he met Sanātana Gosvāmī. Sanātana Gosvāmī took him around the twelve forests of Vraja, and then they stayed together for some time in Gokula Mahavana. Sanātana Gosvāmī used to live on *mādhukarī* (begging for pieces of bread from the local people), but since Jagadānanda

Paṇḍita was not habituated to a wheat-based diet, he went to a local temple and cooked rice. One day, Jagadānanda Paṇḍita invited Sanātana Gosvāmī to eat. A certain *sannyāsī* named Mukunda Sarasvatī had given a red cloth to Sanātana Gosvāmī, which he wore wrapped around his head. When Jagadānanda Paṇḍita saw this, he thought that the cloth must have been given to Sanātana Gosvāmī by Mahāprabhu and was overwhelmed with love. When he learned, however, that it had been given by someone else, he became so angry that he was ready to hit Sanātana Gosvāmī with the rice pot. He criticized Sanātana Gosvāmī:

" 'You are Mahāprabhu's most important associate. No one is dearer to Him than you. How could anyone tolerate you wearing another *sannyāsī*'s cloth around your head?' Sanātana Gosvāmī answered, 'Well said! It is clear, Paṇḍita Mahāśaya, that you are unequalled in your love for the Lord. I could not have learned this lesson from anyone but you, for you alone have such solid faith in the Lord. My purpose in binding the cloth around my head has been fulfilled, for as soon as you saw it, I was able to witness the manifestations of your love for the Lord. A Vaiṣṇava should not wear a red cloth. I will give it to someone else, for I have no farther need for it.' " (*Caitanya Caritāmṛta* 3.13.56-61)

Jagadānanda Paṇḍita offered the food he had cooked to Mahāprabhu and then took *prasāda* with Sanātana Gosvāmī. After staying with him for two months, he started to feel his absence from Mahāprabhu too intensely and asked Sanātana Gosvāmī for permission to return to Puri. Sanātana Gosvāmī bid him goodbye, giving him sand from the place where Kṛṣṇa held the *rāsa* dance, a stone from Govardhan, a garland of *guñja* berries and some dried ripe *pīlu* fruits for Mahāprabhu. Jagadānanda Paṇḍita was delighted to return to Puri and see Mahāprabhu and the other devotees again. Mahāprabhu embraced him tightly and was extremely pleased with the gifts sent by Sanātana Gosvāmī. Most of the devotees did not know how to eat *pīlu* fruits, but because they were from Vrindavan, they relished them anyway.

ADVAITA'S MESSAGE

Mahāprabhu never forgot Śacī Mātā's pure parental affection for Him and would send Jagadānanda Paṇḍita every year to Nabadwip with a piece of Lord Jagannātha's cloth and some *prasāda* sweets. Jagadānanda Paṇḍita would come and talk to her about the Lord and alleviate somewhat the suffering she felt in separation from her son. The last time that he went, he went to Advaita Ācārya's house to ask permission to return to Puri. Advaita gave a cryptic message to deliver to Mahāprabhu. Ṭhe riddle went as follows:

"Convey My millions of obeisances unto His feet. Please inform Śrī Caitanya Mahāprabhu, who is acting like a madman, that everyone here has become mad like Him. Inform Him also that in the marketplace rice is no longer in demand. Further, tell Him that those now mad in ecstatic love are no longer interested in the material world. Also, tell Śrī Caitanya Mahāprabhu that one who has also become a madman in ecstatic love [Advaita Prabhu] has spoken these words." (*Caitanya Caritāmṛta* 3.19.19-21)

Bhaktivinoda Ṭhākura explains this riddle in this way: "Tell Mahāprabhu that everyone has become intoxicated with love for Kṛṣṇa, and so in the marketplace of love, no one is buying the rice of Kṛṣṇa *prema* any longer. Tell Mahāprabhu that the saintly madmen (*āul*) are so intoxicated with love that they are no longer involved in their material duties. Tell

Mahāprabhu that Advaita said this in a state of complete intoxication of *prema*. In short, the message was that the purpose for which Advaita had called Mahāprabhu to earth had been achieved. The Lord may now do as He pleases. "

The date and place of Jagadānanda Paṇḍita's departure from this world are unknown.

Vāsudeva Sārvabhauma Bhaṭṭācārya

bhaṭṭācāryaḥ sārvabhaumaḥ purāsīd gīṣpatir divi

"Sārvabhauma Bhattācārya was formerly Bṛhaspati, the guru of the gods." (*Gaura-gaṇoddeśa-dīpikā* 119)

SĀRVABHAUMA'S SCHOLARSHIP

When Kṛṣṇadāsa Kavirāja Gosvāmī lists Śrī Caitanya's branches, he first names devotees like Paramānanda Purī and Svarūpa Dāmodara, who came to join the Lord in Jagannatha Puri. After them, he enumerates the Bengali devotees who were already living in Puri when the Lord arrived there. Sārvabhauma Bhaṭṭācārya is listed among them.

"One of the Lord's biggest branches was Sārvabhauma Bhaṭṭācārya. Another was Sārvabhauma's brother-in-law, Gopīnātha Ācārya." (*Caitanya Caritāmṛta* 1.10.130)

Śrīla Bhakti Siddhānta Sarasvatī Gosvāmī Ṭhākura has commented on this Bengali verse as follows: "Sārvabhauma Bhaṭṭācārya's given name was Vāsudeva. He was the son of Maheśvara Viśārada, a celebrated resident of Vidyanagar, a village which lies about two and a half miles away from both Nabadwip and Champahati. Sārvabhauma Bhaṭṭācārya was a student of Pakṣadhara Miśra, the head professor of what was at that time India's leading school of logic (Nyāya), in Mithila, Bihar. Sārvabhauma Bhaṭṭācārya memorized the entire body of learning available there and then returned to Nabadwip to establish his own school for the study of logic. This caused a revolution in the history of this branch of learning, as the importance of Mithila was diminished to the profit of Nabadwip, which to this day still has the reputation of being the leading center of Nyāya studies. According to some, the celebrated logician Raghunātha Śiromaṇi, author of the work *Dīdhiti*, studied under Sārvabhauma Bhaṭṭācārya. Sārvabhauma Bhaṭṭācārya had tremendous learning in both Nyāya and Vedānta. Although he was a *gṛhastha*, he took the *kṣetra-sannyāsa*, vowing never to set foot outside of Jagannatha Puri, and taught Vedānta to students there. He gave discourses on Śaṅkarācārya's commentary on the Vedānta to Mahāprabhu Himself until he came to understand its real meaning by the Lord's grace."

Sārvabhauma Bhaṭṭācārya was an aristocratic *brāhmaṇa* of the Rāḍha class. From the *Gauḍīya Vaiṣṇava Abhidhāna*, we learn that he took birth in the first half of the fourteenth century of the Śaka era. We also learn there that when he studied in Mithila, the Nyāya scholars of that city attempted to maintain their monopoly on teaching this branch of philosophy by prohibiting their foreign students from copying the textbooks. For this reason, it was impossible to either teach or study logic in Bengal at that time. Vāsudeva Bhaṭṭācārya was endowed with marvelous powers of retention, and he was thus able to memorize all the texts that he had studied in Mithila. When he returned to Bengal, he was thus able to transcribe these texts and make them readily available to his students. The scholar Dr. Dīneśa Candra Bhaṭṭācārya has argued that this is only a legend. He says that in fact Vāsudeva Sārvabhauma learned the Navya-nyāya ("new logical method") from his father, Viśārada, and never went to Mithila. When Mahārāj Pratāparudra heard of his tremendous learning, he invited him to come to Puri and become the chief scholar of his court.

SĀRVABHAUMA, THE TEACHER OF MĀYĀVĀDA

Even though he was a householder, Sārvabhauma Bhaṭṭācārya was so highly qualified that he became the teacher even of many *sannyāsīs* of the impersonalist school. In fact, the guru of the gods, Bṛhaspati, took birth as Sārvabhauma Bhaṭṭācārya in order to support Mahāprabhu's pastime of delivering the Māyāvādīs. Little wonder that he was an incomparable scholar!

Śrī Caitanya Mahāprabhu and all the Vaiṣṇava *ācāryas* have accepted that the object of worship (*bhajanīya*), the worshipper (*bhajana-kārī*) and the act of worship (*bhajana*) are all eternal principles. Pure devotional service cannot be present if the eternal existence of any one of these three principles is denied. According to the pure and true doctrines of Vaiṣṇavism, the Supreme Lord, who is the object of worship, possesses an eternal identity, and His name, form, qualities and pastimes are all eternal and spiritual in nature. The Māyāvādīs, who follow the path of knowledge, deny the eternal spiritual character of the Lord's identity, name, form, qualities and pastimes. They hold that these are a product of the illusory energy. This is the source of the word "*māyāvāda*", which means "illusory" (*māyā*) "form" (*rūpa*) and "doctrine" (*vāda*). The Māyāvādīs hold that the form of the Lord is a fabrication that is only useful as a meditation aid for less advanced spiritual practitioners. According to them, Brahman, without form, attributes and potency, is the supreme truth. Nothing exists outside of this Brahman, and thus the individual living being is identical with it.

The Māyāvādīs also hold that devotional practice has a momentary value for the less advanced spiritual practitioners to attain the state of identification with Brahman, after which it does not exist. It is clear, then, that such a doctrine interferes with the attainment of the fifth and ultimate goal of life, love of God. The founders of the four schools of Vaiṣṇava thought, Madhvācārya, Rāmānujācārya, Viṣṇu Svāmī and Nimbārka, as well as the Supreme Lord, Śrī Caitanya Mahāprabhu, have thus fought against the Māyāvāda teachings of Saṅkarācārya, characterized by the *vivarta-vāda* (doctrine of the apparent transformation of Brahman). Those who seek their ultimate benefit accept the teaching given by Vedavyāsa himself, known as *śakti-pariṇāma-vāda* (the doctrine of the transformation of the energies of Brahman).

Śrī Caitanya Mahāprabhu appeared in this most fortunate Age of Kālī in order to bestow the most elevated service to Kṛṣṇa in the conjugal mood upon everyone, without any discrimination. Without judging the qualifications of the recipient He gave the supreme gift of love for God that was not given previously. Furthermore, He descended with the intention of destroying the desires which lead the living being away from the Lord and interfere with his attainment of love; He also bestowed upon them the desire for this love and the power through which it can be established in their hearts. Even with all this mercy, the Māyāvāda doctrine remains the biggest obstacle to attaining love for Kṛṣṇa.

Mahāprabhu delivered even Sārvabhauma Bhaṭṭācārya, who was a Māyāvādī. In their biographies of the Lord, both Vṛndāvana Dāsa Ṭhākura, who is not different from Vedavyāsa, and Kṛṣṇadāsa Kavirāja Gosvāmī have described how this took place. The essence of the accounts of the *Caitanya Bhāgavata* and *Caitanya Caritāmṛta* are given below.

SĀRVABHAUMA TAKES THE LORD TO HIS HOUSE

At the age of twenty-four, Mahāprabhu left Nabadwip to take *sannyāsa* from Keśava Bhāratī in Katwa. From there He went to Shantipur and then on to Puri. When He arrived at Atharo Nala, a bridge with eighteen arches that marks the entrance to the town of Jagannatha Puri, the Lord saw the temple spire and had a vision of Kṛṣṇa. He ran toward the temple in a trance of love, and when He entered, ran towards the deity of Lord Jagannātha in order to embrace Him. As He came close to the altar, He fell down in a faint. The temple watchmen and *sevakas* saw Him lying in the temple and prepared to beat Him.

Vāsudeva Sārvabhauma happened to be there, and he stopped them from so doing. He had been impressed by the beauty of the Lord as well as by His manifestations of spiritual ecstasy at the sight of Lord Jagannātha. He could understand that this was no ordinary person. With the help of his disciples and the temple guards, Vāsudeva Sārvabhauma had the unconscious Lord transported to his own home. He was quite anxious about the Lord's condition and placed a tuft of cotton before His nose to see if He was still breathing. He was relieved when he saw the cotton move slightly.

In the meantime, Nityānanda Prabhu, Mukunda Datta, Jagadānanda Paṇḍita and Dāmodara Paṇḍita arrived at the Lion's Gate entrance to the temple. They heard from other visitors to the temple that Mahāprabhu had been taken in an unconscious state to Sārvabhauma Bhaṭṭācārya's house. At that very moment, Sārvabhauma's brother-in-law Gopīnātha Ācārya passed by. Since he too was from Nabadwip, the Lord's devotees instantly recognized him. Mukunda told Gopīnātha everything about Mahāprabhu's *sannyāsa* and His coming to Puri, as well as about His being taken to Sārvabhauma's house. Gopīnātha was thrilled to hear all this news, and he took them to his brother-in-law's house.

The devotees were relieved and overjoyed to see the Lord there. Sārvabhauma then told them to go and take *darśana* of Jagannātha Deva. When they had returned, they began to sing the Holy Names aloud, and this brought Mahāprabhu back to consciousness. In his paternal affection for the Lord, Sārvabhauma Bhaṭṭācārya prohibited Him from going to the temple alone. He invited the Lord and His companions for lunch and sent them to take bath in the ocean. When they returned, he fed them to their full satisfaction with a feast of Jagannātha's *mahā-prasāda*.

When Sārvabhauma Bhaṭṭācārya learned of Mahāprabhu's family background, he was very happy, for his father, Mahesvara Viśārada, had been a good friend of Mahāprabhu's maternal grandfather, Nīlāmbara Cakravartī. Sārvabhauma Bhaṭṭācārya was much older than the Lord, and so he felt protective toward Him. He said, "The name Kṛṣṇa Caitanya which You have been given is a very good name. But You have been initiated into the Bhāratī line of *sannyāsīs*, which has only a moderately good reputation. I shall get You reinitiated into a more prestigious line."

Gopīnātha Ācārya and the other devotees were disappointed to hear Vāsudeva Sārvabhauma make this suggestion. Gopīnātha Ācārya objected, "Śrī Caitanya Mahāprabhu is the Supreme Lord Himself. He does not depend on any *sampradāya*." Sārvabhauma Bhaṭṭācārya and his disciples debated these points with Gopīnātha Ācārya at some length, and this has been described by Kṛṣṇadāsa Kavirāja Gosvāmī in the sixth chapter of the *Caitanya Caritāmṛta*'s *Madhya-līlā*.

Mahāprabhu asked the devotees not to argue with Sārvabhauma Bhaṭṭācārya because he was the Lord's senior and was only advising Him out of affection for Him. How could they object to this? The Lord, setting the example of one who is free from any hankering after prestige and who is ready to give all respect to others, indicated that He was willing to hear Sārvabhauma Bhaṭṭācārya's advice.

Sārvabhauma Bhaṭṭācārya then said to the Lord that he was a handsome young man and that if he wanted to maintain His *sannyāsa* vows, He should study Vedānta diligently. This would awaken the required attitude of renunciation from the world in Him. For the next seven days, he took lessons in Vedānta at his house.

When Sārvabhauma saw that Mahāprabhu was not asking any questions, but simply listening silently, he said, "The study of Vedānta is demanding. A student who wishes to understand the subject properly is generally obliged to ask questions to clarify troublesome areas."

The Lord answered, "You told me to listen, not to ask questions. So I have been listening. I find no difficulty understanding the meaning of the *sūtras*, for they are as self-evident as the sun. On the other hand, your explanations are confusing. I find them to hide the clear meaning of the *sūtras* just like clouds covering the sun."

Sārvabhauma Bhaṭṭācārya felt slighted by the Lord's comments and indeed, somewhat angry. He started to debate the meaning of the word *brahman* with the Lord. Sārvabhauma Bhaṭṭācārya argued that Brahman was without form or qualities, having recourse to various scriptures as evidence. The Lord rebutted his arguments with logic and scriptural references, showing that Brahman possesses form and qualities. The Lord cited the following verse and asked Sārvabhauma to explain it.

ātmārāmāś ca munayo
nirgranthā apy urukrame
kurvanty ahaitukīṁ bhaktim
itthambhūta-guṇo hariḥ

"Even those sages who are established on the path of self-realization, fully self-satisfied and freed from bondage, perform causeless devotional service to Lord Hari, whose pastimes are wonderful, for such is the glorious nature of His qualities." (*Śrīmad Bhāgavatam* 1.7.10)

After Vāsudeva Sārvabhauma had given nine different explanations of the verse, Mahāprabhu put on a display of divine scholarship by explaining the same verse in eighteen ways without even touching on the meanings given by Sārvabhauma Bhaṭṭācārya. The scholar was astounded and speechless. He began slowly to understand that Mahāprabhu was not an ordinary human being, but the Supreme Lord Himself. He started to regret his arrogance and finally fell down at the Lord's feet and begged Him for forgiveness.

SĀRVABHAUMA BECOMES THE LORD'S DEVOTEE

In His kindness, the Lord displayed a number of different divine forms to

Sārvabhauma Bhaṭṭācārya, starting with a four-armed Nārāyaṇa form, then a two-armed Kṛṣṇa form, holding a flute, and finally a six-armed form.

"When Sārvabhauma Bhaṭṭācārya saw the six-armed form of the Lord, as brilliant as a million suns, he fell down in a faint." (*Caitanya Bhāgavata* 3.3.107)

After seeing these divine manifestations, Sārvabhauma Bhaṭṭācārya glorified the Lord in a hundred Sanskrit verses. He inscribed two of these verses on a palm leaf and sent them to Mahāprabhu through Jagadānanda Paṇḍita. Mukunda Datta took the precaution of writing the verses down on the doorway before Jagadānanda Paṇḍita showed them to the Lord, and as a result of this foresight, the verses were preserved, for Mahāprabhu tore the palm leaves up as soon as He saw them. The devotees saw the verses written on the doorframe and memorized them:

vairāgya-vidyā-nija-bhakti-yoga-
śikṣārtham ekaḥ puruṣaḥ purāṇaḥ
śrī-kṛṣṇa-caitanya-śarīra-dhārī
kṛpāmbudhir yas tam ahaṁ prapadye

"Let me take shelter of the Supreme Personality of Godhead, the ocean of transcendental mercy, Śrī Kṛṣṇa, who has descended in the form of Lord Caitanya Mahāprabhu to teach us detachment, real knowledge and His own devotional service."

kālān naṣṭaṁ bhakti-yogaṁ nijaṁ yaḥ
prāduṣkartuṁ kṛṣṇa-caitanya-nāmā
āvirbhūtas tasya padāravinde
gāḍhaṁ gāḍhaṁ līyate citta-bhṛṅgaḥ

"The Supreme Personality of Godhead, who has taken the name of Śrī Kṛṣṇa Caitanya, has appeared to reinstate the devotional service to Himself which had almost been lost due to the influence of time. I pray that the honeybee of my mind will drink deeply of the nectar of His lotus feet." (*Caitanya Caritāmṛta* 2.6.253-4; *Caitanya-candrodaya-nāṭaka* 6.74)

A deity of Mahāprabhu's six-armed form is still worshipped today in the Lord Jagannātha temple at Puri.

SĀRVABHAUMA'S FAITH IN MAHĀ-PRASĀDA

One day not long afterwards, Mahāprabhu came to Vāsudeva Sārvabhauma's house at daybreak with Jagannātha's *mahā-prasāda* and offered it to him. Sārvabhauma had not yet bathed, cleaned his teeth or performed his morning rituals. Despite his ritually impure state, he joyfully honored the *prasāda*, quoting a verse from the *Padma Purāṇa*:

śuṣkaṁ paryuṣitaṁ vāpi nītaṁ vā dūra-deśataḥ
prāpti-mātreṇa bhoktavyaṁ nātra kāla-vicāraṇā

"One should honor *prasāda* as soon as one receives it, whether it is dried up, stale or brought from afar. In this, there should be no consideration of time or circumstances." (*Caitanya Caritāmṛta* 2.6.225)

Mahāprabhu was delighted to see that Sārvabhauma had developed faith in mahā *prasāda* and immediately started to dance in ecstasy. He said:

"Today I have conquered the three worlds and have been taken to Vaikuṇṭha. All My desires have been fulfilled simply because Sārvabhauma Bhaṭṭācārya has developed faith in *mahā-prasāda*." (*Caitanya Caritāmṛta* 2.6.230-1)

When Sārvabhauma Bhaṭṭācārya asked Mahāprabhu about the topmost devotional limb, Mahāprabhu instructed him to perform *nāma-saṅkīrtana*, quoting the following verse from *Bṛhad-nāradīya Purāṇa* (38.126):

harer nāma harer nāma harer nāmaiva kevalam
kalau nāsty eva nāsty eva nāsty eva gatir anyathā

"In this Age of Kālī, there is no other means, no other means, no other means for self-realization than chanting the holy name, chanting the holy name, chanting the holy name of Lord Hari."

SĀRVABHAUMA CHANGES THE WORDS OF THE BHĀGAVATA

Vāsudeva Sārvabhauma's heart was so changed by the Lord's mercy, he recited a verse of the *Śrīmad Bhāgavatam*, but he had altered a word.

tat te 'nukampāṁ susamīkṣamāṇo
bhuñjāna evātmakṛtaṁ vipākam
hṛd-vāg-vapurbhir vidadhan namas te
jīveta yo bhakti-pade sa dāya-bhāk

"One who lives his life while joyfully seeing everything as Your compassion even as he experiences the adverse conditions arising from his past deeds, and who constantly pays obeisances to You with his mind, words and body, is certain to inherit a place at Your lotus feet, the object of all devotion." (*Caitanya Caritāmṛta* 2.6.261)

Sārvabhauma Bhaṭṭācārya had changed the word *mukti-pade* found in the original verse (*Śrīmad Bhāgavatam* 10.14.8) to *bhakti-pade*. Mahāprabhu explained that there was no need to change the words, in as much as *mukti-pada* ("the source of liberation") is an epithet of Kṛṣṇa. Vāsudeva Sārvabhauma answered, "You are quite correct to say that the word *mukti-pade* refers to Kṛṣṇa, but the word *mukti* is used customarily in its sense of impersonal liberation, and thus does not bring as great a pleasure as the word *bhakti*.

When the other scholars in Puri heard that Sārvabhauma Bhaṭṭācārya had been converted to devotion to Kṛṣṇa, they all took shelter of Caitanya Mahāprabhu.

MAHĀPRABHU LEAVES FOR THE SOUTH

Mahāprabhu took *sannyāsa* in the month of Māgha and arrived in Puri in the month of Phālguna. He delivered Sārvabhauma Bhaṭṭācārya in the month of Caitra and left for southern India in the month of Vaiśākha. Nityānanda Prabhu arranged for a certain Kṛṣṇadāsa Vipra to accompany Mahāprabhu as a servant. Before He left, Vāsudeva Sārvabhauma gave the Lord a *kaupina* and *bahirvāsa* and made a special request to the

Lord to visit Rāmānanda Rāya on the banks of the Godavari. At one time, Vāsudeva Sārvabhauma had mocked Rāmānanda Rāya when conversing with him about devotional sentiment. Now, by the mercy of the Lord, he was able to recognize him for what he was, a highly advanced devotee of Kṛṣṇa. Sārvabhauma said to the Lord were:

"Rāmānanda Rāya is the governor of Vidyanagar, on the bank of the Godavari. It is my request that You meet him without fail. Please do not avoid him, thinking that he is a *śudra* who is only interested in material activities. If anyone is fit to associate with You, it is Rāmānanda Rāya. No one in this world is equal to him in the knowledge of the divine sentiments. He is not only a most learned scholar but very knowledgeable in the science of devotional mellows. You will learn the extent of his glories by talking with him. When I first met Rāmānanda Rāya, I could not understand what he was talking about, or his activities, all of which are transcendental. So, I made fun of him because he is a Vaiṣṇava. Now, by Your mercy, I am able to understand his greatness. So too will You, once You converse with him." (*Caitanya Caritāmṛta* 2.7.63-7)

KĀŚĪŚVARA AND GOVINDA COME TO PURI

After Īśvara Purīpāda's disappearance, his two disciples and personal servants, Kāśīśvara and Govinda, came to Puri in order to serve Mahāprabhu, as they had been told to do by their guru. When Sārvabhauma Bhaṭṭācārya learned that Govinda was a *śudra*, he asked Mahāprabhu why His guru had taken a person of a lower caste as a personal servant. Mahāprabhu answered, "The Supreme Lord is completely autonomous, and His mercy does not take anyone's caste or creed into consideration. Service performed out of affection is millions of times better than that which is performed out of a sense of duty or reverence. Kṛṣṇa joyfully took His meal in the home of Vidura. However, as my guru's personal servant, Govinda is an object of reverence and therefore it is improper for Me to accept his service. On the other hand, My guru has ordered him to serve Me, and I cannot ignore My spiritual master's order. What do you think I should do?"

Sārvabhauma Bhaṭṭācārya responded to the Lord's request for advice by saying, "One should never ignore the orders of the spiritual master. Scripture says that this is the supreme guiding principle."

SĀRVABHAUMA SEEKS AN AUDIENCE FOR THE KING

While Mahāprabhu was traveling through the south, Mahārāja Pratāparudra heard a great deal about His glories from Sārvabhauma Bhaṭṭācārya. As a result, the King developed a desire to have an audience with the Lord, but Sārvabhauma Bhaṭṭācārya warned him that the Lord was a *sannyāsī* who had taken strict vows of renunciation, one of which was that he would not grant audiences to kings. Nevertheless, he promised the King that when the Lord returned, he would arrange a meeting with Him by whatever means possible.

After the consultation with the King, Vāsudeva Sārvabhauma deemed Kāśī Miśra's house a fit place Mahāprabhu to stay. After He returned from the south Mahāprabhu stayed there when Sārvabhauma Bhaṭṭācārya introduced the residents of Śrī Kshetra to Him.

All of Sārvabhauma Bhaṭṭācārya's efforts to bring the King into the Lord's presence failed. Subsequently, Nityānanda Prabhu and other devotees glorified the King's qualities to the Lord, but He continued to refuse to give the King an audience. He agreed, however, to give him one of His outer garment. Nityānanda Prabhu gave the Lord's cloth to Sārvabhauma Bhaṭṭācārya to bring to the King. As soon as King Pratāparudra touched the cloth, he experienced the symptoms of love of God.

THE LORD CURES SĀRVABHAUMA'S SON-IN-LAW

When the Lord's Bengali associates had returned home after the *Cāturmāsya* period, Sārvabhauma Bhaṭṭācārya invited the Lord to eat at his house for an entire month. The Lord refused. Sārvabhauma Bhaṭṭācārya reduced his invitation to twenty days, then to fifteen days, but the Lord continued to turn him down, agreeing to go only once. Sārvabhauma Bhaṭṭācārya continued to press Him to accept more than one invitation, and the Lord finally agreed to go for five days. Sārvabhauma Bhaṭṭācārya then asked Paramānanda Purī to also come for five days, Svarūpa Dāmodara for four, and each of the Lord's eight other *sannyāsī* associates for two days each. This way he had invitees for one full month. He told the Lord that it was difficult to offer proper service when there were many guests, so he asked Him to please come alone or with Svarūpa Dāmodara.

Sārvabhauma Bhaṭṭācārya's wife, who was known as "Ṣāṭhī's mother," was very devoted to the Lord and extremely excited to hear that He was going to be coming to their house to eat. She was a very good cook and prepared a large number of vegetable preparations as well as cakes and sweets. Sārvabhauma Bhaṭṭācārya requested the Lord to sit in a place in a quiet room, putting out an uncut banana leaf from a mature tree (which produces a giant banana cluster of thirty-two hands,) upon which he placed all the different preparations.

Mahāprabhu saw the elaborate and unparalleled preparations made for offering to Rādhā and Govinda, and repeatedly praised Sārvabhauma Bhaṭṭācārya for his efforts. When He sat down to eat, Sārvabhauma's son-in-law, Amogha, came to watch. Sārvabhauma Bhaṭṭācārya knew Amogha's fault-finding character and so had kept a stick to chase him away if he came to disturb the Lord. However, when he was so absorbed in serving the Lord, Amogha managed to sneak in without him noticing. Amogha saw the lavish feast, and immediately began to criticize Mahāprabhu:

"There is enough food here to satisfy a dozen people, and yet this *sannyāsī* is going to eat it all by himself?" (*Caitanya Caritāmṛta* 2.15.248)

Sārvabhauma Bhaṭṭācārya flared up in anger, took the stick lying by his side and went after Amogha, who fled as fast as he could. Vāsudeva Sārvabhauma's wife, shocked on hearing her son-in-law insult the Lord, began to flail herself on the head and chest and repeatedly said, "May my Ṣāṭhī become a widow!"

As for the Lord, He laughed off Amogha's trivial criticisms and tried to pacify His hosts. The next day, however, Amogha came down with cholera. Sārvabhauma Bhaṭṭācārya thought that justice was being done, that it was a suitable punishment for the offensive words his son-in-law had spoken. When Gopīnātha Ācārya informed Mahāprabhu that Sārvabhauma Bhaṭṭācārya and his wife were both fasting as a penance for the offense that had taken place in their house and that Amogha was on his deathbed with cholera, the merciful Lord immediately went to Amogha's bedside, placed His hand on his chest and said:

"This *brāhmaṇa*'s heart is naturally holy and is, therefore, a proper place for Kṛṣṇa to sit. Why have you given brutish envy a place in it, allowing it to become contaminated? Fortunately, all your sins have been destroyed by your relationship with Sārvabhauma Bhaṭṭācārya. When the heart is cleansed of all contamination, one is able to chant the name of Kṛṣṇa. So, get up, Amogha, and chant Kṛṣṇa's names! The Supreme Lord will bestow His mercy upon you before long." (*Caitanya Caritāmṛta* 2.15.274-7)

The Lord's touch and His compassionate words had an immediate effect. Amogha rose up and started chanting, "Kṛṣṇa! Kṛṣṇa!" The eight symptoms of ecstatic love manifested on his body. He remembered his offensive words to the Lord and remorsefully began to slap himself repeatedly on the cheeks until his face was swollen and Gopīnātha Ācārya stopped him. The Lord said to Amogha that he was dear to Him because of his relationship with Sārvabhauma.

"I love everyone in Sārvabhauma's house, even his servants. If even his household dog is dear to Me, will I not have affection for his relatives?" (*Caitanya Caritāmṛta* 2.15.284)

The Lord then went to Sārvabhauma Bhaṭṭācārya's house and asked him and his wife to forgive their son-in-law, whose offensive behavior was only the result of immaturity. After convincing them that He was not angry, He had them break their fast.

THE LORD PRAISES SĀRVABHAUMA

Sārvabhauma Bhaṭṭācārya participated in many other activities with the Lord in Puri, such as the water sports and the feasts of *prasāda*. When Vallabha Bhaṭṭa came to Puri, the Lord glorified Sārvabhauma Bhaṭṭācārya to him as follows:

"Sārvabhauma Bhaṭṭācārya is not only such a great scholar in the six philosophical systems that he is a world teacher in these doctrines but is also a foremost devotee of the Lord. He has taught Me the science of *bhakti* yoga. Through his mercy, I have learned that devotion to Kṛṣṇa is the essence of all mystical systems." (*Caitanya Caritāmṛta* 3.7.21-2)

King Śrī Pratāparudra Deva

indradyumno mahārājo jagannāthārcakaḥ purā
jātaḥ pratāparudraḥ san sama indreṇa so 'dhunā

"King Indradyumna, who previously worshipped Lord Jagannātha, appeared as Pratāparudra, with the same opulence as Indra himself."[17] (*Gaura-gaṇoddeśa-dīpikā* 118)

17 In a Satya Yuga during the second half of Brahmā's lifetime, a certain king named Indradyumna was born into the dynasty of the Sun. He ruled over the kingdom of Malwa, with its capital at Avantipur. He was a great devotee of Viṣṇu, as was his priest Vidyāpati. In the first half of Brahmā's life, Lord Jagannātha had appeared in Nilachal as Nīla Mādhava with the purpose of delivering the conditioned souls of this world. He was served by a tribal king named Viśvāvasu. Nīla Mādhava manifested the deity form of Lord Jagannātha through these three persons: Indradyumna, Vidyāpati and Viśvāvasu. The Lord appeared in three forms – Balarāma, Subhadrā and Jagannātha – at the place known as Banki Mohana in order to show His mercy to King Indradyumna.

PRATĀPARUDRA'S ANCESTORS

King Pratāparudra was an independent king of considerable power whose capital city was Cuttack. His ancestors are listed in the Odishan history *Mādalā Pañjī*. There it is said that King Kajjalabhānu, the last ruler of the Gaṅgā dynasty, was overthrown by his minister Kapilendra Deva while absent from the kingdom during wartime. Also known as Kapileśvara, this king founded Odisha's Gajapati dynasty. Kapilendra's Queen was Pārvatī, to whom was born their son and successor, Puruṣottama Deva. Puruṣottama Deva was Pratāparudra's father and, Padmāvatī, or Rupāmbikā, his mother.

Pratāparudra was an important associate of Lord Caitanya Mahāprabhu and is named as a branch of Gadādhara Paṇḍita Gosvāmī. He, his wives and sons were all devotees of Mahāprabhu. His chief wife (or *paṭṭa-mahiṣī*) was named Gaurī. She had five sons, the eldest of whom was named Puruṣottama Jānā. This information is given in *Bhakti-ratnākara* (6.65).

We also learn from Rāmānanda Rāya's *Jagannāth-vallabha-nāṭaka* that Pratāparudra was a mighty and heroic military leader, despite which he maintained a humble demeanor. He was a generous and liberal Vaiṣṇava, devoted to the promotion of learning. Kavi Karṇapūra also writes about Pratāparudra's military qualities in his *Caitanya-candrodaya-nāṭaka*. He protected brahminical culture and was especially benevolent towards the Vaiṣṇava religion. Many books have been attributed to Pratāparudra, such as *Sarasvatī-vilāsa*, *Pratāpa-mārtaṇḍa*, *Kautuka-cintāmaṇi*, and *Nirṇaya-saṅgraha*. In fact, the first two of these books were written by two of his court scholars, Lolla Lakṣmīdhara and Rāmakṛṣṇa, respectively.

PRATĀPARUDRA, KĀŚĪ MIŚRA'S DISCIPLE

King Pratāparudra accepted Kāśī Miśra as his spiritual master and served him with great dedication. While staying at Puri, he would daily go to Kāśī Miśra's house and massage his guru's feet after he had taken his midday meal. While doing so, he would inquire about the state of Lord Jagannātha's service.

"Pratāparudra had a regular duty which he performed whenever he was at Nilachal. He would daily massage Kāśī Miśra's feet and would hear a report on Lord Jagannātha's service." (*Caitanya Caritāmṛta* 3.9.81-2)

Mahāprabhu stayed at Kāśī Miśra's house in a one-roomed cottage on the veranda. In Odisha, such a small cottage is called a *gambhira*.

Many works of Vaiṣṇava history dating to that period have given testimony that Mahāprabhu, Rāmānanda Rāya, Kāśī Miśra and Sārvabhauma Bhaṭṭācārya felt affection for Pratāparudra. Every one of Mahāprabhu's biographies states that Pratāparudra received the Lord's mercy.

There is a legend that when Mahāprabhu left Puri for Vrindavan, Pratāparudra felt such separation that he had a wooden *mūrti* of the Lord made. He assigned fifty-four *brāhmaṇas* to the service of the deity, as well as giving a large tract of land for its maintenance. In the royal palace at Puri, deities of Gaura-Nityānanda Prabhu and Gaura-Gadādhara are worshipped alongside numerous other Deities.

PURUṢOTTAMA FIGHTS FOR LORD JAGANNĀTHA'S HONOR

During Pratāparudra's reign, his kingdom stretched as far as Rajahmundry in modern Andhra Pradesh. It is not necessary to go into detail here, but the following is a brief summary of some of the historical background. Pratāparudra's father, Puruṣottama Deva, retrieved lands which had been lost by his kingdom and expanded Odishan lands as far as Rajahmundry through his own might. He was such a dedicated servant of Lord Jagannātha that Lord Jagannātha Himself appeared on the battlefield to help the king.

On one occasion, marriage was contracted between Puruṣottama and the King of Kanchi's daughter Padmāvatī. The King of Kanchi came to Puri to have a look at the groom. He arrived there during the time of the Rathayātrā and saw his prospective son-in-law sweeping the parade ground before the chariot of the Lord, as was the custom. Though Puruṣottama was sweeping the ground with a golden broom, the King of Kanchi thought that it was an insult to his daughter to marry her to a degraded sweeper. He thus canceled the marriage between them. The King of Kanchi was a devotee of Gaṇeśa, and had no great faith in Lord Jagannātha.

When Puruṣottama heard of the sovereign of Kanchi's faithlessness, he became angry and attacked his territories with a large force. At first, he was unable to secure a victory, so he prostrated himself before Lord Jagannātha and surrendered to Him. This time Lord Jagannātha assured him that He would aid his war effort, and so Puruṣottama took up arms again.

As Puruṣottama passed through the village of Anandpur, about twelve miles from Puri, a milk-maid said to him, "Two horsemen passed through here. They bought milk, yogurt and buttermilk from me and paid for it with a ring. They told me to give you the ring and ask for money in exchange." When Puruṣottama looked at the ring, he was able to recognize that the two horsemen had been none other than Jagannātha and Balarāma. He rewarded the milk-maid and set off for certain victory against Kanchi. He returned with the jewelled throne of that kingdom and offered it to the service of Jagannātha. He also took the Gaṇeśa deity which was worshipped in Kanchi back to Puri. In this way, Jagannātha Deva crushed the arrogant pride of the King of Kanchi. It is said that Gaṇeśa tried to cast obstacles in Puruṣottama's way during the battle. Since he went against his customary role of eliminating obstacles, he was given the name Bhaṇḍa (deceitful) Gaṇeśa.

Kanchi's king personally returned to Puri with his daughter Padmāvatī and offered her as Puruṣottama's bride while he was sweeping the Rathayātrā route for Lord Jagannātha. Thus, Puruṣottama's position was saved by the Lord Himself. He remained King of Puri until 1497 A.D. He was followed by Pratāparudra, who remained on the throne until his death in 1540. Other than the above-mentioned queen Gaurī, he also had four other wives, named Padmā, Padmālayā, Ilā and Mahilā.

PRATĀPRUDRA'S DESIRE TO MEET MAHĀPRABHU

King Pratāparudra was the most fortunate member of the Gajapati dynasty of Odishan kings, for having received the mercy of Śrī Caitanya Mahāprabhu, the combined form of Rādhā and Kṛṣṇa, and for being counted among His associates. Even though Mahāprabhu felt that it was not beneficial for a *sannyāsī* to come into contact with a worldly man like a king, his disdain for him was purely for show. Inwardly, He was won over by the king's pure devotional attitude and generously showered him with His causeless mercy. Kṛṣṇadāsa Kavirāja Gosvāmī has described how the Lord taught the people of this world through King Pratāparudra in his *Caitanya Caritāmṛta*. The story is told in the eleventh chapter of the *Madhya-līlā*.

At first, Pratāparudra approached Sārvabhauma Bhaṭṭācārya to tell him of his desire to meet Caitanya Mahāprabhu. He asked him so many times that finally Sārvabhauma Bhaṭṭācārya asked Mahāprabhu to allow the King to see Him. As soon as he heard the request, however, the Lord covered his ears and said, "For a *sannyāsī* like Myself, to see a king is the same as looking at a woman – it is like consuming poison" (2.11.7). Even though the King was a great devotee, the fact that he was a king made him an object of fear, like a cobra.

PRATĀPARUDRA'S DREAM

In the fifth chapter of the *Antya-khaṇḍa* of the *Caitanya Bhāgavata*, Vṛndāvana Dāsa Ṭhākura has described the King's deep desire to meet with the Lord as well as a dream in which the King saw that Lord Jagannātha and Lord Caitanya Mahāprabhu are nondifferent. The first time the King saw Mahāprabhu dance, however, he had some doubts when he observed His body covered in dust and His mouth filled with frothing saliva from ecstatic dancing.

That very night, Pratāparudra saw Lord Jagannātha in a dream. Lord Jagannātha was also covered in dust and saliva. Then he saw the same dust-covered form of Lord Caitanya Mahāprabhu sitting on Lord Jagannātha's throne along with the deity. From this amazing dream, he understood Lord Caitanya Mahāprabhu's divine nature.

[Lord Jagannātha said,] " 'Just look! My body is covered with dust and spit. You are a king and the son of a king. Surely it is not proper for you to touch someone like Me.' Having said this, Lord Jagannātha looked at His servant and laughed. In that very moment, the King saw Caitanya Mahāprabhu sitting on the altar alongside the Lord." (*Caitanya Bhāgavata* 3.5.175-7)

RĀMĀNANDA AND SĀRVABHAUMA TRY TO INTERVENE

One day, Pratāparudra came to Puri with Rāmānanda Rāya and other members of his retinue. Rāmānanda Rāya knew of the King's eagerness to meet Mahāprabhu, so when he went to visit the Lord, he tried to persuade Him to allow such a meeting to take place, telling Him of the King's deep affection for Him. He added that the King had given him retirement from his job with full pay to allow him to stay with the Lord. When He heard how the King was filled with love for Him and how he had served His devotee, Mahāprabhu replied: "The King has shown so much love for you that the Lord is sure to accept him on the basis of this virtue alone."

ye me bhakta-janāḥ pārtha na
me bhaktāś ca te janāḥ
mad-bhaktānāṁ ca ye bhaktās
te me bhaktatamā matāḥ

"Those who claim to be My devotees are in fact not so. The best of My devotees are those who are devoted to My servants." (*Caitanya Caritāmṛta* 2.11.28)

However, when Sārvabhauma Bhaṭṭācārya again entreated the Lord on the King's behalf to allow such a meeting to take place. The Lord said that under no circumstances would He come face to face with a king, and that if people continued to ask Him to do so, he would leave Puri and go to live elsewhere. When the King heard this, he was devastated. He said:

"The Lord has descended just to deliver all kinds of sinful, low-caste born persons. He has even delivered sinners like Jagāi and Mādhāi.

But it seems that He has made a promise to deliver the entire universe with the exception of Pratāparudra. He may have sworn not to see me, but I have sworn to give up my life if I cannot see Him. Without Śrī Caitanya Mahāprabhu's mercy, my life and kingdom are worthless." (*Caitanya Caritāmṛta* 2.11.45-6, 48-9)

When the Lord returned from His pilgrimage to the south of India, Pratāparudra sent a letter to Vāsudeva Sārvabhauma in which he once again expressed his desire to meet with the Lord. Vāsudeva Sārvabhauma showed the letter to the other devotees, and all were duly impressed by the degree of devotion exhibited by the King. Nityānanda Prabhu decided that He would speak to the Lord, not about meeting the King but simply about his personal qualities and actions. He said the following to the Lord:

"We want to submit everything to You, whether or not it is fitting. The King has decided that he will become a yogi if he cannot meet You. He says, 'I will wear earrings and become a mendicant. I have no desire to enjoy this kingdom without the mercy of Gaura Hari. When will I be able to see the Lord's moonlike face to my full satisfaction, and when will I be able to hold His lotus feet to my heart?' " (*Caitanya Caritāmṛta* 2.12.19-21)

Though the Lord's heart melted listening to the King's mood, He maintained His hard-line position in order to set an example for renouncers of the world. He said that the spiritual injunction is that a *sannyāsī* is forbidden to set sight on a king. Furthermore, the Lord said, Dāmodara Paṇḍita would criticize Him if He were to engage in such forbidden acts. Dāmodara Paṇḍita answered, saying:

"I am merely an insignificant *jīva*, so what power do I have to tell You what to do? I shall see You meet the King of Your own volition. The King loves You very much, and You are influenced by a devotee's feelings of love. It is the power of this love for You that will reward him with the opportunity to touch You. Although You are the Supreme Lord and are completely independent, still it is Your nature to be influenced by the love and affection of Your devotees." (*Caitanya Caritāmṛta* 2.12.27-9)

Nityānanda Prabhu added that people who experience unrequited love tend to commit suicide. Thus, in order to save the King's life, he asked Mahāprabhu to give him a used outer garment (*bahirvāsa*). The Lord could not refuse, so Nityānanda Prabhu asked Govinda for the *bahirvāsa* and sent it to the King via Sārvabhauma Bhaṭṭācārya. The King was overjoyed to receive the cloth, and he began to worship it as nondifferent from the Lord Himself.

MAHĀPRABHU SEES THE KING'S SON

When Rāmānanda Rāya received the King's permission to come to live near the Lord in Puri, he also described Mahārāja Pratāparudra's intense desire to see the Lord and tried to persuade the Lord to fulfill that desire. Mahāprabhu spoke out of a desire to establish the rules of conduct for the renounced order; He said that just as even a slight mark on a piece of white cloth immediately becomes noticeable, the smallest character flaws of a *sannyāsī* are noticed by the general public. A jug full of milk is contaminated by even a drop of liquor; similarly, though it may be true that King Pratāparudra possess all virtues, the very fact that he is a king makes his association undesirable.

However, the Lord was unable to completely ignore Rāmānanda Rāya's request, because of their close friendship. He Himself suggested that He could see the King's son, for according to the maxim *ātmā vai jāyate putraḥ* ("one extends as one's own son"), there is no difference between the father and the son. When he learned of the Lord's will, King Pratāparudra immediately sent his son. When Mahāprabhu saw the teenage prince with his lotus eyes and dark skin wearing a yellow cloth, he immediately thought of Kṛṣṇa. He embraced the lad, making him experience the ecstatic transformations of *prema*. When the prince came back to the palace, the King embraced him and felt the same ecstasies through him. From that day onward, the King's son was considered one of Mahāprabhu's associates.

THE KING'S HUMBLE SERVICE TO LORD JAGANNĀTHA

A devotee who is free from pride, surrendered and without any ulterior motive is eligible to receive the Lord's mercy.

"The Lord bestows greater blessings on the meek and humble. Those of noble birth, the learned and the wealthy are all filled with pride." (*Caitanya Caritāmṛta* 3.4.68)

Mahārāja Pratāparudra was without any pride, even though he had so much material power as well as all good qualities. Mahāprabhu had noticed his willingness to engage in even menial service and was pleased with him and ready to give him His mercy, even though externally He made a show of being hard-hearted.

"King Pratāparudra personally engaged in the Lord Jagannātha's service by cleansing the road with a gold-handled broom. He also sprinkled the road with sandalwood-scented water. Although he sat on the royal throne, he engaged in such menial service for the sake of Lord Jagannātha. Although the King was the most exalted person in the kingdom, he still accepted to do this menial service for the Lord and thus became the recipient of the Lord's blessings. Mahāprabhu was happy to see the King's service to the Lord and it was through this service that he finally received the mercy of the Lord." (*Caitanya Caritāmṛta* 2.13.15-18)

The Lord's mercy has no cause. Only He knows who will receive His blessings and when. He often does so in an indirect manner rather than doing it openly. The Lord was pleased by the King's engagement in a menial service, and even though He did not make a public show of mercy to him, He did reveal His personal form to the King and thus fulfill his deepest desire.

HARICANDANA IS SLAPPED BY ŚRĪVĀSA PAṆḌITA

In the thirteenth chapter of the *Madhya-līlā*, these events are described. During the Rathayātrā festival, the devotees were divided into seven groups for chanting the Holy Names. By the Lord's divine power each one of these groups thought that Mahāprabhu was with them alone. Pratāparudra was able to witness this pastime by the boundless mercy of the Lord and felt wonder and ecstatic love. All this was Mahāprabhu's indirect mercy.

When Mahāprabhu wanted to dance in front of Lord Jagannātha's chariot, He would gather the seven *sampradāyas* together into one *kīrtana* group. Meanwhile, the devotees formed three rings of protection around the Lord. The innermost line of defense was headed by Nityānanda Prabhu, the second by Kāśīśvara Paṇḍita, Mukunda and other devotees. Pratāparudra and his soldiers formed the outermost circle to defend the Lord from the crowds.

Mahārāja Pratāparudra watched mesmerized while the Lord danced, resting his hand on the shoulder of his minister (*mahāpātra*) Haricandana. At that time, Śrīvāsa Paṇḍita, who was also absorbed in watching the Lord's ecstatic dancing, came and stood in front of the King, blocking his vision. Haricandana repeatedly tried to push Śrīvāsa to one side, telling him to let the King see, until finally Śrīvāsa Paṇḍita lost his temper and slapped Haricandana. When Haricandana became angry and was about to respond to Śrīvāsa Paṇḍita's aggression, the King said:

"You are very fortunate, for you have been graced by the touch of Śrīvāsa Ṭhākura. I have not been so fortunate. You should feel obliged to him." (*Caitanya Caritāmṛta* 2.13.97)

PRATĀPARUDRA CATCHES THE LORD

In Mahāprabhu's *līlā*, we find a delightful mixture of the highest manifestations of love, mercy and teachings for the general public. As He pulled the chariot of Lord Jagannātha, Mahāprabhu was absorbed in the mood of Rādhā and the other *gopīs* at their meeting with Lord Kṛṣṇa, who had come to Kurukshetra from Dwaraka on the occasion of the solar eclipse. Thus Mahāprabhu wished to attract Kṛṣṇa (in His Jagannātha form) from the site of His majestic pastimes in Kurukshetra, represented by Nilachal (the Jagannātha temple), to the site of His sweet, loving pastimes in Vrindavan, represented by Sundarachal, or the Guṇḍicā temple. Sometimes, Mahāprabhu would lag behind as He tried to understand the depth of the *gopīs*' loving power; Jagannātha would seem to understand the Lord's emotions and slow down the movement of the chariot. Thus, the Lord danced more frenziedly as He and Lord Jagannātha went deeper and deeper into ecstatic communion. As He danced in this state of transcendental madness (*divyonmāda*), the Lord seemed about to fall down just in the very spot where King Pratāparudra was standing. The alert King immediately held the Lord to keep Him from falling. This was how the Lord blessed the King and allowed him to touch Him, but Mahāprabhu immediately began to rebuke Himself for having allowed a materialistic person to touch Him. The inconceivable activities of the Lord contain both delightful manifestations of emotion and teachings for the world, neither of which are easy to understand.

"When He saw that he was the King, Mahāprabhu condemned Himself, saying, 'O, how pitiful it is that I have touched a person interested in mundane affairs.' Even though the Lord had made up His mind to give the King an audience upon seeing him act as a sweeper in the service of Lord Jagannātha, He still externally expressed feelings of anger in order to warn His personal associates." (*Caitanya Caritāmṛta* 2.13.182, 184-5)

THE LORD EMBRACES THE KING

Vāsudeva Sārvabhauma thought up a way to arrange a meeting between Pratāparudra and the Lord. During the Rathayātrā festival, after having danced in the *saṅkīrtana* with His devotees, the Lord customarily went into a flower garden to rest. Sārvabhauma Bhaṭṭācārya suggested to the King that he take this opportunity to approach the Lord dressed as a commoner and recite a verse of the *rāsa-pañcādhyāya* from the *Bhāgavata*. The Lord would be in a trance-like state and would be transported by the recital of the love of Kṛṣṇa and the *gopīs*. In this condition, He would surely embrace the King. The King was comforted by these words of advice.

There is a spot about halfway between the Lord Jagannātha temple and Guṇḍicā, or halfway between Śraddhā Bālu and Ardhāsanī Devī, which is called Balagandi. On the Rathayātrā day, Lord Jagannātha's chariot stops here at midday. Devotees also take rest here to be freed from their tiredness. The custom is that all devotees, whether important or not, can make food offerings to Him on this occasion. Because of the large crowds which normally accumulate, Mahāprabhu would go to rest in a flower garden by a coconut grove. King Pratāparudra remembered Sārvabhauma Bhaṭṭācārya's counsel and approached the Lord in the dress of a Vaiṣṇava and began to massage His feet. He began to recite the following two verses from *rāsa-pañcādhyāya* of *Bhāgavata*:

jayati te 'dhikaṁ janmanā vrajaḥ
śrayate indirā śaśvad atra hi
dayita dṛśyatāṁ dikṣu tāvakās
tvayi dhṛtāsavas tvāṁ vicinvate

[The *gopīs* said,] "The glories of Vraja-bhūmi have increased ever since You took birth here; ever since then, the goddess of fortune has taken up residence here. O, beloved! We whose lives depend completely on You are searching for You; please show Yourself to us." (*Śrīmad Bhāgavatam* 10.31.1).

tava kathāmṛtaṁ tapta-jīvanaṁ
kavibhir īḍitaṁ kalmaṣāpaham
śravaṇa-maṅgalaṁ śrīmad-ātataṁ
bhuvi gṛṇanti te bhūridā janāḥ

"Nectarean discussions about You give life to those who are suffering from Your separation. The great devotees like Prahlāda, Dhruva and others glorify You always. Such discussions destroy all of one's sins. Listening to them brings auspiciousness and the fortune of love for Kṛṣṇa. Those who distribute these wonderful words throughout the world are the most generous." (*Śrīmad Bhāgavatam* 10.31.9)

As soon as Mahāprabhu heard this verse, He became ecstatic with love and embraced the King, while repeating the word *bhūridā* ("most benevolent") from the verse. Though the Lord is all-knowing, He asked the King his identity. Pratāparudra answered that He was the servant of the servant of the Lord. Satisfied with the King, the Lord revealed to Him a glorious divine form. All the devotees were overjoyed to see that the King had finally received the Lord's mercy.

When the *ratha* was being pulled from Balagandi to Guṇḍicā, it suddenly came to a stop, and even the strongest men and most powerful elephants were unable to move it, much to the worry of Mahārāja Pratāparudra. When the Lord saw that everyone was worried, He told everyone to leave the chariots alone and told His own devotees to man the ropes. Mahāprabhu Himself went behind the chariot and began to push it with His head. In a moment, the chariot began to move with a great rumbling noise. King Pratāparudra and the rest of his entourage marvelled at this feat of the Lord.

PRATĀPARUDRA SEES OTHER WONDERFUL PASTIMES

While spending the four months in Puri, the Bengali Vaiṣṇavas witnessed numerous pastimes of Lord Jagannātha. On the Nandotsava, the day after Kṛṣṇa's appearance ceremony, Mahāprabhu would dress up as a cowherd and put on a play about Kṛṣṇa's Vraja pastimes with His devotees. Pratāparudra also participated in this *līlā*.

When the Lord made His first attempt to go to Vrindavan, He left Puri on Vijayā-daśamī and went to Cuttack, where He met Pratāparudra in a garden under a *bakula* tree. Here too, the Lord saw the great *prema* of the King and embraced him, drenching him in His own tears of love. From that day on, the Lord was given the epithet Pratāparudra-saṁtrātā, "the savior of King Pratāparudra."

At one time, the King's son placed Bhavānanda Rāya's son Gopīnātha Paṭṭanāyaka on the scaffold for having misappropriated state funds. Some devotees came to Mahāprabhu to ask Him to intervene in order to save Gopīnātha's life. The Lord was unhappy at being asked to get involved in such mundane affairs and made up His mind to go to Alalanatha. The King was disturbed at hearing this news and prepared himself to give up everything in order to keep the Lord in Puri. These are all farther proofs of the extent of the King's love for the Lord's lotus feet.

"When King Pratāparudra heard all these details, he felt great pain in his heart. 'I shall give up everything I am owed,' he said, 'if Mahāprabhu will only stay here in Jagannatha Puri. Even a moment's contact with the Lord is worth more to me than millions of *cintamani* jewels. I care nothing for this small sum of 200,000 *kāhans* [a *kāhana* equals 1280 cowries.] I would indeed offer everything not only this but my life and kingdom – for the Lord's lotus feet.' " (*Caitanya Caritāmṛta* 3.9.94-96)

A PRAYER TO RĀDHĀ BY KING PRATĀPARUDRA

In the description of Bengali manuscripts in the Bangiya Sahitya Parishad library in Kolkata, a notice is given of a song with Pratāparudra's signature. There is some doubt as to whether the song is indeed his or not. A portion of that song goes as follows:

I will become an ornament on Your body,
the ankle bells upon Your feet.
I will become the chakora who gazes
at the moons of Your fingernails,
the bee who buzzes around Your lotus feet.
I will become the mirror You look into,
the whisk that fans You.
And I have yet another desire;
Let me become insignificant dust on Your feet.
If I cannot become the dust of Your feet,
then be merciful and do with me as You please,
this is Pratāparudra's prayer.

When Mahāprabhu disappeared, Pratāparudra felt great separation from Him. This is described in the *Bhakti-ratnākara* as follows:

"When the King heard that the Lord had departed, he fell to the ground and began lamenting. Hitting his head again and again, he fell unconscious, and only the association of Rāmānanda Rāya kept him alive. The king was unable to bear the absence of the Lord, and so he left Puri, remaining elsewhere for the rest of his days." (*Bhakti-ratnākara* 3.217-19)

Mahārāj Pratāparudra's descendants are (1) Kāluyā Pratāpa, (2) Kakhāruyā Pratāpa, (3) Govinda Vidyādhara, (4) Chakra Pratāpa, (5) Narasiṁha Deva, (6) Raghurāma Deva, (7) Mukunda Deva Haricandana, (8)

Rāmacandra Deva, (9) Puruṣottama Deva, (10) Nṛsiṁhadeva, (11) Gaṅgādhara Deva, (12) Balabhadra Deva, (13) Mukunda Deva II, (14) Divyasiṁha Deva, (15) Hare Kṛṣṇa Deva, (16) Gopīnātha Deva, (17) Rāmacandra Deva II, (18) Vīrakeśarī Deva, (19) Divyasiṁha Deva II, (20) Mukunda Deva III, (21) Rāmacandra Deva III, (22) Vīrakeśarī Deva II, (23) Divyasiṁha Deva III, (24) Mukunda Deva IV, (25) Rāmacandra Deva IV, (26) Vīrakeśarī Deva III, and (27) Divyasiṁha Deva IV.

Śrī Rāmānanda Rāya

priya-narma-sakhaḥ kaścid arjunaḥ pāṇḍavo 'rjunaḥ
militvā samabhūd rāmānanda-rāyaḥ prabhoḥ priyaḥ
ato rādhā-kṛṣṇa-bhakti-prema-tattvādikaṁ kṛtī
rāmānando gauracandraṁ pratyavarṇayad anvaham
lalitety āhur eke yat tad eke nānumanyante
bhavānandaṁ prati prāha gauro yat tvaṁ pṛthāpatiḥ
gopyārjunīyayā sārdhama ekībhūyāpi pāṇḍavaḥ
arjuno yad rāya-rāmānanda ity āhur uttamāḥ
arjunīyābhavat tūrṇaṁ arjuno 'pi ca pāṇḍavaḥ
iti pādmottara-khaṇḍe vyaktam eva virājate
tasmād etat trayaṁ rāmānanda-rāya-mahāśayaḥ

"There are two Arjunas in Kṛṣṇa *līlā*: one is a *priya-narma-sakhā* in Vraja; the other is one of the Pāṇḍavas. These two combined to become Mahāprabhu's dear companion Rāmānanda Rāya. Rāmānanda was very knowledgeable in the teachings of loving devotion to Rādhā and Kṛṣṇa, which he described to Gauracandra on a daily basis. Some people say that Rāmānanda Rāya was Lalitā Sakhī, while others do not. Mahāprabhu Himself told Bhavānanda Rāya that he was Pāṇḍu, the husband of Kuntī and father of the Pāṇḍavas. *Padmā Purāṇa* states that the Pāṇḍava Arjuna became the *gopī Arjunīyā*. Thus the most aware say that in Rāmānanda Rāya all these three personalities combined." (*Gaura-gaṇoddeśa-dīpikā* 120-124)

As stated in these verses from *Gaura-gaṇoddeśa-dīpikā,* some people hold that Rāmānanda Rāya was an *avatāra* of Lalitā. Some others are of the opinion that he was Viśākhā. In his commentary on *Caitanya Caritāmṛta* (2.8.23), Śrīla Bhaktivinoda Ṭhākura writes, "The love that awakened in Rāmānanda and Mahāprabhu when they met was the same as the love that Viśākhā had for Rādhā and Kṛṣṇa in Vraja, and that which Rādhā and Kṛṣṇa had for Viśākhā." Thus it is clear that Śrīla Bhaktivinoda Ṭhākura saw Rāmānanda Rāya as Viśākhā. Rāmānanda Rāya was one of the Lord's three and a half most intimate associates.

"The Lord accepted that Śikhi Māhiti's sister was one of Rādhā's friends. In the entire world, there were only three and a half devotees who were as worthy. They were Svarūpa Dāmodara Gosvāmī, Rāmānanda Rāya and Śikhi Māhiti. Śikhi Māhiti's sister was the half person." (*Caitanya Caritāmṛta* 3.2.105-6)

RĀMĀNANDA'S SOCIAL STATUS

Rāmānanda Rāya's father was named Bhavānanda Rāya. He was born in a family of the Odishan *karaṇa* caste. Bhavānanda Rāya was previously King Pāṇḍu. He had five sons, of whom Rāmānanda Rāya was the eldest. The other four brothers were Gopīnātha Paṭṭanāyaka, Kalānidhi, Sudhānidhi and Vaṇīnātha Paṭṭanāyaka. The Lord states in *Caitanya Caritāmṛta*: "You are Pāṇḍu himself, and your wife is Kuntī. Your five sons are the five Pāṇḍavas." (*Caitanya Caritāmṛta* 2.10.53)

Manohara Rāya, a descendant of Rāmānanda Rāya, has written his family's history. Śrīla Bhakti Siddhānta Sarasvatī

Gosvāmī Ṭhākura has summarized some details of this account in his *Anubhāṣya*: "Odishan society considers the *karaṇa* community to be part of the *śudra* caste. Rāmānanda Rāya was born into this community. Nevertheless, though he was considered by society to be a *śudra* by birth, he was a de facto *brāhmaṇa*; indeed, as a Vaiṣṇava *paramahaṁsa*, he was a spiritual master to the *brāhmaṇas*."

By Kṛṣṇa's will, the creator Brahmā himself appeared in an outcaste family as Haridāsa Ṭhākura in order to show that one's family and one's race have absolutely no importance. Born as a Muslim, Haridāsa Ṭhākura only enriched Lord Gaurāṅga's pastimes.

"Haridāsa Ṭhākura was born in a low-caste family on the Lord's desire in order to show that caste and class have no importance at all. All the scriptures say that a devotee of Viṣṇu, though born in a lowly family, is still worshipable by all. What will one's caste do for one born in a high caste who does not worship Kṛṣṇa? He will go to hell in spite of his high birth. Haridāsa Ṭhākura took a low birth just to bear witness to these scriptural statements. (*Caitanya Bhāgavata* 1.16.237-240)

A Vaiṣṇava is beyond the qualities of the material nature. Anyone who considers a devotee in terms of his birth or race is destined for a hellish existence.

arcye viṣṇau śīladhīr guruṣu nara-
matir vaiṣṇave jāti-buddhir
viṣṇor vā vaiṣṇavānāṁ kali-mala-
mathane pāda-tīrthe 'mbu buddhiḥ
śrī viṣṇor nāmni mantre sakala-
kaluṣa-he śabda-sāmānya-buddhir
viṣṇau sarveśvareśe tad-itara-
samadhīr yasya vā nārakī saḥ

"Anyone who considers the deity of Viṣṇu to be nothing but stone, the guru to be an ordinary human being, or the Vaiṣṇava to be a member of a particular caste or race, who takes the holy water which has washed Viṣṇu or the Vaiṣnava's feet and can destroy all the sins of the Age of Kālī to be ordinary water, who thinks that the name or *mantra* of Viṣnu, which destroys all evils, is the same as any other sound, or who takes Viṣṇu to be the same as anything other than Him, suffers hellish existence." (*Padma Purāṇa*)

Bhavānanda Rāya made his home in Brahmagiri, or Alalanath, about twelve miles west of Puri. Rāya Rāmānanda was King Pratāparudra's governor in Vidyanagar, and according to some opinions, he was one of his ministers.

According to the *Bhajana-nirṇaya*, Rāmānanda Rāya was the disciple of Rāghavendra Purī and grand-disciple of Mādhavendra Purī.

SĀRVABHAUMA TELLS THE LORD ABOUT RĀMĀNANDA

The Lord took *sannyāsa* in the month of Māgha and arrived in Puri during the month of Phālguna. After celebrating the Dola Yātrā in Puri, Mahāprabhu delivered Sārvabhauma Bhaṭṭācārya in the month of Caitra. In the month of Vaiśākha, He set off on His pilgrimage to South India. Though Mahāprabhu had decided to travel alone, Nityānanda Prabhu convinced Him to take a servant, Kṛṣṇadāsa, as a traveling companion. As He was leaving, Sārvabhauma Bhaṭṭācārya gave the Lord four *kaupins* and *bahirvāsa*, and requested Him to visit Rāmānanda Rāya on the banks of the Godavari.

Sārvabhauma Bhaṭṭācārya said, "My Lord, You must fulfill this request of mine. In the town of Vidyanagar, on the bank of the Godavari, there is a responsible government officer named Rāmānanda Rāya. Please do not neglect him, thinking he belongs to a *śudra* family engaged in materialistic activities. Please take my word for it that You should meet him without fail. If anyone is fit to associate with You, it is he. No other devotee can compare with him in the knowledge of divine sentiments. He has attained the highest limits of learning and is experienced in the science of devotional sentiments. If You converse with him, You will recognize his exalted character. When I first met him, I could not understand that everything he said and did was transcendental. I made fun of him simply because he was a Vaiṣṇava. By Your mercy, I can now understand the truth about Rāmānanda Rāya. In talking with him, You also will acknowledge his greatness." (*Caitanya Caritāmṛta* 2.7.61-67)

Śrīla Bhakti Siddhānta Sarasvatī Prabhupāda has commented as follows (2.7.63): "To superficial understanding, Rāmānanda Rāya was not a *sannyāsī*, wearing a loincloth. In common understanding, those who are courtiers engaged in government service are materialistic, but Rāmānanda Rāya was, in fact, a learned person who was a de facto *sannyāsī*, a perfected human being. Sārvabhauma Bhaṭṭācārya had previously been able to recognize his natural qualities as a Vaiṣṇava, even though he himself was not a Vaiṣṇava at that time. When he took to devotional service by the grace of the Lord, he reconsidered his opinion of Rāmānanda and realized the extent of his qualifications, calling him an *adhikārī rasika-bhakta* – the most highly qualified authority in the matters of devotional sentiment."

Sārvabhauma Bhaṭṭācārya was the *avatāra* of Bṛhaspati and the court Paṇḍita of King Pratāparudra. He was so learned that even though a ḫouseholder, he had *sannyāsīs* as his disciples. Nevertheless, he had been unable to recognize that Caitanya Mahāprabhu was the Supreme Lord Himself, nor was he able to identify Rāmānanda Rāya as His most intimate associate. If he was unable to do so, then how much more difficult it would be for others! No one is able to understand the glories of the Lord and His devotees without being blessed by Their mercy.

"The process of inference is of no value for understanding the nature of the Supreme Lord. Without the Lord's mercy, no person can come to know Him. One to whom the Lord gives even a slight drop of mercy is able to understand His nature." (*Caitanya Caritāmṛta* 2.6.82-3)

MAHĀPRABHU MEETS RĀMĀNANDA

Mahāprabhu set off to the south, blessing the inhabitants of the land by bestowing devotion to Kṛṣṇa on them. He visited Kurmasthan, delivering the *brāhmaṇa* also named Kūrma, and giving everyone the order to preach devotional service to Kṛṣṇa. He saved Vāsudeva Vipra and then went on to Simhachalam, where He danced before the deity of Jiyaḍa Nṛsiṁha. Then He went on to the Godavari River, which in His vision was the Yamuna, and the woods on its banks, Vrindavan. He joyfully crossed the river and came to the place known as Kovoor, where He bathed in the river and waited there, hoping to meet Rāmānanda Rāya. At the same time, Rāmānanda Rāya passed by with fanfare. When he saw Mahāprabhu's supernatural form, he descended from his palanquin and paid his obeisances to the Lord. Though Mahāprabhu recognized him, He asked him to identify himself. Rāmānanda Rāya replied that he was nothing but a lowly *śudra* servant. When the Lord heard him speak in this humble manner, He immediately embraced him.

Both the Lord and His servant felt the onset of divine emotions, and both experienced the eight ecstatic transformations of *prema*. The *brāhmaṇas* who were accompanying Rāmānanda Rāya were astonished to see such a display. They thought:

"This *sannyāsī* is as effulgent as the Brahman. Why is He crying while embracing this *śudra*? The governor, Rāmānanda Rāya, is a scholar and normally very serious. Why has he suddenly become so emotional upon being touched by this *sannyāsī*, as though intoxicated?" (*Caitanya Caritāmṛta* 2.8.26-7)

Seeing that there were outsiders present, the Lord controlled His emotions and told Rāmānanda Rāya that He had been told by Sārvabhauma Bhaṭṭācārya to seek him out. Rāmānanda Rāya replied with humility:

"This is the proof of Your mercy on Sārvabhauma Bhaṭṭācārya: You have touched me, an untouchable, subdued by his love for You. What a difference exists between us – You are the Supreme Lord, Nārāyaṇa Himself, and I, a government servant interested in materialistic activities. Indeed, I am the lowest amongst men of the fourth caste. Even so, You were not contemptuous of my touch, neither did You fear the Vedic injunctions which forbid one to even look upon a *śudra*. Your mercy makes You touch me, even though this activity is condemned both by scripture and by society. You are the Supreme Lord Himself, so who can understand Your intention?" (*Caitanya Caritāmṛta* 2.8.34-7)

Though the *brāhmaṇas* had never shown the slightest interest in *bhakti*, they too were influenced by the sight of the Lord and began to chant the names of Kṛṣṇa, their voices tremulous with divine ecstasy. Rāmānanda Rāya said aloud that Mahāprabhu was the Supreme Lord, both in *ākṛti* (form) and in *prakṛti* (nature). The Lord immediately responded in a way that would show the greatness of His devotee:

[The Lord said:] "You are a great devotee; indeed you are the best amongst them. All those who behold you are immediately affected so that their hearts melt. What to speak of others – I am a Māyāvadī *sannyāsī*, yet I feel the onset of Kṛṣṇa *prema* when I touch you." (*Caitanya Caritāmṛta* 2.8.44-5)

THE LORD LISTENS TO RĀMĀNANDA SPEAK

When Mahāprabhu told him of His desire to hear Kṛṣṇa *kathā* from his lips, Rāmānanda Rāya requested that He stay for a week or longer so that his own wicked mind could be pacified and purified. The two then each went their way to finish their duties, returning to the same spot in the evening. Ordinarily, it is seen that a devotee asks the questions and the Lord answers. This time, however, the roles were reversed, and the Lord asked Rāmānanda to clarify certain spiritual truths and then empowered him to respond. Kṛṣṇadāsa Kavirāja Gosvāmī makes this explicit in the verse which opens the eighth chapter of the *Madhya-līlā*:

sañcārya rāmābhidha-bhakta-meghe
sva-bhakti-siddhānta-cayāmṛtāni
gaurābdhir etair amunā vitīrṇais
taj-jñatva-ratnālayatāṁ prayāti

"Gaurāṅga is like the ocean of spiritual truths; He filled the cloud named Rāmānanda with the nectar of the purest conclusions of devotion to Himself. Rāmānanda then rained down that same nectar on the very ocean from which it had come, producing the jewels of transcendental knowledge." (*Caitanya Caritāmṛta* 2.8.1)

A person who has not taken shelter of the Lord may try to understand the Supreme Truth by using empirical means, without achieving any success. Indeed, he will fall into confusion and be unable to understand the words of the Lord.

Mahāprabhu asked Rāmānanda Rāya to explain to Him, with evidence from the scriptures, the ultimate goal of life. Rāmānanda started his response by explaining that devotion to Viṣṇu is the ultimate aim of human achievement, or *sādhya*. He described progressive path of different practices leading to that theistic goal, starting from the practice of *varṇāśrama-dharma*, to offering the fruits of one's activities to Kṛṣṇa (*karmārpaṇa*), the renunciation of prescribed duties (*karma-tyāga*) and then devotion mixed with knowledge (*jñāna-miśra-bhakti*), offering the scriptural basis for each step. Mahāprabhu rejected each proposal, however, saying that it was superficial or external, for none of these practices had the potential to achieve the pure devotion which He had come to give.

By starting this conversation with Rāmānanda Rāya with *varṇāśrama-dharma*, Mahāprabhu showed that all activities which ignore the Vedic principles or go against them are to be completely rejected. When responding to each of Rāmānanda's suggestings, Mahāprabhu did not say, "Absolutely not!" Rather, He used the words *eho bāhya*, "This is external." The idea is that one must first give up activities which are outside the scope of the Vedic standard. Once one is fixed in these principles, one can progressively gain the qualifications to proceed through each of the various steps described by Rāmānanda Rāya. This holds true even though *bhakti* itself is completely independent and may manifest in an individual through the association of saintly persons despite one's having no prior qualifications not having gone through these prior steps.

When Rāmānanda Rāya finally answered Mahāprabhu's question by saying, "Pure devotional service without any tinge of speculative knowledge (*jñāna-śūnya-bhakti*) is the means to achieve the supreme perfection," Mahāprabhu finally accepted his conclusion. Mahāprabhu's teachings actually begin from this point on. The words *jñāna-śūnya* are meant to completely eradicate any consciousness of the impersonal aspect of the supreme, but not the kind of knowledge of relationships (*sambandha-jñāna*) which is favorable to the attainment of pure devotional service.

Śrīla Bhaktivinoda Ṭhākura writes in his *Amṛta-pravāha-bhāṣya,* "The purport is that sacrificing the results of one's actions is better than merely engaging in one's prescribed duties according to the *varṇāśrama-dharma*; the renunciation of fruitive activities is better than simply giving up the fruits; better than this is the cultivation of knowledge mixed with devotional service. However, despite this progressive improvement in spirituality through these stages, they are all superficial because these four kinds of practices have no power to achieve pure devotion, or *śuddhā bhakti.* The devotions known as *āropa-siddhā* (adding a devotional veneer as an afterthought to another action) and *saṅga-siddha* (devotion alloyed with fruitive activities or speculative knowledge) are never to be considered pure devotional service. Pure devotional service is Svarūpa-*siddhā bhakti*, i.e., it is devotion both in form and in intent. It is entirely and eternally different from these other activities, which have only a superficial relationship to devotional service. The characteristics of *śuddha bhakti* are that it is activity executed uniquely for the pleasure of Kṛṣṇa, devoid of any material desires; it is not hidden by the presence of fruitive intent or identification with Brahman. This is the ultimate goal of spiritual practice, for though it is seen in an aspiring devotee, it is present in its purest form when he reaches the perfection of his practice." (*Caitanya Caritāmṛta* 2.8.68)

As long as Rāmānanda Rāya suggested anything other than following in the footsteps of the great devotees and listening to Kṛṣṇa *kathā* from their lips, Mahāprabhu kept saying, "This is external." Therefore it is to be understood that pure devotion starts from the moment one begins to hear about the activities and teachings of Lord Kṛṣṇa from the lips of a pure devotee. From this point, Rāmānanda Rāya described the various stages of loving devotion, the moods of neutrality, servitude, friendship, parenthood and conjugal love. From there, he went on to describe the supremacy of Rādhā's love as well as both Rādhā's and Kṛṣṇa's characteristics. Then Mahāprabhu asked questions like "What is the essence of education?" and "What kind of fame is best for the living being?" All these things have been extensively described in the eighth chapter of *Caitanya Caritāmṛta*'s *Madhya-līlā*. In order to avoid abnormal expansion of the account of Rāmānanda's life, we will not go into these matters any farther here.

RĀMĀNANDA'S PERCEPTION OF THE LORD'S IDENTITY

The identity of the Lord cannot remain hidden to His devotee. Rāmānanda was able to recognize the Lord for who He was. He said:

"First I saw You as an ordinary *sannyāsī*. Now I see that You are actually a dark-skinned cowherd boy. I see a golden image standing in front of You; its golden luster covers Your entire body." (*Caitanya Caritāmṛta* 2.8.268-9)

Mahāprabhu made an effort to dismiss His identity when He heard this, saying that Rāya Rāmānanda was a great devotee and thus saw Kṛṣṇa everywhere. Rāmānanda, however, clearly stated the primary purpose of the Lord's *avatāra*. Mahāprabhu was pleased with his insightful realization, and He displayed His form as the combination of *rasa-rāja* ("the king of the devotional sentiments") Kṛṣṇa and the embodiment of *mahā-bhāva* ("the supreme devotional mood"), Śrīmatī Rādhārāṇī. When he saw this amazing combined form of the Lord, Rāmānanda Rāya fell to the ground in a faint. When the Lord touched him, he regained consciousness.

Rāmānanda Rāya and the Lord remained together blissfully for ten days before Mahāprabhu continued on His southern pilgrimage. He asked Rāmānanda Rāya to abandon his involvement with government service and join Him in Puri when He returned.

When Mahāprabhu completed His travels in southern India, He met with Rāmānanda Rāya once again on the banks of the Godavari. He showed him the two books, *Kṛṣṇa-karṇāmṛta* and *Brahma-saṁhitā,* He had found in His travels, and which substantiated all that Rāmānanda Rāya had said in their previous conversations. Rāmānanda Rāya copied the two manuscripts himself. The Lord remained another week with Rāmānanda

Rāya, engaging in the pleasure of discussions about Kṛṣṇa before heading back to Nilachal. When Mahāprabhu expressed His desire to take Rāmānada Rāya along with Him to Puri, he delcined to go with the Lord immediately as he was obliged to wait for the king's permission and also would need to take care of other official affairs. He promised to join the Lord in Puri as soon as he was able.

RĀMĀNANDA COMES TO PURI

When the Lord arrived in Puri, He made His permanent residence in the house of Kāśī Miśra. King Pratāparudra had heard about the Lord and was very enthusiastic about meeting Him. Sārvabhauma Bhaṭṭācārya had assured him that once the Lord had returned from His southern pilgrimage, he would somehow or other arrange for him to have His *darśana*. Unfortunately, no matter how hard Sārvabhauma Bhaṭṭācārya tried to convince Him, the Lord insisted that He would not look upon a king. Thus all attempts to arrange a meeting met with failure.

When the King heard that Rāmānanda Rāya wished to return to Puri in order to be close to Mahāprabhu, he was quite happy to grant him permission. He allowed him to leave his duties in the government and continued to pay him a pension. Thus Rāmānanda Rāya first met with the King in Cuttack, and then in Puri, before going to Kāśī Miśra's home to meet with the Lord. Rāmānanda Rāya knew just how eager the King was to encounter Mahāprabhu, but rather than bringing up the matter directly, he simply glorified the King, telling Mahāprabhu how much faith he had in Him, how deep was his devotion to Kṛṣṇa, and how kind he had been to free Rāmānanda Rāya from his governmental duties so that he could serve the Lord directly. By recounting the King's virtues in this way, he was able to soften the Lord's resolve.

In the meantime, Nityānanda Prabhu had sent one of the Lord's *bahirvāsas* (outer garments) to King Pratāparudra as a consolation. Though this gave the King a great deal of joy, his desire to meet the Lord simply increased, and he asked Rāmānanda Rāya to intercede on his behalf and make some kind of arrangement. When Rāmānanda Rāya finally approached the Lord directly, asking Him to be compassionate toward the King, the Lord was not able to refuse him directly. He agreed that the King was no ordinary materialistic person, but nevertheless, the very title Rāja was a type of contamination that He could not overlook. So He agreed to allow the King's son to come and see Him, as the son and father are one, in a sense.

"Mahāprabhu said, 'The King certainly possesses all good qualities, but everything has been ruined simply by his possession of the kingly title. If you are still very eager for the King to meet with Me, then you can bring Me his son in his place. The scripture states that one's self extends to the son; therefore if his son comes, it will be equal to his meeting with Me.' Rāmānanda Rāya then went to inform the King about his talks with the Lord, and, according to his request, brought the King's son to see Him." (*Caitanya Caritāmṛta* 2.12.53-7)

APPRECIATING RŪPA'S PLAYS

Rūpa Mañjarī is the follower of the *sakhīs* Lalitā and Viśākhā, who are not different from Rāmānanda Rāya. Rūpa Gosvāmī discussed the subject of his two plays, *Lalita-mādhava* and *Vidagdha-mādhava*, with Rāmānanda Rāya. When Rāmānanda Rāya asked to hear about the author's worshipable deity, Rūpa

Gosvāmī recited the second verse of the first act, the play's *maṅgalācaraṇa*,

anarpita-carīṁ cirāt karuṇayāvatīrṇaḥ kalau
samarpayitum unnatojjvala-rasāṁ sva-bhakti-śriyam
hariḥ puraṭa-sundara-dyuti-kadamba-sandīpitaḥ
sadā hṛdaya-kandare sphuratu vaḥ śacīnandanaḥ

"May the Supreme Lord who is the son of Śrīmatī Śacī-devī, resplendent with the radiance of molten gold, be always situated in the innermost chambers of your heart. He has appeared in the Age of Kālī by His causeless mercy to bestow that which was never offered before: the most sublime and radiant mellow of devotional service, the treasure of devotion to Him."

When Rāmānanda Rāya heard this verse, he began to praise Rūpa Gosvāmī with what seemed like a thousand tongues. He said that Rūpa Gosvāmī could only have written such an accurate portrayal of such difficult concepts as a result of the Lord's mercy.

PRADYUMNA MIŚRA MEETS RĀMĀNANDA

In order to reveal the extent of Rāmānanda Rāya's transcendental character and identity, Mahāprabhu sent Pradyumna Miśra, who was born in an upper-class *brāhmaṇa* family, to Rāmānanda Rāya to be instructed, even though Rāmānanda Rāya was not of such high caste. Pradyumna Miśra was born in Sylhet, but later made his permanent home in Odisha. He came one day to Mahāprabhu asking to hear some *Hari kathā* and Mahāprabhu sent him to meet Rāmānanda Rāya.

At that time, Rāmānanda Rāya was in the Jagannatha-vallabha gardens, engaged in preparing two young *deva-dāsīs* for a play which was to be given before Lord Jagannātha. He was engaged in bathing, dressing and decorating them and training them in the songs that they would sing and the dance they would perform. The first time that Pradyumna Miśra came to see Rāmānanda Rāya, one of his servants told him that he was busy doing this work and asked Miśra to sit outside and wait. None of Rāmānanda Rāya's servants dared to interrupt him while he was busy preparing the performance which was to be given before Lord Jagannātha. Only after he had finished the rehearsal and come outside did he learn that Pradyumna Miśra had come there to hear about Kṛṣṇa from him.

Rāmānanda Rāya showed the *brāhmaṇa* the appropriate respect and begged forgiveness for the long delay. Miśra realized that it was too late that day for his wish to be fulfilled, and he returned home. Some days later, when Mahāprabhu saw Miśra, He asked him how the meeting with Rāmānanda Rāya had gone and what topics they had discussed. Pradyumna Miśra told Him everything that had happened and told the Lord that some doubts had risen in his mind about Rāmānanda Rāya's activities. The Lord immediately took steps to erase these doubts from the *brāhmaṇa's* mind. He began to glorify Rāmānanda Rāya's extraordinary character with great force. He said:

"I am a *sannyāsī* and consider Myself to be renounced. But if I even hear the name of a woman, what to speak of seeing one, I feel an effect on My mind and body. So who is not moved by the sight of a woman? Listen to Me, everyone. Let Me tell you about Rāmānanda Rāya's activities, even though they are so wonderful and uncommon that they really cannot be properly described. He personally serves Lord Jagannātha's young and beautiful *deva-dāsīs* in every possible way. He personally bathes and dresses them and decorates them with ornaments. While doing so, he naturally sees and touches their bodies, but even so, his mind is never affected. He teaches the girls how to physically express all the moods of love so they can act them out before Jagannātha Deva, but his mind and body are as steady as wood or stone. Indeed, it is amazing that even when he touches such young girls, his mind is not disturbed. Only Rāmānanda has the right to do such things, and when I see him do them, I can understand that his body is not material but has been completely transformed into a spiritual entity." (*Caitanya Caritāmṛta* 3.5.35-42)

Mahāprabhu thus revealed Rāmānanda Rāya's amazing powers to Pradyumna Miśra, and through him, to the world. He told Pradyumna that He himself went to Rāmānanda Rāya to hear about Kṛṣṇa, and advised him to go a second time. This time, Pradyumna was able to hear Rāmānanda Rāya speak about Kṛṣṇa in such depth and with such insight that he was astonished, so astonished in fact that he began to dance in ecstasy.

Bhaktivinoda Ṭhākura has written the following comment on the above pastime: "Rāya Rāmānanda had composed a play known as *Jagannātha-vallabha-nāṭaka*. This play was performed in the Jagannātha temple for His pleasure. Rāya Rāmānanda trained two *deva-dāsī* girls, or "virgins of God" (in Odisha, they are now called *māhārīs*) on how to play the emotions appropriate to the *gopīs* in his drama. Since the two *deva-dāsīs* were playing the roles of chief *gopīs*, Rāmānanda Rāya made no distinction between them and Kṛṣṇa's beloved mistresses. He considered himself to be their maidservant, and in that spiritual identity, engaged in their service by teaching them to dance and sing for their Lord. Because Rāmānanda Rāya knew himself to be one of Śrīmatī Rādhārāṇī's hand-maidens, he was able to project the identity of his worshipable mistress on the two *deva-dāsīs*, and this is why he was able to serve them in this most intimate fashion without experiencing the disturbance of mundane sexual desire." (*Amṛta-pravāha-bhāṣya*, 3.5.20)

"Though a householder, Rāmānanda Rāya is not under the control of the six deadly sins (lust, anger, greed, illusion, pride and malice). Though a so-called materialistic person, he is qualified to instruct those in the renounced order of life. The Lord wished to reveal these qualities of Rāmānanda Rāya, and so He sent Pradyumna Miśra to listen to him speak about Kṛṣṇa. The Lord knows very well how to make His devotee's virtues public. He considers it to be to His personal profit to do so by using various strategies. O devotees, listen carefully to yet another of the Lord's characteristics: He manifests His own majestic nature, though this is usually hidden. He spreads real religious principles through a man from the lowly *śudra class* in order to vanquish the false pride of so-called renunciants and learned scholars. He preached about devotional service, ecstatic love and the Absolute Truth by making Rāmānanda Rāya, a *gṛhastha* born in a low family, the speaker, while He Himself, an exalted *brahmaṇa sannyāsī*, and Pradyumna Miśra, a pure *brāhmaṇa*, both listened and took lessons from him." (*Caitanya Caritāmṛta* 3.5.80-85)

Śrīla Bhakti Siddhānta Sarasvatī Gosvāmī Ṭhākura Prabhupāda comments on these words from the *Caitanya Caritāmṛta* as follows: "To materialistic vision, Rāmānanda Rāya is a *gṛhastha* on the *pravṛtti-mārga*, engaged in an active life in the world and not a self-controlled *brahmacārī*, *vanaprastha* or *sannyāsī*. A materialistic householder is under the control of his senses, and this is the basis of his involvement in worldly activities. A Vaiṣṇava householder who has attained the transcendental state, however, is not at all on the same level, transcending the influences of the six deadly sins and standing aloof from the influence of the senses. Rāmānanda Prabhu accepted the householder state as his role in the pastimes of Śrī Caitanya Mahāprabhu. Ordinary materialistic persons look upon him from a perspective that is tinted by their own desire for sense gratification and thus consider him to be one of their own, but in fact, his mind had been totally spiritualized through being fixed on the supreme worshipable object. He was thus a Kṛṣṇa *viṣayī*, one who seeks only the pleasure of Kṛṣṇa's senses and not his own. He was not an impersonalist or argumentative nihilist opposed to the Lord's transcendental activities. Indeed, he possessed the power to transform the minds of such *sannyāsīs* who had abandoned sense gratification and were absorbed in the undifferentiated Brahman without any appreciation for Kṛṣṇa's form and pastimes, and turn them away from their fundamentally materialistic conception of transcendence, attracting them to the practice of devotional service through hearing and chanting about Kṛṣṇa's name, form and activities."

OTHER ACTIVITIES IN PURI

When Vallabha Bhaṭṭa came to Puri and into contact with Caitanya Mahāprabhu, the Lord kept His own glories hidden from him because He knew him to be proud of his learning. He thus preferred to speak to Vallabha Bhaṭṭa about the qualifications of His entourage. At that time He said of Rāmānanda Rāya that he was expert both in the *sambandha*, or knowledge of the relationships between God and the living entities, and the *prayojana-tattva*, or knowledge of the highest goal of life. Furthermore, He indicated that he was the greatest connoisseur of the pure and sacred raptures of Vrindavan.

"Rāmānanda Rāya is the treasure house of divine sentiments. It was he who disclosed to Me that Kṛṣṇa is the Supreme Personality of Godhead. No one can fully describe the extent of Rāmānanda's spiritual power. Through him, I was able to learn about the pure moods of the devotees of Vraja." (*Caitanya Caritāmṛta* 3.7.23, 37)

"Rāmānanda Rāya had the same type of relationship with Mahāprabhu that Subala, Kṛṣṇa's friend and helper, used to have in Vraja." (*Caitanya Caritāmṛta* 3.6.9)

"Rāmānanda Rāya was also present in Nilachal when Haridāsa Ṭhākura passed away. Mahāprabhu praised Haridāsa Ṭhākura before the devotees, led by Rāmānanda Rāya and Sārvabhauma Bhaṭṭācārya." (*Caitanya Caritāmṛta* 3.11.50)

RĀMĀNANDA DURING THE LORD'S SEPARATION PANGS

When Mahāprabhu spent most of His time in a condition of divine ecstatic madness, He would sometimes disappear from His chambers, even though there were three barred doors through which He had to pass in order to go outside. Once He was found near the Lion's Gate, His joints loosened and taking on a giant, distended form. He was revived and returned to normal by the loud singing of the Holy Names. On another occasion, He was found in the Chataka Parvata, which He had taken in His state of trance to be Govardhan. Once again, He had to be pacified by *saṅkīrtana* and returned to His home. On these occasions, Rāmānanda Rāya was present with Svarūpa Dāmodar. Throughout the ten transformations of the Lord's ecstatic madness (*divyonmāda*), Rāmānanda Rāya would recite verses that fit the Lord's emotional state. In this way, he brought Mahāprabhu pleasure.

"When the Lord acutely felt pangs of separation from Kṛṣṇa, only Śrī Rāmānanda Rāya's talks about Kṛṣṇa and the sweet songs of Svarūpa Dāmodara kept Him alive." (*Caitanya Caritāmṛta* 3.6.6)

"The Lord took Svarūpa Dāmodar and Rāmānanda Rāya by the shoulders and said, 'Listen, Svarūpa and Rāma Rāya! Tell me what I should do. Where should I go in order to find Kṛṣṇa? You can tell me the best thing to do.' In this way, Gaurāṅga would tell His tale of woe to Svarūpa and Rāmānanda and they would console Him in His grief. Svarūpa would sing, and Rāmānanda would recite Sanskrit verses, giving joy to the Lord with poems from *Kṛṣṇa-Karṇāmṛta*, the songs of Vidyāpati and *Gīta Govinda*." (*Caitanya Caritāmṛta* 3.15.24-7)

"Remaining in the company of Svarūpa and Rāmānanda both day and night, Mahāprabhu ecstatically relished the songs of Caṇḍī Dāsa and Vidyāpati and Rāya's plays, as well as *Kṛṣṇa-Karṇāmṛta* and *Gīta Govinda*. (*Caitanya Caritāmṛta* 2.2.77)

Rāmānanda Rāya performed his *bhajana* in the Jagannatha Vallabha garden, a place that was very dear to Mahāprabhu also. As soon as the Lord entered this garden, He would be overwhelmed by feelings of divine love. One day, while the Lord was there, He had a vision of Kṛṣṇa under an *ashok* tree. Then, the vision was suddenly lost to Him, and Mahāprabhu fell to the ground in a faint.

"The main park in Puri is the Jagannatha Vallabha garden. The Lord entered there with His devotees. The trees and flower bushes were in bloom, and it seemed as though it was Vrindavan. The parrots, mynah birds, and cuckoos were singing their songs, and the bees were all buzzing." (*Caitanya Caritāmṛta* 3.19.79-80)

Wandering through the garden, He went from tree to tree. When He came to an *ashok* tree, He suddenly saw Kṛṣṇa standing there. The Lord started to run towards Him, but Kṛṣṇa laughed at Him and disappeared. The Lord was stunned: He had found Kṛṣṇa and then had lost Him again. He lost consciousness and fell to the ground." (*Caitanya Caritāmṛta* 3.19.85-87)

Through Rāmānanda Rāya and Śrī Svarūpa Dāmodara Gosvāmī, Lord Caitanya Mahāprabhu joyfully announced to the world that *harināma-saṅkīrtana* is the best means to attain love of God in this age of quarrel.

"The Lord, in a wave of jubilation, said, 'Listen, Svarūpa Dāmodara and Rāmānanda Rāya! In the Age of Kālī, *harināma-saṅkīrtana* is the supreme means of deliverance.' " (*Caitanya Caritāmṛta* 3.20.8)

There are two opinions about Rāmānanda Rāya's disappearance day: some people say Jyeṣṭha *kṛṣṇa-pañcamī*, others Vaiśākha *kṛṣṇa-pañcamī*.

Śrī Paramānanda Purī

purī paramānando ya āsīd uddhavaḥ purā

"He who was Uddhava in Kṛṣṇa *līlā* came to enrich the pastimes of Gaura as

Paramānanda Purī." (*Gaura-gaṇoddeśa-dīpikā* 118)

Nothing is known about Paramānanda Purī's antecedents or his appearance and disappearance dates. It is known that he was born in Tirhut, the area which surrounds Muzaffarpur, Chapra and Darbhanga in Bihar. Śrīla Bhakti Siddhānta Sarasvatī Gosvāmī Ṭhākura has described him as a *brāhmaṇa* from Tirhut.

Paramananda Purī's *dīkṣā* guru was Mādhavendra Purī, which meant that Mahāprabhu treated him as a very dear superior. Kṛṣṇadāsa Kavirāja Gosvāmī has described Paramānanda Purī as one of the nine *sannyāsī* roots that came out of the trunk of the desire tree of devotion. The first sprout of this desire tree was Mādhavendra Purī; its well-nourished second sprout was Īśvara Purī; its trunk was Caitanya Mahāprabhu Himself. The entire tree stood steadfastly on the strength of nine *sannyāsī* roots: Paramānanda Purī, Keśava Bhāratī, Brahmānanda Purī, Brahmānanda Bhāratī, Viṣṇu Purī, Keśava Purī, Kṛṣṇānanda Purī, Nṛsiṁha Tīrtha and Sukhānanda Purī. Of these nine, Paramānanda Purī is the central root. The great mystery here is that Caitanya Mahāprabhu, through His inconceivable potency, is both the trunk of the tree and the gardener who takes care of it.

"The central root of the tree was the grave and sober Paramānanda Purī. The tree stood solidly on these nine roots." (*Caitanya Caritāmṛta* 1.9.16)

MAHĀPRABHU'S MEETING WITH PARAMĀNANDA PURĪ

When Mahāprabhu left Nilachal to do His pilgrimage to South India in the company of Kṛṣṇadāsa Vipra, He traveled through Kurmasthan, Jiyada Nrisimha, Vidyanagar ,where He met with Rāya Rāmānanda, Gautami Ganga, Mallikarjuna, Ahobala Nrisimha, Siddhavata, Skanda Kshetra, Trimtha, Vriddha Kāśī, Bauddhasthana, Tripati, Trimalla, Pana Nrisimha, Shiva Kanchi, Vishnu Kanchi, Trikalahasti, Vriddhakola, Shiyali Bhairavi, the banks of the Kaveri River, Kumbhakarna Kapala, Shriraṅgam (where He bestowed Kṛṣṇa *bhakti* on Venkata Bhaṭṭa and his entire family). When He arrived at Rishabha Mountain,[18] He met Paramānanda Purī for the first time. Paramānanda Purī was observing the *Cāturmāsya vrata* at this Rishabha Parvata when Mahāprabhu arrived there. The Lord paid His obeisances to Paramānanda Purī, who embraced Him with great affection. The two of them spent three days discussing topics of Kṛṣṇa. When Purī told the Lord of his intention to travel north to Puri and then continue on to bathe in the Ganges, Mahāprabhu invited him to return to Puri afterwards and join Him. He said that He himself would quickly return from Setubandha to Puri, where they would meet again.

"Purī Gosvāmī said, 'I intend to go to Puri. After visiting Puri, I will go on from there to Bengal, where I will bathe in the Ganges.' The Lord said, 'Come back again to Puri afterwards. I will be there soon after I have visited Setubandha. I would like to have your company, so please be kind and come to Puri to take up permanent residence there.' " (*Caitanya Caritāmṛta* 2.9.170-2)

18 Rishabha Parvata is in the state of Tamil Nadu in the Madurai district. Twelve miles north of the town of Madurai is the Anagadamalai Mountain in the forest surrounding Kutakachalam. Ṛṣabhadeva called the forest fire in this very forest to burn His body.The place is known today as Palni Hill, or Varaha Parvata, according to the local people.

PARAMĀNANDA PURĪ GOES TO PURI

When Mahāprabhu returned from His southern tour to Nilachal, Nityānanda Prabhu, Jagadānanda Paṇḍita and other devotees sent Kāla Kṛṣṇadāsa to Nabadwip to announce to Śacī and the other Bengal devotees that He had returned. They were all overjoyed by the news, and then Advaita Ācārya and the others took mother Śacī's permission to visit the Lord in Puri. Paramānanda Purī happened to be in Nabadwip at the time, as he had been walking along the Ganges. He had been staying in Mayapur at Śacī Mātā's house, where she had been taking care of him with great affection. He thus also learnt from Kāla Kṛṣṇadāsa that Mahāprabhu had returned to Nilachal. Feeling an intense eagerness to see the Lord again, he and a *brāhmaṇa* devotee, Kamalā Kānta, immediately left for Puri.

On his arrival, Mahāprabhu respectfully paid obeisances to Paramānanda Purī, who was overwhelmed with feelings of ecstasy and took the Lord in his arms. They told each other how much they desired their association.

"The Lord said, 'I desire very much to remain in your company. I request you to be merciful to Me and take up residence in Nilachal.' Purī answered, 'And I too am very eager to remain in Your company. It is for that reason that I left Bengal to come here to Nilachal.' " (*Caitanya Caritāmṛta* 2.10.97-8)

Mahāprabhu gave Paramānanda Purī a secluded room in Kāśī Miśra's house as living quarters and arranged one devotee as his personal servant. Paramānanda Purī was therefore always present during the *Cāturmāsya* period, participating in all of the Lord's pastimes during that time along with His others associates. We can see from Vṛndāvana Dāsa Thakura's *Caitanya Bhāgavata* just how dear Paramānanda Purī was to Mahāprabhu:

"Mahāprabhu caught sight of Paramānanda Purī from a distance, and He immediately got up respectfully. Joyful to see His devotee, the Lord glorified him and danced in ecstatic love. Lifting His arms, He cried out 'Hari! Hari! I have finally seen Paramānanda Purī with My own eyes! My eyes have been fulfilled!, My life has finally been perfected! All My religious works have finally borne fruit. My *sannyāsa* has been fulfilled. It is as though I am seeing Mādhavendra Purī himself.' Having said this, the Lord embraced His dear devotee and bathed his body with the tears from His lotus eyes. Purī also forgot himself in ecstasy as soon as he saw the Lord's moonlike face. The two paid obeisances to each other for a long time. Paramānanda Purī is the abode of love for Caitanya Mahāprabhu." (*Caitanya Bhagavat* 3.3.168-175)

"Svarūpa Dāmodara is as dear to the Lord as Purī Gosvāmī." (*Caitanya Bhāgavata* 3.10.42)

"Amongst all His *sannyāsī* associates, no one was as dear to the Lord as Purī Gosvāmī. Svarūpa Dāmodara and Paramānanda Purī were the most qualified of the Lord's *sannyāsī* associates. The two of them remained constantly in the Lord's company, taking the staff (*daṇḍa*) of renunciation for the sake of the Lord. Purī engaged primarily in meditation, while Svarūpa Dāmodara was devoted to *kīrtana*. They were like two arms of the Lord's *sannyāsī* form." (*Caitanya Bhagavat* 3.10.46-49)

Vṛndāvana Dāsa Thakura also says that Mahāprabhu spent entire days conversing with Paramānanda Purī about Kṛṣṇa, just as Kṛṣṇa engaged His friend Arjuna in intimate conversation. (*Caitanya Bhāgavata* 3.3.233-4)

PARAMANANDA PURĪ'S ACTIVITIES WITH THE LORD IN PURI

Mahāprabhu ostracized Choṭa Haridāsa for having talked to a woman, refusing him entrance to His house. Choṭa Haridāsa was greatly distressed by this punishment and fasted for three days. Svarūpa Dāmodara and the rest of Mahāprabhu's entourage repeatedly asked the Lord to soften His stance toward Haridāsa, but He would not be shaken. Indeed, He rebuked the devotees for suggesting that He repeal His order. When the devotees learned that Choṭa Haridāsa intended to commit suicide because he was no longer allowed to see the Lord, they came to Paramānanda Purī as a last resort to ask the Lord to forgive him. The Lord considered Paramānanda Purī as worshipable as His own guru, as he was Īśvara Purīpāda's godbrother. The devotees hoped that if he were to approach the Lord on behalf of Choṭa Haridāsa, the Lord would accept his demand.

When Paramānanda Purī came to Mahāprabhu, the Lord said that He was willing to allow Choṭa Haridāsa to return to the Gambhira, but that He Himself would go to Alalanatha. Paramānanda Purī was taken off guard by Mahāprabhu's proposal to leave Puri. He said that He was the independent Lord and that it had been incorrect of him to try to interfere with His decision. He then tried to dissuade Mahāprabhu from going to Alalanatha.

"Mahāprabhu taught by His own behavior that the guru's godbrother is worshipable, like the guru. It is extremely detrimental to one's devotional life to disrespect those who are one's *guru-varga*. The Lord says, 'I cannot tolerate breaches of Vaiṣṇava etiquette.' " (*Caitanya Caritāmṛta* 3.4.166)

Paramānanda Purī participated in nearly all of the Lord's pastimes in Purushottama *dhāma*: the cleaning of the Guṇḍicā temple, the Rathayātrā festival, the water sports in Narendra Sarovara. He was also present at the festival in honor of Haridāsa Ṭhākura after his disappearance. Once, after the Bengali devotees had returned home after the rainy season, Sārvabhauma Bhaṭṭācārya invited either Mahāprabhu or one of His ten *sannyāsī* associates (Paramānanda Purī, Dāmodara Svarūpa, Brahmānanda Purī, Brahmānanda Bhāratī, Viṣṇu Purī, Keśava Purī, Kṛṣṇānanda Purī, Nṛsiṁha Tīrtha, Sukhānanda Purī, and Satyānanda Bhāratī) to take lunch at his house every day for a month. Five of these days were consecrated to nicely feeding Paramānanda Purī with varieties of *mahā-prasāda*.

All the Gauḍīya Vaiṣṇavas and the residents of Puri treated Paramānanda Purī as a senior spiritual leader and gave him all respect. Mahāprabhu Himself followed the etiquette of placing sandalwood paste and giving garlands to Paramānanda Purī and Brahmānanda Bhāratī before anyone else during the Rathayātrā festival.

"Paramānanda Purī and Brahmānanda Bhāratī were overjoyed to receive the sandalwood paste from Mahāprabhu's own hand. Advaita Ācārya and Nityānanda Prabhu were also ecstatic on being touched by the Lord's hand." (*Caitanya Caritāmṛta* 2.13.30-1)

During the Guṇḍicā temple cleaning, He did not engage His *guru-varga* in any of the difficult tasks like carrying buckets of water. Rather, they worked alongside the Lord with the water the other devotees had carried into clean the temple.

"All the devotees carried water except for Nityānanda Prabhu, Advaita Ācārya, Svarūpa Dāmodara, Brahmānanda Bhāratī and Paramānanda Purī." (*Caitanya Caritāmṛta* 2.12.109)

PARAMĀNANDA PURĪ'S WELL

The Vyāsadeva of Lord Caitanya's pastimes, Vṛndāvana Dāsa Ṭhākura, describes Paramānanda Purī's glories in the *Caitanya Bhāgavata* (*Antya-khaṇḍa*, chapter 3), making special mention of his well. Śrīla Bhakti Siddhānta Sarasvatī Gosvāmī Ṭhākura makes the following remarks about Paramānanda Purī's well in his *Bhāṣya* on the *Caitanya Bhāgavata*: "This well is not far along the road leading west from the Jagannātha temple, just next to the police station. Śrīla Bhaktivinoda Ṭhākura identified this well as the one associated with Paramānanda Purī." Being omniscient, Mahāprabhu knew that the water from this well was not good; later He heard the same thing directly from Paramānanda Purī. Lord Jagannātha knew that any living being who touched or drank the water from Paramānanda Purī's well would be freed from all his sins and thus liberated, thus He Himself had made the water of this well muddy in order to discourage anyone from taking it. This was a sign of Lord Jagannātha's miserliness, as He did not seem to want anyone to have such an easy time of attaining liberation. Mahāprabhu thus stood up and prayed with arms upraised, asking Lord Jagannātha to be merciful to the *jīvas*.

"Lord Jagannātha, grant Me this boon: Let the Ganges river enter into this well. Please order the Bhogavati Ganga, which travels underground, to flow into the well." (*Caitanya Bhāgavata* 3.3.242-3)

When the devotees heard the Lord's sweet prayer, they all shouted the names of Hari in joy. Taking the order of the Lord, Gaṅgā Devī entered into the well. The next morning, the devotees, including Paramānanda Purī, were amazed and overjoyed to see that its water had become pure and clear. Mahāprabhu glorified the well, saying that anyone who took a bath with water from it would obtain the same benefits as from bathing in the Ganges and would attain devotion to Kṛṣṇa. Mahāprabhu Himself bathed in the water from this well and drank from it.

Just as the devotee glorifies the Lord, so too does the Lord sing His devotee's glories and seek to increase them. Those who are averse to the Supreme Lord are incapable of understanding the glories of a devotee. The compassionate Lord glorifies the devotees so that everyone can learn that without the association of devotees and without their mercy, there is no auspiciousness for the *jīva*.

"The Lord said, 'I am present on this earth only out of affection for Purī Gosvāmī. I belong to him alone. If he sells Me, I allow Myself to be sold. Anyone who sees Purī Gosvāmī, even once, will receive love for Kṛṣṇa.' " (*Caitanya Bhāgavata* 3.3.255-7)

In the *Gauḍīya Vaiṣṇava Abhidhāna*, it is said that Paramānanda Purī wrote a book named *Govinda-vijaya*.

Śrī Svarūpa Dāmodara

Kṛṣṇadāsa Kavirāja Gosvāmī writes that Śrī Svarūpa Dāmodara Gosvāmī was one of Mahāprabhu's three and a half most intimate associates.

"The Lord accepted that Śikhi Māhiti's sister was one of Rādhā's associates. In the entire world, there were only three and a half devotees who were His intimate devotees. They were Svarūpa Dāmodara Gosvāmī,

Rāmānanda Rāya and Śikhi Māhiti. Śikhi Māhiti's sister was the half person." (*Caitanya Caritāmṛta* 3.2.105-6)

Elsewhere Kavirāja Gosvāmī called Svarūpa Dāmodara the most important of the Lord's companions. "Two persons knew the Lord best: Paramānanda Purī and Svarūpa Dāmodara." (*Caitanya Caritāmṛta* 1.10.124-5)

Mahāprabhu is Kṛṣṇa Himself enveloped by the mood and bodily luster of Śrīmatī Rādhārāṇī. Śrī Svarūpa Dāmodara Gosvāmī was the Lord's alter ego. In Vraja *līlā*, he was also Rādhārāṇī's alter-ego, Lalitā Sakhī. In the *Gaura-gaṇoddeśa-dīpikā* he is identified as Viśākhā Sakhī.

kalām aśikṣayad rādhāṁ yā viśākhā vraje purā
sādya svarūpa-gosvāmī tat-tad-bhāva-vilāsavān

"That same Viśākhā who previously taught Rādhā the arts in Vraja is today Svarūpa Gosvāmī, who rejoices in the moods of Rādhā and Kṛṣṇa."

In either case, Svarūpa Dāmodara had a special affinity for the *madhura-rasa*, in the mood of a *sakhī* of Rādhā. As Kavirāja Gosvāmī says:

"Paramānanda Purī had parental affection for Mahāprabhu; Rāmānanda Rāya had love for Him in pure friendship; Govinda Dāsa's love for Him was as a servant. Gadādhara Paṇḍita, Jagadānanda Paṇḍita and Svarūpa Dāmodara worshipped Him in the ecstasy of the chief *rasa*. Mahāprabhu's heart was won by these four different loving attitudes." (*Caitanya Caritāmṛta* 2.2.78)

Śrīla Bhakti Siddhānta Sarasvatī Gosvāmī Ṭhākura has explained these verses in his *Anubhāṣya* as follows: "Paramānanda Purī, who was Uddhava in Kṛṣṇa *līlā*, loved Mahāprabhu with parental affection; Rāmānanda Rāya, who was either Viśākhā or Arjuna, had the pure sentiment of a close friend; Govinda Dāsa and others were devoted in the pure mood of servitorship (*śuddha-dāsya*). Gadādhara Paṇḍita, Jagadānanda Paṇḍita and Svarūpa Dāmodara served the Lord in the primary sentiment, i.e., that of transcendental conjugal love (*madhura-rasa*). The Lord became obliged to these devotees, for their joyful service and association."

In the last twelve years of His pastimes in Puri, the Lord remained constantly absorbed in the mood of Rādhārāṇī. During this time, Mahāprabhu relished the most confidential mellows of divine love in the company of His two intimate associates Svarūpa Dāmodara and Rāmānanda Rāya.

"Day and night, Mahāprabhu ecstatically relished the songs of Caṇḍī Dāsa and Vidyāpati and Rāmānanda Rāya's plays, as well as *Kṛṣṇa-karṇāmṛta* and *Gīta Govinda* in the company of Svarūpa and Rāmānanda." (*Caitanya Caritāmṛta* 2.2.77)

SVARŪPA DĀMODAR'S KAḌACA

The special intimate relationship that Svarūpa Dāmodara had with the Lord meant that he had deep knowledge of the confidential reason for the Lord's advent and His mystic ecstasies. Kṛṣṇadāsa Kavirāja Gosvāmī writes that Svarūpa Dāmodara is the source of the most confidential knowledge of Lord Caitanya's *avatāra*:

"I have already shown that preaching the *saṅkīrtana* movement was the external cause for the Lord's descent. There is another– the primary purpose of the Lord's *avatāra*. This is the personal work of Kṛṣṇa, the foremost enjoyer of loving exchanges. This very confidential cause is threefold, as has been revealed by Svarūpa Dāmodara Gosvāmī. Śrī Svarūpa Dāmodara Gosvāmī was extremely close to the Lord and thus was able to know all these matters." (*Caitanya Caritāmṛta* 1.4.102-5)

Swarupa Dāmodara was thus the authority through whom the most confidential pastimes of Mahāprabhu came into devotee society.

"Murāri Gupta explained all of the Lord's early pastimes in the form of an outline. Svarūpa Dāmodara did the same for the Lord's later pastimes. The devotees describe the Lord's activities by following the order given in these two outlines." (*Caitanya Caritāmṛta* 1.13.15-17)

Śrīla Bhaktivinoda Ṭhākura has commented on verse 17 as follows: "Murāri Gupta's outline of the Lord's early pastimes are still extant, so devotees were able to expand on the Lord's pastimes after looking at his written text and by listening Svarūpa Dāmodara's *kaḍacā* through Raghunātha Dāsa Gosvāmī."

"Caitanya *līlā* is like the finest of jewels. Śrī Svarūpa Dāmodara Gosvāmī guarded it in his treasure chest and afterwards placed it around Raghunātha Dāsa's neck. I have written down here what I heard from Raghunātha Dāsa to the extent that I have been able, and now make a gift of it to the devotees." (*Caitanya Caritāmṛta* 2.2.84)

Śrīla Bhaktivinoda Ṭhākura says the following of this verse: "Svarūpa Dāmodara noted the Lord's latter pastimes in his *kaḍacā* (notebook). He made Raghunātha Dāsa memorize these verses, and later Kṛṣṇadāsa Kavirāja Gosvāmī spread these accounts of the Lord's activities throughout the world. Thus, though Svarūpa Dāmodara's *kaḍacā* was never published in book form, the *Caitanya Caritāmṛta* itself is its essence." (*Amṛta-pravāha-bhāṣya*)

SVARŪPA DĀMODARA'S KĪRTANA

"Śrī Svarūpa Dāmodara used to make Mahāprabhu very happy by singing the songs of Vidyapati and Caṇḍī Dāsa and the *Gīta Govinda*. He was as expert a musician as the Gandharvas, and in the knowledge of scripture, he was just like Bṛhaspati. No personality was his equal. Śrī Svarūpa Dāmodara was also very dear to Advaita Ācārya and Nityānanda Prabhu, and he was the life and soul of Śrīvāsa Ṭhākura and other devotees." (*Caitanya Caritāmṛta* 2.10.115-7)

Kṛṣṇadāsa Kavirāja Gosvāmī has described the extent to which Śrī Svarūpa Dāmodara Gosvāmī and Rāmānanda Rāya were dear to Mahāprabhu in the fifteenth chapter of the *Antya-līlā*:

"After saying these things, the Lord took Svarūpa Dāmodara and Rāmānanda Rāya by the shoulders and said, 'Listen, Svarūpa and Rāma Rāya! Tell Me what I should do. Where should I go in order to find Kṛṣṇa? You can tell Me the best thing to do.' In this way, Gaurāṅga would tell His tale of woe to Svarūpa and Rāmānanda, and they would console Him in His grief. Svarūpa would sing, and Rāmānanda would recite Sanskrit verses from *Karṇāmṛta*, Vidyāpati and *Gīta Govinda*, giving joy to the Lord." (*Caitanya Caritāmṛta* 3.15.24-7)

A similar passage is found in the twentieth chapter of the *Antya-līlā*:

"This was Mahāprabhu's life in Nilachal. He went through the days and nights absorbed in the anxiety of separation from Kṛṣṇa. Svarūpa and Rāmānanda were always with Him, bringing Him ecstasy with their recitation of songs and verses appropriate to His mood." (*Caitanya Caritāmṛta* 3.20.3-4)

"Vṛndāvana Dāsa Ṭhākura has also named Śrī Svarūpa Dāmodara Gosvāmī as one of Mahāprabhu's principal associates in his *Caitanya Bhāgavata*. He describes there how the Lord would lose external consciousness when hearing Svarūpa Dāmodara's *kīrtana*. When Śrīla Gadādhara Paṇḍita Gosvāmī was living at Ṭoṭa Gopīnātha temple, he would recite *Bhāgavata* while in an ecstatic trance, while Mahāprabhu, Nityānanda Prabhu, Advaita Ācārya Prabhu, Svarūpa Dāmodara, Vakreśvara Paṇḍita, Murāri Gupta and Gadādhara Dāsa would listen." (*Bhakti-ratnākara* 8.278-80)

Mahāprabhu heard Gadādhara Paṇḍita Gosvāmī speak on the sections dealing with the lives of Prahlāda and Dhruva from *Śrīmad Bhāgavatam*. Mahāprabhu would be overcome by the eight ecstatic symptoms on hearing Svarūpa Dāmodara's *kīrtana*, just as He would at Gadādhara Paṇḍita's *Bhāgavatam* readings.

"Gadādhara Paṇḍita was the main expert in the *Bhāgavata*, and Svarūpa Dāmodara in *kīrtana*. Svarūpa Dāmodara would sing *solo* and Mahāprabhu would lose Himself in dance. Mahāprabhu would reveal all the symptoms of ecstatic love such as tears, trembling, laughing, fainting, horripilation and roaring, all of which manifested on His transcendental body as He danced with the devotees. Whenever the Lord heard Svarūpa Dāmodara singing the *kīrtana* aloud, He would lose external consciousness and fall down on the spot. There was no equal to Dāmodara Svarūpa amongst all of the Lord's *sannyāsī* associates. Dāmodara Svarūpa was as dear to Him as Paramānanda Purī. Śrī Svarūpa Dāmodara Gosvāmī was the *avatāra* of the delight of the transcendental song which would make Mahāprabhu dance." (*Caitanya Bhāgavata* 3.10.36-43)

EARLY LIFE AND SANNYĀSA

We have the following information about Śrī Svarūpa Dāmodara Gosvāmī in terms of his bodily identity. Before taking *sannyāsa*, he was known as Puruṣottama Ācārya or Puruṣottama Bhaṭṭācārya. *Gauḍīya Vaiṣṇava Abhidhāna* gives the following account of his antecedents: His father's name was Padmagarbhācārya. His mother's name is not known, but she was the daughter of Jayarāma Cakravartī. Jayarāma's original residence was in the village of Bhitadiya on the banks of the Brahmaputra River in Bangladesh, but he and his family moved to Nabadwip. After arranging for his daughter to be married to Padmagarbhācārya, he made his son-in-law also come to Nabadwip. After Puruṣottama Ācārya was born, Padmagarbha left his wife and child at his father-in-law's house and left for Mithila and Kashi in order to study. Puruṣottama Ācārya was thus raised in his maternal grandparents' home in Nabadwip.

Later, when Mahāprabhu took *sannyāsa*, Puruṣottama was unable to remain in Nabadwip due to the feelings of separation from the Lord, and he departed for Benares, where he also took the renounced order of life. This is described as follows in the *Prema-vilāsa*:

"Puruṣottama became a resident of Nabadwip, staying with his mother's parents. Filled with all virtues, he became Mahāprabhu's dear devotee. When the Lord took *sannyāsa*, he went mad with separation and left for Benares, where he also took *sannyāsa*. Svarūpa Dāmodara is the name he received. He was an intimate devotee of the Lord, an ocean of *rasa*."

Kṛṣṇadāsa Kavirāja Gosvāmī gives a brief account of Śrī Svarūpa Dāmodara Gosvāmī's early life and *sannyāsa* in the *Caitanya Caritāmṛta* (2.10.102-114) when telling of his arrival in Jagannatha Puri:

"Svarūpa Dāmodara was a most intimate friend of the Lord and an ocean of transcendental mellows. Before taking *sannyāsa*, he had resided at Nabadwip in Mahāprabhu's association and was known as Puruṣottama Ācārya. When he saw

Mahāprabhu accept the renounced order, he became like a madman and immediately went to Benares to take *sannyāsa*. His *sannyāsa* guru, Caitanyānanda Bhāratī, ordered him to study the Vedānta and teach it to others. Svarūpa Dāmodara was a great renunciate as well as a learned scholar. He took shelter of Kṛṣṇa's pastimes with heart and soul.

"In his eagerness to worship Śrī Kṛṣṇa without any disturbance, he accepted the *sannyāsa* order in a state of delirium. When taking *sannyāsa*, Puruṣottama Ācārya followed the regulative principles by giving up his tuft of hair and sacred thread, but he did not take the saffron-colored dress. Nor did he take a *sannyāsī* title but rather kept the *brahmacārī* name Svarūpa.

"Svarūpa Dāmodara then took permission from his *sannyāsa* guru and went to Nilachal, where day and night he enjoyed the ecstasies of love for Kṛṣṇa. Though he had attained the peak of learning, he spoke to no one but remained in seclusion and incognito."

Śrīla Bhakti Siddhānta Sarasvatī Gosvāmī Ṭhākura has made the following comments on this section of the *Caitanya Caritāmṛta*: "In the Daśanāmī sect founded by Śaṅkarācārya, the lineages that take the *sannyāsa* names of Tīrtha and Āśrama follow the custom of giving postulants to the renounced order the title *brahmacārī*. Such a postulant is then required to vow to remain celibate for the rest of his life. In Puruṣottama Ācārya's case, the *brahmacārī* title was Svarūpa Dāmodara. *Brahmacārīs* called 'Svarūpa' normally receive the *sannyāsa* title Tīrtha upon taking the saffron cloth, or *yoga-paṭṭa*." (*Anubhāṣya*, 2.10.102).

"In the Daśanāmī sect, certain regulative principles must be followed before taking *sannyāsa*: one must perform eight kinds of offering oblations to one's forefathers, Virajā sacrifice. Then one cuts off the tuft of hair called a *śikhā* and gives up the sacred thread. Svarūpa Dāmodara accepted these preliminary processes to the acceptance of *sannyāsa*, but not the *gurvāhvāna*, or 'call of the guru,' the saffron cloth, a *sannyāsa* title or a *daṇḍa*, and for this reason, he retained his *brahmacārī* name." (*Anubhāṣya*, 2.10.108)

It may be pointed out here that for those who follow the formalities of *tridaṇḍī sannyāsa*, the keeping of the *śikhā*, the sacred thread and saffron cloth are approved by the *Skanda Purāṇa*, which states:

śikhī yajñopavītī syāt tridaṇḍī sa-kamaṇḍaluḥ
sa pavitraś ca kāṣāyī gāyatrīṁ ca japet sadā

"Wearing the *śikhā*, sacred thread and saffron cloth and carrying the *kamaṇḍalu* water pot, a *tridaṇḍī sannyasi* should remain pure in his habits and constantly chant the Gāyatrī *mantra*."

Śrīla Bhaktivinoda Ṭhākura has also commented on the same text in his *Amṛta-pravāha-bhāṣya*: "Puruṣottama Ācārya took Mahāprabhu's example and took *sannyāsa* simply by renouncing his *śikhā* and *sūtra*. His *sannyāsa* name was Svarūpa Dāmodara. He did not accept the formality of the *yoga-paṭṭa* because he wished to avoid any danger of becoming falsely proud of his status that would come with taking *sannyāsa*. He only wished to worship Kṛṣṇa without any worries."

In the *Anubhāṣya* commentary to *Ādi-līlā* (4.105) of *Caitanya Caritāmṛta*, Śrīla Bhakti Siddhānta Sarasvatī Gosvāmī Ṭhākura writes, "Puruṣottama Bhaṭṭācārya was a resident of Nabadwip. Even prior to Mahāprabhu's taking *sannyāsa*, he desired to renounce the world. He left home and went to Benares, where he took up *brahmacārya* in a group of Daśanāmī *sannyāsīs*. He was given the name Śrī Dāmodara Svarūpa. He did not bother completing the *sannyāsa* rituals and came to Nilachal, Jagannatha Puri, where he spent the rest of his life at the Lord's lotus feet. He became Mahāprabhu's constant companion, enhancing the Lord's pleasure by singing the songs requested by the Lord. Svarūpa Dāmodara could understand the deep feelings of Mahāprabhu's heart, and it was by his grace alone that all the Lord's devotees could know this."

SVARŪPA DĀMODARA ARRIVES IN PURI

Mahāprabhu took *sannyāsa* on the full-moon day of the month of Māgha and left for Nilachal in the following month of Phālguna. After delivering Sārvabhauma Bhaṭṭācārya, He left for His pilgrimage to South India in the month of Vaiśākha. Nityānanda Prabhu gave Him a *brāhmaṇa* named Kāla Kṛṣṇadāsa to be His servant and companion on this trip. When Mahāprabhu returned from this journey, after having brought good fortune to the inhabitants of the south through the gift of *Kṛṣṇa prema*, Nityānanda Prabhu sent Kṛṣṇadāsa back to Nabadwip to inform the devotees that the Lord had arrived in Puri. The news brought great joy to Śacī Mātā, Advaita Ācārya, Śrīvāsa Paṇḍita and the other devotees. They immediately started making preparations to visit the Lord in Puri.

Paramānanda Purī, who had been staying in Nabadwip at that time, heard this news from Śacī Mātā and left with a *brāhmaṇa* named Kamalā Kānta. They were thus the first from Bengal to arrive in Puri to meet the Lord. Not long afterwards, Puruṣottama Ācārya, who had taken *sannyāsa* from Caitanyānanda Bhāratī in Benares and received the name Svarūpa Dāmodara, arrived and joyously entered the Lord's entourage. When he first saw the Lord, Śrī Svarūpa Dāmodara Gosvāmī recited the following prayer:

heloddhulita-khedayā viśadayā
pronmīlad-āmodayā
śāmyac-chāstra-vivādayā rasa-
dayā cittārpitonmādayā
śaśvad-bhakti-vinodayā sa-madayā
mādhurya-maryādayā
śrī-caitanya dayā-nidhe tava
dayā bhūyād amandodayā

"O ocean of mercy, Śrī Caitanya Mahāprabhu! May Your unrestrained and auspicious mercy fall upon us, driving away all kinds of material lamentation easily, making everything pure and awakening transcendental bliss, encasing all material pleasures, ending all quarrels and disagreements among different scriptures, pouring transcendental mellows and maddening the minds, stimulating the joy of devotional service constantly, and revealing the extent of the conjugal mood's sweetness." (*Caitanya Caritāmṛta* 2.10.119, *Caitanya-candrodaya naṭaka* 10.8)

Śrī Svarūpa Dāmodara Gosvāmī first received the mercy of the Lord in the form of a heartfelt embrace. Then he paid his obeisances to Nityānanda Prabhu and Paramananda Purī and was introduced to Jagadānanda Paṇḍita and the other devotees. He first met Rāya Rāmānanda when the latter came to Puri with King Pratāparudra. At that time Rāya Rāmānanda paid his obeisance to Paramānanda Purī, Brahmānanda Bhāratī, Svarūpa Dāmodara and Śrīmān Nityānanda Prabhu.

FRIENDSHIP WITH PUṆḌARĪKA VIDYĀNIDHI

In Puri, Śrī Svarūpa Dāmodara Gosvāmī participated in the water sports in Narendra Sarovara at the time of the Chandana *yātrā* and in the Indradyumna Sarovara after the cleaning of the Guṇḍicā temple. He and

Puṇḍarīka Vidyānidhi enjoyed splashing each other.

"The two friends Vidyānidhi and Svarūpa Dāmodara joyously splashed each other and laughed." (*Caitanya Caritāmṛta* 3.8.124)

Lord Jagannātha has an annual festival in Puri named Oḍana Ṣaṣṭhī. On this occasion, Lord Jagannātha's *pūjārīs* dress the deity in cloth which still has the tapioca-based starch (*māṛ*) in it. Śrī Puṇḍarīka Vidyānidhi disliked and condemned this behavior of the *pūjārīs*, as he considered such cloth unclean. He went to Svarūpa Dāmodara and asked him for his opinion on the matter. Svarūpa Dāmodara said to him, "The Lord is completely independent. He is not dependent on the rules regulating deity worship found in the *smṛtis*."

Vidyānidhi immediately answered him. "I accept that Jagannātha is completely independent. That does not mean that the *pūjārīs* are completely independent of the rules and regulations of scripture. They are not *brāhmaṇa*, and they dress the Lord in unwashed cloth. Didn't they know that if they even touch cloth that has *māṛ* in it, they are supposed to wash their hands?"

That night Lord Jagannātha and Lord Balarāma appeared to Śrī Puṇḍarīka Vidyānidhi in a dream and slapped him on his cheeks for having criticized Their servants. By so doing, Lord Jagannātha showed that one is not to criticize His servants for apparent lapses in behavior. The *smārtas* are especially inclined to criticizing Vaiṣṇava behavior for failing to adhere to the arcane standards of the *smṛtis*. Śrī Puṇḍarīka Vidyānidhi, though his cheeks were swollen from the slaps, was overjoyed to have been touched by Their Lordships. Svarūpa Dāmodara also congratulated Vidyānidhi for his good fortune:

"As he looked Puṇḍarīka Vidyānidhi over, Svarūpa Dāmodara felt an affection arise for his friend. Indeed, he started to float in an ocean of ecstasy. A friend always feels joy at the good fortune of a friend. The two of them began to laugh spiritedly, and Svarūpa Dāmodara said, 'Listen, brother. I have never seen or heard of a punishment like this one. The Lord came personally to chastise you in a dream. I never heard of such a thing, but now I see that it has happened to you!' The two friends floated in a feeling of satisfaction. They spent day and night talking about nothing but Kṛṣṇa conscious topics." (*Caitanya Bhāgavata* 3.10.173-7)

GUṆḌICĀ AND RATHAYĀTRĀ PASTIMES

Śrī Svarūpa Dāmodara Gosvāmī was one of the chief participants in the cleaning of the Guṇḍicā temple on the eve of the Rathayātrā. "Other than Nityānanda Prabhu, Advaita, Svarūpa, Brahmānanda Bhāratī and Paramānanda Purī, everyone carried buckets of water." (*Caitanya Caritāmṛta* 2.12.109)

During the washing of the Guṇḍicā temple, a simple but intelligent *brāhmaṇa* who was not aware of the nature of the Vaiṣṇavas' devotional etiquette, took some water, suddenly poured it over the Lord's feet and drank it inside the temple. In view of Mahāprabhu's identity as Supreme Lord Himself, it was certainly no offense to drink the water that had washed His feet even though it was done inside the temple, but here Mahāprabhu acted as an exemplar for the world and showed dissatisfaction at the *brāhmaṇa*'s behavior so that no other person would imitate him and become an offender at the deity's feet. He let His anger be known to Svarūpa Dāmodara, who chastised the Bengali devotee and pushed him out of the temple. The next instant, however, Svarūpa Dāmodara returned to the Lord's side and asked Him to forgive the devotee. Though a Vaiṣṇava may externally appear to be hard-hearted, internally he or she is always filled with compassion and thinks of the welfare of every living being.

Every year during Balarāma, Subhadrā and Jagannātha's Rathayātrā festival, the Lord would offer garlands and sandalwood paste to all the devotees with His own hands. He would then make four *kīrtana* groups with His devotees. Svarūpa Dāmodara would sing in the first of these, with Advaita participating as the principal dancer. With the addition of other *kīrtana* groups from Shantipur, Shrikhanda and Kulina, there were seven *sampradāyas* altogether. In each group, there were two drummers, meaning that there were fourteen altogether. When the *kīrtana* started in each of the seven groups, Mahāprabhu demonstrated His divine powers by appearing simultaneously in the midst of each one of them. Śrīla Bhaktivinoda Ṭhākura writes, "Just as the Lord expands into numerous forms during the *rāsa* dance and to marry the queens in Dwarka, Lord Caitanya expanded in order to be present in the midst of each *sampradāyas' kīrtana*. The members of each group were convinced that the Lord was in his group alone and in none of the others."

When Mahāprabhu wished to dance madly, He would have the seven groups come together and would dance in their midst, appointing nine singers and making Svarūpa Dāmodara the principal singer. As the devotees became progressively intoxicated by the *kīrtana*, Mahāprabhu danced frenziedly for many moments. After this, Mahāprabhu's mood changed. Svarūpa Dāmodara was able to understand the Lord's intention and began to sing:

"I have finally found My life's Lord, for whom I had so long burned in the flames of desire." (*Caitanya Caritāmṛta* 2.1.55)

Bhaktivinoda Ṭhākura writes, "As the Lord's frenzied dancing came to an end, He became absorbed in the mood of Rādhārāṇī at Kurukshetra. This song about meeting the beloved after a long separation manifested naturally." As He felt the mood of union strengthening, the Lord began to loudly recite the following verse:

yaḥ kaumāraharaḥ sa eva hi
varas tā eva caitra-kṣapās
te conmīlita-mālatī-surabhayaḥ
prauḍhāḥ kadambānilāḥ
sā caivāsmi tathāpi tatra
surata-vyāpāra-līlā-vidhau
revā-rodhasi vetasī-taru-tale
cetaḥ samutkaṇṭhate

"That very person who had stolen my heart on the banks of the river Reva during my youth is now my master. The moonlit nights with a fragrance of newly blossomed *mālatī* flowers are also present. The sweet breeze from the *kadamba* tree is also flowing. In our intimate relationship, I am also the same lover, yet still my mind is not happy here. It is very eager to go back to that place on the bank of the Revā under the *vetasī* tree." (*Caitanya Caritāmṛta* 2.1.58)

Bhaktivinoda Ṭhākura writes, "This verse was written about a mundane lover and his mistress, but Mahāprabhu recited it with great respectful feeling. No one could understand His hidden intention other than Svarūpa Dāmodara."

When Rūpa Gosvāmī heard the Lord recite this verse, he himself composed a verse which revealed the deeper meaning which the Lord had envisioned. He wrote it down on a palm leaf and hid it in the roof of his cottage. When Mahāprabhu went to the residence of Śrīla Rūpa Gosvāmī, He accidentally saw the palm leaf on the roof, and thus He read his verse. After reading it, He went into an ecstatic mood, and while He was in that state, Śrī Rūpa Gosvāmī came and immediately fell down on the floor like a stick.

The Lord got up and gave him a slap. Then, He embraced him and began to speak as follows: "No one knows the purport of My verse. How could you understand My intention?"

Saying this, Lord Caitanya Mahāprabhu bestowed various blessings upon Rūpa Gosvāmī, and taking the verse with Him, showed it to Svarūpa Gosvāmī. With great wonder, the Lord asked him how Rūpa Gosvāmī could have understood His mind. Śrīla Svarūpa Dāmodara Gosvāmī replied, "If Rūpa Gosvāmī can understand Your mind, I believe it must be the result of Your special benediction." (*Caitanya Caritāmṛta* 3.1.72-87)

This was Rūpa Gosvāmī's verse:

priyaḥ so 'yaṁ kṛṣṇaḥ sahacari kurukṣetra-militas
tathāhaṁ sā rādhā tad idam ubhayoḥ saṅgama-sukham
tathāpy antaḥ-khelan-madhura-muralī-pañcama-juṣe
mano me kālindī-pulina-vipināya spṛhayati

"O companion! This is my beloved Kṛṣṇa meeting Me here in Kurukshetra; and I am the same Rādhā, and both of us are feeling the joy of union. Even so, My mind wishes for the forest by the banks of the Yamuna where the fifth note of His flute reverberates sweetly within My heart." (*Padyāvalī*, 383)

Mahāprabhu's vision was that the Jagannātha temple was Kurukshetra and the Guṇḍicā temple Vrindavan. He pulled on Jagannātha's chariot in the mood of a *gopi* attracting Him back to Vrindavan. Śrī Svarūpa Dāmodara Gosvāmī was able to understand everything that Mahāprabhu experienced during this time.

"The Lord had relished these topics in His room with Svarūpa Dāmodara for days

and nights. When He was overcome with that mood while dancing before the Lord's chariot, He would repeat this verse while gazing upon Lord Jagannātha's face. No one can describe Śrī Svarūpa Dāmodara Gosvāmī's good fortune, for he was completely absorbed, body, mind and soul, in the Lord. The Lord's senses would become identical with his senses and thus deeply relish his singing." (*Caitanya Caritāmṛta* 2.13.161-4)

Jagannātha Deva lives in Dwarka, but once every year He desires to go to Vrindavan. The Rathayātrā festival, when He travels from the Jagannātha temple (Dwarka) to Guṇḍicā (Vrindavan), symbolizes this desire. Lord Jagannātha does not take Lakṣmī Devī with Him to Vrindavan because Lakṣmī Devī is not qualified to participate in the Vrindavan *līlā*. Only the *gopīs* have such qualifications, and Rādhā is the best of the *gopīs*. Svarūpa Dāmodara explained these things:

"Lakṣmī does not have the right to participate in the pastimes of Vrindavan. Kṛṣṇa's companions in the Vrindavan *līlā* are the *gopīs*, and there are none but they who can enchant His mind." (*Caitanya Caritāmṛta* 2.14.122-3)

"Rādhā is the best among the *gopīs*. She is a treasure chest of jewels of love in the bright and spotless sentiment of conjugal love." (*Caitanya Caritāmṛta* 2.14.160)

Lord Jagannātha mounted His chariot after telling Lakṣmī Devī that He would be back on the very next day. When Lakṣmī Devī saw that the Lord was late in returning, she became angry, and gathering up her forces, sallied forth to attack her beloved. Her servants captured the servants of Lord Jagannātha and brought them to her. Such lovers' quarrels are not heard of anywhere in the world. Nevertheless, the *māna* (loving jealousy) of the *gopīs* is superior to that of Lakṣmī Devī, and of all the *gopīs*, that of Rādhā is the purest. When Mahāprabhu wished to hear about the *gopīs' māna* from Svarūpa Dāmodara, he gave Him great satisfaction by answering in great detail. He was always able to please the Lord in every aspect because he knew His wishes so intimately.

BHAGAVĀN ĀCĀRYA AND HIS BROTHER

Śrī Svarūpa Dāmodara Gosvāmī had a close friendship with the lame Bhagavān Ācārya of Halisahar.

"Bhagavān Ācārya was a great devotee and a scholar – a man of refined habits. He came to Purushottama to be with the Lord. He was an *avatāra* of a cowherd who served Kṛṣṇa in the mood of friendship. His dealings with Svarūpa Dāmodara were also those of a close friend. He was completely surrendered to the Lord's lotus feet, and he occasionally invited Him to eat at his residence." (*Caitanya Caritāmṛta* 3.2.84-6)

Bhagavān Ācārya was a generous and unpretentious Vaiṣṇava. Even so, his father, Śatānanda Khān, was a very materialistic person and his younger brother, Gopāla Bhaṭṭācārya, Māyāvādī. When Gopāla Bhaṭṭācārya came to Puri, the simple, straightforward Bhagavāna Ācārya asked Svarūpa Dāmodara to listen to his brother speak on Vedānta-bhāṣya: "Gopāla has come here after finishing his study of Vedānta philosophy. Come, everyone, and hear him speak on the Vedānta."

Svarūpa Dāmodara Gosvāmī, however, somewhat angry, answered as follows: "You have lost your intelligence in the association of Gopāla, and now you are eager to hear the Māyāvāda philosophy. When a Vaiṣṇava listens to the *Śārīraka-bhāṣya* (the Māyāvāda commentary upon Vedānta-sūtra), he gives up the attitude that the Lord is the master and the living entity His servant. Instead, he considers himself to be the Supreme Lord. The Māyāvāda philosophy is so dangerous that even a highly elevated devotee who has accepted Kṛṣṇa as his life and soul changes his attitude when he reads or hears it."

Bhagavāna Ācārya continued, "We are all fixed at the lotus feet of Kṛṣṇa with our hearts and souls. So the *Śārīraka-bhāṣya* cannot change our minds."

Svarūpa Dāmodara replied, "Maybe so, but when we hear the māyāvāda philosophy, we hear that Brahman is the only spiritual reality and that the universe of *māyā* is false, but we gain no real spiritual understanding. When a devotee hears the Māyāvādī say that the living entity is only imaginary and that the Supreme Lord is a manifestation of ignorance, it breaks his heart." (*Caitanya Caritāmṛta* 3.2.92-99)

SVARŪPA DĀMODARA DISTINGUISHES RASĀBHĀSA

"Śvarūpa Dāmodara was the personification of ecstatic love, fully cognizant of the transcendental mellows in relationship with Kṛṣṇa. He was like a second manifestation of Mahāprabhu. If someone wrote a book or composed verses and songs and wanted to recite them before Śrī Caitanya Mahāprabhu, Svarūpa Dāmodara would have to first examine them before the Lord listened. Mahāprabhu was never pleased to hear books or verses opposed to *siddhānta*, nor did he like hearing *rasābhāsa*, an improper mixture of devotional sentiments. It was the practice of Svarūpa Dāmodara Gosvāmī to examine all works of literature to find out whether their conclusions were correct. Only then would he allow them to be heard by the Lord." (*Caitanya Caritāmṛta* 2.10.110-114)

One day a *brāhmaṇa*, "a so-called" poet, came from Bengal. He had written a play and had read it to Bhagavāna Ācārya, who then asked Svarūpa Dāmodara to give an opinion on it. If Svarūpa Dāmodara approved, then it could be presented to Mahāprabhu. Many of the other Vaiṣṇavas had praised the play's literary qualities, and so after repeated requests from his friend, Svarūpa Dāmodara finally agreed to hear it. But Svarūpa Dāmodara only had to hear the invocation verse to point out numerous faults in it, demonstrating how it contradicted Vaiṣṇava conclusions. All the Vaiṣṇavas were struck with wonder. When he saw the poet's distress at being criticized, however, Svarūpa Dāmodara became compassionate and said:

"Go and study the *Bhāgavata* from a Vaiṣṇava. Take exclusive shelter of Caitanya Mahāprabhu's lotus feet. Always associate with Caitanya Mahāprabhu's devotees. If you do all this, you will be able to plunge into the ocean of His divine teachings." (*Caitanya Caritāmṛta* 3.5.131-2)

It was in Bhagavān Ācārya's house that Choṭa Haridāsa came to beg for fine rice from Mādhavī Devī and engaged in conversation with her. As a result of his conversing with a woman, Mahāprabhu ostracized Choṭa Haridāsa, which led him to undertake a fast. The Lord was as hard as a thunderbolt towards Haridāsa, and Śrī Svarūpa Dāmodara Gosvāmī attempted to intercede, persuading Haridāsa to eat. However, Mahāprabhu remained untouched by Svarūpa Dāmodara's efforts, and a year later, Haridāsa went to Prayag and gave up his life.

SVARŪPA DĀMODARA AND THE GOSVĀMĪS

When Sanātana Gosvāmī came alone to Puri from Mathura, he caught scabies in the Jharikhand jungle. In Puri, he stayed in Haridāsa Ṭhākura's cottage, where Mahāprabhu came to seem him daily, embracing him despite the pus-filled sores that covered his body. Ashamed of his condition, Sanātana Gosvāmī decided to commit suicide but was prevented from doing so by the all-knowing Lord. During his stay in Puri, Sanātana Gosvāmī was introduced to all the devotees of the Lord, including Svarūpa Dāmodara.

Govardhana Majumadāra's son, Raghunātha Dāsa, left his home and tricked his guru and family priest Yadunandana Ācārya. He walked to Puri in only twelve days. There he met Mahāprabhu. Mahāprabhu was extremely merciful to Raghunātha Dāsa and turned him over to Śrī Svarūpa Dāmodara Gosvāmī for tutelage. From that day on he was known as Svarūpa's Raghu.

"When he saw Raghunātha's thin and dirty body, the Lord felt sympathy for him.

He turned to Svarūpa Dāmodara and said, 'I am turning this Raghunātha over to you. I want you to take care of him as though he were your own son and personal servant. I now have three Raghunāthas in My entourage, so henceforth we will call this one Svarūpa's Raghu.' After He had said these words, the Lord took Raghunātha's hand and placed it in that of Svarūpa Dāmodara." (*Caitanya Caritāmṛta* 3.7.201-4)

Raghunātha Dāsa never spoke directly to Mahāprabhu. If he wished to make a submission to the Lord, he made it through either Svarūpa Dāmodara or Govinda. He told Svarūpa Dāmodara repeatedly that he wished to hear some instructions directly from Mahāprabhu.

"After Svarūpa passed this request on to the Lord, Mahāprabhu smiled and told Raghunātha Dāsa, 'I have appointed Svarūpa Dāmodara to be your instructor. You may learn from him about the spiritual practices and their goal. I Myself do not know as much as he. Nevertheless, if you have faith in My orders, you may fix your direction from the following words: Do not listen to gossip or engage in gossip yourself. You should not eat very palatable food, nor should you dress very nicely. Always chant the holy name of Lord Kṛṣṇa without any expectation of honor, while offering all respect to others. Mentally render service to Rādhā and Kṛṣṇa in Vrindavan. I have briefly given you My instructions; you will learn about them in detail from Svarūpa Dāmodara.' " (*Caitanya Caritāmṛta* 3.6.233-8)

On the day of Haridāsa Ṭhākura's disappearance, the Lord initiated *saṅkīrtana*. The devotees surrounded Haridāsa Ṭhākura's body, and Svarūpa Dāmodara sang the Holy Names with the devotees while Vakreśvara Paṇḍita danced. Svarūpa Dāmodara then went to the Jagannātha temple to seek *prasāda* for the feast that followed the *samādhi*, and he joined Jagadānanda Paṇḍita and others to serve the devotees.

Raghunātha Bhaṭṭa Gosvāmī, the son of Tapana Miśra, left his home in Benares to come to Puri via Bengal. When he met Mahāprabhu, the Lord embraced him and introduced him to Svarūpa Dāmodara and the other devotees.

MAHĀPRABHU'S INTENSE AUSTERITIES

At one time, Mahāprabhu went through a period of intense austerity. Constantly crying the names of Kṛṣṇa, due to His feelings of separation, He became leaner day after day. He began sleeping on a bed of plantain bark, taking no notice of the pain that resulted when His bones rubbed against the bark. The devotees, however, were greatly distressed to see His state. Jagadānanda Paṇḍita, in particular, was affected. He obtained some fine cloth and dyed it saffron, and then filled it with cotton from the silk-cotton tree. In this way he made both a mattress and a pillow for the Lord's comfort. Jagadānanda Paṇḍita then asked Govinda Dāsa to give the mattress and pillow to the Lord and Svarūpa Dāmodara to convince Him to use them. The Lord saw the nice bed and asked Govinda Dāsa angrily, "Who has made this bed?" When He heard from Govinda that Jagadānanda Paṇḍita had given it, He hesitated because Jagadānanda Paṇḍita was an *avatāra* of Satyabhāmā, who had quarrelsome nature. Even so, He had Govinda remove the bedding and went to sleep on the plantain-bark bed. When Svarūpa Dāmodara reminded the Lord that Jagadānanda Paṇḍita would be distressed if He did not use his bedding, He answered, "A mattress and pillow? Why don't you just go and get Me a bed? A *sannyāsī* is supposed to sleep on the ground. Jagadānanda wants Me to become a sense enjoyer. This is shameful."

Jagadānanda Paṇḍita was indeed upset when he heard from Svarūpa Dāmodara that Mahāprabhu had refused the bedding. Svarūpa Dāmodara cleverly made a mattress and pillow out of dried banana leaves torn into small pieces and stuffed into pieces of the Lord's used clothes. Despite His reluctance, the Lord accepted this new bedding. This satisfied all the devotees with the exception of Jagadānanda Paṇḍita, who asked the Lord permission to leave for Vrindavan. Mahāprabhu said, "Jagadānanda is angry with Me. That is why he wants to go to Vrindavan." This story gives a brilliant example of Svarūpa Dāmodara's expertise in serving the Lord.

MAHĀPRABHU'S ECSTASIES

As Mahāprabhu's feelings of separation intensified to the point of seeming insanity, He was kept at night in the Gambhīrā, behind three locked doors. One day, Svarūpa Dāmodara and Govinda noticed that even though the doors were still bolted, Mahāprabhu was missing. In great anxiety, the two of them started to look for the Lord everywhere. Finally, they found Him near the Lion's Gate of the Jagannātha temple, lying unconscious on the ground with all His joints loosened, His entire form lengthened. Svarūpa Dāmodara along with the other devotees started to sing the names of Kṛṣṇa into the Lord's ear loudly until suddenly He jumped up, His transcendental body returning to its normal condition, and shouted, "Haribol!" When the Lord returned to normal consciousness, Svarūpa Dāmodara led Him back to the Gambhīrā.

One day, the Lord saw the sand dunes and took them to be Govardhan. He ran towards them, while Svarūpa Dāmodara and Jagadānanda Paṇḍita ran behind Him. His body was overwhelmed by the ecstatic transformations, and He fell to the ground in a faint. When the devotees saw the Lord in this state, they began to cry. He partially regained consciousness when the devotees started to chant the Holy Name aloud. In this state, the Lord started to narrate, "I was at Govardhan. I saw Kṛṣṇa herding the cows and playing the flute. When they heard the flute, the *gopīs* came running toward Him. Śrīmatī Rādhārāṇī was there, and Kṛṣṇa took Her into a grotto. Then suddenly you all started to call Me back here. Why did you do that? Just to bring Me pain?" The Lord began to cry, and the devotees, affected by His great distress at losing His vision, joined Him in shedding tears.

A few days later, Mahāprabhu was in the Gambhīrā in the *divyonmāda* state, the madness of separation. Svarūpa Dāmodara and Rāmānanda Rāya stayed up until the middle of the night with the Lord, relishing discussions of Kṛṣṇa's pastimes. Finally, after a great deal of effort, they managed to persuade the Lord to lie down and take some rest, after which they all returned to their own quarters. Govinda also slept in the Gambhīrā. As He chanted the names of Kṛṣṇa, Mahāprabhu suddenly heard the sound of Kṛṣṇa's flute, and in the ecstasy that overcame Him, He ran out of the Gambhīrā, even though there were three doors bolted from the outside. This time He fell down amongst a herd of *tailaṅgī* cows to the south of the Lion's Gate. When Govinda heard no answer from the Lord, despite calling for Him, he informed Svarūpa Dāmodara of the situation.

Svarūpa Dāmodara organized a search party of devotees with torches, until finally they found the Lord lying unconscious in the midst of the cows. This time, His limbs were retracted into His body, giving it the appearance of a tortoise; His mouth was covered with foam, there were eruptions on His body and His eyes were filled with tears. He looked like a pumpkin, without any limbs. Externally He seemed to be suffering as though poisoned; internally He was experiencing divine ecstasies. The cows had surrounded the Lord and were sniffing His body, and even when the devotees shooed them away, they would come back, attracted by the Lord. After many attempts to arouse the Lord, when the devotees failed to bring Him back to consciousness, they picked Him up and carried Him to the Gambhīrā. There they started loudly singing the Holy Names in *kīrtana*. This continued for some time, until finally the Lord returned to an external state of consciousness, and His body also took on its normal appearance.

Remaining in a trance-like state, Mahāprabhu asked Svarūpa Dāmodara, "Where have you brought Me? I had heard the sound of Kṛṣṇa's flute, and I went to Vrindavan. I saw Kṛṣṇa with the cattle, playing His flute. Rādhārāṇī understood His signal and came to the bower trysting place. I followed them there and felt ecstasy when hearing the sound of her tinkling ornaments and also the voices, laughter and jocular words of the *gopīs*. You forced Me to come back here, and I can no longer hear their humorous conversations or the sound of their ornaments and flute."

Śrī Svarūpa Dāmodara Gosvāmī recognized the Lord's state and sang a verse from the Bhāgavata in his sweet voice:

kā stry-aṅga te kala-padāyata-veṇu-gīta-
sammohitārya caritān na calet trilokyām
trailokya-saubhagam idaṁ ca nirīkṣya rūpaṁ
yad go-dvija-druma-mṛgāḥ pulakāny abibhran

"Dear Kṛṣṇa! What woman within these three worlds would not be captivated by the sweet rhythms of Your wonderful flute-song? What woman would not abandon her vows of chastity as a result? Upon beholding Your beauty, the most sublime in this universe, even cows, birds, trees and animals horripilate in jubilation." (*Śrīmad Bhāgavatam* 10.29.40)

As soon as the Lord heard this verse, He once again merged into the mood of the *gopīs* and began to sing all the statements the *gopīs* made in separation from Kṛṣṇa, known as *citra-jalpa*.

THE LORD JUMPS INTO THE SEA

Kṛṣṇadāsa Kavirāja Gosvāmī has described another extraordinary event of this type. Once, during a full-moon night in autumn, the Lord, accompanied by His devotees, wandered through the Ai Tota garden next to the Guṇḍicā temple, relishing songs about the *rāsa-līlā*. As they approached the seashore, Mahāprabhu took the sea to be the Yamuna River and jumped into it. His body floated toward Konark until a fisherman caught Him in his nets, thinking Him to be a large fish. When he dragged the Lord on board, he saw that all His limbs were distended, transformed into a giant human form. Upon touching Him, the fisherman was immediately infused with *prema* and started crying and calling the name of Kṛṣṇa.

Meanwhile, Svarūpa Dāmodara and the other devotees were desperately seeking the Lord. Finally, they saw the fisherman standing on the shore with the Lord on His shoulders. When Svarūpa Dāmodara saw the fisherman in a state of ecstatic transformation, he came and explained who Mahāprabhu was, but still had to slap him several times before he calmed down. Then the devotees began to sing the Holy Names aloud until the Lord jumped up with a roar. Once again, while in a state of half-absorption in trance, Mahāprabhu recounted everything that He had experienced. Mahāprabhu had been in the world of Kṛṣṇa's *rāsa-līlā* and water sports. When they heard all His ecstatic utterances, the devotees trembled in awareness of the Lord's divine loving madness. Then they led Him back to the Gambhīrā.

THE LORD'S CONCLUDING PASTIMES

When Advaita Ācārya sent the riddle message back from Bengal with Jagadānanda Paṇḍita, indicating that the Lord's pastimes would soon come to an end, Svarūpa Dāmodara became distracted, while the Lord's divine madness became more and more intense. In his instructions to Svarūpa Dāmodara and Rāmānanda Rāya, the Lord made it very

clear that *harināma-saṅkīrtana* is the supreme method for attaining love for Kṛṣṇa.

The Lord, in a wave of jubilation, said, "Listen, Svarūpa Dāmodara and Rāmānanda Rāya! In the Age of Kālī, *harināma-saṅkīrtana* is the supreme means of deliverance. In the Age of Kālī, one who worships Kṛṣṇa by the congregational chanting of His Holy Names is most intelligent and thus attains the lotus feet of Kṛṣṇa. Through the chanting of the Holy Name, all of one's sinful reactions are extinguished and all auspiciousness arises until finally one experiences the joys of love for Kṛṣṇa." (*Caitanya Caritāmṛta* 3.20.8, 9, 11)

After saying this, the Lord recited His own eight verses known as the *Śikṣāṣṭaka.* As He relished them, He felt more and more humble in feelings of separation from Kṛṣṇa. Taking on the mood of Śrīmatī Rādhārāṇī, He became totally absorbed in love for Kṛṣṇa.

Śrī Svarūpa Dāmodara Gosvāmī and Rāmānanda Rāya remained constantly by the Lord's side throughout His ecstasies in *divyonmāda,* calming Him and enriching His feelings of love. Śrī Svarūpa Dāmodara Gosvāmī left the world on the day of Lord Jagannātha's Rathayātrā.

Śrī Mukunda Datta Ṭhākura

vraje sthitau gāyakau yau
madhukaṇṭhamadhuvratau
mukundavāsudevau tau
dattau gaurāṅgagāyakau

"In Vraja, there were two singers named Madhukaṇṭha and Madhuvrata. They appeared in Caitanya *līlā* as two singers, Mukunda Datta and Vāsudeva Datta, who used to sing for Lord Caitanya Mahāprabhu." (*Gaura-gaṇoddeśa-dīpikā* 140)

Śrī Mukunda Datta appeared in the Chittagong district of modern Bangladesh, in the village of Chanhara. This village is situated about twenty miles from Puṇḍarīka Vidyānidhi's Sripat. Vāsudeva Datta Ṭhākura was his elder brother.

"In the district of Chittagong, there is a village named Chakrashala, where lives a respectable family of Amvaṣṭha physicians named Datta. Two great devotees, named Mukunda Datta and Vāsudeva Datta, were born into this family. Both Vāsudeva, the older, and Mukunda, the younger, came to Nabadwip to live." (*Prema-vilāsa*)

"Śrī Mukunda Datta, a class friend of Lord Caitanya, was another branch of the Caitanya tree. Lord Caitanya danced while he sang." (*Caitanya Caritāmṛta* 1.10.40)

MAHĀPRABHU AS CHILDHOOD FRIEND

Mukunda Datta came to Nabadwip from Chittagong and became a fellow student of Mahāprabhu at Gaṅgādāsa Paṇḍita's tola. When Nimāi Paṇḍita, immersed in the joys of learning, roamed around in Nabadwip with thousands of students, none of the scholars other than Gaṅgādāsa Paṇḍita could understand his purports. Nimāi Paṇḍita was the personified form of the god of death for hypocrites, cupid for materialists and Bṛhaspati (the spiritual master of the demigods) for learned scholars.

Many Vaiṣṇavas from Chittagong settled in Nabadwip for learning and to stay near the river Gaṅgā. Every afternoon, they assembled at the house of Advaita Ācārya, where Mukunda Datta sang the hymns about Lord Hari in a sweet, melodious voice that immersed them all in an ocean of bliss. Mahāprabhu was internally very happy with Mukunda, but He would often debate with him by asking tricky questions. Nobody would come close to Nimāi in fear of debates.

One day, to get rescued from the tricky questions about grammar, Mukunda said that grammar was a subject for small children and that Mahāprabhu should answer his difficult questions in *alaṅkāra* (figures of speech). Mahāprabhu answered all the questions perfectly, establishing, refuting, and then again reestablishing the same, which amazed Mukunda.

"Mukunda thought, 'Such a scholarship is impossible for an ordinary human being. There is not one scripture or subject He does not know. He is such a genius. If only He were a devotee of Lord Kṛṣṇa, then I would never leave His company for a moment.' " (*Caitanya Bhāgavata* 1.12.18-9) Devotees were disinterested to hear or speak topics other than Śrī Kṛṣṇa. Therefore at the sight of Nimāi Paṇḍita, they would change their direction and keep a distance from Him.

"One day, Mahāprabhu laughed and said, 'One day he will see how much of a Vaiṣṇava I am. I will become such a Vaiṣṇava that Lord Śiva and Lord Brahmā will come and stand at My doorstep. So, My brothers, now hear from Me carefully. I will become the most famous Vaiṣṇava. Those who run away at My sight now will also sing My glories then.' " (*Caitanya Bhāgavata* 1.11.46-9)

After receiving *dīkṣā* from Īśvara Purīpāda in Gaya, Mahāprabhu returned to Nabadwip. He remained constantly intoxicated by divine love. Mukunda Datta recited *ślokas* and sang *kīrtanas* appropriate for the Lord's particular mood, which gave pleasure to Mahāprabhu. Even Advaita Ācārya and Īśvara Purīpāda were transported by divine ecstasy hearing Mukunda's heartfelt and melodious *kīrtanas*.

MUKUNDA DATTA AND GADĀDHARA PAṆḌITA

Puṇḍarīka Vidyānidhi, King Vṛṣabhānu in Kṛṣṇa-*līlā* and to whom Mahāprabhu had cried "Puṇḍarīka, My father!" came from Chittagong to live in Nabadwip. He stayed there in the guise of a materialist engrossed in sense pleasures. Amongst all, only Mukunda Datta was aware of Puṇḍarīka Vidyānidhi's actual self. One day he took Gadādhara Paṇḍita Gosvāmī, who was extremely detached from the senses since childhood, to have the audience of Puṇḍarīka Vidyānidhi. When he saw Puṇḍarīka Vidyānidhi sitting on comfortable cushions covered in sheets as white as the foam of milk, wearing very expensive clothes and perfumes, chewing betel leaves, and generally surrounded by all the trappings of a sensual lifestyle, he was unable to recognize him as a Vaiṣṇava.

Mukunda saw the doubt written on Gadādhara Paṇḍita's face and decided to reveal Puṇḍarīka Vidyānidhi's true devotional nature to him. He recited a glorification of Kṛṣṇa from *Śrīmad Bhāgavatam*:

aho bakī yaṁ stana-kāla-kūṭaṁ
jighāṁsayāpāyayad apy asādhvī
lebhe gatiṁ dhātry-ucitāṁ tato'nyaṁ
kaṁ vā dayāluṁ śaraṇaṁ vrajema

"How truly amazing! The sister of Bakāsura, the evil Pūtanā, was sent on a mission to kill Kṛṣṇa. Despite her evil intentions, He drank the *kālakūṭa* poison that was mixed with her breast milk, and awarded her the position of a wet nurse [as Ambikā and Kilimbā in Goloka]. Is there anyone else I can take shelter of who is more merciful than this Kṛṣṇa?" (*Śrīmad Bhāgavatam* 3.2.23)

The instant that Puṇḍarīka Vidyānidhi heard this, he began to cry "*Ha Kṛṣṇa!*" and fell to the ground in a faint. Extraordinary ecstatic symptoms began to show on his body. Śrī Gadādhara Paṇḍita Gosvāmī was amazed to see this reaction and began to regret the offensive thoughts he had been having just moments before. He decided that the only way to rid himself of this offense would be to take initiation from Puṇḍarīka Vidyānidhi, and he related this idea to Mukunda. Mukunda was much delighted and communicated his desire to Puṇḍarīka Vidyānidhi, who happily set a date for the auspicious act. Mahāprabhu also gave His approval, and so Gadādhara Paṇḍita took *mantra* initiation from Puṇḍarīka Vidyānidhi.

MAHĀ-PRAKĀŚA-LĪLĀ AT ŚRĪVĀSA AṄGANA

Mukunda was part of Mahāprabhu's *saṅkīrtana* pastimes at Śrīvāsa Aṅgana. He was the lead singer in one of the groups for the morning *kirtans* on the day of Ekādaśī.

"The scriptural injunction is that one should engage in Hari *kīrtana* on Ekādaśī day, also known as Hari-vāsara. On that day from early dawn, Mahāprabhu, the life of the world, began to dance. This auspicious beginning of the *saṅkīrtana* movement took place in the pious Śrīvāsa's courtyard, where the sound of Kṛṣṇa's names Gopāla and Govinda rose to the sky. Different *kīrtana* groups emerged from the assembled devotees. Śrīvāsa Paṇḍita headed one group, and Mukunda headed another." (*Caitanya Bhāgavata* 2.8.138-41)

During Mahāprabhu's twenty-one hour *mahābhāva-līlā* at Śrīvāsa Aṅgana, Mukunda sang *kīrtana* at the transcendental bathing ceremony.

"The devotees of Lord Gaurāṅga are very well versed in chanting Vedic hymns, so they poured water, accompanying the pouring with *mantras*. Mukunda and others were sweetly singing the bathing ceremony song, and other devotees wept or danced with overwhelming happiness." (*Caitanya Bhāgavata* 2.9.31-2)

Śrī Gaura-Nārāyaṇa is the sole proprietor of Vaikuṇṭha, full in six opulences. When He exhibited the *mahā-prakāśa-līlā* for twenty-one hours, taking His position on Lord Viṣṇu's throne, He manifested Himself in different *avatāras* to different devotees depending on their desires and the mellows they belong to. After the devotees completed His *abhiśeka* ceremony, reserved for the king of kings according to the scriptural regulations, Śrī Gaurasundara, bound by deep affection and love, called all the devotees, gave His audience in the form they had desired, and awarded boons to them. But the devotees could not understand why Mahāprabhu was not giving this opportunity to Mukunda, who is in fact very dear to Him.

Śrīvāsa Paṇḍita requested Mahāprabhu to be merciful to Mukunda, to which the Lord replied, "Mukunda is a pretentious wretch. His mind is not fixed. He sometimes is a perfect figure of humility, approaching Me holding straw in his teeth, but the next moment he comes to strike Me with an iron rod. Sometimes he associates with devotees, and other times he associates with nondevotees, striking Me with an iron rod. Therefore he is not eligible for the *darśana* of My divine form as the controller of everything."

Hearing Mahāprabhu's harsh words, Mukunda was deeply aggrieved and decided to quit his body. But before he did, he had Śrīvāsa Paṇḍita inquire from Mahāprabhu if there was any chance of getting His *darśana* ever? Mahāprabhu replied, "He will get My *darśana* after ten million of his births." Hearing Mahāprabhu's reply, Mukunda forgot himself completely and danced while uttering repeatedly. "Mahāprabhu's words will never be untrue". In a moment Mukunda's ten million births got destroyed. Mahāprabhu freed him from his offenses and exhibited him His opulent form at that very moment. Mahāprabhu, accepting His own defeat, said, "I perpetually reside on Mukunda's tongue. Wherever I will appear, you will get the service to sing for Me." (*Caitanya Bhāgavata* 2.10.260)

Mukunda condemned himself for not having any devotion. He sang the glories of devotion and explained through an example the terrifying state of being a nondevotee.

"Mukunda said, 'I am so degraded. I know nothing about devotional service; how can a faithless fool like me experience the bliss of devotion just by seeing You? Duryodhana could easily see Your universal form, whereas scholars study the entire scriptures in order to just perceive that same form. Yet Duryodhana and his entire family were stamped out, undergoing extreme pains, because he lacked the slightest of devotion.' "(*Caitanya Bhāgavata* 2.10.215-17)

MUKUNDA DATTA IS VERY DEAR TO MAHĀPRABHU

Immersed in the loving pastimes of Śrī Kṛṣṇa, one day Mahāprabhu chanted, '*gopī, gopī*' taking their side. One student came there at that time and asked Him to utter the name of Kṛṣṇa. Mahāprabhu was in a devotional trance and ran after that student to beat him with a cane, considering him to be a person of Kṛṣṇa's group. This student, in the company of several others, started to act against Mahāprabhu without understanding His inner mood. To rescue them from committing such an offensive act, Mahāprabhu decided to accept *sannyāsa*, the renounced order of life.

Mahāprabhu went to Mukunda's house where He heard him sing *Kṛṣṇa-maṇgala*. When Mahāprabhu revealed His desire to accept *sannyāsa*, the much aggrieved Mukunda requested Him to postpone His decision for a few days. Also, the thought of Mahāprabhu witha shave head took the devotees in a state of deep anguish. Mukunda along with other devotees sang *kīrtanas* soon after Mahāprabhu's *sannyāsa* at Katwa, much to His pleasure.

Mukunda was amongst the devotees who accompanied Mahāprabhu to Nilachal after His *sannyāsa*. He was present when Nityānanda Prabhu broke Mahāprabhu's *daṇḍa*, at the place of Sārvabhauma Bhaṭṭācārya in Nilachal, and during the water sports in Narendra Sarovara. Mukunda also accompanied the other devotees to Puri every year. During the Rathayātrā festival, Mukunda was the lead singer in the third of the seven groups that performed *saṇkīrtanas* in front of Lord Jagannātha's chariot. Haridāsa Ṭhākura was the principal dancer in this group.

The Lord Himself told the devotees how much affection Mukunda had for Him:

"Mukunda becomes very unhappy when he sees Me follow the *sannyāsa* duties, like lying down on the ground, and taking bath three times a day, even during the winter. Even though he does not say anything, I know that he is very unhappy within, and upon seeing him unhappy, I become twice as unhappy." (*Caitanya Caritāmṛta* 2.7.23-24)

Mukunda met all the chief associates of Mahāprabhu in Nilachal including, Svarupa Dāmodara, Rāya Rāmānanda, and Haridāsa Ṭhākura.

Śrī Mukunda Datta Ṭhākura disappeared on the full-moon day of Jaiṣṭha month, also celebrated as the bathing ceremony of Śrī Jagannātha Deva.

Śrīla Kāśīśvara Paṇḍita

purā vṛndāvane ceṭau sthitau bhṛṅgāra-bhaṅgurau
śrī-kāśīśvara-govindau tau jātau prabhu-sevakau

"Śrīla Kāśīśvara Paṇḍita (also *brahmacārī* or Gosvāmī) was Kṛṣṇa's servant Bhṛṅgāra or the *sakhī* Śasīrekhā." (*Gaura-gaṇoddeśa-dīpikā* 137)

Kāśīśvara Paṇḍita's home was in the village of Chatra in the district of Hooghly, about one mile from the present-day Serampore railway station. His father was Vāsudeva Bhaṭṭācārya, a *brāhmaṇa* of the Vātsya *gotra* in the line of Kañjīlāla Kānu. He also had the title Caudhurī, and hence the place where he established the temple has come to be known as Caudhurī Para. There he installed the deities of Gaurāṅga and Śrī Rādhā Govinda, whose annual festival is held on Dola Pūrṇimā. Kāśīśvara Paṇḍita was especially known for his physical strength. Śrī Rudra Paṇḍita of Ballabhpur was his nephew.

A DISCIPLE OF ĪŚVARA PURĪ

Kāśīśvara Paṇḍita was a disciple of Īśvara Purī who had received much mercy from him. For this reason, he is counted as one of Caitanya Mahāprabhu's branches. Śrī Govinda was also Īśvara Purī's disciple. Both of them devotedly served their spiritual master as long as he was present in this world. Just before he disappeared, he instructed them both to go engage in Mahāprabhu's service. Govinda was the first to come to Puri to serve the Lord after the disappearance of their guru; Kāśīśvara Paṇḍita traveled throughout India on a pilgrimage before finally coming to Mahāprabhu's lotus feet.

"I am a servant of Īśvara Purīpāda; my name is Govinda. On his order, I have come to You. At the time of his departure, my master ordered me: 'Go to Śrī Kṛṣṇa Caitanya and serve Him.' Kāśīśvara will also come after he has seen the pilgrimage sites. I have come directly to You." (*Caitanya Caritāmṛta* 2.10.132-4)

"On another day, Kāśīśvara Gosāi arrived; the Lord greeted him respectfully and gave him a place to stay with Him." (*Caitanya Caritāmṛta* 2.10.185)

Mahāprabhu felt something of a quandary about accepting the service of His guru's servants. He consulted with Sārvabhauma Bhaṭṭācārya, saying, "The servant of My spiritual master is My superior, so how can I accept his service? On the other hand, if I do not obey My guru's order, that too will be an offense. What should I do?" Sārvabhauma Bhaṭṭācārya answered that the spiritual master's order should take priority, and so the Lord followed his guru's directives and accepted Govinda and Kāśīśvara Paṇḍita as His personal servants.

sa śuśruvān mātari bhārgaveṇa
pitur niyogāt prahṛtaṁ dviṣadvat
pratyagrahīd agraja-śāsanaṁ tad-
ājñā gurūṇāṁ hy avicāraṇīyā

"On the order of his father, Paraśurāma killed his own mother, Renuka, as though she were an enemy. When He heard this, Lakṣmaṇa accepted the order of His elder brother, Rāma, for the orders of a guru are not to be debated." (*Raghuvaṁśa*, 14.46)

nirvicāraṁ guror ājñā mayā kāryā mahātmanaḥ
śreyo hy evaṁ bhavatyāś ca mama caiva viśeṣataḥ

"I must follow the order of my guru because he is a great soul. You will certainly benefit from this, but even more so will I." (*Rāmāyaṇa, Ayodhyā-khaṇḍa*, 22.9)

KĀŚĪŚVARA'S SERVICE TO MAHĀPRABHU

Whenever Mahāprabhu went to see Lord Jagannātha, Kāśīśvara would use his physical strength to hold back the crowds, allowing the Lord to pass without being touched by anyone.

"Īśvara Purī's disciples were Kāśīśvara Brahmacārī and Govinda. Being ordered by Īśvara Purī at the time of his departure from this world, they both arrived in Nilachal and met Mahāprabhu. The Lord considered them both to be His superiors because they had personally served His spiritual master, but He nevertheless accepted their service because it was His guru's order. Govinda would engage in personal, bodily service, while Kāśīśvara would go before Him when He went to see Lord Jagannātha. He would push people aside to make a path for the Lord so that He could go through the crowd without being touched." (*Caitanya Caritāmṛta* 1.10.138-142)

"Mahāprabhu joyfully took the devotees to the temple to see Lord Jagannātha. Kāśīśvara led the way, clearing the path, while Govinda followed carrying the Lord's water pot." (*Caitanya Caritāmṛta* 2.12.206-7)

In Puri, when the Lord was dancing in front of Lord Jagannātha's cart, three rings of people would be formed around the Lord in order to hold the people back. The innermost ring consisted of Nityānanda Prabhu and other devotees, the second of Kāśīśvara, Mukunda and others, and the third of King Pratāparudra and his subjects.

"Kāśīśvara, Mukunda and many other devotees held hands to form a second protective circle." (*Caitanya Caritāmṛta* 2.13.89)

Kāśīśvara Paṇḍita was one of the seven persons who would serve *mahā-prasāda* to Mahāprabhu and the other devotees after the *kīrtana* at the Rathayātrā. The others who served *prasāda* were Svarūpa Dāmodara, Jagadānanda Paṇḍita, Dāmodara Paṇḍita, Gopīnātha, Vāṇīnātha and Śaṅkara.

Kāśīśvara Paṇḍita also participated in some of the Lord's pastimes in Nabadwip, such as the *kīrtanas* at Śrīvāsa Aṅgana and bathing in the Ganges. He was also present when the Lord went with *kīrtana* to the house of Śridhara Paṇḍita and drank from his iron pot. He, along with the other devotees present, cried to see the Lord's mercy on that occasion. Govinda, Govindānanda, Śrīgarbha, Śrīmān, Jagadānanda Paṇḍita and Rāma were others present on that occasion. (*Caitanya Bhāgavata* 2.23.451)

Vṛndāvana Dāsa Ṭhākura tells just how dear Kāśīśvara Paṇḍita was to the Lord, calling Mahāprabhu Kāśīśvara's heart on one occasion (*Caitanya Bhāgavata* 2.1.6) and the wealth of Kāśīśvara's life (*Kāśīśvara-prāṇa-dhana*) on another. (*Caitanya Bhāgavata* 2.24.3).

Kāśīśvara Paṇḍita was also present when Mahāprabhu went to greet Advaita Ācārya and the other devotees on their arrival from Bengal.

His disappearance day is on the fourteenth day of the waxing moon (*śukla caturdaśī*) in the month of Kārtika. According to another opinion, it is on the full-moon day of the month of Āśvina, when Rādhā and Kṛṣṇa's Rāsa Pūrṇimā is also celebrated.

Śrī Bhagavān Ācārya

ācāryo bhagavān khañjaḥ kalā gaurasya kathyate

"Khañja Bhagavān Ācārya was said to be Gaurāṅga Mahāprabhu's expansion." (*Gaura-gaṇoddeśa-dīpikā* 74)

ācāryaṁ bhagavantaṁ tu tejomaya-kalevaram
yasya smaraṇa-mātreṇa gaura-prema prajāyate

"I offer obeisances to Bhagavān Ācārya, whose powerful body is filled with effulgence. Just by remembering him, one will develop love for Gaurāṅga Mahāprabhu." (*Śākhā-nirṇayāmṛta*)

Bhagavān Ācārya lived in the town of Halisahar, which is in the twenty-four Parganas district. Kṛṣṇadāsa Kavirāja Gosvāmī writes that he is considered to be Caitanya's branch along with Brahmānanda Bhāratī, Śikhi Māhiti and Murāri Māhiti. (*Caitanya Caritāmṛta* 1.10.136)

It is written in the *Gauḍīya Vaiṣṇava Abhidhāna* that Bhagavān Ācārya appeared in Śrī Dhāma Nabadwip, but left to live in Halisahar. His father, Śatānanda Khān, was a wealthy materialist, while he himself was a scholar and a great Vaiṣṇava who worshipped in the mood of friendship.

"Bhagavān Ācārya was lame and a householder. His son was named Raghunātha

Ācārya who, accompanied Jāhnavā Mātā to Kheturi." (*Bhakti-ratnākara* 10.382)

The following farther information is found in the *Gauḍīya Vaiṣṇava Abhidhāna*: "Bhagavān Ācārya was particularly advanced in the study of logic, so much so that he received the title of Nyāyācārya (preceptor of logic). When his father saw that he was developing the renounced spirit at a young age, he arranged for his marriage to the daughter of Nabadwip's Madhusūdana Ghaṭaka. Despite this, Bhagavān Ācārya overcame the entanglements of his householder life to go to live in Puri with the Lord. Mahāprabhu enjoined him to return to his family, however, and so he went back to Bengal. He had two sons, Raghunātha and Ramānātha. Nevertheless, Bhagavān Ācārya was unable to remain in householder life for long, and he ultimately gave the responsibility for his wife and children to his brother-in-law and disciples. He then took the renounced order and returned to Puri to live with the Lord."

BHAGAVĀN ĀCĀRYA IN PURI

When the devotees heard that Mahāprabhu had returned from South India, they rushed to see Him. Bhagavān Ācārya renounced everything and came to live there near the Lord.

"Rāmabhadra Ācārya and Bhagavān Ācārya came to live near the Lord, giving up all other duties." (*Caitanya Caritāmṛta* 2.10.184)

"Bhagavān Ācārya was a great devotee, a scholar and a man of refined habits. He came to Purushottama to be with the Lord. He was an *avatāra* of a cowherd who served Kṛṣṇa in the mood of friendship. His dealings with Svarūpa Dāmodara were also those of a close friend. He was completely surrendered to the Lord's lotus feet, and he occasionally invited Him to eat at his residence. He made various vegetable preparations, which he personally served to the Lord." (*Caitanya Caritāmṛta* 3.2.84-7)

Bhagavān Ācārya would not brook any materialistic conversation, only listening to Kṛṣṇa's name, form, qualities and pastimes.

"The great personality Bhagavān Ācārya arrived. Mundane topics never entered his ears." (*Caitanya Bhāgavata* 3.3.188)

He was one of the many devotees who came to meet Mahāprabhu in Puri after the Lord delivered Sārvabhauma Bhaṭṭācārya. Bhagavān Ācārya was also present when Mahāprabhu went to greet Advaita Ācārya, along with Kāśīśvara Paṇḍita, Pradyumna Miśra and others. (*Caitanya Bhāgavata* 3.8.57)

He was also present when Mahāprabhu went into an ecstatic trance and fell into the ocean after taking the dunes on the beach to be Govardhan.

"Paramānanda Purī, Brahmānanda Bhāratī and others ran to the beach while Bhagavān Ācārya, being lame, followed them as quickly as he could." (*Caitanya Caritāmṛta* 3.14.90)

One day Bhagavān Ācārya wanted to feed Mahāprabhu nicely and sent the singer Choṭa Haridāsa to beg for fine rice from Mādhavī Devī, the sister of Śikhi Māhiti. While eating, Mahāprabhu learnt of this and became angry and ostracized Choṭa Haridāsa. He said that for a renunciate to talk to a woman is worse than drinking poison.

"The Lord said, 'I cannot look upon the face of someone who after taking the vows of renunciation continues to converse with women.' " (*Caitanya Caritāmṛta* 3.2.117)

BHAGAVĀN ĀCĀRYA'S BROTHER GOPĀLA

Bhagavān Ācārya was a generous and unpretentious Vaiṣṇava. Because of these qualities he was particularly dear to Mahāprabhu. The following account of his simplicity is given in the *Caitanya Caritāmṛta*:

Bhagavān Ācārya's younger brother Gopāla Bhaṭṭācārya had been to Kashi, where he had studied Vedānta. After finishing his studies, he came to Puri to see his elder brother, who was quite pleased to hear that he had become learned in the field. With great enthusiasm, Bhagavān Ācārya brought him to Mahāprabhu. The Lord, being the indweller of all beings, knew that Gopāla was a Māyāvādī, so He was not delighted to meet him. Even so, He formally showed a polite affection. The simple, straight-forward Bhagavān Ācārya went to Svarūpa Dāmodara and requested him: "Gopāla, my younger brother, has come here after finishing his study of Vedānta philosophy. Please come and hear the Vedānta commentary from him."

Svarūpa Dāmodara Gosvāmī, however, somewhat angry due to his love for Bhagavān Ācārya, chastised him as follows:

"You have lost your intelligence in Gopāla's association, and now you are eager to hear the Māyāvādī philosophy. When a Vaiṣṇava listens to the *Śārīraka-bhāṣya*, the Māyāvādī commentary upon *Vedānta-sūtra*, he gives up the attitude that the Lord is the master and the living entity is His servant. Instead, he considers himself to be the Supreme Lord. The Māyāvādī philosophy is so dangerous that even a highly elevated devotee who has accepted Kṛṣṇa as his life and soul changes his attitude if he studies it." (*Caitanya Caritāmṛta* 3.2.94-6)

Bhagavān Ācārya continued, even though he had been chastised by Svarūpa Dāmodara, "The devotees are all fixed at the lotus feet of Kṛṣṇa in heart and soul. Listening to the *Śārīraka-bhāṣya* could not possibly have a negative effect on them."

Svarūpa Dāmodara firmly answered making him understand the needlessness of listening to the heart-wrenching Māyāvādī commentary. He said, "When we hear the Mayavadī philosophy, not only do we hear that Brahman is the only spiritual reality and that the universe of *māyā* is false, but we gain no spiritual understanding. When a devotee hears a Māyāvādī say that the living entity is only imaginary and that the Supreme Lord is a manifestation of ignorance, it breaks his heart and soul." (*Caitanya Caritāmṛta* 3.2.98-99)

Svarūpa Dāmodara's remarks made Bhagavān Ācārya ashamed and a little afraid, so he sent his brother Gopāla back to Bengal.

THE POET FROM EAST BENGAL

One day a poet came to Puri from eastern Bengal who wrote poetry according to his own whim. He had also written a play about Mahāprabhu. Since he knew Bhagavān Ācārya personally, he read the play to him and afterwards to the other devotees, who all praised his work. So they felt that Mahāprabhu should also hear his play. However, only if Svarūpa Dāmodara approved could any work of poetry be presented to Mahāprabhu, as he would examine them for improper presentation of devotional sentiment and doctrine. Since his friend Bhagavān Ācārya had praised the literary qualities of the play, Svarūpa Dāmodara finally agreed to hear it after repeated requests. As soon as the poet read the invocation verse and explained it, however, and even though all the devotees were pleased, Svarūpa Dāmodara pointed out two faults that, in his view, had an offensive character.

The poet's explanation was as follows: "Lord Jagannātha is a most beautiful body, and Śrī Caitanya Mahāprabhu, who is exceptionally grave, is the owner of that body. Śrī Caitanya Mahāprabhu has appeared here in Puri to spiritualize the entire dull material world." (*Caitanya Caritāmṛta* 3.5.114-5)

Svarūpa Dāmodara began to speak in great anger.

"You are a fool and have brought ill fortune upon yourself, for you have no faith in either of the two Lords, Jagannātha Deva or Śrī Caitanya Mahāprabhu. Lord Jagannātha is completely spiritual and full of transcendental bliss, but you have said that He is nothing but a dull, destructible body composed of the inert, external energy. At the same time, you have said that Śrī Caitanya Mahāprabhu, who is the Supreme Personality of Godhead, full in six opulences, is an ordinary living being, a spark of spiritual energy rather than the supreme fire. You have committed offenses to both Lords. This is what happens when someone who knows no theology tries to glorify the Lord.

"Furthermore, you have made another great error. You have made a distinction between the Lord and His body. Such a distinction does not exist, for the Lord's body and His identity are made of blissful spiritual energy. This is a great offense. "(*Caitanya Caritāmṛta* 3.5.117-122)

When one sees a distinction between the body and the identity of the Lord, then he or she commits the mistake of thinking the Lord to be a conditioned living being. When he saw the poet's distress at being criticized, Svarūpa Dāmodara became compassionate and told him to take shelter of a pure devotee,

"Go and study the *Bhāgavata* from a Vaiṣṇava. Take exclusive shelter of Caitanya Mahāprabhu's lotus feet. Associate constantly with the devotees of Caitanya Mahāprabhu. Only then will you be able to understand all the waves of the ocean of Vaiṣṇava philosophy." (*Caitanya Caritāmṛta* 3.5.131-2)

The *brāhmaṇa* poet was amazed, ashamed and afraid, all at once. Svarūpa Dāmodara was kind to him and showed him how his own verse could be reinterpreted to glorify Kṛṣṇa. When he gave an elaborate explanation to the poet, the poet had a change of heart and surrendered to the Lord's devotees.

Śrī Pradyumna Miśra

āvirbhāvo gauraharer nakula-brahmacāriṇi
āveśaś ca tathā jñeyo
miśre pradyumna-saṅgake

"The Lord's *āvirbhāva* (manifestation) took place in Nakula Brahmacārī, and His *āveśa* (empowerment) in Pradyumna Miśra." (*Gaura-gaṇoddeśa-dīpikā* 73-74)

Śrīla Bhakti Siddhānta Sarasvatī Gosvāmī Ṭhākura has written that Pradyumna Miśra was an Odishan (*Caitanya Caritāmṛta* 1.10.131, *Anubhāṣya*). Vṛndāvana Dāsa Ṭhākura has stated the same in *Caitanya Bhāgavata*.

"Many of Mahāprabhu's associates took birth in Odisha. Slowly they came and met with the Lord. Amongst them was Pradyumna Miśra, whose body was solidified *prema*. The great self-controlled devotees Paramānanda Mahāpātra and Rāmānanda Rāya were others." (*Caitanya Bhāgavata* 3.3.183-4)

According to *Gauḍīya Vaiṣṇava Abhidhāna*, Pradyumna Miśra was originally a resident of Sylhet and only later moved to Odisha. He is counted amongst the branches of Caitanya Mahāprabhu. The extent to which he was dear to Mahāprabhu is described in both the *Caitanya Caritāmṛta* and *Caitanya Bhāgavata*:

"Pradyumna Miśra was an ocean of love for Lord Kṛṣṇa, and Lord Gaurasundara put him on the same level as Himself." (*Caitanya Bhāgavata* 3.5.211)

"Chief amongst the loving devotees of the Lord were Kāśīśvara Paṇḍita, Bhagavān Ācārya and Pradyumna Miśra." (*Caitanya Bhāgavata* 3.8.57)

"The Lord felt joy on meeting Kāśī Miśra, Pradyumna Miśra and Bhavānanda Rāya." (*Caitanya Caritāmṛta* 1.10.131)

"All glories to the Lord, the life of Pradyumna Miśra and the wealth of Paramānanda Puri." (*Caitanya Bhāgavata* 1.14.2)

When Mahāprabhu returned from South India, Sārvabhauma Bhaṭṭācārya introduced Pradyumna Miśra to the Lord as a great Vaiṣṇava.

"Pradyumna Miśra is the best of the Vaiṣṇavas. He was Lord Jagannātha's chief cook, also known as Dāsa." (*Caitanya Caritāmṛta* 2.10.42)

Later, Pradyumna Miśra was instructed by Mahāprabhu to go to Rāmānanda Rāya to hear Kṛṣṇa *kathā*. This has been extensively described in the *Caitanya Caritāmṛta*, *Antya-līlā*, chapter 5. Śrīla Bhakti Siddhānta Sarasvatī Gosvāmī Ṭhākura writes in his *Gauḍīya Bhāṣya* to the *Caitanya Bhāgavata* (1.14.2): "Pradyumna Miśra took birth in a *brāhmaṇa* family in Odisha. He led an exemplary pious householder life, showing nobility of character in his adherence to social etiquette. Mahāprabhu gave meaning to this behavioral standard by sending him to the great devotee Rāmānanda Rāya, who though not born in a material *brāhmaṇa* family was the most competent instructor in the matter of *bhakti-rasa*. When Pradyumna Miśra went to this Vaiṣṇava *ācārya* to hear him glorify Kṛṣṇa's pastimes in the attitude of a disciple and thereby received Mahāprabhu's causeless mercy."

PRADYUMNA WANTS TO HEAR HARI KATHĀ

Pradyumna Miśra came one day to Mahāprabhu eagerly asking to hear some Hari *kathā*, The Lord in turn sent him to meet Rāmānanda Rāya. At the time, Rāmānanda Rāya was living in the Jagannatha Vallabha gardens. The service he was engaged in for the pleasure of Lord Jagannātha was beyond the capacity of even great self-controlled sages, what to speak of ordinary human beings. He would prepare two young *deva-dāsīs* for the performance of a play which was to be given before Lord Jagannātha, not only by training them in the songs that they would sing and in the dance they would perform, but also by bathing, dressing and decorating them. While Rāmānanda Rāya was engaged in such service, no one was allowed to interrupt him.

The first time that Pradyumna Miśra came to see Rāmānanda Rāya, one of Rāmānanda's servants told him that he was busy and asked Miśra to sit outside and wait. When Rāmānanda Rāya finished his service and came outside, he learned that Pradyumna Miśra had been waiting there for a long time to hear about Kṛṣṇa from him. He showed the *brāhmaṇa* the appropriate respect and begged forgiveness for his offense in making him wait. Miśra realized that it was too late that day for his wish to be fulfilled, and he returned home.

Some days later, when Mahāprabhu saw Miśra, He asked him how the meeting with Rāmānanda Rāya had gone and what topics they had discussed. At first, Pradyumna Miśra remained silent because of the doubts which he had about Rāmānanda Rāya's behavior. Mahāprabhu, as the *antaryāmī*, was able to understand what was going through his mind and began to glorify Rāmānanda Rāya's extraordinary character with great force. His words are found in the *Caitanya Caritāmṛta*:

"I am a *sannyāsī* and consider Myself to be renounced. But if I even hear the name of a woman, what to speak of seeing one, I feel an effect on My mind and body. So who is not moved by the sight of a woman? Listen to Me, everyone. Let Me tell you about Rāmānanda Rāya's activities, even though they are so wonderful and uncommon that they really cannot be properly described. He personally serves Lord Jagannātha's young and beautiful *deva-dasīs* in every possible way. He personally bathes and dresses them and decorates them with ornaments. While doing so, he naturally sees and touches their bodies' private parts, but even so, his mind is never affected. He teaches the girls how to physically express all the moods of love so that they can act them out before Jagannātha Deva, but his mind and body are as steady as wood or stone. Indeed, it is amazing that even when he touches such young girls, his mind is not disturbed. Only Rāmānanda Rāya has the right to do such things, and when I see him do them, I can understand that his body is not material but a spiritual entity." (*Caitanya Caritāmṛta* 3.5.35-42)

Thus saying that Rāmānanda Rāya was highly qualified to speak on matters connected to Kṛṣṇa, the Lord sent Pradyumna Miśra back again. When he arrived in the Jagannatha Vallabha gardens, Rāmānanda greeted him by paying obeisances. Pradyumna then heard Rāmānanda Rāya explain all the different topics on *sambandha, abhidheya* and *prayojana* which he had recounted to the Lord at Vidyanagar during His trip to South India. Both the speaker and the hearer completely forgot themselves in the ecstasies of Kṛṣṇa *kathā*. The whole day passed in this way. Pradyumna Miśra felt himself to be completely fulfilled by the hearing of all these subjects of Kṛṣṇa, and he went to tell Mahāprabhu about it.

Śrīla Bhakti Siddhānta Sarasvatī Gosvāmī Ṭhākura has made the following commentary on this anecdote in his *Anubhāṣya*: "Ordinarily, the *brāhmaṇa* acts as a preceptor to the three other varṇas, and the *sannyāsī* is the guru of all *brāhmaṇas* in the three other *āśramas*. The Lord wished to curb the false pride arising from these notions by sending Pradyumna Miśra, even though he was a pure *brāhmaṇa*, to take instruction from Rāmānanda Rāya, who belonged to the lowest varṇa, that of the *śudra*, and to the lowest *āśrama*, that of the householder. The Lord Himself, though a *sannyāsī*, also showed the same example by taking instruction personally from him, accepting the conclusions he preached."

Śikhi Māhiti

rāgalekhā kalākelyau rādhā-dāsyau purā sthite
te jñeye śikhi-māhātī tat-svasā mādhavī kramāt

"Śikhi Māhiti and his sister Mādhavī Devī were previously Ragalekhā and Kalākelī, two of Śrīmatī Rādhārāṇī's servants." (*Gaura-gaṇoddeśa-dīpikā* 189)

Śikhi Māhiti was an Odishan, who lived in Purushottama Kshetra. He is considered to be one of Mahāprabhu's most intimate associates and one of His personal branches. He was a servant of the Lord Jagannātha and was a *likhānādhikārī*, in charge of writing. (*Caitanya Caritāmṛta* 2.10.42)

Śikhi Māhiti was a great soul, noted for his great compassion and his pure heart. Besides his devotionally expert sister Mādhavī, he had a brother named Murāri Mahānta or Mahantī, who also had strong faith in Mahāprabhu. Their devotion to Him was spontaneous and unwavering. They never forgot Mahāprabhu for even a moment, and the Lord also poured down unlimited affection on them.

"Lord, this is Murāri Māhiti, the brother of Śikhi Māhiti. He knows nothing other than Your lotus feet." (*Caitanya Caritāmṛta* 2.10.44)

Murāri and Mādhavī became Mahāprabhu's devotees before their elder brother. However, as much as they tried to persuade him, they were not able to convince him to worship Śrī Gaurasundara. In his *Anubhāṣya,* Śrīla Bhakti Siddhānta Sarasvatī Gosvāmī Ṭhākura has described how Śikhi Māhiti finally came to receive Caitanya Mahāprabhu's mercy. The following is a summary of this account:

One day, after his younger brother and sister had spent some time trying to convince him of Mahāprabhu's divinity, Śikhi Māhiti dozed off. Towards the end of the night, he had a dream in which he saw his brother and sister looking upon the feet of Lord Gaurasundara and telling him to wake up. Startled, Śikhi Māhiti opened his eyes and saw that his siblings were indeed before him. The wonderful dream had inspired ecstatic symptoms in him, and his eyes were filled with tears. He ecstatically embraced his brother and sister, who asked him what was the reason for his joy. Śikhi Māhiti saw their wonder and in order to put their minds at ease said to them: "I have just had the most wonderful dream. Listen to me. Today, I have finally become a believer in the glories of the son of Śacī, Śrī Gaurāṅga. In my dream, I saw Mahāprabhu taking *darśana* of Lord Jagannātha in the temple, and as He was doing so, He entered into the body of Lord Jagannātha and then came out again. He did this over and over, and I can still see the Lord doing it. Am I still dreaming? The Lord of unlimited compassion, Gaurasundara, called me by name and then embraced me with His long arms of unblemished beauty."

As he recalled his dream, Śikhi Māhiti became overwhelmed by devotional ecstasy, whereupon Murāri and Mādhavī asked him to accompany them to the temple to behold Lord Jagannātha. Tears flowed down the eyes of Murāri and Mādhavī as they took the Lord's *darsan* and Śikhi Māhiti saw his dream come to life before him. Then Lord Gaurasundara embraced him, saying, "You are Murāri's brother." At the Lord's touch, Śikhi Māhiti fell into an ocean of ecstasy and from that time on, he forgot everything else but the Lord's service.

Kṛṣṇadāsa Kavirāja Gosvāmī's *Caitanya Caritāmṛta,* Vṛndāvana Dāsa Ṭhākura's *Caitanya Bhāgavata* and Narahari Cakravartī's *Bhakti-ratnākara* all describe the extent to which Śikhi Māhiti was dear to Śrī Caitanya Mahāprabhu:

"The Lord joyfully met Svarūpa Dāmodara and then Śikhi Māhiti and Bhavānanda Rāya." (*Caitanya Caritāmṛta* 2.1.130)

"All the devotees joyfully came forward to meet the Lord, and He gave each one of them an embrace of love. Amongst the devotees who were there were Kāśī Miśra, Rāmānanda Rāya, Pradyumna Miśra, Sārvabhauma Bhaṭṭācārya, Vāṇīnātha, Śikhi Māhiti and others." (*Caitanya Caritāmṛta* 2.16.253-4)

Śikhi Māhiti is mentioned as being present at the meeting of the Bengali devotees with those of Puri in *Caitanya Bhāgavata* (3.8.60).

"Śikhi Māhiti and others said that it was time to go and take *darśana* of Jagannātha Deva. (*Bhakti-ratnākara* 8.237)

Śikhi Māhiti was one of Mahāprabhu's three and a half most intimate devotees.

"The Lord accepted that Śikhi Māhiti's sister was one of Rādhā's friends. In the entire world, there were only three and a half devotees who were as worthy. They were Svarūpa Dāmodara Gosvāmī, Rāmānanda Rāya and Śikhi Māhiti. His sister was the half person." (*Caitanya Caritāmṛta* 3.2.105-6)

Śrī Gopīnātha Paṭṭanāyaka

Gopīnātha Paṭṭanāyaka was Bhavānanda Rāya's second son. According to the tenth chapter of the *Ādi-līlā* of *Caitanya Caritāmṛta*, Mahāprabhu says that Bhavānanda Rāya was formerly the King Pāṇḍu and that his sons were the five Pāṇḍavas. All of these five sons were very dear to the Lord.

"Your sons, Rāmānanda Rāya, Gopīnātha Paṭṭanāyaka, Kalānidhi, Sudhānidhi and Vāṇīnātha Nāyaka, are all objects of My affection. Rāmānanda and I are different in body only; in spirit we are one. "(*Caitanya Caritāmṛta* 1.10.133-4)

Brahmagiri or Alalanatha is about twelve miles north of Jagannatha Puri. Bentapur is a small village not far from there. Bhavānanda Rāya was a landowner living in this village. His descendants, who nowadays use the surname Chaudhuri-Pattanayaka continue to reside in this village.

GOPĪNĀTHA FALLS IN ARREARS

Gopīnātha Paṭṭanāyaka was King Pratāparudra's *tahaśīldāra* in Malajathya Dandapata, which is now the district of Midnapur in West Bengal. The *tahaśīldāra's* duty is to collect taxes. On one occasion, there was a shortfall of 200,000 *kāhans* (1 *kāhan* = 16 *paṇas*, 1 *paṇa* = 20 *gaṇḍās*, 1 *gaṇḍā* = 4 cowries) of cowries. In the Odishan language, the crown prince is known as Baḍa Jānā. When Gopīnātha Paṭṭanāyaka could not come up with the tax money, King Pratāparudra's son, the Baḍa Jānā, decided to punish him. At that time, capital punishment was given by throwing the prisoner down from a scaffold to be impaled on swords.

When they saw Gopīnātha in this dangerous situation, some of Bhavānanda Rāya's well-wishers came to Mahāprabhu to appeal to Him to intervene. When Mahāprabhu asked what the reason for Gopīnātha's punishment was, one of the supplicants answered, "Gopīnātha owes the government treasury 200,000 *kāhanas* in back taxes and is unable to make a cash payment. He offered to pay back the money by selling some of his possessions, and for that reason he brought a dozen fine horses to the palace. The King sent one of his princes who was an expert in evaluating horses, but this prince offered a price far below what the horses were actually worth. This prince had a physical quirk by which he repeatedly stretched his neck, looking upward and then from side to side. Gopīnātha was angry at the attempt to cheat him, and so he responded by mocking the prince, saying, "My horses lift their necks, but at least they don't keep looking up in the air! I don't see how they can be worth so little." In other words, he suggested that his horses were more valuable than the prince himself.

The prince was insulted by this comment and decided to take revenge. He went to the King and got permission to put Gopīnātha on the scaffold. The prince was prepared to throw him down on the swords.

Upon hearing this account, Śrī Caitanya Mahāprabhu took an attitude of impartiality and replied with affectionate anger, asking how the King could be at fault if Gopīnātha Pāṭṭanayaka did not pay his dues. How could the King be at fault for punishing someone who has committed an offense? What could He do about that?

THE LORD SAVES GOPĪNĀTHA

However, a few moments later, news came that Bhavānanda Rāya and his entire family had been imprisoned, and Svarūpa Dāmodara Gosvāmī and other close companions of the Lord appealed to Him to do something. Mahāprabhu instructed everyone to take shelter of the lotus feet of Jagannātha Deva, who is able to act freely and can do and undo whatever He likes.

As the Supersoul within the heart, the Lord inspired Haricandana Pātra, one of King Pratāparudra's ministers, to recount Gopīnātha's entire story to the King, asking him to repeal the death sentence which had been given. The King was surprised that he had not been informed of the events and immediately had the death sentence repealed and Gopīnātha released.

"Gopīnātha Paṭṭanāyaka was Rāmānanda Rāya's brother. By the Lord's grace, he was delivered from a royal death sentence." (*Caitanya Caritāmṛta* 2.1.265)

Mahāprabhu inquired about how Gopīnātha's brother Vāṇīnātha, and the other members of their family reacted when they were imprisoned. The messenger replied,

"Vāṇīnātha was without fear; he was constantly chanting Kṛṣṇa's name – 'Hare Kṛṣṇa, Hare Kṛṣṇa.' He counted each *mantra* on the fingers of his hands, and after he had finished chanting a thousand times, he would make a mark on his body."

Mahāprabhu was pleased to hear that Vāṇīnātha was acting in this way. Who can understand the mysterious workings of the Lord's mercy? (*Caitanya Caritāmṛta* 3.9.56-8)

Mahāprabhu complained to the King's priest, Kāśī Miśra, that people were repeatedly coming to disturb Him, trying to get Him to intercede on behalf of Bhavānanda Rāya's family, which was misappropriating state funds. He told him that He was thinking of moving to Alalanath, where He could get some peace. Kāśī Miśra talked Him out of going but told Mahārāja Pratāparudra of how the Lord had been affected by these events. As a result, in order to please the Lord, the King not only pardoned Gopīnātha Paṭṭanāyaka but he forgave him his debt and doubled his salary. Appreciative of the Lord's mercy, Gopīnātha came and placed his head, which had been honored with a silken turban personally wrapped around his head by the King, at the Lord's lotus feet and said:

"The King has pardoned my tax arrears. He has reappointed me to my post and doubled my salary while honoring me with this silken turban. All of this is due to Your mercy. What a difference! One moment I am on the scaffold, preparing myself to die; the next I am being given honors like the silk turban. When on the scaffold, I began meditating on Your lotus feet, and this is the result of that meditation. People are amazed at this turn of events, and they sing the glories of Your mercy. I know, however, my Lord, that these are not the principal results of meditating upon Your lotus feet, but are simply a secondary effect. Material gains are only temporary. Your real mercy has been granted to Rāmānanda Rāya and Vāṇīnātha Rāya, for You have granted them freedom from material sensual entanglements, a blessing that You have not given to me. I pray, O Lord, that You bestow Your pure mercy upon me so that I may also become renounced. I no longer wish for material enjoyment." (*Caitanya Caritāmṛta* 3.9.133-9)

The Lord heard Gopīnātha's heartfelt prayer and answered:

"Whether you remain involved in material activities or become completely renounced, you and your brothers are My eternal servants, birth after birth. But I ask you to obey one order of Mine. Do not spend money which belongs to the King. Pay the King his dues and then spend the balance for religious and fruitive activities. Don't spend a farthing on sinful activities; otherwise, you will be the loser both in this life and the next." (*Caitanya Caritāmṛta* 3.9.141-4)

Śrī Rāmacandra Purī

vibhīṣaṇo yaḥ prāg āsīd rāmacandra-purī smṛtaḥ
uvācāto gaura harir naitad rāmasya kāraṇam
jaṭilā rādhikā-śvaśrūḥ kāryato 'viśad eva tam
ato mahāprabhur bhikṣā-saṅkocādi tato 'karot

"Rāmacandra's dear devotee Vibhīṣaṇa appeared as Rāmacandra Purī. Rādhārāṇī's mother-in-law, Jaṭilā, also entered into him for certain special purposes. On account of him, Mahāprabhu reduced his food consumption." (*Gaura-gaṇoddeśa-dīpikā* 92-3)

taṁ vande kṛṣṇa-caitanyaṁ
rāmacandra-purī-bhayāt
laukikāhārataḥ svaṁ yo
bhikṣānnaṁ samakocayat

"I offer my prayers to Śrī Kṛṣṇa Caitanya, who out of fear of Rāmacandra Purī reduced His eating." (*Caitanya Caritāmṛta* 3.8.1)

RĀMACANDRA PURĪ AS COUNTER-EXAMPLE

Before discussing the character of Rāmacandra Purī, we must remember that the lessons of his life are taught as counter-examples. Anyone who seeks the perfection of his own life should bear in mind that the following lessons are to be learnt from Rāmacandra's actions:

(1) Faultfinding, especially finding fault in Viṣṇu and the Vaiṣṇavas, is extremely detrimental to one's spiritual advancement. A devotional practitioner should look at his own faults rather than at others'. By correcting his own faults, he will be able to make advancement. Anyone who sincerely seeks to achieve pure devotional service should always remember the following teaching of Mahāprabhu to Rūpa Gosvāmī:

"If the maddened elephant of Vaiṣṇava *aparādha* enters the devotional garden, the creeper of *bhakti* will be uprooted and all its leaves will dry up." (*Caitanya Caritāmṛta* 2.19.156)

(2) All the disciples who take initiation from the same guru are not to be considered

equal. Though superficially all may have taken shelter of the spiritual master and received the *mantra* from him, they cannot all be considered true or sincere disciples. The spiritual master rewards the disciple who dedicates himself to affectionate service of the master; such a disciple is furthermore able to recognize the mercy of his spiritual master. A disciple seeking his own perfection will bear in mind that of the sixty-four limbs of devotional service, one of the most important is *viśrambhena guroḥ sevā*, "the service of the spiritual master with firm faith and confidence." The sincere disciple recognizes that the spiritual master's instructions are beneficial both for himself and for others.

(3) To show disrespect to one's spiritual master and to other Vaiṣṇavas has a pernicious effect on one's spiritual life. One should remember that "the Lord cannot tolerate the transgression of the rules of etiquette." (*Caitanya Caritāmṛta* 3.4.166). Unfortunately, some conditioned souls come under the influence of the illusory energy and are so bewildered by a pride in their own knowledge or self-worth that they arrogantly try to correct or instruct the Vaiṣṇava or the guru.

(4) Those who want to progress in devotion should associate with and serve other devotees who are affectionate and who have similar spiritual goals. The tendency to serve Viṣṇu and the Vaiṣṇavas is increased by associating with those who possess this tendency in greater quantities.

(5) Because of his relation to the guru, the guru's godbrother is as worshipable as the guru himself. One must always show him the proper respect. Even if one thinks that his instructions are not correct, one should not be impolite in one's behavior and should not use direct critical speech with him. Mahāprabhu taught this kind of behavior by His own actions.

gorāra āmi, gorāra āmi mukhe balile nāhi cale
gorāra ācāra gorāra vicāra laile phala phale

"Just to repeat 'I belong to Gaura, I belong to Gaura' is not in itself sufficient. One has to follow the practice and the teachings given by Gaura if one wishes to achieve the promised results." (*Prema-vivarta*)

RĀMACANDRA CRITICIZES JAGADĀNANDA PAṆḌITA

Rāmacandra Purī's family background and birthplace are unknown. It is well known that he took initiation from Mādhavendra Purī. Kṛṣṇadāsa Kavirāja Gosvāmī has related his life in the *Antya-līlā* of *Caitanya Caritāmṛta*. Because he was Mādhavendra Purī's initiated disciple, both Mahāprabhu and Paramānanda Purī showed him respect. Nevertheless, despite his relationship to the distinguished master, Rāmacandra Purī associated closely with others who followed the path of dry knowledge and was attracted to doctrines opposed to those of pure devotional service.

One day, in Purushottama dhama, Jagadānanda Paṇḍita saw the Lord, Paramānanda Purī and Rāmacandra Purī paying obeisances to each other, embracing each other and engaging in conversation. He decided to invite the three of them to eat a meal together. He arranged for copious amounts of Lord Jagannātha *prasāda* to be brought for them and fed them very well. When they had finished, Rāmacandra Purī told Jagadānanda Paṇḍita to sit down and take *prasāda*. He took special care of him, personally serving him *prasāda*. After Jagadānanda Paṇḍita had finished eating, however, Rāmacandra Purī criticized Mahāprabhu's followers saying:

"I had heard that Caitanya's followers were big eaters. Now I have seen with my own eyes that this is true. To feed a *sannyāsī* excessively leads to the destruction of religious principles. A renunciate who eats this much will find that his vows will dissipate." (*Caitanya Caritāmṛta* 3.8.15-16)

HOW RĀMACANDRA BECAME A FAULTFINDER

This propensity to find fault with others, to criticize and to give instructions in dry philosophy was the result of offenses Rāmacandra Purī had committed at the feet of his spiritual master. Towards the fag end of Mādhavendra Purī's earthly pastimes in Remuna, he was in the depth of separation from Kṛṣṇa and was crying in the mood of Rādhā after Kṛṣṇa's departure for Mathura. He kept repeating the verse

ayi dīna-dayārdra nātha he
maṭhurā-nātha kadāvalokyase
hṛdayaṁ tvad-aloka-kātaraṁ dayita
bhrāmyati kiṁ karomy aham

"O Lord, whose heart softens at seeing the condition of the unfortunate! O Lord of Mathura, when will I see You? My heart is filled with pain from not seeing You, o My love, and is confused. What can I do?"

Both Īśvara Purī and Rāmacandra Purī were present at this time. Rāmacandra Purī had no understanding of his spiritual master's mood and, treating him like an ordinary human being, arrogantly began to give him instruction. He said, "Remember that you are completely full of the bliss of Brahman. Why are you crying like this despite being knowledgeable of your own Brahma-nature?"

When Mādhavendra Purī heard these words so full of ignorance and effrontery, he became angry and began to rebuke Rāmacandra, saying:

"Get away from me, you most sinful rascal! I am dying from the distress of not having received Kṛṣṇa's mercy, of not having attained Mathura, and you come to add to my misery! Don't show your face again. Go wherever you like! If I see you while I am dying, I will take a lower birth. I am dying from the distress of not having attained Kṛṣṇa, and this lowly fool is teaching me about Brahman." (*Caitanya Caritāmṛta* 3.8.22-5)

As a result of his offenses, Mādhavendra Purī withdrew his blessings from Rāmacandra Purī, who thenceforth started to develop material desires. He became a dry philosopher without any interest in Kṛṣṇa. Not only that, but he became critical of everyone, exclusively devoting himself to faultfinding.

In this connection, Śrīla Bhakti Siddhānta Sarasvatī Gosvāmī Ṭhākura has written, "Even though Rāmacandra Purī saw his own guru suffering of separation from Kṛṣṇa, he was incapable of recognizing the transcendental nature of this transport of emotions. He judged his guru to be an ordinary man and took his mood to be material, the result of some material insufficiency. As a result, he tried to explain to him the value of experiencing the oneness of Brahman. Mādhavendra Purī reacted to his disciple's stupidity and disregard for his instructions and thus stopped wishing for his well-being. He abandoned him and drove him away."

On the other hand, Īśvara Purī not only adhered to his guru's teaching but served him physically and thus received his mercy, thus becoming immersed in the love of Kṛṣṇa.

"Īśvara Purī received his spiritual master's mercy, while Rāmacandra Purī received his rebuke. For the edification of the world, these two served as examples of the guru's blessings and his punishment." (*Caitanya Caritāmṛta* 3.8.32)

RĀMACANDRA PURĪ FINDS FAULT WITH THE LORD HIMSELF

Deprived of his spiritual master's blessings, Rāmacandra Purī became a faultfinder and engaged himself constantly to find out where the *sannyāsīs* stayed, what their activities were, how much they ate, etc. He criticized those in the renounced order for eating sweet-meats, saying that it made it difficult to control the senses. Unable to appreciate the Lord's glories and thinking of Him as an ordinary man, Rāmacandra Purī concerned himself with gathering all sorts of information about His lodgings, His habits, how much He ate and slept and His comings and goings. Though his only goal was to find fault with the Lord, Rāmacandra Purī nevertheless came regularly to see Him. When they met, the Lord would offer him respectful obeisances, in virtue of his position as His spiritual master's godbrother.

One day Rāmacandra Purī came to Mahāprabhu's residence in the morning. On seeing many ants in the Lord's room, he began to criticize Him, saying, "Last night there was surely molasses in here. This is why there are so many ants. Alas, how sad to see such an attachment to sense gratification amongst those in the renounced order of life!"

Though ants quite naturally roam about everywhere, Mahāprabhu became apprehensive as a result of Rāmacandra Purī's accusations. He called Govinda and instructed him to reduce His daily consumption of *prasāda* to a particular proportion. He warned him that if Govinda brought Him more than this amount, He would leave Puri.

When the devotees heard about Mahāprabhu's reduction in *prasāda* consumption, they were thunderstruck. They condemned Rāmacandra Purī, and they themselves stopped eating. When Rāmacandra Purī heard that Mahāprabhu and His devotees had all reduced the amount of food they were taking, he went to see Him and impudently said:

"A *sannyāsī* is not supposed to gratify his senses. He should fill his belly with the bare minimum. I see that You have become thin. Indeed, I have heard that You have cut your eating in half. But this kind of dry renunciation is not the religion of a *sannyāsī*, either. A *sannyāsī* eats as much as is necessary to maintain his body, but without engaging in sense gratification. By so doing, he becomes perfect in the discipline of knowledge."

nātyaśnato 'pi yogo 'sti na caikāntam anaśnataḥ
na cātisvapnaśīlasya jāgrato naiva cārjuna
yuktāhāravihārasya yuktaceṣṭasya karmasu
yuktasvapnāvabodhasya yogo bhavati duḥkhahā

"O Arjuna, yoga practice is impossible for anyone who overeats, eats too little, sleeps too much, or sleeps too little. For a person who eats, relaxes and exerts himself in all duties in a regulated way, the practice of yoga brings about the end of all worldly suffering." (*Bhagavad-gītā* 6.16-17)

Mahāprabhu continued to show Rāmacandra Purī the same respect as before, however, and humbly submitted, "I am just like an ignorant boy, and it is My great fortune that you treat Me like your disciple and instruct Me. I will do my best to follow your instructions."

PARAMĀNANDA PURĪ TRIES TO INTERCEDE

In the meantime, Mahāprabhu heard that the devotees were eating only half as much as usual. Paramānanda Purī and some other devotees approached the Lord with great humility and submission and said, "Rāmacandra Purī is by nature a slanderer. It is not wise to give up eating on his say-so. It is his wont to make someone eat far more than he wants. Then he reproaches that person for overeating."

parasvabhāvakarmāṇi na praśaṁsen na garhayet
viśvam ekātmakaṁ paśyan prakṛtyā puruṣeṇa ca

"One should neither praise nor criticize the nature and activities of others because everything in the universe is a combination of the material nature and the living souls, and is thus controlled by one sole entity". (*Śrīmad Bhāgavatam* 11.28.1)

Śrīla Bhakti Siddhānta Sarasvatī Gosvāmī Ṭhākura comments on this verse by saying, "The abovementioned verse from *Śrīmad Bhāgavatam* gives two injunctions. The first, called *pūrva-vidhi*, is that one should not praise, and the second, *para-vidhi*, is that one should not criticize. It is generally said that the rule which is given later takes precedence over previously given injunctions. From this, we can understand that to praise someone is not so dangerous, while one should avoid calumny. Here, however, Rāmacandra Purī observed the injunction to avoid praising others but did not observe the prohibition against criticism. Thus he neglected the *para-vidhi* but strictly observed the *pūrva-vidhi*. This verse thus has an ironical meaning."

Paramānanda Purī continued: "Rāmacandra Purī does not praise even a person who has hundreds of good qualities; he rather finds some way of calling these qualities a fault. You should not give up eating properly because of his criticism; You should rather accept invitations as before."

Mahāprabhu replied, "There is no reason to get angry at Rāmacandra Purī. A *sannyāsī* should not be lusty after the pleasures of the tongue, but only eat in order to maintain the body."

When the devotees continued to press the Lord, He finally responded to their request by accepting half of the original amount of *prasāda* (rather than a quarter as He was then doing).

"When a *brāhmaṇa* at whose home an invitation could not be accepted invited the Lord, he would pay two *paṇas* of conch shells to purchase the *prasāda*. When a *brāhmaṇa* at whose home an invitation could be accepted invited him, the *brāhmaṇa* would purchase part of the *prasāda* and cook the rest at home." (*Caitanya Caritāmṛta* 3.8.89-90)

RĀMACANDRA LEAVES PURI

At the invitation of Gadādhara Paṇḍita, Bhagavān Ācārya or Sārvabhauma Bhaṭṭācārya on their scheduled date Mahāprabhu would eat as much as they served Him, without any hesitation.

Mahāprabhu sometimes treated Rāmacandra Purī according to worldly etiquette, and sometimes He would ignore him as though he were of no more significance than straw. All the Lord's activities are auspicious and beautiful, in all times and circumstances.

"Sometimes the Lord acted almost like a servant to Rāmacandra Purī. At other times, He treated him like straw. The Lord's activities are beyond human comprehension. Whatever He does, to whomever, is always enchanting." (*Caitanya Caritāmṛta* 3.8.94-5)

Rāmacandra Purī stayed in Jagannatha Puri for some time before departing on pilgrimage. When he left, the devotees felt extremely happy, as if a great load of stones had suddenly been taken from their heads and fallen to the ground. Mahāprabhu once again began to accept invitations as before, and the devotees were able to serve Him without hindrance.

"This is the result of being rejected by one's spiritual master. Eventually, the offense reaches as far as the Supreme Personality of Godhead. Even though the Lord did not consider the offenses of Rāmacandra Purī, considering him to be a senior, through his behavior He instructed everyone about the result of offending the spiritual master." (*Caitanya Caritāmṛta* 3.8.99-100)

MAHĀPRABHU STAYS WITH RĀMACANDRA PURĪ IN BENARES

Vṛndāvana Dāsa Ṭhākura has mentioned that Mahāprabhu hid in Rāmacandra Purī's house in Benares.

"Mahāprabhu remained hidden for two months in Rāmacandra Purī's *maṭha*." (*Caitanya Bhāgavata* 2.19.105)

Śrīla Bhakti Siddhānta Sarasvatī Gosvāmī Ṭhākura writes in his *Gauḍīya-bhāṣya*, "Gaurasundara stayed in the house of Candraśekhara while in Benares. Candraśekhara was a *śūdra* of the *vaidya* caste. Vṛndāvana Dāsa Ṭhākura says that He stayed with Rāmacandra Purī, who is known as a pretentious disciple of Mādhavendra Purī and had a strong preference for the Māyāvāda philosophy. He told people in Benares that He was staying with Rāmacandra Purī while in fact He preferred to spend His time with devotees. Rāmacandra Purī was a *sannyāsī* in one of the ten Śaṅkarite orders; therefore Mahāprabhu stayed with Him to avoid criticism from the nondevotees."

Śrīla Lokanātha Gosvāmī & Bhūgarbha Gosvāmī

lokanāthākhya-gosvāmī śrī-līlā-mañjarī purā

"Lokanātha Gosvāmī was known as Līlā Mañjarī in Kṛṣṇa *līlā*." (*Gaura-gaṇoddeśa-dīpikā* 187)

Lokanātha Gosvāmī is considered to be Mahāprabhu's direct disciple and associate. Prior to coming to Nabadwip, he lived in the village of Talkhori in the Jessore district of present-day Bangladesh. Prior to that, he resided in Kanchna Para. His father's name was Padmanābha Cakravartī, and his mother was Sītā Devī. This is confirmed by the *Bhakti-ratnākara*:

srīmad-rādhā-vinodaika-
sevā-sampat-samanvitam
padmanābha-ātmajaṁ śrīmal-
lokanātha-prabhuṁ bhaje

"I worship Lokanātha Prabhu, the son of Padmanābha, whose life revolved around the wealth of service of his deity Rādhāvinoda." (*Bhakti-ratnākara* 1.297)

The descendants of Lokanātha Gosvāmī's brother Pragalbha Bhaṭṭācārya are still living in Talkhori. Bhūgarbha Gosvāmī was Lokanātha Gosvāmī's closest friend and constant companion. He was Prema Mañjarī in Vraja. (*Gaura-gaṇoddeśa-dīpikā* 187).

bhūgarbha-ṭhakurasyāsīt
pūrvākhyā prema-mañjarī

According to the *Sādhana-dīpikā*, Bhūgarbha Gosvāmī was Lokanātha Gosvāmī's paternal uncle. The *Śākhā-nirṇayāmṛta* adds the following comments on Bhūgarbha Gosvāmī:

gosvāminaṁ ca bhūgarbhaṁ
bhūgarbhotthaṁ suviśrutam
sadā mahāśayaṁ vande
kṛṣṇa-prema-pradaṁ prabhum

śrīla-govinda-devasya
sevā-sukha-vilāsinam
dayāluṁ premadaṁ svacchaṁ
nityam ānanda-vigraham

"I offer my reverence to the illustrious Bhūgarbha Prabhu, who was said to be born from the bowels of the earth. He bestows love of Kṛṣṇa; he takes pleasure in the service of Govinda Deva, is compassionate, simple and always joyful."

Bhūgarbha Gosvāmī's initiating guru was Gadādhara Paṇḍita Gosvāmī. He is therefore considered to be Gadādhara's branch of the Caitanya tree. Śrī Bhāgavata Dāsa, a fellow disciple of Śrīla Gadādhara Paṇḍita Gosvāmī, was his close friend.

"Bhūgarbha Gosvāmī and Bhāgavata Dāsa are branches of Gadādhara Paṇḍita. Both of them went to live in Vrindavan." (*Caitanya Caritāmṛta* 1.12.81)

LOKANĀTHA GOSVĀMĪ AND BHŪGARBHA GOSVĀMĪ GO TO VRAJA

Lokanātha Gosvāmī renounced the householder *āśrama* in 1510 (1431 of the Śaka era) and came to meet Mahāprabhu in Nabadwip. Mahāprabhu immediately told him to go and live in Vrindavan, telling him that it was His own intention to take *sannyāsa* very shortly and go there Himself. Lokanātha Gosvāmī started to cry when he imagined the Lord with His beautiful curly hair shorn and the distress the devotees would feel at His *sannyāsa*. When the Lord saw Lokanātha Gosvāmī's anxiety, He embraced him and consoled him with His mystical words, and Lokanātha Gosvāmī surrendered completely to Him. When Bhūgarbha Gosvāmī saw how unhappy Lokanātha Gosvāmī was, he decided to accompany him to Vrindavan. The two companions walked through Rajmahal, Tajpur, Purnia, Ayodhya, Lucknow and many holy places before finally arriving in Vraja.

Though he had come to Vrindavan on Mahāprabhu's order, Lokanātha Gosvāmī constantly felt intense separation from the Lord, and shed copious tears in his desire to see Him again. When he received the news that Mahāprabhu had taken *sannyāsa* and gone to Puri and from there to the South on pilgrimage, Lokanātha Gosvāmī hurried to southern India in order to join Him. When he arrived in the south, he heard that Mahāprabhu was no longer there, but had gone to Vrindavan. Lokanātha Gosvāmī immediately set off for Vrindavan, hoping to see the Lord there, but by the time he arrived, he heard that the Lord had gone to Prayag. Disappointed, but still determined to see the Lord, Lokanātha Gosvāmī decided to set off again for Prayag.

This time, however, Mahāprabhu appeared to Lokanātha Gosvāmī and in a dream and told him to stop moving about and remain in Vrindavan to perform his *bhajana*. Not long afterwards, Rūpa Gosvāmī, Sanātana Gosvāmī, Gopāla Bhaṭṭa Gosvāmī and other of the Lord's associates started coming to live in Vraja. Their association brought Lokanātha Gosvāmī immense joy.

When Rūpa Gosvāmī was getting old, he found it difficult to walk all the way to Govardhan to take *darśana* of Gopāla. Seeing his intense desire, Gopāla came to stay at the house of Viṭṭhaleśvara in Mathura, ostensibly out of fear of Muslim iconoclasts, but actually to show His mercy to Rūpa Gosvāmī. The deity stayed there for a month, during which time Rūpa Gosvāmī came for His *darśana* with Lokanātha Gosvāmī and other Gauḍīya Vaiṣṇavas.

The extent to which Bhūgarbha Gosvāmī was dear to Lokanātha Gosvāmī is described in *Bhakti-ratnākara*:

"Lokanātha Gosvāmī's affection for Bhūgarbha Gosvāmī was well known everywhere. They only had different bodies, in spirit they were one." (*Bhakti-ratnākara* 1.317)

"Gopāla Bhaṭṭa Gosvāmī was extremely compassionate. Bhūgarbha Gosvāmī and Lokanātha Gosvāmī are a goldmine of virtues." (*Bhakti-ratnākara* 6.510)

Lokanātha Gosvāmī worshipped Rādhā and Kṛṣṇa in deep separation, and with extreme renunciation. He was afraid of the slightest amount of fame. Thus he forbade Kṛṣṇadāsa Kavirāja Gosvāmī to write anything about him in the *Caitanya Caritāmṛta*, with the result that nothing was written about him there other than his name. Sanātana Gosvāmī also mentioned his name in the *maṅgalācaraṇa* to the *Hari-bhakti-vilāsa*, as well as in his *Vaiṣṇava-toṣaṇī* commentary to the Tenth Canto of the *Śrīmad Bhāgavatam*.

vṛndāvana-priyān vande śrī-govinda-padāśritān
śrīmat-kāśīśvaraṁ lokanāthaṁ śrī-kṛṣṇa-dāsakam

"I pay obeisance to Kāśīśvara Paṇḍita, Lokanātha Gosvāmī and Kṛṣṇadāsa Kavirāja Gosvāmī, who have taken shelter of Lord Govinda's lotus feet and to whom residence in Vrindavan is very dear."

LOKANĀTHA GOSVĀMĪ AND RĀDHĀVINODA

Lokanātha Gosvāmī constantly traveled throughout Vraja, ecstatically visiting the various holy places where Kṛṣṇa had engaged in His pastimes. Once, he went to Khadiravan. Then he visited Kishori Kunda, near the village of Umarao by Chatravan. He stayed there for some time to do his *bhajana* in isolation. He developed a deep desire to worship Rādhā and Kṛṣṇa in their deity form.

The Lord knows the desires of His devotees and feels Himself obliged to fulfill them. He came personally to give Lokanātha Gosvāmī a deity, telling him before disappearing that its name was Rādhāvinoda.

Lokanātha Gosvāmī was astonished at seeing the appearance of the deity and started to wonder who gave him the deity. Rādhāvinoda cast His sweet glance on Lokanātha Gosvāmī and said to him, "I have been living in this village of Umarao on the banks of Kishori Kunda. I saw your eagerness to serve Me, and so I came here on My own. Who else but Me could have brought Me to you? I am very hungry. Quickly prepare something for Me to eat."

When Lokanātha Gosvāmī heard these words, tears began to flow from his eyes. He quickly started cooking for Rādhāvinoda and then made an offering that the deity ate with great satisfaction. Lokanātha Gosvāmī then made Rādhāvinoda a bed of flowers upon which he placed Him, fanned Him with branches and joyfully massaged His feet. Lokanātha Gosvāmī devoted himself to Rādhāvinoda in body, mind and soul.

Lokanātha Gosvāmī wondered where he would keep his deity, as he was constantly wandering through the land of Vraja. Finally, he decided to make a large bag which he made into Rādhāvinoda's temple. Wearing the bag around his neck, he was able to keep his worshipable deity close to his heart like a necklace. When they saw the affectionate relationship between Lokanātha Gosvāmī and his Lord, the people of Vraja were attracted to him and asked if they could build a house for him and Rādhāvinoda, but Lokanātha Gosvāmī refused. His spirit of renunciation was so strong that he declined to accept anything but what he absolutely needed for the deity's service.

NAROTTAMA DĀSA BECOMES LOKANĀTHA GOSVĀMĪ'S DISCIPLE

After spending some time at Kishori Kunda, Lokanātha Gosvāmī came to Vrindavan. He learned that Rūpa Gosvāmī and Sanātana Gosvāmī had ended their pastimes in this world and lamented their departure in great sadness. At around this time, Narottama Dāsa, who was the son of Rāja Kṛṣṇānanda Datta of Gopalpur in Rajshahi (now in Bangladesh), came to Vrindavan and met him there.

Many years earlier, Nityānanda Prabhu cried in divine ecstasy on His way to Nilachal. Mahāprabhu stored this divine love with the Padmāvatī River for Narottama Ṭhākura's benefit. Since then, the place has come to be known as Prematali. Years later, when Narottama Ṭhākura took his bath in the river at Prematali, he was immediately overcome with *prema* and was inspired to cut off all family ties and go to Vrindavan.

Upon his arrival in Vraja, Narottama Ṭhākura received the grace of Rūpa Gosvāmī, Sanātana Gosvāmī and Lokanātha Gosvāmī. He received Lokanātha Gosvāmī's special mercy, for he became his one and only disciple. Lokanātha Gosvāmī was extremely renounced and had made a vow not to accept any disciples. But Narottama Dāsa also made a vow – to take initiation from no one other than Lokanātha Gosvāmī. Narottama Ṭhākura repeatedly asked Lokanātha Gosvāmī to give him initiation, but Lokanātha Gosvāmī was firm in his refusal. In order to win his favor, Narottama Ṭhākura went in the middle of the night to clean the area he used as a toilet. Lokanātha Gosvāmī was so surprised to see that the place was being kept clean and free from the bad odor that he became curious to find out who was doing this service. One night, he went and hid there in some bushes, chanting *japa* the entire night.

At midnight, Lokanātha Gosvāmī saw someone come and begin cleaning the place. When he saw who it was, Lokanātha Gosvāmī was astonished that Narottama Ṭhākura, the son of a king, was engaged in doing such a filthy task. He felt embarrassed and asked him what his purpose was in doing it. Narottama Ṭhākura immediately began to cry. He fell at Lokanātha Gosvāmī's feet and said, "My life is useless unless I obtain your mercy." When Lokanātha Gosvāmī saw Narottama Ṭhākura's humility and pain, his resolve to never give anyone initiation softened and he imparted *mantras* to him.

This is a perfect example of how one can win over the worshipable deity through honest and selfless service. Narottama Dāsa took initiation from Lokanātha Gosvāmī on the full-moon day of the month of Śrāvaṇa. Since then Narottama Ṭhākura was engaged in selfless and sincere service to Lokanātha Gosvāmī. However, for the benefit of the entire world, and especially to the people of northern Bengal, Lokanātha Gosvāmī sent Narottama Ṭhākura for preaching there.

Lokanātha Gosvāmī was a much renounced Vaiṣṇava, but he saw in Narottama Ṭhākura someone who not only had a cultured background but an enthusiasm and taste for dealing with people. As a result, he asked him to go back to his homeland to preach Kṛṣṇa consciousness.

When one has taken full shelter of the Supreme Lord and is situated on the transcendental platform in full service to the Lord, then he has no enthusiasm for engaging in activities for the welfare of people on the bodily platform. When a devotee of Narottama Dāsa's caliber goes against this principle, then such activities themselves are honored, and they increase in prestige. So Narottama Ṭhākura returned to northern Bengal on the order of his spiritual master and began to preach pure devotional service and thus delivered the people of his homeland.

In his collection of songs known as *Prārthanā*, Narottama Dāsa Ṭhākura has written:

aneka-duḥkhera pare, layechile vraja-pure
kṛpa-ḍore galāya bāndhiyā
daiva-māyā-balātkāre, khasāiyā sei ḍore
bhava-kūpe kileka ḍāriyā

"After suffering much sadness, O Lord, You brought me to Vraja, pulling me by the rope of mercy, which You had tied around my neck. Māyā and fate forced me back into the well of material existence by cutting loose that rope of mercy."

Lokanātha Gosvāmī left this world somewhere around 1510 Śaka (1589 A.D.) on the eighth day of the dark moon in the month of Āṣāḍha. His *samādhi* tomb is found in the Rādhā Gokulananda temple in Vrindavan. His beloved Rādhāvinoda deity continues to be served in the same temple.

Śrī Subuddhi Rāya

Nothing is known about Subuddi Rāya's birthplace or his parents other than that he was born in a *brāhmaṇa* family and was well known for his scholarship. His life is memorable because he received Mahāprabhu's association and special blessings. In the first part of his life, he briefly took the position as the King of Gauḍa-deśa.[19]

"Formerly when Subuddhi Rāya was a big landowner of Gauda, Hussain Khān Sayyid worked for him." (*Caitanya Caritāmṛta* 2.25.180).

Subuddhi Rāya put Hussain Khān in charge of digging a big pond, but when Hussain made some mistakes, he had him whipped as a

19 According to Āśutoṣa Deva's Bengali dictionary, Gauda was the name of the ancient capital of Bengal in the Malda district, from which the entire Bengali kingdom took its name. On the other hand, in *Gauḍīya-vaiṣṇava-abhidhāna* it is written that, according to the *Skanda Purāṇa*, there were five Gaudas (*pancha-gauda*), by which were meant the kingdoms of Sarasvata, Kanyakubja (Kanauj), Utkala (Odisha), Maithila and Bengal, but that the name was primarily used for the region lying between East Bengal (Baṅga) and Mithila. Vijaya Sen of Karnataka became the King of Gauda, and his descendants were known as *gaudesvara*. Vijaya Sen's son Ballala Sena established the city of Gauda on the banks of the Ganges. The course of the Ganges has since moved. At one time, all western Bengalis were known as Gaudiyas, but the name has become synonymous with Vaiṣṇavas who follow Caitanya Mahāprabhu.

punishment. By the twists and turns of fate, Hussain Khān (Hussain Shah) himself became King of Gauda. Nevertheless, even after becoming king, he continued to treat Subuddhi Rāya with a great deal of respect because of the help he had received from him in the past. The Shah never resented the flogging he had received from Subuddhi Rāya, but even so, the scars remained on his body.

One day Hussain Shah's Queen saw them and asked where they had come from. When the King told his wife the story, she became angry and urged her husband to punish Subuddhi Rāya by putting him to death. Hussain Shah refused to go to such extremes, and so his wife suggested that he punish him by bringing about his caste destruction. The King refused to do this because he knew that doing so would be tantamount to killing him. His wife insisted, however, even threatening to kill herself if he did not do something. Finally, the Shah was obliged to give in to his wife, and he gave Subuddhi Rāya water to drink, which according to the Hindu rules of the time meant that he lost his caste status.

Even prior to these events Subuddhi Rāya had become completely detached from material life. He took this opportunity to leave his home and family and live in Benares. There he inquired from the *smārta brāhmaṇas* how to go about atoning for the loss of caste status. They told him that he should commit suicide by drinking boiling ghee. In the *Gauḍīya Vaiṣṇava Abhidhāna*, it is said that it was common to be told to atone by jumping into a fire of chaff, a fire that is not easily extinguished. Others, however, objected saying that such a heavy punishment did not fit the minor nature of the offense. This difference of opinion amongst the *brāhmaṇas* made Subuddhi Rāya sceptical.

Sometime later, when Mahāprabhu came to Benares, Subuddhi Rāya came to see Him and recounted the whole story from beginning to end. The Lord recommended that he go to Vrindavan and chant the names of Kṛṣṇa. The Lord said, "Leave this place and go to Vrindavan. Chant the Holy Names of Kṛṣṇa constantly. The mere glow of the Holy Name will destroy all sins you may have committed. And if you go on chanting, you will attain Kṛṣṇa's lotus feet. Chanting of the Holy Name is the highest atonement." (*Caitanya Caritāmṛta* 2.25.191-3)

On the Lord's order, Subuddhi Rāya set off for Vrindavan, stopping in Prayag, Ayodhya and Naimisharanya, where he stayed for some time. When he finally arrived in Mathura, he learned that the Lord had already left for Prayag and that he had missed Him. In distress and separation, Subuddhi Rāya took up a life of intense renunciation. He made his living by gathering dry wood from the jungle and selling it in Mathura. He subsisted on the little money that he made from this work, eating only dried chickpeas to maintain his body. Even so, he was able to put some money aside, which he used for serving the Bengali Vaiṣṇavas, feeding them with rice and yogurt.

"Subuddhi Rāya gathered dry wood and sold it in Maṭhura, receiving five or six *paisa* (one rupee = 100 *paisa*) for each load. By eating dried chickpeas, he spent only one *paisa* for food. The rest of the money was kept with a businessman. Whenever he saw Vaiṣṇavas in distress, he would feed them, and when Gauḍīya Vaiṣṇavas arrived in town, he would provide them with rice, yogurt and mustard oil for rubbing on the body." (*Caitanya Caritāmṛta* 2.25.197-9)

Rūpa Gosvāmī was extremely happy when he saw Subuddhi Rāya's renunciation and service to the Vaiṣṇavas. Rūpa Gosvāmī took Subuddhi Rāya with him to visit all the holy sites in Vraja Maṇḍala. (*Caitanya Caritāmṛta*

2.25.207) It is clear from this that service to the Vaiṣṇavas is not restricted to the very rich. Even a poor person will find the means to serve Viṣṇu and the Vaiṣṇavas if he has a sincere desire to do so. By the will of the Lord, he will never have any shortage of means to do so. This is the example set by Subuddhi Rāya's holy life.

When Sanātana Gosvāmī walked from Benares to Mathura, he took the main road from Prayag. The Lord took the road by the banks of the Ganges when He left Vrindavan. In the meantime, Rūpa Gosvāmī and Anupama had taken the same road as the Lord from Prayag. When Sanātana Gosvāmī arrived in Mathura, he learned from Subuddhi Rāya that he had missed all the three of them – Mahāprabhu, Rūpa Gosvāmī and Anupama – which distressed him. Subuddhi Rāya showed a great deal of affection for Sanātana Gosvāmī, as he had known him in his previous life as a government minister. Subuddhi Rāya wanted to serve him, but Sanātana Gosvāmī was too humble to accept his service.

Subuddhi Rāya spent the rest of his life in Vrindavan in the company of the Gosvāmīs, following the order of the Lord by chanting the Holy Names with great faith and living a life of great renunciation. The date of his disappearance is unknown.

Śrīla Rūpa Gosvāmī

śrī-rūpa-mañjarī khyātā yāsīd vṛndāvane purā
sādya rūpākhya-gosvāmī bhūtvā prakaṭatām iyāt

"She who was known in Vrindavan as Rūpa Mañjarī has now appeared as Rūpa Gosvāmī." (*Gaura-gaṇoddeśa-dīpikā* 180)

Lalitā is chief amongst the *sakhīs* who make up Rādhārāṇī's entourage, and Rūpa Mañjarī is the foremost amongst those *sakhīs* who follow Lalitā. It is for this reason that Rūpa Gosvāmī is the chief amongst the six Gosvāmīs in Gaura *līlā*.

RŪPA GOSVĀMĪ'S FAMILY TREE

In the new Bengali dictionary edited by Āśutoṣa Deva, Rūpa Gosvāmī's dates are given as 1489-1558 A.D. or 1410-1479 of the Śaka era. In his earthly pastimes, Rūpa Gosvāmī appeared in a *brāhmaṇa* family of the Bharadvāja *gotra* which hailed from Karnataka, where they had been kings. His father's name was Kumāra Deva. His mother's name is not known. Narahari Cakravartī Ṭhākura has given the names of seven generations of his family in *Bhakti-ratnākara* (1.540-568).

Śrīla Bhakti Siddhānta Sarasvatī Gosvāmī Ṭhākura has summarized this family history in his *Anubhāṣya*: "Sarvajña, a *jagad-guru*, was a great soul who was born in a *brāhmaṇa rājā* family of the Bharadvāja *gotra* in the twelfth century of the Śaka era. His son Aniruddha had two sons, named Rupeśvara and Harihara, neither of whom inherited the land holdings. The older brother Rupeśvara went to live in the mountains, and his son Padmanābha moved to Bengal, taking up residence in the village of Naihati on the banks of the Ganges. Padmanābha had five sons, the youngest of whom was named Mukunda, who fathered the pious Kumāradeva, who had several sons, amongst whom were Sanātana Gosvāmī, Rūpa Gosvāmī and Anupama. Kumāradeva's house was in the village of Bakla in Chandradwip.[20]

20 Chandradwip was the ancient name of a kingdom which now lies in Bangladesh. It included Faridpur, Bakhar Ganj and the southern parts of the Dhaka and Pabna districts.

His house was in the village of Fatehabad in the Jessore district of that time. Three of his sons became Vaiṣṇavas. These three brothers left the Fatehabad home to live in Ramakeli for their work. Jīva Gosvāmī was born there. As a result of their service to the Nawab, all three of them were awarded the Mallika title. Mahāprabhu met Anupama for the first time when He came to Ramakeli. When Rūpa Gosvāmī abandoned his government duties to go to Vrindavan, he was accompanied by Anupama, who was also known as Vallabha." (*Caitanya Caritāmṛta* 1.10.84 *Anubhāṣya*)

RŪPA GOSVĀMĪ'S FIRST MEETING WITH THE LORD

Mahāprabhu met Rūpa Gosvāmī and Sanātana Gosvāmī for the first time beneath *kadamba* and *tamal* trees in Ramakeli village. Rūpa Gosvāmī had a large pond excavated that still exists, named Rupa-sagara. The three brothers were engaged in the service of the contemporary King of Gauḍa, Hussain Shah. Sanātana Gosvāmī was his prime minister, with the title Sākara Mallika, while Rūpa Gosvāmī was also an important minister with the title Dabira Khāsa. We have an indication of this from the *Caitanya Caritāmṛta*, where the Shah addresses him with this title.

When Mahāprabhu arrived at Ramakeli surrounded by countless Hindus, with some concern the Shah summoned Rūpa Gosvāmī to ask him who Mahāprabhu was. Rūpa Gosvāmī glorified Mahāprabhu in such a diplomatic way that the Shah's mind was put at ease.

"The King made private inquiries from Dabira Khāsa, who told him of Mahāprabhu's glories." (*Caitanya Caritāmṛta* 2.1.175)

Vṛndāvana Dāsa Ṭhākura also confirms definitively in the *Caitanya Bhāgavata* that Rūpa Gosvāmī and Sanātana Gosvāmī were named Dabira Khāsa and Sākara Mallika respectively.

In the *Antya-khaṇḍa*, the Lord revealed His divinity to Dabira Khāsa and Sākara Mallika and, recognizing their greatness, released them from their bondage. He then named them Rūpa and Sanātana. (*Caitanya Bhāgavata* 1.2.171-2)

"Then, two great fortunate souls came to the spot where the Lord was. The two brothers were named Sākara Mallika and Rūpa. The Lord looked upon them with compassionate eyes." (*Caitanya Bhāgavata* 3.9.238-9)

Rūpa Gosvāmī and Sanātana Gosvāmī were eternal participants in Kṛṣṇa *līlā*. When the time for them to make their contribution to Gaura *līlā*, Mahāprabhu and His associates arrived in their home village. While performing their earthly pastimes, the Lord and His devotees make an effort to keep their transcendental natures concealed to facilitate spreading of their teachings to the people in this world; however, when they come close to one another, their actual identity could not remain concealed. Thus, as soon as Rūpa Gosvāmī and Sanātana Gosvāmī saw Mahāprabhu, though they were naturally attracted to Him, they behaved in the manner of conditioned souls in order to show the people of this world how to act.

When the Muslim king heard that Mahāprabhu had come to Ramakeli with a company of thousands of Hindus, he was frightened and suspected Mahāprabhu of having a political purpose. A certain Keśava of the *kṣatriya* caste who knew about the Lord explained to the Shah, "He is just a *sannyāsī*, a beggar who is out on pilgrimage. A few people are accompanying Him, but there is no need to be alarmed." The Shah also consulted Rūpa Gosvāmī, who told him of Mahāprabhu's glories and succeeded in calming his fears.

Being desirous of meeting the Lord themselves, Rūpa Gosvāmī and Sanātana Gosvāmī left the palace in the middle of the night and came to Ramakeli. They first encountered Nityānanda Prabhu and Haridāsa Ṭhākura, who brought the two brothers into the presence of the Lord. Rūpa Gosvāmī and Sanātana Gosvāmī placed some grass in their mouths and wrapped cloth around their necks as a sign of humility. They fell down at the Lord's lotus feet and, with tears in their eyes, made the following humble submission:

"We are millions of times more degraded, fallen and sinful than Jagāi and Mādhāi. We have taken a wicked birth, we have become the servants of Muslims and our activities are exactly like those of the Muslims. We constantly associate with people who are inimical toward the cows and *brāhmaṇas*. Due to our abominable activities, we are now bound by the neck and hands and have been thrown into a ditch filled with the excrement of evil sense enjoyment." (*Caitanya Caritāmṛta* 2.1.196-198)

When the Lord heard the extreme humility of the two brothers, He became compassionate. Even so, it is clear from His response to their statement that they were not ordinary conditioned souls, but His eternal associates.

" 'I really had no need to come to Bengal, but I came anyway just to see the two of you. No one knows My purpose, and so people ask Me why I have come to this village of Ramakeli. I am very glad that you have come to see Me. Now you can go home; do not fear anything. You have been My servants life after life, so Kṛṣṇa will deliver you very soon.' After saying this, the Lord placed His hands on the heads of Rūpa Gosvāmī and Sanātana Gosvāmī, and they immediately took the Lord's lotus feet and placed them on their heads." (*Caitanya Caritāmṛta* 2.1.212-6)

The Lord wished to teach that the conditioned soul is delivered by the mercy of the devotees, so He asked Nityānanda Prabhu, Haridāsa, Śrīvāsa, Gadādhara, Mukunda, Jagadānanda, Murāri, Vakreśvara and His other associates to bless the two brothers.

"Sanātana Prabhu then advised Mahāprabhu, 'Dear Lord, you are going to Vrindavan with an entourage of hundreds and thousands of people, and this is not a fitting way to go on a pilgrimage.' " (*Caitanya Caritāmṛta* 2.1.224) As a result of this advice, Mahāprabhu put off going to Vrindavan and turned back after going a little farther, as far as Kanair Natshala.

RŪPA GOSVĀMĪ RESIGNS FROM THE SHAH'S SERVICE

From this meeting at Ramakeli, it is evident that Mahāprabhu intended to teach the people of this world through Rūpa Gosvāmī and Sanātana Gosvāmī. Not long afterwards, an intense spirit of renunciation awakened in the two brothers and they started looking for a way to extricate themselves from their entanglement in the service of the king. They paid two *brāhmaṇas* a large sum of money to perform a *puraścaraṇa* of the Kṛṣṇa *mantra* on their behalf.[21]

---

21 Śrīla Prabhupāda comments: "A *puraścaraṇa* is a ritual performance which consists of worshipping the deity, chanting the *mantra*, offering oblations, performing a fire sacrifice, and feeding the *brāhmaṇas* every morning, noon and evening for a fixed period of time. This is performed for getting desired fruits from the *mantra*. Such performances are not necessary for the *mahā-mantra* of Holy Name, for by even uttering the holy name once one obtains all the results to be obtained from *puraścaraṇa*."

Śrīla Rūpa Gosvāmī finally resigned from his government service, and he deposited 10,000 coins with a grocer in the capital, Gauda, on behalf of his elder brother. Then he took the rest of their accumulated wealth with him in a boat to Bakla Chandradwip, where he divided it up, giving half to the *brāhmaṇas* and Vaiṣṇavas and a quarter for the maintenance of his family, while keeping the rest with a trustworthy *brāhmaṇa* against any future necessity. Then he sent two messengers to Puri to find out when Mahāprabhu intended to travel to Vrindavan by the jungle route through Jharikhand.

In the meantime, Sanātana Gosvāmī had stopped his duties in the court of the Shah. Though he claimed to be ill, he was in fact engaged in an intense study of the *Bhāgavata* with a group of scholars. The Shah first sent a doctor to examine Sanātana Gosvāmī and then, upon learning the truth of the matter, came himself to exhort him to return to work. When Sanātana Gosvāmī showed a continued reluctance to engage in his duties, the Shah had him put in prison. The king then departed to invade Odisha.

RŪPA GOSVĀMĪ MEETS MAHĀPRABHU IN PRAYAG

When Rūpa Gosvāmī received the news from his two messengers that Mahāprabhu had left for Vrindavan, he and Anupama left Bakla to attempt to join Him. He sent a letter to Sanātana Gosvāmī with this message, invoking him to take any necessary steps to free himself and then to come and join them. When Rūpa Gosvāmī arrived in Prayag, he learnt that Mahāprabhu was there at the house of a South Indian *brāhmaṇa*. When Rūpa Gosvāmī found Him there, he was overwhelmed with feelings of love for the Lord. He and Anupama placed straw between their teeth and repeatedly paid their prostrated obeisances to the Lord, chanting various verses of praise and humility. The Lord felt great affection for the two brothers and said, "Kṛṣṇa's mercy is beyond description, for He has delivered you from the blind well of sensual existence."

Mahāprabhu recited verses which stated that a devotee from a family of dog-eaters is dearer to the Lord than even a nondevotee *brāhmaṇa* who knows the four Vedas and that a devotee of the Lord is as worshipable as the Lord Himself. Then He showed His mercy by embracing them and placing His lotus feet on their heads. The two brothers folded their hands and chanted the following verse to show their gratitude to the Lord for His mercy toward them:

namo mahā-vadānyāya kṛṣṇa-prema-pradāya te
kṛṣṇāya kṛṣṇa-caitanya-nāmne gaura-tviṣe namaḥ

"I pay my innumerable obeisances to the lotus feet of the Supreme Lord, who is Kṛṣṇa Himself, whose name is Kṛṣṇa Caitanya, whose complexion is golden and who is most munificent by bestowing *kṛṣṇa-prema*, love for Kṛṣṇa."

Mahāprabhu heard from Rūpa Gosvāmī that his brother Sanātana Gosvāmī had been made prisoner by the king, but predicted that it would not be long before Sanātana Gosvāmī escaped and met Him. The South Indian *brāhmaṇa* invited the two brothers to stay with him that day, and they ate Mahāprabhu's *prasāda* remnants.

MEETING WITH VALLABHA BHAṬṬA

When Vallabha Bhaṭṭa, who lived in the village of Arail on the other side of the Ganges, heard that the Lord had come, he immediately rushed to Prayag to meet Him and fell to the ground in obeisance to Him. Mahāprabhu embraced him, and then the two engaged in conversation about Kṛṣṇa. Vallabha Bhaṭṭa was astonished to see the ecstatic reactions of the Lord in the course of their discussions.

As soon as Rūpa Gosvāmī and Anupama saw Vallabha Bhaṭṭa, they paid obeisances to him from a distance out of humility. When he came forward to touch them, they both reacted by saying, "We are lowly untouchables. You should not contaminate yourself by touching us." They then moved back a certain distance.

Mahāprabhu was pleased by their display of humility, while Vallabha Bhaṭṭa was impressed. The Lord said to Vallabha Bhaṭṭa, "You are an older, aristocratic *brāhmaṇa*, while these two belong to a low caste. You should certainly not touch them." Vallabha Bhaṭṭa was able to divine that there was some hidden meaning to the Lord's utterance, and he asked how they could be considered of a low caste when they chanted the name of Kṛṣṇa constantly.

Vallabha Bhaṭṭa then invited the Lord and His entourage to come to his house to take *prasāda*, and Mahāprabhu was happy to accept. They embarked on a boat, but as they crossed the confluence of the Yamuna and the Gaṅgā, Mahāprabhu was affected by the sight of the waters of the Yamuna and began to dance ecstatically in the boat, causing everyone on board a great deal of anxiety and fear. Finally, Mahāprabhu jumped into the Yamuna's waters and had to be helped on board by all the devotees.

Vallabha Bhaṭṭa took the Lord to his house, washed His feet and then sprinkled this water on his own head. Then he performed an elaborate *pūjā* of the Lord with a variety of ingredients. Then he fed Him with a great feast of numerous preparations and satisfied Rūpa Gosvāmī and Anupama with the Lord's remnants. He gave the Lord a mouth purifier and then a place to rest. When the Lord lay down, he sat beside Him and served Him by massaging His feet. In this way, Vallabha Bhaṭṭa considered himself to have attained the highest good fortune. The Lord told Vallabha to take something to eat himself.

During this time, Raghupati Upādhyāya, a *brāhmaṇa* from Tirhut, arrived there. The Lord was ecstatic to hear the devotional verses which Raghupati Upādhyāya had composed in glorification of Śrī Kṛṣṇa. Mahāprabhu asked him to say what was the Supreme Lord's superlative form, abode, age and last of all, what was the supreme object of worship. Raghupati answered:

"The form of Śyāmasundara is the Supreme form, the city of Mathura is the supreme abode, a meditation on Lord Kṛṣṇa's adolescent form is supreme, and love for Kṛṣṇa in the mood of the *gopīs* is the supreme sentiment." (*Padyāvalī*, 82)

Mahāprabhu was very pleased with this answer and embraced Raghupati Upādhyāya. All the inhabitants of the village became devotees of Kṛṣṇa upon seeing Mahāprabhu. Vallabha Bhaṭṭa then took the Lord back to Prayag by boat.

MAHĀPRABHU INSTRUCTS RŪPA GOSVĀMĪ

Afraid of attracting crowds, Mahāprabhu stayed only ten days in Prayag, remaining incognito at the Dashasvamedha Ghat. The Lord taught Rūpa Gosvāmī the truths about Kṛṣṇa, devotion to Him, and transcendental divine mellows, as well as all other devotional conclusions. He compassionately infused all the supreme sentiments of Vrindavan, which were slowly becoming extinct, into Rūpa Gosvāmī.

The teachings Mahāprabhu gave Rūpa Gosvāmī are known as *Śrī-rūpa-śikṣā*. Śivānanda Sena's son, Kavi Karṇapūra, has described this event extensively in his *Caitanya-candrodaya-nāṭaka*:

kālena vṛndāvana-keli-vārtā
lupteti tāṁ khyāpayituṁ viśiṣya
kṛpāmṛtenābhiṣiṣeca devas
tatraiva rūpaṁ ca sanātanaṁ ca

"In the course of time, tidings of Kṛṣṇa's amusements in Vrindavan had been lost. To make them known again in detail, the Lord drenched Rūpa Gosvāmī and Sanātana Gosvāmī with His mercy." (*Caitanya Caritāmṛta* 2.19.119)

priya-svarūpe dayita-svarūpe
prema-svarūpe sahajābhirūpe
nijānurūpe prabhur eka-rūpe
tatāna rūpe svavilāsarūpe

"The Lord explained the *rasa-śāstra* to Rūpa Gosvāmī in a way He did to no other person, for Rūpa Gosvāmī was the dear friend of Svarūpa Dāmodara, his true identity was that of the Lord's beloved, his nature was that of divine love itself, and he was also possessed of natural physical beauty. Mahāprabhu knew him to be like unto Himself, and indeed, he was verily the expansion of the Lord." (*Caitanya Caritāmṛta* 2.19.121)

ŚRĪ RŪPA-ŚIKṢA

Through Rūpa Gosvāmī, Mahāprabhu taught the world about Kṛṣṇa's Vrindavan pastimes and the process for attaining Vraja-*prema*. Kṛṣṇadāsa Kavirāja Gosvāmī writes, "Through the mercy of Sanātana Gosvāmī I have learnt the devotional doctrines, and by the grace of Rūpa Gosvāmī I have attained the sublime devotional sentiments." (*Caitanya Caritāmṛta* 1.5.203)

"The Lord taught about sacred rapture and Vraja's pastimes of transcendental divine love through Rūpa Gosvāmī. Who can effectively describe the subtleties of Śrī Caitanya Mahāprabhu's *līlā*?" (*Caitanya Caritāmṛta* 3.5.87)

vṛndāvanīyāṁ rasa-kelivārtāṁ
kālena luptaṁ nija-śaktim utkaḥ
sañcārya rūpe vyatanot punaḥ sa
prabhor vidhau prāg iva loka-sṛṣṭim

"Just as the Lord enlightened the heart of Lord Brahmā with the truths about His own self, so did Śrī Caitanya Mahāprabhu eagerly impregnate the heart of Rūpa Gosvāmī with spiritual potency so that he could revive Kṛṣṇa's Vrindavan pastimes, which had almost been lost to memory due to the influence of time." (*Caitanya Caritāmṛta* 2.19.1)

While in Prayag, Mahāprabhu gave Rūpa Gosvāmī the direct order to write *Bhakti-rasāmṛta-sindhu*. This has been stated by Rūpa Gosvāmī himself in the introductory verses to that book:

hṛdiryasya preraṇayā
pravartito 'haṁ varāka-rūpo 'pi
tasya hareḥ pada-kamalaṁ
vande caitanya-devasya

"I worship the lotus feet of the Supreme Personality of Godhead, known as Lord Caitanya-deva, for though I am nothing but an ignorant wretch, I have set out to write this book by His inspiration." (*Bhakti-rasāmṛta-sindhu* 1.1.2)

Particularly relevant in this connection is Śrīla Bhakti Siddhānta Sarasvatī Gosvāmī Ṭhākura Prabhupāda's *Anubhāṣya* (to *Caitanya Caritāmṛta* 2.19.131) on the importance of studying and writing books as an element of devotional practice: "The lives of the Gosvāmīs were exemplary in their renunciation. Sometimes they would engage in chanting the Holy Names of the Lord, sometimes they would worship Him by writing books on divine aesthetics (*bhakti-rasa-śāstra)*, and sometimes they would remember or glorify the pastimes of Lord Caitanya Mahāprabhu. There is an idea which has some currency amongst the *prākṛta sahajiyās* that devotional practice entails the renunciation of studying and writing devotional scriptures, and indeed scriptural discussions should be stopped for their pursuits, which are foolish by nature. Those who follow in the footsteps of Rūpa Gosvāmī have no tolerance to such ideas. However, if a devotional practitioner studies or writes devotional scriptures for the sake of making money through which to satisfy his material senses or attain material fame, respect or any of the other insignificant and superficial goals which are classed as distractions or weeds in the garden of devotional service, then he will not attain the auspicious results which are the real fruit of such activity. A real Rūpānugā (follower of Rūpa Gosvāmī) has no fruitive ambition for such petty results."

When Mahāprabhu was giving Rūpa Gosvāmī the prologue to the characteristics of the different mellows and instructed him how to get an iota of a taste of the fathomless ocean of sacred rapture, He pointed out how difficult it is to attain devotional service to Kṛṣṇa.

The *jīva*, or living entity, is an atomic spark of conscious energy. There are countless *jīvas*, who are divided into two categories – moving and nonmoving. Those that have mobility are again divided into three: those which move on the land, in the air or in the water. Amongst those who live on the land, a small number are human beings, of which only a minority accept the Vedic principles. Outcastes such as *pulindas, mlecchās, shabaras* and Buddhists are in the majority. Of those who accept the Vedas, some do so in name only and engage in sinful activity. Those who practice the Vedic principles are in the minority. Those who are engaged in religious practices toward some fruitive end form the majority in this group.

Amongst millions of such *karma-niṣṭha* followers of the Veda, one person may perhaps attain the level of spiritual knowledge; yet only one of many millions of such *jñanis* will be an actual liberated soul. And out of millions of liberated souls, it will still be difficult to find a devotee of Kṛṣṇa. Devotion to Kṛṣṇa, which is thus so rare, can take birth when a certain merit is attained through great good fortune.

The seed to the devotional creeper comes through the mercy of the Lord and His devotee. The creeper of spontaneous ecstatic devotion does not get shelter anywhere in this world or Virajā, not even in Vaikuṇṭha in the spiritual world, but only in Vrindavan at Kṛṣṇa's lotus feet. Kṛṣṇa's feet are like the wish-fulfilling tree around which the vine of devotion wraps itself and bears fruit. This is described in the clearest and most wonderful manner by Kṛṣṇadāsa Kavirāja Gosvāmī in *Caitanya Caritāmṛta:*

"After wandering through this entire universe, birth after birth, some fortunate souls receive the seed of devotion (*bhakti-latā-bīja)* by the mercy of Kṛṣṇa and the guru. Upon receiving the seed of devotional service, one should take care of it by becoming a gardener and sowing it in his heart. If he waters the seed regularly by the process of *śravaṇa* and *kīrtana* [hearing and chanting], the seed will begin to sprout. As one waters the *bhakti-latā-bīja,* the seed sprouts, and the creeper gradually increases to the point where it penetrates the walls of this universe and goes beyond the

Virajā River between the spiritual world and the material world. The creeper passes through the Brahmaloka, the Brahman effulgence, until it finally reaches the spiritual sky and the spiritual planet Goloka Vṛndāvana, where it takes shelter of the desire tree of the lotus feet of Kṛṣṇa. There the creeper expands greatly and produces the fruit of love for Kṛṣṇa, while the gardener continues to regularly sprinkle the creeper with the water of hearing and chanting here in the material world.

"An offense to the Vaiṣṇavas is like a mad elephant that uproots or breaks the creeper, causing its leaves to dry up. The gardener must, therefore, take care to protect the creeper by making a fence around it so that the elephant of offenses may not enter. Even so, unwanted creepers, such as the weeds of desire for material enjoyment or liberation from the world, may grow along with the creeper of devotional service. Such weeds are countless in their variety. Some examples are forbidden activity, faultfinding and duplicity, causing suffering to other creatures, and seeking wealth, adulation or mundane importance. All these weeds grow alongside the main creeper as one waters it, causing its growth to be curtailed. As soon the devotee sees one of these weeds growing beside the original creeper, he must cut it down instantly. Then the real *bhakti-latā* can grow nicely all the way to Vṛndāvana, where it will find shelter under the lotus feet of Kṛṣṇa." (*Caitanya Caritāmṛta* 2.19.151-61)

Śrīla Bhakti Siddhānta Sarasvatī Gosvāmī Ṭhākura has commented on this passage in his *Anubhāṣya*: "Through the act of watering the creeper of devotional service by hearing and chanting, weeds may also grow, which results in the growth of the *bhakti-latā* being stifled. If one does not avoid bad association, which is the only way to be free of offenses while hearing and chanting, then one becomes attached to sense gratification, the idea of liberation from material bondage, various mystic achievements, or the practice of deception.

"One may also become addicted to the illicit association of women, practice other manifestations of false devotion like the *prākrita sahajiyās*, or become a dweller of the five places given by Parīkṣit to Kālī, namely wherever there is gambling, intoxication, prostitution, animal slaughter or the accumulation of gold. He starts to take the Vaiṣṇavas to be members of a particular race or caste, aspires for honor due to birth in a respected higher caste, and engages in the chanting of Holy Name, *mantra*, deity worship and *Bhāgavata* recitation for making a livelihood. He finds dishonest ways of collecting money or makes a show of practicing spiritual life in seclusion while secretly harboring desires for fame and adulation. The desire for mundane reputation may result in his compromising the philosophy to draw a parallel between the material and transcendental planes, or becoming a supporter of the hereditary caste system by professing discipleship to a so-called guru who opposes Viṣṇu and the Vaiṣṇavas. The sum and substance of these aberrant paths is that one becomes intoxicated in the gratification of one's own senses in pursuit of these superficial and destructive ends. One may pretend to be a great saintly person or as a religious person, but anything less than pure devotion is a hindrance to attaining service to Kṛṣṇa.

"If one uproots the various weeds as soon as one sees them beginning to sprout, then the creeper of devotional service will be able to grow as far as Goloka Vṛndāvana, where it will bear fruits of divine love. If not, one will end up being cut off from the devotional life and, remaining in the material world, whether in the higher or lower planets, will have to suffer its vagaries." (*Anubhāṣya*, 2.19.160-1)

There are twelve devotional sentiments. The five primary sentiments are those of passivity, servitude, friendship, parenthood, and to become a consort. The seven secondary sentiments are humor, astonishment, heroism, compassion, anger, disgust and fear.

"The five primary sentiments remain permanently within the devotee's heart, while the secondary sentiments are adventitious, appearing only when there is a cause." (*Caitanya Caritāmṛta* 2.19.188)

The secondary *rasas* act as supporting elements for the primary sentiments, coming and going under propitious circumstances. After serving their function, they again disappear, whereas the primary sentiments are permanently established in the devotee's heart. In His teachings to Rūpa Gosvāmī, Mahāprabhu established that among the five primary *rasas*, the divine sentiment of conjugal love is foremost. The characteristics of *śānta-rasa* are the abandonment of other desires and steady attachment to Kṛṣṇa. Over and above these characteristics, the possessor of the serving mood has his service, the friend has an intimacy, while the parent has a sense of being the protector. The devotee in *madhura-rasa* has all these qualities with the addition of serving with her own body. Just as all the qualities of the other principal elements of matter starting with ether are added together to be united in the earth, so are all the qualities of the other devotional moods united in the mood of conjugal love. Since all the sentiments are present in *madhura-rasa*, it is the foremost.

RŪPA STARTS WRITING HIS PLAYS

After the Lord had instructed Rūpa Gosvāmī for ten days at Prayag, He prepared to leave for Benares. Rūpa Gosvāmī was eager to accompany Him, but the Lord instructed him to go on to Vrindavan and that he could take the road through Bengal at some later date to see Him in Puri. In keeping with the Lord's order, Rūpa Gosvāmī continued on to Vrindavan and stayed there for one month. Then, he and Anupama set off in search of Sanātana Gosvāmī, hoping to meet him somewhere along the Ganges. However, by the time they reached Prayag, Sanātana Gosvāmī had already left for Mathura by the main highway, so their paths did not cross. When he arrived in Mathura, Sanātana Gosvāmī was able to learn of the news of Rūpa Gosvāmī and Anupama from Subuddhi Rāya.

As the two brothers were traveling along the banks of the Ganges toward Bengal, Anupama departed for the eternal abode of Rāmacandra. Because of Anupama's disappearance, Rūpa Gosvāmī was not able to join the other Bengali Vaiṣṇavas in their annual pilgrimage to Puri, arriving there much later.

While in Vrindavan, Rūpa Gosvāmī had commenced writing a play on Kṛṣṇa *līlā*, and had composed several verses of the introductory portion, known as the *nāndī*. The *nāndī* verses include the obeisance, the blessing and the indication of the play's subject matter. Traveling through Odisha on his way to Puri, he stopped overnight in a village named Satyabhamapur. There he had a dream in which Satyabhāmā Devī appeared to him and told him to write a separate play in her honor.

"The morning after, Rūpa Gosvāmī said to himself, 'Satyabhāmā has ordered me to write a play for her. I had started to write a play which described events from both Vraja and Dwarka, but now I shall do them separately.' " (*Caitanya Caritāmṛta* 3.1.43-4)

When in Puri, Rūpa Gosvāmī would not go into the Jagannātha temple to take *darśana* of Lord Jagannātha. This was because of his great humility. In fact, though there was no impediment to his going there, he would not even enter Kāśī Miśra's house to visit Mahāprabhu out of the same sense of being fallen. Though he had been born into a very respectable *brāhmaṇa* family, he considered himself to be a *mleccha* due to his long association with the Muslim rulers of Bengal. Therefore, he preferred to stay with Haridāsa Ṭhākura at Siddha Bakula. In spite of knowing the supreme eligibility of Rūpa Gosvāmī to see Lord Jagannātha, Mahāprabhu Himself respected his decision and never told him to go to see Lord Jagannātha, for He wished to teach the world humility through Rūpa Gosvāmī's example.

"Through Haridāsa Ṭhākura, the Lord taught forbearance. Through Rūpa Gosvāmī and Sanātana Gosvāmī, he taught humility." (*Bhakti-ratnākara* 1.631)

When Mahāprabhu suddenly came one day to visit Haridāsa Ṭhākura, He was attracted by Rūpa Gosvāmī's humble, pure devotional attitude and embraced him. The Lord then sat down with him and asked him for the latest news about him and Sanātana Gosvāmī, and they talked about these and other things. On another day, Mahāprabhu came there with all of His entourage, and Rūpa Gosvāmī paid obeisances to all of them. Mahāprabhu, out of affection for Rūpa Gosvāmī, had Advaita and Nityānanda Prabhus give him their blessings. Every single day, Rūpa Gosvāmī and Haridāsa Ṭhākura would get the remnants of Mahāprabhu's *prasāda* through Govinda.

"One day, the Lord suddenly said to Rūpa Gosvāmī, 'Never make Kṛṣṇa leave Vraja. Kṛṣṇa never abandons Vrindavan to go elsewhere.' (*Caitanya Caritāmṛta* 3.1.66). As a result of this hint from the Lord, Rūpa Gosvāmī understood that both Satyabhāmā and Mahāprabhu wanted two different dramas, so he composed *Vidagdha-mādhava* exclusively about Kṛṣṇa's pastimes in Vraja and *Lalita-mādhava* about the Dwarka *līlā*.

THE LORD APPRECIATES RŪPA GOSVĀMĪ'S POETRY

By Mahāprabhu's mercy, Rūpa Gosvāmī was able to understand His internal devotional states. While he was in Puri for the Rathayātrā, Rūpa Gosvāmī observed Mahāprabhu standing before the chariot gazing upon Lord Jagannātha. As He stood there, the Lord began to recite a verse from the *Kāvya-prakāśa* in the mood of Rādhā. The verse, though seemingly having nothing to do with Kṛṣṇa, put the Lord in an ecstatic mood, and He began to dance. Other than Śrī Svarūpa Dāmodara Gosvāmī, no one was able to understand the meaning of the verse. Rūpa Gosvāmī, however, also had an insight into the Lord's mood, and he composed an original verse which expressed this sentiment. He wrote the verse down on a palm leaf and tucked it into the thatched roof of Haridāsa Ṭhākura's cottage. Then he went to take his bath in the ocean.

While he was gone, Mahāprabhu came by and found the palm leaf. When He read the verse written upon it, He was astonished to see that Rūpa Gosvāmī had such a clear intuition into His innermost feelings.

priyaḥ so 'yaṁ kṛṣṇaḥ sahacari kurukṣetra-militas
tathāhaṁ sā rādhā tad idam
ubhayoḥ saṅgama-sukham
tathāpy antaḥ-khelan-madhura-
muralī-pañcama-juṣe
mano me kālindī-pulina-vipināya spṛhayati

"O companion! This is the same beloved Kṛṣṇa meeting me here in Kurukshetra, and I am the same Rādhā, and both of Us are feeling the joy of union. Even so, My mind wishes for the forest by the banks of the Yamuna where the fifth note of His flute reverberated sweetly within My heart." (*Padyāvalī* 383)

When Rūpa Gosvāmī returned from bathing, Mahāprabhu gave him an affectionate slap, saying, "How did you know what was in My mind?" Then He embraced him tightly.

"The Lord took the verse and showed it to Svarūpa Dāmodara, asking him to examine it for any possible faults. He asked him, 'How was Rūpa able to know My mind?' Svarūpa Dāmodara answered, 'I believe it must be the result of Your special benediction.' " (*Caitanya Caritāmṛta* 3.1.85-6)

One day, Rūpa Gosvāmī was busy writing *Vidagdha-mādhava.* Mahāprabhu arrived unexpectedly and was impressed by his beautiful handwriting, comparing it to a string of pearls. He read the verse that Rūpa Gosvāmī had composed in the glorification of the Holy Name and was overcome with devotional ecstasy:

tuṇḍe tāṇḍavinī ratiṁ vitanute
tuṇḍāvalī-labdhaye
karṇa-kroḍa-kaḍambinī ghaṭayate
karṇārbudebhyaḥ spṛhām
cetaḥ-prāṅgaṇa-saṅginī vijayate
sarvendriyāṇāṁ kṛtiṁ
no jāne janita kiyadbhir amṛtaiḥ
krṣṇeti varṇa-dvayī

"I do not know out of how much nectar the two syllables of Kṛṣṇa's name have been composed; dancing madly on my tongue, they awaken in me the desire to possess many mouths. As they sprout in my ears, I long for millions of ears; and as they enter into the garden of my heart they overcome the activities of every one of my senses, leaving me inert!" (*Vidagdha-mādhava* 1.15)

Haridāsa Ṭhākura, the *ācārya* of the Holy Name, was amazed to hear such an extraordinary glorification of Kṛṣṇa's name, and he started to dance. He said, "I have heard the glories of the Holy Name from many scriptures and sadhus, but never a description like this of the sweetness of the Name!" (*Caitanya Caritāmṛta* 3.1.101)

On another day, after visiting Jagannātha Deva, Mahāprabhu came to Siddha Bakula with His entire entourage, including Śrī Svarūpa Dāmodara Gosvāmī, Rāmānanda Rāya and Sārvabhauma Bhaṭṭācārya. Svarūpa Dāmodara read the *priyaḥ so'yaṁ* verse quoted above to all the devotees. Upon hearing the verse, Rāmānanda Rāya and Sārvabhauma Bhaṭṭācārya expressed how as a result of Mahāprabhu's special mercy Rūpa Gosvāmī had been able to understand something that even Brahmā and the demigods were unable to comprehend. Then the Lord asked Rūpa Gosvāmī to read the *tuṇḍe tāṇḍavinī* verse glorifying the Holy Name. All the devotees were delighted and said, "How often we have heard about the greatness of the Holy Name. But no one has ever written such a description of its sweetness!" (*Caitanya Caritāmṛta* 3.1.122)

Then Rāmānanda Rāya began discussing the subject matter of Rūpa Gosvāmī's plays with him. He asked to hear the verse glorifying the object of his devotion that would appear at the beginning of the play. At first, Rūpa Gosvāmī was reluctant to recite his composition in front of the Lord. However, when the Lord insisted that he recite, Rūpa Gosvāmī read his verse aloud. Mahāprabhu externally expressed displeasure, saying, "Your praises are overdone. This is an exaggeration," but the rest of the devotees were overcome with ecstatic love. The verse is the second of the first act of *Vidagdha-mādhava*:

anarpita-carīṁ cirāt karuṇayāvatīrṇaḥ kalau
samarpayitum unnatojjvala-rasāṁ sva-bhakti-śriyam
hariḥ puraṭa-sundara-dyuti-kadamba-sandīpitaḥ
sadā hṛdaya-kandare sphuratu vaḥ śacīnandanaḥ

"May the Supreme Lord who is the son of Śrīmatī Śacī-devī, resplendent with the radiance of molten gold, be always situated in the innermost chambers of your heart. He has appeared in the Age of Kālī by His causeless mercy to bestow that which was never offered before: the most sublime and radiant mellow of devotional service, the treasure of devotion to Him."

When Rāmānanda Rāya heard this extraordinary verse, drenched in love for the Lord, he began to praise Rūpa Gosvāmī with what seemed like a thousand tongues.

"Rāmānanda Rāya said to the Lord: 'I wish I had a thousand tongues to glorify Rūpa's poetic ability. This is not poetry; it is a fountain of ambrosia. It is the essence of all ultimate realizations, appearing in the form of plays. His description of transcendental love affairs is truly wonderful. My ears and mind are spinning with delight upon hearing them." (*Caitanya Caritāmṛta* 3.1.192-4)

Once, Kālī Dāsa was considered the greatest Sanskrit poet – that is until Rūpa Gosvāmī began to write his transcendental poetry, deeply imbued with the divine sentiments.

RŪPA IN VRINDAVAN

From Puri, Rūpa Gosvāmī returned to Gaudadesh to arrange for the equitable distribution of his accumulated wealth amongst his family, *brāhmaṇas* and temples and stayed there for nearly a year before going to Vrindavan for good. In the meantime, Sanātana Gosvāmī came to Puri via the Jharikhand path and then returned by the same route to Vraja. When the two brothers met again, it had been more than a year since they had seen each other.

Rūpa Gosvāmī and Sanātana Gosvāmī set an unequalled standard of devotional discipline and an exemplary method of worship:

"These two brothers have no fixed residence, but lie down each night beneath one or the other trees in the forest. They sometimes take a meal at a *brāhmaṇa*'s house, or merely go door to door taking a handful of cooked food from each home. In this way, their meal consists of only some dry bread and fried chickpeas. Their only possessions are their water pots and the quilts and torn clothes they wear. In such a detached state, they constantly chant Kṛṣṇa's Holy Names, discuss His pastimes and dance jubilantly. They engage in Kṛṣṇa *bhajana* for almost twenty-four hours a day, sleeping only an hour and a half. Some days, when they are absorbed in chanting the Holy Names, they do not sleep at all. Sometimes they write books on the divine raptures of devotional service, and other times they spend their time talking or thinking about Caitanya Mahāprabhu." (*Caitanya Caritāmṛta* 2.19.127-31)

Rūpa Gosvāmī is credited with the authorship of sixteen books according to *Bhakti-ratnākara*: (1) *Haṁsadūta*, (2) *Uddhavasandeśa*, (3) *Kṛṣṇa-janma-tithi-vidhi*, (4) *Laghu Radhā-kṛṣṇa-gaṇoddeśa-dīpikā*, (5) *Bṛhat Radhā-kṛṣṇa-gaṇoddeśa-dīpikā*, (6) *Stavamālā*, (7) *Vidagdha-mādhava*, (8) *Lalita-mādhava*, (9) *Dāna-keli-kaumudī*, (10) *Bhakti-rasāmṛta-sindhu* (11) *Ujjvala-nīlamaṇi*, (12) *Prayuktākhyāta-candrikā*, (13) *Mathurā-mahimā*, (14) *Padyāvalī*, (15) *Nāṭaka-candrikā* and (16) *Laghu-bhāgavatāmṛta*.

Other than these sixteen titles, *Upadeśāmṛta*, *Nāmāṣṭaka*, *Siddhānta-ratna* and *Kāvya-kaustubha*, etc., are attributed to Rūpa Gosvāmī.

Raghunātha Dāsa Gosvāmī stayed in Mahāprabhu's association in Puri for sixteen years under the tutelage of Svarūpa Dāmodara Gosvāmī. When the Lord and Svarūpa Dāmodara both ended their pastimes within this world, Raghunātha Dāsa Gosvāmī became so saddened by their departure that he decided to go to Vrindavan to commit suicide by jumping off Govardhan after seeing Rūpa Gosvāmī and Sanātana Gosvāmī one last time. The two brothers were very affectionate to Raghunātha Dāsa Gosvāmī, however, and would not allow him to kill himself. Rather, they adopted him as a third brother and kept him constantly by their side.

Another of the six Gosvāmīs was Raghunātha Bhaṭṭa Gosvāmī, whose father was Tapana Miśra. When Mahāprabhu was in Benares, He stayed and ate at the home of Tapana Miśra, giving the young Raghunātha Bhaṭṭa the opportunity to render Him service by taking His remnants and massaging His feet, etc. When he grew older, he went to see the Lord in Puri and stayed there for eight months. During this time he served Mahāprabhu by cooking various preparations, which gave the Lord great satisfaction. After this, the Lord ordered him to return to Benares to serve his ageing parents, which Raghunātha Bhaṭṭa did for four years. When his parents departed from the material world, Raghunātha Bhaṭṭa returned to Puri, where the Lord told him to go to Vrindavan and follow in Rūpa Gosvāmī's footsteps. Raghunātha Bhaṭṭa followed the Lord's directions and came to Vraja, where, by Rūpa Gosvāmī's mercy, he became infused with love for Kṛṣṇa. He would recite *Śrīmad Bhāgavatam* for Rūpa Gosvāmī's pleasure.

RŪPA GOSVĀMĪ AND GOVINDAJĪ

In Vrindavan, Rūpa Gosvāmī established a temple for Govindajī, and Sanātana Gosvāmī established one for Madana Mohana. The way that Govindajī appeared to Rūpa Gosvāmī is stated in *Bhakti-ratnākara*: Mahāprabhu had given four instructions to Rūpa Gosvāmī: to discover the holy places in the *dhāma* that had become invisible to material eyes, to establish deity worship, to publish scriptures on pure devotional service, and to preach the love of the Holy Name. Rūpa Gosvāmī carried out each of these desires of the Lord to perfection but one. Rūpa Gosvāmī was worried about how he could establish deity worship and started wandering through the villages and forests in the Vraja area in search of Govindajī, but without success.

After the failure of these efforts, he was sitting one day by the banks of the Yamuna, upset and burning up with intense feelings of separation from Kṛṣṇa. Just then, a divine personality taking the form of a handsome Vrajavasi came up to him and asked him in a sweet voice what was the cause of his distress. Rūpa Gosvāmī was attracted by the charming voice and appearance of the Vrajavasi and told him everything that had been troubling him. The Vrajavasi consoled Rūpa Gosvāmī, saying, "There is no cause for worry. Govindajī is secretly residing in the hill named Goma Tila, which is the Yogapitha here in Vrindavan. Every morning a cow goes there and joyfully gives Him milk." Having told him this, the Vrajavasi disappeared.

Rūpa Gosvāmī thought, "Kṛṣṇa came here and spoke to me, and I could not recognize Him," and he fainted. Even so, he was somehow or other able to overcome his feelings of loss at having been unable to recognize Kṛṣṇa and proceeded to the place that the Vrajavasi had indicated. Other residents of the village helped him dig at Goma Tila until they found the deity of Govindajī, more beautiful than a million Cupids. It is said that this Govinda deity had originally been worshipped by Kṛṣṇa's own grandson, Vajranābha.

"After revealing His presence on Goma Tila, Govindajī was first served in a simple thatched hut, but later a disciple of Raghunātha Bhaṭṭa Gosvāmī built a beautiful temple and *kīrtana* hall, etc. "(*Bhakti-ratnākara* 2.404-37)

In 1590, the King of Amber, Man Singh, repaired the existing structure and built additions to this temple, with the result that there stood an exquisite sandstone temple. In his *Mathura Memoir*, Growse has described this temple in the following words: "The temple of Govinda Dev is not only the finest of this particular series but is the most impressive religious edifice that Hindu art has ever produced, at least in upper India."

It is said that the seven-story building was so high that the emperor Aurangzeb could see the temple's pinnacle from his palace in Agra. Out of envy, he destroyed the upper portion of the building. At around this time, Govindajī was moved first to Bharatpur and then later to Jaipur out of fear of Muslim iconoclasm, and He remains in Jaipur to this day.

ŚRĪ RŪPA MAÑJARĪ PADA

Narottama Dāsa Ṭhākura has written and has described Rūpa Mañjarī, or Rūpa Gosvāmī, as his all-in-all in the following song from *Prārthanā*:

śrī rūpa mañjarī pada sei mora sampada
sei mora bhajana-pūjana
sei mora prāṇa-dhana sei mora ābharaṇa
sei mora jīvanera jīvana

sei mora rasa-nidhi sei mora vāñchā-siddhi
sei mora vedera dharama
sei vrata, sei tapa sei mora mantra japa
sei mora dharama karama

anukūla habe vidhi se pade haibe siddhi
nirakhibo ei dui nayane
se rūpa mādhurī rāśī prāṇa kuvalaya-śaśi
praphullita habe niśi-dine

tuwā adarśana ahi garale jārala dehi
ciradina tāpita jīvana
hā hā prabhu koro dayā deha more pada chāyā
narottama laila śaraṇa

"Śrī Rūpa Mañjarī's feet are my only possession. They are my devotional practice, my worship. They are the treasure of my life; they are my ornament, the life of my life.

"They are my treasure house of sacred rapture; they are the fulfillment of my deepest wishes; they are my prescribed duty. They are my religious vow; they are my austerities, my meditation and my *mantra*. They are my religious obligation.

"One day, fate will smile upon me and I will be perfected in a position of service to Rūpa Mañjarī. I will see that form which is an ocean of sweetness, which will cause the moon lotus of my heart to bloom night and day.

"The snake of separation from you spits a venom, which burns my body. I have long suffered in this life as a result. O my Rūpa Prabhu! Please be merciful and give me the shade of your lotus feet. Narottama has taken shelter of you."

Śrīla Bhakti Siddhānta Sarasvatī Gosvāmī Ṭhākura Prabhupāda also considered the dust from Rūpa Gosvāmī's feet to be the most important thing in his life. He often said that he desired nothing other than this.

ādadānas tṛṇaṁ dantair
idaṁ yāce punaḥ punaḥ
śrīmad-rūpa-padāmbhoja-
dhūliḥ syāṁ janma-janmani

"With bunches of straw between my teeth, I pray repeatedly that I may take birth again and again as a particle of dust at the lotus feet of Śrīla Rūpa Gosvāmī." (Raghunātha Dāsa, *Muktā-caritra*)

Rūpa Gosvāmī's main *samādhi* temple and the place where he performed his *bhajan* can be found in the courtyard behind the Rādhā Dāmodara temple in Vrindavan. Other places consecrated to Rūpa Gosvāmī's memory in the Vraja area include his place of worship near Nandagrama, called Teri Kadamba. In this place, Rādhārāṇī came in disguise of a young girl to give Rūpa Gosvāmī milk, rice and sugar so that he could cook a sweet-rice preparation for Sanātana Gosvāmī. When Sanātana Gosvāmī tasted the sweet rice, he felt divine ecstasies invade his body. Upon learning how Rūpa had received the ingredients, however, Sanātana Gosvāmī forbade Rūpa Gosvāmī to ever cook sweet rice again, so that Rādhārāṇī would not have to go to any trouble on his behalf.

Rūpa Gosvāmī's pastimes in this world came to an end in the month of Bhādra, on the twelfth day of the waxing moon, the day after Jhulan Ekādaśī.

Śrīla Sanātana Gosvāmī

yā rūpa-mañjarī-preṣṭhā purāsīd rati-mañjarī
socyate nāma-bhedena lavaṅga-mañjarī budhaiḥ
sādya gaurābhinna-tanuḥ sarvārādhyaḥ sanātanaḥ
tam eva prāviśat kāryān muni-ratnaṁ sanātanaḥ

"Rati Mañjarī, who was previously very dear to Rūpa Mañjarī and was also known by some wise persons as Lavaṅga mañjarī, has become the worshipable Sanātana Gosvāmī, who is nondifferent from Gaura Himself. One of the four sons of Brahmā, Sanātana, has also entered into him to fulfill a certain mission." (*Gaura-gaṇoddeśa-dīpikā* 181)

SANĀTANA GOSVĀMĪ'S LIFE BEFORE MEETING MAHĀPRABHU

According to the *Gauḍīya Vaiṣṇava Abhidhāna*, Sanātana Gosvāmī appeared in around 1410 of the Śaka era (1488 A.D.). Narahari Cakravartī Ṭhākura has described his ancestors in *Bhakti-ratnākara* (1.541), and Śrīla Bhakti Siddhānta Sarasvatī Gosvāmī Ṭhākura has given a summary of this information in his *Anubhāṣya* to *Caitanya Caritāmṛta* (1.10.84), which we have quoted in this book in our discussion of the life of Rūpa Gosvāmī. Other than this, no reliable information about their descendants has been found. Perhaps researchers in Indian history will be able to shed more light on this.

According to the *Gauḍīya Vaiṣṇava Abhidhāna*, the following brief account is given of how Sanātana Gosvāmī's grandfather came to be engaged in the Muslim Shah's service: "During the reign of Barbak Shah (1460-1470 A.D.), Sanātana Gosvāmī's grandfather Mukunda entered the court at the capital city of Gauda. Barbak Shah engaged many Abyssinian slaves and eunuchs in both his court and harem; they were known as *hābsī* [which is now the common Bengali word for any black African]. After the death of Barbak Shah, his son Yusuf became king, and he was followed by his son Fateh Shah. During the reign of Fateh Shah, the *hābsīs* led a coup in which Fateh Shah himself was assassinated. They ruled for five or six years. Hussain Shah was the *vizir*, or prime minister, of the last of the *hābsī* rulers, and he later became himself ruler of Bengal. Mukunda left this world during the rule of Fateh Shah, and Sanātana Gosvāmī was engaged in his place. Sanātana Gosvāmī managed to survive the *hābsī* period, and during Hussain Shah's reign managed to take a higher position on the strength of his personal talents, eventually becoming prime minister. Rūpa Gosvāmī held another ministerial post, possibly as finance minister." Sanātana Gosvāmī's title was Sākara Mallika and Rūpa Gosvāmī's was Dabīra Khāsa.

While Śrī Sanātana Gosvāmī was still young, he studied under the country's leading scholar, named Vidyā Vācaspati, learning many scriptures from him. He was especially attached to the study of the *Śrīmad Bhāgavatam*. Although he had taken birth in a high-class *brāhmaṇa* family, because he had worked for the Muslim government he considered himself to be fallen and always behaved in a most humble manner, as is appropriate for a Vaiṣṇava.

"Sanātana Gosvāmī's teacher, Vidyā Vācaspati, would come to stay in Ramakeli from time to time. Sanātana Gosvāmī studied all the scriptures from him. No one can achieve the depth of devotion that he had for his guru." (*Bhakti-ratnākara* 1.598-9)

"Sanātana Gosvāmī's father would perform atonement rituals even after seeing a Muslim, yet Sanātana Gosvāmī himself would associate constantly with Muslims. Being dependent on them for his livelihood, he would even go into their homes. For this reason, he considered himself to be on the same level as the Muslims and behaved very humbly. Sometimes, when he had fallen into the ocean of humility, he would think of himself as even lower than a *mleccha*. Because he had associated with Muslims and behaved in a lowly manner like them, he would speak of himself in that way. Though born in the highest class family of *brāhmaṇas*, he never thought of himself as a *brāhmaṇa*. (*Bhakti-ratnākara* 1.609-14)

"Through Rāmānanda Rāya, the Lord destroyed Cupid's pride, and through Svarūpa Dāmodara He demonstrated detachment. Through Haridāsa Ṭhākura, He demonstrated forbearance, and through Rūpa Gosvāmī and Sanātana Gosvāmī, He taught humility." (*Bhakti-ratnākara* 1.630-1)

All the participants in Kṛṣṇa's *līlā* also made their appearance in Gaura's *līlā* in order to enrich His pastimes. Through them, the Lord gives various teachings to the people of this world.

"Through Haridāsa, Mahāprabhu revealed the glories of the Holy Name; through Sanātana Gosvāmī, the current of devotional conclusions. Through Rūpa Gosvāmī He taught Rādhā and Kṛṣṇa's pastimes of transcendental love. Who can understand the mysterious workings of the Lord?" (*Caitanya Caritāmṛta* 3.5.86-7)

"Through Sanātana Gosvāmī's mercy, I learnt the foundation of devotional doctrine, while through Rūpa Gosvāmī's mercy, I learnt about the divine devotional sentiments." (*Caitanya Caritāmṛta* 1.5.203)

Thus Sanātana Gosvāmī has been called the *bhakti-siddhāntācārya*, or the teacher of devotional doctrine, by which is meant the teacher of *sambandha-jñāna*, or of the basic relations between God, man and the world. The founder of the worldwide Chaitanya Math and other Gaudiya institutions, my Most Revered Parama-gurudeva Nitya-līlā-praviṣṭa Oṁ 108 Śrī Śrīmad Bhakti Siddhānta Sarasvatī Gosvāmī Ṭhākura Prabhupāda, mercifully gave his disciples a poem entitled "Who is a Vaiṣṇava?" The nectarean instructions found in this poem mention the teachings of Mahāprabhu to Sanātana Gosvāmī from the *Caitanya Caritāmṛta*.

tāi duṣṭa mana nirjana bhajana
pracāricha chale kuyogī-vaibhava
prabhu sanātane parama yatane
śikṣā dila yāhā, cinta sei saba

"So, wicked mind, you have deceptively been preaching *nirjana-bhajana*, or solitary *bhajana*, which is nothing more than a display like that of a misleading yoga practitioner interested in the mystic powers. Study the teachings of the Lord to Sanātana Gosvāmī very carefully and meditate upon them."

Śrīla Prabhupāda thus instructs us all to give great attentionto the teaching the Lord gave to the world through Sanātana Gosvāmī.

FIRST MEETING IN RAMAKELI

After He took *sannyāsa*, Mahāprabhu first went to Shantipur and then to Puri and then on pilgrimage to South India. After completing His pilgrimage and returning to Puri, Mahāprabhu decided to go to Vrindavan via the route which follows the Ganges through Bengal. Great crowds of people accompanied Him, and He eventually decided to turn back from Kanair Natshala. He met Rūpa Gosvāmī and Sanātana Gosvāmī for the first time while passing through the village of Ramakeli[22] on this voyage.

---

22 Ramakeli is in the district of Maldah in West Bengal, about eight miles south of English Bazar, and about five or six miles from the Maldah train station. Ramakeli was made district headquarters during British rule and is also known as Gupta ("hidden") Vrindavan. There are a number of sites which are worth seeing as reminders of Rūpa Gosvāmī and Sanātana Gosvāmī: (1) A *tamāla* and a *kadamba* tree under which Mahāprabhu is said to have been sitting when He met Rūpa Gosvāmī and Sanātana Gosvāmī; a shrine containing the footprints of the Lord has been constructed there as a memorial of that meeting. In this location, the Lord distributed love of Kṛṣṇa to all the devotees. (2) The temple of Madana Mohana. This Madana Mohana deity was personally worshipped by Sanātana Gosvāmī. There are also deities of Nītāi-Gaurāṅga and Advaita Prabhus. (3) There

At first, the Muslim king became concerned when he heard that such great crowds of Hindus had assembled in the nearby village. One of the Hindu members of the Shah's court was Keśava Kṣatriya, who explained to him that there was no reason to fear Mahāprabhu. Rūpa Gosvāmī (Dabīr Khāsa) also glorified Mahāprabhu to the king, telling him of his fortune in having the Lord bless the country by His presence. Keśava Kṣatriya, meanwhile, sent a secret message to the Lord telling Him to go elsewhere because the king could not be trusted.

"The king said, 'Listen, I am also beginning to think that this person must be God Himself. There is no doubt about it.' After having this conversation, the king entered his private quarters, and Dabīra Khāsa also returned to his residence. After returning there, however, he and his brother decided after much consideration to go incognito to see the Lord. Thus, in the dead of night the two brothers, Dabīra Khāsa and Sākara Mallika, went to see Mahāprabhu. First, they met Nityānanda Prabhu and Haridāsa Ṭhākura. Nityānanda Prabhu and Haridāsa then went and told the Lord that Rūpa and Sākara Mallika had come to see Him." (*Caitanya Caritāmṛta* 2.1.180-4)

When Rūpa Gosvāmī and Sanātana Gosvāmī met the Lord, they spoke to Him with extreme humility:

"We two are millions of times more degraded, fallen and sinful than Jagāi and Mādhāi. We are of wicked birth, are servants of Muslims and our activities are exactly like those of the Muslims. We constantly associate with people who are inimical toward the cows and *brāhmaṇas*. Due to our abominable activities, we are now bound by the neck and hands and have been thrown into the ditch filled with the excrement of evil sense enjoyment. There is nobody other than You in the three worlds who can deliver us." (*Caitanya Caritāmṛta* 2.1.196-199)

"It is very distressing to us that we are so unworthy, yet when we see Your merciful qualities, we become desirous of attaining Your blessings. This powerful desire rises up in us like that of a dwarf who wants to touch the moon." (*Caitanya Caritāmṛta* 2.1.204-5)

When the Lord heard the extreme humility of the two brothers, He became compassionate and said to them, "You are My eternal servants. From now on you shall be known as Rūpa and Sanātana. I came to Bengal just so that I could meet you here in Ramakeli village. Kṛṣṇa will deliver you from your entanglements very shortly."

Śrīla Bhakti Siddhānta Sarasvatī Gosvāmī Ṭhākura Prabhupāda has written the following comment in his *Anubhāṣya* (*Caitanya Caritāmṛta* 2.1.208): "Mahāprabhu showed His mercy to Dabīra Khāsa and Sākara Mallika by giving them the spiritual names of Rūpa and Sanātana, respectively. *Nāma-karaṇa* (offering spiritual name) is a type of *saṁskāra* (purification) on the lowest level of qualification. However, those who ignore the mercy that is manifest in the spiritual name have no chance of attaining devotion to Kṛṣṇa but remain intoxicated with material prestige. *Prākṛta sahajiyās* pay no heed to the injunctions of the scripture which state that the minimum characteristics of a Vaiṣṇava are that he wears the symbols of the discus and conch shell and *ūrdhva-puṇḍra* (*tilaka*)

---

are several ponds, which are named Radha Kunda, Syama Kunda, Surabhi Kunda, Lalita Kunda and Vishakha Kunda. (4) A large lake named Rupa Sagara, which is said to have been excavated by Rūpa Gosvāmī himself, and (5) another named Sanātana Sāgara. Rūpa Gosvāmī and Sanātana Gosvāmī built large mansions in both Ramakeli and Fateyabad.

and is awarded a spiritual name. As such, they cannot be qualified as Gauḍīya Vaiṣṇavas. Non-Vaiṣṇavas have not been given a name by the Vaiṣṇava guru and so they continue in the bodily conception of life without any awareness of their relationship with the Lord. They continue to identify themselves with their previous caste according to the name which ties them to their body."

Amongst the Lord's companions present on this occasion were Nityānanda Prabhu, Haridāsa Ṭhākura, Śrīvāsa Paṇḍita, Gadādhara Paṇḍita, Mukunda Datta, Jagadānanda Paṇḍita, Murāri Gupta, Vakreśvara Paṇḍita and many others. The Lord had them all give their blessings to Rūpa Gosvāmī and Sanātana Gosvāmī. As the Lord was departing, the worldly-wise Sanātana Gosvāmī said to Him:

"You should leave this place, Lord. You have no business here. Even though the Shah has faith in You, he is a Muslim and cannot be trusted. To go on pilgrimage with such a large company of devotees is not recommended. You are going to Vrindavan with an entourage of hundreds and thousands of people, and this is not a fitting way to go on a pilgrimage." (*Caitanya Caritāmṛta* 2.1.222-4)

Mahāprabhu continued as far as Kanair Natshala, but as He considered the wisdom of Sanātana Gosvāmī's advice, He decided to turn back, first going to Shantipur and then to Puri.

"After He and His entourage had given their mercy to Rūpa Gosvāmī and Sanātana Gosvāmī, they left Ramakeḷi village." (*Bhakti-ratnākara* 1.635)

SANĀTANA GOSVĀMĪ ESCAPES FROM PRISON

Rūpa Gosvāmī and Sanātana Gosvāmī are the eternal associates of Kṛṣṇa in Vrindavan. They appeared in this world in order to enrich Lord Gaurāṅga's *līlā* by playing the role of aspirants for spiritual perfection (*sādhakas*). After meeting Mahāprabhu, they began to feel very impatient to change their lifestyle. They became very renounced and austere. In order to quickly be united with Mahāprabhu, they engaged two *brāhmaṇas* in the performance of a *puraścāraṇa*.[23]

Śrīla Rūpa Gosvāmī finally resigned from his government service, and he deposited 10,000 coins on behalf of his older brother with a grocer in Gaudadesh. Then he took the rest of their accumulated wealth with him to Bakla Candradvipa, where he divided it up amongst the Vaiṣṇavas, *brāhmaṇas* and his family. He also kept a quarter of it with a trustworthy *brāhmaṇa* against future necessity. He then sent two people to Puri to find out when Mahāprabhu intended to travel to Vrindavan.

Hussain Shah used to treat Sanātana Gosvāmī as his younger brother and had great affection for him. Sanātana Gosvāmī thought that the affection of the king, or indeed of any materialistic person, was a source of material bondage. If the king became angry with him, it would make it easier for him to break away from his entanglements. For this reason, he stopped performing his duties in the Shah's court, pretending to be ill. Though he claimed to be seriously ill, he was in fact engaged in an intense study of *Śrīmad Bhāgavatam* with a group of scholars.

The Shah was disquieted by Sanātana Gosvāmī's illness, and he sent a doctor to examine him. The doctor came back and reported to the king that Sanātana Gosvāmī was in good health and that he was studying the *Bhāgavata* with a group of *paṇḍitas*. When he

23 See footnote 20, in the entry for Srīlā Rūpa Gosvāmī.

heard this, the Shah himself went to Sanātana Gosvāmī and spoke to him very affectionately, trying to convince him to come back to work. Sanātana Gosvāmī refused, however, to return to his ministerial duties and furthermore refused to accompany the Shah in the war he was preparing with Odisha. The Shah became worried about Sanātana Gosvāmī and had him imprisoned.

In the meantime, Rūpa Gosvāmī had received the news that Mahāprabhu had taken the jungle route through Jharikhand to Vrindavan. He himself immediately departed for Vraja with his younger brother, Anupama Mallika. He sent Sanātana Gosvāmī a letter advising him to take any necessary action to free himself and then to come and join them. The letter consisted of the following Sanskrit verse:

yadupateḥ kva gatā maṭhurā purī
raghupateḥ kva gatottara-kośalā
iti vicintya kuruṣva manaḥ sthiraṁ
na sad idaṁ jagad ity avadhāraya

"Where has the Mathura of the Lord of the Yadus gone? And where is the kingdom of Koshala of the Lord of the Raghus? Contemplate this and make your mind steady: Beware, this world will not last forever." (*Amṛta-pravāha-bhāṣya, Caitanya Caritāmṛta* 2.20.3)

"Sanātana Gosvāmī was able to understand the secret meaning of the verse, and was overjoyed. He began to consider how to escape from prison.

Sanātana Gosvāmī knew the Muslim jailkeeper, for Sanātana was the one who had hired him. Sanātana began trying to persuade him to let him go, saying that the Almighty would surely bless him and give him salvation for setting free someone who had been unjustly imprisoned. The jailor remained unconvinced, so Sanātana Gosvāmī tried to win him over by reminding him that he owed him a favor for having given him the job.

When the jail keeper still refused to let him go, Sanātana Gosvāmī offered him a bribe of 5,000 coins. At this, the jailkeeper's resolve began to waver, but he indicated that he was afraid of being caught by the Badshah. Sanātana Gosvāmī told him, "The Shah has gone to war. When he comes back, just tell him that I went to the toilet. Then, I jumped into the Ganges and disappeared. Say that you looked everywhere but couldn't find me."

Sanātana Gosvāmī farther assured him that he would not remain in the area, as it was his intention to become a sufi and go on the Haj to Mecca. Therefore, he need not worry on that account. The jailor remained reticent, however, and finally, Sanātana Gosvāmī had the grocer bring 7,000 coins of the money which Rūpa Gosvāmī had left in his safekeeping and placed it directly in front of him. When he saw the money before him, the jailor became greedy and surrendered to his proposal. He cut Sanātana Gosvāmī's chains and helped him to cross the Ganges.

In general, we consider flattery, asking return for a favor, putting temptation before someone, telling someone to lie, and bribery all to be unethical acts. Sanātana Gosvāmī, however, used all the means at his disposal to escape bondage so that he could join the Lord and engage in His service. To achieve an auspicious end, any means may be permissible. The purity or impurity of a particular means depends on the purity or impurity of the target. In order to serve his master Rāma, the Supreme Brahman, Hanumān burned down Lanka, killing many living beings, but because he was acting for the pleasure of the all-auspicious Supreme Lord, everyone was ultimately benefited by his action, and Hanumān is still considered worshipable to this very day. On the other hand, one can bathe in a holy river three times a day and worship the deity of the Lord and still be completely in the mode of ignorance if his objective is to do harm to other beings.

Even from the worldly point of view, we see that one who commits murder is considered a criminal and is punished by the death penalty, but if one fights on the battlefield to save the nation and kills many members of an enemy army, he is not punished but rather decorated with medals. This is because he is not acting for personal ends, but for a higher purpose. This is easy to understand, yet when one acts not for the limited purposes of serving the country or even the entire world, but for the supremely auspicious owner of unlimited millions of universes, then that is the most justifiable of purposes, and the highest benefits are attained by everyone through such actions. In the *Padma Purāṇa*, it is written:

man-nimittaṁ kṛtaṁ pāpam
api dharmāya kalpate
mām anādṛtya dharmo 'pi
pāpaṁ syān mat-prabhāvataḥ

"Even sinful activities done for My sake are to be considered religious acts. On the other hand, pious activities done while disdaining Me are considered to be a sin. This is the extent of My power."

"Those who chant the Holy Names or make a show of devotion, but in fact are seeking to achieve mundane, egoistic goals, are factually engaged in sin and are destined for a hellish fate. On the other hand, Hanumān had no material identity, nor was his purpose material. Kṛṣṇa also states in the *Bhagavad-gītā*,

yasya nāhaṁkṛto bhāvo buddhir yasya na lipyate
hatvāpi sa imāl lokān na hanti na nibadhyate

"He who is free from egotism (arising from an aversion to the Absolute) and whose intelligence is not implicated in worldly activities does not kill at all – even if he kills every living being in the whole world, nor does he suffer the consequences of murder." (*Bhagavad-gītā* 18.17)

When causeless devotion is manifest in the soul and one's heart has an honest eagerness to serve the Lord, then one gives up all consideration for happiness in this world, for renunciation is a side effect of unmotivated devotion.

ĪŚĀNA NEARLY GETS SANĀTANA GOSVĀMĪ KILLED

Sanātana Gosvāmī had been prime minister, yet he escaped from jail with practically not a penny to his name. He did not take the main highway but traveled as quickly as possible through fields and villages until he reached Patra Mountain, which is part of the Raj Mahal Hills in the Chota Nagpur area in the state of Bihar. He did not know how to get across this mountain, and so requested the aid of a landowner who was also a robber chieftain. Accompanying Sanātana Gosvāmī was a longtime personal servant named Īśāna. Through the help of a palmist, the landowner was able to know that Īśāna had eight gold coins in his possession, so he welcomed Sanātana Gosvāmī into his home and treated him with great hospitality.

Sanātana Gosvāmī was sufficiently experienced from his years in politics to become suspicious of the warm treatment he was getting from his host, and so he asked Īśāna whether he was carrying anything of value. Īśāna answered that he had seven gold coins, keeping his other coin a secret from him. Sanātana Gosvāmī mildly chastised. "Why have you brought this ruination upon us?" He then took the seven coins from him and gave them to his host, asking him to help him get across the mountain.

The landowner then revealed to Sanātana Gosvāmī that he had known all along about the eight gold coins and that it had been his intention to murder them both that night somewhere on the mountain in order to take the money. He was very pleased that Sanātana Gosvāmī had given him the gold and was even ready to return it to him, but Sanātana Gosvāmī refused. He was intelligent enough to understand the adage: *avyvasthita-cittasya prasādo 'pi bhayaṅkaraḥ*, "Even the kindness of an undependable person is dangerous."

dhūrtasya vacane kvāsthā
kvacit satyaṁ kvacin mṛṣā
kvacid raudraṁ kvacid vṛṣṭiḥ
śrāvaṇasya ghano yathā

"How can one have faith in the words of a rascal? He sometimes tells the truth and sometimes falsehoods. It is just as with the clouds of Śravaṇa – sometimes there is sunshine and sometimes rain."

After they had crossed the mountain, Sanātana Gosvāmī told Īśāna to take the remaining gold coin and return home. Īśāna had shown by his attachment to this gold coin that he was still dependent on material conditions and that he was not yet ready to accept a life of renunciation. When unqualified people take the renounced orders, then these orders themselves become contaminated. This is the lesson that Sanātana Gosvāmī gave through his servant Īśāna.

SANĀTANA GOSVĀMĪ MEETS THE LORD IN BENARES

After bidding goodbye to his servant, Sanātana Gosvāmī continued on his way until he arrived at Hajipur on the northern bank of the Ganges near Patna. Sanātana Gosvāmī's brother-in-law, Śrīkānta, made his home there. Though Śrīkānta invited him to stay in his home for a few days to recuperate from the voyage, Sanātana Gosvāmī declined his invitation because of his desire to see the Lord. Śrīkānta gave him a valuable blanket of Bhutanese wool.

Sanātana Gosvāmī then continued on to Benares, where he was overjoyed to learn that Mahāprabhu was staying at the house of the physician Candraśekhara Vaidya. Sanātana Gosvāmī did not go straight into Candraśekhara Vaidya's house but waited on his front porch. The Lord, the indweller of all souls, knew of His devotee's arrival and sent Candraśekhara Vaidya to the door to invite him in. As soon as Sanātana Gosvāmī entered, Mahāprabhu immediately rushed to embrace him. The meeting affected them both so intensely that they were overcome by the transformations of ecstatic love. In His affection for Sanātana Gosvāmī, the Lord made him sit next to Him and started to brush off the dust accumulated on his body from his travels, but this caused Sanātana Gosvāmī to feel uncomfortable. He told the Lord not to touch him, but the Lord answered:

"I touch you in order to purify Myself. Your devotional force is so great that you can purify the entire universe. I look at you, I touch you and I sing your glories. By My so doing, all My senses attain their most perfect use. This is proclaimed in the scriptures." (*Caitanya Caritāmṛta* 2.20.56, 60)

The Lord repeated again and again that He was touching Sanātana Gosvāmī for His own purification and for the purification of the entire universe. Then He immediately added, "Listen, Sanātana. Kṛṣṇa is the ocean of mercy; He saves the most fallen. He has delivered you from the hell known as Raurava."

Sanātana Gosvāmī is, of course, an eternal associate of the Lord, so there is no question of his being truly fallen, but Mahāprabhu wished to make a point for the benefit of the people of the world. He wanted to teach that worldly honor measured in terms of one's fortune and accumulation of sense objects is in truth misfortune since the accumulation of material possessions for the sake of gross or subtle sense gratification ultimately leads to a hellish existence.

Conditioned souls who are bewildered by the illusory energy are constantly busy working hard in order to accumulate wealth, position and influence, whether by fair means or foul. Seldom does one come across an exemplary householder who knows that Kṛṣṇa is the only true enjoyer and engages all his worldly possessions in the Lord's service rather than considering them to be the objects of his own enjoyment.

While Mahāprabhu was in Benares, He stayed with Candraśekhara Vaidya and took His meals at the house of Tapana Miśra. Mahāprabhu introduced Sanātana Gosvāmī to these two devotees, and Tapana Miśra invited Sanātana Gosvāmī to come to his house and take Mahāprabhu's *prasāda* remnants. After many days in prison and traveling, Sanātana Gosvāmī's hair and beard had grown long. The Lord told him to get shaved so that he would look "respectable." Vaiṣṇavas, in general, are clean shaven, growing neither beard nor moustache. With the exception of the *Cāturmāsya* period, when one does not shave or cut the fingernails, this is the accepted practice for Vaiṣṇava men. Vaiṣṇava *sannyāsīs*, however, usually shave only once a month on the full-moon day, as for them to shave daily would be considered to be indulging in unnecessary preoccupation with the body or pleasures.

After being shaved, Sanātana Gosvāmī took his bath in the Ganges. When he came back to the house, Candraśekhara Vaidya wanted to give him a new cloth, but Sanātana Gosvāmī refused it. Later he asked for used cloth from Tapana Miśra. Though he had been rich enough to give clothes to thousands of mendicants, on this day he was reluctant to accept a new cloth for himself. When one's desire to worship the Lord is real, one becomes indifferent to nice clothes or good food. However, accepting gifts from Vaiṣṇavas or taking their remnants does not have the poisonous character that other sense objects have. Every single one of Sanātana Gosvāmī's actions contains an unmatched lesson for the conscientious *sādhaka*.

Mahāprabhu was extremely pleased to see Sanātana Gosvāmī's renunciation. "Renunciation is the predominating characteristic of every one of Mahāprabhu's devotees. When Lord Gaurāṅga sees their renunciation, He is very pleased." (*Caitanya Caritāmṛta* 3.6.220)

When one is intoxicated by material enjoyments and engaged in the competition to attain them, one is destined for a falldown from any spiritual attainment.

There was a Maharashtrian *brāhmaṇa* who invited Sanātana Gosvāmī to come daily to his house to eat for as long as he stayed there. Sanātana Gosvāmī refused, however, saying that he preferred to maintain his life by eating only *mādhukarī*, that is to say, by begging a handful of food from several houses each day. A pure devotee has no desire for bodily comfort.

Sanātana Gosvāmī used the old cloth as his lower cloth (*bahirvāsa*) and upper cloth (*uttarīya*), but even so, he continued to wrap himself in the Bhutanese wool blanket. Mahāprabhu looked repeatedly at this blanket, and Sanātana Gosvāmī realized that Mahāprabhu did not approve of it. That day, when he went to the Ganges and exchanged his expensive blanket with a Bengali mendicant's torn quilt. When Sanātana Gosvāmī came back wearing the threadbare quilt, the Lord was pleased.

"The Lord said, 'I had been thinking about this. Kṛṣṇa has cured you of your disease of attachment to sense enjoyment. Why then would He allow you to hold fast to the last bit of material attachment? After restoring someone to health, a good physician does not allow any trace of the disease to remain. It is contradictory to practice *mādhukarī* while wearing a blanket worth three gold coins. By so doing, you would have lost your spiritual strength and become a laughing stock.' " (*Caitanya Caritāmṛta* 2.20.90-2)

Śrī Caitanya Mahāprabhu is the Supreme Personality of Godhead Himself. Even so, He played the role of the supreme teacher. Just as He set and Himself followed the standards of behavior, so did His associates.

"I shall accept the role of a devotee and shall teach devotional service by practicing it Myself. It is explained in the *Bhāgavata* and the *Bhagavad-gītā* that if one does not oneself practice a religious principle, one cannot teach it." (*Caitanya Caritāmṛta* 1.3.20-1)

yad yad ācarati śreṣṭhas tat tad evetaro janaḥ
sa yat pramāṇaṁ kurute lokas tad anuvartate

"The general masses imitate the ways of great men. They follow whatever the great personality accepts as the right conclusion." (*Bhagavad-gītā* 3.21)

THE LORD'S TEACHINGS TO SANĀTANA GOSVĀMĪ

Being pleased with Sanātana Gosvāmī, Mahāprabhu infused him with spiritual power, giving him the capacity to ask appropriate questions about the practice of true spiritual life. Without the mercy of the Supreme Lord, genuine, honest inquiries on such matters cannot arise in someone's mind. Most people ask questions thinking that they already know the right answer or to exhibit their scholarship, simply as a sort of debating technique. No spiritual benefit arises from such types of questions. Honest inquiries meant to find out doctrinal truths in a mood of submission are called *paripraśna* ("relevant inquiry") in the *Bhagavad-gītā:*

tad viddhi praṇipātena paripraśnena sevayā
upadekṣyanti te jñānaṁ jñāninas tattva-darśinaḥ

"You will be able to attain all this knowledge by taking shelter of the enlightened spiritual master with prostrate obeisances, honest inquiry, and sincere service. Great souls who are most expert in scriptural knowledge and endowed with direct realization of the Absolute will teach you that divine knowledge." (*Bhagavad-gītā* 4.34)

On the day a person undertakes his journey on the road to liberation when his material entanglement is about to start the process of termination, he meets a spiritual master. Sanātana Gosvāmī was himself an ever-liberated soul and a permanent companion of the Lord, but he showed what questions the aspiring practitioner of devotional service should ask his spiritual master on that day. He said to the Lord:

"I was born in a low family and have always associated with low-class men. I am fallen and the lowest of men. Indeed, I have fallen into the well of sinful materialism and passed my whole life there. I have no idea of what is beneficial to me and what is not. In ordinary dealings, people consider me wise, and I have also come to think of myself as such. You have mercifully delivered me from the materialistic path. Now, by the same causeless mercy, please explain to me my duty. I don't know who I am and why the threefold miseries constantly wear me down, so how can I attain the highest good? I do not even know how to inquire about the goal of life and the process for obtaining it. Please bestow Your mercy on me and explain all these things." (*Caitanya Caritāmṛta* 2.20.99-103)

Sanātana Gosvāmī's first question was "Who am I?" This is the first question which arises in the heart of a person seeking the highest good. If one makes a mistake in assessing his true identity, then he will make errors when it comes to determining the ultimate goal of life. If one makes an error in determining the ultimate goal of life, then everything he does, every effort he makes, will be wasted. All of one's duties, religious observations and self-interest rest upon the proper knowledge of oneself. If one takes the body to be the self, then he considers the maintenance of the body and those in relation to the body to be the goal of life, or *prayojana-tattva,* and one's self-interest will be the fulfillment of goals related to the body; duties will also be considered in terms of these ends, and all morality, or the ability to discriminate between good and bad, will be determined purely on the basis of what is good or bad for the body.

On the other hand, if someone takes the subtle body to be the self, then one will consider his personal interests in terms of its development, and he will consider his religious duty to help others to develop in this way. Those who consider the self to be a soul, which exists beyond the gross and subtle bodies, will consider its development to be their self-interest and will consider it their religious duty in terms of helping other people develop their spiritual consciousness. Those whose vision is clear enough to recognize their identity as spirit soul, but find themselves in the undesirable situation of bondage to the gross and subtle material bodies, can still make favorable use of these coverings in the understanding of their true self-interest, which is that of the soul. They avoid the unfavourable use of the gross and subtle bodies.

In His teachings to Sanātana Gosvāmī, Śrī Caitanya Mahāprabhu taught that the living being's true identity is to be Kṛṣṇa's eternal servant. The *jīva* is the Lord's *taṭastha-śakti,* or marginal energy, and is simultaneously one and with different from Him. The Lord taught Sanātana Gosvāmī the *sādhya* and the *sādhana,* the goal of the seeker and the methods by which the seeker achieves his goal. Mahāprabhu summarized the three elements of His teaching as *sambandha,* knowledge of one's relationship with Kṛṣṇa, *abhidheya,* the practice that leads to perfection, or devotion to Kṛṣṇa, and the *prayojana,* the supreme goal of spiritual life, or love for Kṛṣṇa.

"The sum total of the Vedic literature explains three things: *sambandha, abhidheya* and *prayojana.* The living entity's eternal relationship with Kṛṣṇa is called *sambandha.* Devotional service is the process by which one attains the supreme objective, Kṛṣṇa. Devotional service, or activity for the satisfaction of the Lord, is called *abhidheya.* Love of Kṛṣṇa is *prayojana,* the ultimate goal of life. This goal is the living entity's topmost interest and greatest treasure." (*Caitanya Caritāmṛta* 2.20.124-5)

Kṛṣṇadāsa Kavirāja Gosvāmī has explained all these matters at great length in his *Caitanya Caritāmṛta,* from the twentieth to the twenty-third chapters of the *Madhya-līlā,* with copious quotations from scripture. Rather than repeat these teachings in detail here, which would lead to this account of Sanātana Gosvāmī's life becoming overly extensive, we will limit ourselves to a brief summary.

Mahāprabhu told Sanātana Gosvāmī that the various scriptures, in particular, the *śrutī*, contain statements which indicate that the living being is both one with and different from the Supreme Lord. Different *ācāryas* have put forth a variety of doctrines explaining the relation between this oneness and distinction, named *advaita-vāda, dvaita-vāda, viśiṣṭādvaita-vāda, śuddhādvaita-vāda, dvaitādvaita-vāda*, etc. If one accepts the scripture, one must accept it in its entirety. This includes both types of affirmation and involves finding a way to harmonize apparent contradictions. Śrī Caitanya Mahāprabhu's solution to the problem was to establish the doctrine named *acintya-bhedābheda*, "inconceivable oneness and difference." This doctrine has been favorably accepted around the world and created a revolution in theistic thinking.

Mahāprabhu concluded His teachings with a discourse on the *ātmārāma* verse:

ātmārāmāś ca munayo
nirgranthā apy urukrame
kurvanty ahaitukīṁ bhaktim
itthambhūtaguṇo hariḥ

"Self-satisfied sages who are freed from any bondage also engage in the unmotivated service of Śrī Kṛṣṇa, whose activities are all wonderful. Such are the transcendentally attractive features of Hari!" (*Śrīmad Bhāgavatam* 1.7.11)

"Mahāprabhu gave eighteen different explanations of this verse from the *Śrīmad Bhāgavatam* to Sārvabhauma Bhaṭṭācārya. When Sanātana Gosvāmī asked the Lord to allow him to hear them, Mahāprabhu treated him to sixty-one different interpretations.

SANĀTANA GOSVĀMĪ GOES TO VRAJA

After this, Mahāprabhu converted Prakāśānanda Sarasvatī and the other *sannyāsīs* of Benares to Vaiṣṇavism. When He had completed instructing Sanātana Gosvāmī in a most thorough fashion, He sent him to Vrindavan while He himself took the less frequented road to Puri. Sanātana Gosvāmī took the main highway to Vrindavan, where he met Subuddhi Rāya, who was following Mahāprabhu's instructions to atone for his past sins by chanting Hare Kṛṣṇa. Though he was barely able to make a living selling dry wood, Subuddhi Rāya would provide for the Vaiṣṇavas who came to Vraja from Bengal.

Sanātana Gosvāmī took the pilgrimage circuit through the twelve forests of Vraja in the company of Subuddhi Rāya and the Sanoḍiyā *brāhmaṇa*. From them, he learnt that Rūpa Gosvāmī and Anupama had also completed the circuit not long before and had then taken the road along the banks of the Ganges to go to Bengal.

When Mahāprabhu performed Vraja *parikramā*, He discovered Radha Kunda and Shyama Kunda near Arit village. He took *darśana* of Harideva at Govardhan, after which he desired to see Giridhārī Gopāla. The Gopāla deity of Mādhavendra Purī had His temple on top of the hill. Mahāprabhu would not walk on Govardhan. How would He be able to fulfill His desire to take *darśana* of Gopāla? While the Lord was wondering how to solve this problem, Gopāla's *pūjārīs* took Him out of His temple and hid Him in the village of Gatholi in fear of a Muslim attack, thus enabling Mahāprabhu to receive

His *darśana*. From time to time, Gopāla would perform this pastime of being moved to Gatholi in this way. Sanātana Gosvāmī also had the good fortune to be able to visit Gopāla while He was there.

SANĀTANA GOSVĀMĪ VISITS THE LORD IN PURI

It took Rūpa Gosvāmī longer to get to Bengal than he had expected, and so he was unable to join the other devotees on their annual trip to Puri to see the Lord. He, therefore, arrived sometime after the main group and went to stay with Haridāsa Ṭhākura. When Mahāprabhu met Rūpa Gosvāmī, he inquired after Sanātana Gosvāmī and heard from him that the brothers had taken different roads and thus missed each other.

In the meantime, Sanātana Gosvāmī was on his way to Puri after touring Vrindavan, taking the Jharikhand route through the jungle. There he drank some bad water and came down with scabies. He became depressed as a result of the running sores on his body and began to plan suicide in his despondency, thinking that due to his low birth and his now disgusting physical condition, he would not only be unable to go near the temple and see Lord Jagannātha but would also be deprived of Mahāprabhu's *darśana* because He stayed close to the main temple. If Lord Jagannātha's servants should accidentally touch him, he would commit a great offense by rendering them impure. All in all, he thought it would be better to throw himself under the wheels of Lord Jagannātha's chariot and be crushed to death while watching Mahāprabhu dance.

When he finally arrived in Puri, he went directly to see Haridāsa Ṭhākura and paid his respectful obeisances to him. Haridāsa Ṭhākura affectionately embraced him and invited him to stay there with him. This way, whenever Mahāprabhu came to see Haridāsa Ṭhākura, as He was accustomed to doing, Sanātana Gosvāmī would have the opportunity to see Him.

The first time the Lord saw Sanātana Gosvāmī, He was so overcome by divine love that He approached with the intention of embracing him. Sanātana Gosvāmī retreated, however, thinking himself too impure to be touched by the Lord. Nevertheless, Mahāprabhu would not let him escape and took him in His arms by force, holding him so tightly that the fluid oozing from Sanātana Gosvāmī's sores was smeared on His body, the sight of which broke Sanātana Gosvāmī's heart. Mahāprabhu then gave Sanātana Gosvāmī the news of Rūpa Gosvāmī's visit and Anupam's devotion to Lord Rāmacandra and his departure for Lord Rāma's eternal abode.

On another day, the all-knowing Mahāprabhu suddenly confronted Sanātana Gosvāmī about his intention to commit suicide during the Rathayātrā festival. He said:

"My dear Sanātana, if I could attain Kṛṣṇa by committing suicide, then I would give up millions of bodies without a moment's hesitation. But I cannot attain Kṛṣṇa simply by giving up the body, but only through *bhajana*. There are no means by which to attain Kṛṣṇa other than devotional service." (*Caitanya Caritāmṛta* 3.4.55-6)

In this way, Mahāprabhu taught the world through Sanātana Gosvāmī that suicide is an act of the mode of ignorance which cannot be used to attain Kṛṣṇa. It is only through the cultivation of pure devotion in practice that one can attain the Supreme Lord. The best forms of bhajan, or worship, are known as the nine kinds of devotional service, or *nava-vidha bhakti*. The best of these is the congregational chanting of the Holy Names of Kṛṣṇa, *harināma-saṅkīrtana.*

Finally, Mahāprabhu revealed how dear Sanātana Gosvāmī was to Him when He said,

"You have already surrendered yourself to Me, so your body is now My personal property. Why do you want to destroy another's property? Are you unable to distinguish right from wrong? Your body is an important instrument through which I shall accomplish many things." (*Caitanya Caritāmṛta* 3.4.76-8)

During the *Cāturmāsya* period, many Bengali and Odishan devotees would come to Puri to be with the Lord, and that year they also met Sanātana Gosvāmī. Sanātana Gosvāmī was struck with wonder by the Lord's dancing before Lord Jagannātha's chariot. When the Bengali Vaiṣṇavas returned to their homes after the four-month period, Sanātana Gosvāmī remained in Puri.

During the hot season, in the month of Jyaiṣṭha, the Lord stayed at Yamesvara Tota. One day, He called Sanātana Gosvāmī to come and see Him at noontime. Rather than taking the main road leading from the Siṁhadvāra to the seashore, Sanātana Gosvāmī took another path that led across the hot sands of the beach. Though Sanātana Gosvāmī had no consciousness of the burning heat of the sand, his feet were covered in blisters when he arrived.

The Lord asked Sanātana Gosvāmī why he had not taken the road that led directly from the Siṁhadvāra. Sanātana Gosvāmī replied:

"I have no right to pass by the Siṁhadvāra, for the servants of Lord Jagannātha are always coming and going there. Since they are always using that road, I would not be able to pass without touching them. If that should happen, I would be ruined." (*Caitanya Caritāmṛta* 3.4.126-7)

Mahāprabhu was very pleased by Sanātana Gosvāmī's humility and respect for Lord Jagannātha's *pūjārīs*. He answered him as follows:

"My dear Sanātana, you can save the entire universe; and even the demigods and great saints are purified by touching you. Nevertheless, it is in a devotee's nature to observe Vaiṣṇava etiquette. Maintenance of Vaiṣṇava etiquette is the ornament of the devotee. One who transgresses these rules of behavior becomes a laughing stock and is ultimately lost, both in this world and the next. You have brought Me great satisfaction by observing this etiquette. If you did not act in this way, who else would?" (*Caitanya Caritāmṛta* 3.4.129-32)

In His pleasure, Mahāprabhu embraced Sanātana Gosvāmī again and again. Once again the oozing fluids from Sanātana Gosvāmī's blisters oozed all over the Lord's body. The situation so troubled Sanātana Gosvāmī that he went to discuss the matter with Jagadānanda Paṇḍita, asking him for advice on how to free himself from the offenses that he was unwillingly committing. Jagadānanda Paṇḍita suggested that Sanātana Gosvāmī leave Puri and return to Vrindavan.

The next time that Mahāprabhu came to Siddha Bakula and embraced him forcefully, Sanātana Gosvāmī blurted out his distress, saying that he should never have come to Puri as his coming had only resulted in his committing countless offenses. The contaminating impurities from his scabies daily touched the Lord's body, and this was plunging him deeper and deeper into misery. He begged Mahāprabhu for permission to leave for Vrindavan, letting him know that it was Jagadānanda Paṇḍita who had thus advised him.

When Mahāprabhu heard this, He became angry and said,

"Jagadānanda is just a newcomer, a boy. Yet he has become so proud that he thinks he can give advice even to you. You are his guru in every respect, both in material and spiritual terms, and yet he gives you counsel? Doesn't he know his own standing? You are My teacher; you are an authority. And yet, Jagadānanda is giving instructions to the one as qualified as you like an impudent child." (*Caitanya Caritāmṛta* 3.4.158-60)

When Sanātana Gosvāmī heard Mahāprabhu criticize Jagadānanda Paṇḍita in this way, he took it as another sign of the Paṇḍita's great fortune on the one hand and his own misfortune on the other.

"You accept Jagadānanda into Your inner circle while You venerate me. It is as though You were giving him ambrosia to drink and me the bitter juice of neem and *niśindā* leaves." (*Caitanya Caritāmṛta* 3.4.163)

Even after hearing these words, Mahāprabhu continued to take Jagadānanda Paṇḍita's actions as a sign of impudence. Śrīla Bhakti Siddhānta Sarasvatī Gosvāmī Ṭhākura has written in this connection, "If someone thinks that he is more qualified than he really is, he transgresses the prescribed lines of etiquette and gives advice to someone to whom he should rather offer respect. Mahāprabhu did not encourage such transgressions, but rather sought to discourage a younger devotee like Jagadānanda Paṇḍita from behaving in this way."

The Lord farther prohibited anyone from looking upon Sanātana Gosvāmī's body as material.

"You take your body to be disgusting, whereas I think that your body is like nectar. Your body is transcendental, never material, but you conceive of it in material terms." (*Caitanya Caritāmṛta* 3.4.172-3)

When Haridāsa Ṭhākura objected that the Lord was exaggerating out of His own mercy, the Lord laughed and explained to him and Sanātana Gosvāmī as follows:

"I think of you as my children and of Myself as your maintainer. The maintainer never takes seriously any faults of the maintained. I never think of Myself as deserving of respect, but because of affection I always consider you to be like My little boys. A mother never hates her child even when a child passes stool and urine that touch her body. On the contrary, she takes much pleasure in cleansing him" (*Caitanya Caritāmṛta* 3.4.184-6)

Śrī Caitanya Mahāprabhu went on to say, "The body of a devotee is never material. It is transcendental, full of spiritual bliss. At the time of initiation, when a devotee fully commits himself to the service of the Lord, Kṛṣṇa accepts him to be as good as Himself. When the devotee's body is thus transformed into ecstatic spiritual existence, he is able to render service to the lotus feet of the Lord. Kṛṣṇa produced scabies on Sanātana Gosvāmī's body and sent him here to test Me. Had I refused to embrace him out of disgust, I would certainly have committed an offense to Kṛṣṇa Himself. This is the body of an associate of Kṛṣṇa. It has no foul odor coming from it. On the first day that I embraced him, I smelt the aroma of *catuḥsama* [a mixture of sandalwood pulp, camphor, aguru and musk]." (*Caitanya Caritāmṛta* 3.4.191-7)

This time, when the Lord embraced Sanātana Gosvāmī, the foul itches which covered his body immediately disappeared and his skin took on an effulgent golden glow.

JAGADĀNANDA PAṆḌITA AND SANĀTANA GOSVĀMĪ IN VRAJA

Mahāprabhu told Sanātana Gosvāmī to stay in Puri that year before returning to Vrindavan. He bid the Lord goodbye after the Dola Yātrā and set off on the jungle path through Jharikhand. Rūpa Gosvāmī joined him in Vrindavan not long afterwards. When Raghunātha Bhaṭṭa Gosvāmī came to Vrindavan on Mahāprabhu's order, he stayed with Rūpa Gosvāmī and Sanātana Gosvāmī and daily recited *Śrīmad Bhāgavatam* for them in a sweet voice.

Sometime later, Jagadānanda Paṇḍita took permission from Mahāprabhu to come to Vrindavan. When he came there, he met Sanātana Gosvāmī, who was overjoyed to see him. The two of them went together on a tour of the twelve forests of Vraja. Sanātana Gosvāmī encouraged Jagadānanda Paṇḍita to stay with him in Gokula, where he was settled at that time. Even though they dwelt together, they ate separately. Śrīla Bhaktivinoda Ṭhākura writes in his *Amṛta-pravāha-bhāṣya,* "Sanātana Gosvāmī had become habituated to the *mādhukarī* system and lived on a few pieces of bread each day. Jagadānanda Paṇḍita, however, could not live without eating rice, and so he went every day to a nearby temple to cook. In those days, rice and dahl were not regularly offered to the deities in the temples of Vraja."

One day, Jagadānanda Paṇḍita invited Sanātana Gosvāmī to eat with him. Sanātana Gosvāmī desired to show the world the extent of Jagadānanda Paṇḍita's devotion to Mahāprabhu. So when he came to eat Jagadānanda Paṇḍita's offering, he wore around his head a red cloth which had been given to him by a certain Mukunda Sarasvatī. When Jagadānanda Paṇḍita learnt that the cloth was not a gift from Mahāprabhu, he was so angry with Sanātana Gosvāmī that he took the pot in which the rice had been cooking and threatened to hit him with it. He said:

"You are Mahāprabhu's most important associate. No one is dearer to Him than you. How could anyone tolerate you wearing another *sannyāsī*'s cloth around your head?" (*Caitanya Caritāmṛta* 3.13.56-7)

Sanātana Gosvāmī answered by praising Jagadānanda Paṇḍita's exclusive dedication to Gaurāṅga Mahāprabhu:

"Well said! It is clear, Paṇḍita Mahāśaya, that you are unequalled in your love for the Lord. Only from you could I have learnt this lesson, for you alone have such solid faith in the Lord. My purpose in binding the cloth around my head has been realized, for as soon as you saw it, I was able to witness the manifestations of your love for the Lord. A Vaiṣṇava should not wear a red cloth. I will give it to someone else, for I have no farther need for it." (*Caitanya Caritāmṛta* 3.13.58-61)

Jagadānanda Paṇḍita stayed in Vraja for two months, after which he was no longer able to tolerate being separated from Mahāprabhu. He took leave of Sanātana Gosvāmī and headed off in the direction of Jagannatha Puri. As they bid each other goodbye, Sanātana Gosvāmī gave him sand from the place where Kṛṣṇa held the *rāsa* dance, a stone from Govardhan, a garland of *gunja* berries and some dried ripe *pilu* fruits as gifts for Mahāprabhu. Jagadānanda Paṇḍita gave all these gifts to Mahāprabhu upon his arrival in Puri; He and His devotees especially relished the *pilu* fruits in great reverence and were overjoyed.

SANĀTANA GOSVĀMĪ'S SERVICE TO THE LORD

Mahāprabhu gave Sanātana Gosvāmī four responsibilities: (1) to preach pure devotional service by establishing the doctrines of pure devotion; (2) to discover and make known the various places where Kṛṣṇa had His pastimes; (3) to establish the service of the deity of Kṛṣṇa in Vrindavan; and (4) to establish proper Vaiṣṇava behavior through compiling a Vaiṣṇava rule book, or *smṛti*, and in this way create the foundations of a Vaiṣṇava society.

"O Sanātana, you should broadcast the revealed scriptures on devotional service and excavate the lost places of pilgrimage in Mathura. Establish the deity service of Lord Kṛṣṇa in Vrindavan. You should also compile a scripture containing the rules of devotional practice and preach these practices." (*Caitanya Caritāmṛta* 2.23.97-8)

In following the instructions to broadcast the revealed scriptures on pure devotional service and to establish the foundations of proper Vaiṣṇava practice and etiquette, Sanātana Gosvāmī wrote four books, all of which are considered to be jewels by the devotees. He wrote (1) a commentary on the *Hari-bhakti-vilāsa* known as *Dig-darśinī*, (2) a commentary on the tenth canto of the *Śrīmad Bhāgavatam* known as the *Bṛhad-Vaiṣṇava-Toṣaṇī*, (3) *Līlā-stava* or *Daśama-carita*, and (4) *Bṛhad-Bhāgavatāmṛta*, to which he added a commentary. Mahāprabhu Himself personally gave directions to Sanātana Gosvāmī about the contents of the *Hari-bhakti-vilāsa*, which is the *smriti* scripture, or rule book, for the practices to be followed by the devotees.

Sanātana Gosvāmī searched out the various holy spots in the land of Vraja. He also established the service of the Madana Mohana deity. Śrīla Sanātana Gosvāmī founded a Math in Vrindavan at the place known as Dwadashaditya Tila. He first had a temple built there for Rādhā – Madana Mohana. It is said that a rich officer in the Sultan's army named Kṛrishadas Kapoor built the temple and a kitchen and financed an opulent standard of worship for the deity. He later became Sanātana Gosvāmī's disciple.

When Sanātana Gosvāmī was staying in Gokul Mahavan, he saw Madana Gopāla playing with a group of cowherd boys at Raman Reti. Narahari Cakravartī Ṭhākura has given a beautiful description of this vision in his *Bhakti-ratnākara*:

"O Śrīnivāsa, just look at this place. Sanātana Gosvāmī used to live here. All the fortunate residents of Mahavan would be revitalized by seeing him. He joyfully lived in Mahavan in the audience of Madana Gopāla. Madana Gopāla enjoyed playing on the sandy beaches which line the Yamuna, known as Raman Reti. One day He came to that divine riverbank with the children of Mahavan, Himself taking the form of a cowherd boy. Sanātana Gosvāmī watched Him as He played various childhood games with the other children and thought, 'This is no ordinary child.' When the children had finished playing and were leaving, Sanātana Gosvāmī followed them. The child entered the temple, and when Sanātana Gosvāmī followed Him inside, he saw no one but the deity of Madana Mohana. He paid his obeisances to the deity and then returned to his own dwelling without saying anything to anyone. So this is how Madana Gopāla showed Himself to be under the control of Sanātana Gosvāmī's love. Sanātana Gosvāmī's wondrous character has thus filled the three worlds." (*Bhakti-ratnākara* 5.177-186)

SANĀTANA GOSVĀMĪ'S GLORIOUS PASTIMES IN VRAJA

In his *Caitanya Caritāmṛta* Kṛṣṇadāsa Kavirāja Gosvāmī has described how Rūpa Gosvāmī and Sanātana Gosvāmī worshipped Kṛṣṇa in the land of Vraja:

"These brothers have no fixed residence. They spend each night beneath a different tree in the forest, one night under one tree and the next under another. Sometimes, they beg dry food from a *brāhmaṇa*'s house, and other times it is cooked, such as dry bread and fried chickpeas. This is how they have given up all kinds of material enjoyments. They wrap themselves in a quilt and wear nothing but a piece of torn cloth, claiming nothing but a water pot as a possession. They engage almost twenty-four hours daily in rendering service to the Lord by chanting His Holy Names, discussing His pastimes or dancing in great jubilation. They spend only an hour and a half in sleep, and some days, when overcome by the love of chanting the Lord's Holy Name, they do not sleep at all. Sometimes they write transcendental works about divine aesthetics, and sometimes they listen to talks about Śrī Caitanya Mahāprabhu or spend their time thinking about the Lord." (*Caitanya Caritāmṛta* 2.19.127-31)

Sanātana Gosvāmī had another vision of the Lord later in his life. While staying at Chakratirtha near Govardhan, Sanātana Gosvāmī would regularly circumambulate the mountain. As he grew older, he became too weak to circumambulate on a daily basis without becoming excessively fatigued. One day, Gopīnātha Himself came in the form of a cowherd boy to fan him when he became too tired from walking. After refreshing Sanātana Gosvāmī in this way, the boy climbed onto the hill and brought down a stone marked with Kṛṣṇa's footprint. He gave the stone to Sanātana Gosvāmī and said, "You have grown old. There is no longer any need for you to trouble yourself to this extent. I am giving you this stone from Govardhan. If you circumambulate this stone, you can consider yourself to have circumambulated Govardhan itself." Then He disappeared. Sanātana Gosvāmī was overwhelmed with pain and began to cry upon losing sight of the cowherd boy's charming form. (*Bhakti-ratnākara* 5.728-741).

Chakratirtha is on the northern shore of Manasi Ganga. A temple dedicated to Chakleswar Mahadeva stands on the bank. Sanātana Gosvāmī's *bhajana-kutīra* was under a neem tree which stood in front of this temple. Just north of this place is another temple, housing Gaura-Nityānanda Prabhu. The Govardhan *śīlā* worshipped by Sanātana Prabhu is currently being served in the Rādhā-Dāmodara temple in Vrindavan.

There are more stories about the glories of Chakratirtha. When Sanātana Gosvāmī first came to this place, there were so many mosquitos that he was unable to concentrate while meditating on the Holy Name or writing transcendental literature, so much so that he decided to move. That night, Chakleswar Mahadeva appeared to Sanātana Gosvāmī in a dream and told him not to worry about the problem; he would be able to engage in his worship without disturbance. From that night on, there have been no mosquitos at Chakratirtha.

Śrīla Sanātana Gosvāmī also spent some time living in a cottage on the banks of Pavana Sarovara near Nandagram. Here also he was granted a vision of Kṛṣṇa as a cowherd boy who told him to build a hut and engage in His worship there. It is at this place where Rūpa Gosvāmī once wished to prepare sweet rice for Sanātana Gosvāmī. Śrīmati Rādhārāṇī took the form of a young cowherd girl and came to Rūpa Gosvāmī with milk, sugar, rice and ghee, in short, giving him everything he needed to make the preparation for Sanātana Gosvāmī's pleasure. Rūpa Gosvāmī cooked the sweet rice and after offering it to the deity gave the *prasāda* to Sanātana Gosvāmī.

Sanātana Gosvāmī found that after relishing the delicious sweet rice, he was overcome by uncontrollable waves of ecstasy. Suspecting that something unusual had taken place, he asked Rūpa Gosvāmī where the ingredients had come from. When Rūpa Gosvāmī told him about the little cowherd girl, Sanātana Gosvāmī immediately realized that She had been Rādhā. Because Rādhā was their goddess and they were Her servants, the proper relation of served and the servant had been reversed. He therefore strictly forbade Rūpa Gosvāmī from accepting such gifts in the future. (*Bhakti-ratnākara* 5.1311-30)

Another anecdote told about Sanātana Gosvāmī is the following. Once there was a very poor devotee of Śiva whose name, according to the *Bhakta-māla* and *Gauḍīya Vaiṣṇava Abhidhāna*, was Śrī Jīvana Cakravartī. Further, it is stated there that he hailed from the village of Mankar in the Burdwan district in Bengal, but spent many years worshipping Śiva in Benares, praying to him for wealth. Finally, one night Śiva appeared to him in a dream and told him to go to Sanātana Gosvāmī in Vrindavan, for he was in possession of a great wealth which he would share with him.

The poor *brāhmaṇa* immediately set off for Vrindavan, where he found Sanātana Gosvāmī. However, when he saw the Gosvāmī, thin and dressed in a dirty cloth, he began to doubt that he could give him the desired riches. Even so, he told Sanātana Gosvāmī about the dream. Sanātana Gosvāmī heard the *brāhmaṇa* and could not control his laughter. He answered saying that he lived by begging a few crumbs from a number of different houses; how could he possibly give him the riches he desired?

The poor *brāhmaṇa* was disappointed and turned away, thinking that perhaps the message Śiva had given him in the dream had been just an illusion. Meanwhile, Sanātana Gosvāmī pondered why Śiva had sent the *brāhmaṇa* to him. As he ruminated, he remembered a philosopher's stone that was lying in a pile of rubbish and had long been buried in the earth. As soon as he remembered the existence of this valuable jewel, he sent someone to fetch the *brāhmaṇa* and told him to take the jewel from the rubbish heap. When the *brāhmaṇa* saw the touchstone, he was overjoyed and thought,

"Now there will be no one as rich as I in the entire world!" After walking some distance away, however, he began to wonder why Sanātana Gosvāmī had completely forgotten about such a valuable possession. Indeed, if he cared so little for the philosopher's stone, he must have something even more valuable. Perhaps he had been cheated! He wanted to know what riches Sanātana Gosvāmī possessed that he cared so little for the valuable stone.

The *brāhmaṇa* quickly ran back to Sanātana Gosvāmī and expressed his doubts, asking him if he had anything more valuable in his possession. Then Sanātana Gosvāmī told him that there was no greater wealth than love for Kṛṣṇa and that material goods were insignificant and simply a cause of greater distress. The *brāhmaṇa* then bowed his head and prayed to Sanātana Gosvāmī to please give him the wealth which made him consider even a philosopher's stone insignificant. Sanātana Gosvāmī was moved by his prayer and mercifully bestowed upon him the wealth of Kṛṣṇa *prema*.

Sanātana Gosvāmī's *samādhi* is found next to the old Rādhā Madana Mohana temple in Vrindavan. He left this world on the full-moon day of Āṣāḍha in the Śaka year 1480 (1558 A.D.).

Śrīla Raghunātha Bhaṭṭa Gosvāmī

raghunāthākhyako bhaṭṭaḥ purā yā rāga-mañjarī
kṛta-śrī-rādhikā-kuṇḍa-kuṭīra-vasatiḥ sa tu

"In Kṛṣṇa *līlā*, Raghunātha Bhaṭṭa, who made his home in a cottage by Radha Kunda, was Rāga Mañjarī." (*Gaura-gaṇoddeśa-dīpikā* 185)

SERVING THE LORD IN BENARES

In around 1503 A.D. Raghunātha Bhaṭṭācārya appeared as the son of Tapana Miśra, a dear devotee of Śrī Caitanya Mahāprabhu who hailed from the village of Ramapur on the banks of the Padma River in East Bengal. Mahāprabhu first met Tapana Miśra when He went to East Bengal. Tapana Miśra had studied many scriptures but was still bewildered about the purpose of life and what to do to attain it. He had a dream in which he was instructed to go to Nimāi Paṇḍita, who would clarify these matters for him. When Tapana Miśra went to the Lord and told Him of his dream, Nimāi answered that *harināma-saṅkīrtana* was both the purpose of life and the means for attaining it. Tapana Miśra expressed his desire to come and live in Nabadwip near the Lord, but Mahāprabhu told him to go to Benares instead. Several years later, while in Benares, Mahāprabhu stayed at Candraśekhara Vaidya's house and took His meals at Tapana Miśra's house.

"The Lord had three devotees in Benares. One was Candraśekhara Vaidya, another Tapana Miśra. The third was Tapana Miśra's son Raghunātha Bhaṭṭācārya. The Lord met with them when He stopped in Kashi after visiting Vrindavan." (*Caitanya Caritāmṛta* 1.11.152-3)

Śrī Raghunātha Bhaṭṭa Gosvāmī lived at home for about twenty-eight years. During the two months that the Lord spent in Benares, Raghunātha Bhaṭṭa Gosvāmī had the opportunity to personally serve Him and receive His mercy.

"Mahāprabhu stayed in the house of Candraśekhara Vaidya for two months' time, daily taking His meals at Tapana Miśra's residence. Raghunātha was just a boy at the time, but he served the Lord by cleaning His place after He ate and massaging His feet. When he grew up, he went to Puri to see the Lord. He stayed there for eight months, occasionally cooking for the Lord." (*Caitanya Caritāmṛta* 1.11.154-6)

RAGHUNĀTHA BHAṬṬA COMES TO PURI

Out of eagerness to see the Lord, Raghunātha Bhaṭṭa renounced all his materialistic duties and hurried to Puri after visiting Bengal. He was accompanied by a servant who carried his baggage for him. While traveling, he met a certain Rāma Dāsa Visvās, a devotee of Lord Rāma initiated in the Rāmānandī disciplic succession and very learned in scriptures. He was traveling to Puri renouncing his material entanglements to visit Jagannātha Deva. He was constantly chanting Lord Rāma's name. Knowing Raghunātha Bhaṭṭa to be a *brāhmaṇa*, he rendered service to him with great reverence, sometimes massaging his feet, sometimes carrying his baggage on his head. Raghunātha Bhaṭṭa Gosvāmī was somewhat embarrassed that such a rich and important man should be rendering him such menial service, but Rāma Dāsa tried to allay his doubts by saying, "I am a lowly *śudra* and you are a *brāhmaṇa*. It is my duty to serve you. I feel the greatest joy in having this opportunity to serve you."

When Raghunātha Bhaṭṭa Gosvāmī arrived in Puri, he prostrated himself on the ground before the feet of the Lord. The Lord lifted him up with great emotion and embraced him. He inquired after Tapana Miśra and Candraśekhara Vaidya and then sent him to see Lord Jagannātha, telling him to come and eat with Him afterwards. Mahāprabhu had Govinda make housing arrangements for Raghunātha Bhaṭṭa and introduced him to Svarūpa Dāmodara and His other associates.

During the eight months that Śrī Raghunātha Bhaṭṭa Gosvāmī remained in Nilachal, he sometimes had the chance to invite Mahāprabhu for meals. He would take the opportunity to prepare delicious vegetable platters for the Lord's pleasure. He was an expert cook, and the Lord was especially satisfied by the devotional mood in which he prepared these meals. Raghunātha Bhaṭṭa was then fortunate enough to be able to take the Lord's remnants. Rāma Dāsa Visvās also came to meet Mahāprabhu during this time, but the Lord could see through him. He saw that Rāma Dāsa harbored desires for liberation and that he was proud of his learning, and so He did not show him as much mercy as He did to Raghunātha Bhaṭṭa.

After Raghunātha Bhaṭṭa Gosvāmī had been in Puri for eight months, the Lord told him to go back to Kashi to serve his aged Vaiṣṇava parents. He also told him not to get married. The Lord then made him a gift of his own neck beads, which He placed around Raghunātha Bhaṭṭa Gosvāmī's neck, telling him to come to Puri again.

RAGHUNĀTHA BHAṬṬA GOES TO VRINDAVAN

Raghunātha Bhaṭṭa Gosvāmī felt separation from Mahāprabhu and started to weep; however, as per the Lord's order he went back to Kashi and took care of his parents for the remainder of their lives, which was another four years. During this time, he also studied the *Bhāgavata* from a Vaiṣṇava. Raghunātha Bhaṭṭa Gosvāmī had a beautiful singing voice. When he recited the *Bhāgavata*, he would read the same verse in different tunes. This made his readings very attractive to the devotees.

When his parents departed the world, he returned to Puri and stayed with Mahāprabhu. After staying with the Lord for eight months, Mahāprabhu told him to go to Vrindavan and to stay with Rūpa Gosvāmī and Sanātana Gosvāmī. He told him to study the *Bhāgavata* daily as well as to chant the Holy Names. After embracing Raghunātha Bhaṭṭa, the Lord gave him a twenty-one-foot long Tulasī garland which had been worn by Lord Jagannātha as well as unspiced betel. Kṛṣṇadāsa Kavirāja Gosvāmī describes Raghunātha Bhaṭṭa Gosvāmī's voyage to Vrindavan and his life there in the *Caitanya Caritāmṛta*:

" 'Study *Śrīmad Bhāgavatam* and chant the names of Kṛṣṇa continuously. The Supreme Lord Kṛṣṇa will very soon bestow His mercy upon you.' After saying this, the Lord embraced Raghunātha Bhaṭṭa Gosvāmī, who was enlivened with ecstatic love for Kṛṣṇa by His mercy. At a feast, the Lord had been given some unspiced betel and a twenty-one-foot long garland of Tulasī leaves which had been worn by Lord Jagannātha. He gave the garland and betel to Raghunātha Bhaṭṭa, who accepted them as his worshipable deities, taking care to preserve them. Then Raghunātha Bhaṭṭa Gosvāmī took the Lord's permission and departed for Vrindavan.

"When he arrived in Vrindavan, he put himself under the care of Rūpa Gosvāmī and Sanātana Gosvāmī. Whenever he recited the *Bhāgavata* in their company, Raghunātha Bhaṭṭa would be overwhelmed with ecstatic love for Kṛṣṇa. By Mahāprabhu's mercy, he experienced the symptoms of ecstatic love – tears, trembling, and faltering of the voice. His eyes filled with tears, and his throat became so choked that he could not continue his recital.

"Raghunātha Bhaṭṭa Gosvāmī's voice was as sweet as a cuckoo's, and he would recite each verse of the *Bhāgavata* in three or four different tunes. Whenever he recited or heard about Kṛṣṇa's beauty and sweetness, he would be overwhelmed with ecstatic love and become oblivious to the world around him.

"Raghunātha Bhaṭṭa surrendered himself to Govinda's lotus feet, and those lotus feet were the only thing that gave his life meaning. In time, Raghunātha Bhaṭṭa ordered his disciples to construct a temple for Govinda. He himself made various ornaments for the deity, including a flute and dolphin-shaped earrings.

"Raghunātha Bhaṭṭa would never speak or listen to gossip. He would simply discuss Kṛṣṇa and worship Him day and night. He would not listen to criticism of a Vaiṣṇava's misbehavior. He knew only that everyone was engaged in Kṛṣṇa's service. When Raghunātha Bhaṭṭa Gosvāmī was absorbed in remembrance of Lord Kṛṣṇa, he would take the *prasādi* Tulasī garland and the neck beads given to him by the Lord and wear them around his neck. Thus I have described the power of Śrī Caitanya

Mahāprabhu's mercy, by which Raghunātha Bhaṭṭa Gosvāmī experienced unlimited ecstatic love for Kṛṣṇa." (*Caitanya Caritāmṛta* 3.13.121-135)

A farther description of Śrī Raghunātha Bhaṭṭa Gosvāmī is also given in *Bhakti-ratnākara*:

"'As I look upon the *samādhi* of Raghunātha Bhaṭṭa, my heart breaks and my eyes are awash with tears. But who is not overjoyed as soon as he hears Raghunātha Bhaṭṭa Gosvāmī's glories? He was such an expert teacher of all the scriptures that even Bṛhaspati would joyfully cheer upon hearing Raghunātha's explanations of Vaiṣṇava doctrine. There is nothing to which his discourses on the *Bhāgavata* can be compared. Even Vyāsa himself wishes to sit and listen to him speak, knowing that this will bring him happiness. Even the gods were astonished when they observed Raghunātha Bhaṭṭa's devotional practices.' When Śrīnivāsa Ācārya and the devotees heard Śrī Raghunātha Bhaṭṭa Gosvāmī glorified in this way, they fell to the ground and offered their respects. Then they continued on to the Govindajī temple."

Śrī Raghunātha Bhaṭṭa Gosvāmī disappeared in 1580 A.D.

Śrīla Gopāla Bhaṭṭa Gosvāmī

anaṅga-mañjarī yāsīt sādya gopāla-bhaṭṭakaḥ
bhaṭṭa-gosvāminaṁ kecit āhuḥ śrī-guṇa-mañjarīm

"She who was formerly Anaṅga Mañjarī has appeared to enrich Mahāprabhu's pastimes as Śrīla Gopāla Bhaṭṭa Gosvāmī. Some say that Gopāla Bhaṭṭa is actually Guṇa Mañjarī." (*Gaura-gaṇoddeśa-dīpikā* 184)

Śrīla Gopāla Bhaṭṭa Gosvāmī appeared in 1500 A.D. (though, according to some authorities, he appeared in 1503) as the son of Veṅkaṭa Bhaṭṭa in the town of Srirangam in South India. Their residence was in a village not far from Srirangam called Belgundi on the banks of river Kaveri.

According to *Bhakti-ratnākara*, Mahāprabhu gave Gopāla Bhaṭṭa a dream vision through which he could witness all of His Nabadwip pastimes. Though Gopāla Bhaṭṭa Gosvāmī was an eternal associate of Kṛṣṇa, he appeared in a faraway place in order to make a special contribution to Lord Gaurāṅga's pastimes. Thus, even though he was living too far away to know anything about the Lord directly, he was still able to know long before he met the Lord in person that He had appeared and taken *sannyāsa*.

Gopāla Bhaṭṭa did not particularly like the Lord's appearance as a *sannyāsī*. This austere form distressed Gopāla Bhaṭṭa, who was thus crying alone when the Lord appeared to him and gave him this vision of His pastimes in Nabadwip. He then took Gopāla Bhaṭṭa on his lap and drenched him with tears.

"The Lord then embraced Gopāla Bhaṭṭa and drenched him with His tears. He then told Gopāla to keep all these revelations a secret. Gopāla Bhaṭṭa's mind was absorbed in a state of intense joy." (*Bhakti-ratnākara* 1.123-4)

THE LORD'S TEACHINGS TO GOPĀLA BHAṬṬA'S FATHER

In 1510, Mahāprabhu made His auspicious entrance to the pilgrimage city of Srirangam. He was invited by Veṅkaṭa Bhaṭṭa, a Vaiṣṇava of tthe Sri Sampradaya, to spend the four months of the *Cāturmāsya* in his house. Knowing him to be a strict Vaiṣṇava, Mahāprabhu accepted his invitation. In fact, the Lord's pastime of coming to Srirangam and staying at Veṅkaṭa Bhaṭṭa's home was to give His mercy to Gopāla Bhaṭṭa and his family, for the Lord knew that Gopāla Bhaṭṭa, His eternal companion, had appeared there.

At this time, Gopāla Bhaṭṭa was still a young boy. He was fortunate enough to be able to serve the Lord by massaging His feet. Even though He was satisfied with Veṅkaṭa Bhaṭṭa and his family's service, the Lord observed that Veṅkaṭa Bhaṭṭa had an element of pride in his object of worship. He believed that his worshipable deity, Lakṣmī-Nārāyaṇa, was the supreme worshipable object, that Nārāyaṇa was the source of all other *avatāras*, including Kṛṣṇa, Rāma and Nṛsiṁha. His reasoning was that Nārāyaṇa is never born, while Kṛṣṇa and Rāma take birth in the world. He thus thought, "Mahāprabhu worships Kṛṣṇa, the *avatāra* of Nārāyaṇa, while we worship Nārāyaṇa, the source of all *avatāras*."

As Madhusūdana is the destroyer of false pride, Mahāprabhu finally decided one day that He would do so for Veṅkaṭa Bhaṭṭa. He asked him in a mild-humored, witty tone, "Veṅkaṭa Bhaṭṭa, I hear that no one is equal in opulence to your Lord Nārāyaṇa; the same is true for your worshipable goddess Lakṣmī Devī. On the other hand, the object of My worship, Kṛṣṇa, has no opulence of any kind. He wears garlands of wild forest flowers and uses peacock feathers for decoration. He is the son of Nanda Gopa and spends His day grazing the cows with the other cowherd boys. My worshipable goddesses, the *gopīs*, are also nothing but poor cowherd girls. I wonder, therefore, why your worshipable Lakṣmī Devī came to Vrindavan to perform austerities in the hope of gaining Kṛṣṇa's company in the *rāsa* dance."

Veṅkaṭa Bhaṭṭa immediately answered, "What's wrong with that? Rādhā's beloved Kṛṣṇa is not different from Lakṣmī Devī's husband Nārāyaṇa."

siddhāntatas tv abheda 'pi śrīśa-kṛṣṇa-svarūpayoḥ
rasenotkṛṣyate kṛṣṇa-rūpam eṣā rasa-sthitiḥ

"Though according to theological doctrine, Kṛṣṇa and the husband of Lakṣmī are identical in essence, the form of Kṛṣṇa is superior when analyzed from the point of view of divine sentiment." (*Bhakti-rasamrita-sindhu* 1.2.59)

"Since the divine sentiment in Kṛṣṇa is superior, there is no fault if Lakṣmī Devī chooses to seek His association and performs austerities to that end."

Mahāprabhu answered, "I am not saying that there is any fault. I agree that ontologically, Kṛṣṇa and Nārāyaṇa are identical. The difference between them is based on the variety of *rasa* (transcendental taste or mood). When the Lord performs pastimes of opulence, He is Nārāyaṇa. When He performs pastimes of sweetness, He is Kṛṣṇa. She who is Rādhā in Kṛṣṇa's pastimes is Lakṣmī Devī in the pastimes of Nārāyaṇa. Thus, when Lakṣmī Devī performs austerities to have the association of Kṛṣṇa, there is no question of Her breaking Her vows of fidelity to Her husband. Thus, She went to perform these austerities in Vrindavan. But I have another question for you: Why, even after trying so hard through such penances, etc., to enter Kṛṣṇa's *rāsa līlā*, was Lakṣmī Devī still unable to do so?"

Veṅkaṭa Bhaṭṭa was terribly distressed at being unable to give the Lord an answer. Mahāprabhu observed his distress and tried to pacify him by saying, "You yourself said that Nārāyaṇa and Kṛṣṇa are identical ontologically, but that the superiority of Kṛṣṇa is due to the excellence in *rasas*. Nārāyaṇa is involved in two and a half of the five principle rāsas, whereas in Kṛṣṇa there is a complete manifestation of all twelve *rasas*, the five principal and seven secondary sentiments. Since Nārāyaṇa's pastime is primarily one of opulence and majesty, His principal devotee is Lakṣmī Devī, who also worships Him in the appropriate mood of awe and reverence. The same Lakṣmī Devī is Rādhikā in order to heighten the experience of conjugal love. Unless one follows in the footsteps of Rādha and Her expansions, the *gopīs*, who are the repositories of the transcendental divine love, it is impossible to relish Kṛṣṇa's sweet qualities. Lakṣmī Devī, however, did not follow in the *gopīs*' footsteps but continued to perform Her austerities in the mood of awe and reverence. As a result, She repeatedly found Herself in the company of Nārāyaṇa and never in that of Kṛṣṇa. By way of contrast, the *śrutis* followed the *gopīs* in the *rāga-mārga* and so were ultimately able to achieve Kṛṣṇa's service in that mood. As long as one continues to think of Kṛṣṇa in majestic terms as Lord and controller, one cannot possibly worship in the spirit of *rāgānuga bhakti*."

Mahāprabhu said, "Kṛṣṇa has one extraordinary characteristic: by His sweetness, He attracts the minds of the entire world. By taking on the mood of the Vraja *gopīs* one can attain to His lotus feet. The people of Vraja have no idea that Kṛṣna is the Lord and controller. Some think of Him as their son and even tie Him to a mortar, while others take Him to be their friend and climb on His shoulders. The people of Vraja only know Him as the son of Nanda, whereas in the attitude of awe and reverence, the devotee does not have a concept of such a relationship with Him. One who takes the attitude of a resident of Vraja will attain Kṛṣṇa as the son of the King of Vraja in Vrindavan." (*Caitanya Caritāmṛta* 2.9.127-31)

"When the *gopīs*, the objects of My worship, were abandoned by Kṛṣṇa in the *rāsa* dance, they began to cry in the intensity of their distress at not seeing Him. Kṛṣṇa came to them in the form of Nārāyaṇa, but the gopis simply paid their obeisances and moved on in search of Kṛṣṇa, showing absolutely no interest in Him as a lover. When Rādhārāṇī stood before the disguised Kṛṣṇa, however, He could not maintain the four-armed form but once again appeared in His form as the holder of the flute. Such is the power of Rādhārāṇī's love!"[24] (*Bhakti-ratnākara* 5.624-629)

Nanda-nandana Kṛṣṇa is the *avatārī*, or source of all *avatāras*. Nārāyaṇa, Rāma, Nṛsiṁha, etc., are all His *avatāras* and expansions. Kṛṣṇa is *svayaṁ bhagavān*, the Supreme Personality of Godhead.

"Only the Personality of Godhead, the source of all other divinities, is eligible to be designated *svayaṁ bhagavān*, or the primeval Lord." (*Caitanya Caritāmṛta* 1.2.88)

ete cāṁśa-kalāḥ puṁsaḥ
kṛṣṇas tu bhagavān svayam
indrāri-vyākulaṁ lokaṁ
mṛḍayanti yuge yuge

"All of the previously mentioned forms of the Lord are either plenary expansions or partial expansions of plenary expansions, but Kṛṣṇa alone is the original Personality of the Godhead. All of them appear in every age to protect the saints whenever the enemies of the gods disturb them." (*Śrīmad Bhāgavatam* 1.3.28)

GOPĀLA BHAṬṬA'S GURU

24 The place where this happened is near Govardhan and is called Paisa-dhama or Paitha-dhama, which means "the place of entering," because Kṛṣṇa's two extra arms merged back into His body here.

Through the power of Śrī Kṛṣṇa Caitanya Mahāprabhu's merciful association, Veṅkaṭa Bhaṭṭa, his brother Prabodhānanda Sarasvatī, his son Gopāla Bhaṭṭa Gosvāmī, and all the other members of his family were inspired to give up the worship of Lakṣmī-Nārāyaṇa and became engaged in the exclusive devotional service of Rādhā and Kṛṣṇa. Śrīla Gopāla Bhaṭṭa Gosvāmī took initiation from his uncle, Tridaṇḍī Yati Śrīmat Prabodhānanda Sarasvatī. Proof of this is found in the *Hari-bhakti-vilāsa*:

bhakter vilāsāṁś cinute prabodhā-
nandasya śiṣyo bhagavat-priyasya
gopāla-bhaṭṭo raghunātha-dāsaṁ
santoṣayan rūpa-sanātanau ca

"I, Gopāla Bhaṭṭa, the disciple of Prabodhānanda Sarasvatī, who is dear to the Lord, have compiled these most essential and glorious devotional doctrines to satisfy Raghunātha Dāsa Gosvāmī, Rūpa Gosvāmī and Sanātana Gosvāmī." (*Hari-bhakti-vilāsa* 1.2)

"Gopāla Bhaṭṭa's parents were very fortunate, for they surrendered themselves, life and soul, to the feet of Lord Caitanya. They ordered their son to go to Vrindavan before they left this world, absorbed in meditating on the Lord. Gopāla Bhaṭṭa Gosvāmī traveled directly to Vrindava,n where he met with Rūpa Gosvāmī and Sanātana Gosvāmī." (*Bhakti-ratnākara* 1.163-5)

GOPĀLA BHAṬṬA COMES TO VRINDAVAN

When Gopāla Bhaṭṭa Gosvāmī arrived in Vrindavan, Rūpa Gosvāmī and Sanātana Gosvāmī wrote to Mahāprabhu to tell him. The Lord was overjoyed and immediately wrote back telling them to affectionately take care of him as though he were their own younger brother. Śrīla Sanātana Gosvāmī compiled the *Hari-bhakti-vilāsa* and published it in Śrīla Gopāla Bhaṭṭa Gosvāmī's name. Rūpa Gosvāmī considered Gopāla Bhaṭṭa to be as dear to him as his own life and engaged him in the worship of the Rādhā Ramaṇa deity.

Śrīla Gopāla Bhaṭṭa Gosvāmī became one of the six Gosvāmīs, but he always kept an attitude of meekness and humility. Thus, when Kṛṣṇadāsa Kavirāja Gosvāmī approached him for permission to write Śrī *Caitanya Caritāmṛta*, he granted it, but under the condition that he not write about him. Kṛṣṇadāsa Kavirāja Gosvāmī could not go against the order of Gopāla Bhaṭṭa and thus did nothing more than mention his name. Śrī Jīva Gosvāmī writes in the introduction to the *Ṣaṭ-sandarbha* that he wrote it on the basis of an earlier text by Gopāla Bhaṭṭa. Śrīla Gopāla Bhaṭṭa Gosvāmī also wrote a book called the *Sat-kriyā-sāra-dīpikā* ("Light on the Essential Sacraments for the Vaiṣṇavas"). Thus his contribution to Gauḍīya Vaiṣṇava literature was in editing the *Hari-bhakti-vilāsa*, preparing the notes for Jīva Gosvāmī's *Ṣaṭ-sandarbha* and in compiling the *Sat-kriyā-sāra-dīpikā*. He also gave great joy to the community of devotees by writing a commentary on Bilvamaṅgala Ṭhākura's *Kṛṣṇa-karṇāmṛta*.

Amongst his disciples were Śrīnivāsa Ācārya and Śrī Gopīnātha Pūjārī. The following story is told about Gopīnātha Pūjārī becoming Gopāla Bhaṭṭa's disciple. One day, Gopāla Bhaṭṭa went to visit the town of Saharanpur, not far from Haridwar. On that occasion, a simple, devoted *brāhmaṇa* engaged in his service in a most unpretentious manner. He had no children but desired to have a son. Śrīla Gopāla Bhaṭṭa Gosvāmī knew the desire of the *brāhmaṇa* and blessed him that he would have a devotionally-minded male child. The *brāhmaṇa* promised Gopāla Bhaṭṭa that he would give him his first son to be his servant and disciple. This son was Gopīnātha Pūjārī.

It is said that Mahāprabhu had such affection for Gopāla Bhaṭṭa that He sent him His own belt and *kaupīna* as well as a wooden seat which He had used. These items are still worshipped in the Rādhā Ramaṇa temple by the current *sevakas*.

ŚRĪ ŚRĪ RĀDHĀ RAMAṆA

When Śrīla Gopāla Bhaṭṭa Gosvāmī was visiting the pilgrimage centers of northern India, he found a *śālagrāma-śilā* on the banks of the Gandaki River. He took the *śālagrāma-śilā* as Vrajendra-nandana Kṛṣna Himself and worshipped Him. One day he thought that if his *śālagrāma-śilā* were a deity he could dress and decorate the Lord beautifully. On the very next day, he found that the *śālagrāma-śilā* had transformed into the Śrī Rādhā Ramaṇa deity to fulfill the wish of his devotee. This deity stands alone without any form of Rādhā standing by His side. Instead, as a symbol of Rādhārāṇī, a silver crown is placed on His left side.

The story is also told in the following way. It is said that Śrīla Gopāla Bhaṭṭa Gosvāmī used to daily worship twelve *śālagrāmas*. He developed a desire to serve the Lord in the form of a deity, thinking that in this way he would be able to worship him in a much better way. The Lord within his heart knew his feelings and through a rich merchant had many beautiful items used in the worship of the deity, such as ornaments and clothes, sent to him. Gopāla Bhaṭṭa Gosvāmī began to worry that all these beautiful objects could not be used properly unless the *śālagrāmas* took a deity form. That night, he put the *śālagrāmas* to rest, and in the morning he saw that one of them had been transformed into the Śrī Rādhā Ramaṇa deity.

When Rūpa Gosvāmī and Sanātana Gosvāmī heard that Kṛṣṇa had so mercifully appeared to Gopāla Bhaṭṭa, they immediately came with the other devotees for *darśana*, and when they saw Him, they were ecstatic with love. The annual festival commemorating Rādhā Ramaṇa's appearance, when He is bathed publicly, takes place on the full-moon day of Vaiśākha. The Rādhā Ramaṇa temple is considered one of the most important in Vrindavan.

Śrīla Gopāla Bhaṭṭa Gosvāmī ended his earthly pastimes on the *Kṛṣṇā-pañcamī* of Āṣāḍha of 1507 of the Śaka era (1586 A.D.). His *samādhi* temple is behind the current Rādhā Ramaṇa temple. By reading Śrīnivāsa Ācārya's hymn to the six Gosvāmīs, *Ṣaḍ-gosvāmi-aṣṭakam*, we can understand their glories.

Śrīla Raghunātha Dāsa Gosvāmī

dāsa-śrī-raghunāthasya
pūrvākhyā rasa-mañjarī
amuṁ kecit prabhāṣante
śrīmatīṁ rati-mañjarīm
bhānumaty-ākhyayā kecit
āhus taṁ nāma-bhedataḥ

"Three different names are ascribed to Raghunātha Dāsa from his previous identity as a *mañjarī* in Kṛṣṇa *līlā*: Some say he was Rāsa Mañjarī, others Rati Mañjarī, and yet others Bhanumatī." (*Gaura-gaṇoddeśa-dīpikā* 186)

RAGHUNĀTHA DĀSA'S CHILDHOOD

Raghunātha Dāsa appeared in around 1495 A.D. in the village of Krishnapur, which is not far south of the current railway station named Adi Saptagram on the eastern bank of the ancient Sarasvati River. Krishnapur is about a mile from Adi Saptagram station and approximately 1.5 miles from Trish Bigha station.[25]

Śrīla Raghunātha Dāsa Gosvāmī was the son of Govardhana Majumadāra. His mother's name is not known. Govardhana's elder brother, Hiraṇya, was childless. The two brothers belonged to the *kāyastha* caste and were the primary landholders in Saptagram. In those days, the borders of Saptagram stretched from the Jessore Bhairav creek almost up to the Rupa Narayana River. Raghunātha Dāsa lived in Saptagram Krishnapur, his uncle Kālī Dāsa, who was also Caitanya Mahāprabhu's devotee, lived in Shankhanagar. Raghunātha Dāsa's family priest, Balarāma Ācārya, and his guru, Yadunandana Ācārya, lived in the town of Chandpur. Yadunandana Ācārya was an intimate disciple of Advaita Ācārya and a dedicated devotee of Lord Caitanya Mahāprabhu who had also received the special blessings of Vāsudeva Datta Ṭhākura.

After delivering the prostitute sent to tempt him by Rāmacandra Khān, Haridāsa Ṭhākura left Benapole and came to Chandpur, where he stayed with Balarāma Ācārya. Śrīla Raghunātha Dāsa Gosvāmī was just a young boy at this time, but he had the opportunity to see Haridāsa Ṭhākura and receive his blessings. These blessings were the cause of Raghunātha Dāsa Gosvāmī's later being able to attain the association of Mahāprabhu.

"Raghunātha Dāsa was just a little boy engaged in studies when he had the *darśana* of Haridāsa Ṭhākura. Haridāsa was merciful to him and this mercy was the reason that he later was able to attain the company of Lord Caitanya." (*Caitanya Caritāmṛta* 3.3.168-9)

RAGHUNĀTHA DĀSA'S DESIRE TO JOIN THE LORD

Hiraṇya and Govardhana Majumadāra had an annual income of 800,000 coins. At that time, a coin could buy about 650 pounds of rice, which means it had several hundred times the value of a rupee today. Even though Raghunātha Dāsa was the only heir to this great fortune, he was indifferent to riches from his childhood. He had his first opportunity to see Mahāprabhu when the Lord came to Shantipur after taking *sannyāsa*. As soon as he saw the Lord, Raghunātha Dāsa Gosvāmī

25 Saptagram was made up of seven villages: Saptagram, Bangshibati, Shibpur, Vasudevpur, Krishnapur, Nityanandapur and Shankhanagar.

fell to His feet in a transport of divine love. Raghunātha Dāsa's father, Govardhana Majumadāra, always served Advaita Ācārya with faith and devotion, and thus Advaita Prabhu was inclined to show kindness to the young Raghunātha Dāsa Gosvāmī. He thus made sure that Raghunātha Dāsa Gosvāmī received the Lord's remnants for as long as He remained in Shantipur.

When the Lord departed for Puri, Raghunātha Dāsa Gosvāmī returned to his home in Saptagram but was constantly feeling intense separation from the Lord. Seeing him in this condition, his father surrounded Raghunātha Dāsa Gosvāmī by a guard of eleven men, including two *brāhmaṇas*, four servants and five guards. Even so, Raghunātha tried on several occasions to run away in order to join the Lord, but each time was caught and brought back before realizing his objectives. Raghunātha Dāsa Gosvāmī became dejected as a result of this situation. Seeing their son in such a state, his parents were not at all at peace.

When the Lord returned from Kanair Natshala to Shantipur during His attempt to visit Vrindavan, He again stayed there for a short period of time. Raghunātha Dāsa Gosvāmī wanted to see the Lord and this time begged his father to give him permission. Govardhana was worried about the state of his son's mind and finally decided to let him go on condition that he return quickly. He also sent a large entourage of guards to accompany him.

When Raghunātha Dāsa Gosvāmī saw the Lord, it was as though he got a new life. He told the Lord of his intolerable situation and prayed to Him to tell him how he could break free from his material bondage. The all-knowing Lord could understand the depth of Raghunātha Dāsa Gosvāmī's feeling and yet He tried to pacify him with the following instruction:

"Calm yourself and return home. Don't be foolish. It takes time to cross the ocean of material suffering. Don't make a show of *markaṭa-vairāgya* ('monkey renunciation') simply for public display. Accept whatever is required for the body in the worldly life without attachment. Be fixed on Kṛṣṇa internally while externally dealing with the world in the appropriate fashion. It will not be long before Kṛṣṇa delivers you." (*Caitanya Caritāmṛta* 2.16.237-9)

Śrīla Bhakti Siddhānta Sarasvatī Gosvāmī Ṭhākura has made the following comments on the word *markaṭa-vairāgya*: "To a superficial eye, monkeys are engaged in renunciation because they live naked in the forest without any fixed home. In fact, they are only interested in their own sensual enjoyment and have never given it up. Such show-bottle renunciation is called *markaṭa-vairāgya*, 'monkey renunciation.' Real renunciation comes as a side-effect of pure devotion and is long-lasting, and other types of renunciation which arise out of frustration with material pleasures or desires cannot last throughout one's life. Because of its temporary character, such renunciation is therefore called *phalgu*, or false. Such temporary renunciation, or monkey renunciation, is also known as *śmaśāna-vairāgya*, 'the renunciation of the cremation ground.'

"One may accept things which are absolutely necessary in order to serve Kṛṣṇa without becoming absorbed in them or attached to them. If one lives in this way, he will not be under the influence of the karmic reactions. In the *Bhakti-rasāmṛta-sindhu* (1.2.108), it is said:

yāvatā syāt svanirvāhaḥ
svīkuryāt tāvad arthavit
ādhikye nyūnatāyāṁ ca

cyavate paramārthataḥ

"One who knows his purpose should accept only as much as he needs to maintain his existence. If he accepts more or less than that, he will fall from the supreme objective."

"Śrī Jīva Gosvāmī glosses the word *svanirvāhaḥ* in his *Durgama-saṅgamanī* commentary with the words *sva-sva-bhakti-nirvāhaḥ*, i.e., a devotee should accept only those material things that will help him render service to the Lord, according to his own individual needs. In the *Bhakti-rasāmṛta-sindhu* (1.2.256), *markaṭa-vairāgya*, or *phalgu vairāgya*, has been more clearly explained as follows:

prāpañcikatayā buddhyā
hari-sambandhi-vastunaḥ
mumukṣubhi parityāgo
vairāgyaṁ phalgu kathyate

"*Phalgu-vairāgya* is defined as the rejection of something which is related to the Lord in the understanding that it is something material. The seekers of liberation are engaged in such renunciation."

"In other words, it is a mistake to renounce something which is favorable to the service of Lord Kṛṣṇa, thinking it to be an ordinary material sense object.

anāsaktasya viṣayān
yathārham upayuñjataḥ
nirbandhaḥ kṛṣṇa-sambandhe
yuktaṁ vairāgyam ucyate

"*Yukta-vairāgya* is defined as the attitude of one who is detached from the objects of the sense but uses them only in as much as they have utility in the service of Lord Kṛṣṇa."

Hence, devoid of selfish attachment, and endowed with the ability to see things in relation to the Lord, all sense objects are then directly perceived as being Lord Mādhava Himself. Taking Mahāprabhu's instruction to heart, Raghunātha Dāsa Gosvāmī returned home and gave up his desire to renounce material life in madness and instead engaged in his various duties with a sense of detachment. When his parents saw Raghunātha Dāsa Gosvāmī abandon all the external signs of renunciation, they were delighted and they began to think that there was no necessity for such a tight guard around their son.

HIRAṆYA MAJUMADĀRA'S TAX PROBLEMS

In those days, there was an officer of the king with the title Caudhuri, or the present-day *nāyeb*, who acted as an intermediary between the king and the zamindars. He collected taxes from the landowners and received a commission of 25% on them. Hiraṇya Majumadāra, however, paid his taxes directly to the Shah, with whom he had a special agreement, and thus cut out the middle man. On an income of 2,000,000 rupees, Hiraṇya was paying only 1,200,000 rather than 1,500,000. Since the Caudhuri was losing a large amount of commission, he became an enemy to the Majumadāras.

Ever since returning from his meeting with Mahāprabhu, Raghunātha Dāsa Gosvāmī was practicing *yukta-vairāgya* in accordance with the Lord's instructions. However, when he heard that Mahāprabhu had returned from Vrindavan, he started making preparations to join Him in Puri. At that time, the Muslim Caudhuri had started making complaints to the Shah about Hiraṇya Majumadāra out of anger at being cheated of his percentage of the tax revenue. Fearful of arrest, Hiraṇya and Govardhana Majumadāra went into hiding.

When the minister came to investigate the Caudhuri's complaints, he arrested Raghunātha Dāsa, since his father and uncle were not present. The Caudhuri came daily to rebuke and threaten Raghunātha Dāsa Gosvāmī, asking him to reveal their whereabouts. Finally, he decided to have Raghunātha Dāsa Gosvāmī beaten, but when he saw his calm, lotus-like face, he was unable to continue. In fact, though he verbally chastised him, the Caudhuri was afraid to cause him any real harm because Raghunātha Dāsa Gosvāmī belonged to an influential family of the *kāyastha* class. He knew that the *kāyasthas* are intelligent and could plot against him, causing him worse problems.

Raghunātha Dāsa Gosvāmī himself was looking for a way to extricate himself from the situation, and spoke to the Caudhuri in a sweet voice: "My father and uncle are like your brothers. The behavior of brothers is difficult to understand – sometimes they fight amongst themselves, sometimes they are loving to each other. Today you are arguing, but tomorrow, I am sure that you will be reconciled with each other. I am your son as much as I am my father's, and therefore you are my protector. It is not right for one such as yourself to punish his dependent. I need say no more, for you know the scriptures and are practically a living saint, a *pir*."

The Caudhuri was affected by Raghunātha Dāsa Gosvāmī's sweet words and began to cry as he was overcome by affection for him. He said, "From now on, I consider you to be my son. I will find an excuse to have you freed today. Have your uncle meet with me and make arrangements so that I can get my share of the revenues."

Thus Raghunātha Dāsa Gosvāmī was able to appease the Caudhuri by his sweet and diplomatic behavior and bring the dispute between him and his uncle to an end. In the meantime, Raghunātha Dāsa Gosvāmī's father was making arrangements for his son's marriage to an extremely beautiful girl in order to ensure his commitment to the family.

THE DAṆḌA MAHOTSAVA

A year later, Raghunātha Dāsa Gosvāmī once again became anxious to see Mahāprabhu and repeatedly ran away from home in an effort to go to Puri. Each time, he was caught by his father and returned home. Raghunātha Dāsa Gosvāmī's mother thought that her son was going mad and told her husband to bind him with ropes. Govardhana responded in defeated tones:

"He has as much wealth as Indra, the king of the gods, and his wife is as beautiful as the heavenly courtesans. If these things have not been able to capture his mind, then how will mere ropes be able to do so? The father who gives life to a child cannot interfere with the effects of his previous lives' actions. Śrī Caitanya Candra has given His blessings to this boy. Who can keep prisoner one who was been made mad by Lord Caitanya Mahāprabhu?" (*Caitanya Caritāmṛta* 3.6.39-41)

While Raghunātha Dāsa was devising a plan for how he would be delivered from his entanglements, he heard that Nityānanda Prabhu had made an auspicious appearance in the town of Panihati. Thinking that Nityānanda Prabhu was the deliverer of the most fallen and that by His mercy he would surely be able to find his freedom, he went across the Ganges to Panihati where he found the Lord sitting under a tree on an elevated seat, surrounded by His associates. As soon as Raghunātha Dāsa Gosvāmī saw Him from a distance, he fell down like a stick. The merciful Lord Nityānanda Prabhu immediately had him brought close to Him and placed His feet on his head. Understanding the deep-rooted desires of Raghunātha Dāsa Gosvāmī's heart, He arranged for him to perform a service to the Vaiṣṇavas so that he could realize his cherished objective.

" 'Like a thief, you don't come near Me, but simply try to run away. Now that I have caught you, I shall punish you. I want you to feed all My followers chipped rice and yogurt.' When he heard Nityānanda Prabhu's command, Raghunātha's mind was filled with joy." (*Caitanya Caritāmṛta* 3.6.50-1)

The festival which Nityānanda Prabhu ordered Raghunātha Dāsa Gosvāmī to put on is still celebrated as the Panihati Cida-dadhi Mahotsava. Śrī Caitanya Mahāprabhu Himself and His nondifferent manifestation Nityānanda Prabhu celebrated the festival along with Their associates, eating on the banks of the Ganges just as though They were cowherd boys on the banks of the Yamuna River. Śrī Caitanya Mahāprabhu, Nityānanda Prabhu, Their associates, numerous *brāhmaṇas* and countless men and women enjoyed a feast of milk and chipped rice and yogurt and chipped rice. The opportunity to serve the Lord and His devotees in this way was something that could not come about except for some great fortune.

On the following day, Raghunātha Dāsa Gosvāmī distressfully asked Nityānanda Prabhu through Rāghava Paṇḍita how he could possibly gain freedom from his material entanglements and find the association of Mahāprabhu. Like an ocean of mercy, Nityānanda Prabhu placed His feet on Raghunātha Dāsa Gosvāmī's head and said:

"You arranged this feast on the banks of the river, and Mahāprabhu was merciful to you and came here Himself to enjoy it. He blessed you by accepting the offering of chipped rice and yogurt. Then, after watching the devotees' dancing, He took *prasāda* in the evening. Lord Gaurāṅga came here just to deliver you, and now He has removed any impediments which remained. He will turn you over to Svarūpa Dāmodara, and, making you His confidential servant, He will keep you by His side. Go home now and forget your worries. You will soon be able to go to the Lord without any difficulties." (*Caitanya Caritāmṛta* 3.6.139-143)

After discussing with Rāghava Paṇḍita, Raghunātha Dāsa Gosvāmī gave a large sum of money as *dakṣiṇā* ("honorarium") to be paid to Nityānanda Prabhu and His associates. He himself felt as though his life had been fulfilled after receiving Nityānanda Prabhu's blessings. Upon returning to his house, he never again entered the inner quarters but remained outside, where he slept in the Durga Mandapa. Nevertheless, there were always guards posted near him to prevent him from running away.

RAGHUNĀTHA DĀSA ESCAPES

Though Raghunātha Dāsa Gosvāmī knew that the devotees from Bengal were preparing their annual trip to Puri, he was afraid of joining them because he knew that he would easily be caught. One day, at the end of the night, Yadunandana Ācārya came to Raghunātha Dāsa Gosvāmī and told him that a disciple who performed the *pūjā* had abandoned his service and needed to be persuaded to take it up again as there was no replacement.

Raghunātha Dāsa Gosvāmī accompanied his guru while all the guards were still sleeping. After walking away with Yadunandana Ācārya, however, Raghunātha Dāsa Gosvāmī told him to return to his home, saying that he would go alone to the disciple's house and convince him to come and perform his duties. He told him not to worry and bid him goodbye. With no guards or servants around him, Raghunātha Dāsa Gosvāmī realized that he had a golden opportunity to make his escape.

Meditating on Mahāprabhu's lotus feet, he started to walk toward the east. He avoided the main roads for fear of being caught and even the smaller ones that ran through the villages. Despite the difficult route through the jungle, he walked thirty miles on the very first day, finally taking rest in a milkman's cowshed that evening. The milkman saw that he had not eaten for the entire day and gave him some milk.

When Govardhana Majumadāra heard that his son had run away, he immediately sent a group of ten servants with a letter for Śivānanda Sena, who was already on his way to Puri with the devotees, telling him to send Raghunātha back. They caught up with the group of pilgrims but were disappointed to find that Raghunātha was not with them. Meanwhile, Raghunātha Dāsa Gosvāmī was walking at great speed towards Purī, completely oblivious to his own fatigue and hunger.

Raghunātha Dāsa Gosvāmī arrived in Puri after only twelve days, having stopped to eat only three times along the way and resting only infrequently. He came upon Mahāprabhu, who was sitting with Svarūpa Dāmodara, and paid his obeisances to the Lord from a certain distance. Mukunda Datta informed the Lord that Raghunātha had arrived and was paying his obeisances. The Lord told him to approach, and Raghunātha Dāsa fell at His feet. The Lord embraced him, His heart melting with compassion for the exhausted young man. He said, "Nothing is more powerful than Kṛṣṇa's mercy. It has dragged you out of the deep latrine pit of sense gratification." (*Caitanya Caritāmṛta* 3.6.193)

Raghunātha Dāsa Gosvāmī answered the Lord mentally, thinking, "I know nothing about Kṛṣṇa. I believe that it was You who pulled me out of that hole."

Mahāprabhu's maternal grandfather, Nīlāmvara Cakravartī, knew Raghunātha Dāsa Gosvāmī's father and uncle and used to call them *bhāyā* because they were younger than him. They called him *dādā* (older brother) because he was their elder and a *brāhmaṇa*. Knowing that this relationship existed between them, Mahāprabhu joked with Raghunātha, saying:

"Your father and uncle are like worms in the latrine pit of sense gratification. They think that suffering, which comes from sense gratification, is happiness. Even though they believe in brahminical culture and contribute to it, they are not pure Vaiṣṇavas, only imitation Vaiṣṇavas. The nature of the sense objects is that they make one blind; they make one engage in activities which result in material bondage. It is not possible to properly describe Kṛṣṇa's mercy which has delivered you from such bondage." (*Caitanya Caritāmṛta* 3.6.197-200)

Śrīla Bhakti Siddhānta Sarasvatī Gosvāmī Ṭhākura has written the following about Kṛṣṇa's mercy and the suffering caused by the poison of sense gratification: "Kṛṣṇa's mercy is more powerful than the results of one's previous activities. It was this powerful compassion of the Lord which pulled Raghunātha Dāsa Gosvāmī out of the latrine hole of sensual existence. A living entity who is attached to sense gratification does not have the strength to give it up. For the living being who has become a pure devotee of Kṛṣṇa, however, sense enjoyments are like a ditch of stool. Mahāprabhu knew that Raghunātha Dāsa Gosvāmī was completely free from any attachment to sense gratification. Nevertheless, He said this to him as a teaching to the conditioned souls." (*Anubhāṣya* 6.9.193)

Śrīla Bhakti Siddhānta Sarasvatī Gosvāmī Ṭhākura continutes: "Sense objects bring great distress to their so-called enjoyer. Even so, those whose brains are completely immersed in the objects of sense gratification and are entangled in the whirlpool of material existence consider these sources of distress to be happiness. The objects of material sense gratification should be discarded in the same way that one abandons an outhouse, and one whose mind is possessed by the desire for these objects of gratification is like a maggot who feeds off the stools in the latrine. This is how the transcendentalist sees the materialistic person who is trying to extract pleasure from inert matter. He has nothing but disdain for materialistic pleasures, which he sees being exactly like the pleasure a maggot extracts from the taste of rotting excrement." (*Anubhāṣya* 6.9.197)

RAGHUNĀTHA DĀSA'S RENUNCIATION

Mahāprabhu noticed that Raghunātha Dāsa Gosvāmī was extremely weak and so, after accepting him as His own son and servant, entrusted him to Svarūpa Dāmodara, telling him to take responsibility for him and to see to his well-being. From that time on, he was known as Svarūpa's Raghunātha to distinguish him from Raghunātha Vaidya and Raghunātha Bhaṭṭa. The Lord also told Govinda to take care of Raghunātha with great affection. He then told him to go and take his bath in the ocean and go to see Lord Jagannātha, after which he was to join Him for lunch. When Govinda gave Raghunātha Dāsa Gosvāmī the remnants of the Lord's plate to eat, Raghunātha was overjoyed.

Things went on like this for five days, Raghunātha Dāsa Gosvāmī taking the Lord's remnants each day, but on the sixth day, he stopped taking the Lord's *mahā-prasāda*. From that day on, he went to the Jagannātha temple and took *darśana* of the Lord's flower offering at night, after which he would stand at the Lion's Gate and beg *mahā.prasāda*. At night, after they had finished their duties, Lord Jagannātha's servants would pass by on their way home and would customarily give *prasāda* to the hungry Vaiṣṇavas who waited there. In this way, renounced Vaiṣṇavas would maintain their life. This type of renounced attitude was particularly noticeable amongst Mahāprabhu's devotees.

When the Lord asked about Raghunātha Dāsa Gosvāmī and learnt that he was no longer taking *prasāda* in the same way as before, but begging by the Simhadwar, He was satisfied to see that he was taking the renounced way of life so seriously. He said:

"That's very good. He is taking the life of a renunciate seriously. A renunciate should always be engaged in repeating the names of the Lord and should maintain his life through begging. Anyone who takes the renounced order and then becomes dependent on others cannot achieve his ends, and Kṛṣṇa will ignore him. One who becomes a renunciate and then lusts for tasty foods will never attain his spiritual goal and will simply become the slave of his taste buds. A renunciate's duty is to always chant the names of Lord Kṛṣṇa and fill his belly with leaves, fruits and roots. One who runs here and there looking for good things to eat becomes attached to his sex organs and his belly and will never attain Kṛṣṇa." (*Caitanya Caritāmṛta* 3.6.222-7)

Śrīla Bhakti Siddhānta Sarasvatī Gosvāmī Ṭhākura has underscored that Mahāprabhu's associates are extremely detached from material objects and that to chant the names of the Lord is the only duty of such renunciates: "Examining them impartially, both materialistic nondevotees and pure Vaiṣṇavas can see that Mahāprabhu's associates are not attached to the gratification of their material senses. They are indifferent to anything which cannot be used in the service of Kṛṣṇa. Their renunciation for the transcendental service of Śrī Kṛṣṇa, which is unmotivated and uninterrupted, is incomprehensible to the ordinary materialistic person. When Lord Gaurasundara sees a devotee's ingenuity to engage in this kind of devotional service, completely indifferent to sense objects which are outside the scope of his service needs, He feels great love for him.

"The various rituals described in the *Hari-bhakti-vilāsa* are meant for the wealthy householder Vaiṣṇavas who are imperfect but not for those who have renounced everything to take exclusive shelter of the Holy Name. One who chants the Holy Names in the morning, in the middle of the night, in the midday and at sunset, in other words throughout the day and night, is certain to cross over the ocean of material existence. Those pure devotees who are fixed exclusively on the devotional service of the Lord and chant His names and remember Him with love have no duty to perform other than *kīrtana* and *smaraṇa*." (*Anubhāṣya* 3.6.223, translation of *Hari-bhakti-vilasa* 20.366, 379, 382).

Śrīla Raghunātha Dāsa Gosvāmī would never speak to the Lord directly but asked Govinda or Svarūpa Dāmodara to submit any question or request to the Lord on his behalf. One day he asked the Lord through Svarūpa Dāmodara to instruct him personally on his duties. When the Lord heard this, He told Raghunātha Dāsa Gosvāmī that Svarūpa Dāmodara knew far more than He did and that he should take instruction from him about the goal of life and how to attain it. When Raghunātha Dāsa's eagerness to hear from Him directly did not abate, the Lord said, "If he has faith in My words, then let him follow these instructions:

"Do not listen to gossip or engage in gossip yourself. You should not eat very palatable food, nor should you dress very nicely. Always chant the Holy Name of Lord Kṛṣṇa without any expectation of honor, offering all respect to others. Mentally render service to Rādhā and Kṛṣṇa in Vrindavan." (*Caitanya Caritāmṛta* 3.6.236-7)

The Bengali devotees arrived in Puri for Rathayātrā and met Raghunātha Dāsa Gosvāmī, who was particularly fortunate to receive Advaita Prabhu's blessings. Śivānanda Sena told him that his father had been looking for him. After staying four months in Puri, the devotees returned to Bengal, and Śivānanda gave news of Raghunātha Dāsa Gosvāmī to Govardhana Majumadāra, telling him of his determined ascetic spiritual practices. His parents were distressed to hear of his lifestyle and sent a *brāhmaṇa*, two servants and four hundred rupees to Śivānanda for Raghunātha Dāsa Gosvāmī. The following year, Śivānanda took these servants and the money to Puri with him and informed Raghunātha Dāsa Gosvāmī that his father had sent them. Raghunātha Dāsa Gosvāmī would not accept them, but thinking of his father's benefit, he took some of the money and used it to pay for Mahāprabhu's meals twice a month. After doing this for two years, Raghunātha Dāsa Gosvāmī abandoned this practice also. In response to Mahāprabhu's question about why Raghunātha had stopped inviting Him, Svarūpa Dāmodara said that Raghunātha had decided that since his father was a materialistic man, Mahāprabhu was not really pleased to eat the food purchased with his money. By such invitations, his only gain was some fame and status. Furthermore, he thought that Mahāprabhu was only accepting his invitations out of kindness because he was so foolish that he would be unhappy if He refused, but that in fact He was secretly not very pleased by it. Mahāprabhu was greatly satisfied to hear this conclusion and said;

"When one eats food offered by a materialistic person, one's mind becomes contaminated. If the mind is contaminated, one is unable to remember Kṛṣṇa. The food of a materialistic person is infected by the mode of passion, and both the person who offers it and the one who accepts it are mentally contaminated. I accepted his invitation for many days, fearing his displeasure. I am glad that he has realized all this and given up this practice on his own initiative." (*Caitanya Caritāmṛta* 3.6.278-80)

Śrīla Bhakti Siddhānta Sarasvatī Gosvāmī Ṭhākura has commented on the above subject matter as follows: "People who are egotistical and possessive are generally materialistic persons who try to enjoy the world for their own sense gratification. Such persons see their money as a tool for achieving such sense gratification. If they attempt to serve the Lord, the guru or the Vaiṣṇavas, who are beyond the material energy and are transcendental, their only gain will be an increase in material prestige and not the true benefits of such service. One who seeks true auspiciousness should, therefore, with full surrender, engage whatever money one has honestly earned in the spiritual service of Kṛṣṇa, the spiritual master and the Vaiṣṇavas, using his body, mind, words and heart." (*Anubhāṣya* 3.6.275)

"Certain materialistic persons who are intoxicated by high birth, riches, learning or physical beauty may make a show of deity worship and offer the *prasāda* from that worship to Vaiṣṇavas. Due to their ignorance, they are not aware that because they lack devotion, the Lord, who is beyond sensory perception, does not accept their offerings. Because of the taint of the sense enjoyer's false pride which contaminates such offerings, it is often seen that the pure Vaiṣṇava is indifferent to such apparent service to the deity. In other words, a pure Vaiṣṇava who has renounced the life of sense enjoyment does not accept such service. Rich materialistic sense gratifiers are so foolish because of their sense of identification with the body and mind that they become angry with the Vaiṣṇavas and are offended by their behavior." (*Anubhāṣya* 3.6.276)

"Nondevotees and *prākṛta sahajiyās* are considered to be materialistic. Because they offer food without devotion, an aspiring devotee will be contaminated by their association through eating their food. The result of such flaws in association (*saṅga-doṣa*) is that one will develop the same mentality as they. If one engages in even minimal association with materialists or *sahajiyās*, who are materialists in the guise of Vaiṣṇavas, through any of the six kinds of association (exchanging gifts, food or confidences), with even a drop of hidden affection, the result will be that the transcendental devotional service of Lord Kṛṣṇa is transformed into sense gratification, and this will cause the aspiring devotee's falldown. The conclusion is that one whose mind is fixed on the pleasures of the bodily senses and contaminated by the sense objects is too impure to be able to serve Kṛṣṇa through the processes of transcendental remembrance, etc." (*Anubhāṣya* 3.6.278)

Śrīla Bhaktivinoda Ṭhākura has also written about the *rājasika* character of a materialistic person's dinner invitations. He says, "Invitations to dinner are of three kinds, *sāttvika, rājasika* and *tāmasika*. The invitation of a pure devotee is in the mode of goodness, that of a pious materialistic person is in the mode of passion, while the invitation of a very sinful person is in the mode of darkness." (*Amṛta-pravāha-bhāṣya*, 3.6.279)

Raghunātha Gosvāmī's asceticism grew stronger with each passing day. He stopped begging at the Lion's Gate and started going instead to an almshouse. When Mahāprabhu heard this news from Govinda, He asked Svarūpa Dāmodara what the cause was for the change. Svarūpa Dāmodara answered that Raghunātha Dāsa Gosvāmī was finding that a lot of time was being wasted standing in front of the Simhadwar and was going to the almshouse every day at noon instead. Mahāprabhu praised Raghunātha Dāsa Gosvāmī's decision, saying, "Begging by the Simhadwar resembles the behavior of a prostitute."

A prostitute stands around and waits for some man to come and give her some business; a beggar cannot remain indifferent as he waits for someone to be kind to him. Going for handouts at the almshouse does not present the same kind of problem. One simply has to go at the proper time, and one receives enough to keep his body alive. This is useful if one wishes to use one's time in chanting the Holy Names.

The *sannyāsī* Śaṅkarānanda Sarasvatī sent Mahāprabhu a *guṇja-mālā* and a Govardhan *śilā* from Vrindavan. Mahāprabhu cherished the two objects, taking the necklace of *guṇja* beads to be identical to Rādhārāṇī and the Govardhan *śilā* to be identical to Kṛṣṇa. Mahāprabhu would hold the Govardhan *śilā* to His head, to His eyes and to His heart, and this would bring Him great pleasure. After worshipping the necklace and the *śilā* for three years, He gifted them to Raghunātha Dāsa Gosvāmī as a sign of His satisfaction with his devotion. Raghunātha Dāsa Gosvāmī felt honored and delighted by the Lord's gift, and taking them to be the direct representations of Śrī Śrī Gāndhārvikā-Giridhārī, he worshipped them with water and tulasī leaves. When engaged in such loving service, he would go into a devotional trance. After his disappearance, the Govardhan *śilā* was placed in the Gokulānanda temple, where the Lord is still being served.

It is said of Raghunātha Dāsa Gosvāmī's ascetic vows that they were like lines drawn in stone. He spent more than twenty-two hours a day engaged in chanting Kṛṣṇa's names and in *smaraṇa* with, only about one and a half hours for sleep and food. He only ate enough to maintain his body. He allowed no delicious foods to ever touch his tongue and wore only torn cloth.

Finally, he started going at night to gather the *prasāda* which the vendors outside the temple threw away near the Simhadwar after it started to go so bad that even the *tailangi* cows would not eat it. He would wash it to take out the dirt with which it had become mixed until he reached the hard core of the grains, which had not cooked. This is what he would eat, only adding a little salt. One day, Śrī Svarūpa Dāmodara Gosvāmī saw Raghunātha Dāsa Gosvāmī doing this and asked him for some of this *prasāda*, comparing it to the nectar of the gods. Even Mahāprabhu, when He heard about it from Govinda, came and took a handful of Raghunātha Dāsa Gosvāmī's *prasāda*, though Svarūpa Dāmodara prevented Him from taking a second.

" 'What is this all about? You are eating such nice things and not giving any to Me?' Saying this, the Lord snatched a morsel from Raghunātha and ate it. As He was about to take another Svarūpa Dāmodara caught Him by the hand and said, 'It is not fit for You,' and took it away from Him." (*Caitanya Caritāmṛta* 3.6.322-3)

Śrīla Raghunātha Dāsa Gosvāmī has himself summarized Mahāprabhu's mercy on him in his verses called *Caitanya-stava-kalpa-vṛkṣa* ("The Desire Tree of Caitanya Mahāprabhu's glories"), which can be found in the collection called *Stavāvalī*.

mahā-sampad-dāvād api
patitam uddhṛtya kṛpayā
svarūpe yaḥ svīye kujanam api
māṁ nyasya muditaḥ
uro-guñjā-hāraṁ priyam api ca
govardhana-śilāṁ
dadau me gaurāṅgo hṛdaya
udayan māṁ madayati

"By His mercy, Śrī Gaurāṅga took pleasure in delivering me even though I am a fallen soul, the lowest of men, from the blazing forest fire of great material opulence and entrusted me to His personal associate Svarūpa Dāmodara. He gave me the cherished *guñja* garland that He wore on his chest as well as His Govardhan *śilā*. He awakens within my heart and makes me mad after Him." (verse 11)

RAGHUNĀTHA GOSVĀMĪ GOES TO VRINDAVAN

Raghunātha Dāsa Gosvāmī remained under Svarūpa Dāmodara Gosvāmī's tutelage in Puri, thus gaining direct access to Mahāprabhu's confidential service and association. In all, he remained there for sixteen years, until the Lord and Svarūpa Dāmodara Prabhu disappeared to the eyes of this world.

When this event took place, Raghunātha Dāsa Gosvāmī felt that he could no longer live in their absence and decided to go to Vrindavan to commit suicide by jumping from Govardhan Hill. When he arrived in Vraja, he met Rūpa and Sanātana Gosvāmīs. They persuaded him not to put an end to his life, adopted him as their third brother and kept him with them. Rūpa Gosvāmī and Sanātana Gosvāmī were enriched by hearing the nectarean pastimes of Lord Śrī Caitanya Mahāprabhu from Raghunātha Dāsa Gosvāmī.

Raghunātha Dāsa Gosvāmī's separation from Mahāprabhu and Rādhā-Kṛṣṇa became so intense that he gave up eating solid food altogether, only drinking a little buttermilk to sustain himself. He would pay a thousand prostrated obeisances, chant 100,000 Holy Names, serve Rādhā and Kṛṣṇa mentally both day and night, recount the glorious pastimes of Lord Caitanya Mahāprabhu and bathe three times a day without fail in Radha Kunda. This was the exemplary standard of *bhajana* set by Raghunātha Dāsa Gosvāmī in which he served Their Lordships for more than twenty-two hours a day, sleeping only an hour and a half, if at all.

Raghunātha Dāsa Gosvāmī's renunciation may superficially be compared to that of the Buddha, but when examined more closely it will be observed that there are some unique characteristics in Raghunātha Dāsa Gosvāmī's asceticism. The external meaning of renunciation is detachment from sense gratification, but its true meaning is an attachment to the Supreme Person. Raghunātha Dāsa Gosvāmī's strong attachment to the lotus feet of Rādhā and Kṛṣṇa meant that he was completely and naturally detached from anything which was not connected to his worshipable Lords. This kind of renunciation is actual.

RADHA KUNDA

Śrī Raghunātha Dāsa Gosvāmī lived a long life. Śrīnivāsa Ācārya had the chance to receive his blessings before leaving Vrindavan to return to the East with the Gosvāmīs' books. Śrīnivāsa Ācārya was astounded by Raghunātha Dāsa Gosvāmī's powerful asceticism and deep absorption in love. Raghunātha Dāsa Gosvāmī wrote three books: *Stavāvalī, Śrī Dāna-carita* (*Dāna-keli-cintāmaṇi*) and *Muktā-carita.*

He lived in Radha Kunda, where he engaged in his most intense devotional practices. He was blessed there by Nityānanda Prabhu's potency, Jāhnavā Devī, when she visited Radha Kunda.

Earlier when Mahāprabhu Himself visited the village of Arit, He displayed the pastime of bathing in a rice field, by which He indicated the presence of Radha Kunda and Shyama Kunda. Until then, the two ponds had still not been excavated, nor was there a proper bank. Raghunātha Dāsa Gosvāmī thought it would be a good idea to have this work done, but the next moment he became indignant for having desired such. However, one day, a rich merchant who was on a pilgrimage to Badrī Nārāyaṇa with the intention of donating a large sum of money to the temple there. Badrī Nārāyaṇa appeared to him in a dream and told him to fund Raghunātha Dāsa Gosvāmī's vision of a developed Radha Kunda and Shyama Kunda. The merchant came back to Vraja and found Raghunātha Dāsa Gosvāmī in the village of Aarit and recounted the story of the dream to him. Raghunātha Dāsa Gosvāmī thus supervised the excavation of the ponds and the subsequent building of stone step walkways.

Five trees stood on the banks of Shyama Kunda which are said to be the five Pāṇḍavas. Raghunātha Dāsa Gosvāmī had the intention of cutting down these trees so that Shyama Kunda could be made perfectly rectangular. Before this could happen, however, Raghunātha Dāsa Gosvāmī had a dream in which Yudhiṣṭhira appeared to him and told him that the five Pāṇḍavas were present in Radha Kunda in the form of these trees. He immediately stopped the workers from cutting them down. This is why Shyama Kunda was not built as a perfect rectangle.

OTHER LEGENDS ABOUT RAGHUNĀTHA IN VRAJA

Another story is told about Raghunātha Dāsa Gosvāmī. It is said that when he read Rūpa Gosvāmī's play *Lalita-mādhava,* he was submerged in an ocean of separation. Though he was permanently in Rādhārāṇī's association at Radha Kunda, he was unable to tolerate even a moment's separation and was restless always. When he read the *Lalita-mādhava,* which has separation from Kṛṣṇa as its primary subject matter, this mood became so strong that his survival became even more difficult. When Rūpa Gosvāmī saw Raghunātha Dāsa Gosvāmī's response to his play, he gave him the book *Dāna-keli-kaumudī,* which is full of humour and amusing banter, and took back his copy of *Lalita-mādhava.* When Raghunātha read *Dāna-keli-kaumudī,* his feelings of separation vanished.

At first, when staying by Radha Kunda Raghunātha Dāsa Gosvāmī had no fixed shelter. He occasionally stayed with Gopāla Bhaṭṭa Gosvāmī, whose cottage was situated on the banks of the Manasa Ganga in Govardhan. One day he took bath in the Manasa Ganga and then went to sit under a tree surrounded by unkept thickets and began to worship the Lord in a devotional trance. While he was meditating, a tiger came there to drink water. Sanātana Gosvāmī was also present there at the time and observed Raghunātha Dāsa Gosvāmī as he remained unmoved even though exposed to such danger. He instructed Raghunātha Dāsa Gosvāmī to build a cottage in which to live and engage in his devotional activities.

Śrīla Raghunātha Dāsa Gosvāmī had a special affection for a certain Vrajavasi whose name was Dāsa. Raghunātha Dāsa Gosvāmī's daily nourishment consisted of only a leaf bowl of buttermilk. This Vrajavasi was distressed to learn that Raghunātha Dāsa Gosvāmī ate so little, thinking that it was impossible for him to keep alive on such a small amount. One day, when in the place known as Sakhī Sthalī, he was overjoyed to see a *palash* tree with huge leaves. He had a bigger bowl made with these leaves in which he put buttermilk for Raghunātha Dāsa Gosvāmī and then brought it to him.

Raghunātha Dāsa Gosvāmī was quite astonished to see such a large leaf-bowl and asked him where he got it. When he heard the name of Sakhi Sthali, he immediately threw down the bowl. Sakhi Sthali is the home of Candrāvalī, Rādhārāṇī's primary rival for Kṛṣṇa's love. Candrāvalī's *sakhīs*, like Śaibya, are constantly looking for ways to take Kṛṣṇa away from Rādhā's bower and bring him to that of their girlfriend. Just as Rādhārāṇī is distressed by these actions, so are Her girlfriends. Raghunātha Dāsa Gosvāmī was a member of Rādhārāṇī's entourage, and so it was his role to constantly think of how to bring happiness to Her and Her girlfriends. As soon as he heard the name of Sakhi Sthali mentioned, he was transported by anger. This mood is the ultimate stage of love, which envious people who are burdened by material lust can never understand. In the *Bhakti-ratnākara*, it is written:

"After calming down, Raghunātha Dāsa Gosvāmī said to Dāsa, 'That is Candrāvalī's place. You shouldn't ever go there.' Dāsa Vrajavāsī calmed down and recognized that these were the symptoms of spiritual perfection in what was apparently a spiritual aspirant. All these devotees are eternally perfected souls. Ignorant fools cannot understand this." (*Bhakti-ratnākara* 5.572-4)

There is one other extraordinary legend about Raghunātha Dāsa Gosvāmī recounted in the *Bhakti-ratnākara*. One day he was exhibiting pastimes of suffering from indigestion. Viṭṭhalnātha came with two doctors from Ballabhpur to cure Raghunātha Dāsa. After examining him, the doctors said that the indigestion had been caused by eating rice and milk. Viṭṭhalnātha was astonished to hear this diagnosis and said, "This is impossible. This man never eats anything but buttermilk." Raghunātha Dāsa Gosvāmī then spoke up, saying that he had indeed eaten milk and rice in the course of his meditation on the pastimes of Rādhā and Kṛṣṇa.

Śrī Raghunātha Dāsa Gosvāmī left his body on the banks of Radha Kunda where his *samādhi* stands. This took place on the *śukla dvādaśī* tithi of the month of Āśvina.

Śrīla Jīva Gosvāmī

According to the *Gaura-gaṇoddeśa-dīpikā* (195), Śrīla Jīva Gosvāmī was previously Vilāsa Mañjarī in Vraja. In verse 203 of the same book, it is stated that he was the son of Vallabha and a scholar of exemplary character (*suśīlaḥ paṇḍitaḥ śrīmān jīvaḥ śrī-vallabhātmajaḥ*). According to the *Gauḍīya Vaiṣṇava Abhidhāna*, Jīva Gosvāmī was present in this world from 1511 to 1596 (1433 to 1518 Śaka), but some other sources propose that Jīva lived from 1533 to 1618.

JĪVA GOSVĀMĪ'S EARLY LIFE

Śrīla Jīva Gosvāmī appeared in the village of Ramakeli in the district of Maldah as the son of Anupama Mallika (Vallabha), who had made his residence there in order to serve in the government. The name of Jīva Gosvāmī's mother is not known. Narahari Cakravartī in his *Bhakti-ratnākara* (1.540568) has given Jīva Gosvāmī's genealogy going back seven generations. This list, as explained by Śrīla Bhakti Siddhānta Sarasvatī Gosvāmī Ṭhākura, has been given here in this volume in the chapter on Śrīla Rūpa Gosvāmī. Jīva Gosvāmī's father's original name was Vallabha, but Mahāprabhu gave him the name Anupama. (*Caitanya Caritāmṛta* 2.19.36)

Mahāprabhu met Anupam for the first time when He came to Ramakeli. By His will, Rūpa Gosvāmī and Sanātana Gosvāmī abandoned all of their worldly duties and then set off in an effort to be reunited with Mahāprabhu in Vrindavan. The same spirit of renunciation took hold in Jīva Gosvāmī's heart at this time also, as has been vividly described by Narahari in *Bhakti-ratnākara* as follows:

"Śrī Jīva's mind became distracted from the time that his two uncles went to Vrindavan. He abandoned his jewels and fine dress, comfortable bed, food and various amusements. It was as though nothing interested him anymore. He could not bear hearing news of political and other mundane affairs." (*Bhakti-ratnākara* 1.686-8)

Narahari Cakravartī summarizes Jīva Gosvāmī's early life story as follows: In a dream, Jīva Gosvāmī had a vision of Mahāprabhu dancing in the midst of *saṅkīrtana*. He was overwhelmed by feelings of divine love and soon thereafter left his home. He had some companions who went with him as far as Fatehabad from Bakla Chandradwip, but from there he continued alone to Nabadwip. There he met Nityānanda Prabhu in the home of Śrīvāsa Paṇḍita and received His blessings. Nityānanda Prabhu told him at that time that he should go to Vrindavan:

"With fatherly affection, Nityānanda Prabhu touched Śrī Jīva's head with His feet. He showed incomparable mercy toward Śrī Jīva, lifting him from the ground and embracing him tightly. Transported by divine ecstasy, Nityānanda Prabhu said, 'I rushed here from Khardah for your sake alone.' He said other things like this to pacify Śrī Jīva and then made Śrīvāsa Paṇḍita and the other devotees give their blessings to him. After keeping Śrī Jīva there for some time with Him, Nityānanda Prabhu sent him off to the west. He said, 'Hurry off now to Vraja. That is the place the Lord has given over to your family.' " (*Bhakti-ratnākara* 1.765-9, 772)

It is not clear whether Jīva Gosvāmī ever met Mahāprabhu directly. However, there is a hint in the *Bhakti-ratnākara* that Jīva Gosvāmī was a baby when the Lord came to Ramakeli. Jīva Gosvāmī demonstrated an interest in devotion to the Supreme Lord from his early childhood. Even when playing with his friends, he was only interested in games that were connected to the worship of Kṛṣṇa.

"When Śrī Jīva was a little boy, he refused to play any game with other boys that had no relation to Kṛṣṇa. He made deities of Kṛṣṇa and Balarāma and would worship Them with flowers and sandalwood paste and dress and decorate them. He would gaze upon them with unblinking eyes, sitting motionless on the floor like a golden doll. When he paid obeisance to the deities, his eyes filled with tears. He would offer their Lordships sweets and then take the *prasāda* and distribute it to his friends." (*Bhakti-ratnākara* 1.719-23)

JĪVA GOSVĀMĪ GOES TO VRAJA

By Nityānanda Prabhu's grace, Jīva Gosvāmī was able to visit all the sacred sites in Nabadwip *dhāma*. After completing his tour of the dhāma, he traveled to Benares where he studied all the scriptures with Madhusūdana Vācaspati. Then he went on to Vrindavan, where he remained under the tutelage of Rūpa and Sanātana Gosvāmīs.

Śrīla Bhakti Siddhānta Sarasvatī Gosvāmī Ṭhākura Prabhupāda has given the following summary of Jīva Gosvāmī's life in his *Anubhāṣya* to the *Caitanya Caritāmṛta*: "After the disappearance of Rūpa Gosvāmī and Sanātana Gosvāmī, Jīva Gosvāmī was established as the topmost teacher of the Gauḍīya Vaiṣṇavas of Odisha, Bengal and Mathura provinces. He engaged everyone in the worship of Kṛṣṇa through teaching the truths given by Mahāprabhu Himself. He would occasionally perform Vraja *dhāma parikramā* with the other devotees and sometimes would go to visit Viṭṭhalnātha in Mathura.

"Kṛṣṇadāsa Kavirāja Gosvāmī wrote the *Caitanya Caritāmṛta* during Jīva Gosvāmī's lifetime. Not long thereafter, when Śrīnivāsa, Narottama and Duḥkhī Kṛṣṇadāsa came from Bengal, he gave them the titles Ācārya, Ṭhākura and Śyāmānanda, respectively. He then sent them back to Bengal with all the scriptures that had been written by the Gosvāmīs, with instructions to preach the religion of the Holy Names and love of Kṛṣṇa. He received the news of the loss of the scriptures and later of their retrieval. He later gave the title Kavirāja to both Rāmacandra Sena and his brother Govinda. Jāhnavā Devī and other devotees came to Vrindavan during his lifetime. Whenever Bengali devotees came to Vraja, he arranged for *prasāda* and lodgings during their stay." (*Anubhāṣya* 1.10.85)

The loss of the scriptures referred to in the above paragraph took place when agents of King Vīrahāmvīra of Banvishnupur stole them. Later, when the king heard Śrīnivāsa Ācārya speak on *Śrīmad Bhāgavatam*, he was converted to Vaiṣṇavism and took initiation from him. Śrīnivāsa Ācārya thus recovered the books. All this is described in full in this volume in the chapter of Śrīnivāsa Ācārya.

JĪVA'S WRITINGS AND CONTROVERSIES

In the *Bhakti-ratnākara*, a list of twenty-five works ascribed to Jīva Gosvāmī has been given:

(1) *Harināmāmṛta-vyākaraṇa*, (2) *Sūtra-mālikā*, (3) *Dhātu-saṅgraha*, (4) *Kṛṣṇārcana-dīpikā*, (5) *Gopāla-virudāvalī*, (6) *Rasāmṛta-śeṣa*, (7) *Mādhava-mahotsava*, (8) *Saṅkalpa-kalpa-vṛkṣa*, (9) *Bhāvārtha-sūcaka-campū*, (10) a commentary on *Gopala-tāpanī Upaniṣād*, (11) a commentary on *Brahma-saṁhitā*, (12) a commentary on *Bhakti-rasāmṛta-sindhu*, (13) a commentary on *Ujjvala-nīlamaṇi*, (14) a commentary on *Yogasāra-stavaka*, (15) *Gāyatrī-bhāṣya* of *Agni Purāṇa*, (16) *Kṛṣṇa-pada-cihna* of *Padma Purāṇa*, (17) *Śrī Rādhikā-kara-pada-sthita-cihna*, (18) *Gopāla-campū*, *Pūrva* and *Uttara* divisions, (19) *Krama-sandarbha*, (20) *Tattva-sandarbha*, (21) *Bhagavat-sandarbha*, (22) *Paramātma-sandarbha*, (23) *Kṛṣṇa-sandarbha*, (24) *Bhakti-sandarbha* and (25) *Prīti-sandarbha*.

Śrīla Bhakti Siddhānta Sarasvatī Gosvāmī Ṭhākura Prabhupāda has given the following warning in his *Anubhāṣya* to those inexperienced persons who might be deprived of Kṛṣṇa *prema* through the influence of ignorant and offensive *sahajiyā* teachings: "Three slanderous ideas about Jīva Gosvāmī are current amongst the ignorant *prākṛta sahajiyās*. Anyone influenced by these calumnies, which are fundamentally inimical to Kṛṣṇa, the guru and the Vaiṣṇavas, will become increasingly offensive and end up losing his taste for service to the Supreme Lord.

"(1) It is said that a certain *dig-vijayī* scholar, eager to amass mundane prestige, came to Rūpa Gosvāmī and Sanātana Gosvāmī to get their signature as an admission of defeat in the debate. Jīva Gosvāmī's gurus conceded defeat without any argument, and the arrogant scholar proclaimed them to be nothing more than ignorant fools. He then asked Jīva Gosvāmī also to sign such an admission of defeat. Jīva Gosvāmī, however, decided to take on the puffed-up *brāhmaṇa* in debate in order to silence his scurrilous tongue. In this way, he preserved the integrity of his spiritual master's reputation and demonstrated the ideal behavior of one who is *guru-devātma*, (one who recognizes his spiritual master to be his worshipable deity and source of life). Some ignorant *sahajiyās*, however, say that Śrī Jīva's behavior went contrary to Mahāprabhu's teaching of being humbler than a blade of grass and of giving respect to others. Indeed, they say that Rūpa Gosvāmī chastised Jīva Gosvāmī for this very reason and ostracized him for some time, and only when Sanātana Gosvāmī interceded on Jīva Gosvāmī's behalf did he accept him again into his association.

"Only when these enemies of the spiritual master and the Vaiṣṇavas receive Kṛṣṇa's mercy and begin to see themselves as their eternal servant will they also receive Śrī Jīva Prabhu's blessings and be able to understand what it really means to be 'humbler than a blade of grass' and 'a giver of respect to all.' Only then will they be eligible to chant the Holy Names in the proper way.

"(2) Some other foolish *sahajiyās* say that when Jīva Gosvāmī first read the *Caitanya Caritāmṛta* with its clear and brilliant explanation of the divine devotional sentiments of Vraja, he was afraid that it would hamper his own scholarly reputation. He, therefore, threw the manuscript down a well in a spirit of mean-mindedness. Upon hearing of this, Kṛṣṇadāsa Kavirāja Gosvāmī was greatly shocked and immediately gave up his body. Fortunately, Kavirāja Gosvāmī's disciple Mukunda had made a copy of the original manuscript, and thus it was preserved and later published far and wide. Had Mukunda not done so, the *Caitanya Caritāmṛta* would have been lost forever.

This is another contemptible bit of invention based on an inimical attitude to the guru and Vaiṣṇava. It has no basis in reality, and there is no possibility of its being true.

"(3) According to other sense-obsessed fornicators, Śrīla Jīva Gosvāmī should not be accepted as an authority because, in his treatises, he did not accept Rūpa Gosvāmī's *pārakīyā-vāda* idea, but rather supported the *svakīya-vāda*. They say that he cannot be accepted as a *rasika-bhakta*, or a devotee who is knowledgeable in the divine sentiments.

"The fact is that during Jīva Gosvāmī's lifetime, some of his followers demonstrated a preference for the *svakīyā-vāda*. Jīva Gosvāmī recognized their limitations and so, for their benefit and for the benefit of those in the future who would be unable to comprehend the transcendental nature of the *pārakīyā-rasa* and would themselves take up adulterous relationships in imitation of Kṛṣṇa, he gave credence to the *svakīyā* doctrine. This is a sign of his acting appropriately as an *ācārya*. One should not take this as evidence of his being opposed to the transcendental *pārakīyā-rasa*, however, for he is the topmost of Rūpa Gosvāmī's followers and one of Kṛṣṇadāsa Kavirāja Gosvāmī's spiritual teachers." (*Anubhāṣya*, 1.10.85)

RŪPA GOSVĀMĪ'S MERCY TO ŚRĪ JĪVA PRABHU

Narahari Cakravartī has shown how Rūpa Gosvāmī instructed Jīva Gosvāmī, punished him and then blessed him, in a story told in the fifth wave of *Bhakti-ratnākara*:

One hot summer's day, while Rūpa Gosvāmī was writing *Bhakti-rasāmṛta-sindhu* in seclusion and Jīva Gosvāmī was fanning his perspiring body, Vallabha Bhaṭṭa came by to see Rūpa Gosvāmī. After reading some of Rūpa Gosvāmī's introductory verses, he offered to make a few corrections. When Vallabha Bhaṭṭa went to the Yamuna to take a bath, Jīva Gosvāmī followed him on the pretext of going to fetch water. In fact, he was angry because he considered Vallabha Bhaṭṭa's proposal to be arrogant. He asked him what fault he had found in Rūpa Gosvāmī's verse. Vallabha Bhaṭṭa told him, and Jīva Gosvāmī immediately showed him the flaws in his argument. A debate ensued in which Jīva Gosvāmī countered every one of Vallabha Bhaṭṭa's objections. When he came back to Rūpa Gosvāmī's hut, Vallabha Bhaṭṭa told him how impressed he was with Jīva Gosvāmī's scholarship, recounting the entire episode. Rūpa Gosvāmī gently rebuked Jīva Gosvāmī, telling him to return to Bengal and to come back to Vrindavan only when he had calmed down.

Thus banished from his presence, Jīva Gosvāmī left Rūpa Gosvāmī's dwelling and went to Nanda Ghata, a nearby village. Hoping to regain his guru's favor, he began to practice rigorous austerities, worshipping Kṛṣṇa intensely while fasting or eating only a bare minimum. As a result of such severe practices, his body became weak and sickly. One day, Sanātana Gosvāmī happened to come to Nanda Ghata and discovered him in this condition. He was moved and took Jīva Gosvāmī back with him to Rūpa Gosvāmī and appealed to his brother to forgive him. Rūpa Gosvāmī and Jīva Gosvāmī were thus reconciled, and Jīva Gosvāmī once again began to receive Rūpa Gosvāmī's affectionate blessings.

Jīva Gosvāmī's appearance day is on Bhādra *śukla dvādaśī*; his disappearance day is Pauṣa *śukla tṛtīyā*. His deity, Rādhā-Dāmodara, is still being worshipped in the Rādhā-Dāmodara temple in Vrindavan. His *samādhi* tomb is on the grounds of the Rādhā-Dāmodara temple, and his *bhajana kūtīra* is preserved at Radha Kunda, near Lalita Kunda.

Śrīla Prabodhānanda Sarasvatī

tuṅgavidyā vraje yāsīt sarva-śāstra-viśāradā
sā prabodhānanda-yatir gaurodgāna-sarasvatī

"The *gopī* Tuṅgavidyā, who was most learned in all the scriptures, has today become the *sannyāsī* Prabodhānanda, whose words are all used in the glorification of Lord Gaurāṅga." (*Gaura-gaṇoddeśa-dīpikā* 163)

"Veṅkaṭa Bhaṭṭa lived in South India. He held a special position amongst the *brāhmaṇas* as he was very learned in all the scriptures." (*Bhakti-ratnākara* 1.82)

"There was a Vaiṣṇava of the Śrī *sampradāya* named Veṅkaṭa Bhaṭṭa who respectfully invited the Lord to his house." (*Caitanya Caritāmṛta* 2.9.82)

In his commentary on this verse of the *Caitanya Caritāmṛta*, Śrīla Bhaktivinoda Ṭhākura has written: "The three brothers Veṅkaṭa Bhaṭṭa, Trimalla Bhaṭṭa and Prabodhānanda Sarasvatī were previously *ācāryas* of the Śrī *sampradāya*. Gopāla Bhaṭṭa Gosvāmī was the son of Veṅkaṭa Bhaṭṭa."

Śrīla Bhakti Siddhānta Sarasvatī Gosvāmī Ṭhākura Prabhupāda has also commented on the same verse: "Śrī Veṅkaṭa Bhaṭṭa was a *brāhmaṇa* of the Śrī *sampradāya* who lived in Srirangam. Srirangam[26] is situated in Tamil Nadu, where people do not use the names Veṅkaṭa and Tirumalaya (the name of Veṅkaṭa's brother), so it is likely they came from elsewhere. This family had possibly moved to Srirangam not long before Mahāprabhu's visit there. Veṅkaṭa Bhaṭṭa belonged to the Vaḍagalai branch of the Rāmānuja *sampradāya*. One of his brothers was Tridaṇḍī Rāmānujīyārya-svāmī Śrīpāda Prabodhānanda Sarasvatī, who acted as an *ācārya* of the school. Veṅkaṭa Bhaṭṭa's son was Gopāla Bhaṭṭa Gosvāmī."

26 Srirangam is in the current Trichy on the banks of the river Kaveri, or Koliran, about ten miles west of Kubhakonam town in the Tanjavur district. The Raṅganātha temple at this place flourishes as the largest temple in India.

These three brothers were originally worshipers of Lakṣmī-Nārāyaṇa, but they were converted to the worship of Rādhā and Kṛṣṇa by the grace of Śrī Caitanya Mahāprabhu. Kṛṣṇadāsa Kavirāja Gosvāmī has described this conversion beautifully in his *Caitanya Caritāmṛta*.

Śrīla Prabodhānanda Sarasvatī's disciple was his own nephew, Gopāla Bhaṭṭa, one of the six Gosvāmīs.

bhakter vilāsāṁś cinute prabodhā-
nandasya śiṣyo bhagavat-priyasya
gopāla-bhaṭṭo raghunātha-dāsaṁ
santoṣayan rūpa-sanātanau ca

"I, Gopāla Bhaṭṭa, the disciple of Prabodhānanda Sarasvatī, who is dear to the Lord, have compiled these most essential and glorious devotional doctrines to satisfy Raghunātha Dāsa Gosvāmī, Rūpa Gosvāmī and Sanātana Gosvāmī." (*Hari-bhakti-vilāsa* 1.2)

Śrīla Prabodhānanda Sarasvatī wrote a number of books, including *Vṛndāvana-śatakam*, *Navadvīpa-śatakam*, *Rādhā-rasa-sudhā-nidhi*, and *Caitanya-candrāmṛtam*, which are especially loved by *rasika* devotees. Some of his other works as listed in *Gauḍīya Vaiṣṇava Abhidhāna* are *Saṅgīta-Mādhava*, *Āścarya-rāsa-prabandha*, *Śruti-stuti-vyākhyā*, *Gīta-govinda-vyākhyāna* and *Kāma-bīja-kāma-gāyatrī-vyākhyāna*.

IS PRABODHĀNANDA PRAKĀŚĀNANDA?

In his *Gauḍīya-bhāṣya* to *Caitanya Bhāgavata* (2.3.37), Śrīla Bhakti Siddhānta Sarasvatī Gosvāmī Ṭhākura Prabhupāda makes the following observation: "Prakāśānanda was a teacher of the Māyāvāda doctrine and a *sannyāsī*. During his discourses on the Veda, he would cut the Lord's divine and transcendental body into pieces. Some ignorant people say that this Prakāśānanda is the same person as Veṅkaṭa Bhaṭṭa's younger brother Prabodhānanda, who lived on the banks of the Kaveri. This erroneous belief has found its way into the *sahajiyā* text *Bhakta-māla*, and even into the writings of many modern scholars."

Āśutoṣa Deva states in his Bengali dictionary that Prabodhānanda was a Vaiṣṇava philosopher, whose real name was Prakāśānanda Sarasvatī. Caitanya Deva gave him the name Prabodhānanda.

Furthermore, Haridāsa Dāsa has also written in his *Gauḍīya Vaiṣṇava Abhidhāna*: "Some people hold that Prabodhānanda is the Vaiṣṇava name given to Prakāśānanda. It is quite clear from the last verse of the *Rādhā-rasa-sudhā-nidhi* that Prabodhānanda had at one time been a Māyāvādī *sannyāsī*."

We would argue that the words to which Haridāsa Dāsa refers – *māyāvādārka-tāpa-santapta* ("roasted by the burning sun of impersonalism") – are not acceptable as proof of Prabodhānanda's former adherence to the impersonalist philosophy or of his having been a Māyāvādī at one time. Mahāprabhu and all of His followers argued against the impersonal doctrines because of its extreme opposition to devotion. The Lord's deliverance of the Māyāvādīs Sārvabhauma Bhaṭṭācārya and Prakāśānanda Sarasvatī are even greater feats of mercy than the salvation of Jagāi and Mādhāi. In this spirit, Prabodhānanda is simply glorifying Mahāprabhu's quality as the deliverer of the most fallen and drawing attention to just how far-reaching His mercy is.

ŚRĪLA PRABHUPĀDA'S INTRODUCTION TO CAITANYA-CANDRĀMṚTA

The founder of world-wide Sri Chaitanya Math and Sri Gaudiya Math, transcendental personality, the eternal associate of Gaurāṅga Mahāprabhu, dearmost servant of the servants of Śrīmatī Rādhikā, Śrīla Bhakti Siddhānta Sarasvatī Gosvāmī Ṭhākura Prabhupāda, has given an excellent account of Prabodhānanda Sarasvatī's life in his introduction to his edition of *Caitanya-candrāmṛta*. We reproduce it here in full for the benefit of the reader:

In 1512 A.D. Śrī Kṛṣṇa Caitanya went to South India, ostensibly on pilgrimage. In fact, His real purpose was to show His mercy to His devotees. Starting from Puri in Odisha, He traveled southward to the Godavari River and then continued onward through various other holy places in the current Madras area. Mahāprabhu reached Srirangam on the Ekādaśī of the waxing fortnight of the month of Āṣāḍha. The *sannyasis* of the *daśanāmi* order, to which He belonged, normally follow the *Cāturmāsya* vows, and so the Lord decided to spend this four-month period in the town of Srirangam.

Srirangam is the residence of many Vaiṣṇavas of the Śrī *sampradāya*. The Vaiṣṇavas of this school are strict in their practice, and as a result, the *smārta brāhmaṇas* throughout southern India find it difficult to live in villages where they have a strong presence. At the time Mahāprabhu visited Srirangam, it was a holy place inhabited exclusively by Vaiṣṇavas of the Śrī *sampradāya*. He thus considered it to be a most favorable environment for the execution of His four-month vow, and so He spent the period in visiting the temple of Raṅganātha and preaching about Kṛṣṇa.

Three brothers, Tirumalaya, Veṅkaṭa and Prabodhānanda, had recently come from Mysore to live in Srirangam. They were not Tamils but either from Andhra or Uttar Pradesh. The Lord was particularly merciful to this *brāhmaṇa* family and spent the four months of the rainy season in their house. The Vaiṣṇavas of the Śrī *sampradāya* are devoted to the worship of Lakṣmī-Nārāyaṇa. By Mahāprabhu's blessings, the Bhaṭṭa family developed a taste for Kṛṣṇa *rasa*.

The middle brother, Veṅkaṭa, had a son in his boyhood, Gopāla Bhaṭṭa, who later became famous as one of the six Gosvāmīs. The Lord's conversation with Veṅkaṭa Bhaṭṭa is described in the ninth chapter of the *Caitanya Caritāmṛta*'s *Madhya-līlā*. Although we know nothing more about Tirumalaya, we can surmise that he, like his brothers, was totally devoted to Śrī Caitanya Mahāprabhu.

The third brother, Prabodhānanda, was unequalled in his attachment to Śrī Caitanya. Through his pure teachings Veṅkaṭa's son Gopāla Bhaṭṭa later became a great *ācārya* of the Gauḍīya Vaiṣṇava school. Prabodhānanda Sarasvatī himself has a particularly elevated position amongst the followers of Śrī Caitanya. Kavi Karṇapūra identified him as Tuṅgavidyā in his *Gaura-gaṇoddeśa-dīpikā*. In the *Hari-bhakti-vilāsa*, Gopāla Bhaṭṭa Gosvāmī mentioned him as his guru and as extremely dear to Lord Caitanya. In the *Bhakti-ratnākara*, the following passages about him are found:

"Everyone glorified Prabodhānanda's virtues, and thus he was given the title Sarasvatī by which he was known everywhere. Śrī Kṛṣṇa Caitanya is the Supreme Lord and the complete divinity. Prabodhānanda Sarasvatī held Him so dear that he knew nothing but the Lord, even in his dreams. Prabodhānanda Sarasvatī was greatly renounced; he was affection incarnate and handsome, as well as being a great poet and expert in singing, playing musical instruments and dancing. Everyone's joy increased on hearing him speak. These are some of the unlimited glories of Prabodhānanda Sarasvatī". (*Bhakti-ratnākara* 1.149-153)

PRABODHĀNANDA COMES TO LIVE IN VRAJA

A few years after Mahāprabhu had returned to Puri, Prabodhānanda Sarasvatī entered deep into the mode of worship that is dear to Mahāprabhu. He left Srirangam and went to live in Kamyavan in the Mathura region without much delay. Gopāla Bhaṭṭa also gradually developed an intense desire to come and live in Vraja, and so he followed the path taken by his uncle and guru.

Many people ask, "If Prabodhānanda Sarasvatī was so dear to Caitanya Mahāprabhu, why is his name not mentioned anywhere in Kṛṣṇadāsa Kavirāja Gosvāmī's *Caitanya Caritāmṛta*? Would Kṛṣṇadāsa Kavirāja Gosvāmī not have included the pastimes of such a great personality for the pleasure of the Vaiṣṇavas?" We can find an adequate response to this question in the *Bhakti-ratnākara*. Narahari Cakravartī Ṭhākura writes:

"Some people have described the activities of Gopāla Bhaṭṭa, while others have not. Those who cannot understand the reason for this engage in useless argument, with the result that they allow an offensive attitude to take root in them. Previously, great *rasika* devotee poets who were quite capable of describing these things did not do so in order that others would be able to do so in the future. Gopāla Bhaṭṭa enthusiastically gave his approval to the writing of the *Caitanya Caritāmṛta* but would not allow Kṛṣṇadāsa Kavirāja Gosvāmī to write anything about him. Who can understand why he did this? He always considered himself very lowly. Kṛṣṇadāsa Kavirāja Gosvāmī was not able to ignore his command." (*Bhakti-ratnākara* 1.209-223)

PRABODHĀNANDA AND SVAKĪYA-RASA

Some Rūpānuga Vaiṣṇavas say that Prabodhānanda Sarasvatī's writing shows a tendency to the *svakīya* doctrine. They thus do not show a great enthusiasm for studying his books in the conviction that Rūpa Gosvāmī's *pārakīya-vāda* is superior. We hold that anyone who is devoted to Caitanya Mahāprabhu is blessed, and so we simply follow Narahari Cakravartī, a neutral commentator, and avoid a useless argument. And by doing so, we relish the pure surrender mood of Prabodhānanda Sarasvatī towards Mahāprabhu, and the sweetness of servitude of Śrīmatī Rādhikā to Śrī Kṛṣṇa in the *pārakīya* mood.

Prabodhānanda Sarasvatī's writings are rich with transcendental emotions, and the language contains solemnity and the sweetness of divine love in equal measure. Mahāprabhu's devotees take great pleasure in reading Prabodhānanda Sarasvatī's *Vṛndāvana-śataka*. His *Nabadvīpa-śataka* resembles this work, glorifying Nabadwip in the same spirit. His *Rādhā-rasa-sudhā-nidhi* is truly unequalled in the entire world. Those who have appreciation only from a purely literary point of view may not regard this work highly; nevertheless, it is extremely dear to the devotees who are simple, free from hypocrisy and attached to the mellows of devotion to Lord Hari. One experiences a work as being superior or inferior according to one's taste, thus the transcendental moods of Vraja *bhakti* can only have an effect on readers who have accumulated pious activities in their previous lives.

In his notices of manuscripts, Professor Aufret attributes another book, *Viveka-śataka*, to Prabodhānanda Sarasvatī. This manuscript was in the possession of the late Rāma Dāsa Sena of Berhampore. Aufrecht also lists *Saṅgīta-mādhava* as one of Prabodhānanda Sarasvatī's works. We managed to trace this work and published it in *Sajjana-tosani*, Vol. 18, 5-12.

The *Caitanya-candrāmṛta* was widely distributed in Bengal. Even those inimical to Caitanya Mahāprabhu become purified upon reading it and experience a change of heart. It thus goes without saying that those who are His devotees will be immersed in an ocean of indescribable ecstasy when they read it. Indeed, it is not surprising. If the Lord of Goloka comes and stays in someone's house and accepts his service for four whole months, would He not bestow the rarest forms of love of Godhead upon his entire household? The blessed members of such a household naturally possess an abundance of priceless love from which we insignificant living entities, to our great benefit, may hope to gain some leftover crumbs.

PRAKĀŚĀNANDA SARASVATĪ

Some people try to identify Prabodhānanda Sarasvatī with the Māyāvādī *sannyāsī* Prakāśānanda Sarasvatī, who lived in Benares. We do not find their arguments at all convincing for the following reasons:

Prakāśānanda Sarasvatī is first mentioned in the third chapter of the *Madhya-khaṇḍa* in the *Caitanya Bhāgavata*:

"The Lord constantly floated in the joys of devotion along with His followers in Nabadwip. One day, He heard a verse glorifying the Varāha *avatāra*. Roaring ecstatically, He went to Murāri Gupta's house. Murāri Gupta glorified Him with hymns of praise, and this satisfied the Lord. But He began to speak in anger against some portions of the Vedas: 'The Vedas say that I have no hands, feet, face or eyes. This is the way that they make a mockery of Me. There is even a rascal in Kashi named Prakāśānanda who teaches people impersonalism, cutting up My body into little pieces. He states that the Veda does not accept that I have a body. Now his entire body has become infected with leprosy, yet he still does not accept My transcendental form. My body is completely pure, the essence of all sacrifices. Brahmā, Śiva and the other gods all glorify My form and activities. What audacity this rascal has to say that My body is false when one becomes purified and accumulates merit by coming into contact with it.' " (*Caitanya Bhāgavata* 2.3.35-40)

This event took place sometime between 1504 and 1509 A.D. Mahāprabhu came to Srirangam in 1512, which is the first time that He met Prabodhānanda Sarasvatī and his brothers. The three brothers were Vaiṣṇavas following Rāmānuja in the Śrī *sampradāya* and thus accepted the servitude of Lord Nārāyaṇa's eternality. Meanwhile, Prakāśānanda Sarasvatī was a prominent follower of Śaṅkara's doctrine, a Mayavadi *sannyāsī*. It is sheer madness for anyone to claim that these two persons are one and the same person.

Again, in the *Caitanya Bhāgavata*, *Madhya-khaṇḍa*, the following mention is made of Prakāśānanda Sarasvatī:

"As He spoke, the Lord was suddenly possessed by the spirit of the Divinity. Grinding His teeth, He angrily spoke the following words: 'That *sannyāsī* Prakāśānanda is preaching in Kashi in a way that cuts My body into pieces. The rascal teaches Vedānta but does not accept My transcendental form. I have infected his body with leprosy, but still, he does not understand. How can this rascal say that My body, which is the reservoir of unlimited universes, is false? I tell you truthfully, Murāri, for you are My servant, that anyone who denies My transcendental form is destined for destruction. My pastimes and My activities are all real; My abode is real. Anyone who denies them will be struck down. The glories of the Lord will destroy one's ignorance if one hears them, but this sinful professor calls it all false. Anyone who has so little affection for My holy fame will never be able to understand My descent.' " (*Caitanya Bhāgavata* 2.10.31-.44)

At this time, Prakāśānanda Sarasvatī was the leader of the *ekadaṇḍi sannyāsī* followers of Śaṅkara, whereas Prabodhānanda Sarasvatī was a *tridaṇḍi sannyāsī* in the line of Rāmānuja who had moved to Srirangam from Mysore. Śrī Vaiṣṇavas who renounce family life never take the single staff (*ekadaṇḍa*), which is the mark of the Śaṅkarites. Their custom is to take the triple staff (*tridaṇḍa*) and the title Rāmānujīyārya Svāmī. Prakāśānanda was a Māyāvādī living in Kashi, whereas Prabodhānanda was a Vaiṣṇava living in Kamyavan. One was a northerner, the other a southerner. One was an impersonalist and monist, the other a devotee who first followed Rāmānuja's *viśiṣṭādvaita-vāda* and then converted to Mahāprabhu's *acintya-bhedābheda-vāda*. One was inimical to Viṣṇu and the Vaiṣṇavas and only after conversion became a devotee; the other was an eternal associate of Lord Caitanya Mahāprabhu and the guru of Gopāla Bhaṭṭa Gosvāmī, *ācārya* of the Gauḍīya Vaiṣṇava *sampradaya*. Anyone who calls Gopāla Bhaṭṭa Gosvāmī's worshipable guru and uncle a Māyāvādī and opposed to Viṣṇu and the Vaiṣṇavas, a conditioned soul, rather than an eternally perfect devotee of the highest order, is engaging in offensive insults that are sure to lead the one who makes them to a hellish destination.

An extensive description of Prakāśānanda Sarasvatī's conversion is given in two places in the *Caitanya Caritāmṛta*, *Adi-khaṇḍa*, chapter 7, and *Madhya-khaṇḍa*, chapter 25. It is impossible to understand how someone who had been a Māyāvādī from 1504 to 1509 could have become a qualified Śrī Vaiṣṇava in South India in 1512, and then again become the leader of Kashi's Māyāvādīs in 1514. Therefore, any attempt to identify Prakāśānanda with Prabodhānanda is evidence of extreme ignorance. It is no small cause of distress to see the tradition being distorted in this way.

Out of his humility, Prabodhānanda Sarasvatī asked through Gopāla Bhaṭṭa that his own activities not be described in the *Caitanya-caritāmṛta*. Kṛṣṇadāsa Kavirāja Gosvāmī was not able to disobey this order, and so today we have this difference of opinion. If Prabodhānanda Sarasvatī had known that as a result of this silence people would later fall into confusion and identify him with someone who preached against Viṣṇu and the Vaiṣṇavas, he would surely not have instructed Kṛṣṇadāsa Kavirāja Gosvāmī through Gopāla Bhaṭṭa in this way. Anyone who reads the *Bhakti-ratnākara* will understand. The author of that book writes:

"Gauracandra was the wealth of Tirumalaya, Veṅkaṭa and Prabodhānanda's lives. The three of them were worshipers of Lakṣmī-Nārāyaṇa whose preferences changed to Rādhā and Kṛṣṇa as a result of the Lord's mercy. The three of them wondered how they could continue living in the Lord's absence; they wondered who would joke with them and who would accompany them to the Kaveri to bathe in the morning. After four months, when the Lord left, the three brothers began to cry. Mahāprabhu embraced the three brothers and tried to console them. Some people glorified Prabodhānanda's virtues, and thus he was given the title Sarasvatī by which he was known everywhere. Śrī Kṛṣṇa Caitanya is the Supreme Lord and Supreme Absolute Truth. Prabodhānanda held him so dear that he knew nothing but the Lord, even in his dreams." (*Bhakti-ratnākara* 1.83-4, 128-9, 133, 135, 149, 150)

Some people claim upon reading the *Caitanya-candrāmṛta* that Prabodhānanda Sarasvatī had been a worshipper of Brahman, but if we accept this without any supplementary evidence we fall into difficulty.

Śrī Vṛndāvana Dāsa Ṭhākura

vedavyāso ya evāsīd dāso vṛndāvano 'dhunā
sakhā yaḥ kusumāpīḍaḥ kāryatas taṁ samāviśat

"Vedavyāsa became Vṛndāvana Dāsa Ṭhākura. Kṛṣṇa's friend Kusumāpīḍa also entered into him for the sake of Lord's pastimes." (*Gaura-gaṇoddeśa-dīpikā* 109)

Vedavyāsa described Kṛṣṇa's pastimes in the *Śrīmad Bhāgavatam*. Non-different from Vyāsa, Vṛndāvana Dāsa described Mahāprabhu's pastimes in his *Caitanya Bhāgavata*. His book was first called *Caitanya Maṅgala*, but when Locana Dāsa later gave the same name to his biography of the Lord, it was dubbed *Caitanya Bhāgavata*.

VṚNDĀVANA DĀSA'S MOTHER, NĀRĀYAṆĪ

Vṛndāvana Dāsa was born on the *Kṛṣṇa dvādaśī* of the month of Vaiśākha in 1429 of the Śaka era (1507 A.D.). Some say he was born in Mamgachi in the Nabadwip area; others say his birthplace was in Kumarhatta. His father was Vaikuṇṭhanātha Vipra, who originally came from Sylhet; his mother was Nārāyaṇī Devī. Nārāyaṇī was the daughter of Śrīvāsa Paṇḍita's elder brother, Śrī Nalina Paṇḍita. Kavi Karṇapūra has also mentioned her name in his *Gaura-gaṇoddeśa-dīpikā*:

ambikāyāḥ svasā yāsīn nāmnī śrīlakilimbikā
kṛṣṇocchiṣṭaṁ prabhuñjānā seyaṁ nārāyaṇī matā

"Kilimbikā, who used to eat Kṛṣṇa's remnants, was the younger sister of Kṛṣṇa's nurse Ambikā (Śrīvāsa's wife, Mālinī). In Mahāprabhu's *līlā*, she became Nārāyaṇī."

Nārāyaṇī also achieved fame because Gaurasundara bestowed His mercy on her when He gave her His remnants. Nārāyaṇī was only a small child of four when the Lord displayed His divine form in the *mahā-prakāśa* in Śrīvāsa Aṅgana, but the Lord still made her intoxicated with the ecstasy of *prema*.

Whether born in Mamgachi or in Kumarhatta, Vṛndāvana Dāsa spent part of his childhood with his mother in Mamgachi, at the home of his maternal grandparents, where Nārāyaṇī was married. Vṛndāvana Dāsa's Gaura-Nitāi deities are still worshipped at the Mamgachi home. When his father died, he and his mother moved to Śrīvāsa's house, where they received Mahāprabhu's special blessings. Vṛndāvana Dāsa later moved to the village of Denur in the Matresvara precinct of the Burdwan district. Thus Denur is considered to be his Sripat.

VṚNDĀVANA DĀSA WRITES CAITANYA BHĀGAVATA

Vṛndāvana Dāsa received copious blessings from Nityānanda Prabhu, and he is therefore said to have been His initiated disciple.

"Vṛndāvana Dāsa is the recipient of Nityānanda Prabhu's mercy. He is the original Vyāsa of Caitanya's pastimes." (*Caitanya Caritāmṛta* 3.20.82)

He wrote *Caitanya Bhāgavata* in 1535 A.D. Kṛṣṇadāsa Kavirāja Gosvāmī, the author of *Caitanya Caritāmṛta*, praised him and his work in the following words: "Vṛndāvana Dāsa, the son of Nārāyaṇī, wrote the *Caitanya Maṅgala*. Vedavyāsa described Kṛṣṇa *līlā* in the *Śrīmad Bhāgavatam*, and Vṛndāvana Dāsa is the Vyāsa of Caitanya *līlā*." (*Caitanya Caritāmṛta* 1.11.54-5)

"Vedavyāsa told the story of Kṛṣṇa's pastimes in *Śrīmad Bhāgavatam*. "Vṛndāvana Dāsa Ṭhākura is Vyāsadeva of the pastimes of Caitanya. His *Caitanya Maṅgala* annihilates all misfortune. From it, I learnt the wonders of Lord Caitanya and Nityānanda Prabhu and came to know all the subtlest doctrines of devotional service to Kṛṣṇa. Vṛndāvana Dāsa Ṭhākura has summarized the essence of *Śrīmad Bhāgavatam*'s teachings in his *Caitanya Maṅgala*. If even an atheist or a Muslim should listen to *Caitanya Maṅgala*, he immediately becomes a great Vaiṣṇava. An ordinary human being could not have composed such a sublime work; Lord Caitanya Himself has spoken through the mouth of Vṛndāvana Dāsa. I offer millions of obeisances unto the lotus feet of Vṛndāvana Dāsa Ṭhākura, who has delivered the entire universe through his book. He was born in the womb of Nārāyaṇī, who ate the remnants of Śrī Caitanya Mahāprabhu. How wonderful is his description of the activities of the Lord! Simply by hearing them, the three worlds have become sanctified!" (*Caitanya Caritāmṛta* 1.8.34-42)

In the *Caitanya Bhāgavata*, Vṛndāvana Dāsa Ṭhākura primarily narrates Mahāprabhu's early life, such as His childhood, His student life, His chastisement of the Kajī, His departure from Nabadwip, as well as some aspects of His life in Puri. He then became so absorbed in the description of Nityānanda Prabhu's *līlā* that he only gave an abbreviated account of Mahāprabhu's later pastimes. Kṛṣṇadāsa Kavirāja Gosvāmī then elaborated on these undescribed activities in his *Caitanya Caritāmṛta*. Kṛṣṇadāsa Kavirāja Gosvāmī wrote:

"Vṛndāvana Dāsa is the authorized biographer of Śrī Caitanya Mahāprabhu and equal to Śrīla Vyāsadeva. He has described the Lord's pastimes in a very sweet way. He was afraid of excessively enlarging his book and so left some parts of Mahāprabhu's pastimes untold. I shall try as far as possible to fill in these empty spaces." (*Caitanya Caritāmṛta* 1.13.48-9)

VṚNDĀVANA DĀSA'S CRITICISM OF VAIṢṆAVA APARĀDHA

Vṛndāvana Dāsa showed infinite mercy on the fallen souls by warning them:

eta parihāre-o je pāpī nindā kare
tabe lāthi māroṅ tār śirera upare

"If someone still blasphemes the Vaiṣṇavas even after being told how objectionable it is, I will kick him in the head."

These same words are repeated several times throughout the *Caitanya Bhāgavata*. Some foolish and arrogant persons misunderstand such statements and criticize Vṛndāvana Dāsa for having made them. Such criticism leads them to be mired in the bog of Vaiṣṇava *aparādha*.

In this connection, the remarks of Śrīla Bhakti Siddhānta Sarasvatī Gosvāmī Ṭhākura Prabhupāda, the founder of the Sri Chaitanya Math and all the Gaudiya Maths, are well worth studying: "I am even ready to kick the heads of those envious and hellish persons who blaspheme Nityānanda Prabhu, to forever prevent them from repeating their attempts to show disrespect for the Supreme Lord. Not only that, by so doing I can bring about a clear conception of the truth, and I will be offering them the greatest service.

"With these words, the Ṭhākura reveals compassion for even the most atheistic blasphemer with the unswerving faith appropriate to a servant of Nityānanda Prabhu, the supreme guru. By this he instructs that though such people are an object of indifference due to their foolishness, their ignorance of the truth of Nityānanda Prabhu, their insistence on rushing headlong on the path to hell, and their reluctance to act in their own real self-interest, nevertheless, he and other compassionate Vaiṣṇavas like him who practice and preach the

Lord's doctrines act for their welfare selflessly and causelessly. Vṛndāvana Dāsa Ṭhākura is a servant of Nityānanda Prabhu, who is an *avatāra* of Vyāsa and *ācārya* of the Vaiṣṇava faith. If even a single fleck of dust should fall from Vṛndāvana Dāsa's foot onto the head of a sinful blasphemer, then that person will be blessed and all his sinful conditioning will inevitably be eradicated. The compassion of Viṣṇu and Vaiṣṇavas is beyond the comprehension of those who do not know what is truly in their own self-interest. Anyone who follows in the footsteps of Vṛndāvana Dāsa Ṭhākura and both practices and preaches pure devotion to Gaurakṛṣṇa will always be engaged in an effort to bring about everyone's ultimate well-being. Though he may make a show of wanting to punish the enemies of the Lord, he, in fact, harbors a compassion toward them that knows no limit."

Vṛndāvana Dāsa Ṭhākura's disappearance day is the *Kṛṣṇa daśamī* of Vaiśākha. There is some dispute about the exact year of his disappearance, which was likely 1511 Śaka (1589 A.D.).

Kavi Karṇapūra (Śrī Purī Dāsa)

Kavi Karṇapūra is considered a branch of Śrī Caitanya. His father was Mahāprabhu's dear associate Śivānanda Sena. Kavi Karṇapūra himself identifies his parents in *Gaura-gaṇoddeśa-dīpikā*:

purā vṛndāvane vīrā dūtī sarvāś ca gopikāḥ
ināya kṛṣṇanikaṭaṁ sedānīṁ janako mama
vraje bindumatī yāsīd adya sā jananī mama

"The messenger Vīrā, who previously brought all the *gopīs* to Kṛṣṇa, is my father, Śivānanda Sena. My mother was previously Bindumatī in Vraja." (*Gaura-gaṇoddeśa-dīpikā* 176)

PARAMĀNANDA DĀSA, OR PURĪ DĀSA

Kavi Karṇapūra did not give his own identity in *Gaura-gaṇoddeśa-dīpikā*, but from what he has said of his own parents' identity, we can surmise that he too is an associate of Kṛṣṇa in Vraja. In the *Vaiṣṇavācāra-darpaṇa*, we learn:

"Kavi Karṇapūra was Guṇacūḍā Sakhī in Vraja. He is a branch of Caitanya who lived in Kachra Para. He was given the name Purī Dāsa and accumulated great spiritual power from Mahāprabhu when he placed the Lord's big toe in his mouth."

"Kavi Karṇapūra appeared in 1527 in the town of Kanchan Palli, or Kachra Para. His father named him Paramānanda Dāsa, Paramānanda Sena or Purī Dāsa. He was the youngest of Śivānanda Sena's three sons. His older brothers were named Caitanya Dāsa and Rāma Dāsa. All three brothers were devotees of Lord Śrī Caitanya." (*Caitanya Caritāmṛta* 1.10.62)

Śivānanda Sena's entire family was blessed with the Lord's unlimited mercy. The Lord Himself showed His other associates just how dear this family was to Him when He ordered that as long as Śivānanda and his family stayed in Puri, they should receive His remnant *prasāda*. (*Caitanya Caritāmṛta* 3.12.53)

Kavi Karṇapūra received the name Paramānanda Dāsa from Mahāprabhu Himself. The Lord also jokingly called him Purī Dāsa. It is said that he was born as a result of Mahāprabhu's blessing:

"The Lord asked Śivānanda Sena the youngest son's name; Sena answered, 'Paramānanda Dāsa.' The previous time Śivānanda Sena had visited the Lord, the Lord had said to him, 'This time, when your son is born, name him Purī Dāsa.' Śivānanda's wife was pregnant at the time, and she gave birth after Śivānanda returned home. He named the child Paramānanda Dāsa in accordance with the Lord's wishes, and the Lord jokingly called him Purī Dāsa." (*Caitanya Caritāmṛta* 3.12.45-9)

MAHĀPRABHU GIVES THE EPITHET KAVI KARṆAPŪRA

The next year, when Śivānanda Sena brought the baby to Mahāprabhu, the Lord showed the child much mercy by placing his big toe in his mouth. When Purī Dāsa was only seven years old, the Lord himself gave him the title Kavi Karṇapūra upon hearing the wonderful poetry that the child was capable of composing. This has been described by Kṛṣṇadāsa Kavirāja Gosvāmī in the sixteenth chapter of the *Antya-līlā*.

One year, when Śivānanda and his wife were in Puri for the Rathayātrā, they came with Purī Dāsa to see the Lord. The child paid obeisances to Mahāprabhu, and the Lord said to him, "Say the name of Kṛṣṇa! Say Kṛṣṇa!" Though the Lord asked him repeatedly to chant, the boy refused to utter the Holy Name. His embarrassed father also tried to get him to chant, but the child was steadfast in his refusal. Mahāprabhu was astonished at his stubborn attitude and said, "I have made everyone in the universe, even the nonmoving beings, chant the names of Kṛṣṇa, but have been unable to make this little child do so."

Svarūpa Dāmodara suggested: "You have instructed him in Kṛṣṇa *mantra*. Because it is forbidden to repeat the *mantra* one has received from the guru aloud, he is only chanting it mentally. I would guess that this is what he is thinking."

The Lord was happy to see that such a young boy was aware of this scriptural injunction. In his *Anubhāṣya*, Śrīla Bhakti Siddhānta Sarasvatī Gosvāmī Ṭhākura has explained: "The *mantra* which one has received from the guru is not to be revealed to anyone else; otherwise it will lose its potency. We have seen this previously from the life of Gadādhara Paṇḍita."

This is why Purī Dāsa would not repeat the *mantra* which had been given to him by Mahāprabhu. Mahāprabhu asked Purī Dāsa to recite a verse in order to make him break his silence. The child recited the following verse of his own composition:

śravasoḥ kuvalayam akṣṇor
añjanam uraso mahendra-maṇi-dāma
vṛndāvana-ramaṇīnāṁ
maṇḍanam akhilaṁ harir jayati

"All glories to Hari, the ornament for all the beauties of Vrindavan, a blue lotus for their ears, black collyrium for their eyes, and a necklace of blue sapphires to decorate their chest." (*Caitanya Caritāmṛta* 3.16.74)

All those who were present were charmed by the lovely verse. A small boy of seven who had barely commenced his education was yet able to recite a verse of such quality! The demigods like Brahmā and Śiva are unable to understand Mahāprabhu's mercy, what to speak of an ordinary *jīva*!

Though Kavi Karṇapūra received the *mantra* of Kṛṣṇa's name from Caitanya Mahāprabhu, he nevertheless followed the social custom of taking initiation from Śrīnātha Paṇḍita, a sub-branch of Advaita Ācārya on the Caitanya tree. Karṇapūra paid his obeisance to Śrīnātha Paṇḍita in the introduction to his own work

Ānanda-vṛndāvana-campū. Some people say that Śrīnātha Paṇḍita's deities are still being worshipped in Kumarhatta, or Kachra Para.

In another introductory verse to *Ānanda-vṛndāvana-campū*, Kavi Karṇapūra glorified Caitanya Mahāprabhu as his family deity, saying that Mahāprabhu adopted Śivānanda Sena's entire family as His own.

The following is a list of Kavi Karṇapūra's compositions: *Caitanya-caritāmṛta-mahākāvya*, *Ānanda-vṛndāvana-campū*, *Alaṁkāra-kaustubha*, *Caitanya-candrodaya-nāṭaka*, *Gaura-gaṇoddeśa-dīpikā*, *Bṛhad-gaṇoddeśa-dīpikā*, *Ārya-śataka*, *Āhnika-kaumudī*, a commentary on the Tenth Canto of the *Śrīmad Bhāgavatam*, *Caitanya-sahasra-nāma* and *Keśavāṣṭaka*. He was still writing books in 1577 A.D.

"Kavi Karṇapūra was dear to the Lord and became a writer of books in which he revealed the Lord's blessings on Sanātana Gosvāmī." (*Bhakti-ratnākara* 1.657)

Śrī Locana Dāsa Ṭhākura

Locana Dāsa Ṭhākura appeared in 1523 in Kogram, in the Katwa block of the Burdwan district. This village is about ten miles north of Guskar train station. The Ṭhākura's home is situated near the Ajaya River.

His birth *tithi* is given by some as the first day of the fortnight of the waxing moon in Pauṣa. He was born in the Rarha clan of the physician caste (*vaidya*). His father's name was Kamalākara Dāsa, his mother's Sadānandī. He was a very affectionate and lone child of the couple. Locana Dāsa studied while at his maternal grandfather's house. He displayed devotion for Mahāprabhu from his childhood.

Locana Dāsa was married at a very young age, according to the customs of that time. Since he had been married so young, his wife first remained with her parents in the village of Amedpur Kakuta. As he grew older, Locana Dāsa showed a highly renounced attitude to life and spent all his time discussing Kṛṣṇa *kathā* with other devotees of Gaurāṅga.

As the time approached when his wife was to join him, the girl's parents began to worry because of Locana Dāsa's indifference to material life. They approached his guru, Narahari Sarakāra, and told him of their disquiet. As a result, Narahari Sarakāra ordered Locana Dāsa to go to his in-laws' home.

When Locana Dāsa arrived in Amedpur, he was unable to remember where their house was, since it had been so long since he had visited. He asked a young girl in the street for directions, addressing her as "*mā*," or "mother." When he arrived at his in-laws' house, he found out that the girl whom he had addressed as his mother was, in fact, his wife. From that day on, he always looked upon his wife as a mother, worshipping guru and Gaurāṅga in an attitude of renunciation.

THE CAITANYA MAṄGALA

Narahari Sarakāra Ṭhākura, Mahāprabhu's famous associate from Srikhanda, was very affectionate to Locana Dāsa and gave him initiation. Locana Dāsa Ṭhākura enthusiastically took up residence with his guru in Srikhanda and served him. His guru taught him about *kīrtana* and later ordered him to write Mahāprabhu's sacred biography. Locana Dāsa took this order seriously and wrote the *Caitanya Maṅgala*, the events of which are based on Murāri Gupta's *Caitanya-carita*.

The word *maṅgala* means auspicious, and this title reflects the fact that hearing Mahāprabhu Śrī Caitanya's divine pastimes is the most auspicious activity for all the living beings. Vṛndāvana Dāsa Ṭhākura's biography of the Lord was first named *Caitanya Maṅgala* and was only later known as *Caitanya Bhāgavata*. Locana Dāsa gives an indication of this in the introductory portion of his book:

"I attentively pay my obeisances to Vṛndāvana Dāsa Ṭhākura; his *Bhāgavata's* songs have enchanted the entire universe. (*Caitanya Maṅgala, Sūtra khaṇḍa*, 1.35)

Some people believe that Locana Dāsa Ṭhākura and Kṛṣṇadāsa Kavirāja Gosvāmī gave the name *Caitanya Bhāgavata* to Vṛndāvana Dāsa Ṭhākura's book. In the *Caitanya Maṅgala*, Locana Dāsa prays for his guru's blessings as follows:

"Narahari dāsa Ṭhākura is the proprietor of my life, and out of the hope of attaining his lotus feet, I desire to sing the glories of Gaurāṅga, even though I am the lowest of the low. This is my ambition." (*Caitanya Maṇgala, Sūtra-khaṇḍa* 1.9)

"I offer my reverences to Narahari Dāsa, the ocean of Gaurāṅga's qualities. Other than him, I have no friend in the three worlds." (*Caitanya Maṇgala, Sūtra-khaṇḍa* 1.33)

"My lord and master is Narahari Dāsa. I prostrate myself in humility to him. May he fulfill my desires." (*Caitanya Maṇgala Sūtra-khaṇḍa* 1.61)

Locana Dāsa Ṭhākura wrote the *Caitanya Maṅgala* in eastern Bengal's *Pāñcālī* style, completing it in 1537 A.D. There is a legend that he wrote the book while sitting on a stone under a flower tree. In his new Bengali dictionary, Āśutoṣa Deva has underlined Locana Dāsa's contribution by stating that he was the first to write Bengali poetry using vowel-marked meters as well as being one of Bengal's earliest historical writers. The original manuscript of the *Caitanya Maṅgala* is said to be found in the personal library of Prāṇa Kṛṣṇa Cakravartī of Kandra, near the Guskar train station.

Other titles attributed to Locana Dāsa are *Prārthanā, Durlabha-sāra, Padāvalī (Dhāmālī)*, and Bengali verse translations of Rāmānanda's *Jagannātha-vallabha-nāṭaka* and the *Rāsa-pañcādhyāya* of *Śrīmad Bhāgavatam.*

LOCANA DĀSA'S SONGS GLORIFYING NITYĀNANDA

In *Caitanya Maṅgala*, Locana Dāsa Ṭhākura describes his guru, Narahari Sarakāra Ṭhākura, as Mahāprabhu's dearest associate. He does not describe Nityānanda Prabhu's glories as extensively. Fearful that he may have committed an offense by neglecting Nityānanda Prabhu, he later wrote a few songs in His praise. These songs are particularly well appreciated by the devotees.

(1)

nitāi guṇa-maṇi āmāra nitāi guṇa-maṇi
āniyā premera banyā bhāisāla avanī
premera banyā laiyā nitāi āilā gauḍa-deśe
ḍubila bhakata-gaṇa dīna-hīna bhāse
dīna-hīna patita-pāmara nāhi bāche
brahmāra durlabha prema sabākāre yāce
ābaddha karuṇā-sindhu (nitāi) kāṭiyā muhān
ghare ghare bule prema amiyāra bāna
locana bole mora nitāi ye bā nā bhajila
jāniyā śuniyā sei ātma-ghātī haila

"Nitāi is a jewel of virtue! My Nitāi is a jewel of virtue. He brought the deluge of love of God and flooded the world.

"Nitāi brought the deluge of love of God to Gauda Desh and inundated the devotees. The lowly and deprived floated in the flood.

"Nitāi never excluded the lowly and deprived, nor the sinful and atheistic. He freely distributed love of God, which is beyond the reach of even Brahmā.

"Nitāi released the floodgates that held back the ocean of compassion, going from door to door to give everyone the nectar of the love of God.

"Locana Dāsa says that anyone who has not worshipped Nitāi has knowingly committed suicide."

(2)

akrodha paramānanda nityānanda rāy
abhimāna-śūnya nitāi nagare beṛāy
adhama patita jīver dvāre dvāre giyā
harināma mahāmantra dena bilāiyā
yāre dekhe tāre kahe dante tṛṇa kari
āmāre kiniyā laha bhaja gaura-hari
eta boli nityānanda bhūme gaṛi yāy
sonāra parvata yena dhūlāte loṭāy
hena avatāre yāra rati nā janmila
locana bale sei pāpī ela āra gela

"Completely free from anger, Lord Nityānanda Prabhu is the embodiment of supreme joy. He wanders throughout the town without any pride or arrogance.

"He knocks on every fallen soul's door and bestows the *mahā-mantra* of the Holy Names on him.

"Placing straw between His teeth, He says to everyone He sees, 'Worship Gaura Hari and you will purchase Me and make Me your slave.'

"Saying thus, He tumbles on the ground, in an ecstatic fit, looking like a golden mountain rolling in the dust.

"Whoever lacks faith in such a compassionate *avatāra* is a sinner who will die having made nothing of his life, says Locana Dāsa."

(3)

parama karuṇā, pahuṅ dui jana,
nitāi gauracandra
saba avatār sāra śiromaṇi kevala ānanda kanda

"These two lords, Nitāi and Gauracandra, are most compassionate. They are the essence of all other *avatāras* of Godhead, They are the most perfect, for They are the unique source of joy.

bhaja bhaja bhāi caitanya nitāi
sudṛḍha viśvāsa kari
viṣaya chāṛiyā se rase majiyā
mukhe bolo hari hari

"O brothers, worship, worship Caitanya and Nitāi with greath faith. Give up the objects of sense-gratification, absorb yourself in the flavors of Their divine mood, and use your tongue to sing the names of Hari.

dekha are bhāi tribhuvane nāi
emana dayāla dātā
paśu pākhī jhure pāṣāṇa vidare
śuni yāra guṇa-gāthā

"Just look, O my brothers! There is no more compassionate benefactor than Gaura-Nitāi anywhere in the three worlds. Even the birds and beasts shed tears in ecstasy and stones melt when they hear Their virtues.

saṁsāre majiyā rahili paṛiyā
se pade nahila āśa
āpana karama bhuñjāye śamana
kahaye locana-dāsa

"I have fallen into the worldly life, completely absorbed in mundane pursuits, and have never aspired to attaining Them. The god of judgement is making me suffer the consequences of my acts; so sings Locana Dāsa."

Śrīla Locana Dāsa Ṭhākura was present on the occasion of Śrī Narahari Sarakāra Ṭhākura's disappearance festival. In *Bhakti-ratnākara*, it is said that he came there with Yadunandana Ṭhākura, bringing garlands of flowers and sweet-scented sandalwood.

GAURA-NĀGARĪ DOCTRINE CONDEMNED

Followers of certain heterodox groups, or *apa-sampradāyas,* say that the Gaura-nāgara doctrine is found in the *Caitanya Maṅgala.* This is not true. Vṛndāvana Dāsa Ṭhākura writes in his *Caitanya Bhāgavata*: "No one should praise the Lord by calling Him the golden playboy."

Śrīla Bhakti Siddhānta Sarasvatī Gosvāmī Ṭhākura Prabhupāda comments: "Gaurasundara is Kṛṣṇa who has been endowed with Rādhā's bodily hue and Her mood of love. Thus He never abandoned the qualities of the heart of Rādhikā and the other *gopīs*, i.e., the character of the *āśraya* of devotion in the conjugal mood. This means that He never acts like the *viṣaya* ('object') or *bhoktā* ('enjoyer') of *madhura-rasa* by looking at other women in the spirit of a playboy." (*Gauḍīya-bhāṣya* 1.15.30)

Locana Dāsa Ṭhākura ended his pastimes in this world in 1589 A.D. His brick *samādhi* is seen at his Sripat.

Śrīla Kṛṣṇadāsa Kavirāja Gosvāmī

Nothing in connection to the birth and parentage of Kṛṣṇadāsa Kavirāja Gosvāmī, the author of the *Caitanya Caritāmṛta*, is known. In his introduction to the *Caitanya Caritāmṛta*, Śrīla Bhakti Siddhānta Sarasvatī Gosvāmī Ṭhākura Prabhupāda has written the following about him: "We do not know who his parents[27] were, not even their names. Despite recent claims that their names have been discovered, no concrete evidence can be found to substantiate them. Kṛṣṇadāsa is his spiritual name.

"Kṛṣṇadāsa has given us some autobiographical information in the fifth chapter of the *Ādi-līlā*, from which we learn that he was born in Jhamatpur, which is near the present Salar railway station. Jhamatpur is near Naihati village. To this day, Kṛṣṇadāsa's Gaura-Nitāi deities are still worshipped in his hometown, but there do not seem to be any descendants of his family living there.

"Kṛṣṇadāsa was ordered to go to Vrindavan in a dream by Nityānanda Prabhu. He spent the remainder of his life in Vraja dhāma, and his *samādhi* can be seen on the grounds of the Rādhā-Dāmodara temple." (*Bhūmikā*, ii.)

"There is a village near Naihati named Jhamatpur. Nityānanda Prabhu appeared to me in a dream." (*Caitanya Caritāmṛta* 1.5.181)

Śrīla Prabhupāda has established Kavirāja Gosvāmī's dates by collating information from several sources. He concludes that he probably appeared in about 1520 A.D. and disappeared in about 1616 or 1617. Vṛndāvana Dāsa Ṭhākura appeared sometime after 1510 A.D. Kavirāja Gosvāmī's magnificent biography of Caitanya Mahāprabhu was meant to serve as an appendix to his work.

VARṆĀSRAMA STATUS

There is some difference of opinion about Kṛṣṇadāsa Kavirāja Gosvāmī's caste. Once again, Śrīla Prabhupāda Bhakti Siddhānta Sarasvatī Gosvāmī Ṭhākura has discussed this

27 According to Āśutoṣa Deva's Bengali dictionary and Haridāsa Dāsa's *Gauḍīya Vaiṣṇava Abhidhāna*, Kṛṣṇadāsa's parents were named Bhagīratha and Sunandā.

point: "Supporters of different ideas claim that Kṛṣṇadāsa appeared in one of the three upper castes (*brāhmaṇa*, *kāyastha* or *vaidya*). Kavirāja is a title given to those who have proven themselves by composing literary works which have achieved renown for their quality in learned circles. Since this title is also given to Ayurvedic physicians, some people hold that Kṛṣṇadāsa was a *vaidya*. It is difficult to contradict those who claim that he is a *brāhmaṇa* on the basis of his profound skill in *darśana sāstra* and extraordinary mastery of the scriptures and other branches of learning. Nor is the view that he was a *kāyastha* altogether illogical, as he reveals a soft spot for that caste when he praises its intelligence and managerial talents in the chapters about Raghunātha Dāsa Gosvāmī's early life." (*Bhūmikā*, iii.)

From this above discussion, we can see that Kṛṣṇadāsa may have been born in any of these three castes. Whatever the case, all the scriptures say that a Vaiṣṇava is transcendental no matter in what caste he takes his birth.

"All scriptures state that a Vaiṣṇava is transcendental. It does not matter in which caste he takes birth. That most sinful person who judges a Vaiṣṇava in terms of his race or his caste will be born repeatedly in the lowest forms of life." (*Caitanya Bhāgavata* 2.10.100,102)

There is no unanimous opinion about Kṛṣṇadāsa Kavirāja Gosvāmī's marital status, either. Some say that he was a lifelong *brahmacārī* when he went to Vrindavan, for if he had left a wife and family he would likely have mentioned it when telling of his renunciation. Śrīla Prabhupāda writes in this connection, "After arriving in Vrindavan, Kṛṣṇadāsa became totally absorbed in Hari *kathā* and indifferent to talk about his previous family life. This behavior is appropriate for someone in the third or fourth station and completely committed to devotional service. *Caitanya Caritāmṛta* is the composition of someone who has reached the status of a *paramahaṁsa* and is completely beyond the four *āśramas*. He was known as Kavirāja Gosvāmī to his spiritual family. His spiritual identity in Vraja *līlā* is Ratnarekhā Mañjarī, or Kasturī Mañjarī according to *Gauḍīya Vaiṣṇava Abhidhāna*.

From Kṛṣṇadāsa's statements in the *Caitanya Caritāmṛta*, we also learn that he had a brother. Kṛṣṇadāsa does not name him, but Haridāsa Dāsa writes in the *Gauḍīya Vaiṣṇava Abhidhāna* that he was called Śyāma Dāsa Kavirāja.

KṚṢṆA DĀSA'S VISION OF NITYĀNANDA PRABHU

In the course of his glorification of Nityānanda Prabhu in the *Caitanya Caritāmṛta*, Kavirāja Gosvāmī describes the crucial event in his life. He had organized a twenty-four-hour *kīrtana* at his house, and amongst those invited was Lord Nityānanda Prabhu's dear associate Mīnaketana Rāma Dāsa, who also lived in Jhamatpur.

Mīnaketana Rāma Dāsa was a great Vaiṣṇava who was constantly in a state of devotional trance as he chanted the name of Nityānanda Prabhu. While in his ecstatic mood, he would sometimes slap people and sometimes hit people with his flute. In general, his ecstatic behavior was the cause of some astonishment amongst the participants, and most came to pay their obeisances and offer him their respects. Only Guṇārṇava Miśra, who had been engaged as a *pūjārī* of the deities, did not demonstrate a respectful attitude. This behavior was an indication that Guṇārṇava Miśra had no faith in Nityānanda Prabhu. Rāma Dāsa became angry and criticized Miśra, saying:

"Just look! This is a second Romaharṣaṇa Suta, who did not come forward to show respect when he saw Balarāma!" (*Caitanya Caritāmṛta* 1.5.170)

Guṇārṇava Miśra was pleased to have been chastised by Rāma Dāsa. At the end of the *kīrtana* festival, when Guṇārṇava Miśra had left, however, Kṛṣṇadāsa Kavirāja Gosvāmī's brother got into an argument with Mīnaketana Rāma Dāsa about what had happened. Kavirāja Gosvāmī's brother had strong faith in Caitanya Mahāprabhu, but lacked similar faith in Nityānanda Prabhu. Upon hearing this, Rāma Dāsa was deeply wounded, and he became so angry that he broke his flute and left. The result of this curse was that Kavirāja Gosvāmī's brother was doomed to lose whatever devotion he had. In this argument, Kavirāja Gosvāmī took the side of Nityānanda Prabhu's associate and rebuked his brother:

"These two brothers [Caitanya Mahāprabhu and Nityānanda Prabhu] are one body, equal in every respect. If you do not accept the divinity of Lord Nityānanda Prabhu, you will meet with ruin. To have faith in one but to disrespect the other is as logical as only the half of the hen that lays the eggs. Better you should be an atheist and deny the divinity of both than a hypocrite who believes in one and not the other." (*Caitanya Caritāmṛta* 1.5.175-7)

The Lord is influenced by His devotees, and He gives great importance to even the slightest display of attachment to His devotees, bestowing upon those who do so all that they desire. Kṛṣṇadāsa Kavirāja Gosvāmī writes that just for taking the side of Nityānanda Prabhu's associate and chastising his brother, he won the blessings of Nityānanda Prabhu Himself. Nitāi came to him in a dream and ordered him to go to Vrindavan.

" 'O Kṛṣṇadāsa! Have no fear. Go to Vrindavan, for there you will attain all things.' After saying this, He indicated the way to Vrindavan by waving His hand and then disappeared with His associates." (*Caitanya Caritāmṛta* 1.5.195-6)

In contrast, a person who shows all the customary virtues, yet holds devotees in contempt, is eternally deprived of the Lord's blessings. A good example of this is the zamindar Rāmacandra Khān, who committed offenses to Haridāsa Ṭhākura, as a result of which he incurred Nityānanda Prabhu's displeasure and anger. Not only did Rāmacandra lose his family and possessions, but his house was razed, leaving him with nothing. Only a fool who lacks discrimination would be so bold as to behave unjustly toward a saintly person.

With words of profound humility, Kṛṣṇadāsa Kavirāja Gosvāmī proclaims the glories of Nityānanda Prabhu:

"I am more sinful than Jagāi and Mādhāi and lower than a maggot in stool. Whoever hears my name loses the results of his virtuous deeds, and whoever utters my name commits a sin. Other than Nityānanda Prabhu, could

anyone in this world show mercy to one as abominable as me? Nityānanda Prabhu is an *avatāra* of mercy; He is so intoxicated by ecstatic love that He does not discriminate between the superior and the inferior. He delivers anyone who falls down before Him. Therefore, He has delivered such a sinful and fallen person as me." (*Caitanya Caritāmṛta* 1.5.205-9)

KṚṢṆADĀSA WRITES THE FINAL PASTIMES OF THE LORD

Without the mercy of Viṣṇu and the Vaiṣṇavas, it is impossible to describe their glories. It is for this reason that Kṛṣṇadāsa Kavirāja Gosvāmī begins each chapter of the *Caitanya Caritāmṛta* with invocations to Mahāprabhu, Nityānanda Prabhu, Advaita Ācārya, and Their associates and concludes each chapter with a prayer for the service to the feet of Rūpa Gosvāmī and Raghunātha Dāsa Gosvāmī. He thus showed how important it is to carefully avoid any disrespect or offense to the Vaiṣṇavas.

"The activities of Śrī Caitanya Mahāprabhu are by nature wonderful and sweet. When described by Vṛndāvana Dāsa Ṭhākura, they become a shower of nectar. To describe them again would not only be repetition, but a display of arrogance, for I do not possess his powers. I shall thus only present a synopsis of those events already described fully by him in his *Caitanya Maṅgala*. In this book, I shall do my best to fully describe only those incidents mentioned in his outline that he did not develop. I therefore offer respectful obeisances unto the lotus feet of Vṛndāvana Dāsa Ṭhākura, praying that I will not offend his lotus feet by my action." (*Caitanya Caritāmṛta* 2.4.5-9)

"Just as Vyāsadeva compiled Lord Kṛṣṇa's pastimes in *Śrīmad Bhāgavatam*, Ṭhākura Vṛndāvana Dāsa depicted Lord Caitanya's pastimes. I offer millions of obeisances unto the lotus feet of Vṛndāvana Dāsa Ṭhākura, who has delivered the entire universe through his book." (*Caitanya Caritāmṛta* 1.8.35, 40)

"Vṛndāvana Dāsa Ṭhākura is the authorized biographer of Śrī Caitanya Mahāprabhu and equal to Śrīla Vyāsadeva. The way he has described the Lord's pastimes makes them more and more delectable. Afraid that it would become too voluminous, Vṛndāvana Dāsa Ṭhākura left some events out of his book. I shall try as far as possible to fill in these gaps." (*Caitanya Caritāmṛta* 1.13.48-9)

Parampūjyapāda Bhakti Pramode Purī Gosvāmī Mahārāja, the former president of the editorial board of *Caitanya Vāṇī* magazine, explains the above statements in his foreword to the Sri Chaitanya Gaudiya Math edition of the *Caitanya Caritāmṛta*:

"Vṛndāvana Dāsa Ṭhākura gave an outline of Mahāprabhu's *līlā* at the beginning of the *Caitanya Bhāgavata*, but as he started to describe them in more detail he found that the work had become voluminous, resulting in his leaving the events mentioned in the outline unelaborated. He became so absorbed in describing Nityānanda Prabhu's activities that, particularly, the Lord's pastimes after His *sannyāsa* remained incomplete. Mahāprabhu's Vrindavan devotees were extremely eager to listen to those pastimes, and so they approached Kṛṣṇadāsa Kavirāja Gosvāmī, asking him to write down a full version of these events. Kavirāja Gosvāmī then went to the deity of Madana Mohana and asked for permission to do as he had been asked. In front of all the prominent contemporary members of the Gauḍīya community in Vrindavan, Madana Mohana's garland fell from His neck. This was taken by all present as a sign of the Lord's approval, and they let out a joyous cheer. Madana Mohana's *pūjārī* picked up the garland and placed it on Kavirāja Gosvāmī's chest. Accepting it as a symbol of the deity's wishes, he began to write his biography of the Lord. Thus, he has written in great humility,

"*Caitanya Caritāmṛta* is being dictated to me by Madana Mohana. My writing is like the repetition of a parrot. I write as Madana Gopāla orders me, just as a wooden marionette is made to dance by a puppeteer." (*Caitanya Caritāmṛta* 1.8.78-9)

"In writing *Caitanya Caritāmṛta*, Kavirāja Gosvāmī made use of Svarūpa Dāmodara's notes, which Raghunātha Dāsa Gosvāmī had memorized. Śrīla Bhaktivinoda Ṭhākura has described this as follows: "Śrī Svarūpa Dāmodara Gosvāmī wrote an outline of Mahāprabhu's later activities in his diary. He had Raghunātha Dāsa Gosvāmī memorize these events and preached them throughout the world through Kavirāja Gosvāmī. Svarūpa Dāmodara's notes were not published. *Caitanya Caritāmṛta* is the gist of Svarūpa Dāmodara's *kaḍcā*."

"With the blessings of Śrī Caitanya Mahāprabhu, though I am an insignificant living being, I have summarized in writing everything that Svarūpa Dāmodara recorded in his notes about the Lord's pastimes, as well as everything that I heard from the mouth of Raghunātha Dāsa." (*Caitanya Caritāmṛta* 3.3.267-68)

Lord Caitanya Mahāprabhu's glorious name, form, qualities and activities all manifest in Kṛṣṇadāsa Kavirāja Gosvāmī's heart. He then published in the *Caitanya Caritāmṛta*. He himself stated this fact in various places throughout the book:

"I am now an old man and an invalid. My hand trembles as I write, and my memory fails me. I am going blind and deaf, but still I manage to write, and this is a great wonder." (*Caitanya Caritāmṛta* 2.2.89-90)

While Śrīla Bhakti Siddhānta Sarasvatī Gosvāmī Ṭhākura Prabhupāda was once glorifying the supremacy of *Caitanya Caritāmṛta* to his disciples, he instructed them as follows: "If ever a situation were to come where everything in the world were destroyed, leaving only *Śrīmad Bhāgavatam* and *Caitanya Caritāmṛta*, then the people would still be able to achieve the ultimate goal in life. And even if the *Śrīmad Bhāgavatam* were lost, leaving only the *Caitanya Caritāmṛta*, there would be no loss to humanity, for that which has not been revealed in *Śrīmad Bhāgavatam* is found in *Caitanya Caritāmṛta*. Śrī Caitanya Mahāprabhu, the combined form of Radha and Kṛṣṇa, is the Supreme Absolute Truth. *Caitanya Caritāmṛta* is His nondifferent sound manifestation. The most sublime and divine nature of Rādhārāṇī and Her glories are found therein. Can there be any doubt, therefore, of the supreme status of this piece of transcendental literature?"

This statement underscores the supremely special status of Kṛṣṇadāsa Kavirāja Gosvāmī himself. His three books, *Caitanya Caritāmṛta*, *Govinda-līlāmṛta* and a commentary on *Kṛṣṇa-karṇāmṛta*, are all priceless works. *Govinda-līlāmṛta* describes in detail Lord Kṛṣṇa's activities over a twenty-four-hour period. Narottama Dāsa Ṭhākura has therefore stated:

kṛṣṇadāsa kavirāja, rasika bhakata mājh
jiṅho kailā caitanya-carita
gaura-govinda-līlā, śunite galaye śilā
tāhāte nā haila mora cita

"Kṛṣṇadāsa Kavirāja Gosvāmī stands out amongst the devotees who are expert in the knowledge of transcendental divine mellows, for he is the author of the biography of Caitanya Mahāprabhu. Even the stones melt on hearing his descriptions of Gaura's and Govinda's *līlā*. Alas, my mind has still not been attracted by these works." (*Prema-bhakti-candrikā*)

Kṛṣṇadāsa Gosvāmī was honored with the title Kavirāja, "king of poets," for his *Govinda-līlāmṛta*. He is also respected in the Vaiṣṇava world as the best amongst the followers of Rūpa Gosvāmī.

THE AUTHORITATIVENESS OF THE CAITANYA CARITĀMṚTA

From the illustrious commentator Viśvanātha Cakravartī Ṭhākura's words, we can understand that Kṛṣṇadāsa Kavirāja Gosvāmī was an associate of Rādhārāṇī, and that the deepest and most esoteric truths of the Divinity were revealed to him, showing that every word he wrote is to be taken as the supreme spiritual truth. Śrīla Bhakti Pramode Purī Gosvāmī Mahārāja has recounted the following anecdote in his *Caitanya Caritāmṛta* foreword: "Viśvanātha Cakravartī Ṭhākura was unable to understand why Kavirāja Gosvāmī had written that the *kāma-gāyatrī mantra* consists of twenty-four and a half syllables rather than twenty-five. He became so distraught by his inability to comprehend that he finally took a vow to give up his body by the banks of Radha Kunda. As he dozed off in the middle of the night, Rādhārāṇī, the daughter of Vṛṣabhānu, appeared to him in a dream and said, 'O Viśvanātha! O the one dear to Hari! Get up. Kṛṣṇadāsa Kavirāja has indeed written correctly. He is My dear girlfriend, who brings Me much pleasure. I have blessed him so that he can understand the most intimate things about Me. Do not doubt anything he has written.' In the book named *Varṇāgama-bhāsvat*, it is written that whenever the syllable *ya* is followed by the syllable *vi*, it is considered to be only half a syllable."

In the *Bhakti-ratnākara* it is mentioned that Śrīnivāsa Ācārya met Kṛṣṇadāsa Kavirāja Gosvāmī, Raghunātha Dāsa Gosvāmī and Śrī Rāghava Paṇḍita got their blessings. (*Bhakti-ratnākara* 4.392)

On the grounds of Kṛṣṇadāsa Kavirāja Gosvāmī's home in Jhamatpur is a small temple containing Nityānanda Prabhu's footprints. Local legend has it that Kavirāja Gosvāmī received Nityānanda Prabhu's mercy, possibly *mantra* initiation, at this very spot. According to the *Prema-vilāsa*, however, Kṛṣṇadāsa Kavirāja Gosvāmī took initiation from Raghunātha Dāsa Gosvāmī. In the temple, there is a wooden sandal that is said to have belonged to Kavirāja Gosvāmī. His *bhajana-kutīra* and *samādhi* are in Radha Kunda. He disappeared after Raghunātha Dāsa Gosvāmī, on the *śukla dvādaśī tithi* of the month of Āśvina.

Śrīmatī Jāhnavā Devī

śrī-vāruṇī-revata-vaṁśa-sambhave
tasya priye dve vasudhā ca jāhnavī
śrī-sūrya-dāsasya mahātmanaḥ sute
kakudmi-rūpasya ca sūrya-tejasaḥ
kecit śrī vasudhā-devīṁ kalāv-api vivṛṇvate
anaṅga-mañjarīṁ kecij jāhnavīṁ ca pracakṣate
ubhayaṁ tu samīcīnaṁ pūrva-nyāyāt satāṁ matam

"Lord Balarāma's wives Vāruṇī and Revatī became Vasudhā and Jāhnavī, the two wives of Nityānanda Prabhu, in Caitanya *līlā*. Both of them were the daughters of Sūrya Dāsa, who was as effulgent as the sun. He was Kakudmī, the father of Revatī, in Kṛṣṇa *līlā*. According to another opinion, Jāhnavā was the *avatāra* of Anaṅga Mañjarī. Both these opinions are possible, as we have shown that more than one identity can be joined in associates of Caitanya Mahāprabhu." (*Gaura-gaṇoddeśa-dīpikā* 65-6)

Nityānanda Prabhu's *Śakti*, Śrīmatī Jāhnavā Devī appeared on the *śukla navamī tithi* of Vaiśākha. Her father was Sūrya Dāsa Sarakhela. According to the *Gauḍīya Vaiṣṇava Abhidhāna*, her mother's name was Bhadrāvatī. Sūrya Dāsa's Sripat is in the village of Shaligram, which is not far from Nabadwip, close to the Muragacha station on the Eastern Railway. Sūrya Dāsa was the third son of Kaṁsāri Miśra. His older brothers were Dāmodara and Jagannātha, his younger brothers, Gaurī Dāsa, Kṛṣṇadāsa Sarakhela and Nṛsiṁha Caitanya.

"Sūrya Dāsa Paṇḍita made his home in Shaligram, not far from Nabadwip. He held an important post in the service of the King of Gauḍa, as a result of which he was given the title Sarakhela (commander) and earned a large amount of money. Sūrya Dāsa and his brothers were all very pure in their character, and they had a spotless reputation. His virtues are innumerable. His daughters were Vasudhā and Jāhnavā." (*Bhakti-ratnākara* 12.3875-8)

"Sūrya Dāsa Sarakhela and Kṛṣṇadāsa were brothers who both had great faith in Nityānanda Prabhu and were filled with love for Kṛṣṇa." (*Caitanya Caritāmṛta* 1.11.25)

"Sūrya Dāsa Sarakhela was a magnanimous devotee whose brother was Gaurī Dāsa Paṇḍita. Gaurī Dāsa took his permission to come and live in Ambika on the banks of the Ganges." (*Bhakti-ratnākara* 7.330-1)

NITYĀNANDA PRABHU'S WEDDING

Narahari Cakravartī Ṭhākura has written about Jāhnavā Devī's holy life at length in his *Bhakti-ratnākara*. Every manifestation of Viṣṇu-tattva has three energies which are known as Śrī, Bhū and Nīlā or Līlā. Nityānanda Prabhu, the Viṣṇu-tattva, possesses these three energies. In the twlefth *taraṅga* of the *Bhakti-ratnākara*, Lord Nityānanda Prabhu's wedding is described as taking place according to human custom. The essence of that description is as follows.

A certain kāyastha named Kṛṣṇadāsa, the son of Harihoḍa of Borogachi, a village near Shaligram made arrangements for the wedding of Nityānanda Prabhu. A certain elderly *brāhmaṇa* from Shaligram saw that Sūrya Dāsa was worried about finding a suitable husband for his two daughters and made the following suggestion: "In the village of Ekachakra in Rarhadesh are a *brāhmaṇa* couple named Hāḍāi Paṇḍita and Padmāvatī Devī. They were Vasudeva and Rohiṇī in their previous roles in Kṛṣṇa *līlā*. Lord Balarāma has appeared as their son, Nityānanda Prabhu. He traveled to all the places of pilgrimage and performed many austerities. He is a great scholar and Caitanya Mahāprabhu's dearest associate. He is the eternal husband of your two daughters."

In a dream, Sūrya Dāsa also had a vision of Nityānanda Prabhu as Balarāma with Vasudhā and Jāhnavā standing to His left and right in their forms as Revatī and Vāruṇī. When Sūrya Dāsa took the *brāhmaṇa's* advice seriously and offered the two girls to Nityānanda Prabhu's lotus feet, Nityānanda Prabhu mercifully gave him the same vision directly. Sūrya Dāsa forgot himself in ecstasy.

"He saw Vasudhā and Jāhnavā as Vāruṇī and Revatī, whose forms were more effulgent than mountains of gold and *kumkum*. Standing to the left and right of Balarāma, they were decorated in magnificent jewellery and bedecked in fine, colorful clothes. Nityānanda Prabhu revealed this magnificence to His devotee in order to give him joy, and Sūrya Dāsa completely forgot himself in his ecstasy." (*Bhakti-ratnākara* 12.3908-10)

The *adhivāsa* (preliminary function) rituals on the eve of the wedding and the wedding itself were conducted in the house of Kṛṣṇadāsa Sarakhela in Shaligram. All the *brāhmaṇas* of Borogachi and Shaligram were present there.

"The fortunate Sūrya Dāsa Sarakhela gave his two daughters away to Nityānanda Prabhu according to the religious rites and popular custom." (*Bhakti-ratnākara* 12.3983)

At Śacī Mātā's request, Nityānanda Prabhu stayed for some time in Nabadwip after His wedding in Shantipur. He then moved to Saptagram, where He stayed with Uddhāraṇa Datta Ṭhākura, and then established a residence on the banks of the Ganges in Khardah.

Jāhnavā Devi herself had no sons, but Nityānanda Prabhu's other potency, Vasudhā Devī, gave birth to Vīrabhadra (or Vīracandra) Gosvāmī, the manifestation of Kṣīrodakaśāyī Viṣṇu (*Gaura-gaṇoddeśa-dīpikā* 67), and Gaṅgā Devī, the manifestation of river Ganges. According to the *Gaura-gaṇoddeśa-dīpikā* (69), Gaṅgā Devī's husband, Mādhavācārya, is an *avatāra* of King Śāntanu.

JĀHNAVĀ DEVĪ'S GLORIES

Vīrabhadra Gosvāmī was inundated with Jāhnavā Mātā's mercy, becoming her direct initiated disciple. Nityānanda Dāsa writes in his *Prema-vilāsa* that when Vīrabhadra saw Jāhnavā Mātā in a four-armed form, his mind was changed and he took *dīkṣā* from her.

Without the mercy of Nityānanda Prabhu's potency Jāhnavā Devī, no one is able to cross over the ocean of material life, nor can one obtain the service of Nityānanda Prabhu and enter into the loving service of his worshipable Gaurahari and Rādhā-Kṛṣṇa. Śrīla Bhaktivinoda Ṭhākura has written in his *Kalyāṇa-kalpa-taru:*

"O Jāhnavā Devī! Be merciful today to your servant and deliver me from my pain. Give me a place in the boat of your lotus feet so that I can be sure to cross over the ocean of birth and death. You are Nityānanda Prabhu's energy; you are devotion to Kṛṣṇa and my guru. Please give this servant the desire tree of your lotus feet. How numerous are the fallen souls that you have saved? So this fallen beggar seeks a place at your feet."

The great devotee Kṛṣṇadāsa, in his song which begins *jaya rādhe jaya kṛṣṇa jaya vṛndāvan*, has prayed for Jāhnavā Devī's mercy after glorifying Kṛṣṇa's name, abode and associates. "Remembering Jāhnavā Devī's lotus feet, the lowly Kṛṣṇadāsa sings the names of the Lord."

JĀHNAVĀ DEVĪ'S TRAVELS

Jāhnavā Devī was present when Narottama Dāsa Ṭhākura put on a great deity-installation festival at Kheturi village on Caitanya Mahāprabhu's appearance day. Indeed, the installation of the deities took place under her direction. She personally prepared the first offering to the deities and offered it to Them. She then served the *prasāda* to the assembled devotees.

"Early that morning, Jāhnavā Īśvarī rose in great delight, took her bath and did her *mantra* meditation. Then she began to cook innumerable vegetable preparations with great enthusiasm." (*Bhakti-ratnākara* 10.686-7)

"All of Caitanya Mahāprabhu's personal associates from Bengal were very happy to see Narottama Dāsa. Jāhnavā Devī, the daughter of Sūrya Paṇḍita and wife of Nityānanda Prabhu, worshipped by the entire universe, expert in the distribution of the pearl of *prema*, was delighted to hear his name. Her joy increased when she observed his renunciation and uncommon love for Kṛṣṇa. Jāhnavā Devī mercifully came to Kheturi, making everyone happy by being there and giving her *darśana* to all. How can a person as fallen as I describe the compassionate nature of Śrīmatī Jāhnavā Devī?" (*Bhakti-ratnākara* 1.429-34)

Jāhnavā Devī's travels are described in the eleventh *taraṅga* of *Bhakti-ratnākara.* While traveling from Kheturi to Vrindavan, she stopped in a prosperous village where she delivered some atheistic unbelievers and criminals and bestowed Kṛṣṇa *prema* upon them. When she arrived in Vrindavan, she saw the *samādhi* of Gaurī Dāsa Paṇḍita, which moved her to tears. When she was in Vrindavan, the leaders of the Vaiṣṇava community, such as Jīva Gosvāmī, Gopāla Bhaṭṭa Gosvāmī, Lokanātha Gosvāmi, Bhūgarbha Gosvāmī, Madhu Paṇḍita, all came to offer her their and respectful greetings. She took these Vaiṣṇavas and visited the principal temples of Vrindavan – Madana Mohana, Govinda and Gopīnātha – before going to Radha Kunda. There she met Raghunātha Dāsa Gosvāmī, who was engaged in the constant chanting of the Holy Names, and whose body was emaciated by his austerities.

Jāhnavā Devī remained in Radha Kunda for three days, engaged in *bhajana.* She heard the sound of Kṛṣṇa's flute while sitting on the banks of the kuṇḍa and had a vision of Śrī Kṛṣṇa that overwhelmed her with waves of divine love. The ghat where Jāhnavā Devī bathed and had this vision is today known as Sri Jahnava Ghat. She then took the company of Vaiṣṇavas on a *parikramā* of Vraja Mandala. During this *parikramā*, she heard Jīva Gosvāmī speak on *Bṛhad-Bhāgavatāmṛta.*

On the return journey to Gauda Desh, Jāhnavā Devī visited numerous places. She spent three or four days in Kheturi, some time in Budhuri, the place of Nityānanda Prabhu's birth in Ekacakra, Katwa (where Mahāprabhu took *sannyāsa*), Jajigram, Srikhanda, Nabadwip, Sridhama Mayapur, Ambika, and Saptagram (where she visited Uddhāraṇa Datta's house). During her travel, she met Śrī Yadunandana Ācārya and Śrīnivāsa Ācārya in Katwa, Śrīla Narottama Dāsa Ṭhākura and Śrī Rāmacandra Kavirāja in Jajigram and Śrī Raghunandana Ṭhākura in Srikhanda. Finally, she returned to Khardah, where she recounted the story of her entire voyage to Vasudhā and Vīrabhadra Prabhu.

By Jāhnavā Devī's mercy, Nityānanda Prabhu's dear associate Paramesvarī Dāsa Ṭhākura was fortunate enough to see Śrī Gopīnātha united with Śrī Rādhārāṇī in Vrindavan. When he returned to Khardah and told Jāhnavā Devī and Vasudhā what he had seen, Jāhnavā was overwhelmed with feelings of *prema.* She instructed Paramesvarī Ṭhākura to go immediately to the village of Antpur and install deities of Śrī Rādhā Gopīnātha there.

Jāhnavā Devī arranged for Vīrabhadra Prabhu's marriage to Yadunandana Ācārya's two daughters, Śrīmatī and Nārāyaṇī, both of whom became disciples of Jāhnavā Devī.

Śrī Vīracandra Prabhu (Vīrabhadra)

saṅkarṣaṇasya yo vyūhaḥ
payobdhi-śāyi-nāmakaḥ
sa eva vīracandro 'bhūt
caitanyābhinna-vigrahaḥ

"Kṣīrodakaśāyī Viṣṇu, the expansion of Saṅkarṣaṇa who sleeps on the ocean of milk, has become Vīracandra, the son of Nityānanda Prabhu. He is nondifferent from Caitanya Himself." (*Gaura-gaṇoddeśa-dīpikā* 67)

The Supreme Personality of Godhead, Śrī Kṛṣṇa, is the origin of unlimited expansions and *avatāras*. He is the *avatārī*. His first expansion is the root Saṅkarṣaṇa, or Balarāma. This same Balarāma appeared with Lord Caitanya as Nityānanda Prabhu. Balarāma's expansion Mahā-Saṅkarṣaṇa has His abode in the Vaikuṇṭha planets, and He in turn expands as the *puruṣāvatāras* in the work of creation of the universe, first as the Kāraṇādakaśāyī Mahā-Viṣṇu, who lies in the causal ocean, then as Garbhodakaśāyī Viṣṇu, who lies in the ocean within the individual universes, and finally as the Ksīrodakaśāyī Viṣṇu, who not only lies in the ocean of milk, but is the director of the individual universe and is present as the indweller of every living being within the universe. Also known as Aniruddha, Ksīrodakaśāyī Viṣṇu appeared in the course of Mahāprabhu Śrī Caitanya's pastimes as Vīrabhadra Prabhu, the son of Lord Nityānanda Prabhu and His energy Vasudhā Devī.

Kṛṣṇadāsa Kavirāja Gosvāmī has written in his *Caitanya Caritāmṛta* that Vīrabhadra is the best of all the branches of the Nityānanda Prabhu trunk of the Caitanya tree.

"The best of all of Nityānanda Prabhu's branches is Vīrabhadra Gosvāmī. The sub-branches which grew out of His are unlimited in number." (*Caitanya Caritāmṛta* 1.11.56)

As with all Viṣṇu-tattvas, the three energies Śrī, Bhū (Bhakti), and Nīlā (Līla) *śaktis*, were all present in Vīrabhadra Prabhu's life. His Śrī *śakti* was named Śrīmatī, who appeared in the village of Jhamatpur in the Hooghly district as the daughter of Yadunandana Ācārya and Vidyunmāla (Lakṣmī).

"Yadunandana's wife, Lakṣmī, was extremely chaste and devoted to her husband. Two daughters were born to her, Śrīmatī and Nārāyaṇī, both of whom were startlingly beautiful. At Jāhnavā's behest, the fortunate *brāhmaṇa* gave both of his daughters in marriage to Virabhadra." (*Bhakti-ratnākara* 13.251-3)

Though Vīrabhadra Prabhu belongs to the category of Viṣṇu-tattva, He performed His pastimes like a devotee:

"The greatest branch coming out of the trunk named Nityānanda Prabhu is Vīrabhadra Gosvāmī, who also has innumerable branches and sub-branches. It is not possible to describe them all. Although He is the Lord of the creation, Vīrabhadra Prabhu presented Himself as a great devotee. Though transcendental to all Vedic injunctions, He strictly followed the Vedic prescripts. Though the power of God was operating within Him, out of sight to the world, He showed no pride. He is the main pillar holding up the edifice of devotional service to Śrī Caitanya Mahāprabhu. It is by the glorious mercy of Śrī Vīrabhadra Gosāi that people all over the world now have the chance to chant the names of Caitanya and Nityānanda Prabhus. I, therefore, take shelter of the lotus feet of Vīrabhadra Gosvāmī for by His mercy all desires are fulfilled." (*Caitanya Caritāmṛta* 1.11.8-12)

Śrī Narahari Cakravartī Ṭhākura has written the following about Vīrabhadra Prabhu in his *Bhakti-ratnākara*:

"Vīrabhadra Prabhu, the son of Nityānanda Prabhu, was an ocean of virtue and redeemer of the world. There is no limit to His glories, so who can sufficiently glorify Him? He is famed as the branch of Nityānanda Prabhu. The root of all joy, He is sometimes known as Vīrabhadra and sometimes as Vīracandra. If anyone sees Him even once, he will give up everything and make His lotus feet his all-in-all." (*Bhakti-ratnākara* 9.413-4, 420-1)

Vīrabhadra Prabhu took initiation from Jāhnavā Devī. In his *Anubhāṣya*, Śrīla Bhakti

Siddhānta Sarasvatī Gosvāmī Ṭhākura has written, "Vīrabhadra Gosvāmī had three disciples who were later celebrated as his sons – Gopījana-vallabha, Rāmakṛṣṇa and Rāmacandra. The youngest, Rāmacandra, belonged to Khardah. The eldest disciple, Gopījana-vallabha, was a resident of a village known as Lata, near the Mankor railway station in the district of Burdwan. The second, Ramakṛṣṇa, lived near Maldah, in a village named Gayeshpur."

According to the thirteenth chapter of the *Bhakti-ratnākara,* Vīrabhadra Prabhu took permission from his mother, Vasudhā, to go to Vrindavan. Upon arriving there, he performed *Vraja-dhāma-parikramā* with the blessings of Bhūgarbha Gosvāmī and Śrī Jīva Gosvāmī.

The old Śyāmasundara temple in Khardah has a manuscript of *Śrīmad Bhāgavatam* that is hand copied by Vīrabhadra Prabhu. Some hold that this was actually written by Nityānanda Prabhu Himself. Vīrabhadra Prabhu personally brought a piece of stone from which the deities Śyāmasundara, Rādhāvallabha, and Nandadulāla became manifest. These deities are still worshipped in Khardah. The ghat where this stone arrived is known as Śhyamasundara Ghat. Vīrabhadra Prabhu established the custom of celebrating the birth of Nityānanda Prabhu at Khardah. During His time, the offerings during the festival were prepared using sixty kgs of rice and equal amounts of other materials. The current managers of the Khardah temple tell many other legends about the life of Vīrabhadra Gosvāmī.

The date of Vīrabhadra's appearance is given as Kārtika *kṛṣṇa navamī.* The *Gauḍīya Vaiṣṇava Abhidhāna*, however, gives the date as Agrahāyaṇa *śukla caturdaśī.*

Śrīla Gopāla Guru Gosvāmī

Gopāla Guru Gosvāmī's name is found in neither the *Caitanya Caritāmṛta* nor the *Caitanya Bhāgavata*, but information about his life has been preserved in the histories of the Rādhā Kānta Math in Puri.

Gopāla Guru was born in an Odishan *brāhmaṇa* family. His father's name was Murāri Paṇḍita. His mother's name is unknown. While still a child, he had the good fortune to serve Mahāprabhu through His servant Govinda. His original name was Makaradhvaja Paṇḍita, but Mahāprabhu used to affectionately call him Gopāla.

Makaradhvaja Paṇḍita was the disciple of Vakreśvara Paṇḍita, one of the Lord's close associates living in Jagannatha Puri. This is confirmed in the book *Vakreśvara-carita*, where the following passage is found:

"There are five branches in the lineage descending from Vakreśvara Paṇḍita – those coming from Candraśekhara, Śaṅkarāraṇya Ācārya, Govindānanda, Devānanda and Gopāla Guru, whose qualities are beyond description."

From the book *Guru-praṇālī* published by the Rādhā Kānta Math, we learn that Gopāla Guru Gosvāmī was the *sakhī* Mañjumedhā in Vraja *līlā*.

HOW HE GOT THE NAME GOPĀLA GURU

There is a legend surrounding the addition of the word *guru* to Gopāla's name.

There was once a devotee in Puri who was particularly attached to the chanting of the Holy Names. The chanting had become automatic for him, so that his tongue uttered the Holy Names incessantly. One day Gopāla saw this devotee on his way to the toilet, holding his tongue between his fingers because he did not wish to chant the Holy Name while engaged in an impure act. Gopāla was just a lad, but he was able to understand why the devotee was doing this and he said to him, "What are you doing? Don't you know that there are no regulations governing the time and place for chanting the Holy Name? One should chant the Name in all times and any circumstance, pure or impure. If you were not able to chant while defecating, how would you be able to have an auspicious death should death suddenly come upon you at that time?"

Mahāprabhu overheard Gopāla's words of the highest wisdom and was very impressed. He announced to all His devotees that Gopāla was doing the work of a guru. From that day on, the young Makaradhvaja Paṇḍita was known to the Vaiṣṇavas as Gopāla Guru. The name was appropriate because he both preached and practiced and was factually acting as an *ācārya* or guru.

It did not take long for his fame to spread through the Vaiṣṇava world. Abhirāma Ṭhākura had the reputation of being able to verify whether a stone was a real Viṣṇu-śilā or *śālagrāma-śilā* by paying his obeisances to the *śilā*. If not real, it would crack or turn into dust. Only a pure Vaiṣṇava would be able to tolerate his obeisances; otherwise, they could prove fatal. When the Vaiṣṇavas heard that Abhirāma Ṭhākura had come to Puri to test Gopāla Guru, they were anxious for the boy for whom they felt great affection. Mahāprabhu realized that everyone was troubled, and so He placed His foot on Gopāla's forehead, thus creating the distinctive *tilaka* marking of the Lord's foot that is used to this day by those in Gopāla Guru's spiritual lineage. Even so, Gopāla was still frightened, and so he sat in the Lord's lap for protection. Abhirāma Ṭhākura's obeisances could thus do him no harm.

THE SERVICE OF RĀDHĀ KĀNTA DEVA

Mahārāja Pratāparudra's father, Puruṣottama Deva, brought several deities back from Kanchi with him after defeating that city's king. Among these deities was the *mūrti* of Rādhā Kānta. This deity was first placed in a small temple on the northwestern corner of Jagannātha's Chatrabhoga temple, but later, Pratāparudra's guru, Kāśī Miśra, asked to be given the deity for his personal service. Kāśī Miśra had bequeathed everything he possessed to Mahāprabhu. Kāśī Miśra had no children of his own, so Mahāprabhu gave the service of Rādhā Kānta, his temple and the surrounding gardens, etc., to Gopāla Guru. His guru, Vakreśvara Paṇḍita, never sat on the *gādī*, or in other words, never acted as *ācārya*, at Rādhā Kānta Math. Rather, he stayed absorbed in *kīrtana* and danced in the company of Mahāprabhu.

The *tithi* marking Mahāprabhu's bestowal of Rādhā Kānta's service on Gopāla Guru is celebrated on the *śukla dvādaśī* of Māgha. On this day, he also gave him the post of the first *ācārya* of the Rādhā Kānta Math, and the occasion is marked annually by an *abhiśeka* of the present-day head of the Math.

Śrīla Bhaktivinoda Ṭhākura has written the following about Gopāla Guru Gosvāmī: "Vakreśvara Paṇḍita's disciple Gopāla Guru Gosvāmī is currently head of Mahāprabhu's own *maṭha* in the house of Kāśī Miśra in *Purushottama*. He has completely memorized the teachings of Śrī Svarūpa Dāmodara Gosvāmī." (*Jaiva Dharma*)

Svarūpa Dāmodara Gosvāmī's method of worshipping in the *madhura-rasa* was spread through the world through two different lines: one through Raghunātha Dāsa Gosvāmī, which was carried through Kṛṣṇadāsa Kavirāja Gosvāmī, the other through Vakreśvara Paṇḍita and Gopāla Guru Gosvāmī. Gopāla Guru wrote two books on the subject, *Smaraṇa-krama-paddhati* ("a guidebook to the steps to remembering"), or *Sevā-smaraṇa-paddhati* ("a guidebook to remembering and service"), and *Gaura-govindārcana-paddhati* ("a guidebook to Gaura-Govinda's deity worship").

From the time of Gopāla Guru, Kāśī Miśra's house was known as Rādhā Kānta Math. During Kāśī Miśra's lifetime, the deity of Kṛṣṇa was worshipped alone. While Gopāla Guru was in charge of the temple, however, a deity of Rādhā was placed at Rādhā Kānta's left side and a deity of Lalitā on His right. Deities of Gaurāṅga and Nityānanda Prabhu were also installed, and the temple buildings were repaired and enlarged during this time, between 1539 and 1549 A.D.

In the Odishan language, a small separate room situated on temple grounds is given the name *gambhīrā*. Srila Bhaktivinoda Ṭhākura has written, "In the customary architecture of a temple in Odisha, the deity room itself has a verandah (*alinda*) facing it. Facing the verandah is a paved and covered area known as the *dālāna*. A small room within this area is given the name *gambhīrā*." The Gambhīrā at Kāśī Miśra's house marks the place where Mahāprabhu performed His *bhajana* and where He slept. Gopāla Guru kept Mahāprabhu's wooden shoes and a quilt, which was made either by Svarūpa Dāmodara Gosvāmī or Jagadānanda Paṇḍita, in the Gambhīrā, where they are worshipped. The water pot made of clay from the Vraja area which Mahāprabhu used is also kept there, along with a wooden water pot that was placed there in later times.

From *Bhakti-ratnākara* (8.382, 389) we learn that when Narottama Dāsa Ṭhākura visited Puri, he came to Kāśī Miśra's house and met Gopāla Guru who affectionately took Narottama Ṭhākura on his lap and wept loudly.

A FEW MIRACULOUS EVENTS

A few accounts of miraculous events are told about Gopāla Guru. When Gopāla Guru grew old, he turned the responsibility for the Rādhā Kānta Math over to his disciple Dhyāna Candra Gosvāmī. Not long after he left his body, his successor was overcome with grief. He took his guru's body to the Svarga Dwara for final rites.

While he and other disciples of Gopāla Guru Gosvāmī were at the cremation ground, some representatives of a government department barricaded the temple, claiming that the transfer of authority to Dhyāna Candra Gosvāmī had been done without ministerial sanction. When Dhyāna Candra Gosvāmī heard that this was going on, he fell at the lotus feet of his guru's body, tears flowing from his eyes. Gopāla Guru's body was already on the funeral pyre, but the prayers of his dear disciple reached him, and he was revived. He rose up, chanting the Holy Names in *saṅkīrtana*.

As soon as the government representatives heard of this event, they became fearful and abandoned their effort to take over Rādhā Kānta Math and fled away from there. Gopāla Guru returned to the temple and made a legal written transfer of ownership to his disciple before disappearing finally sometime later on the Kārtika *śukla navamī*.

A year after Gopāla Guru disappeared, when some devotees who had made the trip from Vraja for the Rathayātrā returned home, they were amazed to see Gopāla Guru sitting under a *pakur* tree in Vamsi Vat, chanting *japa*. They sent the message to Dhyāna Candra Gosvāmī in Puri, and he immediately hurried to Vrindavan to see his guru. He fell down at his feet and begged him to come to stay in Puri; however, Gopāla Guru rejected the proposal. Finally, Gopāla Guru told his disciple, "If you feel such separation from me that you are unable to tolerate it, then have an deity of me made out of a neem tree and place it in front of the altar room of the temple and worship the deity." This is what was done, and the deity of Gopāla Guru Gosvāmī is worshipped at the Rādhā Kānta Math to this day.

GOPĀLA GURU GOSVĀMĪ'S ŚUCAKA KĪRTANA

āre mora gopāla guru bhakati kalapa taru
makara-dhvaja nāma jāṅhāra
śrī kṛṣṇa caitanya jāṅke gopāla baliye ḍāke
dekhi śiśu caritra udāra

gaurāṅgera sevā-rase sadāi ānande bhāse
gorā binu nāhi jāne ān
tileka nā dekhi jāṅre dhairaja dharite nāre
gorā jena gopālera prāṇ

gopāla śiśura prati śiksā dila eka rīti
prabhu premāveśe ḍhuli ḍhuli
kahe sabe āre āre āji haite gopālere
ḍākibā gopāla guru bali

gopāle karuṇā dekhi sabāra sajala āṅkhi
sukhera samudra uchalila
sabe kahe anupāma śrī gopāla guru nāma
prabhu datta jagate vyāpila

gopālera guru-bhakti kahite nāhika śakti
sadāi prasanna vakreśvara
mahāmatta nija-gīte nāhika upamā dite
sarva cittākarṣa kalevara

dekhila sakala ṭhāṅi emana dayālu nāi
kebā nā jagate yaśa ghoṣe
sabe kaila prema-pātra haila vañcita mātra
narahari nija karma doṣe

"O Gopāla Guru, you are my devotional desire tree. Your name was previously Makaradhvaja, but Śrī Kṛṣṇa Caitanya called you Gopāla because of your noble behavior as a child.

"You were alway absorbed in the joy of serving Gaurāṅga; indeed you knew nothing other than Him. You could not tolerate being separated from the Lord for even a moment; it was as if Gaura was Gopāla's very life.

"One day, Gopāla was explaining some devotional practices to another child. The Lord was so ecstatic when He saw this that He said to everyone, 'From today on, all of you call Gopāla, "Gopāla-guru." '

"Tears filled the devotees' eyes when they saw how merciful the Lord was to Gopāla; it was as though the ocean of joy was overflowing.

Everyone said that Gopāla Guru was an extraordinary name, and he became famous by the name given by the Lord Himself.

"I am incapable of describing Gopāla's devotion to his guru, Vakreśvara, who was always pleased with him. The incomparable Gopāla Guru, whose appearance was attractive to everyone, was always intoxicated in singing his own devotional songs.

"Everyone recognized that no one was as merciful as he. Who in the world did not sing his glories? He made everyone worthy of loving ecstasy. Only I, Narahari, have been deprived of it because of my own misdeeds."

Śrīnivāsa Ācārya

Śrīnivāsa Ācārya was born in 1530 A.D. on the full-moon day of the month of Vaiśākha combined with Rohiṇī *nakṣatra*, in the village of Chakhandi, which lies just north of Agradwip in the district of Nadia. His father, Gaṅgādhara Bhaṭṭācārya, was a *brāhmaṇa* of the Rarha class. The *Bhakti-ratnākara* describes how this came about:

"Gaṅgādhara was overcome with grief when Mahāprabhu took *sannyāsa* in Katwa, and he began to cry constantly while calling out the names '*Ha Caitanya! Ha Caitanya!*' When the other devotees saw him intoxicated in divine love for Mahāprabhu, they nicknamed him Caitanya Dāsa, a name that stuck with him for the rest of his life."

Caitanya Dāsa was indifferent to the things of this world, but one day he suddenly felt a strong wish to have a son and told this to his wife, Lakṣmī Priyā. She responded by telling him to go immediately to Puri to submit to Mahāprabhu. The couple left for Puri, first stopping for a few days in Jajigram at the house of Lakṣmī Priya's father, Balarāma Vipra.

When they arrived in Puri, Caitanya Dāsa and his wife paid their obeisances to Mahāprabhu. Before they could speak, the Lord Himself spoke, understanding their wish to have a son: "Jagannātha Deva will surely fulfill all your desires."

The other devotees were curious about what desire Mahāprabhu was talking about. Mahāprabhu called Govinda and said in a deep voice, as if from a trance state: "Caitanya Dāsa desires to have a child. Indeed, his wife will soon give birth to a jewel of a son, who will be named Śrīnivāsa. He will be the manifest form of My love and will increase everyone's enthusiasm for devotion. I will bring scriptures into the world through Rūpa Gosvāmī and others; through Śrīnivāsa, I shall distribute them. Śrīnivāsa is the embodiment of pure love for Me. All minds will be enthused upon seeing him." (*Bhakti-ratnākara* 2.120-3)

Once they had received Mahāprabhu's blessing, Caitanya Dāsa and his wife returned to their home, and when the auspicious moment came, a son was born to them. Caitanya Dāsa immediately consecrated the child to Mahāprabhu.

The baby went through the early childhood rituals of the first feeding of solid food, name-giving, tonsure, and sacred thread ceremony. The associates of Mahāprabhu, such as Govinda Ghoṣa and residents of Srikhanda such as Narahari and Raghunandana poured affectionate blessings on the child.

EARLY EDUCATION AND TRAVELS

Śrīnivāsa Ācārya was devoted to his parents. He was fortunate to hear about Mahāprabhu's divine glories as well as Rādhā and Kṛṣṇa's Vrindavan pastimes from Caitanya

Dāsa. Father and son would go into an ecstatic state as they discussed these transcendental topics. His mother trained him in various forms of *nāma-saṅkīrtana.*

He studied grammar, literature and poetic theory from Dhanañjaya Vidyā Vācaspati, and quickly acquired mastery of these subjects.

Śrīnivāsa's father left the world while he was still quite young. The loss of his father's association greatly affected Śrīnivāsa, but the other devotees made a concerted effort to console him and his mother in their grief.

Śrīnivāsa took his mother and moved from Chakhandi to his maternal grandfather's house in Jajigram, where the villagers were overjoyed to see him. Shortly after moving to Jajigram, he went to visit Narahari Sarakāra in nearby Srikhanda. From Narahari Sarakāra he learnt that Mahāprabhu would shortly be ending His earthly pastimes. This news made Śrīnivāsa determined to see the Lord before it happened. He quickly returned to Jajigram and took permission from his mother to make the trip to Puri. He then joined the devotees on the annual pilgrimage. It was the fifth day of the waxing moon.

Before Śrīnivāsa arrived in Puri, however, the news that Mahāprabhu had indeed ended His *līlā* reached the party of pilgrims. Śrīnivāsa Ācārya fainted at hearing this report, and when he came back to consciousness, he decided to commit suicide. However, the Lord Himself appeared to him in a dream and told him to complete his journey to Puri. Once in Puri, he again had a dream, in which he saw Jagannātha, Baladeva and Subhadrā as well as Caitanya Mahāprabhu with His associates.

In Puri, Śrīnivāsa met Śrīla Gadādhara Paṇḍita Gosvāmī, the *avatāra* of Mahāprabhu's pleasure potency, and both of them were immersed in an ocean of ecstasy. He also met Rāya Rāmānanda, Paramānanda Purī, Śikhi Māhiti, Sārvabhauma Bhaṭṭācārya, Vakreśvara Paṇḍita, Govinda, Śaṅkara Paṇḍita, and Gopīnātha Ācārya and received blessings from them all.

Śrīnivāsa stayed in Puri for some time, hearing *Śrīmad Bhāgavatam* from Gadādhara Paṇḍita Gosvāmī, and was enchanted. Gadādhara then told him to return to Gauda.

While on his way to Bengal, Śrīnivāsa learnt that Advaita Ācārya and Nityānanda Prabhu had also wound up their earthly pastimes. Once again he determined to end his life in Their separation, but the two Prabhus appeared to him in a dream to assuage his grief and persuaded him to give up his resolve.

When he arrived in Nabadwip, Śrīnivāsa was once again plunged into an ocean of despondency at the loss of Caitanya Mahāprabhu. Vaṁśīvadana Ṭhākura saw him in this condition and approached Viṣṇupriyā Devī and asked her to grant Śrīnivāsa an audience and to bless him. Śrīnivāsa Ācārya was amazed to see Śrīmatī Viṣṇupriyā Devī's deep faith in Mahāprabhu's worship and her intense renunciation. While in Nabadwip, he had a dream of Śacī Devī and received blessings from her, too. Śrīnivāsa then wandered throughout Bengal, going to all the Sripats of the associates of Mahāprabhu and Nityānanda Prabhu, seeking their blessings. In this way, he visited Shantipur, Khardah, Khanakul Krishnanagar, and Srikhanda. Among the *pārṣadas* he met were Murāri Gupta, Śrīvāsa Paṇḍita,

Dāmodara Paṇḍita, Śuklāmvara Brahmacārī, Gadādhara Dāsa, Paramesvarī Dāsa, Jāhnavā Devī, Vasudhā Devī, Vīrabhadra, Abhirāma Ṭhākura, Narahari Sarakāra Ṭhākura, and Raghunandana Ṭhākura. All these great personalities witnessed Śrīnivāsa's intense devotion and told him to go to Vrindavan. Śrīnivāsa then went to his mother and repeatedly asked her for permission to make the trip. His mother could not refuse when she saw his eagerness.

ŚRĪNIVĀSA ARRIVES IN VRAJA

Śrīnivāsa then traveled through Agradwip, Katwa, Maureshwar, and Ekachakra, and then went to Kashi, Ayodhya, and Prayag. He spent a long time visiting all these holy places before he finally arrived in Vraja. There he learnt that Rūpa Gosvāmī, Sanātana Gosvāmī, Kāśīśvara Paṇḍita and Raghunātha Bhaṭṭa Gosvāmī had all disappeared. Raghunātha Dāsa Gosvāmī, Gopāla Bhaṭṭa Gosvāmī and Jīva Gosvāmī were still living, however. Śrīnivāsa met all three of them and received their blessings. He was initiated by Gopāla Bhaṭṭa Gosvāmī and took instruction in the Vaiṣṇava scriptures from Jīva Gosvāmī. In great affection for Śrīnivāsa, Jīva Gosvāmī commended him to his deities, Rādhā-Dāmodara. Śrīnivāsa met Raghunātha Dāsa Gosvāmī and Kṛṣṇadāsa Kavirāja Gosvāmī in Radha Kunda and received their blessings. One day Śrī Jīva Gosvāmī heard Śrīnivāsa explain a verse from *Ujjvala-nīlamaṇi* and was so impressed by his erudition that he bestowed the title Ācārya upon him. Jīva Gosvāmī also gave the titles Ṭhākura to Narottama and Śyāmānanda to Duḥkhī Kṛṣṇadāsa. Jīva Gosvāmī ordered Śrīnivāsa Ācārya Prabhu to tour all of Vraja's pilgrimage sites with Rāghava Gosvāmī.

THE RETURN TO BENGAL

Śrī Jīva Gosvāmī and the other Vaiṣṇavas in Vraja ordered Śrīnivāsa Ācārya, Narottama Ṭhākura and Śyāmānanda Prabhu to take manuscripts of the invaluable Gosvāmī's literature to Bengal in an ox-cart. They placed them in a chest that was offered to them by a rich merchant in Mathura back to Bengal in an ox-cart. They set off on the *śukla pañcamī* of Agrahāyaṇa month. It was a long and dangerous trip, but they were able to cover the greater part of the distance without any trouble. Upon arriving in the Hindu kingdom of Ban Vishnupur, they felt that the danger was over. However, the rumor had reached the capital of Vishnupur that a rich merchant was traveling to Puri with a valuable cargo of merchandise.

Vīrahāmvīra, the ruler of Ban Vishnupur, was also the leader of a gang of highwaymen. When he heard that a cargo of great value was passing through his territory, he asked an astrologer to confirm the truth of the rumors. The astrologer confirmed that the chest being carried on the ox-cart was indeed of great value. The king immediately sent a group of robbers to steal the chest, thinking that it contained gold and jewels. He specified to the robbers that they should kill no one.

The robbers first worshipped the goddess Caṇḍī, then sent out a spy, who returned to tell them that everyone in the group accompanying the ox-cart was sleeping in exhaustion after eating their evening meal. The robbers felt that Caṇḍī had mercifully given them a golden opportunity to make the raid. They stole the chest of books and turned them over to the King of Vishnupur.

When Vīrahāmvīra saw the large chest, he was delighted at the prospect of finding large booty inside. How disappointed he must have been to see nothing but books! He turned to the astrologer and asked him how he could have made such a mistake. The astrologer answered, "I can't understand it. Every time I made my calculations I came up with the same conclusion: this chest is full of priceless jewels! It is incredible, I don't know why my calculations have gone wrong!"

The mere sight of the holy books had a purifying effect on the king, however, and he regretted having stolen them. Indeed, he desired to meet with the *ācārya* who owned them. That night he had a dream in which this *ācārya* appeared to him, and this pacified him somewhat.

The next morning, Śrīnivāsa Ācārya, Narottama Ṭhākura and Śyāmānanda Prabhu awoke to find the chest of books missing. They searched everywhere, but when they failed to find any clue of the books' whereabouts, they felt so depressed that they considered killing themselves. Some local villagers saw the distressed condition of the three Vaiṣṇavas and immediately suspected the robber king, Vīrahāmvīra, and rebuked him. Śrīnivāsa Ācārya made some farther inquiries and was assured that he would be able to find more information from the king himself. The three Vaiṣṇavas felt some hope and abandoned their suicidal intentions. Śrīnivāsa Ācārya decided to remain in Vishnupur in the hope that he would be able to recover the manuscripts, but he sent Narottama Dāsa Ṭhākura to Kheturi and Śyāmānanda Prabhu to Odisha.

THE CONVERSION OF VĪRAHĀMVĪRA

While staying in Vishnupur, Śrīnivāsa Ācārya heard from a *brāhmaṇa* named Kṛṣṇavallabha that Vīrahāmvīra liked to listen to *Śrīmad Bhāgavatam* and daily attended its recital. One day, Śrīnivāsa Ācārya went with this *brāhmaṇa* to the place where the *Bhāgavata* was recited. The *brāhmaṇa* introduced Śrīnivāsa Ācārya to the king as a great Vaiṣṇava, and the king indeed observed the characteristics of a great person in him and was attracted to him. The king expressed a desire to hear Śrīnivāsa Ācārya speak on the *Bhāgavata,* and Śrīnivāsa Ācārya agreed, thinking that this might be a good opportunity to recover the books. So he started to speak on the *Bhāgavata* on a daily basis. The king was enchanted by Śrīnivāsa Ācārya's unprecedented explanations of the *Bhāgavata* in his sweet voice.

Śrīnivāsa Ācārya preached Mahāprabhu's teachings both through speaking on the *Bhāgavata* and by *kīrtana*, while Narottama Ṭhākura and Śyāmānanda Prabhu primarily used the medium of *kīrtana*. Each of them had his own particular style of singing *kīrtana*, by which they intoxicated their listeners with devotional ecstasy. The styles that these three *ācāryas* used respectively were named *manohara-sāhī*, *garāṇahāṭī*, and *reṇeṭī.*

Vīrahāmvīra arranged for a secluded dwelling to be given to Śrīnivāsa Ācārya. One day, when he had the opportunity to find the king alone in his apartments, Śrīnivāsa Ācārya recounted the entire story of his journey from Vraja and the theft of the manuscripts. The king immediately confessed, showing great sorrow for his misdeed, and had the chest of books returned to him. Greatly relieved, Śrīnivāsa Ācārya immediately sent messengers to Vrindavan, Narottama Ṭhākura and Śyāmānanda Prabhu with the good news. In the course of time, Vīrahāmvīra and his entire entourage all took initiation from Śrīnivāsa Ācārya and dedicated their entire lives and wealth to him. At initiation, Vīrahāmvīra was given the name Caitanya Dāsa.

ŚRĪNIVĀSA ĀCĀRYA'S MARRIAGE

After staying in Ban Vishnupur for some time, Śrīnivāsa Ācārya returned to his maternal grandfather's house in Jajigram. Then he set off on another tour of Katwa, Nabadwip and other towns in Bengal. Śrīnivāsa Ācārya respected Narahari Sarakāra of Srikhanda greatly and was also very devoted to his saintly mother. When Narahari Sarakāra heard Śrīnivāsa Ācārya's mother express her desire to see her son married, he gave him the order to do so. Even prior to receiving this order, Śrīnivāsa Ācārya had received the same command from Advaita Ācārya in a dream. Though he felt somewhat ashamed, he realized that he could not ignore the wishes of Advaita Prabhu, Narahari Sarakāra and his mother. He thus agreed to get married and was wed to Īśvarī, the devoted daughter of Gopāla Cakravartī of Jajigram.

It is not always easy to understand the divine activities of Mahāprabhu's devotees. Only someone who is totally surrendered to the Lord and His devotees can comprehend their glories.

ŚRĪNIVĀSA ĀCĀRYA'S PREACHING ACTIVITIES

Śrīnivāsa Ācārya started to teach the Gosvāmīs' books to his disciples in Jajigram. One of his most important disciples was Rāmacandra Kavirāja, the son of Srikhanda resident Cirañjīva Sena. Śrī Jīva Gosvāmī Prabhu gave Rāmacandra the title Kavirāja after hearing his poems. Narottama Ṭhākura had a close friendship with Rāmacandra Kavirāja and even wrote about it in one of his songs:

dayā kara śrī-acārya prabhu śrīnivāsa
rāmacandra sanga māge narottama dāsa

"O my master, Śrīnivāsa Ācārya! Please be merciful to me. I, Narottama Dāsa, beg you to give me the association of Rāmacandra."

When Śuklāmbara Brahmacārī, Gadādhara Dāsa, Narahari Sarakāra and Dvija Haridāsa Ācārya all ended their earthly activities, Śrīnivāsa Ācārya was once again overcome by grief and made another trip to Vrindavan. Rāmacandra Kavirāja and Śyāmānanda Prabhu also joined Śrīnivāsa Ācārya in Vraja on this occasion. Śrīnivāsa Ācārya met with Gopāla Bhaṭṭa Gosvāmī and Śrī Jīva Gosvāmī, as well as with Bhūgarbha Gosvāmī and Lokanātha Gosvāmī, and these great devotees encouraged him and diminished his feelings of loss.

When he returned to Gauda, Śrīnivāsa Ācārya joined in the festivities occasioning the departure of Gadādhara Dāsa in Katwa, Narahari Sarakāra in Srikhanda and Dvija Haridāsa Ācārya in Kanchan Gariya. From there he went to Budhari village, where Rāmacandra Kavirāja and Govinda Kavirāja hosted him in great opulence.

Narottama Dāsa Ṭhākura had also left Vrindavan on Lokanātha Gosvāmī's orders, returning to Kheturi. On the full-moon day of Phālguna, he established the worship of six sets of deities in the temple there: Śrī Gaurāṅga, Śrī Vallabhī Kānta, Śrī Vraja Mohana, Śrī Kṛṣṇa, Śrī Rādhā Kānta, and Śrī Rādhā Ramaṇa. Śrīnivāsa Ācārya performed the installation ceremony and the first *pūjā*.

Jāhnavā Devi was also present at this great event. After the festival, she went on to Vraja with her entourage. Upon her return, she met with Śrīnivāsa Ācārya at Katwa and then went with him to Jajigram, where she spent some time as his guest.

Śrīnivāsa Ācārya made another trip to Nabadwip with Narottama Ṭhākura and Rāmacandra Kavirāja, performing the *parikramā* of the nine islands, each of which represents one of the limbs of devotional service.

When Raghunandana Ṭhākura entered the *nitya-līlā*, Śrīnivāsa Ācārya went to Srikhanda and participated in the disappearance festival. He returned with a heavy heart to Jajigram, and from there went to Ban Vishnupur. The king and the other residents of the town were excited by his visit and received him with great pomp. In Vishnupur, Śrīnivāsa Ācārya received an order from Mahāprabhu in a dream to accept the hand of Gaurāṅga Priyā, the daughter of a certain Rāghava Cakravartī. Rāghava Cakravartī and his wife, Mādhavī, had been searching for a suitable husband for their daughter. They had simultaneously received the order to give their daughter in marriage to Śrīnivāsa Ācārya in a dream. Śrīnivāsa Ācārya thus married for the second time.

Pure devotees have no objective in life other than to fulfill the desires of the Supreme Lord. They are thus ready to do anything if it pleases the Lord. None of their activities has the slightest hint of material desire in it. Śrīnivāsa Ācārya is the *śaktyāviṣṭa avatāra* of Mahāprabhu, and only a person who has received his special blessings can describe his transcendental activities.

Śrīla Narottama Dāsa Ṭhākura

ākumāra-brahmacārī sarva-tīrtha-darśī
parama-bhāgavatottamaḥ śrīla-narottama-dāsaḥ

"Narottama Dāsa was a *brahmacārī* throughout his entire life. He visited all the places of pilgrimage. He was on the highest platform of devotional achievement." (*Bhakti-ratnākara* 1.279)

Narottama Ṭhākura was Campaka Mañjarī in Kṛṣṇa *līlā*. Eternally assisting Rūpa Mañjarī in her service to Rādhā and Kṛṣṇa, Campaka Mañjarī had mercy on the conditioned souls of this earth and appeared as Narottama Ṭhākura in the village of Kheturi, about twelve miles from Rampur Bowalia in the Gopalpur subdivision of the Rajshahi district. This took place on the full-moon day of the month of Māgha sometime around the middle of the fifteenth century of the Śaka era.

"Narottama was born on the *māghī pūrṇimā*. From that day on he thrived and grew like the waxing moon." (*Bhakti-ratnākara* 1.281)

Narottama Ṭhākura's father was Rāja Kṛṣṇānanda Datta, the zamindar of the Gopalpur area. His mother's name was Nārāyaṇī Devī. Rāja Kṛṣṇānanda had an elder brother (according to others' opinion a younger brother) named Puruṣottama Datta, who had a son named Santoṣa Datta. In order to show that His associates can take birth in any caste, Lord Kṛṣṇa had Narottama Ṭhākura take birth in a *kāyastha* family.

A Vaiṣṇava is beyond the qualities of the material nature. In order to teach this to the world, the Lord had Haridāsa Ṭhākura take birth in a *mleccha* family. Anyone who considers a devotee in terms of his birth or race is destined for a hellish existence.

arcye viṣṇau śīladhīr guruṣu nara-
matir vaiṣṇave jāti-buddhir
viṣṇor vā vaiṣṇavānāṁ kali-mala-
mathane pāda-tīrthe 'mbu buddhiḥ
śrī viṣṇor nāmni mantre sakala-
kaluṣa-he śabda-sāmānya-buddhir
viṣṇau sarveśvareśe tad-itara-
samadhīr yasya vā nārakī saḥ

"Anyone who considers the deity of Viṣṇu to be nothing but stone, the guru to be an ordinary human being, or the Vaiṣṇava to be a member of a particular caste or race, who takes the holy water which has washed Viṣṇu or the Vaiṣṇava's feet and can destroy all the sins of the Age of Kālī to be ordinary water, who thinks that the name or *mantra* of Viṣnu, which destroys all evils, is the same as any other sound, or who takes Viṣṇu to be same as anything other than Him, suffers hellish existence. " (*Padma Purāṇa*)

From his early childhood, Narottama Ṭhākura began to show signs of his future greatness. Everyone was amazed to see his great intelligence and devotional demeanor. He was constantly absorbed in meditation on the wonderful qualities of Śrī Caitanya Mahāprabhu and Nityānanda Prabhu and had not an iota of interest in the opulence of his father. The Lord and His associates appeared to him in his dreams.

"As tears poured from his eyes, Narottama would offer prayers of surrender to Śrī Kṛṣṇa Caitanya, Nityānanda Prabhu, Advaita and the other associates of the Lord. Finally, the Lord and His associates appeared to him in a dream and consoled him with kind words." (*Bhakti-ratnākara* 1.285-6)

MAHĀPRABHU LEAVES PREMA BEHIND FOR NAROTTAMA

According to the *Prema-vilāsa*, when Mahāprabhu passed through Kanair Natshala, as He was dancing ecstatically in *kīrtana*, He began to call out Narottama's name. When Nityānanda Prabhu asked Him why He was calling out this name, Mahāprabhu answered, "My Lord, You do not know Your own glories. On Your way to Jagannatha Puri, You shed tears out of divine love, day after day. I managed to capture Your divine love and save it. Now I wish to place it here by the Padmavati River in safekeeping for Narottama Dāsa."

Mahāprabhu then went to the place known as Kutubpur on the Padmavati River, where He bathed and sang and danced in ecstasy. He then called out to the river, "O Padmavati! Take this love and keep it here in strict confidence. When Narottama comes and bathes here, give it to him."

Padmavati inquired, "How will I recognize him?"

Mahāprabhu answered, "You will have no trouble recognizing Narottama, for as soon as he enters your waters, you will overflow."

The place where Mahāprabhu placed *prema* for Narottama Ṭhākura's sake was later given the name Premtoli. When Narottam Ṭhākura was twelve years old, he had a dream in which Nityānanda Prabhu told him to bathe in the Padmavati and take the *prema*, which had been stored there for him. One day he went to the Padmavati, and as soon as he put his foot in the water, the river started to overflow. The Padmavati then remembered Mahāprabhu's words and gave Narottama Ṭhākura the *prema* she had guarded for all that time.

NAROTTAMA LEAVES HOME

As soon as he experienced the ecstasies of *prema*, Narottama Ṭhākura's character, his appearance, everything about him changed. His parents noticed the transformation and did everything they could to bring him back to his normal state but failed. Having drunk the wine of divine ecstasy, Narottama had become intoxicated, and the bonds of family life could no longer hold him back.

Narottama began to wonder how he could escape from his material entanglements. Finally, one day when his father and uncle were away on official business, he practiced some deception on his mother and tricked his bodyguards so that he could leave his family for Vrindavan. This event took place on Kārtika *pūrṇimā*.

According to others, Narottama Ṭhākura waited to go to Vrindavan until after the death of his father and handing over the responsibility for the zamindari to his cousin Santoṣa. Even though he was the son of a rich zamindar, in his desire to unite with the Lord he was ready to abandon the pleasures of the body in a moment. Day and night, walking barefoot, crying, forgetting to eat and drink, finally, he fell unconscious under a tree. A golden-skinned brahmana came and offered him a cup of milk and said to him in a sweet voice, "O Narottama, drink this milk. Your cuts and bruises will go away. Your journey will be comfortable."

After saying this, the *brāhmaṇa* vanished, and the exhausted Narottama fell asleep. That night, he dreamt of Rūpa Gosvāmī and Sanātana Gosvāmī. The two Gosvāmīs placed their hands on his chest and fed him the milk that Mahāprabhu Himself had brought him. All of Narottama's fatigue disappeared.

NAROTTAMA IS INITIATED BY LOKANĀTHA GOSVĀMĪ

The *Prema-vilāsa* also describes how Narottama Ṭhākura took initiation from Lokanātha Gosvāmī in Vrindavan. Narottama Ṭhākura was born on the full-moon day of Māgha, his renunciation took place on the full-moon day of Kārtika, and he was initiated by Lokanātha Gosvāmī on the full-moon day of Śrāvaṇa.

Lokanātha Gosvāmī is a direct disciple and a personal associate of Śrī Caitanya Mahāprabhu. Indeed, he was the first Gauḍīya Vaiṣṇava to be instructed by the Lord to go to Vrindavan, along with Bhūgarbha Gosvāmī. Lokanātha Gosvāmī set the standard for worship in a spirit of renunciation while in the Holy *dhāma*. He was a *viviktānandī* Vaiṣṇava, i.e., a hermit one who worships the Lord in solitude. In this spirit, he had vowed not to take any disciples. Narottama Dāsa too made a vow – to take initiation from no one other than Lokanātha Gosvāmī. Though he was the son of a *rāja*, Narottama Ṭhākura's desire to receive Lokanātha Gosvāmī's mercy was so great that he went in the middle of every night to clean the place he used as a toilet. He would also leave fine earth and water for him to clean himself afterwards. This is described as follows in the *Prema-vilāsa*:

Narottama went to the place where the Gosvāmī performed his bodily functions and did a special job of cleaning it. He sifted the earth to make fine, clean earth with which Lokanātha Gosvāmī could clean his hands. He would hide his coconut-leaf broom and take it out each night to sweep the place clean, his heart filled with joy. All these things he did as a regular service. He considered himself to be fortunate to have this service and that it made his body worthwhile. He would hold the broom to his chest, repeating, "This is the power that will help me attain my Lord's lotus feet." As he said these words, he cried, and torrents of tears washed over his chest.

Lokanātha Gosvāmī was astonished to see that the place was daily being kept clean and free from foul smell. He became curious to find out who was doing it, and so, one evening, he went and hid in the jungle, chanting *japa* the entire night in wait for the anonymous benefactor. At midnight, he saw someone engaged in cleaning the place and asked him who he was. When he found out that Narottama, the son of a king, was doing this task, he felt embarrassed and told him to desist. Narottama, however, immediately fell at Lokanātha Gosvāmī's feet and began to cry. When Lokanātha Gosvāmī saw Narottama Ṭhākura's humility and pain, his resolve softened, and he finally gave him initiation. Thus Narottama Ṭhākura gave an outstanding example to the world of how one should serve one's spiritual master.

"Narottama went there and engaged in whatever service was necessary to his guru, performing it with great enthusiasm. Lokanātha Gosvāmī was pleased by Narottama's service and showed him the greatest mercy by initiating him in the *mantra*." (*Bhakti-ratnākara* 1.345-6)

"Without caring for his youth or his looks, he left home on the full-moon day of the month of Kārtika. After wandering through many pilgrimage places, he finally came to Vrindavan where he became Lokanātha Gosvāmī's disciple. On the auspicious day of *Śrāvaṇī pūrṇimā*, Lokanātha Gosvāmī initiated Narottama Ṭhākura. (*Bhakti-ratnākara* 1.292-4)

Narottama Dāsa Ṭhākura was thus Lokanātha Gosvāmī's one and only disciple. Śrīla Bhakti Siddhānta Sarasvatī Gosvāmī Ṭhākura Prabhupāda, the founder of world-wide Śrī Chaitanya Math and Śrī Gaudiya Maths, demonstrated similar one-pointed faith in service to the lotus feet of his spiritual master, and perseverance and patience in order to obtain his mercy. Gaura Kiśora Dāsa Bābājī Mahārāja, like Lokanātha Gosvāmī, had vowed to take no disciples. He refused Śrīla Prabhupāda three times, but this did not break Prabhupāda's will. When Gaura Kiśora Dāsa Bābājī Mahārāja saw his humility and intense desire, he finally relented and gave him *mantra dīkṣā*. Śrīla Prabhupāda was Gaura Kiśora Dāsa Bābājī Mahārāja's only disciple.

After the disappearance of Rūpa and Sanātana Gosvāmīs, Śrī Jīva Gosvāmī became the Gauḍīya Vaiṣṇava *sampradāya*'s undisputed *ācārya* throughout Mathura, Bengal and Odisha and the chief of the universal court of Vaiṣṇavas at Vrindavan – the *Viśva-vaiṣṇava-rāja-sabhā*. Śrīnivāsa, Narottama and Duḥkhī Kṛṣṇadāsa all studied the scriptures under Jīva Gosvāmī, receiving detailed personal instruction from him. Jīva Gosvāmī gave them the titles of Ācārya, Ṭhākura and Śyāmānanda, respectively.

NAROTTAMA RETURNS TO BENGAL

Jīva Gosvāmī sent his three students to Bengal with the Vaiṣṇava scriptures. Śrī Jīva Gosvāmī heard the news that the books had been stolen in Ban Vishnupur and then later that they had been recovered by Śrīnivāsa Ācārya. This story has been told in this book in the chapter on Śrīnivāsa Ācārya.

Lokanātha Gosvāmī considered Narottama Ṭhākura's previous life as a wealthy zamindar to be particularly suitable for preaching in his home area of northern Bengal and thought that with his status he would be able to teach the standards of renounced devotional behavior. Out of compassion for that country's people, he ordered Narottama Ṭhākura to return to his home-town of Kheturi. Śrīnivāsa Ācārya was aware of Lokanātha Gosvāmī's intention, so when the books were stolen, he told Narottama Ṭhākura to continue on his way to preach in Kheturi and north Bengal. Śrīnivāsa Ācārya said, "Go quickly to Kheturi and carry out Lokanātha Prabhu's orders." (*Bhakti-ratnākara* 7.119)

Anchorite devotees (*viviktānandīs*), being absorbed in the intimate service of the Lord on the transcendental platform, normally have no taste for engaging in any welfare activity which brings only temporary succor to materialistic persons, bound by *māyā* and absorbed in their bodily identification. Materialistic welfare activities are considered to be of great value only when there is a misunderstanding about the real goal of life – service to Kṛṣṇa. Lokanātha Gosvāmī taught the world through his disciple, on the principle that "a housewife teaches the daughter-in-law by instructing the daughter." Though Narottama Ṭhākura himself was distraught with separation from his spiritual master, he nevertheless took his order seriously and returned to Kheturi, where he began preaching the doctrines of pure devotional service to the people of northern Bengal. Narottama Ṭhākura's humility and sorrow were expressed in his *Prārthanā*:

aneka duḥkhera pare, layechile vraja-pure
kṛpa-ḍora galāya bāndhiyā
daiva-māyā balātkāre, khasāiyā sei ḍore
bhavakūpe dileka ḍāriyā
punaḥ yadi kṛpā kari, e janāre keśe dhari
ṭāniyā tulaha vraja-dhāme
tabe se dekhiye bhāla, natubā parāṇa gela
kahe dīna dāsa narottame

"After I had suffered for such a long time, You finally tied the rope of mercy around my neck and dragged me to Vraja dhāma. But now, the forces of fate and illusion have loosened that rope, and I have been thrown back down the well of material existence.

"If You would only be merciful to me and grab me by the hair, pulling me back into Vraja *dhāma*, then everything will seem right once again. If not, Narottama says, my life is over."

On Lokanātha Gosvāmī's orders, Narottama Ṭhākura installed six sets of deities in his temple in Kheturi: Śrī Gaurāṅga, Śrī Vallabhī Kānta, Śrī Vraja Mohana, Śrī Kṛṣṇa, Śrī Rādhā Kānta, and Śrī Rādhā Rāmaṇa. The great festival which he held on that occasion is still remembered in the Vaiṣṇava world.

"Narottama Ṭhākura arrived in the land of Gauda (Nabadwip). He had been ordered by Lokanātha Gosvāmī to establish the deity service of both Gaurāṅga and Kṛṣṇa, to serve the Vaiṣṇavas and to preach the congregational chanting of the Holy Names. He immediately dedicated himself to carrying out these orders. First, he set about establishing the service of six sets of beautiful deities, whose names, taken together, bring joy to the heart of the devotees.

gaurāṅga vallabhī-kānta
śrī-kṛṣṇa vraja-mohana
rādhā-ramaṇa he rādhe
rādhā-kānta namo 'stu te
(*Bhakti-ratnākara* 1.422-6)"

THE GREAT FESTIVAL AT KHETURI

Prior to the Kheturi-mahotsava, Narottama Dāsa Ṭhākura traveled throughout Bengal and Odisha, visiting various places where Mahāprabhu had performed His pastimes, meeting the Lord's associates and receiving their blessings. Amongst the places he visited were Uddhāraṇa Datta's home in Saptagram; Khardah, where he met Paramesvarī Dāsa Ṭhākura and Nityānanda Prabhu's *śaktis*, Jāhnavā and Vasudhā; Khanakul Krishnanagar, the home of Abhirāma Ṭhākura; Śyāmānanda Prabhu's home in Nrisinghapur; the Sripats of Narahari Sarakāra Ṭhākura and Raghunandana Ṭhākura in Srikhanda; the birthplace of Nityānanda Prabhu in Ekacakra *dhāma*; and in Jagannatha Puri, Gopīnātha Ācārya's home, Haridāsa Ṭhākura's *samādhi* temple, Gadādhara Paṇḍita's place of worship, the Jagannātha temple and Guṇḍicā temple, the Jagannātha-vallabha gardens, Narendra-sarovara, etc.

Most of the associates of Mahāprabhu of that time and other leaders of the *sampradāya* came to Kheturi on the occasion of the festival organized by Narottama Dāsa Ṭhākura. A list of these has been given by Narahari Cakravartī in his books *Bhakti-ratnākara* and *Narottama-vilāsa*: Śyāmānanda Prabhu, Jāhnavā Devī, Parameśvarī Dāsa, Kṛṣṇadāsa Sarakhela, Mādhava Ācārya, Raghupati Vaidya, Mīnaketana Rāma Dāsa, Murāri Caitanya Dāsa, Jñāna Dāsa, Mahīdhara, Śrī Śaṅkara, Kamalākara Pippalāi, Gaurāṅga Dāsa, Nakaḍi, Kṛṣṇadāsa, Dāmodara, Balarāma Dāsa, Śrī Mukunda, Vṛndāvana Dāsa Ṭhākura; Raghunandana Ṭhākura and other devotees from Srikhanda; Śrīnivāsa Paṇḍita's brothers Śrīpati and Śrīnidhi from Nabadwip, Advaita Ācārya's sons Acyutānanda, Gopāla Miśra and Kṛṣṇa Miśra came from Shantipur; Hṛdaya Caitanya Prabhu and other devotees from Ambika Kalna.

Śrīnivāsa Ācārya acted as the officiating priest at the festival and performed the rituals installing the deities. In the *kīrtana* festival held by Narottama Ṭhākura, Mahāprabhu and His associates appeared.

"Who can describe the joy of that *kīrtana*? Mahāprabhu Himself descended with all His associates in its midst just like lightning in a conglomeration of rainclouds."(*Bhakti-ratnākara* 10.571-2)

"The *kīrtana* was amazing: you could see Nityānanda Prabhu and Advaita Ācārya overcome with ecstasy and Gauracandra encircled by the devotees. What wonderful compassion the Lord displayed on that day! Who can understand these wonderful pastimes? What blessings He poured on Narottama and Śrīnivāsa, for they and their companions found the fulfillment of all their desires." (*Bhakti-ratnākara* 10.605-7)

After the Kheturi festival, Narottama Ṭhākura's fame spread throughout the Vaiṣṇava world. Prominent *brāhmaṇas* like Rāmakṛṣṇa Ācārya and Gaṅgā Nārāyaṇa Cakravartī became his disciples.

NAROTTAMA'S PREACHING ADVENTURES

Narahari Cakravartī extensively described Narottama Ṭhākura's activities in his *Narottama-vilāsa*. One can understand his outstanding accomplishments by reading this book. Some of these are given here.

In Gopalpur village lived a *brāhmaṇa* named Vipra Dāsa. He had a poisonous snake living in his wicker grain-storage bin (*golā*). When Narottama Ṭhākura visited Vipra Dāsa's house, the snake vanished, and deities of Gaura and Viṣṇupriya appeared in its place. "Gaurasundar and His beloved Viṣṇupriya came out of the *golā* and climbed into Narottam's lap in plain view of everyone." (*Bhakti-ratnākara* 10.202)

Everyone was quite amazed. These same deities are being served today in Gambhila.

A certain *smārta brāhmaṇa* scholar blasphemed Narottama Ṭhākura, calling him a *sūdra*. The result of this offense was that he was attacked by leprosy. After suffering for some time, he was given a vision of the Goddess in a dream. She told him to fall at Narottama Dāsa's feet and beg for forgiveness, and it was only after he followed this advice that the *brāhmaṇa* was freed from his terrible disease.

Harirāma Ācārya and Rāmakṛṣṇa Ācārya, the sons of Śivānanda Ācārya, were taking a goat and a buffalo to be offered as a sacrifice to the Goddess on the order of their father. They met Narottama Ṭhākura and Rāmacandra Kavirāja on the way and were attracted by their effulgent beauty. Narottama Ṭhākura advised the two young *brāhmaṇas* to abandon worship in the modes of passion and ignorance that entailed violence to animals and to worship the Supreme Lord without any desire. The brothers immediately let the goat and buffalo go and bathed in the Padmavati River. They then took initiation from Narottama Ṭhākura and dedicated their lives to the service of Lord Kṛṣṇa and His devotees.

Śivānanda Ācārya became angry when he heard about this. He called a *smārta* scholar from Mithila named Murāri to come and defeat Narottama Ṭhākura's Vaiṣṇava philosophy. However, Harirāma and Rāmakṛṣṇa were given divine blessings by their guru and were able to defeat every one of the *smārta's* arguments with scriptural evidence. Defeated, Śivānanda Ācārya went to pray to the Goddess. She appeared to him that night in a dream and rebuked him for his enmity toward the Vaiṣṇavas and told him to cease all such behavior.

In the course of time, Gaṅgā Nārāyaṇa Cakravartī, Jagannātha Ācārya and other well-known *brāhmaṇas* started to become Narottama Ṭhākura's disciples. This caused a stir in the *smārta* community, and out of jealousy they went to complain to Rāja Narasiṁha: "Narottama is a *śūdra* who makes disciples of *brāhmaṇas*. He is using some kind of mystic powers or hypnotism to convert them. He should be stopped."

After a discussion of the matter with Rāja Narasiṁha, it was decided that a scholar named Rūpa Nārāyaṇa should be summoned to debate Narottama Ṭhākura. This *brāhmaṇa* had won numerous debates of this sort and was known as a *mahā-digvijayī*. The Rāja himself would set off with Rūpa Nārāyaṇa toward the village of Kheturi. Rāmacandra Kavirāja and Gaṅgā Nārāyaṇa Cakravartī were upset to see the wicked intentions of the Rāja and his *paṇḍita*. When they heard that the Rāja and his entourage were resting overnight in Kumarpur village, they went in disguise as a potter and a *pāna*-seller and set up stalls in the village market. When the students of the *smārta brāhmaṇas* came through the market, Rāmacandra and Gaṅgā Nārāyaṇa spoke with them in Sanskrit. The *brāhmaṇas* were astounded that even ordinary stall-keepers in the village were able to speak in Sanskrit. Rāmacandra and Gaṅgā Nārāyaṇa began a debate with the *brāhmaṇas*, defeating every *smārta* argument that they put forward. The Rāja and other *brāhmaṇas* were amazed to hear this and personally came there, only to be defeated in their arguments. Rāmacandra Ācārya and Gaṅgā Nārāyaṇa Ācārya established the pure doctrine of devotional service.

The Rāja and his *digvijayī paṇḍita* were rendered speechless by the scholarship of the two ordinary stall-keepers. When they learned that the two men were disciples of Narottama Dāsa Ṭhākura, the king said to his *paṇḍita*, "If Narottama Ṭhākura's common disciples can defeat you in a debate, there is no need of going to see him."

But once again, the Goddess appeared to King Narasiṁha and Rūpa Nārāyaṇa and ordered them to go to Narottama Ṭhākura and pray for forgiveness for their offenses. The two of them did so and became devotees of Rādhā and Kṛṣṇa.

TWO SONGS BY NAROTTAMA

In the *Gauḍīya Vaiṣṇava Abhidhāna*, the following comments are found: "Narottama Ṭhākura's *āśrama* was in a place called Bhajanatuli, about two miles from the capital city, Kheturi. Narottama Ṭhākura did his preaching through *kīrtana*. He created an amazing melody of kīrtana known as *garāṇahāṭī*. He wrote two books, *Prārthanā* and *Prema-bhakti-candrikā*, which are the very life of the devotees. He has written songs which are appropriate for every devotional mood, and this is what touches the devotees' hearts. These two books are so popular that they have been published countless times. Narottama Ṭhākura's influence can be appreciated even in distant Manipur, where everyone agrees that the Vaiṣṇava religion spread through His spiritual potency. His devotional songs are sung in every home throughout Manipur state."

Śrīnivāsa Ācārya's disciple Rāmacandra Kavirāja was Narottama Ṭhākura's dearest companion. Narottama Ṭhākura received news of Rāmacandra Kavirāja's disappearance first; not long afterwards, he heard of Śrīnivāsa Ācārya's disappearance. He wrote the following song in the mood of separation. It is capable of melting even a stone-like heart.

je ānila prema-dhana karuṇā pracura
hena prabhu kothā gelā ācārya ṭhākur
kāhāṅ mora svarūpa rūpa, kāhāṅ sanātana?
kāhāṅ dāsa raghunātha patita-pāvana?
kāhāṅ mora bhaṭṭa-yuga, kāhāṅ kavirāja?
eka-kāle kothā gelā gorā naṭarāja?

pāṣāṇe kuṭiba māthā anale paśiba
gaurāṅga guṇera nidhi kothā gele pāba
se saba saṅgīra saṅge je kaila vilāsa
se saṅga nā pāiyā kānde narottama-dāsa

"Where has Ācārya Ṭhākura, who out of great mercy for the world brought the wealth of love, gone? Where are my Svarūpa and Rūpa, Where is Sanātana? Where has Raghunātha Dāsa, the deliverer of the most fallen, gone? Where are Raghunātha Bhaṭṭa and Gopāla Bhaṭṭa? Where is Kṛṣṇadāsa Kavirāja? Where has the king of the dance, Gaurāṅga, suddenly disappeared to? I will beat my head against the rocks or enter the flames – but where can I go to find that ocean of virtue, Gaurāṅga? Deprived of the association of all those companions of the Lord, Narottama Dāsa can do nothing but cry."

Narottama Dāsa Ṭhākura was the topmost of the followers of Rūpa Gosvāmī, Mahāprabhu's close associate. His unparalleled devotion to Rūpa Gosvāmī can be recognized from the following song:

śrī rupa mañjarī pada sei mora sampada
sei mora bhajana pūjana
sei mora prāṇa-dhana sei mora ābharaṇa
sei mora jīvanera jīvana

sei mora rasa-nidhi sei mora vāñchā-siddhi
sei mora vedera dharama
sei vrata, sei tapa sei mora mantra japa
sei mora dharama karama

anukūla habe vidhi se pade haibe siddhi
nirakhiba ei dui nayane
se rūpa mādhurī-rāśī prāṇa-kuvalaya-śaśī
praphullita habe niśi-dine

tuwā adarśana ahi garale jārala dehi
cira-dina tāpita jīvana
hā hā prabhu kara dayā deha more pada-chāyā
narottama laila śaraṇa

"Śrī Rūpa Mañjarī's feet are my treasure; they are my object of worship; they are my devotional service. They are the wealth of my life; they are my ornament; they are the life of my life.

"They are my ocean of nectar; they are the perfection of my desire; they are my Vedic prescripts. They are my vow; they are my austerity; they are the *mantra* that I chant. They are my religious duty.

"When providence is kind to me, I will find perfection by attaining Śrī Rūpa Mañjarī's feet and will be able to behold them with my own eyes. The abundant sweet beauty of her lotus feet will shine like the moon upon the lily of my heart, causing it to blossom in jubilation day and night.

"The snake of your absence has burned up my body with its poison; I have suffered this pain for so long. O my master, be merciful to me. Give me the shade of your feet, for I, Narottama, seek refuge there."

NAROTTAMĀŚTAKA BY VIŚVANĀTHA CAKRAVARTĪ

śrī-kṛṣṇa-nāmāmṛta-varṣi-vaktra-
candra-prabhā-dhvasta-tamo-bharāya
gaurāṅga-devānucarāya tasmai
namo namaḥ śrīla-narottamāya

"I offer my repeated obeisances to Śrīla Narottama Dāsa Ṭhākura, the glorious follower of Gaurāṅga, who completely destroys the darkness of ignorance of the living entities at its root with the nectarean rays of Kṛṣṇa's Holy Name, which emanate from His moon-like face.

saṅkīrtanānandaja-manda-hāsya-
danta-dyuti-dyotita-diṅ-mukhāya
svedāśru-dhārā-snapitāya tasmai
namo namaḥ śrīla-narottamāya

I offer my repeated obeisances to Śrīla Narottama Dāsa Ṭhākura, who lights up every direction with the effulgence of his teeth, revealed as he laughs out of the joy of Harināma-*saṅkīrtana* and is bathed in torrents of tears and perspiration out of Divine Love.

mṛdaṅga-nāda-śruti-mātra-cañcalat-
padāmbujāmanda-manoharāya
sadyaḥ samudyat-pulakāya tasmai
namo namaḥ śrīla-narottamāya

"I offer my repeated obeisances to Śrīla Narottama Dāsa Ṭhākura, whose body is covered with horripilation and whose lotus feet dance enchantingly, being set into motion as soon as he hears the sweet sound of the *mṛdaṅga*.

gandharva-garva-kṣapaṇa-svalāsya-
vismāpitāśeṣa-kṛti-vrajāya
sva-sṛṣṭa-gāna-prathitāya tasmai
namo namaḥ śrīla-narottamāya

I offer my repeated obeisances to Śrīla Narottama Dāsa Ṭhākura, whose fame has spread through the songs he has written and whose dance and song – indeed, whose every action in *kīrtana* – amazes even the most proficient and brings shame to the Gandharvas.

ānanda-mūrcchāvanipāta-bhāta-
dhūlī-bharālaṅkṛta-vigrahāya
yad-darśanaṁ bhāgya-bhareṇa tasmai
namo namaḥ śrīla-narottamāya

"I offer my repeated obeisances to Śrīla Narottama Dāsa Ṭhākura, who can be seen only by one who has unlimited good fortune, and whose figure is decorated with the dust that covers it as he falls to the ground unconscious in divine ecstasy.

sthale sthale yasya kṛpā-prapābhiḥ
kṛṣṇānya-tṛṣṇā jana-saṁhatīnām

nirmūlitā eva bhavanti tasmai
namo namaḥ śrīla-narottamāya

"I offer my repeated obeisances to Śrīla Narottama Dāsa Ṭhākura, who established almshouses of mercy everywhere, causing every person's desires, other than those for service to Kṛṣṇa, to be uprooted.

yad-bhakti-niṣṭhā pala-rekhikeva
sparśaḥ punaḥ sparśa-maṇīva yasya
prāmāṇyam evaṁ śrutivad yadīyaṁ
tasmai namaḥ śrīla-narottamāya

"I offer my repeated obeisances to Śrīla Narottama Dāsa Ṭhākura, whose devotional faith is like a line scratched in a stone, whose touch is like that of the philosopher's stone that fulfils all desires and whose every word is as authoritative as that of the Veda.

mūrtaiva bhaktiḥ kim ayaṁ kim eṣa
vairāgya-sāras tanumān nṛloke
saṁbhāvyate yaḥ kṛtibhiḥ sadaiva
tasmai namaḥ śrīla-narottamāya

"I offer my repeated obeisances to Śrīla Narottama Dāsa Ṭhākura, who forever appears to the fortunate learned scholars of transcendental knowledge as devotion itself incarnate, or as the embodiment of the essence of renunciation in this mortal world."

Śrīla Narottama Dāsa Ṭhākura performed the pastimes of disappearance on the *kṛṣṇa-pañcamī* in the month of Kārtika.

Śrī Rāmacandra Kavirāja

svardhunyās tīra-bhūmau
sarajani-nagare gauḍa-bhūpādi-pātrād
brahmaṇyād viṣṇu-bhaktād
api suparicitāt śrī-cirañjīva-senāt
yaḥ śrī-rāmendu-nāmā samajani paramaḥ
śrī-sunandābhidhāyāṁ
so 'yaṁ śrīmān narākhye sa hi kavi-nṛpatiḥ
samyag āsīd abhinnaḥ

"Rāmacandra, a great devotee with an attractive form, was born in the town of Sarajani on the banks of the Ganges as the son of Sunandā and Cirañjīva Sena, a well-known minister of the King of Gauda, a devotee of the *brāhmaṇas* and Viṣṇu. Rāmacandra was not in any way different from Narottama Dāsa Ṭhākura, the king amongst the poets." (*Saṅgīta-mādhava-nāṭaka*, quoted at *Bhakti-ratnākara* 1.270)

"Cirañjīva Sena was a resident of Srikhanda. His wife's name was Sunandā. They had two virtuous sons, the elder was Rāmacandra, the younger Govinda. Rāmacandra was a disciple of Śrīnivāsa Ācārya, and received the title Kavirāja. His *siddha* name was Karuṇā Mañjarī." (Verses quoted in *Gauḍīya Vaiṣṇava Abhidhāna.*)

Rāmacandra Kavirāja was born in *vaīdya* family. After the death of his father, he went to live in Kumar Nagar with his maternal grandfather, Dāmodara Kavirāja, who was a disciple of Narahari Sarakāra. Later he went to live with his younger brother Govinda Kavirāja in the village of Telia Budhari in the Murshidabad district. This place has the distinction of being his Sripat. Śrīla Bhakti Siddhānta Sarasvatī Gosvāmī Ṭhākura, however, mentioned that Rāmacandra Kavirāja's Sripat is in Kumar Nagar.

RĀMACANDRA'S WEDDING

Śrīla Bhakti Siddhānta Sarasvatī Gosvāmī Ṭhākura has written that Rāmacandra Kavirāja was a lifelong renunciate and never married. Haridāsa Dāsa, on the other hand, writes in his

Gauḍīya Vaiṣṇava Abhidhāna that Rāmacandra did get married, but never lived with his wife. Śrīnivāsa Ācārya saw Rāmacandra as a groom and said a few words to him about the temporary nature of material life, thus awakening within him an indifference to worldly life such that he never took up the duties of householder life. This story has been taken from a book which is not accepted as authoritative by everyone. The following quote is taken from there:

[Śrīnivāsa Ācārya said,] "Just look at how much enthusiasm everyone has for this wedding! They are spending so much money, and for what? Just to purchase illusion and quarrel. They don't know that *māyā* has placed a noose around their neck, and so they take great interest in the auspicious invocatory rituals. People celebrate weddings thinking that they are auspicious when they are not and that they have been fulfilled when they have not."

THE KAVIRĀJA TITLE

Śrīnivāsa Ācārya was so overcome with affection for Rāmacandra that he gave him the *dīkṣā mantra* and engaged him as his personal servant. He had unparalleled devotion to his guru and would follow his guru's words without any kind of reservation. Though Vīrahāmvīra became Śrīnivāsa Ācārya's disciple, Rāmacandra Kavirāja acted as his *śikṣā-guru*. Rāmacandra Kavirāja also visited Vrindavan, where he associated with Jīva Gosvāmī and the other Vaiṣṇavas, receiving their blessings. They were very pleased to hear his poetry, so much so that Jīva Gosvāmī gave him the Kavirāja title. He was thus one of the eight Kavirājas (*aṣṭa-kavirāja*). He was Narottama Ṭhākura's favored companion for preaching activities and spiritual association.

"Paramānanda Bhaṭṭācārya, an ocean of love, Jīva Gosvāmī and the other residents of Vraja listened to Rāmacandra recite his own poetic compositions and they joyfully awarded him the title of Kavirāja. Rāmacandra Kavirāja is full of all virtues, and is Narottama Dāsa's second self." (*Bhakti-ratnākara* 1.267-9)

Kaṁsāri Sena, Rāma Sena, Rāmacandra Kavirāja, and the three Kavirājas – Govinda, Śrīraṅga and Mukunda – are Nityānanda Prabhu's branches." (*Caitanya Caritāmṛta* 1.11.51)

Rāmacandra wrote several books, including *Smaraṇa-camatkāra*, *Smaraṇa-darpaṇa*, *Siddhānta-candrikā* and *Śrīnivāsa-ācāryera-jīvana-racita*.

RĀMACANDRA IN VRINDAVAN

Narahari Cakravartī has written an extensive description of Rāmacandra and his visit to Vrindavan in the ninth wave of his *Bhakti-ratnākara*. Everyone would get attracted by his unblemished divinely effulgent form. When Rāmacandra visited the Rādhā-Dāmodara temple with Jīva Gosvāmī and saw the deities and Rūpa Gosvāmī's *samādhi*, he experienced ecstatic transformations that were a source of amazement to all. Gopāla Bhaṭṭa Gosvāmī, Lokanātha Gosvāmī and Bhūgarbha Gosvāmī gave him their blessings. He went to bathe in Radha Kunda and Shyama Kunda and met Raghunātha Dāsa Gosvāmī there. When he paid obeisances to Dāsa Gosvāmī, the venerable saint affectionately embraced him and felt ecstasy.

Śrī Narottama Dāsa Ṭhākura has prayed for the association of Rāmacandra Kavirāja in his *Prārthanā*:

dayā kara śrī-ācārya prabhu śrīnivāsa
rāmacandra saṅga māge narottama dāsa

"Please be merciful, Śrīnivāsa Ācārya Prabhu! Narottama Dāsa begs for Rāmacandra's association."

yau śaśvad-bhagavat-parāyaṇa-
parau saṁsāra-pārāyaṇau
samyak sātvata-tantra-vāda-
paramau niḥśeṣa-siddhāntagau
śaśvad-bhakti-rasa-pradāna-rasikau
pāṣaṇḍa-hṛn-maṇḍalāv
anyonya-priyatābhareṇa yugalī-
bhūtāv imau tau numaḥ

"I pay my obeisances to Narottama and Rāmacandra Prabhus, who are always fond of dedication towards devotion to the Supreme Lord, who help people to cross over the ocean of material life, who know all the scriptures completely and have understood all the transcendental doctrines, who are the most generous with the distribution of *bhakti rasa* who won the hearts of the atheists, and who are constantly attached to each others' affectionate company. (*Saṅgīta-mādhava-nāṭaka*, quoted at *Bhakti-ratnākara* 1.277)

Rāmacandra Kavirāja's disappearance day is the *kṛṣṇa tṛtīyā* in the month of Māgha. He disappeared in Vrindavan after the disappearance of Śrīnivāsa Ācārya.

Śrī Śyāmānanda Prabhu

Śrī Śyāmānanda Prabhu was a servant of a servant of Subala in Kṛṣṇa *līlā*. He was the disciple of Hṛdayānanda, or Hṛdaya Caitanya, a disciple of Gaurī Dāsa Paṇḍita, who is Subala in Kṛṣṇa *līlā*.

yaṁ lokā bhuvi kīrtayanti
hṛdayānandasya śiṣyaṁ priyaṁ
sakhye śrī-subalya yaṁ bhagavataḥ
preṣṭhānuśiṣyaṁ tathā
sa śrīmān rasikendra-mastaka-
maṇiścitte mamāharniśaṁ
śrī-rādhāpriya-narma-marmasu
ruciṁ sampādayan bhāsatām

"Śrī Śyāmānanda was known in this world as Hṛdayānanda's dear disciple. He was a follower of Subala Sakhā, and he became the grand-disciple of Lord's dear associate. May he, the crest-jewel of the connoisseurs of divine love, appear day and night in my mind, bringing me a fondness for the service of Śrī Śrī Rādhā-Mādhava's confidential joyous pastimes." (*Śyāmānanda-śataka*)

Śyāmānanda Prabhu was born on the full-moon day of Caitra in 1456 of the Śaka era (1535 A.D.) in the town of Dharenda Bahadurpur, which is near the Khargapur railway station in Midnapore. His father was Śrī Kṛṣṇa Maṇḍala, and his mother, Durikā. Kṛṣṇa Maṇḍala's hometown was Dandeshwar, which lies on the banks of the Subarnarekha River. The following statement is found in the *Gauḍīya Vaiṣṇava Abhidhāna*: "Śrī Kṛṣṇa Maṇḍala used to live in a place called Ambua, near Dandeshwar. He formerly lived in Gauda (the part of Bengal which lies on the banks of the Bhagirathi River) and only later moved to Dandeshwar, just across the present-day border in Odisha. Śyāmānanda Prabhu's Sripats in the towns of Dharenda, Bahadurpur, Rayni or Rohini, Gopiballabhpur and Nrisinghapur are very dear to his disciples."

Śyāmānanda Prabhu was born in the *sadgopa* subcaste (which fits in the category of *jala-cala*, i.e., *brāhmaṇas* who are permitted to only take water touched by its members). Of course, a Vaiṣṇava is beyond the material qualities and may take birth in a family of any race or caste. Anyone who thinks badly of

Vaiṣṇavas or judges them on the basis of their race or caste is destined for hell.

arcye viṣṇau śīladhīḥ guruṣu
naramatir vaiṣṇave jāti-buddhir
viṣṇor vā vaiṣṇavānāṁ kali-mala-
mathane pāda-tīrthe 'mbu buddhiḥ
śrī viṣṇor nāmni mantre sakala-
kaluṣa-he śabda-sāmānya-buddhir
viṣṇau sarveśvareśe tad-itara-
samadhīr yasya vā nārakī saḥ

"Anyone who considers the deity to be nothing but stone, the guru to be an ordinary human being, or the Vaiṣṇava to be a member of a particular caste or race, who takes the holy water which has washed Viṣṇu or the Vaiṣnava's feet and can destroy all the sins of the Age of Kālī to be ordinary water, who thinks that the name or *mantra* of Viṣnu, which destroys all evils, is the same as any other sound, or who takes Viṣṇu to be equal to anything other than him, has a hellish nature." (*Padma Purāṇa*)

"One who takes birth in a low-class family is not disqualified from performing devotional service, nor is one who born in a pure, high-class brahminical family automatically qualified for such service. Whoever engages in the worship of the Lord is a great person; one who does not worship is rejected. There is no consideration of caste or creed in Kṛṣṇa *bhajana*." (*Caitanya Caritāmṛta* 3.4.66-7)

na me bhaktaś caturvedī
mad-bhaktaḥ śvapacaḥ priyaḥ
tasmai deyaṁ tato grāhyaṁ
sa ca pūjyo yathā hy aham

"Simply being a knower of the four Vedas does not make someone My devotee. An outcaste who is My devotee is dear to Me. One should exchange gifts and food, etc., with such a devotee for he is verily as worshipable as I am." (*Itihāsa-samuccaya*, quoted in *Hari-bhakti-vilāsa*, 10.127.)

Śyāmānanda's parents had lost several children in childbirth, and they vowed to surrender their next child to Viṣṇu if it survived. Having suffered so much grief in the loss of their previous children, they first named Śyāmānanda as Duḥkhī, or "unhappy," to ward off farther distress.

"Śyāmānanda's parents, Durikā and Śrī Kṛṣṇa Maṇḍala, made their home in Dandeshwar. His father was the best of the *sadgopa* caste, of impeccable character. Kṛṣṇa was everything to him, and Kṛṣṇa's devotees very dear. We cannot describe the virtues of his parents for fear of increasing the volume of this book. They had previously lived in Dharenda-Bahadurpur, and people say that Śyāmānanda was born there. Though his brothers and sisters had all died in childbirth, nothing could stop him. Even so, his parents brought him up in sadness, and they called him Duḥkhī. (*Bhakti-ratnākara* 1.351-5, 359)

Śyāmānanda Prabhu's parents performed the appropriate rituals when their time came, such as the first eating of solid food and the cutting of hair. As he grew older, he studied Sanskrit grammar, etc. His parents were overjoyed to see his talents and his religious proclivity. Śyāmānanda Prabhu listened attentively to devotees when they spoke of Gaurāṅga and Nityānanda Prabhu's glories and would repeat them to others constantly. Whenever he listened to the activities of Gaura-Nitāi or Rādhā and Kṛṣṇa, tears would flow in torrents from his eyes.

Duḥkhī served his parents devotedly, and they told him to get initiated so that he could fully commit himself to the service of the Lord. Duḥkhī agreed and told them that he wished to take *dīkṣā* from Hṛdaya Caitanya in Ambika Kalna. Going there would also give him the chance to see the Ganges and bathe in it. His parents happily gave him permission to go.

When Duḥkhī arrived in Ambika Kalna, he threw himself at the feet of Hṛdaya Caitanya, who upon becoming acquainted with him, happily gave him Kṛṣṇa *mantra*. He gave Duḥkhī the Vaiṣṇava name Kṛṣṇadāsa, and so he was known from then on as Duḥkhī Kṛṣṇadāsa. Hṛdaya Caitanya ordered him to go to Vrindavan and take up a life of intense *bhajan*. Though Duḥkhī Kṛṣṇadāsa did not like being separated from his *gurudeva*, following his order he set off for Vraja, first visiting Nabadwip and other places in Gauda Mandala, where he sought the blessings of the Vaiṣṇavas. After spending much time on pilgrimage, he finally arrived in Vrindavan, where he became completely absorbed in the worship of Śrī Rādhā Śyāmasundara.

In Vrindavan, Duḥkhī Kṛṣṇadāsa studied the Vaiṣṇava scriptures under Śrī Jīva Gosvāmī, who was the leading scholar of the *sampradāya*. When Hṛdaya Caitanya heard of the enthusiasm with which Duḥkhī Kṛṣṇadāsa was leading the devotional life in Vraja, he wrote a letter to Jīva Gosvāmī in which he said that Jīva Gosvāmī should accept Duḥkhī Kṛṣṇadāsa as his own disciple. Just as he gave titles to his other prominent students (the Ācārya title to Śrīnivāsa, and Ṭhākura title to Narottama), Jīva Gosvāmī gave the name Śyāmānanda to Duḥkhī Kṛṣṇadāsa. The reasoning behind this name was that he brought great joy to Śrī Rādhā Śyāmasundara.

"He brought great joy to Śyāmasundara, and hence he was given the new name Śyāmānanda in Vrindavan. Seeing his sincere endeavor in devotion, Śrī Jīva Gosvāmī taught him devotional scriptures." (*Bhakti-ratnākara* 1.401-2)

Jīva Gosvāmī sent Śrīnivāsa Ācārya, Narottama Dāsa Ṭhākura and Śyāmānanda Prabhu back to Bengal with the Vaiṣṇava scriptures written by the Gosvāmīs in 1504 of the Śaka era (1582-3 A.D.). The idea was to spread the teachings found in these books throughout Bengal and Odisha. We have already related the events that took place when Vīrahāmvīra had these books stolen. Narottama Ṭhākura went to northern Bengal, and Śyāmānanda Prabhu went to Odisha. The Midnapore district was previously under the rule of the Odishan king.

RĀDHĀRĀṆĪ'S SPECIAL MERCY ON ŚYĀMĀNANDA

Even though Śyāmānanda Prabhu was Hṛdaya Caitanya's initiated disciple, his guru had entrusted him to the care of Jīva Gosvāmī Prabhu. Through the association of Jīva Gosvāmī and service to him, Śyāmānanda Prabhu developed a taste for serving Rādhā and Kṛṣṇa in the conjugal mood. Hṛdaya Caitanya Prabhu himself was a disciple of Gaurī Dāsa Paṇḍita, who was one of the twelve *gopālas*, Subala Sakhā. He thus worshipped Gaura-Nitāi in the mood of friendship. Those who think that Śyāmānanda Prabhu committed an offense to his initiating spiritual master by

abandoning his mood and by serving Kṛṣṇa in a different mood are wrong. The mood of friendship is contained within the conjugal mood. If a disciple makes farther progress in spiritual life, it enhances the reputation of his teacher.

An extraordinary incident, which took place in Vrindavan prior to his being ordered by Jīva Gosvāmī to return to Odisha, demonstrates how dear Śyāmānanda Prabhu was to Rādhārāṇī. One day, Śyāmānanda Prabhu was sweeping the *rāsa maṇḍala* in Vrindavan, absorbed in an ecstatic trance. Suddenly, by Rādhārāṇī's transcendental mercy, he found Her ankle bracelet (*nūpura*) lying on the ground. In his excitement, he touched the ankle bracelet to his forehead, where it left a mark, which is preserved to this day as the *tilaka* marking of the disciple descendants of Śyāmānanda Prabhu. It is known as *nūpura-tilaka*.

ŚYĀMĀNANDA PRABHU'S PREACHING

Śrīnivāsa Ācārya, Narottama Ṭhākura and Śyāmānanda Prabhu primarily preached the message of Mahāprabhu through *kīrtana*. The styles that these three *ācāryas* used respectively were named *manohara-sāhī*, *garāṇahāṭī*, and *reṇeṭī*. They would enchant the listeners with their heartfelt singing of *kīrtana*. Unfortunately, these styles of *kīrtana* are no longer extant.

As a result of Śyāmānanda Prabhu's preaching in Odisha, many Muslims also became his disciples. The most important of his innumerable disciples was Rasika Murāri, or Rasikānanda. Rasikānanda was the son of Acyutānanda, the zamindar of Rohini village. He had another name, Murāri, and was thus most commonly known as Rasika Murāri. He was a very powerful preacher, and his fame is still widespread throughout the villages of Odisha.

A list of some of Śyāmānanda Prabhu's prominent disciples is given in the *Bhakti-ratnākara*:

"Śyāmānanda made disciples all over the place. A person can be purified by hearing their names: Rādhānanda, Puruṣottama, Manohara, Cintamaṇi, Balabhadra, Jagadīśvara, Uddhava, Akrūra, Madhuvana, Govinda, Jagannātha, Gadādhara, Ānandānanda, and Rādhā Mohana. Śyāmānanda was constantly immersed in the joys of *kīrtana* in the association of these disciples. Poets have described his wonderful pastimes for the pleasure of everyone." (*Bhakti-ratnākara* 15.62-66)

Another of Śyāmānanda Prabhu's notable disciple was a yogi named Dāmodara whom he converted to Vaiṣṇavism. Narahari Cakravartī has written the following account of that conversion:

"Śyāmānanda mercifully flooded the yoga practitioner named Dāmodara with devotional *rasa*. After becoming his disciple, Dāmodara constantly cried and chanted the names of Nitāi-Caitanya. Who could remain untouched by his ecstatic absorption? He danced, crying out 'Bhakti is the best of all!' After delivering Dāmodara, Śyāmānanda continued to travel about, distributing the jewel of devotion to everyone." (*Bhakti-ratnākara* 15.55-8)

Śyāmānanda Prabhu put on a large festival at Dharenda with Rasika Murāri and Dāmodara that is still remembered today by his descendants. When he left the world, Śyāmānanda Prabhu turned over the service of Śrī Govinda at Gopiballabhpur to his dear disciple Rasikānanda Deva Gosvāmī. Śyāmānanda Prabhu's disciples and their descendants still worship his deity Rādhā Śyāmasundara in Vrindavan. This temple is still one of the principal pilgrimage sites in Vrindavan.

Śyāmānanda Prabhu lived the last part of his life in Nrisinghapur in Odisha, where he continued preaching Vaiṣṇavism. His earthly pastimes came to an end on the first day of the waning moon in the month of Āṣāḍha in 1552 of the Śaka era (1631 A.D.) To preserve his holy memory, the branch of the Gaudiya Math in Midnapore city was named Shyamananda Gaudiya Math.

Śrīla Rasikānanda Deva Gosvāmī

Śrīla Rasikānanda Deva Gosvāmī was born in 1512 of the Śaka era (1591 A.D.) in the village of Rohini, or Rayni, in the Midnapore district. This village is situated at the confluence of the Subarnarekha and Dolanga rivers. His father's name was Rāja Acyutānanda, and his mother, Bhavānī Devī. The Subarnarekha River crosses back and forth across the present-day Bengal-Odisha border. The Midnapore district used to be a part of the Odishan kingdom. Rāja Acyutānanda was an Odishan of the *karana* caste, the equivalent of the *kāyasthas* in Bengal. A Vaiṣṇava is beyond the material qualities and should not be judged in terms of his caste origins. Rāja Acyutānanda and Rasikānanda were born in the *karaṇa* caste in order to bless it.

We can assume that Rasikānanda Deva Gosvāmī was a female servitor belonging to the conjugal loving mood in Kṛṣṇa *līlā*. Though his spiritual master, Śyāmānanda Prabhu, had himself been initiated by Hṛdaya Caitanya Gosvāmī, who worshipped the Lord in the mood of friendship, he later took shelter of the conjugal mood due to the association of Jīva Gosvāmī. Śyāmānanda Prabhu thus initiated Rasikānanda into the worship of Rādhā and Kṛṣṇa.

Rasikānanda was also known by the name Rasika Murāri. In *Prema-vilāsa* (20) it is written that Śyāmānanda Prabhu had two principal disciples, one named Rasikānanda, the other Murāri, both of whom lived in Rayni, and whose glories are sung by everyone in Odisha. But Narahari Cakravartī indicates clearly in *Bhakti-ratnākara* that both names refer to the same individual:

"In the village of Rayni lived the famous son of Acyutānanda. He had two names: Rasikānanda and Murāri. Thus he was also known as Rasika Murāri. He became learned in the scriptures in his childhood." (*Bhakti-ratnākara* 15.27-8)

We learn from the *Bhakti-ratnākara* that when the son of King Daśaratha, Lord Rāmacandra, was exiled from Ayodhya, He spent some time with Lakṣmaṇa and Sītā in the village of Barajita, not far from Rayni.

He there established the Śiva *liṅga* named Rāmeśvara.

Acyutānanda was a benevolent landowner who strictly followed religious principles and took good care of his subjects. His wife also had a good reputation as a faithful and loyal wife. Rasika Murāri served his parents very expertly, bringing them much satisfaction. *Bhakti-ratnākara* also notes that he had a devoted wife, name, Icchāmayī Devī or Icchādei, from the village of Ghantashila. This village also has a certain history as a place where the Pāṇḍavas stayed during their exile. It was in this village that Rasika Murāri first met his guru and received his grace, an event that has been elaborately described in the *Bhakti-ratnākara*.

RASIKA MURARI MEETS ŚYĀMĀNANDA PRABHU

One day, while in Ghantashila, Rasika Murāri was anxious to find a spiritual master and went to a solitary place to meditate. He had just entered into a very deep trance when he heard a voice from an unseen source say,

"Murāri! You need be anxious no longer. Your guru is Śyāmānanda, and you will meet him very shortly. Take shelter of him, and your life will be successful."

Upon hearing this divine message, Murāri began chanting the name of Śyāmānanda with joyful enthusiasm. He spent the entire night crying out of eager expectation to meet his guru, until finally at the end of the night, he had a dream vision of Śyāmānanda Prabhu, who said to him, "Don't worry any longer, for you will meet me this very day."

At dawn, Rasika Murāri was on the lookout for his guru when he saw the tall figure of Śyāmānanda Prabhu approaching him, as effulgent as the sun. Surrounded by disciples like Kiśora Dāsa, he was dancing in a state of absorption in divine love while chanting "*Ha Kṛṣṇa Caitanya! Ha Nityānanda!*". Rasika Murāri had been waiting anxiously for so long to encounter his guru that he immediately fell down at his feet. Śyāmānada Prabhu affectionately lifted him up, embraced him and drenched him with tears. Then, after giving him the Rādhā-Kṛṣṇa *mantra*, he offered him up to Caitanya and Nityānanda Prabhus. This whole event reveals how we can find a guru through sincere prayers.

RASIKĀNANDA BECOMES A POTENT PREACHER

Rasikānanda Deva Gosvāmī fully committed himself in body, mind and soul to the service of his guru. Indeed, he served him so well that in a short time he was recognized as Śyāmānanda Prabhu's chief disciple, a very powerful preacher and, *ācārya* himself. In fact, it is a truism that a good disciple becomes a good teacher. A spiritual master may have innumerable followers who call him their guru, but are disciples in name only. Only a true disciple who has dedicated himself completely to his spiritual master is imbued with all the powers of the guru. Śyāmānanda Prabhu invested Rasikānanda Deva with such spiritual powers that he was able to convert many criminals, atheists, Muslims, and other fallen souls to the path of devotion, bestowing the jewel of *prema* upon them all.

On one occasion, a wicked Muslim tried to silence Rasika Murāri by having him attacked by an intoxicated elephant, but Rasikānanda Prabhu was able to transform even the elephant into a disciple and engage him in the service of Viṣṇu and the Vaiṣṇavas. All who witnessed this amazing event were overwhelmed with astonishment at Rasika Murāri's spiritual power, and the evil Muslim zamindar himself came and surrendered to him.

"Śyāmānanda Prabhu turned the service of his personal Govinda deity in Gopiballabhpur over to Rasikānanda. He delivered unlimited living beings without any consideration of their caste or religious background. He preached in every village accompanied by his disciples, thus delivering innumerable living beings. He remained constantly intoxicated in *harināma-saṅkīrtana*. Who will not be overcome with emotion on reciting his virtues?" (*Bhakti-ratnākara* 15.81-6)

The *Prema-vilāsa* corroborates this account in the nineteenth chapter: "He delivered many criminals and Muslims."

The Rāja of Mayurbhanj, Vaidyanātha Bhañja, Gajapati, the zamindar of Patashpur, Candrabhānu, the Rāja of Maynar, Harinārāyaṇa, the Rāja of Pancheta, Śrī Bhīma and Śrīkara (the zamindars of Dharenda), Ahmed Beg, the son-in-law of Ibrahim Khān, and the governor of Odisha were all attracted to the transcendental power of Rasikānanda Prabhu and became his disciples.

Rasikānanda Deva Gosvāmī wrote *Śyāmānanda-śataka, Bhakta-Bhāgavatāṣṭaka,* and *Kuñjakeli-dvādaśaka.*

Rasikānanda Prabhu met Śyāmānanda Prabhu after a long gap when the latter arrived from Ban Vishnupur and stayed in Nrsinghapur. Rasikānanda Prabhu and all others extremely rejoiced at having their guru's audience. *Bhakti-ratnākara* 9.256-8 describes this event:

"Śyāmānanda Prabhu, accompanied with many disciples, went to Odisha from Ban Vishnupur for a few days. As soon as the news spread, everyone rushed to have his audience. Rasikānanda and others were extremely pleased to see Śyāmānanda Prabhu in Nrsinghapur."

Śyāmānanda Prabhu put on a large festival at Dharenda with Rasika Murāri and Dāmodara that is still remembered today by his descendants.

RASIKĀNANDA'S DISAPPEARANCE

"It is said that just prior to Rasikānanda Deva Gosvāmī's disappearance, he went with seven of his disciples to a village named Bansdaha near Jaleswar. Mahāprabhu passed through this village when traveling to Puri with Nityānanda Prabhu." (*Caitanya Bhāgavata* 3.2.263-4)

Rasikānanda Deva Gosvāmī and his disciples walked from there to Remuna, chanting *kīrtana* the whole way. When they arrived in the courtyard of the famous Ksīracora Gopīnātha temple, Rasikānanda Prabhu suddenly merged into the Gopīnātha deity. His disciples also left their bodies in the same place. Rasika Murāri's flower *samādhi* and those of his seven associates are still maintained in the courtyard of the Ksīrcora Gopīnātha temple.

An annual festival lasting twelve days is held in Remuna to celebrate his disappearance. This takes place starting from the day after *śiva caturdaśī* in the month of Māgha.

Viśvambharānanda Deva Gosvāmī, the author of the celebrated *Āstikya-darśana,* was Rasikānanda Deva Gosvāmī's descendant.

Śrī Gaṅgā Mātā Gosvāmīnī

Gaṅgāmātā Gosvāmīnī was initiated by Haridāsa Paṇḍita Gosvāmī into the line of Gaurāṅga's *Śakti*, Śrīla Gadādhara Paṇḍita Gosvāmī. Kṛṣṇadāsa Kavirāja Gosvāmī himself has described Paṇḍita Haridāsa's character in his *Caitanya Caritāmṛta*:

"Śrī Haridāsa Paṇḍita was the head priest of the Govinda temple. His virtues and good fame are known all over the world, for he was gentle, tolerant, peaceful, magnanimous, grave, sweet in his words, very sober in his endeavors, and wise. He was respectful to everyone and worked for the benefit of all. Diplomacy, envy and jealousy were unknown to his heart. The fifty general qualities of Lord Kṛṣṇa were all present in his body. Paṇḍita Haridāsa's spiritual master was Gadādhara Paṇḍita's disciple Ananta Ācārya. Ananta Ācārya was always absorbed in love of Godhead, magnanimous and advanced in all respects. He too was a reservoir of all good qualities whose greatness cannot be fathomed by anyone." (*Caitanya Caritāmṛta* 1.8.547, 5960)

Śrīla Bhakti Siddhānta Sarasvatī Gosvāmī Ṭhākura writes in his *Anubhāṣya*: "During the advent of Lord Śrī Kṛṣṇa, Ananta Ācārya was Sudevī, one of the eight *gopīs*. This is stated in the *Gaura-gaṇoddeśa-dīpikā,* verse 165, as follows: *anantācārya-gosvāmī yā sudevī purā vraje.* According to the disciplic succession descending from him at the famous Gaṅgā Mātā monastery in Puri, he is known as Vinoda Mañjarī and his disciple Haridāsa Paṇḍita Gosvāmī, who is also known as Śrī Raghu Gopāla, as Śrī Rāsa Mañjarī. Haridāsa Paṇḍita had two important disciples: Lakṣmī Priyā and her niece, Gaṅgā Mātā, daughter of the King of Puntia."

More is learnt about Gaṅgā Mātā's holy life from Haridāsa Dāsa's *Gauḍīya Vaiṣṇava Abhidhāna* and from Sundarānanda Vidyavinoda, who has given a detailed account of her life in his *Śrī Kṣetra.*

ŚACĪ DEVĪ GOES TO LIVE IN VRAJA

Gaṅgā Mātā Gosvāmiṇī's original name was Śacī Devī. She was born in Puntia, which is in the Rajashahi district of present-day Bangladesh. Her father was Rāja Nareśa Nārāyaṇa. Śacī Devī was indifferent to family life and devoted to Kṛṣṇa from her early childhood. When her parents wanted to get her married, Śacī Devī told them that she refused to accept any mortal as her husband, making them worried for her. When her mother departed from the mortal world, Śacī Devī left home and set out on a pilgrimage which led her first to Puri and then to Vrindavan.

Upon her arrival in Vrindavan dhāma, she met Haridāsa Paṇḍita Gosvāmī and felt blessed. She became anxious to receive initiation from him, but he hesitated at first because of her wealthy family background. Later, however, when he saw her asceticism and her unswerving determination to engage in pure devotional activity, he gave her initiation in the eighteen-syllabled *mantra.* This event took place in the Govindajī temple that year on Wednesday, the Caitra *śukla ekādaśī.*

After having received these blessings from her guru, she began to engage in intense *bhajana*, subsisting through *mādhukarī* (by begging for morsels of food from door to door). After a year of this intense devotional activity, she was told by her spiritual master to live in Radha Kunda with her spiritually advanced and soft-hearted godsister Lakṣmī Priyā, who regularly chanted 300,000 names every day. As a part of their regular spiritual practice, the two of them daily circumambulated Govardhan together.

After several years of such practice at Radha Kunda, when Śacī Devī had become very advanced in her devotional life, her guru sent her to Purusottama Kshetra to recover the home of Sārvabhauma Bhaṭṭācārya, which had fallen into disrepair. Taking the command of her spiritual master as her all in all, Śacī Devī came to Jagannatha Puri and took the *kṣetra-sannyāsa* vow. At that time, all that remained of Sārvabhauma Bhaṭṭācārya's house was a single rundown building which housed his Rādhā Dāmodara *śālagrāma-śilā*.

Even while she had lived at home in Puntia, Śacī Devī had studied the scriptures with rapt attention. In Vrindavan, furthermore, she had thoroughly studied the *Bhāgavata Purāṇa* in the company of Vaiṣṇavas. In order to salvage Sārvabhauma Bhaṭṭācārya's residence, she set out to preach. Her transcendental qualities and discourses on the *Bhāgavata* made such an impression on the public that she began to attract large audiences. It did not take long before her fame had spread so widely that the King of Odisha himself, Mukunda Deva, came to listen to her speak on the *Bhāgavata*. He too became a devoted follower after being impressed by her devotional qualities and her learning.

THE SHWETA GANGA

According to the *Utkala-khaṇḍa*, there was a King Śveta in the Tretā Yuga who was a devotee of Lord Jagannātha. He made arrangements for Lord Jagannātha's *bhoga* just as Indradyumna had done. One morning he came to the temple and saw the offerings which were made by the gods – thousands and thousands of wonderful gifts which were beyond the power of any mortal to present to the Lord. King Śveta became disturbed at the insignificance of his own offerings and stood at the temple door, his head hung in shame. As he was meditating on his own insignificance, he had a vision in which he saw Lakṣmī Devī herself taking his food offerings and feeding them to the main Lord Jagannātha deities as well as to the *vijaya-vigraha*, who were eating them with great enthusiasm. The king immediately thought himself consummated by this vision, and he continued to serve Lord Jagannātha with unflagging enthusiasm. Lord Jagannātha eventually granted him the boon of being liberated in a spot which faces Matsya Mādhava, halfway between Akshaya Bata and the ocean, which was subsequently named Shweta Madhava in his honor. The pond excavated here was also named Shweta Ganga (the white Ganges). On the banks of this pond, deities of Śveta Mādhava, Matsya Mādhava and the nine planets are still worshipped.

One night, the King of Odisha, Mukunda Deva, had a dream in which Jagannātha Deva appeared to him and told him to give Śacī Devī a tract of land bordering on this Shweta Ganga. The next morning, the king joyfully came to see Śacī Devī and told her about the dream. Though she had no interest in increasing her worldly possessions, Śacī Devi decided to accept the king's gift for the sake of her guru-given mission to improve the condition of Sārvabhauma Bhaṭṭācārya's house. She performed the service of the deities at this place by begging from door to door. Wherever there is true devotion to the Lord and the service to the devotees is the real interest, the trouble which one accepts in service is not seen as trouble, but rather as a special opportunity and a source of joy.

HOW ŚACĪ DEVĪ CAME TO BE KNOWN AS GAṄGĀ MĀTĀ

Not long afterwards, a miraculous occurrence took place. One *kṛṣṇa trayodaśī*, an opportune moment came for the Maha Varuni Ganges bath. Many people who seek to accumulate pious credits make the trip to the Ganges for this auspicious occasion. Indeed, many people asked Śacī Devī to accompany them, but she could not abandon her *kṣetra-sannyāsa* vows or her service to the deities, so she was obliged to plead that it was impossible for her to go.

Even though she did not really want to go, Jagannātha Deva Himself made arrangements for her to bathe in the Ganges. That night He appeared to her in a dream and told her to take bath in the Shweta Ganga in the middle of the night. Śacī Devī followed His instructions, but as soon as she entered the water, Ganga appeared there. She was carried away in a strong river current and she suddenly found herself inside the Jagannātha temple. She could see herself bathing in the midst of the other residents of Puri *dhāma*. She could hear the joyful noise of the bathing crowds.

The temple gatekeepers awakened on hearing this commotion and called the temple superintendent. They, in turn, gave a report to the king himself, who ordered them to open the temple doors. When they finally flung the doors open, they saw no one but Śacī Devī standing there alone. Lord Jagannātha's *pūjārīs* were confused and at first, did not know what to do. They assumed that Śacī Devī had hidden herself in the temple with the intention of robbing the deities' valuables and that they had caught her red-handed, but by their suspicions and accusations they committed an offense to this great devotee. As a result, they were attacked by various diseases and distresses, so much so that the service to Lord Jagannātha was affected.

Jagannātha Deva finally appeared to King Mukunda Deva again and told him what had really happened. Being influenced by Śacī Devī's pure devotional attitude, Lord Jagannātha Himself had made the Ganges flow from His feet to bathe Śacī Devī directly in those currents. The King and the other servants of the Lord could only be freed from their offenses if they apologized to Śacī Devī and took initiation from her.

King Mukunda Deva went to Śacī Devī with his entourage, the temple guards and servants. They paid her their prostrated obeisances and begged for her forgiveness. Though the King and all the *pūjārīs*, etc., asked her for initiation, she only gave the *mantra* to the King in obedience to Lord Jagannātha's order. The King wanted to give a large amount of land as *guruda-kṣiṇā*, but Śacī Devī refused it. When the King continued to beg for an opportunity to render service, she finally said that every midday he could send two containers of *prasāda* rice and one of the vegetables, a cloth and 160 *paisa* for the service of the Vaiṣṇavas. From that day onward, Śacī Devī was known as Gaṅgā Mātā and Sārvabhauma Bhaṭṭācārya's house as Gaṅgā Mātā Math, and to this day, after the midday offering at the Jagannātha temple, these same items are sent to the Gaṅgā Mātā Math.

Another of those who were blessed by initiation from Gaṅgāmātā Gosvāminī was a certain smārta *brāhmaṇa* named Mahīrath Śarmā from Dhananjaypur.

RASIKA RĀYA

There was a deity of Kṛṣṇa named Rasika Rāya in the house of Candra Śarmā, a resident of Jaipur in Rajasthan. As a result of *sevāparādha*, offenses in the performance of service to this deity, this *brāhmaṇa* had no descendants to continue the family line. Jagannātha Deva appeared to him in a dream and told him to bring the deity to Puri and to give it to Gaṅgā Mātā if he wished to be rid of the effects of his offenses. The *brāhmaṇa* did as he was told and appeared at Gaṅgā Mātā's door to offer her the service of Rasika Rāya and Rādhārāṇī. At first, she was not ready to accept, as it was impossible for her to give the kind of royal service which was due to such a deity. Finally, the *brāhmaṇa* simply hid the deity amongst the Tulasī bushes and went away. Rasika Rāya appeared to Gaṅgā Mātā in a dream and told her that He wanted her to accept and serve Him. Having been so ordered, Gaṅgā Mātā joyfully accepted the deity service and organized a festival in His honor.

At present, there are five pairs of deities in the Gaṅgā Mātā Math: Śrī Śrī Rādhā Rasika Rāya, Śrī Śrī Rādhā Śyāmasundara, Śrī Śrī Rādhā Madana Mohana, Śrī Śrī Rādhāvinoda and Śrī Śrī Rādhāramaṇa. Other than these, the Dāmodara *śālagrāma-śilā* of Sārvabhauma Bhaṭṭācārya, a dancing figure of Gaurāṅga and a Gopāla deity are also present on the altar there.

According to the information given by the Math, Gaṅgā Mātā was born on the *śukla daśamī* of Jyaiṣṭha in A.D. 1601 and entered the eternal pastimes in A.D. 1721. Branches of her Math are found in Jagannatha Puri at the Haveli Math and Gopāla Math, as well as the Gopāla Math in Tangi village in the Cuttack district.

Devotees of Kṛṣṇa may be born in any race, in any caste, or indeed in either sex. They are to be considered the best of all and worshipable by all. Gaṅgā Mātā Gosvāminī is a perfect example of that. There are many examples of women who attained the supreme achievement of pure devotional service to the Lord, such as the wives of the Vedic *brāhmaṇas* in Dvāparayuga who due to their pure *bhakti* ignored the orders of their husbands to serve Kṛṣṇa. In the Kali Yuga, also, as a result of the blessings of Haridāsa Ṭhākura, a prostitute was transformed into a renowned Vaiṣṇavī, and many great devotees went to seek audience with her in order to receive her saintly association.

Śrīla Viśvanātha Cakravartī Ṭhākura

viśvasya nātha-rūpo 'sau
bhakti-vartma-pradarśanāt
bhakta-cakte vartitatvāt
cakravarty-ākhyayābhavat

"Because he revealed the path of devotion, he is considered to be identical with the Lord of the universe, Viśvanātha; and because he was prominent in the circle of Vaiṣṇavas, he held the title Cakravartī."

VIŚVANĀTHA'S BIRTH AND DISCIPLIC SUCCESSION

Viśvanātha took birth in a family of *rāḍhīya brāhmaṇas* in the village of Devagram in the Nadia district in about 1560 of the Śaka era (1639 A.D.) Some others suggest 1576 (1655 A.D.) as his year of birth. The *Gauḍīya Vaiṣṇava Abhidhāna* identifies his father as Rāma Nārāyaṇa Cakravartī. His mother's name is unknown. He had two older brothers, Rāmabhadra and Raghunātha. His spiritual master was Rādhāramaṇa Cakravartī, a disciple of Kṛṣṇacaraṇa Cakravartī. Kṛṣṇacaraṇa Cakravartī was a disciple and, according to some, adopted son of Gaṅgā Nārāyaṇa Cakravartī. Viśvanātha Cakravartī has summarized his *guru-paramparā* at the beginning of the *Rāsa-pañcādhyāya* section of his *Sārārtha-darśinī* commentary on the *Śrīmad Bhāgavatam.*

śrī-rāma-kṛṣṇa-gaṅgā-caraṇān
natvā gurūn uru-premṇaḥ
śrīla-narottama-nātha-śrīgaurāṅga-
prabhuṁ naumi

In this verse, Rādhāramaṇa Cakravartī's name is abbreviated as Rāma, Kṛṣṇacaraṇa's name as Kṛṣṇa, and Gaṅgā Nārāyaṇa's name as Gaṅgā. The word *nātha* refers to the guru of Narottama Ṭhākura, Lokanātha Gosvāmī, whose guru was Gaurāṅga Mahāprabhu. Thus the entire disciplic succession of Viśvanātha Cakravartī has been given in this one single verse.

VIŚVANĀTHA'S STUDIES AND WRITINGS

After completing his studies of grammar in Devagram, Viśvanātha Cakravartī went to Saiyadabad in the Murshidabad district to study devotional scriptures from his guru. According to the *Gauḍīya Vaiṣṇava Abhidhāna*, he was married. Although he was married according to the rites, he never showed the slightest attachment for family life. It is said that before he left home, he taught his wife the *Bhāgavata*, giving her a taste for its nectar, and instructed her to devote herself to the worship of the Lord.

Śrīla Viśvanātha Cakravartī Ṭhākura followed the example of the Gosvāmīs and went to live in Vrindavan, where he could dedicate himself to the devotional life. As a result of his commitment to following the orders of his spiritual master, he received many blessings from him. These blessings took shape in his good fortune to be able to live in various spots in Vraja *dhāma* and write a great number of books on Gauḍīya Vaiṣṇava subjects, which are considered to be a great treasure by those in the *sampradaya*. All his books and his commentaries on the *Bhagavad Gītā* and *Bhāgavata* are written in a Sanskrit which is clear and simple but at the same time full of the nectar of devotion.

In the Sri Chaitanya Gaudiya Math edition of the *Bhagavad-gītā*, some remarks have been made about Viśvanātha Cakravartī under the heading,"A Description of the Commentary." Those comments have been reproduced here:

"Cakravartī Ṭhākura has an important place in Gauḍīya Vaiṣṇava history as the guardian and chief teacher of the middle period between the life of Mahāprabhu and His associates and the modern period. Amongst Vaiṣṇavas of our day, a saying has been preserved about three of his works: *kiraṇa-bindu-kaṇā, ei tin niye vaiṣṇava-paṇā* – 'Viśvanātha Cakravartīpada's resumes of Rūpa Gosvāmī's *Ujjvala-nīlamaṇi* (*Ujjvala-nīlamaṇi-kiraṇa*), *Bhakti-rasāmṛta-sindhu* (*Bhakti-rasāmṛta-sindhu-bindu*) and *Laghu-bhāgavatāmṛta* (*Bhāgavatāmṛta-kaṇa*) are the source of transcendental joy for the Vaiṣṇavas; studying them makes one a Vaiṣṇava.'

"After the disappearance of Mahāprabhu's Vrindavan associates, Śrīnivāsa Ācārya,

Narottama Ṭhākura and Śyāmānanda Prabhu preserved the pure devotional stream and expanded the movement in Bengal. Viśvanātha Cakravartī Ṭhākura is the fourth descendant of the disciplic line from Narottama Ṭhākura. Few *ācāryas* of the Gauḍīya Vaiṣṇava school have produced such works in Sanskrit as he. Besides producing a large corpus of books, Cakravartī Ṭhākura also made other major contributions related to preaching and *kīrtana*.

"Rūpa Kavirāja, who was excommunicated from Vaiṣṇava society, was the founder of an *apasampradaya*, *atibaḍī*, which taught that only renunciates were eligible to act as *ācārya* and that all householders are disqualified. He preached a distorted doctrine of *rāgānugā bhakti* by completely negating the value of *vidhi-mārga*, and by minimizing the importance of hearing and chanting. To the benefit of the general public, Viśvanātha Cakravartī Ṭhākura has argued against this doctrine in the *Sārārtha-darśinī* commentary on the Third Canto of the *Bhāgavata*. Rūpa Kavirāja holds that no householder can take the Gosvāmī title. Viśvanātha Cakravartī Ṭhākura counters this proposition by stating, on the basis of scripture, that any member of a dynasty of gurus who has the proper qualifications is entitled to be called a Gosvāmī – i.e., he can do the work of a guru or *ācārya*. However, to call one's unworthy children Gosvāmī simply for the purpose of accumulating wealth and disciples is opposed to the scriptural conclusions and is to be considered unlawful, even if the children are born in a family with a tradition of acting gurus.

"Viśvanātha Cakravartī Ṭhākura wrote Bengali songs under the pen name of Harivallabha Dāsa. Some people say that this name was given to him when he took the dress of a renunciate. In all respects, Viśvanātha Cakravartī Ṭhākura is worthy of superlatives, whether in his scholarship, his expertise in philosophical conclusions, his knowledge of the Vaiṣṇava scriptures, or his poetic talent.

"It is said of Viśvanātha Cakravartīpada that at the place where he wrote the *Bhāgavata*, even if it rained the water would not wet the leaves on which he wrote. Thus, the ink did not run, and the text remained intact.

"The following is a list of the books written by Viśvanātha Cakravartī Ṭhākura: (1) *Vraja-rīti-cintāmaṇi*, (2) *Camatkāra-candrikā*, (3) *Prema-samputam*, (4) *Gītāvalī*, (5) *Subodhinī* commentary to *Alaṅkāra-kaustubha*, (6) *Ānanda-candrikā* commentary on *Ujjvala-nīlamaṇi*, (7) a commentary on *Gopāla-tāpanī Upaniṣad*, (8) *Śrī-Kṛṣṇa-bhāvanāmṛta-mahā-kāvyam*, (9) *Śrī-Bhāgavatāmṛta-kaṇa*, (10) *Ujjvala-nīlamaṇi-kiraṇa-leśa*, (11) *Bhakti-rasāmṛta-sindhu-bindu*, (12) *Rāgavartma-candrikā*, (13) *Aiśvarya-kādambinī*, which appears to have been lost, (14) *Mādhurya-kādambinī*, (15) *Bhakti-sāra-pradarśinī*, a commentary on *Bhakti-rasāmṛta-sindhu*, (16) a commentary on the *Dānakeli-kaumudī*, (17) a commentary on the *Lalita-mādhava*, (18) an incomplete commentary on *Caitanya Caritāmṛta*, (19) a commentary on the *Brahma-saṁhitā*, (20) *Sārārtha-varṣiṇī*, a commentary on the *Bhagavad-gītā*, and (21) *Sārārtha-darśinī*, a commentary on the *Śrīmad Bhāgavatam*.

He also wrote a number of small works which have been brought together in the collection known as *Stavāmṛta-laharī*: (1) *Guru-tattvāṣṭakam*, (2) *Mantra-dātṛ-gurorаṣṭakam*, (3) *Parama-guror-aṣṭakam*, (4) *Parātpara-guror-aṣṭakam*, (5) *Parama-parātpara-guror-aṣṭakam*, (6) *Śrī-Lokanāthāṣṭakam*, (7) *Śrī-*Narottamāṣṭaka, (8) *Śrī-Śacīnandanāṣṭakam*, (9) *Śrī-Svarūpa-caritāmṛtam*, (10) *Svapna-vilāsāmṛtam*, (11) *Śrī-Gopāladevāṣṭakam*, (12) *Śrī-Madana-mohanāṣṭakam*, (13) *Śrī-Govindāṣṭakam*, (14) *Śrī-Gopīnāthāṣṭakam*,

(15) *Śrī-Gokulānandāṣṭakam*, (16) *Svayaṁ Bhagavad-aṣṭakam*, (17) *Śrī-Rādhā-kuṇḍāṣṭakam*, (18) *Jaganmohanāṣṭakam*, (19) *Anurāgavallī*, (20) *Śrī-Vṛndādevī-aṣṭakam*, (21) *Śrī-Vṛndāvanāṣṭakam*, (22) *Śrī-Rādhikā-dhyānāmṛtam*, (23) *Śrī-Rūpa-cintāmaṇi*, (24) *Śrī-Nandīśvarāṣṭakam*, (25) *Śrī-Govardhanāṣṭakam*, (26) *Śrī-Saṅkalpa-kalpa-druma*, (27) *Śrī-Nikuñja-virudāvalī*, (28) *Śrī-Surata-kathāmṛtam*, and (29) *Śrī-Śyāmakuṇḍāṣṭakam*."

VIŚVANĀTHA'S STUDENT BALADEVA

When Viśvanātha Cakravartī Ṭhākura was old and hampered in his ability to travel, the ācaryas of the Rāmānuja *sampradāya* in the Galta village of Jaipur attempted to convert the King of Jaipur to their school by accusing that the Gauḍīyas did not have a tie to any one of the four Vaiṣṇava disciplic successions. They advised the King of Jaipur to take initiation from someone in the Rāmānuja line. The King was confused by their arguments and asked Viśvanātha Cakravartī Ṭhākura, who was the most prominent *ācārya* of the Gauḍīya school at that time, to come to Jaipur and answer the questions posed by the Rāmānuja group. Due to his advanced age, Viśvanātha Cakravartī Ṭhākura was unable to go, but in his stead he sent his student of *Bhāgavata*, Baladeva Vidyābhūṣaṇa, to defend the line.

Kṛṣṇa Deva, a disciple of Viśvanātha Cakravartī Ṭhākura, accompanied Baladeva Vidyābhūṣaṇa. One of the arguments of the Rāmānujīs was that the Gauḍīya school had no commentary of its own on the Vedānta and hence could not be accepted as an authentic lineage. Baladeva Vidyābhūṣaṇa Prabhu asked the accusers for some time – seven days according to some, three months according to others – to write a Gauḍīya commentary on Vedānta. He was given the time, and then he went to the Govinda temple and prayed to his guru and to the Lord to give him the power to write such a commentary. Govindajī's garland fell from around His neck, and the *pūjārīs* placed it on Baladeva Vidyābhūṣaṇa Prabhu's chest.

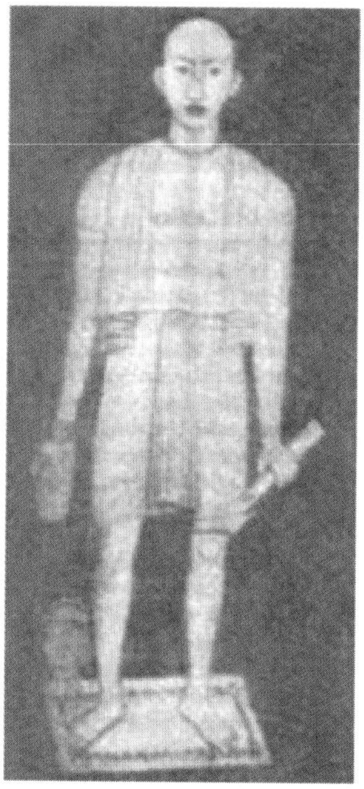

With the guru's, Vaiṣṇava's and Lord's blessings, even the impossible becomes possible. Baladeva Vidyābhūṣaṇa Prabhu undertook the writing of comments on the five hundred *sūtras* of the *Brahma-sūtra* with the subtle aspects of the divine aesthetics revealed in the pure devotional line of Gauḍīya Vaiṣṇava thought, completing it in the limited time given him. When he went to Galta, the scholars of the other *sampradāyas* were astonished to hear his commentary, which has the highest divine sentiment. Because Govindajī Himself had ordered its writing, the commentary became known as the *Govinda-bhāṣya*. It was after completing this commentary that Baladeva received the Vidyābhūṣaṇa title.

Viśvanātha Cakravartī Ṭhākura established the service of Gokulānanda that still stands in the Gokulānandajī temple in Vrindavan. He left this world in Radha Kunda in around 1630 of the Śaka era (1709 A.D.) The *tithi* was either the *śuklā* or *kṛṣṇa pañcamī* of the month of Māgha.

Śrīla Baladeva Vidyābhūṣaṇa

The exact time and place of Śrī Baladeva Vidyābhūṣaṇa Prabhu's birth are unknown. Perhaps one day historians will be able to establish these facts beyond any doubt. From the little information that we do have about his life, we can conjecture that he was born in the eighteenth century of the modern era. Though we do not know the name of the exact village where he took birth, it was likely in the Balasore district of Odisha, somewhere near Remuna. From the date given in his commentary on Rūpa Gosvāmī's *Stavamālā*, namely *Stavamālā-vibhūṣaṇa*, it is clear that Baladeva Vidyābhūṣaṇa Prabhu was still living after the Battle of Plassey in 1757.

We know that Baladeva Vidyābhūṣaṇa Prabhu studied in Vardhisnu village on the banks of Chilka Lake, where the scholars used to live. There he learned grammar, poetics and logic, achieving expertise in all these subjects. He began his studies of the Vedas there, but in order to study various commentaries on Vedānta in greater depth, he went to Mysore. He was there particularly impressed by the logical consistency of Madhvācārya's *śuddha-dvaita* commentary on the Vedānta *sūtras* and became a disciple of that school and began living in a Tattvavādī monastery. After taking *sannyāsa*, he moved to Purusottama Kshetra, where he defeated many of the local scholars in debate, demonstrating the depth of his scholarship. His fame soon spread everywhere.

Later, however, he met Rādhā Dāmodara Gosvāmī, a scholar from Kanauj under whose direction he studied Jīva Gosvāmī's *Ṣaṭ-sandarbha* in great detail. When he was convinced of the supremacy of the Gauḍīya Vaiṣṇava philosophy, he took initiation from Rādhā Dāmodara Gosvāmī. He was thus initiated in Nityānanda Prabhu's line. The following is his disciplic succession: (1) Gaurī Dāsa Paṇḍita, (2) Hṛdaya Caitanya Prabhu, (3) Śyāmānanda Prabhu, (4) Rasikānanda Deva Gosvāmī, (5) Nayanānanda Gosvāmī, (6) Rādhā Dāmodara Gosvāmī, (7) Baladeva Vidyābhūṣaṇa.

Baladeva Vidyābhūṣaṇa Prabhu then continued his studies of the Gauḍīya literature under Pītāmvara Dāsa and later studied the *Bhāgavata Purāṇa* under Viśvanātha Cakravartī Ṭhākura. He also took the Vaiṣṇava *vairāgi's* dress, at which time he was given the name Ekāntī Govinda Dāsa.

BALADEVA'S LITERARY WORKS

He was ordered by Viśvanātha Cakravartī Ṭhākura to go to Jaipur, where he prayed to Rūpa Gosvāmī's Govindajī deity for the authorization to write a commentary on the Vedānta-sūtra. He then composed the *Govinda-bhāṣya* and took it to Galta, where he defeated the other *sampradāyas* in a debate, preserving the reputation of the Gauḍīya school. After this episode, he was given the title Vidyābhūṣaṇa. This story has been told in greater detail in the previous chapter on Viśvanātha Cakravartī Ṭhākura.

It is said that Baladeva established the worship of the Vijaya Gopāla deity in Galta. His two most prominent disciples were Uddhava Dāsa and Śrī Nanda Miśra.

The following is a list of Baladeva Vidyābhūṣaṇa Prabhu's written works:

(1) A commentary on the *Brahma Sūtras*, *Govinda-bhāṣya*, (2) *Siddhānta-ratna*, (3) *Vedānta-syamantaka*, (4) *Prameya-ratnāvalī*, (5) *Siddhānta-darpaṇa*, (6) *Sāhitya-kaumudī*, (7) *Kāvya-kaustubha*, (8) *Vyākaraṇa-kaumudī*, (which appears to have been lost) (9) *Pada-kaustubha*, (10) *Vaiṣṇavānandinī*, a commentary on the Tenth Canto, (11) a commentary on *Gopāla-tāpanī Upaniṣad*, (12) commentaries on the *Īśa* and nine other *Upaniṣads*, (13) *Gītā-bhūṣaṇa-bhāṣya*, a commentary on *Bhagavad-gita*, (14) *Nāmārtha-sudhā*, a commentary on the Viṣṇu-*sahasra-nāma*, (15) *Sāraṅga-raṅgadā*, a commentary on the *Laghu-bhāgavatāmṛta*, (16) A commentary on *Tattva-sandarbha*, (17) *Stavamālā-vibhūṣaṇa*, a commentary on *Stavamālā*, (18) a commentary on Rūpa Gosvāmī's *Nāṭakā-candrikā* (which appears to have been lost,) (19) a commentary on *Chandaḥ-kaustubha*, (20) a commentary on Rasikānanda's *Śyāmānanda-śataka*, (21) a commentary on *Candrāloka* (which appears to have been lost,) (22) *Kṛṣṇānandinī*, a commentary on *Sāhitya-kaumudī*, (23) *Govinda-bhāṣya-ṭīkā*, a commentary on his own *Govinda-bhāṣya, and* (24) a commentary on *Siddhānta-ratna*

Other than these, it is claimed that Baladeva Vidyābhūṣaṇa Prabhu also wrote an *Aiśvarya-kādambinī* which is different from that written by Viśvanātha Cakravartī Ṭhākura. In the *Aiśvarya-kādambinī* by Viśvanātha Cakravartī Ṭhākura, there is a discussion of the *dvaita* and *advaita* doctrines, which is missing from Baladeva Vidyābhūṣaṇa Prabhu's work of that name.

In the succession of bona fide gurus who make up the Mādhva-Gauḍīya-Sārasvata *sampradāya*, Baladeva Vidyābhūṣaṇa Prabhu is to be remembered regularly. Simply demonstrating a connection through initiation to a family succession of initiating spiritual masters does not make one a bona fide guru. One must demonstrate complete dedication to the supreme truth, *brahma-niṣṭhā*. Only a pure devotee can be called a bona fide guru. Therefore Bhakti Siddhānta Sarasvatī Ṭhākura Prabhupāda wrote, "I pay obeisances to Viśvanātha and all his disciples, like Baladeva, Baladeva's disciple Jagannātha Dāsa Bābājī and his dearmost follower Bhaktivinoda Ṭhākura."

Śrī Jagannātha Dāsa Bābājī Mahārāja

gaurāvirbhāva-bhūmestvaṁ
nirdeṣṭā sajjana-priyaḥ
vaiṣṇava-sārvabhauma
śrī-jagannāthāya te namaḥ

"I offer my obeisances to Śrī Jagannātha Dāsa Bābājī Mahārāja, who was adored by the Vaiṣṇava community as a perfect realized one, who is dear to all the Vaiṣṇavas, and who is the foremost Vaiṣṇava, Vaiṣṇava Sārvabhauma. Through your divine vision, you designated the place where Mahāprabhu appeared in this world."

JAGANNĀTHA DĀSA' POSITION IN THE DISCIPLIC SUCCESSION

Throughout the world, any devotee who comes in the disciplic succession following Śrīla Bhakti Siddhānta Sarasvatī Gosvāmī Ṭhākura daily remembers Śrī Jagannātha Dāsa Bābājī Mahārāja and prays for his mercy.

viśvanātha bhakta sātha, baladeva jagannātha
tāṅra priya śrī bhaktivinoda
mahā-bhāgavata vara, śrī-gaura-kiśora-vara
hari-bhajanete yāṅra moda
śrī-varṣabhānavī-varā, sadā sevya-sevā-parā
tāṅra dayita-dāsa nāma

"[I offer respects to] Viśvanātha Cakravartī Ṭhākura along with his devotees, to Baladeva Vidyābhūṣaṇa and to Jagannātha Dāsa Bābājī Mahārāja, whose dear disciple is Bhaktivinoda Ṭhākura, and to Śrī Gaura Kiśora Dāsa Bābājī Mahārāja, the great devotee, whose great pleasure is the worship of the Lord. Rādhārāṇī is the daughter of Vṛṣabhānu and is always fixed in service to her Lord. I am the servant of him who is dear to her."

There is also a Sanskrit version of the disciplic succession, where Jagannātha Dāsa Bābājī Mahārāja is mentioned in the following way:

vaiṣṇava-sārvabhaumaḥ śrī-
jagannātha-prabhus tathā
śrī-māyāpura-dhāmnas tu
nirdeṣṭā sajjana-priyaḥ

"Next in the line is Jagannātha Prabhu, known as Vaiṣṇava Sārvabhauma. Very dear to the saintly, he designated the Sri Mayapur *dhāma*."

There were four dark ages in the history of Gauḍīya Vaiṣṇava lineage: (1) preceding the appearance of Caitanya Mahāprabhu; (2) following the disappearance of the six Gosvāmīs; (3) after the disappearance of Śrīnivāsa Ācārya, Narottama Dāsa Ṭhākura, Śyāmānanda Prabhu, and Rasikānanda Deva Gosvāmī; and (4) following the disappearance of Viśvanātha Cakravartī Ṭhākura and Baladeva Vidyābhūṣaṇa Prabhu.

One should not think that the Mādhva-Gauḍīya disciplic succession following in the spirit of Rūpa Gosvāmī has been disrupted on account of these periods of darkness. Sometimes spiritual masters in the disciplic succession are individual performers of solitary *bhajana* (*viviktānandī*), and sometimes preachers who delight in increasing the size of the congregation (*goṣṭhyānandī*). To the untrained eye, it seems that one can measure the strength of an *ācārya* by the number of disciples he makes, but this is not an appropriate criterion for judgement.

Baladeva Vidyābhūṣaṇa Prabhu's disciple was Uddhava Dāsa, or Uddharan Dāsa. This Vaiṣṇava had a disciple also named Uddhava Dāsa, who gave the renounced order to Madhusūdana Dāsa. This Madhusūdana Dāsa Bābājī was famed throughout the Vaiṣṇava world as the Siddha Madhusūdana Dāsa Bābājī from Surya Kunda. Madhusūdana Dāsa Bābājī gave the *paramahaṁsa-veṣa* (*bābājī* initiation) to Jagannātha Dāsa Bābājī. Śrīla Bhakti Siddhānta Sarasvatī Gosvāmī Ṭhākura wrote: "All of these Vaiṣṇavas adopted the lifestyle of the *paramahaṁsa*, preaching the path of pure devotion by their example. They are thus the objects of the greatest faith and reverence in the Gauḍīya Vaiṣṇava *samprādaya*."

From this statement of Śrīla Prabhupāda, we learn that all these *bhajanānandīs* not only practiced the anchorite life of solitary worship but engaged in preaching activities as well, serving as *ācāryas*.

BĀBĀJĪ MAHĀRĀJA'S LIFE IN VRINDAVAN

Bābājī Mahārāja was born in a respectable family in the Tangail district in what is today Bangladesh, in around 1780 A.D. According to some people he was born into a family of Vārendra Kāyasthas in Taras village in the Pabna district. The names of his parents are unknown.

After taking the *pāramahaṁsya-veṣa,* Jagannātha Dāsa Bābājī set the exemplary standard of intense *bhajana* in Nabadwip and Vrindavan, so much so that he was accepted by all the *bhajanānandī* Vaiṣṇavas as their leader. He remained in this world for more than a century.

Bābājī Mahārāja performed loving service to Śrī Rādhā Kṛṣṇa during eight periods in a day, following the path of Rūpānuga devotees, while staying in Radha Kunda. On one occasion when he was engaged in *bhajana* in Vraja with other *bhajanānandī* Vaiṣṇavas, a certain professional speaker on the *Bhāgavata* from Katwa decided to move to Vrindavan to make his living, looking for gold and glory. Even though he gave an excellent discourse on the *Bhāgavata,* the renounced Vaiṣṇavas showed no enthusiasm for them. When he inquired into the reasons for this, Bābājī Mahārāja and the other Vaiṣṇavas told him any discourse on the *Bhāgavata* by someone who has other goals in mind cannot be called a true explanation of the *Bhāgavata.* His words can have no beneficial effect on anyone, not even himself. Indeed, such discourses have a negative effect on the consciousness of the listener. The Vaiṣṇavas led by Bābājī Mahārāja thus advised the professional speaker to give up the business of giving *Bhāgavata* discourses as a means of making his living. By their grace, this money-minded Vaiṣṇava was completely transformed, and he gave up his false pride in his learning and high birth. He became a great devotee with such humility that he paid prostrated obeisances to every creature living in the holy dhāma.

Bābājī Mahārāja was himself a dedicated and intense *bhajanānandī,* but he did not believe that disciples who were unqualified and filled with material desires should be allowed to act in ways detrimental to service to Viṣṇu and the Vaiṣṇavas on the pretext of engaging in the service of the Holy Name. He engaged his less qualified disciples who had taken the renounced order in working in the garden next to his cottage so that he could offer vegetables to the deity and the Vaiṣṇavas. If the senses are not engaged in the service of Viṣṇu and the Vaiṣṇavas, one does not develop the qualifications necessary to chant properly and it is impossible to experience the power of the Holy Name. When an individual engages the senses and sense objects in relation to the body and bodily relations, then attachment for these naturally arises. When we are fixed in the consciousness that our very self, including our body and senses, belong to the Lord, and we engage our senses in the service of the Lord and His devotees, then our feelings of love and possessiveness for Him increase.

BĀBĀJĪ MAHĀRĀJA MEETS BHAKTIVINODA ṬHĀKURA

Bhaktivinoda Ṭhākura met Jagannātha Dāsa Bābājī Mahārāja for the first time in 1880 A.D. Their second meeting took place in the village of Amlajora in Burdwan district in 1891. On this occasion, they spent the entire night (Ekādaśī day) discussing the topics of Gaura Kṛṣṇa. Jagannātha Dāsa Bābājī Mahārāja encouraged Bhaktivinoda Ṭhākura to preach Gaura's name and abode.

Ṭhākura Bhaktivinoda gave an account of this eventful night in his *Sajjana-toṣaṇī* magazine: "After spending the whole night in the Ekādaśī vigil, people from the entire village gathered together at 8 AM to go on the *nagara saṅkīrtana* through its streets. Placing the venerable Jagannātha Dāsa Bābājī Mahārāja at the head of the group, they made their way to the Prapannāśrama. It is impossible to describe Bābājī Mahārāja's ecstatic transformations during this *kīrtana*. Though he is over a hundred years old, he dances like a lion, sometimes singing out the couplet,

nitāi ki nāma eneche re nāma eneche nāmer hāṭe,
śraddhā mūle nāma diteche re

" 'What divine name is this that Nitāi has brought? He has brought the name to the marketplace and is distributing it for the price of faith!'

"As Bābājī Mahārāja sang, he cried and fell to the ground in ecstasy. I then saw something transpire which I had never seen before. All present were affected by his mood: their eyes filled with tears and their hairs stood on end, and even though they could barely sing, they remained absorbed in the *kīrtana* and danced wildly."

Śrīla Bhaktivinoda Ṭhākura has also written about Jagannātha Dāsa Bābājī Mahārāja in his autobiography: "In 1892, Jagannātha Dāsa Bābājī Mahārāja and many other Vaiṣṇavas participated in the *saṅkīrtana* festival in Godruma and then in Sri Mayapur. In the month of Māgha in 1299 (Bengali), Bābājī Mahārāja came from Kuliya-Nabadwip with his associates to my residence, Surabhi Kunja, in Godrumdwip. A great *saṅkīrtana* festival was held there on Wednesday, the 27th of Māgha."

BĀBĀJĪ MAHĀRĀJA DESIGNATES MAHĀPRABHU'S BIRTH SITE

A physically powerful Vrajavasi named Bihārīdāsa Bābājī was Jagannātha Dāsa Bābājī Mahārāja's personal servant. He used to place Bābājī Mahārāja in a large wicker basket and carry him from place to place. Even though Bābājī Mahārāja was very aged, his sight was still good. His eyelids drooped, however, covering his eyes, and he had to lift them in order to see. It is said that when Bihārīdāsa Bābājī carried Bābājī Mahārāja in the wicker basket to the birthplace of Caitanya Mahāprabhu, Bābājī Mahārāja got out of the basket and began to dance madly, singing the names *Jaya Śacīnandana Gaura-Hari*. Everyone was amazed to see the old *bābājī* dance in this way. Through his divine vision, Bābājī Mahārāja pointed out the site of Mahāprabhu's birth and then later Khola-bhāṅgāra Dāṅgā, the site where the Kājī broke a *mṛdaṅga*, that is, Śrīvāsa Aṅgana.

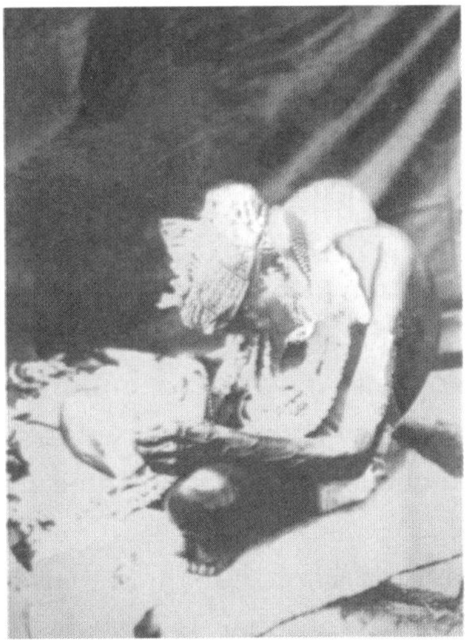

Śrīla Bhaktivinoda Ṭhākura has described these events in *Sajjana-toṣaṇī*, 4th Khaṇḍa, pg. 234-5, as follows: "At eleven o'clock in the morning on Thursday, the 20th of Phālguna in 1299 of the Bengali era (1892 A.D.), devotees filled three boats on the west bank of the Ganges in Nabadwip town. Mahendra Bābu, a well-known devotee, brought them from the western bank. The great devotee Jagannātha Dāsa Bābājī Mahārāja was carried in a palanquin. By the time the party reached Mayapur it was impossible to count the number of people who had gathered. Śrī Dvārika Bābu and a party of devotees carrying colorful flags were waiting for the renounced Vaiṣṇavas with a joyous *kīrtana* at Mahāprabhu's birthplace. When all these devotees had gathered in the raised area where Mahāprabhu was born and started to dance, it was such a wondrous sight as had likely not been seen in Nabadwip *dhāma* for nearly four hundred years. Later the devotees sat down and, after discussing the matter, decided that deity service should be established both at the birthplace and at Śrīvāsa Aṅgana. Jagannātha Dāsa Bābājī Mahāśaya proposed that Jagannātha Miśra and Śacī Devī should be worshipped in one building and Mahāprabhu with Lakṣmī Devī and Viṣṇupriyā standing on His either side in another. On the other hand, deities of the Pañca Tattva should be consecrated in Śrīvāsa Aṅgana."

In those days, there was a large *kadamba* tree at the birth site in Mayapur. Bābājī Mahārāja came and danced under this tree. Śrī Gaura Kiśora Dāsa Bābājī used to sit under that tree, chanting the Holy Name in a deep trance.

Jagannātha Dāsa Bābājī Mahārāja spent many years in a cottage in Koladwip named Bhajana Kutira. This is where Bābājī Mahārāja's *samādhi* is now situated. Śrīla Bhaktivinoda Ṭhākura had a concrete veranda built for this cottage.

BĀBĀJĪ MAHĀRĀJA IN KOLKATA

Bābājī Mahārāja also came to visit Śrīla Bhaktivinoda Ṭhākura in his house, Bhakti Bhavana, in Ram Bagan in Kolkata. There he also met Śrīla Bhakti Siddhānta Sarasvatī Gosvāmī Ṭhākura, upon whom he showered unlimited affection. When he learned that Sarasvatī Ṭhākura was an expert in astrology, he asked him to publish an almanac based on the Vaiṣṇava *siddhānta*. Later, Srila Prabhupāda published *Nabadvīpa-Pañjikā* from the Chaitanya Math.

Though Bābājī Mahārāja would not allow anyone to take his photograph, Śrīla Bhaktivinoda Ṭhākura was able to arrange to have one taken when he came to visit Bhakti Bhavana. It shows Bābājī Mahārāja sitting on a wooden seat with his worshipable Giridhārī deity on his chest. If Śrīla Bhaktivinoda Ṭhākura had not done this, we would be eternally deprived of knowing what Jagannātha Dāsa Bābājī looked like.

Bābājī Mahārāja deeply loved Bhaktivinoda Ṭhākura. We have heard that he later gave his Giridhārī to Bhaktivinoda and that this deity is still being served in Bhakti Bhavana.

BĀBĀJĪ MAHĀRĀJA'S DISAPPEARANCE

When approaching the end of his sojourn in this world, Bābājī Mahārāja became hunched and tiny looking. Nevertheless, when he danced in *kīrtana* in a divine intoxicated state, he appeared to his full height of six feet. When absorbed in the ecstatic mood of *kīrtana*, he would sometimes jump five or six feet into the air. With his tall figure and long arms, he made people think of Mahāprabhu.

Jagannātha Dāsa Bābājī Mahārāja's disappearance took place on the *śukla pratipad* of the month of Phālguna, Monday, February 25, 1895. Śrīla Bhaktivinoda Ṭhākura wrote of it in *Sajjana-toṣaṇī* (Year:2, page:2): "At ten o'clock in the morning of the 14th of Phālguna in 1301 of the Bengali era, in the Bhajana kutira in Koladwip in Nabadwip town, the old general of the Vaiṣṇavas went to his eternal abode. Siddha Bābājī Mahāśaya went to the spiritual world, leaving this world in darkness. Our mundane eyes will no longer be able to see his ecstatic dancing in *kīrtana*. May he bestow his blessings on us from his place in the eternal abode."

Rāsavihārī Gosvāmī of Puruniya in the Burdwan district was Jagannātha Dāsa Bābājī Mahārāja's initiated disciple. Rāsavihārī Gosvāmī initiated the independent King of Tripura, Rāja Īśāna Candra Maṇikya Bāhādura. Rasavishari Gosvāmī's deity, Rāsavīharī Jīu, is worshipped to this day in the Rāja's palace.

ŚRĪ-ŚRĪLA-JAGANNĀTHĀṢṬAKAM

rūpānugānāṁ pravaraṁ sudāntaṁ
śrī-gauracandra-priya-bhakta-rājam
śrī-rādhikā-mādhava-citta-rāmaṁ
vande jagannātha-vibhuṁ vareṇyam

"I venerate Jagannātha Prabhu, the best of the Vaiṣṇavas, the foremost of the followers of Śrīla Rūpa Gosvāmī, the King of Lord Gauraṇgacandra's dear devotees, who takes pleasure in remembering Rādhikā and Mādhava.

śrī-sūrya-kuṇḍāśrayiṇaḥ kṛpālor
vidvad-vara-śrī-madhusūdanasya
preṣṭha-svarūpeṇa virājamāṇaṁ
vande jagannātha-vibhuṁ vareṇyam

"I venerate Jagannātha Prabhu, the best of the Vaiṣṇavas, who was the dearest associate of Śrī Madhusūdana Dāsa Bābājī, the most merciful resident of Surya Kunda.

śrīdhāma-vṛndāvana-vāsi-bhakta-
nakṣatra-rāji-sthita-soma-tulyam
ekānta-nāmāśrita-saṅgha-pālaṁ
vande jagannātha-vibhuṁ vareṇyam

"I venerate Jagannātha Prabhu, the best of the Vaiṣṇavas, who stood out from the rest of the devotees of Śrī Dhāma Vrindavan just like the moon amongst the stars. He was the protector of the assembly of Vaiṣṇavas who are uniquely dedicated to the chanting of the Holy Name.

vairāgya-vidyā-hari-bhakti-dīptaṁ
daurjanya-kāpaṭya-vibheda-vajram
śraddhā-yuteṣv ādara-vṛttimantaṁ
vande jagannātha-vibhuṁ vareṇyam

"I venerate Jagannātha Prabhu, the best of the Vaiṣṇavas, aglow with devotion to Hari, endowed with knowledge and renunciation, a veritable thunderbolt to those who are wicked and pretenders and ever affectionate to the faithful.

saṁ prerito gaura-sudhāṁśunā yaś
cakre hi taj-janma-gṛha-prakāśam
devair nutaṁ vaiṣṇava-sārvabhaumaṁ
vande jagannātha-vibhuṁ vareṇyam

"I venerate Jagannātha Prabhu, the best of the Vaiṣṇavas, who was directed by Gaurāṅga Himself to point out the place where He appeared on this earth. He is worshipped by even the gods as the sovereign of the Vaiṣṇavas on this earth.

sañcārya sarvaṁ nija-śakti-rāśiṁ
yo bhakti-pūrṇe ca vinoda-deve
tene jagatyāṁ hari-nāma-vanyāṁ
vande jagannātha-vibhuṁ vareṇyam

"I venerate Jagannātha Prabhu, the best of the Vaiṣṇavas, who infused the devoted Bhaktivinoda Ṭhākura with all of his own potency, and through him unleashed the flood of *harināma* throughout the universe.

śrī-nāma-dhāmnoḥ prabala-pracāre
ihāparaṁ prema-rasābdhi-magnam
śrī-yoga-pīṭhe kṛta-nṛtya-bhaṅgaṁ
vande jagannātha-vibhuṁ vareṇyam

"I venerate great Jagannātha Prabhu, the best of the Vaiṣṇavas, always immersed in the ocean of sacred rapture and engaged in forcefully preaching the Holy Names and the Lord's abode. He danced ecstatically in the Yogapīṭha at Mayapur.

māyāpure-dhāmani sakta-cittaṁ
gaura-prakāśena ca moda-yuktam
śrī-nāma-gānair galad-aśru-netraṁ
vande jagannātha-vibhuṁ vareṇyam

"I venerate Jagannātha Prabhu, the best of the Vaiṣṇavas, who is totally attached to the holy *dhāma* of Mayapur, who is joyful from the vision of Gaurāṅga, and whose eyes flow with tears from the chanting of the Holy Names.

he deva he vaiṣṇava-sārvabhauma
bhaktyā parābhūta-mahendra-dhiṣṇya
tvadegātra-vistāra-kṛtiṁ supuṇyāṁ
vande muhur bhaktivinode-dhārām

"O lord! O sovereign of the Vaiṣṇavas! Through your devotion, you have overcome even the rulers of demigods. I constantly venerate the most pious line of Bhaktivinoda Ṭhākura that has grown out from your body and works."

JAGANNĀTHA DĀSA AND THE BĀBĀJĪ COMMUNITY

The book *Śrī-Sarasvati-Jayaśrī*, published by the Bagh Bazar Gaudiya Math in 1934, gives an account of the transcendental life and instructions of Vaiṣṇava Sārvabhauma Jagannātha Dāsa Bābājī Mahārāja. Most Revered Srila Bhakti Pramode Purī Gosvāmī Mahārāja, the chairman of the editorial board of *Caitanya-vāṇī* magazine, wrote an article that included some portions of the book as well as about the *svapna-samādhi* of Śrīla Prabhupāda. It is presented below for the benefit of a sincere reader.

"On Sept. 28, 1922, after the Kolkata Gaudiya Math's annual festival, Śrīla Prabhupāda traveled to Vrindavan, where he arrived on Saturday, Sept. 30. That was the appearance day of Śrī Madhvācārya and Vijaya-daśamī. Through the efforts of Dr. Bala Haridāsa, he and his disciples stayed at the Ghoṣa family residence opposite the Lāla Bābu temple. On Oct. 3, Śrīla Prabupāda went for *darśana* of Rūpa Gosvāmī's beloved deities, Rādhā and Govinda. He and his disciples went to look at a few places, seeking a site to establish a Math in Vrindavan.

"On hearing of Prabhupāda's arrival, Paṇḍit Madhusūdana Gosvāmī Sārvabhauma of the Gopāla Bhaṭṭa Gosvāmī's family lineage came to visit him from Rādhā Rāmaṇa Gherā. They discussed scriptural matters for about two hours, and Prabhupāda presented him with the latest copy and a few back issues of *Gauḍīya* magazine. Madhusūdana Gosvāmī was very pleased with the high caliber of discussion found in *Gauḍīya* and stated that one day it would be the guiding publication for all Gauḍīya Vaiṣṇavas.

On Oct. 4, Śrīla Prabhupāda visited Madana Mohana, the beloved deity of Sanātana Gosvāmī. On his way back, he visited the famous Paṇḍita Rāmakṛṣṇa Dāsa Bābājī in Madana Mohana Ṭhora, near the walled garden of the Rādhā Vallabha temple. In the discussion that followed, Paṇḍita Bābājī claimed that the chanting of the Holy Name is on the same level as any other devotional activity and that all the various songs, even those that contradict the Gosvāmīs' teachings, are equivalent to the *nāma-saṇkīrtana*. He also stated that unless one was educated in the study of logic, or *nyāya*, one could not be qualified for the study of Vedānta. He also argued that it was unnecessary to discuss mundane and spiritual matters.

"Śrīla Prabhupāda replied in accordance with the teachings of the Gosvāmīs, as furthered by Viśvanātha Cakravartī Ṭhākura, Baladeva Vidyābhūṣaṇa Prabhu, Jagannātha Dāsa Bābājī Mahārāja and Gaura Kiśora Dāsa Bābājī Mahārāja. He said, 'The Gosvāmīs have taught, following the order of Mahāprabhu, that the chanting of the Holy Names is the primary devotional practice as well as being the goal of all such practice. Divine remembrance of the Lord and His pastimes comes naturally to one who is engaged in such chanting. Discussions of transcendental topics characterized both Mahāprabhu and His followers, the Gosvāmīs. If one does not have an acute sense of discrimination between the spiritual and mundane, then one equates the debauchery of the *sahajiyās* with devotional activity. This is the royal road to self- and mass deception.' "

"Siddha Jagannātha Dāsa Bābājī's teachings were in line with those of Rūpa Gosvāmī: he would in no way embrace any snappy jingles that made a confusion of the divine sentiments. Offenses to the Holy Name can in no way be equated with the pure name. The scriptures talk about the positive effects of chanting either with faith or without it, but this is not at all the same as chanting without giving up the ten offenses. It is self-deception to think that you can allow yourself to commit any one of the ten offenses, knowingly or unknowingly, and still chant the Holy Names effectively." (*Sarasvatī-jaya-śrī, Vaibhava Parba*, 1st Khāṇḍa, 27th Vaibhava)

Vaiṣṇava Sārvabhauma Srila Jagannātha Dāsa Bābājī Mahārāj was particularly inclined to chant the *mahā-mantra*, comprising of thirty-two syllables and sixteen names, as propagated by Mahāprabhu Himself. Other than this, he did not give leniency to chant any composition by the modern and imaginative faculty that is contradictory to pure devotional conclusions and is defected with an improper mixture of devotional sentiments. Such chanting is nothing but *nāma-aparādha*.

THE VIŚVA VAIṢṆAVA RĀJA SABHĀ

According to *Sarasvatī-jaya-śrī*, 6th Vaibhava, page 41, it was Jagannātha Dāsa Bābājī Mahārāja who identified the *śukla pañcamī* of the month of Māgha as the appearance day of Viṣṇupriyā Devī, the potency of Śrī Caitanya Mahāprabhu. He told this to Bhaktivinoda Ṭhākura, and from him the custom was established throughout the Vaiṣṇava world so that everyone honors Viṣṇupriyā Devī on this day.

Śrīla Bhakti Siddhānta Sarasvatī Gosvāmī Ṭhākura chose Viṣṇupriyā Devī's appearance day to reinstate the Viśva Vaiṣṇava Rāja Sabhā, or World Vaiṣṇava Association. This was done in the midst of a *kīrtana* on Feb. 5, 1919 at the Ultadanga Math, also known as the Bhaktivinoda Āsana. The following article appeared in *Amrita Bazar Patrika*, a Kolkata English-language daily, on the 10th of February:

"On Wednesday last (5th instant) was celebrated with great eclat the Advent Ceremony of Śrī Śrī Viṣṇupriyā Devī at the same Āsana (7 Ultadanga Junction Road). The occasion was solemnised by the reinstitution of Śrī Viśva Vaiṣṇava Rāja Sabhā as inaugurated by no less a Personage than Śrīla Jīva Gosvāmī himself eleven years after the passing of Śrī Śrī Mahāprabhu and as given fresh impetus by Śrī Bhaktivinoda Ṭhākura 33 years ago."

Śrīla Prabhupāda gave an explanation of the history of the Viśva Vaiṣṇava Rāja Sabhā, which was published in *Sajjana-toṣaṇī,* vol. 21, no. 9.

ŚRĪLA PRABHUPĀDA'S SVAPNA-SAMĀDHI

After the disappearance of Śrīla Bhaktivinoda Ṭhākura and Śrīla Gaura Kiśora Dāsa Bābājī Mahārāja, the grief-stricken Śrīla Prabhupāda stayed in Mayapur in the place called Vraja-pattana (now a part of the Caitanya Math grounds). He wondered, "How can I fulfill the desires of my gurus by preaching the pure doctrine of Śrī Caitanya Mahāprabhu throughout the world. I have no followers to help me and no money to speak of. I have no great learning by which I can enchant the mundane. I have no assets of any kind which qualify me to perform this herculean task. It seems that I will not be able to fulfill the desires of my gurus."

Śrīla Prabhupāda exhibited the pastimes of entering into a state of deep depression, thinking that it would be impossible for him to continue the preaching mission. His work on writing a commentary on Rūpa Gosvāmī's *Upadeśāmṛta* also came to a halt after only eight verses.

One night, however, Prabhupāda had a *svapna-samādhi* (a transcendental divine vision while dreaming) in which he saw all the members of the Pañca Tattva, being led by Mahāprabhu in *saṅkīrtana,* dancing and approaching toward the birthplace at the Yogapīṭha in Mayapur, from the eastern side of its *naṭya-mandira.* They were followed by the six Gosvāmīs and by Vaiṣṇava Sārvabhauma Jagannātha Dāsa Bābājī, Bhaktivinoda Ṭhākura, Gaura Kiśora Dāsa Bābājī Mahārāja and other *guru-varga* members of the disciplic succession, all appearing in effulgent, divine forms. They consoled Prabhupāda, saying, "Why are you worrying? Get the task of preaching pure devotion underway. Preach Mahāprabhu's message everywhere: spread service to *Gaura-dhāma* (Mahāprabhu's abode), *Gaura-nāma* (His name), and *Gaura-kāma* (His desire or work). All of us are at the ready to support you at every turn. We will help you at every moment in your efforts to preach pure devotional service. Countless people, unlimited wealth and extraordinary scholarship are all waiting for you to call for them. Whenever you need anything at all, it will come to you to be engaged in the service of the preaching mission. Simply go forward to preach the message of love of God as given by Caitanya Mahāprabhu, giving it your total effort. No worldly force will be able to disrupt this effort. We are with you always."

The following morning, Śrīla Prabhupāda joyfully told Paramānanda Prabhu and some other faithful followers about his dream. From that day onward, he displayed an unbounded enthusiasm for the worldwide preaching of Mahāprabhu's message. He completed his *Anuvṛtti* of the *Upadeśāmṛta.* These efforts have borne fruit in as much as those seeking service to the divine throughout India have been washed up in the flood of pure devotional preaching he started. The flood has even begun to inundate the West. It thus seems to me that Śrīla Prabhupāda is constantly repeating Mahāprabhu's instructions to all of us:

yāre dekho tāre kaho kṛṣṇa upadeśa
āmāra ājñāya guru hañā tāro ei deśa
ihāte nā bādhibe tomāra viṣaya taraṅga
punarapi ei ṭhāñi pābe mora saṅga

"Instruct whomever you see on the orders of Kṛṣṇa. Become a spiritual master on My order and deliver everyone in this land. Do this and you will never again be entangled in the waves of materialistic life. Indeed, you will have My company again, here in this very place." (*Caitanya Caritāmṛta* 2.7.128-9)

Śrīla Saccidānanda Bhaktivinoda Ṭhākura

namo bhaktivinodāya
saccidānanda-nāmine
gaura-śakti-svarūpāya
rūpānuga-varāya te

"I offer my obeisances to Śrīla Saccidānanda Bhaktivinoda Ṭhākura, who is an embodiment of the transcendental potency of Śrī Caitanya Mahāprabhu and the best of the followers of Rūpa Gosvāmī."

BHAKTIVINODA ṬHĀKURA'S SPIRITUAL IDENTITY

Śrīla Bhaktivinoda Ṭhākura's transcendental identity is revealed to the members of his spiritual family who are blessed. He is the best of the followers of Śrī Rūpa Mañjarī, who is dearest to Śrī Lalitā Sakhī, the foremost of Rādhārāṇī's eight confidants (*sakhīs*). In various places in his own writings, Śrīla Bhaktivinoda Ṭhākura has indicated this divine identity:

yugala-sevāya, śrī-rāsa-maṇḍale,
niyukta kara āmāy
lalitā-sakhīra, ayogya-kiṅkarī,
vinoda dhariche pāy

"Praying, 'Engage me in the service of the Divine Couple in the circle of the divine *rāsa-maṇḍala*,' Bhaktivinoda, the most unworthy servant of Lalitā Sakhī, holds tight to Your lotus feet." (*Kalyāṇa-kalpa-taru*)

Śrīla Bhaktivinoda Ṭhākura also gives his eternal spiritual identity as Kamala Mañjarī, the servant of Śrī Rūpa Mañjarī, in the song *Siddhi-lālasā* in his *Gīta-mālā*. Her *kuñja* is in the bower of Lalitā, Śrī Vraja-svānanda-sukhada-kuñja, where she sets the standard of worship to the Divine Couple.

varaṇe taṛit, vāsa tārāvalī,
kamala-mañjarī nāma
sāṛe bāro varṣa, vayas satata,
svānanda-sukhada dhāma

"I am Kamala mañjarī. My bodily hue is like that of lightning, and I wear a sari the color of a clear night sky sprinkled with stars. I am twelve and a half years old, and I live in Svānanda-sukhada-kuñja."

THE NEED FOR BHAKTIVINODA ṬHĀKURA'S APPEARANCE

After the disappearance of Śrī Kṛṣṇa Caitanya Mahāprabhu, Svarūpa Dāmodara, Rāmānanda Rāya, the six Gosvāmīs, Śrīnivāsa Ācārya, Narottama Dāsa Ṭhākura and Śyāmānanda Prabhu, a dark age descended on the world of Gauḍīya Vaiṣṇavism. Those unable to understand the transcendental purity of Mahāprabhu's teachings of divine love started numerous pseudo sects, or *apasampradāyas*. Toṭārama Dāsa Bābājī Mahārāja named thirteen such pseudo sects:

āula, bāula, kartābhajā, neḍā, daraveśa, sāiñ
sahajiyā, sakhībhekī, smārta, jāta-gosāi
atibāṛī, cuṛādhārī, gaurāṅga-nāgarī
totā kahe ei teror saṅga nāhi kari

Educated upper-class Bengali society, by seeing the odious practices of these pseudo sects, came to identify Mahāprabhu's religion with the lower classes, the uneducated and immoral. People of the educated classes thus had no understanding of faith in Mahāprabhu's true religion. The most munificent form Śrī Caitanya Mahāprabhu took pity on the living entities and in order to bring about their greatest welfare sent His personal associate Śrīla Bhaktivinoda Ṭhākura into this world. Possessed of divine prowess, Śrīla Bhaktivinoda Ṭhākura wrote more than a hundred books in several different languages with the goal of defeating all the unorthodox views opposed to the true doctrines of Mahāprabhu's religion. The result was that many members of discerning society and others from all over the world came to recognize the unequalled value of Mahāprabhu's teachings. The founder of the Sri Chaitanya Math and the worldwide Sri Gaudiya Maths, Śrīla Bhakti Siddhānta Sarasvatī Gosvāmī Ṭhākura Prabhupāda, based his mission on the books and teachings given by Śrīla Bhaktivinoda Ṭhākura and accomplished the fulfillment of Mahāprabhu's message, found in the *Caitanya Bhāgavata*:

pṛthivī paryanta āche yata deśa-grāma
sarvatra sañcāra haibeka mora nāma

"My name will pervade every village and country in the world." (*Caitanya Bhāgavata* 3.4.126)

Śrīla Bhaktivinoda Ṭhākura thus made an unequalled contribution to the ultimate, spiritual welfare of humankind. Śrīla Bhakti Siddhānta Sarasvatī Gosvāmī Ṭhākura Prabhupāda wrote in his preface to *Jaiva-dharma*: "Śrīla Bhaktivinoda Ṭhākura is an extremely dear associate of Śrī Caitanya Candra. In the course of time, when those who preached the message of Caitanya Deva had left this world to enter the Lord's eternal pastimes, the Gauḍīya Vaiṣṇava sky slowly darkened, covered by the thick clouds of sensual enjoyment and false renunciation. The sky was covered and the world was bereft of the rays of light coming from the *saṅkīrtana* propagated by Śrī Caitanya Mahāprabhu. One by one, the sun, the moon and the bright stars of that sky faded from view, leaving only the flash of lightning to disrupt the unending darkness of ignorance. Almost 350 years after the appearance of Caitanya Mahāprabhu, Śrīla Bhaktivinoda Ṭhākura came to illuminate the Gauḍīya sky in Birnagar village in Nadia district.

"All the great virtues are present in the body of a Vaiṣṇava. All the good qualities of Kṛṣṇa are seen in His devotees. All these transcendental qualities are the characteristics of pure Vaiṣṇavas, and they cannot be fully explained, but I shall try to point out some of the most important. Devotees are always merciful; they are not bellicose. They are truthful, equal to all, faultless, generous, mild and clean. They are without material possessions, and they work for the welfare of all. They are peaceful, surrendered to Kṛṣṇa and desireless. They are indifferent, resolute, and completely control the six character flaws of lust, anger, greed and so forth. They eat only as much as required and are prudent, respectful, and free from false prestige. They are grave, compassionate, friendly, poetic, expert and silent." (*Caitanya Caritāmṛta* 2.22.75-80)

"All of these qualities of the devotees were perfectly displayed in the pure devotional life of Śrīla Bhaktivinoda Ṭhākura. The ocean of compassion, Śrī Gaurahari, displayed this never-ending merciful nature to the conditioned souls in nine different ways. The same kind of distribution of mercy is seen in the life and work of Śrīla Bhaktivinoda Ṭhākura."

THE SAMPRADĀYA'S DEBT TO ŚRĪLA BHAKTIVINODA ṬHĀKURA

Śrīla Bhaktivinoda Ṭhākura is the root of the daily activities in the Sri Chaitanya Math, Śrī Gaudiya Math, the Sri Chaitanya Gaudiya Math , and its sister institutions. The Gaudiya Math institutions cannot be separated from Śrīla Bhaktivinoda Ṭhākura. These institutions are entirely indebted to his sublime contributions.

Śrīla Bhakti Siddhānta Sarasvatī Gosvāmī Prabhupāda has written, "Devotees in the line of Śrīla Rūpa Gosvāmī do not put faith in their own powers, but rather attribute everything to its original source. We also do everything for the sake of Śrī Kṛṣṇa Caitanya, Śrī Rūpa Gosvāmī, Śrīla Bhaktivinoda Ṭhākura and our divine spiritual master." (From *Patrāvalī*, Śrīla Prabhupāda's letters, vol. 3, p. 89.)

Devotees of Śrī Brahma-Mādhva-Gauḍīya-Sārasvata *sampradāya* pay their respects daily to Śrīla Bhaktivinoda Ṭhākura as follows:

śuddha-bhakti-pracārasya
mūlībhūta ihottamaḥ
śrī-bhaktivinodo devas
tat-priyatvena viśrutaḥ

"Śrīla Bhaktivinoda Ṭhākura is the transcendental personality who is the root of the preaching movement of pure devotion. He is renowned as one who is dear to Śrī Caitanya Mahāprabhu."

HYMNS TO ŚRĪLA BHAKTIVINODA ṬHĀKURA

Two of Śrīla Bhakti Siddhānta Sarasvatī Gosvāmī Ṭhākura's most prominent disciples, Pujyapāda Śrīla Bhakti Rakṣaka Śrīdhara Deva Gosvāmī Mahārāja and Pujyapāda Śrīla Bhakti Vichar Yayavar Gosvāmī Mahārāja, wrote hymns in praise of Śrīla Bhaktivinoda Ṭhākura, the former in Sanskrit, the latter in Bengali. These have been given below:

vande bhaktivinodeṁ śrī-
gaura-śakti-svarūpakam
bhakti-śāstra-jña-samrājaṁ
rādhā-rasa-sudhā-nidhim

"I bow to Śrī Ṭhākura Bhaktivinoda, Mahāprabhu's divine energy personified. He is the emperor of Vaiṣṇava scholars and possesses the ambrosial treasure of Śrī Rādhā's sacred rapture.

bhakativinoda prabhu, dayā koro more
tava kṛpā bale pāī śrī-prabhupādere
bhakati-siddhānta sarasvatī prabhupāda
jagate āniyā dile kariyā prasāda
sarasvatī kṛṣṇa-priyā, kṛṣṇa-bhakti tāṅra hiyā
vinodera sei se vaibhava
ei gītera bhāvārtha, prabhupāda para-artha
ebe morā kari anubhava

"O Bhaktivinoda Prabhu, be merciful to me, for by your blessings I can attain Śrīla Prabhupāda, Bhakti Siddhānta Sarasvatī Ṭhākura. Out of compassion for the world, you brought him whose heart is filled with devotion to Kṛṣṇa and who is His dear one. This is the glory of Bhaktivinoda Ṭhākura. The purpose of this song is to find complete dedication to Śrīla Prabhupāda, and this is what I now experience.

śrī-caitanya-janma-sthāna śrī-māyāpura
tomāra pracāre ebe jānila saṁsāra
śikṣāmṛta, jaiva-dharma, ādi grantha śata
sajjana-toṣaṇī-patrī sarva-samādṛta
ei saba grantha-patrī kariyā pracāra
lupta-prāya śuddha-bhakti karile uddhāra
jīvere jānāle tumi hao kṛṣṇa-dāsa
kṛṣṇa bhajo kṛṣṇa cinto chāṛi anya āśa
kṛṣṇa-dāsye jīva saba parānanda pāy
sakala vipad ha'te mukta haye jāy

"The whole world has come to know the birthplace of Śrī Caitanya in Mayapur on account of your preaching efforts. Your more than one hundred books, such as *Śrī-Caitanya-Śikṣāmṛta, Jaiva Dharma,* etc., and your magazine *Sajjana-toṣaṇī* are valued by all. You preached by means of these books and magazines and by so doing were able to restore the religion of pure devotion, which had almost been lost. You told the fallen souls that they were in truth servants of Kṛṣṇa, and you told them to worship Kṛṣṇa, to think of Kṛṣṇa and to give up all other ambition. Through service to Kṛṣṇa, the living being finds full happiness in life and freedom from all danger.

āpani ācari dharma śikhāle sabāre
gṛhe kimvā dhāme thāki bhajaha kṛṣṇere
gadādhara-gaurahari-sevā prakāśile
śrī-rādhā-mādhava-rūpe tāṅdera dekhile
gosvāmi-gaṇera grantha vicāra kariyā
susiddhānta śikhāyeche pramāṇādi diyā
tāhā paṛi śuni loka ākṛṣṭa hailā
jaga-bhari tava nāma gāhite lāgilā
vyāsera abhinna tumi purāṇa prakāśa
śukābhinna prabhupāda śrī-dayita-dāsa

"You taught everyone by your own example that they should worship Kṛṣṇa whether they are living as a householder or residing in the *dhāma.* You consecrated deities of Gadādhara-Gaurāṅga, seeing Śrī Rādhā Mādhava in Them. You studied the scriptures of the Gosvāmīs and preached the pure doctrines with the appropriate evidence. Those who heard and read these doctrines were attracted and began to sing your glories throughout the world. You are like Vyāsadeva, who published the *Purāṇas*, and Śrīla Prabhupāda, Śrī Dayita Dāsa, your son, is like Śukadeva Gosvāmī.

vaiṣṇavera jata guṇa āchaye granthete
sakala prakāśa hailā tomāra dehete
śrī-gauṛa-maṇḍala mājhe śrī-bīranagar
tava āvirbhāva sthāna sarva-śubhaṅkara
vandi āmi nata-śire sei puṇya-kṣetra
mastake dhāraṇa kari se dhūli pavitra
tomāra kṛpāya īśodyāne sthāna pāi
bhāgavata-maṭhe basi tava nāma gāi
tomāra dāsānudāsa yati yāyāvāra
prārthanā karaye dhāma-vāsa nirantara

"All the Vaiṣṇava qualities described in the scriptures are manifest in you. You appeared in Gauda Mandala, in the village of Birnagar, a place that is auspicious for all. I worship that holy spot with my head bowed low, taking its holy dust on my head. By your mercy, I have found a place in Ishodyan, the divine garden of Mayapur, and here in the Bhagavat Math, I glorify your name. The servant of your servants, the *sannyāsī yāyāvara*, prays to you to grant him eternal life in the holy *dhāma.*"

ŚRĪLA BHAKTIVINODA ṬHĀKURA'S FAMILY HISTORY

Just as the Supreme Lord Śrī Kṛṣṇa's highest perfection is in His activities in a human form, so similarly His eternal associates also act in human-like ways when they descend to the worldly platform for the benefit of the fallen living entities. Even though they appear to be ordinary human beings, they are in fact never touched by the illusory nature and always remain transcendental to it. They may be situated in householder life, but they are never entangled in material sensual desires like an ordinary conditioned soul because of their deep attachment and love for the Lord. They are simply engaged in a pastime whereby they imitate the activities of the rest of mankind for the sake of exchanging with them for the purposes of benefiting them. Those who have surrendered with sincerity to Viṣṇu and the Vaiṣṇavas are able to recognize the transcendental character of these personalities.

The King Ādisūra invited *brāhmaṇas* and other upper-class Hindus to Bengal, amongst whom was Śrī Puruṣottama. His seventh- and eighth-generation descendants were Śrī Vināyaka and Śrī Nārāyaṇa, who became government ministers. The fifteenth-generation descendant was Mahāprabhu's contemporary Rāja Kṛṣṇānanda Datta, a devotee of Kṛṣṇa. Nityānanda Prabhu came to stay in his home with His entourage and bestowed profuse blessings on him. Descendants of Kṛṣṇānanda Datta include Govinda Śaraṇa Datta, who founded the village of Govindapur. Kalighat, Sutanuti and Govindapur are the three villages that formed the central core of Kolkata.

Govinda Śaraṇa Datta's grandson was Rāmacandra. His grandson was Madana Mohana Datta, who donated Kolkata's Hedua pond to the municipality for public use. Madana Mohana Datta also spent a great deal of his personal wealth to build steps at Gaya's Pretashilā Tirtha and Candranatha Mountain. His grandson was Rājaballabha Datta, whose son Ānanda Candra Datta was very religious and detached from material life. Ānanda Candra married Jaganmohinī Devī, the daughter of the celebrated zamindar of Ula village in Nadia district, Īśvara Candra Mustaufī.

Śrīla Bhaktivinoda Ṭhākura accepted Ānanda Candra Datta and Jaganmohinī Devī as his parents and appeared in Ula-Birnagar in the home of his maternal grandfather. It was the 352nd year after the birth of Caitanya Mahāprabhu, Sunday, Sept. 2, 1838; the *tithi* was *śukla trayodaśī* of Bhādra. His parents gave him the name Śrī Kedāranātha.

ŚRĪLA BHAKTIVINODA ṬHĀKURA'S CHILDHOOD

Śrīla Bhaktivinoda Ṭhākura composed his first poem when he was only two years old. This extraordinary display of talent gave an indication of his future vocation and the transcendental devotional songs he would write later in his life. Songs full of devotion to the Lord and sacred sentiment like his are not the result of any worldly scholarship or creativity but are self-manifested in the eternally perfect associate of the Lord. The words of the residents of Vaikuṇṭha are all not different from the object of their speech, the Supreme Lord. They can in no way be compared to any mundane sound vibration. Every word used by Śrīla Bhaktivinoda Ṭhākura is divine ambrosia which awakens the mood of love for the Lord and is full of the flavors of devotional sentiment.

At only six, he had learnt all the details of the historical epics, *Mahābhārata* and *Rāmāyaṇa*. Is an ordinary six-year-old capable of such a feat? Without divine mercy, it is impossible to understand the purports of all the devotional scriptures, which are nondifferent from the Lord Himself. They are not accessible to mere scholarship. The meaning of the scriptures was revealed in the heart of the Ṭhākura on its own. Thus, there is a basic difference between his explanations of scripture and those derived from a mundane scholarly analysis.

According to his autobiography, Śrīla Bhaktivinoda Ṭhākura began researching astrological texts when he was nine years old, but he left them to inquire into spiritual truth at the age of ten. Though he was naturally fixed in eternal transcendental understanding at every moment, he displayed these pastimes in order to demonstrate the special character of human life. At this time, he began to mix with people in order to find out what preoccupied them and what guided them in life. He won over everyone he encountered with his sweet words and respectful attitude. As a result, no one ever felt angry or disappointed, even when he pointed out flaws in their argument. This was not within the capacity of an ordinary restless boy of ten years.

The following is Śrīla Bhaktivinoda Ṭhākura's account of several childhood events from his autobiography: "I would go whenever a festival was held at someone's house. There were often such religious festivals at the *brahmacārī's* residence. There was a nice temple on the outside and inside a flower garden and an altar for fire-sacrifice. The *brahmacārī* worshipped according to the *tāntrika* cult. He kept a human skull in a small, hidden room. Some people said that if you give water and milk to a human skull, it will smile. I took the skull down and gave it water, but I did not see any smile.

"Nearby there was also an astrologer's house where I would listen to singing performances. One old carpenter was engaged to paint backdrops for the image during the Durgā *pūjā*. I sat near him while he worked and asked him many questions, which he always answered. I asked, 'When does the spirit of the god enter into the image?' The carpenter answered, 'When I paint its eyes, the god will come and take up residence in the image.' The day that he was actually going to paint the deity's eyes, I eagerly came, but I never saw the god actually appear. I said, 'Goloka Pāla made this image. He first tied bundles of straw and then covered it with clay. You covered it with chalk and then painted it. There is no god anywhere in this statue at all, is there?' The old carpenter then said, 'When the *brāhmaṇas* consecrate the deity then the god incarnates and enters the form.' I observed this consecration ceremony carefully, but I was never able to see any divine manifestation. I thought that the carpenter was a fairly wise fellow and so I went to his house and asked him to explain again. He then said to me, 'I have no faith in this worship of idols. My belief is that the *brāhmaṇas* simply use this as a means of deception for taking money from gullible people.' The carpenter's words brought me great pleasure, and I asked him to tell me something about the Supreme Lord. He said, 'Say what you will, I believe in nothing other than the one Supreme Lord, Parameśvara. The gods and goddesses are all imaginary. I worship that Parameśvara every day.' These words of the old man gave me faith.

"I became even more inquisitive. The Muslim footman Golāma Khān used to guard the treasury. Once in response to my questions, he said, 'God's name is Khodā. At one time he was alone and there was no one and nothing but him. Then he took the dirt from his body and made a pancake out of it which he threw into the single ocean. The upper part of the pancake became the sky and the lower part became the earth. He then created humankind, starting with Adam and Eve. We are all the descendants of Adam and Eve.' After hearing this myth, I asked him, 'Who do you think Rāma is?' He said, 'Rāma and Rahim are one. That is Khodā.' Then I learned from him about a spell which chases ghosts. Golāma Khān said,

'Ghosts are the descendants of Satan. They are afraid of the name of Rahim.' These teachings gave me great pleasure.

"My maternal uncle Paraśurāma Mustaufī was studying law at that time. At first, he had some faith in God but later dismissed the idea. While he was a believer, my other uncles Raghu and Naśu were his followers. When he stopped believing in the personal god, he started calling Rāma Mohana Rāya his guru. I was very troubled because, being just an ignorant child, I was uncomfortable having a difference of opinion with him. Uncle Paraśurāma said, 'Everything in the world is a product of natural forces. There is no such thing as a God outside of nature.' When I heard this, I went to see some Bhaṭṭācārya in his school and asked him to respond to it. His answers caused me to become more confused. Though I was confused, I never gave up chanting the name of Rāma."

From all these stories, we can draw the lesson that in an immature state, rather than entering into the confusing business of reasoning out an absolute conclusion about the relation between the divine and creation, one should simply chant the Holy Name with faith. At one point, Mahāprabhu also bound His books in their cloth wrappers and told His students to simply chant the Holy Name. Absolute truth will be revealed through the Holy Name and not through mental speculation, for by this method one is bound to arrive at a mistaken conception of God.

HIS MARRIAGE

When Śrīla Bhaktivinoda Ṭhākura was only eleven years old, his father died. According to the custom prevalent at that time, his mother arranged for him to be married to a five-year-old girl from nearby Ranaghat. Śrīla Bhaktivinoda Ṭhākura has the following to say about his marriage: "It was just like a doll's play-marriage. Because I would not be able to stay alone at my in-laws' house, my parents sent my nanny to accompany me." Though the Ṭhākura had knowledge of the human predicament, in order to perceive it directly he did nothing to protest the marriage which was customary.

STUDIES

At six years of age, Kedāranātha went to study Sanskrit at the home school of Vidyā Vācaspati. Then at the age of seven, his grandfather sent him to study at Krishnanagar College. At that time, the college principal's name was Captain D. L. Richardson, and the main native professor was Rāmatanu Lāhiḍī. The next year, an English-language school was established in Ula in which Kedāranātha was enrolled. While studying at Krishnanagar College, one of his fellow students was the King of Coochbihar, who was still a child at the time.

When his maternal grandfather died, he and his mother came to live in Kolkata at the family home at the corner of Beadon Street and Hedua. He recommenced his studies at the Hindu Charitable Institution. After four years there, he was admitted to the Hindu School in 1856.

Śrīla Bhaktivinoda Ṭhākura was one of the first students of Īśvara Candra Vidyāsāgara's, whom he held in great affection. One day, Śrīla Bhaktivinoda Ṭhākura visited the great scholar in his house in Kolkata. Vidyāsāgara Mahāśaya said to him, "Since none of us has ever seen God, it is best that we not talk about him." Though he was his student, Bhaktivinoda Ṭhākura did not refrain from speaking the truth to the venerated teacher. He asked, "Paṇḍita Mahāśaya, why then did you write in your [children's] book *Bodhodaya* that God is formless, having pure consciousness. If you haven't seen God, then why have you written this about Him? God is omnipotent. Don't you think that if He can do anything, then He has the power to maintain a form? The Supreme Lord is our eternal master, and we are His eternal servants. The natural affection that we have for the Supreme Lord is called *bhakti, brahma-vidyā* or *para-vidyā* in the Veda. This is real knowledge, the realization of which means that there is no dearth of any knowledge."

Those who are always engaged in a direct relationship with the Absolute Truth, the Supreme Lord, are immediately able to recognize any statement which goes contrary to the Absolute truth. There is a complete difference between knowledge which has been garnered from the reading of books and the knowledge which arises from the revelation of the self-effulgent truth.

Kolkata University was founded in 1856, and entrance exams held for the first time. Amongst Śrīla Bhaktivinoda Ṭhākura's fellow students were Satyendranātha and Gaṇendranātha Ṭhākura, Tāraka Nātha Pālita and Navagopāla Mitra. Principal Clint, Reverend Duff, George Thompson, and Keśava Candra Sena were attracted by the young man's mastery of the English language and literature. Toward the end of 1856, Śrīla Bhaktivinoda Ṭhākura published an English poem, *The Poriade,* which was well received in educated circles in Kolkata. All the Ṭhākura's English poems were published in the paper *Library (Literary) Gazette.* He delivered a lecture to the British Indian Society in 1856 on the philosophical truths which was much applauded.

During this time, the Ṭhākura also studied Brāhmo Dharma, Christianity, the Bible and Quran and many other religious traditions and books. He considered Christianity superior to the Brāhmo religion because of its acceptance of God's eternal personality. In 1857, the Sepoy Mutiny broke out. He spent some of this time traveling and lecturing.

THE PREDICTION OF GRANDFATHER RĀJAVALLABHA

In 1858, Śrīla Bhaktivinoda Ṭhākura started from Bengal to reach Nilachal. On the way, he stopped at Chutigram near Jajpur, where his grandfather Śrī Rājavallabha Datta was living. His grandfather prophetically stated that the Ṭhākura would be a great Vaiṣṇava. Immediately upon making this prediction, his life airs passed out through the top of his head. From Cuttack, the Ṭhākura moved on to Puri by foot to be present at the time of Lord Jagannātha's Candana Yātrā. He remained in Puri for a few more days before continuing through Cuttack, Bhadrak, and Midnapore to Kolkata.

THE TITLE BHAKTIVINODA

On Śrī Īśvaracandra Vidyāsāgara's recommendation, Śrīla Bhaktivinoda Ṭhākur took a job teaching at the Cuttack Government Secondary School and shortly thereafter, the headmaster's position at a school in Bhadrak. During this time, he wrote a book on the various religious institutions of Odisha, *Maths of Odisha,* which Sir William Hunter made much use of as a reference in his work *Odisha.* He also wrote a work named *Śrī-Caitanya-Gītā* under the pen name Saccidānanda Premālaṅkāra. He was given the title Bhaktivinoda by the Śrī Gauḍīya Gosvāmī Saṅgha on the 400th anniversary of Mahāprabhu's appearance (1885). From this time on, Śrī Kedāranātha Datta was known as Śrī Saccidānanda Bhaktivinoda Ṭhākura.

TRAVELS AND PREACHING

The Ṭhākura also taught at a school in Midnapore. One day a follower of the Brāhmo religion, Rājanārāyaṇa Basu, heard him speak at a literary society meeting on the truth of religion and was deeply moved. During his time in Midnapore, the Ṭhākura's first wife died and he married for a second time, to Bhagavatī Devī. From Midnapore, he went to Burdwan to preach. While there, he published an English book, *Our Wants*. On the request of the local residents, he took part in the arguments between the Brāhmo Samāja and Christians and tried to mediate between the two religions. In two lectures he showed the problems with both groups' positions. While in Burdwan, he started a group called the Bhrātṛ-samāja. At one of the meetings of this group, he gave a learned speech on the soul which attracted the attention of a certain Mr. Heiley.

From Burdwan, the Ṭhākura went to Chuadanga and Ranaghat before going to live temporarily in Chapra in Bihar. While living there, he made his first visit to Vrindavan, traveling through Kashi, Mirzapur, Prayag, Agra, etc. While in Chapra, the Ṭhākura studied Urdu and Persian and mastered these languages. He also gave a speech on Gautama while there.

From Chapra, he went to Purniya and then to Dinajpur, where he was engaged as Deputy Magistrate. In Dinajpur, he found that there was a dispute between Hindus and Brāḥmos in which he intervened, giving a speech on The *Bhāgavata: Its Philosophy, Its Ethics and Its Theology*.

In June of 1868, he visited Rūpa and Sanātana Gosvāmī's home in Ramakeli as well as Rajmahal, etc. Thereafter he returned to Kolkata, where he undertook research to find copies of *Caitanya-caritāmṛta* and *Śrīmad Bhāgavatam*. After much work, he finally found copies at the Bot Tola publishing house. With these valuable editions, he went to Purushottama *dhāma*. He was engaged as a director of the temple to oversee its management. He lived in Puri continuously for over five years, over five years beginning in 1869.

PUNISHING VIṢAKIṢAṆA FOR DECEPTION

In Śrīla Bhaktivinoda Ṭhākura's life, we find that he personified the description of a Vaiṣṇava as one who is gentler than a rose, yet more terrible than the thunderbolt. Although he was generally kind and gentle, he gave no quarter to dishonesty. One event in his life which took place while he was in Odisha is an indication of this. In 1871, a member of the Khaṇḍāit family lineage and the Ativāḍī sect named Viṣakiṣaṇa who had gained some mystic powers through yogic practices proclaimed himself to be an incarnation of Mahā-Viṣṇu. He was staying with his followers at the edge of the jungle near the town of Bhubaneshwar. He announced that on the thirteenth of Caitra, he would reveal a four-armed form and destroy all the *mlecchas*, restoring the true religion. His announcement was written in Odishan verse:

banere achi biṣakiṣaṇa
guptare achi na jānai āna
tera mīnare ārambhiba raṇa,
caturbhuja hoi nāśiba mleccha-gaṇa!

"In the forest am I hiding, and no one else knows me, but on the thirteenth of Mīna I will begin the war. Taking on a four-armed form, I will destroy the *mlecchās*."

Through his mystic powers, he had been able to cure incurable diseases, and these powers had won for him a large following. One day he announced that on the full-moon day he would perform the *rāsa-līlā* and invited the girls of a nearby village to come and join him. The Caudhurīs of the Bhringar clan found that he had polluted their womenfolk and went to complain en masse to the district commissioner, Mr. Ravenshaw. The commissioner gave the task of investigating the matter to Bhaktivinoda Ṭhākura, who went personally into the jungle to meet with Viṣakiṣaṇa and told him to refrain from such improper deeds. Viṣakiṣaṇa told Bhaktivinoda Ṭhākura that he was the living Mahā-Viṣṇu and that Jagannātha Deva was nothing but a lifeless wooden statue. He tried in various ways to flatter the Ṭhākura and win him over. When he saw that Viṣakiṣaṇa had no intention of stopping his efforts to deceive the people, Bhaktivinoda Ṭhākura had him arrested and brought him to Puri.

The Ṭhākura proceeded to investigate the background of Viṣakiṣaṇa by going to many villages and Buddhist *vihāras* in the Khandagiri area of the Puri district. After accumulating a mass of evidence showing the extent to which this yogi was cheating people, he had him brought to court. While the case was being heard, the yogi used his mystic power to cause Bhaktivinoda Ṭhākura and his family to be attacked by various illnesses, in an effort to intimidate him, but without success. The Ṭhākura overcame all oppressions and gave him a sentence of one and a half years. Viṣakiṣaṇa went for twenty-one days without food or drink and then left his body.

In the months which followed, another rascal in Jajpur proclaimed himself to be the *avatāra* of Brahmā, while someone else in Khorda said that he was a manifestation of Balarāma. Bhaktivinoda Ṭhākura quickly thwarted their efforts to cheat the populace.

OTHER ACTIVITIES OF THE THAKUR IN PURI

While living in Puri, Śrīla Bhaktivinoda Ṭhākura took the opportunity to study the *Bhāgavata*, the *Six Sandarbhas* of Jīva Gosvāmī, and the *Govinda-bhāṣya, Siddhānta-ratnam and Prameya-ratnāvalī* of Baladeva Vidyābhūṣaṇa. He also studied Rūpa Gosvāmī's *Bhakti-rasāmṛta-sindhu* in great detail. By making a display of intense study, he demonstrated the necessity of cultivating an understanding of the scriptures in order to learn the truths about pure devotion contained therein. Mahāprabhu indicated that one of the five principal limbs of devotional service is hearing the *Bhāgavata*. Jīva Gosvāmī indicated that this is the best of all devotional activities. In order to proclaim this same truth, Śrīla Bhaktivinoda Ṭhākura founded a regular group for discussion of the *Bhāgavata called*, *Bhāgavata-saṁsat*, which was held in the Jagannatha Vallabha gardens in Puri.

Many of the leading Vaiṣṇavas in Puri, such as Nityānanda, Paramānanda and others, Mahānta Nārāyaṇa Dāsa, and Harihara Dāsa of Uttara Pārśva and others were attracted to hearing the *Bhāgavata* from his lips. Just as Mahāprabhu performed the pastime of hearing *Bhāgavata* from Śrīla Gadādhara Paṇḍita Gosvāmī, Śrīla Bhaktivinoda Ṭhākura also listened to discourses given by Śrī Gopīnātha Paṇḍita.

A certain renounced Vaiṣṇava, Raghunātha Dāsa Bābājī of Hati Akhra, objected to the Ṭhākura's speaking on *Bhāgavata* and was attacked by disease. After Jagannātha Deva appeared to him in a dream and ordered him, he went and begged Śrīla Bhaktivinoda Ṭhākura for forgiveness, after which he was cured.

When the Ṭhākura went to the Jagannātha temple, he did not sit in the Mukti Maṇḍapa, where Māyāvādī scholars discussed their philosophy. He would sit by the Lakṣmī temple and the place where Mahāprabhu's footprints are enshrined and discussed devotional doctrines there. Many of the Māyāvādīs also attended and were attracted by his discourses. Soon the place became known as the Bhakti Maṇḍapa or the Bhakti Prāṅgaṇa.

During this time, Śrīla Bhaktivinoda Ṭhākura studied Kṛṣṇadāsa Kavirāja Gosvāmī's *Caitanya Caritāmṛta and* Narahari Cakravartī's *Bhakti-ratnākara*, but he did not accept Jayānanda's *Caitanya-maṅgala* as being authoritative. He associated with a perfected Vaiṣṇava named Svarūpa Dāsa Bābājī, discussing scripture with him. While at Puri, he also wrote the Sanskrit work *Datta-kaustubha* and composed many Sanskrit verses of *Śrī-kṛṣṇa-saṁhitā*.

THE BIRTH OF BHAKTISIDDHĀNTA SARASVATĪ ṬHĀKURA

A wealthy family in Puri had leased land along the Grand Road from the Dakṣiṇa Pārśva Math and built a house on it. Śrīla Bhaktivinoda Ṭhākura and his family resided in this building, which is not far from the Jagannātha temple, next to the Narayana Chata. This house was reclaimed by Paramapujyapāda Śrīmad Bhakti Dayita Mādhava Gosvāmī Mahārāja Viṣṇupāda and now houses a Sri Chaitanya Gaudiya Math with a beautiful temple building, where a deity of Śrīla Prabhupāda is worshipped.

After 3:30 pm on Friday, February 6, 1874, on the *Kṛṣṇa pañcamī* of Māgha month, an effulgent and beautiful child was born to Bhagavatī Devī in this home, while the Ṭhākura and other family members sang the names of the Lord. Everyone was amazed to see natural marks of a sacred thread around the child's body. He was named after the divine energy of Jagannātha Deva, Vimalā Devī, as Bimala Prasad. His first solid food was Lord Jagannātha's *maha-prasāda*. When he grew up, this child became the founder of the Chaitanya Math and the worldwide Gaudiya Maths, Śrīla Bhakti Siddhānta Sarasvatī Gosvāmī Ṭhākura Prabhupāda.

Śrīla Bhaktivinoda Ṭhākura was Jagannātha Deva's own man. It was by Lord Jagannātha's arrangement that he was brought to Puri to see to the smooth management of His service. After the appearance of Śrīla Bhakti Siddhānta Sarasvatī Gosvāmī Ṭhākura, the preaching of Mahāprabhu's message spread over the entire planet. This gave meaning to the words written by Vyāsadeva in the *Padma Purāṇa, hy utkale puruṣottamāt*, "out of Purushottama in Odisha."

Ten months after Bimala Prasad's birth, Śrīla Bhaktivinoda Ṭhākura was reposted to Ranaghat, so he and his family returned to Bengal, traveling overland by palanquin.

BHAKTIVINODA ṬHĀKURA'S INCOMPARABLE CONTRIBUTION

Vedavyāsa and the scriptures he wrote are the foundation of all those who follow the *Sanātana-dharma*. He himself practiced and preached the means by which humankind can attain the supreme peace. He divided the Veda, wrote the eighteen *Purāṇas* and the *Mahābhārata* including the *Bhagavad -gītā*, but remained unsatisfied. Finally, while at Badrikashram, Nārada Muni instructed him to glorify the activities of Śrī Kṛṣṇa for His pleasure. After writing the twelve cantos of the *Śrīmad Bhāgavatam*, Vedavyāsa finally found the peace he had been looking for.

Mahāprabhu Śrī Caitanya preached the *Bhāgavata* religion found in this text. After the disappearance of Mahāprabhu and His associates, however, the path of pure devotion became covered with thorns until Bhaktivinoda Ṭhākura appeared to write many books and to preach the pure doctrine of devotional service to Kṛṣṇa. Through his tireless efforts, all the heretical doctrines were shown to be empty, and the path of supreme auspiciousness and compassion was again revealed to the world. These efforts can only be said to constitute an unequalled and certainly unsurpassed mercy towards all the living beings. No one can spread the message of pure devotion without being empowered by Kṛṣṇa Himself. Were Bhaktivinoda Ṭhākura not a direct associate of Gaurāṅga Mahāprabhu and Śrī Kṛṣṇa, he would never have been able to make such a show of empowerment.

Externally Bhaktivinoda Ṭhākura was a householder with family obligations, a government servant engaged in the administrative service, but despite these responsibilities, he was still able to write over a hundred books in several different languages and preach. One cannot fail to be impressed by this monumental achievement. Every word he wrote is scripture; every word awakens the spirit of devotion to Lord Adhokṣaja (one who reserves the right of not being exposed to human senses). Mundane scholars could not have achieved a fraction of his literary accomplishments. None of his writings are a product of an imaginative brain but are spontaneous and self-manifest. His writings are a permanent display of compassion to the fallen souls. Paramārādhya Śrīla Gurudeva Bhakti Dayita Mādhava Gosvāmī Mahārāja used to say to his disciples, "You need do nothing else other than translate Bhaktivinoda Ṭhākura's books into the world's various languages. By doing so, you will perform the greatest act of welfare for the people of the world." Whatever the Gaudiya Math and its numerous branches throughout the world have achieved is built on the foundation established by Śrīla Bhaktivinoda Ṭhākura.

BHAKTIVINODA ṬHĀKURA'S TRAVELS AND PREACHING ACTIVITIES

After the appearance of Śrīla Bhakti Siddhānta Sarasvatī Gosvāmī Ṭhākura, Śrīla Bhaktivinoda Ṭhākura returned to Bengal. From then on he engaged in preaching the doctrine of pure devotional sservice as well as traveling throughout India for pilgrimage. We will give a brief summary here of all the places he visited between 1877 and 1910, whether for the sake of pilgrimage or for preaching. He went to Amta in the Uluberiya subdivision, to Abhirāma Ṭhākura's Sripat in Khanakul Krishnanagar, Shyampur, Bhadrak in Odisha, Narail in the Jessore district, Kolkata, Prayag, Vrindavan (where he met Śrī Jagannātha Dāsa Bābājī Mahārāja for the first time), Sri Radha Kunda, Sri Govardhan (where he broke up the Kanjhara dacoit gang that was harassing pilgrims to the *dhāma*), Mathura, Lucknow, Faizabad, Goptar Ghat, Ayodhya and Benares.

He then returned to Kolkata, where in 1882 he started construction of Bhakti Bhavana at 181 Maniktola Street. While eorkers were digging the foundations for the building, a deity of Kūrma Deva was found. Śrīla Bhaktivinoda Ṭhākura gave this deity to Śrīla Bhakti Siddhānta Sarasvatī Gosvāmī Ṭhākura and taught him how to worship it. He also visited Barasat and Mayapur.

The Ṭhākura was then engaged as deputy collector in the Barasat subdivision. Then he was transferred to Sriramapur, Vaidyanatha, Bakipur, and Gaya, where he saw the steps on Pretashila constructed by his great-grandfather, Madana Mohana Datta. He returned to Naral, Barasat, Memari, Kulingram, Bandel, and

Saptagram. In Kulinagram he lectured on the Holy Name, distinguishing between the pure name, *nāmābhāsa* and *nāmāparādha*. There he also gave Śrīla Bhakti Siddhānta Sarasvatī Gosvāmī Ṭhākura initiation in the Holy Name and the Nṛsiṁha *mantra*.

Śrīla Bhaktivinoda Ṭhākura established the Caitanya Yantra printing press. The Vishva-Vaishnava Raja Sabha was established under his guidance at the Durga Mandapa of Rāma Gopāla Basu in Krishna Singha Gali off Bethun Row Road. There he gave lectures on *Caitanya Caritāmṛta* and *Bhakti-rasāmṛta-sindhu*. At this time he also had a meeting with the famous Rāmakṛṣṇa Paramahaṁsa, during which he countered his impersonal philosophy and explained the truth of pure devotion.

DISCOVERY OF MAHĀPRABHU'S BIRTHPLACE

Śrīla Bhaktivinoda Ṭhākura visited Tarakeshwar, where Lord Śiva appeared to him in a dream and said, "You want to go to Vrindavan, but there is much work left to do in Nabadwip *dhāma*, which is nearby. What have you done there?"

The Ṭhākura then visited Kuliya, where the modern city of Nabadwip stands. He went on the roof of his place of stay to take a view of the *dhāma*'s beauty. At about ten o'clock at night, when thick clouds darkened the sky, he saw an illuminated building on the other side of the river. His son Kamalā Prasāda was accompanying him and also saw this light, much to his surprise. On inquiry the next day, they learnt that the light was coming from a place known as Ballala Dighi. On going later to Ballala Dighi, they learnt from the elderly residents of the village that this was Caitanya Mahāprabhu's birthplace. Intrigued, Bhaktivinoda Ṭhākura began to research old maps and documents and was able to establish conclusively that Mahāprabhu's birthplace was indeed at Ballala Dighi.

Śrīla Bhaktivinoda Ṭhākura continued to maintain his Kolkata home, where he installed the Giridhārī Śilā given to him by Jagannātha Dāsa Bābājī Mahārāja. In 1888 he purchased a property in Godrumdwip, which he named Surabhi Kunja. While stationed at Krishnanagar, he was also able to visit his birthplace at Ula.

Śrīla Bhaktivinoda Ṭhākura later visited the Netrakona subdivision in the Mymensingha District, Nārāyaṇa Ganj, Mymensingha city, the Garo Hills, where he blessed the people of the Hajong tribe, and Gowalanda. Upon his return to Kolkata, he visited Tangail, Burdwan, Shantipur, Kalna, Baghna Para, Koigram, and Denur, the site of Vṛndāvana Dāsa Ṭhākura's Sripat.

He then again visited Kuliya, where he met Jagannātha Dāsa Bābājī Mahārāja at his *bhajana kutira*. He rendered service to Bābājī Mahārāja by arranging for a concrete veranda to be built for him. While in Burdwan, he also performed *kīrtana* with the devotees of Amlajora village and visited Gopalpur, Raniganj, Barakar, Durgapur, and Dinajpur.

When in Kolkata, he met the famous newspaper publisher Śiśira Ghoṣa, who considered him a guru, even calling him "the seventh Gosvāmī." Śiśira Ghoṣa would come regularly to visit him at Bhakti Bhavana, and at the Ṭhākura's direction, started chanting *japa* on Tulasī beads. He was not able to accept the principles of Vaiṣṇava behavior in their entirety, however.

During this period Śrīla Bhaktivinoda Ṭhākura also visited Ramjivanpur in the Midnapore district, where he discussed with Sitānatha Mahāpātra and also preached the glories of the Holy Name at a nearby place.

He then visited Ghatal in the Midnapore district and Kayapat Badna Ganj in the Hooghly district. From there he returned to Krishnanagar, staying once again in Surabhi Kunja. He arranged for some large assemblies to be called in Krishnanagar, at which he spoke. A number of Englishmen, including Messrs. Mulrow, Wallace and Butler, were regular attendants at these meetings.

At Amaljora on March 9, 1892, he participated in a *Harivāsara* (Ekādaśī) program at which Jagannātha Dāsa Bābājī Mahārāj was present. From there he traveled to Vrindavan, stopping at Buxar (Bihar) and Prayag. He was in Vraja from March 21 to 29, during which time he managed to visit Bilvavana, Bhandiravana, Mathavana, Mana Sarovara, Mathura, Gokula, Madhuvana, Tālavana, Kumudavana, Bahulāvana, Radha Kunda, Govardhan, etc. He then returned to Kolkata via Kanpur and Allahabad.

In Kolkata, Śrīla Bhaktivinoda Ṭhākura was engaged in preaching the message of Śrī Caitanya Mahāprabhu at Bhakti Bhavana, as well as continuing to hold assemblies at Krishnanagar. In February 1893, he held a *kīrtana* festival at Godrumdwip under the guidance of Jagannātha Dāsa Bābājī Mahārāja. During this time, Jagannātha Dāsa Bābājī Mahārāja indicated the exact spot where Mahāprabhu had first appeared in this world.

At this time, the Ṭhākura had an argument with a certain member of a Gosvāmī family who held that one of Mahāprabhu's closest associates was a *śūdra*. Śrīla Bhaktivinoda Ṭhākura was very displeased when he heard this and warned him and those who carry such opinion with the words:

vaiṣṇava-caritra, sarvadā pavitra,
jei ninde hiṁsā kari
bhakativinoda, na sambhāṣe tāre,
thāke sadā mauna dhari

"A Vaiṣṇava's character is always spotless. I, Bhaktivinoda, always remain silent and never speak to those who criticize Vaiṣṇavas out of spite."

Also at about this time, Śrīla Bhaktivinoda Ṭhākura wrote down his *guru-paramparā* and hung it on the outside of Bhakti Bhavana. He also did some preaching of Mahāprabhu's doctrines of love in Bihar, in the towns of Sasaram, Nasirganj and Dihiri.

In January of 1894, Śrīla Bhaktivinoda Ṭhākura held another large meeting at the A.V. School in Krishnanagar. At this meeting, it was decided that deities should be installed at Mahāprabhu's birthplace. At the same time, the Nabadwip Pracāriṇī Sabhā was formed to preach the newly discovered birthsite. Naphara Candra Pāla Bhakti Bhūṣaṇa, the zamindar of Natudaha in the Nadia district, was elected executive secretary of the Sabhā. Dvarikā Bābu, Naphara Bābu, and other members of the Sabhā decided that a thatched cottage would be constructed on the site and would house deities of Gaurāṅga and Viṣṇupriyā. These deities were consecrated on Friday, March 21, 1894 (Caitra 9, 1300 Bengali), on the Phālgunī *pūrṇimā*, in the midst of a rousing *kīrtana* during a lunar eclipse. For the maintenance of the deities, a committee was formed (Śrī Mayapur Sevā Samiti) which had many distinguished Vaiṣṇavas as its members, including Śyāmalāla Gosvāmī, Śaśībhūṣaṇa Gosvāmī, Rādhikānātha Gosvāmī, Bipina Bihārī Gosvāmī, Mahāmahopādhyāya Paṇḍita Ajitanātha Nyāyaratna, Mahendranātha Bhaṭṭācārya Vidyāraṇya, Satyajīvan Lāhiḍī, Vanamālī Rāya Bāhādura of Taras in the Pabna district, Śiśira Kumāra Ghoṣa, Matilāla Ghoṣa, Yatīndranātha Rāya Caudhurī, the engineer Dvārikānatha Sarakāra, Surendranātha Pāla Caudhurī of Ranaghat, Mahendranātha Majumadāra, the advocate Kiśorīlāla Sarakāra,

Nalinākṣa Datta, Kānāilāla Dey Bāhādura, Deputy Magistrate Navīna Candra Sena, and Jagaccandra Rāya.

BHAKTIVINODA ṬHĀKURA RETURNS TO PURI

On October 4, 1894, Śrīla Bhaktivinoda Ṭhākura retired from government service and came to Surabhi Kunja in Godrumdwip, where he gave discourses on Vaiṣṇava scriptures for one month. Sometime after the disappearance of Jagannātha Dāsa Bābājī Mahārāja in February of 1895, he accepted the invitation of the independent Rāja of Tripura, Vīracandra Devavarmaṇa Mānikya Bāhādura, to go to Agartala. He went there with Śrīla Bhakti Siddhānta Sarasvatī Ṭhākura in July 1895 and enchanted the Rāja with his discourses on pure devotional service. Later, in 1896, he took Śrīla Bhakti Siddhānta Sarasvatī Ṭhākura to Karshiyang, in the Himalayan foothills. In 1898, he revealed Godruma Svananda Sukhada Kunja and later took Śrīla Bhakti Siddhānta Sarasvatī Ṭhākura to Benares and Prayag.

In 1899, when the building was finished in Svananda Sukhada Kunja, Śrīla Bhaktivinoda Ṭhākura came to perform his *bhajana* there. Gaura Kiśora Dāsa Bābājī Mahārāja was a regular visitor, coming to hear the Ṭhākura's *Bhāgavata* lectures, and it was here that Śrīla Bhakti Siddhānta Sarasvatī Gosvāmī Ṭhākura first met his guru.

In 1900, Śrīla Bhaktivinoda Ṭhākura traveled with Sarasvatī Gosvāmī through Balasore, Remuna, Bhubaneshwar, and Sakshi Gopala to Puri. Śrīla Bhakti Siddhānta Sarasvatī Gosvāmī Ṭhākura displayed a deep desire to engage in *bhajana* near Haridāsa Ṭhākura's *samādhi* on the beach and his father arranged with Puri's sub-registrar, Jagabandhu Paṭṭanāyaka, for him to be given the service of the Giridhārī Āsana at the Sātāsana Math. In March of 1901, they came to Puri again, and in 1902 the construction of Bhakti Kutira was begun. At this time the Rāja of Kashimbazar, Manindra Chandra Nandi, took instruction in devotional service from the Ṭhākura.

In 1903, Bhakti Siddhānta Sarasvatī Gosvāmī would regularly read and give discourses at Bhakti Kutira on *Caitanya Caritāmṛta* in the presence of the Ṭhākura. The famous Rādhāramaṇa Caraṇa Dāsa Bābājī came to visit Bhaktivinoda Ṭhākura during this time, and they discussed devotional doctrines. Śrīla Bhakti Siddhānta Sarasvatī Gosvāmī Ṭhākura disproved Caraṇa Dāsa's anti-devotional activities and teachings through reference to the scriptures. Later, after Śrīla Bhaktivinoda Ṭhākura had returned to Nabadwip, Caraṇa Dāsa opined to the Ṭhākura that Sarasvatī Gosvāmī would be the only shelter for pure devotional doctrines going forward. Caraṇa Dāsa also indicated his desire to participate in the Nabadwip *parikramā* inaugurated by the Ṭhākura, but unfortunately left his body before he was able to do so. During this time the Ṭhākura also met Śrī Vaṁśīdāsa Bābājī Mahārāja.

THE ṬHĀKURA RETURNS TO GODRUMDWIP

In 1906, Śrīla Bhaktivinoda Ṭhākura gave a lengthy discourse on Mahāprabhu's teachings at the house of zamindar Yatīndranātha Rāya Caudhurī in Taki, fifty Km east of Kolkata. On February 26, 1906, the Ṭhākura came to Kolkata again and from there to Swarup Ganj in Godrumdwip, where he engaged in his devotional activities at Svananda Sukhada Kunja. While there, a certain Tāraka Brahma Gosvāmī of the village Harinadi in Jessore came to him and asked him to accept his

Rādhā-Mādhava deities, which the Ṭhākura installed in Mayapur. Tāraka Brahma Gosvāmī moved close to this temple place with his wife and family, but after a short time, it became clear that his behavior was at odds with the standards expected of them, and they were obliged to leave. On April 29, 1906, however, the Śrī Dhāma Pracāriṇī Sabhā decided to award an annual stipend of five hundred rupees to the temple for the service of Śrī Śrī Rādhā Mādhava.

In 1908, Śrīla Bhaktivinoda Ṭhākura took the dress of a renounced Vaiṣṇava, a *bhāgavata-paramahaṁsa*, in order to dedicate his life to deeply relishing the sacred nectar of Rādhā and Govinda's intimate pastimes.

On March 25, 1910, which was Phālgunī *pūrṇimā* (the appearance day of Lord Caitanya Mahāprabhu), Jagadīśa Bhakti Pradip, at that time still a householder, visited Śrīla Bhaktivinoda Ṭhākura at Mayapur and five days later received initiation from him at Godrumdwip. Another disciple, Kṛṣṇadāsa Bābājī Mahāśaya, was also living with the Ṭhākura at Svananda Sukhada Kunja at that time.

Śrīla Bhaktivinoda Ṭhākura preached that the rules of the *daiva-varṇāśrama-dharma* should always be followed. Thus, he upheld the directives of the *Sat-kriyā-sāra-dīpikā* in giving the sacred thread to Jagadīśa Bhakti Pradīpa (who after taking *sannyāsa* from Śrīla Bhakti Siddhānta Sarasvatī Gosvāmī Ṭhākura became Śrīmad Bhakti Pradīpa Tirtha Mahārāja), Sītānātha Mahāpātra, Vasanta Kumāra Ghoṣa, and Manmathanātha Rāya.

In this connection, it is worth examining the following words written by the Ṭhākura: "The *varṇāśrama-dharma* current in today's society is quite distinct from the transcendental dharma of exclusive devotion to Kṛṣṇa. The practice of Varṇāśrama dharma on its own does not result in full surrender to the Lord. The ultimate instruction of the *Bhagavad-gītā* is to discard all the principles related to the *varṇas* and *āśramas*, in short, all activities based on bodily identification, and to engage in cultivation of devotional activities based on the natural constitution of the soul, which is pure love and without an ulterior motive. The standard of this transcendental Vaiṣṇava *dharma* is supremely high. The pure and causeless devotional doctrines of Gauḍīya Vaiṣṇavism cannot be comprehended even by scholars dedicated to *nyāya* philosophy such as Rāghavācārī."

BHAKTIVINODA ṬHĀKURA SENDS SARASVATĪ GOSVĀMĪ TO BALIGHAI

In 1910, while still at Svananda Sukhada Kunja, Śrīla Bhaktivinode Ṭhākura was engaged in writing his *Sva-niyama-dvādaśaka* when suddenly he displayed the pastimes of falling extremely ill. Śrīla Bhakti Siddhānta Sarasvatī Gosvāmī Ṭhākura and other dear disciples and followers gathered around him, afraid that he was about to enter the *nitya-līlā*. Even in this state of extreme physical discomfort, however, the Ṭhākura's enthusiasm for preaching Lord Caitanya's message was unabated. Though unable to walk, he indicated that he wished to be taken from place to place on horseback so that he could continue to spread Mahāprabhu's teachings.

Three years before the Ṭhākura's disappearance, he was extremely anxious as to who would take up the task of defeating all the heterodox doctrines that go against pure devotional service, thereby bringing about the ultimate welfare of the living entities. Śrīla Bhakti Siddhānta Sarasvatī Gosvāmī Ṭhākura indicated to him that though he felt himself to be an unworthy servant, he would take up this work. Bhaktivinoda Ṭhākura was greatly delighted to hear his son's determination, and when Gopiballabhpur's Śrī Viśvambharānanda Deva Gosvāmī invited him to participate in a conference in Balighai-Uddhavpur, Midnapore, he sent Śrīla Bhakti Siddhānta Sarasvatī Gosvāmī Ṭhākura and Sureśa Candra Mukhopādhyāya in his place. The conference took place Sept. 8-11, 1911. Many respected and well-reputed scholars of the *sampradāya* were present, including Madhusūdana Gosvāmī Sārvabhauma of the Rādhā Ramaṇa Gherā in Vrindavan.

Śrīla Sarasvatī Ṭhākura gave a talk on the distinctions between a Vaiṣṇava and a *brāhmaṇa*, clearly demonstrating a great amount of research, and left the assembly of scholars enchanted and speechless. A year later, when Madhusūdana Gosvāmī visited Śrīla Bhaktivinoda Ṭhākura at the Bhakti Bhavana, he enthusiastically proclaimed Śrīla Sarasvatī Gosvāmī Ṭhākura to be Bhaktivinoda Ṭhākura's worthy successor in his work of protecting the Gauḍīya *sampradāya* and in carrying forward his mission.

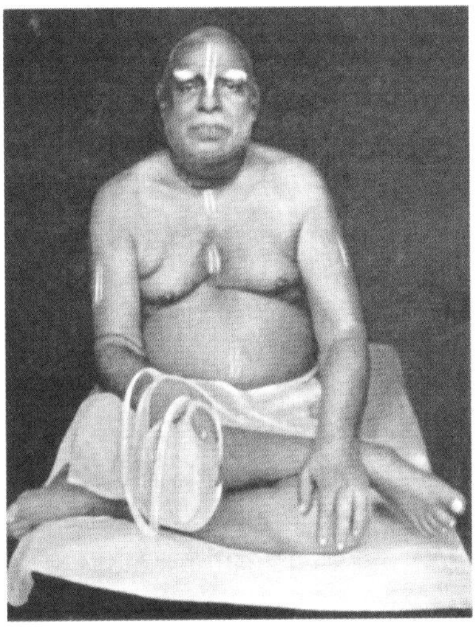

In 1913, Sarasvatī Gosvāmī wrote a commentary on the *Caitanya Caritāmṛta*, which was meant to accompany Bhaktivinoda Ṭhākura's *Amṛta-pravāha-bhāṣya.* He read several passages of this *Anubhāṣya* to the Ṭhākura, giving him indescribable pleasure.

BHAKTIVINODA ṬHĀKURA'S ENTRY INTO THE ETERNAL PASTIMES

A few days before his disappearance, Śrīla Bhaktivinoda Ṭhākura left Godrumdwip to come to Bhakti Bhavana. On June 23, 1914, on the disappearance day of Gaura's *śakti*, Śrīla Gadādhara Paṇḍita Gosvāmī, in his Kolkata Bhakti Bhavana, Śrīla Bhaktivinoda Ṭhākura entered the midday pastimes of Śrī Śrī Rādhā and Govinda at Radha Kunda. Six years later, his wife Śrī Bhagavatī Devī, the worshipable Mātā Ṭhākurāṇī, left her body at Bhakti Bhavana.

ŚRIMAD-BHAKTIVINODA-VIRAHA-DASAKAM

(Ten verses describing the feelings of separation from Śrīla Bhaktivinoda Ṭhākura written for the occasion of his disappearance day by Śrīmad Bhakti Rakṣaka Śrīdhara Dev Gosvāmī)

hā hā bhaktivinoda ṭhākura
guro dvāviṁśatis te samā
dīrghād-duḥkha-bharād aśeṣa-
virahād duḥsthīkṛtā bhūr iyam
jīvānāṁ bahu-janma-puṇya-
nivahākṛṣṭo mahīmaṇḍale
āvirbhāva-kṛpāṁ cakāra ca bhavān
śrī-gaura-śaktiḥ svayam

"Alas! Alas! My guru Bhaktivinoda Ṭhākura! It is now twenty-two long years that the world has been burdened with the grief of your separation. You are the personification of Śrī Gaurāṅga's energy, and you mercifully appeared in this world after being attracted by the living beings' many lifetimes of pious activities.

dīno 'haṁ cira-duṣkṛtir na hi
bhavat-pādābja-dhūli-kaṇā-
snānānanda-nidhiṁ prapanna-śubhadaṁ
labdhuṁ samartho 'bhavam
kintv audārya-guṇāt tavāti-yaśasaḥ
kāruṇya-śaktiḥ svayaṁ
śrī-śrī-gaura-mahāprabhoḥ prakaṭitā
viśvaṁ samanvagrahīt

"Being most fallen and possessing nothing but sinful activity in my past, I have not been able to attain the joyful treasure of being bathed in the dust of your lotus feet, which brings all auspiciousness to the surrendered. Even so, you are deservedly renowned for your magnanimity. You are the personification of Lord Śrī Caitanya Mahāprabhu's compassionate powers and have appeared in this world in order to bestow your divine blessings upon it.

he deva! stavane tavākhila-
guṇānāṁ te viriñcādayo
devā vyartha-manorathāḥ kimu
vayaṁ martyādhamāḥ kurmahe
etan no vibudhaiḥ kadāpy
atiśayālaṅkāra ity ucyatāṁ
śāstreṣv eva 'na pāraye 'ham' iti
yad gītaṁ mukundena tat

"O lord! The gods led by Brahmā are frustrated for their inability to glorify your unlimited virtues. What then can low-born humans such as we accomplish? This is no rhetorical exaggeration, as some scholars may claim, for even Mukunda Himself has said the same.

dharmaś carmma-gato 'jñataiva
satatā yogaś ca bhogātmako
jñāne śūnya-gatir japena tapasā
khyāti-jighāṁsaiva ca
dāne dāmbhikatā 'nurāga-
bhajane duṣṭāpacāro yadā
buddhiṁ buddhimatāṁ bibheda hi
tadā dhātrā bhavān preṣitaḥ

"You were sent by the Lord when even the most intelligent people's wisdom had been ruined through religious activities that seek only bodily pleasures, by constant ignorance, by yoga that has sense enjoyment as its goal, by the idea that the goal of knowledge is the void, by the desire to destroy individual consciousness through prayer and austerity, by arrogant pride in giving charity, and by immoral practices spread in the name of *rāgānuga-bhajana*.

viśve 'smin kiraṇair yathā himakaraḥ
sañjīvayann auṣadhīr
nakṣatrāṇi ca rañjayan nija-
sudhāṁ vistārayan rājate
sac-chāstrāṇi ca toṣayan budha-
gaṇaṁ sammodayaṁs te tathā
nūnaṁ bhūmi-tale śubhodaya
iti hlādo bahūḥ sātvatām

"Just as the moon gives life to the world's vegetation, revitalizes the constellations and spreads its own nectar with its rays, so too, your auspicious appearance on earth brings fulfillment to the holy scriptures, joy to the intelligent and abundant ecstasy to the Vaiṣṇavas.

lokānāṁ hita-kāmyayā bhagavato
bhakti-pracāras tvayā
granthānāṁ racanaiḥ satām
abhimatair nānāvidhair darśitaḥ
ācāryaiḥ kṛta-pūrvam eva kila tad
rāmānujādyair budhaiḥ
premāmbhonidhi-vigrahasya bhavato
māhātmya-sīmā na tat

"Wishing to bless everyone in the world, you demonstrated how to preach devotion to the Supreme Lord through writing a multitude of books, all appreciated by the saintly. Śrī Rāmānuja and several other *ācāryas* have done that before. But your glorious achievements are unlimited, for you are the embodiment of the ocean of *prema*.

yad-dhāmnaḥ khalu dhāma caiva
nigame brahmeti saṁjñāyate
yasyāṁśasya kalaiva duḥkha-
nikarair yogeśvarair mṛgyate
vaikuṇṭhe para-mukta-bhṛṅga-
caraṇo nārāyaṇo yaḥ svayaṁ
tasyāṁśī bhagavān svayaṁ rasa-
vapuḥ kṛṣṇo bhavān tat-pradaḥ

"You came to give the Supreme Person Kṛṣṇa Himself, whose body is the form of sacred rapture, the effulgence of whose abode is known in the Veda as Brahman, whose mere partial expansion is the goal of the great yogis' austere practices, who is the source of Nārāyaṇa Himself, and whose lotus feet are surrounded by the most advanced, bee-like liberated souls in Vaikuṇṭha.

sarvācintya-maye parātpara-
pure goloka-vṛndāvane
cil-līlā-rasa-raṅginī parivṛtā sā rādhikā śrī-hareḥ
vātsalyādi rasaiś ca sevita-tanor
mādhurya-sevā-sukhaṁ
nityaṁ yatra madā tanoti hi bhavān
tad-dhāma-sevā-pradaḥ

"You bestowed service to the completely inconceivable divine abode of Goloka Vṛndāvana, which lies beyond the other spiritual worlds, where Śrīmatī Rādhikā, surrounded by Her *sakhīs*, whose pleasure is in the transcendental nectar of the spiritual pastimes, constantly and joyfully serves in the loving mood, Śrī Hari, who is also worshipped in other moods, like parenthood.

śrī-gaurānumataṁ svarūpa-
viditaṁ rūpāgrajenādṛtaṁ
rūpādyaiḥ pariveśitaṁ raghu-
gaṇair āsvāditaṁ sevitam
jīvādyair abhirakṣitaṁ śuka-śiva-
brahmādi-sammānitaṁ
śrī-rādhā-pada-sevanāmṛtam
aho tad dātum īśo bhavān

"You are perfectly competent to give the nectar of service to Śrī Rādhārāṇī's feet, which was approved by Gaurāṅga Mahāprabhu, which was understood by Svarūpa Dāmodara, adored by Sanātana Gosvāmī, distributed by Śrī Rūpa Gosvāmī, relished by Raghunātha Dāsa Gosvāmī and the rest of Śrī Rūpa Gosvāmī's followers, and which is held aloft by Śrī Śukadeva Gosvāmī, Lord Śiva and Lord Brahmā.

kvāhaṁ manda-matis tv atīva patitaḥ
kva tvaṁ jagat-pāvanaḥ
bho svāmin kṛpayāparādha-nicayo
nūnaṁ tvayā kṣamyatām
yāce 'haṁ karuṇā-nidhe varam
imaṁ pādābja-mūle bhavat-
sarvasvāvadhi-rādhikā-dayita-
dāsānāṁ gaṇe gaṇyatām |

"I am a wicked-minded fallen soul, so far from you who purify the entire universe. O master! Please forgive me all my offenses out of your great compassion. I beg you, O ocean of mercy, to grant me this boon – that I be included amongst the followers of Śrīla Bhakti Siddhānta Sarasvatī Gosvāmī Ṭhākura, for whom your lotus feet are everything."

ŚRIMAD-BHAKTIVINODA-DAŚAKAM

This poem, also by Śrīla B.R. Śrīdhara Gosvāmī Mahārāja, was published in *Gauḍīya* magazine, July 1939, 7.47.

amanda-kāruṇya-guṇākara śrī-
caitanya-devasya dayāvatāraḥ
sa gaura-śaktir bhavitā punaḥ kiṁ
padaṁ dṛśor bhakti-vinoda-devaḥ

"You are an embodiment of the most magnanimous Caitanya Deva's mercy. You are the energy of Gaurāṅga. O lord Bhaktivinoda, when will you again be visible to me?

śrīmaj-jagannātha-prabhu-priyo ya
ekātmako gaura-kiśorakena
śrī-gaura-kāruṇya-mayo bhavet kiṁ
nityaṁ smṛtau bhakti-vinoda-devaḥ

"When will Bhaktivinoda Prabhu, the embodiment of Mahāprabhu's blessings, remain fixed in my memory? He is dear to Jagannātha Prabhu and is not different from Gaura Kiśora Dāsa Bābājī Mahārāja.

śrī-nāma-cintāmaṇi-sampracārair
ādarśam ācāra-vidhau dadhau yaḥ
sa jāgarūkaḥ smṛti-mandire kiṁ
nityaṁ bhaved bhakti-vinoda-devaḥ

"When will Bhaktivinoda Prabhu, who gave us the example how to act by preaching the jewel of the Holy Name, remain alive in the temple of my memory?

nāmāparādhai rahitasya nāmno
māhātmya-jātaṁ prakaṭaṁ vidhāya
jīve dayālur bhavitā smṛtau kiṁ
kṛtāsano bhakti-vinoda-devaḥ

"When will Bhaktivinoda Prabhu, who displayed his utmost mercy to all living beings by revealing the glories of the Holy Name, void of any offenses, take his place in the throne of my mind?

gaurasya gūḍha-prakaṭālayasya
sato 'sato harṣa-kunāṭyayoś ca
prakāśako gaurajano bhavet kiṁ
smṛtyāspadaṁ bhakti-vinoda-devaḥ

"When will I remember Bhaktivinoda Prabhu, the member of Gaurāṅga's entourage who revealed His hidden birthplace, to the joy of the saintly and the envious reaction of the wicked?

nirasya vighnān iha bhakti-gaṅgā-
pravāhanenoddhṛta-sarvalokaḥ
bhagīratho nitya-dhiyāṁ padaṁ kiṁ
bhaved asau bhakti-vinoda-devaḥ

"Like King Bhāgīratha, he saved the entire world by destroying all impediments and allowing the Gaṅgā of pure devotion to flow. When will Bhaktivinoda Prabhu be the permanent object of my meditation?

viśveṣu caitanya-kathā-pracārī
māhātmya-śaṁsī guru-vaiṣṇavānām
nāma-grahādarśa iha smṛtaḥ kiṁ
citte bhaved bhakti-vinoda-devaḥ

"When will I remember Bhaktivinoda Prabhu, who preached the message of Caitanya Mahāprabhu throughout the world, who glorified the guru and the Vaiṣṇavas and who set the example for chanting the Holy Name?

prayojanaṁ sann abhidheya-bhakti-
siddhānta-vāṇyā samam atra gaura-
kiśora-sambandha-yuto bhavet kiṁ
cittaṁ gato bhakti-vinoda-devaḥ

"When will Bhaktivinoda Prabhu, himself the representative of the *proyojana-tattva*, appear in my mind, accompanied by Gaura Kiśora Dāsa Bābājī, the personification of the *sambandha-tattva*, and by Bhakti Siddhānta Sarasvatī, the manifestation of the *abhidheya-tattva*.

śikṣāmṛtaṁ sajjana-toṣaṇīṁ ca
cintāmaṇiṁ cātra sajaiva-dharmam
prakāśya caitanya-prado bhavet kiṁ
citte dhṛto bhakti-vinoda-devaḥ

"When will Bhaktivinoda Prabhu, who made people conscious of Śrī Caitanya Mahāprabhu through his publications *Caitanya-śikṣāmṛta*, *Sajjana-toṣaṇī*, *Harināma-cintāmaṇi*, and *Jaiva Dharma*, be held constantly in my mind?

āṣāḍha-darśe 'hani gaura-śakti-
gadādharābhinna-tanur-jahau yaḥ
prapañca-līlām iha no bhavet kiṁ
dṛśyaḥ punar bhakti-vinoda-devaḥ

"When will Bhaktivinoda Prabhu appear to us again? Being nondifferent from Gaura *śakti* Gadādhara Paṇḍita, he left the material world on the same day as he, the dark-moon-day of Āśaḍha month."

SRI GODRUMA-CANDRA-BHAJANOPADEŚAḤ

"Instructions to worship the Moon of Godruma". These verses written by Śrīla Bhaktivinoda Ṭhākura were published posthumously for the first time in 1950 in *Gauḍīya* magazine, 18.47-8, pp. 757-8.

yadi te hari-pāda-saroja-sudhā-
rasa-pāna-paraṁ hṛdayaṁ satatam
parihṛtya gṛhaṁ kali-bhāra-mayaṁ
bhaja godruma-kānana-kuñja-vidhum

"If your heart wishes to always drink the nectar of Hari's lotus feet, then abandon your household life which is oppressed with the spirit of Kālī and worship the moon of Godrum's forest bowers.

dhana-yauvana-jīvana-rājya-sukhaṁ
nahi nityam anukṣaṇa-nāśa-param
tyaja grāmya-kathā-sakalaṁ viphalaṁ
bhaja godruma-kānana-kuñja-vidhum

"All the joys you get from wealth, youth, life and power are temporary and susceptible to destruction at any moment. Give up all your useless mundane conversations and worship the moon of Godrum's forest bowers.

ramaṇī-jana-saṅga-sukhaṁ ca sakhe
carame bhayadaṁ puruṣārtha-haram
hari-nāma-sudhā-rasa-matta-matir
bhaja godruma-kānana-kuñja-vidhum

"O friend! The joys of your company with beautiful women are ultimately a source of fear, for they prevent the achievement of life's real goal of life. Become intoxicated with the nectar of the Holy Names and worship the moon of Godrum's forest bowers.

jaḍa-kāvya-raso nahi kāvya-rasaḥ
kali-pāvana-gaura-raso hi rasaḥ
alam any-kathādy-anuśīlanayā
bhaja godruma-kānana-kuñja-vidhum

"The taste of mundane poetry does not afford the sweet taste of actual poetry. The sweet mellows of true poetry are found in the descriptions of the purifier of the Age of Kālī, Gaura. Give up the study of all other subjects and worship the moon of Godrum's forest bowers.

vṛṣabhānu-sutānvita-vāma-tanuṁ
yamunā-taṭa-nāgara-nanda-sutam
muralī-kala-gīta-vinoda-paraṁ
bhaja godruma-kānana-kuñja-vidhum

"Worship the moon of Godrum's forest bowers, the son of Nanda, the transcendental playboy who sports on the Yamuna's banks with the daughter of Vṛṣabhānu at His left side, joyfully playing wonderful songs on His flute.

hari-kīrtana-madhyagataṁ svajanaiḥ
pariveṣṭita-jāmbunadābha-hariṁ
nija-gauḍa-janaika-kṛpā-jaladhiṁ
bhaja godruma-kānana-kuñja-vidhum

Worship the moon of Godrum's forest bowers, the ocean of mercy for His own companions from the land of Gauḍa; He dances in the midst of Hari *kīrtana*, surrounded by these associates, His effulgent form appearing to be of refined gold.

girirāja-sutā-parivīta-gṛhaṁ
nava-khaṇḍa-patiṁ yati-citta-haram
sura-saṅgha-nutaṁ priyayā sahitaṁ
bhaja godruma-kānana-kuñja-vidhum

"Worship the moon of Godrum's forest bowers – Lord Caitanya, who along with His beloved wife Viṣṇu Priyā is glorified by all demigods and saintly persons. His home, Nabadwip, is surrounded by the river Gaṅgā, the daughter of the Himalayas. He is the Lord of Nabadwip and the stealer of the hearts of all *sannyāsīs*.

kali-kukkura-mudgara-bhāva-dharaṁ
hari-nāma-mahauṣadha-dāna-param
patitārta-dayārdra-sumūrti-dharaṁ
bhaja godruma-kānana-kuñja-vidhum

"Worship the moon of Godrum's forest bowers, who has taken the mood of the hammer-wielding chastiser of the Kālī-dog, who distributes the great panacea of the Holy Name, and whose form is soaked in tearful compassion for the fallen.

ripu-bāndhava-bheda-vihīna-dayā
yad abhīkṣṇam udeti mukhābja-tatau
tam akṛṣṇam iha vraja-rāja-sutaṁ
bhaja godruma-kānana-kuñja-vidhum

"His mercy makes no distinction between friend and foe. Though His bodily hue is not black, He is the son of the king of Vraja. Worship the moon of Godrum's forest bowers.

iha copaniṣat-parigīta-vibhur
dvija-rāja-sutaḥ puraṭābha-hariḥ
nija-dhāmani khelati bandhu-yuto
bhaja godruma-kānana-kuñja-vidhum

"Worship the moon of Godrum's forest bowers – He whose glories are sung in the *Upaniṣads* and is now a son of the best of *brāhmaṇas* with a golden bodily hue, playing in His own *dhāma* with His eternal associates.

avatara-varaṁ paripūrṇa-phalaṁ
para-tattvam ihātma-vilāsa-mayam
vraja-dhāma-rasāmbudhi-gupta-rasaṁ
bhaja godruma-kānana-kuñja-vidhum

"Worship the moon of Godrum's forest bowers, who is the best of the *avatāras* of the Supreme, who brings the ultimate fruit of spiritual life, who is the Supreme Truth come into this world out of His own pleasure and who relishes a taste hidden in the ocean of rapture that is Vraja *dhāma*.

śruti-varṇa-dhanādi na yasya kṛpā-
janane balavad-bhajanena vinā
tam ahaituka-bhāva-pathā hi sakhe
bhaja godruma-kānana-kuñja-vidhum

"Learning, high birth or wealth are useless in bringing about His mercy without intense *bhajana*. O friend, worship the moon of Godrum's forest bowers without any motivation.

api nakra-gatau hrada-madhya-gataṁ
kam amocayad ārta-janaṁ tam ajam
avicintya-balaṁ śiva-kalpa-taruṁ
bhaja godruma-kānana-kuñja-vidhum

"This same Lord also once liberated a distressed elephant (Gajendra) from a crocodile within a lake. He is the unborn one, possessing inconceivable power, and is truly a desire tree of pure auspiciousness. Just worship the beautiful moon of Godrum's forest bowers.

surabhīndra-tapaḥ-pariuṣṭa-mano

vara-varṇa-dharo harir āvirabhūt
tam ajasra-sukhaṁ muni-dhairya-haraṁ
bhaja godruma-kānana-kuñja-vidhum

"When His mind was pleased by the austerities of Indra and Surabhī, He appeared in a golden form before them. Worship the moon of Godrum's forest bowers, who brings unlimited pleasure and who disturbs the calm minds of the silent sages.

abhilāṣa-cayaṁ tad abheda-dhiyam
aśubhaṁ ca śubhaṁ tyaja sarvam idam
anukūlatayā priya-sevanayā
bhaja godruma-kānana-kuñja-vidhum

"Give up all your desires for sense enjoyment. Give up the idea that you are identical with the Lord. Abandon both auspicious and inauspicious works. Only worship the moon of Godruma's forest bowers with acts favorable with His pleasure and by serving those dear to Him.

hari-sevaka-sevana-dharma-paro
hari-nāma-rasāmṛta-pāna-rataḥ
nati-dainya-dayā-paramāna-yuto
bhaja godruma-kānana-kuñja-vidhum

"Become fixed in the religion of serving the servants of Hari. Be fixed in drinking the nectar of the Holy Names. Always be fixed in respect, humility and compassion. Worship the moon of Godrum's forest bowers.

vada yādava mādhava kṛṣṇa hare
vada rāma janārdana keśava he
vṛṣabhānu-sutā-priyanātha sadā
bhaja godruma-kānana-kuñja-vidhum

"Sing the names of Yādava, Mādhava, Kṛṣṇa and Hari. Sing the names of Rāma, Janārdana and Keśava. Always sing the name of the dearest Lord of the daughter of Vṛṣabhānu. Worship the moon of Godrum's forest bowers.

vada yāmuna-tīra-vanādri-pate
vada gokula-kānana-puñja-rave
vada rāsa-rasāyana gaura-hare
bhaja godruma-kānana-kuñja-vidhum

"Sing the name of the Lord of the forests by the Yamuna banks. Sing the name of the sun which lights up the gardens of Gokula. Sing the name of Gaurahari, the knower of sacred rapture. Worship the moon of Godrum's forest bowers.

cala gaura-vanaṁ nava-khaṇḍamayaṁ
paṭha gaurahareś caritāṇi mudā
luṭha gaura-padāṅkita-gāṅga-taṭaṁ
bhaja godruma-kānana-kuñja-vidhum

"Go live in Gaurāṅga's forest with its nine divisions. Joyfully study Gaurahari's life. Roll about in the dust by the banks of the Ganges marked with Gaurāṅga's footprints. And worship the moon of Godrum's forest bowers.

smara gaura-gadādhara-keli-kalāṁ
bhava gaura-gadādhara-pakṣa-caraḥ
śṛṇu gaura-gadādhara-cāru-kathāṁ
bhaja godruma-kānana-kuñja-vidhum

"Remember always the enchanting pastimes of Gaura-Gadādhara. Become a follower of Gaura-Gadādhara. Always listen to the enchanting topics of Gaura-Gadādhara. Worship the moon of Godrum's forest bowers."

A LIST OF BHAKTIVINODA ṬHĀKURA'S WRITTEN WORKS

Other than the titles already mentioned, Śrīla Bhaktivinoda Ṭhākura wrote numerous works from 1866 to 1907 which are listed here as far as possible.

(1) *Balid-e-registry* (Urdu), 1866.
(2) *Speech on Gautam* (English), 1856.

(3) Speech on the *Bhāgavatam* (English), 1869.
(4) *Garbha-stotra-vyākhyā* (Bengali), 1870.
(5) *Reflections* (English), 1871.
(6) *Ślokas of Haridāsa Thākura's Samādhi* (English), 1871.
(7) *Jagannātha Mandir of Purī* (English), 1871.
(8) *Akhras of Purī* (English), 1871.
(9) *Vedāntādhikaraṇa-mālā* (Sanskrit), 1872.
(10) *Datta-kaustubham* (Sanskrit), 1874.
(11) *Datta-vaṁśa-mālā* (Sanskrit), 1876.
(12) *Bauddha-vijaya-kāvyam* (Sanskrit), 1878.
(13) *Śrī-Kṛṣṇa-saṁhitā* (Sanskrit with Bengali translation), 1880.
(14) *Kalyāṇa-kalpa-taru* (Bengali songs), 1881.
(15) *Śrī-sajjana-toṣaṇī* (Bengali monthly magazine), 1881–1898.
(16) Review of *Nitya-rūpa-saṁsthāpana* (English), 1883.
(17) *Śrimad-Bhagavad-gītā*, with *Viśvanātha Cakravartīpāda*'s commentary, and *Rasika-rañjana* translation (Bengali), 1886.
(18) *Śrī-Caitanya-śikṣāmṛta* (Bengali), 1886.
(19) *Sammodana* commentary to *Śikṣāṣṭaka* (Sanskrit), 1886.
(20) *Manaḥ-śikṣā-padyānuvāda* (Bengali), 1886.
(21) *Daśopaniṣad-chūrṇikā* (Sanskrit), 1886.
(22) *Bhāvāvalī*, verses and commentary (Sanskrit), 1886.
(23) *Prema-pradīpa* (Bengali novel), 1886.
(24) *Viṣṇu-sahasra-nāma* with Baladeva's commentary (Sanskrit), 1886.
(25) Published Satyarāja Khān's *Śrī-Kṛṣṇa-vijaya*, 1886.
(26) *Chaitanyopaniṣat* with *Caitanya-caraṇāmṛta* commentary (Sanskrit), 1887.
(27) *Vaiṣṇava-siddhānta-mālā* (Bengali), 1888.
(28) *Śrī-Āmnāya-sūtram* (Sanskrit *sūtras*, Bengali explanation), 1890.
(29) *Śrī-Nabadvīpa-dhāma-māhātmya* (Bengali), 1890.
(30) *Siddhānta-darpaṇa* translation (Bengali), 1890.
(31) *Śrīmad-Bhagavad-gītā, Bengali translation (Vidvad-rañjana-bhāṣya) and Baladeva's Sanskrit commentary (Bengali)*, 1891.
(32) *Śrī-Harināma* (Bengali), 1892.
(33) *Śrī-Nāma* (Bengali), 1892.
(34) *Śrī-Nāma-tattva* (Bengali), 1892.
(35) *Śrī-Nāma-mahimā* (Bengali), 1892.
(36) *Śrī-Nāma-pracāra* (Bengali), 1892.
(37) *Śrīman-Mahāprabhura Śikṣā* (Bengali), 1892.
(38) *Tatta-viveka* (Sanskrit verses and Bengali commentary), 1893.
(39) *Śaraṇāgati* (Bengali songs), 1893.
(40) *Śoka-śātana* (Bengali song), 1893.
(41) *Jaiva-dharma* (Bengali), 1893.
(42) *Tattva-sūtra* (Sanskrit and Bengali commentary), 1894.
(43) *Īśopaniṣat Vedārka-dīdhiti-vyākhyā* (Bengali), 1894.
(44) *Tattva-muktāvalī* or *Mayavāda-śata-dūṣaṇī* (Bengali commentary), 1894.
(45) *Amṛta-pravāha-bhāṣya on Śrī Caitanya-caritāmṛta* (Bengali), 1895.
(46) Śrī-Gaurāṅga-smaraṇa-maṅgala-stotram (Sanskrit), 1896.
(47) *Life and Precepts of Śrī Caitanya Mahāprabhu* (English), 1896.
(48) *Śrī-Rāmānuja-Upedeśa* (Bengali), 1896.
(49) *Artha-pañchaka* (Bengali), 1896.
(50) Bengali translation of *Brahma-saṁhitā*, 1897.
(51) *Kalyāṇa-kalpa-taru* (Revised), 1897.
(52) Translation and commentary on *Kṛṣṇakarṇāmṛtam* (Bengali), 1898.
(53) Translation and *Pīyūṣa-varṣiṇī* commentary on *Upadeśāmṛtam* (Bengali), 1898.
(54) *Bhagavad-gītā* with Mādhva's commentary (Bengali), 1898.

(55-56) Śrī Sanātana Gosvāmī Prabhu's *Bṛhad-Bhāgavatāmṛta* in two volumes (Bengali translation), 1898.
(57) Narahari Ṭhākura's *Bhajanāmṛtam* (Bengali commentary), 1899.
(58) *Nabadvīpa-bhāva-taraṅginī* (Bengali verse), 1899.
(59) *Śrī-Harināma-cintāmaṇi* (Bengali verse), 1900.
(60) *Tattva-vaṁśa-mālā* (Bengali), 1900.
(61) *Bhāgavatārka-marīchi-mālā* (compilation and Bengali translation), 1901.
(62) *Śrī-saṅkalpa-kalpadruma* (Bengali commentary), 1901.
(63) *Padma Purāṇa* (edited in Bengali), 1901.
(64) *Bhajana-rahasya* (collection of verses and Bengali verse translation), 1902.
(65) *Vijana-grāma o sannyāsi* (Bengali verse, revised edition), 1902.
(66) *Śrī-Kṛṣṇa-saṁhitā* (Sanskrit and Bengali, revised), 1903.
(67) *Sat-kriyā-sāra-dīpikā* (Bengali, edited), 1903.
(68) *Śrī-Caitanya-śikṣāmṛta* (Bengali, revised and expanded), 1905.
(69) *Prema-vivarta* (Bengali, edited), 1906.
(70) *Sva-niyama-dvādaśakam* (Sanskrit verse), 1907.
(71) *Śrī-Nimbārka-daśa-ślokī* (Bengali trans. and comment), 1907.
(72) *Śrī-Gītamālā* (Bengali songs), 1907.
(73) *Śrī-Gītāvalī* (Bengali songs), 1907.
(74) *Hari kathā* (Bengali verse), 1850.

Śrīla Bhaktivinoda Ṭhākura wrote *Śrī-Kṛṣṇa-saṁhitā* and *Kalyāṇa-kalpa-taru* and started publishing the monthly magazine, *Sajjana-toṣaṇī,* while living at Naral in the Jessore district, from 1878 to 1881. He published an English edition of *Sajjana-toṣaṇī* in 1883 while in Barasat. Then in 1886, when in Serampore, he published his translation-commentary to the *Bhagavad-gītā*, *Rasika-rañjana marmānuvāda,* with Viśvanātha Cakravartī Ṭhākura's commentary *Sārārtha-darśinī.* While in Serampore, he also wrote *Caitanya-śikṣāmṛta,* the *Sanmodana-bhāṣya* commentary to Mahāprabhu's *Śikśaṣṭaka*, and a book named *Bhaktivinoda.* In 1887, while in Sambalpur, he published *Chaitanyopaniṣat* after receiving a unique hand-written manuscript from a disciple named Madhusūdana Dāsa. Later in the same year, while living in Krishnanagar, he started work on *Āmnāya-sūtra* and published his *Nabadvīpa-dhāma-māhātmya.* In 1896, after returning to Kolkata from Tripura, he wrote and published his English book *Life and Precepts of Śrī Caitanya Mahāprabhu* and the Sanskrit *Gaurāṅga-smaraṇa-maṅgala-stotra.*

Śrīla Gaura Kiśora Dāsa Bābājī

namo gaura-kiśorāya
sākṣād vairāgya-mūrtaye
vipralambha-rasāmbhodhe
pādāmbujāya te namaḥ

"I bow to your lotus feet, Śrīla Gaura Kiśora Dāsa Bābājī, the embodiment of renunciation and the ocean of sacred rapture in separation."

EARLY LIFE

Paramahaṁsa Śrīla Gaura Kiśora Dāsa Bābājī Mahārāja was born on the banks of the Padma River in Bagayan village in the Faridpur district in what is now Bangladesh. The names of his parents are unknown. His given name was Vaṁśī Dāsa. He was born sometime in the middle of the nineteenth century. He was the *dīkṣā-guru* of Śrīla Bhakti Siddhānta Sarasvatī Gosvāmī Prabhupāda, founder of the Śrī Chaitanya Math and the worldwide Gaudiya Maths.

Vaṁśī Dāsa's parents had him married at an early age according to the custom of the time, but he always remained detached from householder life. His main interest was always worshipping the Lord. When his wife died, he left home, and in order to perform *bhajana* in solitude with extreme renunciation, he went to Vrindavan, where he took the *paramahaṁsa veṣa* from Śrīmad Bhāgavata Dāsa Bābājī (a disciple of Śrīla Jagannātha Dāsa Bābājī Mahārāja) and took the name Gaura Kiśora Dāsa Bābājī Mahārāja.

BĀBĀJĪ MAHĀRĀJA COMES TO NABADWIP

After being initiated into the Bābājī order, Bābājī Mahārāja spent thirty years in Vraja engaged in intense devotional practice. He also traveled outside of the Vraja area, visiting northern India and Bengal. While in the east, he met many of the leading Vaiṣṇavas of Bengal and Odisha, such as Svarūpa Dāsa Bābājī of Puri, Bhagavān Dāsa Bābājī of Kalna and Caitanya Dāsa Bābājī of Kuliya.

In 1893, after the birthplace of Caitanya Mahāprabhu was consecrated at the Sri Mayapur Yogapitha, Jagannātha Dāsa Bābājī Mahārāja ordered Gaura Kiśora Dāsa Bābājī Mahārāja to stay in Nabadwip. This is where he remained for the rest of his life. He saw all the residents of Nabadwip with transcendental eyes, considering them to be divine beings. He thus accepted *mādhukarī* from them, cooking everything in a rejected clay bowl. It is said that sometimes he would subsist on nothing but Ganges water and mud. Sometimes he would go for long periods without eating, chanting the Holy Names constantly. He set the standard for those in the renounced order who live the life of solitary worship, remaining completely independent of others.

Mahāprabhu's personal envoy Śrīla Bhaktivinoda Ṭhākura was extremely impressed by Bābājī Mahārāja's extraordinary renunciation, his pure devotion and his attachment to the Lord. Bābājī Mahārāja would often go to Śrīla Bhaktivinoda Thakura's home in Godrumdwip, Svananda Sukhada Kunja, where he would listen to him speaking *Śrīmad Bhāgavatam* and discuss Vaiṣṇava theology with him.

SARASVATĪ ṬHĀKURA MEETS BĀBĀJĪ MAHĀRĀJA

Bābājī Mahārāja never accepted service from anyone. He constantly chanted the Holy Name, sometimes counting the names on a Tulasī *mālā*, at other times by making knots on long strips of an old cloth. His favorite texts were Narottama Ṭhākura's *Prārthanā* and *Prema-bhakti-candrikā,* which he considered to be his all-in-all. His renunciation resembled that of Raghunātha Dāsa Gosvāmī, and he possessed the same attachment to Kṛṣṇa.

In 1898, Śrīla Bhakti Siddhānta Sarasvatī Gosvāmī Ṭhākura got the first *darśana* of Śrīla Gaura Kiśora Dāsa Bābājī Mahārāja at Svananda Sukhada Kunja in Godrumdwip. Sarasvatī Ṭhākura was enchanted and overcame with ecstasy by Bābājī Mahārāja's heartfelt emotional *kīrtana.* He wrote the *kīrtana* song down and later made it available to the devotees. The song describes Śrīla Raghunātha Dāsa Gosvāmī's ecstatic separation from Śrīmatī Rādhārāṇī.

kothāy go premamayi rādhe rādhe
rādhe rādhe go, jaya rādhe rādhe
dekhā diye prāṇa rākha rādhe rādhe
tomāra kāṅgāl tomāy ḍāke rādhe rādhe
rādhe vṛndāvana-vilāsini rādhe rādhe
rādhe kānu-mano-mohini rādhe rādhe
rādhe aṣṭa-sakhīra śiromaṇi rādhe rādhe
rādhe vṛṣabhānu-nandini rādhe rādhe
(gosāi) niyama kare sadāi ḍāke rādhe rādhe
(gosāi) ekabāra ḍāke keśī-ghāṭe
ābāra ḍāke vaṁśī-vaṭe rādhe rādhe
(gosāi) ekabāra ḍāke nidhuvane
ābāra ḍāke kuñja-vane rādhe rādhe
(gosāi) ekabāra ḍāke rādhākuṇḍe
ābāra ḍāke śyāma-kuṇḍe rādhe rādhe
(gosāṣī) ekabāra ḍāke kusuma-vane
ābāra ḍāke govardhane rādhe rādhe
(gosāṣī) ekabāra ḍāke tāla-vane
ābāra ḍāke tamāla-vane rādhe rādhe
(gosāṣī) maline vasana diye gāya,
vrajera dhulāya gaṛāgaṛi jāya rādhe rādhe
(gosāṣī) mukhe rādhā rādhā bole
bhase nayanera jale rādhe rādhe
(gosāṣī) vṛndāvane kulikuli
keṅde beṛāya rādhā boli rādhe rādhe
(gosāṣī) chāpānna daṇḍa rātri dine, jāne nā
rādhā-govinda bine rādhe rādhe
tāra para cāri daṇḍa śuti thāke svapne
rādhā-govinda dekhe rādhe rādhe

"Where is the abode of all love, Rādhā! Glories to Rādhā! Show Yourself to me, O Rādhā, and save my life. Your beggar is calling for You, O Rādhā. O Rādhā, You enjoy pleasure pastimes in Vrindavan, You enchant Kṛṣṇa's mind, You are chief amongst the eight *sakhīs*, and are the daughter of Vṛṣabhānu.

"Raghunātha Dāsa Gosvāmī regularly, constantly calls out to You, O Rādhā. He calls for You in Keshī Ghat, in Vamshī Vat, Nidhuvana, Kunjavana, in Radha Kunda and Shyama Kunda, in Kusumavana and Govardhan, in Talavan and Tamalavan. He calls out wearing only a worn and dirty cloth and rolling in the Vrindavan dust. The names of Rādhā on his lips, his eyes are filled with tears. He wanders through every part of Vraja, calling Rādhā's name and weeping. Night or day, for twenty-three hours he thinks of nothing but Rādhā-Govinda, and when he sleeps, he dreams of Rādhā-Govinda."

BĀBĀJĪ MAHĀRĀJA INITIATES ŚRĪLA PRABHUPĀDA

In January 1900, Śrīla Bhakti Siddhānta Sarasvatī Gosvāmī Ṭhākura took initiation from Gaura Kiśora Dāsa Bābājī Mahārāj in Godrum Svananda Sukhada Kunja on the instructions of Śrīla Bhaktivinoda Ṭhākura. Śrīla Bhakti Siddhānta Sarasvatī Gosvāmī was Bābājī Mahārāja's only disciple. Bābājī Mahārāja was an anchorite who had sworn not to take any disciples, but he was forced to change his decision when he saw Sarasvatī Ṭhākura's determination and devotion.

The story is told that Śrīla Prabhupāda asked Gaura Kiśora Dāsa Bābājī Mahārāja several times to give him initiation. The first time he asked, Bābājī Mahārāja told him, "If Mahāprabhu tells me to, I will."

The second time Bābājī Mahārāja told him that he had forgotten to ask Mahāprabhu. Śrīla Prabhupāda did not give up and came a third time. Bābājī Mahārāja said, "Virtuousness, scholarship and other qualities are not the means to attain the Lord. They do not give you any right to initiation."

Though he had been turned back by Bābājī Mahārāja repeatedly, Śrīla Prabhupāda did not abandon his resolution. Rāmānujācārya was turned back eighteen times before receiving the mercy of Goṣṭhīpūrṇa. Śrīla Prabhupāda, similarly, showed his qualities of patience and determination and continued to come before Bābājī Mahārāja. He humbly entreated him to give him initiation until finally, his heart melted, and out of great affection Bābājī Mahārāja mercifully initiated Śrīla Prabhupāda by sprinkling the dust of his lotus feet on his head.

Bābājī Mahārāja would never allow any materialistic persons touch his feet. If they did so, he would make a show of anger, saying, "You are doomed!" Most people were thus afraid to attempt it. On this occasion, however, he himself offered the dust of his feet to his dear disciple and smeared it on his body. From Śrīla Prabhupāda's disciples, it is heard that he was turned back twelve times before Bābājī Mahārāja became compassionate and initiated him at his thirteenth request. Others say that it happened on the fourth time. This story reminds one of Narottama Dāsa Ṭhākura's initiation by Śrīla Lokanātha Gosvāmī. Unswerving dedication to the guru is the sign of a true disciple. Afterward, Bābājī Mahārāja, judging Śrīla Prabhupāda to be eminently qualified for the task, blessed him and ordered him to preach Mahāprabhu's message all around the world.

ŚRĪLA PRABHUPĀDA DESCRIBES HIS GURU

Śrīla Prabhupāda wrote the following words about his guru, with exemplary humility, in order to show the world definitively the path of auspiciousness: "In order to complete the gaping needs that I felt, I was busily trying to get my hands on everything under the sun. I thought that possessions would fulfill my needs. Over time, I had indeed accumulated a great number of rare possessions, but I was not able to rid myself of the sense of being unfulfilled. I had encountered many personalities who were reputed to be great saints but saw various deficiencies in every one of them and so was unable to give them my full respect. Seeing my pitiful and gloomy state, fortunately, the supremely merciful Śrī Gaurāṅga Mahāprabhu allowed two of his dearest companions to show their kindness to me. I was egotistically so self-absorbed that I had completely lost any sense of where my well-being could be found. Even so, due to past pious activities, I was able to get the association of Śrīla Bhaktivinoda Ṭhākura, who was my ever well-wisher. My Prabhu often came to visit him and sometimes stayed overnight at his house. Out of mercy to me, Śrīla Bhaktivinoda Ṭhākura introduced me to my Prabhu. From the time that I first met my Prabhu, my stubborn egoism started to diminish. Previously, I used to think that everyone who took birth in a human body was filled with the same faults that I had, but upon seeing my Prabhu's divine character I realized that there truly were flawless Vaiṣṇavas in this world who matched the ideal."

Śrīla Prabhupāda farther wrote, "Many people who saw Gaura Kiśora Dāsa Bābājī Mahārāja, whether innocent or experienced, young or old, learned or ignorant, or proud of their being advanced devotees, were not able to truly see him. This is the divine power of Kṛṣṇa's devotees. Hundreds of people came to him seeking help in fulfilling their material desires ,and he would give them advice, but this was a kind of deception. There are countless persons who take on the dress of a saintly person and make a show of acting like a saintly person, but on closer analysis are far from the standard. My Prabhu was not a cheater like them. It is clear from his spiritual activities that he identified complete honesty with the truth. His sincere affection was incomparable; it proved that the attainment of mystical (yogic) powers is a deception. He showed no enmity for those who opposed him or disagreed with him; similarly, he made no particular external show of affection for those who were objects of his compassion. He used to say, 'I neither love nor hate anyone in this world; everyone is the object of my respect.'

"Amazingly, Prabhu would be surrounded by people with no understanding – fakers and materialists inimical to the path of pure devotion who thought themselves to be recipients of such a saintly person's mercy but continued to engage in sensual activities. My Prabhu never openly rejected any of these people, but he never openly accepted any of them, either."

BĀBĀJĪ MAHĀRĀJA'S DISAPPEARANCE

Bābājī Mahārāja was an expert judge of character and had highly developed forcsight and clairvoyance, often foretelling events in the distant future.

On the 30th of Kārtika in 1322 Bengali (1915 A.D.), Paramahaṁsa Śrīla Gaura Kiśora Dāsa Bābājī Mahārāja entered the eternal pastimes of the Lord. At the time, he was residing at Rahira Dharmahala in Kuliya. When Śrīla Bhakti Siddhānta Sarasvatī Gosvāmī Ṭhākura received the news of his disappearance, he was overcome with feelings of separation from his guru and immediately hurried to the site of his departure. He was heart-broken to see that *mahānta bābājīs* (abbots) of various *ākhaṛās* (*āśramas*) were busily arguing about where and how to perform Bābājī Mahārāja's *samādhi* rites. Their idea was to lay claim to any future *samādhi* temple of such an advanced devotee as such a temple would be an attractive pilgrimage site and a possible source of money-making. Śrīla Prabhupāda alone stood up and spoke out against this rascaldom. As things heated up, the Nabadwip chief of police, Yatīndranātha Siṁha Rāya Bāhādura, came to maintain the peace.

At that time, Śrīla Prabhupāda had not yet taken *tridaṇḍa sannyāsa*. The *bābājīs* argued that as they had taken the renounced order, they had the right to perform the last rites for one of their order. As this was not the case for Śrīla Prabhupāda, he had no rights. Śrīla Prabhupāda displayed his spiritual strength and stated that he was Bābājī Mahārāja's one and only disciple. He then asked them if there was any amongst them who had not had illicit sexual relations in the previous one year, six months, three months, one month, or even in the previous three days. He who had so done would be doomed if he touched Bābājī Mahārāja's divine remains.

When he heard Śrīla Prabhupāda make this challenge, Yatīndra Bābu asked how anyonc could prove whether or not he had had illicit sexual relations. Śrīla Prabhupāda answered that he would take anyone who came forward at his word. When the *bābājīs* looked at the effulgence of pure spiritual practice emanating from Śrīla Prabhupāda, they slowly slunk away, one by one. The chief of police was embarrassed at this sight, and he paid his obeisances to Śrīla Prabhupāda and then left himself.

Some residents of Kuliya told Śrīla Prabhupāda what Bābājī Mahārāja had said about his last desires. Apparently, he had stated that he wished his body to be dragged through the streets of Nabadwip so that it would be covered by the dust of the holy *dhāma*. Śrīla Prabhupāda replied, "This is my gurudeva. Even Kṛṣṇa is honored to carry him on His shoulders and carries him like a crown upon His head. He said these things to confound the pride of the materialists with his humility. We may be inexperienced fools and offenders, but we should still make an effort to understand his intention. When Haridāsa Ṭhākura entered his eternal pastimes, Lord Gaurāṅga took his transcendental body to His chest and danced with it. What a precedent He set for honoring the perfected soul's departure! We would rather follow Mahāprabhu's example and carry Bābājī Mahārāja's divine remains on our head."

On the first day of Agrahāyaṇa in Kuliya's Nutan Chada, Śrīla Prabhupāda performed the *samādhi* rites for Śrīla Gaura Kiśora Dāsa Bābājī Mahārāja according to Vaiṣṇava *smṛti* injunctions during the noon. It was *utthāna-ekādaśī-tithi*. A certain Poddara Mahāśaya of Lohagada in the Jessore district gave the land for the *samādhi*, renouncing any claims on the property. Later, however, he reneged on his promise and came to live there himself and engaged in various illicit activities on the site. During the Ganges floods one season, the *samādhi* site gradually started to drown into the river. On the fifth of Bhādra, 1339 Bengali (1932 A.D.) Śrīla Bhakti Siddhānta Sarasvatī Gosvāmī Ṭhākura retrieved the *samādhi* remains from the Ganges bed and took them to the Chaitanya Math, where he established a *samādhi* temple on the banks of Radha Kunda. The site was consecrated on the second of Āsvina, 1339, and in the course of time, a small temple housing a Śrī mūrti of Gaura Kiśora Dāsa Bābājī Mahārāja was constructed there. The Śrī mūrti's *nitya-sevā* has continued ever since.

BĀBĀJĪ MAHĀRĀJA'S TEACHINGS

Śrīla Bhakti Siddhānta Sarasvatī Gosvāmī Ṭhākura's disciples recounted some events from Bābājī Mahārāja's divine life which are full of import for the practitioner of devotional life.

(1) On one occasion, a certain *bābājī* came to visit Śrīla Gaura Kiśora Dāsa Bābājī with some of his followers in tow. These acolytes began glorifying their guru to Bābājī Mahārāja. "Our Prabhu is so merciful. He takes so much trouble to travel from place to place to deliver the poor, fallen souls. If he did not travel, what would be the destiny of these forsaken places?" Bābājī Mahārāja immediately became cross and answered, "If someone makes a pretence of delivering the world when in fact he is only interested in making money and garnering prestige, he not only does no one any good but falls down for having cheated others."

(2) One day, a few devotees were describing the expertise of a particular lecturer on *Śrīmad Bhāgavatam*. Bābājī Mahārāja, as an indweller of the heart, knew that this individual did *Śrīmad Bhāgavatam* recitation to earn money. He said, "This fellow does not explain the *Śrīmad Bhāgavatam* or the scriptures of the Gosvāmīs. He is simply speaking on the sense-gratificatory scriptures. He isn't chanting 'Gaura, Gaura!' or 'Kṛṣṇa, Kṛṣṇa!', but 'Money! Money!' It has nothing to do with *bhajana*. The end result is that the true Vaiṣṇava *dharma* is obscured. Nothing good can come from it; indeed, the world will be harmed by such preaching."

(3) One day Bābājī Mahārāja was chanting *japa* in Nabadwip. At 10 o'clock in the night,

he suddenly jumped up and exclaimed, "Did you see that? Did you see? A professional speaker on the *Śrīmad Bhāgavatam* has gone to Pabna district and has just made a chaste widow break her vows! What a shame! These rascals are giving a bad name to *dharma*." He spoke as if he were personally witnessing the event.

(4) The owner of the Nabadwip Dharmashala was a certain Giriśa Bābu. One day, his wife offered to build a cottage for Bābājī Mahārāja. He answered, "I have no problem sleeping under the straw shelter under a boat. The only problem I have is that so many rascals are constantly coming to me asking me to bless them. They disturb my chanting. They don't really want my blessings because they don't really want what is best for them, but still, they come to disrupt my chanting the Holy Name. If you give me your brick outhouse, I will be able to chant in peace. No one will come to bother me there." When he realized that Bābājī Mahārāja was serious, Giriśa Babu immediately had the outhouse purified with cow dung and brought in a mason to completely redo the building.

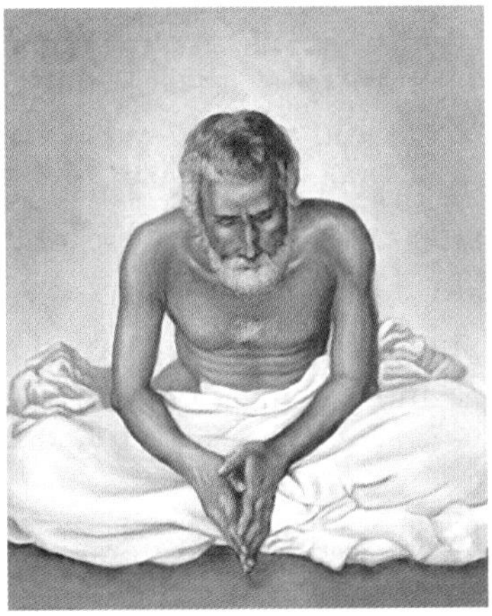

(5) One day during the cold season, a devotee made a gift of a quilt to Bābājī Mahārāja, but rather than wrapping himself in it, he simply draped it over the tiny bamboo shelter. When asked why he did that, he answered that the cold would go away simply upon seeing the quilt.

(6) One day the Rāja of Kashim Bazaar, Sir Manīndra Candra Nandī Bāhādura, invited Bābājī Mahārāja to his palatial residence for a Vaiṣṇava assembly. Bābājī Mahārāja answered, "If you want my association, leave all your riches and come and live under a bamboo shelter like mine. You won't have to worry about food. I will beg enough to feed both of us. If I go to stay in your palace, it won't be long before I start desiring to enjoy sense gratification. I will start thinking about how I can accumulate a property for myself. Then before you know it, I will become your enemy. If you want to preserve our friendship and if you wish to be kind to me as your Vaiṣṇava friend, then you will come to the *dhāma* and join me in worshipping the Lord and eating *mādhukarī*."

GAURA KIŚORA DĀSA BĀBĀJĪ MAHĀRĀJA'S FAVORITE SONG

Narottama Dāsa Ṭhākura's songs were much beloved of Bābājī Mahārāja. He was often heard to sing one of them in particular. All the Vaiṣṇava teachings can be found in this one song:

gaurā pahū nā bhajiyā moinu
prema ratana dhana helāya hārāinu

"Due to my neglect in not worshipping Lord Caitanya, I have carelessly cast away the treasure of love for Kṛṣṇa.

adhane yatana kari dhana teyāginu
āpana karama-doṣe āpani ḍubinu

"I have rejected the real purpose of my life and given my attention to worthless things. I am drowning because of my own misdeeds.

satsaṅga chāṛi kainu asate vilāsa
te-kāraṇe lāgila je karma-bandha-phāṅsa

"Disregarding the association of the holy, I have amused myself in the company of the wicked. Because of this there is a noose of karmic bondage around my neck.

viṣaya viṣama viṣa satata khāinu
gaura kīrtana rase magana nā hainu

"I have constantly drunk the most dangerous poison of sense gratification and so could not absorb myself in the taste of Mahāprabhu's divine *saṅkīrtana*.

keno vā āchaye prāṇa ki sukha pāiyā
narottama dāsa kena nā gela mariyā

"What pleasure keeps me still alive today? Narottama Dāsa wonders, 'Why have I not died from this misery?' "

Śrīla Vaṁśī Dāsa Bābājī

This article is based on other articles that previously appeared in the old *Gauḍīya* magazine and various statements made by Śrīla Bhakti Siddhānta Sarasvatī Gosvāmī Ṭhākura and his disciples.

THE PARAMAHAṀSA AVADHŪTA

Śrīla Vaṁśī Dāsa Bābājī Mahārāja appeared in the village of Majidpur in the Mymansingh district of current Bangladesh, near the city of Jamalpur. The names of Bābājī Mahārāja's parents are not known.

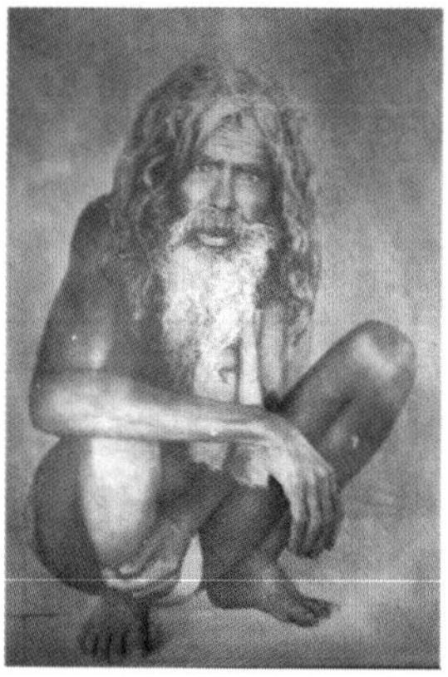

Bābājī Mahārāj came to Nabadwip from East Bengal. He was a *paramahaṁsa* Vaiṣṇava who acted in the manner of an *avadhūta*[28].

Vaṁśī Dāsa Bābājī lived in Nabadwip under a tree on the banks of the Ganges, demonstrating a very high standard of renunciation. Śrīla Bhakti Siddhānta Sarasvatī Gosvāmī Ṭhākura was attracted by his *paramahaṁsa* Vaiṣṇava behavior and his disregard for the rules and regulations of society at large. Śrīla Prabhupāda himself paid his obeisances to Bābājī Mahārāja from a distance but did not allow his disciples to go near him. For though Bābājī Mahārāja was a *paramahaṁsa* Vaiṣṇava, an ordinary beginner in devotional practice would likely misunderstand his indifference to the rules and regulations and end up committing offenses at his feet.

28 The word *avadhūta* refers to one who has shaken free from all worldly feeling and obligation. He does not care for social conventions, particularly the Varṇāśrama Dharma, and he is quite eccentric in his behavior. Nityananda Prabhu is often characterized as an *avadhūta*.

The primary purpose of the rules and regulations is to bring pleasure to Śrī Śrī Rādhā Govinda. A practitioner who has not yet overcome his mundane conditioning may very well judge an advanced Vaiṣṇava according to rules and regulations which were designed to help him advance to the next level of spiritual realization. If he measures a perfected soul by the standards which have been set for the beginner, as a result of committing offenses he falls down from the devotional path.

It is said that Bābājī Mahārāja had two cloth bags. He kept his Nitāi-Gaura deities in one, Rādhā Govinda in the other. He regularly worshipped Them, taking Them out of the bags and serving them mentally with *mantras*. Then, after the worship, he would place the deities back in their bags. On occasion, he would leave Them outside so that people could look at them. Once in a while, he would offer tobacco to Rādhā Govinda in a hookah – but not to Nitāi-Gaurāṅga. Many people would come bringing offerings of rice, fruits, vegetables, flour, or bananas, but Bābājī Mahārāja would ignore them. When he noticed an accumulation of such offerings, he would mentally offer them to his deities and then distribute the remnants to whoever happened to be present. Who can understand such enigmatic behavior? Bābājī Mahārāja was tall enough to be able to pick fruits for his *pūjā* from the high branches of a tree without making use of ladders or other paraphernalia. On one occasion, he fell from a tree, and from that time on he took on the guise of a lame person. He only wore a *kaupīn*, a strip of cloth covering his private parts, and left his hair and beard uncut and unkempt.

BĀBĀJĪ MAHĀRĀJA'S VOYAGE TO VRAJA

Bābājī Mahārāja did not stay exclusively in the Nabadwip area but traveled to many holy places where he also performed his spiritual practices. He embodied the verse *kṛṣṇa-bhakti-rasa-bhāvita-matiḥ*, and wherever he went he always remained immersed in the ocean of Kṛṣṇa *rasa*. Therefore, everything reminded him of Kṛṣṇa *līlā*, but especially the banyan tree. Whenever he saw a banyan tree, he would sit under it, taking it to be the Vamshi Vata under which Kṛṣṇa played His flute to attract the *gopīs*. Once he had stationed himself there, it would be difficult to get him to move.

On the twelth of Phālguna, 1347 (Monday, Feb. 24, 1941), Bābājī Mahārāja left Nabadwip city and headed for Vrindavan. He sometimes walked, sometimes He traveled by ox-cart and sometimes by rail. He first went to Katwa where he stayed for two days under a *vaṭa* tree near the train station. Then he took the train to Bhagalpur, where he stayed for one day under a *vaṭa* tree near the station and for four days by the Ganges. Then he traveled on to Gaya, where he remained on the banks of the Phalgu River for three days. He also stayed on a boat in the Ganges near Dashshvamedha Ghata in Benares for three days, spent another three days in Ayodhya by the Sarayū River, including three hours under a *vaṭa* tree, at the Triveni confluence at Prayag for ten days, two days at the Vishrama Ghata in Mathura, eight days at the Vamshi Vata in Vrindavan, nine days at the Madhyacada on the banks of the Yamuna, one day at the Govindajī temple, two days at Kaliyadaha, eight days under a tamal tree on the east bank of Surya Kunda at Nandagram, two days at Pavana Sarovara, four days at the foot of a *pīlu* tree, and then another nine days at Vamshī Vata Ghata in Vrindavan. Everywhere he went, he remained absorbed in chanting the Holy Names and meditating on Kṛṣṇa's form and pastimes. After three months, he returned to Nabadwip Dhāma, in the month of Jyaiṣṭha.

Those who traveled with Bābājī Mahārāja recounted that when wandering through Vraja-mandala, he would sometimes sing songs about Kṛṣṇa's pastimes, sometimes glorify Nabadwip *dhāma*, sometimes chant loudly, sometimes laugh madly. Sometimes, he would babble incoherently, and oftentimes he would remain completely silent. When visiting a temple, he was often seen muttering confidentially to the deities, disclosing some personal sentiment to them. All in all, his companions were charmed by his devotional absorption.

In the old *Gauḍīya* weekly magazine, farther accounts of Bābājī Mahārāja's travels were given. It is stated there that between 1943 to 1944, he traveled to Ambika Kalna, Kharagpur, Baleshwar, Soro, Bhadrak, Khorda Road and Purushottama *dhāma*. Afterwards, he again visited Gaya, Kashi, Saidpur, Patna, Munger, etc.

After traveling to all these places, some devotees from his birthplace in Majidpur invited him to come for a visit. He acquiesced to their enthusiasm but found little pleasure in going. He said that it was a place which the Pāṇḍavas had neglected.

ŚRĪLA MĀDHAVA GOSVĀMĪ MAHĀRĀJA'S ENCOUNTER WITH BĀBĀJĪ MAHĀRĀJA

The founding *ācārya* of the Sri Chaitanya Gaudiya Math, my spiritual master, Nitya-līlā-praviṣṭa Oṁ Viṣṇupāda Śrīmad Bhakti Dayita Mādhava Gosvāmī Mahārāja, told his disciples a story about a personal encounter he had with Vaṁśī Dāsa Bābājī Mahārāja. Gurudeva founded an *āśrama* in Midnapore city, Sri Shyamananda Gaudiya Math, with the help of two of his godbrothers, Śrīla Bhakti Vichar Yayavar Mahārāja and Śrīla Bhakti Kumud Santa Mahārāja. On one occasion, Bābājī Mahārāja was traveling and passed through Midnapore. When Gurudeva received the news that Bābājī Mahārāja was coming with a group of devotees by ox-cart, he immediately sent a disciple to invite him and his other companions to visit the Math. Bābājī Mahārāja promised the disciple that he would come, and so Gurudeva started to make preparations to receive the party of pilgrims. However, after the midday offering and *ārati*, no one from Bābājī Mahārāja's party came. Śrīla Gurudeva waited for some time and finally took several of his disciples and went looking for him.

When Bābājī Mahārāja had entered the city with his party, he had seen a *vaṭa* tree and had taken it to be Vamshī Vata. He had camped there and planned for to make an offering to his deities and feed his party there. When he saw Gurudeva, Bābājī Mahārāja remembered his affection for Śrīla Prabhupāda and offered him some sweet-rice *prasāda*, which Gurudeva accepted respectfully. I often heard Gurudeva say how delicious the sweet rice tasted that day.

ŚRĪLA PURI GOSVĀMĪ MAHĀRĀJA'S REMINISCENCES

Our *śikṣā-guru*, most revered Śrīla Bhakti Pramode Purī Gosvāmī Mahārāja, also told us a few anecdotes about Bābājī Mahārāja, incidents that he had witnessed personally: "Once, a pile of fruit intended for the service of the deities had accumulated at Bābājī Mahārāja's cottage by the Ganges, and Bābā would not let anyone lay a finger on it. One day, however, a cow entered the cottage and ate all the fruits. Though they tried, no one was able to drive the cow away. Meanwhile, Bābājī Mahārāja watched and laughed, clapping his hands. Out of curiosity, I asked Bābā's disciple, whose name was Pūrṇa or Puṇya, why Bābā was laughing. He said, 'Last night a thief stole all the deities and cooking pots. Now a cow has come and eaten all the fruits. So he is beside himself with joy and is laughing and saying, "One thief gives and another thief takes away!" 'Kṛṣṇa is the supreme thief.'

[Bhakti Dayita Mādhava Mahārāja continues:] "Bābājī Mahārāja never allowed anyone to touch his feet, except once, on the day after Phālgunī *pūrṇimā*, the festival celebration of Jagannātha Miśra. Bābājī Mahārāja was so ecstatic that he forgot his rule and became as generous as a desire tree. So on that day, I was fortunate enough to get the dust of his lotus feet. I also had the good fortune of getting his *prasādi* leftovers.

"We have heard that Śrīla Bābājī Mahārāja took *bābājī veṣa* from our Paramgurudeva, Śrīla Gaura Kiśora Dāsa Bābājī Mahārāja.

"Bābājī Mahārāja relished hearing devotional songs. One day, he heard Śrīla Bhaktivinoda Ṭhākura's couplet *tyajiyā śayana sukha, vicitra pālaṅka, kabe vrajer dhulāya dhūsara habe aṅga* – 'When will I give up the pleasure of sleeping in a comfortable bed and roll in the dust of Vrindavan?' Tears rolled down from his eyes and his voice choked. Bābājī Mahārāja said, 'You are only singing a song. It only bursts open for those who have burst open.' In other words, we only sing the songs of the Mahājanas, but we feel no emotion. When the dust of the holy places covers our bodies, we only think of brushing it off. We have no real idea of its value.

"Another day, however, someone started singing one of these new-fangled, invented *mantras* that contradicts *siddhānta* and divine sentiment. Bābājī Mahārāja said, 'That Name is not allowed here.'

"One gentleman often came to visit Bābājī Mahārāja and kept asking him for his mercy. One day, Bābā finally became impatient; he took off his *kaupina* and handed it to the gentleman and said, 'You want my mercy? Here it is – take it.' The visitor was frightened by the manner in which Bābā challenged him. We have heard that all perfections come from the grace of the Vaiṣṇavas, but we do not have the sincerity necessary to really take their blessings when they are given. What is the use of repeatedly imploring them to be merciful if we don't mean it?

"We had an elderly godbrother named Gokula Dāsa Bābājī. His family home was not far from that of Bābājī Mahārāja. Gokula Dāsa Bābā went frequently to see Vaṁśī Dāsa Bābājī Mahārāja, and when they got together, they would joyfully converse about Kṛṣṇa in their Mymensingha dialect."

BĀBĀJĪ MAHĀRĀJA'S TEACHINGS

Bābājī Mahārāja was normally occupied with his devotional activities; he minded his own business and spoke little. He would talk to his deities, sometimes laughing, sometimes crying desperately, but he did not speak much to others. Many people would come to him; often they would ask him questions. Mostly he remained silent, and if he took any notice at all, he would usually answer indirectly. If he did give spiritual instruction, he would rarely cite scripture, but always spoke from his personal realization. In two or three short phrases, he would make a deep impression on the listener.

Once, he had a regular visitor who kept asking him, "How can we attain God?" Bābājī Mahārāja just remained silent, giving the questioner no answer. One day, he suddenly looked at this visitor and asked him, "What do you want?" The fellow replied, "I want to find God." Bābājī Mahārāja answered in one word, "Cry."

Those who visited him occasionally reported the short answers that he gave to their questions. Some of these were noted down and are given here.

Q: Bābā, what should we do?
A: If you worship Nitāi, you will get Gaura. All your unhappiness will disappear and you will begin to feel real joy.

Q: How can one become free from the demands of the senses?
A: *śuniyā govinda-rab, āpani palābe sab, siṁha-rabe yathā kari-gaṇ* – "They will all flee at the sound of Govinda's name just as the deer flee at the sound of the lion's roar." (*Prema-bhakti-candrika* – Narottama Dāsa Ṭhākura)

Q: Bābā, is there no happiness even in your world?
A: There is no joy here unless you worship Gaura-Nitāi. This is my eternal world, while this world of yours is an illusion. Happiness in this world is like the laughing or crying of a dreaming baby.

Q: How can we tell if we have received the blessings of Kṛṣṇa or the Vaiṣṇavas?
A: *je kare tomāra āśa, tāre koro sarva-nāśa* – "You ruin everything for someone who aspires to attain You." *kāhāke-o ṭākā dey, kāhāro ṭākā nei* – "To some He gives money, while He makes others penniless." *Tomā sthāne aparādhe nāhi paritrāṇa* – "There is no pardon for an offense at your (Vaiṣṇava Ṭhākura's) feet." Why false vanity? Who will deliver you? To whom should I explain who will understand? I haven't got the slightest bit of attachment to the Vaiṣṇavas.

Q: How will I attain Kṛṣṇa's mercy?
A: You will get His mercy by crying. Who really cries? If you cry with tears of love, you will get the Lord's mercy. *Mukhe boli hari, kāje anya kari, prema-vāri cokhe elo nā* – "I recite Hari's names, but I act otherwise. So the tears of love do not well up in my eyes."

Q: How can we be happy? In renunciation or in enjoyment?
A: There are saintly persons on the Sarayu River who chant the names of Sītā Rāma. They are happy, they know no distress. Those who stay with King Duryodhana know no joy. Those who were with King Yudhiṣṭhira are happy. Happiness and distress – enjoyment and renunciation – are twins. Some people enjoy and some renounce.

Q: Have you ever been to Mayapur?
A: Yes. Some call it Mayapur, some call it Nabadwip. There are buildings all over the Mayapur temple site and the deity is worshipped under a neem tree. I once went to Mayapur with a torn wrapper and a water pot. Śacīnandana Gosāi (Mahāprabhu) came and took my water pot. I sat down and waited, and a few minutes later Śacīnandana Gosāi came and gave it back. Then I came back here.

Bābājī Mahārāja's disappearance day was the *Śravaṇa Śukla Caturthī.*

Śrīla Bhakti Siddhānta Sarasvatī Gosvāmī Ṭhākura Prabhupāda

APPEARANCE IN PURI DHĀMA

On Friday, February 6, 1874 (Māgha 25, 1280 Bengali, 1795 Śaka), at 3:30 P.M., in the home of Śrīla Bhaktivinoda Ṭhākura, Oṁ Viṣṇupāda Śrīla Bhakti Siddhānta Sarasvatī Gosvāmī Ṭhākura appeared from the womb of Bhagavatī Devī as an effulgent, golden-skinned child. It was *kṛṣṇa pañcamī* of the month of Māgha. This house, adjacent to Narayana Chata, is situated not far from the Jagannatha Temple on the Grand Road in Puri and was constantly reverberating with the sound of *harināma*. Those who saw the newborn child were amazed to see a natural symbol of a sacred *brāhmaṇa* thread around his shoulder. Śrīla Bhaktivinoda Ṭhākura named the child after Jagannātha Deva's *parā śakti*, Bimalā, calling him Bimalā-prasāda (Bimala Prasad).

THE CHILD'S PREFERENCE

Six months after the appearance of the child, it was time for the Rathayātrā festival. That year, by Lord Jagannātha's desire, His chariot stopped in front of Śrī Bhaktivinoda Ṭhākura's house and simply would not move forward. Lord Jagannātha Deva stayed there for three whole days. Under Bhaktivinoda Ṭhākura's direction, a *kīrtana* festival was held in front of the deity for the entire three-day period. During one of these days, the six-month-old baby came before Lord Jagannātha in the arms of his mother, grabbed Jagannātha Deva's feet and took the garland from around the deity's neck. Bhaktivinoda Ṭhākura gave the child Jagannātha *prasāda* for the *anna-prāśana* ritual in which a child eats its first solid food.

The child stayed in Purushottama *dhama* for ten months after his birth, after this he went with his mother in a palanquin by land to Ranaghat in Bengal. He went through his entire childhood in the midst of an extended festival of *harināma-saṅkīrtana*.

INITIATION IN HARINĀMA AND NṚSIṀHA MANTRA

While Śrīla Bhaktivinoda Ṭhākura was living in Serampore, he came back one day from a visit to Puri with Tulasī beads. He gave them to Bimala Prasad, who was a seventh-grade student at the time, and initiated him in the chanting of the Holy Name and the Nṛsiṁha *mantra*. While he was in the fifth grade, the boy had invented a type of phonetic writing which he called Bicanto or *vikṛnti*. Śrīla Bhaktivinoda Ṭhākura read him the *Caitanya-śikṣāmṛta*.

WORSHIP OF ŚRĪ KŪRMA DEVA

In 1881, Śrīla Bhaktivinoda Ṭhākura started construction of Bhakti Bhavana in Kolkata's Ram Bagan. During the digging of the building's foundations, a deity of Kūrma was found. Śrīla Bhaktivinoda Ṭhākura taught his seven-year-old son the rules for worshipping a deity and the Kūrma *mantra*, after which Bimalā Prasad started to regularly wear *tilaka* and to perform the deity's *pūjā*. In 1885, a center for publishing Vaiṣṇava literature named "The Vaiṣṇava Depository" was opened at Bhakti Bhavana. From this time, the boy started to gain experience with the printing press and helped with proofreading and other tasks. Śrīla Bhaktivinoda Ṭhākura also resumed publishing his monthly magazine *Sajjana-toṣaṇī* in that year. He also traveled with his father to many of the Sripats of some of Mahāprabhu's associates, such as Kulinagram and Saptagram, where he heard his father lecture on the doctrines of the Holy Name.

RECEIVES THE TITLE SIDDHĀNTA SARASVATĪ

When Bimala Prasad was a fifth-grade student, he began to show a natural talent for mathematics and astrology. He went to study the astrological texts with the great scholar Maheśa Candra Cūḍāmaṇi from the Siyakhala village on the Tarakeshwar railway line. In a very short time, he mastered the arts of calculating astrological charts. Later he went on to advanced studies of astrology with Aloya resident Sundara Lāla Paṇḍita.

Cūḍāmaṇi Mahāśaya was astounded by the talents of the fifteen-year-old boy. From this young age, he was called Śrī Siddhānta Sarasvatī by his teachers. After taking *sannyāsa* in 1918, he took on the name Parivrājākācārya Śrī Bhakti Siddhānta Sarasvatī. At other times, he identified himself as Vārṣabhānavī Dayita Dāsa.

THE WORLD VAIṢṆAVA ASSOCIATION

In 1885, 399 years after the appearance of Śrī Caitanya Mahāprabhu, Śrīla Bhaktivinoda Ṭhākura formed the Vishva Vaishnava Raj Sabha, or World Vaiṣṇava Association, at the home of Rāma Gopāla Basu in Krishna Singh lane, which is today known as Bethune Row. The association organized the 400th-anniversary celebrations of Mahāprabhu's appearance the following year. Some of its well-known members were Madana Gopāla Gosvāmī, Nīla Kānta Gosvāmī, Bipin Bihari Gosvāmī, Rādhikā Nātha Gosvāmī, and Śiśira Kumāra Ghoṣa. Śrī Sarasvatī Ṭhākura attended the Association's weekly meetings every Sunday in the company of his father and carried his father's copy of *Bhakti-rasāmṛta-sindhu* for him. He would listen attentively to the discussion of scripture which took place at these meetings.

DISTASTE FOR BAD COMPANY AND MATERIAL LEARNING

While Sarasvatī Ṭhākura was a student, he never mixed with children who were ill-natured. Thus from his very early life, the determination to avoid *asat-saṅga* and to associate exclusively with genuine saintly persons was evident in his character. In the early years of high school, he spent more time studying astrology and Vaiṣṇava scriptures than the prescribed curriculum. In fact, he had a hard time maintaining interest in his school's textbooks. He felt it was unnecessary to even touch these books once outside the school grounds. His reading material consisted mainly of Narottama's *Prārthanā* and *Prema-bhakti-candrikā*, and the books written by his father.

THE AUGUST ASSEMBLY

While still a student, Sarasvatī Ṭhākura published *Sūrya-siddhānta*, *Bhakti-bhavana-pañjikā*, and other books related to astrology. In the afternoons, he would go to Kolkata's Beadon Square and engage in debate with other students about religion. In 1891, this debating society took the name "The August Assembly," and all its members took the vow to never get married. People of all ages, including many highly educated and respected members of society, attended the Assembly's meetings.

AT THE SANSKRIT COLLEGE

In 1892, Sarasvatī Ṭhākura was admitted to the Kolkata Sanskrit College. There once again, instead of studying the books which were on the curriculum, he started systematically reading all the books in the library. Other than the college hours, he spent most of his time studying the Veda with the scholar Pṛthvīdhara Śarmā. A few years later, in 1898, when teaching Sanskrit at the Sārasvata Catuṣpāṭhī in Bhakti Bhavana, he studied *Siddhānta-kaumudī* with the same Pṛthvīdhara Śarmā, and in a brief period went through the entire text. Pṛthvīdhara Śarmā advised him to devote his life to the study of *Siddhānta-kaumudī*, but Sarasvatī Ṭhākura disagreed with him, saying that human life was meant for worshipping the Supreme Lord and not for studying grammar manuals with their verb roots and conjugations, nor for reading mundane poems.

SARASVATĪ ṬHĀKURA ABANDONS MUNDANE LEARNING

While studying at the Sanskrit College, Sarasvatī Ṭhākura also came into public disagreement with the opinions of a student of the renowned scholar from Kashi Bāpudeva Śāstrī and with the professor Pañcānana Sāhityācārya.

We can see parallels in the life of Sarasvatī Ṭhākura and Śrī Caitanya Mahāprabhu, for Sarasvatī Ṭhākura first engaged in the delights of study and debating during his student life but then turned to exclusively chanting and preaching the Holy Names. In his autobiography, he wrote, "'If I go on to study at the university, my family will inevitably harass me terribly to get married. On the other hand, if I present myself to the world as a useless fool, no one will try to interest me in that kind of life.' This was the reasoning that led me to quit the Sanskrit College. I then started looking for an honest means of making my livelihood with minimum effort so that I could lead a life of devotion to the Lord."

IN TRIPURA

In 1895, Sarasvatī Ṭhākura took a job with the royal family of Tripura, which was then an independent state. He was engaged as associate editor of the royal family's history, *Rāja-ratnākara*. While there, he had the opportunity to study many important books held in the royal library. When the king, Vīracandra, left this world on December 11, 1896, Rādhā Kiśora Māṇikya Bāhādura was placed on the throne. The new king engaged Sarasvatī Ṭhākura as the Sanskrit and Bengali tutor for the crown prince, Vrajendra Kiśora. Later, he sent Sarasvatī Ṭhākura to Kolkata with various responsibilities. When Sarasvatī Ṭhākura expressed a desire to permanently leave the employ of the royal family in 1905, the king gave him a full pension equal to the salary which he had been earning. Sarasvatī Ṭhākura received this pension until 1908.

SĀRASVATA CATUṢPĀṬHĪ

In 1897, the Sarasvata Catuṣapāṭhī Sanskrit school was established at the Bhakti Bhavana. Many educated and important people came there to study astrology, including Lālā Haragaurīśaṇkara, Dr. Ekendranātha Ghoṣa, M.B., Sātakaḍi Caṭṭopādhyāya Siddhānta Bhūṣana, Śyāmalāla Gosvāmī (the noted scholar of the Nityānanda Prabhu family), Śarat Candra Jyotirvinoda, etc. From the Sārasvata Catuṣpāṭhī, Sarasvatī Ṭhākura published the monthly magazines *Jyotirvid* and *Bṛhaspati*, as well as many ancient astrological works.

ON PILGRIMAGE WITH ŚRĪLA BHAKTIVINODA ṬHĀKURA

In October of 1898, Sarasvatī Ṭhākura set off on a pilgrimage with Śrīla Bhaktivinoda Ṭhākura during which they visited Kashi, Prayag and, on the way back, Gaya. While in Kashi, he met Rāma Miśra Śāstrī, with whom he discussed many aspects of the Rāmānuja *sampradāya*. On this occasion also, Sarasvatī Ṭhākura began to show the spirit of renunciation which ran throughout his life. Starting in 1897, he had begun to follow the rules of *Cāturmāsya* according to the Vaiṣṇava scriptures, cooking *haviṣyānna* (boiled food without salt or spices) himself, which he would eat directly off the floor without using a plate, and sleeping on the ground without a pillow.

AN INVESTIGATION OF THE ŚRĪ SAMPRADĀYA

Sarasvatī Ṭhākura first started his fundamental study of Rāmānujācārya and his *sampradāya* while in Bengal, and he published books and articles as the results of his research. In 1898, he wrote about Śrīnātha Muni, Śrī Yamunācārya and other *ācāryas* of this school in a series of articles which appeared in *Sajjana-toṣaṇī.* Prior to this, he had books in the four South Indian languages provided to him by Sundareśvara Śrauti, from which he learned about the Rāmānuja and Mādhva schools.

In 1899, he wrote articles on spiritual matters for the weekly magazine *Nivedana,* and in 1900, he published a book, *Baṅge Sāmājikatā* ("Bengali Social Customs"), a study of religious and social behavior in Bengal, which was the fruit of a great deal of research.

FIRST ENCOUNTER WITH HIS GURU

In 1897, Śrīla Bhaktivinoda Ṭhākura established his place of worship in Nabadwip's Godrumdwip area, near the Sarasvati River, and called it Svananda Sukhada Kunja. It was there, in 1898 during the winter season, that Sarasvatī Ṭhākura first saw Śrīla Gaura Kiśora Dāsa Bābājī Mahārāja. He was attracted by the transcendental character of this Vaiṣṇava *paramahaṁsa*, who was indifferent to all social conventions, and later, in the month of Māgha (January-February), 1900, on the order of Śrīla Bhaktivinoda Ṭhākura, took *bhāgavatī dikṣā* (initiation into Bhāgavata *paramparā*) from him.

SĀTĀSANA MATH AND BHAKTI KUṬĪ

In March of 1900, Sarasvatī Ṭhākura accompanied Śrīla Bhaktivinoda Ṭhākura on a trip to Baleshwar and Remuna, where he had *darśana* of Kṣīracorā Gopīnātha. Then they traveled on to Bhubaneshwar and Puri. On this occasion, Sarasvatī Ṭhākura deepened his attachment to the holy city of Puri. When he expressed a wish to establish a *maṭh* near the *samādhi* of Haridāsa Ṭhākura, the local sub-registrar, Jagabandhu Paṭṭanāyaka, and other prominent citizens asked him to take over the service of one of the seven seats of the Sātāsana Math, that of Giridhārī. In 1902, Śrīla Bhaktivinoda Ṭhākura himself started construction of a residence not far from Haridāsa Ṭhākura's *samādhi* and named it Bhakti Kuṭī. During this time, Kashim Bazaar's king, Maṇīndra Candra Nandī Bāhādura, in mourning at the loss of a loved one, came to live in a tent on the beach near to this site. He came frequently to hear Bhaktivinoda Ṭhākura and Sarasvatī Ṭhākura speak on the Vaiṣṇava scriptures. Sarasvatī Ṭhākura also regularly read and spoke on the *Caitanya Caritāmṛta* in the presence of his father.

COLLECTING MATERIALS FOR MAÑJUṢĀ

While in Puri, Sarasvatī Ṭhākura engaged in collecting materials for his book *Vaiṣṇava-mañjuṣā*. He was introduced to the abbot of the Govardhan Math, Madhusūdana Tīrtha, with whom he had many philosophical discussions. Tīrtha Svāmī held Sarasvatī Ṭhākura in high esteem. Other people whom he met in Puri and with whom he engaged in scriptural discussions included Śrī Vāsudeva Rāmānuja Dāsa and Śrī Dāmodara Rāmānuja Dāsa of Samadhi Math; Śrī Raghunandana Rāmānuja Dāsa of Emāra Math, Jagannātha Dāsa of the Jamāyet (Rāmānandī) *sampradāya*'s Pāpaḍiyā Math, Oṁkāra Japī Vriddhatāpasa of Svargadvāra Chātā, the scholar Sadāśiva Miśra, the lawyer Hariśacandra Basu, Śrī Bihārīdāsa Pūjārī of Gaṅgā Mātā's Math, Rādhā Kānta Math's abbot Narottama Dāsa, Ananta Caraṇa Mahānti, etc.

During this time, he would preach door to door to prominent people in Puri, out of which many difficulties and dangers arose. Problems also came up in the responsibilities, which he had accepted at the Giridhārī Āsana of Sātāsana Math. Sarasvatī Ṭhākura showed the same attitude as Prahlāda Mahārāja, however, demonstrating exemplary fortitude and turning a deaf ear to the foul-mouthed accusations made against him. In these circumstances, Śrīla Bhaktivinoda Ṭhākura advised him to go to Mayapur and worship in solitude, just as Rāmānujācārya had done at Tirunarayanpur.

MAHĀTMĀ VAṀSĪ DĀSA

When he arrived in Nabadwip, Sarasvatī Ṭhākura was introduced to Vaṁsī Dāsa Bābājī Mahārāja by Śrīla Bhaktivinoda Ṭhākura. Not long afterwards, Caraṇa Dāsa Bābājī along with Kalna's Viṣṇu Dāsa and many others, went with a *kīrtana* party to Mahāprabhu's birthplace in Mayapur to participate in the Dola Pūrṇimā festival there. The following year, Caraṇa Dāsa Bābājī announced to Śrīla Bhaktivinoda Ṭhākura that he wished to take a party on a tour of Nabadwip Dhāma every year. Unfortunately, his disappearance in 1906 made it impossible for him to carry out this wish.

WINNING AN ASTROLOGICAL DEBATE

On January 2, 1903, Sarasvatī Ṭhākura engaged in a debate with an accomplished student of Bāpudeva Śāstrī, a professor at a Sanskrit college, and an instructor to a very prominent astrologer. Rāya Bāhādura Rajendra Candra Śāstrī, President of the Royal Society, presided over the debate in which Sarasvatī Ṭhākura so badly defeated his opponent that he passed stool and urine in the assembly out of shock.

MORE PILGRIMAGES

In January of 1904, Sarasvatī Ṭhākura visited Sita Kunda and Candranatha. In December of the same year he went to Puri, and on February 23, 1905, he went on a pilgrimage to South India. He visited Singhachalam, Rajahmundry, Madras, Perembadur, Tirupati, Kanjivaram, Kumbhakonam, Srirangam, Madurai, etc., before returning to Kolkata and Sri Mayapur. In Perembadur, he learned the scriptural rules and regulations surrounding Vaiṣṇava *tridaṇḍa-sannyāsa* from a member of that order in the Rāmānuja *sampradāya*.

THE VOW TO CHANT A BILLION HOLY NAMES

While staying in Mayapur in 1905, Sarasvatī Ṭhākura began preaching the message of Caitanya Mahāprabhu and, following in the footsteps of Śrī Haridāsa Ṭhākura, he undertook a vow of chanting a billion (ten crores) of Holy Names, chanting a minimum of three lakhs (300,000) every single day. In 1906, Rohiṇī Kumāra Ghoṣa, the nephew of Justice Candra Mādhava Ghoṣa, had an extraordinary dream telling him to go to Sarasvatī Ṭhākura and take initiation from him. Rohiṇī Kumāra Ghoṣa thus became his first initiated disciple.

In 1909, Sarasvatī Ṭhākura had a cottage in Vraja-pattan built on the site of Candraśekara's house, where he continued to engage in his *vrata*, visualizing himself on the banks of Radha Kunda.

VICTORIOUS IN DEBATE

A crisis arose for the Vaiṣṇava world in 1911. The *smārta brāhmaṇas* were engaged in a concerted attack on the Vaiṣṇava religion and its *ācāryas*. Those who claimed descent from Advaita Ācārya and other associates of Caitanya Mahāprabhu had taken the side of the *smārtas* in the hope of extracting some advantage from the alliance. Śrīla Bhaktivinoda Ṭhākura was performing pastimes of illness at the time, so when an assembly of hundreds of scholars and *paṇḍitas* was called in Midnapore at Balighai village to debate the issues, he sent Sarasvatī Ṭhākura in his place. In the debate, which was presided over by Viśvambharānanda Deva Gosvāmī, Vrindavan scholar Madhusūdana Gosvāmī invited him to speak. Sarasvatī Ṭhākura read an article and gave a discourse on the distinction between *brāhmaṇas* and Vaiṣṇavas which completely destroyed the arguments of the materialistic *karmī smārtas*.

In the same year, at Bada Akhda in Nabadwip town, a debate was held on the Gaura *mantra*. Sarasvatī Ṭhākura established on the basis of the Atharva Veda's *Caitanyopaniṣad* and other scriptural evidence that a special *mantra* for worshipping Gaurāṅga Mahāprabhu was eternally valid.

On March 21, 1912, Sarasvatī Ṭhākura went to a religious conference held at Kashim Bazaar where he gave a speech, establishing the characteristics of pure devotional service and criticizing the materialistic ambitions and sycophancy of those who claimed to be the leaders of the Gauḍīya Vaiṣṇava religion. In order to demonstrate noncooperation with the so-called leaders of the school, he fasted for the four days he was there before returning to Mayapur, where he resumed taking *prasāda*.

PILGRIMAGE THROUGH THE GAUDA MANDALA

On November 4, 1912, Sarasvatī Ṭhākura took a small group of devotees on a tour of Srikhanda, Jajigram, Katwa, Jhamatpur, Akai Hat, Chakhandi, Dai Hat and other places where Mahāprabhu's associates had had their homes. In every place, he preached the gospel of pure devotional service.

THE PUBLICATION OF ANUBHĀṢYA

In April of 1913, Sarasvatī Ṭhākura established a publishing house named Bhāgavata Yantrālaya in Kolkata's Kalighat area. The first book printed was *Caitanya Caritāmṛta* with his *Anubhāṣya* commentary. Others which followed were the *Bhagavad-gītā* with Viśvanātha's commentary and the *Gaura-kṛṣṇodaya-mahā-kāvya* of the Odishan poet Govinda Dāsa.

After Śrīla Bhaktivinoda Ṭhākura's disappearance on June 23, 1914, Sarasvatī Ṭhākura took over the editorship of *Sajjana-toṣaṇī*, the monthly magazine founded by his father. In January of 1915, the press was moved to Vraja-pattana in Mayapur and more books continued to be printed. On June 14, 1915, the *Anubhāṣya* commentary to *Caitanya Caritāmṛta* was completed at Vraja-pattana. In July of 1915, the printing press was again moved to Krishnanagar, and *Sajjana-toṣaṇī* and various books written by Śrīla Bhaktivinoda Ṭhākura were published from there.

THE DISAPPEARANCE OF GAURA KIŚORA DĀSA BĀBĀJĪ

On November 17, 1915, *utthāna ekādaśī*, Śrīla Gaura Kiśora Dāsa Bābājī Mahārāja entered into his eternal pastimes. Śrī Sarasvatī Ṭhākura established his *samādhi* in the Nutana Cadaya neighborhood of old Kuliya (the present-day town of Nabadwip) according to the prescriptions of Gopāla Bhaṭṭa's *Saṁskāra-dīpikā*.

SARASVATĪ ṬHĀKURA TAKES TRIDAṆḌA SANNYĀSA

On March 7, 1918, on the occasion of Śrī Caitanya Mahāprabhu's appearance day, Sarasvatī Ṭhākura took *tridaṇḍa-sannyāsa* in Sri Mayapur as per the Vedic tradition. Although as an eternally perfected soul, he had already achieved the goals of the renounced order, he took this step in order to preach the gospel of Lord Caitanya everywhere without restriction, to crystallize the conception of the *daiva-varṇāśrama* social system, and to demonstrate the transcendental character of the *paramahaṁsa* (Bābājī) dress taken by his gurus, Jagannātha Dāsa Bābājī Mahārāja, Saccidānanda Bhaktivinoda Ṭhākura and Gaura Kiśora Dāsa Bābājī Mahārāja.

On the same day, he consecrated the deities of Guru-Gaurāṅga and Rādhā-Govinda at the house of Candraśekhara Ācārya and established the Sri Chaitanya Math. The Sri Chaitanya Math became the headquarters for the branch Gaudiya Maths throughout the world, the flagship of which is situated in Kolkata.

At the end of March, Sarasvatī Ṭhākura gave an exhaustively researched lecture on Vaiṣṇava philosophy in the Krishnanagar town hall. In May, he went to Daulatpur and other places to deliver Hari *kathā*.

VISIT TO SRI KSHETRA

On June 2, 1918, Sarasvatī Ṭhākura and a group of twenty-three devotees left Kolkata for Puri. They stopped at Sauri, Kuamara and other places along the way to preach. As they followed the route Mahāprabhu had taken to Puri, Sarasvatī Ṭhākura was overcome with ecstatic feelings of separation from the Lord. The party stopped at Remuna, where they saw Kṣīracorā Gopīnātha, and then at Baleshwar, where he gave a lecture on Mahāprabhu's *Śikṣāṣṭaka* to the town's Hari Bhakti Pradāyiṇī Sabhā. He was welcomed to Baleshwar by the Subdivisional Magistrate, Rāya Saheba Gauraśyāma Mahānti, and other distinguished personalities of the town. At Cuttack, he was invited by Diwan Bāhādura Śrī Kṛṣṇa Mahāpātra to stay at his home and preach on the topics of *Bhāgavata* there. Then in Puri, the party stayed at Bhakti Kuṭī and did the *parikramā* of Sri Kshetra Mandala. Once again, Sarasvatī Ṭhākura was in a state of ecstatic separation the whole time.

The former collector and present Deputy magistrate of Puri Aṭala Bihārī Maitra, had heard Sarasvatī Ṭhākura explain *Caitanya Caritāmṛta* and *Śrīmad Bhāgavatam*. In a great meeting held on the grounds of Hariballabha Basu Rāya Bāhādura's house, Śaśi Bhavana, Sarasvatī Ṭhākura gave a lecture on the difference between personal and impersonal conceptions of the Absolute Truth. He wrote a Sanskrit poem of a few verses about the memorial to Mahāprabhu's lotus feet enshrined in the Jagannātha temple.

SILENCING ENEMY TONGUES

In August and September of 1918, a spokesman for a group of atheists with little philosophical knowledge sent a list of twenty-nine questions challenging the Vaiṣṇava faith and its *ācāryas*. Sarasvatī Ṭhākura silenced these critics with answers based on scriptures. The questions and his answers were published in the name *Pratīpera praśnere pratyuttararūpe*, "Answering the Enemy's Questions."

BHAKTIVINODA ĀSANA AND VIŚVA VAIṢṆAVA RĀJA SABHĀ

To increase the preaching activity in Kolkata, in November of 1918, Sarasvatī Ṭhākura established a center at 1, Ultadanga Junction Road, which he named Śrī Bhaktivinoda Āsana. From there, he traveled to various towns in the Jessore and Khulna districts for preaching. On February 5, 1919, he reestablished the World Vaiṣṇava Association under the name Viśva Vaiṣṇava Rāja Sabhā at the Bhaktivinoda Āsana. On June 27, 1919, he consecrated a deity of Śrīla Bhaktivinoda Ṭhākura at Svananda Sukhada Kunja in Godrumdwip. The first month-long *kīrtana* festival was held at the Bhaktivinoda Āsana from August 18 to September 18, 1919.

PREACHING IN EAST BENGAL

On October 4, 1919, on the appearance day of Madhvācārya, Sarasvatī Ṭhākura set off on a preaching trip to north and eastern Bengal. In April of 1920, he and the other leaders of the Viśva Vaiṣṇava Rāja Sabhā sent a letter with seven questions to the Mahārāja of Kashim Bazaar's annual convocation of Vaiṣṇava scholars, challenging them to clarify the distinction between pure and blemished devotion.

Six years to the day after the disappearance of Śrīla Bhaktivinoda Ṭhākura, on June 23, 1920, Sarasvatī Ṭhākura's mother, Bhagavatī Devī, left for her eternal abode.

THE FIRST GAUDIYA MATH

On September 6, 1920, deities of Guru and Gaurāṅga and Rādhā and Govinda were installed at the Bhaktivinoda Āsana, and the first Gaudiya Math was established at that time.

VAIṢṆAVA MAÑJUṢĀ

At the request of Śrīla Bhaktivinoda Ṭhākura and Śiśira Kumāra Ghoṣa, Sarasvatī Ṭhākura had been working on the compilation of a Vaiṣṇava encyclopedia, for which he had visited Purushottama *dhama* and various places of South India and Gauda Mandala since 1900 and collected necessary information. In October of 1920, he came to Kashim Bazaar at the invitation of Mahārāja Sir Maṇīndra Candra Nandī Bāhādura, to whom he described the scope of this Vaiṣṇava encyclopedia. The Mahārāja agreed to donate a monthly stipend for the publication of the encyclopedia, but in the end was unable to fulfill his commitments.

Sarasvatī Ṭhākura left Kashim Bazaar and went with his party to Saidabad, Nowallis Para, Kheturi and other places in the area that had been blessed by the touch of Mahāprabhu's associates. Everywhere he went, he preached Mahāprabhu's message.

THE FIRST SANNYĀSA DISCIPLE

On November 1, 1920, Sarasvatī Ṭhākura initiated Śrīla Bhaktivinoda Ṭhākura's disciple Jagadīśa Bhakti Pradip, Vaiṣṇava-siddhānta-bhūṣaṇa, Sampradāya-vaibhavācārya, B.A., in the renounced order as a *tridaṇḍa-sannyāsī.* He was thus the first member of the order in the Viśva Vaiṣṇava Rāja Sabhā and was known thenceforth as Tridaṇḍi Svāmī Bhakti Pradīp Tīrtha Mahārāja.

On March 14, 1921, Sarasvatī Ṭhākura revived the annual *parikramā*, or circumambulation of Nabadwip *dhāma.* At the end of March, he left again for Puri on a preaching trip. Meanwhile, Śrīla Bhakti Pradīp Tīrtha Mahārāja published the book *Ācāra o Ācārya* ("Standards of Conduct and the Spiritual Master") with a profound reflection which caused a great stir amongst the caste Gosvāmīs, most of whom were acting as professional gurus.

PREACHING AND ESTABLISHING MATHS IN EAST BENGAL

Afterwards, Sarasvatī Ṭhākura visited Dhanbad, Katrasgarh and Dhaka. In Dhaka, he spoke on the Bhāgavata's *janmādyasya* verse for an entire month, explaining it in thirty different ways. On October 13, 1921, he established the Madhva Gaudiya Math in Dhaka. On October 31, deities were installed and a great feast held in Their honor. From Dhaka, he went on to Mymensingha for preaching.

After this, he returned to Nabadwip, where he reestablished the worship of Gaura Gadādhara at Champahati, as well as a deity installation at the birthplace of Vṛndāvana Dāsa Ṭhākura in Modadrumdwip. Then he returned to Kolkata to preach there and in the surrounding area.

SRI PURUSHOTTAM MATH

According to Vedavyāsa, *hy utkale puruṣottamāt*, the pure message of the Vaiṣṇava religion would spread out of Jagannatha Puri. In order to do honor to this prediction, Sarasvatī Ṭhākura established the Sri Purushottam Math at Bhakti-kuṭī on June 9, 1922, installing a deity of Gaurāṅga Mahāprabhu. Then, in the spirit of Mahāprabhu, he and his followers participated in the cleaning of Guṇḍicā, did the *parikramā* of Jagannatha Puri and went to Alalanatha during Jagannātha Deva's *anavasāra* period during which He does not give *darśana.* He established an annual memorial festival at the Purushottam Math in honor of Śrīla Bhaktivinoda Ṭhākura and Śrīla Gadādhara Paṇḍita Gosvāmī.

He also sent disciples to Cuttack, Baripada, Kuamara, Udala, Kaptipada, and Nilgiri, etc., to preach Mahāprabhu's gospel of pure devotion.

GAUḌĪYA MAGAZINE

On August 19, 1922, the monthly magazine of the Gaudiya Math, the *Gauḍīya,* was published for the first time from the Bhāgavata Press.

VISIT TO VRAJA MAṆḌALA

On September 28, 1922, Sarasvatī Ṭhākura left for Vraja Maṇḍala with the intention of establishing a preaching center. Accompanied by his disciples, he visited Mathura, Vrindavan, Radha Kunda, and other important holy sites connected to Kṛṣṇa's pastimes. He gave a speech on Mahāprabhu's teachings and the Vaiṣṇava *dharma* at an assembly of learned Vaiṣṇavas at Lālā Bābu's temple in Vrindavan town.

On his return to Bengal during the month of Kārtika, he came to Dhaka, where he once again outlined the true character of devotional service. After this, he went to Kuliya, where he revealed the site where Mahāprabhu forgave Devānanda Paṇḍita and Cāpāla Gopāla their offenses. From there, he went on to the Santal Paragana to preach Hari *kathā.*

THE CONSTRUCTION OF THE TEMPLE AT THE CHAITANYA MATH

On the appearance day of Caitanya Mahāprabhu, March 2, 1923, work began on the construction of a temple at the Chaitanya Math. It was to be built according to Sarasvatī Ṭhākura's original idea of having deities of Guru-Gaurāṅga and Rādhā-Govinda installed in the main deity room, while placing images of the founders of the four *sampradāyas* (Lakṣmī, Brahmā, Rudra, the four Kumāras) and their *ācāryas* (Rāmānuja, Madhva, Viṣṇusvāmī, Nimbārka) in shrines on the temple's four corners.

IN PURI

After preaching in West and East Bengal, Sarasvatī Ṭhākura returned again to Puri for the annual festival and, emulating the pastimes of Mahāprabhu in separation from Kṛṣṇa, danced in front of the Rathayātrā cart. He also preached to large numbers of devotees, including Rāja Maṇīndra Candra Nandī, Śaśīmohana Gosvāmī of Bhadrak, etc. He sent preachers to Mayurbhanj and Madras Presidency to spread Mahāprabhu's gospel and himself took a party of devotees to Amlajora in Burdwan and then to Banari Para in the Barisal district.

PREACHING THE BHĀGAVATA

In 1923, just before the annual festival at the Gaudiya Math in Kolkata, the Gaudiya Printing Works was established and the first fascicules of the *Śrīmad Bhāgavatam* were published with the *Gaura Kiśorānvaya* (word-by-word translation), *Svānanda-kuñjānuvāda* (translation), and the *Ananta-gopāla-tathya* and *Sindhu-vaibhava* commentaries.

VYĀSA PŪJĀ

On February 24, 1924, on the *tithi* commemorating the fiftieth anniversary of Sarasvatī Ṭhākura's appearance in the world, the first Vyāsa Pūjā in his honor was held at the Kolkata Sri Gaudiya Math. The speech that he gave on that occasion stands as an immortal jewel in the history of Vaiṣṇava literature.

Not long thereafter, on the occasion of Mahāprabhu's appearance day, the first edition of the *Śrī Caitanya Bhāgavata* was published from the Sri Madhva Gaudiya Math in Dhaka.

TRIDANDI MATH AND SĀRASVATA ĀSANA

On July 9, 1924, Sarasvatī Ṭhākura established the Tridandi Math in Bhubaneshwar in Odisha. From there he went to preach in the Madras Presidency, where he established the Sārasvata Āsana. There he gave instructions to his disciples and preached Bhaktivinoda Ṭhākura's writings extensively. In the first part of September of the same year, many distinguished persons came to hear him speak, including Rāut Rāya of Mayurbhanj, His Excellency General Puṇya Samsera Rāṇā Jaṇg Bāhādura of Nepal, Justice Manmathanātha Mukhopādhyāya, etc.

In October, he set foot in Dhaka for the fifth time and spoke extensively on the Mādhva *sampradāya*, giving a learned explanation of the differences between the Madhva and Pūrṇaprajña doctrines, Madhva's vision of varṇāśrama *dharma*, and the doctrines of Śrī Mādhva-Gauḍīya lineage.

AT BENARES HINDU UNIVERSITY

On December 16, Sarasvatī Ṭhākura came to the Benares Hindu University to lecture on the place of Vaiṣṇavism in the world's religions. Amongst those in the audience who greeted his lecture with enthusiasm were the director of the Department of Western Philosophy, Pramathanātha Tarkabhūṣaṇa, and Professor Phaṇī Bhūṣaṇa Adhikārī, M.A. Afterwards, he and his followers went to places in Kashi visited by Mahāprabhu, then to Prayag, where he indicated the exact spot (Dashashvamedha Ghata) where Rūpa Gosvāmī had taken instruction from Mahāprabhu, and then to Arail, where Mahāprabhu had met with Vallabhācārya.

PILGRIMAGE THROUGH GAUDA MANDALA

On January 29, 1925, Sarasvatī Ṭhākura took a large group of devotees on a tour of Gauda Mandala to visit the various sites made holy by Mahāprabhu and His associates. Overcome with divine inspiration, he lectured on *bhakti* in all these places.

In the same year, during the Nabadwip *parikramā*, deities of Śrī Śrī Rādhā Govinda were carried on the back of an elephant through the streets of Koladwip. The envious leaders of those in the guru business incited a number of ruffians to throw bricks at the deities and the devotees who were accompanying them, including Sarasvatī Ṭhākura, at Podama Tala. One witness of the event was quoted in the next day's (Phālguna 24, 1331) *Ananda Bazaar Patrika* as saying, "Today I witnessed the same pastime that was enacted about four hundred years ago when Nabadwip's two thugs named Jagāi and Mādhāi tried to cause injury to Avadhūta Nityānanda Prabhu."

MADANA MOHANA MĀLAVIYA

On April 17, 1925, Paṇḍita Madana Mohana Mālaviya, the leader of the Hindu Mahasabha, a nationalist organization, came to the Kolkata Sri Gaudiya Math and heard Sarasvatī Ṭhākura explain the *daiva-varṇāśrama* system according to the book, *Āgama prāmānya.*

Sarasvatī Ṭhākura sent preachers to Sylhet and other places.

BHAGAVAT JANANANDA MATH

In 1926, a three-day sacrifice to the Holy Name was performed in Mayapur to commemorate the appearance of Nityānanda Prabhu. In April of the same year, a maṭha was founded in Chirulia (Midnapore) and given the name Bhagavat Janananda Math. Sarasvatī Ṭhākura sent his *tridaṇḍi-sannyāsīs* throughout India to Bengal, Bihar, Odisha, and north and west India to preach the message of pure devotion, while he himself spoke and lectured throughout Midnapore. This is the time when the large-scale expansion of the Gaudiya Math really started.

TRAVELING AND PREACHING THROUGHOUT INDIA

In the beginning of November 1926, Sarasvatī Ṭhākura started on a trip throughout India, when he would meet with various learned persons to discuss scriptures and gather information. He was also preaching the message of Caitanya Mahāprabhu to the people in large assemblies. The *ācāryas* of many schools acclaimed him as the leading *ācārya* of the Gauḍīya Vaiṣṇava school. The Mahānta of Nathdwar, Gokulanātha Gosvāmī Mahārāja of Bombay, the abbot of the Udupi monastery of the Mādhva *sampradāya* and the abbot of the Salimabad seat of the Mādhva *sampradāya* all received him with the honor due to the spiritual master of a Vaiṣṇava *sampradāya*.

While on this trip, he established a Maṭh in Naimisharanya called Paramhamsa Math. Upon his return, he opened the Paravidyā Pīṭha school in Mayapur, as well as the newly completed twenty-nine-towered temple at the Chaitanya Math. Deities of the *ācāryas* and Rādhā Govinda were installed there.

THE HARMONIST

On June 15, 1927, Sarasvatī Ṭhākura started publishing *Sajjana-toṣaṇī* in three languages – English, Sanskrit and Hindi. The English edition was given the name *The Harmonist.* On September 17, 1927, in Dumurkonda in the Manbhoom district, the Sri Chaitanya Gaudiya Math was founded.

At the end of September, Sarasvatī Ṭhākura set out again on a preaching tour of northern India. He visited Kashi, Kanpur, Lucknow, Jaipur, Galta Parvat, Salimabad, Pushkar, Ajmer, Dwarka, Sudamapuri, Girnar Parvat, Prabhas, Avanti, Mathura Mandal, Indraprastha, Kurukshetra, and Naimisharanya and preached the message of Caitanya *vāṇī.*

In 1928, during the Gaudiya Math festival period, he spoke at Kolkata's Albert Hall and in other public places, giving access to Mahāprabhu's message to the common people. The fourth edition of the *Caitanya Caritāmṛta* was published. On September 26, the foundation of the Bagh Bazaar Gaudiya Math was laid near the banks of the Ganges. On October 7, he went with a large party of devotees to Assam for preaching. From there he went to Shillong, where he spoke to several large assemblies. Amongst those who came to hear him explain the unexcelled doctrines of Caitanya Mahāprabhu was the Rājarṣi Kumāra Śaradindu Nārāyaṇa Rāya.

AT KURUKSHETRA FOR THE SOLAR ECLIPSE

On November 4, following the mood of separation that was experienced by the *gopīs* and by Mahāprabhu during the Rathayātrā, Sarasvatī Ṭhākura went with a party of devotees to Kurukshetra at the time of a solar eclipse. Hundreds of thousands of pilgrims who had also come there had the good fortune to hear the Gaudiya Math devotees singing the names of Gaura. Deities of Gaurāṅga were installed at the Sri Vyasa Gaudiya Math, and a spiritual diorama exhibition (the *Bhāgavata Pradarśinī*) was opened.

THE OPENING OF THE EKAYANA MATH

On December 30, the great scholar Pramathanātha Tarka Bhūṣaṇa came to the Gaudiya Math and heard an extended explanation of the *daiva-varṇāśrama* system from Sarasvatī Ṭhākura.

In January of 1929, Sarasvatī Ṭhākura established the Ekayan Gaudiya Math in Krishnanagar. At the opening ceremony, he gave a lecture with an original explanation showing that the single path of exclusive devotion (*ekāyana*) is the trunk and the various other paths (*bahvayana*) are the branches of the Vedic tree.

On January 14, 1929, Sarasvatī Ṭhākura met Professor Albert E. Suthers of Ohio State University and explained to him how the Vaiṣṇava religion was an extended and perfected Christianity. On January 16, Sarasvatī Ṭhākura was in New Delhi to open the Delhi Gaudiya Math, creating the opportunity for Mahāprabhu's gospel to be spread to thousands of respectable people in India's capital.

A SPEECH IN THE KRISHNANAGAR TOWN HALL

On March 30, 1929, Sarasvatī Ṭhākura gave a lecture on the Holy Name in the Rāma Gopāla Town Hall building. In May of the same year, he was in Puri, where he started Gaurasundara's Candana Yātrā festival. At the same time, he started repair work on the Alalanatha temple. On August 11, he spoke at Kolkata's Albert Hall on the Gauḍīya *darśana*.

SHRINES OF MAHĀPRABHU'S FOOTPRINTS

It was Sarasvatī Ṭhākura's wish to establish 108 shrines throughout India as memorials to the places Mahāprabhu had sanctified by the touch of His lotus feet. These shrines, or *pāda-pīṭhas*, would house prints of Gaurasundara's feet stamped in marble. For this purpose, he went to Kanair Natshala on October 13, 1929, and to Mandar two days later. From there he went on to Rajmahal, Bhagalpur, Nalanda and Rajgiri to preach Mahāprabhu's message. Then he went on to Kashi, where he discoursed on Mahāprabhu's teachings to Sanātana Gosvāmī.

He was welcomed by many educated and respectable people to Kashi, Faizabad, Ayodhya, Naimisharanya, Karauna, Mishrik, Sitapur and Lucknow. Many seekers of the truth were initiated by him into the religion of pure devotion. The widely renowned bar-at-law Mr. A. P. Sena, the professor Dr. Rādhā Kumuda Mukhopādhyāya, Dr. Rādhā Kamala Mukhopādhyāya, Dr. A. N. Sena Gupta and many other highly regarded citizens came to hear him speak.

THE SRI MAYAPUR POST OFFICE

On June 1, 1929, a temporary post office was opened at Sri Mayapur and made into a permanent branch on November 1. During this time, Sarasvatī Ṭhākura had his devotees establish the "Lord's garden" (*Īśodyāna*) that Śrīla Bhaktivinoda Ṭhākura had desired in Mayapur. He also had electricity brought to Mayapur and electric lights placed on the pinnacle of the Chaitanya Math temple.

MAHĀ MAHOPĀDHYĀYA HARAPRASĀDA ŚĀSTRĪ

On January 8, 1930, the great scholar Dr. Haraprasāda Śāstrī visited Sarasvatī Ṭhākura and discussed many matters with him regarding the history of the various Vaiṣṇava *sampradāyas* including the Gauḍīya, the dates of many *ācāryas*, the Pañcarātra, and Śrī Caitanyadeva.

In the middle of January, Sarasvatī Ṭhākura went to the Pūrṇa Kumbha Melā in Prayag. He engaged the Chaitanya Math's preachers in talking about Mahāprabhu's teachings to Rūpa Gosvāmī. He installed deities of Rādhā Govinda, the life and soul of Śrī Rūpa Gosvāmī, at the confluence of the three rivers, triveṇī. By the grace of the best of Rūpa Gosvāmī's followers, the pilgrims who came to Prayag to bathe in the confluence of the holy rivers were fortunate to be able to hear the message of pure devotion.

EXHIBITION IN ŚRĪ DHĀMA MAYAPUR

From February 3 to March 17, 1930, Sarasvatī Ṭhākura held an unprecedented spiritual diorama exhibition in Nabadwip-Mayapur. It was opened by the famous chemist Dr. Prafulla Candra Rāya. On February 18, on the occasion of Vyāsa Pūjā, a shrine to the *ācārya*'s feet was inaugurated at the Chaitanya Math.

On May 4, Mr. I. H. Napier came to hear about Indian spiritual philosophy from Sarasvatī Ṭhākura. On May 25, Sarasvatī Ṭhākura went to Chatrabhoga, a place that Mahāprabhu visited on His way to Puri, and blessed many seekers of the truth. In July, he went to the Saccidananda Math in Cuttack and spoke on Kṛṣṇa to both learned and general audiences. On August 22, he traveled to Allahabad, where he stayed with his entourage at the house of retired sessions judge Manomohana Sānnyāla. He spoke there for several days, attracting Mr. Sānnyāla to Caitanya Mahāprabhu's lotus feet. He also resolved many of the questions asked by educated citizens of the town, especially Professor Dr. P. K. Ācārya.

SPIRITUAL ASSEMBLY

On October 5, 1930, the move with the devotees and deities was made from the Ultadanga Junction Road Math to the new buildings at Bagh Bazaar. At the same time, a festival was held in honor of Rādhā Madana Mohana, Rādhā Govinda and Rādhā Gopīnātha. A transcendental diorama exhibition was also opened, and a great spiritual conference was called at the same time. The chief contributor to the construction of the temple, Jagabandhu Bhakti Rañjana, left the world on November 19 of the same year.

On December 25, Sarasvatī Ṭhākura was in Jajpur; on the 26th, in Kurmakshetra; on the 27th in Singhachalam; Kovvur on the 29th and on the 31st in Mangalagiri. In all these places, he installed shrines of Caitanya Mahāprabhu's lotus feet and preached His gospel. Sir P. S. Shivaswami Iyer, K.C.S.I.,[29] Dr. U. Ram Rao and P. N. Subrahmanya Iyer were among the distinguished persons who were attracted by Sarasvatī Ṭhākura's preaching.

THE BHAKTIVINODA INSTITUTE

On April 3, 1931, Sarasvatī Ṭhākura opened the Bhaktivinoda Institute in Sri Mayapur, and to the large assembly of people present for the occasion, spoke on the difference between material and spiritual learning. On May 3, he went to Darjeeling to preach in that district. On June 28, he officially accepted responsibility for the management of the Sripat of Nityānanda Prabhu's associate Maheśa Paṇḍita, in Chakdah. At the opening

29 Knight Commander of the Star of India.

ceremonies, he spoke to a large crowd of seekers.

On July 12, he installed the deity of Gaurāṅga named Gauḍīyanātha at the Brahma-Gaudiya Math in Alalanatha. Five days later, he set the foundations of the Purusottam Math temple on land which had been donated by the King of Mayurbhanj. From there he went on to Cuttack, where he spoke on Kṛṣṇa at the Sacchidananda Math. He sent a party of preachers to Simla in northern India.

On July 30, he spoke Hari *kathā* to an audience including the well-known professor Kālidāsa Nāga of Calcutta University at the Bagh Bazaar Gaudiya Math. On September 5, Honorable Justice Manmathnātha Mukhopādhyāya came to listen to Sarasvatī Ṭhākura speak at the Gaudiya Math.

THE SPIRITUAL EDUCATION EXHIBITION IN KOLKATA

At the time of the Gaudiya Math's annual festival, on September 6, Sarasvatī Ṭhākura opened a spiritual education exhibition (*Sat-śikṣā Pradarśinī*) in Kolkata. Over the next few weeks, some of the prominent people who came to hear him speak were Yatindranātha Basu, M.A., M.L.C., Dr. Dīneśa Candra Sena Rāya Bāhādura, Vīrāja Mohana Majumadāra, the Vice Principal of University Law College, Dr. Magnus Hirschfeld, the German scholar and world-traveler, and Dr. Stella Kremrisch of Calcutta University.

Sarasvatī Ṭhākura spoke at the Gaudiya Math's many festivals. On September 29, he spoke on the nature of spiritual sound to the principal of the Calcutta Medical College, Colonel Dvārakāprasāda Goyel, I.M.S. and to the American traveler and scholar A. J. Jacobs on October 9. On October 11, in Prayag, he met Allahabad University Vice-Chancellor Dr. Gaṇgānātha Jha, and Allahabad Divisional Commissioner Vināyaka Nanda Śaṅkara Mehta, I.C.S., and answered their questions on spiritual life.

THE HINDI MAGAZINE BHĀGAVATA

On October 16, Sarasvatī Ṭhākura was welcomed to Benares by its distinguished citizens and stayed and spoke at the king's Mint Palace. On the 19th and 20th, he spoke at length on Vaiṣṇava philosophy and Kṛṣṇa *līlā* to Vasanta Kumāra Cattopādhyāya, Deputy Accountant and General of Bengal literary. From there he went on to Lucknow on Oct. 31, and then to Naimisharanya, where on November 9 on *āmāvasyā tithi*, he introduced the new Hindi fortnightly, *Bhāgavata*, published from the Paramhamsa Math.

In the beginning of November, Sarasvatī Ṭhākura sent preachers to the princely state of Bhajji in Simla for propagating the gospel of Mahāprabhu. On November 14, he sent preachers to New Delhi to tell the Viceroy, Lord Willingdon, about the Math's preaching activities. On November 17, he established the annual festival at the Delhi Gaudiya Math and spoke to many distinguished personalities about the life of Caitanya Mahāprabhu. He also gave a speech about *bhakti* at the Gurudwar Bungalow Saheb Hall in New Delhi. On November 29, a great spiritual assembly was held in the garden of Honorable Council of State member Rāya Bāhādura Lālā Jagadīśa Prasāda, at which Sarasvatī Ṭhākura gave a speech. Then on November 30, he went with his entourage to Sukartal, the place where Śrī Śukadeva Gosvāmī first narrated the *Bhāgavatam*, and he himself spoke from the *Bhāgavatam*.

On December 6, he installed Rādhā-Govinda deities in the Delhi Gaudiya Math.

On the 9th, he came to Kolkata to speak at the first annual memorial service in honor of Jagabandhu Bhakti Rañjana, the builder of the Bagh Bazaar Gaudiya Math buildings. The Honorable Justice Manmathanātha Mukhopādhyāya presided over the assembly. On the 13th, Mr. Mukhopādhyāya visited Mayapur, where he again heard Sarasvatī Ṭhākura speak. He also visited the *dhāma* and the Bhaktivinoda Institute.

PREACHING IN MADRAS

On January 10, 1932, Sarasvatī Ṭhākura went with a party of twenty devotees to Madras. A large group of devotees and dignitaries, including Madras Corporation President, T. S. Ramaswami Iyer, the Honorable T. Rajan, Mr. S. V. Ramaswami Mudaliyar, the honorable Diwan Bahadur Ji, Nārāyaṇa Svāmī Chetiyar, C.I.E. [Companion of the Indian Empire], and T. Punurulla Pillai, etc., greeted him at the Basin Bridge Station and accompanied him in a huge *saṅkīrtana* procession back to the Gaudiya Math, which at that time was situated in the North Gopalpuram neighborhood. In the assembly which followed, the honorable Diwan Bahadur Kumarswami Reddiyar offered a speech in which he indicated the depth of his esteem for the *ācārya*, Śrī Sarasvatī Ṭhākura.

On January 14, Madras High Court Justice Diwan Bahadur Sundaram Chettiyar visited Sarasvatī Ṭhākura at the Madras Gaudiya Math and was satisfied by answers to his questions on spiritual matters. On January 23, deities were installed in the Madras Gaudiya Math. On the same day, the cornerstone for a new Math was laid in the Raipetta Palli. On January 24, a huge meeting was held with many important personalities as guests, including Sir P. S. Shivaswami Iyer. Sarasvatī Ṭhākura spoke and attracted many of these people to Mahāprabhu's teachings. On January 27, the governor of Madras Presidency, Sir George Frederick Stanley, laid the cornerstone for the Śrī Kṛṣṇa *Kīrtana* Hall at the Madras Gaudiya Math.

On January 29, Madras City Corporation gave an official welcome to Sarasvatī Ṭhākura. He gave a speech of thanks in the Corporation's Rippon Building.

On the 30th, Sarasvatī Ṭhākura went to the town of Eluru in the West Godavari district, where he was greeted by a huge *saṅkīrtana* party of townspeople. He received an official letter of welcome from the Janardana Prārthanā Samāja. He gave a speech and then initiated and inspired a large number of people from that region in the practice of pure devotional service. On his fifty-eighth birthday, he wrote a speech which was sent to Kolkata to be read at the Vyāsa Pūjā festivities there.

Sarasvatī Ṭhākura returned to Mayapur before the 1932 Nabadwip Parikramā. On the occasion of Mahāprabhu's appearance day, he laid the cornerstone for a new temple building at Advaita Ācārya's house. He gave a speech at the annual meeting of the Śrī Dhāma Pracāriṇī Sabhā as well as instituted the examinations for *Bhakti-śāstrī* and *Bhakti-vaibhavācārya* degrees. On April 3, he presided over the annual award-giving ceremony at the Bhaktivinoda Institute, where he gave a speech on "Altruism and Extended Altruism".

MADRAS, UDAGAMANDALAM, MYSORE AND KOVVUR

On May 23, 1932, Sarasvatī Ṭhākura returned to Madras. This time he had the opportunity to explain the particularities of the Gauḍīya Vaiṣṇava *sampradāya* to the religious leaders and scholars of the Śaṅkara, Rāmānuja and Madhva schools. On May

25, he spoke to a group of questioners led by Prof. K. Panchapagesan of Pudukottai College and settled their doubts. On May 29, he was welcomed to Coimbatore by its citizens. He spoke there and on the banks of the Bhavani River to the people of the town of Mettuppalaiyam. From there he went to Udugamandalam in the Nilgiri Hills, where he stayed at the Raṅgavilāsa Bhavana. He stayed there long enough to revise Prof. Niśikānta Sānnyāla's English book *Śrī Kṛṣṇa Caitanya*, as well as completing his own English translation of *Brahma-saṁhitā*, his *Gauḍīya Bhāṣya* commentary on the *Caitanya Bhāgavata*, and a short English book on the life of Rāmānanda Rāya.

While in Udagamandalam, several distinguished people came to visit Sarasvatī Ṭhākura and had the opportunity to hear his teachings through his principal disciples. They included Sir Kishan Prasad, G.C.I.E. (Knight and Grand Commander of the Indian Empire), prime minister to the Nizam of Hyderabad, Hyderabad zamindar Dhanaraj Girji, Sir P.S. Shivaswami Aiyar, and the honorable Diwan Bahadur P. Muniswami Naidu.

On June 17, the King of Mysore, Sir Krishnaraj Vadhiyar, G.C.S.I. [Knight and Grand Commander of the Star of India], G.B.E. [Grand Cross of the British Empire] invited Sarasvatī Ṭhākura and his disciples to Mysore, where they stayed as his guests in the Rāma Mandir and tirelessly preached the Caitanya gospel throughout the area. On the way from Udagamandalam to Mysore, Sarasvatī Ṭhākura visited various places such as the Liṅgaits temple Śrī Kanṭhasvara and the Mādhva Math, etc., in Nanjangar. On June 19, Sarasvatī Ṭhākura visited Krishnaraj Sagar and Srirangapattanam (20 km north of Mysore).

In the morning on June 20, Sarasvatī Ṭhākura visited the Mysore Sanskrit College and spoke to the professors on Kṛṣṇa *bhakti*. That afternoon he was invited to the king's palace, where he gave a discourse on Caitanya Mahāprabhu and answered the king's questions.

From there, Sarasvatī Ṭhākura went to Kovvur, the place on the banks of the Godavari where Mahāprabhu met with Rāmānanda Rāya for the first time. On July 5, he installed deities at the Rāmānanda Gaudiya Math. Hundreds of thousands of people come around at that time to take bath in the Godavari on the occasion of the *Puṣkara* and were blessed by the chance to hear the chanting of Gaurāṅga's names. Sarasvatī Ṭhākura spoke on the gradual process of spiritual life and its ultimate goal to the educated people of the locality.

GAURA KIŚORA DĀSA'S SAMĀDHI IS TRANSFERRED

By August 16, Sarasvatī Ṭhākura returned to Kolkata, and Sir Deva Prasāda Sarvādhikārī came to hear him speak on "Śrī Caitanya *prema*." On the 28th, during the annual festival held at the Gaudiya Math, he gave a lecture entitled "Relative Worlds" at the Gauḍīya Sārasvata Śravaṇa Sadana.

On August 21, 1932, upon hearing that the *samādhi* of his guru, Śrīla Gaura Kiśora Dāsa Bābājī Mahārāja, was about to fall into the Ganges, Sarasvatī Ṭhākura sent disciples to arrange to have his transcendental *samādhi* transferred in its entirety to the Chaitanya Math in Mayapur.

In the beginning of September, publication of a monthly magazine in the Assamese language, *Kīrtana*, was begun out of the town of Dhuburi on Sarasvatī Ṭhākura's orders. On September 3, Sarasvatī Ṭhākura gave a lecture entitled "The Ultimate Goal of Life" at the Kolkata Sri Gaudiya Math. On the 4th, the Calcutta University professor Sunīti Cattopādhyāya and Nadia District Magistrate T. C. Rāya came to the Sri Gaudiya Math to hear him speak. On Sept. 11th, he gave a lecture on the Vedānta. These three lectures were later published. Then on the 16th, Sarasvatī Ṭhākura came to Mayapur to inaugurate the *samādhi* temple of Gaura Kiśora Dāsa Bābājī Mahārāja on the banks of Radha Kunda.

ŚRĪ VRAJA MAṆḌALA PARIKRAMĀ

On October 9, the appearance day of Śrī Madhvācārya, Sarasvatī Ṭhākura and countless devotees undertook the 84-*krośa* pilgrimage tour of Vraja Mandala. Stopping at every place where Kṛṣṇa had engaged in His pastimes, Sarasvatī Ṭhākura and his disciples preached in various different languages for the benefit of the devotees coming from many different places. On the holy place of the confluence of Sri Radhā Kunda and Shyāma Kunda, he himself lectured on Rūpa Gosvāmī's *Upadeśāmṛta* to a large assembly of Vraja residents and scholars.

On November 4, after finishing the *parikramā*, he went to Haridwar-Mayapur, where he laid the cornerstone for the Sri Saraswata Gaudiya Math. Then on Nov. 21, in Prayag, the cornerstone for Sri Rupa Gaudiya Math was laid at his invitation and in his presence by the governor of the United Provinces, Sir William Malcolm Haley. On the 24th, deities of Śrī Rādhā-Govinda were installed in the Sanatan Gaudiya Math in Benares.

On November 27, the second annual memorial festival in honor of Jagabandhu Bhakti Rañjana was held in Kolkata Sri Gaudiya Math, with Sir Manmathanātha Rāy Caudhurī Rāja Bāhādura presiding at the meeting. On December 4, Krishnanagar College professor Dr. Sudhīndra Kumāra Dāsa and Viśvambhara Vyākaraṇatīrtha, Vedānta-śāstrī of Radha Kanta Math in Puri, came to Mayapur, where they learnt much about the different Vaiṣṇava *sampradāyas* throughout India.

A SPIRITUAL EDUCATIONAL EXHIBITION IN DHAKA

On December 12, Sarasvatī Ṭhākura came to Dhaka to open a diorama exhibition. He remained there for longer than a month, until January 30, 1933, during which time many of the most respectable members of the learned community came to see him and hear his teachings. The diorama exhibition with the theme of spiritual education, unprecedented in Dhaka, was opened on January 6 in the Math in Purana Paltan. His lecture on that occasion, entitled "Exhibition speech," created a change in the ideas of his listeners about the true nature of religion and its doctrines.

On February 2, on his return to the Kolkata Gaudiya Math, he explained the difference between *eka-daṇḍa sannyāsa* and *tri-daṇḍa sannyāsa* after being questioned on the subject by Satīśacandra De, dean of Narasingha College in Howrah, and Professor Raṇadā Caraṇa Cakravartī. On the 8th, Sarasvatī Ṭhākura went to Sri Mayapur to celebrate Nityānanda Prabhu's appearance day, Vyāsa Pūjā and the appearance day of Śrī Caitanya Mahāprabhu.

PREACHING ENVOYS TO EUROPE

On Mahāprabhu's appearance day, 1933, Prof. Niśikānta Sānnyāla's English-language book *Śrī Kṛṣṇa Caitanya* was released for distribution. After this event, Sarasvatī Ṭhākura decided that it was now time to preach Mahāprabhu's message in Europe. He selected three preachers for the job: Śrīmad Bhakti Pradīp Tīrtha Mahārāja, Śrīmad Bhakti Hridoy Bon Mahārāja, and Samvidānanda Dāsa, M. A., Bhakti-Śāstrī. On March 18, in a meeting presided over by Yatīndranātha Basu M.L.C [Member of Legislative Council], Sarasvatī Ṭhākura gave a farewell speech called "My Message" (*Āmāra Kathā*), in which he praised these three disciples, bidding them bon voyage before they left to carry out the European mission.

The first news of results of their preaching in London was received at the beginning of May: a preaching center had been opened at 39 Drain Gardens, Kensington, S.W. 10. On May 31, Sarasvatī Ṭhākura answered inquiries on spiritual matters sent from London by the Marquess of Ludian and Lord Zetland, a former governor of Bengal. On June 15, Lord Zetland presided over a meeting of the Society for the Study of Religion at Bedford Square, in which Sarasvatī Ṭhākura's disciples spoke on the glories of Śrī Caitanya Mahāprabhu.

On June 23, a meeting was held at the London Gaudiya Math in honor of Śrīla Bhaktivinoda Ṭhākura. Many distinguished guests, including the Honorable Justice Bistrow, came there to hear about Śrīla Bhaktivinoda Ṭhākura's teachings. In the month of July, Sarasvatī Ṭhākura received letters from several distinguished British citizens thanking him for the great work the Gaudiya Math had undertaken in Great Britain. They included Lord Irwin's private secretary, Mr. R. A. Butler, the Marquis of Ludian, Sir Stanley Jackson, and *Times* editor Mr. Brown.

On July 5, former Viceroy of India Lord Irwin, his wife and representatives of the Joint Select Parliamentary Committee heard from the Gaudiya Math missionaries about their objectives in preaching Mahāprabhu's message in Europe. At 4 P.M. on July 20, the Secretary of State for India, Sir Samuel Hoare, introduced the Gaudiya Math preachers to Emperor George V and Empress Mary in Buckingham Palace. They had the opportunity to offer him their respects and to tell him the purpose of the Gaudiya Mission. On July 14, they met with the head of the Church of England, the Archbishop of Canterbury. Then on October 7 and 8, a large meeting was held for the professors and students of Oxford University, in which the Gauḍīya Vaiṣṇava doctrine of the Holy Names was explained.

The Gaudiya Math's European preachers gave lectures on Caitanya Mahāprabhu's gospel at the Eastbourne Theosophical Society on November 24-25, then at the Deutsch Akademi in Munich, Germany, on December 10; at Humboldt House in Berlin on December 12; Koningsburg on the 14th, at the Institut de la Civilization Indienne in Paris between December 16 and 18. On December 20, the London Gaudiya Math moved to 3 Gloucester House, Cornwall Gardens, S.W. 7.

PREACHING ACTIVITY IN BOMBAY AND OTHER CITIES

While this was going on, Sarasvatī Ṭhākura opened the Śrī-Kṛṣṇa Kīrtana Hall in Madras. From there he went to Bombay, where he met with the Nepali professor Sañjīva Kumāra Caudhurī, M.A., and answered his three sincere questions.

Not long afterwards, he opened the Gaudiya Math's Bombay office in the Jangu Villa on Babul Nath Road. While staying there, he made great efforts to preach Mahāprabhu's message in the large city. On May 20, in response to a question by a distinguished relative of Dādābhāi Nārajī, he gave his resolution of the problem of the movement for the admission of untouchables into Hindu temples.

Meanwhile, on June 16, Sarasvatī Ṭhākura spoke on the uniqueness of the *Śrīmad Bhāgavatam* at the Krishnanagar Town Hall. The occasion was a memorial meeting in honor of Śrīla Bhaktivinoda Ṭhākura, which was presided over by Ksitipati Nātha Mitra and Dīnanātha Sānnyāla Rāya Bāhādura.

On July 3, Sarasvatī Ṭhākura installed deities of Gaurasundara and Rādhā-Govinda in the newly finished temple at the Tridandi Gaudiya Math in Bhuvaneshwar. This was followed by a *kīrtana* festival.

In August, on the occasion of a solar eclipse, a spiritual diorama exhibition was held for the second time at Kurukshetra. During the time of the Bagh Bazaar Math's annual festival, a large *kīrtana* procession was taken through many Kolkata neighborhoods. On August 12, Sarasvatī Ṭhākura spoke on "The Ultimate Goal of Human Life", on the 20th, on "The Uniqueness of Śrī Caitanya Mahāprabhu", and on the 27th, in English on "The Vedānta, Its Morphology and Ontology". On September 7, he went by motor launch to Nabadwip, bringing *saṅkīrtana* to various places along the Ganges.

On October 27, Sarasvatī Ṭhākura made his auspicious entrance into the city of Patna to preach Mahāprabhu's message to the local populace. Some of the distinguished people who came to hear his instructions were Amarendranātha Dāsa Rāya Bāhādura; Gaṇeśa Candra Canda, the government archeological superintendent for the region of Bihar, Odisha, and Chota Nagpur; the barrister P. R. Dāsa; advocate Nabadvīpa Candra Dāsa; District and Session Judge Śivapriya Cattopādhyāya. On November 14, Darbhanga Mahārāja, Sir Kāmeśvara Singh Bāhādura, K.C.S.I., opened the diorama exhibition in Patna, attracting some of the most distinguished citizens of that town.

On November 19, the third annual memorial meeting for Jagabandhu Bhakti Rañjana was presided over at the Kolkata Sri Gaudiya Math by Sir Vijaya Prasāda Siṁha Rāya. At the end of November, the *Bhakti-sandarbha*, edited by Sarasvatī Ṭhākura, was published in its entirety. On November 24, he spoke Hari kathā in Tetiya Palli near Nrisimha Palli in Nabadwip *dhāma*. On November 26 and 27, he took part in a *saṅkīrtana* festival at the Ekayan Math in Krishnanagar. By his grace, there was also preaching activity in Amarshigram in Midnapore at this time as well.

During this time, preaching activity was also being conducted in Karachi, now in Pakistan. On December 24, the spiritual exhibition was opened in Benares in the Michir Pokra neighborhood by Saravati Ṭhākura's supporter District Magistrate and Collector Mr. Pannalal, I.C.S. [Indian Civil Service].

THE KING OF TRIPURA VISITS THE GAUDIYA MATH

On January 15, 1934, the King of the independent state of Tripura, Vīravikrama Kiśora Devavarma Maṇikya Bāhādura, visited the Kolkata Sri Gaudiya Math with his entourage. He showed his reverence for the Ācārya and at a great assembly that evening gave a speech praising the work of the Gaudiya Math. On February 2, Hetampur's Kumāra Bāhādura Rādhikā Rañjana Cakravartī, B.A., his private secretary and retinue came to visit Sarasvatī Ṭhākura and to receive his instructions.

On February 4, on his sixtieth birthday, the Vyāsa Pūjā ceremony was held and printing of a book written by his disciples in glorification of his life, *Sarasvatī Jayaśrī*, was begun. On Feb. 2, in London, a meeting in honor of the Ācārya was held at Grosvenor House in London's Park Lane, presided over by Lord Zetland.

On February 25, in Modadrumdwip, the new temple at Vṛndāvana Dāsa Ṭhākura's birthplace was inaugurated. That year, the Nabadwip *dhāma parikramā* and festival celebrating the appearance of Caitanya Mahāprabhu were held as usual, temple buildings at the site of Śrīvāsa Aṅgana and Gaura Kiśora Dāsa Bābājī's *samādhi* were consecrated, three devotees were initiated into the *tridaṇḍa-sannyāsa* order, and Sarasvatī Ṭhākura gave regular lectures in the Bhakti Vijaya Bhavana as well as at the annual meeting of the Nabadvīpa Dhāma Pracāriṇī Sabhā. Amongst the notable visitors to the Chaitanya Math during this time were Rājarṣi Kumāra Śaradindu Nārāyaṇa Rāya and Rāya Bāhādura Ramā Prasāda Candra, who came on February 19 and visited many of the holy places in Māyāpura besides coming to see the Ācārya.

On March 5, Sarasvatī Ṭhākura headed a large preaching party which went to Chanchuri Puruliya in Jessore, the home village of the Gaudiya Math temple manager, Mahā Mahopadeśaka Ācāryatrika Kuñja Bihārī Vidyābhūṣaṇa Mahāśaya. He spent five days there constantly preaching the message of Lord Caitanya.

THE NEW TEMPLE AT THE MAYAPUR YOGAPĪṬHA

On March 18, the foundations were laid for the proposed temple at the birthplace of Caitanya Mahāprabhu, as well as for a temple at Murāri Gupta's house. Three months later, at 10 A.M. on June 13, 31 Jyaiṣtha, the four-armed form of Viṣṇu known as Adhokṣaja was found in the ground while digging the foundations for the new temple at the Yogapīṭha, made possible by the donations of Śrī Sakhīcaraṇa Rāya Bhakti Vijaya Mahāśaya. This was the same deity worshipped by Jagannātha Miśra in his home.

THE GAUDIYA MISSION SOCIETY IN LONDON

On April 2, Sarasvatī Ṭhākura established a shrine to Mahāprabhu's lotus feet in Chatrabhoga. The villagers there awarded him special recognition, and he gave a speech in response. On April 8, he gave *sannyāsa* to several disciples. On the 20th he went to Puri from Kolkata.

On April 24, in Westminster's Caxton Hall, a general meeting presided over by Lord Zetland was held to inaugurate the foundation of the Gaudiya Mission Society.

On May 6, the archeologist Rāma Prasāda Canda Rāya Bāhādura gave a lecture on "Nabadvīpa at the Time of Lord Caitanya" at a meeting presided over by Yatīndranātha Basu, M.L.C.

IN PURI

Throughout the month of May, Sarasvatī Ṭhākura met with a number of important people and spoke to them about Kṛṣṇa. They included the chief lecturer of the Āyurveda department at the Puri Sanskrit College, Ānanda Mahāpātra; the novelist Śacīśacandra Cattopādhyāya, the abbot of Emar Math, Gadādhara Rāmānuja Dāsa; Hanuman Khuṇtiyā; Rāya Bāhādura Gaura Śyāma Mahānti; Rādhā Śyāma Mahānti; Professor Junākara of Dhaka University; Puri Deputy Magistrate Revatīnātha Cattopādhyāya and Magistrate Narendranātha Datta Bāhādura, the founder of the Bodhana Ashram, Girijā Prasanna Mukhopādhyāya; Khagendranātha Mitra.

On June 27, the Gopīnātha deity was consecrated by Sarasvatī Ṭhākura at the

Alalanatha Brahma Gaudiya Math along with festive *kīrtana*. The revised and expanded edition of the book *Brāhmaṇa o Vaiṣṇava* was released on this day.

On July 12, he installed a deity of Gaura Kiśora Dāsa Bābājī in Mayapur. On August 13, he preached to the son of the illustrious O. N. Mukhārjī, Yāminī Mohana Mukhopādhyāya. On August 14, he installed deities at the Patna Gaudiya Math.

At the annual Gaudiya Math festival, once again *harināma-saṅkīrtana* was held in the streets of Kolkata. On September 1, on the day of Kṛṣṇa Janmāṣṭamī, the book *Sarasvatī Jayaśrī* was released. On September 4, the English language fortnightly *Harmonist* was published in a new format.

On September 16, Sarasvatī Ṭhākura spoke at the Sri Gaudiya Math on Rādhāṣṭamī in an assembly presided over by Dvārakānātha Mitra, M.A., D.L. Countless visitors to the temple heard Sarasvatī Ṭhākura speak on topics related to Kṛṣṇa.

THE MONTH OF KĀRTIKA IN MATHURA

Starting October 17, Sarasvatī Ṭhākura spent the month of Kārtika observing the *vrata* in Mathura with a large group of disciples and followers. During this time, he set the example of discussing Śrī Rādhā-Kṛṣṇa's *Aṣṭakālīya-līlā* (remembrance of pastimes during eight periods of the day). On October 29, he discovered the place in Mathura city, in the Sataghara neighborhood, where Rūpa Gosvāmī would come for *darśana* of Gopāla.

In the third week of October, his representative preachers visited several German universities to preach the message of pure devotion.

On November 1, Sarasvatī Ṭhākura and his party visited Chandra Sarovara, Parasauli, Gauri Tirtha, and Paitha Grama, and he was inspired to talk on the *līlās* which took place in these spots. On November 17, he gave *tridaṇḍa sannyāsa* to a *brahmacārī* disciple.

On November 29, at the Rajendra Bhavana in New Delhi, he spoke on "The Duty of Human Life" and "Mahāprabhu's Mercy and His Teaching" to an audience which included N. Chatterjee and Dr. J. K. Sena.

CAITANYA-ŚIKṢĀMṚTA IS TRANSLATED INTO TELUGU

On December 6, Rāja Bhūpendra Nārāyaṇa Siṁha Bāhādura presided over the fourth annual memorial assembly in honor of Jagabandhu Bhakti Rañjana. At this time, on his order, Sarasvatī Ṭhākura's Andhra disciple Y. Jagannatham, B.A., published *Śrī Caitanya-Śikṣāmṛta* in the Telugu language. Meanwhile, the English edition of *Jaiva-dharma* was also in publication.

THE GOVERNOR OF BENGAL VISITS MAYAPUR

On January 15, 1935, the Governor of Bengal, Sir John Anderson, came to visit the birthplace of Śrī Caitanya Mahāprabhu in Mayapur and, after hearing about the site from Sarasvatī Ṭhākura, himself gave a speech.

Sarasvatī Ṭhākura's sixty-first birthday was celebrated with Vyāsa Pūjā on February 23 in his birthplace, Puri, amidst the sand dunes near the ocean (Chataka Parvata). A huge assembly was held at which the King of Puri, Gajapati Rāmacandra Deva Bāhādura, presided. The following day, Sarasvatī Ṭhākura led a *parikramā* around Puri and gave a lecture for the occasion. In preparation for the Dola

Pūrṇimā festivities, Śrī Sakhī Caraṇa Rāya Bhakti Vijaya Mahodaya had electric lights installed in the Yogapīṭha temple building. On March 4, Sir. B. L. Mitra came to hear Sarasvatī Ṭhākura speak on Caitanya Mahāprabhu.

March 20, Dola Pūrṇimā, the birthdate of Caitanya Mahāprabhu was marked by the inauguration of the newly finished temple. The King of Tripura, Sir Vīravikrama Kiśora Devavarma Maṇikya Bāhādura, came to Mayapur for the occasion and officially opened the temple doors.

PREACHING TOUR IN EAST BENGAL

On March 24, the Gaudiya Math Ācārya went with a party of devotees to Deruli in the Khulna district, where he addressed several massive gatherings. On March 31, the King of Burdwan, Sir Vijaya Cāṇḍa Mahātāv, came to the Kolkata Gaudiya Math and heard the Ācārya speak.

On April 8, the Ācārya came to Dhaka and placed the foundation for the proposed new temple building of the Madhva Gaudiya Math in Narinda Palli. The residents of Dhaka and Narain Ganj welcomed him and eulogized him.

On April 12, Sarasvatī Ṭhākura installed deities at the Jagannath Gaudiya Math in Mymensingha. He stayed there until the 15th at Shashi Lodge on the invitation of the King, Śaśīkānta Ācārya, and preached to many learned and distinguished citizens of the district.

FOUNDING THE GAYA GAUDIYA MATH

On April 19, Sarasvatī Ṭhākura traveled to Gaya, where he visited all the places that Mahāprabhu had been to and constantly spoke to many educated and respectable people. On the 22nd, he established the Gaya Gaudiya Math. On April 30, he sent a few preachers to Burma for propagating Mahāprabhu's message. On May 31, he was in Darjeeling with a group of devotees and spoke constantly on topics related to Kṛṣṇa. Then on June 9 and 10, in large assemblies presided over by Sir Yadunātha Sarkāra and Colonel Upendranātha Mukhopādhyāya, he had his leading disciples speak. On June 9, he spread Caitanya's gospel on the Indian Broadcasting Service Center's radio network.

On June 28, at the Kolkata Gaudiya Math, he received the Cooch Bihar Queen, Indirā Devī, the princesses Elā Devī and Gāyatrī Devī, prince Indrajitendra Nārāyaṇa Bāhādura, and the French intellectual Maximilian Poitiers, PhD, all of whom heard from the Ācārya about Vaiṣṇava philosophy.

On July 8, he installed deities at the Bombay Gaudiya Math on Proctor Street and in a meeting held at the People's Jinnah Hall spoke on the *Bhāgavata* and *Pañcarātra*. At this time, Sarasvatī Ṭhākura's disciple Samvidānanda Dāsa, M.A., Bhakti Śāstrī, the expert archeologist, received his doctorate from the University of London in Vaiṣṇava history and literature. From the end of July to the middle of August, the Ācārya was preaching in different places in the Nabadwip area.

PREACHING THE GOSPEL OF LORD CAITANYA ON THE RADIO

Every Sunday beginning with the annual Gaudiya Math festival, street *saṅkīrtana* was held and programs about Janmāṣṭamī, Nandotsava, Rādhāṣṭamī and Bhaktivinoda Ṭhākura's appearance day were given on the radio. From Balarāma's appearance day, the Ācārya spoke on the *Bhāgavata* for sixteen consecutive days. During the festival itself, at the great assembly presided over by the Kashim Bazaar king, Śacīndra Nandī Bāhādura, he spoke on "Devotion and the Material World," and in the assembly presided over by Hiraṇyakumāra Mitra he spoke on "Devotion and Worldly Indifference."

In Kolkata on September 18, the people of Kolkata welcomed and gave a special letter of appreciation to returning preacher Śrīmad Bhakti Hridoy Bon Mahārāja and two German devotees, who arrived from London.

On September 12, the full-moon day of the month of Bhādra, twelve cantos of *Śrīmad Bhāgavatam* with the *vivriti* commentary by Śrīla Sarasvatī Ṭhākura got published, and he gave a lecture on the completion of this service.

NIYAMA SEVA IN RADHA KUNDA

From October 1 to 7, Sarasvatī Ṭhākura was on a preaching engagement in New Delhi. Then, from the 8th, he spent more than a month in Radha Kunda to keep the vows for the month of Kārtika (*niyama-sevā)*. During this time, he spoke daily on the *Upaniṣads*, *Caitanya Caritāmṛta*, *Śrīmad Bhāgavatam*, as well as circumambulating the *kuṇḍa*, and hearing and chanting about Kṛṣṇa's *aṣṭakāliya-līlā*. A committee was founded to improve opportunities to serve the holy *dhāma* of Vraja named the Vraja Dhāma Pracāriṇī Sabhā.

On November 4, Sarasvatī Ṭhākura installed deities at the Kunja Bihari Math at Radha Kunda, and two days later, Śrīla Bhaktivinoda Ṭhākura's *puṣpa-samādhi* memorial and *bhāva-sevā* at Vraja Svananda Sukhada Kunja.

On November 7, he traveled to Seshshayi in Punjab and then on to Delh,i where he preached at the annual festival on the 10th. On the 11th, he was in Gaya, where he stayed, telling the good news of Mahāprabhu's mercy to the people of that town, until the 15th. On the 13th, he installed deities in the Gaya Gaudiya Math. During this period, the preaching activity in Burma was meeting with great success.

On December 23, the King of Tripura, Vīravikrama Kiśora Devavarma Māṇikya Bāhādura, presided over the fifth annual memorial festival to Jagabandhu Bhakti Rañjana. After the assembly, the Ācārya met with Dr. Henry Hand and Mr. S. V. Rossetto of California, barrister S. N. Rudra, retired judge Lalita Mohana Basu and others, preaching to them about knowledge beyond the sense perception.

DIORAMA EXHIBIT AT PRAYAG

On December 27, Sarasvatī Ṭhākura traveled to Patna, where he spoke at the Gaudiya Math. On the 30th, he went on to Allahabad, where he spoke on Mahāprabhu's teachings to Rūpa Gosvāmī.

On January 7, 1936, he opened the transcendental diorama exhibition at Prayag, after which he gave the presidential speech in English before an assembly of learned persons.

A DEVOTIONAL LIBRARY AND SOCIETY FOR PROMOTING DAIVA VARṆĀŚRAMA

On January 11, Sarasvatī Ṭhākura returned to Mayapur, where he remained for a full two months, preaching daily to the devotees living at the Chaitanya Math and the birth site of Gaurāṅga Mahāprabhu.

On February 12, in celebration of his sixty-second birthday, he established the Bhaktivinoda Ṭhākura Research Institute or the Kṛṣṇānuśīlanāgāra ("Library for Kṛṣṇa Culture"), and the Daiva Varṇāśrama Saṅgha.

The Vyāsa Pūjā was held at Śrīvāsa Aṅgana. The appearance day of the Ācārya was also celebrated in London with the London Gaudiya Mission Society chairman, The Right Honorable Sir Sadilal, presiding.

Starting from February 25, Sarasvatī Ṭhākura started establishing deities of the *viṣaya* and *āśraya-vigrahas* of each of Nabadwip's nine islands. On March 1, he went to Suvarna Bihara where he established the Suvarna Bihara Gaudiya Math and installed deities. On March 5, he opened the Sarvabhaum Gaudiya Math in Vidyanagar, also installing deities there. On the 7th, the Rudradwip Gaudiya Math was opened along with deity service.

On March 8, the appearance day of Śrī Caitanya Mahāprabhu, on the Ācārya's direction the Burmese education minister, Dr. Bame, opened the Rangoon office of the Gaudiya Math at 29 Brooking Street. At the London Gaudiya Math also, the devotees gave speeches in honor of Mahāprabhu's appearance, with Dr. Parhi presiding.

On March 15, the Ācārya traveled to Assam, where deities were installed at the Sarbhog Gaudiya Math. The residents of Sarabhog gave him a warm welcome and bestowed honors on him.

THE HUNDRED-DAY KĪRTANA FESTIVAL IN ORISSA

On March 27, Sarasvatī Ṭhākura traveled to Cuttack, where he preached to distinguished people of that town. From March 29, he stayed at Chaṭaka Parvata in Puri, establishing a residence for devotees and a temple with deities of Śrī Rādhā-Govinda. In a speech before many learned people of the city, he inaugurated a hundred-day *saṅkīrtana* festival. On May 4, he celebrated Nṛsiṁha Caturdaśī at Alalanatha, at the Brahma Gaudiya Math. On May 30, he initiated several *brahmacārī* preachers into the order of *tridaṇḍa-sannyāsa*.

BALIYATI, GODRUM, DARJEELING AND BOGRA

On June 7, Sarasvatī Ṭhākura went to Dhaka, where he stayed at the home of Supati Rañjana Nāga M.A., B.L., where he spoke on topics of Kṛṣṇa to an audience of distinguished persons. He also initiated a number of truth-seekers in the service of Lord Śrī Kṛṣṇa Caitanya.

On June 9, he arrived in Baliyati village in the Dhaka district, accepted the welcome of the villagers and gave a speech in thanks. On June 10, he installed deities of Śrī Rādhā-Govinda in the newly constructed Gadai Gauranga Math temple. On the 13th and 14th, he had his *sannyāsī* preachers and one of his German disciples speak at Dhaka University and the Dhaka Bar Library.

On June 19th, he celebrated the twenty-second anniversary of Śrīla Bhaktivinoda Ṭhākura's disappearance at Svananda Sukhada Kunja in Godrumdwip. He spoke on renouncing the company of nondevotees and held a *saṅkīrtana* festival. On the same day, the Gaudiya Math devotees gave the opportunity to thousands of pilgrims who had assembled at Kurukshetra for the solar eclipse to hear Mahāprabhu's gospel by visiting the diorama exhibition, Sat Śikṣā Pradarśinī.

On the 27th, Sarasvatī Ṭhākura went to Darjeeling, where he stayed at the Gaudiya Math office. He spoke and had his disciples speak Hari *kathā* to their distinguished guests. He installed Śrī Rādhā-Govinda deities there on July 19, taking the opportunity to speak himself to the assembled guests.

On July 24, he came to Bogra on the insistent invitation of its people. He was given a warm welcome, and at the local Hindu Sabhā meeting, he spoke on the need for preaching Gauḍīya Vaiṣṇavism in northern Bengal, which had previously been blessed by Narottama Dāsa Ṭhākura.

THE PURUṢOTTAMA VRATA IN VRINDAVAN

After celebrating the appearance day of Balarāma and Janmāṣṭamī in Kolkata, Sarasvatī Ṭhākura decided to spend the month of Puruṣottama (the supplementary month irregularly added to the Hindu calendar to balance the lunar and solar years, also known as *mala-māsa*) in the Mathura area. He left Kolkata on August 12, 1936. He first stayed in Mathura Cantonment at a building by the name Śivālaya. From there, he went to Vrindavan, where he stayed at Madhumangala Kunja, speaking regularly on *Śrīmad Bhāgavatam*. He inaugurated a place of worship in Govardhan. He returned to the Kolkata Gaudiya Math on September 9 for the annual festival.

THE GAUḌĪYA SAṄGHA PRESIDENT SENT TO GREAT BRITAIN

On October 16, Sarasvatī Ṭhākura spoke for nearly an entire hour to Dr. Śivapada Bhaṭṭācārya, M.B. On the 23rd, he bestowed the responsibility for preaching Mahāprabhu's message in Great Britain and America on Bhakti Sāraṇga Prabhu. He blessed him and gave him instructions in the worship of Gomati, Śālagrāma- and Govardhan-śilā before leaving for London. Sarasvatī Ṭhākura also gave a speech at the Sārasvata Śravaṇa Sadana.

INTIMATIONS OF SARASVATĪ ṬHĀKURA'S DEPARTURE

On October 24, he left for Puri. On November 1, Sarasvatī Ṭhākura's dear disciple Tridaṇḍi Svāmī Bhakti Srirup Purī Mahārāja left this world.

While at Chaṭaka Parvat, Puri's nondifferent manifestation of Govardhan Hill, he celebrated the appearance of Madhvācārya and performed Govardhan Pūjā, which he performed with the hymns composed by Rūpa and Raghunātha Gosvāmīs. He also observed a festival of separation from his dear lord, Śrīla Gaura Kiśora Dāsa Bābāji Mahārāja. Each day, his disciples and guests were refreshed after bathing in the holy waters of his discourse. While in Puri, he constantly warned everyone, "Worship the Lord without duplicity, for not much time is left." He constantly repeated few lines written by Rūpa and Raghunātha Gosvāmīs:

pratyāśāṁ me tvaṁ kuru govardhana pūrṇām

"O Govardhan, fulfill every one of my wishes!" (Śrī Rūpa Gosvāmī's *Govardhanāṣṭakam*)

nija-nikaṭa-nivāsaṁ dehi govardhana tvam

"O Govardhan, please give me residence near to you." (Śrī Raghunātha Dāsa Gosvāmī's *Govardhana-vāsa-prārthanā-daśakam)*

Śrīla Prabhupāda returned to Kolkata on December 9 and spoke Hari-*kathā* to his disciples without cessation.

ŚRĪLA PRABHUPĀDA'S FINAL INSTRUCTIONS

On December 23, 1936, a few days prior to the setting of the blazing sun of the Gauḍīya Vaiṣṇava *sampradāya*, Oṁ Viṣṇupāda Śrīla

Bhakti Siddhānta Sarasvatī Gosvāmī Ṭhākura, spoke to a gathering of his disciples in the morning, at which time he said the following words:

"I have given trouble to many persons. As I have been compelled to speak the undeceitful truth, and have urged persons to worship God (Śrī Hari) sincerely without deceitfulness, many persons may even have considered me to be their enemy. By inspiring them to be eagerly devoted to Śrī Kṛṣṇa sincerely without ulterior desires and deceitfulness, they will someday be able to understand why I have given trouble to them.

"All should propagate the teachings of Rūpa-Raghunātha with great enthusiasm. The ultimate object of our desires is to become specks of dust at the lotus feet of the followers of Śrī Rūpa Gosvāmī. Remain united in following the *āśraya-vigraha* in order to satisfy the transcendental senses of the one, nondual Supreme Truth. Make your way through this impermanent, transitory life in whatever way you can, keeping the goal of worshipping the Lord foremost in your minds. Don't abandon this goal, even in the face of hundreds of dangers, insults, or persecutions. Don't lose your spirit if you see that the majority of people cannot accept the principle of selfless service to the Supreme Lord. Never abandon your *bhajana*, hearing and chanting Kṛṣṇa *katha*, the be-all and end-all of your devotional life. Please always chant the name of the Lord, being humbler than a blade of grass and more tolerant than the tree.

"This body is like the ageing cow which in ancient times was meant to be offered up in sacrifice. Only we desire to offer the body to Kṛṣṇa in the sacrifice of the Holy Name established by Śrī Kṛṣṇa Caitanya and His associates. We do not seek to become heroes performing great works or religious deeds; our true being and our identity is that of a speck of dust at the lotus feet of Śrī Rūpa Prabhu, life after life. The stream which flows from Śrīla Bhaktivinoda Ṭhākura will never be dammed up. Remember this and vow to double your efforts to fulfill Śrīla Bhaktivinoda Ṭhākura's desires. Amongst you are many capable and worthy individuals. We seek nothing for ourselves; our only motto is:

ādadānas tṛṇaṁ dantair
idaṁ yāce punaḥ punaḥ
śrīmad rūpa-padāmbhoja-
dhūliḥ syāṁ janma-janmani

"Taking grass between my teeth, I pray repeatedly that I may become a speck of dust at Śrī Rūpa Gosvāmī's lotus feet, birth after birth." (Raghunātha Dāsa Gosvāmī, *Mukta-carita.*)

"While living in the world, we encounter many difficulties; but there is no need for us to be bewildered by these difficulties – nor need we make any effort to remove them. What is necessary for us, while we are still here, is to learn what will remain after we have removed all those difficulties – what will be the nature of our eternal life. There are so many things, which we want or don't want, but we have to come to terms with this duality of attractions and repulsions. The more we distance ourselves from Kṛṣṇa's lotus feet, the more these things will draw us in. We can only begin to comprehend the exquisite taste of service to Kṛṣṇa's lotus feet after transcending these worldly attractions and repulsions and being attracted by His Holy Name. The doctrines of Kṛṣṇa-*bhakti* seem startling at first, perhaps even perplexing. Knowingly or unknowingly, every human being is struggling to eliminate the adventitious elements in life which interfere with his direct experience of eternal fulfillment. Our only obligation is to go beyond duality and to enter the world of that eternal fulfillment.

"We have no attachment for anyone in this world, nor any hostility. Whatever arrangements we make in this world last but a moment, while the need to search out the supreme fulfillment is equally unavoidable for everyone. May all of you work united and in harmony toward the same goal: to earn the right to serve the root *āśraya-vigraha*. May the current of ideas propagated by Śrī Rūpa Gosvāmī flow throughout the world. May we never under any circumstances become indifferent to the seven-tongued sacrificial flame of the Holy Name. If our attraction to it remains ever increasing, we will achieve all perfection. Remain one-pointedly faithful to Śrī Rūpa Gosvāmī's followers and preach Rūpa-Raghunātha's message enthusiastically and fearlessly."

ON THE DAY OF HIS ENTERING INTO ETERNAL PASTIMES

In the morning of the day on which he disappeared, Śrīla Prabhupāda asked Tridaṇḍi Svāmī Śrīmad Bhakti Rakṣaka Śrīdhara Mahārāja to sing Narottama Dāsa Ṭhākura's song *Śrī Rūpa Mañjarī Pada,* and Śrīpāda Navīna Kṛṣṇa Vidyālaṇkāra Prabhu to sing the song *Tuhun Dayā Sāgara Tārayite Prāṇī* from Bhaktivinoda Ṭhākura's translation of the second verse of the *Śikṣāṣṭaka.* Prabhupāda expressed satisfaction and thanks to Śrī Bhakti Sudhakar Prabhu (Prof. Niśikānta Sānnyāla) for his service. He also told Patna's Śrī Vrajeśvarī Prasāda Prabhu to remain enthusiastic in his service.

At about four o'clock in the afternoon, he called Śrī Sakhī Caraṇa Rāya Bhakti Vijaya to tell him that he was very fortunate because of the service he had rendered to Sri Mayapur. Later in the afternoon, he said to Śrī Bhakti Vivek Bhāratī Mahārāja, "You are a competent person. Take care of the mission. It is good to have a single and specific purpose for love of Godhead. Narottama Dāsa Ṭhākura adopted Rūpa and Raghunātha's understanding. It is best if we live according to that understanding."

Then Śrīla Prabhupāda said to everyone, "I give my blessings to all who are present here and to those who are absent. Remember always that our only duty and religion is to propagate the service of the *Bhāgavata* and of Bhagavān."

ENTERING THE ETERNAL ABODE

At about 5:30 A.M., on Thursday, January 1, 1937, on *kṛṣṇā caturthī,* Śrīla Prabhupāda entered the eternal abode, joining Śrī Rādhā-Govinda in the predawn pastimes (*niśānta-līlā*). At the end of every night, Śrī Rādhā-Kṛṣṇa lie intertwined in an embrace, becoming as one body. It is at this moment, when Their united form of Śrī Gaurasundara is eternally manifest, that Vārṣabhānavī Dayita Dāsa, Their servant, joined them.

namaste gauravāṇī-śrī-mūrtaye dīna-tāriṇe
rūpānuga-viruddhāpa-siddhanta-dhvānta-hāriṇe

"Obeisances to you who are the embodiment of Śrī Gaurāṅga Mahāprabhu's gospel, the deliverer of the fallen and the destroyer of the darkness of unorthodox doctrines which oppose the conclusions given by Śrī Rūpa Gosvāmī and his followers."

ANNOUNCEMENT OF SRILA PRABHUPĀDA'S DEPARTURE IN GAUḌĪYA MAGAZINE

"Last Nārāyaṇa 4, 450 of the Caitanya era, at the end of the Thursday night, Pauṣa 16, 1343 of the Bengali calendar, on Friday morning, January 1, 1937, Paramahaṁsa Parivrājakācārya Oṁ Viṣṇupāda Śrīla Śrīmad Bhakti Siddhānta

Sarasvatī Gosvāmī Prabhupāda joined his eternal service in the predawn pastimes (*niśānta-līlā*) of Śrī Rādhā-Govinda. This is the same hour that his own *gurudeva*, Oṁ Viṣṇupāda Śrī Śrīla Gaura Kiśora Prabhu entered into *nitya-līlā*. Prabhupāda was the great Ācārya of the Gauḍīya Vaiṣṇava *sampradāya* and its only protector, the ninth in descent from Śrī Caitanya Mahāprabhu, and the best of the followers of Śrī Svarūpa Dāmodara and Śrī Rūpa Gosvāmī.

"The meaning of entering into eternal pastimes (*nitya-līlā*) at this hour is understood clearly by those who are intimate with him for it is directly experienced in their hearts, but a hint, based on the words of realized souls, is being given here. At the end of the night, Śrī Rādhā-Govinda are locked in a divine unbreakable embrace, *gāḍhāliṅgana-nirbhedam āptau*. Jayadeva Gosvāmī has indicated this situation with the word *naktaṁ* in the first verse of *Gīta Govindam*, which begins *meghair meduram ambaram*. When Śrī Rādhā-Govinda are joined together like this, They take on Their combined form of Śrī Gaurasundara. It is this auspicious moment that Śrī Vārṣabhānavī Dayita Dāsa Prabhu chose to make his entry into Their pastimes.

"Śrīla Prabhupāda is like the sun of the Gauḍīya *sampradāya*, as he is identical with its *ācāryas* Śrī Rūpa and Śrī Svarūpa Dāmodara. But now that this sun of Śrī Caitanya Mahāprabhu's *sampradāya* has set, darkness has descended not only on the preachers in the sky of the Gauḍīya lineage but on the entire world. It seems that the direct light of unadulterated devotion will once again be hidden from the view of the world's people. Our only hope is that this luminary amongst spiritual teachers sufficiently inspired his sincere followers with such an unparalleled desire to serve the feet of the Lord Adhokṣaja, with such ever-fresh enthusiasm, and instilled in them such paramount and rare ideals of practice and preaching, that the stream which passed through Śrī Svarūpa and Śrī Rūpa and then through Bhaktivinoda Ṭhākura will only continue to gather more force and flow into the world. In our hearts, we consider nothing else to be possible even in our worst imaginings. From the blessings that he gave just before entering into his eternal service, we know that by adhering faithfully to his teachings and propagating them, we will be able to get his direct, personal association and will be able to find all the strength we need. Furthermore, by preaching fearlessly, without any expectation, and with the force of character that comes of sincere service and fidelity, we will be able to practice and preach the gospel of Śrī Gaurasundara, our master's master, throughout the world. By so doing, we are assured that his blessings will continue to rain down on us even more profusely. This faith is the sole lamp post illuminating the path of pure devotion, which is strewn with countless obstacles.

"We, the *Gauḍīya's* writers, are today without any shelter, as we will no longer be able to show our articles to him who was the preserver of Svarūpa Dāmodara and Rūpa Gosvāmī's devotional doctrines. Śrīla Prabhupāda would eagerly read every article which was to be published in the *Gauḍīya*. He would give us blessings and show the deepest satisfaction with our efforts. Now, even though we will no longer be able to experience this directly, we will not be entirely devoid of his blessings nor of the spiritual strength arising from his mercy. We are not without succour, for he left us the gift of service to those who know the doctrines of pure devotion as taught by Bhaktivinoda Ṭhākura, and hence we are not deprived of his eternal blessings and mercy.

"Śrīla Prabhupāda wrote the following words in *Sajjana-toṣaṇī* after the disappearance of Oṁ Viṣṇupāda Śrīla Bhaktivinoda Ṭhākura:

" 'The purpose of the *Sajjana-toṣaṇī* remains unchanged. Ṭhākura Mahāśaya has entered the *nitya-līlā*, but by his blessings, this magazine will continue to bring joy to the pious through Hari *kathā*, just as before.

" 'Some think, accepting the opinion of the material sensualists, that the path of *bhakti* is advanced by eliminating the idea of pure devotion; others tarnish pure devotion's beauty by accepting the facile path of the materialistic devotees as the standard.'

"Śrīla Bhaktivinoda Ṭhākura has sung in his *Kalyāṇa-kalpa-taru*,

bhakti-bādhā jāhā ha'te se vidyāra mastakete
padāghāta kara akaitava
sarasvatī kṛṣṇa-priyā kṛṣṇa-bhakti tār hiyā
vinodera sei se vaibhava

" 'Fearlessly stomp on any learning which causes obstacles on the path of devotion. The goddess Sarasvatī is dear to Kṛṣṇa, and her heart is full of devotion to the Lord. Such devotion is my wealth and glory.'

"Śrīla Prabhupāda, Bhaktivinoda Ṭhākura, and Śrīmān Gaurāṅga Mahāprabhu can condone neither any words which contradict devotional service, nor any which compromise with it. This, we have always experienced, is the matchless characteristic of those teachings. Śrī Caitanya-Sarasvatī (Śrīla Prabhupāda), who is most dear to Kṛṣṇa, as Śrī Bhaktivinoda Ṭhākura's wealth, is the expansion of the lotus feet of the original *āśraya-vigraha*, Śrīmatī Rādhārāṇī. The daughter of Vṛṣabhānu has expanded as Mahāprabhu's gospel, *gaura-vāṇī*, through Bhaktivinoda Ṭhākura. Thus, service to Gaura's teachings is identical with the service to Rādhā and Govinda in obedience to the guru, and with service to Śrī Gopī-Gopīnātha in compliance with Śrī Rūpa Mañjarī.

"Śrīla Prabhupāda has shown the path of the bower where Śrī Gaurāṅga of Śrī Bhaktivinoda Ṭhākura's teachings reside and illuminated it – by the lamp of devotion – to the ears of eternally conditioned souls like us and has revealed the order of Gaura-Sarasvatī, the goddess of learning: 'Be the servant of Śrī Svarūpa Dāmodara and Śrī Rūpa Gosvāmī's followers and always chant the Holy Name.'

"We pray to remain constantly dedicated to the glorification of that abode of virtue, Gaurāṅga, who is Kṛṣṇa Himself residing in that message-bower, with single-minded commitment and great gusto. On this day, we pray to all the Vaiṣṇavas who are obedient to the preceptors in the line of Śrī Svarūpa Dāmodara and Śrī Rūpa Gosvāmī for this blessing."

SOME OF ŚRĪLA PRABHUPĀDA'S TEACHINGS

1. Caitanya Mahāprabhu has revealed our supreme worshipable object in His *Śikṣāṣṭaka*: *paraṁ vijayate śrī-kṛṣṇa-saṅkīrtanam*. (From *Patrāvalī*, vol. 3, page 38)
2. Only Kṛṣṇa, the object of devotion (*viṣaya-vigraha*), is the enjoyer (*bhogī*); everyone else is the enjoyed (*bhogya*). (Ibid., 58)
3. Everyone but the worshipper of Hari is a suicidal fool. (Ibid., 76)
4. One of the Matha's residents' chief duties is to learn tolerance. (Ibid., 88)
5. The followers of Rūpa Gosvāmī do not place their faith in their own powers, but rather attribute all glory to the fountainhead of those powers. (Ibid., 89)

6. Taking the Holy Name and the direct experience of God are one and the same thing. (*Patrāvalī*, vol. 2, page 3)
7. Those who follow a jumbled syncretic religious path cannot engage in the service of the Lord. (Ibid., 13)
8. True service to Sri Mayapur will be achieved through the establishment of printing presses, the distribution of devotional literature and the establishment of Nāma Haṭṭa preaching centers. (Ibid., 51)
9. Stay united and cooperate in the common purpose of serving Hari. (Ibid., 53)
10. A holy place is where the topics of Kṛṣṇa are being discussed. (Ibid., 82)
11. We perform neither pious works nor engage in sinful activity; we are neither learned nor ignorant. We are simple carriers of genuine devotees' sandals, and are initiated in the *mantra kīrtanīya sadā hari*. (Ibid., 104)
12. My advice is that you not calumniate other people's nature but rectify yourselves. (Ibid., 106)
13. In the precepts set forth by Mahāprabhu, I cannot find the precepts of the *kṣatriyas*, *vaiṣyas*, *śūdras* or Muslims. From His teachings, I understand that He adopted the highest standards of the seers, the rishis. Following in His footsteps, we also will adopt this religion of the *Bhāgavata* based on brahminical moral principles. (*Patrāvalī*, vol. 1, page 27)
14. Our ultimate duty is to serve the residents of Vraja in their mood of intense separation from Kṛṣṇa after He had departed for Mathura. (Ibid., 46)
15. The *mahā-bhāgavata* knows that everyone is his guru, and that is why he is guru to the whole world. (Ibid., 58)
16. If I seek the path leading to the ultimate good, I must ignore the countless voices of popular wisdom and listen to that of the realized souls – the *śrauta-vāṇī*. (Lecture, Āṣāḍha 22, 1333 Bengali era)
17. The truly beneficial should only be pleasing. (Lecture, Kārtika 2, 1333)
18. A confidential devotee is greedy for nothing but service to the followers of Rūpa Gosvāmī. (*Sajjana-toṣaṇī*, 19.10, 380)
19. If, in order to carry out the orders of a Vaiṣṇava guru, I must act arrogant or impolite, or even if I must go to hell for all eternity, I agree to sign the contract. I am arrogant enough to say that on the strength of my guru's lotus feet, I have the knockout punch for all the world's spurious philosophies. (Lecture, Āṣāḍha 25, 1334)
20. Other than the ear, there is no route to a vision of the transcendental Supreme Entity. (Lecture, Phālguna 18, 1334)
21. Once we are bereft of a protector, everything around us will turn into a hostile force ready to attack. Our only protection is the Hari *kathā* of a genuine saintly person. (Ibid.)
22. A flatterer is neither a guru nor a preacher. (Lecture, Caitra 12, 1334)
23. Better to take birth as an animal or a bird, a worm or an insect, rather than be a hypocrite. Only one who is free from hypocrisy can attain auspiciousness. (Lecture, Phālguna 18, 1334)
24. Simplicity by another name is Vaiṣṇavism. The servants of a *paramahaṁsa* Vaiṣṇava

are unpretentious. This means that they are the best of *brāhmaṇas*. (Ibid.)

25. The most charitable person is the one whose only duty is to reform the misleading tastes and tendencies of the conditioned souls. If one single person can be rescued from Mahāmāyā's fortress, then we will have done a charitable work-of-infinite-folds than that of opening a hundred million hospitals. (Ibid.)
26. Every selfless welfare worker in the Gaudiya Math should be prepared to expend two hundred gallons of his own blood to nourish the spiritual body of every person in this human society. (Caitra 12, 1335)
27. Every last farthing of the money collected by the volunteer servants of the Gaudiya Math from dawn to dusk with great effort is used for the satisfaction of Kṛṣṇa's senses, and thus brings an end to material sense gratification, which, based on an error, is a source of suffering. (Ibid.)
28. Those whose tendency to serve the Supreme Lord is not constantly awakened before the one who knows the self are not desirable company, however pleasing their association may be. (*Patrāvalī*, Vol. 1, 73)
29. Preaching without practice should be considered to be nothing more than an aspect of *karma*. (Speech, Oct. 23, 1936)
30. We have not established the *maṭha* to provide fuel for the sense enjoyer or to follow the clever speculative reasonings of a philosopher. Our assets are not measured in the one or two rupees we collect for the benefit of the *maṭha*. If we are able to do some real good for someone, then he or she will contribute to the *maṭha*, which does everything for the service of Kṛṣṇa. (*Patrāvalī*, Vol. 3, 70)
31. Śrīla Bhaktivinoda Ṭhākura identified himself as the sweeper in the marketplace of the Holy Name. This is a transcendental *līlā*, and the work that takes place in cleaning up the material world has countless aspects in which we are engaging our hundreds of followers. Though this and our refusal to imitate the undesirable example of nondevotees may make us unattractive to the worldly, it is through this work that our ultimate good will be achieved. (Introduction to *Gauḍīya-kaṇṭha-hāra*)
32. As one serves the Lord and His devotees, one's entanglement in family duties diminishes. (*Patrāvalī*, Vol. 3, 74)
33. Our basic disease is nothing but the accumulation of things devoid of any relation to Śrī Kṛṣṇa. (Ibid., 83)
34. We have not come to this world to be bricklayers or carpenters; we are peons of Lord Caitanya's message (Lecture, November 8, 1936)
35. We will not remain much longer in this world. If this body should drop while we are engaged in chanting the Holy Names, our life will have been worthwhile. (Ibid.)
36. The only thing we want in our life is the dust of the lotus feet of Rūpa Gosvāmī, who fulfilled the desires of Lord Caitanya. (Ibid.)

"BRINGING IN THE NEW YEAR"

The following is a translation of, *Hayanodghata*, the last article of Śrīla Prabhupāda published in *Gauḍīya* magazine, in Vaiśākha of 1936.

"*Gauḍīya* magazine today enters its fifteenth year. For fourteen years, *Gauḍīya* has sung Goloka's incomparable glories just as Lakṣmaṇa served Rāma during His exile. May the readers and hearers of *Gauḍīya* find eternal ecstasy in joyfully relishing the fruits born by this fifteen-year-old tree. We ask that everyone join us in praying for Lord Gaurasundara's mercy so that Gauḍīya's message will soon spread to America. This message is being discussed in Europe, particularly in London, so why should America be left behind?

"May Śrīla Bhaktivinoda Ṭhākura's songs and transcendental literature, which contain the same essence as those of Narottama Dāsa Ṭhākura's *Prārthanā*, be distributed in huge numbers throughout Bengal, Odisha and Assam. The translations of *Śaraṇāgatī* into Tamil and *Caitanya Śikṣāmṛta* into Telugu will certainly help the people of those regions find direction to the highest spiritual truth.

"May the *tridaṇḍi-sannyāsīs* of the Gaudiya Math bring joy to *Gauḍīya* magazine. May Gauḍīyas in every stage of life find firm faith in the service of Lord Caitanya.

pṛthivīte jata kathā dharma nāme cale
bhāgavata kahe tāhā paripūrṇa chale

'Whatever is spread in the name of religion in this world is said by the *Bhāgavatam* to be a complete fraud.'

"May this statement become the standard by which religons all over the world are measured. May the world's intelligentsia come to adore *Jaiva-dharma* and *Śrī Caitanya Śikṣāmṛta*. May they then raise the victory flag of the truly nonsectarian religion and learn that Śrī Kṛṣṇa Caitanya, *harināma* and *Śrīmad Bhāgavatam* are identical with each other. May the Gauḍīya devotees along with the rest of the world's people hear, chant and study *Śrīmad Bhāgavatam*. May this institution for Śrī Rūpa Gosvāmī's followers be eternally engaged in Śrī Caitanya Mahāprabhu's service. May all fraudulent conclusions about spiritual life disappear like a fog from the heart of the human race with the rising of the sun of the *Śrīmad Bhāgavatam*."

ARTICLES BY ŚRĪLA PRABHUPĀDA PUBLISHED IN GAUḌĪYA

YEAR I (1922-3)

Śrī-Kṛṣṇa-janma – "The birth of Śrī Kṛṣṇa"
Madhura-lipi – "A sweet Letter"
Loka-vicāra – "Public Opinion"
Paramārtha – "The Highest Purpose"
Purāṇa-samvāda – "The Message of the *Purāṇas*"
Nīti-bheda – "Ethical Differences"
Ruci-bheda – "Differences in Taste"
Śrī Jīva Gosvāmī – "Śrī Jīva Gosvāmī"
Gauḍiye Prīti – "Affection for Gauḍīya Magazine"
Durgā-pūjā – "Durgā *Pūjā*"
Śāradīya vāhana – "Durgā's Carrier"
Je dike bātāsa – "Whichever Way the Wind Blows"
Mārute secana – "Drying in the Wind"
Smārtera Kāṇḍa – "The Tricks of the *Smārtas*"
Vicāra Ādālata – "The Courthouse"
Sevāpara Nāma – "The Name Devoted to Service"
Tridaṇḍi Bhikṣu Gīti – "The Song of the Tridaṇḍi Sannyāsī"
Śrī Madhva Janma-tithi – "The Appearance Day of Madhvācārya"
Varṇāśrama – "The Social and Religious Order"
Aprakaṭa-tithi – "Disappearance Days"
Vraje Bānara – "Vraja's Monkeys"
Sāmājika Bheda – "Social Differences"
Cyuta-gotra – "The Fallible Family Line"

Nṛmātrādhikāra – "The Heritage of Every Human Being"
Bhṛtaka-srotā – "The Hired Audience" (or "Hearing from the Salaried")
Vaiṣṇava o abhṛtaka – "The Vaiṣṇava and One Not Hired"
Dīkṣa-vidhāna – "Initiation regulations"
Āsurika pravṛtti – "Demonic tendencies"
Śrī Baladeva Vidyābhūṣaṇa – "Śrī Baladeva Vidyābhūṣaṇa"
Sadācāra-smṛti – "Scriptures Prescribing Saintly Behavior"
Pañcārātra – "The Pañcārātra"
Nigama o āgama – "Vedic and Tantrik Scriptures"
Śrī Viśvanātha Cakravartī – "Visvanath Cakravartī"
Vaiṣṇava darsana – "Vaiṣṇava Philosophy"
Varṇāntara – "Changing Caste"
Paricaye praśna – "A Question About Identity"
Asatye ādara – "An Attachment for Untruth"
Ayogya Santāna – "An Unworthy Child"
Aśūdra dīkṣā – "Initiation for Non-śudras"
Pūjādhikāra – "The Right to Perform Deity Worship"
Anātma-jñāna – "Knowledge of the Nonself"
Nija paricaya – "One's Own Identity"
Vaṁśī-praṇālī – "Family Disciplic Lineages"
Gaura-bhajana – "Worshipping Mahāprabhu"
Dhānya o Śyāmā – "Rice and Wild Rice"
Tṛtīya janma – "The Third Birth"
Avaidha sādhana – "Illegitimate Practices"
Vaija-brāhmaṇa – "The Vaidya Caste's Claims to Brahmanahood"
Pracāre bhrānti – "Mistakes in Preaching"
Bhāgavata-śravaṇa – "Listening to the Bhāgavata"
Maṭha ki? – "What is a Maṭh?"
Āche adhikāra – "We Have the Right"
Śrīdhara Svāmī – "Śrīdhara Svami"
Vyavahāra – "Behaviors and Custom"
Kaminā – "Ignobility"
Śakti-sañcāra – "Finding the Energy"
Varṣa-parīkṣā – "Annual Exam"
Ekajāti – "One Race"
Ihaloka Paraloka – "This World and the Next"

SECOND YEAR (1923-1924)

Varṣa-praveśa – "The new year"
Brahmaṇya-deva – "The Lord of Brahminical society"
Guru-bruva – "So-called Spiritual Masters"
Kīrtane-vijñāna – "A Scientific Approach to Chanting"
Āvirbhāva-tithi – "Appearance Days"
Maṭhera utsava – "Maṭh Festivals"
Gosvāmī-pāda – "Gosvāmī Status"
Kṛṣṇe bhoga-buddhi – "The Enjoyer Mentality Directed to Kṛṣṇa"
Dīkṣītā – "The Initiated Person"
Gauḍīya bhajana-praṇālī – "The Process of Performing Bhajana in the Gauḍīya *Sampradāya*"
Śrī-vigraha – "The Divine Form"
Jābālā kathā – "The Story of Jabala"
Smārta o Vaiṣṇava – "Smārta Brāhmaṇas and Vaiṣṇavas"
Sāmājika ahita – "Unbeneficial Acts to Society"
Prakṛta bhokta ke? – "Who is the Real Enjoyer?"
Gauḍīyera veśa – "The Gauḍīya Dress"
Pratisambhāṣaṇa – "A speech in Response to an Honor"
Sūtra-vidveṣa – "Enmity of the Sūtras"
Sāmayika-prasaṅga – "Essays on Timely Subjects" (No. 49-50)

THIRD YEAR (1924-1925)

Gauḍīya hāsapātāla – "Gauḍīya Hospitals"

Sāmayika prasaṅga – "Essays on Timely Subjects" (No. 7)
Bhāgavata-vivṛti – "Explanations of the *Bhāgavatam*"
Śrī Kulaśekhara – "Śrī Kulashekhar"
Meyeli Hinduyānī – "Effeminate Hinduism"

FOURTH YEAR (1925-1926)

Madhura lipi – "A Sweet Letter"
Śrī Vyāsa-pūjāya abhibhāṣaṇa – "Address on the Occasion of Vyāsa Pūjā"
Prapta-patra (rahasya) – "Receipt of a Mysterious Letter"
Asrauta-darsana – "Philosophy Without Revelation"
Vedānta-tattva-sārer upodghāta – "Introduction to the Vedānta-tattva-sāra"

FIFTH YEAR (1926-1927)

Patrāvalī – Collected Letters
Darśane bhrānti – "Philosophical Misconceptions" (No.38)
Vaiṣṇava-śrāddha-vyavasthā – "Śrāddha Regulations for the Vaiṣṇava"
Alocaker alocana – "Criticizing the Critics"
Nyākābokara Svarūpa – "The Description of a Real Simpleton"

SIXTH YEAR (1927-1928)

Māna-dāna o hāni – "Offering Respects and its Dangers"
Pratinivedana – "A Counter-request"
Paramārtha – "The Spiritual Goal of Life"
Gauḍapura – "The City of Gauḍa"
Āsala o nakala – "Real and Counterfeit"
Ahaituka dhāma-sevaka – "A Selfless Servant of the Dhāma"
Sarva-pradhāna vivecanāra visaya – "The Most Important Thing to Consider"
Bhāi Kutārkika – "Brother Quibbler"
Kṛṣṇa-bhakta nirbodha nahena – "A Devotee of Kṛṣṇa is Not a Fool"
Prācīna Kuliyāya sahar Navadvīpa –"The City of Navadwip in Old Kuliya"
Kapatatā daridratāra mūla – "The Source of All Poverty is Deceitfulness"
Ekaścandra – "Ekashchandra"
Puṇyāraṇya – "Punyaranya"
Goḍāya galada – "A Basic Error"
Nīlācale Śrīmat Saccidānanda Bhaktivinoda – "Śrīmad Saccidānanda Bhaktivinoda in PurI"

SEVENTH YEAR (1928-1929)

Sāmayika prasaṇga – "A Timely Subject" (No. 1)
Virakta jaghanya nahe – "The Renunciate is Not Contemptible"
Āmi ei nai, āmi sei – "I am Not this One, I am He"
Vyavasādārera kapatatā – "The Duplicity of the Merchants"
Haṁsajātira itihāsa – "The Story of the Swans"
Patrāvalī – "Letters"
Mantra-saṁskāra – "The Sacrament of Receiving the *Mantra*"
Bhoga o bhakti – "Sense enjoyment and Devotional Service"
Suniti o durnīti – "Good and Evil Policies"
Kṛṣṇa-tattva – "Kṛṣṇa, the Ultimate Truth"
Śridhāma vicāra – "Conclusions About the Holy Dhāma"
Ekāyana-sruti o tad-vidhāna – "The Ekāyana Scriptures and their Prescriptions"
Pratīcye Kārṣṇa sampradāya – "The School of Devotion to Kṛṣṇa in the West"
Vijñapti – "An Announcement"
Pañcarātra – "Pancharatra"
Nīlācale Śrīmad Bhaktivinoda – "Śrīmad Bhaktivinoda Ṭhākura in PurI"

Tīrtha Pāṇḍharapura – "The Holy Site of Pāṇḍarapur (Maharasthra)"
Māṇikya bhāskara – An Article Praising the King of Tripura
Vaiṣṇava-smṛti – "Scriptures Governing the Rules of Vaiṣṇava Behavior"
Mahānta Guru-tattva – "The Doctrine of the Highly Elevated Guru" (No. 42)
Boṣṭama Parliament– "The Parliament of the So-called Vaiṣṇavas
Alaukika Bhakta-caritra – "The Transcendental Life of a Devotee" (No. 48)

EIGHTH YEAR (1929-1930)

Śridhāma Māyāpura kothāya?--
"Where is Śridhāma Māyāpura?"
Gauḍācale Śrī Bhaktivinoda – "Śrī Bhaktivinoda Ṭhākura in *Gaudadesh*"
Sātvata o asātvata – "Sātvata Devotees of Kṛṣṇa and Non-Sātvatas"
Bhārata o paramārtha – "The Supreme Goal of Life and India"
Paramārthera Svarūpa – "The Nature of the Supreme Goal of Life"
Patrāvalī – "Letters"
Vyāsa-pūjāya pratyabhibhāṣāṇa – "Speech in Response to the Vyāsa Pūjā Offerings"
Prācīna Kuliyāya Dvārabheta – "Charging Admission to Nabadvīpa's Temples"
Śikṣaka o Śikṣita – "The Educator and the Educated"
Viṣayāra Kṛṣṇa-prema – "*Kṛṣṇa-prema* of a Sense Enjoyer"
Ātmahārā Pāṭhaka – "The Ecstatic Lecturer"
Āsramera veṣa – "The appropriate dress of the different stages of life"

NINTH YEAR (1930-1931)

Śrī-bhakti-mārga – "The Holy Path of Devotion"
Pāramārthika sammilanīra sabhāpatira abhibhāṣaṇa – "The Presidential Address at the Spiritual Conference"
Bhava-rogīra Hāsapātāla – "A Hospital for those with the MaterialDSisease"
Jagabandhura Kṛṣṇānuśīlana – "Jagabandhu's Way of Serving Lord Kṛṣṇa"
Patrāvalī – "Letters"

TENTH YEAR (1931-1932)

Gauḍīya mahimā – "In Praise of Gauḍīya Magazine"
Patrāvalī – "Letters"
Sat-śikṣārthira vivecya – "What Every Honest Student Should Consider"
Nimbarbhāskara – "Nimbarka"
Ajña o vijñera narma kathā – "The Conversation of a Fool and a Wise Man"
Vaiṣṇava-vaṁsa –"The Vaiṣṇava dynasty"
Vārṣika abhibhāṣaṇa – "Speech Made at Madras on the Occasion of the Vyāsa Pūjā"
Kanph-ucora vicāra – "The Philosophy of Confucius"
Patra – "A letter"

ELEVENTH YEAR (1932-1933)

Ekādasa prārambhikā – "Entering the Eleventh Year of Gauḍīya"
Patrāvalī (1) – "Letters"
Vaiṣṇave jāti-buddhi – "Ascribing Caste to a Vaiṣṇava"
Mādhukara bhaikṣaya – "Begging From Door to Door"
Pradarsakera abhibhāṣaṇa – "The Exhibitor's Speech"
Patravalī (2) – Letters
Dṛṣti-vaiklavya – "The Defective Sight" (No.28)
Āmāra Kathā – "My Message"

Sat-śikṣā pradarśanī – "The Spiritual Education Exhibit" (No. 35)
Kṛṣṇa bhakti-i soka-kāma-jādyāpahā-- "Devotion to Kṛṣṇa is the Only Way to Get Rid of Suffering, Desire and Lethargy"
Kṛṣṇe matir astu – "May You Always Think of Kṛṣṇa"

TWELFTH YEAR (1933-1934)

Kṛpāśīrvāda – "Merciful Blessings"

THIRTEENTH YEAR (1934-1935)

Sva-para maṅgala – "Auspiciousness for Onself and for Others"
Vaikuṇṭha o guṇa-jāta jagat – "The Difference Between Vaikuṇṭha and the World Born of Nature's Modes"
Bhogavāda o bhakti – "Hedonism and Devotion"

FOURTEENTH YEAR (1935-1936)

Nava-varṣa – "The New Year"
Patravalī – "Letters"
Baḍa āmi o bhāla āmi – "I am Great and I am Good"
Tad-vana vāstava-vastu – "The Factual Substance"

FIFTEENTH YEAR (1936-1937)

Hāyanodghāta – "Bringing in the New Year"
Patra – "A Letter"

Other than these, Śrīla Prabhupāda wrote many other articles, letters, autobiographical accounts, diaries, commentaries, explanations, books and literature. All of these have been preserved in the *Gauḍīya* head office. Śrīla Prabhupāda also wrote many articles which were published in *Nadīyā Prakāśa* and *The Harmonist*.

MAGAZINES AND NEWSPAPERS FOUNDED BY PRABHUPĀDA

1. *Sajjana-toṣaṇī* or *The Harmonist* – Śrīla Sarasvati Ṭhākura restarted publication of this magazine in March of 1915 after Śrīla Bhaktivinoda Ṭhākura's disappearance.
2. *Gauḍīya* – a Bengali weekly published from the Kolkata Gaudiya Math, starting August 19, 1922.
3. *Dainika Nadīyā Prakāśa* – A Bengali daily published from Mayapur starting March 1926. At first it appeared twice a week in English and Bengali editions. From February 28, 1928, however, it was made into a daily at Śrīla Prabhupāda's wish.
4. *Bhāgavata* – A Hindi monthly published from the Naimisharanya Paramahamsa Math, starting in 1931.
5. *Kīrtana* – An Assamese monthly published from Goalpara Prapannashram, starting in 1932.
6. *Paramārthī* – Odishan fortnightly, published from the Cuttack Sacchidananda Gaudiya Math, starting in 1932.

MAGAZINES ON ASTROLOGICAL MATTERS

1. *Bṛhaspati* or *Scientific Indian* – A monthly in English and Bengali on astrological matters. First appeared in October, 1896.
2. *Jyotirvid* – A monthly magazine devoted to astrological matters. Published from Manik Tala Street in Kolkata. The first issue came out in April, 1901.
3. *Nivedana* or *Sign Board* – A weekly published starting in 1899.

PRINTING PRESSES ESTABLISHED BY ŚRĪLA PRABHUPĀDA

1. Bhāgavata Yantra, Krishnanagar – In 1913, *Caitanya Caritāmṛta* was published here with Śrīla Prabhupāda's *Anubhāṣya* commentary. In January 1914, the Bhāgavata Yantra was moved to Mayapur in Vraja Pattan. It was moved back to Gowari Krishnanagar in July of 1915 and took the name Bhāgavata Press.
2. Gauḍīya Printing Works, Kolkata, 1923.
3. Nadīyā Prākāśa Yantrālaya, Śrī Dhāma Mayapur, 1928.
4. Paramārthī Printing Works, Cuttack, 1936.

MATHS AND PREACHING CENTERS ESTABLISHED BY ŚRĪLA PRABHUPĀDA

1. Sri Chaitanya Math (Parent Maṭh), Sridhama Mayapur, Nadia.
2. Sri Gaudiya Math, P.O. Bagh Bazaar, Kolkata.
3. Sri Yogapith Śrī Mandir, Sridhama Mayapur, Nadia.
4. Sri Advaita Bhavan, Sridhama Mayapur, Nadia.
5. Sri Srivas Angan, Sridhama Mayapur, Nadia.
6. Caṇḍa Kazi's *Samādhi*, Sridhama Mayapur, Nadia.
7. Sri Murari Gupta's Sripat, Sridhama Mayapur, Nadia.
8. Paravidyapith, Sridhama Mayapur, Nadia.
9. Thakur Bhaktivinoda Institute, Sridhama Mayapur, Nadia, 1931.
10. Thakur Bhaktivinoda Research Institute, Sridhama Mayapur, Nadia.
11. Jayadeva Gaudiya Mathalaya, Srinathpur, Nadia.
12. Svananda Sukhada Kunja, Godrum, P.O. Swarup Ganj, Nadia.
13. Suvarna Bihar Gaudiya Math, Nadia.
14. Sri Kunja Kutir, Krishnanagar, Nadia.
15. Tetiya Kunja Kanan, P.O. Krishnanagar, Nadia.
16. Sri Bhagavat Asan, Krishnanagar, Nadia.
17. Śrī Gaura Gadadhar Math, Champāhati, P.O. Samudra Garh, Burdwan.
18. Sri Modadrum Chatra, Mamgachi, P.O. Jannagar, Burdwan.
19. Sarvabhauma Gaudiya Mathalay, Vidyanagar, Burdwan.
20. Sri Rudradwip Gaudiya Math, P.O. Śrī Māyāpura, Nadia.
21. Sri Ekayan Math, Govindapur, P.O. Hanskhali, Nadia.
22. Sri Mahesh Pandit's Sripat, Kanthalpuli, P.O. Chakdaha, Nadia.
23. Sri Madhva Gaudiya Math, Dhaka.
24. Sri Gopalji Math, Kamalapur, P.O. Dhaka.
25. Sri Gadai Gauranga Math, P.O. Baliyati, Dhaka.
26. Sri Jagannath Gaudiya Math, Bara Bazaar, P.O. Mymensingha.
27. Amlajora Prapannashram Math, P.O. Rajbandh, Burdwan.
28. Sri Chaitanya Gaudiya Math, Dumurkonda, P.O. Chirkunda, Manbhoom (Bihar).
29. Sri Bhagavat Janananda Math, Chirulia, P.O. Basudevpur, Midnapore.
30. Amarshi Gaudiya Math, P.O. Amarshi, Midnapore.

31. Brahmanpara Prapannashram Math, Brahmanpara, P.O. Maju, Howrah.
32. Darjeeling Gaudiya Math, August Villa, Darjeeling.
33. Ranaghat Gaudiya Mathasan, Nadia.
34. Punra Sri Gaudiya Math, 24 Paraganas.
35. Goalpara Prapannashram, Assam.
36. Sarabhoga Gaudiya Math, P.O. Chakchaka, Kamrup (Assam).
37. Sri Purushottam Math, Chataka Parvat, Puri.
38. Bhakti Kuti, Swarga Dwar, Puri.
39. Tridandi Gaudiya Math, P.O. Bhubaneshwar, Puri.
40. Sri Brahma Gaudiya Math, Alalanath, P.O. Brahmagiri, Purī.
41. Saccidananda Math, Bansgali, P.O. Oriya Bazaar, Cuttack.
42. Baleshwar Gaudiya Math Pith.
43. Sri Ramananda Gaudiya Math, P.O. Kovvur, West Godavari.
44. Chennai Gaudiya Math, P.O. Raipetta, Chennai.
45. Patna Gaudiya Math, P.O. Bankipur, Kadamkua.
46. Danapur Gaudiya Mathalay.
47. Gaya Gaudiya Math, Ramna Road, Gaya.
48. Sri Sanatan Gaudiya Math, 42, Faridapur, Benares City, U.P.
49. Sri Rupa Gaudiya Math, Allahabad, U.P.
50. Sri Paramahasa Math, P.O. Nimsar, Naimisharanya, Sitapur, U.P.
51. Bhagavat Path Shala, Naimisharanya, U.P.
52. Sri Vyas Gaudiya Math, Kurukshetra, Thaneshwar, Karnal (H.P.)
53. Sri Saraswata Gaudiya Math, Haridwar, Saharanapur, Uttarakhānd.
54. Sri Krishna Chaitanya Math, Purana Sahar, Śrī Dhāma Vrindavan, Mathura, U.P.
55. Sri Mathura Gaudiya Mathalay, Vishram Ghat, Mathura, U.P.
56. Sri Kunja Bihari Math, Radha Kunda, Mathura, U.P.
57. Sri Vraja Svananda Sukhada Kunja, Radha Kunda, Mathura, U.P.
58. Sri Radha Kund Gosthobati, Radha Kunda, Mathura, U.P.
59. Sri Sanket Bihari Math, P.O. Barshana, Mathura, U.P.
60. Sri Nandagram Gaudiya Mathalay, Mathura, U.P.
61. Barshana Gaudiya Mathalay, Maṭhura, U.P.
62. Sri Gosthabihari Math, Sesh Shayi, P.O. Hodol, Gurgaon (Punjab).
63. Delhi Gaudiya Math, 43, Hanuman Road, New Delhi.
64. Bombay Gaudiya Math, Kalyan Das Building, Gwalior Trunk Road.
65. London Gaudiya Mathalay, 3 Gloucester House, Cornwall Gardens, S.W.7, London.
66. Rangoon Gaudiya Mathalay, 224 Lewis St., Rangoon (Burma).

SHRINES TO MAHĀPRABHU'S FEET ESTABLISHED BY PRABHUPĀDA

1. Mandar. October 13, 1929.
2. Kanair Natshala. October 15, 1929.
3. Yajpur. December 25, 1930.
4. Kurmakshetra. December 26, 1930.

5. Singhachalam. December 27, 1930.
6. Kovur. December 29, 1930.
7. Mangalgiri. December 31, 1930.
8. Chatrabhog. April 2, 1934.

OTHER PREACHING INSTITUTIONS, COMMITTEES, MEETINGS AND SOCIETIES FOUNDED BY ŚRĪLA PRABHUPĀDA

1. Śrī Bhaktivinoda Āsana, founded in Kolkata in November, 1918.
2. Śrī Viśva Vaiṣṇava Rāja Sabha, first established by Śrī Rūpa and Śrī Sanātana Gosvāmīs, and then reestablished on February 5, 1919, in Kolkata.
3. Śrī Saraswat Asan, July 1924.
4. Gaudiya Sampadak Sangha (The editorial board of *Gauḍīya*), August 15, 1925.
5. Nikhil Vaishnav Sammilani, March 18, 1927. This meeting of Vaiṣṇavas was held on Gaura Pūrṇimā in Mayapur.
6. Paramarthik Alochana Sammilani. A nine-day meeting held at the Kolkata Gauduya Math, starting October 24, 1930.
7. London Gaudiya Mission Society. Established in London for preaching in Europe at a meeting on April 24, 1934, with India Secretary, Lord Zetland, presiding.
8. Sri Vraja Dham Pracharini Sabha ("Society for the Promotion of Vraja Dhāma"). Established October 9, 1935 at Radha Kunda.
9. Anukul Krishna Anushilnagar (Bhaktivinoda Research Institute), Founded at Sri Mayapur on February 12, 1936.
10. Daiva Varṇāśrama Saṅgha ("Association for Promoting the Spiritual Varnashram Social System"). Established at Sri Mayapur on February 12, 1936.

SPIRITUAL DIORAMA EXHIBITIONS

1. Kurukshetra Gaudiya Pradarshini. Opened on November 4, 1928.
2. Sri Dham Mayapur-Navadwip Pradarshini. February 9, 1930.
3. Kolkata Sri Gaudiya Math Paramarthik Pradarshini. November 5, 1930.
4. Kolkata Sri Gaudiya Math Sat-Siksha Pradarshini. September 6, 1931.
5. Dhaka Sat-Siksha Pradarshini. January 6, 1933.
6. Kurukshetra Gaudiya Pradarshini. August 21, 1933.
7. Patna Paramarthik Pradarshini. November 14, 1933.
8. Kashi Paramarthik Pradarshini. December 24, 1933.
9. Prayag Sat-Siksha Pradarshini. January 7, 1936
10. Kurukshetra Sat-Siksha Pradarshini. June 19, 1936.

Śrīla Bhakti Dayita Mādhava Gosvāmī Mahārāja

nama oṁ viṣṇupādāya rūpānuga-priyāya ca
śrīmate bhakti-dayita-mādhava-nāmine

"Obeisances to Oṁ Viṣṇupāda Śrīla Bhakti Dayita Mādhava Gosvāmī Mahārāja, the one who is dear to the followers of Rūpa Gosvāmī.

kṛṣṇābhinna-prakāśa-śrī-mūrtaye dīna-tāriṇe
kṣamā-guṇāvatārāya gurave prabhave namaḥ

"Obeisances to you, the spiritual guide, the nondifferent manifestation of Supreme Lord Śrī Kṛṣṇa, the redeemer of the fallen souls and the personification of the quality of forgiveness.

satīrtha-prīti-saddharma-guru-prīti-pradarśine
īśodyāna-prabhāvasya prakāśakāya te namaḥ

"Obeisances to you, who by rendering affectionate service to godbrothers, you demonstrated your loving attachment to guru and who manifested the glory of Iśodyan at Śrī Māyāpur.

śrī-kṣetre prabhupādasya sthānoddhāra-sukīrtaye
sārasvata-gaṇānanda-saṁvardhanāya te namaḥ

"Obeisances to you, who increased the joy of those devoted to Śrīla Bhakti Siddhānta Sarasvatī Gosvāmī Ṭhākura by recovering his birthplace in Puri, for which you are justly renowned.

śrī-bhakti-dayitaṁ nāmācārya-
varyaṁ jagad-gurum
vande śrī-mādhavaṁ deva-
gosvāmi-pravaraṁ prabhum

"I worship my Lord, Śrīla Bhakti Dayita Mādhava Gosvāmī Mahārāja, teacher of the Holy Name and spiritual master to the universe."

APPEARANCE OF ŚRĪLA BHAKTI DAYITA MĀDHAVA GOSVĀMĪ MAHĀRĀJA

Tenth in the preceptorial line from Śrī Kṛṣṇa Caitanya, Paramahaṁsa Parivrājakācārya Oṁ 108 Śrī Śrīmad Bhakti Dayita Mādhava Gosvāmī Mahārāja Viṣṇupāda, the a dear associate of Prabhupāda 108 Śrī Śrīla Bhakti Siddhānta Sarasvatī Gosvāmī Ṭhākura, who was the founder of the Chaitanya Math and the Gaudiya Maths throughout the world, Śrī Śrīmad Bhakti Dayita Mādhava Gosvāmī Mahārāja was himself the founder of the Sri Chaitanya Gaudiya Math throughout India and my own spiritual master. He appeared in this world at 8:00 A.M. on Friday, Agrahāyaṇa 3, 1311 (Bengali), or November 18, 1904, *utthāna ekādaśī*, in the village of Kanchanpara in the Madaripur subdivision of the Faridpur district in East Bengal.

Utthāna ekādaśī is the *tithi* which marks the end of the *Caturmāsya* period, when Lord Viṣṇu performs the pastimes of waking up from his four-month-long sleep. It is thus a day that brings joy and auspiciousness to the world. Similarly, the appearance on that *tithi* of the most compassionate dear associate of Lord Hari, our most worshipable Śrīla Bhakti Dayita Mādhava Gosvāmī Mahārāja, had the effect of bringing joy and good fortune to the world's conditioned souls who are suffering from the threefold miseries. It is also significant that our *parameṣṭhī-guru*, the *avatāra* of extreme renunciation Paramahaṁsa Vaiṣṇava Śrīla Gaura Kiśora Dāsa Bābājī entered the eternal pastimes on this same *tithi*.

GURUDEVA'S BIRTHPLACE AND FAMILY

Kanchanpara village is in a pure and beautiful area on the banks of the Padma River near its mouths in the precinct of Bhedara Ganj. The distintion of the Padma River is to award *prema bhakti* but it is sometimes called the Kirtinasha River, "the river which destroys all glories," because its annual flooding washes away so many villages and towns. Further upstream, there is a place called Prema Tali, where Nityānanda Prabhu once bathed, depositing divine love of God for Narottama Dāsa Ṭhākura.

The village was prosperous and home to a large number of *brāhmaṇas*. It was also the residence of my Gurudeva's maternal uncles, who were of a prominent wealthy family in the area. Though they were *talukdars*, or subsidiary landholders, they were given respect equal to that of zamindars. The British rulers of the day decorated them with the title Rāja-cakravartī; thus, although the family name was Bandyopādhyāya, their home came to be known as "Cakravarti Badi." The village is known to his disciples as "Gurudeva's *mātulālaya*."

The following is known about Śrīla Gurudeva's paternal family. His grandfather was named Śrī Caṇḍīprasāda Devaśarmā Bandyopādhyāya, his father Śrī Niśikānta Devaśarmā Bandyopādhyāya. They lived in the village of Bharakar in the precinct of Tangibari in the Bikramapur subdivision of the Dhaka district. Both Śrīla Gurudeva's father and grandfather were well known in the district as pious men. Śrīla Gurudeva's mother, Śaibālinī Devī, was an extremely devoted woman who dedicated herself to the service of God, the *brāhmaṇas* and holy men.

Śrīla Gurudeva lost his father at the age of four, after which his mother took him and returned to her brothers' home, which is where he was raised. His uncles' great affection for him played an important part in his upbringing. The name given him by his father was Śrī Heramba Kumāra Bandyopādhyāya, but he was known by his nickname Gaṇeśa.

GURU MAHĀRĀJA'S CHILDHOOD

Śrīla Gurudeva began to display extraordinary qualities from a very early age. Under no circumstances would he tell a lie. He would furthermore explain the moral value of truthfulness to his friends and companions. Everyone was impressed by the young lad's character.

Even when very young, Śrīla Gurudeva showed no interest in material enjoyments. He distinguished himself from the other children by his desire to lead an orderly and disciplined life. Not only did he himself act in this way, but he encouraged the other children to do the same. He always tried to alleviate the sufferings of others and bring them happiness, even if it meant undergoing difficulty himself. People who observed the extent of his generosity and wisdom were convinced that he would grow up to be a great personality of extraordinary virtue.

I personally heard from Śrīla Gurudeva's mother that whenever she gave him some special delicacy or sweet, he would only eat whatever was left after he had called his friends and distributed it amongst them.

At school, his teachers were astonished to hear him say things which showed a level of wisdom beyond his years. The following story can serve as an example: One day, he and some of his fellow students were playing the way boys of that age do. They were engaged in various competitions of speed and strength, including a running race. Śrīla Gurudeva quickly took the lead, but tripped on a root and fell with great force, causing him to bleed profusely. When his school teachers and other guardians heard, they rushed to the scene and applied medicines to his cuts and bruises. They also said many things to calm him, but he answered, "You need not worry on my account. I will get better soon. The Lord does everything for our good. I could have injured my eyes, ears or broken my nose, but nothing serious like that happened. I no doubt committed so many sins in previous lives that I should have suffered a more serious accident, but God is so merciful that He did not allow it to happen." When the school teachers heard him say these things, they immediately realized that he was no ordinary child.

While in high school, Śrīla Gurudeva started a library for the benefit of his poorer classmates and lent books to them without cost. At all ages, in his boyhood, adolescence or youth, Śrīla Gurudeva was a natural leader as a result of his tall, handsome figure, his charismatic personality, his extraordinary honesty and patience. He never had to apply or stand for election to leadership positions; wherever he chose to participate, others would unfailingly be impressed by his qualities and acclaim him as their leader. What is more, they were satisfied with his performance afterwards. In truth, leadership is the result of an individual's depth of character, exemplary behavior and competence. Tall and strong, Śrīla Gurudeva also excelled in sports and was regularly made captain of his teams. He also participated in dramatic presentations. There was no area in which he did not excel, and thus he was always involved in directing any set-up meant for the social well-being. He even played a role in the independence movement.

BEGINNINGS OF A SPIRITUAL CALLING

Śrīla Gurudeva was exemplary in his devotion to his mother. She would read to him and have him read various scriptures so that he became conversant with subjects related to religion and imbued with faith in God. She made him read the *Bhagavad-gītā* daily, so that by the age of eleven, Śrīla Gurudeva had memorized all of its verses.

He finished his primary and secondary education in Kanchanpara and Bhatagram. Then for higher education he went to Kolkata. While in Kolkata his feelings of separation from the Lord intensified. He stayed with a relative named Nārāyaṇa Candra Mukhopādhyāya, who later took *sannyāsa* from him and was given the name Bodhāyana Mahārāja. Nārāyaṇa Candra Prabhu recounted that he often saw Śrīla Gurudeva calling out the names of the Lord and crying in the middle of the night. He would eat only *haviṣyānna* (an unspiced khichuri) once a day. In this state of absorption in the Lord, he one day had a dream in which Nārada Muni came to reassure him. Nārada Muni gave him a mantra and told him that by chanting it he would achieve all perfection. However, upon awakening, try as he might Śrīla Gurudeva was unable to recall the *mantra* in its entirety. The loss of the *mantra* bewildered and distressed him immeasurably. His impatience with household life reached an intolerable degree, and he became determined to leave it behind. With this in mind, he went to ask the blessings of his widowed mother, who at that time was living in Gosain Durgapur in the Nadia district. She made no effort to oppose his wishes. So, with an intense desire to have the company of the Supreme Lord, Śrīla Gurudeva set off for the Himalayas. Just as iron filings attracted by a magnetic force cannot be thwarted, the individual soul who has been attracted to the Supreme Soul allows nothing of this world, whether friends or family, to interfere with his calling.

ŚRĪLA GURUDEVA GOES TO HARIDWAR

Śrīla Gurudeva's intense desire for the Lord brought him first to Haridwar and from there into the mountains, though he was alone and in a state of indigence. High up in the Himalayan jungle, he fasted for three days from food and water and did not sleep, all the time calling out anxiously to the Lord. When he had practically lost all awareness of the external world, he was given a divine order to seek out a spiritual master. He was also told that his guru would appear to him in the very place he had left.

Taking the divine order as his imperative, he came down from the mountain to the banks of the Ganges in the holy town of Haridwar, where he decided to stay for a few days. While there, he met a saintly person to whom he recounted all that had happened on the mountain. When he asked this *sādhu* for advice, he was told to return home and that he would meet a bona fide spiritual master there.

Śrīla Gurudeva made up his mind that he would return to Kolkata after spending a few more days in the pilgrimage town, but his stay in Haridwar was disturbed when a rich businessman and his wife from North India came there on pilgrimage. The couple, which was childless, saw the handsome figure of Śrīla Gurudeva when bathing in Brahma Kunda, and were attracted to him. They gave him a gift of fruit and sweets and insisted that he visit them in their lodgings. When this happened almost every day, out of courtesy Śrīla Gurudeva acceded to their request.

At their place of residence, they once again fed him copiously and generally treated him with great affection. Finally, they proposed that he become their adopted son, which meant that he would eventually inherit their substantial wealth. Śrīla Gurudeva was unprepared for such an offer and began to think, "I came here with the intention of abandoning family life. Now *māyā* has devised another way to ensnare me."

Śrīla Gurudeva politely refused their proposal and left their home, but the businessman and his wife were so enamored of him that they came each day and repeatedly put pressure on him to accept their offer. One who has a sincere eagerness to attain the Supreme Lord, however, cannot be swayed by any amount of material temptation. Someone filled with desires for sense enjoyment would have found it impossible to resist such an opportunity to become heir to a fortune, but Śrīla Gurudeva had no such yearnings. Because of his sincere aspiration to worship the Lord, he considered the couple's invitation to be dangerous and rejected it out of hand. Consequently, he found it impossible to remain in Haridvāra and returned to Kolkata without any farther delay. These events took place sometime around 1925.

ŚRĪLA GURUDEVA MEETS ŚRĪLA PRABHUPĀDA

That same year, Śrīla Gurudeva came to visit Mayapur for the first time with Nārāyaṇa Candra Mukhopādhyāya and some other friends. There they saw Śrīla Bhakti Siddhānta Sarasvatī Gosvāmī Ṭhākura Prabhupāda and were attracted by his divine personality. During their conversation, Śrīla Prabhupāda said that it was all right to visit the deity form in the temple, but that one has to learn to see it first. One cannot really see it with eyes that are blinded by material desire, but only with the eyes of love. On that same day Śrīla Prabhupāda initiated Dr. S. N. Ghoṣa and his wife.

After returning to Kolkata, Śrīla Gurudeva started visiting the Gaudiya Math on Ultadanga Road to hear Śrīla Prabhupāda speak Hari *kathā*. Understanding that through service to the Vaiṣṇavas one can clear the path to the Lord and receive His mercy, or perhaps wishing to teach that same principle to the world, Śrīla Gurudeva sent much money and material for the *maṭh* without any fanfare. During this period, he also spent much time in studying the scriptures.

After hearing the Vaiṣṇava doctrines from Śrīla Prabhupāda, he became convinced of their rationality and superiority over other religious dogmas. He took shelter of Śrīla Prabhupāda and on September 4, 1927, on Rādhāṣṭamī, received initiation in the Holy Name and *mantra* at the Ultadanga Math. After initiation, he was known as Hayagrīva Dāsa Brahmacārī. Ācārya Dāsa Deva Śarmā was the officiating priest at the Vaiṣṇava fire sacrifice.

LIFE AND SERVICE IN THE GAUDIYA MATH

Not long after being initiated, Śrīla Gurudeva decided to commit himself completely to the service of Kṛṣṇa and His devotees by moving into the *maṭh*. He thus took the great vow of remaining a lifelong celibate, or *naiṣṭhika-brahmacārī*. It was not long before Śrīla Gurudeva was counted amongst Śrīla Prabhupāda's leading disciples as a result of his dedicated service to his guru, his unflagging enthusiasm and his competence in a variety of services. Śrīla Prabhupāda used the words "volcanic energy" to describe Śrīla Gurudeva's unflinching resolve, application and success in all endeavors entrusted to him.

Śrīla Gurudeva was one of the leading collectors whose service was essential for maintaining Śrīla Prabhupāda's vast movement and especially the efforts made toward preaching Mahāprabhu's message in the West. Anyone who saw Śrīla Gurudeva's golden form and heard him speak Hari *kathā* could not fail to be attracted. Many people came forth spontaneously and made donations to him.

On Śrīla Prabhupāda's order, Śrīla Gurudeva spent a long time at the Madras Gaudiya Math, where he was chiefly responsible for the purchase of land and the construction of the temple, *nat mandir* and residences. During this time he was particularly encouraged by his senior godbrothers Śrīla Bhakti Rakṣaka Śrīdhara Mahārāja and Śrīla Bhakti Hridoy Bon Mahārāja. In the course of collecting funds for this project, Śrīla Gurudeva met with the leading citizens of Madras and became closely acquainted with many of them.

ŚRĪLA PRABHUPĀDA'S ADVANCE MAN

In order to awaken a consciousness of the Lord amongst the people at large, Śrīla

Prabhupāda traveled to Kolkata, Dhaka, Patna, Allahabad, Benares and other important places throughout India and held spiritual exhibitions. He organized preaching festivals as well as *parikramās* of Vraja and Navadwip *dhāmas*, established preaching centers and *maṭhs*, spreading the message of Śrī Caitanya Mahāprabhu in various cities within India as well as outside the country, putting on programs and sending out street *saṅkīrtana* parties. He also established shrines of Mahāprabhu's feet (*pāda-pīṭhas*) in many of the places that the Lord had visited, restored other holy sites, and published transcendental books, magazines and newspapers in a variety of languages in order to spread the message of pure devotion. Śrīla Gurudeva was a leading participant in this colossal preaching movement of Śrīla Prabhupāda.

Śrīla Prabhupāda generally sent Śrīla Gurudeva as the advance man to do the groundwork for these events. He had complete faith that whatever task he gave him would be carried out to completion. Śrīla Gurudeva was one of the principal devotees charged with building the Ramananda Gaudiya Math in memory of Mahāprabhu's intimate associate Rāmānanda Rāya. He was involved in purchasing land in Andhra Pradesh, near Goṣpada Tīrtha in the Rajmundry district, where Rāmānanda's meeting with Lord Caitanya took place, and in supervising the construction of the buildings.

Anyone, no matter how important a person, who met Śrīla Gurudeva – with his handsome features and imposing physique, pleasant manner, extraordinary personality, facility with modern reasoning and ability to convince by means of irrefutable scriptural evidence – would become enchanted and quite happy to do anything requested of him. Śrīla Gurudeva's entire being--his meditation, his thoughts, his *japa*, everything – was fully devoted to fulfilling Śrīla Prabhupāda's desires. Today's volunteer workers cannot even imagine the extent of his commitment to service, for which he gave up eating and sleeping, working through the night if necessary to achieve his goals.

Śrīla Gurudeva's single-minded allegiance to his spiritual master is an example to be followed by everyone. He never undertook any task without the express direction of his spiritual master. As a result of his full surrender to Śrīla Prabhupāda's lotus feet, he came to inherit his divine potency for spreading Lord Caitanya's mission in its entirety.

ŚRĪLA PRABHUPĀDA'S VISIT TO ASSAM

We can know the degree to which Śrīla Prabhupāda trusted Śrīla Gurudeva and considered him to be a responsible servant and intimate associate from comments he made in March of 1936, on the occasion of the installation of Śrī Śrī Guru-Gaurāṅga-Gāndharvikā-Giridhara deities at the Sarbhog Gaudiya Math (Assam).

The Sarbhog Gaudiya Math in Assam's Kamrup district (at present in the Barpeta district) was one of the sixty-four *maṭhs* and preaching centers that were established during Śrīla Prabhupda's time. Śrīla Prabhupda sent Śrīla Gurudeva along with his senior godbrother Śrīla Bhakti Rakṣaka Śrīdhara Mahārāja, Janaki Vallabh Dāsa Brahmacārī and others in advance to prepare for the deity installation ceremony. At that time, the *maṭh* was under the direction of Śrīla Gurudeva's senior godbrother, Tridaṇḍi Svāmī Bhakti Viñjāna Āśrama Mahārāja. Śrīla Gurudeva's party arrived in Sarbhog only a few days before the festival date and was shocked to find that little or nothing had been done in preparation for Śrīla Prabhupāda's coming and the installation of the deities.

Śrīla Gurudeva's transcendental nature was such that he would never lose enthusiasm or stop working until his desired goals were achieved. He immediately brought all his efforts to bear on finding temporary quarters for Śrīla Prabhupāda and the other devotees who would be coming with him.

When Śrīla Prabhupāda arrived at the Sarbhog rail station at 6:30 AM on Sunday, March 15, 1936, he was greeted by a large party of devotees and local citizens. Noteworthy amongst those who accompanied him were Kuñja Bihārī Vidyābhūṣaṇa Prabhu, Paramānanda Vidyāratna Prabhu, Vāsudeva Prabhu, Kīrtanānanda Brahmacārī, Sajjana Mahārāja, and Kṛṣṇa Keśava Brahmacārī. On each of the three days that Śrīla Prabhupāda remained in Sarbhog, thousands of men, women and children were satisfied with varieties of *maha-prasāda*.

On the following day, Śrīla Prabhupāda ordered Tridaṇḍi Svāmī Bhakti Rakṣaka Śrīdhara Mahārāja to make final arrangements for Śrī Śrī Guru-Gaurāṅga-Gāndharvikā-Giridhara's installation rituals, over which he was to officiate. As a part of these arrangements, Śrīla Śrīdhara Mahārāja dressed the deities and decorated them with flower garlands and other ornaments. At the auspicious moment at 10 o'clock in the morning, upon being told that everything was ready, Śrīla Prabhupāda entered the temple room, took *darśana* of the garlanded deities and paid his prostrated obeisances to them. He said, "The deities have already been installed." On hearing this, Śrīla Śrīdhara Mahārāja immediately became remorseful, thinking that he had committed an offense by doing something that Śrīla Prabhupāda had intended to do himself. Despite his faux pas, the installation of the deities was performed in great splendor according to the regulations of the Vaiṣṇava *smṛitis* and in the midst of joyous *saṅkīrtana*.

At the end of the installation ceremony, Āśrama Mahārāja repeatedly asked Śrīla Gurudeva to tell Śrīla Prabhupāda that Nīmanānda Brahmacārī had not carried out his duties. Śrīla Gurudeva was reluctant to do anything which would be displeasing to Śrīla Prabhupāda, and so at first refused. Upon being pressed, however, he felt obliged to do as he was asked out of respect for his senior godbrother.

Later that day, Śrīla Gurudeva followed Śrīla Prabhupāda when he went out for a walk, fanning him to keep insects away. As they were talking, he told Prabhupāda of Āśrama Mahārāja's complaint. As soon as Śrīla Prabhupāda heard it, he became angry and chastised Śrīla Gurudeva, who felt extremely sorry at having displeased him. Śrīla Prabhupāda, however, seeing the effect his words had on Śrīla Gurudeva, immediately changed his mood and began to praise him affectionately. Śrīla Gurudeva was not happy at hearing such praise either, because he took it to mean that Śrīla Prabhupāda felt he would not be able to take criticism. However, Śrīla Prabhupāda took the opportunity to give him many valuable personal instructions that showed the extent to which he held his disciple dear.

Śrīla Prabhupāda first said, "Why do you want so much? And why do you let it bother you that much? It is not proper to expect so much service from any person. Your service to your spiritual master and all its details are your responsibility alone. You should be grateful if anyone else contributes to it in any way. Kṛṣṇa's 'major domo' is Śrīmatī Rādhikā. She knows that She alone is entirely responsible for Kṛṣṇa's pleasure. If anyone comes forward to help Her, She is filled with gratitude."

Here, it is apparent that Śrīla Prabhupāda was saying that it was up to Śrīla Gurudeva to take full responsibility for his service in its entirety. If anyone should assist him in the fulfillment of that responsibility, he should be grateful. From this statement it is clear that Śrīla Prabhupāda considered him to be a confidential associate. Because of this affectionate relationship and the physical similarity of Śrīla Gurudeva to the tall, light-skinned Śrīla Prabhupāda, people often mistook him to be his son.

Śrīla Gurudeva often recounted the story of the Sarbhog Gaudiya Math when he wished to give an example of the process of surrender to his disciples. We have already stated that Śrīla Śrīdhar Mahārāja humbly felt as though he had committed an offense for having garlanded the deities in the place of Śrīla Prabhupāda. Śrīla Śrīdhar Mahārāja asked Śrīla Gurudeva to approach Śrīla Prabhupāda and ask him for forgiveness on his behalf, saying that he made the mistake unintentionally. Having been so entreated by Śrīla Śrīdhar Mahārāja, Śrīla Gurudeva wrote a letter to Śrīla Prabhupāda in which he prayed for forgiveness on Śrīla Śrīdhar Mahārāja's behalf. Śrīla Prabhupāda answered that a surrendered soul never commits offenses. The Lord never sees the faults of one who is surrendered to Him, always forgiving him, for the surrendered person has given up everything for the service of the Lord without any ulterior motive. On the other hand, someone who has ulterior motives and is not surrendered must fear offenses at every moment.

ŚRĪLA GURUDEVA HAPPY FOR NOT GOING TO ENGLAND

Śrīla Prabhupāda was eager to preach Mahāprabhu's message in the western world and had chosen Śrīla Gurudeva as one of his missionaries because of his competence. By Śrīla Prabhupāda's order he and two other godbrothers had their photos taken and passports made in preparation for the trip. When everything was ready, Rājarśi Śaradindu Nārāyaṇa Rāya said to Śrīla Prabhupāda, "England is a land full of heavenly nymphs. I don't think it is a good idea to send handsome young men there to preach. It would be better to send a more mature disciple."

Śrīla Prabhupāda thought the Rajarṣi's suggestion had merit and so decided to send Śrīla Bhakti Pradīp Tīrtha Mahārāja in Śrīla Gurudeva's place. He gave Śrīla Gurudeva the responsibility of collecting money for the preaching mission.

Śrīla Gurudeva was afraid that Śrīla Prabhupāda would not remain in the world much longer and had been worried that if sent to England he might never see him again. He was thus relieved when Śrīla Prabhupāda changed his mind about sending him there on the Rājarṣi's advice.

MEETING WITH PAÑCĀNANA TARKARATNA

Śrīla Prabhupāda recognized that Śrīla Gurudeva possessed a great talent for persuading others with his humble and respectful manner of defeating their arguments. As a result, on October 4, 1936, he decided to send him to Bengal's leading religious scholar, Pañcānana Tarkaratna of Bhattapara in Naihati. Pañcānana Tarkaratna was very proud of being a *brāhmaṇa* and a learned scholar and had forcefully criticized the *daiva-varṇāśrama* system preached by Śrīla Prabhupāda. Śrīla Prabhupāda was afraid that his criticisms could cause untold harm to countless people seeking the ultimate good and thus gave Śrīla Gurudeva the responsibility of trying to change his opinion. Pañcānana Tarkaratna was reluctant to give proper respect to anyone who was not born in the *brāhmaṇa* caste. For this reason, Śrīla Prabhupāda told Gurudeva to go without Vaiṣṇava *tilaka* and give his identity as a high-caste *brāhmaṇa.*

On the given day, at 8:30 in the morning, Śrīla Gurudeva came to Pañcānana Tarkaratna's house accompanied by Praphulla Candra Caṭṭopādhyāya of Naihati's Kanthalpara. He first met with the *paṇḍita's* highly qualified son, Śrī Jīva Nyāyatīrtha, and then spent two hours in scriptural discussions with the *paṇḍit* himself. Śrīla Gurudeva often recounted the experience that he had to his disciples: "It is true that Pañcānana Tarkaratna possessed vast learning. He had memorized large numbers of verses from scripture, but in some cases was not able to come to logical conclusions or to harmonize the apparent inconsistencies. In his arguments he would go down a blind alley and not be able to give a proper answer when questioned."

When asked how such a great scholar could end up this way, Śrīla Gurudeva would answer, "Paṇḍita Mahāśaya had never had the opportunity to associate with a pure devotee or a real saintly person. Only by following a pure devotee or through associating with saintly persons can one arrive at the right conclusions."

Śrīla Gurudeva's long conversation with Pañcānana Tarkaratna resulted in an article which headlined the *Gauḍīya*, the Math's Bengali weekly, 15.13-15 (1936).

ŚRĪLA GURUDEVA MEETS DR. C. V. RAMAN

The following events took place in 1930 while Śrīla Prabhupāda was still present. A month-long festival was being held at the Kolkata Bagh Bazaar Gaudiya Math for Janmāṣṭamī. Each day a different dignitary was invited to sit as honorary chairman of the evening meeting. Some students of world-renowned scientist C. V. Raman were amongst those who came regularly to listen to the lectures of the Gaudiya Math saints. One day, these students came to see Śrīla Prabhupāda and complained that every day a different distinguished person was being made honorary chairman, but their professor, whose fame had spread throughout the world, had not even been invited.

Śrīla Prabhupāda answered that he had no objection to having Dr. Raman be honorary chairman one evening. He asked Śrīla Gurudeva to take charge of inviting him. Śrīla Gurudeva first went to Dr. Raman's house but did not find him there. His wife sent him with an orderly to Dr. Raman's laboratory on Circular Road. There, Śrīla Gurudeva met with the scientist on the second floor, where he was sitting in a corner of a huge loft, engaged in his research activity. Dr. Raman spoke neither Bengali nor Hindi, and so their conversation took place in English.

Upon being asked by Dr. Raman the reason for his coming, Śrīla Gurudeva answered, "A large month-long religious gathering is being held by the Bagh Bazaar Gaudiya Math at Janmāṣṭamī. On each day, a different dignitary of the city is invited to grace the chairman's seat, and we humbly invite you to do the same."

Dr. Raman answered, "I do not believe in your Keṣta-Biṣtu. I have no faith in anything that cannot be confirmed by direct sensory experience. I cannot waste my valuable time with imaginary things. I value my time. I would prefer to attend any conference dealing with science or education, but not a religious one."

Śrīla Gurudeva said, "Your own students have been coming regularly to listen to the Math's *svāmījīs* speak. It was their desire that you be honored in the same way that so many other eminent persons of Kolkata have been. I have been asked by my Gurudeva to invite you, so please accept our invitation."

Dr. Raman then challenged Śrīla Gurudeva: "Can you show me your God? If you can show him to me, I will go."

One side of the lab room in which the conversation was being held was a windowless, doorless wall, on the other side of which lay the whole of north Kolkata. Śrīla Gurudeva asked, "I can see nothing on the other side of this wall, but if I say that there is nothing there, will that be true?"

Dr. Raman answered, "Perhaps you cannot see what is there, but I could with the appropriate instruments."

Śrīla Gurudeva then asked him, "There is a limit to what your instruments can do. You can only see as far as they allow you. Can you say that there is nothing beyond these limits?"

Dr. Raman replied, "Never mind. I will not waste my time on this. I will not give my attention to anything which is not within my sense experience. I will only spare my valuable time if you can actually show me your God. Can you do it?"

Śrīla Gurudeva: "If your students were to say to you that they will study your scientific findings only if you can show them the truth of what you have realized through your experiments, what would you say?"

Dr. Raman: "I would make them realize it!"

Śrīla Gurudeva: "Can you make them realized before teaching them?"

Dr. Raman: "No, I would first have to show them the process by which I have come to realize the truth. They will have to follow that process if they want to have the same realization. First, they have to earn their B.Sc. degree, then their M.Sc. Then they will have to study with me for another five years. Then I will be able to make them understand."

Śrīla Gurudeva: "If that is true for you and your scientific knowledge, then can the seers of ancient India not say exactly the same thing? Follow their process and see whether or not you experience the existence of soul, supersoul and God. You are not able to show the scientific truths you profess to your students until they have adopted your process. Similarly, if you want to experience or understand God, you have to follow the process by which that is accomplished. If it does not happen, then you can deny His existence. But how can you deny His existence without following the process?"

Dr. Raman could not answer. After a few moments of silence, he said, "I know nothing about Kṛṣṇa. If I go, I will be able to say nothing. You would be better off inviting someone who knows something about these matters."

Śrīla Gurudeva's quick-wittedness and presence of mind was such that it was impossible to get away with an illogical statement in his presence. Such capacity does not come with simple book-learning. Only one who has surrendered himself to his spiritual master and has come to direct realization of the truth through his mercy can display such divine power. To such a person, a display of intelligence without any basis in realization cannot get very far.

AFTER THE DISAPPEARANCE OF ŚRĪLA PRABHUPĀDA

Śrīla Prabhupāda instructed all of his disciples to follow *āśraya-vigraha* (Śrī guru) in preaching the message of Śrī Rūpa and Raghunātha Gosvāmīs, and that they should work together to achieve this one purpose.

From the superficial point of view of a short-sighted pessimist, the events which followed Śrīla Prabhupāda's disappearance seem to have contradicted his wishes, but whatever comes about as a result of the all-auspicious Lord Hari's desire is for the good of everyone. If we are unable to see the truth of this basic tenet of spiritual life we become incapable of reconciling things and become unhappy as a result. Nothing takes place contrary to the will of the Lord; one who believes that He is all-auspicious must also accept that whatever takes place is somehow working toward the fulfillment of some larger, auspicious purpose. The short-sighted are only able to realize this after much water has flowed under the bridge.

Mahāprabhu said, "My name will be preached in every town and village throughout the world." In order to bring this prophecy to fruition, it was His will and that of His *abhinna-prakāśa-mūrti* (nondifferent manifestation) Śrīla Prabhupāda, that those leading disciples who had been enriched by their blessings should be inspired to work to that end independently. Śrīla Prabhupāda did not wish that those worthy disciples of his who had attained the qualifications to act as *ācārya* should be restricted or limited in their activities. As a result of their being empowered by him to spread Mahāprabhu's message, the movement has today been acknowledged and adopted by many persons throughout the world, fulfilling the Lord's prediction. If Prabhupāda's disciples were ordinary flawed living beings who disregarded the wishes of their spiritual master, then such widespread successes would not have been possible. When those hapless people who are ignorant of the overall intention of the Supreme Lord praise one of Śrīla Prabhupāda's disciples and condemn another, they fall from the path of spiritual life and into the mire of Vaiṣṇava *aparādha*.

All of Śrīla Prabhupāda's associates tried or are trying to sincerely follow his orders to the extent of their abilities. As a result of these sincere efforts, great numbers of wretched souls have been attracted to the teachings of Lord Caitanya Mahāprabhu and have accepted the discipline of Vaiṣṇava *sad-ācāra*. They have been engaged in the worship of Lord Kṛṣṇa according to the doctrines of pure devotional service and have thus made their lives successful.

OPENING THE SHYAMANANDA GAUDIYA MATH

In 1942, just prior to taking the vows of *tridaṇḍī-sannyāsa*, Śrīla Gurudeva worked together with his godbrothers, particularly Tridaṇḍi Svāmī Śrīmad Bhakti Bichar Jajabar Mahārāja and Tridaṇḍi Svāmī Śrīmad Bhakti Kumud Santa Mahārāja, to establish a *maṭh* in the city of Midnapore. This *maṭh* was named the Shyamananda Gaudiya Math. As a result of the preaching efforts of these godbrothers, many men and women of the city became attracted to Mahāprabhu's message and took up the regulative principles of Vaiṣṇava *sad-ācāra* and the path of devotional service as ordained by Śrī Caitanya. The Gaudiya Math's good name spread throughout the region, and many wealthy citizens of Midnapore city took up the task of establishing a permanent branch there. With their help, land and a large two-storey building were purchased in the Shiva Bazaar area for the *maṭh*.

Śrīla Gurudeva told the story of how one of the chief donors, Govardhana Piḍi, came into contact with the *maṭh* and the amazing change in his life as he renounced all sinful activity to engage in the service of Kṛṣṇa and the devotees. When Śrīla Gurudeva was in search of donations for the establishment of the *maṭh*, he suggested going to visit Govardhana Piḍi, but local people counselled him not to. They described him as a great miser who would not give a *paisa* to a poor person in need. They told Śrīla Gurudeva that if he went to see him, he was sure to be insulted.

Śrīla Gurudeva answered, "A *sādhu* shouldn't be bothered by the fear of insults, nor should he seek praise. If Govardhana Piḍi is a miser, then the *sādhus* should make an effort to see that he changes his ways. There is no need to change a good person. We can see the real results of preaching when bad people change and become good."

One day, Śrīla Gurudeva went to Govardhana Piḍi's office and was greeted cordially and given a suitable seat. When he heard from Śrīla Gurudeva that he was trying to open a preaching center through which the ultimate good for the *jīvas* could be achieved through spreading Śrī Caitanya Mahāprabhu's teachings, Govardhana Bābu responded by saying that his family had worshipped Rādhā and Kṛṣṇa for generations and that they continued to serve the deities in his home. He invited Śrīla Gurudeva to come and see them and took him to his roof-top temple to take *darśana* of his deities. Śrīla Gurudeva was very pleased to see the beautiful Rādhā-Kṛṣṇa deities and said, "Rādhā and Kṛṣṇa are the object of our worship. As yet we have no deities in our preaching center. We would be very grateful if you gave us these deities for our temple."

Govardhana Bābu answered, "These are our family deities, and They have a great deal of land in Their name. It is impossible for us to part with Them. However, if you want to have deities brought for your temple, I will pay the cost."

Śrīla Gurudeva told him that the Gaudiya Math imported their deities of Rādhā and Kṛṣṇa from Jaipur, but Govardhana Bābu was not deterred and continued to agree to bear all the expenses. When Śrīla Gurudeva returned to the *āśrama* and told his companions about Govardhana Bābu's offer, they were all dumbfounded. Govardhana Bābu paid not only for the deities, but for their service, their dress and ornaments, the installation ceremony and the feast which followed it. He also began coming regularly to hear Hari *kathā* in the temple. In time, as a result of the association of devotees, he came to realize that materialistic life was without substance and gave up all sinful practices. Understanding that true happiness could only be found in worshipping the Lord, he took initiation in the Holy Name and the *mantra* and adopted a regulated Vaiṣṇava life.

When the local people saw the amazing change in Govardhana Bābu's behavior, they were astonished and overjoyed. One day his wife came to the *maṭh* and in an outburst of emotion, fell at Śrīla Gurudeva's feet and said, "Ever since you came, my husband has been returned to me. All our family problems have disappeared."

We cannot say how many people's lives were affected by coming in contact with Śrīla Gurudeva and having sweet dealings with him. This is only a single small example of how one person's life was completely changed.

ŚRĪLA GURUDEVA TAKES SANNYĀSA

Immediately prior to taking *sannyāsa*, Śrīla Gurudeva went on a preaching tour of the Bankura and Midnapore districts, visiting Kether Danga, Onda, Jhanti Pahari, Bankura city, Gadbeta, and other places. People everywhere were impressed by his personality, his upstanding character and his powerful Hari *kathā* and became attracted to the gospel of Lord Caitanya Mahāprabhu. Accompanying him on this trip were Kṛṣṇa Keśava Brahmacārī, Rāma Govinda Brahmacārī, Kuñjalāla Prabhu, Hari Vinod Prabhu and other Godbrothers. Helping the preaching work in Kether Danga and Onda were Rādhā Govinda Sīṭa and Avināśa Pāla, respectively.

Although Śrīla Prabhupāda had intended to give Śrīla Gurudeva *tridaṇḍi-sannyāsa*, he never did so because of the important role he played in fundraising. Not long after Śrīla Prabhupāda's disappearance, however, a large group of Gurudeva's godbrothers appealed to him to take the renounced order. Amongst them were Śrīmad Kuñja Bihārī Vidyābhūṣaṇa Prabhu, Śrīmad Bhakti Prakaś Araṇya Mahārāja, Śrīmad Bhakti Sarvasva Giri Mahārāja, Śrīmad Bhakti Svarūpa Parvata Mahārāja, Śrīmad Bhakti Prasun Bodhayan Mahārāja,Śrīmad Kṛṣṇa Keśava Brahmacārī, and Śrīmad Sundar Gopal Brahmacārī. Thus, at the age of forty, to fulfill Śrīla Prabhupāda's command to preach Mahāprabhu's message, he took *sannyāsa* according to the Vaiṣṇava rituals from Śrīmad Bhakti Gaurava Vaikhānasa Mahārāja on the grounds of the Tota Gopinath temple in Purushottama *dhāma*. It was the Phālgunī Pūrṇimā of 1944, the 457th anniversary of Mahāprabhu's appearance. He was henceforth known as Parivrājakācārya Tridaṇḍi Svāmī Śrīmad Bhakti Dayita Mādhava Gosvāmī Mahārāja. Other important godbrothers present on that occasion were Śrīmad Kuñja Bihārī Vidyābhūṣaṇa Prabhu, Śrīmad Paramānanda Vidyarāatna Prabhu, Śrīmad Parvat Mahārāja, and Śrīmad Bodhayan Mahārāja.

After taking *sannyāsa*, Śrīla Gurudeva returned to the Shyamananda Gaudiya Math in Midnapore, where he was greeted with great pomp by the members of the Viśva Vaiṣṇava Rāja Sabha. The Viśva Vaiṣṇava Rāja Sabha presented him with a special certificate in which they praised him for his fearlessness, saintly courage, ability to enchant people when speaking on religious topics, and above all, his affection for the devotees, by which he gave great joy to Śrīla Prabhupāda.

Of all of Śrīla Gurudeva's virtues, his attachment to his spiritual master and his affection for his godbrothers were exemplary. After Śrīla Prabhupāda's disappearance, whenever any of Śrīla Gurudeva's godbrothers were faced with hardship, he would immediately step forward to give them a helping hand without considering his own happiness or distress. Many of Prabhupāda's worthiest disciples were unable to come to terms with the turmoil in which the Math found itself after his disappearance and either returned to householder life or considered doing so. Śrīla Gurudeva took a lot of trouble to find such devotees, seeking them in their home and persuading them to return to the Math and to lead a life of service to the Lord. Some of those he brought back subsequently took the role of *ācārya*!

Devotees are a manifestation of Kṛṣṇa; affection for them accurately demonstrates the extent of one's affection for Kṛṣṇa, Similarly, the guru's disciples are the manifestations of the guru himself, and affectionate behavior towards them demonstrates the depth of one's love for the guru. Śrīla Gurudeva's exemplary love for his Godbrothers was evident to the very last days of his presence in this world.

PREACHING ACTIVITIES IN EAST PAKISTAN

After Śrīla Gurudeva took *sannyāsa*, just prior to Indian independence (1947) and afterward he went on an extended preaching tour throughout India and East Pakistan (modern Bangladesh). Accompanying him were Mihir Prabhu, Saṅkarṣana Prabhu, Kṛṣṇa Keśava Brahmacārī, Rāma Govinda Brahmacārī, Trailokya Prabhu, Mahendra Prabhu, Brahma, Pyārī Mohan Brahmacārī, Śrī Yajñeśvara Dāsa Bābājī Mahārāja, and others. Some of the important places he visited in Dhaka and Mymensingha districts were Baliyati, Nawabganj, Kalakopa village, Jamurki, Pakulla, and Churain.

While in Jamurki-Pakulla in the Mymensingh district, Śrīla Gurudeva gave a lecture in a large gathering at the local high school. He often talked about this event later. In the audience that gathered, more than a thousand people of both Hindu and Muslim faiths were present. Many students and teachers from the school also came. Several local policemen gave Śrīla Gurudeva the friendly warning that following partition of India and Pakistan, the situation was tense for the Hindus in the Muslim-dominated country. He was told to be careful about what he said and did because the government was watching him. If complaints were made that something he said went against Pakistan's interests, he could be jailed. After having received this warning and seeing the large numbers of police officers present in the crowd, Śrīla Gurudeva started to worry about the difficulties of being put in prison, where contact with many untouchable foodstuffs would be inevitable. Seeking to avoid any possibility of trouble, he requested the listeners to save their questions, for which he would leave fifteen to twenty minutes at the end of his discourse. He furthermore said he would entertain any inquiries on matters not related to his lecture at his quarters at another time. He asked that no one interrupt the lecture to ask questions, for it would disrupt the proceedings and cause distress to the other listeners.

Despite this request, however, after Śrīla Gurudeva had been speaking for half an hour, a mullah stood up and asked, "What is the reasoning behind the Hindu custom of worshipping idols?" Many of the people in the audience were irritated by the interruption and told him to hush up and Śrīla Gurudeva not to answer. But Śrīla Gurudeva welcomed the mullah's question by praising it, saying that it was deserving of an answer from which everyone present could profit. Furthermore, by answering it he would not wander from the subject under discussion, but would rather enrich it.

He then proceeded to deal with the mullah's question as follows. He said that before answering him, he wished to ask him a question: "Do you believe in God (*khudā*)?" The mullah said, "Of course I do." Śrīla Gurudeva then asked, "Do you believe that Khudā's almighty?" The mullah loudly declared, "Khudā is all-powerful!" Śrīla Gurudeva then laughed and said, "There you have your answer."

Not realizing the implications of the word "omnipotent," the mullah was at first confused by Śrīla Gurudeva's answer. So Gurudeva started to clarify by asking, this time with the help of an example: "Is God powerful enough to take a Mymensingh (very large) elephant and push him through the hole of the smallest needle without even harming a hair on his body?"

When the mullah remained silent, Śrīla Gurudeva continued, "Perhaps Maulvi Sāheb does not know the extent of Khudā's powers, but the fact is that nothing is impossible for the omnipotent Lord. *Kartum akartum anyathā kartuṁ yaḥ samarthaḥ sa eva īśvaraḥ*. He can do whatever He wishes, not do something if He does not wish to do it, or undo or change whatever He has done. The Supreme Lord is all-powerful and nothing is beyond His abilities. The omnipotent Lord is not limited to the powers that we ascribe to Him. That is not what is meant by omnipotence. The *sarva-śaktimān* is one who possesses all powers imaginable and unimaginable. Once we have accepted that the Supreme Lord is omnipotent, we cannot say, 'He can do such and such, but not this or that.' In accordance with the wish of His devotees, the supremely powerful Lord can appear in any form He desires, at any time, with His full complement of powers. If you say that He cannot, then there is no point in claiming that He is all-powerful.

"Any figure that a man may create out of the five elements, or any entity that he imagines with his material mind – whether with form or formless – is all material. That is what we call a *putula*, or an idol. There is no regulation in the Sanātana Dharma for the worship of such idols. What is ordained, rather, is service to the Lord's deity form, or *śrī-vigraha*. The *śrī-vigraha* is that form which the all-powerful Supreme Lord feels obliged to accept as a result of His devotee's love for Him. There is a gulf of difference between an idol and the Lord's deity form. Even though the Lord's deity form is purely spiritual and blissful, *cid-ānanda-maya*, a materially conditioned soul is unable to recognize Him, just as he would be unable to recognize the Lord if He appeared directly before him. One can only perceive the Lord's divine form with the eyes of pure devotion. A vision of the Lord which has not been earned is not a true vision of the Lord."

PREACHING IN ASSAM

After East Pakistan, Śrīla Gurudeva took his party into Assam, recalling that Śrīla Prabhupāda had once directly ordered him to preach there, as the Assamese people are simple and have faith in *sādhus*. To fulfill Prabhupāda's order, Śrīla Gurudeva first went to Sarbhog near Barpeta in the Kamrup district. Accompanying him were Bhuvana Prabhu, Uddhāraṇa Prabhu, and Kṛṣṇa Keśava Brahmacārī Prabhu.

Because of problems in the Sri Gaudiya Math, due to the change in the management subsequent to the disappearance of Śrīla Prabhupāda, Śrīla Gurudeva stayed at the house of Kṛṣṇa Keśava Brahmacārī's brother rather than in the *maṭh*. As there had been torrential rains and extensive flooding in the area, the devotees had to put all their bedding in an ox-cart and walk through knee-deep water to get there. As the veranda and ground floor of the house were under water, the party had to construct a bamboo platform on which to sleep, while another such platform served as a toilet. Even in these difficult circumstances, Kṛṣṇa Keśava Prabhu's devout mother daily cooked meals for the Vaiṣṇavas.

The war with Japan was at its height during this period, and the Japanese army had already conquered Burma and crossed the border into Assam. The British Indian government's War Ministry had ordered many homes throughout Assam to be requisitioned for quartering Indian army troops. Kṛṣṇa Keśava Brahmacārī's family home was one of those taken over for this purpose, and Śrīla Gurudeva and his party were obliged to stay in some village not far from Sarbhog. This is just a small example of how Śrīla Gurudeva was prepared to accept any difficulty to follow the orders of his own spiritual master and bring auspiciousness to those who had forgotten Kṛṣṇa.

Śrīla Gurudeva preached in these untoward circumstances for seven days before moving to Sarbhog, where he stayed in Gopāl Prabhu's house. While there, he gave daily

Bhāgavatam lectures at the house of a local high school teacher and leading citizen, Cintā Haraṇa Pātagiri. Those who became Śrīla Gurudeva's disciples during his preaching activities in Sarbhog were Gopāla Dāsādhikārī and Acyutānanda Dāsādhikārī.

A local youth named Kamalā Kānta Gosvāmī was a regular attendant at Śrīla Gurudeva's *Bhāgavata* lectures. He was so attracted by Mahāprabhu's teachings that he decided to leave home and join his preaching party. Śivānanda Prabhu and his nephew enthusiastically invited Śrīla Gurudeva to visit their village, Bhavanipur Tapa, where he stayed for a few days. Kamalā Kānta Gosvāmī accompanied the Vaiṣṇava group to Tapa, but when his father, Ghana Kānta Gosvāmī, found out, he came there, severely chastised him, and took him back home.

Ghana Kānta was conditioned to believe in the superiority of *brāhmaṇas*. He did not accept the rationale behind the *daiva-varṇāśrama* taught by the Gaudiya Math. He considered that his son had lost his caste status by eating the food of the devotees, and he instructed him to remain outside the house until he had atoned. Kamalā Kānta had been born in a very high caste, but after hearing the pure scriptural doctrines from Śrīla Gurudeva about the differences between a Vaiṣṇava and a *brāhmaṇa*, about the superiority of the Vaiṣṇava and about how a Vaiṣṇava can be born in any race or caste, he could not understand what fault there was in taking food which had been cooked and served by Vaiṣṇavas who followed the religious practices prescribed in the scriptures. He could not approve of his father's attitude, which was disrespectful to the Vaiṣṇavas, and in order to avoid offenses, he left home again the very next day and came back to Tapa to surrender to Śrīla Gurudeva. Though Kamalā Kānta wanted to take initiation, Śrīla Gurudeva worried that his father and family might cause trouble, and thought it better to not give him *harināma* and *mantra* on that occasion.

In Tapa, several wealthy Marwari businessmen were attracted to Śrīla Gurudeva and took great care to serve the Vaiṣṇavas and help the preaching of Mahāprabhu's gospel with great sincerity. Śivānanda Prabhu was very renounced, even though married, spending most of his time in devotional activities. He gave his worthy son, Lokeśa, to Śrīla Gurudeva to be fully engaged in the service of guru and Gaurāṅga. It is rare to see a father give his own son over to devotional service in this way. Śivānanda Prabhu's nephew Śrī Lohita and son Lokeśa were initiated in the Holy Name at the house of Tulārāma Bābu in Tapa. Just before leaving for Kolkata, Śrīla Gurudeva also initiated Kamalā Kānta Gosvāmī, Rāma Prasāda and Bhavānanda in the Holy Name. He gave *dīkṣā mantra* to Śrī Lohita, Lokeśa and Kamalā Kānta when they arrived in the Midnapore *maṭh*. They were given the names Lalitā Caraṇa Brahmacārī, Lokanātha Brahmacārī and Kṛṣṇa Prasāda Brahmacārī, respectively. All three of these devotees later took *sannyāsa* from Śrīla Gurudeva and were known thereafter as Tridaṇḍi Svāmī Śrīmad Bhakti Lalita Giri Mahārāja, Tridaṇḍi Svāmī Śrīmad Bhakti Suhṛd Dāmodara Mahārāja, and Tridaṇḍi Svāmī Bhakti Prasāda Āśrama Mahārāja.

BHĀGAVATA DISCOURSES AT THE CHIEF MINISTER'S HOUSE

Before returning to Kolkata, Śrīla Gurudeva spent a few days in the Assamese capital, Gauhati. Through the efforts of Kṛṣṇa Keśava Brahmacārī and Cintā Haraṇa Pātgiri, he had the opportunity to meet many of Assam's leading citizens and preach to them. Amongst these people were Assam's chief minister, Gopīnātha Bardalai, Durgeśvara Śarmā, Kumudeśvara Gosvāmī, Bhuvana Gosvāmī, Kanakeśvara Gosvāmī, Rohiṇi Caudhurī, Navīna Bardalai, Girijā Dāsa, Dhīrena Deva, Caritra Bābu, Narendra Bābu, and others.

Arrangements were made for Śrīla Gurudeva to speak on the *Bhāgavata* at the Chief Minister's house. The people who came there to hear him speak the pure doctrines of the *Bhāgavata* through unprecedented reasoning were enchanted. One day, after Gurudeva's lecture, Gopīnātha Bardalai came to him with great enthusiasm and praised his explanation of *siddhānta*. He said, "Upon hearing your *Bhāgavata-pāṭha*, I am convinced that your objectives and those of Mahatma Gandhi are the same. You give so many examples from scripture and explain everything logically, and then you make people chant the names of Kṛṣṇa. Gandhiji also ends his speeches, in which he has talks about so many different things, by engaging everyone in *Rāma-dhun*. So both of you have the same goal – to make people chant the names of God. I don't see any difference between your messages. What do you think of this opinion?"

Śrīla Gurudeva recognized that Gopīnātha Bardalai had great faith in and affection for him. He did not wish to disturb his mind by saying something that would hurt him, so he decided to instruct him according to his level of understanding. He smilingly said, "If you don't mind, then I will tell you what I think."

The Chief Minister said, "I have been illuminated by all your valuable instructions. I have never heard such a learned discourse on the *Bhāgavata* from anyone else before. How could I mind if you say anything at all for my benefit? Speak freely and say whatever you wish to say."

Guru Mahārāja then said, "Before I entered the *maṭh*, I used to take part in the freedom movement. Gandhi's Sabarmati Ashram used to publish an English newspaper called *Young India*, which I often read. I remember once that Gandhiji told his audience in a speech that he was ready to abandon even the chanting of the Holy Name for the sake of his country. As far as I can remember, his exact words were, 'I can even sacrifice *Rāma-dhun* for my country.'

"We, on the other hand, say exactly the opposite: 'We can sacrifice our country for *Rāma-dhun*.' Our worshipable Lord Rāma is not there for us and our ends. He is for Himself, and everything exists for Him. Western philosophers have defined the Absolute by saying, 'The Absolute is for itself and by itself.' We do not have an 'It-God.' Our Lord is the Supreme Person, the 'He-God.' So we prefer to say, 'The Absolute is for Himself and by Himself.' The unlimited universes come out of Him, they exist within Him, and they are maintained by Him. So their existence is uniquely to fulfill His ends. If anyone wishes to worship the Lord, he must have a proper theological understanding."

Gopīnātha Bardalai was so influenced by Śrīla Gurudeva's powerful personality that he told him his resolve to abandon householder life and live in the *maṭh*, dedicating his entire life to the service of the Lord. Unfortunately, his associates would not let him leave politics. Not long afterward he died and so was never able to do as he had wished. Politics are so entangling that once one has gotten involved in them, it is very difficult to extricate oneself.

As a result of the influence Śrīla Gurudeva had on all these important people in Guwahati, he became well known both in the city and outside it. After completing his preaching activities there, he returned to Kolkata.

BHAKTI BALLABH TIRTHA MAHĀRĀJA TAKES SHELTER

In 1947, Śrīla Gurudeva returned to Assam, this time to Goalpara. He was invited by the Gaudiya Math household devotee Śrī Rādhāmohana Dāsādhikārī Prabhu. Accompanying him were Śrī Kṛṣṇa Keśava Brahmacārī, Śrī Uddharan Brahmacārī, Śrī Mādhavānanda Vrajavāsī, and Śrī Ratharūḍha Dāsa Brahmacārī. Śrīla Gurudeva and his companions headquartered in Rādhāmohana Prabhu's house and held meetings in various parts of the town. At Harisabha in Goalpara a special assembly was held in which the town's leading barrister, Kṣīroda Sena, was made president. Amongst the other important people who were present were the local district attorney, Kāmākhyā Caraṇa Sena, and the pleader for the Mechpara estate, Priya Kumāra Guha-Rāya.

Śrī Kāmākhyā Caraṇa Guha-Rāya, son of Śrī Dhīrendra Guha-Rāya, first met Śrīla Gurudeva at Rādhāmohana Prabhu's house in Goalpara. He later took initiation and became known as Śrī Kṛṣṇa Ballabh Brahmacārī, and after *sannyāsa*, Tridaṇḍi Svāmī Śrīmad Bhakti Ballabh Tirtha Mahārāja. He came with his friend Devavrata (Ravi) to ask some questions about spiritual life, as he wished to establish clearly by what method he could attain the Lord. When he first saw Śrīla Gurudeva's sitting on an elevated seat and paid his obeisances to him, Kāmākhyā Caraṇa felt his blessings being showered on him, and his entire body erupted with horripilation. He asked him the following question: "When I chant the Holy Name, I feel as though I will see the Lord any minute. Then I will have to leave my home and family, giving up all the love I feel for them. This troubles me so much that I stop chanting. Please give me some advice so that I won't stop chanting when these thoughts start bothering me."

Even though the question did not show great intellectual depth, Śrīla Gurudeva praised it to give enthusiasm to the questioner. He then said, "A few geese used to live by a lake which was really nothing more than a stinking, stagnating little waterhole. They lived quite happily there, eating the plentiful snails, clams, worms and shrimp. One day, they saw a flock of their cousins, the swans, flying overhead. The large birds looked so beautiful with their sparkling white wings that the geese began to think that the place where they were heading must surely be much more wonderful than their waterhole. If they could only live there, surely they would become as beautiful as the swans and be as happy as they.

"The swans had been to the sea and were now on their way to Mana Sarovara in Himalayas. One of them saw the geese looking at them so pitifully and felt compassion for them. He came down to land near the geese, who were astonished by the swan's beauty. They asked him if he could take them with him to his home. The swan said that he had come precisely for that reason, to take them away from that putrid place. But when he told them to follow him, the poor geese pleaded that they were unable to fly very far. The swan felt so sorry for them that he told them to climb on his back and that he would carry them.

"The geese then started to wonder whether they would be able to find the snails, clams, worms and shrimp they were used to eating once they were at Mana Sarovar. The swan answered that such disgusting things were not available there and that the swans lived on lotus stems. The geese began to shriek as if with one voice, 'Then how will we survive?' And so they decided not to go at all.

"The geese's attachments to other things kept them from going to live in a very beautiful place like Mana Sarovar. Similarly, our attachment to this perishable body and everything connected with it is an impediment to our going to join the Lord. The Lord is all-auspicious and free from any material defects, He is the embodiment of ultimate joy, and so is His abode. There is no place there for the despicable aspects of transitory material life. Anyone who is unable to abandon his attachments to things unconnected to the Lord and wishes to hang on to those things is unable to attain Him. The Lord and *māyā* are opposites. Supreme auspiciousness cannot be had unless one is freed from material wants through the association of advanced devotees.

tato duḥsaṅgam utsṛjya
satsu sajjeta buddhimān
santa evāsya chindanti
mano-vyāsaṅgam uktibhiḥ

"An intelligent person should therefore avoid bad company and associate only with devotees. With their realized instructions, such saints can cut through the knots of material attachments."(*Śrīmad Bhāgavatam* 11.26.26)

Rādhāmohan Prabhu was Śrīla Bhakti Siddhānta Sarasvatī Gosvāmī Prabhupāda's initiated disciple. He had stayed as a *brahmacārī* in the Gaudiya Math for a while before entering householder life. People of the region held him in high esteem because of his knowledge of Vaiṣṇava philosophy, his high standards and his personal character. In Goalpara he was known as Rāmamohana Dā. He worked as a clerk in the office of Kāmākhyā Caraṇa's uncle. The affection and kindness he had showered on Kāmākhyā Caraṇa by showing him the devotional path is exceptional. He was thus the *vartma-pradarśaka* guru who brought Śrīla Bhakti Ballabha Tirtha Mahārāja to the Gaudiya Math. Because of this, he had to face much opposition and criticism. Śrīla Gurudeva's letters for Kāmākhyā Caraṇa were sent to Śrī Rādhāmohan Prabhu's address. The affection of Śrī Rādhāmohan Prabhu's pious wife and family for Kāmākhyā could never be repaid.

In his letters, Śrīla Gurudeva advised Kāmākhyā to study Śrīla Bhaktivinoda Ṭhākura's *Jaiva-dharma* in order to eradicate all doubts. As a result of reading this book, Kāmākhyā Caraṇa indeed found that the doubts which he had harbored for so long were effaced. In another letter, Śrīla Gurudeva said that if he planned to follow a life of renunciation, the *nivṛtti-mārga*, and dedicate his life to the worship of the Lord, then it made no sense to take a government job. On the other hand, if he wished to follow the path of action, the *pravṛtti-mārga*, and worship the Lord while staying at home, he should take the job. Kāmākhyā realized that it would not be possible for him to engage in pure devotional service in his family environment, and so he made up his mind to leave.

PREACHING ACTIVITIES IN HAULI

My *parama-gurudeva*, Śrīla Bhakti Siddhānta Sarasvatī Gosvāmī Ṭhākura, visited Goalpara on only one occasion. He ordered his householder disciple Nimānanda Prabhu to establish a Gaudiya Math near the banks of the Brahmaputra River, in a beautiful spot on Hulukanda Hill. The Math was given the name Prapannashram and was considered a branch of the Gaudiya *maṭh*. In the course of time, however, due to the unavailability of personnel and other problems, the institution was lost. Later, Goalpara resident Śarat Kumāra Nātha offered to give a building and land for the establishment of a *maṭh* in the town. Śrīla Gurudeva understood that this was

Śrīla Prabhupāda's desire, and so he accepted the offer. He established a branch of the Sri Chaitanya Gaudiya Math there in 1969.

Some of the other places Śrīla Gurudeva visited while preaching in Assam were Bijani, Bhatipara, Hauli, and Barpeta. In Hauli a great meeting was held where thousands of men and women, both of the Hindu and Muslim faiths, were present. Śrīla Gurudeva asked the audience to save its questions, for which he would leave fifteen to twenty minutes at the end of his discourse. However, a Muslim scholar interrupted to ask during the course of the lecture, "Has anyone ever seen the soul or God? What is the proof that you are not simply deceiving everyone when you talk about the soul and God?"

The audience asked Śrīla Gurudeva not to answer as the question had been asked breaking the discipline requested by him, but he thought that if he did not respond, the ignorant would think that he had no answer. He saw that the maulvī was carrying a book, and he asked him what its name was. The *maulvī* called the book a *kitāb* and gave its name. Though Śrīla Gurudeva knew several languages, including Bengali, Assamese, Hindi and English, and though his eyes were in perfect condition, he said he could not recognize the title of the book. He asked the *maulvī* if he was not deceiving him by giving him some false name. How could he prove that it was not so?

The *maulvī* asked the people sitting around him to confirm that the title he had given was indeed correct. Śrīla Gurudeva said, perhaps the group was in collusion to deceive him. Maulvī Sāheb was surprised by his statement and asked him what he saw. Śrīla Gurudeva said that it looked like footprints of a crow. *maulvī* replied that he evidently did not know Urdu, and Śrīla Gurudeva confessed that indeed he did not. The *maulvī* then asked him, if he did not know Urdu how could he expect to know what was written there? He would first have to learn Urdu, then he would be able to confirm that he had been told the book's correct title.

Śrīla Gurudeva then took the *maulvī's* own words to explain to him what he was getting at. "Even if someone knows many languages, he won't be able to understand Urdu unless he has learnt it. Even if one has good eyesight, unless he knows Urdu, he will neither be able to recognize what sounds are represented by its script, nor what the meaning of those sounds is. The same thing goes for understanding the soul and the Supersoul. Even if one has great learning and experience in this world, unless he has specifically earned the qualifications to experience the Lord, he will not be able to experience Him.

"There are two kinds of vision, one based on Vedic knowledge (*veda-dṛk*), the other on simple sensual capabilities (*māṁsa-dṛk*). The physical eye can only see physical objects and nothing else. Things which are beyond matter and the senses are self-revelatory and can only be seen with His blessings. The truth is revealed in the heart of the surrendered soul."

A few people took shelter of Śrīla Gurudeva in Hauli became fixed in Vaiṣṇava practices and took the vow to worship the Lord according to the teachings of Lord Caitanya Mahāprabhu. Most noteworthy amongst these was Rāmeśvara Barmaṇa, who was known after initiation as Rāmeśvara Dāsādhikārī.

PREACHING IN HYDERABAD

The notable citizens of Hyderabad, the fortress of Advaita-Māyāvādīs (monist philosophers), responded overwhelmingly in a positive manner to the pure devotional teachings of Śrīla Gurudeva when He arrived there in 1959. They were immediately attracted to Him due to His beautiful and effulgent saintly appearance and even more so by the magnetic effect of His compelling words. Seeing their sincerity to serve the *sādhus* and also by their request, Śrīla Gurudeva decided to open a branch of Sri Chaitanya Gaudiya Math to spread the doctrines of *prema*-bhakti as enunciated by Śrī Caitanya Mahāprabhu. Accordingly, a center was founded in the Pattharghati locality of Hyderabad. At first, it began to function from rented quarters adjacent to the main road, but later it was shifted to larger premises in Urddugali. Here, at the house of Lālā Fakirchand Agarwāl, the property consisted of a courtyard, balcony and four rooms. In the *maṭh*, daily *pūjā* was offered to Śrī Giridhārī and Śrī Nārāyaṇa Śālagrāma. *Kīrtanas* were performed at dawn and dusk, and festivals like Śrī Janmāṣṭamī, Śrī Annakūṭa, Śrī Gaurāvirbhāva, and so on were observed in an opulent manner. In July 1961, the assistant secretary of the *maṭh*, Śrī Maṅgala Nilaya Brahmacārī, organized a special religious meeting. This was attended by the Mayor of the Corporation of Hyderabad, as well as the Āchārya of the Madhvācārya Sampradāya Pejāvara Maṭh of Uḍupi, Śrīmad Viśveśa Tīrtha Śrīpādaṅgalāvaru, and the Accountant General of Andhra Pradesh, Śrī R. N. Chatterjee. Many eminent persons came to visit the *maṭh* during this time.

Upon Śrīla Gurudev's next arrival to Hyderabad, on August 1, 1961, the city's notable citizens welcomed him grandly. This time he stayed in the well-known Balaji Bhavan in Himayet Nagar. Mr. Arbamuda Ayangar, the former minister of law of Hyderabad Nizam, Mr. Ved Prakash, the Mayor of Hyderabad Corporation, Mr. P. Chandra Reddy, the Honorable Chief Justice of the Andhra Pradesh High Court, respectively, were the honorary chairmen during each day of the three-day function that started on August 5, 1961.

To participate in the installation of the holy deities of Śrī Śrī Guru-Gaurāṅga-Rādhā-Vinoda-Jīu at the Hyderabad *maṭh*, Śrīla Gurudeva arrived there accompanied by Pūjyapāda Tridaṇḍi Svāmī Śrīmad Bhakti Gaurava Vaikhānasa Mahārāja and other saintly persons on Tuesday, June 28, 1962. The head of the *maṭh*, Śrī Maṅgala Nilaya Brahmacārī, received them at the railway station. The welcoming party consisted of notable citizens carrying an umbrella (*chatra*) and fans (*cāmara* and *vyajana*). A western-style band played music while intense *saṅkīrtana* was being performed. Many Marwari devotees accompanied Śrīla Gurudeva from the station, singing *kīrtana*.

On Monday July 9 (24 Āśāḍha), Śrīla Gurudeva saw to the installation of the deities according to the injunctions of *Śrī Pañcarātra* and *Śrī Bhāgavata*. Śrīmad Bhakti Gaurava Vaikhānasa Mahārāja was the chief preist, whereas Śrīmad Bhakti Bhudeva Srauti Mahārāja assisted. An eight-day special religious congregational program starting from July 8 was organized. On each of these eight days special dignitaries were invited to take the chair, and many notable saints of the *maṭh* spoke on various devotional subjects. On Sunday July 15 (30 Āṣāḍha), the deities were mounted on elaborately decorated chariots (*rathas*) and taken around the main thoroughfares of the city accompanied by a very impressive procession of devotees loudly singing *kīrtana*. This was the first time that such an event had taken place in Hyderabad, and it evoked a tremendous and enthusiastic response from all who had the good fortune to witness it. Stopping at certain places along the way, the devotees offered worship to Their

Lordships, the holy deity forms of the Supreme Lord and also to Śrīla Gurudeva.

On July 3, a few days prior to the deity installation festival, a cultural group from the United States, accompanied by Dr. P Śrīnivāsāchāra, came to visit and was given a warm reception by the head of the *maṭh*, Śrīpāda Maṅgala Nilaya Brahmacārī. The American party consisted of professors from different universities across the United States. They met and exchanged cordial greetings with Śrīla Gurudeva, who, upon their request, enlightened them with a talk on the subject of the life and teachings of Śrī Kṛṣṇa Caitanya Mahāprabhu. The following contains the gist of His discourse.

"Śrī Kṛṣṇa Caitanya Mahāprabhu appeared on this earth in 1486 A. D. in Sridhama Mayapur, in the district of Nadia. From childhood, He came to be known as Nimāi Paṇḍita all over India due to His unparalleled scholarship (Nimāi meaning one born beneath the *nīma* tree, Paṇḍita meaning scholar). At the age of twenty-four, He took the vow of renunciation (*sannyāsa*) and proceeded to the holy city of Puri. From there He traveled for six years to various places of pilgrimage in both North and South India. During that time, He spread *kṛṣṇa-bhakti* in the hearts of all living beings – man, bird or beast – especially the most fallen. He was intent upon saving them from the grip of *māyā*. He then returned to Puri, where He remained up to the time of His disappearance from this world. At Puri, He was constantly immersed in *kṛṣṇa-prema* and tasted the *bhāva* (transcendental mood) of Śrīmatī Rādhārāṇī, together with His intimate devotee associates Śrī Rāya Rāmānanda and Svarūpa Dāmodara. He terminated the visible display of His pastimes at the age of forty-eight.

"Śrī Caitanyadeva has pointed out that the sole objective of our lives is to achieve love of God (*kṛṣṇa-prema*). Attachment to objects of an impermanent nature with materialistic yearnings is the root cause of our bondage and all sorrows. Eternal peace can never be attained by amassing material ego and sensory pleasures. We can reach the shores of eternal peace only by turning the mind away from all that is perishable and instead, placing it at the lotus feet of Śrī Bhagavān, who is the form of all-existence, all-knowledge and all-bliss (*sac-cid-ānanda*). Citing the evidences from the scriptures, Śrī Kṛṣṇa Caitanya Mahāprabhu negated the arguments for *nirviśeṣa* (impersonalism) and established *saviśeṣa* (personalism) to be the Ultimate Causal Reality. Because Śrī Bhagavān, possessing a transcendental form, is devoid of mundane distinctive features, He is sometimes referred to as *nirviśeṣa*. Moreover He is *saviśeṣa* for He possesses transcendental supramunane qualities. It would be foolish to equate the mundane, base features of the material world with those of Śrī Bhagavān's pure, transcendental, spiritual form. One need not be concerned that attributing variegatedness and personality to Śrī Bhagavān will, in some way, negate the concept of God's being infinite. Without a doubt, Bhagavān should be understood to be infinite and eternal.

"His potency knows no bounds, but it can be seen that there are three manifestations of that potency that are prominent: (1) the internal potency (*antaraṅgā-śakti*); (2) the external potency (*bahiraṅgā-śakti*); and (3) the marginal potency (*taṭasthā-śakti*). All living beings are of the nature of the *taṭasthā-śakti* of the Lord. They are thus free to choose to live either under the umbrella of Śrī Kṛṣṇa's internal potency (the spiritual realm) or in the temporary material world, which constitutes Śrī Kṛṣṇa's external potency. Those who choose to turn away from Śrī Bhagavān, mesmerized by His external potency, begin to think of themselves as lord and master of all they survey. This is ignorance. The ego of false enjoyerhood inevitably leads to hatred, aggression and malice. Śrī Bhagavān is the only true master and enjoyer. All energies, including all living beings, are under His dominion. The *jīvātmā* (living entity) is an infinitesimal particle (*aṁśa*) of the potency of Śrī Bhagavān. It goes without saying that a part cannot be happy independently, having separated itself from the whole. If attraction to material enjoyment persists and no attempt is made to turn toward Śrī Bhagavān, then neither the individual, nor the family, nor even society as a whole will ever attain true and lasting peace. Where there are many centers of interest, conflict becomes inevitable. If, however, love for Bhagavān becomes the focal point for all, then immediately all are seen as being related to each other. Then love and a sense of unity become spontaneous as a natural consequence. It can be seen that love for one's own family can easily lead to a clash with the family of another. If one's interest is pivoted to one particular locality, province or country, this will lead to disputes with other localities, provinces or countries. However, being in a relationship of love with Śrī Bhagavān, who is the shelter of all, one will have no quarrel with anyone.

"In the modern world, the powerful nations are engaged in the highly competitive production of nuclear weapons and the launching of satellites into space. The consequences of this could be disastrous. The founding of the whole world as a single powerful nation may solve these problems, but without offering worship to Śrī Bhagavān, everlasting peace which transcends the mundane plane will forever remain elusive and altogether impossible."

Śrīla Gurudeva concluded by expressing the hope that the bonds between America and India could be strengthened by means of cultural exchange programs. The professors were delighted to hear the *bhajana-kīrtana* and *nāma-kīrtana* interwoven with the glories of Śrī Gaurasundāra. To fulfill their desires, they were happily presented with a pair of *karatālas* (brass hand cymbals used in worship) to remember the special musical quality of the *bhajana-kīrtanas*. The devotees were happy to see how the guests, who were unacquainted with Indian manners and customs, had quickly adjusted to the situation, sitting on floormats and partaking of the Lord's *prasāda* (foodstuffs which have been offered to the Lord).

On July 15, upon the invitation of the Governor of Andhra Pradesh, Śrī Bhīmsen Sāchār, Śrīla Gurudeva along with his *sannyāsī* Godbrothers and *brahmacārīs* went to the Rāja Bhavana (Governor's house) and spoke Śrī Hari *kathā*. Highlights of this lecture appear below.

"Śrī Kṛṣṇa Caitanya Mahāprabhu has stated that *nāma-saṅkīrtana* is the ultimate goal of mankind. Initially, the tongue, which is coated with the bile of ignorance, might fail to relish the exquisite flavor of Śrī Kṛṣṇa's Holy Name. However, by the gradual practice of recitation, it will become possible to do so. Analogously, even the best sugar candy seems bitter to a jaundiced tongue, coated with bile. However, by regularly tasting it, the tongue gradually experiences its sweetness. Similarly, the Holy Name of Śrī Bhagavān will slowly but surely cure all ailments and reveal its inner greatness and magnificence.

syāt kṛṣṇa nāma caritādi sitāpyavidyā
pittopatapta rasanasya na rocikā nu
kitvādarād anudinaṁ khalu saiva juṣṭā
svādvī kramād bhavati tad gada mūlahantrī

"The holy name, character, pastimes and activities of Kṛṣṇa are all transcendentally sweet like sugar candy. Although the tongue of one afflicted by the jaundice of *avidyā* [ignorance] cannot taste anything sweet, it is wonderful that simply by carefully chanting these sweet names every day, a natural relish awakens within his tongue, and his disease is gradually destroyed at the root." (*Upadeśāmṛta*, Verse 7)

"Each and every living being has the right to listen to and chant the Holy Name of Śrī Bhagavān, but this is not so in the case of customary Vedic religion, which is inhibited by a bewildering array of rules and regulations. Thus, if Śrī Bhāgavata-dharma in the form of *śrī nāma-saṅkīrtana* penetrates the hearts of the masses at large, then a firm bond of unity will arise. Cursed by the nature of the present age, Kālī Yuga, mankind is madly attracted to material objects, completely lacks control over the senses and is perverted with sicknesses of all kinds. Consequently, the *yuga-dharmas* of the previous three ages, namely *dhyāna* (meditation) for the Satya Yuga, *yajña* (sacrifice) for the Tretā Yuga and *arcana* (deity worship) for the Dvāpara Yuga, cannot be applied effectively in this era. Taking into account the seriousness of the malady, we can see that the prescribed medicine is proportionate in strength. Thus, the scriptures advise us to take the medicine of the Holy Name:

harer nāma harer nāma harer nāmaiva kevalam
kalau nāsty eva nāsty eva nāsty eva gatir anyathā

" 'In the Age of Kālī, there is no other way, there is no other way, there is no other way (for attaining the ultimate goal) than the chanting of the Holy Name, the chanting of the Holy Name, the chanting of the Holy Name.' (*Bṛhan-naradīya Purāṇa*)"

SPIRITUAL SUMMIT CONFERENCE AT KOLKATA

The "Temple of Understanding" of Washington, D.C., in the USA organized a historic five-day Spiritual Summit Conference starting from October 22, 1968 at the Birla Academy of Art and Culture. The purpose of the conference was to bring unity among world religions. It was attended by religious leaders representing Hindus, Muslims, Christians, Buddhists, Jains, Sikhs, Baha'is, Jews, Confucians, Zoroastrians, etc. The Hindus were represented by Most Revered Śrīla Gurudeva Oṁ 108 Śrī Śrīmad Bhakti Dayita Mādhava Gosvāmī Mahārāja Viṣṇupāda, Svāmī Śrī Cinmayānanda Jī, Dr. Rāghavan, Śvāmī Lokeśvarānanda of the Rāmakṛṣṇa Mission and Professor Amiya Cakravartī of New York State University. The chairman of the International Committee of the Temple of Understanding was the wife of Śrī B. K. Birla, Śrīmatī Saralā Birla. Many prominent personages from the USA, China, Japan, Sri Lanka, Africa, Tibet, Thailand and other countries of the world, as well as from different provinces of India, participated in the conference. The B. K. Birla family took on the responsibility of seeing to the accommodation of the guests who had come from outside.

Invited by the Birlas, Śrīla Gurudeva visited their residence on Gurusaday Road to discuss topics related to the forthcoming summit. Mr. Finley P. Dan (Executive Director of the Temple of Understanding) and Mr. V. G. Rathi came to Sri Chaitanya Gaudiya Math at 35 Satish Mukherjee Road to formally invite Śrīla Gurudeva. They had a long discussion on how an atmosphere of understanding could be created among the different faiths. Śrīla Gurudeva also discussed this same issue with Mrs. Dickerman Hollister at Birla Academy.

A brief synopsis of the recorded lectures was later published in Washington under the title "The World Religions Speak on the Relevance of Religion in the Modern World."

For the promotion of peace, the representatives gathered on Friday October 25 at Shivpur Botanical Gardens and offered prayers. Present with Śrīla Gurudeva were Pūjyapāda Tridaṇḍi Svāmī Śrīmad Bhakti Pramode Purī Mahārāja and the secretary of the *maṭh*, Tridaṇḍi Svāmī Śrīmad Bhakti Ballabh Tīrtha Mahārāja. Śrī B. K. Birla had arranged for a car to be at the disposal of Śrīla Gurudeva around the clock. Unable to refuse the persistent invitations of Mr. Birla and his wife, Śrīla Gurudeva attended the afternoon celebrations at their house. However, since it was the occasion of Kārtika *vrata*, He only partook of fruits. The hospitality of the Birla family is praiseworthy.

Śrīla Gurudeva delivered the following speech in English at the Birla Academy of Art and Culture:

"I heartily welcome the organizers of this symposium in their attempt to explore an impartial and liberal approach to different views of religious faiths in this world and to find out how a world fellowship of different religions or a unity of hearts amongst human beings can be promoted. There are two methods of approach: (1) the sincere, real and practical approach relating to the actual state and nature of human beings; and (2) an idealistic approach having little or no practical value, merely indulging in the luxury of high-sounding words. If we sincerely wish to obtain real and abiding effect, we should face the facts boldly. The truth is that there exists no one hundred percent identity amongst individuals, as they are all conscious units possessing independence of thinking, feeling and willing. Individuals, as a result of their different actions, achieve separate environments and paraphernalia. Every individual has his peculiar nature distinct from any other. So, obviously, individuals will vary in their opinions and tastes and this is quite natural. It is unnatural to attempt to forcibly encage individuals into one fold, faith or particular ideology. Accordingly, cultivation of tolerance of others' views is essential for world peace and unity. Indian sponsors of religion appeared to have that insight and tolerance; hence, many independent views have cropped up in India and have flourished simultaneously. Want of tolerance makes us sectarian, and that spirit motivates us toward the forcible conversion of others, which brings turmoil and unrest to the world. Religion should give equal scope to all individuals for their respective spiritual development according to their attributes. Indian saints have classified the nature of human beings into three broad groups: *sāttvika*, *rājasika* and *tāmasika*. *Sāttvika* people are wise, sincere, generous and nonviolent. As such, they have an altruistic mentality and render disinterested service. *Rājasika* people are egoists; however, they are active and do good to others with the motive of getting a return of their actions for self-aggrandizement. They won't tolerate harm to themselves and have the spirit of taking revenge. *Tāmasika* people are indolent, out and out egoists and are of violent temperament. They are indiscriminate in their pursuit of enjoyment. They completely disregard the interest of others and will do anything to fulfill their selfish desires. So, *sāttvika*, *rājasika* and *tāmasika* people vary in their tastes, habits and nature. Three forms of teaching religion have been prescribed for these three groups, according to their eligibility, giving them scope for gradual elevation. These three modes of teaching are related to the apparent self and, as such, are changeable. There are still higher states of religious existence which transcend those three qualities and relate to the eternal, natural function of the real self. If we want quantity, we must sacrifice quality, and if we want quality, evidently we shall have to sacrifice quantity – both cannot be achieved at one time. However, the primary point to be noted here is that there should be tolerance amongst sponsors of different religious views and respect for others' views, as well as equal scope given to all for their spiritual upliftment from their respective statuses. Another point to be noted here is that we should have the patience to understand the underlying spirit of different religious faiths and not merely indulge in disputes in regard to the ritualistic aspects of religions, which will certainly vary in different parts of the world in accordance with the change of climatic conditions and environments.

Nowadays, we find lack of discipline rampant in every sphere of human life – political, social, economic, and even in education. Student unrest (youth unrest) is one of the most serious problems of the day. It is extremely difficult to proceed with constructive work when people are prone to indiscipline. To fight against disruptive tendencies and indiscipline, a radical treatment of the minds of the people is required. Here we feel the necessity of moral and spiritual values in human life. There are two ways of treating diseases – pathologically and symptomatically. In pathological treatment, the root cause of the disease is ascertained first and then the remedy is prescribed. The process of symptomatic treatment may be easier, but it does not have a lasting effect. It may give temporary relief, while treatment through the pathological process brings about permanent relief.

"To determine the root cause of unrest, we ought first to determine the meaning of the self. I strongly believe that ignorance of our real self is the cause of unrest, discord and anxiety. The real self is not the physical tabernacle; it is something other than the gross and subtle bodies. We consider the body to be the person as long as we observe consciousness in it. The moment the body is bereft of consciousness, it loses its personality. I am 'I' when the conscious entity (i.e., the entity that thinks, feels and wills) is present in me, and I am 'not-I' when it is absent in me. Hence, the entity whose presence and absence makes me 'me' and 'not-me' respectively must be the person. This conscious entity (the soul) is designated as *ātmā* in Indian scriptures. *Ātmā* is indestructible; it has no origin and no end. If we plunge deep into the matter, we can trace our existence to the Absolute Conscious Principle, whom we call Godhead, the fountain source of innumerable conscious units. Godhead is termed *sac-cid-ānanda,* i.e., He is All-Existence, All-Knowledge and All-Bliss. Individuals are points of rays emanating from Him and, as such, are one of His eternal and coexisting potencies. Individuals cannot live independently; they are all interconnected and coexisting though retaining their own individual characteristics.

"It has already been stated that differences between individuals are unavoidable as they are conscious units. Now, the problem is to find a common ground and interest for the solution of these differences. A sense of common interest can be fostered among individuals if they know that they are interconnected, are parts of the one organic system, and are the sons and daughters of the one Father. Here is the task of all religions – to teach people that all beings of the world are closely interrelated. Although steadfastness or firm belief in God (*niṣṭhā*) according to some particular faith and eligibility of the individual is congenial for healthy spiritual growth of every individual, religious bigotry which begets enmity is condemnable, as it is against the real interest of the individual and society. Real religion teaches love for one another.

"Lord Śrī Kṛṣṇa Caitanya Mahāprabhu propagated the cult of all-embracing divine love, which brings universal brotherhood on a transcendental plane. According to Him, forgetfulness of our eternal relation with the Supreme Godhead, Śrī Kṛṣṇa, is the root cause of all afflictions. Śrī Kṛṣṇa is the God of all gods, the Supreme Person having all-existence, all-knowledge and all-bliss. He is Beginningless, yet the beginning of all and primal cause of all causes. The word *Kṛṣṇa* means one who attracts all and pleases all by His wonderful enchanting beauty, majesty, munificence and supremacy. This denotes the highest conception of Godhead with all perfections. He is the object of all-love. So, remembrance of Śrī Kṛṣṇa, or God, is the divine panacea of all evils. The easiest and most effective way of remembering God is chanting of the holy name, which can be practiced by all, at any place or any time, irrespective of one's caste, creed, religion, age, health, or economic, social or educational status.

"In Vedic culture, we find the theory of the cycle of time, within the period of infinite time, which has four stages in accordance with the predominance of religiousness and irreligiousness. The four ages are designated as Satya, Tretā, Dvāpara and Kālī. In Satya Yuga (the first age of the cycle of time), wisdom predominated in men, and as such, they were aware of the painful and transitory nature of the world and thereby were not fascinated by it. Concentration without interruption was possible, and meditation (*dhyānam*) was prescribed as the common religion suitable for all. In Tretā Yuga (the next spiritually degraded age of the cycle of time), when the spirit of activity predominated and people were attached to worldly objects, *yajña* (sacrifice, i.e., offering of the things of attachment to the Lord) was prescribed as the common religion to divert the attention of the people from material objects of attachment and turn their minds towards Him. In Dvāpara Yuga (the next and still more degraded age), when people were addicted to worldly objects and sensualism, *arcana* (worship of deities) was prescribed as the common religion for gradual attainment of concentration of the mind by directing all the senses and objects of attachment to His service. In the present age, Kālī Yuga (the last and most spiritually degraded age of the cycle of time), when people are firmly attached to worldly objects, are too much given to sensualism and are always diseased, they are incapable of performing *dhyānam* (meditation), *yajña* (sacrifice) or *arcana* (deity worship) rightly, and as such, the chanting of the Holy Name of God is prescribed for them.

"Today the world is making tremendous scientific strides. Modern scientists are performing wonders. But in spite of their marvellous accomplishments and pride in twentieth-century civilization, it is puzzling to see that science is so much engaged in inventing destructive weapons like atom bombs, etc., and thereby imperiling the whole human race. At any moment there may be a conflagration, and the whole world may perish. Saints are deeply concerned as to how to avert such a calamity. Mere material scientific accomplishments are unable to save the world from such danger. Of course, scientific inventions or achievements as such are not condemnable. Everything depends on the proper use of things. Science may be used for the good of humanity and also may be misused for the destruction of human civilization. It is imperative to consider the problem and diagnose the disease of conflicts and mutual distrust amongst nations and individuals. So long as nations and individuals have separate centers of interest, tension is inevitable. Nobody can avoid it.

"This world is limited. When there are many claimants for one limited object, disputes among these claimants are unavoidable. It is because of this that Indian saints differ from the leaders of the West or from the westernised leaders of our own country in their manner of tackling the problem of peace. In fact, genuine saints of the world are wise enough to see the fundamental defect in the attempt of the so-called best brains to achieve world peace. They assert with great emphasis that a practical solution of the problem is not possible so long as individuals do not change their present craving for sensuous enjoyment and greediness for mundane wealth, and direct their attention towards the Unlimited, the Infinite and the Absolute. The heads of different religious groups should clearly and emphatically point out and teach their followers the painful and perishable character of worldly objects and the futility of sensuous enjoyment. They should create interest in man for the worship of God, which brings about real happiness.

"Unless and until the eternal relationship of the people is known to them and they realize that they cannot exist or be happy without the Godhead, who is all-bliss, the natural inclination of the people towards the Godhead and diversion of their attention from the material aspects of life cannot be effected. As long as people do not have this realization, they will maintain the conviction that their only satisfaction lies in the realm of one's own gross and subtle senses. This is termed 'lust.' Hindrance to the fulfillment of lust breeds anger, and that in turn brings conflict and malice amongst individuals and nations.

"So long as people do not understand that they are inseparably connected, and until the activities of the people are God-centered, mere sentimentalism or fictitious ideals will not be able to foster real love amongst individuals.

"If we believe that our interest lies in material prosperity and sensuous enjoyment (lust), discord cannot be avoided. Want of patience and tolerance originates from lust. Mere belief in the existence of God will be of great benefit to humanity by restraining them from committing sins and teaching man to do good to others. They will have fear of punishment for bad deeds and encouragement to seek rewards for good deeds. Any activity which leads to the infliction of harm to other animate beings is detrimental to our own interest and will bring harm in return; we will not be encouraged to harm any individual, not even any sentient being of this world.

"If we can love the Absolute Whole – the Godhead – we cannot have the impetus to injure any of His parts. So, according to me or the teachings of Lord Gaurāṅga, divine love is the best solution to all the problems of the world."

MORE PREACHING IN ASSAM

Remembering Śrīla Prabhupāda's instructions, Śrīla Gurudeva returned to Assam nearly every year with a force of disciples and Godbrothers in all situations of life. The immense efforts paid off as hundreds of men and women took to following the regulative principles and became his disciples.

In some places, extremely unfavorable circumstances presented themselves. Nevertheless, Śrīla Gurudeva remained undisturbed and continued to preach fearlessly.

The great devotees who have completely surrendered to Kṛṣṇa go wherever they wish without any worry. Nothing can impede their tendency to serve the Lord. Because their service has no basis in personal desire, it is and so it is unstoppable.

tathā na te mādhava tāvakāḥ kvacid
bhraśyanti mārgāt tvayi baddha-sauhṛdāḥ
tvayābhiguptā vicaranti nirbhayā
vināyakānīkapa-mūrdhasu prabho

"O Mādhava! Your pure devotees have got firm love for you. They never deviate like strivers who are falsely thinking to be emancipated, so they do not fall down. The pure devotees being well-protected by you can move in this world without any fear over the heads of the leaders of the impeding persons." (*Śrīmad Bhāgavatam* 10.2.33)

Śrīla Gurudeva wandered from village to village simply to bring the greatest good to every living being, to turn them toward Kṛṣṇa. Despite the difficulties, he traveled, sometimes by foot and sometimes by ox-cart, in order to deliver the Lord's message. Some of the places he visited were Goalpara, Dhubaṛi, Basugaon, Bilasipara, Kashikotra, Sidali, Agiya, Depalchong, Bardamal, Lakshmipur, Krishnai, and Dudhnai in the Goalpara district; Guwahati, Sarbhog, Chakchaka Bazaar, Ketaki Bari, Hauli, Barpeta, Barpeta Road, Pathshala, Tihun, Bijani, Rangia, Nalbari, Jalaha Ghat, Bhantipara, Unnikuri, and Amingaon in the Kamrup and Barpeta districts; Tezpur, Tangla, Bindukuṛi, Rangapara, Dhekiajuli, and Mangaldai in the Darranga district; Silchar and Hailakandi in the Kachar district; Sibsagar, Lakhimpur, and other important towns in estern Assam, etc., and Shillong in Meghalaya state.

Most Assamese tribals are traditionally followers of the *Bhāgavata* religion. Many Vaiṣṇava *ācāryas* such as Śaṅkara Deva, Mādhava Deva, Dāmodara Deva and Hari Deva, preached the *Bhāgavata dharma* throughout Assam. The topmost leader or *satrādhikārī*, of Śaṅkara Deva's school at that time, Nārāyaṇa Deva Miśra, had great faith in our worshipable Śrīla Gurudeva. Nārāyaṇa Deva Miśra was the priest when Śrīla Gurudeva came to Barpeta to preach in a vast assembly at the local school and college. He was especially attracted by Śrīla Gurudeva's scholarship and his force of character and invited him to his home. While in Barpeta, Śrīla Gurudeva stayed at the house of Amiya Kānti Dāsa and Hare Kṛṣṇadāsa, who were later initiated and given the names Aghadamana Dāsa and Haridāsa. When Śrīla Gurudeva went to Barpeta from Hauli in 1945, Śrī Kṛṣṇa Keśava Brahmacārī, Śrī Gopāla Kṛṣṇadāsādhikārī, Śrī Trailokyanātha Vrajavāsī, Śrī Mādhavānanda Vrajavāsī and Śrī Bhuvana Mohana Dāsādhikārī were in his party.

Another important individual who was attracted by Śrīla Gurudeva's personality was Jīveśvara Gosvāmī of Tihun. He confessed to Śrīla Gurudeva that he had been disenchanted with the Gaudiya Math after hearing one of its fiery householder preachers criticize another religious denomination and its doctrines. He praised Śrīla Gurudeva, saying that though he said the same things, he did it in such a way that it was pleasing and he felt none of the same disturbance that he did before. Such sweetness of expression was only possible for a transcendental personality of extraordinary character.

As a result of his tremendous preaching efforts, Śrīla Gurudeva established three *maṭhs* in Assam – the first in Tezpur, then Guwahati and finally in Goalpara.

No mundane efforts can diminish the glory of a true guru or devotee. For the benefit of the world's conditioned souls, Mahāprabhu took Śrīla Gurudeva out of a restrictive situation so that he could act freely to spread His gospel of pure devotional service everywhere. Though Śrīla Gurudeva left the Chaitanya Math at a fairly advanced age, he organized a great preaching effort throughout India by which countless men and women were attracted to the pure devotional religion which had been practiced and taught by Śrī Kṛṣṇa Caitanya Mahāprabhu. In a very short time, he established major centers throughout India. Without the divine power invested in him by the Supreme Lord, this would never have been possible. Just as a wisp of cloud cannot hide the sun, no amount of envious disruptions can hold back the brilliant manifestation of a bona fide guru. Anyone who tries to do that will fall into the swamp of Vaiṣṇavā *aparādha*.

KOLKATA

Two distinguished residents of Kolkata, Maṇikaṇṭha Mukhopādhyāya and the president of the Homeopathic Factory, Dr. S. N. Ghoṣa, were influenced upon hearing Śrīla Gurudeva's vigorous delivery of Hari *kathā*. They came forward in a time when Śrīla Gurudeva was in apparent difficulty and became his right- and left-hand men, taking the responsibility for the management and improvement of all the temples which he had established. Later, Kolkata lawyer Jayanta Kumar Mukhopadhyaya was attracted by Śrīla Gurudeva's effulgence, character and words to take up many of the service opportunities sincerely in Sri Chaitanya Gaudiya Math for its all-round progress.

OTHER PREACHING ACHIEVEMENTS

One of Śrīla Gurudeva's extraordinary achievements was to pierce the fortress of impersonalist philosophy in the Punjab and in Hyderabad. Hundreds of men and women in these places accepted the pure doctrines of Mahāprabhu's religion and Vaiṣṇava *sadācāra* and took the vow of worshipping the Lord in the manner ordained by Mahāprabhu.

Śrīmad Atul Kṛṣṇa Gosvāmī of Śrī Rādhā Ramaṇa temple in Sridhama Vrindavan held a high opinion of Śrīla Gurudeva, saying that he had never seen a "gigantic spiritual personality" of equal stature.

As a result of his force of personality, Śrīla Gurudeva acquired the land and buildings on the birth site of his own spiritual master, the founder of the worldwide Sri Chaitanya Math and Sri Gaudiya Math, Śrīla Bhakti Siddhānta Sarasvatī Gosvāmī Ṭhākura, in Puri; established centers in Sector 20-B in Chandigarh and in the Tripura capital of Agartala, where he took over the service of the Lord Jagannātha temple. He was the chief organizer of the India-wide festivities celebrating Śrīla Prabhupāda's 100th birthday, in which all of his Godbrothers took part.

It seemed that no personality of any significance, whether president, state governor, judge, minister, barrister, lawyer, vice-chancellor, professor, mayor, chief commissioner, doctor, inspector general of police, wealthy citizen, Westerner or member of other religious denominations participating in interfaith conferences was not attracted to Śrīla Gurudeva once he came into contact with him. A full account of his transcendental activities and contributions can be found in his full biography, which has been published as a separate volume.

His extraordinary and exemplary character, his unbound warmth and affectionate behavior, his outstanding tolerance and forgiveness were qualities which attracted educated and influential people, many of whom left material life to take *tridaṇ-ḍisannyāsa* and dedicate their lives to the service of Kṛṣṇa and the devotees. It was for this reason that the Sri Chaitanya Gaudiya Math could have such wide results in such a short time.

ŚRĪLA GURUDEVA'S GURU PŪJĀ LECTURE

Śrīla Gurudeva gave the following nectarine instructions to his disciples in the evening religious assembly at Kolkata Math, 35 Satish Mukherjee Road, on November 12, 1967. It was *utthāna ekādaśī*, his appearance day:

"Today, *utthāna ekādaśī*, is also the *tithi* when we worship our predecessor *ācārya*, Śrīmad Gaura Kiśora Dāsa Bābājī Mahārāja, for it is his disappearance day. You have heard a great deal about Bābājī Mahārāja's transcendental activities and teachings from the venerable Śrīmad Purī Mahārāja. As I utter his name, I beg for his blessings, and I also pray for the blessings of my Guru Mahārāja, who is nondifferent from him.

"Coincidentally, this also happens to be my own birthday. Those who love me have taken this opportunity to give me their profuse blessings. Who is such a fool that he will not accept blessings when they are given? Who will not take the opportunity to make spiritual advancement when it comes? I therefore humbly accept all of your blessings. May every one of my senses be constantly engaged in the service of Kṛṣṇa and His devotees by your mercy.

"It is the custom for those in the renounced order to worship the guru on their own birthday. So, today, I make this my personal duty. I have three types of gurus: (1) The word *gu-ru* means 'the destroyer of ignorance.' The embodiment of unlimited knowledge is the Lord himself, whose appearance destroys all ignorance. The Lord Himself is thus the root of the truth that is guru. (2) The second is he who personally attracted me and engaged me in the service of the Lord, who is himself another form of the Lord – he who founded the worldwide Chaitanya Maths and Gaudiya Maths, my Gurudeva Nitya-līlā-praviṣṭa Prabhupāda Śrīla Bhakti Siddhānta Sarasvatī Gosvāmī Ṭhākura. (3) Thirdly, all the Vaiṣṇavas are my gurus.

"What do the Vaiṣṇavas do? Just as it is the guru's job to constantly engage the disciple in the service of the supreme object of service, the Lord, similarly the Vaiṣṇavas keep us engaged in the service of our worshipable Lord. Disciples are also another form of guru as they too engage us in the service of our guru. It is impossible to get away with any aberrant behavior. If you deviate in any way, they will catch you. So, I also include my disciples amongst my gurus.

"Today my disciples performed worship through *kīrtana*. By listening to their *kīrtana*, I performed worship. If by listening I had any untoward motives, if I had tried to 'pocket' it, then there would have been no *pūjā*. Just as *kīrtana* is a devotional activity, so listening is also a devotional activity. However we express it, they are all my masters, whom I must serve. But even though they are my masters, the objects of my service, the great affection I have for them makes me instruct them, take care of and protect them in the same way that Yaśodā Mātā and Nanda Mahārāja punished Gopāla, instructed and took care of Him. When Yaśodā Mātā bound little Gopāla to the mortar, she did not do so because she considered Him to be the 'object of her service,' she did it because she considered Him to be her child. The object of service can be both the one who protects and the one who is protected, the one who takes care and the one who is taken care of. Therefore both attitudes are found in a pure devotee.

"Śrīla Prabhupāda called his disciples *prabhu*; he called even his most junior disciples *prabhu* and used the polite form of the pronoun *āpni*. He used the more intimate pronouns, *tui* and *tumi*, with only very few of his disciples; he was never condescending. But he would chastise and instruct even those disciples whom he addressed as *prabhu*, using the respectful pronoun *āpni*. When one calls someone *prabhu*, or 'master,' is it not paradoxical to then discipline him? Some might even consider it to be a kind of hypocrisy. But this is not hypocrisy on his part: when he calls his disciple 'master,' he means it. On the other hand, when the other mood comes on him, he disciplines his disciple. In one way of looking at things, the spiritual master is a disciplinarian, in another, he is the disciple's dearmost friend and well-wisher.

"I am most grateful to all those who have blessed me today. May the result of their blessings be that my every thought and instinct be directed toward the service of Kṛṣṇa and His devotees. And if anyone was really worshipping me, then he should know that he has in fact worshipped my spiritual master, who is the real object of worship. Service to the guru is service to God. I never saw anything in my guru other than the desire to achieve the pleasure of the Lord. He never for a moment thought that anything other than devotion to Kṛṣṇa was in the true interest of the conditioned souls. Had he thought thus, he would not have been able to keep someone like me in the *maṭh*.

vāco-vegaṁ manasaḥ krodha-vegaṁ
jihvā-vegam udaropastha-vegam
etān vegān yo viṣaheta dhīraḥ
sarvām apīmāṁ pṛthivīṁ sa śiṣyāt

" 'A sober person who can tolerate the urges of speech, the mind and anger, as well as the urges to taste nice food, to fill the belly and to satisfy the genitals, is qualified to become master of the entire world. (*Upadeśāmṛta* 1)'

"Those who have controlled the six urges are qualified to discipline others. Śrīla Bhaktivinoda Ṭhākura considered the above instruction to be directed towards householders and not to renunciates, because unless one has already been able to control the six urges, he is not qualified to leave the householder *āśrama*. Why then did Śrīla Prabhupāda make me a *tyāgī*, when I have not been able to master the six urges? Perhaps I can make a mistake, but he certainly could not have made one. As my well-wisher, as my protector and master, why did he keep me in the *maṭh*? The reason is that he knew with certainty that there is no other way for anyone to achieve the ultimate good without associating with Vaiṣṇavas and engaging in the service of the Supreme Lord.

Through association with the devotees, by hearing the scriptures, one is able to experience the greatness of the Lord. This gives him the impetus to serve the Lord. There is no guarantee that simply by superficially controlling the senses one will become a devotee. There are many eunuchs in the world who would have become devotees if that were the case. Such sense control or renunciation has no standing unless there is love for the guru, Kṛṣṇa and Rādhā. Without love for Kṛṣṇa, without service to my Lord, then all this renunciation is not worth a plugged nickel; it is false renunciation.

"A renunciate or celibate who has no interest in service to the Lord is nowhere near as dear to us as someone who has dedicated himself to the Lord's service; he is by far superior. This is because even though at first he may be somewhat erratic in controlling his senses, through the higher taste his senses will ultimately be completely mastered and he will have no interest in anything but Kṛṣṇa. Nothing else will enchant him.

viṣayā vinivartante
nirāhārasya dehinaḥ
rasa-varjaṁ raso'py asya
paraṁ dṛṣṭvā nivartante

"Although a person of gross corporeal consciousness may avoid sense objects by external renunciation, his eagerness for sense enjoyment remains within. However, inner attachment to sense objects is spontaneously denounced by the person of properly adjusted intelligence, due to his having had a glimpse of the all-attractive beauty of the Supreme Truth. (*Bhagavad-gītā* 2.59)' "

"One may fast, but does that stop one from desiring food? Even if one stops sense activities, the tendency to engage in such activities is not stopped. When one experiences a higher taste, however, one loses one's interest in the lower taste. When one has the experience of the joys of love for Kṛṣṇa, then the inferior pleasures of the world cease to hold any charm. This is called *yukta-vairāgya*. This is why Nārada Muni instructed Mahārāja Yudhiṣṭhira: *tasmāt kenāpy upāyena manaḥ kṛṣṇe niveśayet*: 'O Mahārāja Yudhiṣṭhira! Engage your mind in Kṛṣṇa by any means possible.' (*Śrīmad Bhāgavatam* 7.1.32)

"I may be renounced, but my mind is still accepting and rejecting thoughts and desires constantly. So, I am associating with my mind, not with Kṛṣṇa. What benefit can come of that? It is of no benefit to me to associate with someone who simply praises and flatters me. It is far more beneficial to find the company of someone who will discipline me, who will instruct me and show me my mistakes.

"Devotion to Kṛṣṇa has no relation to worldly learning or ignorance. If it did, then scholars and *paṇḍitas* would all be devotees. Whoever has realized that the ultimate goal of life is Kṛṣṇa's pleasure alone does not need to waste his time in studies. I remember an event which took place when I was at the Madras Gaudiya Math, where I spent about ten years of my life. Through the efforts of Śrīpāda Śrīdhara Mahārāja, Śrīpāda Bon Mahārāja, other venerable godbrothers and me, we were able to build the Madras temple. Rāmacandra Aiyar, the son of the man who had donated the land for the temple, Sadāśiva Aiyar, advised us to learn Tamil so that we could preach to the general populace of the city. He even took steps to help us learn. I had been studying Tamil for only three days when a telegram came telling me to go to Puri. When I saw Prabhupāda, I told him that it would take about six months to learn Tamil. Śrīla Prabhupāda said, 'Kṛṣṇa *bhakti* is not transmitted by language. Through it, you may be able to transmit learning or scholarship, but that is all. Love for Kṛṣṇa is communicated by one who possesses love for Kṛṣṇa. Preach in whatever languages you already know. I don't advise you to lose your valuable time learning other languages.'

"The *maṭh* is there for culturing one's inherent love for Kṛṣṇa. Through such culture, one feels happiness, and he communicates that happiness to others. One who loves Kṛṣṇa loves every single living being. Devotion to the Lord is awakened by associating with saintly devotees:

saṅgena sādhu-bhaktānām īśvarārādhanena ca
(*Śrīmad Bhāgavatam* 7.7.30)

"I may be incapable, but my worshipable Lord is not. If any of you engage me in the service of Kṛṣṇa and His devotees, then my worshipable Lords, Śrīla Prabhupāda, Mahāprabhu and Rādhā-Kṛṣṇa, will surely give you Their combined blessings. May all of you be successful; may Śrīla Prabhupāda be pleased with you all."

REGISTRATION OF SRI CHAITANYA GAUDIYA MATH

In order to assure the proper management of the Sri Chaitanya Gaudiya Math, Śrīla Gurudeva had the society officially registered according to the Registration of Societies, West Bengal Act XXVI of 1961. This was done on August 9, 1976. Not long thereafter, he wrote the following letter:

"To the members and associates of the Sri Chaitanya Gaudiya Math, as well as to all my disciples:

"My physical condition is worsening, and I do not know where I will be when I leave my body. In view of my imminent departure, I make the following submission to my disciples, whether renounced or householder, as well as to my affectionate Godbrothers, that I have registered all of my *maṭhs* and temples according to the Society Registration Act. The society has twelve trustees. None of these trustees can be changed unless it is proved that they have committed a serious fault contrary to the principles of pure devotion or some act which is against the interests of the *maṭh* and its preaching activities. If one of the trustees leaves of his own will, then someone else must be chosen to replace him according to the rules. I have chosen Tridaṇḍi Bhikṣu Śrīman Bhakti Ballabh Tīrtha Mahārāja to be president and *ācārya* of the Sri Chaitanya Gaudiya Math after my departure. I will be happy if everyone works toward the maintenance of the institution, preaching pure devotion and maintaining its principles under his leadership.

"The humble petitioner,

Tridaṇḍi Bhikṣu, Śrī Bhakti Dayita Mādhava,

Dec. 27, 1976."

ŚRĪLA GURUDEVA'S LAST INSTRUCTIONS

The following lecture was delivered at the Kolkata Sri Chaitanya Gaudiya Math on the morning of Saturday, December 30, 1978. Tridaṇḍi Svāmī Bhakti Ballabh Tīrtha Mahārāja told Śrīla Gurudeva that a devotee inexperienced in the Gaudiya Vaiṣṇava *siddhānta* had come to Kolkata from Chandigarh in order to receive personal instructions from Śrīla Gurudeva himself. The devotee had been there for several days, but since the doctor had forbidden Gurudeva to talk excessively, he had had no opportunity to hear him speak. It would be nice if Gurudeva could say something to him. Our most worshipable Śrīla Guru Mahārāja then started to speak, directing his words to that devotee who had taken shelter of him.

EXCLUSIVE DEVOTION TO KṚṢṆA

"I am not well, and the doctor has warned me not to speak too much. It is quite possible that I will not stay much longer in this world. I am telling you that to engage in a proper practice of devotional service, you must be fixed in the worship of the ultimate object of your devotion. When a woman is not faithful to her husband, when she loves someone else, she cannot give herself to his service. Infidelity and exclusive devotion cannot go together. For this reason, a faithful and devoted wife will never allow anyone to take the place of her husband, nor will she criticize anyone else. She will not condemn her brother-in-law, her mother-in-law or her father-in-law, or anyone else who is related to her husband, but will rather give each of them his or her due respect. In the same way, if you wish to advance in devotional service, worship Kṛṣṇa alone. Do not criticize the other gods and goddesses, but think of them as servants of Kṛṣṇa and give them their due respect in that consciousness. But be careful to never give them the place which is due to the ultimate object of your devotion. I am giving you this instruction. Give this matter a little thought. You are a competent person, you are highly qualified, but you don't understand this tradition yet.

"In the Gauḍīya *sampradāya*, in the lineage of Śrī Caitanya Mahāprabhu, in the religious tradition of devotion to Kṛṣṇa, dedicated devotees worship Kṛṣṇa exclusively. If you put other gods and goddesses on the same level as Kṛṣṇa, you are making a mistake. Don't forget this. Not all gods and goddesses are equal, nor all *avatāras* of Viṣṇu. *Ete cāṁśa-kalāḥ puṁsaḥ kṛṣṇas tu bhagavān svayam* (*Srimad Bhagavatam* 1.3.28). After discussing all the different *avatāras* – Matsya, Kurma, Rāma, Nṛsiṁha, etc. – Vedavyāsa says that none of these *avatāras* is Kṛṣṇa Himself. Some of Them are expansions, some are partial manifestations, but Kṛṣṇa is the Supreme Personality of Godhead.

jaṅra bhagavattā haite anyer bhagavattā
svayaṁ bhagavān śabder tāhātei sattā

The epithet *svayaṁ bhagavān* can only be used for Him from whom the characteristics of Godhead are derived. (*Caitanya Caritāmṛta* 1.2.88)' "

"No one is equal to Kṛṣṇa. Everyone should keep this in mind and worship Kṛṣṇa exclusively and with dedication. Devotion will not increase by making a great sound and fury. Everyone should remember this. We will not condemn any other gods or goddesses, but will pray to them to give us the blessing that we remain fixed on our supreme object of worship, Kṛṣṇa."

INSTRUCTIONS FOR THE MAṬH AFTER HIS DEPARTURE

"I have registered the *maṭh*. The *maṭh* is no one's personal property. But that doesn't mean that each of us becomes boss or becomes indisciplined. By doing so, this life will have been wasted. Therefore a management scheme is necessary for the proper running of the *maṭh*. One person will be named Ācārya; he will be the head man or president.

"When I am gone, one person will take my place. Who will that be? My spiritual master did not like the idea that there should be a vote to decide the matter. To elect an *ācārya* is not in accordance with the principles of Hari *bhakti*. God Himself will decide who is the *ācārya*. The *ācārya* is the person who is most dear to the Lord. Who will make that decision? The proper arrangement is when the Lord Himself says, 'This person is the one who is most dear to Me.' Therefore the rule of the disciplic succession is that the choice should come from above. The correct process is that the order should be given from higher up. From the worldly point of view, everyone can get together to elect a leader, but the correct process is that the Lord Himself indicates which devotee is filled with love for Him, and He makes him the *ācārya*. This is the process approved by scripture.

"When Śrīla Prabhupāda was exhibiting pastimes of illness, he asked the solicitor, Mr. J. N. Basu, to write up a constitution. We heard that the constitution could be made according to one of two methods, by nomination or by election. Finally, the constitution was written according to the latter method. But Śrīla Prabhupāda did not like it, and he rejected it. I and two or three others were personally present when it happened. You cannot decide who is a *sādhu*, an *ācārya* or realized soul by taking a vote on the matter. Someone will say one thing, another something else and the debate will simply go on. Therefore the proper method is that the Lord Himself will choose which person will be honored with the position of *ācārya*. The scripture enjoins us to respect this process.

"This process is not followed only in the Gauḍīya *sampradāya*; it can be seen in every Vaiṣṇava *sampradāya*, the Rāmānuja, Madhva, Nimbārka and Viṣṇusvāmī lineages. This is the way that the disciplic succession is maintained. Therefore, the process ordained in the disciplic succession must be followed. I have therefore discussed with my senior godbrothers who are a part of the Gaudiya Math brotherhood, and I have decided to make Śrīmān Bhakti Ballabh Tīrtha Mahārāja my successor and president in my absence.

When I have gone, that does not give you all an excuse to behave just as you please. The defining characteristic of a Vaiṣṇava is following a devotee. The highest-order devotee is the one who follows the footsteps of a devotee for the pleasure of the Supreme Lord. The Lord's blessings follow the blessings of the devotee. When a devotee is merciful to someone, the Lord's mercy follows. This is the essence of my instruction to you; please follow it. I have written in more detail elsewhere.

"It will not be correct if you try to expel someone out of the *maṭh* as soon as there is some discord. That will result in chaos. You first have to explain and try to clarify the situation. If that still doesn't work, then give the devotee who is causing problems some money and a letter and send him to another *maṭh*. Do not act impetuously but try to work together and follow the person who has been made leader. It is not proper to ignore his commands and to do as one pleases. One has to follow the directions of the temple commanders. All his commands are given for the service of the Lord; bear that in mind."

THREE IMPEDIMENTS TO DEVOTIONAL SERVICE

"I want to say one more thing. We have come here to engage in devotional service to Kṛṣṇa. There are three principal impediments we have to watch out for.

"The first is the desire for sense gratification. The first obstacle to devotional service is *kanaka*, gold – the greed to accumulate lots of money. Your attention, your attachment, should be fixed on Kṛṣṇa's lotus feet. If you become attached to anything else, you will fall down. You should not think that because outsiders will not understand, you should save money for a rainy day. Mendicants beg; that is their duty. But they should turn whatever money they collect over to the *maṭh*.

"The temple managers should note that they must arrange for treatment if any temple devotee falls ill. If necessary, they should borrow money, but they must see that the devotee is taken care of. I can remember a time in the *maṭh* when we didn't even have money for groceries. Then I borrowed money from someone without telling any of the devotees and went and bought food from the market. Only Uddhāraṇa Prabhu knew about it. Uddhāraṇa Prabhu would also go to a householder's place and borrow money from him. The householder was Govinda Bābu. If Govinda Bābu didn't have any money, he borrowed it from his wife. Later I paid all the money back. How many people know about that?

"Śrīpāda Gosvāmī Mahārāja, Śrīpāda Nemi Mahārāja and I did all the collecting. I would put on a waistcoat and would go out to collect. Then I would come back and give all the money to the temple. Śrīmad Bhakti Pradīp Tīrtha Mahārāja, Yayavar Mahārāja and Śrīdhara Mahārāja would accompany me. Whenever they needed something, I would buy it, but I never spent the temple collection money for myself.

"When I was at the Kolkata *maṭh*, I would say to Kunja Da, "Is there any cloth in the *maṭh*? If there is, let me have one." But I would never ask for anything that I did not need, just for pleasure. None of you should set aside money that was collected for the temple. That will disrupt your devotional life. It doesn't really matter to the *maṭh* if you decide to hold some of the money for yourself, because the *maṭh* is protected by Kṛṣṇa, the devotees, the Vaiṣṇavas. But if you try to build up a savings account with that money, your spiritual life will go to hell and you will not last long in devotional service. So please don't set money aside for your personal use; give everything to the temple manager. If there is any problem, tell the temple manager. The desire for money is an obstacle to devotional service.

"The next obstacle is association with women. Both direct association and subtle association are a hindrance. It goes without saying that you don't engage in gross sexual activity, but you shouldn't even think about it, because we have given up everything to come here and engage in the service of the Lord.

"The third obstacle is the desire for personal aggrandizement. Śrīla Gurudeva wrote:

kanaka kāminī pratiṣṭhā bāghinī
chāṛiyāche jāre sei to vaiṣṇava
sei anāsakta, sei śuddha bhakta,
saṁsāra tathāya pāy parābhava

" 'Someone who has given up the tigresses of gold, women, and fame is a true Vaiṣṇava. He is unattached and a pure devotee. He has overcome the illusory power of the material world.'

"Prabhupāda here compares the desires for wealth, women and fame to a tigress. The desire for fame and good reputation are very strong and problematic, but even someone who does not seek fame finds that it comes to him of its own accord when he engages in true service to the Lord. People naturally give him their respect. People will always give respect to a true devotee.

pratiṣṭhāra bhaye purī gela palāṣā
kṛṣṇa-preme pratiṣṭhā cale saṅge gaṛāṣā

" 'Mādhavendra Purī ran away, afraid of being distracted by fame. But when one has love for Kṛṣṇa, fame flows alongside him.' (*Caitanya Caritāmṛta* 2.4.147)

"So, you avoid these three obstacles. It is not an easy thing to do, for they draw the mind. The conditioned soul lives for money, women and fame. They are *anarthas* that remain to a greater or lesser extent in the mind of the practitioner, but we should not tolerate their presence or approve of them.

"Tīrtha Mahārāja cannot always stay here. So Jagamohana Prabhu has to run the *maṭh*. Don't be offended if I am rough with you. Forgive me. Vaiṣṇavas are my object of worship. I want to serve all of you.

"Worship the Lord with unflinching dedication. Don't stop worshipping Him, no matter what situation you are in. This is my prayer to you, my appeal and my instruction. Chant the Holy Name in all circumstances. Worship Kṛṣṇa always. Always respect the best Vaiṣṇava, and don't hesitate to do so. May all auspiciousness follow you all.

vāñchā-kalpa-tarubhyaś ca
kṛpā-sindhubhya eva ca
patitānāṁ pāvanebhyo

vaiṣṇavebhyo namo namaḥ

" 'I offer my respectful obeisances unto all the Vaiṣṇava devotees of the Lord. They are just like desire trees which can bestow all that is wished for, they are oceans of compassion who purify the fallen souls.' "

ŚRĪLA GURUDEVA'S DISAPPEARANCE

On Tuesday, February 27, 1979 (Govinda 26, 492 of the Caitanya era; Phālguna 14, 1386, Bengali), at 9 A.M., in the midst of the singing of the Holy Names, Śrīla Gurudeva entered the eternal pastimes of the Lord at the time of His morning pastimes with Rādhā. He left his Godbrothers and disciples in an ocean of grief. It was also the disappearance day of Jagannātha Dāsa Bābājī and Rasikānanda Deva Gosvāmī and the first day of the bright fortnight. Śrīla Gurudeva was in his own room at the Kolkata *maṭh*, situated at 35 Satish Mukherjee Road. At four o'clock in the afternoon on the same day, the devotees left Kolkata with his transcendental body in the accompaniment of the Holy Names and came to Mayapur, where he was placed in *samādhi* at the end of the night according to the scriptural directions. The officiating priest at his *samādhi* festival was Śrīla Bhakti Pramode Purī Gosvāmī Mahārāja, and on March 1, 1979, a festival of separation was held in his honor at the headquarters of the Sri Caitanya Gaudiya Math at Īśodyāna in Mayapur.

On Thursday, March 22, 1979, a memorial assembly was held in the *saṅkīrtana* hall at the Kolkata *maṭh* on 35 Satish Mukherjee Road, under the direction of Parivrājakācārya Tridaṇḍi Svāmī Bhakti Hridoy Bon Mahārāja. The guest of honor was the publisher of the Amrita Bazaar Patrika, Tuṣāra Kānti Ghoṣa. Many of Śrīla Gurudeva's Godbrothers and leading citizens of Kolkata were present at the assembly.

A LIST OF MAṬHS AND INSTITUTIONS ESTABLISHED BY ŚRĪLA GURUDEVA

Here is a list of the many *maṭhs*, schools, libraries, free clinics, and printing presses – the great drums of the modern *saṅkīrtana* movement. This list is given in chronological order.

1. 1942. Shyamananda Gaudiya Math, Midnapore (W.B.) This temple was established by Śrīla Gurudeva with the help of his two Godbrothers Śrīla Bhakti Vichar Yayavar Mahārāja and Śrīla Bhakti Kumud Santa Mahārāja.
2. 1948. Sri Gaudiya Math, Tezpur (Assam).
3. 1953. Sri Chaitanya Gaudiya Math. Paltan Bazaar, Gauhati-8 (Assam).
4. 1955. Sri Chaitanya Gaudiya Math. 86A Ras Bihari Avenue, Kolkata-26.
5. 1956. Sri Chaitanya Gaudiya Math. Īśodyāna, Sri Mayapur, Nadia (W.B.).
6. 1956. Sri Chaitanya Gaudiya Math. Sarveshwar Haveli, Vrindaban (U.P.)
7. 1960. Sri Chaitanya Gaudiya Math. Goari Bazaar, Krishnanagar, Nadia (W.B.)
8. 1960. Sri Chaitanya Gaudiya Math. Mathura Road, Vrindaban (U.P.).
9. 1961. Sri Chaitanya Gaudiya Math. 35 Satish Mukherjee Road, Kolkata-26. The new temple was opened in 1967.
10. 1961. Sri Gaudiya Sevashram. Madhuvana Mahauli, Mathura (U.P.)
11. 1962. Sri Chaitanya Gaudiya Math. Urdu Gully, Patharghati, Hyderabad (A.P.).
12. 1962. Śrīla Jagadīśa Paṇḍita's Sripat, Jashra, Nadia (W.B.).

13. 1967. Sri Vinoda Vani Gaudiya Math. 32 Kaliya Daha, Vrindaban (U.P.).
14. 1969. Sri Chaitanya Gaudiya Math. Goalpara (Assam).
15. 1970. Sri Chaitanya Gaudiya Math. Sector 20B, Chandigarh.
16. 1972. Sri Chaitanya Gaudiya Math. Divan Deori, Hyderabad (A.P.)
17. 1974. Sri Chaitanya Gaudiya Math. Grand Road, Purī (Odisha).
18. 1975. Sri Chaitanya Gaudiya Math. Gokula Mahavan, Mathura (U.P.).
19. 1976. Sri Chaitanya Gaudiya Math. Śrī Jagannātha Mandira, Agartala (Tripura).
20. 1977. Sri Chaitanya Gaudiya Math. 187 D.L. Road, Dehradun (U.P.).

SCHOOLS

1. 1946. Sri Chaitanya Saraswat Catushpathi. Shyamananda Gaudiya Math, Midnapore.
2. 1959. Sri Siddhānta Sarasvatī Prāthamika Vidyālaya. Īśodyāna, Śrī Mayapur (Nadia).
3. 1959. Sri Gaudiya Sanskrit Vidyāpīṭha, Īśodyāna, Śrī Māyāpura (Nadia).
4. 1961. Sri Chaitanya Gaudiya Vidyamandira. (Primary and secondary). 86A Rash Bihari Avenue, Kolkata-26.
5. 1967. Sri Chaitanya Gaudiya Pashcatya Bhasha Shikshalaya (western languages school). 86A Rash Bihari Avenue, Kolkata-26.
6. 1968. Sri Chaitanya Gaudiya Sanskrit Mahavidyalaya. 86A Rash Bihari Avenue, Kolkata-26.
7. 1972. Sri Chaitanya Gaudiya Sanskrit Vidyālaya Sector 20-B, Chandigarh.
8. 1972. Sri Chaitanya Gaudiya Antahpradeshika Bhasha Shikshalaya (Indian languages school). Sector 20-B, Chandigarh.

LIBRARIES (GRANTHĀGĀRA)

1. 1970. Sri Chaitanya Gaudiya Math Granthagara (for comparative religious studies). 86A Rash Bihari Avenue, Kolkata-26.
2. 1972. Sri Chaitanya Gaudiya Math Granthāgāra. Sector 20-B, Chandigarh.

FREE CLINICS (DĀTAVYA-CHIKITSĀLAYA

1. 1959. Sri Chaitanya Gaudiya Math Datavya Chikitsālaya. Īśodyāna, Śrī Mayapur, Nadia.
2. 1972. Sri Chaitanya Gaudiya Math Datavya Chikitsalaya. Sector 20-B, Chandigarh.
3. 1978. Sri Chaitanya Gaudiya Math Datavya Chikitsalaya. Grand Road, Purī (Odisha).

PRINTING PRESS

1. 1964. Sri Chaitanya Vani Press. 25/1, Prince Golam Mohammad Road, Tollygunge, Kolkata-33. Was moved in 1966 to 34/1A, Mahim Haldar Street, Kolkata-26.

MONTHLY MAGAZINE

1. 1961. *Śrī Caitanya Vāṇī Patrikā*. 35, Satish Mukherjee Road, Kolkata-26.

OTHER TEMPLES THAT CAME UNDER GURUDEVA'S MANAGEMENT

1. 1955. Sarbhog Śrī Gaudiya Math. P.O. Chakchaka Bazzar. Kamrup (now Barpeta), Assam.
2. 1955. Śrī Gadai Gauranga Math. P.O. Baliati. Dhaka district, Bangladesh.

Śrīla Bhakti Pramode Purī Gosvāmī Mahārāja

In the early years of this century, Śrīla Prabhupāda Bhakti Siddhānta Sarasvatī Gosvāmī Ṭhākura set into motion a devotional revival that rapidly spread through Bengal, India, and eventually the world. He put into question the very foundations of present-day theistic thought in a way that has little comparison anywhere in the spiritual record, East or West. Through him, the world was awakened to the teachings of Śrī Caitanya Mahāprabhu and the movement of pure devotion, *śuddha bhakti.*

In orchestrating this modern *bhakti* revolution, Śrīla Prabhupāda gathered some of the greatest spiritual luminaries in contemporary history into his circle. Such a convergence of exalted spiritual personalities can only be compared to the coming together of Śrī Caitanya's direct followers in the sixteenth century. One of the devotional giants who entered Śrīla Prabhupāda's orbit was His Divine Grace Bhakti Pramode Purī Gosvāmī Mahārāja.

We cannot describe the life of Śrīla Purī Gosvāmī Mahārāja without emphasizing his contribution to the spiritual movement in which he was so integrally involved. The depth of his accomplishments cannot be fathomed outside the context of Sri Gaudiya Math. With his fellow Godbrothers, he shared an indomitable faith in the service of his guru and the message of Śrī Caitanya Mahāprabhu. This service was the sole purpose and highest aspiration of his being. This conviction led him to spend his entire life in the pursuit of Śrīla Prabhupāda and Mahāprabhu's pleasure and the fulfillment of their desires. If we examine his life in this setting, we will see more than just numbers, dates, places and names. We will see how he embodied the very life current that his spiritual preceptors came to give the world.

Śrīla Purī Gosvāmī Mahārāja took birth in the village of Ganganandapur in the Jessore district (in present-day Bangladesh) on October 8, 1898. His parents, Tarini Charan Chakravarti and Srimati Ram Rangini Devi, named him Śrī Pramode Bhushan Chakravarti. During his childhood, he met his *vartma-pradarśaka* guru ("one who opens the door to the path of devotion"), Śrīla Bhakti Ratna Ṭhākura, a Godbrother and *siksha* disciple of Ṭhākura Bhaktivinoda, the legendary architect of the present Gaudiya Vaiṣṇava movement. Through Bhakti Ratna Ṭhākura he was introduced to *Sajjana-toṣaṇī,* Bhaktivinoda Ṭhākura's own Vaiṣṇava periodical, which was filled with Bhaktivinoda's commentaries and holy teachings. In this way Śrīla Purī Mahārāja became familiar with the seminal works of the *śuddhā bhakti* tradition, such as *Caitanya Caritāmṛta*, *Caitanya Bhāgavata* and the *Śrīmad Bhāgavatam*. It was also through Bhakti Ratna Ṭhākura that he first learned of his future guru, Śrīla Bhaktisiddhānta Sarasvatī Gosvāmī Prabhupāda.

Śrīla Purī Mahārāja was still a young university student when he first came before Śrīla Prabhupāda at the Yoga Pith in Sri Mayapur in 1915. It was a significant occasion, for Śrīla Prabhupāda's *dikśa* guru, Paramahaṁsa Ṭhākura Śrīmad Gaura Kiśora Dāsa Bābājī, had entered his eternal abode only the day before. Śrīla Purī Mahārāja often recounted that as soon as he saw Śrīla Prabhupāda and paid his obeisances to him for the first time, he knew in his heart that this was his spiritual master. Some years later, on the auspicious day of Śrī Kṛṣṇa Janmāṣṭamī in 1923, he accepted both *harināma* and *mantra dikśa* from Śrīla Prabhupāda and was given the name Praṇavānanda Brahmacārī.

At the time, Sri Gaudiya Math was rapidly establishing itself as a bona fide manifestation of Indian religious culture and transforming the caste-conscious socio-religious world of Hinduism. Śrīla Prabhupāda Sarasvatī Ṭhākura was bringing together his intimate associates to share the wealth of Śrī Kṛṣṇa *saṅkīrtana*. He had accepted *tridaṇḍī-sannyāsa* in 1918 and by the early 1920's had already assumed a formidable position in the Bengali spiritual firmament. He was fearless when it came to upholding true religious principles. The students and practitioners of the Gaudiya Math aligned themselves with this attitude and led most exemplary lives of devotion, imbued with austerity, discipline and in-depth scriptural learning. This high standard of religious life was the hallmark of Sri Gaudiya Math and would be the thread that guided all of Śrīla Prabhupāda's disciples, including Srimad Purī Gosvāmī Mahārāja.

The keystone of success in devotion is to perfectly hear the holy words spoken by one's spiritual preceptor. Śrīla Prabhupāda would often say, "All that is required of you is that you lend me your ears." Śrīla Purī Mahārāja was fully committed to this maxim. He had the great good fortune to associate closely with Śrīla Prabhupāda for thirteen years, and during that time he served him personally by recording his lectures and conversations, which were later published. The greater part of Śrīla Prabhupāda's spoken words we are left with today come from the transcriptions of these notes. At the same time, Śrīla Purī Mahārāja cultivated a deep knowledge of the Vaiṣṇava scriptures, with the result that he became a veritable storehouse of the wealth of the preceptorial line coming from Śrī Caitanya and His followers. This led him to become one of the most prolific writers and influential teachers in all of Gauḍīya Vaiṣṇava history. His writings reflect the disciplined eye of a scholar who expresses with grace and directness the purest scriptural conclusions supported by his own uncommonly profound realization.

Following Śrīla Prabhupāda's directives, our Gurudeva edited, wrote for, published and helped distribute countless spiritual publications. He was initially inspired and directed by Śrīla Prabhupāda to start writing and contributing articles to the *Gauḍīya* magazine, the backbone of the Gaudiya Math's missionary work. For seven years he served as a proofreader and as one of its primary editors. In 1926, he was charged with running the world's only daily Vaiṣṇava newspaper, *Dainika Nadiyā Prakāśa*. He held this service for two years, publishing all of his preceptor's daily discourses along with articles by fellow students and other contemporaries. His service and learning did not pass unnoticed by Śrīla Prabhupāda who awarded him the titles of Mahā-Mahopadeśaka ("great instructor") and Pratna-Vidyālaṅkāra ("keeper of the wisdom of the ancient scriptural lore").

After the disappearance of his Gurudeva in 1937, Srila Purī Mahārāja continued his vocation of spreading the teachings of Śrī Caitanya through the *Gauḍīya* magazine, first out of the Bagh Bazaar Gaudiya Math and then later the Sri Chaitanya Math in Mayapur. After he founded the Sri Chaitanya Gaudiya Math, Srila Purī Gosvāmī Mahārāja's Godbrother, Srimad Bhakti Dayita Mādhava Mahārāja, invited him to head the editorial board of *Caitanya Vāṇī* magazine in 1964. Purī Mahārāja served in this capacity for thirty-three years, furthering his life's work of preserving the teachings of his spiritual lineage. Through *Caitanya Vāṇī*, he continued to make a deep impact on the devotional world.

In all, our venerable teacher's wisdom is embodied in over sixty years of writings on Vaiṣṇava philosophy and theology. He penned a rich variety of texts, bringing the Bhāgavata *dharma* to life through hundreds of poems, essays, narratives, diaries, editorials and personal letters, thus creating a storehouse of the wealth of pure devotion for his disciples and the world at large.

In 1942, Srila Prabhupāda appeared to Srila Purī Mahārāja in a dream vision and imparted to him the *sannyāsa mantra*, ordering him to accept the renounced order. After accepting *tridaṇḍī-sannyāsa* from his godbrother Bhakti Gaurava Vaikhānasa Mahārāja in Champahati in August of 1946, he toured parts of India with other godbrothers such as Bhakti Hridoy Bon Mahārāja and Bhakti Dayita Madhāva Mahārāja. In the meantime, he continued to write and lecture with dedication. At the behest of his godbrother Tridaṇḍi Svāmī Bhakti Vilāsa Tīrtha Mahārāja, he also served for seven years as chief pūjārī for the Yoga Pith temple, the birth site of Śrī Caitanya Mahāprabhu.

Śrīla Purī Mahārāja took up a more solitary life of worship in the 1950's. He moved to a humble cottage on the banks of the Ganges in Ambika Kalna. The King of Burdwan was extremely impressed by his saintly ascetic character and, on the appearance day of Śrīmatī Rādhārāṇī in 1958, presented him with the ancient Ananta Vāsudeva temple in Kalna.

In 1989, at the age of 91, Śrīla Purī Gosvāmī Mahārāja established the Sri Gopinath Gaudiya Math in Ishodyan, Sri Mayapur, for the service of their divine Lordships Śrī Śrī Gaura-Gadādhar, Jagannātha Deva, Rādhā-Gopīnātha and Lakśmī-Nṛsiṁha Deva. In the following years, he established other temples in Jagannath Puri, Vrindavan, Calcutta and Midnapore.

Śrīla Purī Mahārāja taught through his every action. He excelled in all aspects of devotional practice, and there was perhaps no area in which he did not exhibit utmost expertise, diligence and foresight. This ranged from his encyclopedic knowledge of scripture, to maintaining the printing press, to his beautiful singing of *kīrtana*. He was especially recognized for his sensitivity and attention to detail in the performance of deity worship and devotional rites and was thus widely called upon to be the head priest in most of the Gaudiya Math's deity installations and ceremonial functions. He was rarely known to rest; his service was an uninterrupted flow. Even in his later years, he would remain awake, writing and chanting through the night while all his youthful disciples were still asleep. When his personal servants came in the morning, they would inevitably find him arisen before everyone else in the ashram, chanting the Holy Name.

Śrīla Bhakti Pramode Purī Mahārāja had outstanding love for his godbrothers and was inspired in his glorification of others. He found richness in everyone he met. He had the quality of making one feel so much wanted and their life so much valued. At the same time, he paid the least attention to himself. He was an emblem of humility and simplicity, and his generosity of spirit and kindness touched the hearts of the whole Vaiṣṇava community. Among his lifetime, intimate companions were Śrīla Bhakti Rakṣaka Śrīdhar Deva Gosvāmī Mahārāja, Srila Bhakti Prajñana Keśava Mahārāja, and Srila Akiñcaan Kṛṣṇa Dāsa Bābājī Mahārāja. Toward the end of his sojourn in this world, he was honored by the Gaudiya Vaiṣṇava community for his learning, long life of service and devotion and made president of the World Vaiṣṇava Association in 1995.

"He has love for his guru; and let it be known that his life is one with his words." This tribute, coming from Śrīla Prabhupāda himself, is the most revealing statement about Srila Purī Gosvāmī Mahārāja's personality and qualities. He gave credit for all of his accomplishments to the mercy of his Gurudeva alone. Through the blessings of Srila Bhaktisiddhānta Sarasvatī Gosvāmī Ṭhākura, Srila Bhakti Pramode Purī Mahārāja attracted the hearts of so many to the *Bhāgavata* religion. People from so many different backgrounds and countries found in him a true spiritual guide and shelter. He upheld the principles of pure Vaiṣṇavism and delineated the path of *śaraṇāgati*. He so embodied pure devotion and service to his spiritual master that one of his disciples once remarked that he was able to "silently lay down Śrīla Prabhupāda's entire *siddhānta*."

We are greatly indebted to His Divine Grace for his gift—a lifetime of pure devotion, spanning over a century, which we can aspire for, learn from, and discuss about for our own spiritual nourishment. Śrīla Purī Mahārāja departed this world for the eternal abode in the predawn hours of Nārāyaṇa *caturdaśī*, October 21, 1999, one day before the Rāsa Pūrṇimā. His divine body was transported from Jagannath Puri to the Gopinath Gaudiya Math in Ishodyan and there placed in his eternal *samādhi* shrine. Prior to his departure from this world, Śrīla Purī Gosvāmī Mahārāja appointed his intimate disciple, Śrīpāda Bhakti Bibudh Bodhayan Mahārāja as his successor and President Acārya of Sri Gopinath Gaudiya Math.

In years to come as more of his words and vision are translated, the world outside of Bengal and India will come to know the spirit of the true Vaiṣṇava religion that he tirelessly shared. May the gentle rain of nectar of his perfect teachings continue to bring auspiciousness into this world.

Śrīla Bhakti Rakṣaka Śrīdhara Deva Gosvāmī Mahārāja

Śrīla Bhakti Rakṣaka Śrīdhar Deva Gosvāmī Mahārāja was born in Hapaniya, West Bengal, in 1895. The pastimes of his youth were spent in learning, and he naturally excelled in every subject that he took up. From his childhood, his tendency was towards the culture of faith in God and the study of the Vedas, *Upaniṣads* and other scriptures. He received the sacred thread according to his family tradition when fourteen years old, and his affinity for the divine world kept on increasing. In his early years he was especially attracted to Lord Rāmacandra, but later, when he came in contact with the doctrine of Śrī Caitanya Mahāprabhu, he began to read *Bhagavad-gītā* and developed an attraction for Lord Kṛṣṇa.

After completing his primary and secondary education, Śrīla Śrīdhar Mahārāja entered Krishnanath College in Berhampore (District Murshidabad), Bengal. After four years of study, he graduated with a bachelor of arts degree in philosophy. For some time Śrīla Śrīdhar Mahārāja was searching for a sadhu from whom he could take initiation, but could not find anyone to his liking. Then, by the grace of the Almighty, Śrīla Śrīdhar Mahārāja met his eternal guide and preceptor, Śrīla Bhakti Siddhānta Sarasvatī Ṭhākura, and in 1927 became his initiated disciple.

In 1930 Bhakti Siddhānta Sarasvatī Ṭhākura awarded Śrīla Śrīdhar Mahārāja *sannyāsa* and bestowed upon him the name Bhakti Rakṣaka, meaning "guardian of devotion." Bhakti Siddhānta Sarasvatī Ṭhākura saw in Śrīla Śrīdhar Mahārāja the ability to perfectly protect the Gauḍīya Vaiṣṇava line from misrepresentation and misconception. After reading Śrīla Śrīdhar Mahārāja's Sanskrit compositions glorifying Bhaktivinoda Ṭhākura, Bhakti Siddhānta Sarasvatī Ṭhākura remarked, "Now I am satisfied that, after I leave, there will be at least one man who can represent my conclusions (*bhakti-siddhānta*)."

Śrīla Śrīdhar Mahārāja was recognized for his vast understanding and realization of the *śastra,* and thus his guru also awarded him the title Śāstra-Nipuṇa, meaning one who is very expert or intelligent in understanding the meaning of *śastra.* Not only was Śrīla Śrīdhar Mahārāja recognized by his guru for his

advancement in Kṛṣṇa consciousness, but he was also recognized by many of his affectionate godbrothers for his seniority. Many of them, such as Śrīla A. C. Bhaktivedanta Swami Prabhupāda, Śrīla Bhakti Prajñana Keśava Mahārāja, Śrīla Bhakti Sāraṅga Gosvāmī Mahārāja, Śrīla Bhakti Dayita Mādhava Mahārāja, Śrīla Bhakti Pramode Purī Gosvāmī Mahārāja and many others, considered him to be their *sikṡa* guru.

Once in a letter Śrīla A. C. Bhaktivedanta Swami Mahārāja Prabhupāda commented as follows: "What Śrīpād Śrīdhar Mahārāja has directed, I take it on my head. He is my ever well-wisher. After the departure of Prabhupāda (Sarasvatī Ṭhākura) it is appropriate that I should accept his direction. I got direction from him that I shall live in this country forever."

Sometime after the passing away of Bhakti Siddhānta Sarasvatī Ṭhākura in 1936, Śrīla Śrīdhar Mahārāja established his own temple, Sri Chaitanya Saraswata Math, on the banks of the sacred Ganges in Nabadwip *dhāma*, the holy land of Śrī Caitanya Mahāprabhu. Having deeply assimilated the teachings of Śrī Caitanya, Śrīla Śrīdhar Mahārāja began composing original texts. His first work, *Śrī-śrī-prapanna-jīvanāmṛta*, was a comprehensive scriptural study of sharanagati (surrender). Śrīla Śrīdhar Mahārāja composed numerous songs, prayers, and commentaries in Bengali and Sanskrit. Among these important works are his commentaries on Bhaktivinoda Ṭhākura's *Śaraṇāgati*, Bengali translations of *Bhagavad-gītā* and *Bhakti-rasāmṛta-sindhu*, and his own original Sanskrit poem summarizing Caitanya *līlā*, *Prema-dhāma-deva-stotram*. An outstanding contribution to the Rūpānuga Gauḍīya *sampradāya* is Śrīla Śrīdhar Mahārāja's commentary on Gāyatri *mantra*, *Gāyatrī-nigūḍhārtha*, following the *siddhānta* of *Srimad Bhāgavatam*.

The senior members of the Gaudiya Vaiṣṇava community deeply appreciated all the literary works of Śrīla Śrīdhar Mahārāja. The well-known, if not famous, disciple of Sarasvatī Ṭhākura, Śrīla Akiñcana Dāsa Bābājī Mahārāja, used to say, "I find the writings of Śrīpāda Śrīdhar Mahārāja to be not different from those of Narottama Dāsa Ṭhākura."

Many enlightened souls have proclaimed the greatness of the *Gāyatrī-nigūḍhārtha* as the supreme wealth of the Gauḍīya Vaiṣṇavas. Śrīla Bhakti Pramode Purī Gosvāmī Mahārāja wrote: "Śrīdhar Mahārāja's explanation of Brahma-gāyatri, the mother of all the Vedas, indicating how it is centred on the meditation of Śrīmatī Rādhārāṇī, was revealed to him in the depth of his realization. It is the result of Paramārādhya Śrī Śrīla Prabhupāda (Bhakti Siddhānta Sarasvatī Ṭhākura's) divine grace on him. This explanation is deeply appreciated by those fortunate, intelligent devotees who are aware of the relishable beauty of pure devotional service.

"Parama-pūjyapāda Śrīdhar Deva has presented the world with this most beautiful, full-fledged explanation of Gāyatri, the mother of *śruti*, after realizing the deepest meaning of *Śrīmad Bhāgavatam*. He has shown us the treasure of the most beautiful opulent wealth of the supreme reality: that the loving adoration of *vareṇya bhargo*, who is the supreme loving worshipper, ecstasy giver and internal potency of the supremely worshipable Śrī Līlā Puruṣottama Deva, is the best way to attain the grace of Śrī Kṛṣṇa. Gāyatri is the benevolent source of pure devotional inspiration and intelligence required to attain the grace of Śrī Kṛṣṇa, the Divine Lord of this universe, and is the exclusive meaning of the expression *śavalāc chyāmalaṁ prapadye* (*Upaniṣads*)."

In the *Gāyatrī-nigūḍhārtha* Śrīla Śrīdhar Mahārāja has written:

bhv-ādes tat-savitur-vareṇya-vihitaṁ
kṣetra-jña-sevy-arthakam
bhargo vai vṛṣabhānu-jātma-
vibhāvaikārādhana-śrī-puram
bhargo jyotir acintya-līlana-
sudhaikārādhana-śrī-puram
bhargo dhāma taraṅga-khelana-
sudhaikārādhana-śrī-puram
bhargo dhāma sadā nirasta-
kuhakaṁ prajñāna-līlā-puram
devasyāmṛta-rūpa-līlā-rasadhera
radha-dhiḥ-preṣiṇaḥ
devasyāmṛta-rūpa-līlā-puruṣasya
radha-dhiḥ-preṣiṇaḥ
devasya dyuti-sundaraika-
puruṣasyārādhya-dhiḥ-preṣiṇaḥ
gāyatrī-muralīṣta-kīrtana-dhanaṁ
rādhā-padaṁ dhīmahi
gāyatrī-gaditaṁ mahāprabhu-
mataṁ rādhā-padaṁ dhīmahi
dhīr ārādhanam eva nānyad iti
tad rādhā-padaṁ dhīmahi

"With all of your thoughts and heart's desire, fully engage yourself in the pure devotional service and worship of *bharga*, the supreme goddess Śrīmatī Rādhārāṇī, who is the unlimited origin and possessor of the *svarūpa-śakti* of Kṛṣṇa, the Supreme Beautiful Godhead (*deva*). Being the ultimate and all-harmonizing potency of Kṛṣṇa, She remains His eternally unexcelled beloved servitor. In order to fully enrich and promote His *līlā-vilāsa*, She manifests Herself in variegated congenial forms. It is She who manifests Herself as *dhāma* (Goloka) the abode of Kṛṣṇa, in the form of beautiful effulgence (*saundarya-jyotiḥ*) and opulence (*vaibhava*), adorning and glorifying Him all around. It is She who extends Herself as *līlā-śakti* (the potency principle which promotes the bliss-giving pastimes of Śrī Kṛṣṇa in variegated colorful, tasteful, mystically opulent and beautiful ways). She is the unlimited ocean of Love of Kṛṣṇa personified (*mahābhāva-svarūpiṇī*). Therefore adore Her as the supreme goal of life, who gives venerable, blessed intelligence, realization and taste of enhanced loving worship towards Her and Her eternal beloved deva, Śrī Kṛṣṇa, the all fulfillment of life.

"The sound of Gāyatri is none other than the divine flute song of Kṛṣṇa. This flute song is naturally filled with Rādhā-prema and dedicated to serve pleasure unto Her. What is the special characteristic of this all-attractive flute song in the life of devotional aspirants? It deeply attracts all souls to the unending beauty, glories and qualities of His eternal beloved Śrīmatī Rādhārāṇī, and situates them correctly in their own respective positions in Her eternal ecstatic service. Kṛṣṇa's flute song thus deeply inspires the devotees to embrace an artist-servitor in the divine service-concert of His eternal consort Śrīmatī Rādhārāṇī through harmonious service performance. The innermost meaning of this flute song for all devotees is *rādhā-padaṁ dhīmahi*, which means to wholeheartedly embrace and engage yourself in the service of the lotus feet of Srimati Radharani with all devotional love. The highest and innermost instruction of Śrī Caitanya Mahāprabhu is *rādhā-padaṁ dhīmahi*."

Kṛṣṇa is *deva*, the Supreme Personality of Godhead, who reveals His pastimes of love in the eternal Goloka Vṛndāvana surrounded by His devotees imbued with wonderful love of God. The honorific suffix *deva* was given to Śrīla Śrīdhar Mahārāja's name, as Śrīdhar *deva* Gosvāmī, due to his ability to reveal the inner meaning of the Supreme Lord's divine pastimes of love to the sincerely aspiring devotee. The way that Śrīla Śrīdhar Mahārāja spoke of the Supreme Lord's pastimes was absolutely wonderful. His voice and every movement were filled with divine love for Godhead. He was, as one disciple exclaimed, "beauty, sweetness, and charm in motion."

At an advanced age, in his fully matured stage of realization, Śrīla Śrīdhar Mahārāja spoke extensively before devotees who had come from around the world to hear the teachings of Bhakti Siddhānta Sarasvatī Ṭhākura and the great predecessor *ācāryas* from him. These talks were recorded on audio and videotape and transcribed. They continue to be published by Sri Chaitanya Saraswata Math and Srila Sridhara Mahārāja's many affectionate followers and admirers.

During the last days of his manifest pastimes, Śrīla Śrīdhar Mahārāja remained always absorbed in deep moods of devotional separation and hankering for the divine service of Śrī Śrī Rādhā Govinda. Then in 1988, on the Amavasya, or the dark-moon night, of the month of July, Śrīla Śrīdhar Mahārāja withdrew his manifest presence from this earthly plane to enter the *nitya-līlā* (eternal pastimes) of the Supreme Lord.

At present the teachings of Śrīla Śrīdhar Mahārāja are being spread throughout the world through the noble efforts of his many loyal and dedicated followers. Gaura Haribol!

Śrīla A. C. Bhaktivedanta Swami Prabhupāda

His Divine Grace A. C. Bhaktivedanta Swami Prabhupāda was a *rasika-ācārya*, an expert in relishing the mellows of pure devotion as taught by Śrī Caitanya Mahāprabhu. Such a capacity to relish hearing and chanting of the Godhead's transcendental name, form, attributes, and pastimes is uncommon. The great *Śrīmad Bhāgavatam* (6.14.5) informs us:

muktānām api siddhānāṁ
nārāyaṇa-parāyaṇaḥ
sudurlabhaḥ praśāntātmā
koṭiṣv api mahā-mune

"Out of thousands of perfected souls, it is very rare to find one who is a pure devotee of God."

Perfection, or self-realization, is indeed a noteworthy accomplishment, yet it pales in comparison to unalloyed devotion. One need not fully surrender to God to achieve liberation from the flawed existence of material life. Any number of techniques may be employed in this attempt, but absolute humility of heart is not a requirement. Pure devotion, on the other hand, acknowledges no technique, while humility and absolute surrender are the stage on which the drama of divine love is eternally performed. His Divine Grace had such humility, such surrender, although he was at the same time often very demanding, insisting on a high standard from his disciples. His assertiveness was all on behalf of Godhead and therefore justified. It was an example of the dynamic face of humility, not an abstract, sterile humility, but the concrete and productive humility of doing God's bidding.

Śrīla Prabhupāda came to America in 1965 "as an aggressor." Aggression against illusion is the highest service to humanity. The cost of this war is absolute humility, for souls in this world are often less than thankful, unaware as they are of their own self-interest. The reward, however, is great. It is the dignity of the soul. This was the work of His Divine Grace: to bring dignity to all souls, and he did so with all of the humility at his command. It has been said that what Mohammed did with the sword, what Christianity did with wealth, he did with a humble heart – inundating the entire planet

with love of God. The day will come when all men, women, and children from all races, countries, and creeds sing his praise.

For twelve years, beginning in 1965 until he disappeared from mortal vision in 1977, His Divine Grace circled the globe transplanting what was thought by many to be an Indian religion onto foreign soil. He demonstrated practically that Gauḍīya Vaiṣṇavism is not a product of a particular culture, but the *dharma* of the soul. He took the living conception of what he called Kṛṣṇa consciousness and extended its life beyond what the greatest Gauḍīya thinkers and practitioners of the time imagined even remotely possible. Deep realization lies within the ability to adapt the spiritual reality to diverse material circumstances, making it accessible to one and all. This is the work of an *ācārya*, who teaches by both precept and example. The *ācārya* is not frozen in time. He is melted in love of Godhead, and flows without restriction to anyone and everyone who shows even the slightest interest in pure devotion. This was the work of His Divine Grace. He left a legacy of love, not law, for any and all of his immediate followers to embrace and continue. He gave to all, and looked for one – one who could actually understand his message.

Who was His Divine Grace? Founder-*ācārya* of the International Society for Krishna Consciousness, father, friend, and *śaktyāveśa-avatāra* (empowered incarnation of a particular potency of God,) *nityānandāveśa* the empowerment of Śrīpād Nityānanda Prabhu, the Lord Himself in His most merciful disposition – these can only describe what we could see of him with the outer eye atuned to the spiritual mind. The inner truth of Śrīla Prabhupāda's eternal form and personality will forever remain concealed to those who fail to embrace not merely the form, but the substance of all that he taught and all that he exemplified. The *darśana* (spiritual revelation) of his inner identity is his prerogative. May His Divine Grace mercifully bestow that most precious vision upon all who follow him with steadfast intelligence.

Index of Associates

1	Śrī Jayadeva Gosvāmī
7	Śrī Mādhavendra Purī
16	Śrī Īśvara Purīpāda
19	Śrī Raṅga Purī
20	Śrī Jagannātha Miśra
25	Śrīla Jagadīśa Paṇḍita
29	Śrīmad Advaita Ācārya
43	Śrīla Nāmācārya Haridāsa Ṭhākura
59	Śrī Gaṅgā Dāsa Paṇḍita
62	Śrīvāsa Paṇḍita
70	Śrī Murārī Gupta
74	Śrī Vāsudeva Datta Ṭhākura
76	Śrīla Gadādhara Paṇḍita Gosvāmī
82	Śrī Buddhimanta Khān
83	Śrī Nandana Ācārya
87	Śrī Candraśekhara Ācārya
90	Śrī Puṇḍarīka Vidyānidhi
96	Śrī Śuklāmbara Brahmacārī
98	Śrī Sadāśiva Paṇḍita
99	Śrīdhara Paṇḍita
104	Śrī Vakreśvara Paṇḍita
106	Śrī Devānanda Paṇḍita
109	The Ghoṣa Brothers
111	Śrīmatī Viṣṇupriyā Devī
114	Śrī Īśāna Ṭhākura

116	Śrī Vaṁsīvadanānanda Ṭhākura
118	Śrīla Narahari Sarakāra Ṭhākura
121	Śrīla Raghunandana Ṭhākura
123	Śrī Śivānanda Sena
129	Śrī Acyutānanda
132	Śrī Rāghava Paṇḍita
136	Śrī Kālī Dāsa & Jhāru Ṭhākura
139	Śrī Pradyumna Brahmacārī (Nṛsiṁhānanda)
141	Śrī Gadādhara Dāsa
144	Śrīla Maheśa Paṇḍita
145	Śrī Gaurī Dāsa Paṇḍita
146	Śrī Abhirāma Ṭhākura (Śrī Rāma Dāsa)
148	Śrī Parameśvara Dāsa Ṭhākura (Parameśvarī Dāsa)
150	Śrī Uddhāraṇa Datta Ṭhākura
154	Śrī Puruṣottama Dāsa
155	Śrī Kamalākara Pippalāi
157	Śrī Sāraṅga Ṭhākura
158	Śrī Kālīya Kṛṣṇa Dāsa (Kāla Kṛṣṇa Dāsa)
159	Śrīla Dhañaṣjaya Paṇḍita
160	Śrī Sundarānanda Ṭhākura
161	Śrī Mīnaketana Rāma Dāsa
163	Kūrma Vipra
163	Śrī Uddhava Dāsa
165	Śrī Vāsudeva Vipra
167	Śrī Raghupati Upādhyāya
168	The Sanoḍiya Vipra
171	Śrī Bijlī Khān (The Pāṭhāna Vaiṣṇava)
173	Śrī Dāmodara Paṇḍita
178	Śrī Jagadānanda Paṇḍita
187	Vāsudeva Sārvabhauma Bhaṭṭācārya

195	King Śrī Pratāparudra Deva
204	Śrī Rāmānanda Rāya
214	Śrī Paramānanda Purī
218	Śrī Svarūpa Dāmodara
232	Śrī Mukunda Datta Ṭhākura
236	Śrīla Kāśīśvara Paṇḍita
238	Śrī Bhagavān Ācārya
241	Śrī Pradyumna Miśra
243	Śikhi Māhiti
245	Śrī Gopīnātha Paṭṭanāyaka
247	Śrī Rāmacandra Purī
252	Śrīla Lokanātha Gosvāmī & Bhūgarbha Gosvāmī
256	Śrī Subuddhi Rāya
258	Śrīla Rūpa Gosvāmī
272	Śrīla Sanātana Gosvāmī
291	Śrīla Raghunātha Bhaṭṭa Gosvāmī
294	Śrīla Gopāla Bhaṭṭa Gosvāmī
298	Śrīla Raghunātha Dāsa Gosvāmī
311	Śrīla Jīva Gosvāmī
315	Śrīla Prabodhānanda Sarasvatī
321	Śrī Vṛndāvana Dāsa Ṭhākura
324	Kavi Karṇapūra (Śrī Purī Dāsa)
326	Śrī Locana Dāsa Ṭhākura
329	Śrīla Kṛṣṇadāsa Kavirāja Gosvāmī
334	Śrīmatī Jāhnavā Devī
337	Śrī Vīracandra Prabhu (Vīrabhadra)
339	Śrīla Gopāla Guru Gosvāmī
343	Śrīnivāsa Ācārya
348	Śrīla Narottama Dāsa Ṭhākura
357	Śrī Rāmacandra Kavirāja

359	Śrī Śyāmānanda Prabhu
363	Śrīla Rasikānanda Deva Gosvāmī
366	Śrī Gaṅgā Mātā Gosvāminī
369	Śrīla Viśvanātha Cakravartī Ṭhākura
373	Śrīla Baladeva Vidyābhūṣaṇa
374	Śrīla Jagannātha Dāsa Bābājī Mahārāja
383	Śrīla Saccidānanda Bhaktivinoda Ṭhākura
407	Śrīla Gaura Kiśora Dāsa Bābājī
414	Śrīla Vaṁśī Dāsa Bābājī
418	Śrīla Bhakti Siddhānta Sarasvatī Gosvāmī Ṭhākura Prabhupāda
458	Śrīla Bhakti Dayita Mādhava Gosvāmī Mahārāja
498	Śrīla Bhakti Pramode Purī Gosvāmī Mahārāja
501	Śrīla Bhakti Rakṣaka Śrīdhara Deva Gosvāmī Mahārāja
505	Śrīla A. C. Bhaktivedanta Swami Prabhupāda

Author

Śrīla Bhakti Ballabh Tīrtha Gosvāmī Mahārāja

His Divine Grace Śrīla Bhakti Ballabh Tīrtha Gosvāmī Mahārāja is one of the foremost spiritual leaders of the mission of Śrī Caitanya Mahāprabhu and His associates in the modern world. He is the dearly beloved disciple of His Divine Grace Śrīla Bhakti Dayita Mādhava Gosvāmī Mahārāja, who is in turn the equally beloved disciple of His Divine Grace Śrīla Bhakti Siddhānta Sarasvatī Gosvāmī Prabhupāda.

His Divine Grace Bhakti Ballabh Tīrtha Gosvāmī Mahārāja appeared in 1924 in Assam, India, on Rāma-navamī, the most auspicious appearance day of the Supreme Lord Kṛṣṇa in His form as Rāmacandra. Having been brought up in a pious environment, he developed a strong inclination to search for the ultimate goal of life, which led him to take up the study of philosophy at Calcutta University. While studying at the university, he came in contact with his spiritual master, His Divine Grace Śrīla Bhakti Dayita Mādhava Gosvāmī Mahārāja, and immediately became attracted by his transcendentally powerful personality. After completing his Master's degree in philosophy in 1947, Śrīla Bhakti Ballabh Tīrtha Mahārāja wholeheartedly and unreservedly dedicated his life to the service of his spiritual master.

His service attitude was so exemplary that soon Śrīla Mādhava Mahārāja established him as the secretary of the devotional institution known as Sree Chaitanya Gaudiya Math, which has over twenty *āśramas* in India alone. He was awarded *sannyāsa*, the order of renunciation, in 1961. Eventually, Śrīla Mādhava Mahārāja, seeing his disciple's degree of dedication and sincerity combined with an astute and practical mind, selected him as his worthy successor. After the disappearance of his beloved spiritual master, Śrīla Mādhava Gosvāmī Mahārāja, in 1979, Śrīla Tīrtha Mahārāja was appointed as President-Ācārya of the *maṭh*. He received the fortunate blessings and great affection of many of Śrīla Bhakti Siddhānta's prominent followers, such as Śrīla Bhakti Rakṣaka Śrīdhar Deva Gosvāmī Mahārāja, Śrīla Bhakti Pramode Purī Gosvāmī Mahārāja, Śrīla Bhakti Hridaya Vana Gosvāmī Mahārāja, Śrīla Bhakti Akiñcan Kṛṣṇa Dāsa Babaji Mahārāja, Śrīla Bhakti Kumud Sant Gosvāmī Mahārāja and many others.

For the last five decades, Śrīla Tīrtha Mahārāja was engaged in the propagation of the all-embracing doctrine of transcendental divine love of Śrī Chaitanya Mahāprabhu to counter the present trend of violence and cruelty, and to bring about unity of hearts among all, irrespective of caste, creed or religion. "Example is better than precept" was his way of preaching. He would always practice what he preached. Śrīla Tīrtha Mahārāja is known for not even deviating one inch outside of the four corners of the prescripts of the holy scriptures. His Divine Grace is a renowned authority on Gauḍīya Vaiṣṇava philosophy, and he is beloved by thousands of devotees throughout the world as the very embodiment of humility and spiritual affection.

Even at a very advanced age, inspired by the grace of his Gurudeva, Śrīla Tīrtha Mahārāja was always on the move, going from town to village in India and also abroad, propagating the divine message of *Bhagavad-gītā* and *Śrīmad Bhāgavatam*.

At the behest of his beloved *śikṣā-guru* (instructing preceptor), His Divine Grace Śrīla Bhakti Pramode Purī Gosvāmī Mahārāja, Śrīla Tīrtha Mahārāja preached the message of Śrī Caitanya Mahāprabhu throughout the world, beginning with a tour of the United States in 1997.

As well as being the President-Ācārya of the Sree Chaitanya Gaudiya Math devotional institution, he was also the Founder of GOKUL (Global Organisation of Kṛṣṇa Chaitanya's Universal Love). His Divine Grace Śrīla Bhakti Ballabh Tīrtha Gosvāmī Mahārāja also served as the President of the World Vaiṣṇava Association (WVA).

His Divine Grace was always engaged in writing articles and books of a profoundly spiritual nature in several Indian languages, as well as English, for the eternal benefit of the conditioned souls of the world. To date, his books in English include *Suddha Bhakti, Sages of Ancient India, A Taste of Transcendence, The Holy Life of Śrīla Bhakti Dayita Mādhava Gosvāmī Maharaja, Guru Tattva, Daśāvatāra, Path of Pure Devotion, Philosophy of Love, Teachings of Bhagavad-gita, Hari Katha* and *Vaiṣṇava Aparadha, Affectionately Yours*, the present book (*Sri Chaitanya & His Associates*), and a number of others still to be published.

On April 21, 2017, on the *navamī* of the second fortnight of the Vaiśākha month, one of the greatest saints of the modern era, His Divine Grace Śrīla Bhakti Ballabh Tīrtha Gosvāmī Mahārāja, left this world and entered into the eternal transcendental pastimes of Śrī Śrī Rādhā-Kṛṣṇa.